FIFTH EDITION

Social Psychology

Kay Deaux
Graduate Center of City University of New York

Lawrence S. Wrightsman
University of Kansas

In collaboration with Carol K. Sigelman and Eric Sundstrom

Brooks/Cole Publishing Company
Pacific Grove, California

Brooks/Cole Publishing Company
A Division of Wadsworth, Inc.

© 1988 by Wadsworth, Inc., Belmont, California, 94002. All rights reserved. No part of this book may be reproduced, stored in a retrieval system, or transcribed, in any form or by any means—electronic, mechanical, photocopying, recording, or otherwise—without the prior written permission of the publisher, Brooks/Cole Publishing Company, Pacific Grove, California 93950, a division of Wadsworth, Inc.

Printed in the United States of America
10 9 8 7 6 5 4 3

Library of Congress Cataloging-in-Publication Data
Deaux, Kay.
   Social psychology.
     Rev. Ed. of: Social psychology in the 80's. 4th ed. © 1984
     Bibliography: p.
     Includes index.
     1. Social psychology. I. Wrightsman, Lawrence S.
II. Deaux, Kay. Social psychology in the 80's.
III. Title. [DNLM: 1. Psychology, Social. HM 251 D285s]
HM 251.D358   1987   302   87-15798
ISBN 0-534-08226-2

Sponsoring Editor: *Claire Verduin*
Editorial Associate: *Linda Ruth Wright*
Production Editor: *Ellen Brownstein*
Manuscript Editor: *Barbara Salazar*
Permissions Editor: *Carline Haga*
Interior and Cover Design: *Katherine Minerva*
Cover Art: Alex Katz: *One Flight Up*, 1968. Oil on aluminum cutout, 67¾ x 180 x 47 inches overall. Reproduced by permission of the artist. Photo courtesy Robert Miller Gallery.
Art Coordinator: *Lisa Torri*
Interior Illustration: *Wayne Clark, Cyndie Clark-Huegel*
Photo Researcher: *Lindsay Kefauver*
Typesetting: *Graphic Typesetting Service, Los Angeles, CA*
Cover Printing: *Phoenix Color Corporation, Long Island City, NY*
Printing and Binding: *R. R. Donnelley & Sons Company, Harrisonburg, VA*

PREFACE

Social psychology is thriving. As a relative youngster on the psychological block, social psychology had some difficult developmental periods. By attempting to formulate a perspective on human social behavior that would, in the early view of Gordon Allport, consider the influence of other people on thoughts and feelings as well as on behavior, social psychology set itself an ambitious and challenging agenda. Many investigators have been drawn to this agenda over the years, hoping to provide a better understanding of the human being as a social animal.

The enthusiasm reflected in the developing field of social psychology in the 1960s was followed by a somewhat turbulent period in the 1970s, as critics found fault with many of the awkward moves of the still-youthful discipline. As the field has continued to develop, much of this adolescent awkwardness has fallen away. Now, in the late 1980s, the strengths of an increasingly mature field are apparent.

The vigor and development of social psychology was evident to us when we wrote the previous edition of this textbook four years ago. Now the signs of health are unmistakable. On numerous fronts, social psychologists are extending their investigations and our understanding of how people act and interact. This activity represents more than just an increase in numbers of studies or papers. Current work in social psychology demonstrates an increased awareness of how various pieces of the puzzle fit together and faddishness seems less apparent than it was a decade or two ago. Traditional work in attitude structure and change, for example, is being tied to more recent cognitive work. Questions of self and identity are framed not only in individual terms, but are related to issues of group identity and social categorization. And work in these and other areas moves freely between laboratory and field, from basic research questions to practical applications, in a way that seemed improbable just 15 years ago.

As the field of social psychology has developed and strengthened, so has this text. There is much new material in the present edition that reflects this growth. The greater understanding of the ways in which social knowledge is represented and used is evidenced in several chapters: Most centrally in Chapter Four, which is concerned with social cognition, but also in Chapter Three's treatment of self-knowledge and Chapter Seven's coverage of attitude structure. Other issues of self-definition and identities are also added to the treatment of self in Chapter Three. Current social psychology is not just an individualistic endeavor, however. Work on expectancy confirmation and self-fulfilling prophecies, covered in Chapter Five, reflects an increasing appreciation of the interactive nature of human behavior. Additional coverage of roles, norms, and status characteristics in group behavior (Chapter Fourteen) echoes this theme. Intergroup behavior, a chapter introduced in the previous edition, is explored further in this edition with more discussion of social identity and categorization. Also added to this chapter are the topics of prejudice and discrimination, including both racism and sexism as case examples. Finally, the specific applications of social psychological principles to areas such as health, law, and energy use are covered with increasing detail.

Every chapter in this edition has been revised, and in many cases the revisions are substantial. More than 500 new references testify to the extent of the new material. The organization of chapters has been altered as well. As one example, the topics of attitudes and attitude change are introduced earlier in the sequence of chapters, allowing the links with work in social cognition to be established more clearly. At the same time, each chapter stands as an independent unit, and instructors may find other sequences serve their purposes better. To allow this flexibility, we have included some glossary terms in more than one chapter and we have cross-referenced textual discussions that benefit from other material.

With each new edition of this book, we try to make the learning process more effective and more engaging. As in previous editions, each chapter opens with a chapter outline and closes with a summary. Important terms in each chapter are boldfaced and are defined in the Glossary, which follows Chapter Eighteen. A study guide and an instructor's manual accompany the text. The instructor's manual provides multiple-choice and discussion questions for each chapter, as well as extensive suggestions for further reading, classroom discussion, demonstrations, and individual-involvement exercises. The study guide includes the following for each chapter: A chapter preview; a list of basic terms, concepts, and theories; a set of completion items; and sample-multiple choice and short-answer questions. Prepared by Glenn Littlepage, this workbook gives students the opportunity to evaluate their understanding of the material presented in the text.

Just as generations of social psychological investigators have provided the material on which this book is based, so have many groups of instructors and students helped to shape this book's identity. We hope that you, the instructors and students using this edition, will benefit from these past contributions. Further, we hope that in reading this text you will experience some of the challenge and excitement of social psychology that has kept both of us involved in the field for so long.

Acknowledgments

As *Social Psychology* has continued to evolve, now manifesting itself in a fifth edition, the list of people who have contributed to its development lengthens. No longer can we identify, or even remember, every individual contribution. Over the course of the past nearly 20 years, hundreds—perhaps thousands—of people have made suggestions, contributed effort, and helped to shape the book that we have written. These people include the students who have filled out questionnaires included in the text, the professors who offered their reactions in both written comments and personal conversations, and the many dedicated editors and production people at Brooks/Cole. Without doubt, the book is better as a result of these varied contributions.

When we began to plan this revision, we asked a number of colleagues to comment on the previous edition and to recommend changes for this edition.

For their helpful reviews, we thank the following people: Dorothea Braginsky, Fairfield University, Fairfield, Connecticut; Mark K. Covey, University of Idaho at Moscow; Francis Dane, Clemson University; Jayne Gackenbach, University of Northern Iowa at Cedar Falls; Glen Littlepage, Middle Tennessee State University at Murfreesboro; Richard Moreland, University of Pittsburgh; Charlan J. Nemeth, University of California at Berkeley; and Ronald W. Rogers, University of Alabama. Their suggestions, even those not ultimately adopted, made us think and rethink the best ways to present an accurate and engaging portrait of social psychology today. Tory Higgins, New York University, and Eliot Smith, Purdue University, read selected chapters of the revised text and offered helpful advice.

We also wish to thank the following people, who examined the complete revised manuscript for the fifth edition: Don Bauman, University of Texas at Austin; Eugene Borgida, University of Minnesota at Minneapolis; Martin Chemers, University of Utah at Salt Lake City; Steve Slane, Cleveland State University; and Jim Weyant, University of San Diego.

Almost all of this book was written while Kay Deaux was a Fellow at the Center for Advanced Study in the Behavioral Sciences in Stanford, California. Although the idyllic setting and stimulating companionship of fellows from other disciplines often threatened to distract the author from her task, the Center itself provided an environment and resources that made the task easier and the product far better than it would otherwise have been. In particular, we would like to thank Margaret Amara and Rosanne Torre for their enormous help in gathering material and doing the kind of sleuth work that makes good librarians invaluable.

The enthusiasm and dedication of the Brooks/Cole staff continues to be a source of invigoration and pleasure. Many people in the Brooks/Cole family are a part of this book, even if they were not directly involved in the current edition. For the present edition, however, we must give particular recognition and thanks to a number of people. Claire Verduin has continued as sponsoring editor of *Social Psychology*, a role she has so ably played for four editions. Neither she nor we are willing to disengage ourselves from a book that has been so special to us all. For this edition, Linda Ruth Wright ably managed to keep communication flowing between editor and authors. As production editor of this edition, Ellen Brownstein was marvelous, seemingly missing no beats despite the most challenging of schedules. Barbara Salazar did superb work as a copy editor and increased the clarity of our thoughts and the effectiveness of our words. Permissions were handled expertly by Carline Haga. Developing the art program for this book was a particular pleasure, thanks to a number of people. Lindsay Kefauver, who first joined the *Social Psychology* team on the third edition, returned to the project as photo researcher, contributing her imagination, artistic sensitivity, and enthusiasm. At the Brooks/Cole offices, Katherine Minerva created a wonderful design for this edition and Lisa Torri ably coordinated the art program. Outside of Brooks/Cole, still others contributed to this project. We thank Marie Hibbard for assisting in preparing the index and Mary Kite for her contributions to the Instructor's Manual. In addition, Glenn Littlepage deserves considerable credit for preparing a Study Guide that will enhance students' understanding and appreciation of the material we present here.

To all of these people, and to others whose contributions are not listed here, a heartfelt thanks.

Kay Deaux
Lawrence S. Wrightsman

BRIEF CONTENTS

ONE
Theories as Explanations of
Social Behavior 2

TWO
Methods of Studying Social Behavior 28

THREE
The Self 60

FOUR
Social Knowledge 92

FIVE
Communication 126

SIX
Attitudes & Behavior 158

SEVEN
Attitude Change 182

EIGHT
Social Influence & Personal
Control 210

NINE
Affiliation, Attraction, & Love 238

TEN
The Social Psychology of
Sexual Behavior 270

ELEVEN
Aggression & Violence 298

TWELVE
Prosocial Behavior 334

THIRTEEN
Group & Individual Differences 374

FOURTEEN
Behavior in Groups 402

FIFTEEN
Leadership 434

SIXTEEN
Intergroup Relations 460

SEVENTEEN
Interpersonal Behavior & the Physical
Environment 494

EIGHTEEN
Social Psychology & Society 536

CONTENTS

CHAPTER ONE
Theories as Explanations of Social Behavior 2

A History of Social Psychology 5
Theories in Social Psychology 10
Role Theory 12
Learning Theory 15
Cognitive Theory 20
A Comparison of Theories 23
Summary 26
Glossary Terms 27

CHAPTER TWO
Methods of Studying Social Behavior 28

Formulating Hypotheses 30
Testing Hypotheses 32
Major Methods of Social-Psychological Research 36
Some Issues in Research 53
Ethics of Research 56
Summary 58
Glossary Terms 59

CHAPTER THREE
The Self 60

The Nature of the Self 63
Becoming Aware of the Self 69
Dealing with the Self 73
Relating to Others 81
Summary 90
Glossary Terms 91

CHAPTER FOUR
Social Knowledge 92

Forming Impressions of People   95
Organizing Impressions   101
The Process of Social Cognition   111
Explaining Behavior: Attributions of Causality   115
Summary   124
Glossary Terms   125

CHAPTER FIVE
Communication 126

The Meaning of Communication   128
Channels of Communication   130
Patterns of Communication   144
Deceptive Communication   150
Communication and Social Interaction   152
Summary   155
Glossary Terms   157

CHAPTER SIX
Attitudes & Behavior 158

The Nature of Attitudes   160
The Formation of Attitudes   164
The Structure of Attitudes   170
Attitudes and Behavior   174
Summary   180
Glossary Terms   181

CHAPTER SEVEN
Attitude Change   182

The Process of Attitude Change   185
Theories of Attitude Change   193
When Attitudes Don't Change   205
Summary   207
Glossary Terms   209

CHAPTER EIGHT
Social Influence & Personal Control   210

Conformity   212
Compliance   216
Obedience   222
The Sense of Control   226
Reactions to a Loss of Control   230
Summary   236
Glossary Terms   237

CHAPTER NINE
Affiliation, Attraction, & Love   238

Alone or Together?   240
Attraction   247
Close Relationships   256
Falling Out of Love   262
Summary   268
Glossary Terms   269

CHAPTER TEN
The Social Psychology of Sexual Behavior 270

The Study of Sexual Behavior 272
Theoretical Issues in Sexual Behavior 278
Sexual Behavior in Relationships 284
Sexual Behavior and Contraception 288
Erotic Material and Sexual Arousal 291
Summary 296
Glossary Terms 297

CHAPTER ELEVEN
Aggression & Violence 298

Aggression and Human Nature 301
Conditions That Influence Aggression 307
Violence and the Mass Media 319
Violence in Society 325
How Can Aggression Be Controlled? 328
Summary 332
Glossary Terms 333

CHAPTER TWELVE
Prosocial Behavior 334

Prosocial Behavior and Human Nature 338
Why Do We Help? Models of Helping Behavior 342
Situational Influences on Prosocial Behavior 349
Personal Influences on Prosocial Behavior 357
Seeking and Receiving Help: The Recipient's Perspective 364
Toward a Prosocial Society 367
Summary 371
Glossary Terms 373

CHAPTER THIRTEEN
Group & Individual Differences   374

Similarities and Differences among Groups   377
Cross-Cultural Comparisons   381
Demographic Categories   385
Personality Variables   390
Personality and Social Behavior   396
Summary   400
Glossary Terms   401

CHAPTER FOURTEEN
Behavior in Groups   402

The Influence of Other People   405
Group Composition and Structure   411
Interaction in Groups   416
Group Socialization   427
Summary   432
Glossary Terms   433

CHAPTER FIFTEEN
Leadership   434

The Search for Leadership Traits   436
What Do Leaders Do?   443
Contingency Models of Leadership   448
The Interaction of Leaders and Followers   454
Summary   458
Glossary Terms   459

CHAPTER SIXTEEN
Intergroup Relations 460

Prejudice and Discrimination 463
In-Groups and Out-Groups 475
Strategies of Interaction 479
Reduction of Intergroup Conflict 487
Summary 491
Glossary Terms 492

CHAPTER SEVENTEEN
**Interpersonal Behavior &
the Physical Environment
494**

Ambient Environment 497
Settings for Conversation 503
Architecture and Interaction 509
Privacy 514
Crowding 518
Attachment to Places 524
Summary 532
Glossary Terms 534

CHAPTER EIGHTEEN
Social Psychology & Society
536

Pure Science or Applied Science—or Both? 539
Health Care and Medical Practice 542
Energy Use 550
The Legal System 554
From Problems to Solutions 560
Summary 570
Glossary Terms 571

Glossary 573
References 583
Author Index 627
Subject Index 639

FIFTH EDITION

Social Psychology

*The purpose of psychology is
to give us a completely different idea
of the things we know best.*
Paul Valéry

Scientists know nothing for certain.
Gerald Piel

Isabel Bishop, *High School Students #2*, 1973. Courtesy of Midtown Galleries, New York.

CHAPTER ONE

Theories as Explanations of Social Behavior

I. A History of Social Psychology
II. Theories in Social Psychology
III. Role Theory
   Basic Assumptions and Concepts
   Contributions to Social Psychology
IV. Learning Theory
   Basic Assumptions and Concepts
   Contributions to Social Psychology
V. Cognitive Theory
   Basic Assumptions and Concepts
   Contributions to Social Psychology
VI. A Comparison of Theories
VII. Summary

*I*magine, if you will, the following scene, drawn from the realm of science fiction but illustrative of the domain of social science.

It is a Saturday morning in spring. You are still lying in bed, slowly rousing yourself after a Friday-night party. The sun shines through your bedroom window and you hear birds singing. Yet something seems strange; the neighborhood is more quiet than usual. You glance out the window and see no one, even though your neighbors warned you they would be working on their car fairly early this morning. Could they have finished the repairs so quickly and left for the weekend? Moving more rapidly now, you grab your robe and head for the front door. Looking outside, you find the world looks the same, except for one thing—there are no people in sight. What's going on? Unusual events are always explained on television, you know, so you quickly flip through the channels. Only snow and static, except for the 24-hour test pattern that appears as distinctly and dully as ever. No help from the radio, either; it lights up but produces no intelligible sound.

Call someone on the phone. You are relieved to get a dial tone when you pick up the receiver and you hurriedly call a friend who lives a few blocks away. You hear ring after ring, but no answer. You make other phone calls to other friends, but still get no answer. You call your parents in Idaho, but still hear only the interminable ring of an unanswered phone. Increasingly panicked, you get dressed and literally run to the nearest shopping district, seeing no one as you dash through empty streets. The supermarket looks open—lights are on and the doors are open. But no one is inside. There is food, there is electricity, there are telephones—but there are no people. The physical world is intact, but the human world is gone.

How would you react to this situation? Try to consider what life without people would be like. No television, no radio, no newspapers or magazines, for they all require human effort to produce. Perhaps you could continue your work, but only if other people were not involved. The university would continue to exist as a physical plant, but no teaching or learning could occur. No Monday-night football, no high school reunions, no Thanksgiving dinners. No spouses or lovers, no friends or enemies, no parents or children.

And no social psychology. As a discipline, social psychology focuses on human social interaction, exploring all of the ways in which our behaviors affect and are affected by other people. As Gordon Allport has suggested, social psychologists "attempt to understand and explain how the *thought, feeling,* and *behavior* of individuals are influenced by the *actual, imagined,* or *implied* presence of others" (1985, p. 3). In this well-accepted definition, the term *implied presence* refers to the fact that people's behavior is often shaped by their awareness that they belong to particular cultural, occupational, or social groups. Furthermore, even when we are alone, our behavior may be influenced by our awareness that we are performing a role in a complex social structure, thus reflecting the implied presence of others.

But what if those others are gone? What if the cultural, occupational, and social groups no longer exist? Imagining the total absence of people, as in this science fiction scenario, may give you some sense of just how pervasive the influence of others can be. With no other people, there could be no group effort—everything you did would be an individual project. Aggression and violence would be impossible, but so would love and friendship. There would be no one to give you orders, but no one to give social support and comfort either. Decisions that seemed easy before might become more difficult, as there would be no one to give you needed information. And the absence of others would make it difficult for you to judge your own condition, as the answer to "How am I doing?" often depends on an assessment of how others are doing in the same situation. Human beings are indeed social animals, and a life without others would be severely restricted.

Not all activities carried out by humans are social behaviors. For example, if you pick an apricot off a tree, eat it, immediately get sick, and thereafter avoid eating apricots (at least those straight off the tree), your reactions occur whether other people are present or not and probably do not reflect an awareness of others. Reflex actions, such as removing your hand from a hot stove, are nonsocial; the immediate physical response is the same regardless of the presence or the awareness of others. However, your oral response to touching a hot stove may well be colored by the presence of others. Certain internal responses—glandular, digestive, excretory—are generally considered to be beyond the realm of social psychology. Yet nausea, constipation, and other physical responses may result from feelings associated with the actions or presence of other people. Even the time of dying may be a response to social considerations. David Phillips (1970, 1972) has suggested that Jews postpone the date of dying until after significant events, such as Yom Kippur, the Day of Atonement. In Jewish populations in both New York City and Budapest, he found a "death dip"—a significant decrease in death rates—during the months leading up to Yom Kippur. Thus a great deal of any person's behavior—perhaps more than you first realized—is social.

A History of Social Psychology

To understand modern-day social psychology, we should look, if only briefly, at the roots of this science. As Box 1–1 suggests, social psychology is often said to have originated in 1908, the year in which two textbooks, both titled *Social Psychology,* were published in the United States, calling attention to a newly defined field. Yet the fact that these books had anything at all to say suggests that relevant research had been under way before that date, that people were thinking about issues that would eventually fit under the rubric of social psychology.

During the 19th century, both philosophical thought

Box 1–1
Milestones in
social psychology

1908 Edward Ross and William McDougall each publish a textbook titled *Social Psychology.*
1918–1920 W. I. Thomas and F. Znaniecki's five-volume study, *The Polish Peasant in Europe and America,* makes attitude a central concept for social psychology.
1921 The *Journal of Abnormal Psychology* becomes the *Journal of Abnormal and Social Psychology.*
1924 Floyd Allport publishes an influential text on social psychology.
1934 George Herbert Mead's book *Mind, Self, and Society* is published, stressing the interaction between self and others.
1935 The first *Handbook of Social Psychology,* edited by Carl Murchison, is published.
1936 Muzafer Sherif explains the process of conformity in *The Psychology of Social Norms.*
1939 Kurt Lewin, together with his students Ronald Lippitt and Ralph White, reports an experimental study of leadership styles, showing how social issues can be studied in the laboratory. In the same year, John Dollard and his associates introduce the frustration-aggression theory.
1941 In *Social Learning and Imitation,* Neal Miller and John Dollard present a theory that extends behavioristic principles to the realm of social behavior.
1945 Kurt Lewin founds the Research Center for Group Dynamics.
1954 The first edition of the modern *Handbook of Social Psychology,* edited by Gardner Lindzey, is published.
1957 Leon Festinger publishes *A Theory of Cognitive Dissonance,* presenting a model that stresses the need for consistency between cognition and behavior.
1958 Fritz Heider lays the groundwork for attribution theory with the publication of *The Psychology of Interpersonal Behavior.*
1959 John Thibaut and Harold Kelley publish *The Social Psychology of Groups,* a foundation for social exchange theory.
1960 The *Journal of Abnormal and Social Psychology* splits into two separate publications, the *Journal of Abnormal Psychology* and the *Journal of Personality and Social Psychology.*

and psychological experimentation presaged the development of the science of social psychology. Such well-known philosophers as G. W. F. Hegel and Auguste Comte were introducing ideas about the relation of people to their society. The French philosopher Gabriel Tarde dealt at length with the concept of imitation, to which he attributed conformity in human social behavior (Allport, 1985). In fact, Tarde's book *Etudes de psychologie sociale* serves as an early marker of the field, antedating the better-known textbooks of Edward Ross and William McDougall by ten years (Pepitone, 1981).

The developing field of experimental psychology also recognized social variables. Empirical studies of hypnosis by the British physician James Braid have sometimes been considered early evidence of social-psychological problems (Haines & Vaughan, 1979). More often, people have pointed to the work of Norman Triplett (1898), who investigated how the presence of other people affects motor performance (the phenomenon now known as **social facilitation**,[1] which will be discussed more thoroughly in Chapter Fourteen). Yet Triplett himself did not discuss the events he investigated as social phenomena, nor did the first textbooks of social psychology recognize his work as falling within their domain (Haines & Vaughan, 1979; Pepitone, 1981). Clearly, exactly what was and what was not social psychology was still in the process of being defined.

The two textbooks mentioned earlier, by Ross and by McDougall, presented quite different pictures of social psychology, reflecting the differing intellectual traditions of their authors. Edward Ross was a sociologist, and he endorsed the concept of a group mind as proposed by Emile Durkheim, Gustave Le Bon, Gabriel Tarde, and others (Pepitone, 1981; Post, 1980). Imitation and suggestibility figured largely in his accounts, and the chapters of his textbook dealt with such topics as the mob mind, public opinion, and social conflicts. William McDougall, in contrast, came from a psychological tradition that focused on instincts as the major explanation of human behavior. Accordingly, McDougall emphasized the biological basis of individual motivations and sentiments.

The influence of both of these approaches was short-lived. Their global concepts—the group mind in the case of Ross and instinct for McDougall—were too general to be useful, particularly for the increasingly popular experimental methods of psychology. During the early years of the 20th century, two other major theories began to dominate psychological thought: the **psychoanalytic theory** of Sigmund Freud and the **behaviorism** of John B. Watson. Between the experimental concerns of behaviorism, which focused on learning and the role of external stimuli, and the more internally directed speculations of psychoanalytic theory, social psychology began to define its domain. Both of these reigning viewpoints had an effect on social psychology. Psychoanalytic theory, for example, raised a concern with the process of **socialization** and the limits of rationality (see Box 1–2). Behaviorism stressed the importance of experimental methods and the influence of environmental factors on behavior.

The shape of modern social psychology became much clearer in 1924 with the publication of Floyd Allport's social psychology text (Post, 1980). Unlike the earlier works of Ross and McDougall, this new social psychology book offered experimental work as well as theoretical development. A new rigor was evident in this presentation, and Allport's discussions of such topics as social influence were early signs of an increasingly vital social psychology discipline.

In the 1930s, social psychology became more articulate about the distinctly social aspects of human behavior. Although the first social psychology handbook, published in 1935, still showed some uncertainty about the new discipline's boundaries (including discussions of insect populations and domesticated animals, as well as the "black man," the "yellow

---

[1] Terms printed in **boldface** type are listed in the "Glossary Terms" section at the end of each chapter and are defined in the Glossary, which follows Chapter Eighteen.

Box 1–2
Psychoanalytic theory

Sigmund Freud
(1856–1939)

Psychoanalytic theory, which was developed by Sigmund Freud and his followers, is a theory of personality that grew out of psychotherapy. In conceptualizing the structure of personality, Freud posited three sets of forces—called the **ego,** the **id,** and the **superego**—that are constantly in conflict over the control of behavior. According to Freud, when the ego has control over the two other sets of forces in the personality, the person has made a rational adjustment to his or her environment. Even though unconscious id forces, such as aggressive and sexual urges, will continue to seek discharge, they will be released in healthful, socially acceptable ways if the ego is in control. Dreams and slips of the tongue, for example, are means by which such unconscious urges express themselves. The ego manages to deny reality by means of devices called **defense mechanisms,** which operate at an unconscious level. These defense mechanisms enable the ego to reduce tensions that might otherwise build up between the id and the superego.

Some elements of psychoanalytic theory can be found in social-psychological models. For example, discussions of aggressive behavior sometimes invoke psychoanalytic concepts of instinct and defense mechanisms. A more general influence derives from the emphasis of psychoanalytic theory on **socialization**—the process of acquiring behaviors that are considered appropriate by society. For example, how does a child learn to be a responsible, moral person? According to Freud, the superego develops as a result of early socialization processes. The substance of the superego is distilled from the teachings and admonitions of parents, teachers, other authorities, and peers. Eventually these messages become internalized as *conscience*. This development has been offered as one explanation of altruistic behavior.

Although psychoanalytic concepts rarely contribute to modern social-psychological theory, psychoanalysis' emphasis on internal processes and on conflicts between the individual and society still informs our thinking about human behavior.

man," and the "red man"), activity in the next few years did much to solidify social psychology's base. In 1934 the sociologist George Herbert Mead's book laid the groundwork for **symbolic interaction,** a theory that deals with the importance of interactions between oneself and other people. Two years later, Muzafer Sherif published *The Psychology of Social Norms,* which described the dramatic laboratory demonstration of the social process of conformity to group norms. Still in that decade, John Dollard and his associates introduced frustration-aggression theory, an explanation of human aggression that showed the influence of both psychoanalytic thought and the experimental method. The value of the experimental method for analyzing social issues was further shown by Kurt Lewin and his colleagues, who compared the consequences of authoritarian, democratic, and laissez-faire leadership styles in a laboratory setting. Lewin further capped the developments of the 1930s by introducing **field theory,** a model of social behavior that incorporates both person and environment (see Box 1–3). Lewin defined the basic assumptions of this new field by calling for a constant interchange between laboratory and field work and between theoretical formulations and practical problems.

The potential practical value of social psychology was tested and proved during World War II. The U.S. Army called on psychologists to assess the effectiveness of its morale and propaganda films. Other government agencies wanted to persuade consumers to eat unusual foods, such as sweetbreads, in order to reserve beef for the fighting forces. In

> **Box 1-3**
> Kurt Lewin's field theory
>
>
>
> Kurt Lewin
> (1890-1947)
>
> The fundamental contribution of **field theory,** as developed by Kurt Lewin (1951), is the proposition that human behavior is a function of both the person and the environment; expressed in symbolic terms, $B = f(P,E)$. Thus one's behavior is related both to one's personal characteristics (heredity, abilities, personality, state of health, and so on) *and* to the social situation in which one finds oneself (for example, the presence of others or the extent to which one's goals may be blocked). Although this proposition may seem obvious to us now, its statement in the early development of social psychology marked a clear shift from the individual emphasis of psychoanalytic theory on the one hand and the external emphasis of behaviorism on the other.
>
> In defining his view of social psychology, Lewin stressed several properties of field theory. All actions, he suggested, are influenced by the field in which they take place. Thus analysis must be based on the situation as a whole and must consider the dynamic interchange between parts of the system. The more current *general systems theory* is based on a similar assumption.
>
> The most basic construct in field theory is the **life space,** the total subjective environment that each of us experiences (Lewin, 1938). All psychological events—including thinking, acting, and dreaming—are a function of the life space, "which consists of the person and the environment viewed as one constellation of interdependent factors" (Deutsch, 1968, p. 417).
>
> Another major emphasis of field theory is the *here and now.* To Lewin, psychological events must be explained by the properites of the life space that exist in the present. According to field theorists, if a 29-year-old man is unmarried, shy, and self-deprecatory in his relationships with others, the fact that an auto accident permanently disfigured his face at age 12 is not sufficient explanation for his later behavior. The young man's current reluctance to date is a function of only contemporary properties of the field—properties that may, however, include his current feelings about his appearance or his memories of humiliating comments about his face. The past can influence current behavior only indirectly, in the form of representations or alterations of past events carried into the present.
>
> The specific theoretical constructs that Lewin introduced are not often used in current social-psychological theorizing, but the general orientation that he espoused is very much in evidence. The belief that social-psychological phenomena can be studied experimentally, that psychological events must be studied in relation to one another, that both the individual and the group are important—these ideas are a part of the Lewinian legacy and continue to influence both theory and research.

these and other efforts, persuasion and social influence became major areas of applied research. After the war, theory and research in attitude change continued, led by Carl Hovland and others who had participated in the war effort (Jones, 1985; Pepitone, 1981).

Since the end of World War II, research and theorizing in social psychology have accelerated. Work on such problems as conformity, aggression, and the interaction of society and self has continued, building upon the efforts of the pioneering investigators and revealing more complex patterns of behavior. Many new questions about human behavior have also been raised—the nature of love and close relation-

"I'm a social scientist, Michael. That means I can't explain electricity or anything like that, but if you ever want to know about people I'm your man."

ships, the processes of communication, the ways in which we perceive other people and process information about our social environment. Concern for social problems has generated new research as well, on such issues as the impact of media violence, the consequences of crowding and stress, and the willingness of people to help others in emergencies. With the proliferation of research has come growth in theoretical work as well—efforts to give us a way to view and interpret the wealth of data that are now available.

Theories in Social Psychology

Anyone who offers an explanation of why a social relationship exists or how it functions is, at one level, reflecting a theory of social behavior. In this sense, we are all theorists forming explanations for the events that occur around us, although our theories may be vague, idiosyncratic, and not verifiable.

Within science, the term *theory* is used more specifically, and theories are considered essential to the scientific enterprise. Generally speaking, we can consider a theory to be a set of conventions created as a way of representing reality (Hall & Lindzey, 1978). A more formal definition of *theory* is "a set of interrelated hypotheses or propositions concerning a phenomenon or set of phenomena" (Shaw & Costanzo, 1982, p. 4).

Every theory makes a rather arbitrary set of assumptions about the nature of the behavior it seeks to describe and explain. It also contains a set of empirical definitions and **constructs.** Theories developed by different groups of scientists vary in their assumptions, constructs, and emphases, yet all theories serve common purposes. One of these purposes is to organize and explicate the relation between diverse bits of knowledge about social phenomena (Hendrick & Jones, 1972). We all have a tremendous accumulation of knowledge about human behavior. Some of this knowledge is based on personal experience; some is based on recent public events; and some is based on what we glean from books, movies, or the accounts of friends. Similarly, the scientists of human social behavior have an extensive set of observations and empirical data, and theory provides a convenient way of organizing them (Shaw & Costanzo, 1982). In short, a theory integrates known empirical findings within a logically consistent and reasonably simple framework (Hall & Lindzey, 1978).

Another vital function of any theory in social psychology is to indicate gaps in knowledge, so that further research can lead to a more comprehensive understanding of social phenomena. Theory guides future investigations; it provides a source of **hypotheses** to test predictions about the world. Theory may also anticipate kinds of events that we can expect to occur, even if the particular conditions have not yet been encountered (Shaw & Costanzo, 1982). In the physical sciences, for example, theoretically derived hypotheses that were made decades ago by Albert Einstein about the relation between space and time have been tested only recently, since the advent of supersonic travel.

Data generated by a theory may not always support the original theoretical framework—the research may, in fact, show that the theory has to be revised or even rejected. A theory is simply a model of behavior, and as such it may have a limited life span. Without the use of some theory, however, the task of understanding the variety of social behavior would be tremendously difficult.

Judging the ultimate validity or "goodness" of a theory is difficult and often requires the accumulation of considerable data. Marvin Shaw and Philip Costanzo (1982) have suggested three necessary characteristics of a good theory: (1) the propositions of a theory must be logically consistent among themselves, (2) the theory must agree with known facts and with future observations, and (3) the theory must be able to be tested in order to determine its usefulness. Other desirable characteristics of a theory noted by Shaw and Costanzo include simplicity, ease of relating to real-world observations, and usefulness in generating further research.

By these criteria, some theories are better than others. Yet it is also true that several theories may meet these criteria. No one theory adequately accounts for all social phenomena, and each of several theories may do a good job of explaining a single phenomenon. In other words, there is no one perfect theory. The social scientist may use a variety of perspectives to generate hypotheses and to interpret events (Georgoudi & Rosnow, 1985; Gergen, 1985). As William McGuire has said in explaining his use of the term *perspectivism,* "any one theoretical viewpoint depicts the known just from one perspective and . . . a creative scientist should view it from multiple theoretical perspectives" (1984, p. 29).

In this chapter we shall describe three broad theories of social psychology: role theory, learning theory, and cognitive theory. Each of these theories has a different orientation, set of assumptions, and set of constructs. Within each of these general theoretical approaches, it is possible to develop more limited models (sometimes called "minitheories") that attempt to explain a much narrower range of human behavior. Many of these more limited theories will be discussed here and in subsequent chapters.

We hope to show how the theoretical approach that an investigator adopts will lead that investigator to ask certain kinds of questions about the behavior he or she is researching and to ignore others. Some theories will focus on the individual, while others will emphasize the situation or the social structure. A person's present circumstances will be emphasized by some theories, while others will pay more attention to early learning or to biological causes. In discussing the three most prominent orientations of social psychology, we will first consider the basic concepts

Photo 1–1   People perform a series of roles every day.

and assumptions of each theory. Then we will give examples of research that has been guided by each theoretical perspective. And finally, we will provide some comparisons of the three theories.

Role Theory

Basic Assumptions and Concepts

Role theory has its origin in the theatrical conception of roles as parts that actors play in a dramatic presentation (Shaw & Costanzo, 1982). This concept, which can be traced back to classical times, has more recently been found useful by sociologists. George Herbert Mead, for example, as we noted earlier, talked about the development of self in relation to the social structure. Other uses of the concept of role can be found in anthropology, sociology, philosophy, and psychology.

Although we are using the term *role theory* as if it were a single model, the concept of role is in fact shared by a variety of theoretical perspectives (Stryker & Statham, 1985). These different models do have a number of things in common, however. Generally, role theory does not consider such individual determinants of behavior as personality, attitudes, and motivation. It explains behavior mainly by reference to the roles, role expectations and demands, role skills, and reference groups operating on the participants in a social interaction. Further, in contrast to the more psychological theories that we will discuss later, role theory gives particular attention to large social networks and organizations.

What is a **role**? Following the lead of Shaw and Costanzo, we can define a role as "the functions a person performs when occupying a particular [position] within a particular social context" (1982, p. 296). For a look at the concept of roles, consider Figure 1–1. To gain additional understanding of the concept of role, let's look at a student named Gloria McWilliams.

As a student, Gloria McWilliams performs certain behaviors—she attends classes, prepares assignments, makes an application for graduation, and so on. When interacting with Gloria in her role as a student, other people assume that she will act in certain ways. Their assumptions about her behavior are called **role expectations.** Professors, for example, expect their students to attend class with some regularity and to show some concern about grades. Some instructors may expect a certain amount of deference from their students, whereas others may not. (Similarly, students may have role expectations in regard to their professors, expecting them to be

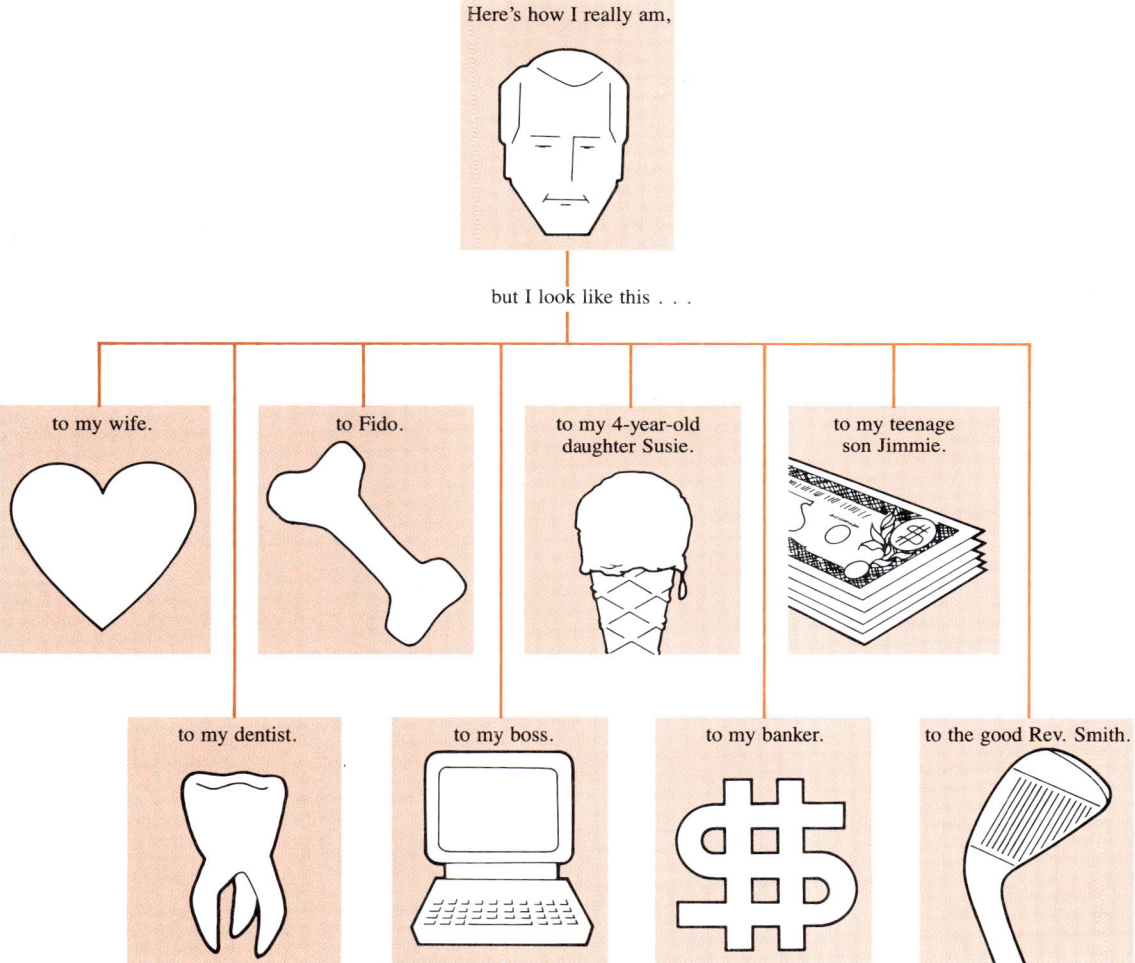

Figure 1–1 One person can play many roles.

on time for class, to be dynamic lecturers, to be experts on the topic, and to be understanding when an exam is missed). **Norms** are more generalized expectations about behavior that are learned in the course of socialization (Biddle & Thomas, 1966). We may, for example, hold general norms about the appropriate interactions between women and men, or between authority figures and their subordinates, which have developed from experience with more specific role relationships.

Role conflict results when a person holds several positions that make incompatible demands (*interrole conflict*) or when a single role involves expectations that are incompatible (*intrarole conflict*). Of course, we all fill a variety of roles every day. While studying for an important final exam, for example, Gloria

McWilliams may receive a call from the local kindergarten teacher reporting that her son is ill and must be taken home from school. At the same time, her husband may come home and announce that his boss is coming over for dinner. As the roles of student, mother, and wife cannot be satisfied at the same time, interrole conflict is produced. In contrast, Gloria would experience *intrarole* conflict if she had to choose between studying for a history exam and typing a psychology term paper that was due the same day.

To say that people "perform a series of roles" does not mean that people are pretending; nor does it mean that they are being deceitful or deceptive. To a significant extent, we behave in ways that are in agreement with the settings we are in and the positions we hold. Of course, the range of behaviors that are considered acceptable in a particular setting is fairly broad; even an occasional sleeper may be tolerated in some large classes if he or she does not snore too loudly! But the role defines the limits of what is appropriate in the setting.

Contributions to Social Psychology

The concept of role has been used often in social psychology: such terms as *role model, role playing,* and *role taking* appear frequently in the literature. This concept helps us to understand why people's behavior may change when their position in a social system is altered.

A vivid demonstration of the effect of roles is seen in Lieberman's (1965) study of the attitudes of factory workers. In an initial testing phase, Lieberman assessed the attitudes of virtually every worker in a midwestern home-appliance factory toward union and management policies. About a year later he went back to the same factory and again assessed workers' attitudes—this time selecting two specific groups of workers. In the intervening year, members of the first group had been promoted to foreman, a position that should ally them more closely to management. The second group of workers had been elected as stewards in their union. Did the attitudes of these workers change as a function of their new roles in the organization? In both cases, the answer is yes, when the responses were compared with those of a control group of workers who had retained their previous positions. Workers who became foremen expressed more positive attitudes toward management officers and became more favorable toward the incentive system, a policy that paid workers according to what they produced. Workers who had been elected union stewards, in contrast, became more positive in their attitudes toward union officers and favored the seniority system over performance criteria. In each case, attitudes shifted according to the new role the worker occupied.

Eighteen months later, the researchers returned to the factory again. By this time some of the foremen had been returned to nonsupervisory jobs and some of the stewards had also returned to their original positions. Once again shifts in attitudes were detected. The former foremen once again were less positive toward management, and the former stewards were now somewhat less strongly in favor of union officers. Thus this study strikingly demonstrates the influence of roles on our attitudes and beliefs.

In recent years the general ideas of role theory have been evident in the increasing concern with concepts of the self. The concept of self is not a new one for social psychologists. In 1922 Charles Cooley discussed the self-concept as a "looking-glass self," presenting the idea that the self is defined on the basis of our interactions with others. George Herbert Mead also made important contributions to our understanding of the self as a product of social interchange. In Chapter Three we will discuss recent developments in the study of the self.

Models of *self-awareness* point to conditions in which we become most aware of ourselves. Analyses of *self-discrepancies*—such as the difference between what we think we are and what we wish we were—help us understand our emotional experiences.

The concept of *self-monitoring* focuses on the tendency of some people to monitor the way they are perceived by others, often choosing particular behaviors in response to the social context. At a more general level, theories of *self-presentation* and impression management show how many actions may be chosen for their usefulness in achieving particular goals. In other words, the role we elect to play may depend on what we want and what the situation allows.

The insights of role theory provide a basis for understanding aspects of the communication process (discussed in Chapter Five). Role theory can also help us understand the positions of leaders and subordinates in an organization (discussed in Chapter Fifteen), where behavior may be influenced by a person's position in the organizational structure. In each case we will see the influence of role theory on the formulation of research questions.

Looking back at our science fiction scenario, we can see that the role perspective would predict some serious distortions in a person's life. If the self is a product of interactions with others, how can one evaluate one's own behavior in the absence of other people? And if one plays out roles in larger social structures, what would a world without groups, communities, and organizations mean for the solitary individual? Only one's memories of those relationships would be influential, and in time presumably their influence would wane, leaving an individual without any guides for behavior.

Learning Theory

Basic Assumptions and Concepts

A second approach to social behavior relies on the psychological principles of reinforcement and learning. As we noted earlier, experimental psychologists in the early years of the century were strongly influenced by the behaviorist principles of John Watson. Later psychologists such as Clark Hull, Kenneth Spence, and B. F. Skinner elaborated the process by which learning takes place. The central focus of **learning theory** is an analysis of the relation between stimuli and responses. A **stimulus** is an external or internal event that brings about an alteration in a person's behavior (Kimble, 1961). This alteration in behavior is called a **response.** If a response leads to a favorable outcome for the person, a state of **reinforcement** then exists; that is, the person has been rewarded for his or her response. As the sociologist George Homans has written, in applying reinforcement theory to social behavior, "if a man takes an action that is followed by a reward, the probability that he will repeat the action increases" (1970, p. 321). Actions that are not rewarded, in contrast, tend to be discarded, and actions that are punished may be actively avoided.

Early reinforcement theorists, including Ivan Pavlov, extended their power of explanation by developing the concepts of generalization and discrimination. **Stimulus generalization** is a "process whereby a novel stimulus evokes a response which had been previously learned to a separate but similar stimulus" (Shaw & Costanzo, 1982, p. 33). In other words, if you have been reinforced for being nice to your Aunt Julia, reinforcement theory would predict that you might be nice to your Uncle Pete as well, even if you had not been reinforced for that behavior in the past. This principle allows reinforcement theorists to explain a wider range of behaviors than they could if each single behavior had to be reinforced separately. The flip side of generalization is **stimulus discrimination,** a process of learning to make distinctions among stimuli. Thus, through experience we may learn that Uncle Pete is pleasant but Uncle Al is a bit gruff. Our ability to make such distinctions allows us to develop more complex ways of responding to our social environment.

Basic reinforcement theorists (sometimes called S-R theorists, for *stimulus-response*) traditionally have little interest in what goes on between the stimulus and the response—that is, the cognitive and phenomenological experience of the organism itself. Theirs is a "language of observables" (Lott & Lott, 1985, p. 110) that deals with specific antecedent and consequent events. Learning theorists want to know how a particular behavior was learned and how it is maintained. Their emphasis is therefore on past events as determinants of current behavior.

The basic ideas of reinforcement theory have continued to be influential, but in general social psychologists have moved beyond the simple S-R model. One major development has been increased reliance on cognitive principles, with the functioning person considered as an intermediary step between the stimulus and the response. Such a model is sometimes called an S-O-R model, where *O* refers to the human organism. We will look at two types of learning theory that are prominent in social psychology: social learning theory and social exchange theory.

Social learning theory. In 1941 Neal Miller and John Dollard laid the foundations for modern social learning theory by proposing that imitation could be explained by basic principles of stimulus, reward, and reinforcement. Their basic assumptions were (1) that imitation, like most other human behavior, is learned and (2) that social behavior and social learning can be understood through the use of general learning principles. Miller and Dollard gave imitation a central place in their explanation of how children learn to behave socially and, specifically, how

Photo 1–2 Imitation is important in maintaining conformity to societal norms.

they learn to talk—which is, after all, a social act. Furthermore, they proposed that imitation was important in maintaining discipline and conformity to the norms of a society. Suppose, for example, that a young boy waits with his older brother for their father to arrive home from work. It is the father's custom to bring each son a piece of candy. The older brother runs toward the garage when he hears a car pull up in the driveway. The younger child imitates his brother's response and discovers that he is rewarded for doing so. The younger son continues to emulate his brother's behavior in other situations: he reacts to frustration by screaming, as his brother does; he combs his hair the same way; he begins to use the same four-letter words.[2] Imitation having been rewarded, the imitative response has become generalized to many situations.

More recently, Albert Bandura (1973, 1977) has developed a broader **social learning theory.** According to this theory, social learning can occur directly through the consequences of responses or, more frequently, through observation of the behavior of others. The behavior of another person (termed a *model*) serves as a source of information. The observer then uses this information to decide whether or not to perform the same behavior, even if no reinforcement is present. In fact, Bandura and his colleagues would argue that reinforcement has its major influence in determining whether or not a behavior is performed—but not in determining whether it is initially learned. Such learning can have embarrassing outcomes; as Kaufmann (1973) notes, a 5-year-old boy may hear certain obscenities but give no evidence of having learned them until he shouts them out in front of his teacher and class.

As we suggested, this modern version of social learning theory assumes that a number of cognitive processes accompany learning. Box 1–4 illustrates some of the hypothesized steps in the sequence of observational learning. First, the observer must pay attention to the model. The attention paid is influenced by characteristics both of the model (is the model someone you like, is that person's behavior relevant to your own concerns?) and of the observer

[2]This story is adapted from Miller and Dollard (1941).

> **Box 1–4**
> Observational learning
>
> How do we learn all the things we know? Sometimes, as either children or adults, we must be carefully taught—how to do multiplication tables, how to drive a car, how to manage a good serve in tennis. But much of our learning is acquired less formally, through the process of observing other people doing things that we would like to do.
>
> Parents often serve as models for their children's behavior, either intentionally or unintentionally. A mother completing her makeup, for example, may be unaware that she is serving as a teacher in her child's learning. Wanting to look like "Mommy," her daughter watches closely and then tries to duplicate the behavior. Although the final result may be a bit sloppy the first few times—as anyone who has been around young children will recognize—the elements of the behavior have been established, and practice will refine the skills.

(is the observer alert, aware of what's going on?). At the retention stage, cognitive processes come into play strongly; Bandura suggests that the individual may code the observed event, organize it in terms of past experience, and symbolically rehearse the behavior. Motor reproduction, the third stage in Box 1–4, depends in part on the person's ability actually to perform the observed behavior. I may carefully observe Martina Navratilova play tennis, for example, and rehearse in my mind how she serves, yet when I get out on the court I may be quite incapable of duplicating her behavior. Finally, the presence of reinforcements—either from others or from oneself—will determine whether the learned behavior will actually be performed.

Social learning theory allows for much more complicated forms of learning than the earlier reinforcement models did. Yet like its predecessors, social learning theory is centrally concerned with the stimuli that elicit social behaviors and the reinforcements that the individual anticipates. And like basic learning theory, this is primarily a model of individual behavior.

Social exchange theory. The second theory that relies on principles of reinforcement is focused more strongly on the interactions between two people. According to **social exchange theory,** such interactions depend on the rewards and costs involved—people will seek out those relationships that promise greater rewards than costs and will avoid relationships whose costs exceed their rewards.

George Homans (1958, 1974), who presented one of the first models of social exchange, assumes that people are basically hedonistic—in other words, they seek to maximize pleasure and minimize pain. In interacting with one another, people make exchanges to achieve pleasure. Exchanges can consist of either material or nonmaterial goods: approval and prestige, for example, are nonmaterial goods; money is considered a material reward. An exchange often encompasses both domains. You may give money to your favorite political candidate, for example, in order to gain prestige or influence in the community. For Homans, a basic principle of social exchange is **distributive justice**—a rule that says a reward should be proportional to one's investment. Within this model, the principle of distributive justice is believed to apply equally well to workers in an employment setting and to spouses in a domestic relationship.

John Thibaut and Harold Kelley present a more complex version of social exchange theory—in their terms, a theory of interdependence (Kelley & Thibaut, 1978; Thibaut & Kelley, 1959). Their theory emphasizes the dynamic aspects of dyadic interaction—a process in which a person who is acting with and reacting to another person may be affected by that person's actions. A critical element that distinguishes their model from Homans' simpler framework is the assumption that people make comparisons between their present outcomes and other possible alternatives (Jones, 1985). In other words, one not only evaluates the costs and rewards involved in a current exchange but also considers the costs

Figure 1–2 A social exchange outcome matrix. The words to the right of the diagonal in each of the four quadrants describe the costs and rewards that Ann finds attached to the particular combination of behaviors. The words to the left (or below) the diagonal describe Lisa's costs and rewards.

and rewards that might be attached to a different relationship.

To analyze the interaction process, Thibaut and Kelley introduced the outcome matrix (see Figure 1–2). Basically, this matrix suggests that each person in an interaction confronts a set of alternatives that entail varying costs and rewards. The process of interaction depends on maximizing the satisfaction of *both* participants. If the values of only one person were considered in isolation from the other, the interaction would break down.

Let's consider a simple example to see how the outcome matrix is used. Ann and Lisa, who are roommates, are trying to decide how to spend a Saturday. Ann observes that their apartment is a mess, and suggests that they clean it together. Lisa has planned to go cycling for the day and suggests that Ann join her. For our purposes we will assume that those are the only two options available for each— cleaning and cycling. For Lisa, cycling is more rewarding; for Ann, cleaning is more rewarding. If these two women were not interacting, there would be no question about which choice would be made— Lisa would grab her bike and Ann would grab her broom. Yet, because the outcomes of these choices are related, we have to consider each in relation to the other. For Lisa, guilt might be a cost of the choice to cycle, for she would realize that Ann was doing more than her fair share of the work. Ann, in turn, would find the situation negative because of the resentment aroused by Lisa's pleasure-seeking. In exchange relationships, therefore, the participants must calculate the rewards and costs attached to each possible combination of actions, in order to determine which outcome will be most beneficial for both.

Thibaut and Kelley's model, which can be applied to much more complicated interchanges, considers also how relationships change over time as the participants take account of each other's preferences and the outcomes of their exchanges.

Contributions to Social Psychology

Social psychologists have applied the principles of learning theory to a wide variety of areas. Perhaps the best example is seen in the study of aggressive behavior. The frustration-aggression theory of John Dollard and his associates (Dollard et al., 1939) borrowed many concepts from the behaviorist models current at the time. More recently, psychologists studying the development of aggressive behavior in children have shown how important observational learning can be, whether the models are present or seen on television. Other attempts to understand the occurrence of aggression and violence have pointed to the reinforcements that people sometimes receive—

messages that aggression pays off. These and other explanations of aggressive behavior will be discussed more thoroughly in Chapter Eleven.

Just as learning principles have been applied to the question of why people hurt each other, so they have been used to explain why people help one another. Again, both direct reinforcement and observational learning can help us understand how people learn to be helpful and the conditions under which they are most likely to do so (see Chapter Twelve). Why do people like each other? Some scientists suggest that a major reason is the reinforcement provided by the realization that we are similar to another person (see Chapter Nine). Learning models have also been used to show why the presence of an audience sometimes facilitates performance and at other times impairs it (Chapter Fourteen). Many of our basic attitudes may be acquired through a process of learning and reinforcement, a process that will be described further in Chapters Six and Seven.

Social exchange theory, as a version of learning theory, has similar versatility when we think about actual social interactions. Cooperative and competitive behavior, power relationships, bargaining and negotiation can all be informed by the principles of social exchange theory. Such interactions may occur in a marital relationship (Chapter Nine) or in confrontations between groups, classes, or governments (Chapter Sixteen).

What would learning theory do with the sole survivor in our science fiction scenario? Traditional behaviorism would probably be more successful, in that it could look to behaviors acquired in the past as a key to current behavior. Even so, behaviorist models would agree that as people can act as stimuli for behaviors, many behaviors would be less likely to occur in the absence of other people. Social learning theory, with its emphasis on other people as models for behavior, would predict more limitations for the survivor's behavior. Social exchange theory, which rests on the interaction between people, offers little basis for predicting behavior of any kind.

Cognitive Theory

Basic Assumptions and Concepts

In the history of psychology, many people have reacted against the behaviorist, or learning, orientation. Rather than shunning mentalistic concepts, many psychologists have seen such concepts as absolutely necessary for understanding human behavior. *Gestalt* psychologists, led by Kurt Koffka and Wolfgang Köhler in the 1930s, were one such group. Taking their name from the German word for shape or form (*Gestalt*), these psychologists stressed perception and thought. In making the basic assumption that "the whole is greater than the sum of its parts," they moved beyond the simple associations proposed by the behaviorists. Their studies of problem solving, for example, led Gestalt psychologists to argue that people learn not only by a repetitive, trial-and-error process but often by experiencing sudden insights that involve broad reorganization of cognitive structures. Thus Gestalt psychologists moved away from an analysis of observable stimuli and responses, toward the inference of internal cognitive processes.

The **phenomenological approach** also represents a reaction against behaviorist principles. According to this view, we can understand a person's behavior only if we know how that person perceives the world. Previous stimuli and responses are influential only if they are represented in a person's consciousness. Kurt Lewin's field theory (see Box 1–3), emphasizing the notion of life space, is also related to the phenomenological approach.

Gestalt psychology, the phenomenological approach, and Lewin's field theory all provide a background for current cognitive models of social psychology. Work in cognitive psychology has also provided a framework for social psychologists to use. To understand more about this approach, we need to understand some basic terms. The word *cognition* itself derives from a Latin word (*cognoscere*) that means to become acquainted with or to know. Accordingly, psychologists use the term *cognition* to refer to thinking or knowing, as distinguished from feeling and behaving (Landman & Manis, 1983).

Cognitive psychologists are interested in two basic issues: mental representation and mental processing. A representation is something that stands for something else; thus when we talk about mental representation, we are asking how an event or an experience is represented in the mind (Markus & Zajonc, 1985). We can think of representations more graphically as building blocks (Landman & Manis, 1983). The term **cognitive structure** refers to the organization of these building blocks—to the set of principles that organizes our cognitive experience (Shaw & Costanzo, 1982). This brings us to the second issue, mental processing. Cognitive psychologists want to know how the mind works—how we perceive, how we remember, and how cognition leads to action. In other words, cognitive processes deal with how the building blocks are put together and what they do.

Social cognition is a special form of cognitive psychology, one that deals specifically with the ways in which we think about people and the social aspects of our environment (thoughts about objects, numbers, and nonsocial things are left to the cognitive psychologist). The world of objects and the world of people differ in many respects (Fiske & Taylor, 1984). People can influence their environment, for example, in a way that objects cannot. Social cognition is also a mutual process, in that the target of your perception is probably looking back at you in a way that a rock could not. People are also flexible, changing from situation to situation and from year to year in a way that most objects do not. So the process of social cognition differs from and in many ways is more complex than the more basic process of cognition.

What assumptions are made by social psychologists who rely on cognitive theory? Generally, such theorists are not concerned with such concepts as reinforcement and learning. Instead they refer to types of cognitive structures and the processes by which such structures are formed. One of the most widely used of the concepts referring to cognitive structure is that of a **schema,** defined as an organized configuration of knowledge derived from past experience that we use to interpret our current experience. In other words, a schema both reflects what we have already experienced and influences our perception

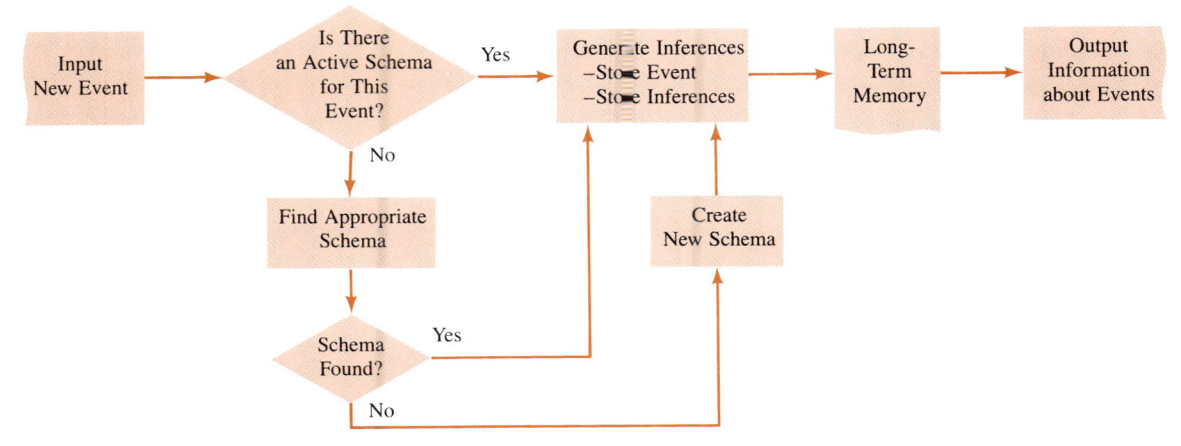

Figure 1-3 Flow chart representing the ways in which schema operate in the social cognition process. Stimuli and events occur at the left end of the diagram (the input), and recall is represented at the right end (the output). In between, inferences are made and stored in memory.

of new events. Figure 1-3 shows how this process is represented. As you might guess, computer analogies are often used to describe cognitive structures.

It has been said that social psychology has been cognitive for a very long time (Zajonc, 1980). Indeed, the newer models of social cognition follow a well-established tradition of using cognitive variables to explain social behavior. These newer models differ from older ones, however, in their emphasis on process as well as on structure. Current cognitive theory also places an even greater emphasis on the individual, paying relatively little attention to ongoing interaction or to social and cultural systems.

Contributions to Social Psychology

It is easy to find examples of cognitive theorizing throughout the history of social psychology, from the early interest in attitudes through the work of Muzafer Sherif and Kurt Lewin's emphasis on life space. Cognitive variables will be evident in many of our later chapters. Chapters Six and Seven, for example, explore the idea of an attitude and consider some of the theories that have been developed to predict when and how our attitudes change. Cognitive consistency theories, for example, assume that we want our various attitudes, or our attitudes and our behaviors, to be consistent with one another. When they are not consistent, we are motivated to make changes. Suppose, for example, that you admire football heroes and oppose the use of drugs. How do you reconcile your attitudes when you read about drug use among professional football players? This contradiction might cause some shift in your attitudes, either away from football players ("They're not so great after all") or toward drug use ("Maybe the dangers have been exaggerated")—changes that may not be directly observable but can be inferred if we rely on cognitive theory.

The ways in which our thoughts can influence our behaviors will be demonstrated in other chapters as well. The communication process (Chapter Five), for example, is fueled by our beliefs about the person we talk with, and discriminatory behavior can be understood, in part, as a consequence of our stereotyped beliefs (Chapter Sixteen). Even more centrally, our beliefs about ourselves reflect the functioning of cognitive variables (see Chapter Three). We will see the analysis of cognitive processes most directly in Chapter Four, when we discuss in more detail the assumptions of cognitive theories.

Table 1–1 A comparison of three theories in social psychology

	Role Theory	Learning Theory	Cognitive Theory
Central concept or unit of analysis	Role	Stimulus-response unit	Cognitive structure and process
Causes of behavior (historical or contemporary)	Contemporary ("You are the role you hold now")	Both—past reinforcement history and present reinforcement contingencies are equally important	Both—memories and cognitive structure influence behavior, as do current events
Internal processes or external events emphasized	Roles and situations	External stimuli	Internal processes
Emphasis on individual or social structure	Social structure	Individual learning	Individual cognitions
Assumptions about human nature	People act in response to the expectations associated with the roles they hold	People's behaviors are determined by patterns of reinforcement	People are cognitive beings, who form cognitive structures and act on the basis of their cognitions

Because cognitive theories are so individualistic, they may seem likely to predict little disruption for the individual who has suddenly lost his or her society. To some extent that is true. Cognitive theories say far less than role and learning theories about the actual interchange of human life. Yet social cognition theories suggest that past schemas would soon prove ineffective in our science fiction scenario, and that the sole survivor would have to create new schemas to deal with the new experiences. Beliefs about the self might shift to incorporate increasing evidence of self-reliance; schemas about the environment would focus on animals rather than people. How the individual would act would then depend on the characteristics of the new schemas adopted to deal with this unprecedented situation.

A Comparison of Theories

Each of the three major theories that we have discussed makes certain assumptions about human behavior, defining some variables as important and others as incidental. Each theory points an investigator in certain directions, suggesting some questions to ask and ignoring others. Having considered the central features of each theory separately, let's now compare them directly. Table 1–1 summarizes these comparisons across five dimensions: the unit of analysis, historical or contemporary emphasis, internal or external emphasis, individual or social-structural emphasis, and assumptions about human nature.

Unit of analysis. Each of the three theories that we have examined points to one concept as its centerpiece. For role theory, this concept is roles, formed as people interact with one another in a social system. Learning theory explains social behavior by looking at specific stimulus-response-reinforcement connections. Although the more contemporary learning theories, such as social exchange and social learning, consider rather complex units, their focus is still on discrete behaviors. For cognitive theory, the basic units are cognitions or, more specifically, cognitive structures and processes.

Historical versus contemporary emphasis. The three theories diverge somewhat in the extent to which they emphasize historical versus contemporary causes of behavior. Role theory places the greatest weight on the present. (Lewin's field theory, presented in Box 1–3, was also very contemporary in its emphasis.) Both reinforcement theories and cognitive theories give more attention to historical antecedents of current behavior. Neither, however, emphasizes historical factors as strongly as psychoanalytic theory (briefly described in Box 1–2), which explains nearly all behavior on the basis of events that occurred when a person was very young. Both reinforcement and cognitive theories assume that behavior can and does change with new reinforcements or new experience.

Internal versus external events. A third dimension on which theories differ is the emphasis they place on internal and external events. Role theory tends to stress external roles and situations (although, as we shall see in Chapter Three, the current emphasis on the self-concept allows a great deal of consideration of internal events as well). Classical reinforcement theory is concerned only with external events; it is uninterested in and even antagonistic to the notion of "mentalistic" concepts. More contemporary versions of reinforcement theory, such as social learning and social exchange theories, give more attention to internal thoughts, expectancies, and mediating cognitions. Cognitive theories are very internal in their focus, stressing internal cognitive structures almost exclusively.

Individual versus social structure. Although learning and cognitive theories differ in the extent to which they consider external events, they are alike in their emphasis on the individual as opposed to the social structure. Learning theories give more attention to individual learning histories and, in the case of social learning and social exchange theories, to individual differences in cognitive abilities and in interaction goals. Cognitive theory puts more emphasis on the individual than on the social structure, reflecting psychologists' continuing interest in analyzing individuals rather than groups. Role theory, in contrast, virtually ignores individual differences; it looks instead at the common features of roles, role conflicts, and role expectations as the determinants of behavior.

Assumptions about human nature. Both classical reinforcement theory and role theory assume that human nature lacks an essence; rather, people act in reponse to stimuli (reinforcement theory) or in response to the expectations of the roles they are fulfilling (role theory). In both cases, however, recent modifications have inserted the person more directly into the theory, acknowledging an organism (an *O* between the stimulus and response) in the case of reinforcement theory and giving greater attention to the self-concept in the case of role theory. Cognitive theory, in contrast, rests its case on the human being as a cognitive being—thinking, interpreting, and finding meaning in events. At the same time, cognitive theory has been accused of giving too little attention to other aspects of human behavior, such as emotion and action, and allowing the analogy of the computer to direct attention away from these other basic features of human nature.

Clearly these three theories differ considerably in

Box 1–5
Sociobiological theory

Sociobiology has been defined by its original proponent, Edward O. Wilson, as "the systematic study of the biological basis of all social behavior" (1975, p. 4). According to the sociobiologists, genetic determinants of social behavior have evolved over the life of each species. This theory is an extension of Darwinian evolutionary theory, which introduced the principles of natural selection and survival of the fittest. Sociobiology differs in assuming that it is the fittest genes, defined as those that increase the probability of the offspring's survival, rather than the fittest individuals that nature selects to survive.

Aggression and altruism have been of particular interest to sociobiologists, but ambitious scientists in the field have ventured much further, looking at behaviors as diverse as the communication of deceptive messages, the nature of physical attractiveness, and gender differences in social behavior. The basic argument in each case is that social behavior is substantially determined by one's genetic makeup, and that behaviors that an individual or species displays have evolved because they are genetically adaptive. In other words, sociobiologists base their inferences regarding the causes of a behavior on their observations of the behavior's effects.

Not surprisingly, this theory is very controversial (Kitcher, 1985). First of all, it is difficult to test. Experiments that can be performed rather quickly with several generations of insects cannot, for reasons of time or ethical considerations, be performed with humans. Second, the fact that a behavior exists or is displayed does not guarantee that it was a result of adaptation. It has been amply demonstrated that characteristics may survive in a species for a variety of reasons, not just because they are adaptive (Dumont & Robertson, 1986; Gould, 1986). Third, the dependence of an organism on its biological makeup generally decreases as the complexity of the brain increases. In other words, a human being has much more latitude than a simpler organism in deciding whether to respond to external events, internal goals, or biological drives.

Despite these criticisms of sociobiological theory, we recognize that social psychologists have probably paid less attention to biological determinants than they might have. Certainly the potential for some forms of behaviors is influenced by biological factors. Physical size, for example, may be related both to the amount of harm an individual can do and to other people's reactions and expectations. Sexual behavior certainly has important biological components. To acknowledge some influence of biological factors, however, is not to claim that all social behavior is biologically based. Demonstrating the link between the potentials or possibilities that genetics and biology may establish and the actual display of social behavior remains one of the challenges of biologically based theories.

what they consider important and how they think social behavior develops. As we suggested earlier, none of these theories is sufficient in itself to explain the broad range of behavior that social psychology incorporates. Each perspective offers us valuable insights; at the same time, there are facets of behavior that none of these theories really comes to grips with. The possible biological determinants of behavior, for example, are not really considered by either role, learning, or cognitive theory (see Box 1–5). Nor, with the possible exception of role theory, do these theories give much attention to the influence of groups and cultures on our behavior. Some people would prefer to leave such concerns to anthropologists. Yet a discipline rooted in sociology as well as psychology might well pay attention to the group as well as to the individual (Jahoda, 1986; Pepitone, 1981).

"A theory is a guide to tell you where to look for what you want to observe," observed Runkel and McGrath (1972, p. 23). Depending on the theoretical orientation we adopt, we may observe quite diverse aspects of human behavior. The importance of being aware of our assumptions and of their consequences is perhaps the most important lesson to be learned. At that point we can begin to recognize the full complexity of human social behavior.

Summary

Social psychology is the field of study concerned with interpersonal behavior. Its concerns include not only actual interpersonal behavior but any behavior in which the presence of others is imagined or anticipated. Imagining what the world would be like without any other human beings gives you some sense of how broad the concerns of social psychology are.

Although the writings of early philosophers and the experiments of 19th-century psychologists indicate an interest in social behavior, the beginning of social psychology as a recognized discipline is often set at 1908, when two textbooks titled *Social Psychology* were published. During the next 30 years, many important developments set the tone for modern social psychology as a research-based discipline, and both research and theory have continued to accelerate.

Theories are sets of hypotheses formulated to explain phenomena. The three theoretical approaches that dominate current social psychology are role theory, learning theory, and cognitive theory.

Role theory seeks to explain social behavior by an analysis of roles, role obligations, role expectations, and role conflicts. A role is a socially defined pattern of behavior that accompanies a particular position within a social context. In recent years, concepts derived from role theory have been used to explain a variety of phenomena related to the self and the self-concept.

Learning theory originally limited its concerns to stimuli, responses, and reinforcements, concentrating only on events external to the person. More recent offshoots of reinforcement theory include social learning theory and social exchange theory, both of which include numerous cognitive concepts in their models. Thibaut and Kelley's theory of interdependence has shifted the focus from the individual to the interacting dyad, considering the rewards and costs for both partners in an interaction.

Cognitive theory finds some roots in early work by both Gestalt and phenomenological theorists. It has developed much more elaborate concepts of cognitive structure, however, often borrowing models from the field of computer technology. *Social cognition* refers specifically to the ways in which we think about people and the social aspects of our environment.

Theories can be compared on a number of dimensions, including their units of analysis, emphasis on historical or contemporary situations, focus on internal or external events, emphasis on individuals or social structures, and basic assumptions about human nature.

Each theory offers a unique perspective on social behavior, and no single theory explains everything. Our understanding is often increased when we take several different perspectives into account.

Glossary Terms

behaviorism
cognitive structure
constructs
defense mechanisms
distributive justice
ego
field theory
hypothesis
id
life space
norms
phenomenological approach
psychoanalytic theory
reinforcement
response
role
role expectations
schema
social exchange theory
social facilitation
socialization
social learning theory
sociobiology
stimulus
stimulus discrimination
stimulus generalization
superego
symbolic interaction

Research is the invasion of the unknown.
DeWitt Stetton, Jr.

*The whole of science is nothing more
than a refinement of everyday thinking.*
Albert Einstein

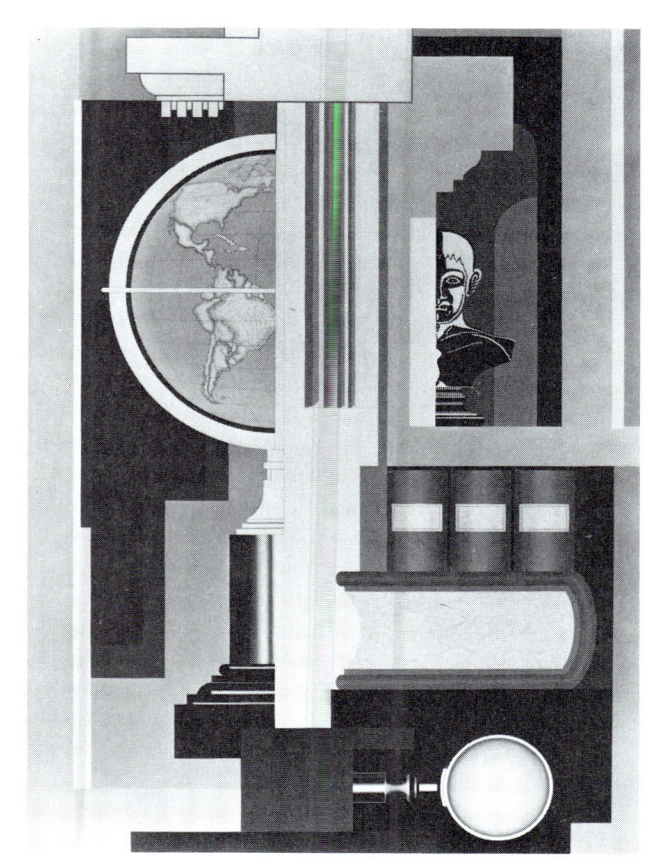

Gerald Murphy, *Bibliotheque*, 1926–27. Courtesy of Southern Bell Corporation Collection, St. Louis.

CHAPTER TWO

Methods of Studying Social Behavior

I. Formulating Hypotheses
II. Testing Hypotheses
   The Hypothesis
   A Laboratory Investigation
   A Field Investigation
   A Cross-Cultural Investigation
   Choice of a Method
III. Major Methods of Social-Psychological Research
   The Laboratory Experiment
   The Field Experiment
   Quasi-Experimental Research
   The Field Study
   Archival Research
   Simulation and Role Playing
   Surveys and Interviews
IV. Some Issues in Research
   Selection of Method and Setting
   Units of Analysis
V. Ethics of Research
VI. Summary

*T*heories give us ways to look at the world. They provide a general framework for our understanding, and they also tell us what specific events to look for. As we saw in Chapter One, a social learning theorist may look for people in the present environment who influence a person's behavior, whereas the investigator with a Freudian bent may turn to early childhood experiences to find the causes of adult behavior. It has been said that "we are prone to see what lies behind our eyes rather than what appears before them" (Beveridge, 1964, p. 99).

"Behind our eyes," however, encompasses a lot of territory, and it is from this territory that experimental hypotheses emerge. Social psychologists, like other scientists, begin their pursuit of knowledge with an idea and then proceed to test that idea to determine its validity. All the research that will be discussed in this book began with an idea—sometimes a formally derived hypothesis, sometimes an intuitive leap, and sometimes just a lucky happenstance. How ideas develop will be the first topic of this chapter; how ideas are translated into scientific study will be our focus in the rest of the chapter.

Formulating Hypotheses

Where do ideas come from? Curiosity and observation are the starting points in the research process (Silverman, 1977). The curiosity of social psychologists is concerned with human behavior; their observations focus on people and their interactions. Research ideas may develop from a general interest in some topic, such as persuasion or group processes or love. In other instances, a specific event may be perplexing, and, like Sherlock Holmes, the social psychologist will try to unravel the mystery and arrive at a solution. In still other cases, an investigator may be involved in one project and, like the fabled princes of Serendip, accidentally discover some other significant information about human behavior, quite removed from the original research focus. In each case, however, curiosity and observation are at the root of the investigation.

William McGuire (1973) has suggested some specific ways in which testable hypotheses about human behavior may be derived (see Table 2–1 on p. 31). Some of these approaches are based on a consider-

30

Table 2-1 Some approaches to hypothesis generation

1. Intensive case study
   Example: Most psychoanalytic theory began with the extended analysis of individual patients. In treating a hysterical patient named Dora, for instance, Freud developed some of his theories about unconscious sexual impulses.
2. Accounting for a paradoxical incident
   Example: A cult of Illinois citizens in the mid-1950s fervently predicted the end of the world. When the designated day arrived and the world did not end, the enthusiasm of the believers for their cause did not wane (Festinger, Riecken, & Schachter, 1956). This incident led to a hypothesis about the effects of commitment on subsequent behavior.
3. Use of analogy
   Example: Borrowing from the medical principles of immunization as a means of resisting disease, William McGuire (1964) developed research showing how familiarity with attitudinal issues could increase later resistance to persuasion.
4. Hypothetico-deductive method
   Example: In this more formal method, the investigator combines a number of principles derived from previous research and, through logical deductive methods, arrives at a set of predictions. Hullian learning theory exemplifies this approach.
5. Functional or adaptive approach
   Example: The investigator considers a particular pattern of events and then generates the principles that must be operating in order for the event to occur. Matina Horner (1972) did this when she suggested that a "fear of success" keeps many people who have high achievement needs from actually meeting their goals.
6. Analyzing the practitioner's rule of thumb
   Example: Television commercials and magazine advertisements frequently show a celebrity praising a product. This observation, which suggests that advertisers believe that status sells products, could lead to a series of hypotheses about the effects of the communicator's status on attitude and behavior change.
7. Trying to account for conflicting results
   Example: Many people believe, and research often shows, that our first impressions of a person have the most lasting effect. Yet other research indicates that the most recent information carries the greatest weight. Research hypotheses have been developed to predict when "primacy" will be important and when "recency" will be important.
8. Accounting for exceptions to general findings
   Example: Most research shows that a performance by a woman will be rated less favorably than an equivalent performance by a man. Yet on a few occasions such devaluation will not occur (Taynor & Deaux, 1973). These exceptions to the rule provide an intriguing source of hypotheses.
9. Reducing observed complex relationships to simpler component relationships
   Example: The complex process of attitude change can be broken down into separate stages, as the investigator may form hypotheses about the initial reception of the message, the cognitive processing of the arguments, or the long-term retention of change.

able body of past research; the investigator builds on past theory and data to develop increasingly complex hypotheses. Other approaches begin from more direct observation of people's behavior, as the investigator tries to define the basic psychological processes that may underlie the observed events. The latter approach is seen in attempts to analyze the practitioner's rule of thumb (see no. 6 in Table 2-1).

Consider the door-to-door encyclopedia representative. You yourself may have been on the receiving end of such house calls. The seller customarily begins the pitch with a simple request. Having granted the sales representative five minutes of your time, you may find yourself two hours later still listening to a talk on the virtues of the books. Such an experience, annoying as it is at the time, could be the source of an experimental hypothesis if you were a social psychologist. In fact, research on this very issue has been conducted, and the findings have identified what is referred to, not inappropriately, as the foot-in-the-door effect. Social psychologists have learned that a large request is more likely to be granted if it is preceded by the granting of a small request than if no request precedes it (Freedman & Fraser, 1966).

This particular issue of compliance will be discussed at greater length in Chapter Eight. For the present, it serves to illustrate how mundane the sources of some experimental ideas can be.

Other hypotheses may be developed from much more sophisticated theoretical networks or from a large body of previous research. Some of the approaches that McGuire suggests deal with these more developed bases of hypothesis generation. The hypothetico-deductive method, for example, is perhaps best represented by Clark Hull's learning theory, which formulated numerous postulates. These postulates permitted the prediction of specific relationships, such as the relationship between level of hunger and speed of learning a response.

Each of the approaches that McGuire suggests can be used to develop a hypothesis. But once you have a hypothesis, how do you know if the idea is a good one? It has been said that "most of the knowledge and much of the genius of the research worker lie behind [the] selection of what is worth observing" (Beveridge, 1964, p. 103). Just how does the scientist decide what is worth observing? The social psychologist Bibb Latané suggests four criteria. First, the problem should be theoretically interesting; second, the problem should suggest an advance in methodology; third, a well-designed experiment should follow from the problem; and fourth, the issue should have social relevance (Hunt, 1985). Not all research can satisfy each of these criteria, but some does. For example, Latané and John Darley developed a very productive research program that investigated the conditions under which people are willing to help other people in emergencies. Prompted by a widely reported incident in New York in which many people witnessed a long-drawn-out murder but none called for help, Latané and Darley designed a set of research studies to answer the question "Why don't people help?" (Latané & Darley, 1970). Their work showed, among other things, that the presence of other people can diffuse the individual's sense of responsibility, making a victim less likely to receive help in a crowd. (Chapter Twelve will describe this area of research in more detail.) Latané and Darley's work addressed questions that have both theoretical and practical importance. At the same time, their work made methodological contributions to both laboratory and field research, and the experiments were unquestionably sound in their design.

As this example suggests, formulating a hypothesis and devising a means to test that hypothesis are closely linked processes. The hypothesis-generation phase provides the initial direction, but the latter stages of the research process are no less critical. Nor are they simple or automatic, as Box 2–1 illustrates.

Testing Hypotheses

There is no one right way to test a hypothesis. Social psychologists have developed a warehouse of methods, many of which may be appropriate for any single question. Every method has strengths and weaknesses, and the ultimate strategy of the scientist should

Box 2-1
If at first you don't succeed . . .

Research reports in professional journals often make the research process sound easy. Apparently the investigators came up with a good hypothesis, tested it, obtained interesting results, and then quickly published their findings. In truth, the course of research is not so smooth.

Alan Gross and Anthony Doob (1976) provide an interesting account of their attempts to test the frustration-aggression hypothesis in a natural setting. Though inexperienced, they decided to move outside the laboratory to see whether experiencing frustration leads people to become more aggressive. After considerable thought, they decided that traffic jams were a good source of frustration, and although they did not think it reasonable to cause a series of major traffic jams, it seemed possible to arrange for a single driver to stall a car at a traffic light. The honking that occurs on such occasions could serve as a likely measure of aggression—but what factors might influence the arousal of aggression? Various bumper stickers on the stalled car were one possibility; the number of people in the car was another. Finally Gross and Doob decided on the status of the car, suggesting that people would be less likely to honk at a high-status car than at a low-status car. For graduate students, finding a low-status car was no problem; a high-status car was harder to come by. A rented Chrysler proved to be the solution.

After a few more practical problems were encountered and solved, the field experiment was conducted. Data were collected and analyzed, and the statistical analyses showed that the data supported the initial hypothesis: people were less likely to honk at the driver of stalled high-status car. So far, so good. But when the report was written up and submitted to a journal, the editor of that journal found the study uninteresting. The editor of a second journal concurred. Fortunately, however, this study has a happy ending. On their third try, Doob and Gross had a positive response, and the study of horn honking now occupies a place in the social psychology literature (Doob & Gross, 1968).

---

be to test a single hypothesis through a diversity of methods, thereby increasing one's confidence in the validity of the hypothesis. Before delving into the characteristics of each method, however, let us consider how a single hypothesis might be tested in a variety of settings: the laboratory, the field, and across cultures.

The Hypothesis

The behavior of the individual in a group is one of the central issues of social psychology. Although the effects of a group are numerous, let us for the moment consider only one aspect: **deindividuation.** This term refers to a state of relative anonymity, in which the group member does not feel singled out or identifiable (Festinger, Pepitone, & Newcomb, 1952). In the late 19th century, Gustave LeBon (1896) observed crowd behavior and postulated a similar notion to explain why persons in a mob lose their sense of responsibility. From such general observations, then, it is possible to develop a specific hypothesis concerning the effects of anonymity on subsequent behavior. Let us focus on the following hypothesis: An increase in anonymity will result in greater frequency of antisocial behavior.

Formulating such a hypothesis represents the first stage of the research process. The next step is to develop a means of testing the validity of that hypothesis. As we noted before, a single hypothesis can be tested in many ways. To demonstrate the truth of this assertion, we will describe three different studies in three different settings, each of which was designed to test the relationship between anonymity and antisocial behavior.

A Laboratory Investigation

In a psychology laboratory at New York University, Philip Zimbardo (1970) conducted a study in which four students were asked to share the responsibility for giving another student a set of electric shocks, under the pretext that the experimenter was interested in people's reactions to the pain of another person. In fact, however, the experimenter was interested in the level of aggressive behavior (as measured by the duration of electric shocks given) as a function of anonymity. (We will discuss the issue of deception later in this chapter.) To vary the conditions of anonymity, Zimbardo dressed half of his subjects in hoods. These students never gave their names, and they performed the experiment in the dark. The other half of the subjects in this experiment had their individuality emphasized: they were greeted by name, were given large name tags, and got to know one another on a first-name basis. Subjects in both groups were free to give as much or as little shock to the other student as they wished.

In this laboratory setting, the deindividuation hypothesis was confirmed: subjects in the anonymity condition gave more shock to the other student than did subjects in the individuated condition. Although the laboratory has been the setting most frequently used by social psychologists to test their hypotheses, it is certainly not the only setting available. Let us consider two other settings that were used to test the same hypothesis.

A Field Investigation

The social psychologist who moves outside the laboratory to test a hypothesis is basically concerned with increasing the natural quality of the situation: the naturalness of the behavior, the setting, and the treatment (Tunnell, 1977). Often the investigator's role in such a study is simply to observe what occurs, with little or no intervention. To test the hypothesis concerning deindividuation, one might therefore look for natural settings that would differ in the degree of anonymity they provided. We might expect anonymity to be much more pervasive in a large urban center than in a small university town, where people are more likely to be acquainted. Thus our hypothesis would predict greater antisocial behavior in the large city than in the small town.

To test the deindividuation hypothesis in these circumstances, Zimbardo and Fraser bought a used car and left it on a busy street adjoining the Bronx campus of New York University. At the same time, a similar car was left on a street near the Stanford University campus in Palo Alto, California. Within 26 hours the car in New York was stripped of battery, radiator, air cleaner, radio antenna, windshield wipers, side chrome, all four hubcaps, a set of jumper cables, a can of car wax, a gas can, and the one tire worth taking. In Palo Alto, meanwhile, the second

Table 2-2 Relationship between changes in physical appearance before battle and extremity of aggression in warfare among 23 linguistically and geographically independent cultures

Aggression	Deindividuation	
	Changed Appearance	Unchanged Appearance
High	12	1
Low	3	7

NOTE: $N = 23$; $\chi^2 = 7.12$, $df = 1$, $p < .01$.

car remained unharmed. In fact, one day when it rained, a passerby lowered the hood so the motor would not get waterlogged!

Although automobile-parts thieves and hooded students are obviously quite different, from the point of testing a hypothesis the conclusion remains the same: the greater the anonymity, the greater the frequency of antisocial behavior.

A Cross-Cultural Investigation

What is true in industrialized countries may not be true in other parts of the world. Consequently, experimenters who want to determine the universality of their hypotheses often look to other societies as a means of testing their ideas. One source for such tests is the Human Relations Area Files (HRAF), a collection of information assembled by ethnographers on more than 200 cultures throughout the world.

Robert Watson, Jr. (1973) used the material available in these files to test the anonymity/antisocial-behavior hypothesis in yet another context. He assumed that the extensive use of masks and of face and body paint by warriors serves as a guarantee of anonymity. Consequently, he hypothesized that societies in which use of paint and disguise was extensive would have a tradition of more aggressive and ferocious warfare than societies in which disguise was less frequent. To test the hypothesis, Watson simply categorized societies described in the HRAF on two dimensions: intensity of warfare (as indicated by reports of such practices as torture, sacrifice of prisoners, headhunting, and fighting to the death in all battles) and the presence or absence of paints and disguise as a prelude to battle. Once again the hypothesis concerning anonymity and aggression was supported: those societies that engaged in more aggressive forms of warfare were also more likely to don heavy disguises than were the more peaceful cultures (see Table 2-2).

It is more difficult to determine the direction of cause and effect in Watson's study than in the laboratory experiment, for example. The **correlational method** (the study of the interrelationship between two sets of events) may tell us that two factors are associated, but we don't generally know which factor causes which. It could be, as hypothesized, that anonymity leads to aggression. It is also possible, however, that aggressive people are more likely to seek anonymity. Or, as a third possibility, perhaps some other factor, such as climate, leads both to aggression and to a desire for anonymity. The experimenter in the laboratory, in contrast, first manipulated anonymity and then measured aggression, so that we are quite certain which factor came first and hence is the cause.

Choice of a Method

The three studies discussed above show that there are many ways and places to test a single hypothesis. Given such abundance, how does the investigator decide on one way to test a hypothesis? There are many reasons for any particular choice, including convenience, a particular investigator's preference, and the history of past research in the area. In actual practice, most social scientists use a variety of methods as they seek to understand a particular phenomenon. Whatever the choice, the investigator must carefully consider the strengths and weaknesses of each method as they may affect the outcome. Let us now look more carefully at each of the methods.

Major Methods of Social-Psychological Research

Social psychologists have developed an extensive repertoire of methods to help them answer questions about human behavior. We will discuss seven of these methods: laboratory experiments, field experiments, quasi-experimental research, field studies, archival research, simulation and role playing, and surveys and interviews. In each case, we will consider both the advantages and disadvantages of the method.

The Laboratory Experiment

Zimbardo's study of the effect of anonymity on students' willingness to shock another student is one example of a laboratory experiment. As another example, consider the following study by John Darley and Paget Gross (1983). Princeton University students volunteered to take part in a study that allegedly would determine the reliability of forms that elementary school teachers could use to determine appropriate programs for individual pupils. The Princeton students were asked to observe a videotape of a nine-year-old girl named Hannah and then to make some judgments about her capabilities. Approximately half of the students first saw a scene of Hannah in a home environment that was decidedly upper middle class—a suburban neighborhood with large five- and six-bedroom homes, a modern school, and tree-lined parks. These subjects were told that Hannah's parents were both college graduates and currently employed as professionals, he as an attorney and she as a freelance writer. The remaining subjects in these experiments were given a different impression of Hannah's environment. A run-down urban neighborhood was shown, the schoolyard was asphalt enclosed by a chain-link fence, and the parents were described as people of little education who worked as a meat packer and a seamstress.

In such laboratory experiments the researcher's aim is to test the effects of one or more independent variables on one or more dependent variables. **Independent variables** are those factors that are controlled or arranged by the experimenter. Ideally, they are independent of all sources of variation except those controlled by the experimenter (Aronson, Brewer, & Carlsmith, 1985). **Dependent variables** are the subject's behaviors that are observed or recorded by the experimenter; the form or pattern of those behaviors is presumably dependent on or caused by the events that have preceded them.

In Darley and Gross's experiment, the expectancy in regard to Hannah's ability was an independent variable. This expectancy, established by the videotape and the supplemental information about the parents, was either positive (the first description) or negative (the second description). This experiment included a second independent variable as well. Before the subjects made their judgments, half of those in each expectancy condition were given additional performance information in the form of a 12-minute videotape of Hannah performing a series of achievement-test tasks. The other half of the subjects (again, half in the positive expectancy condition and half in the negative expectancy condition) made their judgments without the benefit of this additional information on Hannah's performance. The dependent variables in this experiment included several questionnaire ratings of Hannah's ability, motivation, and academic potential.

What did Darley and Gross learn from their experiment? People who had been given positive expectancies about the child's performance *and* had had the opportunity to view a tape that could be used to support their expectancies rated Hannah more favorably than did people who had been given negative expectancies, even though both groups had seen the same taped performance. Without the additional "evidence" provided by the performance tape, however, the two groups of subjects did not differ in their judgments, possibly because they were unwilling to make such judgments on obviously inadequate evidence.

Characteristic of the laboratory experiment is the investigator's ability to control the independent variables. Indeed, this aspect of control is one of the most important features of the laboratory experiment because it allows the investigator to draw conclusions about the cause-and-effect relationship. Darley and Gross specifically designed the information their subjects received. Hannah was portrayed by the same child in all of the videotapes, so that the child's appearance did not vary in any particular in the two experimental conditions. Furthermore, the fact that the videotaped performance sequence was identical in the positive and negative expectancy conditions allowed the experimenters to conclude that subjects were indeed reading into the film what they expected to see, rather than responding simply to what was there. Darley and Gross could exercise similar control of the dependent variables, asking the subjects precisely what they wanted to know about the judgments people will make in such a situation.

In addition to control, the laboratory experiment offers another important advantage: the ability to assign subjects randomly to conditions. If investigators are to be able to draw firm conclusions about cause and effect, they must make sure that the pattern of results is not due to some systematic differences between the groups being compared. By randomly assigning subjects to either the positive or negative expectancy condition, Darley and Gross could control for the possibility that some people are predisposed to favor members of a particular social class. On the average, this procedure of **randomization** distributes subject characteristics evenly across the various experimental conditions.

One other characteristic of the laboratory experiment should be mentioned—the **manipulation check.** Although experimenters are able to control the independent variable, it is still important for them to be sure that the subjects in the experiment perceive the manipulation as it is intended to be perceived. Darley and Gross, for example, asked their subjects to identify Hannah's socioeconomic class in order to be sure that the subjects had perceived the difference between the two expectancy conditions.

Advantages. The major advantages of the laboratory experiment have been summarized above. Principal among them is the ability of the experimenter to control the independent variables and to assign subjects randomly to conditions. These two capabilities provide some basis for drawing conclusions about cause and effect. Furthermore, the laboratory allows the investigator to "sort out" factors—to simplify the more complex events of the natural world by breaking them down into their component parts.

Other advantages of the laboratory experiment are somewhat more mundane, convenience being one of the major ones. Most psychological laboratories are located on university campuses, where there is an abundant supply of students to serve as subjects and where the experimenter has easy access to facilities. As procedures at many universities make a "subject pool" readily available, the investigator is spared the difficulty of recruiting subjects individually.

Disadvantages. Although the laboratory experiment has many advantages, it has some substantial disadvantages as well. In recent years these disadvantages have become a subject of considerable debate. Three issues of concern have been the possible irrelevance of the laboratory setting, the reactions of subjects to the laboratory setting, and the possible influence of experimenters on their results. (Questions of deception and ethics, though focused primarily on certain laboratory experiments, are not exclusive to this method and will be discussed in more general terms in a later section of this chapter.)

The issue of irrelevance concerns the artificiality of the laboratory setting and the fact that many of the situations created in the laboratory bear little direct relation to the situations a person encounters in real life. Aronson, Brewer, and Carlsmith (1985) have distinguished between **experimental realism** and **mundane realism.** *Experimental realism* refers to the amount of impact inherent in the situation—that is, the extent to which the subject is involved in the situation and paying attention to it. *Mundane realism* refers to the similarity of the situation to real-world events. Aronson and his colleagues contend that in the laboratory one can devise situations that have impact and that evoke valid psychological processes (experimental realism), even if the situation itself does not look like the real world (mundane realism). Zimbardo's laboratory study of deindividuation, for example, undoubtedly aroused a considerable sense of involvement in its subjects, even if, because few of us sit around in hooded robes, its mundane realism was low. Yet despite the persuasiveness of these arguments, it remains true that many laboratory tasks seem suspiciously artificial and that their **external validity** has not been demonstrated. *External validity* refers to the "generalizability" of research findings to other populations, treatment variables, and measurement variables (Campbell &

Stanley, 1966). Although this criterion must be applied to all social-psychological studies, it is in the case of laboratory experiments that its applicability has been questioned most vigorously. Thus, although college students' evaluations of the performance of another student on an object-perception task may parallel the judgments of a supervisor rating male and female employees in an organization, we cannot be absolutely certain that the situations are sufficiently similar to ensure external validity.

Indeed, critics have argued that reliance on college students as subjects in academic laboratories can seriously distort our understanding of human behavior (Sears, 1986). Compared to the general population, college students may be more cognitive, more concerned with material self-interests, less crystallized in their attitudes, and responsive to particular situational pressures that are not likely to bother other people. Very different people in very different settings need to be studied, Sears suggests, if we are to understand the full range of human experience.

A second criticism of the laboratory experiment focuses on the reactions of subjects to the laboratory setting. These reactions may involve **demand characteristics** and **evaluation apprehension**. The first term refers to the fact that the experimental setting may evoke certain demands—that is, feelings on the part of subjects that they ought to act as they think the experimenter wants them to act (Orne, 1969). For example, if you were in a psychology experiment in which somebody asked you to indicate your attitude toward nuclear disarmament, then asked you to listen to a speech in which nuclear disarmament was advocated, and then once again asked for your attitude, you might suspect that the experimenter was concerned with attitude change. A subject in this situation who wanted to please the experimenter or do the "right thing" might well indicate on paper a change of attitude that had not really occurred. Such a response would reflect the influence of the demand characteristics of the situation rather than the influence of the experimenter's intended variable.

Evaluation apprehension refers to a subject's concerns about being observed and judged in the laboratory setting. Some people are afraid to be studied—perhaps the psychologist will discover that they're "crazy" or "stupid." Because subjects come to a laboratory experiment knowing that the investigator is interested in some aspect of their behavior, they may try to present themselves in a favorable light. (This specific problem is related to the more general issue of impression management, which will be discussed in Chapter Three.) Again the issue is the veridicality of subjects' behavior; that is, are the subjects acting as they normally would in such a situation, or are they modifying their behavior *because of* the laboratory setting?

In an interesting experiment that examined the problem of evaluation apprehension (Sigall, Aronson, & Van Hoose, 1970), subjects were faced with a choice: they could cooperate with the experimenter by conveying negative information about themselves or they could reject the experimenter's demands and look good. Most subjects chose to look good. Their choice points out the importance of self-presentation strategies and also suggests that the experimenter has only limited power to elicit behaviors that conflict with the subject's own aspirations.

A final criticism of the laboratory experiment concerns **experimenter expectancies** (Rosenthal, 1966). It has been shown in a variety of situations that an experimenter, knowing the hypothesis of the study, can unwittingly influence the results of the study. In tests involving rats running down an alley, for example, Rosenthal and his colleagues found that experimenters who believed their rats were the faster group obtained results that supported their belief—even though their rats were in fact no more predisposed to speed than the other group of rats. The experimenter's expectation is even more likely to influence results when human interaction is involved. Through vocal inflection or subtle facial movements, an experimenter may unconsciously influence the subject's behavior and thus bias the results. In this instance, we are questioning the **internal validity** of the experiment (Campbell & Stanley, 1966): are the results due to the independent variables that were manipulated or to some other, uncontrolled element in the situation?

Social psychologists can generally find ways to avoid these potential threats. Instructions can be tape-recorded in advance, for example, to ensure that they are exactly the same for all subjects. Other effective techniques include the use of a "blind" experimenter, one who is not informed of the experimental hypothesis and therefore is unlikely to bias the results in any systematic way.

In summary, the laboratory experiment offers the most precise control of variables and the greatest ability to isolate those factors that are believed to be important, uncontaminated by extraneous variables and competing events. At the same time, however, the artificiality of the laboratory setting can create another set of problems that reduce the correspondence between laboratory-obtained findings and real-life behavior.

The Field Experiment

It's Saturday evening, you've been studying all day, and the urge for a pizza grows strong. You call your favorite pizza parlor, order a large pizza with everything on it but anchovies, and are told that it will be delivered in 45 minutes. Thirty minutes later your phone rings. Delivery will be delayed, you are told, because the driver got mixed up on one of his deliveries. When the pizza finally arrives, what kind of tip will you give the driver?

This scenario, perhaps not unfamiliar to you, was part of a recent field experiment by Clive Seligman and his colleagues (Seligman, Finegan, Hazlewood, & Wilkinson, 1985). Thirty customers of a local pizza parlor were told that the delivery of their pizzas would be delayed. Thirty other customers, randomly selected, were called and told that delivery would be early. The reasons given for the change in delivery time varied: in some cases the driver was credited with being ahead of schedule or blamed for being behind; in other cases such circumstances as traffic conditions were said to be the cause. What kinds of tips did the driver receive in each of these situations? Figure 2–1 shows the results. Tips were not affected by delivery time when the change was attributed to

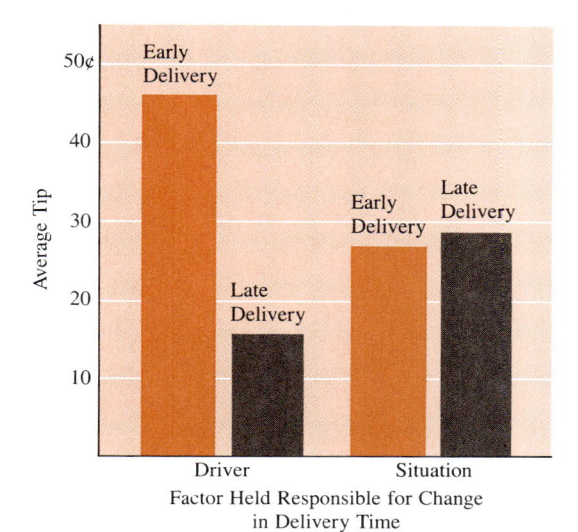

Figure 2-1 The effect of explanations given for early and late deliveries on driver's tips: A field experiment

situational factors, but the driver who was held to be responsible for the time change either benefited or suffered, depending on the direction of the change.

This study is a typical field experiment. In the field as in the laboratory, the experimenter has control of the independent variables and the random assignment of subjects to conditions. In this study there were two independent variables: time of delivery and reason for the change. Customers were randomly assigned to conditions, and to control for bias, the delivery person did not know which condition a particular customer was assigned to.

Advantages. The advantages of the field experiment are probably obvious. Experimenters who focus on behavior in a natural setting can be reasonably confident of the external validity of their findings. Furthermore, because subjects are generally unaware of their status as subjects, the problems of reactivity and the subjects' desire to be seen in a positive light are eliminated. In addition, because control over the independent variable and principles of randomization are maintained, the field experi-

ment allows the same possibilities for conclusions about cause and effect as the laboratory experiment does.

Disadvantages. Although the field experiment may seem to offer an ideal combination of the strict rules of experimentation and the realism of natural behavior settings, it too has some disadvantages. These potential problems concern the nature of the independent variable, the nature of the dependent variable, the ethics of the experiment, and the practical difficulties involved.

Because the experimenter is working in a complex natural setting where many events may be occurring simultaneously, the independent variable in the study must be fairly obvious. Suppose you wanted to see whether people would help a person who dropped some packages. If the packages were dropped in the middle of a crowded rock concert, the incident would probably go unnoticed by the majority of people in the audience. Thus the investigator conducting a field experiment must be sure that the independent variable is sufficiently strong to make an impact on potential subjects. Otherwise, a failure to respond will be difficult to interpret.

The dependent variable in a field experiment must also be selected carefully. The experimenters must be able to observe the dependent-variable behavior readily and judge it reliably. In the pizza delivery experiment, it was very easy for the experimenters to record each customer's tip. If they had been interested in more subtle facial reactions that might indicate satisfaction with the delivery, their task would have been much more difficult. Because of such difficulties, the dependent variables in field experiments tend to be rather simple behaviors, frequently scored as either present or absent. (We will discuss the statistical limits of such measures later in this chapter.)

An additional problem in field experimentation concerns ethics. Is it reasonable for a social psychologist to involve individuals in an experiment without their knowledge or permission? This question has been discussed extensively (Aronson, Brewer, & Carlsmith, 1985; Kelman, 1968; Selltiz, Wrightsman, & Cook, 1976). Although there is no simple answer, most social scientists would agree that field experiments are reasonable if the independent variables are normal occurrences in a person's daily life and if the setting is a public one. The less the experimenter's intervention inconveniences the subjects or involves them emotionally, the less serious the ethics question becomes. An experiment in which someone drops packages on the street raises fewer ethical questions than one in which people are accosted by a stranger who is apparently having an epileptic seizure. The latter situation would probably be ruled out by most investigators, whereas the former would be ethically acceptable. Many situations, however, are not so easily evaluated. On each occasion the investigator must carefully consider the harm or inconvenience that an experimental intervention could cause.

Finally, the field experiment often poses practical problems. In contrast to the laboratory scientist, the investigator in the field has no control over the majority of events in the environment; unexpected events may reduce or destroy the effectiveness of the manipulation. A pizza parlor may have more than one person making deliveries, a major fire may prevent any driver from getting through, or the management may refuse to cooperate. A field experimenter must study the setting carefully before the research begins and must be aware of as many contingencies as possible. Often the experimenter must also get permission from store owners or from the local police force beforehand to ensure that the events to be staged will not be misinterpreted and will not violate local laws.

In summary, the field experiment has many advantages, combining control and randomization principles with a realistic setting. At the same time, because the field experimenter cannot control the environment, the precision of laboratory experiments cannot be attained.

Quasi-Experimental Research

Not all patients experience the same outcome from the same medical procedures. Patients whose kidneys fail to function normally face several treatment options, one of which is renal transplantation from a cadaver. For some patients this treatment succeeds; for others it does not. Interested in how one's own experience affects one's judgments of other events, Clark McCauley and his colleagues (McCauley, Durham, Copley, & Johnson, 1985) asked kidney patients to estimate the general survival rates of people who have had kidney transplant operations. They focused on two groups of patients: patients in one group had received donor kidneys successfully, while the other group had been returned to kidney dialysis because the transplant operation failed. A key dependent measure in this study was the patient's response to the following question: "What percentage of kidney transplants from an unrelated person (cadaver) are functioning successfully one year after the transplant operation?" The two groups of patients differed markedly in their answers. On average, successfully treated patients estimated that 53% of transplants were successful, while the unsuccessfully treated patients guessed a more pessimistic 29%. Thus one's own experience does affect one's judgments of population trends.

This study is an example of quasi-experimental research. The investigator who engages in quasi-experimental research does not have full experimental control over the independent variables—in this case, who receives a kidney transplant—but does have a choice about how, when, and for whom the dependent variable is measured. Generally, such experiments involve behavior in a natural setting and focus on the effect of intervention in a system of ongoing behavior. Sometimes the intervention results from a policy decision by a government agency. In other cases, the intervention may be a natural disaster, such as a flood, earthquake, or tornado. A power blackout in New York or Chicago, for example, could serve as the independent variable in a study of reactions to stressful events, as could the increase in radiation levels in northern Europe following the nuclear disaster at Chernobyl. The experimenter would have no control over the independent variable, but he or she could carefully select a set of dependent variables to measure the effects of stress.

Advantages. One unique advantage of quasi-experimental research conducted in a natural setting is that it allows us to study very strong variables that cannot be manipulated or controlled by an experimenter. In the wake of a tornado, for example, the investigator can study reactions to distressing events much more consequential than anything that could be produced in the laboratory. Often, too, quasi-experimental research deals with policy decisions that have consequences for very large numbers of people. The broad impact of such decisions gives the research findings a measure of external validity rarely matched in the more limited laboratory or field experiment.

Disadvantages. Because the investigator has no control over the independent variable in quasi-experimental research, it is always possible that other uncontrolled variables are affecting the dependent-variable behavior. In the study of kidney patients, for example, it is possible that certain differences among patients influenced both their judgments of events and their responsiveness to their operations. Random assignment of subjects to conditions can rarely be assumed in the quasi-experimental design. However, there are a number of statistical procedures by which investigators can increase their confidence in the validity of the proposed cause-and-effect relationship (see Campbell & Stanley, 1966; Cook & Campbell, 1979).

When a natural disaster is the independent variable, the investigator faces the additional problem of preparation. Natural disasters usually arrive with little or no warning, thus giving the investigator little time to design a study and to prepare appropriate measuring instruments. Often such research must be done on the run. Furthermore, the arbitrariness of events in the quasi-experimental world does not allow the experimenter to vary factors according to any theoretical model. It is difficult to predict how people will respond to stress, for example, before one knows the magnitude of the stressful event. As it is clearly impossible for experimenters to control such a variable, they must accept the level of stress inherent in the situation they find.

In summary, quasi-experimental research offers some clear advantages to investigators in the impact and complexity of situations that can be studied; in addition, it allows investigators to study some situations that cannot be studied in any other way. At the same time, experimenters have less control in this situation than in the true experiment, and they must interpret results more cautiously.

The Field Study

A 12′ × 57′ steel cylinder, placed 205 feet below the surface of the Pacific Ocean, provided the site for an exotic field study by Roland Radloff and Robert Helmreich (1968). This cylinder, capable of sleeping ten persons, was named SEALAB II and was designed by the U.S. Navy to study human capabilities of living and working underwater (see Figure 2–2). Radloff and Helmreich were interested in the effects of psychological stress on human behavior, and they obtained the permission of navy officials to observe the aquanauts in their undersea world.

The conditions in SEALAB II were undoubtedly stressful. In addition to the potential danger of a ruptured wall or broken porthole, the living conditions themselves were unpleasant. The space inside the capsule was extremely confined and crowded, and there was little privacy. To make matters worse, the habitat rested unevenly on the ocean floor at a 6° angle, causing drawers to slide open or shut and objects to slide off tables. In addition, the aquanauts were expected to make a series of diving expeditions outside the capsule, where they were subjected to the typical hazards of deep-sea diving at 200 feet.

In their intense study of this small group of men, Radloff and Helmreich collected hundreds of pieces of information. Some of this information consisted of objective behavioral measures—for example, number of excursions made outside the capsule, number of telephone calls made to the surface, and types of activities conducted within SEALAB. Other dependent measures were collected by questionnaires that measured various personality characteristics and moods before and after dives. Still other information consisted of such background data as birth order, marital status, age, and years of diving experience.

These measures enabled the investigators to gain a wealth of information about the behavior of groups of men in a stressful situation and the factors that may predict success or failure in attempts to adjust

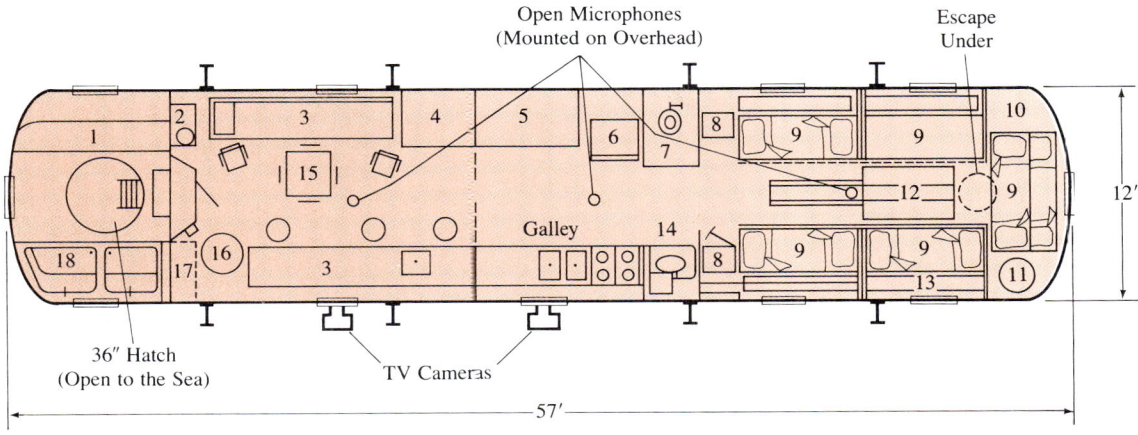

SEALAB II. Interior Arrangement: Top Removed—Looking Down.

1. Swim Gear Stow
2. TV
3. Lab Bench
4. Fan Room
5. Electric Power and Light
6. Reefer
7. Head
8. Locker
9. 2-Berths
10. Stowage
11. CO_2 Can
12. Table
13. Bench
14. Lavatory
15. Table and Chairs
16. Water Heater
17. Can Stowage
18. Tub and Shower

Figure 2–2 Diagram of SEALAB II

to such a situation. They found, for example, that men born in small towns adjusted better to the SEALAB environment than men raised in urban areas. At the group level, they observed an increase in camaraderie as the test period wore on.

Not all field studies are conducted in such exotic locales. Barker and Schoggen (1973), for example, focused their study on the residents of a small midwestern town, population 830, and compared behaviors observed there to those seen in an English village of similar size. A major goal of this research was to make a complete classification of each town's behavior settings, defined as public places or occasions that evoke their own typical patterns of behavior. Theodore Newcomb (1961) conducted a year-long field study of students at Bennington College in Vermont, focusing on the change in students' values and attitudes from the beginning of the year to the end.

Most field studies are characterized by their in-depth consideration of a limited group of people. The investigator plays a more reactive role in this setting than in the field experiment. Rather than manipulating some aspect of the environment and observing the changes that occur, the investigator who engages in a field study records as much information as possible about the situation without altering it in any substantial way. People in the environment are usually aware of the investigator's presence and the general purpose of the investigation. Many investigators become **participant observers**—that is, they actively engage in the activities of the group while at the same time maintaining records of the group members' behaviors.

Observation is the key element of the field study. Because people-watching is a fairly common activity for most of us, it is often hard to appreciate how difficult systematic scientific observation can be. First, one must become very familiar with the environment and aware of the kinds of behaviors that are most likely to occur. Next, one must decide which types of behavior are to be recorded. For example, should one focus on easily recorded behaviors, such as (in the case of the SEALAB study) telephone calls made from the underwater laboratory or excursions taken outside the laboratory? Or is one interested in charting the locations frequented and the number of people in each location? Or is the interest in smaller units of behavior, such as facial expressions and vocal pitch? The choice of one or more of these categories depends on the questions that the investigator has posed. Although investigators do not purposely manipulate conditions in field studies, they are no less likely than experimenters in other settings to have a specific set of questions formulated in advance of the actual study. Without such questions, field observation becomes mired in a hopeless array of competing events.

Once categories of behavior are selected for observation, the investigator must devise specific methods of recording the desired information. Finally, the observer must conduct a series of preliminary investigations to determine the **reliability** of the measures. In other words, it must be demonstrated that a series of different observers watching the same event and using the same methods will code the behavior in the same way. Without such reliability, a coding system merely reflects one observer's biases and cannot become the basis of a scientific statement.

Advantages. The major advantage of the field study is its realism. The focus of the study is on events as they normally occur in a real-life setting. Furthermore, because most field studies take place over an extended period, they provide information about the sequence and development of behaviors that cannot be gained in the one-shot observation typical of field and laboratory experiments. Additionally, the duration of the field study generally allows collection of several types of dependent measures. The study of aquanauts, for example, yielded observations, responses to questionnaires, and demographic information. Such a variety of measures, when they are directed at the assessment of a limited number of concepts, gives us greater confidence in the conclusions than we could derive from any one measure taken alone.

Disadvantages. Although well-conducted field studies furnish a wealth of data, the lack of control in such settings can be a problem. Because there is no controlled independent variable, it is difficult to form conclusions about cause and effect. Although some statistical techniques can be useful in the attempt to distinguish cause from effect, the process is more difficult here than in the controlled experimental design.

A second potential problem in the field study is the subjects' awareness of the investigator's observations. When subjects know they are being observed, their behavior may be reactive—that is, influenced by the process of observation. Most experienced observers believe that in the course of a long-term field study the subjects become indifferent to the observer's presence, but the problem remains a serious one in briefer studies.

In summary, the field study allows the investigator to study intensively a series of events in a real-life setting. Although field studies are not always the best means of testing particular experimental

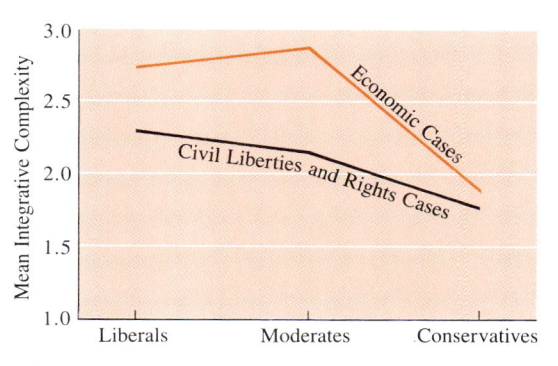

Figure 2–3 Mean integrative complexity of U.S. Supreme Court justices

hypotheses, they may serve as a rich source of information that can provide the basis for more stringent experimental tests.

Archival Research

Although Supreme Court justices may make every effort to be objective in their rulings, they are human like the rest of us, and their opinions are influenced by their personal values and preferences. Individuals vary in their integrative complexity—the degree to which they consider multiple dimensions of issues and a variety of evidence in arriving at judgments. Philip Tetlock and his colleagues (Tetlock, Bernzweig, & Gallant, 1985) were curious as to whether the political stances of judges—whether liberal, moderate, or conservative—were related to the complexity of their judicial decisions. To answer this question, they studied the verbatim records of judicial opinions written by justices on the U.S. Supreme Court between 1946 and 1978. In order to get a broad perspective they selected two kinds of cases, those dealing with civil liberties and with economic issues, and they used an accepted coding procedure to assess integrative complexity. They then compared the complexity scores of justices in the three political groupings. As Figure 2–3 shows, the opinions of justices who were politically liberal or moderate revealed greater complexity than those of conservative justices—but only when economic issues were at stake. In the area of civil liberties and rights, the written opinions of justices of all political persuasions were equally complex.

Archival research refers to the analysis of any existing records that have been produced or maintained by persons or organizations other than the experimenter. In other words, the original reason for collecting the records was not a social-psychological experiment. Government documents, such as Supreme Court decisions, are one example. Other sources of material include newspaper reports, records of private organizations, books and magazines, folk stories, personal letters, and speeches by public figures. The study of the use of war paint and societal aggression discussed earlier provides another example of archival research. In this case, the material in the Human Relations Area Files was originally compiled by social scientists (generally anthropologists) but not for the purpose of testing the hypothesis of deindividuation and aggression.

Advantages. Archival research has a number of advantages. First of all, it allows the investigator to test hypotheses over a wider range of time and societies than would otherwise be possible. Many records date back for centuries, a period of time beyond the scope of the other methods we have discussed. A hypothesis shown to be valid in several cultures and historical periods can be accepted with much greater confidence as a description of human behavior in general than can one that has been tested only in a single society at one point in time.

A second advantage of the archival method is that it uses **unobtrusive measures**—measures that did not cause reactivity in the participants at the time they were collected (Webb, Campbell, Schwartz, & Sechrest, 1966). Because the information used in archival research was originally collected for some other purpose, there is little or no chance that demand characteristics or evaluation apprehension will be problems for the present investigator.

Disadvantages. Although people engaged in archival research do not collect the data personally and thus are spared the problems of reactivity, they may have difficulty locating the kind of data they need to test a hypothesis. Not being able to design the dependent measures, they find themselves at the mercy of the people who collected the data. Sometimes, of course, creativity and ingenuity help investigators to locate the kinds of data they need; in other cases, however, missing or inaccurate records prevent an adequate experimental test. Even if the material is available, it is sometimes difficult to categorize it in a way that will yield an answer to the research question. Careful methods of content analysis must be developed for material that is nonquantitative, much as categories are developed for observational research. Such procedures are time-consuming, although the development of computer programs has provided a welcome assist in many instances.

In summary, archival research offers the investigator tremendous opportunities to examine data from a wide range of times and places. Although reliance on data that were collected for another purpose may cause problems for the investigator, the appeal of archival research, particularly when it is used in conjunction with other research methods, is strong.

Simulation and Role Playing

One of the most dramatic studies in social psychology is the prison **simulation** experiment (see Photo 2–1) conducted at Stanford University by Phillip Zimbardo and his colleagues (Haney, Banks, & Zimbardo, 1973). The simulation began with wailing police sirens as nine young men were picked up at their homes, spread-eagled and frisked, handcuffed, taken to the police station and booked, and finally driven blindfolded to a "prison" in the basement of the Stanford psychology building. There three other young men dressed as guards supervised the "prisoners'" activities in a small area of the building that had been outfitted with typical prison cells, a small "yard," and even a solitary-confinement "hole."

The subjects in this research project were college students who had answered a newspaper ad for volunteers to take part in a psychological study of prison life. All applicants were screened before acceptance, and those selected were judged to be the most stable, most mature, and least antisocial of the volunteers. All of those selected agreed to serve as either guards or prisoners and were randomly assigned to one of the two roles by the experimenter. Conditions at the Stanford University "prison" were made as realistic as possible. Prisoners were referred to only by number; their meals were bland and their toilet visits were supervised; they were assigned to work shifts and were lined up three times a day for a count. The guards were allowed to devise most of their own rules for running the prison, although neither punishment nor physical aggression was permitted. The project was scheduled to run for two weeks.

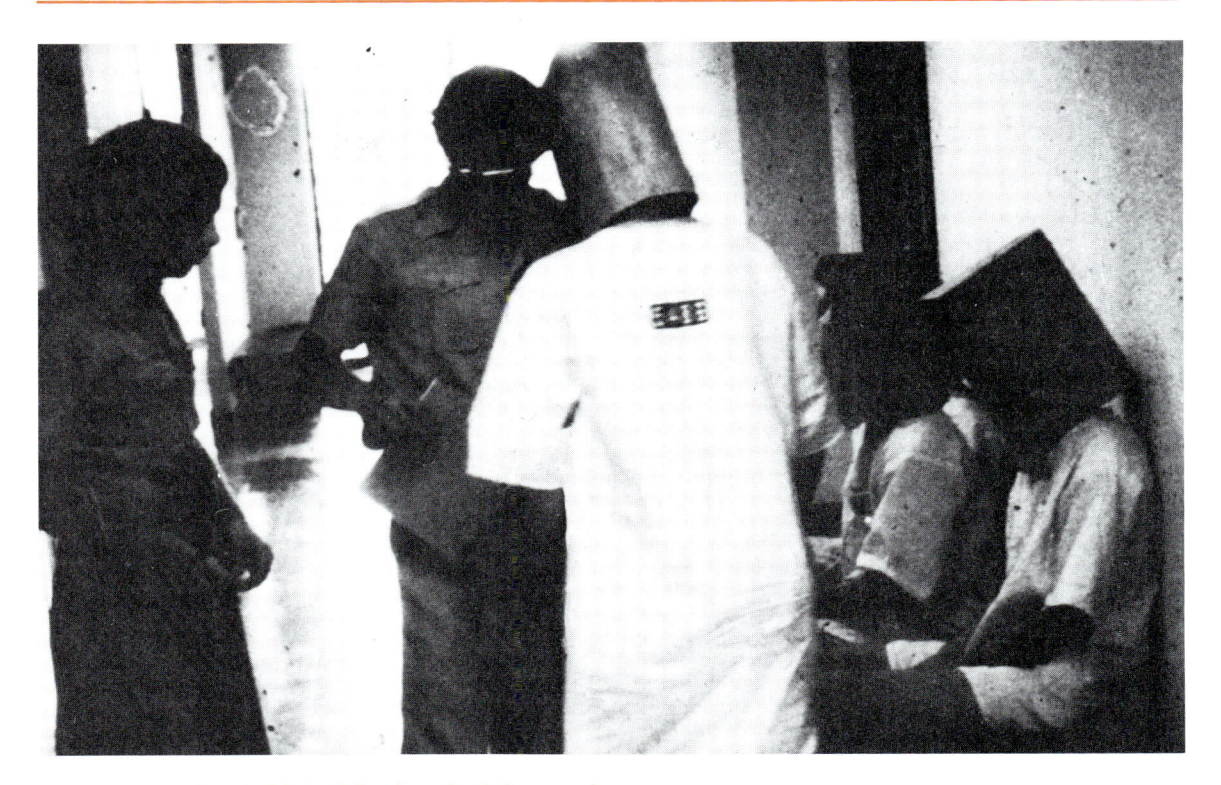

Photo 2–1 Subjects in Zimbardo's prison simulation experiment

The experimenters maintained constant observation of the situation by means of audio- and videotape equipment, and they administered a series of questionnaire measures as well. Their observations prompted them to terminate the intended two-week simulation study abruptly at the end of six days.

Within that six-day period, the behavior of the college men had degenerated. Guards increasingly enjoyed their power; they issued arbitrary commands to do pushups, for example, and refused requests to go to the toilet. Prisoners lapsed into depression and helplessness and began to develop symptoms of both physical and emotional distress. It was clear to the experimenters that the reality of a prison had indeed been created, and the situation was too dangerous to continue. After terminating the experiment, the researchers held several sessions with the participants to deal with their emotional reactions to the experience, and they maintained contact with each student for a year after the study to ensure that the negative effects of the prison simulation did not persist.

Not all simulation studies are so dramatic. Subjects may simply be brought to a bare room, given a description of an experimental setting, and asked to act as if they were in the real situation. In this case, the participants in the simulation play the roles of subjects rather than such dramatic roles as prisoners and guards. Somewhere between these two extremes are studies that simulate international decision making, in which subjects are given a large playing board and asked to make political and economic decisions for imaginary countries (Streufert, Castore, & Kliger, 1967). In still another form of simulation, computer programs are developed to model some aspect of behavior, and hundreds or thousands of hypothetical subjects (or computer runs) may be used to test a hypothesis.

Although simulation studies take many forms, all are designed to imitate some aspect of a real-world situation in order to increase our understanding of psychological processes.

Advantages. The success of a simulation or role-play study depends greatly on the degree of involvement that the experimental setting can engender (Geller, 1978; Greenwood, 1983). If the subjects get deeply involved in the setting, then the simulation may well approximate the real-life conditions that it intends to match. Furthermore, because participants are fully informed of the purposes of the study in advance, they basically take on the role of co-investigator, a role that is both ethically and humanistically more satisfying in many respects than the more typical experimental subject role, in which the subject is unaware of many of the experimenter's intentions (Kelman, 1968). An additional advantage of the simulation is that it may allow the investigator to study in the laboratory phenomena and situations that are difficult to study in the real world. It is difficult for social scientists to gain access to prisons or to negotiations between warring countries, for example, but they can simulate such situations in the laboratory or on the computer and enjoy the additional advantages of experimental control of variables and random assignment of subjects.

Disadvantages. In spite of their advantages, simulation and role playing are among the most controversial methods in the social-psychological repertoire (Cooper, 1976; Forward, Canter, & Kirsch, 1976; Hendrick, 1977; Miller, 1972). Critics of the method claim that when one asks subjects to act as if they were in a certain role, the subjects will do only what they think they *might* do, not necessarily what they *would* do in the real situation (Carlsmith et al., 1976).

In addition, the problems of experimental demands and evaluation apprehension, discussed earlier in relation to laboratory experiments, are even more serious when the subject is fully informed of the purposes of the study. Proponents of role playing argue, however, that to some degree the participant in an experiment is always playing a role, whether it is the general role of subject or a more specific role defined by the investigator. Computer simulations avoid these particular criticisms, but questions can be raised about their correspondence to actual behavior.

This controversy is difficult to resolve and will probably continue for several years. Some of the issues in the controversy can be resolved empirically by experiments focused on the methodological practices themselves. Other aspects of the argument may be more philosophical and, like the theories of Chapter One, may reflect overriding views of human nature.

Surveys and Interviews

An assessment of the quality of life in the United States was the objective of a large-scale interview study conducted by Campbell, Converse, and Rog-

Photo 2-2 During an interview, a researcher asks predetermined questions and records the responses.

ers (1976). After carefully selecting a sample of 2164 persons aged 18 years or older and representing all segments of the population and all regions of the country, these investigators conducted lengthy interviews to determine how satisfied people were with their lives in general and with such particular aspects as job, marriage, and health. The initial findings of the study indicated that most people were reasonably happy with their lives. A closer analysis, however, showed that subjective feelings of satisfaction are very clearly related to objective characteristics of the life situation. Degree of marital satisfaction, for example, is related to educational level, as Figure 2-4 indicates. People with less education are more likely to report that they are completely satisfied with their marriage than those with more education. It is also worth noting that the differences between men and women in reported marital satisfaction are greatest at the two extremes of educational level.

This study of the perceived quality of life is an example of an **interview** survey, in which a researcher questions people according to a predetermined schedule and records their answers. A similar procedure is the **questionnaire** survey, in which respondents read the questions themselves and provide written answers. Social psychologists often use questionnaires in conjunction with other procedures, but surveys and interviews rely *solely* on this type of information. In both cases, the investigator defines an area for research and designs a set of questions that will elicit the beliefs, attitudes, and self-reported experiences of the respondent in relation to the research topic.

Designing a good questionnaire is not as easy as it may seem. Considerations that enter into the design include the wording of questions, the provision of sufficient alternative responses, and the format of the questionnaire itself. The wording of a question,

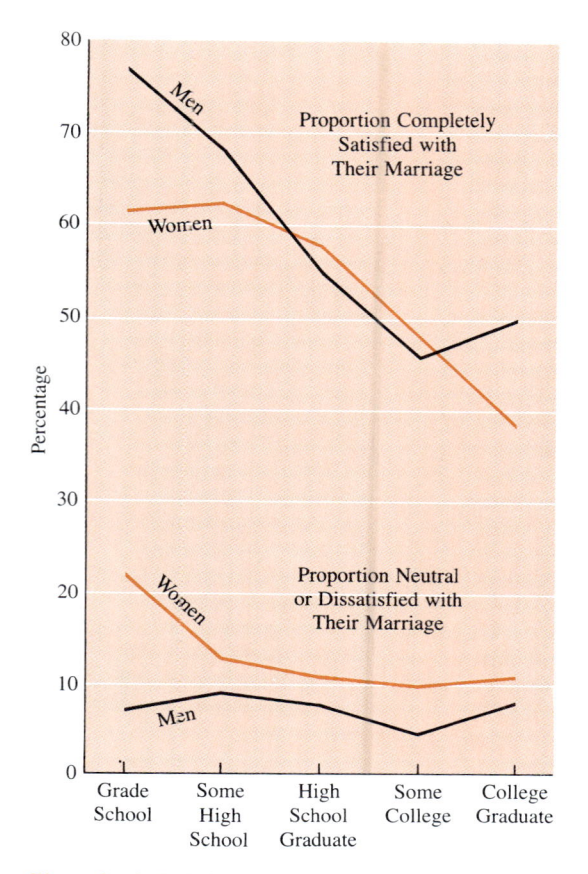

Figure 2–4 Relationship of marital satisfaction to educational level

for example, may systematically bias the answers. Politicians often use this tactic to their advantage. A question that begins "I agree that Candidate X . . . ," for example, is more likely to receive a positive response than a question that begins "Does Candidate X . . ." Considerable pretesting is necessary to ensure that the questions are objective, unbiased, understandable to the average respondent, and specific enough to elicit the desired information (Schuman & Kalton, 1985, offers much more detail).

Additional precautions must be taken when the interviewer administers the questionnaire. Experimenter bias, discussed earlier in relation to laboratory experiments, can be a problem if the interviewer consciously or unconsciously encourages some responses and discourages or seems uninterested in others. Hence interviewers must be carefully trained to standardize their delivery of questions. In addition, the interviewer must be able to develop rapport with respondents, so that they will be willing to answer questions straightforwardly and honestly.

Both questionnaires and interviews require the investigator to be concerned with *sampling procedures*. If the researcher wants to generalize to a larger population—for example, the entire population of the United States and Canada—it is not necessary to contact every member of that population. A sample or a subset of perhaps 2000 people can, if selected properly, be an accurate representation of the total population. Improper sample selection, however, is almost certain to produce inaccurate results. Many televised news programs, for example, feature a roving reporter who asks passing pedestrians their opinion on some topical issue. Such samplings are not systematic and probably tell us very little about the attitudes of the general population.

Advantages. A major advantage of both survey questionnaires and interviews is that they can be very straightforward and specific. Rather than devising a situation to elicit desired behavior or finding a natural situation in which to observe that behavior, constructors of questionnaires directly question people about the topic under investigation. In some cases, this is the only practical approach to desired information. If, for example, you were interested in the events of a person's childhood, directly asking the person about those events may be the only way to find out.

Interviews and questionnaires also have their own particular advantages and disadvantages, which tend to balance out. For instance, survey questionnaires are easier and more economical to use than interview procedures. In addition, they provide greater anonymity for the respondent, which is important when sensitive or personal issues are being examined. Face-to-face interviews, however, allow the interviewer to gather additional information from observation. Furthermore, the interviewer can clarify questions that may be confusing to the respondent and can also be sure which person in the household is answering the questions.

Disadvantages. Perhaps the major difficulty with self-report data, whether from interviews or surveys, is the issue of accuracy. When asked about childhood events, for example, a respondent may or may not recall what actually happened. Even when more recent events are discussed, either unintentional or deliberate bias may intrude. Surveys of sexual behavior are frequently questioned on these grounds: critics suggest that people may be less than honest in describing their own sexual practices. Other topics may lead to embellishments as the respondent attempts to create a favorable impression. (This process is a form of evaluation apprehension, discussed earlier in relation to the experimental method.)

Survey questionnaires and interviews have opposite sets of weaknesses. The survey questionnaire gives the investigator less control over the situation and cannot guarantee the conditions under which the questionnaire is being administered, who is answering it, and that the respondent fully understands the questions. For its part, the interview is more costly, more time-consuming, and more susceptible to examiner bias.

In summary, questionnaire and interview methods allow the investigator to ask directly about the issues of concern. Questionnaires in particular permit very large-scale studies and thus allow greater generalizability of the results. Both methods, however, rely on the accuracy and honesty of the respondent and depend on self-reports of behavior rather than observations of the behavior itself.

Some Issues in Research

Social psychologists have a variety of research methods at their disposal, just as they have innumerable questions that they can ask. Research requires investigators to put many pieces together, and in the process they must make many judgment calls, to use the sports terminology (McGrath, Martin, & Kulka, 1982). Far from being an orderly process, research is often accidental and always to some degree opportunistic. Some authors have even suggested that a garbage can may be the most accurate model of the research process, representing the accidental conjunctions of methods, theories, resources, and solutions that take place (McGrath et al., 1982).

Selection of Method and Setting

Each method has its own set of advantages and disadvantages, and in the abstract, there is no best method.

In the initial stages of research, questions may be only vaguely defined. An investigator may be interested in something concrete, such as communes, the jury system, or a particular religious group. Such topics would probably guide the investigator to the natural setting—that is, to a field study—or to the use of a survey or interview method. In other cases, the investigator's questions may involve something more abstract—for example, why people like each other, what causes aggression, or how we attribute intentionality to others' behavior. Here the possibilities for study are much more numerous.

Phoebe Ellsworth (1977), in discussing the selection of a research method, notes some basic concerns that the investigator always has. "In brief, one wants an instance that is capable of disconfirming the hypothesis, that allows for fairly precise specification of both independent and dependent variables, that is free of serious confounds, and that is informative, allowing the investigator to collect supplementary data that will be helpful in understanding the results" (p. 606).

The possibility of disconfirming the hypothesis is important. Although scientists, like most other people, enjoy finding out that they are right, it is crucial that their experiments be not simply a demonstration of what was known all along but rather a true questioning process. As the eminent biologist Albert Szent-Györgyi once stated, "research means going out into the unknown with the hope of finding something new to bring home. If you know in advance what you are going to do or even find there, then it is not research at all: then it is only a kind of honorable occupation" (1971).

Sometimes an investigator will begin in the laboratory, testing a theory under highly controlled conditions, and then move out to the field to see whether the same principles hold. On other occasions a reverse strategy is used, as when relationships observed in a field study are then taken back to the laboratory for testing with the hope of more precisely defining cause-and-effect relationships. Such a back-and-forth strategy was, in fact, prescribed by Kurt Lewin, often considered the forefather of modern social psychology.

The advantages of such a strategy should be evident after our discussion of the various research methods. Because each method has its own particular set of weaknesses, it is impossible to rely on any single one for a full understanding of a phenomenon. Thus the question is not which method is best but which set of methods will be best. As Eugene Webb and his colleagues note, "if a proposition can survive the onslaught of a series of imperfect measures, with all their irrelevant error, confidence should be placed in it" (Webb et al., 1966, p. 3). This principle of *triangulation*—of focusing on a single concept from a variety of vantage points—represents a key strategy in the conduct of social-psychological research.

Units of Analysis

An investigator's decisions do not end with the definition of a question and the choice of a research method. The next decisions to be made concern the types of data that will be collected and the procedures to be used for analyzing those data. Depending on the way a hypothesis is framed, an investigator may be interested in the *frequency,* the *rate,* or the *level* of a particular behavior. For example, we might ask how often married couples engage in physical aggression or what percentage of people are willing to help a person who has fallen down in a subway. These are questions about frequency of occurrence. On other occasions, the concern may be with the rate of a behavior, as measured in units of behavior per person or per segment of time. For example, we might want to know how many contacts a kindergarten teacher has with pupils each day. Still other questions might focus on the specific level of a behavior, as when one measures the degree of attraction between two persons or the level of shock a subject administers in an aggression experiment.

A second and related issue is the way the data we collect are to be analyzed. Although this is not the place for an elaborate discussion of statistics, a few basic concepts will help you to understand the research discussed in later chapters. In general, four types of questions may be asked about data: they involve central tendency, variability, association, and measures of difference.

In the case of *central tendency,* we are asking what the average response for a group of people is. What, for example, is the average income of a college graduate? What is the average attitude of Canadians on the issue of independence for Quebec?

Variability refers to the dispersion of responses. Rather than the average opinion of Canadians about independence for Quebec, it might be more helpful to know the degree to which those opinions vary. Are most Canadians generally favorable toward the separatist movement, or do the opinions vary widely from strong opposition to strong support?

A third question that the investigator may ask involves the *association* between two variables. In the study of Supreme Court decisions, for example, the analysis dealt with the relationship between two types of data—complexity of ideas and political ideology.

Finally, an investigator may be concerned with the *differences* among two or more groups. "Are men more satisfied with marriage than women?" is a question of this type. Another such study might ask whether speakers of high or low status were more effective in changing listeners' attitudes. In each of the last two examples we are concerned with only one factor: sex in the first case, and the prestige of the communicator in the second. Often, however, social psychologists are interested in looking at the effects of two or more independent variables simultaneously. Earlier we described Darley and Gross's experiment in which subjects were asked to evaluate a young girl after they had been led to have either a positive or negative expectancy and either had or had not observed the child in actual performance. This was a 2 × 2 factorial experiment: one factor was the expectancy (positive or negative) and the other factor was performance information (present or not). Such experiments often give us more information than we would have if we studied only one variable at a time. Their results frequently take the form of an **interaction,** as shown in Figure 2–5. *Interaction* is a statistical term referring to the fact that the effect of one variable depends on the level or state of the other variable. Thus, in Figure 2–5, grade-level placements recommended by subjects depended on both expectancy and the availability of additional information. Only when subjects had both a negative expectancy *and* additional observation did their judgments show bias. In such a case, information about the **main effect**—the effect that either one of the variables has by itself, without consideration of the other factor—is much less informative than the combined information represented by the interaction.

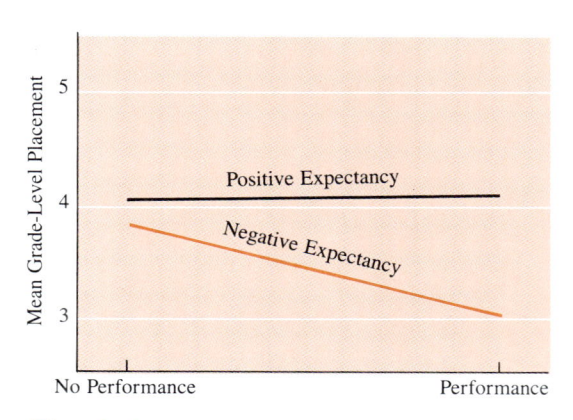

Figure 2–5 Mean grade-level placements in mathematics made by subjects in four experimental conditions

Ethics of Research

Beyond the technical issues already discussed, another set of concerns must be considered before an investigator conducts an experiment—its ethical aspects. Social psychologists have become increasingly aware of the ethical questions involved in research. Pressures for such consideration have come in part from the federal and state governments. The U.S. Department of Health and Human Services, for example, has issued a set of guidelines that all recipients of grants and contracts must follow. There has been considerable concern within the profession as well, evidenced in numerous books and articles (for example, Carlsmith et al., 1976; Cook, 1976; Kelman, 1968; Schlenker & Forsyth, 1977) and by a set of guidelines developed by the American Psychological Association (1973). In fact, social psychologists tend to subject research practices to far more stringent ethical evaluation than other academicians, law professors, and the students who frequently participate in such research (Rugg, 1975; Schwartz & Gottlieb, 1981).

The ethical issues involved in research are numerous and complex, and they cannot be fully resolved here. A few important points, however, should be considered briefly.

One concern is the level of pain or stress that a subject experiences. This question is more prominent in the medical and biological sciences because experimentation with new drugs or surgical procedures can produce irreversible damage. Social psychologists are generally more concerned with psychological than with physical harm. An investigator interested in the effects of negative personal evaluation on subsequent interaction, for example, may purposely expose a subject to uncomplimentary information. Such information can cause considerable stress. In other experimental situations the subject may be instructed to administer increasingly intense electrical shocks to another person. In such cases, even if no shock is actually delivered, subjects may get very upset as they try to comply with the experimenter's demands.

An experimenter should always try to minimize the amount of stress that a subject experiences. At the same time, it is difficult to argue that stressful events should never be studied (West & Gunn, 1978). Although it is certainly more pleasant to focus one's research attention on positive forms of human behavior, humans do display undesirable behavior as well. The social psychologist who seeks to understand the full range of human behavior is obligated to consider both positive and negative aspects of human interaction.

One solution is to rely on *informed consent*. Insofar as possible, the experimenter should inform subjects in advance about the requirements of the experiment and obtain their consent to participate. Thus, if a subject is to be exposed to electrical shock, it is the experimenter's obligation to inform the subject of that fact in advance. Informed consent is important in any area of study, and it is particularly so when the potential for stress or pain is great.

Informed consent procedures are relatively easy to institute in the laboratory experiment, in which the investigator has a great deal of control over the total situation. But what of the field experiment? As we noted earlier, field experiments are generally carried out without the knowledge of the participants. For that reason, the investigator must plan field experiments carefully. *Invasion of privacy* is an important consideration. If a subject has been fully informed of procedures and has given consent, the experimenter will probably not be intruding unfairly. In a situation such as the field experiment, however, where the revelation of the information necessary to obtain informed consent would defeat the purposes of the study, the investigator must be particularly concerned about unreasonable intrusion. Although it is difficult to formulate specific criteria for an acceptable field experiment, we saw earlier that similarity to a normal situation is a working rule of thumb.

In the field study, in which the experimenter does not tamper with the environment, some of the ethical concerns are resolved. Even in this setting, however, investigators must consider carefully the potential for invading the privacy of individuals.

Another ethical concern of experimenters relates to the practice of deceiving subjects, either by withholding certain information or by purposely misleading them. Such procedures are fairly common in social-psychological research (Gross & Fleming, 1982). Scientifically, there is some justification for such procedures. The problems of demand characteristics and evaluation apprehension, discussed earlier, lead many investigators to develop elaborate scenarios so that the subject will be unaware of the true purpose of the experiment. Although deception can occasionally be justified, however, the technique has been abused.

Subjects are less likely to be deceived when informed consent is required. If deception is a necessary part of the procedure, it is critical that the experimenter undertake a thorough debriefing of all participants as soon as the experiment is completed. **Debriefing,** a term borrowed from the military, refers to the process whereby an experimenter reveals the complete procedure to the subject. An investigator should be certain that subjects are not permanently harmed by their experience and that they leave the laboratory feeling no worse than they did when they arrived.

A final ethical concern of the social psychologist concerns the confidentiality of the data that are obtained and the anonymity of the participants. Investigators should protect subjects' confidentiality routinely, and the subjects should be assured that confidentiality will be preserved.

Few questions of ethics are easily resolved, and the investigator must carefully weigh the question of scientific value against the rights of the subject. Ultimately, investigators must decide for themselves whether or not to conduct an experiment, although numerous checks exist in the form of sanctions by colleagues and review committees.

Each time a study is begun, the investigator must consider all the available options and determine the best way to answer the research question, keeping a multitude of complex factors in balance.

Venturing into any unknown territory is a complex but exciting process. The investigator must make numerous judgment calls along the way, and each one will contribute to the ultimate success or failure of the project. Not all questions are easily answered; their solutions may take dozens of studies and years of effort by many investigators. The results of many such efforts are the basis of this book.

Summary

Research is an exacting and exciting endeavor. The process of research is a lengthy one, beginning with an idea and moving through decisions on how to test the idea, completion of the actual research, and, finally, analysis and interpretation of the data. Each of these stages is important to the final product, which is the answer to some question about human behavior.

Sources for experimental hypotheses are numerous, ranging from casual observation to complex hypothetico-deductive systems. Once a question is formulated, there are many ways to attempt to answer it. Any question can be answered by several methods.

At least seven specific methods are available to the social-psychology researcher: laboratory experiments, field experiments, quasi-experimental research, field studies, archival research, simulations and role playing, and surveys and interviews. Each of these methods has certain advantages and disadvantages.

The selection of any one research method depends in part on the question being asked. In the long run, it is important for the investigator to test each question with a variety of methods, thereby canceling out the disadvantages of each single method and gaining confidence in the validity of the research results. Further, different techniques of statistical analysis are required to test different hypotheses.

Finally, investigators must give careful thought to ethical issues. Social-psychology research involves people, and the rights of these participants in the research process must be recognized and protected at all times.

Glossary Terms

archival research
correlational method
debriefing
deindividuation
demand characteristics
dependent variables
evaluation apprehension
experimental realism
experimenter expectancies
external validity
independent variables
interaction
internal validity
interview
main effect
manipulation check
mundane realism
participant observer
questionnaire
randomization
reliability
simulation
unobtrusive measure

*Show me the sensible person who likes
himself or herself! I know myself too
well to like what I see. I know but too
well that I'm not what I'd like to be.*
Golda Meir

*The image of myself which I try to create
in my own mind that I may love myself
is very different from the image which I
try to create in the minds of others in
order that they may love me.*
W. H. Auden

George Tooker, *Mirror No. 2*, 1964. Addison Gallery of American Art, Phillips Academy, Andover, Massachusetts.

CHAPTER THREE

The Self

I. The Nature of the Self
   Theories of the Development of Self
   The Structure of the Self-Concept
   Influences on Self-Definition
II. Becoming Aware of the Self
   A Theory of Self-Perception
   States of Self-Awareness
   Individual Differences in Self-Awareness
III. Dealing with the Self
   Self-Esteem
   Experiencing Emotions
   Evaluating Abilities
IV. Relating to Others
   Presenting the Self
   The Goals of Self-Presentation
   Tactics of Self-Presentation
   Individual Differences in Self-Presentation
V. Summary

"*B*egin at the beginning," the King of Hearts tells the White Rabbit in *Alice in Wonderland*. And so we begin our understanding of social behavior with the self.

The concept of the self is one of the oldest and most enduring in psychology, dating from the first definitions of the field. Yet it is an idea not limited to psychology. Early philosophers advised us to "know thyself," and poets have told us, "To thine own self be true"; more recent scribes have written hundreds of books dealing with systems of self-knowledge. Further reflecting this interest, the *Oxford English Dictionary* lists more than one hundred words that focus on the self, from *self-abasement* to *self-wisdom*.

How often do you think about aspects of yourself? When you decided to go to college, did you wonder whether you had the ability or the drive to succeed? When you go out with someone, do you worry whether your date will find you charming, interesting, and fun to be with? When you're alone in your room at night, do you ever introspect, weighing your good and bad points? Such moments come frequently to most of us.

The self is clearly important—but is it a topic for social psychology? Yes, as we shall see, it is, for the self is a *social* construct, formed on the basis of our interaction with others. Not only is the self defined in the process of such interactions, but it can affect a wide range of social behaviors. How we judge other people, how we communicate with them, whether we choose to be leaders or followers, when we are willing to help a person in need—each of these behaviors can be influenced by our view of ourselves.

Later chapters will deal with some of these consequences of self-reference. Here we shall consider how the notion of a self develops and what influences self-definitions. Then, recognizing that people are not always introspective, we will describe some of the situations that tend to make people aware of themselves. We shall then consider how people deal with various aspects of themselves—how they regard themselves, how they experience emotions, and how they evaluate their abilities and the situations in which they find themselves. Finally, we will look at the self in social interaction, describing the ways people choose to present themselves to other people.

The Nature of the Self

How do you think about yourself? What image do you have of yourself? What talents do you think you have? What do you regard as your weak points? All such thoughts constitute your **self-concept.** The self-concept can be defined more precisely as the totality of the thoughts and feelings that have reference to the self as an object (Rosenberg, 1979). But where do these thoughts come from? How do we come to have certain beliefs about ourselves and certain ways of dealing with the world? These are some of the questions that social psychologists ask as they try to understand the self.

Theories of the Development of Self

The philosopher and psychologist William James was one of the most articulate theorists of the self, and his writings still influence current thought. James defined the self in the broadest possible terms. The self, according to James, includes body and mind, clothes and house, spouse and children, ancestors and friends, reputation and possessions (James, 1890). Experiences that involve any one of these elements, he believed, affect one's sense of well-being and self-worth. Nearly 100 years later, most contemporary psychologists would agree that the self is constructed of many elements and that almost any experience we have may affect our self-concepts.

James also believed that the experience of selfhood is very much a social experience—that is, our personal identities are critically dependent on our relationships with other people. In fact, it was James who first sensitized us to the identity-threatening consequences we would suffer if our relationships with other people were eliminated:

> If no one turned around when we entered, answered when we spoke, or minded what we did, but if every person we met "cut us dead," and acted as if we were nonexisting things, a kind of rage and impotent despair would ere long well up in us, from which the cruelest bodily tortures would be a relief; for these would make us feel that, however bad might be our plight, we had not sunk to such a depth as to be unworthy of attention at all. [1890, 1: 293–294]

James was not alone in recognizing that the self is a product of social interaction. Charles Cooley (1902/1964), a sociologist who wrote at the turn of the century, used the term "looking-glass self" to convey the idea that self-concepts reflect the evaluations of other people in the environment. This idea, elaborated by George Herbert Mead (1934) and Harry Stack Sullivan (1953), has come to be known as the principle of *reflected appraisals*. This principle suggests that we see ourselves as others see us. *Which* others is a critical question, as different people may have contradictory views of us. Some people may be more important at one point in our life than at others. The views of our parents are usually paramount when we are young, for example, and the views of our spouse are likely to be most important when we are older. Even at the same period in the time span, different people may use different points of reference. In a study of high school students, for example, Jon Hoelter (1984) found that girls relied more on the evaluations of peers while boys looked to parental appraisals.

Other people are important to the development of a self-concept, but they are not the only influences. Not only do we respond to the views of others, but we take actions ourselves, and the outcomes of those actions help to define the self. This kind of action has been referred to as *effectance* or *self-efficacy*, terms that stress the individual as controlling and influencing his or her environment (Gekas, 1982; Gekas & Schwalbe, 1983). When we decide to learn to play the piano, for example, we discover something about our musical ability, our finger dexterity, and our willingness to commit time to practice. Each of these pieces of information can become part of our self-concept.

The Structure of the Self-Concept

One way to think about the self-concept is as a type of cognitive structure (Greenwald & Pratkanis, 1984; Kihlstrom & Cantor, 1984). In Chapter One we introduced the concept of a **schema**—an organized configuration of knowledge that we use to interpret our experience. The concept of schema can also be applied to the self as what we will call a **self-schema.** As Hazel Markus defines them, self-schemas are "cognitive generalizations about the self, derived from past experience, that organize and guide the processing of self-related information contained in the individual's social experiences" (1977, p. 64).

The contents of self-schemas vary from individual to individual. Some people think of themselves as very independent, others as rather dependent; for the self-concepts of still other people, the dimension of independence/dependence is irrelevant. To understand how these different self-schemas can affect the organization of information, Markus (1977) selected three groups of people who defined themselves differently in terms of independence: some rated themselves as extremely independent, some as extremely dependent, and others more neutrally, suggesting that neither end of this dimension was particularly central to their self-concepts. Markus then asked each of these groups to participate in a series of tasks that included making judgments about the self and providing descriptions of behavioral events that related to independence or dependence. Her results showed how the self-schema can affect the processing of information. People who described themselves as independent, for example, showed much faster agreement when asked whether a list of adjectives that related to independence applied to themselves. They were also able to think of more specific incidents of their own independent behavior than people in either of the other groups were—and they recalled fewer occasions when they had been dependent. People who had described themselves as dependent showed just the opposite pattern, responding well when dealing with dependency but taking more time with independence and providing fewer examples of it. The aschematics—people who did not clearly define themselves as either independent or dependent—showed no differences in information processing between the two kinds of tasks.

Independence is just one dimension that has been used to illustrate the operation of the self-schema. In fact, almost any personality trait is probably central to the schemas of some people and irrelevant to others. Honesty may be the organizing principle for some people, while masculinity or femininity may be a central concept for other people (Markus, Crane, Bernstein, & Siladi, 1982).

Nor are self-schemas limited to verbal material. Part of our self-concept also involves visual images—for example, what we look like (or how we would like to look). Investigators have found that people are more likely to remember photographs of themselves that most closely resemble their physical self-image than to remember pictures that are more discrepant from that self-image, even though all the photos were taken at the same time (Yarmey & Johnson, 1982). If you think of yourself as a serious person, for example, you might be more likely to remember a picture that portrayed you without a smile than one that showed you laughing merrily at the camera. Thus our visions of ourselves affect our visions of the world in a variety of ways.

The self-concept is multifaceted. One way to describe the various aspects of the self is in terms of multiple schemas, as we have just done. This description reflects the assumptions of cognitive theories, outlined in Chapter One. Another approach, borrowing more from the language of role theory, is to talk about *multiple identities* or *multiple selves*.

Consider the identities that you yourself have. You probably define yourself as a student, as a son or daughter, and as a citizen of your country. You may also have an identity as a wife or husband, as a member of a particular religious group, or as someone with a particular ethnic identity. Perhaps you also think of yourself as an athlete, as a bookworm, or as a musician. These different roles may vary in their importance to you—some may frequently guide your thoughts and behavior, while others may come to mind only on rare occasions. One way to think of these roles is in terms of a hierarchy, with the most important ones at the top of a pyramid and less important roles falling lower on the scale (Rosenberg & Gara, 1985; Stryker, 1982). Each identity also has a set of characteristics associated with it. With the identity of athlete, for example, one may think of oneself as strong, limber, and adventurous. As a son, the same person may be most aware of his obedience and respectfulness. Of course, roles may share certain characteristics, representing the continuity in one's personality. As a daughter, as a wife, and as a mother, for example, a woman may consider herself equally caring and warm.

The more important an identity is, or the higher it stands in the hierarchy, the more likely it is to influence our choices and our behavior. Consider, at a very general level, a person whose identity is defined primarily in personal terms (for example, his own feelings, emotions, and goals) versus a person who thinks of herself in more social terms (as a popular person, say, as a member of a certain group, as a friend of specific people). How might these two people differ in their activities? Mark Leary and his colleagues considered this question in the context of sports interests (Leary, Wheeler, & Jenkins, 1986). As they suspected, people whose identities were defined primarily in personal terms were much more likely to engage in individual sports than in team activities. They ran and they swam, but they were less likely to play volleyball. Just the reverse was true of individuals who defined themselves in social terms. Their reasons for engaging in the sports of their choice differed as well. Individuals who scored high in personal identity said they felt better physically and they got a feeling of self-satisfaction from participation in sports; people who scored high in social identity were more likely to say that they liked others to know that they were physically active, or that they enjoyed competing and exercising with other people.

Our self-concept consists not only of various identities that we currently possess but of selves that we would like to be or that we imagine we might be. These "potential selves" (James, 1890; Markus & Nurius, 1986) can include ideals that we would like to attain and standards that we feel we should meet (sometimes termed the "ought self"), and can originate from our own thoughts or from the messages of others (Higgins, in press). As Morris Rosenberg has observed, "the ability and even the propensity to imagine ourselves as other than we are is a remarkable feature of the human mind" (1979, p. 38).

You might think that this diversity of selves would be problematic, perhaps causing what is sometimes called an "identity crisis." In fact, it is just the opposite: diversity and complexity of the self-concept reduce stress. As Patricia Linville (1985; in press) has suggested, greater self-complexity provides a buffer against stressful events. If an individual has only one or two major identities, any negative event is going to have an impact on most aspects of the self-concept. The woman who sees herself primarily as a wife, for example, is likely to be devastated if her husband says he wants an immediate divorce. In contrast, the individual who has a more complex representation of self may be more protected from negative events that primarily involve only one or two of several roles. The woman who sees herself not only as wife, but also as a mother, lawyer, friend, and tennis player, will have other roles to fall back on when impending divorce threatens the role of spouse. Linville's research has shown that people with more complex self-concepts are less prone to depression and illness; they also experience less severe mood swings following success or failure in one particular area of performance.

Influences on Self-Definition

The concepts of self-schemas and multiple identities are general, describing the structure of anyone's self-concept. The content of a specific self-concept, in contrast, depends very much on one's particular experiences and characteristics. Even the historical era in which one lives may influence the nature of the self-concept (see Box 3–1).

Some of a person's characteristics—whether one

Box 3–1
Historical selves

Roy Baumeister (in press) has recently taken a historical look at the self-concept. Over the centuries, he observes, societies have stressed quite different aspects of the self. Indeed, they have differed in whether they consider self-conceptions and self-knowledge important at all. Literature suggests that in the late medieval period, for example, people did not engage in a great deal of introspection. More recently, Freudian psychoanalytic theory proposed that it is impossible to know the self totally, as unconscious forces set barriers to self-inquiry. Today self-knowledge is believed to be not only within reach but of critical importance. There is even a magazine called *Self*, which provides information for those who a short time ago were called the "me" generation.

As concern with self-knowledge varies across historical periods, so do the dimensions that are considered most important for self-definition. The themes of self-reliance and individualism characteristic of the Victorian period (mid- to late-19th century) were replaced by concerns for socioeconomic status in the early 20th century. Which themes are central now? External guidelines are less apparent today, Baumeister suggests, and more responsibility lies with the individual to develop his or her own criteria for self-evaluation.

---

is male or female, for example—are almost inevitably part of that person's self-concept. **Gender identity** has been defined as a "fundamental, existential sense of one's maleness or femaleness" (Spence, 1985). Although this sense of being male or female is probably always with us, its significance may change over the life course. In childhood, for example, one's identity as a girl or a boy may influence one's choice of playmates and preferences among toys; in later life, one's gender identity can affect occupational choices and marital roles (Katz, 1986). Another basic influence on the self-concept is one's **racial identity,** defined as one's sense of belonging to a particular racial or ethnic group. Like gender, this sense of one's identity develops early. When Black children are asked whether a White or a Black doll looks most like them, for example, most will select the Black doll by the age of about 5 (Clark & Clark, 1947; Fine & Bowers, 1984).

Race and gender are likely to be salient elements of one's self-concept because they usually are the most visible of one's attributes. Identifying us on the basis of these characteristics, people may shape their behavior toward us in accordance with their beliefs about people of our race and sex (an instance of stereotyping, which we will discuss in Chapter Four). In fact, any visible characteristic is likely to influence other people's views of us and our views of ourselves as well (Herman, Zanna, & Higgins, 1986; Jones et al., 1984). Height, weight, physical appearance—each of these characteristics will probably be part of our self-concept.

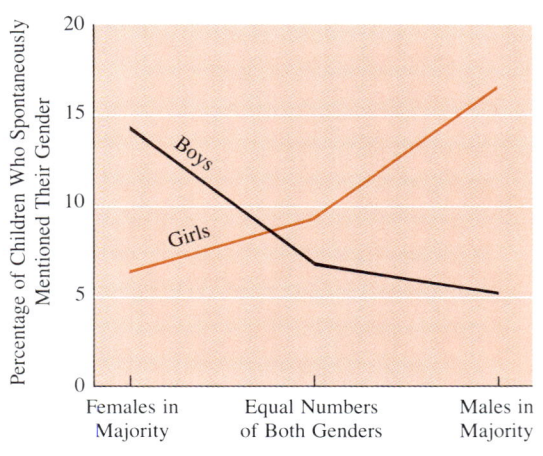

Figure 3-1 Prominence of gender in the self-concept in relation to gender composition of respondents' households

Obvious physical characteristics are particularly likely to be part of the self-concept if they serve to mark us as different from those around us. William McGuire and his colleagues have shown that the self-concept often reflects features of identity that make people distinctive (McGuire & McGuire, 1981). When fourth-graders were asked to tell investigators about themselves, as Figure 3–1 indicates, the children were much more likely to mention their gender spontaneously when they came from households in which that gender was in the minority. Being female, for example, was a particularly important feature of the self-concepts of girls whose families included more males than females. If a girl came from a family that had a larger proportion of females, in contrast, she was much less likely to mention that she was a girl when asked for a self-description.

The spontaneous self-concept can also be influenced by immediate circumstances. McGuire has found, for example, that children who are taller or shorter than average are more likely to mention their height than are children of average height; children who are older or younger than most of their classmates are more likely to mention age (McGuire & Padawer-Singer, 1976). College students in a psychology laboratory are sensitive also to the sex of their companions. Even in groups of only three people, students who are asked to describe themselves are more likely to mention their sex if they are the sole representative of their sex in that group than they are if the other two members are of the same sex (Cota & Dion, 1986).

Particular experiences and environments also affect our thoughts about ourselves. Research shows, for example, that our self-evaluations are influenced by the self-appraisals of our friends (Felson & Reed, 1986). Thus if we associate with people who tend to stress athletics and card games, those dimensions are likely to find their way into our own self-concept as well. Of course, the causal direction goes both ways. A person in whose self-concept athletics is prominent is likely to seek out friends who share an interest in active sports. The broader cultural context may also influence the contents of the self-concept. When Michael Bond and Tak-Sing Cheung (1983) compared Japanese students with students from Hong Kong and the United States, they found numerous differences in the kinds of descriptors used in self-description. Japanese students were more likely than the others to describe personal aspirations and choices (what we might call possible selves or ideal selves) and less likely to mention psychological attributes.

Clearly, many things influence the self-concept, and it is easy to see why a concept of multiple selves or multiple self-schemas is more useful than the notion of a single self-concept. When and how these various selves come to the forefront is the next issue to consider.

Becoming Aware of the Self

Although the self is always with us, our awareness of and concern with our self-concept may vary from time to time. If you are in the habit of walking immediately to the television set after you get up in the morning, switching on the national news, and then walking into the kitchen for coffee, you probably do not engage in much self-reflection when you follow this routine for the 50th day in a row. Ellen Langer (1978a) has called such behaviors "mindless," suggesting that the self is not engaged in sequences of behavior that are overlearned. In other situations, as in the deindividuation studies discussed in Chapter Two, particular circumstances may minimize attention to the self, creating a sense of anonymity. In contrast, if you walk into a party filled with people you have never met, all of whom turn to stare at you as you enter, you will probably engage in considerable self-reflection, wondering how you look and what your next move should be. In this second case, we see how important the environment can be to our awareness of our selves.

A Theory of Self-Perception

Daryl Bem (1967, 1972) has proposed a **self-perception theory** that suggests we become aware of ourselves simply by watching what we do. As Bem has described this process, "individuals come to 'know' their own attitudes, emotions, and other internal states partially by inferring them from observations of their own overt behavior and/or the circumstances in which this behavior occurs" (1972, p. 5). In other words, he suggests that people don't have a great deal of inside information about who they are or why they do things. Rather, much as an outside observer would do, people look at what they are doing and infer a reason for that behavior.

Bem's theory, which relies greatly on the behaviorist principles of B. F. Skinner, assumes that we are generally aware of *reinforcement contingencies* that affect our behavior. Suppose you spend two hours every day doing weight-reducing exercises. Why are you spending so much time on this activity, and what does it say about you? Perhaps, when you stop to think about it, you realize that you have been sweating vigorously ever since your favorite date said that he or she liked only thin and well-conditioned people. In that case, you may conclude that the extrinsic reinforcement from your favorite date is the main cause of your behavior. But what if your date doesn't care a bit about your physical condition? Without this external motivator, you—and a neutral observer as well—may conclude that exercise reflects an internal value or attitude of your own—perhaps a belief in the importance of fitness. Thus observing your own behavior leads to inferences about the self. Bem does not claim that all aspects of the self depend on this after-the-fact observation process, but he claims that the process does operate whenever internal cues are weak or ambiguous.

Can we also learn about ourselves from being aware of what we don't do? If I find myself jogging every morning, I may well conclude that jogging reflects something about my self-definition. But what if I don't jog—does that say something as well? Earlier research in the psychology of problem solving sug-

Photo 3–1 Some people choose to make their self-evaluations public.

gested that people are less adept at using negative instances of an event than at using positive instances when they try to find a solution, even if instances of both types provide the same amount of information. The same tendency seems to operate in the self-perception process, as people tend to infer characteristics about themselves more on the basis of what they have done than on the basis of what they have not done (Fazio, Sherman, & Herr, 1982). Thus, if I am a regular jogger, I may well see myself as energetic and athletic. If I do not jog or engage in other sports, however, I am not likely to label myself unathletic or lazy, even though I may well be both.

Behavior is only one source of information about our selves; thoughts and feelings provide insight as well. In fact, as Susan Andersen and her colleagues have shown, people are often more influenced by these cognitive and affective elements than by behavioral factors (Andersen, Lazowski, & Donisi, 1986). In one study, students were asked to respond to statements that concerned either religious behaviors (for example, I prayed) or thoughts and feelings about religion (for example, I have felt like praying). The statements presented to some students were worded in a positive way, such as "I have devoted time to religious or spiritual activities." Other students read a negative form of the same statement: "I fail to devote time to religious or spiritual activities." After responding to these statements, the students were asked to indicate their overall degree of religiosity. The results showed that students were more likely to be influenced by the positive or negative phrasing of cognitive and affective statements than by that of behavioral statements. Thus, Andersen and her colleagues reasoned, self-perception may be affected less by thinking about our behavior than by thinking about what we feel and believe with regard to those behaviors. Justification by faith may be more crucial than justification by deed, at least in our own self-awareness.

States of Self-Awareness

How often do people think about themselves in the course of the day? Do people think about themselves more often than they think about their families, for example, or their jobs or their favorite TV shows? To answer such questions, two investigators recently asked 107 persons, ranging in age from 19 to 63 and in occupation from clerical worker to manager, to record their thoughts at selected times each day for one week (Csikszentmihalyi & Figurski, 1982). Subjects did not know when they would be asked to reflect on their thoughts; they responded whenever they heard a beep from an electronic paging device that they had been asked to carry with them. Approximately 45 times during the course of the week, each person recorded his or her thoughts and feelings, for a total of more than 4700 observations.

As Figure 3-2 shows, the self was not at the top of the list. People reported thinking more often about their work or about chores and home, or they reported having no thoughts at all. However, thoughts about the self were more common than thoughts about food, about television and radio, or about the research project itself. The investigators also asked their subjects to describe how they felt at the moment—how happy they felt, how active and alert they felt, and whether they would rather be doing something else at that time. Responses made to these questions when subjects were thinking about themselves suggest that self-reflection is not necessarily a pleasant activity. When subjects were thinking about themselves they reported being less happy and less active than when they were thinking about other topics, and they more often wished they were doing something other than thinking about themselves. These patterns were found only when subjects had been engaging in some voluntary activity, however, not when they had been doing something they were obliged to do.

Robert Wicklund and his associates have proposed a theory of self-awareness that predicts when people will focus attention on themselves and what happens when they do (Wicklund, 1975; Duval & Wicklund, 1972; Wicklund & Frey, 1980). Wicklund defines self-awareness—sometimes called **objective self-awareness**—as "focused attention directed toward just one facet of the self" (Wicklund & Frey, 1980, p. 36). Self-awareness can be aroused in many ways. Laboratory investigators have used a variety of techniques, from placing a mirror in front of the subject to playing a tape recording of the subject's own voice and confronting the subject with a

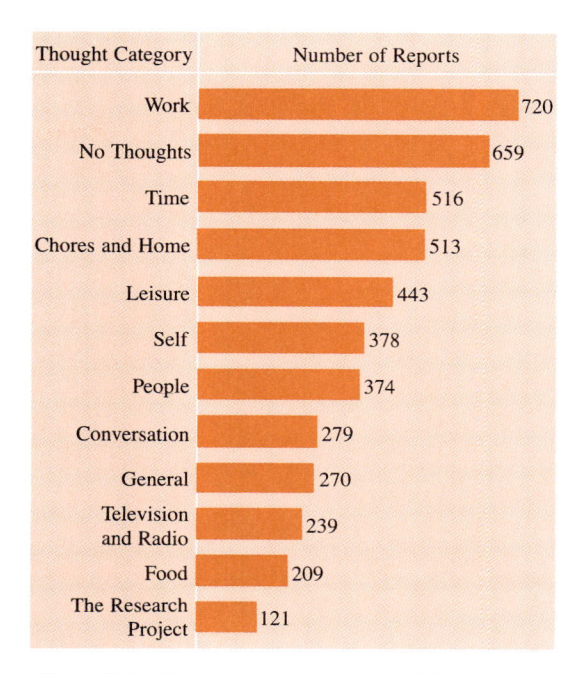

Thought Category	Number of Reports
Work	720
No Thoughts	659
Time	516
Chores and Home	513
Leisure	443
Self	378
People	374
Conversation	279
General	270
Television and Radio	239
Food	209
The Research Project	121

Figure 3-2 Most common categories of thought reported by Csikszentmihalyi and Figurski's subjects

camera. Self-awareness can also be induced by an unfamiliar and unstructured situation, similar to the party situation we described earlier.

What happens when a person is in a state of self-awareness? According to Wicklund, a person will engage in a process of self-evaluation, considering how his or her behavior measures up to some internal rule or standard. If there is a discrepancy between behavior and standard—as there often is—then the person will experience some negative feelings and frequently will try to avoid further self-reflection. In one experiment, subjects who had experienced a discrepancy between their own performance and an ideal standard left the experimental laboratory more quickly than subjects who either had not engaged in self-focusing or had not experienced a discrepancy between their performance and the standard (Duval & Wicklund, 1972).

Self-awareness can also lead to changes in behavior, often in a positive direction. Thus, if a person becomes self-aware while making a decision about how to act, the behavior may well reflect the person's concern with meeting some internal standard. Subjects in an experiment reported by Duval, Duval, and Neely (1979) watched a videotape about epidemics of venereal disease either immediately before or after a period of self-focused attention. When asked whether they would be willing to assist in a program designed to prevent such an epidemic, subjects in both groups were much more likely to volunteer their services than were subjects who had seen the videotape but had not been focused on themselves. Thus self-awareness may be aversive, but it may also be a guide for behavior that reflects the internalized norms and values of a society.

The aspect of the self that comes into self-awareness depends on the immediate situation. Just as a discussion of venereal disease makes behavior in regard to that issue salient, so standing on a football field may make you think about your athletic ability. Cognitive psychologists talk about variations in the *accessibility* of self-schemas—how readily they come to the forefront of our thinking (Higgins & King, 1981; Wyer & Srull, 1981). One factor that influences accessibility is **priming,** defined as the effects of prior context on the retrieval of information (Fiske & Taylor, 1983, p. 231). (Think of the prime coat of paint on a house, applied to get the surface in shape to receive the final coat.) If a movie on television had just reminded you of your father, for example, you would be more likely to think of yourself as a son or daughter than you would if you had not seen that movie. Even casual comments at a party may trigger particular self-concepts, predisposing you to evaluate yourself on the characteristic that was mentioned.

Research has often focused on awareness of one particular aspect of the self at one particular point in time, but shifts in self-focused attention are much more fluid than such research suggests. In fact, some recent investigators have suggested that self-attention can best be represented as a continual adjustment process. In this model (Carver & Scheier, 1981, 1982), comparisons between behavior and internal standards constitute a series of feedback loops, paralleling the *cybernetic* models of control developed in communication. Faced with one situation and with a focus on one internal standard, the person will make adjustments until the particular discrepancy is eliminated. Given another set of cues and/or focus on a different aspect of the self, the feedback process will begin anew.

Individual Differences in Self-Awareness

As we have seen, self-awareness can be induced by various manipulations in the laboratory. Self-focused attention does not require such techniques, however, and some people are more likely than others to engage in this process. To measure these natural tendencies, Fenigstein, Scheier, and Buss (1975) developed what they termed a "Self-Consciousness Scale." **Self-consciousness** is defined as a disposition to focus attention inward on the self and can be further analyzed in terms of its public and private aspects. *Private self-consciousness* involves a focus on personal aspects of the self, such as bodily sensations, beliefs, moods, and feelings. *Public self-consciousness* relates to a more outward concern, involving an awareness of how one is seen as a social object by others (Scheier & Carver, 1981). Box 3–2 provides more information on the measurement of these dispositions.

People who differ in their level of self-consciousness, as measured by scales such as the ones described in Box 3–2, show other differences as well. People who score high on measures of *private* self-consciousness, for example, are more aware of their internal feelings and more quick to make self-descriptive statements (Carver, 1979; Mueller, 1982).

Because individuals who score high in private self-consciousness can be considered well aware of their true feelings, it is perhaps not surprising that they and their close friends tend to agree as to what they are really like (Franzoi, 1983). Such people also tend to be aware of changes in their internal bodily states (Scheier, Carver, & Gibbons, 1979). It has been suggested that such people may tend to be healthier than others because they can recognize stresses to their bodies and take action before the stress is physically damaging (Mullen & Suls, 1982).

Whereas *private* self-consciousness relates to behaviors that reflect the inner self, *public* self-consciousness is linked to the social world. People high in public self-consciousness tend to be more sensitive to social rejection (Fenigstein, 1979), while people low in public self-consciousness show less concern for this kind of evaluation (Franzoi & Brewer, 1984).

Dealing with the Self

The self-concept, as described so far, may appear to be rather passive, neutral, and quite rational. Indeed, the description may suggest a piece of computer hardware, storing experiences and responding to input in an orderly fashion. But this analogy would be misleading. In fact, the self-concept is active, it is evaluative, it is a source of emotions, and it can be described as more than occasionally nonrational. Let us see now how individuals deal with their concepts

Box 3–2
Assessing public and private self-consciousness

Do the following exercise. With your dominant hand (the hand that you normally write with), print a capital letter E on your forehead.

This simple exercise provides one clue as to whether you are low or high on the dimension of public self-consciousness. Think about which direction your *E* faced. Was it oriented so that someone looking at you would have seen it in its correct position? Or was it turned so that you, if you had eyes inside your head, would see it in its normal position? If the first of these alternatives is the case, it is likely that you are high in public self-consciousness, according to a study by R. Glen Hass (1984). People who are low in public self-consciousness are more likely to draw an *E* from an internal perspective.

The "draw an *E*" test is only a rough assessment of public self-consciousness. Alan Fenigstein and his colleagues (Fenigstein, Scheier, & Buss, 1975) have developed more exacting questionnaire measures to assess both public and private self-consciousness. Among the items developed to assess public self-consciousness are the following:

- I'm concerned about what other people think of me.
- I'm self-conscious about the way I look.
- I'm concerned about my style of doing things.

Private self-consciousness refers to an inward focus, a concern with private feelings and beliefs. Among the items that assess this dimension of self-awareness are the following:

- I'm always trying to figure myself out.
- I reflect about myself a lot.
- I'm generally attentive to my inner feelings.

Although these statements represent only a portion of the actual measures developed, they may give some indications as to whether you would score high on public self-consciousness, on private self-consciousness, on both, or on neither.

---

of themselves. We will consider specifically the concept of self-esteem, how and why emotions are experienced, and how individuals evaluate their abilities and explain their behavior.

Self-Esteem

The singer Pearl Bailey once said, "There's a period of life when we swallow a knowledge of ourselves and it becomes either good or sour inside." What she described in very graphic terms is what social psychologists call **self-esteem**—the evaluation of oneself in either a positive or a negative way.

Social psychologists have developed a variety of measures to assess self-esteem, asking people to respond to such questions as "On the whole, I am satisfied with myself" (Rosenberg, 1979). In general, these measures assume that a person's self-esteem is relatively stable. In other words, it is believed that some people tend to feel good about themselves most of the time, while others rate themselves more negatively a good part of the time.

These evaluations of the self are based on a variety of experiences. Earlier we discussed the notion of *efficacy*—the sense of control we achieve when our actions lead to the outcomes we desire. Such

"Call it vanity, call it narcissism, call it egomania. I love you."

outcomes tend to result in positive self-esteem, while negative self-esteem tends to follow from repeated unsuccessful outcomes (Gekas & Schwalbe, 1983). Satisfaction with one's current activities, friendships, and romantic involvements contributes to positive self-esteem, while deficits in such areas lower one's self-esteem (Bohrnstedt & Fisher, 1986). Physical characteristics and facial appearance also affect a person's self-esteem (see Box 3–3). Men's self-evaluations have been found to be related to their muscular strength, for example (Tucker, 1983). Some of these areas of self-evaluation may be more important to self-esteem than others. Among sixth-grade children, for example, the roles of athlete, son or daughter, and student seemed to have the greatest impact on overall self-esteem, while the areas of friendship and club membership were less influential (Hoelter, 1986). And of course people vary in the values they attach to specific areas. Whereas one person's self-esteem may be linked primarily to facial attractiveness, another person may rely primarily on academic achievement as a yardstick of self-worth.

Positive self-esteem is generally considered a good thing, the mark of a healthy person. And indeed, there is considerable evidence that self-esteem is associated with a variety of positive outcomes. Rebecca Ellis and Susan Taylor (1983) looked at the effects of college students' self-esteem in a very practical situation—the job search process. First these investigators assessed the self-esteem of 86 college seniors who were preparing to look for jobs upon graduation. Then, four months later, the investigators came back to find out how the students had gone about their job searches and what the outcomes had been. They found that students who differed in level of self-esteem had quite different experiences. Students with low self-esteem tended to use formal resources, such as newspaper ads and employment agencies, to identify job possibilities. Students with high self-esteem tended to shun these traditional resources, yet they had more job offers than did students who used them. The fact that the students with high self-esteem were rated more favorably by the organizational recruiters who interviewed them sug-

Box 3–3
Mirror, mirror on the wall . . .

Many people find their physical appearance an important source of self-esteem. This link between self-evaluation and external appearance is reflected in the culture as a whole. Consider the amount of money that people spend on cosmetics, physical fitness programs, plastic surgery, and toothpastes that promise sex appeal. Perhaps because our society places so much emphasis on physical appearance, investigators have found that people tend to see themselves as more attractive than other people consider them (Pittenger & Baskett, 1984). At the same time, other people's opinions have a strong influence on our judgments of our own attributes—the effect of reflected appraisals. Indeed, the opinions of others may be particularly influential in the case of physical appearance, where the objective criteria are not altogether clear (Felson, 1985). Judgments of one's attractiveness can also be influenced by one's immediate circumstances. Imagine that you are in a room filled with beautiful people. If someone asked you to rate your attractiveness, you might give yourself a lower rating than you ordinarily would. Such downgrading would be less likely if the beautiful people were professionals—models, for example—than if you saw them as peers (Cash, Cash, & Butters, 1983). Once again we see clearly that the self is a social construct.

---

gests that such people have superior social skills. Even the loss of a job, a serious setback for most people, can be buffered by high self-esteem (Shamir, 1986).

Experiencing Emotions

High self-esteem is pleasurable and satisfying, and it is not surprising that many theorists have considered it a dominant human goal (Rosenberg, 1979). Most people would prefer to be in a positive state and to experience positive emotions. In fact, people report that they do experience more positive than negative emotions. Shula Sommers (1984) asked college students to describe their experiences on a typical day, using a list of adjectives that referred to positive and negative emotions. By a large margin, students believed that mildly positive emotions best characterized a typical day. When they were asked to use the same set of adjectives to describe an atypical day, they chose adjectives that applied to mildly negative emotions most frequently (see Figure 3–3).

Often the unpleasant emotions that we experience are a consequence of negative self-evaluation. Possible selves—identities that we believe we might take on—can be a cause of substantial negative emotion (Markus & Nurius, 1986). Thus if I fear that I may become an accountant when I really want to be a lawyer, or worry that I may have a mental breakdown, my vision of such an outcome can create feelings of distress.

The kind of emotion we feel depends on the particular standard we are using to evaluate ourselves. According to a theory proposed by Tory Higgins (in press), most of us use two major standards to evaluate ourselves: (1) an *ideal* self, which is an image of what we would like to be (or what someone else would like us to be), and (2) an *ought* self, which represents what we feel we should be (or what some other significant person thinks we should be). Discrepancies between the actual self and one of these standards will cause negative emotions, with the kind of emotion felt depending on the type of discrepancy. Higgins shows that dejection and disappointment are most likely if the discrepancy is between an actual self and an ideal self. For the sake of argument, assume that you would like to be an effective leader of your organization—your ideal self is a natural leader. In fact, however, you have to admit that your leadership qualities are not terribly strong, and other members of your group are regularly sought for leadership roles before you are. How will you feel? In all likelihood you will feel downcast, sad, and dejected because you are failing to gain the positive rewards that you want.

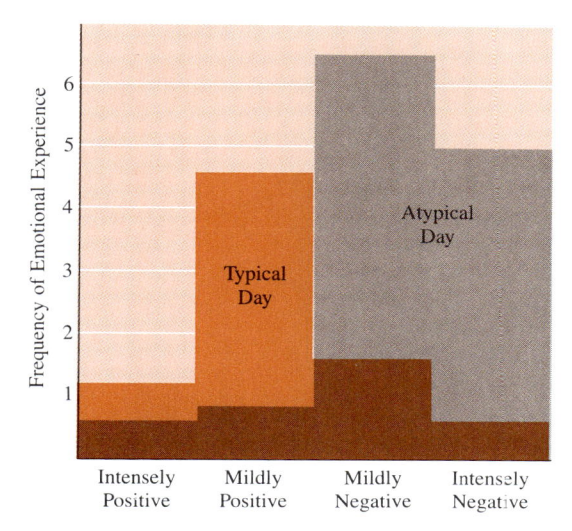

Figure 3–3 Reported emotional experiences of typical and atypical days

Discrepancies between one's actual self and an ought self produce a more agitated state. This time let's assume that you believe you ought to be an honest person on all occasions. As you talk with your professor the day before an exam, you see a copy of the exam on the desk. The phone rings and the professor is distracted for a few minutes. You unobtrusively make notes on the questions you see on the exam so you can prepare answers for use the next day. How do you feel about the discrepancy between what you think you ought to be (honest) and what you have done (a dishonest act)? Guilt, uneasiness, possibly self-contempt—each of these emotions results from a state of fearing some negative consequence or possible punishment.

Reductions in such discrepancies may, to turn the issue around, be a source of positive emotions. If you as a would-be leader begin to develop more effective leadership skills and are selected increasingly often to lead your group, you will probably experience a sense of elation or satisfaction. Thus self-evaluation is an important process in the generation of both positive and negative emotions.

Just how people interpret their emotional experiences is subject to some variability. Emotional experience depends on both a state of physiological arousal and on an appropriate cognitive label for that arousal (Schachter & Singer, 1962; Zillmann, 1978). In other words, how a person interprets an event influences how and what emotions will be experienced. "Butterflies in the stomach" can be interpreted both as excitement and anticipation at an important social occasion and as fear and apprehension when being called into the supervisor's office after a major account is lost. These variations in interpretation, like the evaluations discussed in the next section, demonstrate how influential and how flexible beliefs about oneself can be.

Evaluating Abilities

Mayor Ed Koch of New York City made the phrase "How'm I doin'?" his byline, urging citizens on the streets and reporters in his office to provide some evaluation of his performance. Like Mayor Koch, most of us seek information that will give us a sense of where we stand.

Some judgments about ourselves are easy to make. There is little room for error in deciding whether one's hair is red or black or how old or tall one is. Such objective judgments are quite easy to make, and there is generally very little disagreement between a person's self-description and an outside observer's description of the same person. In other areas, though, judgments cannot be made with so much certainty because there are no objective standards on which a person can rely.

One way to find out more about one's abilities is to gain some experience. People are more likely to seek out tasks that test abilities about which they are uncertain than tasks that call for skills they are quite certain they lack (Trope & Ben-Yair, 1982). If Mack is uncertain about his ability to solve crossword puzzles, for instance, he may do one every day for a week to find out just how well he can perform. With more experience at the task, he will be in a better position to evaluate his ability. After a week of doing crossword puzzles, Mack may be quite certain that he has no talent or liking for those black and white boxes. His attempts at self-evaluation on that particular dimension may cease. In fact, people who believe they have little ability at a task will avoid situations that would provide additional feedback (Meyer & Starke, 1982). At the same time, people who have considerable ability may sometimes continue to seek opportunities for evaluation, perhaps still seeking to learn just how good they are.

As we have indicated, some characteristics, such as hair and eye color, can be evaluated with little or no reference to other people. Similarly, it is easy to know whether or not you have completed a crossword puzzle. Many skills, aptitudes, and values, however, can be evaluated only by comparing oneself with other people. Leon Festinger (1954) developed **social comparison theory** to explain this process. The theory states that, in the absence of a physical or objective standard of correctness, we will seek other people as a means of evaluating ourselves. Whether the issue is our attitudes toward Iranians or a new dress style or the latest rock group, we are often motivated to evaluate our beliefs and abilities by comparing them with social reality (Goethals, 1986; Latané, 1966; Suls & Miller, 1977).

Self-evaluation through social comparison is more fruitful when we choose to compare ourselves with people who are generally similar to us (Castore & DeNinno, 1977; Goethals & Darley, 1977). Similarity, in this case, is gauged on the basis of characteristics related to the task in question (Wheeler, Koestner, & Driver, 1982). If Anita is trying to evaluate her tennis game, for example, she probably will not choose to compare herself with top-seeded Martina Navratilova, nor is she likely to choose a 6-year-old who has just picked up a racket. She is much more likely to compare herself with someone just slightly better than she is, reflecting what Festinger (1954) termed a *unidirectional drive upward*. When she chooses such a "comparison other," Anita is selecting a standard that she may be able to match in the future. Later, if her tennis game improves, her standard of comparison will probably rise as well.

The sex of the comparison other has been found to be an important dimension of comparison. When subjects in an experiment were allowed to choose one person with whose performance they would like to compare their own, both males and females generally showed a strong preference for someone of the same sex (Suls, Gaes, & Gastorf, 1979; Zanna, Goethals, & Hill, 1975). The choice of someone of the same sex for purposes of comparison is particularly likely if the task is somehow related to gender and if the individual has a strong tendency to refer to gender in processing information (Miller, 1984). Thus, people seek relevant others with whom to compare their performances, and similarity often serves as a cue for potential relevance.

Our curiosity about ourselves often goes beyond

deciding how we feel, what we believe, and how well we did in comparison with other people. Many times we want to figure out *why* we acted in a particular way or why a certain outcome occurred. This process of explaining or inferring the causes of events has been termed **causal attribution.** (As we shall see in Chapter Four, causal attributions are made in regard to the behavior of other people as well.)

Fritz Heider, whose work (1944, 1958) serves as the mainspring for much of the work on attribution processes, suggested that we all act as "naive psychologists," trying to discover cause-and-effect relations in the events that occur around us. These attempts to make sense of our work are the central focus of attribution theory.

Any event can have a variety of possible causes. To create some order in this abundance, Heider (1958) suggested that the causes to which we attribute events may be either of two basic types: *dispositional* (or personal) and *situational* (or environmental). In the cartoon on p. 80, for example, Lois has come up with a variety of situational causes for her first gray hair. Each of these claimed causes is external to her—some person or event in the environment. Alternatively, it would be possible for Lois to assign a dispositional cause to the event (such as the fact that she is growing older).

"Growing old" is an attribution that would require some change in Lois's self-concept—a change that many people find aversive. People often avoid making such attributions, preferring to accentuate the positive and eliminate the negative, at least when it comes to themselves. This tendency to accept greater personal responsibility for positive outcomes than for negative outcomes has been termed the **self-serving attribution bias.** And a pervasive bias it is. Miron Zuckerman (1979), analyzing several dozen studies that looked at people's explanations of their own performance, found a systematic tendency for people to claim that success on a task is due to their ability or the amount of effort they exerted—qualities that are associated with the people themselves. People are much more likely to seek situational causes when they fail, preferring to look outside themselves for an explanation. The self-serving bias is also in evidence when people estimate their own effect on other people's outcomes. A professor, for example, is more likely to claim responsibility when his or her students do well than when they do poorly (Arkin, Cooper, & Kolditz, 1980).

Not everyone is given to self-serving attributions. People who suffer from depression (as a pervasive condition, not as an isolated reaction to an unfortunate turn of events) are likely to explain events in just the opposite way (Sweeney, Anderson, & Bailey, 1986): after negative outcomes, the depressive person is likely to offer explanations that stress dispositional and stable causes. "It's all my fault," the depressive tends to claim. Furthermore, depressive people often use global or general reasons, suggesting that a particular factor could cause the same outcome in many other situations. People who are not depressed are more likely to offer specific explanations, not generalizing them to other possible events. The depressive's explanations for positive outcomes are also the reverse of those predicted by the self-serving model. Now the depressive turns to situational, temporary, and very specific factors as the

Attributions of causality

responsible agents. Good things may happen, but for the depressive person, they are not really under one's own control.

These patterns of explanation are interesting, but are they important? Does it make a difference how a person interprets events? Attribution theorists have always assumed that there is a connection between the explanations that people offer and their subsequent behavior (Jones et al., 1972), and several studies support this assumption. A particularly relevant case is the work of Timothy Wilson and Patricia Linville (1985) in investigating the explanations offered by first-year college students who did poorly in their initial studies. They wanted to see if they could help those students who were below the class median (below a 3.0 or B average, in this case) and who reported being worried about their academic performance. Their strategy was to give students information that might alter their attributions. Students in the treatment condition listened to upper-class students talk about their academic experiences. The advanced students revealed that they, too, had had poor grades during their first year, but that steady improvement had followed. This information was designed to show the faltering first-year students that their performance was fairly typical and was subject to change. A control group of first-year students, with whom the investigators proposed to compare the students in the treatment condition, received no such information. Did the information have any effect on the subsequent performance of the students?

Wilson and Linville sought to answer this question in two ways, looking at both short-term and long-term performance. Short-term effects were assessed by the students' performance on questions from the Graduate Record Examination, administered immediately after the interview sessions. The intervention proved to be effective for male students but to make no difference for female students. More important, perhaps, were the effects on long-term performance, reflected in the grades the students earned in the semester following the study. These results are shown in Figure 3–4. Again the program seemed to be more effective for male students, whose performance improved dramatically in comparison with that of the control group. In a somewhat different pattern, all of the women students improved, although the amount of improvement was greater for women in the treatment condition, who had initially had lower grades than those in the comparison group. Why the difference between women and men? Wilson and Linville suggest that women may typically engage in more discussion of their problems and more comparison with others. Thus women in the control group may have gained on their own much of the same information that the investigators were providing the treatment group.

Attributional effects go beyond the classroom. When Antonia Abbey and her colleagues interviewed law school students who were looking for jobs, they found that students who believed that their ability to find a job was contingent on personal and dispositional factors reported being much happier than their peers who made situational attributions (Abbey, Dunkel-Schetter, & Brickman, 1983). And although these particular investigators did not follow

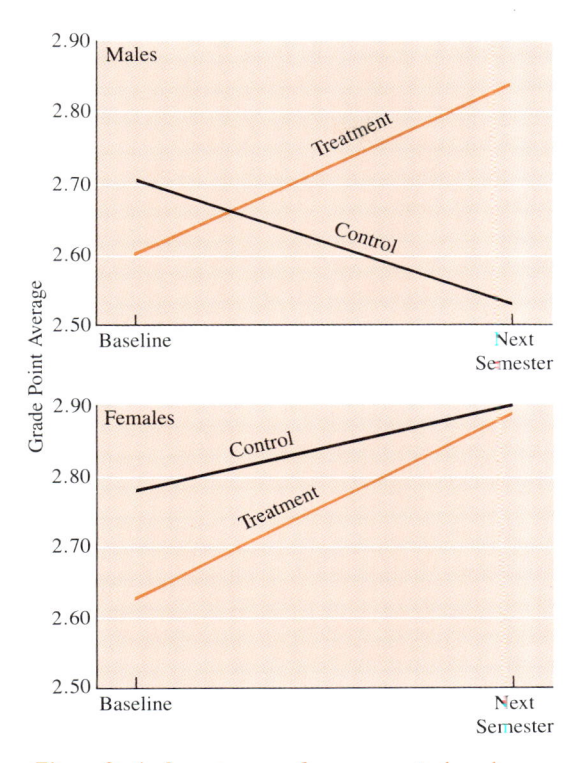

Figure 3–4 Long-term performance: actual grades achieved by students before and after Wilson and Linville conducted their studies (on a 4-point scale, where 4.0 = A, 3.7 = A−, 3.3 = B+, 3.0 = B, etc.)

the students to find out how successful their job searches were, the study of self-esteem and job success that was described earlier suggests that these dispositional attributors probably did better in the search. That suggestion is given further support by a study of life insurance sales agents (Seligman & Schulman, 1986), who were classified into two groups on the basis of their general attributional style: in one group were those who tended to explain unfortunate events as we have seen depressive people do (offering dispositional, stable, and global explanations); in the other group were people who did not typically give such explanations. Following the progress of these agents over a one-year period, the investigators learned that the agents in the latter group were much more likely to keep their jobs and sold considerably more insurance than their more depressive counterparts.

We cannot say that the way one explains events is always going to have such major consequences. But it is an important factor not only in what we think about ourselves but in the way we deal with the people and events in our world as well.

Relating to Others

Knowing oneself is no easy task. As individuals, we attempt to evaluate our worth, understand our emotions, and explain our outcomes. But individuals are more than self-contained units. Each of us is part of an ongoing social process, an interaction between the self and others. And in those interactions we make many choices as to how we wish to represent ourselves to others.

Presenting the Self

As we have suggested, the self is best represented as a variety of self-schemas or identities. Given this multiplicity of selves, how does the individual decide which self to present? The general process by which people behave in particular ways to create a desired social image has been called **impression management**. Barry Schlenker defines impression management as "the conscious or unconscious attempt to

Person Wandering Through Indistinct Identities

control images that are projected in real or imagined social interactions" (1980, p. 6). In other words, people are often concerned about the image they present to others. Different situations may arouse different identity concerns; people's goals may vary from one situation to the next. These and other factors affect the presentation of the self.

The sociologist Erving Goffman (1959, 1967) drew analogies to the world of theater in formulating his theory of the *presentation of self in everyday life*. Goffman described social interaction as a theatrical performance in which each individual presents a "line"—a set of carefully chosen verbal and nonverbal acts that express one's self. One major feature of a person's line, which Goffman termed the "face," is the positive social value gained by one's interaction. For Goffman, one of the fundamental rules of social interaction is mutual commitment. By this he meant that each participant will work to keep all members of the interaction "in face" through their self-presentation. Each person has a repertoire of face-saving devices, an awareness of the interpretation that others place on his or her acts, a desire to sustain each member's face, and the willingness to use his or her repertoire of impression-managing techniques.

Maintaining face is not the goal of social interaction; rather, it is a necessary background that permits social interaction to continue. Incidents that threaten the face of a participant also threaten the survival of the relationship. Consequently, when events challenge the face of a participant, corrective processes called *face-work* are initiated to avert any embarrassment that might interfere with the conduct of the relationship. Thus we conspicuously overlook or help others apologize for the social blunders and potentially embarrassing faux pas they commit. In short, for Goffman, social interaction requires its participants to be able to regulate their self-presentation so that it will be perceived and evaluated appropriately by others.

Some people think of impression management as a deliberate strategy of manipulation, as opposed to expressing one's true inner feelings and beliefs. That notion is usually mistaken (Tetlock & Manstead, 1985). In choosing which aspect of the self to present in a particular situation, an individual may be choosing among equally true selves. Indeed, a common goal pursued in social interaction is self-verification—presenting the self as one believes it to be (Swann, 1986).

The Goals of Self-Presentation

The choice of self-presentation strategies depends on the individual's goals. Some goals may suggest that certain attributes of the self are most important to display, while other goals may call for a different presentation of self. Edward Jones and Thane Pittman (1982) have identified five major strategies of self-presentation, each designed to help the individual attain a particular sort of goal. These five tactics are ingratiation, intimidation, self-promotion, exemplification, and supplication. Let us look at each of these tactics in detail.

1. *Ingratiation*. Perhaps the most common of presentation techniques, ingratiation consists of behaviors that are "designed to influence a particular other person concerning the attractiveness of one's personal qualities" (Jones & Wortman, 1973, p. 2). In other words, the main goal of the ingratiator is to be seen as likable.

One can approach this task in a variety of ways. One common tactic is to compliment the other person. Another ingratiation tactic is to conform to the other person's opinions and behaviors. As one character says in Molière's play *The Miser*, "I find the best way to win people's favor is to pretend to agree with them, to fall in with their precepts, encourage their foibles, and applaud whatever they do." This view assumes, correctly, that we tend to like people whose beliefs, attitudes, and behaviors are similar to our own (see Chapter Nine). Such a tactic will not work, however, if the target suspects that one is deliberately being ingratiating (Kauffman & Steiner, 1968). The ingratiating person is often a *reactor*, responding to the comments and actions of the other person (Godfrey, Jones, & Lord, 1986). The ingra-

tiator can be friendly, a good listener, and willing to look for common ground in a conversation.

2. *Intimidation*. In contrast to the goal of affection sought by the person who relies on ingratiation, the goal of the person who uses intimidation as a strategy is to arouse fear. By creating the image of a dangerous person, the intimidator tries to control an interaction by the exercise of power. Jones and Pittman (1982) offer the example of a sidewalk robber, who attempts to create fear in the victim and thereby gain money or jewelry. One can also think of cases in which a parent presents such an image to a child or a professor to a student. Threats are obviously not very pleasant and may cause the other person to try to escape the situation. For this reason, Jones and Pittman suggest that intimidation may be used most often in relationships that are in some respects involuntary, from which escape is not easy.

3. *Self-promotion*. If a person's goal is to be seen as competent, either on some general quality, such as intelligence, or in some specific skill, such as playing the banjo, self-promotion is the tactic most often used. In contrast to the reactive ingratiator, the self-promoter tends to be proactive (Godfrey, Jones, & Lord, 1986). Self-promoters take the lead in conversations, describing their strengths and attempting to impress others with their accomplishments. Sometimes self-promoters acknowledge minor flaws in order to be more credible when they claim skills in areas that are important (Jones, Gergen, & Jones, 1963). Similarly, the self-promoter may acknowledge weaknesses if they are already known to the target person, and then go on to emphasize positive

traits that the person was not aware of (Baumeister & Jones, 1978). A danger in self-promotion is the possible mismatch between claims of competence and reality. If I claim that I am a great racketball player, for example, I had better either be good or avoid getting on the court with the person on whom I used this tactic.

4. *Exemplification.* "You go on home. I'll stay here at the office and work four more hours to finish this project, even though I may have to miss my daughter's birthday party." This is an example of exemplification, a tactic designed to elicit perceptions of integrity and moral worthiness—and often to arouse guilt in the target person as well. The exemplifier may be a martyr or the leader of a revolutionary cause or simply a person who likes to appear as a sufferer. In each case, the goal is to influence the impressions that others form and, in turn, their behaviors in regard to either the person or the cause.

5. *Supplication.* In this fifth form of self-presentation, a person advertises his or her weakness and dependence on another person. Unlike the exemplifier, who is seeking respect, the supplicant is seeking sympathy. Jones and Pittman suggest that supplication is often the person's last hope, tried when other goals appear unattainable. Although it may not be the preferred tactic, we can think of many occasions when people may resort to it. The man who claims to be "all thumbs," for example, may get someone else to sew a button on his shirt; the woman who expresses fear of electricity may avoid the task of repairing a broken lamp; the student who claims ignorance of typing skills may prompt a generous roommate to offer to type a term paper. In each case, the person is presenting an image of helplessness in the hope of arousing a sense of obligation in the target.

Many other goals are possible when people decide how they want to present themselves to others. Often it is important to present oneself as a member of a particular group, or to affirm some central aspect of one's personality. Gender identity is one such case. Although one's basic sense of masculinity or femininity is probably quite stable, the importance of that identity may vary. In some situations, a person may feel it is very important to be seen as particularly masculine or feminine; in other circumstances, this particular self-presentational goal may not exist (Deaux & Major, in press).

Consider an experiment in which female job applicants were scheduled to be interviewed by male interviewers, described either as valuing the traditional female stereotype of emotionality and deference or as favoring more independent, career-oriented women (von Baeyer, Sherk, & Zanna, 1981). When the women arrived for their scheduled interviews, the experimenters carefully observed what they wore and recorded their answers to the interviewer's questions. The values that the women expected the interviewer to hold clearly affected the self-presentation strategies they chose. Women who expected a traditional interviewer looked more "feminine," not only in their overall appearance and demeanor but also in their use of makeup and choice of accessories. These women also gave more traditional responses to questions about marriage and children. Women who expected an interviewer who favored career-oriented women tended less to fulfill the traditional female stereotype in their behavior and appearance.

Such tailoring of one's sex-role image is not limited to women. Similar studies have found that men also alter their presentation to fit the presumed values of another person (for example, Jellison, Jackson-White, Bruder, & Martyna, 1975). Other basic characteristics can also be subject to self-presentational concerns. A Black person, for example, may choose to speak and dress differently with a predominantly Black group than with a predominantly White group. Similarly, a White may follow the same kind of strategy in an attempt to create a positive impression on one or the other group. In these and many other cases, concerns with self-presentation may cause marked shifts in behavior as a person moves from one audience to another.

Tactics of Self-Presentation

The tactics of self-presentation are as various as its goals. One widely used tactic, particularly when perceived competence is the goal, is the **self-handicapping strategy.** As Stephen Berglas and Edward Jones define it, a self-handicapping strategy is "any action or choice of performance setting that enhances the opportunity to externalize (or excuse) failure and to internalize (reasonably accept credit for) success" (1978, p. 406). Think of a student who approaches an exam with the following story: "I didn't get any sleep last night. The phone kept ringing, two cats were fighting in the alley, the people upstairs had the stereo blasting for hours. How could I study or sleep? I'll never do well on this exam." Such a student is carefully setting up excuses in preparation for possible failure on the exam.

In an empirical demonstration of self-handicapping strategies in action, Berglas and Jones (1978) asked two groups of college students to work on a problem-solving task. One group received problems that could be solved, while the other group had to work on problems that had no solutions. Before proceeding to a second problem-solving session, subjects were given a choice of two drugs that were ostensibly of interest to the experimenter. One of these drugs was supposed to enhance performance; the other was described as impairing performance. Subjects who had previously worked on solvable problems generally chose the drug that would improve their performance. The other group of subjects, whose experience probably led them to believe that they might not do well on the next task either, showed a strong preference for the interfering drug. By handicapping themselves through the use of a drug, they provided themselves with a convenient excuse in case they did poorly on the second task. In the language of attribution theory, they had prepared a situational explanation for their possible failure and thus would be able to avoid negative dispositional explanations. (For another example of self-handicapping strategies, see Box 3–4.)

Box 3–4
Self-handicapping in the swimming pool

Do athletes engage in self-handicapping strategies? Would a top tennis player slack off in practice before a big tournament? Would a star receiver stay out too late before the big football game? Such behavior is hardly calculated to help one achieve a great performance—yet some players deliberately handicap themselves in this way in an attempt to protect their self-esteem in case they lose.

Frederick Rhodewalt and his students observed the performance of 27 members of the Princeton men's swimming team to learn more about self-handicapping strategies (Rhodewalt, Saltzman, & Wittmer, 1984). Using a scale that has been developed to assess people's general tendencies to handicap themselves, the investigators divided the swimmers into two groups—high self-handicappers and low self-handicappers. Records of attendance at practice were kept during each week leading up to a meet. In addition, the swimming coaches were asked to evaluate the practice performance of each swimmer during each of the weeks.

We would expect swimmers who have strong tendencies to handicap themselves to practice less before a meet than those low in such tendencies. By cutting back on practice, high self-handicappers give themselves an excuse for poor performance. Such differences should be particularly strong when the upcoming meet is an important one, because more self-esteem is at stake. The results of the Rhodewalt study are shown below. Although high and low self-handicappers differed little in regard to

continued

A person who has taken no self-handicapping actions before a failure may try to find some excuse for the failure afterward. As we saw earlier, people's attributions are often self-serving: they tend to take credit for their successes and to avoid the blame for failure. One may make such attributions in order to convince not only oneself but an audience as well. A good excuse dissuades an audience from linking a person with an undesirable outcome (Snyder, Higgins, & Stucky, 1983). Excuses take many forms. A person who has failed may try to convince an audience that his or her performance is highly inconsistent, thus suggesting that no single failure should be taken too seriously. Or a person may claim that this one particular situation was unique, thus preventing generalization of the outcome to his or her overall competence (Mehlman & Snyder, 1985).

Even the distant past may be appealed to when excuses are needed. People may claim that they are not responsible for their outcomes because of early traumatic experiences. As the psychoanalyst Alfred Adler once said, "the neurotic does not suffer from his reminiscences, he makes them. He raises them to rank and dignity" (quoted in DeGree & Snyder, 1985, p. 1512). Nor is it only the neurotic who makes such excuses. College students who faced probable failure on a task reported more adversity in their backgrounds when such a tactic seemed to provide a suitable excuse for failure (DeGree & Snyder, 1985).

Sometimes the desire for favorable self-presentation leads people to associate themselves with the success of others. Have you ever told people that you come from the same town as a well-known television personality, that you went to school with a prominent politician, or that you are distantly related to a famous historical figure? Such attempts to *bask in reflected glory* can be seen on many college campuses the Monday morning after a big football game (Cialdini, Borden, Thorne, Walker, & Freeman, 1976). Students are more likely to wear clothing and buttons that associate them with their school after a victory than after a defeat. "We won," they say after a winning game, but "They lost" after the other team won. "Cutting off reflected failure" coexists with basking in glory as a self-presentation strategy (Snyder, Lassegard, & Ford, 1986).

Box 3–4
continued

practice before unimportant meets, differences increased—both in actual attendance and in the coach's ratings—before important meets.

Presumably collegiate swimmers are not alone in these tendencies. In fact, Rhodewalt and his colleagues have found similar tendencies among professional golfers, and we suspect that the self-handicapping net spreads to other sports as well.

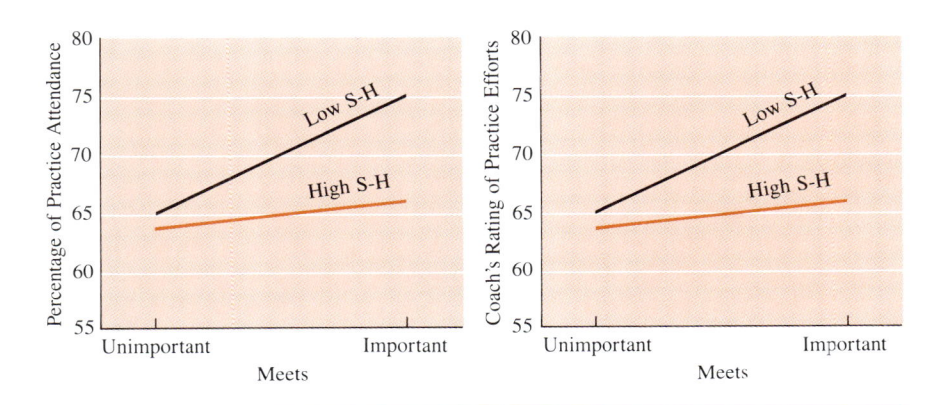

These various tactics of self-presentation are designed to present a particular face to an audience (and to oneself) on a specific occasion. But do they have any lasting effect? Does the image we present on one occasion have any impact on our private self-conceptions? Frederick Rhodewalt and his colleagues have shown that self-presentation strategies can have *carryover effects* (Jones, Rhodewalt, Berglas, & Skelton, 1981; Rhodewalt, in press; Rhodewalt & Agustsdottir, 1986). They suggest that the phenomenal self-concept—the aspects of the self that one is immediately aware of—can be influenced by self-presentations. Referring back to our earlier discussion of self-schemas, we can think of particular aspects of the self as being more accessible after they are presented, and hence more likely to influence our future sense of self. In this case, we are suggesting that images of the self that were already part of the self-concept become more prominent as a result of self-presentation. At the same time, self-concepts can be changed by self-presentation as well. When an individual chooses to engage in a behavior that conflicts somewhat with his or her previous sense of self, that behavior can cause an alteration in the way the self is conceived. The fact that an individual's sense of self may be changed by the very means chosen to express the self testifies to both the stability and the flexibility of the self-concept.

Individual Differences in Self-Presentation

Everyone engages in self-presentation behaviors from time to time; yet there are important differences in the extent to which people can and do control their presentations. Some people engage in impression management more often and with greater skill than others. Professional actors are trained to manipulate the images that they project to the audience. Successful politicians, too, have long practiced the art of wearing the right face for the right constituency (see Box 3–5).

People outside these professional realms also vary in the extent to which they can and do exercise control over their verbal and nonverbal self-presentation. These variations are captured by the psychological construct of **self-monitoring** (Snyder, 1979,

Photo 3–2 A person's sense of self can be changed by the very means used to express oneself.

1987). High self-monitoring persons are particularly sensitive to the expressions and self-presentations of others in social situations, and they use these cues in monitoring their own self-presentation for purposes of impression management. High self-monitoring persons are identified by their high scores on the Self-Monitoring Scale (Snyder & Gangestad, 1986). The high self-monitoring person endorses such statements as these:

1. In different situations and with different people, I often act like very different persons.
2. I'm not always the person I appear to be.
3. I may deceive people by being friendly when I really dislike them.

High self-monitoring persons are good at learning what is socially appropriate in new situations, have good control of their emotional expressions, and can effectively use these abilities to create the impressions they want. In fact, they are such polished actors that they can effectively adopt the mannerisms of a reserved, withdrawn, and introverted person and then do an abrupt about-face and portray themselves, equally convincingly, as friendly, outgoing, and extroverted (Lippa, 1976, 1978a). In self-presentation situations, high self-monitoring persons are quite likely to seek out and consult social-comparison information about appropriate patterns of self-presentation. They invest considerable effort in attempting to "read" and understand others (Berscheid, Graziano, Monson, & Dermer, 1976; Jones & Baumeister, 1976).

You may detect similarities between the concept of self-monitoring and that of public self-consciousness, discussed earlier. In fact, the two concepts are related, though only moderately so (Scheier & Carver, 1980). The person high in self-consciousness may be aware of the impression that he or she is making but does not necessarily act on that information. High self-monitors, in contrast, use this information to guide their self-presentations in order to gain approval or power in an interaction. In other words, a high degree of self-consciousness may be necessary for self-monitoring behavior, but it is not sufficient for impression management.

Let's consider an experiment by Mark Snyder and Thomas Monson (1975) to see how self-monitors operate. In this study, group discussions sensitized individuals to different peer reference groups that could provide cues to the social appropriateness of one's self-presentation. High self-monitoring persons were keenly attentive to these differences, as

Box 3–5
Presidential rhetoric: Self-presentation in action

Campaign promises made by candidates as they run for election often seem to be forgotten when they take office. One possible explanation for these apparent shifts in position is that new information leads to a real change in opinion. According to this *cognitive adjustment* interpretation, the officeholder may be exposed to arguments that did not surface during the campaign and may be forced to alter his or her view of the proper course. A second, more cynical explanation is that politicians never intend to fulfill their campaign promises. Rather, the claims they present on the campaign trail may simply represent a self-presentation strategy, designed to make a favorable impression on their audiences—and win their votes.

To test these competing hypotheses, Philip Tetlock (1981) compared preelection and postelection statements by 20th-century U.S. presidents. Preelection statements were made during the five months before the election; postelection statements were gathered at three points in time—one month after the president took office, during the second year of office, and during the third year. Tetlock reasoned that if cognitive adjustment were the major reason for shifts in policy, then changes should be gradual as the president acquired increasing amounts of information. The self-presentation hypothesis, in contrast, predicts more rapid changes in policy statements, changes that should be evident during the first month in office. To assess these possible changes, Tetlock evaluated the complexity of statements the presidents made, ranging from simple, unidimensional statements at one end of the scale to more complex, multidimensional statements at the other end.

Tetlock's findings give strong support to the self-presentation interpretation. Presidents' policy statements became significantly more complex immediately after they took office and did not change much over their first three years. The suddenness of this shift and the level pattern after election are not consistent with a gradual accumulation of information leading to cognitive adjustment. The trends were very similar for all the presidents during the 20th century with one exception: statements made by Herbert Hoover became simpler after he took office than they had been before.

But what if an elected official planned to run for reelection? Under these conditions, the self-presentation hypothesis predicts, statements would once again be simplified as the election drew near. And that is exactly what Tetlock found. Concentrating only on presidents who decided to run for reelection after their first term, he compared statements made in their next-to-last year in office with statements made in the last year before the election. The complexity of their statements was found to decline significantly as these candidates prepared once again to present themselves to the voters.

Figure 3–5 indicates. They were conforming when conformity was the most appropriate interpersonal orientation and nonconforming when reference-group norms favored autonomy in the face of social pressure. Low self-monitoring persons were virtually unaffected by the differences in social setting. Presumably their self-presentations were accurate reflections of their own personal attitudes and dispositions. In a similar study, high self-monitoring subjects were more likely to be cooperative when they expected future interaction with a partner than when they did not, while low self-monitors did not vary their behavior in response to such prospects (Danheiser & Graziano, 1982).

Self-monitoring may be a useful skill in the work world. Some positions in organizations have been

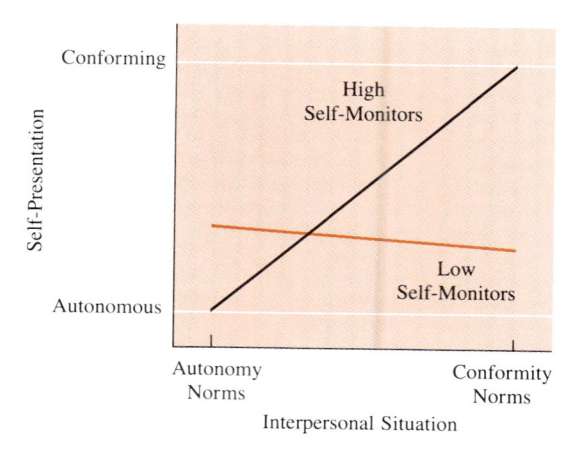

Figure 3-5 Autonomy and conformity in self-presentations of high self-monitoring and low self-monitoring persons when faced with group norms calling for autonomy or conformity

called "boundary-spanning" positions. As people who hold such positions are responsible for filtering and transmitting information across organizational boundaries, they must be able to adapt to a variety of pressures and competing opinions. David Caldwell and Charles O'Reilly (1982) reasoned that persons who score high in self-monitoring should be more successful in such positions because they have the ability to perceive cues and modify their behavior accordingly. They measured the self-monitoring tendencies of 93 field representatives whose jobs required boundary spanning and assessed their job performance. High self-monitors did indeed do better in these jobs, and the differences were particularly important during the early stages of employment. These findings are important, for they suggest that self-monitoring, far from being a skill to be cultivated only by people who wish to deceive, can be helpful to anyone in an environment that contains a complex mix of people and policies.

Is impression management good or bad? Clearly it can be either. Erving Goffman pointed out both the potentials and the pitfalls:

> Too little perceptiveness, too little *savoir faire* [that is, too little impression management], too little pride and considerateness, and the person ceases to be someone who can be trusted to take a hint about himself or give a hint that will save others embarrassment. Such a person comes to be a real threat to society; there is nothing much that can be done with him.... Too much *savoir faire* or too much considerateness, and he becomes someone who is too socialized, who leaves the others with the feeling that they do not know how they really stand with him, nor what they should do to make an effective long term adjustment. [Goffman, 1955, p. 227]

The same tactic of self-presentation can foster an honest image or a deceptive one, can influence others for altruistic purposes or for exploitive ones. We may or may not approve of a particular goal served by self-presentation, but certainly the presentation of self is an integral part of everyday social interaction.

Summary

Social knowledge and social behavior begin with the *self-concept,* the totality of an individual's thoughts about the self. As such early social scientists as George Herbert Mead and Harry Stack Sullivan pointed out, we learn about ourselves from the reflected appraisals of others. We also learn about ourselves through the outcomes of actions we take.

Self-schemas are cognitive generalizations about the self that influence the way we organize and remember events and experiences. The self-concept consists of multiple schemas. We may usefully think of the self as consisting of multiple identities arranged in a hierarchy of importance. The self-concept also includes ideas about what we would like to be or think it possible to become. Certain of a person's characteristics are likely to affect the definition of self. Both *gender identity* and *racial identity* are important aspects of the self.

Self-perception theory says that we become aware of ourselves by watching what we do, much as outside observers form judgments of us on the basis of what they see. Certain conditions can create a state of *objective self-awareness*; at such times we focus attention on some aspect of the self. The particular aspect of self that is salient depends in part on the accessibility of that aspect, which can be affected by *priming*. People who are high in *self-consciousness* are more likely to engage in this process than people who are low in self-consciousness.

Because the concept of self is an active one, it is important to consider the processes involved. *Self-esteem* refers to the evaluation of oneself, an assessment of how good or bad one is. Negative emotions are generally aroused when there is a discrepancy between the perceived self and some standard of comparison (an ideal self, an ought self, or a possible self).

To evaluate their abilities, people often engage in *social comparison,* looking to other people as a way of gauging their own performance. People also make *causal attributions* to explain their outcomes. Frequently such attributions are *self-serving,* designed to permit us to take credit for positive outcomes and to avoid blame for negative ones. Attributions are important because they can affect subsequent choices and actions.

The attempt to control the images of the self that are presented to others is called *impression management*. Such self-presentation can serve many goals and people can use a variety of strategies in pursuing them. People who anticipate failure, for instance, may resort to *self-handicapping strategies*. Although all people engage in some impression management, people who score high in *self-monitoring* are more attuned to this process than people who score low in it.

Glossary Terms

causal attribution
gender identity
impression management
objective self-awareness
priming
racial identity
schema
self-concept
self-consciousness
self-esteem
self-handicapping strategy
self-monitoring
self-perception theory
self-schema
self-serving attribution bias
social comparison theory

*To know one's self is wisdom, but to know one's
neighbor is genius.*
Minna Antrim

The cause is hidden, but the result is well known.
Ovid

Lisa Kanemoto, *Mother's Day 1980*.

CHAPTER FOUR

Social Knowledge

I. Forming Impressions of People
   Physical Appearance
   Character Traits
   The Question of Accuracy
II. Organizing Impressions
   Implicit Personality and Social Theories
   Schemas, Prototypes, and Scripts
   Stereotypes
III. The Process of Social Cognition
   Encoding: Getting the Information In
   Storage and Retrieval: Getting the Information Out
   Errors and Biases
IV. Explaining Behavior: Attributions of Causality
   Covariation and Causal Schemas
   Correspondent Inference
   Causes of Success and Failure
   Belief in a Just World
V. Summary

*K*nowing ourselves is one form of understanding. Knowing about other people is another. Perhaps, as Minna Antrim suggests, truly knowing another person requires genius. If that is true, then most of us spend a great deal of time aspiring to genius status.

Why do we constantly try to understand and interpret the behavior of the people around us? Because we know that those people can affect our lives. The ability to predict whether an approaching stranger is a harmless beggar or a dangerous mugger may enable us to avoid theft and injury. If we seek out new people at a party, we may find love or rejection. The actions of other people have such important consequences to us that the ability to interpret their behavior is crucial to our well-being.

Just how do we think about people? What do we notice and what do we remember? How is information about other people represented in our memories? Are our impressions of other people generally accurate, or are we prone to certain biases? And how does the knowledge that we have affect our judgments of and interactions with others? Suppose that you are sitting in a chair reading a book, and you happen to glance out the window toward the house next door. Suddenly you see a person run out through the front door, jump into a car in the driveway, and speed away. What would you notice first? Probably you would notice first whether the person was a man or a woman. Having established that it was a woman, you would note her approximate height and weight and perhaps her ethnicity. If she was someone you had seen before, these features might help you to identify her. Ah, yes, it's Susan, your neighbor's sister. But why did she seem in such a hurry to leave? Why didn't your neighbor come out to say good-bye? These questions could lead you to engage in a process of causal attribution as you attempted to find explanations for the event that you had just witnessed.

Now let's change this scenario slightly. Suppose that you haven't recognized the person you've seen, but you're sure it was a middle-aged White man. Soon you find out that a burglary has been discovered next door, and you are called to the police station. Will you recognize the man in a police lineup? In this case, the concern is not with interpreting events but with recognizing an individual you have seen before. And later, as you think about these events, what do you recall? In succeeding months, can you recreate the scene that you witnessed? Does your account of the event change with the passage of time? These and other questions are the domain of social cognition.

As we noted in Chapter One, cognitive theories in general emphasize the ways in which experiences are represented and information is processed. In this chapter the cognitive approach will be very much in the foreground as we consider how social knowledge develops.

Forming Impressions of People

First impressions are important, we are often told. And although we are also advised never to judge a book by its cover, there is considerable evidence that people do just that—make judgments on the basis of appearance alone. Such judgments involve a set of inferences as to what the person we see is like "underneath." How accurate are such inferences? To answer these questions, let's look first at the raw material that goes into the impressions on which we base our initial judgments.

Physical Appearance

When we meet someone for the first time, appearance provides the first and most obvious information that we have about the person. Some characteristics, such as sex and race, are almost always noted and remembered (Grady, 1977; Kessler & McKenna, 1978; McArthur, 1982). Such physical features as height and weight are also likely to be noticed, particularly if the person varies strikingly from the average on one of these dimensions (DeJong & Kleck, 1986; Roberts & Herman, 1986). Thus we are unlikely to overlook the girth of a fat person, nor can exceptionally tall or short persons fail to draw comments.

To note a stranger's appearance is almost automatically to make an initial judgment on the person's physical attractiveness. It is reported that Queen Victoria once said, "An ugly baby is a very nasty object" (quoted in Langlois, 1986), making clear both her awareness of appearance and her feelings about it. Although most of us are less outspoken, our first impressions of people, adults as well as babies, are strongly influenced by the degree of their physical attractiveness (Dion, 1986; Freedman, 1986; Patzer, 1985).

Why are physical features so central a part of first impressions? As people's physical features are immediately apparent, we generally know whether they are tall or short before we know whether they are honest or conniving. It has also been suggested that we are attuned to physical features because we believe that they provide information about people's underlying characteristics and thus about their probable behavior (McArthur & Baron, 1983). In ecological terms, it is adaptive to pay attention to these physical signs.

In studies designed to explore this ecological interpretation, Leslie McArthur and her colleagues have investigated people's perceptions of faces of infants (Berry & McArthur, 1985, 1986; McArthur & Apatow, 1983/1984). Certain characteristics of

Figure 4–1 These three faces differ in the placement and size of the features. Which face looks youngest? Oldest? In what ways do the features vary from one face to another? Leslie McArthur and Karen Apatow used faces like these in their research, with the face on the left representing babyish features and the face on the right mature features. They used the face in the center, representing features midway between extreme youth and maturity, as a control.

the infant face are distinctive. Infants' heads are larger in relation to their bodies than adults' are, for example, and their eyes are larger in relation to their faces. A baby's features are lower on the face, giving the impression of a large forehead and a tiny chin. (The relative placement of the features of very youthful and mature faces is seen in Figure 4–1.) In ecological terms, these features serve as cues to inform people that this person is an infant, and so in need of attention and protection. In other words, people may infer from certain physical characteristics a set of behavioral tendencies, in this case helplessness and dependency.

Such inferences can be overgeneralized, however, as McArthur and her colleagues have shown. Adults whose features resemble those of infants—large eyes placed low on the face, for example, as in the left-hand face in Figure 4–1—are judged to have childish traits as well (Berry & McArthur, 1985; McArthur & Apatow, 1983/1984). They are assumed to be weaker, less dominant, and less intellectually astute than the average adult. At the same time, such adults are also judged to be exceptionally honest, kind, and warm—a judgment that reflects the widespread belief in the naiveté of childhood. As a poten-

tial roommate, the person with childlike features is seen as likely to respond to friendly conversation but unlikely to be able to move heavy boxes of books. All in all, a large set of inferences to draw from a small set of physical signs!

Infantile features are not the only physical characteristics with which people tend to associate psychological traits. Indeed, almost every physical feature has accumulated a history of associations, from the nose (a long one has been seen as a sign of energy) to wrinkles (which presumably testify to depth of character) (Berry & McArthur, 1986). At one time or another, tall people have been assumed to be delicate, introverted, stupid, and intelligent, while short people have been said to be passionate, pettish, and given to negativity (Roberts & Herman, 1986). Perhaps most studied by psychologists are the inferences we make about physically attractive people. Considerable research has shown that "what is beautiful is good," at least in a great many minds.

In fact, it is difficult to overestimate the effect of another person's physical appearance on our initial impressions. Studies have shown that the highly attractive person is more likely to be recommended for hiring after a job interview (Dipboye, Arvey, &

Photo 4–1 We rely on physical features when we first judge others.

Terpstra, 1977; Dipboye, Fromkin, & Wiback, 1975), to have his or her written work evaluated favorably (Landy & Sigall, 1974), to be seen as an effective psychological counselor (Cash et al., 1975), and less likely to be judged maladjusted or disturbed (Cash et al., 1977). Such studies powerfully demonstrate our reliance on physical appearance when we judge others. On the reverse side of the coin, those whose physical features are less admired are often judged to be less admirable, and the outcomes of their encounters with others tend to be less satisfying than those of people who are considered more attractive (Jones et al., 1984).

In summary, physical features are an important ingredient of first impressions. Not only are they a source of information in themselves, but they also serve as clues to the characteristics presumed to underlie them.

Character Traits

The inferences people draw from surface characteristics are often concerned with personality traits. Is a person honest or sneaky, kind or stingy, assertive or shy? Because descriptions of this kind are so common, social psychologists have taken great interest in the role played by traits in the formation of initial impressions.

Some of the first research on impression formation was done by Solomon Asch, who explored the way various pieces of information combine to form a first impression. Asch (1946) observed that when we form an impression of another person, some pieces of information carry so much more weight than others that they are able to modify the whole picture. Asch (1946) called such influential characteristics **central traits.** Asch showed that the warm/cold dimension could strongly affect the organization of people's impressions. For example, when the adjective *cold* was included in a list of seven stimulus words that purportedly described a person, only about 10% of the subjects believed that the person in question was also likely to be generous or humorous. When *warm* replaced *cold,* however, about 90% of the subjects described the person as generous, and more than 75% described the person as humorous. When, by contrast, the words *polite* and *blunt* were substituted for *warm* and *cold,* the resulting impressions differed little from each other. Asch therefore concluded that warmth/coldness was a central trait but that politeness/bluntness was not.

These apparently minor differences in description can have pronounced effects. In an extension of Asch's work, Harold Kelley (1950) introduced a guest lecturer to several university classes after leading some students to believe that the lecturer was a rather warm person, others that he was rather cool. The lecturer then gave the identical talk to all groups. The impressions that class members reported after the lecture varied considerably, however, and were consistent with the initial description of him as warm or cold. Furthermore, class members who had been led to expect a warm person interacted more with the lecturer in discussion.

More recent research has shown that the role of central traits is not quite so simple as Asch thought. The centrality of any particular trait depends on the information that is presented about a person and on the judgments that the subject is asked to make (Wishner, 1960). The specific effect of *warm* or *cold* may be weak if other information supplied implies warmth or coldness. Thus the information that someone is warm adds little to your impression if you already think the person is good-natured, happy, and helpful. If most of the information that you have relates to the person's intellectual abilities, however, then information about warmth will add a dimension to your mental picture of the person. Both of these dimensions—intellectual competence and interpersonal warmth—can be central, and in fact they are two of the most important dimensions of judgments about people (Rosenberg et al., 1968).

Another important feature of trait descriptions, in addition to their degree of centrality, is the extent to which they can be confirmed or disconfirmed (Rothbart & Park, 1986). The confirmability of a trait depends on a number of things. First, some traits are more commonly displayed than others. Thus it is probably easier to know whether someone is cheerful than whether someone is musical. Second, some traits require more evidence than others before we can conclude that they are present. The sight of a disordered room may or may not lead us to conclude that its occupant is basically a messy person; a single instance of cheating, in contrast, may be enough to convince us that the cheater is dishonest. Finally, some traits are simply more concrete than others; that is, the behaviors that indicate the traits are easy to identify. It is quite clear, for example, whether or not a person is talkative; it is less easy to say whether someone is imaginative. Traits vary not only in the ease with which we can confirm them but also in their ability to be disconfirmed. In general, favorable traits are hard to acquire but easy to lose, while unfavorable traits are easy to acquire and hard to

Table 4-1 The likableness of words describing personality traits

What is the best thing you can say about someone's personality? What is the worst? Norman H. Anderson (1968) obtained likableness ratings of 555 words that describe personality traits; that is, subjects rated each word on a 7-point scale ranging from "least favorable or desirable" to "most favorable or desirable." Each word was assigned a value for use in research, determined by the average of the ratings it received from 100 college students. The list below shows only the relative rankings; the numerical values are omitted. Such a list is tremendously useful in research on impression formation, for it gives us an empirical indication of the values associated with various traits. Of course, these likableness ratings are colored by the particular group of raters; some other group might rate *polite* as more or less favorable than this group (which made it 53rd in the list of 555 terms).

Such a list is interesting in what it reveals about our preferences. *Sincere* is rated most favorably of all 555 terms, while *liar* and *phony* receive the lowest ratings. These rankings say something about our values. Interestingly, the very middle term in the list (278th in rank) is *ordinary*. The entire list cannot be reproduced here, but some extremes and highlights serve to indicate the traits Americans tend to find desirable and undesirable.

Rank	Term	Rank	Term	Rank	Term
1	sincere	53	polite	531	loud-mouthed
2	honest	80	ethical	540	greedy
3	understanding	100	tolerant	546	deceitful
4	loyal	150	modest	547	dishonorable
5	truthful	200	soft-spoken	548	malicious
6	trustworthy	251	quiet	549	obnoxious
7	intelligent	278	ordinary	550	untruthful
8	dependable	305	critical	551	dishonest
9	open-minded	355	unhappy	552	cruel
10	thoughtful	405	unintelligent	553	mean
20	kind-hearted	465	disobedient	554	phony
30	trustful	500	prejudiced	555	liar
40	clever	520	ill-mannered		

lose (Rothbart & Park, 1986). Thus to be convinced that someone is truthful (a positive trait, as Table 4-1 indicates), we would probably want to observe the person in a variety of situations on numerous occasions; yet one incident of dishonesty would probably be enough to alter our impression of that person. For the reverse case, consider an unfavorable characteristic, such as cruelty. The sight of an individual kicking a dog on a single occasion would probably stick with us, and repeated evidence of kindness would not wipe out the impression of cruelty.

Information about a person's personality doesn't always come in a tidy package. When we ask what someone is like, we are often given a list of personality traits that presumably describe the person. For example, your roommate may tell you that your blind date for Friday night is "open-minded, clever, and modest, but kind of quiet." How do you integrate these pieces of information? Social psychologists have developed two basic models to explain how this kind of information is combined: the *additive model* and the *averaging model*. To illustrate how these models work, let us consider your hypothetical blind date. Would your impression of the person differ if you had been told only that the date was open-minded and clever?

The *averaging model* claims that we use the mean value of the traits provided to form our impression of a person (Anderson, 1965, 1974). The averaging model predicts that you would have a more favorable impression of your blind date if you were given only the description "open-minded and clever," because both of these terms describe very desirable traits and thus have high values, or scores near the top of the ranked list in Table 4-1. The inclusion of "modest" and "quiet" would reduce the average, as they describe less attractive traits and have low values, or scores near the bottom of the ranked list.

The *additive* (or *summation*) *model,* in contrast, predicts that one's judgment is based on the sum of the values assigned to the descriptors rather than on the average value. According to this model of information integration, adding the values of "modest" and "quiet" to the values of "clever" and "open-minded" would increase the favorability of the overall evaluation. Table 4–2 shows more precisely how these two models work.

Which model is correct? Most of the available evidence tends to support the averaging model. However, a simple average is not always the best solution. Some traits have more influence on our impressions in some situations than in others. The qualities that interest you in a potential roommate, for example, may have no relevance to your assessment of someone you hire to mow your lawn. To account for these variations, Norman Anderson has proposed a *weighted averaging model,* which predicts impressions on the basis of an average of scores that have been assigned weights in accordance with their importance. This more complicated version of the averaging model appears to account best for our integration of information about people.

The Question of Accuracy

Observations of physical appearance and inferences about character traits may be combined to form an impression of someone. But are these impressions accurate? That question is not so easy to answer as it may appear at first glance.

Thirty years ago, the study of social perception focused mainly on the issue of accuracy of impressions. Despite a great deal of research, the overall result was frustration, resulting in part from methodological dead ends. Traits, after all, are not concrete entities that can be weighed and measured; rather, they are psychological constructs. Therefore, to determine whether a judgment is accurate, we must first have a reliable way of assessing the presence or absence of a given trait in the person being judged.

Even when an observer is asked to make judgments about objective events, accuracy is elusive. In jury trials, eyewitness testimony is often introduced as evidence against the defendant (Loftus, 1979; Wells & Loftus, 1984). Research by social psychologists, however, suggests that such reports may often be in error. A television news program provided one researcher with an opportunity to assess the accuracy of eyewitness reports. Viewers witnessed a street mugging in New York and then saw a police lineup of six persons, one of whom was the mugger. Only 14% of the viewers who called the station in response to a request by the announcer correctly identified the mugger. Participants in a legal conference who watched the same film did only slightly better; just under 20% made the correct identification (Buckhout, 1980). It should be noted that people often think their ability to recall what they have seen is greater than these figures indicate. Indeed, witnesses often swear that their identification of a suspect cannot be mistaken. Such statements of certainty or confidence, however, bear little relation to the actual accuracy of eyewitness reports (Wells & Murray, 1984).

Table 4-2 Adding versus averaging in the integration of impressions

When we see a list of adjectives that describe another person, how do we integrate the information conveyed by these descriptors? The additive model and the averaging model agree that in effect we assign a value to each descriptor. But the models differ in the way these values are integrated.

Consider the data below, bearing in mind that we have assigned relative likableness values to each descriptor. Let us say that the following words are said to describe two men:

Gary		Steve	
Understanding	(+3)	Understanding	(+3)
Poised	(+2)	Sharp-witted	(+2)
Confident	(+1)	Congenial	(+2)
		Resourceful	(+2)
		Loud-mouthed	(−3)

The additive model would sum the values for each person, giving each a score of +6. Thus the additive model would predict that our overall impressions of the two men would be equally favorable. The averaging model would determine the mean value of the words applied to each man, giving Gary a +2 and Steve a +1⅕. The averaging model would predict that our overall evaluation of Gary would be more favorable than our assessment of Steve.

Are there conditions under which a person is more likely to make an accurate identification? Peter Shapiro and Steven Penrod (1986) considered this question, surveying the findings of more than 100 relevant studies. Several factors appear to influence the accuracy of identifications, including the similarity between the original situation and the later situation in which the judgment is requested. If the person's physical appearance has changed in the interval, as by a change in hairstyle or clothing, then, not surprisingly, identification is more difficult. If people are asked to make judgments in the same context as the event witnessed, their judgments are more accurate.

Context is also important when we consider the more general question of accuracy of personality judgments. People don't always act the same in all situations. Thus it is possible to form an accurate impression of someone on the basis of his or her behavior in the dormitory and be quite wrong in predicting how that person will behave at a job interview. Here we see the difference between circumscribed accuracy and global accuracy (Swann, 1984). *Circumscribed accuracy* refers to impressions that are based on specific traits that a person displays in specific situations. You might predict, for example, how talkative a fellow student will be in classroom discussions. This kind of accuracy is probably easier to attain. *Global accuracy*, in contrast, suggests an ability to form impressions that are valid in many situations and on many occasions. Would the same person be talkative with family members, on a date, and at a job interview? Accuracy of this kind, as the early investigators discovered, is more difficult to achieve.

Organizing Impressions

In coming to know other people, we do not respond simply to their external characteristics or to the traits that are ascribed to them. Rather, we approach the world with certain assumptions about people, based on our experience. At a general level, we may have overriding **philosophies of human nature**—expectancies that people will possess certain qualities and will behave in certain ways (see Box 4–1). At a more specific level, psychologists have been trying to understand how social knowledge is organized. As we have already mentioned, one of the major interests of cognitive social psychologists is the representation of social knowledge—the analysis of the structures of the mind. A number of concepts or categories have been identified, including implicit theories, schemas and scripts, and stereotypes.

Box 4–1
Philosophies of human nature

An analysis of writings by philosophers, theologians, and social scientists suggests that our beliefs about human nature have six basic dimensions (Wrightsman, 1964). These dimensions define a basic framework, or template, by which we judge the actions and characteristics of others. The first four dimensions listed below can be combined to show a generally positive or negative view of the world; the fifth and sixth dimensions are concerned with multiplexity, or beliefs about the extent of individual differences in human nature.

1. Trustworthiness versus untrustworthiness. On the one hand, we may generally believe that people are trustworthy, moral, and responsible, echoing the beliefs of the psychotherapist Carl Rogers that such attributes as "positive, forward-moving, constructive, realistic, trustworthy" qualities are "inherent in [the] species" (1957, p. 200). On the other hand, we may endorse the more pessimistic view that "with a few exceptions, human nature is basically worthless" (E. L. Freud, 1960, p. 79). Of course, many people's beliefs lie between these extremes.

2. Strength of will and rationality versus lack of willpower and rationality. Many people believe that human beings can control their outcomes and that they understand themselves. This view is reflected in the beliefs expressed by the luminaries of the self-help movement, from Mary Baker Eddy to Dale Carnegie to Werner Erhard. In contrast, others adopt the view that people are basically irrational and lack self-determination.

continued

Implicit Personality and Social Theories

Through development and experience, each of us develops his or her own **implicit personality theory**—a set of unstated assumptions about what personality traits are associated with one another. Such theories are considered implicit because they are rarely stated in formal terms and are often not part of conscious awareness; nonetheless, they dominate our judgments of other people (Schneider, 1973; Wegner & Vallacher, 1977).

When college students describe the people they know, they use the terms *intelligent, friendly, self-centered, ambitious,* and *lazy* with the greatest frequency (Rosenberg & Sedlak, 1972). Use of these terms is not random, however. People described as intelligent are also likely to be described as friendly and are rarely described as self-centered. Thus many people apparently hold to an implicit personality theory that says intelligence and friendliness go together, whereas intelligence and self-centeredness do not. The accuracy of such theories may be measured against the actual occurrence of such characteristics in real life. In fact, however, one of the things that distinguishes implicit personality theories from more formal psychological theories is the lesser likelihood of their being tested and found incorrect. Because we may not even be aware that we make an association between, for example, intelligence and friendliness, we may be unlikely to notice exceptions to the rule.

Each of us probably has his or her own implicit personality theory, which could be assessed by reference to conversations and letters or to free descriptions elicited by experimenters. In an interesting application of the archival method, Rosenberg and Jones (1972) showed that it is possible to assess the implicit personality theories of historical figures, in

3. Altruism versus selfishness. Do you believe that people are basically altruistic, unselfish, and sincerely interested in others? Or are you more likely to think that people are generally selfish and that they are interested only in themselves and are unconcerned about the fate of others?

4. Independence versus conformity to group pressures. One perspective says that people are generally independent and able to maintain their beliefs in the face of group pressures to the contrary. A more pessimistic view says that people readily give in to the pressures of other individuals, groups, and society at large.

5. Variability versus similarity. Some people believe that people are quite different from one another in personality and interests and that people can easily change. Others believe that people are similar and can change very little. Personality theorists who adopt the *idiographic* approach assume the uniqueness of each individual (Allport, 1962), while those who take the *nomothetic* approach classify people in large groups or categories when they attempt to explain behavior.

6. Complexity versus simplicity. One way of viewing people is to believe that they are basically complicated and hard to understand. Alternatively, we may take the position that people are rather simple and quite easy to understand. Probably many psychologists would endorse the view that people are rather complex.

Beliefs about human nature can vary widely from one individual to another and from one group of people to another. What are your philosophies of human nature?

---

this case the writer Theodore Dreiser. Analyzing *A Gallery of Women* (1929), a collection of sketches about 15 women, these investigators tabulated all the traits that Dreiser ascribed to the women in his sketches; Table 4–3 summarizes the 99 descriptors Dreiser used most frequently. By statistical analysis, Rosenberg and Jones reduced these traits to three basic dimensions: hard/soft, male/female, and conforms/does not conform. Hardness was closely related to maleness in Dreiser's implicit theory but not identical with it; sex and conformity, in contrast, seemed to be quite independent characteristics. It is interesting to consider this pattern of Dreiser's in conjunction with current stereotypes of men and women. Dreiser was clearly concerned with the outward physical characteristics of women, as evidenced by the relative frequencies of the descriptions listed in Table 4–3. Although such descriptions might suggest a rather superficial view of women, he deviated from at least one aspect of the commonly held stereotype: he did not associate women with conformity.

Just as people have implicit personality theories about how individual character traits go together, so they have implicit social theories about how events are related. More specifically, we can define a **social theory** as a belief "about how and in what way variables in the social environment are related" (Anderson & Sechler, 1986, p. 24). Social psychologists, of course, develop social theories on the basis of research and experimentation. The lay person's social theory may relate the same kinds of events but be based less on formal theory than on casual observation. Like implicit personality theories, these implicit social theories are often unstated. Social theories typically imply a cause-and-effect relationship. Thus a person may have beliefs about the relationship between capital punishment and murder rates,

Table 4–3 The 99 most frequently occurring trait categories in *A Gallery of Women*, by Theodore Dreiser

Trait Category	Frequency	Trait Category	Frequency
Young	100	Colorful, graceful, intelligent, poor, reads, religious, studies, tall	15
Beautiful	67		
Attractive	44	Fool, good-looking, literary, pagan	14
Charming, dreamer	41	Aspirant, determined, good, had means, sad, society person, not strong, tasteful	13
Poetic	39		
Interesting, worker	32	Ambitious, careful, defiant, different, erratic, genial, happy, lonely, man, varietistic	12
Artistic	29		
Gay	26	Clever, genius, indifferent, Irish, manager, nice, old, pale, quiet, restless, serious, shrewd, sincere, successful, suffering, sympathetic, thin, understanding	11
Practical, romantic, writer	25		
Conventional, girl	24		
Free, strong	23		
Woman	22	American, communist, crazy, critical, emotional, enthusiastic, fearful, fighter, forceful, great, handsome, hard, lovely, had money, painter, physically alluring, playful, repressed, reserved, skilled, sophisticated	10
Unhappy	20		
Intellectual, radical, sensitive, sensual	19		
Kind, cold	18		
Vigorous	17		
Able, drinker, generous, troubled	16		

between child-rearing practices and moral development, or between diet and mental health.

Another approach to understanding people's implicit theories is represented in the work of the psychologist George Kelly. In developing a cognitive theory of human behavior, Kelly was concerned about the links between our perceptions and our behavior. A crucial mediating link in this chain is our interpretation of the events and stimuli in our world. As Kelly asserts:

> [People] look at [their] world through transparent patterns or templates which [they] create and then attempt to fit over the realities of which the world is composed. . . . Let us give the name constructs to these patterns that are tried on for size. They are ways of construing the world. [1955, 1:8–9]

Construct is a key term for Kelly. A construct is a way of interpreting the world and a guide to behavior. Kelly's fundamental assumption is that we are all scientists. Just as a scientist tries to understand and predict events, each human being tries in the same way to choose constructs that will make the world understandable and predictable. According to Kelly's theory, people do not strive for reinforcement or seek to avoid anxiety; instead, they try to *validate their own construct systems*. Furthermore, Kelly has discarded the notion of an objective, absolute truth in favor of a phenomenological approach—that is, conditions have meaning only as they are construed by the individual.

Such implicit theories and construct systems reflect our need to simplify and integrate information in order to deal effectively with the complexities of human interaction. Given a limited amount of information, we fill in the details in order to make people and events more comprehensible. When people are confronted with two essentially random events and are asked to imagine a link between them, they are more likely than not to believe that the events are indeed related (Anderson & Sechler, 1986). Implicit personality and social theories persist, even in the face of contradictory evidence, because people develop a rationale for the theories that they form (Anderson, Lepper, & Ross, 1980).

Schemas, Prototypes, and Scripts

Discussions of implicit theories and construct systems emphasize certain elements that enter into our judgments of other people. More recently social psychologists have begun to use such terms as *schemas, prototypes,* and *scripts* to describe the way we interpret the world around us. Actually, the concept of a schema is not a new idea. In 1932 the psychologist Sir Frederick Bartlett introduced the term *schema* as a way of representing the memory process. In doing so, he was arguing against the then-dominant associationist (or S-R) school of thought, suggesting that some form of meaning structure needed to be hypothesized in order to account for alterations in memory between the presentation of a stimulus and its recall. In other words, people do not simply respond to what they see; rather, they interpret it on the basis of previous experience—experience that is represented in memory as a schema.

The concept of a **schema** was defined in Chapter One as an organized configuration of knowledge derived from past experience which we use to interpret our current experience. One particular set of schemas, those related to the self, were discussed in Chapter Three. Just as we have schemas in regard to the self, we also have schemas in regard to other people. In fact, the two sorts of schema may be quite similar, as factors that enter into self-definitions may be applied to other people as well (Fong & Markus, 1982; Markus, Smith, & Moreland, 1985).

Schema is a very general term. Yet, despite a certain vagueness that often makes the concept difficult to pin down, many investigators believe that it is useful in our attempts to explain how we form impressions and react to other people's behavior (Hastie, 1981). We can think of many forms of schemas—those based on verbal material, those based on visual material, those dealing with individual persons, and those dealing with social groups.

A somewhat more specific concept to describe the categorization of social knowledge is the **prototype,** defined as "an abstract set of features commonly associated with members of a category, with each feature assigned a weight according to degree of association with the category" (Cantor, 1981, p. 27). In other words, for any particular category that you think of, such as rock star, a set of characteristics may come to mind. Some of these characteristics may seem to you to have a high probability of being found in a rock star—such people generally wear wild clothes and jewelry, for example. Other characteristics you may think are sometimes associated with rock stars, but not so often—taking drugs, for example.

Prototypes can be associated with situations as well as with people (Cantor, Mischel, & Schwartz, 1982; Schutte, Kenrick, & Sadalla, 1985). Thus you may associate a particular set of characteristics with a baseball field, a concert hall, or a dormitory room.

Prototypes can also operate at different levels of categorization. Thus, under the general idea of extroversion, you may think of a comic joker or a public relations type. At an even more specific level, you may think of different types of comic jokers—a circus clown, a popular comedian, or the practical joker in a local fraternity. One of the tasks of cognitive social psychologists is to determine which of these levels is most important in person perception: at which level do people tend to categorize others? Research has shown that people will use the level that provides the greatest differentiation between

Photo 4–2 Prince is a prototype of a rock star.

concepts while providing the most meaningful, or "richest," definition within concepts.

A third concept that has been used to categorize our experiences is the **script.** A script (sometimes called an event schema) consists of a sequence of events. More specifically, a script has been defined as a "conceptual representation of a stereotyped event sequence" (Abelson, 1981, p. 715). To take a common example, we can think of a restaurant script. When you first enter a restaurant, this particular cognitive representation will probably be activated: you will get a menu from the waiter, decide what to order, place your order, and then wait for your food. These are events that typically occur in a standard order, and if you have been to restaurants before, the script will come to mind immediately. As another example, consider the script for a first date described in Box 4–2.

Each of these concepts—schema, prototype, and script—is a way of representing our organization of social knowledge. All are considered important, not just because they are ways of organizing knowledge that we already have but because they affect future action as well. These categories influence us in at least four ways (Markus & Zajonc, 1985). First, schemas, prototypes, and scripts affect the initial coding of new information. Schemas and other categories incorporate certain information that is available in memory. When a particular schema is activated (or made accessible, to foreshadow a discussion in the next section), it is likely to influence the way an event or an object is interpreted. Such influences are particularly likely if the new event is ambiguous, capable of being interpreted in a variety of ways (Higgins & Bargh, 1987).

Second, these cognitive categories influence memory. In general, people are more likely to remember events that are consistent with their existing cognitive structures, although there are some exceptions to this rule. If a friend's description of her visit to a new California-style restaurant included some events that fitted your restaurant script and others that did not, you would be more likely to remember the events that coincided with your script than those that deviated from it (Higgins & Bargh, 1987).

Box 4–2
The dating script

Most people have dozens of scripts in their memory, perhaps hundreds. Of course, not all people share the same scripts. Some may have a "taking the car to a repair shop" script, for example, while others do not. Even when people have scripts for the same situation, the scripts are likely to differ in detail, depending on each person's experience in that situation. John Pryor and Thomas Merluzzi (1985) looked at one particular script for an experience that varies widely in detail among individuals: the first date script. Below are listed the elements of that script identified by students at Notre Dame. The figure in parentheses after each statement represents the percentage of students who mentioned that particular action, indicating the range in belief about this particular script. How many of these actions would be part of your dating script?

1. Male arrives (55%).
2. Female greets male at the door (33%).
3. Conversation with date after arrival (43%).
4. Introduce date to parents/roommates and leave the house (36%).
5. Discuss where you will go (16%).
6. Talk about common interests: "small talk" (33%).
7. Go to a movie (43%).
8. Male buys refreshments at movie (16%).
9. Go to get something to eat and drink while talking (23%).
10. Male takes female home (65%).
11. Male walks female to door (20%).
12. Complimentary summary of evening (27%).
13. If interested ask to call/hope he asks to call again (53%).
14. Kiss (71%).
15. Say "good night" and thank date for the evening (34%).
16. Male returns home (25%).

Individuals differ also in their familiarity with a particular script. Those who have dated many people could be considered to have more expertise with the dating script than those who have had few dates. How would this difference in expertise be shown? Pryor and Merluzzi asked two groups of students, one consisting of men who had dated six or more women in the past year ("experts") and the other of men who had dated three or fewer women ("novices"), to arrange in order a randomly listed set of statements from the dating script. Experts did the job faster, a finding that supports the idea that available schemas affect information processing.

Third, these categories influence judgments, evaluations, and predictions. People generally anticipate that individuals and events will fit their already-established framework for understanding human behavior. If I have a script on the way professors act on the first day of class, then I will expect the unknown Professor Jones to act in accordance with my script. If I believe that most plumbers are talkative, then I will probably anticipate a long conversation while the sink is being repaired.

Finally, it is believed that schemas have an influence on behavior. My belief in the talkativeness of plumbers may lead me to seek out information to support that belief. This link to action is more difficult to establish because so many factors can influence behavior, but cognitive organization certainly plays a major part in its determination.

Stereotypes

A **stereotype** can be thought of as one particular type of schema—a schema about members of an identifiable group (Hamilton, 1979, 1981). Thus when I see a person with red hair, I may activate my "red-haired person" schema, reacting to that person on the basis of my more general beliefs and experiences regarding this category of person.

It was the journalist Walter Lippmann (1922) who first introduced the term *stereotype* to the social science literature, describing stereotypes as "pictures in our heads." In many respects, this idea of a picture or template is similar to the more recent notion of schema. Yet, whereas the word *schema* is not pejorative, Lippmann viewed stereotypes in negative terms, seeing them as a means by which people protect their relative standing in society. In a society in which White people are dominant, for example, they may use negative stereotypes of Blacks to justify their position. Psychoanalytic theorizing reinforced this idea of the stereotype as a defense mechanism, emphasizing stereotypes as products of unconscious needs and defensive drives. In the 1950s, work by Theodore Adorno and his colleagues on the authoritarian personality firmly placed stereotypes in the category of bad things to have.

Stereotypes often do contain negative elements. White persons in the United States, for example, often describe Blacks in more negative terms than they do Whites. In cognitive terms, we can say that the schematic representation of Blacks contains more negative elements than the schematic representation of Whites. How would one demonstrate this difference? One method that cognitive psychologists have developed relies on reaction time—the length of time it takes a person to respond to some kind of information. The assumption is that people will respond more quickly to information that fits a category that is available in memory. In a study based on this assumption, John Dovidio and his colleagues asked people to decide whether a series of positive and negative adjectives did or did not apply to a Black and a White person (Dovidio, Evans, & Tyler, 1986). Their results showed the predicted differences in reaction times. Subjects in the study (all White) responded more quickly to descriptors of positive traits in reference to a White person and to descriptors of negative traits in reference to a Black person.

It would be a mistake, however, to assume that stereotypes are always negative. Some of the information they contain is positive and some is quite neutral. A stereotype, like other cognitive categories, embraces the range of our information about a particular group and our associations with it. Consider the stereotypes that many people hold regarding women and men, for example. As Figure 4–2 shows, people are more likely to think that men are independent and competitive and that women are warm and emotional. None of these traits is necessarily bad, however. When you think about stereotypes, you should keep in mind the notion of probabilities, suggested by the concept of prototypes. For as Figure 4–2 also shows, people in general do not

Personality Traits

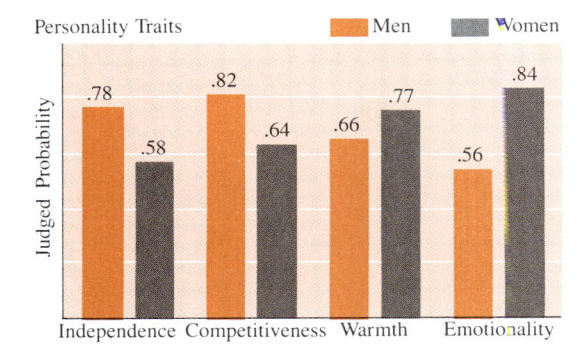

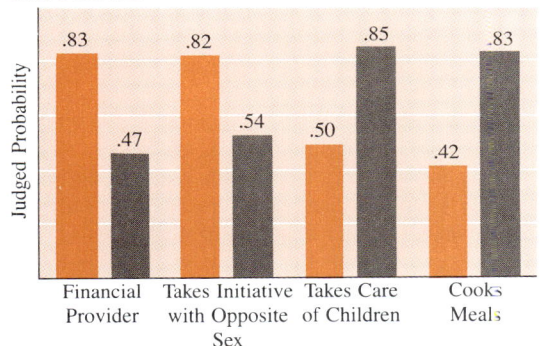

	Independence	Competitiveness	Warmth	Emotionality
Men	.78	.82	.66	.56
Women	.58	.64	.77	.84

Role Behaviors

	Financial Provider	Takes Initiative with Opposite Sex	Takes Care of Children	Cooks Meals
Men	.83	.82	.50	.42
Women	.47	.54	.85	.83

Physical Characteristics

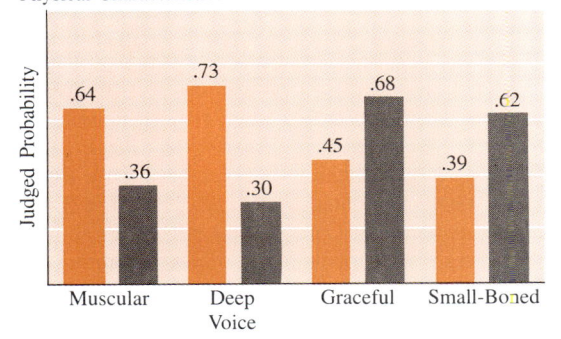

	Muscular	Deep Voice	Graceful	Small-Boned
Men	.64	.73	.45	.39
Women	.36	.30	.68	.62

Figure 4–2 Stereotypes of women and men

think it impossible that women are independent or that men are warm; rather each trait is simply seen as more likely in one sex than in the other.

In discussing person prototypes, we suggested that there are various levels of categorization—for example, an extroverted person, a comic, and a TV comedian. Stereotypes operate in the same way. In the case of gender stereotypes, we have found that four types of women come readily to people's minds: housewives, athletic women, businesswomen, and sexy women. Types of men that are frequently considered are businessmen, macho men, blue-collar workingmen, and athletic men (Deaux, Winton, Crowley, & Lewis, 1985). Even more specific types of men and women may emerge on a college campus, such as fraternity men or bookworms. Other groups of people are also differentially conceptualized; among the elderly, for example, we find the grandmother, the senior citizen, and the elder statesman (Brewer, Dull, & Lui, 1981).

The existence of such subtypes testifies to the fact that people recognize that their existent stereotypes don't always fit. When such a mismatch occurs, one can either alter the general stereotype or develop more specific beliefs about certain types of individuals within that general category. If you met a husband who did all the family's cooking, you could decide that most men really like to cook or you could instead develop a stereotypic category for "gourmet chefs" or "men who are married to professional women who can't cook." The more deviant the observed individual is from the general stereotype of his or her category, the more likely subtypes are to form (Weber & Crocker, 1983).

Sometimes, as we have just seen, stereotypic categories may form to account for individuals we have actually observed. At other times, however, stereotypic beliefs may be the result of false inferences about what we have seen. Such is the case of the **illusory correlation,** defined as an overestimation of the strength of a relationship between two variables (Chapman, 1967). The variables in an illusory correlation may not be related at all, or the relationship may be much weaker than it is believed to be. One explanation for this kind of bias relates to the frequency or the distinctiveness of the events that we try to explain (Hamilton, 1981). If two types of information both occur infrequently, we will tend to make an association between them even if no real association exists. In a demonstration of this bias, subjects were given a set of descriptive statements about a variety of people (Hamilton & Gifford, 1976). Two-thirds of these people were identified as being members of group A, while the remaining third were identified as members of group B. In addition to their group identification, each person was described by a single behavior, either a desirable behavior (for example, "John visited a sick friend in the hospital") or an undesirable behavior (for example, "John always talks about himself and his problems"). Approximately two-thirds of the members of both group A and group B were described by positive behaviors and approximately one-third by negative behaviors. Thus the subjects of this experiment were given two kinds of information: group membership and type of behavior. When asked to make judgments about the typical member of each group, subjects showed evidence of the illusory correlation. They judged members of group B to be less likable than members of group A, suggesting a perceived link between frequencies. The smaller number of people in group B was associated with the smaller number of undesirable behaviors, even though the proportions of undesirable behaviors were identical for the two groups.

The key issue here is the distinctive character of the behaviors (Hamilton, Dugan, & Trolier, 1985). We pay more attention to events that we see infrequently simply because they are unusual. Put two such events together and the distinctiveness is particularly great. If the minority position on a political issue is voiced by a citizen of a small town, for instance, that association is more likely to be remembered than the majority position taken by a citizen of either a large or a small town or than a minority protest by a citizen of the large town (Spears, van der Pligt, & Eiser, 1985).

As we suggested earlier, schemas affect our judgments and actions. To consider just one example, in this case the influence of a stereotype, imagine that you have been watching a debate between a Black and a White candidate for political office. The Black candidate appears to lose, and the person sitting next to you takes that opportunity to make an ethnic slur on Blacks in general. Will your evaluation of the Black candidate differ in any way from the judgment you would make if *(a)* the Black candidate won or *(b)* you heard no ethnic slur? Jeff Greenberg and Tom Pyszczynski (1985) predicted that an ethnic slur uttered in such a situation would activate any negative stereotype of Blacks (to the extent that stereotypes were present) and that the evaluation of the Black candidate would be lower in this situation than in condition *a* or *b*. That is exactly what happened.

It is important to recognize, however, that several conditions were necessary for this effect to occur: neither the ethnic slur nor the losing performance was sufficient in itself to cause the Black candidate to be judged more negatively than the White candidate. Once the stereotype was activated, however, the negative evaluation resulted.

Stereotypes are not solely based on individual experience. Although our own observations and inferences are important sources of information about people and the groups they represent, stereotypes also are the product of social learning. As children mature, they acquire information about categories of people that tend to be shared by members of their culture. In other words, an individual's categories may share many features with those categories used by other members of the society.

Our beliefs about members of recognizable groups come into play on numerous occasions. In Chapter Five we will consider how communication between people is influenced by the beliefs that each person holds. Later on, in discussing the ways in which groups of people interact (Chapter Sixteen), we will again have occasion to think about stereotypes and their consequences. First, however, we need to think more about how information is actually processed.

The Process of Social Cognition

Schemas, stereotypes, and similar concepts represent ways of thinking about the structure of social knowledge—an issue of *what* the categories of thought are. The other question that needs to be considered is a *how* question—how do we think about other people, how do the categories work, how do we process information? We will consider the answers to these questions in three stages. First, we will ask how information gets into the system—a process that can be called encoding. Second, we will consider how information is retrieved, or how information gets out of the system. And third, we will consider some of the errors and biases in the process— ways in which humans are far from the rational processors of information that the computer analogy might suggest.

Encoding: Getting the Information In

Encoding is the process of taking in external stimuli and creating internal representations of them (Fiske & Taylor, 1983). The correspondence between these two elements of the process is not necessarily one-to-one. As we form internal representations of a stimulus, we may omit details, change features, and even invent elements that were not present. What we store depends on the attention that we pay to the event itself. Several factors can affect our attention and thus the schemas that are activated.

The vividness or prominence of a person or event is one such factor. **Vividness** refers to the intensity or emotional interest inherent in a stimulus (Fiske & Taylor, 1983). A movie filmed in color, for example, is more vivid than a black-and-white film. Or consider the following two statements, used in a recent experiment by Jonathan Shedler and Melvin Manis (1986):

1. Mrs. Johnson sees to it that her child washes and brushes his teeth before bedtime.
2. Mrs. Johnson sees to it that her child washes and brushes his teeth before bedtime. He uses a Star Wars toothbrush that looks like Darth Vader.

Which description is more vivid, creating a clearer image in your mind? Although the effects of vividness are not always apparent (Taylor & Thompson, 1982), there is evidence that people are more likely to pay attention to vivid information and to encode it more readily. Hence vividly presented information is more likely to be *available* in memory later. Vivid information also leads people to be more extreme in their judgments. Mrs. Johnson was judged to be a more suitable parent, for example, when positive information was presented in vivid form (Shedler & Manis, 1986).

A second factor that affects encoding is the distinctiveness of a stimulus or event. *Distinctiveness* refers to the degree to which a stimulus stands out in relation to its context. A 6'8" basketball player stands out in a roomful of midgets, and so would be distinctive in that context, but not on a professional basketball court. A woman would be distinctive at an otherwise all-male meeting of a corporate board of directors but would not be readily distinguished at a professional women's luncheon. Distinctive stimuli attract our attention by virtue of being different in some way from their surroundings. Distinctive events are those that are unexpected—those that are generally not predictable on the basis of our prior knowledge. If a person or event is distinctive, we evaluate it more extremely and recall it more readily (Fiske & Taylor, 1983).

It is also true, however, that when we already have a schema in our memory for a certain class of people or events, our encoding of new information will be influenced by those expectancies (Higgins & Bargh, 1987). We tend to encode events that fit into an existent category as additional evidence of the validity of that schematic representation.

Emotional and motivational factors can also affect the encoding process. Alice Isen and her colleagues have found, for example, that people create and use more inclusive categories when they are in a positive mood than when their mood is more neutral (Isen & Daubman, 1984). People asked to sort color chips into as many or as few categories as they wished created fewer categories when they had just viewed a funny film; subjects were more likely to say that such things as camels, feet, and elevators were good examples of the category "vehicle" after they had viewed a comedy than after a sobering documentary.

People's goals in a situation also influence the way they encode information. Imagine that you are given a written description of a person named Wanda. First you read the description to yourself and then you are asked to describe Wanda to Mr. Jones. Now add one other detail. You are told either that Mr. Jones likes Wanda or that he dislikes her. Would this information affect not only what you said about Wanda but what you actually coded in memory about her? Yes, if your behavior is anything like that of the subjects studied by Tory Higgins and Douglas McCann (1984). Either immediately or several days later, subjects remembered the individual more positively when they had tailored their description to a favorable audience.

Storage and Retrieval: Getting the Information Out

Although it is easy to conceptualize the difference between encoding processes and retrieval processes, it is somewhat more difficult to measure the difference. If you, an eyewitness to a burglary, cannot remember what the burglar looked like, have you failed to encode the information or are you simply unable to retrieve it from memory? Cognitive psychologists have developed a variety of techniques to tease out these different processes. For example, if you watch a film of a couple having dinner and are told in advance that the woman is a librarian, you will presumably encode information about her in terms of your schema (or, at a more specific level, your stereotype) of librarians, and you may recall information in terms of that same schema. But what if you learn that she is a librarian only after you have seen the film? Under these conditions, your initial encoding could not have been affected by the schema, but your recall could. Both processes will affect the degree to which you remember information. However, schemas appear to exert more influence on encoding than on retrieval (Cohen, 1981).

Recall can also be affected by **priming**. As we saw in Chapter Three, *priming* refers to the effects of prior context on the retrieval of information. Thus a schema is more likely to be used if it has been activated recently; it is more *accessible* than some other schemas that have not been primed by recent use.

In one study that showed this memory effect, people first read a list of words that described either positive traits, such as adventurousness, or more negative characteristics, such as recklessness. Shortly after seeing these words, in what they believed to be an unrelated task, they read a story about a man named Donald who enjoyed such activities as skydiving and demolition derbies. Evaluations of Donald were affected by the prior, and presumably unrelated, information. When an "adventurous" schema had been primed, people viewed Donald more favorably than when a "reckless" schema had been primed (Higgins, Rholes, & Jones, 1977). Another way of viewing the priming effect is to think of a storage bin of schemas. If a memory has been called up recently, the corresponding schema will probably be at the top of the bin, ready to be used if a suitable situation arises (Wyer & Srull, 1981).

Many factors can affect the accessibility of a schema, and hence its influence on information retrieval. Tory Higgins and Gillian King (1981) distinguish between chronic and momentary accessibility. Momentary accessibility depends on the situation or the context, as in the Donald study above. Chronic accessibility, in contrast, involves the individual's own stable set of categories and beliefs. If Lisa is an active campaigner against smoking, she will be more likely than Pam, a heavy smoker, to remember and be able to retrieve information that deals with the hazards of cigarettes. She will refer to that particular category so frequently that it will be readily accessible in her memory.

Errors and Biases

Already you may have noted that the acquisition and use of social knowledge is not an automatic process. Some events stand out and are readily coded; others fade into the background and are effectively ignored. Events that fit a preexisting schema may be recalled more rapidly than events that are not so easily categorized. These are only some of the ways in which the representation of social knowledge is shaped and molded. In fact, a whole host of biases, shortcuts, and misplaced assumptions influence our interpretation of social life.

Heuristics. The amount of information that a person receives or is exposed to is tremendous. If the human brain were a computer of infinite capacity, all of this information could be input and the individual could determine exactly what events had occurred and were likely to occur. But neither human nor computer capacity is infinite. Furthermore, all of the relevant information is not always available. As a result, people have developed rules of thumb, or **heuristics,** for estimating the likelihood of events. Heuristics are mental shortcuts that reduce complex problem solving to simpler judgmental operations, and they are part of the routine business of social perception and judgment.

Consider two heuristics in particular that Amos Tversky and Daniel Kahneman (1974) have identified: the *representativeness heuristic* and the *availability heuristic*. The first term refers to the fact that we tend to consider some events more representative of the total population than they are. Suppose you are asked to predict Jenny's grade point average. All you know about Jenny is her score on a humor test (let's say she scored well above average). What would you predict about her GPA? Subjects asked to make this prediction typically surmise that Jenny's GPA is well above average. What these subjects (and perhaps you as well) seem to be doing is assuming that a high score on one measure is representative of Jenny's performance in general—even though humor and grades are probably not at all related. A better bet, given no other information, would be that Jenny's performance is average, as statistically that is the most likely event. Consider another example. You are given information about Henry, who belongs to a club whose membership consists of 25 engineers and 5 artists. Henry is described as flamboyant, creative, bearded, and rarely seen in a suit. Is Henry an engineer or an artist? Although the odds (5 to 1) suggest that Henry is probably an engineer, most people peg Henry as an artist. Again, information about the base rate or the overall distribution tends to be ignored in favor of one's own beliefs about people and the perceived similarities of their behavior.

The availability heuristic (which in fact might be better termed the accessibility heuristic) suggests that we tend to be biased by events that are readily accessible in our memory. If you were asked whether the average musician is rich or poor, for example, what would you say? If you had seen a lot of rock concerts or read about the lavish lifestyle of popular musicians, you might be inclined to answer "rich." On the other hand, if you had more experience hanging around the musicians' union hall and listening to stories of unemployment, your answer might be quite different. As in the case of priming, where the accessibility of a schema can affect one's interpretation of an event, so people's *predictions* of events are influenced by their schemas.

People can of course learn to use statistics when they are aware of the advantages of doing so (Nisbett et al., 1983). When it is obvious that an event is determined by chance, for example, people are more likely to use statistical heuristics. And in fact, when people are asked to estimate the distribution of other people's beliefs and attitudes, for example, they can often judge the general range of such attitudes quite accurately (Nisbett & Kunda, 1985).

False consensus bias. Although people are generally aware that other people's opinions on issues cover a wide range, they also tend to think that other people are more similar to themselves than they actually are. This tendency to believe that others share our attitudes and behaviors is called the **false consensus bias.** Evidence indicates that we tend to see our own behaviors and judgments as quite common and appropriate, and to view alternative responses as uncommon and often inappropriate (Ross, Greene, & House, 1977). This bias is evident even in regard to simple and minor issues. College students who preferred brown bread, for instance, estimated that 52% of students also prefer brown bread; students who preferred white bread put the estimate at 37%. Although some people have suggested that this egocentric bias may be a self-presentation strategy—an attempt to demonstrate that one is like others—the evidence suggests that it is basically a cognitive and perceptual error (Mullen et al., 1985).

Explaining Behavior: Attributions of Causality

Social cognition, as we have described it so far, deals with the *what* and the *how* of social knowledge. What are the structures of knowledge and how does the process operate? Whereas researchers may ask what and how, people are more likely to view events with *why* questions. Why did Amy move to the country? Why did Tony drop off the football team? Such questions provide the impetus for **causal attribution**—the process of explaining or inferring the causes of events.

In Chapter Three we considered the process of causal attribution as it operates in people's attempts to explain their own behavior and outcomes. The same general principles apply when we consider how people explain the behavior of other individuals. In their simplest form, causal attributions consist of distinguishing between *dispositional* (or personal) causes and *situational* (or environmental) causes, as Fritz Heider first suggested. Yet this distinction, although quite useful, is too simple to describe the sometimes elaborate explanations that people devise.

More recent theorists have offered a number of detailed models that attempt to map the causal attribution process.

Covariation and Causal Schemas

Harold Kelley assumes that we try to explain events in much the same way as a scientist would; armed with a series of observations of people's behavior, we try to figure out what might be responsible for a particular action. According to the principle of *covariation,* "an effect is attributed to the one of its possible causes with which, over time, it varies" (Kelley, 1967, p. 108). In other words, Kelley believes that we look for a systematic pattern of relationships and infer cause and effect from that pattern. This model obviously assumes that we have more than one opportunity to observe a particular person, and that we have observed other people in similar situations as well.

Building on Heider's general distinction between dispositional and situational causes, Kelley has pointed to three general types of explanations that people may offer when they try to interpret someone's behavior: an attribution to the *actor,* or the person who is engaging in the behavior in question; an attribution to the *entity,* or person who is the target of the actor's behavior; and an attribution to the *circumstances,* or the particular setting in which the behavior occurs (Kelley, 1967). Thus, if Susan runs away from Joe at a restaurant, we might attribute the event to something about Susan ("She is basically a hysterical person"), to something about Joe ("He is an insulting boor"), or to the particular circumstances ("The restaurant's vichyssoise had mold in it, and it made Susan sick").

Each of these explanations is reasonable; the trick is to decide on one as *the* explanation. Kelley suggests that to reach this decision we use three basic kinds of information: consensus, consistency, and distinctiveness. *Consensus* information consists of our knowledge about the behavior of other actors in the same situation. If everyone in the restaurant jumped up and ran out, we would say the behavior had high consensus; if Susan ran out alone, her behavior would have low consensus. The second source of information, *consistency,* is our knowledge about the actor's behavior on other occasions. Does Susan habitually run out of restaurants and out of movies and concerts as well, or is this the only time that she has created such a scene? Finally, one can use distinctiveness as a source of information. *Distinctiveness* is concerned with the variation in behavior among different entities, or targets. Does Susan run away only from Joe, or has she also run away from Rita, Peter, and Lila on other occasions?

Kelley suggests that if we have information about each of these three factors, our causal explanations will be quite predictable. These predictable explanations, which have been confirmed by subsequent research (Major, 1980; McArthur, 1972; Orvis, Cunningham, & Kelley, 1975), are outlined in Table 4–4. Depending on the particular combination of information we have about the people involved, we will explain the event by attributing it to the actor, to the entity, or to the circumstances. When the pat-

Table 4–4 Kelley's model of attribution: Why did Professor Martinez criticize Paul?

Attributions are made to the actor when:
  Consensus is low.
  Consistency is high.
  Distinctiveness is low.
Example: No other professors criticize Paul (low consensus); Professor Martinez criticized Paul last year, last month, and twice last week (high consistency); and Professor Martinez criticized every other student in the class as well (low distinctiveness). Conclusion: The behavior is attributed to Professor Martinez—for example, "Professor Martinez is a mean professor."

Attributions are made to the entity when:
  Consensus is high.
  Consistency is high.
  Distinctiveness is high.
Example: Every other professor criticizes Paul (high consensus); Professor Martinez criticized Paul last year, last month, and twice last week (high consistency); and Professor Martinez was friendly to all the other members of the class (high distinctiveness). Conclusion: The behavior is attributed to Paul—for example, "Paul is stupid and lazy."

Attributions are made to the circumstances when:
  Consistency is low.
Example: Professor Martinez has never criticized Paul before (low consistency). Conclusion: The behavior is attributed to a particular set of circumstances and not to either Paul or Professor Martinez—for example, "Paul said something today that Professor Martinez misinterpreted."

tern of information is less clear than that outlined in Table 4–4, we may base our explanations on some combination of these three factors.

Although the covariation model has a kind of precise elegance, it is clearly an idealized model. Often we do not have available the kinds of information the model requires: we may not have observed a person on previous occasions, or we may not know how other people have behaved in the same situation. What do we do in such cases if we want to explain behavior? Kelley (1972) suggests that we rely on causal schemas. According to Kelley, a **causal schema** is "a conception of the manner in which two or more causal factors interact in relation to a particular kind of effect" (1972, p. 152). (A causal schema can be considered one particular form of a social theory, as described on page 103.) Our observations of people lead us to develop certain beliefs about causes and effects. We then explain a particular person's behavior on the basis of those beliefs, or schemas. In other words, Kelley is suggesting that in the absence of all possible information about one person in one situation, we rely on some general beliefs when we attempt to explain a particular behavior.

As an example of a general causal schema, consider the *multiple sufficient-cause model*. When we follow this model, we decide that any number of factors may be responsible for a particular event. If we saw a father give his son an affectionate hug, we could decide either that the father was generally a warm person or that the son had just done something special. Either of these explanations is possible; the one we select will depend on the information we have available. If we knew that the son had done nothing special, we would decide that the father was an affectionate person; if we knew that the father was generally inhibited about showing affection, we would conclude that the son had done something unusual to deserve the hug. The point here is that either attribution would be sufficient to explain the event.

In other cases, we follow a *multiple necessary-cause model*. In this model at least two causes are necessary to explain the event. Often we refer to the multiple necessary-cause model to explain fairly extreme events. For example, Howard suddenly starts fighting with Tom. Did Tom do something to provoke Howard, or is Howard the kind of person who is likely to start a fight? In such a case, most people would conclude that both statements were true: Tom provoked Howard, and Howard is the kind of guy who starts fights. It takes two people to start an argument, so the saying goes; or, in other terms, it takes two causes to explain an effect.

In summary, causal schemas are a kind of shorthand. If we have unlimited information, the covariation model may represent our inference processes accurately. But in many situations we try to explain events without having all the information, and in such cases we will rely on a causal schema to make sense of the behavior we observe.

Correspondent Inference

In our attempts to explain the events that occur around us, we do, as the covariation and causal schema models suggest, make a general distinction between dispositional and situational causes. Beyond this general process, however, we also make some very specific attributions about the personal characteristics of the actor. Edward Jones and his colleagues (Jones & Davis, 1965; Jones & McGillis, 1976) have focused on the way we make these dispositional attributions—that is, on the way we observe an event and infer the intentions and characteristics of the actor.

If you are watching someone act in a certain situation, you are probably aware not only of the behavior itself but also of some of the consequences of that behavior. If you see John give Maria a bouquet of flowers at the office, for example, you may also observe that Maria is very pleased by the gift. Perhaps, you may infer, John's intention was simply to make Maria happy. However, if you happen to know that Maria is the vice-president's executive secretary and that John is trying to get a promotion, you may begin to suspect that the intended consequences of John's actions were not simply to please Maria. This scenario illustrates one of the factors that Jones and his colleagues believe are most important in our inference process: the consequences of an action. Jones suggests that when we observe a person's behavior, we consider not only the effects of that behavior itself but also the possible effects of alternative behaviors that the person might have engaged in. If you knew that John had two tickets for a hit play but did not ask Maria to go with him, you might suspect that making Maria happy was less important to John than being seen as a friendly person around the office. In this analysis, the impression John makes in the office would be a *noncommon effect*—that is, a consequence that he could achieve only by giving the flowers to Maria at work—whereas the effect of making Maria happy could have been achieved in at least two ways. The fewer the noncommon effects, the more likely those effects are to be influential in our attribution of characteristics to the actor (Newtson, 1974).

The tendency to infer dispositional causes for another person's behavior is influenced by what we initially expect the actor to do. As a general case, unexpected events are most likely to elicit a search for explanations. Faced with a novel event, a person will encode the event in some detail (Hastie, 1984). If a particular person does something quite divergent from what we expect, we are much more likely to wonder why the event happened and to seek an explanation in the personality of the actor. If we are familiar with the setting in which this unexpected event occurs, person attributions are apt to be particularly strong (Lalljee, Watson, & White, 1982). For example, the action of someone who comes into your room and recites Hamlet's soliloquy is much more likely to invoke a person attribution than the same behavior at a party in an unfamiliar locale (unless you are an actor, accustomed to dramatic monologues recited in your room).

We form two basic kinds of expectancies. The first, *category-based expectancies,* are assumptions we make on the basis of the individual's membership in a particular group or category. Stereotypes, discussed earlier, are one form of such category-based expectancies. If we assume that most men are not gentle, then we would probably take particular note of a man who was playing gently with children and would tend to attribute his behavior to something special about his personality. *Target-based expectancies* are based on information we have about the particular individual in other situations. For example, having seen Lionel behave gently with many children on many occasions, we would probably expect Lionel to be gentle, no matter what our expectations of men in general might be.

You may notice that these two kinds of expectancies are very similar to the concepts of consensus and consistency, discussed earlier. Both category-based expectancies and consensus involve information we have about a group of people, from which we may infer the causes of a particular person's behavior. Similarly, target-based expectancies and consistency both rely on our information about the particular actor.

Although the attribution models of Kelley and Jones are similar in some respects, Jones pays much more attention to specific dispositional attributions. To use his terms, the concern is with the *correspondence* between a behavior and a dispositional attribution. If John performs a friendly act, do we infer that John is a friendly person? As we have seen, in making this inference we look to the consequences of the action—that is, to the number of noncommon effects and to the expectedness of the effects. When both of these factors are low, we are likely to infer that the person intended the behavior, and in turn we will infer that the intention was a result of a particular personality disposition—in this case, friendliness. Under other conditions, as when the behavior is expected and the noncommon effects are numerous, correspondence may be low, and we will not infer a particular personality disposition in order to explain the behavior. Thus the Jones model takes us one step further in the process of explaining behavior, from pointing generally to something about the person to labeling the specific traits that are believed to be responsible.

Overestimating dispositional causes. The tendency to look to the individual for an explanation can be exaggerated. In fact, this tendency to overemphasize the actor as a cause of events has been called the **fundamental attribution error,** in recognition of its pervasiveness (Ross, 1977).

As an example of this bias, imagine yourself watching a quiz show in which a woman is asked to make up questions and a man is asked to answer them. The questioner, drawing on her own area of expertise, poses a difficult set of questions, and the respondent is only moderately successful in providing answers. If you were asked to judge the general intellectual ability of each contestant, whom would you rate more favorably? If you are like the subjects in an experiment conducted by Ross, Amabile, and Steinmetz (1977), you would probably rate the questioner as more intelligent than the respondent. Yet in making this judgment you would be neglecting an important situational factor—the control and choice assigned to the questioner, which allowed her to select particular areas and avoid others. Had the roles in the situation been reversed, so that the woman became the respondent and the man became the questioner, the man might well have displayed similar finesse, and your judgments of intelligence would have been reversed.

You may have experienced this same phenomenon in playing a game of trivia with a friend. When you tap your own area of expertise, you feel quite intelligent as your friend fails to answer several questions in a row. Yet, when your friend takes over the questioning, he or she appears to be the intelligent one. Ross and his colleagues point out the pervasiveness of this particular error in judgments of the powerful and the powerless: we tend to overestimate the capability of those in power, forgetting to consider the role requirements that give the powerful an advantage over the powerless.

What accounts for the fundamental attribution error? One explanation, suggest Jellison and Green (1981), is the fact that people in Western society tend to have a strong belief in personal responsibility: people should be held accountable for their own outcomes. Internally caused outcomes are therefore valued while externally caused ones are disparaged. In support of this argument, there is evidence that cultures do vary in such normative beliefs. In a crosscultural study comparing Americans and Indians, Joan Miller (1984) found that as American children grew older they increasingly referred to internal dispositions in their explanations of outcomes. Hindu children of India, in contrast, tended to base their explanations on context.

Another reason for the fundamental attribution error was originally suggested by Fritz Heider: we simply pay more attention to the behavior of the actor than to the surrounding context. Focusing on the actor and ignoring background factors, we then place undue reliance on what we have observed most closely.

Another source of bias occurs when we are asked to make judgments about people who have some relation to us. Jones and Davis (1965) have pointed to two factors that increase our tendencies to make dispositional attributions: hedonic relevance and personalism. **Hedonic relevance** refers to the extent to which a person's actions are rewarding or costly to the observer. To the extent that Anna's behavior has a direct effect on you, you are more likely to attribute causality to Anna than you would be if her actions did not affect you. **Personalism** is a closely related concept that refers to the perceived intentionality of a person's actions, or the degree to which a perceiver believes that another's behavior is directed at him or her. The greater your belief that Anna intended to affect you by her behavior, the stronger your attributions of causal responsibility to Anna.

Is the tendency to emphasize dispositional factors really an error? As we noted earlier, accuracy in such matters is elusive. Just as it is difficult to determine exactly what traits a person has, so it is difficult to say what the "true" cause of an event is. When situational constraints are really strong, however, the tendency to rely on dispositional causes may certainly be questionable.

Causes of Success and Failure

Bernard Weiner has developed a model of attribution that refers to a much more specific area of behavior than do the models of Kelley and Jones. Weiner's model deals with the explanations we arrive at for people's success and failure at particular tasks (Weiner, 1974; Weiner et al., 1972). Why did Linda get promoted so quickly? Why did David flunk the calculus exam? These are the kinds of questions that Weiner's model attempts to answer.

Like Kelley's and Jones's models, Weiner's basic model rests on the foundations established by Fritz Heider. Like Kelley, Weiner believes that one of the dimensions of our judgments is a comparison between dispositional and situational causes, which he refers

	Temporary/Stable Dimension	
Internal/External Dimension	Temporary	Stable
Internal	Effort, Mood, Fatigue	Ability, Intelligence, Physical Characteristics
External	Luck, Chance, Opportunity	Task Difficulty, Environmental Barriers

Figure 4–3 Weiner's model of causal attribution, showing typical attributions that represent each category

to as the *internal/external* dimension. In addition, he posits a second dimension, called *temporary/stable*. Weiner suggests that these two dimensions are independent of each other and that therefore we can describe causal explanations by means of a two-by-two table (see Figure 4–3).[1]

Each category contains a variety of possible explanations to account for someone's performance (including our own). The two dimensions have different consequences. The temporary/stable dimension is most important in the formation of expectancies, or predictions of how someone will do in the future (Valle & Frieze, 1976). For example, if we believe that Linda's excellent job performance was due to her ability or to the ease of the assignment, we would expect her to do well again if she were given the same assignment. If we decide that the reason for her success was something temporary, such as a fleeting good mood or pure chance, we would be less confident of her future success. The same principles hold when we try to explain failure. Failure that is attributed to stable factors is likely to yield predictions of future failure, whereas failure

---

[1] More recently Weiner has suggested that a third important dimension—intentionality—cross-cuts the other two. Because less work has dealt with this dimension, however, we shall limit our discussion to the internality and stability factors.

that is attributed to more temporary factors allows the possibility of future improvement.

The second dimension of causal attribution in Weiner's model—internal versus external explanation—relates primarily to the rewards or punishments that follow a performance. We are more likely to reward people if we believe that their success was of their own making—due to their ability, for example, or to their hard work—than if we think that chance or some other external factor was responsible. Punishment is also more likely when failure is attributed to an internal rather than an external cause. If David failed his exam because he didn't try hard enough, we are likely to be much more critical of him than we would be if we thought his failure was the consequence of an unreasonably hard test.

Our choice among these possible causes can be affected by a variety of factors. Initial expectancies may be important, for example, in decisions between a stable cause and a more temporary cause. If we expected someone to do well, then we will probably attribute that person's success to ability or skill. If we expected the person to fail, in contrast, then we are more apt to attribute the person's success to some more temporary cause. Category-based expectancies in regard to members of a particular group may affect attributions as well. For example, people are more likely to attribute a woman's success to temporary factors but to attribute a man's similar success to his ability (Deaux, 1976). Similarly, Whites are more likely to see ability as responsible for the success of a White than of a Black (Yarkin, Town, & Wallston, 1982); both Blacks and Whites are more likely to attribute failure to a lack of ability in the out-group than in their own group (Whitehead, Smith, & Eichhorn, 1982).

Such biases in evaluation are important in their own right. They become even more important when we realize that attributions are not the end of the line, that the explanations we form may influence other kinds of behavior. Madeline Heilman and Richard Guzzo (1978) have provided a vivid demonstration of some of these consequences. In a simulated organizational setting, business students were asked to assume the role of an employer and to decide on the raises and promotions to be given to a set of hypothetical employees. The information provided about the employees included one of four explanations for their recent successful job performance: superior ability, considerable effort, a relatively easy assignment, or pure chance. The behavior of the role-playing supervisors strongly supported the validity of Weiner's two dimensions. Supervisors recommended raises only to those employees whose performance had been explained by either ability or effort; in other words, rewards were given for internally caused success but were not given when external factors were believed to be responsible. Promotion was reserved for those employees who were said to be superior in ability. Presumably subjects believed that future performance could be ensured only if the employee had superior ability (an internal *and* stable characteristic) but not necessarily if exceptional effort (a more temporary characteristic) had been shown.

Weiner's model of attribution is more limited than the others we have considered, focusing strictly on explanations for successful and unsuccessful performances in an achievement context. In any case our reactions to events and our explanations of them may be more complicated than the simple fourfold table suggests. Nevertheless, Weiner's model is an important approach because it points more clearly than the others to some of the behavioral consequences that attribution patterns may have.

Belief in a Just World

Explanations of the outcomes of individual events may reflect a more general view of the way the world works. The social psychologist Melvin Lerner has suggested that many people have a **belief in a just world**—a belief that "there is an appropriate fit between what people do and what happens to them" (Lerner, 1966, p. 3). For Lerner, the belief in a just world is not only a cognitive principle; it develops out of a motivational context as well. Lerner suggests that we develop a sense of our own deservingness, and that in order to maintain that comforting belief we need to believe that others also get what they deserve in the world.

But what happens if situations appear to be unjust? Lerner suggests that such events threaten our belief in a just world and that accordingly we will try to correct the situation in some way (Lerner, 1975, 1977; Lerner, Miller, & Holmes, 1976). On some occasions we may rectify the situation by compensating the victim of injustice—by giving aid to refugees, for example. At other times we may try to punish the harmdoer (if we can find one). And if we cannot reestablish justice, we may convince ourselves that no injustice has occurred.

By blaming the victim, we can maintain our belief that people get what they deserve (Ryan, 1971). Martin Symonds (1975), a psychiatrist, has interviewed hundreds of victims of rapes, assaults, and kidnapings and finds that many of these victims receive censure instead of sympathy. When a person has been mugged, for example, friends, family, and the police frequently interrogate the person relentlessly about *why* he or she got into such an unfortunate situation. "Why were you walking in that neighborhood alone?" "Why didn't you scream?" "Why were you carrying so much money?" Such reactions reflect our pervasive need to find rational explanations for apparently senseless events. Observers are particularly likely to place the responsibility for rape on the victim. This tendency is most pronounced when other explanations for the attack are not apparent. For example, a victim who is unacquainted with her assailant is seen as more responsible for a rape than one who is acquainted with him (Smith et al., 1976). In general, men are more likely to attribute responsibility to the female victim than women are (Feild, 1978; Selby, Calhoun, & Brock, 1977). The same type of rationale has been used by some people to account for the assassination of public figures (see Photo 4–3).

We do not always blame the victim, however. Indeed, we are particularly unlikely to do so when the victim's suffering threatens our own feelings of deservingness and justice. Observers who are told to expect a fate similar to that of the victim are less likely to malign the victim (Sorrentino & Boutilier, 1974). Subjects in their experiment observed a female undergraduate receive a series of electrical shocks

Photo 4-3 Martin Luther King, Jr., victim of assassination. In April 1968, right after Dr. King's murder, a representative sample of 1337 American adults were asked: "When you heard the news [of the assassination], which of these things was your strongest reaction: (1) anger, (2) sadness, (3) shame, (4) fear, (5) he brought it on himself?" About one-third (426) of the respondents chose the response "brought it on himself" (Rokeach, 1970). For these respondents, Lerner's "just world" hypothesis applies: since Dr. King was killed, he must have deserved to be killed.

as a "learner" in a teaching-effectiveness project. Some of the subjects were told that they would also serve as learners later; others were told that they would not. Anticipation of a similar fate led to a significant reduction in the assignment of negative characteristics to the learner. Such a pattern is, of course, consistent with the sex differences in attribution of responsibility for rape, a case where we can assume that women are more likely than men to anticipate a similar fate.

At a more general level, Lerner (1977) has suggested that the individual's first concern is his or her own deservingness and the ability to believe in a world where justice prevails. Often this belief leads a person simply to ignore evidence of injustice. Thus we may skip articles in the newspaper that deal with suffering in other countries, and we may avoid neighborhoods in our own town where evidence of poverty is prominent. Yet many of those same occasions may lead us to offer direct assistance—perhaps because they represent only a minimal threat to our sense that justice prevails in our own lives. Not being personally threatened, we may feel free to offer assistance in order to correct the injustices suffered by others. When we see a threat to our own state of deservingness, though, we are much more likely to choose other strategies, such as blaming the victims and seeing them as directly responsible for their own misfortunes, thereby sparing ourselves the fear that a similar fate may befall us.

Summary

Understanding other people is a useful skill that makes the world more predictable. Our initial impressions of other people are often based on surface characteristics, such as physical appearance, which are immediately visible. We infer a person's character traits and personality from the characteristics we see.

Some traits, which have appropriately been called

central traits, are more important than others in the process of impression formation. Traits also vary in the degree to which they can be confirmed or disconfirmed by observation. In combining a series of trait descriptors, people tend to average their values to arrive at an overall judgment. Accuracy of impressions is an elusive issue, as eyewitness testimony in the courtroom has demonstrated.

The mental categories that represent social knowledge may be conceptualized in several ways. Most people have a set of *implicit personality theories* and *social theories* that represent their understanding of human behavior. More specific events are represented by *schemas, prototypes,* and *scripts.* A *stereotype* is a schema that summarizes beliefs about members of a particular group. In some instances, particularly in the case of a negative belief, a stereotype may reflect an *illusory correlation* between two actually unrelated factors.

The processes of social cognition include the initial encoding of information and the subsequent retrieval of information from memory. Both the *vividness* and the distinctiveness of an event will affect its encoding. Moods, goals, and emotional states are also influential. *Priming* can affect the accessibility of a particular social category.

Because social information is so extensive, people have developed a set of *heuristics* or shortcuts to make their task simpler. The social inference process is also subject to a number of biases, including the *false consensus bias.*

The specific form of social inference that concerns explanations for the outcomes of events is called *causal attribution.* In general, actions may be attributed to either a dispositional factor or a situational factor. Several models have been developed to explain various aspects of the attribution process. Biases are evident in our attributions as well. We tend, for example, to overestimate the influence of dispositional factors (the *fundamental attribution error*). At a more general level, explanations of events often reflect a *belief in a just world.*

Glossary Terms

belief in a just world
causal attribution
causal schema
central traits
false consensus bias
fundamental attribution error
hedonic relevance
heuristics
illusory correlation
implicit personality theory
personalism
philosophies of human nature
priming
prototype
schema
script
social theory
stereotype
vividness

Language exists only when it is listened to as well as spoken. The hearer is an indispensable partner.
John Dewey

Those of us who keep our eyes open can read volumes into what we see going on around us.
E. T. Hall

David Fredenthal, *The People*, The University of Arizona Museum of Art. Gift of Leonard Pfeiffer.

CHAPTER FIVE

Communication

I. The Meaning of Communication
II. Channels of Communication
    Language and Paralanguage
    Gaze
    Facial Expressions
    Body Movements and Gestures
    Touch
    Interpersonal Distance
    Combining the Channels
III. Patterns of Communication
    Basic Dimensions of Communication
    Equilibrium and Arousal Models
    Conversational Patterns
    Conversation in Close Relationships
IV. Deceptive Communication
    Those Lying Ways
    Detecting Deception
V. Communication and Social Interaction
VI. Summary

*I*n Chapter Three we described the self as a social entity, the product of social experiences and interaction. There we considered how individuals present themselves to other people, choosing particular strategies of self-presentation that may help them to be liked, to be rewarded, or to attain other desirable goals. In Chapter Four our perspective shifted from the self to the observer as we considered how people form impressions and explain the behaviors of other people. Each of those chapters considered only one side of an interaction. Now it is time to put those two pieces together and look at the communication process as a whole.

Communication is an interaction in which two or more people both send and receive messages, and in the process both present themselves and interpret the other. Just how these messages are conveyed is the concern of this chapter. In fact, communication is fundamental to most of the social processes that will be discussed in the remainder of this text. Expressions of friendship, affection, and love depend on people's ability to communicate their feelings; so do expressions of anger, mistrust, and hatred. Relationships falter as people claim they can't communicate anymore; negotiations between the superpowers are bedeviled by "communication breakdowns."

In this chapter we will consider the foundations of these larger phenomena. What does it mean to communicate? How are messages sent and how are they received? What are the channels of communication through which messages flow? When we understand the elements of the process, we can then look at specific kinds of communication situations, from those in which people try to be very open and honest with one another to those in which they aim not to communicate clearly but rather to deceive. Finally, the issues of self, social knowledge, and communication will be linked together in a general model of social interaction.

The Meaning of Communication

It has often been said that one can't *not* communicate. In other words, although a particular interaction may be filled with so much tension and stress that verbal communication actually ceases, the communication process continues. Signs and messages continue to be transmitted between one person and the other, even if the goals of the interaction may have changed.

The term *communication* is widely used and has

```
Information          Message                  Signal            Noise         Received            Message
  Source          ─────────▶   Transmitter  ────────▶   Source   Signal    Receiver  ─────────▶  Destination
                                                              ────────▶
```

Figure 5–1   A simple model of communication

been applied to situations ranging from information processing within the individual to large-scale sociocultural systems, mass communication and influence, and communication networks. We will focus primarily on a phenomenon somewhere between those extremes: interpersonal communication—that is, the interactions that take place between two persons.

Communication theorists have developed many models in an attempt to represent the communication process. An early and influential model proposed by Shannon and Weaver (1949) is represented in Figure 5–1. According to this model, the communication process has five necessary components: source, transmitter, channel, receiver, and destination. Shannon and Weaver introduced in addition, the concept of *noise*, defined as any disturbance that interferes with transmission. Later this model was revised to include the concept of *feedback*, which attempted to deal with the fact that the receiver may not always receive the same message that the transmitter has sent.

Shannon and Weaver's model had a tremendous influence on the early analysis of communication, particularly in the then-developing field of computer science. More recent communication theorists, however, have had some problems with models as simple as this. One problem lies in the one-way assumptions they made, illustrated by the arrows in Figure 5–1. Can communication be accurately described as a one-way street? Probably not. As we suggested earlier, communication involves at least two people, both of whom are simultaneously sending and receiving messages.

A second problem with the early models is that they treat the speaker and the receiver as isolated individuals, devoid of a social context. In emphasizing the basic structures and elements by which communication takes place, a model such as the one depicted in Figure 5–1 ignores the ways in which particular people, topics, and situations may shape the process (Clark, 1985).

More recent work makes a number of assumptions about the interpersonal communication process. First, it is assumed that communication represents an interaction between two parties, both of whom have speaking and listening parts to play. From this viewpoint, communication is seen as a shared social system rather than as a one-way street (Scott, 1977). Second, as co-actors in this system, both parties bring to their interaction a set of expectations and understandings that shape the nature of their communication with each other—what have been called the rules of the communication game (Higgins, 1981). It is easy to demonstrate that such expectations affect communication (Krauss & Glucksberg, 1977). If you were asked how today's history lecture was, for example, would you respond in the same way to a friend as you would to the university president? The question might be the same, but the form of your answer could differ substantially. For communication to flow most effectively, speakers must share what Herbert Clark (1985) has termed a common ground. In other words, the participants must share certain beliefs and suppositions that will enable them to coordinate their communicative efforts.

A third assumption that most current communication experts share is that verbal and nonverbal communications are part of the same system.

Although it is sometimes useful to focus on one or the other, it is important to remember that communication takes place through many channels simultaneously. A person who is speaking, for example, is also displaying some facial expression, is standing in a particular way, and may be using a particular set of gestures. Sometimes the communications sent through these channels may parallel each other, conveying the same message, while at other times they may be contradictory, so that interpretation becomes more difficult.

Channels of Communication

When the word *communication* is mentioned, many people think automatically of language. Speech has, after all, often been designated as a unique ability that distinguishes humans from other primates. Yet messages may be exchanged through many other channels of communication—facial expressions, eye contact, physical touch, body gestures, even the distance that we put between ourselves and others. Because speech is the most obvious of the communication channels, however, we shall begin there.

Language and Paralanguage

"When I use a word, it means just what I choose it to mean, neither more nor less," said Humpty-Dumpty in Lewis Carroll's classic *Through the Looking Glass*. Such confidence in the encoding of one's message is admirable but perhaps not realistic. Although the choice of words and the combination of these words into sentences represent our most controlled form of communication, the levels of meaning involved in such choices are numerous.

All of the models developed by linguists to represent the language process have many elements, and we can deal with those components only briefly. At the most basic level are *phonemes*—that is, the elementary sounds of any language, such as the soft *b* sound of Spanish or the *th* of English. At a slightly higher level are *morphemes*, the minimum meaningful forms in the language (Brown, 1965); in somewhat oversimplified terms, morphemes are the basic word forms in a language. *Dog, chase*, and *cat* are morphemes. At a higher level, the linguist deals with grammar, which combines a set of rules for the construction of words (morphological rules) and a set of rules for the construction of sentences (syntactic rules).

These concepts are basic to linguistic analysis. Our own concern, however, really lies at the level of *semantic analysis*—what is the meaning transmitted through our verbal language?

The philosopher John L. Austin (1962) pointed out that communication operates at a number of levels. At the simplest level, an *utterance* is a sound that one speaker makes to another. One step further in the communication process, a *locution* consists of words placed in some sequence—a sentence that conveys a particular content. For example, someone might say, "It's cold in this room." The literal meaning of that sentence is clear. But what is the intended

> **Box 5–1**
> Social registers
>
> The social psychologist Roger Brown (1986) has used the term *social register* to refer to a way of expressing a message addressed to a particular type of listener. A classic example of such stylized ways of talking, which combine linguistic and paralinguistic cues, is baby talk. Listen carefully to someone talking to a very young child. Typically the pitch will be higher than normal, the sentences very simple, and the intonation exaggerated. These characteristic features of the baby talk register have been noted in countries throughout the world and can easily be spotted by a listener who cannot actually see the speaker's target.
>
> Is such speech limited to babies? Not exclusively, Lynn Caporael (1981) found when she studied the speech of caregivers in nursing homes. Speech directed by staff members to elderly patients bore a striking resemblance to the speech of adults to children, suggesting similarities in the assumed dependency of these two groups.

message? For this level of meaning, the term *illocution* has been used. Hearing your companion say "It's cold," you may need to consider whether the intended message is (*a*) "Shut the door behind you"; (*b*) "I know you just turned down the heat, but would you please turn it up again?"; (*c*) "This is a crummy, drafty apartment"; or any of a host of other possibilities.

What sorts of meanings do people intend to convey by their language? According to the linguist John Searle (1979), there are five general possibilities: (1) to say how something is; (2) to get someone to do something; (3) to express feelings and attitudes; (4) to make a commitment; and (5) to accomplish something directly. The listener's job is to decide which of these intentions motivated the speaker's utterance. To make such determinations people rely on a variety of implicit rules and agreements that are shared in the society—the common ground that we referred to earlier. Thus the speech act, like any other action, is subject to interpretation by those who witness it.

Not all verbal communication is expressed in words and sentences; communication can also be made through vocal sounds and modifications that are not considered language but nonetheless convey meaning. These sounds are called **paralanguage**. The study of paralanguage deals with *how* something is said, not *what* is said (Knapp, 1978). Examples of paralanguage include speech modifiers such as pitch, rhythm, intensity, and pauses, as well as vocalizations such as laughing, crying, yawning, groaning, sneezing, and snoring (Trager, 1958). Each of these paralanguage forms can convey meaning. The person who yawns while you are talking, for example, sends a very clear message of boredom; less obviously, perhaps, the person who speeds up his or her speech while talking to you may be conveying either anxiety or excitement. (See also Box 5–1.)

Recently, glowing claims have been made that spoken lies can be detected by the analysis of the speaker's voice patterns. Proponents of the spectrographic analysis of vocal stress patterns have argued for this method as a reliable lie detector. Although such claims appear to be exaggerated, it is true that we can transmit a considerable amount of information through paralinguistic cues. Low voice pitch, for example, tends to convey pleasantness, boredom, or sadness, whereas high pitch conveys anger, fear, surprise, or general activity. Moderate variations in pitch may communicate anger, boredom, or disgust, whereas more extreme voice variations indicate pleasantness, happiness, and surprise (Knapp, 1978; LaFrance & Mayo, 1978).

Even though we know that words sometimes fail us, it may seem as if the tremendous variety of linguistic and paralinguistic forms of communication should be sufficient to communicate virtually any thought or feeling. Yet beyond these verbal forms of communication lies a wealth of nonverbal communication modes that sometimes support, sometimes contradict, and sometimes go beyond the verbal message.

Gaze

"Drink to Me Only with Thine Eyes," "the eyes of a woman in love," "seeing eye to eye"—all such expressions and songs testify to the importance of eyes as communicators. The pervasiveness of optic symbols in myth and religion also testifies to the importance we assign to this mode of communication. In some cultures, for example, people wear veils to protect themselves against the "evil eye" (Kleinke, 1986). Indeed, we perhaps depend more on the eye behavior of other people than on any other form of nonverbal communciation, although, as we shall see later, this dependence sometimes causes problems.

Gazing behavior,[1] and indeed all nonverbal behaviors, can serve a variety of purposes. Miles Patterson (1982, 1983) has identified five specific functions of such behaviors: (1) to provide information; (2) to regulate interaction; (3) to express intimacy; (4) to exercise social control; and (5) to facilitate the accomplishment of a task.

Providing information. People convey information by the amount and pattern of their gazing behavior. A gaze can communicate liking, attentiveness, competence, and credibility (Kleinke, 1986). Our dependence on the eyes as a source of information is manifested in the discomfort we feel when we converse with people who are wearing opaque sunglasses. "I can't tell what they're thinking" is a frequent complaint.

People tend to look more at people they like than at people they dislike. Even the belief that another person has gazed at us can often engender liking. In a demonstration of this effect, Chris Kleinke and his colleagues (Kleinke et al., 1973) asked male and female subjects to engage in a ten-minute conversation. At the end of the period, the subjects were told that their partner had gazed at them far more or far less often than the average number of times, without regard to the actual frequency of gazes. Subjects who were told that the gaze frequency was lower than normal rated their partners as less attentive. Interestingly, reports of supposedly above-average rates of gazing produced different effects on men than on women. When women thought their male partner had looked at them more than might be expected, their attraction to him did not increase. A similar belief had the opposite effect on men: they were more attracted to women who they believed had gazed at them more than the average number of times.

Gaze is also an important indicator of status differences in a relationship. Ralph Exline and his colleagues have explored the gaze patterns of high- and low-status people interacting with each other (Exline, 1971; Exline, Ellyson, & Long, 1975). In some of

---

[1] The term *eye contact* is often used interchangeably with *gaze* (a fixed look directed at the face of another person) and *mutual gaze* (the fixed looks of two persons directed at each other). Most investigators prefer the latter terms, however, because actual eye contact is difficult to measure in the laboratory: a look in the general direction of someone's face cannot be distinguished from direct eye-to-eye contact.

Photo 5-1 Gazing behavior is an important means of communication.

their studies, status differences were manipulated by the experimenter; in other studies, the investigators looked at real-life status relationships, such as that between an ROTC officer and a cadet. In all cases, the low-status person gazed at a partner more than the high-status person did.

Nancy Henley (1977) has suggested that these status differences may be related to the pervasive sex differences in eye behavior. In general, women engage in much more eye contact than men do (Duncan, 1969), consistent with the finding that the lower-status person looks directly at others more often than a higher-status person (in this case, the man). Women are also less likely to engage in staring and are more apt to avoid the gaze of the other (Henley, 1977).

Regulating interaction. Gaze serves an important role in initiating communication and in maintaining a conversation once it has begun. For example, if your professor is looking around the classroom for someone to supply the correct answer, you are likely to avoid eye contact if you failed to read the material the night before; however, you will probably return the professor's gaze if you know the correct answer and can discuss it. Similarly, you will probably ignore a gaze from a stranger at a bar if you don't want to be bothered, but you might return the look if you were interested in establishing a new relationship.

Observing unacquainted college students meet in a laboratory setting, Mark Cary (1978) found that mutual gaze predicted the beginning of conversations. If students looked at each other at their first encounter, they were likely to engage in conversation. If they looked at each other again, as one student entered the room where the other one was sitting, conversation was even more likely.

Once a conversation has begun, gaze continues to play an important role in the course it takes. Consider these figures from a study of typical two-person conversations (Argyle & Ingham, 1972). One or both participants are gazing at the other approximately 61% of the time during such conversations, and mutual gaze accounts for 31% of the total interaction time. The average length of an individual gaze is about three seconds, whereas the average duration of mutual gaze is slightly more than one second. White adult speakers tend to gaze at the other person more often when they are listening (75% of the time) than when they are speaking (41%). This pattern is reversed among Blacks, although the overall amount of gaze remains the same (LaFrance & Mayo, 1976; see Figure 5-2).

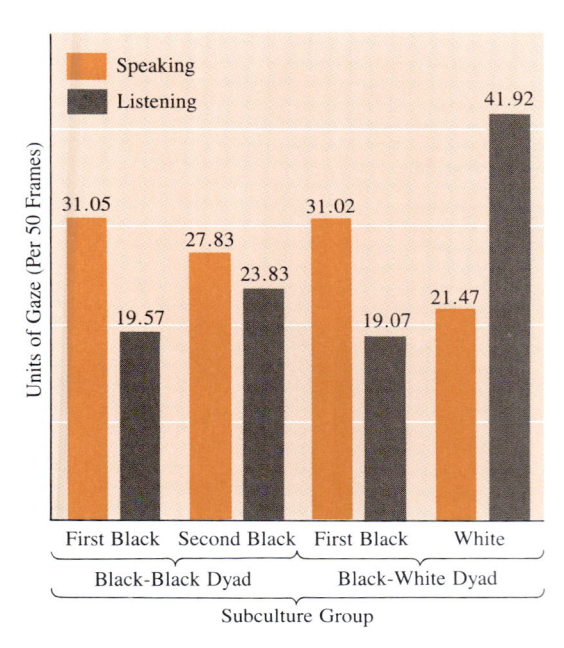

Figure 5-2 Mean other-directed gaze in film frames per 50 frame units. The bar graph shows the results of a study by Marianne LaFrance and Clara Mayo (1976). When two Blacks were talking to each other, both looked at each other more while they were talking than while they were listening. In contrast, when a Black and a White were paired with each other, the White person gazed at the other person much more while listening (about 80% of the time), whereas the Black person looked at his or her partner primarily while talking. As a result, while the White was talking and the Black was listening, little eye contact occurred.

Ethnic differences in typical patterns of gaze can create substantial problems in communication. Marianne LaFrance and Clara Mayo observed, for example, that when Blacks and Whites converse, they often misinterpret the signals for taking turns in the conversation. "When the White listener . . . encountered a pause with sustained gaze from a Black speaker, the White was cued to speak, and both found themselves talking at once. In the obverse situation, by directing his gaze at the Black listener, the White speaker often did not succeed in yielding the floor and had to resort to direct verbal questioning" (LaFrance & Mayo, 1976, p. 551). Such differences can certainly create discomfort in a conversation, and they may cause errors in judgment about the other person's intentions and motives as well.

Expressing intimacy. A third function of gaze is to express intimacy in a relationship. People look more at others whom they like than at those they dislike (Exline & Winters, 1965). This gaze pattern has been observed in the laboratory in people who have interacted only briefly. It has also been observed in dating couples, whose interactions are obviously much more extensive. Couples who score high on a measure of romantic love (see Chapter Nine) spend more time looking at each other than those who report being less involved in a relationship (Rubin, 1970).

In addition to conveying positive feelings, extended gaze may indicate the intensity of a relationship. Kimble and Forte (1978) asked women to communicate either a positive or a negative message to a male assistant. When the women were asked to act as if they were strongly involved in the message, they looked at the assistant more than when they were instructed to appear less certain about the message. This effect of intensity was found whether messages were positive or negative. In fact, it was slightly stronger when the messages were negative.

Exercising control. Gaze can also serve as a means of controlling an interaction, or at least it often accompanies attempts to exert control. People gaze more when they are attempting to be persuasive; they also gaze more when they are attempting to ingra-

tiate themselves with the other person (Kleinke, 1986). Phoebe Ellsworth and her colleagues have shown that a stare can also cause flight. When drivers are stopped at an intersection, for example, a stare from a person standing on the corner causes them to depart much more rapidly than they do when no one is staring at them (Ellsworth, Carlsmith, & Henson, 1972).

Although higher-status people tend to gaze at a partner less often than people of lower status, a specific pattern of gaze behavior is seen in high-status people when they wish to exert control. The *visual dominance behavior* characteristic of people in high-status positions involves a tendency to look at the other person more fixedly when they speak than when they listen. The effectiveness of this visual dominance pattern was demonstrated convincingly by Ralph Exline in a field study of ROTC officers at their training camp (Exline et al., 1975). Those leaders who showed a visual dominance pattern were given the highest leadership ratings, whereas those officers who engaged in a lower ratio of direct gaze while speaking to direct gaze while listening were rated less favorably on leadership abilities. This study gives no indication, of course, whether individuals who engage in visual dominance behavior are more likely to be selected as leaders or whether the holding of a leadership position encourages the development of visual dominance behavior. Nevertheless, the effectiveness of such behavior in communicating power and status is clear.

Facilitating task accomplishment. Gaze can facilitate communication between people who are working together on the same project (Patterson, 1983). If you and a friend are sailing a boat, for example, some decisions or agreements may be made primarily by an exchange of gazes. In service relationships, such as that between a doctor and a patient, a person's gaze may transmit information that is not easily expressed in words. A patient's eyes may indicate fear or acceptance or a variety of other responses to a doctor's explanation of the problem. When speech is impossible, as when a patient is in a dentist's chair, gaze may be a major medium of communication.

Overall, it is evident that eye contact or gaze provides substantial amounts of information in the communication process. The eyes are not the only channel, however; other nonverbal channels also convey information effectively.

Facial Expressions

The scientific study of facial expressions has a long history, dating from the classic work of Charles Darwin, *The Expression of the Emotions in Man and Animals* (1872). Darwin believed that there are evolutionary connections between animal and human facial expressions and that certain facial expressions may serve to communicate the same message across species.

Investigators since Darwin have continued to be interested in the ways in which facial expressions convey emotions. Most investigators have focused their attention on six primary emotions: surprise, fear, anger, disgust, happiness, and sadness. An extensive research program conducted by Paul Ekman and his colleagues has provided an exact description of the facial expressions that accompany each of these emotional states (Ekman, 1972; Ekman & Friesen, 1975; Ekman, ed., 1982). A person caught by surprise, for example, will typically raise the eyebrows and drop the jaw; horizontal wrinkles will appear across the forehead; the upper eyelid will be raised while the lower lid is drawn down, and the white of the eye will show above the iris and often below as well. Subtle muscular activity, detectable with a technique called *facial electromyography,* also differentiates the various emotions (Rinn, 1984; Schwartz, 1982). Ekman uses the term **facial affect program** to designate the pattern of facial-muscle activity that accompanies a particular emotional experience.

In support of the universality of emotional expression postulated by Darwin, Ekman and others have also shown that members of very different cultural groups demonstrate consistency in associating facial expressions with emotions. Samples of people in Europe, South America, and preliterate societies of New Guinea all were able to identify correctly most of the primary emotions displayed in photographs of faces of North Americans (Ekman, 1972; Izard, 1969).

In a more realistic demonstration of the same phenomenon, Robert Krauss and his colleagues compared the reactions of Japanese and American viewers of soap operas (Krauss, Curran, & Ferleger, 1983). The Japanese subjects understood both English and Japanese; the American subjects knew only English; and excerpts from both American and Japanese soap operas were shown to both groups of subjects. The subjects then interpreted the facial expressions that they viewed. If the understanding of emotional expression is culture-specific, then we would expect the Japanese and American viewers to be similar in their interpretations of the shows that originated in the United States, whose language and culture were familiar to both groups, but to differ in their interpretations of programs taped in Japan, whose language and culture were unfamiliar to the American subjects. The results? The two groups gave very similar interpretations of both American and Japanese shows, a finding that supports the universalist argument.

However, the fact that an emotion can be recognized by respondents of different cultures does not mean that the same emotion will always be displayed in similar circumstances. In some societies, for example, it is not considered appropriate to display emotional reactions in actual communication, even though such emotions may be experienced. Similarly, even within our own society, certain situations may call for restraint in the expression of an emotion. Consider what your reaction would be to the sight and smell of an overflowing and odorous garbage can in a neighbor's kitchen. Although you might experience disgust, it is also quite likely that you would mask your emotional expression as you talked with your neighbor. These qualifications of emotional expression, which Ekman terms **display rules,** can stem from personal habits, situational pressures, or cultural norms.

The recognition of display rules brings us closer to the central issue of this chapter—namely, communication. Although the abstract expression of emotions is of interest in its own right, it is the ways in which we transmit those emotions to the other person that affect the communication process. This distinction between the expression and the communication of emotion is an important one. Consider a series of studies conducted by Kraut and Johnston (1979) on smiling behavior. Exploring a wide range of natural settings, including bowling alleys, hockey arenas, and public walkways, these investigators observed the frequency of smiling and attempted to relate those occasions to simultaneously occurring events. Their findings indicated that people were most likely to smile when they were talking with other people; they were far less likely to smile when an event caused them to experience positive emotions while they were alone. Figure 5–3 shows the results of two of these studies, which dealt with reactions to scores at a bowling alley and weather conditions in Ithaca, New York.

Kraut and Johnston's findings suggest that a major function of the smile is to *communicate* happiness to other persons. In other words, facial expressions such as a smile may be less an automatic response to a particular stimulus than a conscious choice to affect the communicated message. This idea, of course, allows for the possibility that a smile may be used to mask some other emotion that is being experienced, and, as we shall see later, such masking attempts are common.

Body Movements and Gestures

Other parts of the body get involved in the communication process as well. Movements of the head, hands, legs, feet, and torso can all serve to com-

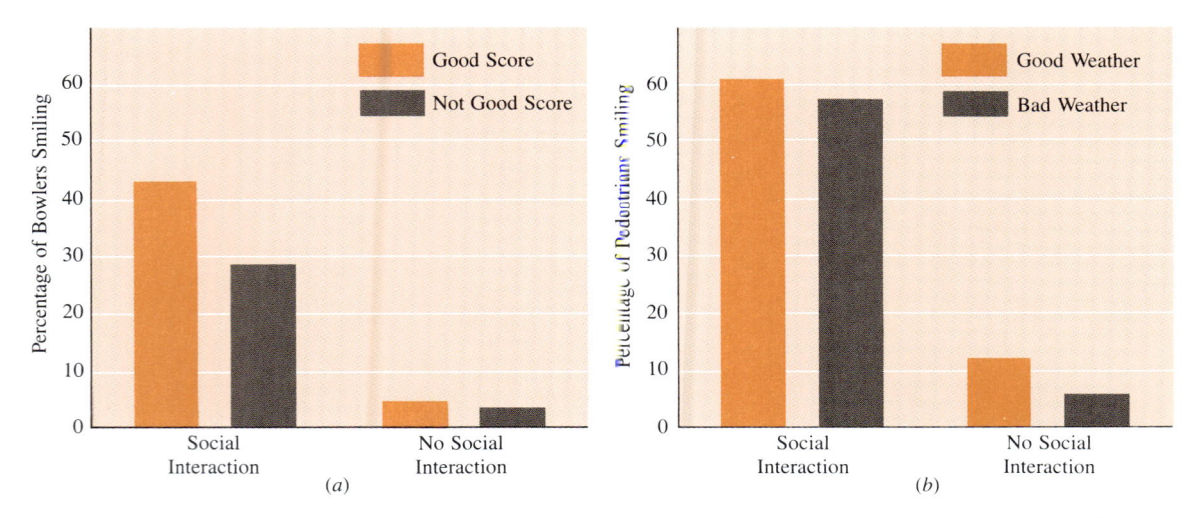

Figure 5–3 (a) Percentage of bowlers who smiled after a good or other score, when the bowlers were facing the pins and when they faced their teammates; (b) percentage of pedestrians who smiled in good weather or in bad weather, when they were alone or in context with another person.

municate messages. To impose some order on the multitude of possible body movements, Ray Birdwhistell (1970) proposed a model called **kinesics**, in analogy with *linguistics,* the term that designates the study of human language. Continuing the linguistics/kinesics analogy, Birdwhistell proposed the terms *kinemes* and *kinemorphs* to represent basic units of body movement (these terms are similar in meaning to *phonemes* and *morphemes,* discussed earlier). On the basis of extensive observations, mostly in the United States, Birdwhistell proposed that there are approximately 50 to 60 basic kinemes—that is, classes of body movements that form the core of nonverbal body language. He suggests that there are four basic kinemes of the nose area, for example: a wrinkled nose, compressed nostrils, both nostrils flared, and a single nostril flared. Continuing the parallel to linguistics, Birdwhistell suggests that kinemes, like phonemes, rarely occur in isolation. Instead, several basic units may occur simultaneously to produce a kinemorph. Although Birdwhistell's ambitious approach to classifying body movements has its supporters, it has not escaped criticism. A major point of argument is whether kinesics describes a separate language or whether kinemes depend in large part on their verbal context. Nonetheless, whether the analogy holds or not, Birdwhistell has made an important contribution to the study of communication by categorizing the many varieties of movements made by the human body.

Nonverbal behaviors that are directly linked with spoken language have been termed **illustrators** (Ekman & Friesen, 1972). If you are asked to direct someone to the library, for example, it is likely that you will gesture as well as use verbal explanations. Other research has shown that speech and movements are tightly bound together; if a person is unable to use one channel (gestures, for example, when one talks on the telephone), the other channel may be used more extensively (Graham & Heywood, 1975).

Not all body gestures accompany verbal language, however. Sometimes a gesture substitutes for a spoken phrase. Such gestures, termed **emblems,** are nonverbal acts that are clearly understood by the majority of the members of a culture (Johnson, Ekman, & Friesen, 1975). A wave of the hand in greeting, for example, is widely recognized in our society. Less friendly gestures may be equally well recognized. Other emblems may be shared by smaller groups, such as the two-fingered horns sign of Texas football fans. As you might suspect, the meaning conveyed by an emblem can vary dramatically across cultures. A single gesture may covey two quite different meanings, and a single meaning may be translated into different gestures. Because emblems replace rather than accompany other forms of communication, these disparities in meaning can cause much confusion among members of different cultures.

So far we have discussed body language as an accompaniment to or a substitute for particular verbal utterances. In addition to serving this function, body movements and gestures can also indicate the nature of the relationship between two persons in a conversation. Status differences in a relationship, for example, are often communicated by body position. The higher-status person in a relationship will generally look more relaxed: arms and legs in asymmetrical positions and a backward lean to the body. The lower-status person is more likely to maintain a fairly rigid position, with body upright, feet together and flat on the floor, and arms close to the body (Mehrabian, 1972). Once again, these status differences in nonverbal behavior frequently parallel observed sex differences in body language (Henley, 1977): men are far more apt to adopt an open stance, whereas women more frequently adopt the closed positions typical of a lower-status person.

Attraction can also be conveyed through body movements and gestures. People who like each other are more likely to lean forward, to maintain a body orientation directly toward the other person, and to take a more relaxed body position (Mehrabian, 1972). These signs are clearly interpreted, and may arouse feelings of liking or disliking in the other person (Clore, Wiggins, & Itkin, 1975).

Touch

Perhaps one of the most basic means of communication is touch. Long before a child has developed language skills and learned body illustrators and emblems, he or she communicates through tactile contact. The parent and child depend on touch for much of their early communication (see Photo 5-2).

Touch takes different forms in different kinds of relationships. At a professional or functional level, we may be touched by a barber, a dentist, or a tennis pro without giving the contact much thought. Social-polite touch is more personal but not intimate, exemplified by routine handshakes when people first meet. Other forms of touch may involve more intimate interactions, as in friendship, love, or sexual involvement.

Even seemingly accidental touches can have an effect on behavior. In a restaurant, for example, a waitress may briefly touch a customer on the hand or the shoulder when she returns the change from the customer's payment. Can such a brief touch make a difference? Apparently so, according to a study by April Crusco and Christopher Wetzel (1984): both male and female customers left larger tips when they had been touched than when they had not.

Men and women do not always respond in the same way, however. In a study conducted at the Purdue University library, for example, students who

Photo 5–2 Touch is a major channel of communication between this father and his young child.

checked out books were briefly touched or not touched on the hand by the library clerk (Fisher, Rytting, & Heslin, 1976). The female students who were touched briefly responded positively: they liked the clerk and even the library more than those who had not been touched. Men, however, did not respond to touch with similar increases in liking. An even more striking demonstration of sex differences in reaction to touch is provided by Sheryl Whitcher and Jeffrey Fisher (1979). Male and female patients in an eastern U.S. university hospital were either touched or not touched during a preoperative teaching interaction with the nurse. The touches themselves were relatively brief and professional—a light touch on the patient's hand and an approximately one-minute contact on the patient's arm. The dependent measures in this study included both questionnaire responses and physiological measures taken immediately after surgery. The findings constituted striking evidence of the positive effects of touch on women. Female patients who had been touched reported less fear and anxiety on the questionnaire measures, and their blood pressure readings after surgery were lower. The nurse's brief touch produced negative effects in the male patients; these men indicated less positive reactions than a no-touch control group and had higher blood pressure readings.

In general, women react more positively than men to touch (Major, 1981; Stier & Hall, 1984). Brenda Major (1981) has suggested that the existence of such a sex difference is dependent upon differences in status. When the status of two persons is approximately equal or when their status is ambiguous, Major argues, the reactions of men and women differ in the way we have just described—women's reactions are positive and men's are negative. When the toucher is clearly higher in status than the recipient, however, both men and women react positively to touch.

Touch can in itself convey information about status. As observers, we are more apt to attribute dominance and high status to the person who initiates a touch, while attributing submissiveness and low status to the person who receives the touch (Major & Heslin, 1982).

Interpersonal Distance

The forms of communication discussed so far have all involved some part of the body as a means of transmitting messages. At this point we turn to something more abstract—the distance between bodies as a mode of communication. The anthropologist Edward Hall (1959, 1966) is probably the individual most responsible for pointing out how the *interpersonal distance* established between two or more persons can communicate a variety of messages. On the basis of extensive observations, primarily within the United States, Hall has proposed a categorization of *distance zones* to describe the patterns typically found in different types of interactions. The four major zones are termed *intimate, personal, social,* and *public*. *Intimate zones* range in distance from actual physical contact to about 18 inches (approximately 0.5 meter). In the intimate zone "the presence of the other person is unmistakable . . . because of the greatly stepped-up sensory inputs. Sight (often distorted), olfaction, heat from the other person's body, sound, smell, and the feel of the breath all combine to signal unmistakable involvement with another body" (Hall, 1966, p. 116). This zone generally indicates a high level of intimacy between the participants, although there are exceptions, as when strangers are crowded together in an elevator. In the latter instance, the distance is uncomfortable because it conflicts with the feelings that may be aroused in the occupants by close physical contact with total strangers.

The *personal distance zone* extends from 1½ to 4 feet (about 0.5 to 1.25 meters) and typifies the distance that we usually maintain between ourselves and friends (at the closer end) and ourselves and acquaintances in everyday conversations, for example (at the farther end).

Greater distances, ranging from 4 to 12 feet (1.25

Photo 5–3 We often use distance to send messages to other people.

to 3.5 meters), represent the *social distance zone* and are typically found in business interactions or very casual social interactions. Your interactions with a clerk at the bookstore probably fall into this category, as do typical professor/student interactions.

Finally, Hall describes a *public distance zone,* in which interpersonal distance ranges from 12 to 25 feet (about 3.5 to 7.5 meters). Interactions at these distances are typically quite formal, as at a public address or in an interaction with a judge or celebrity.

As Hall's categorization indicates, greater liking is usually communicated by smaller interpersonal distance. The optimal distance between friends, for example, tends to be less than the distance between two strangers who interact (Hayduk, 1983).

Because intimacy and interpersonal distance are so closely related, we often use distance to send messages to other people. If you want to communicate liking for another person, for example, you will probably decrease the interpersonal distance. If you're not fond of a person, you will probably choose instead to "keep your distance." In a demonstration of this behavior, Howard Rosenfeld (1965) asked female students to talk with another student (actually a confederate of the experimenter) with the goal either of appearing friendly or of avoiding the appearance of friendliness. Approval-seeking women placed their chairs an average of 4.75 feet from the confederate; students seeking to avoid affiliation placed their chairs an average of 7.34 feet away.

Interpersonal distance can convey status messages as well as affiliative messages. In general, peers stand closer together than do people of unequal status (Mehrabian, 1969b). When Lott and Sommer (1967) observed seating patterns of students of different academic rank, they found that seniors sat closer to other seniors than to either first-year students or professors. In a field study, Dean, Willis, and Hewitt (1975) observed conversations between military personnel. Navy men maintained a greater distance when they initiated a conversation with a superior than when they initiated a conversation with a peer, and this difference grew larger as the difference in rank increased. Such differences were not observed among the superiors, however, an indication of the freedom of the higher-status person to define the boundaries of the conversation.

Combining the Channels

Communication is a multichanneled process. In only the most unusual cases do we rely on just one form of communication; most often messages are transmitted back and forth through a variety of verbal and nonverbal modes.

Thus far we have assumed, to paraphrase Gertrude Stein, that a channel is a channel is a channel. In other words, we have acted as if all the channels of communication were equally important. But is that assumption true? What if communication cues are not consistent with one another? Which ones do we rely on the most?

There is no single answer to these questions. The particular channel of communication that is most effective depends on several factors, including the truthfulness of the speaker, the topic of conversation, and the kind of judgment that is being made (O'Sullivan et al., 1985). There is evidence, however, that people tend to rely more on facial cues than on vocal cues or on the verbal message itself (Mehrabian & Weiner, 1967; O'Sullivan et al., 1985).

In one series of experiments, Bella DePaulo and her colleagues paired various combinations of auditory and visual messages and examined their effects in the communication of dominance and liking (DePaulo et al., 1978). Visual cues proved to be more influential than vocal cues. The subjects' preference for visual information was most noticeable when facial expressions were paired with auditory cues; body gestures did not exert as strong an effect as facial cues. These investigators also found that visual cues are more significant when people are interpreting liking messages than when the messages concern status or dominance. Finally, women revealed a greater reliance on visual messages than men did.

In some instances, however, the visual message may be discarded in favor of the spoken message. Consider a series of studies by Daphne Bugental and her colleagues (Bugental, Kaswan, & Love, 1970; Bugental, Love, & Gianetto, 1971). These investigators asked children to interpret situations in which either a woman or a man was conveying one message with the face while expressing a contradictory verbal message. In judging women, the children tended to believe a negative verbal message and ignore an accompanying smile. With men, in contrast, the children relied more on the facial expression than on the verbal message. Why would the children react differently to men than to women? To explore this question, Bugental and her colleagues observed the behavior of fathers and mothers with their children. They found that mothers tended to be less consistent in combining channels of communication—they were just as likely to smile when saying negative things as when saying positive things. Fathers were more consistent, smiling when they said positive things and not smiling when they said negative things. As a result, children may learn to disregard the facial channel of their mothers' communication, because it is a less reliable indicator of meaning, and pay more attention to their fathers' facial messages.

Patterns of Communication

The channels that we have described, both verbal and nonverbal, are the tools of communication. People learn to use these tools to convey messages and to give meaning to their utterances. It is time, then, to look more closely at the patterns of communication—to the ways in which one person relates to another.

Basic Dimensions of Communication

Although the ways we communicate with other people may seem to have endless variety, investigators have discovered that there are three major dimensions of communicative behavior. Osgood, Suci, and Tannenbaum (1957), who concentrated mainly on verbal material, defined these three dimensions as general *evaluation, social control,* and *activity.* Early investigators of facial movements and the expression of emotion also defined three dimensions: pleasantness/unpleasantness, sleep/tension, and attention/rejection (Schlosberg, 1954). More recently, Albert Mehrabian (1969a) analyzed a variety of nonverbal behaviors and, through a statistical technique known as factor analysis, described three similar factors. As Table 5–1 indicates, Mehrabian relates evaluation or liking to a series of immediacy cues, social control or status to relaxation cues, and responsiveness to activity cues.

Thus, according to Mehrabian, when you are attracted to someone, you are most likely to communicate this feeling through a variety of immediacy cues—by touching, by decreasing the distance between yourself and the other person, by leaning forward, and by maintaining eye contact. You would communicate dislike in just the opposite way—by refraining from physical contact, increasing the interpersonal distance, leaning away, and avoiding eye contact. In a similar manner, status relationships can be communicated by a combination of relaxation cues. In general, Mehrabian proposes that the greater the communicator's status in relation to the addressee, the greater the relaxation of the communicator. Finally, Mehrabian suggests that the responsiveness of one person to the other is communicated mainly by activity cues, including amount of facial activity and rate of speech.

Equilibrium and Arousal Models

The ways in which channels of communication combine is further explained by two models, the *equilibrium model* and the *arousal model,* both of which look at the ebb and flow of interactions. According to Argyle and Dean (1965), who proposed the equi-

Table 5–1 Nonverbal cues of liking, status, and activity

IMMEDIACY CUES (indicate like or dislike for the other person)
  Touching (as in holding hands or touching shoulders)
  Distance (physical distance separating the two persons)
  Forward lean
  Eye contact
  Orientation (facing directly or angled away from the other person)
RELAXATION CUES (indicate status differences between two persons)
  Arm-position symmetry or asymmetry (clasped hands or arms folded symmetrically, for example, indicate lower status)
  Sideways lean
  Leg-position symmetry or asymmetry (crossed legs, for example, indicate higher status)
  Hand relaxation
  Neck relaxation
  Reclining angle
ACTIVITY CUES (indicate responsiveness to the other person)
  Movements
    Trunk swivel movements
    Rocking movements
    Head-nodding movements
    Gesticulation
    Self-manipulation
    Leg movements
    Foot movements
  Facial expressions
    Facial pleasantness
    Facial activity
  Verbalization
    Communication length
    Speech rate
    Halting quality of speech
    Speech error rate
    Speech volume
    Intonation

librium model, every interpersonal encounter engenders pressures toward both approach and avoidance; a person may seek friendship or security while at the same time fearing rejection. Depending on the situation, an appropriate balance, or state of equilibrium, will be established by regulation of the nonverbal channels of communication. Argyle and Dean suggest that if this equilibrium is disturbed, as when one person presses for more intimacy than the other wants, the latter person will alter the messages conveyed through some of the nonverbal channels to restore the equilibrium. During a casual conversation, for instance, an acquaintance may sit much closer to you than seems appropriate. Such an imbalance would probably lead you to alter your own nonverbal communication—either by increasing the distance between the two of you or perhaps by avoiding eye contact, orienting your body away from the person, or making facial signs that indicate discomfort. Thus the model's basic assumption is that loss of equilibrium created by a message conveyed through one channel can be compensated for by alterations in the messages sent through other channels—in other words, the model proposes a set of compensatory functions.

To test this model, investigators have manipulated one of the communication channels and looked at the effects of these manipulations on another channel. For example, investigators may vary the distance between persons and then assess the amount of eye contact or gaze between participants. As people interact at closer distances, amount of eye contact tends to decrease (Argyle & Dean, 1965; Russo, 1975). In similar fashion, body orientation becomes less direct as interpersonal distance decreases (Patterson, Mullens, & Romano, 1971). Still other research has shown that as an interviewer's questions become increasingly personal, the interviewee will initiate less eye contact with the interviewer (Carr & Dabbs, 1974; Schulz & Barefoot, 1974).

Not all research supports the equilibrium model,

however. For example, men and women often react differently to disturbances of equilibrium in a relationship (Aiello, 1977a, 1977b). The model is generally supported by the behavior of men—they increase their gaze behavior as the distance between them and another person increases—but a different pattern is seen in women's behavior. When the distance between participants is greater than 6 to 8 feet, women no longer increase their gaze behavior, as Figure 5–4 indicates. Cultural differences also affect the way in which equilibrium is established, as described in Box 5–2.

A further problem for the equilibrium model is the fact that compensation is not the only response to a change in equilibrium. Sometimes an increase in the level of intimacy initiated by one person is reciprocated rather than avoided. When you are with someone you like in a romantic setting, aren't you more apt to respond positively to increases in intimacy than to try to reduce the intimacy level?

To account for either reciprocal or compensatory reactions to a loss of equilibrium, Miles Patterson (1976) has proposed an *arousal model* (see Figure 5–5). Patterson suggests that small changes in the intimacy level of an interaction will probably not be noticed, and hence no behavior changes will occur. At some threshold point, however, a sufficient change in the intimacy level of the interaction will be noticed, and consequently some behavioral adjustment will be necessary.

The precise adjustment that will be made, however, depends on the way one labels the state of arousal. Patterson assumes that a given state of arousal can be labeled either positive or negative, depending on the circumstances. In the romantic setting suggested earlier, physical contact or intensified gazes initiated by your lover would probably be a positive experience and would lead you to reciprocate the behavior. The same behavior displayed by a stranger on a park bench would most likely be labeled negatively and so would lead to compensatory adjustments on your part—turning your body away, avoiding the gaze, or getting up and leaving. The arousal model of intimacy incorporates the equilibrium principles proposed by Argyle and Dean (1965) but adds another dimension as well. This model permits us to predict that a change in the behavior of one person may lead to any of a variety of reactions in the other person, depending on situational factors.

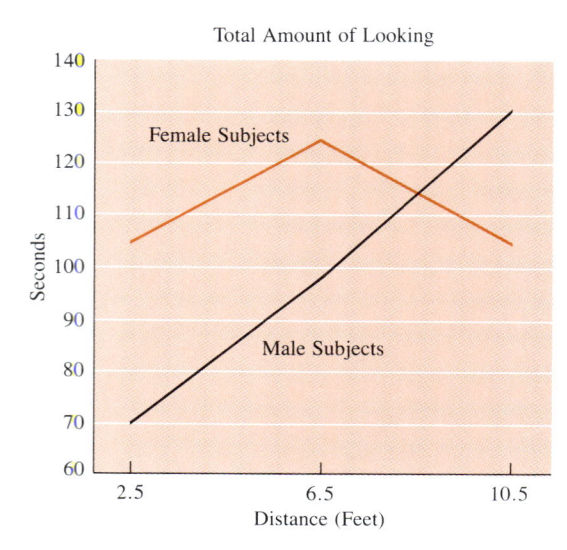

Figure 5–4 Sex differences in gaze as a function of distance. The pattern of gaze behavior exhibited by women differs from that of men as the distance between them increases.

Conversational Patterns

Nonverbal channels combine to provide one of the rhythms of communication. Verbal patterns also exist, often regulated by conversational rules and conventions. In its simplest form, a conversation between

Box 5–2
Bilingualism and nonverbal behavior

Nonverbal communication behaviors common in one culture often differ from those found in another. But what of the person who is bilingual? In a fascinating demonstration of the close connection between verbal and nonverbal channels of communication, Grujic and Libby (1978) studied French-Canadians who were equally proficient in French and English. The investigators varied both the spoken language in a 30-minute conversation and the ethnic identification of the partner. Thus some subjects spoke French with a person identified as of English heritage, other subjects spoke English with a person identified as of English heritage, and so on. The findings indicated that the ethnic identification of the partner had no effect on the nonverbal behavior of the speaker, but the language of the conversation did. When French was spoken, subjects sat closer to their partner at the beginning of the conversation, moved closer during the course of the conversation, gestured more, and interacted longer.

This study suggests that the means employed to establish intimacy vary in accordance with the language being spoken: those associated with English differ from those associated with French. When they spoke English, subjects maintained intimacy more by looking at the partner than by smiling. When they spoke French, just the reverse pattern was found: there was more smiling and less gaze. Thus in both cases some intimacy was established—but the language of the conversation had strong effects on the nonverbal channels that were used.

---

two people can be divided into three parts: an opening section, the body of the conversation, and a closing section (Clark, 1985).

To open a conversation, people must first recognize each other as potential conversants and make some kind of contact or gaze at each other (Schiffrin, 1977). Initial greetings begin the interchange: "Hello," "How are you doing?," "What's happening?" Once conversation is initiated, it proceeds according to a set of more or less strict rules. Among the numerous characteristics of the typical conversation, Harvey Sacks, Emanuel Schegloff, and Gail Jefferson (1974) have identified the following:

1. Length of conversation is not specified in advance.
2. Occurrences of more than one speaker at a time are common but very brief.
3. Turn order and size are not fixed, but vary.
4. Turn allocation techniques are used.

The taking of turns, a fundamental principle of conversation, can be effected in a number of ways. Direct questions may shift the focus from one partner to another, as may a pause at the end of a sentence.

Paralinguistic cues play an important role in the management of conversation. Turn-taking often depends more on vocal cues than on the actual content of the communication (Duncan & Fiske, 1977; Wiemann & Knapp, 1975). If you want to keep talking even though you sense that the other person wants to take a turn, you may increase the volume and rate of your speech and decrease the frequency and duration of pauses (Knapp, 1978). At the same time, the other person may persist in an attempt to gain entrance by using vocal "buffers" ("Ah . . ." or "Er . . .") or by increasing the rapidity of responses, as if to say, "Hurry up so I can talk."

As we noted earlier, communication requires the participants to share some common ground (Clark, 1985). Conversation can develop quickly between two people who already know one another, for they have a common store of shared experiences and past conversations. People who are not acquainted, however, need to engage in certain preliminaries to determine just where the common ground may lie (Maynard & Zimmerman, 1984). Upon first meeting, for example, two new students may try to find

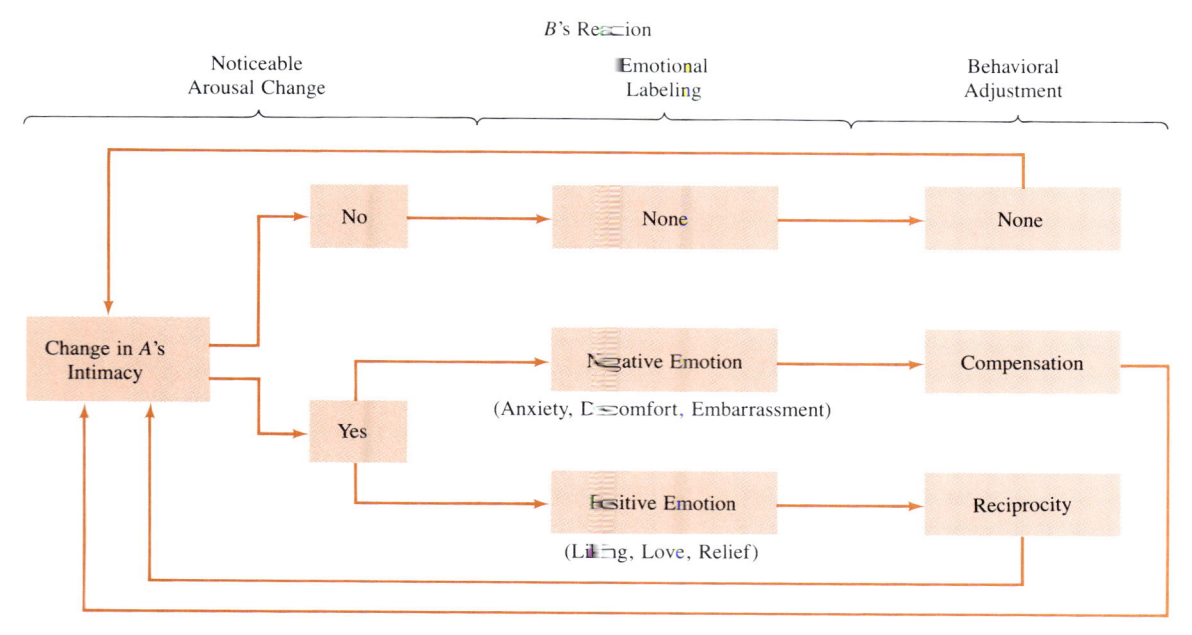

Figure 5–5 Arousal model of interpersonal communication

out about each other's living quarters, hobbies, or hometown in order to establish areas of common experience.

Participants in a conversation make certain assumptions about the nature of their interaction. People adhere to what the philosopher H. P. Grice (1975) has called the *cooperative principle*. Grice suggests that each participant assumes the other person to be informative, truthful, relevant, and concise. Thus, if you ask your roommate what he or she thinks of Professor Wong, you anticipate that the answer will be governed by each of these criteria. "Professor Wong is a good lecturer, but he makes the exams too hard" would fulfill your expectations. But what if your roommate answered, "He wears elegant ties"? Such a response would probably lead you to seek an alternative explanation for the response (which Grice has termed a *conversational implicature*); perhaps your roommate wants to avoid a truthful answer or is being sarcastic. In other words, people take from conversation not only what the other person is literally saying but what is implied as well. The implications we discern derive from our beliefs about ourselves, the other person, and people's behavior in general. (For another way of looking at conversational meanings, see Box 5–3.)

The ending of a conversation also follows some predictable patterns. The topic of conversation is exhausted, the participants prepare to leave, and the contact ends (Clark, 1985). A preclosing statement, such as "Well, I gotta go now" may signal that one person wishes to end the conversation. People may also make statements that point to future interaction, assuring the partner that the break is only temporary. Nearly every language has a set of ritualized phrases that signal a temporary end: *au revoir, hasta la vista, auf Wiedersehen, so long*.

Conversation in Close Relationships

Conversations between people who know each other well tend to follow a slightly different pattern. In

> **Box 5–3**
> **Relational analysis**
>
> Relational analysts believe that each individual message can be described by one of three control dimensions (Rogers & Farace, 1975). A "one-up" message represents an attempt to gain control in an exchange; a "one-down" message indicates that one is yielding control by either seeking or accepting the control of the other person; and a "one-across" message represents a movement toward neutralizing the control in the interaction. To see how these dimensions work, consider the following conversation between a husband and wife. The arrow after each statement indicates whether the statement is coded as one-up (↑), one-down (↓), or one-across (→).
>
> *Wife:* We don't do anything together any more. ↑
> *Husband:* What do you mean? ↓
> *Wife:* Well, as a family we don't do very much. ↑
> *Husband:* Oh, I don't know. →
> *Wife:* Don't you feel I do the major portion of the disciplining of the children? ↓
> *Husband:* The times we're together you don't. ↑
> *Wife:* Well, just for the record, I have to disagree. ↑
> *Husband:* Well, just for the record, you're wrong. ↑
> *Wife:* Well, then, we completely disagree. ↑

general conversation, for example, good friends tend to raise more topics and are generally more responsive to one another, asking more questions in reaction to the other person's statements (Hornstein, 1985). Close friends are also more likely to engage in **self-disclosure**, or the process of revealing information about the self.

Not all information about oneself is equally likely to be revealed in the process of self-disclosure. Sidney Jourard (1971) found that people reveal more information about their attitudes and opinions than about their personalities and their bodies. Sex differences are also apparent in self-disclosure: women report more self-disclosure than men, and the things they talk about tend to differ from the topics introduced by men.

In studying communication between pairs of best friends, Davidson and Duberman (1982) found that although women and men were equally likely to talk about topical issues, such as politics, current events, work, and movies, the sexes differed in their discussion of relational and personal topics. Women were more likely to talk specifically about their relationship with their friend and were also more likely to talk about personal aspects of their lives. These same women also reported much more reliance on nonverbal cues in communicating with their best friends.

Although men's and women's communications may differ in content, they are alike in their evidence of reciprocity in self-disclosure. In other words, if one person increases the intimacy of the disclosures, the other person is likely to respond with a similar increase in intimacy (Cozby, 1973).

In longer-term relationships, however, strict reciprocity is no longer the rule in communication (Altman, 1973; Morton, 1978). Although the overall intimacy level tends to be higher in such exchanges than in those of new relationships, there does not seem to be a one-for-one exchange of intimate information in any single conversation. Over the course of many conversations, however, the self-disclosures of one partner tend to balance those of the other. Thus the specific rules of communication may change considerably as we move from the initial encounter to more stable relationships.

In marriage, one of the most intense and intimate of human relationships, communication is a central process. Patricia Noller (1984) has investigated the ways in which married couples communicate, looking at both the encoding and decoding abilities of the partners. To study encoding abilities, she presented one partner with a description of a situation and a hypothetical reaction to that situation. For example, the wife might be told to imagine that she was sitting alone with her husband on a winter evening and felt cold. She would be asked also to assume that she wondered whether her husband was cold as well and to say, "I'm cold, aren't you?"

It was then the other partner's task to decode the message. Noller provided this second partner with three possible interpretations of the message and asked him to select one on the basis of his understanding of his wife's statement. Possible interpretations of "I'm cold" might be the message actually intended (she wondered whether he, too, was cold), a request for physical affection, or an accusation that the partner showed a lack of consideration in keeping the house too cold.

How did couples do at this task? Couples who scored high on a measure of marital adjustment communicated significantly better than couples who scored low on this measure, a finding that testifies to the association between effective communication and marital happiness. As for the encoding of the messages they wished to send, women were generally better than men at this task. This superiority was especially evident in the sending of positive messages, which men encoded surprisingly poorly.

Why were the men, particularly men in less satisfactory marriages, not effective in this communication task? Perhaps they simply lacked communication skills in general. Another explanation focuses on the marital relationship itself, suggesting that these men tended to show communication deficits only in interaction with their wives. To answer this question, Noller asked the same subjects to decode messages sent by strangers. In this case, the men had few problems. Thus the ability to decode messages is not just a general trait but can be sharply influenced by particular features of a relationship. Husbands and wives may indeed experience failures of communication, but such failures are more apt to be a consequence than a cause of the problem.

Deceptive Communication

Not all communication is intended to convey accurate information from one person to another. Political scandals, criminal proceedings, and extramarital affairs are often occasions for determined attempts to tell another person something other than the truth.

It is often believed that such deceptive communications are easily detected. In 1905, for example, Sigmund Freud suggested that "he that has eyes to see and ears to hear may convince himself that no mortal can keep a secret. If his lips are silent, he chatters with his fingertips; betrayal oozes out of him at every pore" (Freud, 1905/1959). More recently, the trial lawyer Louis Nizer (1973) has pointed to cues that are associated with witnesses' attempts to deceive jurors. Among such cues are a tendency to look at the ceiling, a self-conscious covering of the mouth before answering questions, and crossing of the legs. Are these beliefs in the detectability of deception justified? Do liars regularly expose themselves through the various communication channels? To answer these questions we must determine whether people who lie communicate that fact reliably through the verbal and nonverbal messages they send and then we must find out whether an observer can reliably interpret those cues.

Those Lying Ways

Many communicative cues accompany deception. Although a liar may control the verbal content of a message, many of the other communication channels leak information.

The content of the speech of people who are being deceptive tends to vary from the norm: they make fewer factual statements than usual, they are prone to vague, sweeping statements, and they frequently leave gaps in their conversation, apparently in an attempt to avoid saying something that would give them away (Knapp, Hart, & Dennis, 1974). The voice alters as well, in that liars tend to speak at a higher pitch than truthtellers (Ekman, Friesen, & Scherer, 1976). An increase in manipulative gestures also accompanies lying in many instances: the deceiver is more apt to touch the face with the hand, for example (Ekman & Friesen, 1974)—a finding that echoes the observations of Louis Nizer—or to play with glasses or some other external object (Knapp et al., 1974).

Facial expression is somewhat less reliable as an indicator of deception. This finding may be explained in part by the fact that people are more aware of their facial expressions than they are of some of the other nonverbal channels, and thus they can attempt to control the face that they present to others. People also vary considerably in the face that they present: some people smile while they are lying, for example, whereas others maintain a placid expression. Some other facial signs may indicate emotion, but do not reliably point to the specific emotion that calls them forth. The blinking rate or the extent of pupil dilation may increase when a person is lying, for example, but the same signs may accompany general nervousness as well. The face gives more microscopic cues that are less easily controlled (Ekman, 1985), but such cues are not so readily interpreted by the average observer.

Some people are better at lying than others. Recalling the discussion of self-monitoring in Chapter Three, you might expect that persons high in self-monitoring would be more successful in controlling at least some of the cues of deception. Aron Siegman and Mark Reynolds (1983) found that to be the case when they looked at the ability to control the temporal pacing of speech: people high in some aspects of self-monitoring can speak at the same pace when they lie as when they tell the truth. People who are highly motivated to lie—because they believe, for example, that the ability to lie is related to career success—tend to be good at controlling the verbal aspects of their presentation. The same people are apparently less successful in controlling the other nonverbal channels, however, a failing that often permits their deception to be detected (DePaulo, Lanier, & Davis, 1983).

Detecting Deception

Just how well can people detect deception? Although liars give a large variety of nonverbal cues to their deceit, observers do not use all of this information. Even those whose occupation relies on the ability to detect deception are not necessarily very good at the task. U.S. Customs officers, for example, would be expected to be particularly skillful in distinguishing travelers who are likely to be carrying contraband, yet a study that compared a sample of these workers with a random group of college students indicated no superiority in the customs agents (Kraut & Poe, 1980).

Why should our ability to detect deception be so poor? For one thing, observers tend to rely on the verbal message, often to their detriment. People given both vocal and facial cues, for example, are no better at detecting deception than people who only hear the deceptive message (Zuckerman, DePaulo, & Rosenthal, 1981). Reliance on verbal cues may make people inattentive to channels through which more reliable information is being conveyed. Of course, when only the verbal message is available, detection of deceit is particularly difficult. Reading the transcript of a trial, for example, is probably not a very good way to tell if a witness was lying. People may also rely on their own theories as to which cues are relevant, and those theories may be wrong. If nervous blinking is not a valid indicator of lying, for example, then it will not do much good to pay attention to that sign. Yet another reason for our poor hit rate where lying is concerned is that we often do not receive the feedback that would permit us to know whether our assumptions were right or wrong. In the absence of such feedback, faulty theories can persist. Some conditions that make the detection of deception less difficult are listed in Box 5–4.

Yet just as some people can lie more successfully than others, so we can more readily detect deceit in some people than in others. Lies told by women, for example, seem to be more readily detected than lies told by men. Further, lies told by a person of the other sex are more easily spotted than lies told by someone of our same sex (DePaulo, Stone, & Lassiter, 1985). Exactly why these disparities are found is not clear, but they suggest that our experience may be more beneficial in some areas than in others.

Communication and Social Interaction

As we noted at the beginning of this chapter, communication links the self with another person. Looking inward, the self is concerned with its own identities, goals, and motivations. Looking outward, the individual has a set of beliefs and theories about other people, both as individuals and as groups. It is through communication that these identities and beliefs take shape.

Individuals often approach other people with some

Box 5–4
When it is relatively easy to detect a lie

The psychologist Paul Ekman has studied deceptive communication for years and has written a book (1985) that can help people detect deception in others. Some of the conditions he has found under which lying is relatively easy to detect are:

1. The liar does not anticipate exactly when he or she has to lie.
2. The lie involves emotions felt at the moment.
3. Amnesty is available to the liar who confesses.
4. The punishment that will follow discovery is severe.
5. The liar and the target are personally acquainted.
6. The lie is not authorized by some official body.
7. The liar is not practiced in lying.
8. The liar does not have a good memory.
9. The liar is not convinced that what he or she is saying is absolutely true.
10. The liar has not successfully deceived the target before.

---

prior expectations. As we saw in Chapter Four, such beliefs or expectations are not necessarily valid. Yet the process of communication and interaction may tend to confirm one's initial expectations. This general phenomenon is known as the **self-fulfilling prophecy**—the fact that a perceiver's beliefs about another individual may elicit from that person behavior that confirms the initial expectation. Researchers have looked closely at the process by which we elicit reactions that conform to the expectations we have conveyed (Jones, 1986; Miller & Turnbull, 1986; Snyder, 1984). John Darley and Russell Fazio (1980) have termed this process the *expectancy confirmation sequence*.

As Figure 5–6 indicates, the expectancy confirmation sequence involves five steps. For convenience, the person who initiates this sequence (the perceiver) is designated *A*; the target or recipient of communication is designated *B*. In fact, of course, both people in an interaction are simultaneously perceivers and targets.

In the first two steps of the sequence, the perceiver has a set of beliefs about the target and behaves toward the target on the basis of those beliefs. As we saw in Chapter Four, a perceiver's beliefs may stem from any of numerous sources. They may be based on past interaction with the target. The wife of 20 years may know from experience, for example, that her husband will get angry when she tells him he needs a haircut or that he will smile when she talks about their daughter's progress in school. Alternatively, beliefs about an individual may derive from stereotypes about a group to which the individual belongs. Whatever the beliefs, it is quite likely that the perceiver will communicate them in some way to the target.

This communication sequence has been confirmed by numerous studies. Mark Snyder and William Swann (1978), for example, told subjects that their partner in a competitive game was either hostile or nonhostile. Perceivers who believed their partner was hostile acted more competitively toward the partner than did subjects who had no such belief. In another study demonstrating the influence of initial expectations, male students engaged in a ten-minute telephone conversation with a female student whom they believed to be either physically attractive or unattractive (Snyder, Tanke, & Berscheid, 1977). Analysis of conversations revealed that men who believed they were interacting with an attractive woman were friendlier, more outgoing, and generally more sociable than those who believed their partner was less attractive.

How do perceivers communicate such beliefs to their targets? As we might expect, they make use of both verbal and nonverbal channels. Monica Harris and Robert Rosenthal (1985) identify the following behaviors as those that convey a positive expectancy:

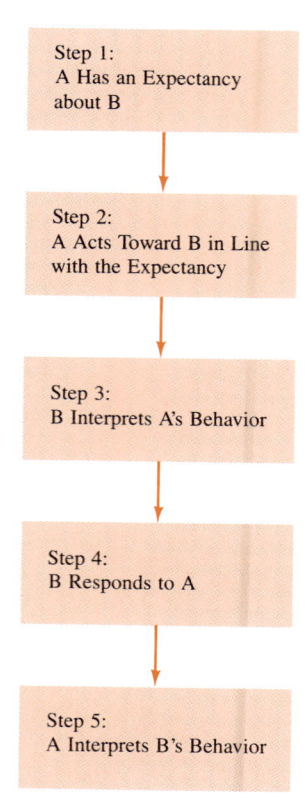

```
Step 1:
A Has an Expectancy
about B
    ↓
Step 2:
A Acts Toward B in Line
with the Expectancy
    ↓
Step 3:
B Interprets A's Behavior
    ↓
Step 4:
B Responds to A
    ↓
Step 5:
A Interprets B's Behavior
```

Figure 5–6 The expectancy confirmation sequence

maintaining closer physical distances, having longer interactions, interacting more often, encouraging more, engaging in more eye contact, smiling more, and praising more.

The target who receives such a communication then faces a number of questions. First (step 3 in Figure 5–6), the target must interpret exactly what the perceiver is doing. Of course, such an interpretation may or may not be correct, but in either case, the target's response is based on what he or she believes the perceiver has communicated. The target's response, whether in words or in action, in turn sends a message back to the perceiver. Sometimes the response confirms the perceiver's initial belief.

Such *behavioral confirmation* is an instance of the self-fulfilling prophecy. In Snyder and Swann's study of competitive behavior, for example, targets whose partners thought they were hostile, and accordingly acted hostile, tended to respond in a hostile manner. Similarly, the women in the telephone conversation study whose partners believed they were attractive responded with more sociability, poise, and humor than did women who were believed to be unattractive—even though the women in the two conditions actually differed not at all in degree of physical attractiveness. And in yet another demonstration of the expectancy confirmation effect, people in a study of conversational interchange were told that their partners either liked them a lot or didn't particularly like them. People who believed they were liked responded in kind: they disclosed more information about themselves, they had a more pleasant tone of voice and general attitude, and they were less likely to disagree or express feelings of dissimilarity in later conversations (Curtis & Miller, 1986). The results? Their partners really did like them better than partners who had been described as less approving.

The expectancy confirmation sequence has been shown to affect interaction in the classroom as well. Rosenthal and Jacobson (1968) found that teachers' beliefs about the abilities of their students could affect the performance of those pupils. When teachers were led to believe that a (randomly selected) group of students were brighter than average, the students scored higher on an intelligence test at the end of the school year than another group of randomly selected students who had not been so identified. In such situations, as subsequent research confirms, the expectancy confirmation sequence is played out: first, the teachers develop expectations; second, their behavior toward the students is colored by their beliefs; and third, the students tend to react to the differential treatment in ways that confirm the initial beliefs (Jussim, 1986). Such is the power of beliefs.

It would be a mistake, however, to assume that a perceiver can always shape the behavior of a target. Targets are, after all, individuals with their own self-identities and goals, and they may just as easily choose to disconfirm a perceiver's expectancies (Miller & Turnbull, 1986). Predicting just when a target will and will not confirm a communicated expectancy is one of the challenges of this particular approach (Deaux & Major, in press). Investigators have identified some conditions that favor nonconfirmation. When a perceiver's expectation is quite discrepant from the target's firmly held self-conception, for example, the perceiver's beliefs are likely to be ineffective in eliciting the expected response (Swann & Ely, 1984). Also, if the perceiver's beliefs are made quite explicit, the target is better able to ignore them (Hilton & Darley, 1985). Nonconfirmation is particularly likely when the perceiver has conveyed a negative expectation, which most of us would be unlikely to endorse.

The final step in the expectancy confirmation sequence is the perceiver's interpretation of the target's behavior. This perception may accurately reflect the target's response. Sometimes, however, perceivers elect to maintain their initial beliefs, even in the face of nonconfirming evidence, through a process of *cognitive confirmation*. In other words, a perceiver may choose to see what he or she believes, ignoring information that tends to be inconsistent with that belief (Darley & Gross, 1983).

The sequence of expectancy confirmation does not necessarily stop when a particular conversation ends (Jones, 1986). If people treat you as competent, for example, and you act competently in response, you may begin to see yourself as a competent person. This self-conception of competence may cause you to act more confidently in the future, continuing the sequence a step further.

Communication processes form the core of social interaction. As later chapters will show, liking and hating, helping and harming are all influenced by the messages that are communicated. Communication constantly shapes our views of ourselves and of others, defining present realities and laying the groundwork for future interaction.

Summary

Communication is fundamental to most social behavior. Although the forms of communication are varied, it has been truthfully said that we can't *not* communicate. Early models of the communication process described a one-way flow from a transmitter to a receiver. More recent models stress that communication is a shared social system, with both partners bringing a set of expectations and understandings to the interaction. Both verbal and nonverbal communications are part of this shared system.

We communicate through many channels, including language and paralanguage, gaze, facial expressions, body movements and gestures, touch, and interpersonal distance. The study of our use of language, the most obvious form of communication, reveals how important intention and interpretation can be. The nonverbal behaviors, including gaze, serve a variety of purposes. Five specific functions are (1) to provide information, (2) to regulate interaction, (3) to express intimacy, (4) to exercise social control, and (5) to facilitate the accomplishment of tasks.

Facial expressions convey a variety of emotions, and these basic emotional expressions can be identified by people in very different cultures. Cultures may differ, however, in the *display rules* that govern the circumstances in which an emotion will be expressed. Interpersonal distance is a more abstract form of communication, but it, too, is an important means of conveying information. Four major zones (intimate, personal, social, and public) define the distances between people which accompany different types of interchange.

All of these verbal and nonverbal channels combine in the process of communication to convey meaning. Three major dimensions of communication have been identified (liking, status, and responsiveness), each of which is associated with a distinctive set of nonverbal cues. Two models have been proposed to explain how nonverbal cues are combined to convey liking. The *equilibrium* model proposes that participants in an interaction seek to achieve a balance between pressures toward approach and avoidance, and compensate for an excess of pressure in one direction by sending nonverbal messages designed to restore the balance. The *arousal model* suggests that the way a change in arousal level is interpreted depends on the way the situation is defined. Sometimes compensation will be the rule, and at other times reciprocity is more likely.

Conversations have a regular structure, and the elements of that structure—an opening, a body, and a close—are typically regulated by a set of rules or conventions. Conversations between partners in a close relationship tend to follow somewhat distinctive rules. Self-disclosure, for example, is both more common in such conversations and less subject to rules of strict reciprocity.

Deceptive communication is accompanied by specific patterns of verbal and nonverbal behaviors. Although deceit may be leaked, however, observers are often unable to distinguish the truthteller from the liar.

Self and social knowledge combine in the communication process. Often a person's beliefs about another can influence that other person's behavior, creating a *self-fulfilling prophecy*. Five steps comprise the expectancy confirmation sequence, in which beliefs of the perceiver are conveyed to a target, who interprets the message and then acts in accordance with that interpretation. The target's response may thus tend to confirm the perceiver's beliefs. In other circumstances the target will disconfirm expectations in order to communicate some other message back to the perceiver.

Glossary Terms

display rules
emblems
facial affect program
illustrators
kinesics
paralanguage
self-disclosure
self-fulfilling prophecy

*People are disturbed not by things but by the views
that they take of them.*
Epictetus

*We have too many high sounding words, and too
few actions that correspond with them.*
Abigail Adams

Robert Eckert / EKM Nepenthe

CHAPTER SIX

Attitudes & Behavior

I. The Nature of Attitudes
   Definitions of Attitudes
   Components of Attitudes
   Measurement of Attitudes
II. The Formation of Attitudes
   Encountering the Attitude Object
   Parents and Peer Groups
   Media Influence
III. The Structure of Attitudes
   Complexity and Values
   How Attitudes Interrelate
   Attitudes and Information
IV. Attitudes and Behavior
   What Attitude and What Behavior?
   A Theory of Reasoned Action
   How Do Attitudes Influence Behavior?
V. Summary

*F*ew people were aware of the existence of atomic bombs in 1940. Nor did many people have an understanding of the potential of nuclear power. That situation changed with the bombings of Hiroshima and Nagasaki. People who a short time before had never heard of atomic fission now formed strong opinions on both sides of the issue. Most Americans supported President Truman's decision to use atomic weapons. Questioned in a public opinion poll in 1945, 93% of a random sample of the U.S. population said that they would have used the bomb in some circumstances (Fiske, Fischhoff, & Milburn, 1983). Attitudes had shifted somewhat by 1982, although a majority of U.S. citizens still supported Truman's decision. Asked whether it was necessary and proper to have dropped the atomic bombs on Japan during World War II, 63% said it was, while 26% said they thought it was wrong. An additional 11% were not sure whether it was right or wrong. Different distributions of attitudes could undoubtedly be found outside of the United States, reflecting different experiences with nuclear power.

Nuclear power is only one of many issues on which people form opinions and take a stand. What do you think about gun control, abortion, space exploration, social science research, and the killing of whales? Attitudes are equally pervasive in less controversial realms. What kind of ice cream do you prefer, which television shows do you watch the most, who is your favorite recording star, and what brand of toothpaste do you like? Each of these questions is a question about your attitudes.

Attitudes serve as an index of individuals' thoughts and feelings about the people, the objects, and the issues in their environment. In addition, they provide clues to future behavior, predicting how people will act when they encounter the objects of their beliefs. In this chapter we consider just what an attitude is, how attitudes develop, and how they relate to other beliefs and to behavior. In Chapter Seven we will see how attitudes change under the influence of persuasion.

The Nature of Attitudes

More than 50 years ago the distinguished Harvard psychologist Gordon Allport described attitudes as "the keystone in the edifice of American social psychology" (1935, p. 798). But just what is this concept that not only is central to social psychologists but is part of the common language as well?

Definitions of Attitudes

In one of the earliest uses of the word, *attitude* meant a physical posture or body position. In early experiments on reaction time, for example, experimenters talked about a subject's attitude when they referred to a readiness to respond to the onset of a stimulus (Himmelfarb & Eagly, 1974b). In more recent times the term has generally been limited to mental states. In this sense, attitudes are not directly observable events but rather are mediating constructs (like the schemas discussed in Chapters Three and Four) which can represent internal structures and processes.

The term *attitude* is widely used by psychologists and the public alike, and many different definitions have been offered. These definitions often reflect particular theoretical positions that are accepted by some investigators but rejected by others. To avoid such disputes, we will accept the working definition offered by William McGuire, that attitudes are "responses that locate objects of thought on dimensions of judgment" (1985, p. 239). By *objects of thought*, we mean the issues or people about which people have opinions. *Dimension of judgment* designates the range over which evaluations extend, as from good to bad or from positive to negative. Thus a person may think that volleyball is a good sport, cats are so-so pets, and anchovies are a distasteful food. Each of these thoughts represents an attitude, an evaluation of the object on a particular dimension.

Two other terms should be mentioned before we go further into the nature of attitudes. *Values* are broad, abstract goals that lack a specific object or reference point. Bravery, beauty, and freedom are values. They serve as dimensions of judgment or as abstract standards for decision making, through which the individual may develop specific attitudes and beliefs (Rokeach, 1973). Thus, if beauty is one of your primary values, many of your beliefs may be based on judgments as to whether a particular object is beautiful. The value of practicality or efficiency may be more important to other people, and so their attitudes and beliefs in regard to the same object may differ sharply from yours.

Opinion is a less easily defined term that has often been used interchangeably with *attitude*. The term is closely associated with public opinion polling, which focuses on the shared attitudes and beliefs of large groups of people. In other words, public opinion represents a summation of individual attitudes.

Components of Attitudes

Many theorists have proposed that attitudes have three basic components: the cognitive, the affective or emotional, and the behavioral (Katz & Stotland, 1959). As McGuire (1985) has noted, the proposition that people take three existential stances in regard to the human condition—knowledge, feeling, and acting—has been advanced by philosophers throughout history. As far back as Plato, terms designating *cognition, affect,* and *conation* were used to refer to the three components of what we call attitude (Oskamp, 1977). The cognitive component consists of the beliefs and ideas a person has about some attitude object. For example, the beliefs that women are more intuitive than men, that all cab drivers are talkative, and that Germans are always methodical represent the cognitive aspect of attitudes toward objects. The affective component of an attitude is the emotional feelings one has about the attitude object or one's liking or dislike for the object. Positive feelings include respect, liking, and sympathy; negative feelings may be contempt, fear, and revulsion. The behavioral, or conative, component of an attitude is one's action tendencies in regard to the object. For example, does a legislator vote for or against a balanced-budget amendment? Does an individual donate money to the cancer society?

It is useful to keep these distinctions in mind, because the affective, cognitive, and behavioral components of one person's attitude do not always match those of the same attitude held by another person. Two people may share a belief that jogging is an aerobic exercise, for example, but may differ sharply in their feelings about jogging. It is possible for a person to feel positively about recycling but, for various reasons, never quite get around to taking the bottles and papers down to the local recycling center. As we will see later when we discuss the relationships of attitudes and behaviors, these distinctions are important ones. Public opinion polls often emphasize only one of these three elements. Consider the following three questions about a hypothetical candidate X: (*a*) Do you like candidate X? (*b*) Do you think candidate X is well informed on education issues? (*c*) If the election were held today, would you vote for candidate X? The answer to each of these questions would provide some information about people's attitudes toward candidate X, but some of the answers might be more predictive of actual voting behavior than others.

Measurement of Attitudes

Attitudes, as we said earlier, are not observable entities. You can't see, smell, or touch an attitude; it is an underlying construct that must be inferred. To make such inferences, psychologists have developed many methods of measurement, all designed to tap people's underlying attitudes toward various objects and issues in their environment (Dawes & Smith, 1985).

In its simplest form, such a method might consist of open-ended questions—for example, "What do you think about space exploration?" Such questions have the advantage of eliciting a broad range of respondent views and sometimes more detail than some of the other forms. However, open-ended questions also have the disadvantage of low reliability (a person may answer quite differently on different occasions), and it is difficult to compare the answers of different respondents because their answers may vary so widely. Although open-ended questions can be quite useful in the initial stage of an investigation—when you are not sure of all the issues that may be involved—later stages of attitude research generally call for more closed-ended questions that allow more precision.

Many types of questionnaires and rating scales have been developed to measure attitudes more precisely. To give you an idea of what these scales look

| "Nuclear power plants are a safe means of energy production." ||||||
| Strongly Disagree (1) | Disagree (2) | Undecided (3) | Agree (4) | Strongly Agree (5) |

Figure 6–1 A sample item from a Likert scale of attitude measurement

like, we will discuss two types of scales in some detail—the Likert method and the semantic differential technique.

The Likert method of summated ratings. In 1932 Rensis Likert proposed a procedure for measuring attitudes which has been widely used ever since. A **Likert scale** consists of a set of declarative statements with which subjects are asked to indicate the degree of their agreement or disagreement. A sample item from such a scale is shown in Figure 6–1. The number of categories (possible answers to each question) may vary, but five or seven is probably the most common number.

A Likert scale will contain a series of such items, and a person's final attitude score will be the sum of the responses to all items. For example, if there are 20 items on the scale, each with 5 categories, a person's score can range from 0 to 100. In refining a Likert scale, an investigator will generally do an item analysis to determine which questions are the best measures of the attitude being studied. Specifically, the investigator will determine the correlation of each item with the total score and will keep only those items that yield a substantial correlation with the total score.

The semantic differential technique. The Likert method requires the investigator to create a series of items specific to the issue at hand and then to determine whether the items are indeed good measures of attitudes toward the issue. The **semantic differential technique**, in contrast, relies on a scale that is general enough to be applied to any topic (Osgood, Suci, & Tannenbaum, 1957).

This method, which was originally developed to measure the meaning of an object (hence the term *semantic*), requires a person to rate a given concept on a series of 7-point bipolar rating scales, as shown in Figure 6–2. This format can be used to rate any concept—a person, a political issue, a work of art, or anything else.

The adjective scales that are used in this format have been found to represent three distinct dimensions of judgment: evaluation (as represented by such pairs as good-bad and clean-dirty), potency (for example, weak-strong), and activity (such as active-passive or fast-slow). Investigators are usually interested in the evaluative dimension when they assess attitudes, but at times the other dimensions may be of interest as well.

There are less direct ways to assess attitudes than the use of scales such as the two described. Reactivity, as discussed in Chapter Two, can be a problem if respondents feel a need to express a position that they think the interviewer favors rather than state their true opinion. In other words, self-report always must be treated with caution.

One indirect measure of attitudes is the *lost-letter procedure*, conceived by Stanley Milgram and his colleagues (Milgram, Mann, & Harter, 1965). Stamped letters or postcards addressed to organizations associated with the issue that interests the researcher are dropped in parking lots and on street corners, and the experimenter waits to see how many are picked up and mailed to their destinations. If you

The subject is asked to rate a given concept (such as nuclear energy) on a series of seven-point bipolar rating scales. Any concept—a person, a political issue, a work of art, a group, or anything else—can be rated. In the usual format, the respondent places an *X* at one of the seven points on the scale to indicate his or her rating of the item on each bipolar dimension.

Nuclear Energy

Fair	_ _ _ _ _ _ _	Unfair
Large	_ _ _ _ _ _ _	Small
Clean	_ _ _ _ _ _ _	Dirty
Bad	_ _ _ _ _ _ _	Good
Valuable	_ _ _ _ _ _ _	Worthless
Weak	_ _ _ _ _ _ _	Strong
Active	_ _ _ _ _ _ _	Passive
Cold	_ _ _ _ _ _ _	Hot
Fast	_ _ _ _ _ _ _	Slow

Figure 6–2 A sample item from a semantic differential scale of attitude measurement

wanted to know how residents of a community felt about the issue of gun control, for instance, you could address 100 letters to the National Rifle Association (NRA) and another 100 letters to the National Committee to Ban Handguns (NCBH). (So that you could keep track of the outcome, the address on both sets of envelopes would be your own or a post office box that you rented.) If more letters were mailed to the NCBH than to the NRA, you might conclude that community opinion tended to favor gun control. Of course, this method has its problems as well. Letters may not be returned for many reasons, including loss or destruction by the weather; conversely, many people would probably mail the letter no matter what they felt about the organization to which it was addressed. Thus, although it avoids the problems of self-report, the lost-letter technique is at best a rather crude measure of attitudes.

Other indirect measures of attitudes rely on responses over which people have little control, such as pupil dilation or skin conductance (Dawes & Smith, 1985). The mere fact that a measure does not require self-report, however, does not necessarily mean it is better than one that does. Ultimately, the technique must show that it measures attitude-related behaviors—the only reason to measure attitudes at all.

The Formation of Attitudes

People have attitudes about a great many things. But where do these attitudes come from? As you might suspect, there is no single answer to this question. Some attitudes are based on direct experience with the attitude object, while other attitudes may be acquired less directly. A person may develop an attitude toward pizza, for example, as a result of eating pizza, while the same person could develop an attitude toward squid without ever actually tasting it. Attitudes can be learned through direct reinforcement or may be acquired by means of imitation and social learning (see Chapter One). In short, there are a great many routes to attitude formation.

Encountering the Attitude Object

Perhaps the most obvious way to develop an attitude toward some object or issue is by personal experience, an experience that engenders either positive or negative reactions. You taste your first piece of pizza, you like the taste, and you develop a positive attitude toward pizza. Conversely, your first taste of squid may be so unpleasant that a negative attitude is formed. Both of these cases illustrate quite simple processes by which an attitude can be acquired. Sometimes the single event is more dramatic (McGuire, 1985). A religious experience, a childhood trauma, a wartime bombing—such incidents can create quite strong attitudes toward relevant issues and objects.

Sometimes attitudes are acquired by virtue of their objects' association with other objects that arouse attitudes or feelings. Such are the principles of classical conditioning. Building on earlier work by Leonard Doob (1947), Arthur Staats (1967) used a classical conditioning model, like that developed by Pavlov with his dogs, to explain the acquisition of attitudes. In the now-familiar experiments associated with Pavlov, an unconditioned stimulus (UCS) is paired with a new stimulus, called the conditioned stimulus (CS). Through the process of association, the animal learns to make the same response to the CS as it previously did to the UCS (see Figure 6–3). This new response is called a conditioned response (CR), and Staats defines an attitude as such a response—a conditioned evaluative response to some object in the environment.

To apply these principles to the acquisition of attitudes, consider your associations with the word *seedy*. Most people would react to this description rather negatively. Now assume that a particular politician is always described in the same breath with seedy people. Presumably you would learn to evaluate that politician negatively as well.

A simple encounter with an object does not necessarily lead a person to develop an attitude toward that object. Every day the average person comes into contact with innumerable objects, issues, and groups, many of which may call forth no attitude at all. You may walk into a large department store, for example, and encounter hundreds of different products. Do you have an attitude toward each of them? Probably not. If an employee of the department store approaches you and asks what you think of portable vacuum cleaners, however, you may form an opinion on the spot. In other words, direct questioning may cause

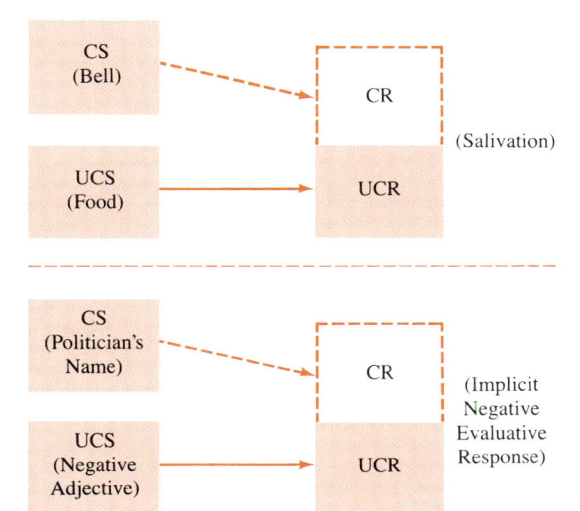

Figure 6–3 Classical conditioning model. The original Pavlovian situation is represented in the top half of the diagram; the parallel process for social attitudes is shown in the lower half. (CS = conditioned stimulus; UCS = unconditioned stimulus; UCR = unconditioned response; CR = conditioned response.)

attitudes to form. Even the expectation that one will be asked about a particular object or issue in the future seems to be enough to cause attitudes to develop (Fazio, Lenn, & Effrein, 1983–1984). Presumably such anticipation is functional, allowing an individual to be prepared to understand and react to situations that would otherwise be unfamiliar.

Parents and Peer Groups

Many attitudes are acquired from other people. Parents are the earliest and most obvious sources of acquired attitudes. The political attitudes of children, for example, are remarkably similar to those of their parents on the average (McGuire, 1985). Peers are also a major influence on attitude acquisition, as the cycles of teenage fads testify. Attitudes toward music, clothing styles, hair styles, and many other things develop in the context of interaction with peers. Children's ideas about smoking are related to the opinions of both parents and peers. A study

Photo 6–1   Parents are a major influence on their children's attitudes.

of British 15-year-olds, for example, indicated that boys who smoked were more likely to have fathers and friends who smoked. Further, according to their reports, their parents were more tolerant of smoking than those of boys who did not smoke (Eiser & van der Pligt, 1984).

Various principles of learning can help to explain how such attitudes and the correspondent behaviors are acquired. Principles of operant reinforcement apply to the situation in which a reward immediately follows the expression of an attitude. Imagine that you express an opinion about nuclear disarmament and a listener excitedly says, "You're right!" Would you be more likely to endorse that opinion in the future?

A classic study of the role of reinforcement in attitude acquisition was conducted at the University of Hawaii (Insko, 1965). Students were phoned by an interviewer who sought their opinions about "Aloha Week" (festivities held every fall in Honolulu). To half the students, the investigator responded with "Good" when the student indicated a favorable opinion of Aloha Week; the other half received a "Good" response following statements of negative attitudes toward Aloha Week. By this means, verbal conditioning was instituted—positive attitudes were reinforced in some of the students, negative attitudes in others.

About one week after the telephone calls, the same students completed an apparently unrelated "Local Issues Questionnaire" in their regular class meeting, and one of the items in this questionnaire asked for their attitudes toward Aloha Week. Students in the group whose positive attitudes had been verbally reinforced by the telephone interviewer expressed more favorable views than subjects in the group that had been verbally reinforced for negative attitudes. The effect of verbal reinforcement thus appeared in another setting one full week later.

Why does a verbal response such as "Good" have an effect on expressed attitudes? One possibility is that the response leads the person to believe that conformity to his or her current opinion will result in a variety of future reinforcements. Some people have questioned whether the reinforcement itself is really the cause of changes in attitudes, suggesting that *demand characteristics* may be a more reasonable explanation. It is possible that students who participated in Insko's study expressed either more favorable or more unfavorable attitudes toward Aloha Week on the Local Issues Questionnaire because they felt they were supposed to rather than because any true shift in attitude had occurred (Page, 1974).

Although demand characteristics may account for some experimental findings, there is little doubt that attitudes can be conditioned. A child who knows that her parents approve when she says school is good and disapprove when she says school is bad is aware of what her parents want to hear (their demands); yet it is still possible that a positive attitude toward school which the child develops in response to her parents' attitudes may be due in part to the reinforcement she receives. In a similar manner, praise and approval from friends and relatives can effectively mold attitudes.

The principles of **social learning theory** also help to explain how some attitudes are formed. As we saw in Chapter One, people can learn simply by observing the behaviors of others. Those other people (termed models) can express particular attitudes, which then may be adopted by the individual who witnesses their expression. In the case of parents and children, observational learning is at least as important as direct reinforcement, and probably more common. Similarly, people probably acquire many of their attitudes through imitation of their peers without having any direct experience with the targets of the attitudes.

Media Influence

Parents and peers are not the only models that affect the formation of attitudes. The media, and in particular television, are another powerful source of attitudes (Roberts & Maccoby, 1985). Research has shown that the media can both create attitudes and reinforce those that already exist. In one study, for example, Eskimo children were exposed to television for the first time when they saw a series about other cultures and values. Children who watched this series underwent significant changes in their beliefs about other cultural groups (Caron, 1979). In the case of sex-role stereotypes, amount of television viewing has been shown to affect the sexism scores of adolescent girls. Heavy television viewing increased sexism scores, particularly among girls of middle-class families. Interestingly, this effect was not found among boys. Although boys who initially were more sexist in their views did watch more television, their attitudes were not altered by their viewing experience (Morgan, 1982).

Political campaigns, and particularly U.S. presidential campaigns, are increasingly dependent on television to create positive attitudes toward the candidates. The attempts to create favorable attitudes are not always successful, of course. On occasion an advertising campaign has backfired, fostering negative rather than positive attitudes.

People who report the actions of political candidates, such as news broadcasters, affect the development of attitudes as well. As we suggested earlier, an attitude can be considered a process of locating an attitudinal object on some dimension of judgment. On just which dimension or dimensions the object will be judged, among the many that may be appropriate, is a question that can affect the final outcome. Television news programs can affect such decisions. Relying on principles of social cognition, which indicate that the concepts or schemas most likely to affect judgments are those that are accessible, Shanto Iyengar and his colleagues designed an experiment that considered the effects of news programs on viewers' attitudes (Iyengar et al., 1984). Students at Yale University watched televised evening newscasts that covered a variety of issues, including civil rights, U.S.-Soviet relations, and energy problems. The students were divided into three groups, differing only in the level of exposure to stories about energy (none, intermediate, or high). The investigators predicted that students who were exposed more frequently to energy stories would be more likely to evaluate the performance of the president, Jimmy Carter, on this dimension, because it would be more accessible to them. Their findings supported the hypothesis. The students who had high exposure to the energy issue based their overall evaluation of President Carter primarily on their beliefs about his performance on energy issues. If they thought he was good in this area, they rated his overall performance favorably; if they thought he was weak in this area, his overall performance was devalued. Other issues were less important for these subjects. Students who had less exposure to energy stories, in contrast, did not base their overall evaluation on this issue. Thus television broadcasters, by making some issues more salient than others, can influence the dimensions on which potential voters base their attitudes. This influence of the media is a fairly subtle one, affecting the dimensions of judgment rather than the evaluation of the candidate

Box 6-1
Can a smile elect a president?

The television newscaster David Brinkley was once quoted as saying, "I am not objective. . . . There are a great many things I like and dislike, and it may be that at times some indications of this appear in my facial expression" (quoted in Mullen et al., 1986). Whether newscasters are biased in their presentations, particularly when political candidates are concerned, has been a topic of heated debate for years. Studies of the verbal content of news programs have produced mixed results, some suggesting bias while others find no evidence of it. David Brinkley's comments, however, suggest a more subtle form of influence. As communication takes place through a variety of channels, a newscaster may, inadvertently or not, indicate approval or disapproval by signs that are not at all obvious.

Brian Mullen and his colleagues considered this possibility in the context of the 1984 U.S. presidential election coverage. As a first step, these investigators analyzed a series of news segments broadcast by the anchors of the three major networks: Peter Jennings (ABC), Dan Rather (CBS), and Tom Brokaw (NBC). Their specific interest was the degree to which these newscasters displayed positive or negative facial expressions when they reported on the activities of Ronald Reagan and Walter Mondale. In two cases they found no difference. The facial expressions of Peter Jennings, however, were significantly more positive when he talked about Reagan than when he reported on Mondale.

Can such differences in style of presentation affect the voter? This was the next question that Mullen and his colleagues asked. They conducted a telephone survey of potential voters in four cities (Cleveland, Ohio; Rolla, Missouri; Williamstown, Massachusetts; and Erie, Pennsylvania) to see if there was any relationship between the television news broadcast that a person watched and that person's voting behavior. There was: people who regularly watched Peter Jennings on ABC were more likely to report having voted for President Reagan than were people who watched the other two network broadcasts.

Can we conclude that Peter Jennings was influential in the election outcome? Not really. When we find such a correlation, it is not possible to make reliable judgments about the direction of cause and effect. It is equally possible that people who favored Reagan chose to watch Peter Jennings because they perceived him to be more favorable to the candidate they preferred. Or perhaps something else about ABC programming in general had more appeal for Reagan voters. Thus, although the relationship reported by these investigators is an interesting one, suggesting some qualifications to claims of unbiased news coverage, the findings also demonstrate how complicated the relationships between attitudes and behavior can be.

directly. For a different form of influence, consider the study described in Box 6–1.

In summary, individual attitudes can be formed in many ways. Some attitudes may be developed through the operation of basic learning and reinforcement principles; others may be formed as a person acquires information about new topics. Once formed, attitudes are then in a position to have their own effects, on other attitudes and on behavior as well.

The Structure of Attitudes

Attitudes are pervasive, encompassing a broad spectrum of topics and issues. Although it would be fairly easy to study attitudes if each attitude were self-contained, the situation is in fact complex. Sets of attitudes tend to be interrelated, and any attempt to change an attitude, as we will discuss in the next chapter, must recognize these interrelationships. Also, like the schemas that were discussed in Chapters Three and Four, attitudes affect the processing of related information. Here we shall consider some of these structural issues.

Complexity and Values

One way to think about the structure of attitudes is in terms of their complexity and flexibility. Two people can have the same general attitude on a particular issue, for example, yet differ greatly in the way they express that attitude. One person may be rigid in defense of the attitude and never question it; the other person may have developed the same general attitude after frequent questioning and consideration of alternative views. The differences to be found among members of political elites in regard to complexity of thought has been a major question for the psychologist Philip Tetlock. In Chapter Two, when we discussed archival research, we looked at Tetlock's study of the decisions of Supreme Court justices. Tetlock has investigated other decision makers as well, including members of the British House of Commons (Tetlock, 1984). Once again his interest was in what he calls integrative complexity—the degree to which people have multidimensional views of an issue and integrate a variety of information in arriving at their position. Consider the following statements, representing the two extremes of this dimension, made by two parliamentarians who were interviewed about their views on the economy.

Person A: The key problem is that we have been living way beyond our means for far too long. We have to tighten our belts. Nobody likes to face this unpleasant truth, but that's the way it is.

Person B: We always have to deal with competing priorities in making up the budget. Most basically, we face the tension between the need to fund social welfare programs to which we are committed and the need to stimulate private sector expansion. But there is no simple rule to resolve that tension.   [Tetlock, 1984, p. 369]

Person A represents a simplified position in this case, while person B reveals that he has considered more than one dimension of the problem. (It is, of course, a matter of debate as to which style of thought is better or more effective.)

The politicians investigated in the course of this study were classified in four groups on the basis of their political stance: extreme socialists, moderate socialists, moderate conservatives, and extreme conservatives. As Figure 6-4 shows, the level of attitudinal complexity varied with the political stance of the parliamentarians. Those who took extreme positions, to either the right or the left, were more

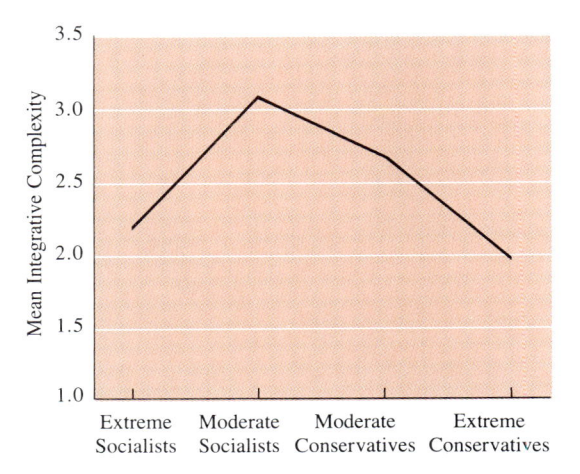

Figure 6-4 Attitudinal complexity and political beliefs of British parliamentarians

unidimensional in their attitudes than the more moderate politicians.

Why should moderates differ in complexity from those who take more extreme attitudinal positions? Tetlock suggests that one needs to look at the values that underlie attitudes. In the case of political attitudes, at least two values are paramount in a democracy—equality and freedom. Tetlock suggests that people who take extreme positions clearly favor one of these values over the other. Freedom is more important than equality to the conservative; equality is more important than freedom to the socialist. Given such clear priorities, attitudes in regard to a particular position should be quite clear. Moderates of both persuasions, in contrast, attach more nearly equal importance to both values (although the moderate socialists in Tetlock's study approached this mean position more closely than the moderate conservatives). Consequently, many issues arouse in such people a conflict between two fundamental values, thus complicating the process of arriving at a final position. *Value pluralism* is the term that Tetlock gives to this model. The more equal weight people give to potentially conflicting values, the more complex their attitudinal positions tend to be.

Value pluralism is not an issue for political elites alone. As Tetlock (1986) has shown, the complexity of many attitudes can be understood in terms of value conflict. College students who value highly both a world of beauty and personal prosperity, for example, are more likely to have complex attitudes toward the issue of opening public lands to mining and drilling operations. Such conflicts may be a major factor in the moderation of the attitudes of the people who experience them (Chaiken & Stangor, 1987).

How Attitudes Interrelate

Attitudes toward seemingly different topics are not always independent of one another. Basic values that underlie a set of attitudes provide a kind of glue that holds those attitudes together. Thus the person who values equality highly may see women's rights, homosexual rights, and rights for aliens as interrelated issues. Attitudes may also be held together by their connection to a general world view. David Buss and Kenneth Craik (1983) have identified two contemporary world views that tie together beliefs on such diverse issues as economic growth, societal goals, and world responsibility. Items that are characteristic of each of these views are shown in Table 6–1. World view *A* endorses high growth and high technology. Proponents of this view tend to take a pro-business stance and favor rational, quantified decision-making processes. World view *B*, in contrast, suggests that material and technological growth should level off. Proponents of this view are concerned with redistribution of wealth from richer to

Photo 6–2 Leaders of the Soviet Union and the United States often disagree.

poorer nations, with the social and environmental impacts of growth, and with decentralization of control and decision making.

People who endorse these two different world views differ in a number of other ways. Proponents of world view *B*, for example, are more likely to anticipate catastrophic outcomes from a variety of modern technologies (such as X rays and pesticides). The urban setting appeals to people who hold world view *A*; the *B*'s prefer open spaces and natural environments. These general patterns are important, Buss and Craik suggest, because they can guide the formation of new attitudes. People do not necessarily form individual attitudes in regard to each new form of technology that arises. Confronted by a particular technology, however, the individual may rely on his or her general world view to come to terms with it.

Attitudes relate not only to other attitudes but to

Table 6-1 Contemporary world views: Sample items from two orientations

WORLD VIEW *A*
1. A high-growth, high-technology society provides the best hope for raising the poor to a high state of material and social well-being.
2. Some of the decentralization talk heard nowadays is romantic nonsense; we can never go back to the family farm.
3. On the whole, centralization promotes efficiency and effective management.

WORLD VIEW *B*
1. The social and environmental costs of continued technological growth and rising per capita energy consumption are intolerably high.
2. Decision making in our society should be made as participative as possible and guided more by humane criteria.
3. The rich nations of the world consume far more than their fair share of the earth's limited resources and contribute far more than their share of environmental damage.

general moods and feelings as well. Beliefs about the use of nuclear power and the possibility of nuclear war, for example, not only relate to each other but form a general cluster that has been termed nuclear anxiety (Newcomb, 1986). People who are characterized by this cluster of attitudes tend to feel a greater sense of powerlessness and depression and to be less satisfied with their lives generally. Further, such people—particularly men—have a greater tendency to use drugs on a regular basis. Thus ways of coping with life may be related to particular attitudinal positions.

Attitudes and Information

An attitude, once formed, influences the way related information is perceived. Having established an attitudinal position on a particular issue, people often interpret new information in ways that will be consistent with their beliefs. They also are more likely to remember information that is consistent with their particular beliefs (Roberts, 1985). Memory is not always so selective, however, and in some circumstances people may pay especially close attention to information that contradicts their beliefs (Chaiken & Stangor, 1987).

Enjoyment of support for one's attitudes leads to other behaviors as well. For example, people sometimes actively look for information that will support their beliefs. At the same time, they will take steps to avoid encountering information that contradicts those beliefs. Such behavior is termed **selective exposure.**

Political attitudes are often held with a great deal of fervor, and it is not surprising that selective exposure operates here. Consider the case of the U.S. voter who, in the 1972 election, voted either for George McGovern or for the successful candidate, Richard Nixon. Six months later the U.S. Senate opened its hearings on the Watergate break-in, investigating President Nixon's involvement in or knowledge of the illegal activities of the Republican re-election committee. Would McGovern and Nixon supporters be equally likely to watch the televised hearings? The selective exposure hypothesis predicts not. Paul Sweeney and Kathy Gruber (1984) conducted a series of interviews to test this hypothesis and found support for selective exposure. McGovern supporters reported paying more attention to the hearings and being more interested in politics than they had been previously. Nixon supporters, in contrast, reported a significantly lower level of interest in the Watergate coverage. Supporting a selective exposure interpretation, the findings of this study also revealed that McGovern supporters could recall the names of more people involved in the scandal than could Nixon supporters, as well as the names of members of the investigating committee and of witnesses who testified before the committee. Thus the supporters of both McGovern and Nixon showed evidence of selective exposure: McGovern supporters by seeking out information that damaged the opposition candidate and Nixon supporters by avoiding information that threatened their beliefs. Such activities help to maintain the attitudes people already have.

Attitudes and Behavior

Do attitudes predict behavior? People who study attitudes have traditionally assumed that the answer is yes. Find out a person's attitude and you should be able to predict what that person will do. If you assess a person's attitude toward environmental protection and find that it is positive, for example, then you might expect the person to save bottles and newspapers for recycling. But would your prediction be accurate? Not necessarily.

What Attitude and What Behavior?

Fairly early on in the history of attitude research, investigators learned that attitudes and behaviors were not always directly related. Early evidence that called such linkage into question was provided by Richard LaPiere (1934). In the early 1930s there were strong feelings against Orientals in the United States, particularly along the West Coast. LaPiere, a highly mobile sociologist, took a Chinese couple on a three-month automobile trip, twice across the United States and up and down the West Coast. The trio stopped at 250 hotels and restaurants during their trip, and only once were they refused service. Later LaPiere wrote to each of these establishments, asking whether it would accept Chinese patrons. Only about half of the proprietors bothered to answer, but of those who did, 90% said that they would not serve Chinese! In a similar study, Kutner, Wilkins, and Yarrow (1952) arranged for a Black woman to join two White women seated in a restaurant, repeating this procedure in 11 restaurants. In no case was the Black woman refused service. However, later telephone calls requesting reservations for an interracial party produced six refusals and only five grudging acceptances of the reservation.

These studies suggest some discrepancy between behavior and attitude, but some problems can be seen in both of them. In neither case, for example, was attitude actually assessed. Instead, an indication of intended behavior was compared with an actual behavior. Furthermore, there is no way of knowing whether the person who refused the reservation by letter or by phone was the same person who had admitted the Chinese or Black persons when they visited the establishment. If they were not the same people, then it makes no sense to talk about inconsistency. An additional question raised by these studies concerns the existence of other attitudes that might be relevant to the behavior. The hotel and restaurant personnel might also have had attitudes in regard to embarrassing people or filling empty hotel rooms and restaurant tables, or other beliefs that took precedence at the time (Dawes & Smith, 1985).

In the face of failures (some more sophisticated than the LaPiere study) to find expected relations between measured attitudes and observed behavior, many social psychologists began to believe that the concept of attitude was not useful in their attempts to understand human behavior. Other investigators, however, rather than throwing the baby and the bath water out together, have pointed to a number of reasons that the expected relationship may not always be strong and, at the same time, have charted new directions for the investigator of attitudes. Let us consider some of these reasons for the weakness of the relationship found.

First, consider the *level of specificity* at which attitudes and behaviors are defined. Investigators have often used a very general measure of attitudes (for example, attitudes toward psychology) and then looked at a very specific measure of behavior (such as willingness to enroll in a social psychology course taught at Classic University by Professor Knowlittle). It is not surprising that such a general measure of attitude has little power to predict such a specific behavior. Experiments in which the measure of attitude is more specific have had much more success in predicting specific behavior. For example, Weigel, Vernon, and Tognacci (1974) measured people's attitudes toward general issues, such as the environment, and toward more specific objects, such as the Sierra Club. Later they gave subjects the opportunity to volunteer for activities of the Sierra Club. Although no relation between general environmental attitudes and Sierra Club activities was found (correlations were .06), there was a strong relation between the more specific attitudinal measures and the actual behavior.

A related issue in regard to the attitude/behavior relation is the question of single acts versus multiple acts. Investigators have generally selected a single behavior to test their predictions. Yet if we are interested in a general issue, such as attitudes toward the environment, then it probably makes more sense to look at a series of possible behaviors. In other words, although a person's general attitude toward the environment may not be an accurate predictor of his or her response to any single activity such as joining the Sierra Club or recycling bottles, that attitude may be a much more accurate predictor when a whole series of behaviors related to the environment is taken into account. Many factors can influence a decision to engage in any single act; over a wide range of behaviors, however, the general attitude is likely to exert a more powerful influence.

One of the reasons for seeking a broader range of indexes is that behavior is complex and multidetermined. Our attitude toward an object will affect some of our behavior, but other factors can influence our behavior as well. Suppose an elderly White man tells his friend, "The less contact I have with Blacks, the better," and then boards a bus. Noting that all the seats but one are occupied, the man takes the available one—next to a Black. We cannot conclude that his verbal statement is false just because his choice of seats has repudiated it. Even the apparently simple action of taking a seat may be multidetermined.

Although the old man might rather not sit next to a Black, perhaps his feet hurt so much that sitting anywhere is preferable to standing. Observation of future behavior, however, might prove more enlightening. Perhaps the man would refuse to take that bus again or would change his schedule to avoid traveling when the bus was crowded. Other situations involving the man's interactions with Blacks might show a consistency between expressed attitude and actual behavior. In short, one-shot measures of behavior don't give us much information about the strength of the attitude/behavior relation.

Situational factors also influence behavior. When situational pressures are strong, people of widely differing attitudes may act in a similar way. If a Vietnamese child were about to be hit by a car, for example, most people, no matter what their attitude toward Vietnamese, would probably try to save the child. Yet in other situations that did not involve a threat to life, varying attitudes toward Vietnamese might influence one's reaction to a Vietnamese child. In general, we can say that the stronger the situational pressures toward some behavior, the less likely individual differences in attitudes are to affect the behavior. (We shall have reason to return to this general point in Chapter Thirteen.)

A related issue in regard to the attitude/behavior relation is that a given behavior may be related to more than one attitude. In the case of the Vietnamese child about to be struck by a car, a person might have one set of attitudes toward Vietnamese and another set of attitudes toward children. Which attitude would best predict behavior? Thus the relation between behavior and a single attitude may appear inconsistent because other attitudes have greater influence.

A Theory of Reasoned Action

Our ability to predict when and how attitudes influence behavior has been increased tremendously by the work of Martin Fishbein and Izek Ajzen (Fishbein & Ajzen, 1975; Ajzen & Fishbein, 1980). These investigators have developed what they call a theory of "reasoned action." The term *reasoned action* implies that most behaviors are carried out for a reason—that people think about the consequences of their actions and make deliberate decisions to achieve some outcomes and avoid others.

The elements of the Fishbein and Ajzen model are shown in Figure 6–5. This model has two major components, a personal component (Aact) and a social component (SN), which combine to predict a *behavioral intention*, which then predicts the behavior itself. It is important to note that Fishbein and Ajzen have defined their task very precisely: they are concerned with the prediction of very specific behaviors on the basis of attitudes. They thus assess each of the model's components in terms of the specific behavior with which they are concerned. Nearly any behavior and its correspondent behavioral intention could be studied within this framework, from a decision to use birth control to the choice of a particular toothpaste.

The personal component of the model, Aact, is a measure of a person's attitude toward engaging in a specific behavior. This attitude is the product of two

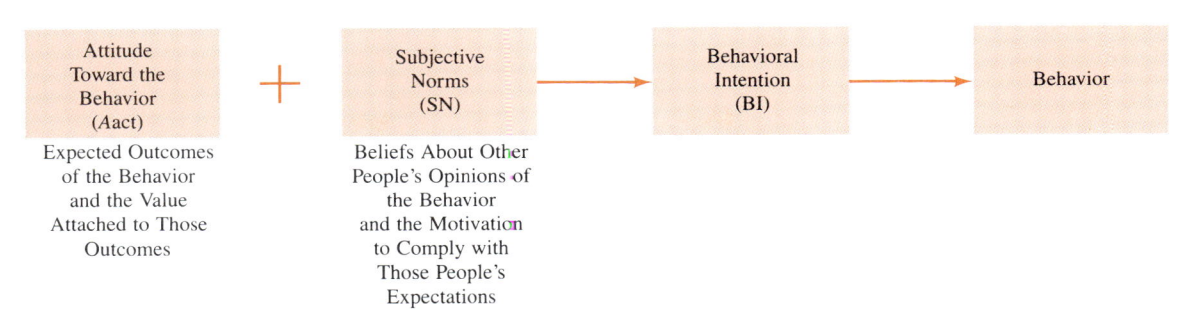

```
┌─────────────┐     ┌─────────────┐     ┌─────────────┐
│  Attitude   │     │  Subjective │     │  Behavioral │
│ Toward the  │  +  │    Norms    │ →   │   Intention │ →   Behavior
│  Behavior   │     │    (SN)     │     │    (BI)     │
│   (Aact)    │     │             │     │             │
└─────────────┘     └─────────────┘     └─────────────┘
Expected Outcomes   Beliefs About Other
 of the Behavior    People's Opinions of
 and the Value        the Behavior
 Attached to Those   and the Motivation
   Outcomes           to Comply with
                      Those People's
                      Expectations
```

Figure 6–5 A theory of reasoned action

factors: (1) the individual's beliefs about the consequences of that specific behavior and (2) his or her evaluation of those possible outcomes. Each of these factors varies among individuals, as do behaviors. Consider the decision of a person to spend an additional 10 hours a week studying. Two people may agree on the likely outcomes of this behavior—better grades and less time to spend with friends, for example—but differ in their evaluation of those outcomes. Julie may value a higher grade point average much more highly than time spent with friends. Consequently, her attitude toward the additional study will be more positive than that of Hal, who views friendships as very important and grades as only moderately so.

The second component of the model, subjective norms (SN), introduces a social element: the person's beliefs about what other people think he or she should do, and the strength of the person's motivation to comply with those expectations. Julie and Hal, for example, may consider the expectations of their parents, their friends, and perhaps their favorite professor when they decide whether to spend more time studying. Julie may be sure her parents favor study and be motivated to comply with their expectations, while Hal may have the same perception of his own parents but not care about complying with their wishes. Similarly, the expectations of friends and peers influence some people more than others.

These two factors, Aact and SN, combine to determine a person's intention to perform the behavior in question—Fishbein and Ajzen call it a *behavioral intention*. The relative importance of these two components will vary from issue to issue, as considerable research has shown. Individuals also vary in the weight they attach to the two factors, as Lynn Miller and Joseph Grush (1986) have demonstrated. They reasoned that the personal attitude should be most influential for people who tend to be very aware of their own attitudes and who also are relatively unconcerned about the behaviors and opinions of others. Such people can be identified by high scores on a measure of private self-consciousness and low scores on a measure of self-monitoring (as discussed in Chapter Three). Indeed, Miller and Grush found that the attitude component was more strongly related to the behavior of this group of individuals, whereas they found greater correspondence between subjective norms and behavior among other people they studied.

The theory of reasoned action assumes that behavioral intentions have a direct bearing on behavior, and that in most cases one would need to look no further for the cause. Other factors, however, do affect behavior. Past behavior, for example, is often the best single predictor of future behavior, independent of expressed attitudes and normative concerns (Chaiken & Stangor, 1987). The move from a behavioral intention to an actual behavior can also be affected by perceptions of control over the action and the obstacles that may intervene. A person may, for example, have a positive attitude toward donating money to charity and believe that others also endorse such action. Yet if that person is poor and has no money to spare, then the behavioral intention will not be manifested in action (Ajzen, 1986).

In summary, the theory of reasoned action has proved very useful in efforts to predict behavior in relation to a wide range of issues and objects. It does not predict all behavior, but it does quite well. What the theory does not do, however, is tell us *how* and *why* attitudes do or do not influence behavior. For an answer to those questions, we need to think about the processes involved.

How Do Attitudes Influence Behavior?

Confident that attitudes do indeed predict behavior, investigators have begun to consider the hows and the whys of the attitude-behavior relationship. In other terms, investigators are looking at the process by which an attitude in the mind is translated into a behavior that can be objectively observed.

Not all attitudes are expressed in behavior on all occasions. You may have a positive attitude toward the use of seat belts, for example, yet fasten the belt in your car only some of the time. What determines whether your attitude toward seat belts affects your actual behavior? One of the major factors, as the research of Russell Fazio (1986) has shown, is whether a particular attitude is active in working memory. As we saw earlier when we discussed the general processes of social cognition, some schemas or knowledge structures in an individual's memory may not be immediately accessible. If an attitude is made accessible, however, then it is much more likely to guide behavior. In that case, the behavior is consistent with the attitude.

What kinds of events are likely to make attitudes accessible? A variety of cues in the environment can make a person think about a particular topic. The sight of your class notebook, for example, could make you think about studying, just as signs announcing a nuclear disarmament rally might activate your attitudes toward nuclear energy. A direct request that you think about your attitudes toward some issue will, not surprisingly, make that attitude more accessible. So, too, will performing a behavior that has implications for an attitudinal position. As we saw in Chapter Four, **self-perception theory** suggests that we sometimes infer our attitudes from observations of our own behavior. Thus helping a friend stuff envelopes for a student government campaign will make a person think about his or her attitudes toward the candidate. Furthermore, as Fazio and his colleagues have shown, this inference process not only makes attitudes accessible at the moment but also increases the accessibility of that attitude in the future (Fazio, Herr, & Olney, 1984).

The accessibility of an attitude is determined by its overall strength as well as by immediate events. The stronger the attitude, the more likely it is to become available, virtually automatically, when the attitude object is present (Fazio et al., 1986). Several factors contribute to the strength of an attitude and hence to its general accessibility (measured in laboratory experiments by the speed of reaction time). Attitudes that have been expressed often, for example, are more likely to be accessible than attitudes that are rarely expressed. Attitudes that are formed on the basis of direct experience are also more readily accessed than attitudes that are formed more indirectly.

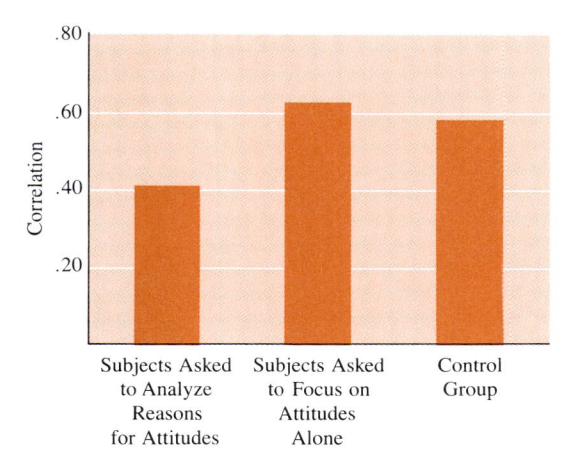

Figure 6-6 Correlations between attitudes toward beverages and consumption of beverages

Variations in the chronic strength of an attitude, and thus in its accessibility, influence the attitude-behavior relationship, just as circumstantial events may do. To see what the practical implications of this relationship are, consider a study of the 1984 U.S. presidential election conducted by Russell Fazio and Carol Williams (1986). In June and July 1984 these investigators interviewed 245 residents of voting age in Bloomington, Indiana, about a variety of issues, including their attitudes toward the two presidential candidates. The critical statements presented for agreement or disagreement were: (1) A good president for the next four years would be Ronald Reagan; and (2) A good president for the next four years would be Walter Mondale. A special recording device enabled the investigators to record the speed with which respondents answered questions about the candidates, and thus provided a measure of attitude accessibility. Respondents answered the questions in a Likert-scale format, like the one shown in Figure 6-1, by pushing a button on the recording apparatus.

Three to four months later the same respondents were asked whether they had watched the presidential debates on television, and if so, which candidate they thought was more impressive. Finally, following the election, the respondents were asked whom they had voted for. If the accessibility of an attitude, as determined by its strength, increases the relationship between attitude and behavior, then we would expect the association between the attitudes, as measured in the summer, and the later perceptions and voting behavior to be stronger for respondents whose attitudes were more accessible. In general, that was the case. Respondents whose attitudes were stronger were more likely to view their candidate's performance in the debates as more persuasive and were more likely to have voted for that candidate.

Although consideration of one's attitude will often increase the correspondence between attitude and behavior, a more careful look at issues of process indicates that this is not always the case. Asking people to analyze the reasons for their attitudes may actually weaken the relationship. In one study conducted in a university dining hall, for example, female students were asked about their attitudes toward a variety of beverages, such as milk, diet colas, and iced tea (Wilson & Dunn, 1986). In one condition, the students were first asked to *analyze the reasons* why they liked or disliked various beverages before indicating their attitude. In a second condition, the students were asked simply to think about how much they liked each beverage. A third set of students, in a control condition, received neither set of instructions. All students then were asked their attitudes toward the beverages, and later their actual choice of beverage during dinner was assessed. As Figure 6-6 indicates, consistency of attitude and behavior differed among the three groups. The attitudes expressed were less closely related to actual behavior among students who first analyzed the reasons for their attitudes than among students in the other two groups.

Why should a request that one analyze one's reasons for an attitude have this effect? An important distinction, it appears, is between the cognitive and affective elements of an attitude (recall the discussion on p. 161). Wilson and Dunn suggest that bringing cognitions to mind may increase the discrepancy between the cognitive and affective elements, thus making the attitude measurement less stable. Furthermore, if an attitude happens to be based primarily on affect, then bringing cognitions to the forefront may simply muddy the waters. In other words, it may be important for the attitudinal component to match the kind of behavior that is called for. If a heavily cognitive behavior is of interest, then instructions that require a person to focus on relevant cognitions will increase attitude-behavior consistency. If, in contrast, a more affective response is of interest, then an emphasis on the affective basis of the attitude will produce greater correspondence (Millar & Tesser, 1986).

Given some of these complexities, it is not surprising that early investigators sometimes despaired of finding a relationship between attitudes and behavior. Yet our understanding of just how and why attitudes influence behavior has improved considerably, thanks in large part to advances in our understanding of cognitive processes. Attitudes will continue to be a central issue for social psychologists because their consequences for social behavior are so extensive. And, as the next chapter will discuss, the attempts made by various people, institutions, and media to change our attitudes makes our understanding of the attitude formation process all the more important.

Summary

The many definitions of *attitude* that have been offered through the years have referred to both physical and mental states. As a working definition, we can consider attitudes to be responses that locate objects of thought on some particular dimension of judgment. The attitudes of a large group of people are referred to collectively as *public opinion*.

Most attitudes have three components: a cognitive or belief aspect, an affective or feeling aspect, and a behavioral or conative component. Different questions and measures may emphasize different aspects of an attitude. Two major measurement techniques are the Likert method and the semantic differential technique. Among the numerous other measures that have been developed, some are rather indirect indexes of attitudes.

Attitudes are formed in a variety of ways. Direct experience with the attitude object itself is a common means of developing an attitude, and learning theory principles can help to explain the acquisition process. Attitudes are also influenced by the opinions and behaviors of parents and peers and by the communications media. The media's influence can be explained by social learning theory.

Attitude structure refers to the makeup of attitudes. Attitudes vary, for example, in their complexity. *Value pluralism* suggests that attitudinal complexity is a result of the amount of conflict between competing values that are relevant to a particular issue. Attitudes are related not only to basic values but to other attitudes as well. They also affect the ways in which other information is selected and retained in memory, so that it often supports existent attitudes.

A major issue is the relationship between assessed attitudes and observed behaviors. Some early investigators found little relationship between the two, but more recent work has substantially advanced our understanding of when and how such relationships will be found. The *theory of reasoned action* bases predictions of behavioral intentions, and in turn behavior, on two factors: one's attitude toward the behavior and subjective norms in regard to that behavior.

An understanding of the relationships between attitude and behavior entails an understanding of the processes involved. Advances in social cognition have helped to develop such understanding. The accessibility of an attitude is a major determinant of its ability to predict behavior, and conditions that make attitudes accessible are being specified.

Glossary Terms

Likert scale
selective exposure
self-perception theory
semantic differential technique
social learning theory

*Some praise at morning what they blame at night,
But always think the last opinion right.*
Alexander Pope

We are incredibly heedless in the formation of our beliefs, but find ourselves filled with an illicit passion for them when anyone proposes to rob us of their companionship.
James Harvey Robinson

Jeff Albertson / Stock, Boston.

CHAPTER SEVEN

Attitude Change

I. The Process of Attitude Change
   The Sequence of Attitude Change
   Elements of Persuasion
   Thinking about Attitude Change
II. Theories of Attitude Change
   Social Judgment Theory
   Balance Theory
   Cognitive Dissonance Theory
   Functional Theories
III. When Attitudes Don't Change
   Anticipatory Attitude Change
   Resistance to Persuasion
IV. Summary

Some of our attitudes are challenged virtually every day. Consider a few moments in the life of a young woman named Joan Siegal. It is a dreary Monday morning. Joan drags herself out of bed and flips on the television. She hopes the early-morning program will provide some provocative piece of news that she can share with people at the office. Instead, a commercial praises a new hair rinse that promises to transform her into the essence of charm, popularity, and sexuality. That's the last thing she needs, Joan thinks—to heighten her sexuality. The phone rings—it's Ernie, still trying to persuade her to go away with him for the weekend. But Joan is resistant; she's never *done* that before. She finally terminates the conversation by telling Ernie that she'll see him at lunch and discuss it further then. She sighs for a moment, then quickly prepares her breakfast, swallows her sugar-coated corn flakes, and scans the front page of the newspaper. The headlines are about efforts to persuade Congress to pass a new nuclear arms agreement. Joan wonders how persuaded her own congressional representative has been. As she leaves for work, the mail arrives, but it contains nothing but some throwaway ads.

If Joan had nothing else to do all day, she might be able to keep track of the number of efforts made to change her attitudes or behavior. On this particular morning, she has already been inundated by advertisements emanating from several media—even the cereal box! It may seem to her that every story in the newspaper is concerned with changing attitudes or behavior—whether it's pressures on a president or prime minister, a local petition campaign to build a new park, or a terrorist's threats to destroy a hijacked plane unless certain demands are met. And then there's always Ernie and his constant persuasion campaign.

Persuasion of course operates in both directions. Not only do other people attempt to persuade us, but we also try to persuade others to change their beliefs and behaviors. To understand more about the occurrence of attempts to persuade, Brendan Rule and her colleagues asked students at the University of Alberta two questions: "Who tries to persuade you in the course of your everyday life?" and "Who do you try to persuade in the course of your everyday life?" (Rule, Bisanz, & Kohn, 1985). Their answers are shown in Table 7–1. Interestingly, people on the average reported more people trying to persuade them (mean = 5.8) than people whom they tried to persuade (mean = 4.6). Perhaps, as this difference suggests, we may be seen as attempting to persuade without necessarily attempting to do so.

Because attempts at persuasion are so common, social psychologists have taken a great deal of interest in the phenomenon. Numerous theories have been developed to predict and explain the process of attitude change, and we will discuss several of them in this chapter. The theories differ in the mechanisms that they consider important in the attitude change process. Some theories emphasize processes of perceptual judgment, others emphasize cognitive prin-

Photo 7–1 Persuasion operates in both directions.

ciples of consistency in beliefs, and still others look to motivations and the functions that beliefs serve. In each case, the principles can be applied to persuasion that occurs not only in the psychological laboratory but in such areas as advertising, health care, and politics as well. Before turning to these specific theories, however, we must first consider some general features of the attitude change process.

The Process of Attitude Change

During the late 1940s and 1950s, a highly energetic and productive group of social psychologists gathered at Yale University under the direction of Carl Hovland. Together these investigators conducted a massive amount of research on the process of attitude change. Their theoretical perspective on the process was based on reinforcement principles. They believed, for example, that the laws that govern the acquisition of verbal and motor skills could shed light on attitude formation and change as well (Hovland, Janis, & Kelley, 1953).

The Sequence of Attitude Change

Using the stimulus-response terminology of learning theory, Hovland and his colleagues proposed the sequence that is shown in Figure 7–1. Although many modern investigators of the attitude change process have abandoned the learning theory terminology, many still find it useful to think of attitude change as a series of stages: attention, comprehension, and acceptance.

The first stage, *attention*, recognizes the fact that not all message stimuli that we may encounter are noticed. Driving down a highway lined with billboards, for example, you may notice only a fraction of the persuasive messages that you pass by. Lacking

Table 7–1 The targets of persuasion: Percentage of responses in nine categories

	"Who tries to persuade you?"	"Whom do you try to persuade?"
Immediate family	27%	35%
Extended family	7	5
Close friends	18	24
Circumstantial friends	7	12
Instructors	13	7
Sales people	11	2
Other professionals	10	3
Trait-defined people (e.g., religious people)	5	9
Goal-defined people (e.g., people who are trying to impress me)	2	3

your attention, the attempted persuasion will very likely not be successful. But even when an appeal is noticed, it may not be effective. The second stage posited by Hovland and his colleagues, *comprehension,* recognizes that some messages may be too complex or too ambiguous for their intended audience to understand. A highly complex treatise on the balance-of-payments deficit, for example, may be totally ineffective in persuading the economic novice to vote for or against a particular bill. Finally, in the third step, a person must decide to accept the communication before any real attitude change takes place. From the perspective of the reinforcement theorist, the degree of *acceptance* depends largely on the incentives that are offered. A message may provide arguments or reasons for accepting the advocated point of view, or it may engender expectations of rewards or other pleasant experiences. For example, the billboard on the highway may tell you that a nationally known restaurant is only minutes off the highway, thus promising you something better than you had planned to get at the next truck stop.

Later investigators have retained the idea of a sequence of stages, but have elaborated on just what those stages are. William McGuire (1968a), for example, talks of a five-stage sequence, consisting of (1) attention, (2) comprehension, (3) yielding, (4) retention, and (5) action. In this formulation, the acceptance stage of the early Hovland model has been broken down into two separate stages: first, the act of being persuaded by the message, and second, the retention of that changed belief. Further, in adding an action stage, McGuire has pointed to the importance of considering behavior as well as internalized beliefs. Even more detailed analyses of this sequence are possible, as McGuire has shown in his more recent writings (1985). Drawing on some of the more recent work in cognition, he has proposed a 12-stage model that considers how beliefs are stored in and retrieved from memory during the course of attitude change.

One important assumption made by most of these sequence models is that the stages are dependent on one another. In other words, each preceding stage is necessary before the next one can take place. Comprehension cannot occur unless a person has paid attention to the message; yielding is dependent on prior comprehension; and so forth.

Elements of Persuasion

A major contribution of the Yale communication program was its specification of factors that may influence the acceptance of a persuasive communication. As journalism students are often told, a good news article should identify "who said what to whom under what circumstances." In a similar fashion, the Communication Research Program at Yale identified four elements that are involved in most persuasive

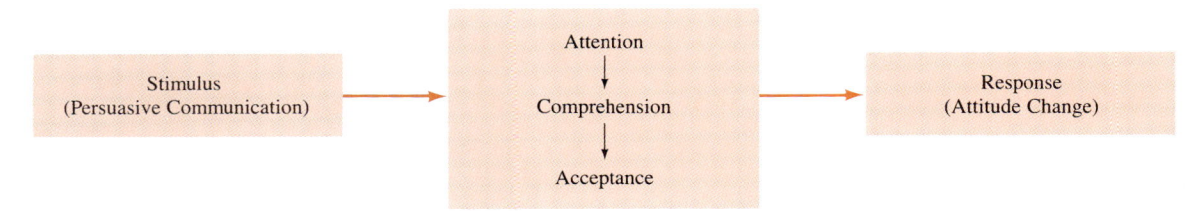

Figure 7–1 A model of attitude change

situations: (1) the source of the persuasive communication, (2) the characteristics of the message, (3) the context in which the message is delivered, and (4) the personality of the recipient of the message. Interest in these four elements has motivated considerable research, both by the original Yale group and by investigators who have followed their lead.

Source. *Who* says something may be just as important as what is said. Hovland and his colleagues (1953) suggested that the credibility of a source would affect the incentives for changing one's attitude. Therefore, the more believable the source, the more likely a change in attitude. In the early research that tested this hypothesis, the manipulations of credibility were quite strong. For example, Hovland and Weiss (1951) contrasted the effectiveness of the American physicist Robert Oppenheimer with that of the Soviet newspaper *Pravda*. Not surprisingly, U.S. subjects were more persuaded by a message from Oppenheimer.

Recent research has considered more specific components of a communicator's credibility, including expertise, trustworthiness, attractiveness, and similarity to the recipient (Petty & Cacioppo, 1981). Each of these factors has been shown to affect attitude change. For example, a message advocating a certain number of hours of sleep was more effective when the source was a Nobel Prize–winning physiologist than when the source was a YMCA director. A communicator may also be more effective when we believe that the person is arguing *against* his or her best interest (Walster, Aronson, & Abrahams, 1966), presumably because the person is seen as more trustworthy. Alice Eagly and her colleagues have discussed this process in terms of attribution theory, noting two kinds of biases that the recipient may perceive (Eagly, Chaiken, & Wood, 1981). When we perceive *knowledge bias,* we believe that the source's knowledge is inaccurate and biased. For example, I might suspect that a millionaire does not know how poor people live. We perceive *reporting bias* when we suspect that the source is simply not willing to report the known facts. Politicians are often accused of this kind of bias. In either case, we are making attributions about the source, and our attributions will determine how effective the source will be. Messages that seem unlikely to reflect the communicator's self-interest are much more credible and therefore much more apt to change attitudes.

Both the physical appearance of communicators and their similarity to us can also affect attitude change. After the 1960 U.S. presidential election, many commentators attributed John Kennedy's victory to the fact that he appeared more attractive on the televised debates than did his opponent, Richard Nixon (McGinniss, 1970). Closer to home, Shelly Chaiken (1979) asked students to persuade other undergraduates to sign a petition. Physically attractive sources were more effective than less attractive sources. In trying to explain this effect, Chaiken found that the more attractive student sources had a number of other characteristics as well, such as better communication skills and higher SAT scores, all of which may have contributed to their greater effectiveness.

The degree to which the attractiveness or likability of a communication source will be influential depends on the medium of communication. If a persuasive message is presented through either a visual or an auditory medium, the likability of a communicator affects the amount of attitude change that occurs. Persuasive messages transmitted in written form, in contrast, seem to be less affected by these characteristics of the source (Chaiken & Eagly, 1983).

People are also more easily persuaded if the source is similar to them in ways that are relevant to the issue (Berscheid, 1966). The importance of this similarity factor was demonstrated by Dembroski, Lasater, and Ramirez (1978). Studying ways to increase toothbrushing behavior, these investigators found that when the target group was Black, a Black communicator was much more effective than a White communicator.

Advertisers make extensive use of these various source characteristics in planning their advertising campaigns. It is quite common for a famous person from the world of sports or entertainment to be shown endorsing a product (see Photo 7–2). Presumably the credibility or trustworthiness or attractiveness of the source makes the message more convincing. Other ads attempt to create a feeling of similarity between the viewer and the source. Someone who acts just like your neighbor or your parents should be more persuasive than someone who appears quite different.

Message. Imagine that you were asked to persuade an audience of the virtues of yearly medical checkups. Assume that you know everything there is to know about the topic. How would you organize your arguments? What medium would you use? What particular appeals would you stress? These questions deal with the messages themselves, which can vary in content, organization, and the medium used.

One major issue in regard to the content of persuasive messages has been the effectiveness of fear-arousing appeals. In our example of yearly medical examinations, would it be wise to describe serious diseases? Or would it be better to stress the positive effects of having a medical exam—improved health, greater self-assurance, and the like?

In an early experiment, Irving Janis and Seymour Feshbach (1953) presented subjects with a message designed to encourage proper dental care. The level of fear aroused by the content of the message ranged

Photo 7–2 People are more easily persuaded if the source is familiar to them.

from low (some small cavities might occur) to high (pictures of advanced gum disease were shown). These investigators found the greatest reported change among those subjects who had been exposed to material designed to arouse low levels of fear. More recent evidence contradicts this conclusion, however; investigators often find greater attitude change following high-fear appeals (Higbee, 1969; Leventhal, 1970).

These contradictions suggest the need to look more carefully at the content of fear-arousing messages. Ronald Rogers (1975) proposed that three factors are important in any fear appeal: (1) the magnitude of unpleasantness of the event described, (2) the probability that the event will really occur if the recommended action is not taken, and (3) the perceived effectiveness of the recommended action. For example, most people probably see the chances of developing severe gum disease as slim, even though they may forget to brush their teeth for days. Other people may disregard antismoking campaigns that warn of lung cancer and heart attacks, assuming that they are not going to die in the near future whether or not they quit smoking.

In general, then, fear appeals will be most persuasive if the described event is relatively unpleasant, if the person believes that the event will really occur, and if the recommended action sounds effective. In addition, there is a fourth factor that is important—*self-efficacy,* or the degree to which a person believes that he or she will be effective in taking the recommended action (Maddux & Rogers, 1983). A person may know that quitting smoking is an effective way to reduce the probability of lung cancer, for example, but believe that he or she will find it very difficult to quit. Fear-arousing communications may be less effective with this person than with one who anticipates a relatively easy time of it.

Another issue in regard to the content of persuasive messages is the question of one-sided communications versus two-sided communications. For example, if you are arguing in favor of reduced television time for children, should you present only arguments that are favorable to your position, or should you acknowledge and attempt to refute an opposing viewpoint? In answering this question, we again see that few answers are "all or none"; instead, specific conditions must be considered in each case. As Karlins and Abelson put it:

> When the audience is generally friendly, or when your position is the only one that will be presented, or when you want immediate, though temporary, opinion change, present one side of the argument. [But when] the audience initially disagrees with you, or when it is probable that the audience will hear the other side from someone else, present both sides of the argument. [1970, p. 22]

If on some occasions it is most effective to present both sides of an argument, which side should be presented first for maximum impact? In general, the answer to this question depends on the time intervals involved—the time between the two messages and the time between the messages and the measurement of attitude (Petty & Cacioppo, 1981). Figure 7–2

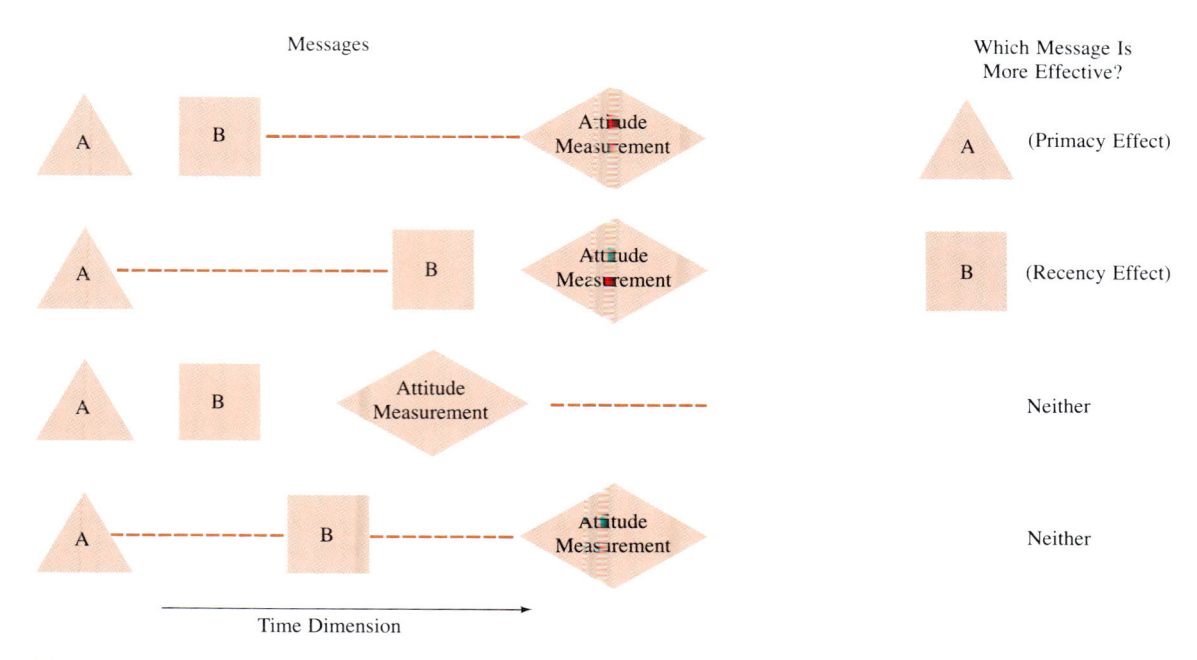

Figure 7–2 Effects of order of presentation of two messages and of timing of attitude measurement

shows how these factors interact. As can be seen, sometimes there is a primacy effect, sometimes there is a recency effect, and sometimes there is no effect at all.

A third question, in addition to the content and organization of the persuasive message, concerns the medium by which the message is delivered. Does the effectiveness of a message vary with the modality of transmission, for example, an audio versus a video presentation? The answer is not a simple "one is better, one is worse." It depends in part on whether one is considering the comprehending or the yielding stage of the attitude change process (Chaiken & Eagly, 1976). A written communication may be more effective in conveying information, particularly information that is complex and difficult to grasp. More direct communications, such as videotaped or live presentations, may be more effective when the focus is on yielding rather than comprehension. Therefore, if you want to present a complex proposal to your supervisor at work, written communication may be preferable in the initial presentation stage. Later, however, when the options have been reduced to yes and no, a face-to-face presentation should be more effective.

Context. Up to this point, we have discussed persuasive communications as though they took place in a vacuum. Some laboratory experiments have structured situations in just that way, but in a real-life persuasion context, many factors often operate at the same time. For instance, a television commercial suggesting that you buy a particular brand of aspirin may have to compete with a family argument, the stereo in the next room, and a knock at the door. What effect do distractions have on the effectiveness of a persuasive message?

You might think that any distraction would reduce the effectiveness of a persuasive message, but that is not necessarily true. Apparently distraction inhibits the thoughts that we have and mentally rehearse while we listen to a communication (Petty, Wells, & Brock, 1976). If a message is one with which we are in sympathy, distraction prevents us from rehearsing supportive arguments; therefore, the communication proves to be less effective than it would be under more neutral circumstances. If a message contradicts our beliefs, however, distraction reduces our ability to generate arguments.

When investigators want to distract subjects in the laboratory, they generally ask them to do two tasks simultaneously. A more natural version of distraction can be seen in the political heckler, who makes comments from the audience while a speaker tries to present an argument. Studies of heckling have found that this form of distraction, in contrast to the laboratory situation, generally reduces the persuasiveness of a message among listeners who are initially neutral, although it may serve to moderate positions that were originally extreme (Silverthorne & Mazmanian, 1975; Sloan, Love, & Ostrom, 1974). Why do these findings differ from those of laboratory-based studies of distraction? One reason may be that a heckler not only serves as a distractor (as a competing laboratory task does) but also provides information and an opposing viewpoint. When uninvolved members of an audience are presented with another side of an argument, the speaker's position may seem much less convincing than it otherwise would. Consistent with the research on two-sided communications, however, a speaker who responds to hecklers in a calm and relevant manner apparently can overcome their effects (Petty & Brock, 1976).

Recipient. Are some people, by the nature of their personalities, more responsive than others to an attempt to change their attitudes, regardless of the source, the content, or the context of a message? Conversely, are some people able to resist efforts—even the best-designed and most appropriate ones—to change their attitudes? The answer is yes, to a slight degree (McGuire, 1968a, 1968b). In the majority of cases, however, the personality of the recipient interacts with other factors to determine whether a change in attitude will take place.

Early attempts to relate personality to persuadability focused on single variables, such as intelligence, self-esteem, the need for social approval, and gender. Generally, these simple approaches met with little success. For example, despite the frequently held belief that women are more easily persuaded than men, systematic reviews find that in the standard attitude change setting, men and women have nearly equal tendencies to change their attitudes (Eagly & Carli, 1981). Although early research suggested that people low in self-esteem would automatically be more prone to change their attitudes (Janis & Field, 1959), this assumption proved to be inaccurate when it was subjected to a wider range of tests (Bauer, 1970).

One alternative to this simple but unsuccessful approach has been proposed by McGuire (1968b). As we noted earlier, the learning model considers three distinct stages in the attitude change process—attention, comprehension, and acceptance, or yielding to the message. If we look at each of these stages separately, we may find that a personality variable has different effects at different stages. For example, people of high intelligence may be able to comprehend a complex message more easily than persons of lesser intellectual endowment; or more intelligent people may be less prone to yield to persuasion because they have greater confidence in their own critical abilities. In testing this hypothesis, Eagly and Warren (1976) found that high intelligence is related to attitude change when a message is complex—highly intelligent people changed their attitudes more than less intelligent people. When a message is weak and unsupported by arguments, only people of lower intelligence are likely to change their attitudes.

Personality differences among people, such as the factor of *self-monitoring* (described in Chapter Three), also affect the type of message that people prefer. Consider the case of advertising. Two general approaches to advertising are often identified within the trade, the soft sell and the hard sell. The major emphasis of the soft-sell approach is on the visual image—the form, color, and appearance of the ad—and there is relatively little concern with the qualities of the product itself. Consider the man in the Hathaway shirt and the Marlboro cigarette man: the depicted individuals get most of the attention. A hard-sell approach, in contrast, emphasizes the characteristics of the product—its quality, its value, its utility. A soft-drink producer, for example, may emphasize the taste of the beverage, and a manufacturer of automobile tires may stress their safety features and durability. Mark Snyder and Kenneth DeBono (1985) suspected that individuals who differ in their tendencies toward self-monitoring may prefer different advertising approaches. According to their analysis, high self-monitoring individuals, who are more sensitive to the demands of situations, should be more sensitive to the soft-sell approach, with its stress on images. In contrast, the low self-monitoring person, who relies more on internal attitudes and dispositions as guides, may be more influenced by those ads that stress the characteristics of the product itself. Their hunch was correct. Not only did high self-monitoring individuals evaluate image-oriented advertisements more favorably, but they were also more willing to try products that were marketed with an appeal based on image and to pay more money for such products. Low self-monitors, as predicted, were more influenced by claims of quality than by projected images.

Thinking about Attitude Change

When people do change their attitudes, just how much thought do they give to the process? Is attitude change a logical process, in which individuals systematically evaluate information and decide which attitudinal position is best? Sometimes attitudes do change in this way. This manner of change has been termed systematic processing or central processing (Eagly & Chaiken, 1984; Chaiken & Stangor, 1987; Petty & Cacioppo, 1986). In the *central processing* mode, people are motivated to engage in systematic thinking about the issues. They pay attention to the arguments presented in the persuasive message and they evaluate the implications of those arguments. A number of factors can increase the likelihood of central processing. If an issue has a great deal of personal relevance to an individual, for example, central processing is more likely. Written messages are more likely than broadcast messages to engage central processing. Moreover, some people are generally disposed to analyze messages in this way and

Box 7–1
Items from a scale to measure the need for cognition

An individual with a high need for cognition would be more likely to agree with each of the statements below than would a person low in need of cognition.

1. I really enjoy a task that involves coming up with new solutions to problems.
2. I usually end up deliberating about issues even when they do not affect me personally.
3. I am an intellectual.
4. I prefer my life to be filled with puzzles that I must solve.

An individual with a low need for cognition would be more likely to endorse the following statements:

1. Ignorance is bliss.
2. Simply knowing the answer rather than understanding the reasons for the answer to a problem is fine with me.
3. I prefer to think about small, daily projects rather than long-term ones.
4. Thinking is not my idea of fun.

---

tend to treat most persuasive communications as an intellectual challenge. Such people, considered high in need for cognition, can be identified by their answers on a scale developed by John Cacioppo and Richard Petty (1982; Cacioppo, Petty, & Kao, 1984). Some of the items from this scale are shown in Box 7–1.

Not all persuasive messages are processed in this systematic way, however. Sometimes, as Shelly Chaiken has suggested, people use **heuristics** to judge a persuasive message (Chaiken, 1980; Chaiken & Stangor, 1987; Eagly & Chaiken, 1984). As we saw in Chapter Four, heuristics are mental shortcuts or simplified decision rules that people use. In the case of persuasion, a person may rely on a rule that says "the statements of experts can be trusted" or "statistics don't lie." In such cases, the person is associating certain message cues (such as the presence of statistics in an argument) with the judged validity of that message. With such decision rules in hand, the individual may not bother to think carefully about the issues, but rather may come to a conclusion that fits the rule. Sometimes heuristics are applied without conscious recognition that they are being used. On other occasions, a person knows that he or she is, for example, taking the word of an expert on faith, but in lieu of more detailed understanding of the issue, that choice appears most reasonable. A newcomer to the stock market, for instance, may find it necessary to rely on the broker's advice because the amount of potentially relevant information seems overwhelming.

Heuristic processing is one kind of attitude change that involves no systematic analysis of the message and the relevant issues. More generally, the term *peripheral processing* has been used to describe attitude change in which little thought is given to the message itself. Instead, tendencies to change are affected more by external characteristics, such as the attractiveness of a source or the rewards associated with a particular attitudinal position, than by the message. Even the simple frequency with which an object is encountered may cause attitude change (see Box 7–2). Models of attitude change that stress simple conditioning of attitudes, as described in Chapter Six, can also be considered to emphasize peripheral processing. For the practitioner of attitude change, one of the challenges is knowing how and when central versus peripheral mechanisms of persuasion will be engaged.

Theories of Attitude Change

Many theories have been developed to explain just how and when attitude change occurs. Some of these theories emphasize central processing, focusing on

Box 7-2
Effects of mere exposure on voting behavior

Because of the increased use of television in recent political campaigns, many investigators have begun to focus on the effects that exposure alone can have on voting behavior. Laboratory research by Robert Zajonc (1968) has shown that mere exposure to a stimulus can increase our positive feelings about that stimulus. In other words, the more we see something, the more we are apt to like it. Apparently this simple principle applies to political elections. Grush, McKeough, and Ahlering (1978) predicted 83% of the winners in the 1972 U.S. congressional primaries by calculating the amount of media coverage devoted to each candidate. In light of this finding, it isn't surprising that Grush and his colleagues have found that wealthy candidates are very likely to win elections (Grush & Scherching, 1978). With enough money, a candidate can buy extensive television coverage. The frequency of exposure in the media apparently provides a strong force for attitude change—specifically, a vote for the candidate on election day.

Yet there may be some limits to this effect. In the 1982 U.S. elections, for example, more candidates spent more money than ever before. But many of the highest-spending candidates did not win, a finding that suggests there may be a limit to the effectiveness of mere exposure—at some point, any candidate is seen often enough.

---

the way individuals analyze incoming information and judge it against their own beliefs. Other theories pay more attention to the peripheral processes, stressing learned habits or perceptual judgments. Although their emphases differ, all of these theories identify some important factors in the broad process of attitude change.

Social Judgment Theory

Social judgment theory emphasizes the individual's perception and judgment of a persuasive communication, and it views such judgments as mediators of attitude change. The theory assumes that people know what their attitudes are, where they stand along a continuum of positions, what other attitudes they are willing to accept, and which attitudes they would reject. These cognitive judgments are assumed to precede any actual changes that occur. At the same time, social judgment theory assumes that emotional involvement in an issue can affect attitudes and attitude change. Thus cognitive and affective components are intertwined in this theory, and each may affect the other.

The major developer of the social judgment approach to attitude change has been Muzafer Sherif (Sherif & Hovland, 1961; Sherif, Sherif, & Nebergall, 1965). In developing his theory, Sherif borrowed some concepts from psychophysics. One such concept is that of an **anchor**, defined as a reference point used in making judgments. Two other principles that he used in his social judgment theory are **assimilation effects** and **contrast effects**. *Assimilation effects* refer to shifts in judgments *toward* an anchor point; *contrast effects* refer to shifts in judgments *away from* an anchor point. Applying these principles to the attitude change process, Sherif suggested that persuasive communications that are similar to our own view (an internal anchor) will be judged as more similar than they really are. Communications at some distance from our own position will be contrasted with our own view, or judged to be farther away from it than they actually are. To explain how these judgments of assimilation and contrast are related to actual attitude change, Sherif introduced three new concepts: *latitude of acceptance, latitude of rejection,* and *latitude of noncommitment* (Sherif & Hovland, 1961; Sherif et al., 1965). The principle of latitudes reflects Sherif's belief that a person's attitude cannot be represented by a single point on a scale; rather, an attitude consists of a range of acceptable positions. For example, if you were presented with a set of statements on a particular issue, you would be asked to indicate all the statements that you felt were consistent with your attitude on the issue. These statements would constitute your latitude of acceptance (see Figure 7–3). The range of statements that a person finds unacceptable or objectionable is defined as the latitude of rejection, and statements that are neither acceptable nor unacceptable constitute the latitude of noncommitment.

When a person encounters a persuasive communication, his or her first reaction is to make a judgment on where this communication falls on the dimensions in question and specifically whether it falls inside or outside the latitude of acceptance. Once this judgment is made, attitude change may or may not occur. Social judgment theory states that attitude change is most likely to occur when a communication falls inside a person's latitude of acceptance (Atkins, Deaux, & Bieri, 1967). Attitude change has also been shown to occur when the message falls within an individual's latitude of noncommitment, approaching but not within the latitude of rejection (Peterson & Koulack, 1969).

Research done within the framework of social judgment theory has concentrated on two issues: (1) What are the effects of ego involvement in an issue on the latitudes of acceptance and rejection and hence on attitude change? (2) How much is attitude change influenced by the discrepancy between the communication and the recipient's position?

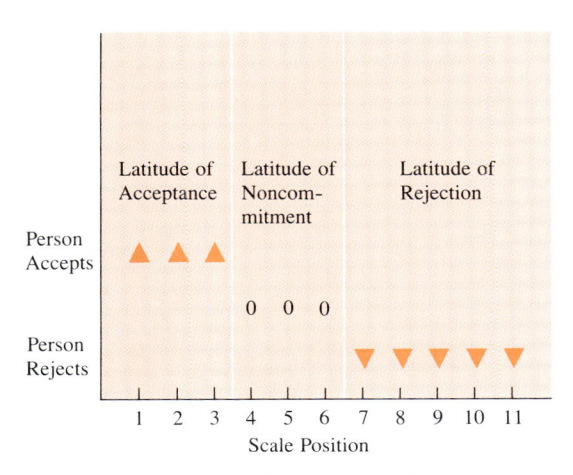

Figure 7–3 Latitudes of acceptance, rejection, and noncommitment. Each number represents a particular statement that the person is asked to accept or reject. For example, if the issue were birth control, a statement at 1 might be "Birth control devices should be available to everyone, and the government and public welfare agencies should encourage the use of such devices." A statement at the other extreme might be "All birth control devices should be illegal, and the government should prevent them from being manufactured." In the example depicted here, our hypothetical person favors positions in support of birth control and rejects positions opposed to it.

Ego involvement and the latitudes. If you are extremely committed to an issue, will you be apt to find a smaller range of positions acceptable than you would if your concern were less intense? Surprisingly, Sherif and his colleagues found no difference in the size of the latitude of acceptance as a function of a person's involvement in an issue. People who were strongly committed to either a Republican or a Democratic position did not differ from uncommitted or neutral people in the size of their acceptable range of positions (although obviously the content of statements within those ranges did differ considerably). Differences did occur in the width of latitudes of noncommitment and rejection. People at either extreme of the scale found considerably more positions unacceptable and were neutral or uncommitted on far fewer items. In other words, the person who is a fanatic about some issue, such as gun control, will not necessarily find any fewer positions acceptable than will a less ego-involved advocate—but that person will reject more positions at the opposite end of the gun-control spectrum and be neutral about very few positions. Not all research is consistent with Sherif's findings, however, and the exact relation between ego involvement and size of latitudes is still uncertain (Eagly & Telaak, 1972; N. Miller, 1965)

The question of the size of the latitude of acceptance is important in Sherif's theory because it serves as the basis for predictions of attitude change. A person with a narrow latitude of acceptance would not be expected to change his or her position easily, whereas the person with a wider range of acceptance should find more persuasive messages falling at or near the boundaries of acceptability.

Effects of discrepancy between communication and recipient's position. On the basis of the principles of the latitudes, social judgment theory predicts a curvilinear relation between discrepancy and attitude change. If you consider the implications of the various latitudes, the reasons for this prediction become clear. Messages that fall very close to the person's own position should be assimilated, and no real change will be necessary. At the other end, messages that are highly discrepant with one's own position will probably fall within the latitude of rejection and will not be acceptable or effect any change. Between these two extremes, when messages fall somewhere in the latitude of noncommitment, their persuasive impact should be the greatest. Research findings generally support this prediction (Hovland, Harvey, & Sherif, 1957; Peterson & Koulack, 1969).

Although there have been some applications of social judgment theory, it has not been used so extensively in the practical arena as some other models. The theory is somewhat limited, dealing only with the variables of message discrepancy and a person's ego involvement in the issue. Furthermore, because the measurement procedures are somewhat cumbersome, other methods and theories are often preferred. The main attraction of social judgment theory is its recognition of an optimum distance between the subject's attitude position and the position of the persuasive communication.

Balance Theory

Balance theory relies on the principle of cognitive consistency to explain attitude change. (Cognitive dissonance theory, which we will discuss in the next section, also emphasizes this principle.) Consistency theories assume that we are aware of our attitudes and behaviors and, more important, that we want these various aspects of ourselves to be consistent with each other. Holding inconsistent attitudes is assumed to be an uncomfortable experience that leads to attitude change.

Although consistency theories assume that we are thoughtful, they do not necessarily posit that we are rational. Indeed, Robert Abelson and Milton Rosenberg (1958) have coined the term *psycho-logic* to refer to the process whereby we may alter our beliefs so that they are psychologically consistent without necessarily following the strict rules of formal logic. For example, if you know that cigarettes can cause cancer and yet continue to smoke, the belief and the behavior are inconsistent. To resolve this uncomfortable state of inconsistency, you may deny that cigarettes have anything to do with disease. Such a choice is not totally rational, yet the denial allows your continued smoking behavior to be consistent with your beliefs.

Fritz Heider (1946, 1958) was the first to develop a theory based on a principle of consistency to explain how people view their relationships with other people and with their environment. For simplicity, Heider limited his analysis to two persons (P and O) and to one other entity (X). The person P is the focus of analysis, and O represents some other person; X can be an idea, a person, a thing, or any attitude object. Heider's goal was to discover how the relationships among P, O, and X are organized in P's cognitive structure. Heider proposed that two possible relationships could exist among these three elements—a *unit relationship*, which refers to the extent to which two elements belong together, as in ownership or membership in similar groups, and a *liking relationship*. We will concentrate on the liking relationship, which includes all forms of positive or negative sentiments, or affect, between two or more elements.

In formulating **balance theory**, Heider proposed that the relations among P, O, and X may be either balanced or unbalanced, depending on the pattern of like and dislike links among elements. Consider the following example. Paul (P), who has spent all summer as a volunteer worker for the Republican presidential candidate, enters the state university as a freshman in the fall. His faculty adviser is Professor O'Hara (O). When they meet to plan a first-semester schedule, Paul observes that Professor O'Hara is wearing a campaign button for the Democratic candidate. Will Paul like Professor O'Hara? Will Paul think much of the professor's recommendations about which courses to take? Probably not—because Paul does not feel comfortable in unbalanced relationships. If X in this example stands for the Democratic candidate, a balanced state exists when Paul likes Professor O'Hara, Paul likes Democrats, and O'Hara likes Democrats. As long as Paul dislikes Democrats and the professor disagrees, the only way a balanced state can exist within Paul's cognitive structure is for Paul to dislike Professor O'Hara. Paul can say, in effect, "Professor O'Hara is no good, which figures because she's a big supporter of the Democratic candidate."

Heider proposed that balanced states exist either when all three relations are positive (as in liking) or when two relations are negative (disliking) and one is positive (see Figure 7–4). The preceding example fits the latter possibility. Of course, if Paul had found that his adviser was a Republican and if he had come to like her, then balance theory would describe the relationship as "P likes O, P likes X, and O likes X." As Figure 7–4 indicates, unbalanced states do occur; people do like other people who differ in their attitudes toward important issues or objects. The reverse situation is also possible: you may discover

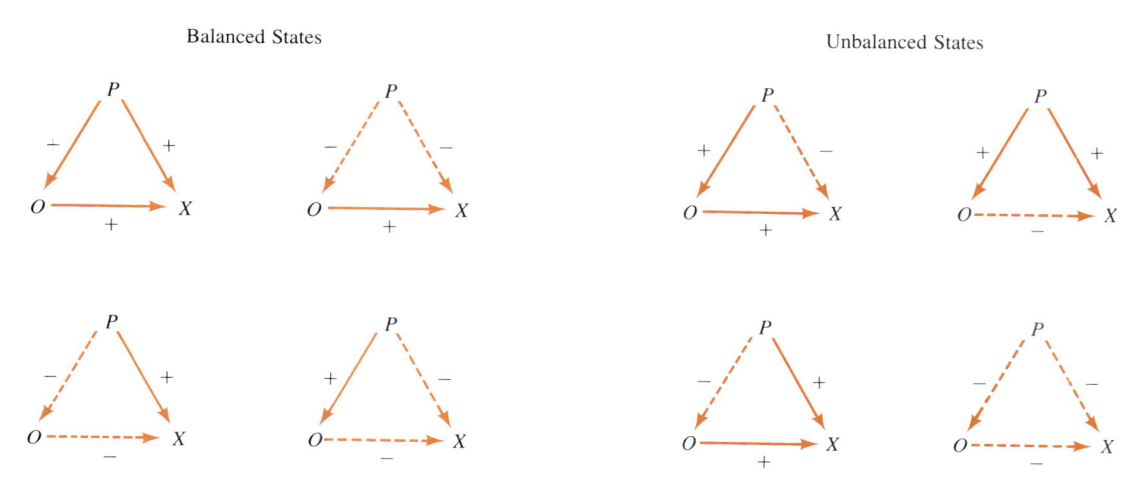

Figure 7-4 Heider's balance theory: Examples of balanced and unbalanced states according to Heider's definition of balance. In each case, *P* is the person whose attitudes are of concern. *P* can either like or dislike *O*, and both *P* and *O* can have either positive or negative attitudes toward *X*. Can you find any pattern in the definition of balanced and unbalanced states?

that someone you hate intensely likes the same rather obscure artworks that you do. What do you do about such a state? Heider proposes that such unbalanced states produce tension and generate forces to achieve or restore balance.

In the realm of political opinion, balance theory can often explain how voters view candidates and their positions. Donald Kinder (1978) studied voters' perceptions of the 1968 U.S. presidential candidates—Nixon, Hubert Humphrey, and George Wallace. At the same time, he asked the voters about their own stands on a number of current issues, such as the problem of urban unrest. In line with balance theory, voters who thought that the solution to urban unrest was the use of more force also tended to see their preferred candidate as having similar views on the issue. Other voters who were opposed to the use of force saw the same candidate as sharing their views. In other words, people were attempting to achieve a balanced relationship among the triad consisting of (1) their attitude toward an issue, (2) their attitude toward a candidate, and (3) the candidate's attitude toward that issue.

Not only do people's attitudes toward a candidate influence their perceptions of the candidate's position, but they bias their expectations in regard to the outcome of the election. When Donald Granberg and Edward Brent (1983) studied U.S. election survey data collected between 1952 and 1980, they found that voters systematically biased their estimates of which candidate would win. By a ratio of about 4 to 1, they thought their candidate would win. In the 1932 election, 93% of the voters who preferred Franklin Roosevelt believed that Roosevelt would win. In contrast, only 27% of Herbert Hoover's supporters thought that Roosevelt would win. Using the framework of balance theory, we can consider *P* to be the individual voter, *O* to be the general electorate, and *X* to be the issue of who should be president. Balance would occur if all views were consistent—if *P* liked a particular candidate, had faith in the electorate, and believed that his or her candidate would be elected by the voters.

Balance theory, as described here, is a fairly simple approach to the understanding of attitude change. More complicated versions of the theory incorporate more elements and more complicated relationships among the elements (Insko, 1981, 1984). The basic principles, however, remain the same, stressing the importance of consistency among various beliefs.

Cognitive Dissonance Theory

Another type of consistency theory, first proposed by Leon Festinger (1957), is **cognitive dissonance theory.** In its original form, the idea of cognitive dissonance is quite simple, as Figure 7–5 indicates. Cognitive dissonance is said to exist when a person has two cognitions that contradict each other. Cognitions are thoughts, attitudes, beliefs, and also behaviors of which the person is aware. For example, the following statements could be considered cognitions: "It's a nice day today," "I am a thoughtful person," "I believe that schools are repressive institutions," and "I forgot my father's birthday." According to Festinger, such cognitions can be either relevant or irrelevant to each other. For example, "It's a nice day today" and "Schools are repressive institutions" would probably be considered irrelevant, in that the one cognition does not imply anything about the other. In contrast, "I am a thoughtful person" is relevant to "I forgot my father's birthday" because the one cognition relates to the other in a psychological sense. Two relevant cognitions may exist either in a state of *consonance* or in a state of *dissonance*. When dissonance occurs, exemplified by the conjunction of "thoughtful person" and "forgetting father's birthday," the two elements do not fit with each other—or, to use a term of Festinger's, the one element implies the obverse of the other. Dissonance, the theory suggests, is an uncomfortable state

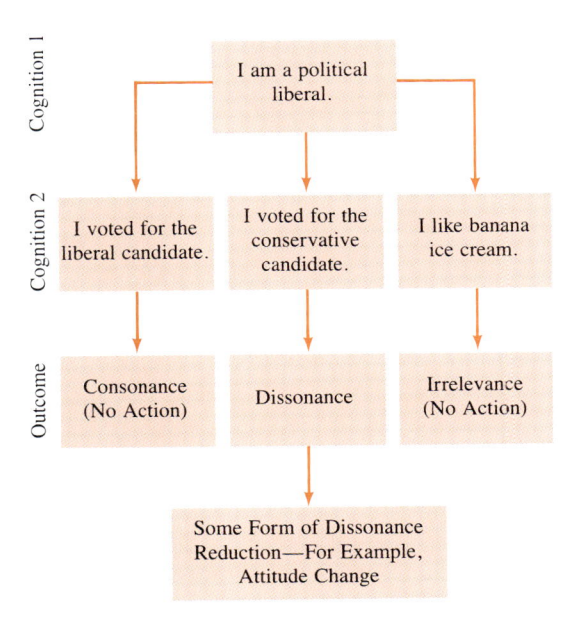

Figure 7–5 Basic elements of cognitive dissonance theory

from which the individual will try to escape by altering some of his or her cognitions or behaviors.

We often think of attitudes as preceding behavior. Thus if you want to change someone's behavior, you will probably try first to change his or her attitude. One of the intriguing features of cognitive dissonance theory is its consideration of the possibility that a change in behavior may lead to a change in attitude. If a person behaves in a way that is contrary to his or her beliefs, cognitive dissonance theory predicts, the person will change those attitudes so that they will be consistent with the behavior already engaged in. One of the classic demonstrations of this effect is the *forced-compliance* experiment. Dissonance theory proposes that when a person is forced to take a public position contrary to his or her private attitude, the conflict will lead to attitude change (usually in the private attitude). The theory also makes the somewhat surprising prediction that the smaller the inducement to advocate a public position that violates a private attitude, the more likely a shift in the privately held attitude. In the first test of this prediction, Leon Festinger and Merrill Carlsmith (1959) paid male students either $1 or $20 to lie to other students. After participating for an hour in a series of dull, meaningless tasks (for example, putting 12 spools in a tray, emptying the tray, and then refilling it, time and time again), the student was paid to tell a prospective subject that the experiment was interesting, educational, and highly worthwhile. Later, on a questionnaire that presumably was not part of the experiment, each subject who had lied for either $1 or $20 indicated his private attitudes toward the experiment. Festinger and Carlsmith found that students who had been paid only $1 rated the experimental task as more enjoyable than did students who were paid $20. Presumably the students who were paid $20 for the lie could easily justify their behavior—money did talk, in this instance. The other students, who received only $1 in payment, had to find some other reason for their behavior. Hence the attitude change: they said that the experiment was enjoyable because they believed it must have been.

This study was a dramatic demonstration of what can happen when behavior and attitudes are inconsistent. It was particularly striking because it appeared to contradict basic principles of reinforcement, which suggest that the greater the reward, the greater the attitude change. But was inconsistency the only factor that caused the apparent attitude change? And is it true that inconsistency alone, as the original cognitive dissonance model suggested, will always cause attitude change? These are the questions that have interested investigators in the 30 years since Festinger introduced dissonance theory. And as these investigators have discovered, a number of conditions are necessary before dissonance is aroused. They are depicted in Figure 7–6.

Joel Cooper and Russell Fazio (1984) have found that the arousal of dissonance depends on two critical conditions. First, the consequences of the behavior must in some way be aversive; the behavior must lead to "an event that blocks one's self-interest or an event that one would rather not have occur" (p. 232). In the case of Festinger and Carlsmith's experiment, for example, lying to a fellow student would be aversive to most people, especially in combination with the knowledge that they were leading that student on to a very boring experience. In contrast to this situation, imagine that you are alone in your room, reading out loud a speech with which you disagree. Would you experience dissonance? Probably not, because the event would be less aversive and, equally important, you could easily change your speech and your mind without any aversive consequences.

A second condition that is necessary for the arousal of dissonance, according to Cooper and Fazio, is the assumption of personal responsibility. To experience dissonance, a person must attribute the event to some personal and internal factor (as we saw in Chapter Three). Such personal attributions are most likely when people believe that they had a choice in making the event happen, and that they were able to foresee the consequences. When these conditions are not met, dissonance is unlikely to be aroused. In experimental studies of cognitive dissonance, investigators are careful to give subjects the appearance of

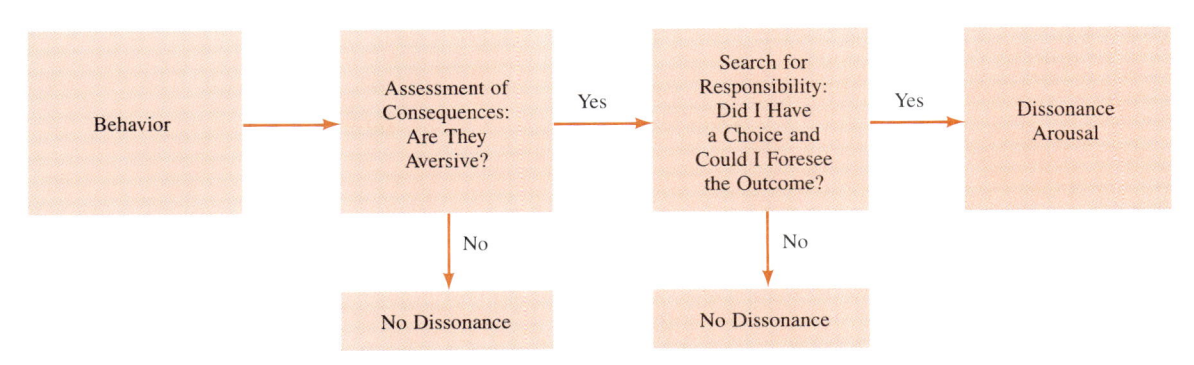

Figure 7–6 Conditions of dissonance arousal

choice in order to create the conditions necessary for the arousal of dissonance. If both of these general conditions are met—a person perceives the consequences of a behavior as aversive and accepts responsibility for the event—then dissonance is likely to be aroused. But just what does dissonance arousal mean?

As we suggested earlier, dissonance is considered to be an unpleasant state. In fact, an actual physiological state of arousal or tension accompanies the dissonant condition (Croyle & Cooper, 1983). Whether this state of arousal leads to behavior designed to reduce dissonance, as by changing one's attitude, depends on how the state of arousal is explained. Under some conditions, a person who experiences a physiological arousal state may attribute it to some external event, thus putting the locus of causation outside the self. In that case, the motivation to change one's attitude may not develop.

Some people have found that alcohol enables them to ignore contradictions between their attitudes and behavior. Claude Steele and his colleagues considered this effect in a series of laboratory experiments (Steele, Southwick, & Critchlow, 1981). They recruited college students who were at least 21 years old and who had experience with alcohol for a study presumably concerned with beer tasting. The experimenters initially created dissonance by asking these students to write a counterattitudinal essay—an essay in favor of increased tuition, which most students in fact opposed. Having created this inconsistency between behavior and belief, the experimenters then gave subjects the opportunity to sample a variety of beers. Although dissonance did not affect the amount of beer that students drank, it did affect their subsequent attitudes. Students who drank beer after writing the counterattitudinal essay were less likely to change their attitudes than subjects who indicated their attitudes immediately after completing the essay, before drinking any beer. In a further demonstration of the specific effect of alcohol, these investigators found that neither water nor coffee had any noticeable effect on attitudes. Thus, alcohol may serve many people as a means to reduce uncomfortable tension and to avoid recognizing the contradictions between their behaviors and their beliefs.

More than most other theories of attitude change, dissonance theory has been concerned with the effects of making a decision on subsequent attitudes and behavior. According to the theory, any time one is forced to choose between two attractive options, postdecisional dissonance is aroused (Festinger, 1957). The more difficult or important the decision, the more likely a person is to find reasons that support the choice that was made and to minimize the attractive qualities of the foregone choice. For example, if you are undecided about which of two persons to invite to the Super Bowl game, dissonance theory predicts that once you have made your choice, you will find many ways of "spreading apart" the alternatives—your chosen date will seem more attractive than he or she did before, and the rejected date will seem less attractive than before. This same strategy has been evidenced in a variety of settings, including election polling areas and race tracks (see Box 7–3).

Behavior following a decision takes other forms as well. **Selective exposure**, a concept introduced in Chapter Six, was a phenomenon predicted by cognitive dissonance theorists. Specifically, they predicted that people would prefer supportive information and would avoid information that contradicted existent cognitions. Such selective information seeking does not always occur (Frey, 1986). If people know they can effectively refute some discrepant information, for example, they may seek it out for the sheer pleasure of refuting it. Similarly, most people are fairly rational about their needs, and if they realize that future decisions will require familiarity with the dissonant information, they will pay attention to it. Thus there appear to be limits to the selective exposure effect, but within those limits, biased information search often occurs.

Cognitive dissonance theory has been applied to many practical problems, and in the process has shed light on the relationship between attitudes and behaviors. Principles of cognitive dissonance have been used, for example, to predict how psychotherapy can affect weight loss. Psychotherapy requires effort, and most people who undertake it look for some explanation to justify the considerable effort they must exert. In an early experiment within the cognitive dissonance tradition, Elliot Aronson and Judson Mills (1959) found that people who had to exert great effort in order to join a group liked that group more than potential members who had to exert less effort. Using this same logic, Danny Axsom and Joel Cooper (1985) proposed that patients in a weight therapy program who were required to exert a great deal of effort on a task—even a task that had no apparent relation to the therapy program—would justify their effort by becoming more committed to the goal of the program, and consequently would lose more weight. The results of this experiment were striking, even when they were assessed 6 and 12 months after the effortful procedures had taken place. Six months later, for example, patients who had completed the more effortful series of tasks over a four-day period had lost an average of 8.5 pounds, while patients whose tasks had been relatively easy lost virtually no weight. In this case, behavior affected behavior, through the mediation of attitudinal processes.

In another practical demonstration of the consequences of cognitive dissonance, consumers of electric power in Australia were given one of several kinds of information about their use of energy (Kantola, Syme, & Campbell, 1984) All of the subjects were heavy users of electricity, and their behavior in this regard was inconsistent with their belief that energy should be conserved. How might people resolve such inconsistency? Faced with a contradiction between an important value and the evidence that they were consuming large amounts of energy, consumers might try to alter their future behavior, essentially in an attempt to prove that their behavior was really in line with values they expressed. To explore this possibility, the Australian investigators aroused dissonance in some consumers by pointing

Box 7–3
Postdecisional dissonance reduction at posttime

"Put your money where your mouth is" was an admonition followed by Robert Knox and James Inkster (1968), who were not content to test cognitive dissonance theory only under controlled laboratory conditions. These researchers went to a race track in Vancouver and interviewed bettors at the $2 window about the chances of their horse's winning. Subjects who were interviewed as they stood in line waiting to place their bets thought their horse had a little better than fair chance to win. Subjects interviewed right after they had placed their bets were significantly more confident, rating their chances as good. These findings suggest that the act of committing oneself by placing a bet creates dissonance and leads to a dissonance-reducing boost in confidence in one's choice. A similar process was observed by Frenkel and Doob (1976) at polling areas during a Toronto election. Voters polled after they had cast their ballot were more likely to believe that their candidate was best and that he or she would win than voters polled before they entered the polling area.

out the contradiction, but did not mention the contradiction to another group. Even though both groups were given feedback on their use of energy and tips on reducing it, only the dissonance arousal group showed a significant decrease in energy consumption. Interestingly, the attitudes of people in this experiment did not change, an indication that not all attitudes are readily changed.

Functional Theories

A fourth type of attitude change theory, functional theory, emphasizes individual differences in human nature. Whereas other theories tend to emphasize the common factors in attitude change, **functional theory** looks at the assumptions and needs on which individual attitudes are based—at the functions the attitudes serve (Katz, 1960; Smith, Bruner, & White, 1956).

The basic proposition of a functional theory of attitude change is simple: people hold attitudes that fit their needs, and in order to change those attitudes, we must determine what their needs are. The functional approach is a phenomenological one; it maintains that a stimulus (for example, a television commercial, a new piece of information, or an interracial contact) can be understood only within the context of the perceiver's needs and personality. Different people may have quite different needs, and consequently a message that some people find persuasive may not be equally effective for others.

A variety of functions served by attitudes have been identified, some of which are listed in Table 7–2. Attitudes that have a knowledge function, for example, "give meaning to what would otherwise be an unorganized chaotic universe" (Katz, 1960, p. 175). The attitude serves much the same function as the cognitive schema described in Chapters Three and Four, organizing information and providing some stability. Some other functions of attitudes are more emotional than cognitive. An attitude may serve to ensure rewards, for example, or to avert punishments. Reinforcement theories talk a lot about this type of attitude, learned on the basis of past experience. Ego defense is a more psychoanalytic function. In this case, it is assumed that an attitude is formed to help an individual cope with some internal anxieties. Derogatory attitudes toward out-groups and minority groups, for example, may convince one of one's own worth, and thus may serve to resolve certain insecurity problems.

Gregory Herek (1986) has suggested that it may be useful to think of two general classes of attitude functions, based on the type of benefit they provide. The first class, which he calls *evaluative*, includes attitudes toward objects that themselves provide some rewards or punishments. The expectation of such rewards and punishments may be based on past expe-

Table 7−2 Some functions of attitudes

Type of Attitude	Function Served by Attitude
Knowledge	Categorizing and organizing of information
Instrumentality	Maximizing of rewards and minimizing of punishments
Ego defense	Help in coping with intrapsychic conflict
Social adjustment	Mediation of interpersonal relationships
Value expression	Expression of important aspects of self-concept

riences with the attitude object: for example, a person may develop a positive attitude toward Asian-Americans if people of that group always provided help with homework during high school. Anticipated rewards and punishments may also engender evaluation-based attitudes. If, for example, a person anticipates getting good job offers from computer companies upon graduation, a generally positive attitude toward that segment of the economy may develop. In sum, the object of an evaluative attitude is an end in itself.

Attitudes in the second general class identified by Herek, *expressive* attitudes, are directed toward objects that are means to an end. By expressing the attitude, the individual gains some desired end, such as increased self-esteem, reduced anxiety, or greater social support. (This class includes the last three types listed in Table 7−2.)

The important feature of the functional approach is that it requires the investigator to determine just what function a particular attitude serves for a particular individual. A number of investigators have tried to make such determinations by classifying individuals into groups on the basis of the functions that their attitudes are presumed to serve. In an early test of functional theory, subjects were assessed on two general personality measures (need for conformity and ego defensiveness) and then presented with one of several messages concerning prejudice (McClintock, 1958). One message was informational, stressing the cultural relativism arguments against prejudice; another was interpretational, focusing on the internal dynamics that can lead to prejudice. McClintock predicted that subjects high in conformity would be more susceptible to the informational appeal, whereas subjects high in ego defensiveness would be more persuaded by the interpretational appeal. Among subjects who read the informational message, more high-conformity subjects than low-conformity subjects changed their attitudes. In contrast, high-ego-defensive persons were less likely to change their attitudes than low-ego-defensive persons. The interpretational message yielded much less consistent results. No relationship was found between conformity and attitude change; as for ego defensiveness, the greatest change was shown by subjects in the middle range of the scale. Although some might argue that those high in ego defensiveness are simply too rigid to make any changes, at least in such an impersonal setting, we must conclude that the findings do not provide wholehearted support for functional theory.

The study of the reactions of high and low self-monitors to hard-sell and soft-sell advertisements, discussed on page 192, is a more recent attempt to understand how the functions of attitudes differ among people (Snyder & DeBono, 1985). In this case, the attitudes of both groups were serving a general expressive function. The attitudes of the high self-monitors, however, served their need for social adjustment and approval, whereas those of the low self-monitors tended to express their individual values.

One difficulty with both of these studies is that

they assume that an individual's attitudes will generally develop to serve only one function. The situation is probably more complicated than that. Different attitudes probably serve different functions for individuals, so that a person may have some evaluative attitudes, some expressive attitudes, and so forth. Herek (1986) suggests that the functions of attitudes vary not only among individuals but among situations and attitude domains as well. Attitudes that are related to one's social class or occupational group, for example, are more likely to be based on value-expressive functions, whereas attitudes related to sexuality may be more closely tied to defensive needs.

The functional theory of attitudes, with its recognition of multiple functions and variations among personalities, situations, and domains, does not offer easy strategies for attitude change. It does, however, directly confront the fact that people hold attitudes for very different reasons. Consequently, any particular campaign designed to change attitudes will probably be effective for only some of the people, and then perhaps only some of the time. And that is, of course, exactly the case.

When Attitudes Don't Change

Discussions of theories of attitude change often convey the impression that all people change their attitudes almost all the time. That is not the case. Shifts in attitude are often quite temporary; sometimes people strongly resist any attempt to change their attitudes. Let us look more carefully at some of the cases in which attitudes do not change.

Anticipatory Attitude Change

Attitudes can change even before a person receives a persuasive message. In the initial demonstration of *anticipatory attitude change,* McGuire and his colleagues observed that people who expected a persuasive message shifted their attitudes in the direction of the forthcoming message before it was even presented (McGuire & Millman, 1965; McGuire & Papageorgis, 1962).

Are such changes in attitude real? If so, why do they occur in the absence of any actual persuasion? Early explanations of this phenomenon stressed self-esteem, suggesting that people change their attitudes in advance of a communication in order to avoid appearing gullible later (Deaux, 1968; McGuire & Millman, 1965). More recently, investigators have stressed two factors in attitude change. First, as Robert Cialdini and his colleagues have described it, there is "elasticity" in a person's attitudes (Cialdini et al., 1973, 1976). In response to various pressures, people moderate their position within a limited range (perhaps comparable to the latitude of acceptance); however, when the outside pressures disappear (for example, when the promise of a persuasive speech is withdrawn), their attitudes snap back to their original positions. Cialdini and his colleagues raise the possibility that most of the attitude change observed in the laboratory reflects this principle of elasticity rather than any real change.

At a more general level, we can think of such anticipatory changes as a form of impression management (Hass, 1975; Hass & Mann, 1976). In other words, when people anticipate a persuasive message, they may try to manage the impression that others are forming and moderate their original position in an attempt to appear broad-minded. Such strategies are no doubt common in real life as well as in the laboratory. Consider the way you would state your opinion about a longer school year if you were discussing that issue with a friend who was in favor of the extension. Concerns with appearing moderate and reasonable may occur, however, only when people have no personal investment in an issue. Indeed, Cialdini and his colleagues (1976) found that when an issue is of great importance to a subject, anticipatory shifts are in the direction of greater polarization rather than greater moderation. Furthermore, the subjects who had initially polarized their attitudes maintained this more extreme position even when the threat of persuasion was removed, a finding that suggests continued vigilance on their part.

Resistance to Persuasion

Although a forewarning of an attempt to persuade may lead to some initial shifts in the direction of the forthcoming communication, some evidence suggests that in the long run, forewarning encourages resistance to the attempt—or, in the words of Richard Petty and John Cacioppo (1977), "forewarned is forearmed."

In an experiment conducted during the months preceding President Truman's announcement that the Soviet Union had produced an atom bomb, Arthur Lumsdaine and Irving Janis (1953) considered whether one-sided or two-sided messages would be more likely to encourage resistance to subsequent counterpropaganda. Their findings indicated that two-sided communication was more effective in inducing resistance to propaganda, and they suggested that the presentation of counterarguments initially serves to "inoculate" subjects against later attempts to persuade them.

McGuire (1964) pursued this explanation in a more elaborately designed set of studies. Before hearing a persuasive message, his subjects were presented with arguments that supported their initial beliefs, arguments that refuted the counterarguments that would be used in the subsequent persuasion, or arguments that refuted counterarguments that would not be used in the actual communication. Subjects who had heard only the arguments that supported their initial position showed the least resistance to subsequent persuasion. In contrast, subjects who had already been exposed to a weakened form of the counterarguments resisted the actual message when it was presented (see Figure 7–7). Using a medical analogy, McGuire suggests that exposure to weakened forms of a message can be effective in producing defenses. In other words, the exposure inoculates a person against the subsequent attack. Presumably this strategy is most effective when a person's initial position is relatively "germfree"— when it hasn't been questioned.

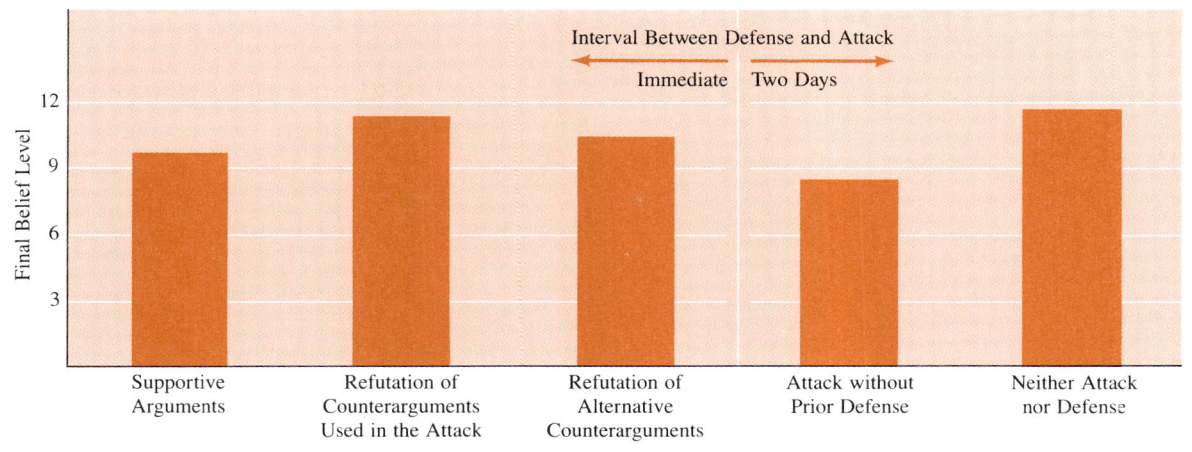

Figure 7-7 Persistence of the resistance to persuasion conferred by three types of prior belief defense. Numbers represent level of belief, with 15 representing complete endorsement of the initial belief and 1 complete acceptance of the persuasive message.

Applying this same rationale to a marketing context, Szybillo and Heslin (1973) studied the effectiveness of various defenses when people were exposed to arguments favoring the installation of inflatable air bags in cars. They, too, found that prior arguments could increase resistance to persuasion and that refutational arguments were more effective than supportive arguments in building up resistance.

Even when counterarguments are not supplied, forewarning can be effective in allowing people to muster their own counterarguments and build up resistance to later attacks. Petty and Cacioppo (1977) have found, for example, that when people are warned of a forthcoming message and are given time to think about the issue, they consider their own positions and alternative positions, and they generate cognitive defenses against the impending assault. Therefore, one of the most effective ways of encouraging resistance to persuasion is to warn a person that an attempt to persuade is about to be made and to identify the specific content of a message (so that counterarguments can be rehearsed). A somewhat similar strategy for increasing resistance to persuasion is to encourage people to think about behaviors that are relevant to the attitude. When people were asked to think about how often they had brushed their teeth in the past two weeks, for example, they were more resistant to a persuasive message that questioned the effectiveness of toothbrushing (Ross et al., 1983). Given these findings, it isn't surprising that commercials are often introduced with little warning or that government leaders often call surprise press conferences to announce new policy initiatives.

Summary

The process of attitude change can be considered as a sequence of steps. In its simplest form, this sequence consists of attention to, comprehension of, and acceptance of a persuasive message. The major elements in persuasion are the source, the message, the context, and the recipient. Many studies have been conducted to show how variations in each of these elements can affect the amount of attitude change that occurs.

Although we often think of attitude change as a rational, logical process in which information is carefully considered, that is not always the case. In what is called central processing, information is systematically evaluated. In other cases, however, the route is peripheral, and characteristics other than the message itself become important. The use of heuristics—reliance on simple decision rules—is one form of peripheral processing.

Many theories have been developed to predict when attitudes will and will not change. Among them are social judgment theory, balance theory, cognitive dissonance theory, and functional theories.

Social judgment theory emphasizes the individual's perception and judgment of a communication as prerequisites to attitude change. Attitudes are described by a range of positions along a scale, called the latitude of acceptance. Other opinion points on the scale may fall either in the latitude of rejection or in the latitude of noncommitment. Attitude change is believed most likely to occur when a persuasive communication falls in or near a person's latitude of acceptance. Research within the social judgment framework has focused on two major variables: (1) the effects of a person's ego involvement in an issue and (2) the amount of discrepancy between a persuasive communication and the person's own position.

The consistency theories of attitude change include Heider's balance theory and Festinger's cognitive dissonance theory. Common to these theories is an assumption that people change their attitudes in order to reduce or eliminate inconsistency between conflicting attitudes and behaviors. Although these theories assume that we are thoughtful, they do not require that we be rational either in our perception of inconsistency or in its resolution.

Balance theory deals with the relationship among a person (P), another person (O), and some object (X). If there is an imbalance among these elements, then attitude change is expected to occur.

Cognitive dissonance theory is also based on the principle of consistency, but it deals with behaviors as well as attitudes. In its simplest form, the theory holds that dissonance is aroused when a person's behavior is inconsistent with his or her attitude. Such dissonance is believed to be uncomfortable, and the resultant discomfort motivates the person to eliminate the dissonance by changing either the behavior or the attitude. Inconsistency is not sufficient in itself to arouse dissonance, however. The behavior must have aversive consequences, and the individual must accept personal responsibility for the outcome. Under those conditions, dissonance will be aroused and a person will be motivated to reduce it. A variety of techniques to reduce dissonance are available; other tactics, such as selective exposure, serve to justify a decision already made.

Functional theories of attitude change assume that people hold attitudes that fit their needs, and that to change those attitudes we must determine what the particular needs are. Some attitudes are evaluative, based on the rewards and punishments associated with the attitude object itself; others are expressive, directed toward objects that are means to a desired end.

Although emphasis has been placed on the factors

that bring about change, we should consider also the factors that increase resistance to change. Studies of anticipatory attitude change suggest that some changes may simply reflect "elasticity," that people consciously present their opinions as moderate in order to appear flexible. When a person is forewarned of a persuasive communication, he or she may be inoculated against subsequent change as a result of that warning.

Glossary Terms

anchor
assimilation effects
balance theory
cognitive dissonance theory
contrast effects
functional theory
heuristics
selective exposure
social judgment theory

*As for conforming outwardly, and living your own
life inwardly, I do not think much of that.*
Henry David Thoreau

Don't compromise yourself. You are all you've got.
Janis Joplin

Ben Shahn, *No Man Can Command My Conscience!*, © 1968. New Jersey State Museum Collection, Trenton. Gift of Bernarda Bryson Shahn.

CHAPTER EIGHT

Social Influence & Personal Control

I. Conformity
   The Asch Situation
   Why Do People Conform?
   Influences on Conformity
II. Compliance
   The Foot-in-the-Door Effect
   The Door-in-the-Face Effect
   The Low-Ball Procedure
   The Generality of Compliance
III. Obedience
   Laboratory Studies of Destructive Obedience
   Criticisms of the Obedience Studies
IV. The Sense of Control
   The Illusion of Control
   Consequences of a Belief in Control
   Individual Differences in Perceptions of Control
V. Reactions to a Loss of Control
   A Theory of Reactance
   Learned Helplessness
   Self-Induced Dependence
VI. Summary

*A*ttitude change is one reflection of social influence. As its operation relies on verbal comprehension, it is generally assumed that human behavior has a cognitive basis. Of course others can influence us in many other ways—by power strategies, direct orders, requests, and even simple example. In many cases, to succumb to social influence is simply to adapt oneself to the world as one finds it; driving on the right side of the road in the United States and Canada, for example, is a simple matter of safety, just as it is wise to drive on the left in Great Britain. In other cases, the wisdom of conformity behavior may be questionable, as when members of a junior high school clique determine what clothes are acceptable to wear and reject people who choose a different dress style. The way we respond to the requests or orders of others will vary across a wide range of situations; we do not respond the same way to a friend who asks us for a favor, a door-to-door salesperson who's pressuring us to buy a gadget we don't need, and a dictator in a repressive society.

Each time we encounter an attempt to influence our behavior or attitudes, we must decide whether to comply or resist. At the heart of this process is the issue of control—the degree to which we feel we have control over our own lives versus the degree to which others have the power to determine our behavior.

This very basic issue of influence and control is the focus of this chapter. First we will consider the various forms of control—conformity, compliance, and obedience. Then we will look more carefully at why control is an important issue and how people respond to a loss of control in their lives.

Conformity

The Asch Situation

A male college student has volunteered to participate in a research project. He is to be a subject in a visual perception experiment. Along with six other "subjects" (who are in fact confederates of the researcher), he is seated at a round table. The group members are shown a vertical line and then asked which of three other vertical lines match it in length. (All lines are in view at the same time.) One of these lines is identical in length to the first line; the others differ enough so that in controlled tests (taken individually, not in groups) more than 95% of subjects make correct judgments about the length of the lines. In the group experiment, the subjects are asked to state their choices out loud, one at a time. The participants are seated so that the real subject is always the next-to-last person to respond. On the first and second trials, everyone gives the same response, the obviously correct one. (The volunteer begins to think that this task is easy.) The same outcome occurs on several more trials. Then, on a subsequent trial—when the choice appears as clear-cut as those before—the first confederate gives a response that is obviously incorrect. All the other confederates follow suit, giving the wrong response. When it is the subject's turn to respond, all the preceding respondents at the table have given an answer that he believes is wrong. What does he do? Does he stick to his convictions, remain independent, and give the correct response? Or does he conform to the group, giving an answer that he knows is wrong? Or does he convince himself that he must be wrong and that the group's answer is correct?

This was the procedure used in an early set of studies on conformity by the social psychologist Solomon Asch (1951, 1956, 1958), and it illustrates some of the basic characteristics of the process of influence and control. In its most basic sense, **conformity** is a yielding to group pressures when no direct request to comply with the group is made. Thus, in the Asch situation, the confederates did not directly ask the subject to go along with their judgment. Nevertheless, the subject undoubtedly per-

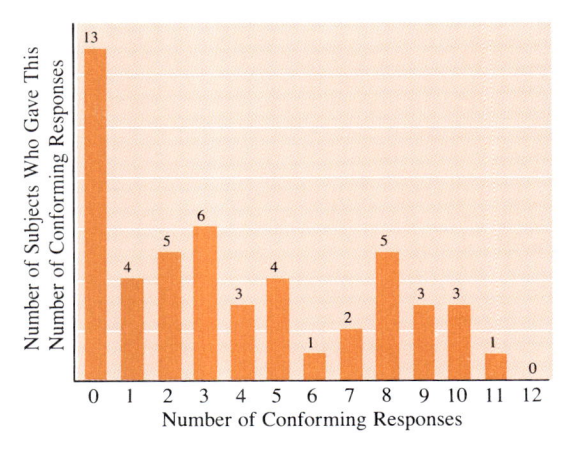

Figure 8–1 Distribution of conformity responses in Asch's study

ceived some real pressures to conform his judgment with those of the other group members.

How did Asch's subjects respond? Asch's standard procedure consisted of 12 critical trials on which confederates gave the wrong response, interspersed with a large number of trials on which all confederates gave the correct answer. The conformity behavior of 50 subjects is shown in Figure 8–1. When we consider the responses of subjects on all the critical trials, we find that 32% of the responses were conforming: subjects, on the average, conformed on 3.84 out of 12 possible trials. But the averages are deceiving; in Asch's study the distribution of conforming responses is important because of the great range of individual differences. Notice in Figure 8–1 that 13 of the 50 subjects never yielded to the majority on any of the critical trials, whereas 4 subjects yielded on 10 or more of those trials. Thus, although some conformity is certainly evident, many of Asch's subjects responded with little or no conformity.

Asch's work on conformity was influenced by the even earlier studies of Muzafer Sherif (1935) on the **autokinetic effect.** If you look at a stationary light in an otherwise completely dark room, the light will appear to move, because your eyes have no other reference point. Sherif capitalized on this phenomenon to study the effects of another person's response and found that a subject's reports of movement were highly influenced by other people's estimates. In this case, it is not surprising that some conformity occurred; the stimulus was ambiguous, and there was no other source of information. The results of Asch's studies are more surprising, because the correct response was so clear and the subjects were not exposed to group pressure.

Why Do People Conform?

What can explain this tendency to conform to other people's opinions? It is not hard to understand in Sherif's subjects, for whom the reality of the situation was quite uncertain. Given a collection of people, none of whom is certain about which answer is the correct one, a group consensus or group norm forms. Together, people establish a frame of reference on which to base subsequent judgments. Something slightly different seemed to be happening in Asch's experiments. There the reality was much clearer: most people could easily tell which line was equal to or longer or shorter than the standard. Yet the group opinion still exerted considerable influence.

Two different types of social influence are seen in these two situations. *Informational* influence is based, as the term suggests, on facts or knowledge about what is true or correct in a situation. A group is an effective source of influence in this case because it constitutes an objective source of information on which the individual can base his or her opinion. The second type of social influence, *normative* influence, is social pressure exerted by a group. In this case, the individual adapts to the group position because of a desire to be like the group members and to avoid appearing deviant (Deutsch & Gerard, 1955).

Conformity in behavior does not always reflect private acceptance of the position it implies. A person may conform to the group's opinion without believing that position to be correct. Put in another situation, this person may behave quite differently. We can easily imagine a person who says she dislikes rock music when she is among friends who are devoted to classical music but who also dances up a storm when she is with other friends at a disco. The public conformity of such a person tells us very little about her private beliefs.

If conformity is public behavior that yields to group pressure, what is the opposite of conformity? We may think of two different types of opposing nonconformity responses. One is *independence,* defined as behavior that does not correspond to group norms. The person who wears blue jeans when they are popular and continues to wear them when the styles change is demonstrating independence—he does his own thing. **Anticonformity,** in contrast, is characterized by opposition to the majority response on all occasions. The anticonformist may choose to wear blue jeans when more formal clothes are in style but switch to more formal wear when blue jeans become popular (see Cartoon 8–1). Thus the actions of two persons may appear similar in some situations but may actually reflect quite different motives. When psychologists investigated the reasons that some U.S. prisoners of war did not collaborate with their Communist Chinese captors during the Korean war, they identified two types of resisters. Some prisoners resisted because they knew that admitting guilt for

"I just got damn well fed up with being formal all the time"

the war and broadcasting peace appeals were wrong; these men were labeled independent resisters. Another group of men had a long history of unwillingness to accept any kind of authority; they did not conform to the commands of their officers in the U.S. Army *or* to orders from the Chinese (Schein, 1957). These men displayed anticonformity, or counterconformity.

It is important to recognize that some people do not conform to group pressures, whether for normative or for informational reasons. It is also important to recognize, as the French psychologist Serge Moscovici (1985) has frequently pointed out, that social influence in a group works both ways. Not only can the majority influence an individual or a small minority, but the minority can affect the beliefs and behaviors of the majority as well. While the phenomenon of conformity helps us to understand the general regularity of social life, the frequent successes of minority groups in their efforts to influence the majority prove that the group that sets the norms can shift its position. We will consider the influence of the minority in more detail in Chapter Fourteen, when we talk about group behavior more generally.

Influences on Conformity

Many factors affect the extent to which behavior will conform to a group norm. The size of the group is one such factor. In general, the larger the group, the more influence it exerts (Tanford & Penrod, 1984). There are two explanations for this effect, both related to the issues of normative and informational influence discussed above. First, a person's concern about being liked increases with the size of the group, up to a point. Second, as the number of people expressing an opinion increases, the consensus becomes stronger, and so do the pressures to be right (Insko et al., 1985).

The effectiveness of numbers diminishes when the group is larger than three. Furthermore, if the group is not unanimous, conformity behavior is dramatically reduced. In this case, the behavior of those who do not go along with the majority becomes a source of influence in its own right.

An important factor in the effect of group size is the extent to which members of the group are regarded as a single unit (Wilder, 1977). Consider the difference between a situation in which four individuals all give the wrong answer, apparently independently, and one in which those four persons are viewed as a single group or club. In the latter case, conformity pressures are less effective and more closely approximate the pressure exerted by a single individual. In other words, the four opinions are actually considered to represent only one voice, and hence the size of the majority becomes less important.

The position that the majority espouses also affects the amount of conformity shown. The more discrepant a group's position is from one's own, the more pressure one will feel to move toward the group norm. And people tend to succumb to conformity pressures more readily when the group's position becomes more discrepant over time than they do when the group's position becomes increasingly similar to their own (Campbell, Tesser, & Fairey, 1986).

The wide variation in responses to Asch's task led many investigators to explore the various personality types that may be susceptible to pressures to conform. A number of differences were reported. Richard S. Crutchfield (1955), for example, reported that independent businessmen and military officers demonstrated "more intellectual effectiveness, ego strength, leadership ability, and maturity of social relations, together with a conspicuous absence of inferiority feelings, rigid and excessive self-control, and authoritarian attitudes," than their more conforming colleagues (p. 194). Other researchers have found that conforming subjects have a stronger need for affiliation (McGhee & Teevan, 1967) and stronger tendencies to blame themselves (Costanzo, 1970). People who are given reason to doubt their ability to judge a particular task are, not surprisingly, more likely to conform, relying on the group to supply the information that they lack (Campbell, Tesser, & Fairey, 1986).

Women are somewhat more conforming than men in situations that involve face-to-face interaction (Eagly & Carli, 1981). One possible explanation for this difference is that women are more concerned about group harmony—when group pressure is exerted, they tend to go along with the group rather than assert their own judgment and risk disharmony.

None of these individual characteristics, however, can predict all conformity behavior. If the laboratory research on conformity has demonstrated anything, it is that situational factors are of great importance in eliciting conformity behavior. It is also important to consider the reasons for individual choices. Conformity is one outcome of an attempt to solve problems and reach conclusions about one's surroundings. Such a perspective should be considered before one too quickly adopts the judgment that conformity is always and forever bad. As Barry Collins has stated:

> It would be a mistake to oversimplify the question and ask whether conformity is good or bad. A person who refused to accept anyone's word of advice on any topic whatsoever . . . would probably make just as big a botch of his life . . . as a person who always conformed and never formed a judgment on the basis of his own individual sources of information. [1970, p. 21]

Compliance

The term **compliance** has often been used interchangeably with *conformity*. Here, however, we will use the term in a more specific sense, limiting its use to situations in which a direct request is made and the person agrees to behave in accordance with that request. In contrast to conformity, which is a response to indirect pressure, compliance is a response to direct pressure to comply with a request. Such demands are made of us daily. A professor may ask you to stop by after class, a door-to-door salesperson may suggest that you buy a new vacuum cleaner, a panhandler may stop you on the street and ask for a quarter. Many experimental studies of compliance have, in fact, taken their lead from these common events.

The Foot-in-the-Door Effect

The **foot-in-the-door effect** is well known to salespeople. The sales lore suggests that once the seller has his or her foot in the door, a sale will be no problem. In social-psychological terms, a person who complies with one small request is likely to comply later with a larger and more substantial demand.

In an initial test of this hypothesis, Jonathan Freedman and Scott Fraser (1966) arranged for two undergraduate experimenters to contact suburban women in their homes—first with a small request and later with a larger one. The women were first asked either to place a small sign in their window or to sign a petition about driving safely or keeping California beautiful. Two weeks later, a different experimenter returned to each home and asked each subject to place a large and unattractive billboard promoting auto safety on her lawn for the next couple of weeks—a rather substantial request. A second group of homemakers (the control group) was contacted only about the second, large-billboard request. The results showed a very strong foot-in-the-door effect—those subjects who had complied with the earlier trivial request were much more likely to comply with the larger request several weeks later. More intriguing yet was the apparent generality of the effect; signing a petition to "keep California beautiful" led to greater compliance with a different experimenter on a different issue.

What causes the foot-in-the-door effect? One explanation stresses people's perceptions of themselves (see Chapter Three). Having once agreed to help, a person may decide that he or she is basically a helpful person. A second request—even a burdensome one—may then be granted because the person wishes to maintain that image of helpfulness. Considerable evidence supports this interpretation (DeJong, 1979). However, at least two conditions are necessary to produce the effect. First, the initial request must be large enough to cause people to think about the implications of their behavior. Offhandedly telling someone the correct time, for example, might not be enough to cause you to think about yourself, whereas giving a set of complicated directions to someone who was lost might lead to self-perceptions. A second necessary condition is a perception of free choice. If a person feels forced to comply, then there is no reason to attribute one's compliance to any internal disposition. In fact, any external justification for the compliance will weaken or eliminate the foot-in-the-door effect. For example, homemakers who were offered money for agreeing to a 5-minute telephone interview were no more likely to comply with a later request for a 25-minute interview than women who did not receive the initial request. Demonstrating the foot-in-the-door effect, women not offered the monetary justification were more likely to agree to the later request (Zuckerman, Lazzaro, & Waldgeir, 1979).

What about people who refuse the initial request? The self-perception explanation suggests that these people should be *less* likely to comply with subsequent requests. In contrast to people who agree to help, these noncompliers should view themselves as unhelpful people and act accordingly on future occasions. Labels can also be provided by others, as Robert Kraut (1973) has shown. In this experiment, subjects who gave to charity were either labeled as charitable or not labeled. Subjects who gave a donation might be told, for example, "You are really a generous person. I wish more people were as charitable as you are." Similarly, subjects who refused to give to charity were either labeled as uncharitable or not labeled. All subjects were later asked by another canvasser to contribute to a second charity. Subjects who had been labeled as charitable gave more and subjects labeled as uncharitable gave less than their respective unlabeled peers.

Thus, consistent with sales lore, there is considerable evidence in support of the foot-in-the-door effect. A "foot in" makes future compliance more likely; conversely, "no foot in" should reduce future compliance. But does such a reduction in compliance always occur?

The Door-in-the-Face Effect

Robert Cialdini and his co-workers (1975), who coined the term **door-in-the-face effect,** suggested that on some occasions people who refuse an initial request may be *more* likely to agree to a subsequent request. These researchers approached college students with a socially desirable but highly demanding request: Would they serve as voluntary counselors at a county juvenile detention center for two years? Virtually everyone politely refused, thus in effect slamming the door in the face of a demanding request for compliance. However, when a second and smaller request was made—specifically, to chaperon juveniles on a trip to the zoo—many subjects readily agreed.

Why wasn't there less compliance in this case, as the self-perception explanation would predict? Apparently, investigators have concluded, the door-in-the-face effect depends on a particular set of circumstances (DeJong, 1979). First, the initial request must be very large—so large that the people who refuse make no negative inferences about themselves. Thus the people who declined two years of voluntary service would probably conclude that hardly anyone would agree to such a large request and would feel no compulsion to think of themselves as unhelpful. Second, for the door-in-the-face effect to occur, the second request must be made by the same person who makes the first request. According to Cialdini and his colleagues, subjects view the toned-down request as a concession by the experimenter, and they then feel pressure to reciprocate that concession. If a different person makes the second request, however, such conciliatory behavior is not necessary.

The door-in-the-face technique has been applied in a business context as well (Mowen & Cialdini, 1980). Pedestrians selected at random were more likely to agree to fill out an insurance-company survey when the initial request had been for a much longer survey. In this case, however, the second request had to be part of the first request for the tactic to be successful. In other words, a door slammed in the face could be reopened only if the topic of the second survey was the same.

Closely related to the door-in-the-face technique is what the psychologist Jerry Burger (1986) has called the "that's not all" technique. Imagine that you are sitting at home and hear a knock at your door. A boy and a girl from the local high school are there, selling candles to raise money for a band trip. "We're selling the candles for $3 apiece," the boy says. Before you have a chance to say yes or no, the girl jumps in to say that they'll let you have them for only $2. Would you be more likely to buy a candle now than you would be if they had originally been offered to you at $2 apiece? Yes, according to Burger's research. Notice that the major difference between "that's not all" and the door in the face is that in the latter case the consumer, or subject, has the opportunity to refuse; in "that's not all," a more favorable offer is made before any refusal (or acceptance) occurs. In a comparison of the two techniques, Burger found "that's not all" to be the more effective, inducing greater compliance.

The Low-Ball Procedure

Yet another investigation of compliance that was inspired by a practitioner's rule of thumb is the low-ball procedure (Cialdini et al., 1978). Presumably widespread (especially among new-car dealers), the technique of "throwing a low ball" consists in inducing the customer to buy a car by offering an extremely good price (for example, $500 below what competitors are offering). Once the customer has agreed to buy the car, the conditions of the deal are changed, resulting in a higher purchase price than the customer originally agreed to. Reported techniques include a refusal to approve the deal by the salesperson's boss, a reduction in the trade-in figure given by the used-car manager, and the exclusion of various options from the purchase price offered.

As Cialdini and his colleagues demonstrated, this technique of inducing compliance works beyond the new-car showroom. University students, for example, were more likely to show up for an experiment at 7 A.M. if they had first agreed to participate in a general way than if they were initially told of the early hour. Although this technique of inducing compliance is in many ways similar to the foot-in-the-door procedure, there is at least one important difference. In low-balling, the initial commitment is to the behavior to be performed; in the "foot" procedure, the commitment is first to a different and less demanding behavior.

Why does the low-ball technique work? Cialdini (1985) suggests that after receiving the initial offer, people make a commitment, and then they develop a set of justifications for that commitment. When the initial justification—the low price—is then taken away, they still have supports for their decision to buy the product—even if those reasons were developed late in the game.

Box 8–1
Strategies used to obtain compliance

The following strategies for obtaining compliance are listed in the order in which a group of students at the University of Alberta thought it likely they would be used.

1. Ask (either directly or indirectly).
   Example: "Would you please . . ."
2. Invoke personal expertise.
   Example: "I read in *Consumer Reports* that . . ."
3. Offer a personal reason.
   Example: "I need . . ."
4. Invoke a role relationship.
   Example: "If you were my friend, you would . . ."
5. Bargain for a favor.
   Example: "If you'll do this for me, I promise I'll . . ."
6. Invoke a norm.
   Example: "Everyone is doing it."
7. Invoke a moral principle.
   Example: "It would be the right thing to do."
8. Invoke altruism.
   Example: "The health of other people depends on you."
9. Butter them up.
   Example: "You look so attractive today."
10. Bargain for an object (or bribe).
    Example: "I'll give you $100 if you will . . ."
11. Appeal to their emotions.
    Example: "I'm going to cry if you don't . . ."
12. Offer a personal criticism.
    Example: "You're so stingy, you probably wouldn't . . ."
13. Try deception.
    Example: "The boss told me to tell you . . ." (when the boss never said a word about it).
14. Threaten.
    Example: "I'm going to tell father if you don't . . ."
15. Use force.
    Example: "Do it right now!" (accompanied by physical shaking).

The Generality of Compliance

In a normal day, many requests are made of each of us. People use a variety of strategies in their attempts to get others to comply. Box 8–1 shows 15 possible tactics.

In some instances a decision to comply with a request may be a rational choice, arrived at after careful consideration of the pros and cons of the request. Often, however, our willingness to comply with a request may be much less considered. Ellen Langer has argued that many such behaviors are essentially "mindless"—in other words, we go along with the request without much thought (Langer, 1978b).

Although compliance may sometimes be mind-

Table 8-1 Forms of power and their bases

Form	Basis
Coercive power	Agent's ability to administer punishment
Reward power	Agent's ability to give rewards
Expert power	Target's belief that agent has superior knowledge, ability, or expertise
Legitimate power	Target's belief that agent is authorized by a recognized power structure to command and make decisions
Referent power	Target's identification with, attraction to, or respect for agent

less, studies of power strategies suggest that at other times we are quite sensitive to the form in which compliance is requested. John French and Bertram Raven (1959) have identified five forms of power, or ways in which one person can induce compliance by another. These five forms of power are defined in Table 8-1. You can probably think of instances when others have exercised each of these types of power in an effort to gain your compliance. The parent who promises use of the car in return for some behavior, for example, is using reward power, while the parent who threatens "grounding" is using coercive power. A professor may gain compliance through the use of expert power, whereas a friend may be powerful because he or she is someone you would like to emulate (referent power). Corporate officers and elected officials are said to have legitimate power and gain compliance because it is agreed that they have a right to expect it. Of course, it is possible that one person may have several bases of power; an admired professor, for example, may be able to reward and punish by means of grades and may be an important role model and source of expertise as well.

The likelihood of compliance varies with the form of power exercised, although in practice it is often difficult to isolate the effect of a single power type when multiple forms are being used (Podsakoff & Schriesheim, 1985). Coercive power may be quite effective if the power source is present, for example, but may be less effective if that person is not present when the behavior is to be performed. Furthermore, people's explanations for their compliance depend on the power strategy that is being used. When either referent or reward power is used, for example, compliance is generally explained by reference to characteristics of the person who performs the compliant behavior. When either coercive or legitimate power is used, in contrast, explanations for compliance generally focus on the person who has made the request (Litman-Adizes, Raven, & Fontaine, 1978). Thus, recalling the discussions in Chapters Three and Four, we see that attributional patterns may influence the extent of future compliance once the agent who has made the request is no longer present.

People may be willing to comply with the request of another person for many reasons. At one extreme is the mindless response: we comply almost automatically, giving little thought to the reasons we should or should not agree to carry out the behavior. This form of compliance is most likely to occur when the response is overlearned, so that it requires little conscious monitoring on our part. At the other end of the spectrum are situations in which we carefully weigh the reasons for compliance and act accordingly. Yet, although rational thought enters into the picture on many occasions, the sheer force of the request often determines our response. As we shall see in the case of obedience, once legitimate power has been established, a person may refuse to question the reasons for the agent's request and simply carry out orders because they are given.

Obedience

A special form of compliance, in response to a request made in the form of an order, is **obedience.** All of us feel some degree of pressure to obey certain symbols of authority, such as parents, police officers, and traffic lights. But can obedience lead us to take extreme actions against our better judgment? Can obedience be carried to destructive lengths? The cases of Lieutenant William Calley and Adolf Eichmann are relevant. When he was tried for killing 22 South Vietnamese villagers, U.S. Army Lieutenant Calley stated that he was simply following orders. Adolf Eichmann, in charge of exterminating 6 million Jews during World War II (as well as gypsies, homosexuals, political prisoners, and others deemed unacceptable by the Third Reich), also did what he was told. At his trial for war crimes, Eichmann denied any moral responsibility. He was, he said, simply doing his job.

Laboratory Studies of Destructive Obedience

Are Eichmann and Calley unusual cases? Stanley Milgram, a social psychologist, attempted to determine whether people in more normal circumstances will obey an authority even when they believe they are endangering the life of another person.

Through advertisements and direct-mail solicitations in New Haven, Connecticut, Milgram (1963) gathered 40 men of various ages and occupations for paid participation in a research project at Yale University. When each subject arrived for the experiment, he was introduced to the experimenter and another subject (actually an accomplice of the experimenter). The subjects were told that the purpose of the experiment was to determine the effects of punishment on learning. Subjects drew lots to determine who would be the teacher and who the learner, but the drawing was rigged so that the true subject was always the "teacher" and the accomplice was always the "learner." Then the learner was strapped to a chair, electrodes were attached to his wrist, and the subject was instructed in his task.

The lesson to be "taught" by the subject was a verbal learning task. The teacher was told to administer a shock to the learner in the next room each time he gave a wrong answer by operating a shock generator with 30 switches. The switches presumably controlled electric current that increased by 15-volt increments from 15 to 450 volts and were labeled from "Slight shock" at the low end to "Danger: severe shock" and finally an ominous "XXX" at the highest end. In fact, this equipment was a dummy generator and the confederate never received an actual shock, but its appearance was quite convincing.

After each wrong answer (of which the accomplice intentionally gave many), the experimenter instructed the subject to move one level higher on the shock generator. When the subject reached 300 volts, the accomplice began to pound on the wall between the two rooms, and from that point on, he no longer answered any question posed by the subject. At this point subjects usually turned to the

Photo 8–1 Milgram's obedience experiment

experimenter for guidance. In a stoic and rather stern way, the experimenter replied that a failure to answer should be treated as a wrong answer and that the learner should be shocked according to the usual schedule.

Milgram's basic question was simply how many subjects would continue to administer shocks to the end of the series, following the experimenter's orders. Table 8-2 presents the results. Of the 40 subjects, 26 (65%) continued to the end of the shock series. Not a single subject stopped before administering 300 volts—the point at which the learner began to pound on the wall. Five refused to obey at that point; at some point 14 of the 40 subjects defied the experimenter. Milgram concludes that obedience to commands is a strong force in our society, since nearly two-thirds of his subjects obeyed the experimenter's instructions even though they were led to believe that they were hurting another human being. In the words of Milgram himself:

> If in this study an anonymous experimenter could successfully command adults to subdue a fifty-year-old man, and force on him painful electric shocks against his protests, one can only wonder what government, with its vastly greater authority and prestige, can command of its subjects. [1965, p. 75]

Milgram (1965, 1974) extended his research program to study some of the situational factors that may lead subjects to obey or to refuse to obey when the experimenter (the authority figure) tells them to hurt another person. He found, for example, that the closer the victim was to the subject, the more likely subjects were to refuse the command of the experimenter. Thus, when the victim was in the same room as the subject and only 1½ feet away, only one-third of the subjects were willing to go to the maximum shock level. Milgram also found that obedience was less frequent when the experimenter was not physically present but issued his commands either by telephone or by tape recording. In fact, when the experimenter was absent, several subjects administered shocks of a lower voltage than was required, thus defying the authority of the experimenter. In an interesting reversal of the typical procedure, Milgram also demonstrated that authority could be a force for good. In this case, the learners insisted that the shocks be continued, citing a commitment to the experiment and a challenge to their masculinity. But when the experimenter repeated his command to stop, the subjects stopped, again showing their adherence to the commands of an authority.

In the years since Milgram's original demonstration of obedience in the laboratory, numerous other researchers have investigated the conditions under

Table 8–2 Distribution of breakoff points in Milgram's study of obedience

Voltage Level	Number of Subjects for Whom This Was Maximum Shock
"Slight shock" (15–60 volts)	0
"Moderate shock" (75–120 volts)	0
"Strong shock" (135–180 volts)	0
"Very strong shock" (195–240 volts)	0
"Intense shock" (255–300 volts)	5
"Extreme-intensity shock" (315–360 volts)	8
"Danger: severe shock" (375–420 volts)	1
"XXX" (435–450 volts)	26

which obedience occurs. Similar findings have emerged from a variety of countries and age groups (Miller, 1986). Thus obedience is not a peculiarity of the German people or of New Haven men. It is a behavior that can be observed in most of us, encouraged or discouraged by situational factors.

Criticisms of the Obedience Studies

Provocative as these findings are, the obedience studies have not escaped criticism. In fact, they have been a focus of considerable controversy within the social sciences (Miller, 1986). Consider the following statements, which reflect the tone of the debate. First, from the psychiatrist Bruno Bettleheim: "These experiments are so vile, the intention with which they were engaged in is so vile, that nothing these experiments show has any value" (quoted in Miller, 1986, p. 124). The other pole of the debate is exemplified by a statement by the social psychologist Alan Elms:

> Milgram, in exploring the external conditions that produce such destructive obedience, the psychological processes that lead to such attempted abdications of responsibility, and the means by which defiance of illegitimate authority can be promoted, seems to me to have done some of the most morally significant research in modern psychology. [Quoted in Miller, 1986, p. 132]

Two major issues are at stake in this often heated debate: the ethics of the experiments and the generalizability of their findings.

Ethics of the experiment. One criticism of Milgram's obedience studies is that the subjects' rights were not protected. Subjects were not told that the experiment would arouse distressful conflict and the experimenters did not ask them for permission to put them in such a situation. In fact, it is unlikely that the exact procedures of Milgram's studies could be replicated today. In part because of the public reaction to these studies, experimenters are required to give subjects more information before they consent to participate than Milgram gave his subjects.

A second criticism is that participation in these experiments could have had long-term effects. The subjects could have lost their trust in experimenters, the university, or science in general. The subjects' self-concepts might also have suffered long-term effects. Until the experiment, most subjects probably saw themselves as persons who would not deliberately inflict pain unless the circumstances were extreme. As a result of the experiment, they would have to believe otherwise. One can certainly argue that such self-education might be beneficial, but it is probably not within the province of the experimental social psychologist to force such education on anyone.

Milgram has argued that debriefing at the end of the experiment was sufficient to eradicate any tensions, doubts, or resentment that subjects experienced. In describing the debriefing procedure, Milgram stated: "After the interview, procedures were undertaken to assure that the subject would leave the laboratory in a state of well-being. A friendly reconciliation was arranged between the subject and the victim, and an effort was made to reduce any tensions that arose as a result of the experiment" (1963, p. 374). Milgram further reports (1974) that interviews by psychiatrists and follow-up questionnaires completed by the subjects indicated no long-term deleterious effects.

Generalizability of the findings. People have also questioned whether the extreme degrees of obedience found in Milgram's subjects can be generalized to the real world. For example, trust in and obedience to the authority figure may be demand characteristics that are especially salient for subjects in experiments (Orne & Holland, 1968). In other words, subjects who will do as they are told in an experiment may disobey another authority figure, such as the physician who tells them to exercise daily or the employer who tells them to fire a popular co-worker. Along with this criticism goes the claim that the prestige of Yale University contributed to the high obedience rate; subjects may have assumed that any study carried out at Yale must be scientifically and socially acceptable—hence they were more inclined to obey. However, the available evidence contradicts this last claim. Milgram repeated the experiment with another group of men in a run-down office building in a deteriorating area of Bridgeport, Connecticut. Here he found that almost 50% of the men obeyed the experimenter to the end of the shock series. Although the prestige of Yale apparently accounted for some obedience, the phenomenon still occurred in a blatantly nonuniversity setting. Furthermore, many people would argue that the influence of authority is considerable in any organization that has a powerful hierarchy. Individuals often do agree to fire popular subordinates if their superior tells them to do so, and carry out other orders that are contrary to their own inclinations. As a further argument in support of the generalizability of the obedience experiments, one must consider the reactions of subjects in the experiment. Whereas ethical questions can surely be raised about the stress that was created, the evidence of stress testifies to the impact of the procedures and the reality of the subjects' experience (Miller, 1986).

Despite the legitimate criticisms, Milgram's work has demonstrated that obedience is a much more pervasive phenomenon than had been thought. Neither a group of undergraduates nor a group of psychologists and psychiatrists, when told of the procedures, predicted that subjects would continue to obey when the high voltage levels were reached. Assumptions about human nature were more favorable than the actual outcomes.

Photo 8–2 A lottery provides the illusion of control.

The Sense of Control

Theories of human behavior differ in their assumptions about human nature and hence are divided on the issue of personal control. Humanistic approaches to social behavior often rest on the assumption that we humans have almost complete control over our behavior. B. F. Skinner and his followers, in contrast, take the position that stimuli in the environment determine our behavior—that we are controlled by external rewards and punishments and that free will is merely a figment of our imagination (Skinner, 1971). Between these two positions lie a number of variations, which social psychologists have explored.

The issue of control is particularly relevant when we talk about social influence. As we have seen, people will conform to group pressure, comply with requests, and obey orders in a variety of circumstances. In each case external forces appear to regulate the behavior, and the element of individual control seems peculiarly absent. Yet many people fervently believe that we do have nearly complete control over our behavior, and even those who, like Skinner, disagree nevertheless admit that most people believe in a sense of personal control.

The remainder of this chapter will consider the general issue of control—how we develop illusions of control, how a belief in control affects our behavior, and how we react to a loss of control in our lives.

The Illusion of Control

Magicians entertain by appearing to control events in a way we cannot explain. Although most of us cannot make rabbits appear out of hats or people float in air, we do believe in our ability to control more mundane events. We even develop an illusion of control over the outcomes of events that we know are determined purely by chance. Ellen Langer (1983) and her colleagues have presented the most persuasive evidence in support of these beliefs.

The lottery is a situation in which the likelihood of winning is determined solely by chance—the "luck of the draw" allows little room for an individual to influence the outcome. To illustrate the illusion of control, Langer (1975) gave people the opportunity to buy $1 football lottery tickets with the chance of winning a $50 prize. To vary the illusion of control, the experimenters allowed one group of people to select the ticket they wanted. Other participants received randomly selected lottery tickets from the experimenter (identical to those chosen by the first group). Before the random drawing of the prize ticket, the experimenter approached all subjects and asked whether they would be willing to sell their ticket to someone who would pay more than the going price for it. Subjects who had been given no choice were willing to sell their tickets for an average of $1.96. In contrast, subjects who believed that they had had some choice demanded an average of $8.67 for their tickets, presumably because they believed they had a better chance of winning the random draw than did those subjects who had not exercised a choice.

Many factors can increase our belief in control. In general, the more similar a purely chance situation is in appearance to a real skill situation, the more likely we are to believe in our own ability to control the outcome. Competition, for example, increases our belief in control. We will be much more confident of our success when we are paired with a seemingly incompetent competitor than when the competitor appears competent, even though the outcome is determined purely by chance (Langer, 1975). Playing a slot machine when a 5-year-old is playing at the next stand, for example, would probably lead us to believe that we had greater control over our outcome—even though the machines themselves are obstinately beyond our control. Similarly, involvement in the task, knowledge about the procedures involved, and practice in performing the task all lead us to believe that we have more control than we in fact possess. Success at a task may also create the illusion of control. In another study, Langer and Roth (1975) asked subjects to predict coin tosses and structured the outcome so that people experienced either early success and later failure, early failure and later success, or a purely random outcome. In each case, however, the number of correct predictions was the same and did not differ from what could be expected by chance. People who experienced early success were much more confident of their ability at the task, predicting more future successes for themselves and viewing themselves as more skilled. Early experience with success apparently created a belief in the ability to control the outcome, a finding that is probably quite similar to the case of the novice gambler who hits the jackpot the first time around—and then proceeds to lose far more than was initially won!

Belief in one's ability to control events is not limited to the realm of coin tosses and lottery tickets. People believe that they have control over many events in their lives (Wright, Zautra, & Braver, 1985). Belief in control is not uniform across the board, however. People believe that they have more control over positive events than over negative events, and more control over events that seem likely to recur in the future than over events that they do not expect to recur (see Figure 8–2). This pattern of belief is consistent with some of the self-enhancement behaviors that we discussed in Chapter Three: people take credit for positive events and deny responsibility for negative events.

Such findings do not mean that we never have real control over situations and outcomes. It is apparent, however, that our belief in the extent of our control may far outstrip our actual ability to determine the course of events.

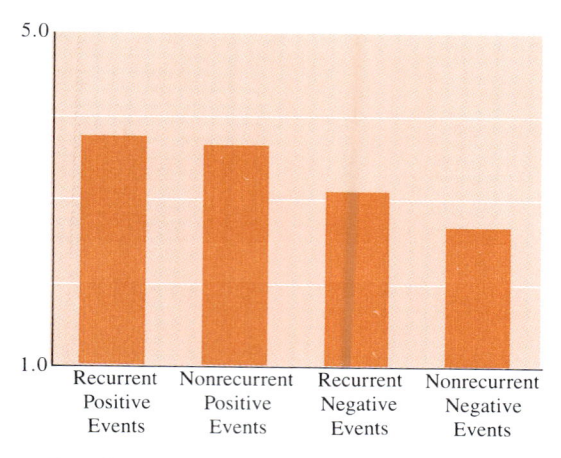

Typical Recurrent Positive Events
Study habits improved
Family became closer
Accomplished a goal in a hobby
Found a bargain

Typical Nonrecurrent Positive Events
Found a valuable object
Graduated from high school
Became an aunt or uncle
Acquired a pet

Typical Recurrent Negative Events
Had trouble sleeping
Family increased pressure to do well in school
Had serious conflict with roommate
Relationship with boyfriend or girlfriend became less satisfying

Typical Nonrecurrent Negative Events
Was put on academic probation
Lost a close friend
Received ticket for traffic violation
Was hospitalized with a serious illness

Figure 8–2 Ratings of personal control

Consequences of a Belief in Control

Why do we believe so strongly in our ability to influence events, often in the face of evidence suggesting that we in fact have little or no control? One reason is that a belief in such control makes the world seem more predictable. If we are expecting to interact with someone in a competitive situation, for example, we would like to be able to predict that person's behavior so that we can determine our own outcomes. Experiments have shown that we may exaggerate our ability to make such predictions. In one study, subjects who expected to compete with another subject were more certain that they would be able to infer the personality of their competitor than were subjects who expected only to observe the interaction (Miller, Norman, & Wright, 1978). Yet the belief in control is not solely a fantasy. Behavior, too, is altered when we believe that we have control over our circumstances.

Performance on routine tasks was found to be better when people believed that they could control a loud noise to which they were subjected before the performance, even when they did not actually exercise any control over it (Glass & Singer, 1972). People who can control their environment perceive conditions to be less crowded than do those who feel that they have no control; further, they consider their surroundings more pleasant and their own mood more positive (Rodin, Solomon, & Metcalf, 1978). In general, over a wide range of circumstances, we react more positively when we believe we have some control than when we do not.

Perhaps one of the most dramatic demonstrations of the power of a belief in control is a study of aged people in institutions by Ellen Langer and Judith Rodin (Langer & Rodin, 1976; Rodin & Langer, 1977). These investigators suggested that one of the reasons for the debilitated condition of many elderly residents of institutions is their perception of having no control. When they had lived in their own homes, dozens of decisions had been required of them every day; the typical institution is a decision-free envi-

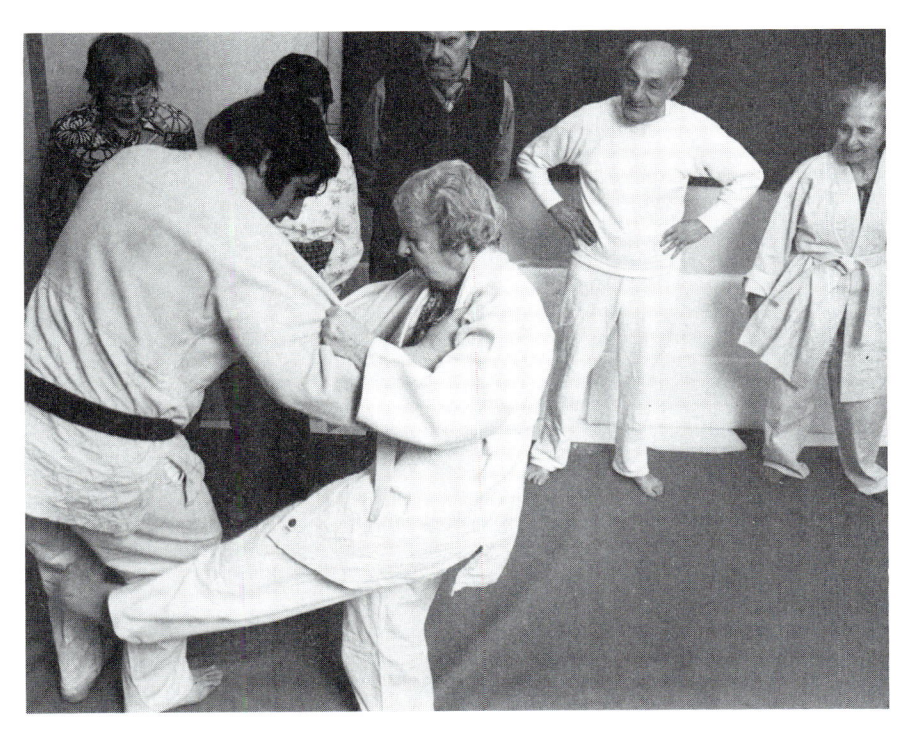

Photo 8–3 Belief in control can alter behavior.

ronment where all the control resides in others. Such psychological factors may be as important as physical factors, or more so, in determining well-being.

To test this hypothesis, Langer and Rodin (1976) gained the cooperation of the staff of a Connecticut nursing home, divided the residents into two groups, and administered one of two communications. Residents of one floor received a message that stressed the staff's responsibility for them and for their activities. Residents were given a plant but were told that the nurses would care for it; they were informed that they would be allowed to see a movie but that the staff would determine what day the movie would be shown. This message minimized the residents' sense of control (and probably paralleled the situation in most nursing homes). Members of the other group, in contrast, were given a communication that emphasized their own responsibility. The message stressed the things that they could do for themselves, from arranging the furniture in their room to deciding how to spend their time, and encouraged the residents to make their complaints known if they were not satisfied with the current arrangements. Members of this group were also given a plant, but they were allowed to pick the plant they wanted and were told that it would be their responsibility to take care of it. Finally, these residents were told that a movie would be shown and that they could decide when and whether they would view it.

In many respects, the communication provided to the experimental group seems quite weak. The defined areas of responsibility are, after all, ones that most of us take for granted. It may be difficult to believe that a specific reminder would have much effect. But it did. Members of the group whose message had stressed personal control reported significant increases in happiness when they were questioned three weeks later. Nurses judged the mental outlook of these residents to be improved and reported substantially increased activity among the group—talking with other patients, visiting people from outside the nursing home, and talking to the staff. Even attendance at the promised movie was greater among those residents who could decide when they would see the film.

More dramatic evidence of the effects of control was found when Rodin and Langer (1977) returned to the nursing home 18 months later. Nurses continued to rate the group whose responsibility had been encouraged as more active, more sociable, and more vigorous; physicians rated their health as better. Most striking of all was the difference in mortality rates. Whereas 30% of the patients in the control group had died in the intervening months, only 15% of the residents in the responsibility group had died. These results provide powerful evidence for the importance of control in a person's life.

Individual Differences in Perceptions of Control

Situational factors can forcefully affect the extent to which we believe we have power over events. It is also true, however, that people vary widely in their general beliefs about control. The general question of individual differences in behavior will be discussed much more extensively in Chapter Thirteen. Here, however, we should give some notice to the idea of **locus of control,** originally proposed by Julian Rotter (1966). Rotter suggested that people have a general tendency to believe that control of the events in their lives is either internal or external. Internal people tend to believe in their own ability to control events; external people believe that other people or events are the primary influences on their own circumstances. Figure 8–3 shows some items from the scale that Rotter developed to measure these general orientations. Although Rotter's ideas are accurate in a general sense, they may be too simplified. A belief in external control, for example, can imply a number of different beliefs: in fate, in powerful others, in a difficult world, in a politically unresponsive world (Collins, 1974; Gurin et al., 1969; Mirels, 1970).

Although the concept of locus of control is not without ambiguity, considerable research has shown that people do differ, often dramatically, in their approach to the world and in their feelings of effectiveness over their environment (Phares, 1976; Strickland, 1977). Individual differences in such beliefs must ultimately be considered in conjunction with those situational factors that make us feel more or less in control of our world.

Reactions to a Loss of Control

Most of us would like to believe that we have control over events, yet such control is not always possible. Often we are faced with situations in which someone else or something else appears to be in control of our fate, and our own freedom of choice is severely limited. In some cases, this sense of another's control may simply be exasperating or frustrating. The social critic L. Rust Hills (1973), for example, con-

The concept of *internal versus external locus of control* (also called "internal versus external control of reinforcement") developed from Julian Rotter's social learning theory (Rotter, 1954; Rotter, Chance, & Phares, 1972).

Rotter's Internal-External (I-E) scale contains pairs of statements about both oneself and people in general. In each case, a respondent is asked to indicate which of the two statements he or she believes more strongly.

1. a. People's misfortunes result from the mistakes they make.
   b. Many of the unhappy things in people's lives are partly due to bad luck.
2. a. With enough effort we can wipe out political corruption.
   b. It is difficult for people to have much control over the things politicians do in office.
3. a. There is a direct connection between how hard I study and the grades I get.
   b. Sometimes I can't understand how teachers arrive at the grades they give.
4. a. What happens to me is my own doing.
   b. Sometimes I feel that I don't have enough control over the direction my life is taking.

Figure 8–3 Internal versus external locus of control

cluded that several "cruel rules" govern social life in the contemporary United States. One of these rules is that "(a) whenever you really feel like going out you don't have an invitation; and in converse: (b) whenever you are invited to go out, you feel like staying at home" (p. 15). In this case, although the belief in control by others may not be overpowering, it can be a source of some annoyance—especially on a Saturday night. In other cases, a perception that others have control over our lives may be much more pervasive. Citizens living under a repressive dictatorship, for example, may feel that they have little control over their daily activities, their conversations, and even their thoughts. How do people cope with such perceptions of loss of control?

A Theory of Reactance

The social psychologist Jack Brehm (1966; Brehm & Brehm, 1981) has proposed the concept of psychological **reactance** to explain some of our reactions to a loss of control or of freedom of choice. According to Brehm, reactance is a motivational state that is aroused whenever a person feels that his or her freedom has been abridged or threatened. Consider the following fairly commonplace example:

> Picture Mr. John Smith, who normally plays golf on Sunday afternoons, although occasionally he spends Sunday afternoon watching television or puttering around his workshop. The important point is that Smith always spends Sunday afternoon doing whichever of these three things he prefers; he is free to choose which he will do. Now consider a specific Sunday morning on which Smith's wife announces that Smith will have to play golf that afternoon since she has invited several of her lady friends to the house for a party. Mr. Smith's freedom is threatened with reduction in several ways: (1) he cannot watch television, (2) he cannot putter in the workshop, and (3) he must (Mrs. Smith says) play golf. [Brehm, 1966, p. 2]

Given this threat to his freedom, reactance theory predicts that Mr. Smith will attempt to restore his personal freedom. He might choose to stay in his workshop, for example, perhaps creating a clamor of protest in the process. Threats to freedom, according to this theory, create a psychological state of reactance, and this motivational state leads the person to take actions that will help to retain control and personal freedom.

The exact actions that the person chooses depend on the nature of the threat and the freedom being threatened. In the face of a threatening communication, for example, a person might change an attitude in a direction opposite to that advocated, thus confirming a sense of independence and control. Another instance of reactance is seen in a situation in which certain alternatives are eliminated, so that our ability to choose freely is threatened. In one experiment, subjects were initially given a choice of record albums and then later told that certain albums would not be available. In reaction to this threat to their freedom, the subjects' feelings toward the threatened options became increasingly positive (Brehm et al., 1966). The effects of restrictions on people's feelings are seen with striking clarity in the case of limitations on the availability of pornography. According to reactance theory, material that is restricted or censored becomes increasingly appealing; in fact, censorship of a message can cause a potential audience to change their attitudes in the direction of the position advocated by the communication, as well as to develop a greater desire to hear the communication (Worchel, Arnold, & Baker, 1975).

Clee and Wicklund (1980) have reviewed a wide variety of areas of consumer behavior in which feelings of reactance may play a role. The high-pressure salesperson, for example, may create reactance by pushing a particular product too hard, thus leading the consumer to prefer an alternative product. Similarly, government regulations or bans may increase the desire for the prohibited product or policy.

We can imagine many other situations in which a threat to freedom or a perception of external control may lead to actions geared to restoring a sense of personal control. A child who is told not to touch the stereo, for example, is likely to make a game of touching the forbidden object. Teenagers show similar behavior when they break a parent's imposed curfew, not because they lost track of time or were involved in anything of interest but simply as a means of demonstrating that they, not their parents, control their activities. Thinking back on your own behavior, you can probably easily think of cases in which reactance was operating, when the sheer sense of control was more important than the particular action you took.

Of course, it is not always to our advantage to be perceived as in control of a situation. If a man pointed a gun in your face and demanded your money, would you try to show that you were in control by wrestling with him? In such cases, in which an attempt to reestablish control could lead to personal injury, people are often willing to acknowledge the other person's control (Grabitz-Gneich, 1971). In still other cases, personal harm may not be likely, but the responsibility for harm to someone else may be equally discomforting. "Passing the buck" is a case in point. Here people voluntarily relinquish control in order to avoid responsibility for some unpleasant outcome (Feldman-Summers, 1977). Thus, in situations that involve negative outcomes and personal responsibility for them, we are willing to forgo a sense of control; in many other cases, however, in which outcomes are positive or simply neutral, we actively attempt to reassert control and preserve our sense of personal freedom.

Learned Helplessness

One aspect of our belief in personal control rests on the fact that outcomes are predictable—the issues of predictability and control are very closely related. Many routines in our life are based on a sense of predictability. If you live in a city that has a subway system, you have probably learned to expect that every time you put a token in the turnstile, it will click, turn, and allow you to board the next train. A failure of the stile to turn when the coin is dropped almost inevitably results in frustration. Such a break in the normal routine threatens both predictability and control. On the one hand, the turnstile did not react as you predicted it would, and, on the other, its recalcitrance casts doubt on your ability to control your own outcomes.

Consider the adventures of Alice in Wonderland. Finding herself in a strange environment, Alice quickly discovers that all is not as she has learned it to be. When she drinks the contents of a bottle labeled "Drink me," she quickly shrinks to a mere ten inches in height. Trying another bottle similarly labeled, Alice grows to gigantic proportions. Such fictional adventures illustrate the principle of *noncontingency:* similar actions do not lead to similar outcomes. There are many situations in life in which people experience such unexpected outcomes.

The result of such experiences is a state that the psychologist Martin Seligman (1975) has termed **learned helplessness,** defined as a belief that one's outcomes are independent of one's actions. The first research on this problem was done with animals. It

Photo 8–4 The adventures of Alice in Wonderland: Experiences with noncontingency

was found that animals that were first exposed to shock that they could not avoid were later unable to learn how to avoid shock when it actually could be avoided. Seligman suggested that three kinds of deficits result from experiences with uncontrollable outcomes. First, motivation is lost: the animal does not *try* to learn new behaviors. The failure to try leads to a cognitive deficit: the animal fails to learn from its experiences. Finally, the learned-helplessness hypothesis suggests that repeated experiences of this kind lead to an emotional deficit: the animal becomes depressed by the inability to control outcomes.

Although this phenomenon would seem to be applicable to humans as well, we cannot make the transfer without considering one additional element—the factors to which a person attributes responsibility for his or her situation. Imagine that you have taken two biology exams and failed them both. In one case you studied hard, and in the other you just glanced at your notes. Nevertheless, you failed both times. Would you experience a state of learned helplessness and depression? The answer depends on the attributions you make to explain your failure. If you made external attributions—for example, the tests were unfair and everyone else failed, too—then you might feel helpless, but you would not take the failure personally. However, if you made an internal attribution, seeing the failure as specific to yourself and not shared by others, then your reaction would probably be more severe. Such attributions to personal helplessness lead to a fourth deficit—lowered self-esteem—and make depression more likely (Abramson, Seligman, & Teasdale, 1978; Peterson & Seligman, 1984).

Thus the experience of learned helplessness in humans depends on a complicated pattern of explanations. Depression will be most severe if unwanted outcomes are attributed (*a*) to internal factors, so that helplessness becomes one's personal problem; (*b*) to stable factors, so that helplessness becomes chronic; and (*c*) to global factors, so that helplessness is generalized to other situations. If you attributed your failure in the exams to your general stu-pidity, you might then avoid not only biology courses but the college curriculum in general.

A crowded environment may affect a person's ability to regulate social control and thus contribute to a feeling of learned helplessness. Rodin (1976), for example, found that children who lived in a high-density residence were less likely to assume control of outcomes than children who lived in less densely populated settings, and they performed more poorly on puzzles. Patients in hospitals, who have little control over their environment, show progressively greater deficits in performance as the length of their hospitalization increases, even though their physical condition may be improving (Raps et al., 1982).

But why do people fall with such apparent ease into a state of learned helplessness? Why don't they react against the situation, as reactance theory suggests they should? Sometimes they do. In a situation in which the person had no initial belief in control, learned helplessness may be the immediate response (see Figure 8–4). In contrast, Camille Wortman and Jack Brehm (1975) predict that "reactance will precede helplessness for individuals who originally expect control" (p. 308). In a field study of this hypothesis, Andrew Baum and his colleagues selected residents of college dormitories who lived either in large or in moderate-sized groups and for whom the architecture of the building (long- or short-corridor design) either facilitated a sense of control and predictability in their interactions or diminished such a sense of control (Baum, Aiello, & Calesnick, 1978). Taking these subjects into the laboratory to perform a standard social task that allowed either cooperation or competition, the experimenters considered the per-

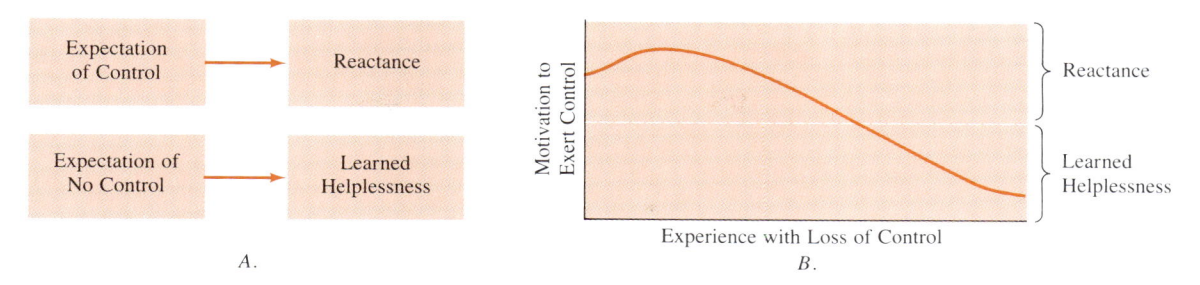

Figure 8–4 Reactance and learned helplessness. The basic principle, as shown in panel *A*, is that a person who expects to be able to control a situation will experience reactance, while a person who does not have such expectations will experience learned helplessness. As the graph in panel *B* shows, the shift from reactance to learned helplessness may be gradual.

formance of subjects as a function of the length of time they had lived in the residence halls—either one, three, or seven weeks. Students who had lived in the long-corridor dormitories for shorter periods of time (either one or three weeks) reported negative feelings about their living conditions, but at the same time they engaged in highly competitive behavior, which suggested an attempt to assert control. After living in the low-control situation for several more weeks, however, the students seemed to abandon some of their attempts at control. They became less negative and more accepting of the conditions, and their play in the game became less competitive, less involved and motivated, and more withdrawn. Thus in the initial weeks the students appeared to experience reactance—they attempted to restore their belief in freedom and their feeling of control. But because their attempts presumably led to little success, the outcomes regulated by the facts of the dormitory design, attempts to gain control were replaced by feelings of resignation and helplessness. Residents of short-corridor dormitories, in contrast, perceived no problems of control, and their behavior was more adaptive than the other residents' and did not change over the course of the study.

Self-Induced Dependence

Uncontrollable outcomes are one source of feelings of a loss of control. Other situations can also create such feelings, and the illusion of incompetence as well. Other people, for example, may imply or suggest directly that a person is incompetent, and that belief may be incorporated by the person himself or herself. Ellen Langer (1983) has suggested that part of the apparent dysfunction of the elderly may result directly from the experience of being labeled as incompetent. As a society, we tend to disparage the elderly, assuming that they are past their prime, incapable of any significant physical or mental activity, and generally dependent on the aid of friends, relatives, and institutional personnel. Such assumptions not only are inaccurate, Langer argues, but may create the conditions that they presuppose. The elderly themselves, labeled as dependent, may come to believe the label.

The reality of such self-induced dependence is made clear in a study by Langer and Benevento (1978). They gave male high school students the opportunity to perform a set of word-hunt problems and to experience success at the task. In a second phase, each boy worked in a team with another male (actually a confederate of the experimenter). By a predetermined draw, the student was assigned the role of assistant, and the confederate was assigned the role of boss. After working on a second task in the role of assistant, the subjects once again worked individually on the word-hunt task they had performed earlier. As Figure 8–5 shows, the performance of these boys dropped by 50%—they located only half as many roles—after they had experienced a dependent role. In contrast, boys who had not par-

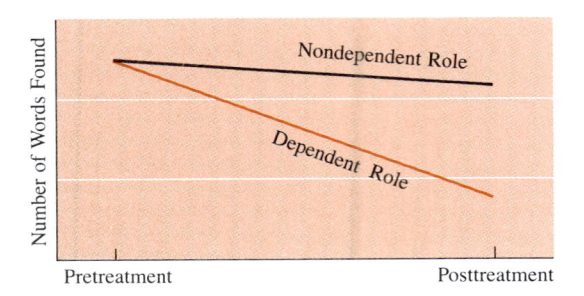

Figure 8–5 Effect of experience in a dependent role on performance on a word-hunt task

ticipated in the assistant role performed as well as they had earlier.

Perhaps the most surprising aspect of this experiment is how strong the performance effects were after only a brief experience in the role of assistant. We can easily imagine how pervasive and powerful induced dependence effects can be in the elderly and in other people who are forced to adopt a dependent role.

Summary

The issues of social influence and personal control are central to human behavior.

Conformity is a yielding to group pressure when no direct request to comply with the group is made. Asch conducted some of the earliest studies demonstrating the effect of a group's judgments on the behavior of the individual. A group can exert two kinds of influence on the individual: informational influence, based on facts, and normative influence, based on social pressure.

Nonconformity behavior can be of two types. Independent behavior is that which occurs with no reference to the group position. A person who engages in anticonformity behavior, in contrast, does exactly the opposite of what the group does; thus the group is still serving as a reference point for the individual's behavior. Later investigators have shown that a variety of situational factors—such as group size, number of persons who agree with the individual, status of the group members, and type of task—can affect the degree of conformity.

Compliance is behavior that occurs in response to a direct request. The foot-in-the-door technique consists of a small request followed by a substantially larger one. Agreement with the first request increases the probability of compliance with the second request. The door-in-the-face effect works in the opposite way. In this case, the person who initially refuses a fairly large request is more likely to agree to a subsequent smaller request. A third technique for inducing compliance is the low-ball procedure, in which initial commitment to a behavior correlates with increased probability of compliance when the costs are increased.

Although compliance with some requests appears to be relatively mindless, occurring without conscious thought, other acts of compliance evidence considerable thought, as when we evaluate the kind and amount of power that the agent has over our own situation.

Obedience studies show that most people readily follow orders even when their compliance may cause harm to another person. Obedience declines when the victim is near to the subject and when the person who has issued the orders is not physically present.

Criticisms of the obedience studies focus on ethical questions and on their generalizability.

In the face of pressures for conformity, compliance, and obedience, people maintain a pervasive belief in their own control. Even when outcomes are obviously determined by chance, people have an illusion of control. Some of the factors that strengthen this illusion are competition, involvement in the task, knowledge and practice, and the similarity of the situation to a task requiring skill.

Belief in personal control improves performance and makes feelings more positive. Individuals vary in their perceptions of control; some people are inclined to believe in external control, and others believe strongly in internal control.

Because belief in personal control is so pervasive, people often react strongly to a perceived or real loss of control. Psychological reactance is a motivational state that is aroused whenever a person feels that his or her freedom has been abridged. According to reactance theory, people will attempt to restore their sense of freedom when they perceive such threats. In some cases, however, as when insistence on control may bring harm to oneself or to others, people are often willing to accept the control of others.

Learned helplessness is induced by situations in which outcomes are not contingent on one's own behavior. People who experience such apparently random outcomes may develop the belief that their own responses have no effect on subsequent outcomes. A variety of deficits may result—motivational, cognitive, emotional, and loss of self-esteem, depending on the factors to which one attributes one's loss of control.

Self-induced dependence may develop even when outcomes are not random. Labeling people as dependent can cause decrements in subsequent behavior, apparently because the labeled person begins to believe that the outcomes of his or her own behavior depend primarily on the actions of others.

Glossary Terms

anticonformity
autokinetic effect
compliance
conformity
door-in-the-face effect
foot-in-the-door effect
learned helplessness
locus of control
obedience
reactance

Nobody loves me well do I know,
Don't all the cold world tell me so?
Hattie Starr

Love is much nicer to be in than an automobile
accident, a tight girdle, a higher tax bracket, or a
holding pattern over Philadelphia.
Judith Viorst

Constantin Brancusi, *The Kiss*, 1908. Philadelphia Museum of Art, The Louise and Walter Arensberg Collection.

CHAPTER NINE

Affiliation, Attraction, & Love

I. Alone or Together?
   Loneliness
   Reasons for Affiliation
   Affiliation Patterns and Social Networks
II. Attraction
   The Basis of Initial Attraction
   Theoretical Models of Attraction
III. Close Relationships
   Friendship
   Conceptions and Measurements of Love
   Mate Selection
   Stages in the Development of Love
IV. Falling Out of Love
   Breaking Up Is Hard to Do
   Inequity and Impermanence
   Marriage and Divorce
V. Summary

"People who need people are the luckiest people in the world," a popular song tells us. But doesn't everyone need people? In the science fiction scenario presented in Chapter One, we imagined a world in which a single person existed. Many of the social behaviors that we have already considered would be difficult or impossible in such a world: impressions of others, communication, persuasive messages, and power relationships would make no sense in the absence of others. We truly need people, for we are social beings.

Interpersonal relationships take many forms. Some people are only casual acquaintances; others become spouses or lovers. Some relationships last; others end in boredom or distress. And sometimes we may be lonely, wanting relationships we do not have. These many forms of interpersonal involvement are the concern of this chapter.

Alone or Together?

Suppose you have been offered $50 a day to remain in a room by yourself. You are free to leave whenever you want. The room has no windows but is equipped with a lamp, a bed, a chair, a table, and bathroom facilities. Food is brought at mealtime and left outside your door, but you see no one. You are allowed no companions, no telephone, no books, magazines, or newspapers, and no radio or television. If you were to volunteer for such a project, how long could you remain?

In an effort to understand people's need to affiliate with other people, Stanley Schachter (1959) placed five male students in a setting similar to the one described. All the participants were volunteers. One of them was able to remain in the room for only 20 minutes before he had an uncontrollable desire to leave. Three volunteers remained in their rooms for two days. Afterward, one of these students said that he had become quite uneasy and would not want to do it again, but the other two seemed rather unaffected by their isolation. The fifth volunteer remained in isolation for eight days. On his release the student admitted that he was growing uneasy and nervous, but no serious effects from the isolation were observed.

These five students differed in their reactions to isolation—in this case, isolation in a strange room arranged by an experimenter. In other circumstances, people also have varying reactions to isolation. Some people, as Peter Suedfeld (1982) notes, seek out isolation, finding it exhilarating, stimulating, or

Photo 9–1 Being alone is not the same as being lonely.

Loneliness

Being alone is not the same as being lonely. Aloneness is an objective state, easily assessed by any observer. Loneliness is a subjective experience and depends on our interpretations of events. Many definitions of loneliness have been offered (Peplau & Perlman, 1982). Although the definitions vary in subtle ways, most of them touch on three particular elements. First, as we have indicated, loneliness is a subjective experience; we cannot measure it by simply observing whether someone is alone or with other people. Second, loneliness generally results from some deficiencies in a person's social relationships. Third, loneliness is unpleasant. It plunged Holden Caulfield, in J. D. Salinger's *Catcher in the Rye*, into despair: "I was crying and all. I don't know why, but I was. I guess it was because I was feeling so damn depressed and lonesome" (Salinger, 1953, p. 138). Although a feeling of loneliness does not always lead to such anguish, it is, by definition, always an unpleasant experience.

Carin Rubenstein and Phillip Shaver (1982) asked people to describe in detail the feelings they experienced when they were lonely. Four general factors emerged from these descriptions: desperation, in the sense of being panicked and helpless; depression; impatient boredom; and self-deprecation. Although each of these factors taps a slightly different emotion, all of them reflect the unhappiness inherent in being lonely.

Why do people get lonely? Robert Weiss (1973) has suggested that there are two general types of loneliness: emotional and social. *Emotional loneliness* is caused by the lack of a close, intimate attachment to one particular person. Anyone who does not have such a relationship but wishes to have one is subject to this type of loneliness. The recently widowed or divorced person is especially prone to this

conducive to religious experience. The explorer, the artist, the mystic may all seek extensive amounts of time to be alone. Yet other people find that being isolated from other people can be deeply disturbing.

form of loneliness. *Social loneliness* results from an absence of friends and relatives, or of some form of social network in which activities and interests can be shared. One kind of loneliness can be quite independent of the other type (Russell et al., 1984). A student may live in a dormitory, for example, eating, studying, and having bull sessions with friends, and yet feel emotionally isolated without an intimate relationship with one special person.

Just as the causes of loneliness vary, so do people's reactions to it. Some people, particularly those who are severely lonely, are likely to sink into a sad passivity. Crying, sleeping, drinking, taking tranquilizers, and just watching television aimlessly are typical responses. Other responses to loneliness may be more active and probably more helpful. Some people, despite their solitude, engage in activities, such as working on a hobby, studying, exercising, or going to a movie; others (particularly those with high incomes) go on shopping sprees; still others attempt social contact, calling someone on the telephone or paying a visit (Rubinstein & Shaver, 1982).

Some types of people are more prone to loneliness than others; some types of situations are more likely to cause feelings of loneliness than others. An important distinction to be made here is the difference between *trait loneliness* and *state loneliness* (Shaver, 1982). Trait loneliness is a stable pattern of feeling lonely, which often changes little with the situation. In general, people who are low in self-esteem, generally viewing themselves in negative terms, are more likely to report being lonely (Jones, Freemon, & Goswick, 1981; Peplau, Miceli, & Morasch, 1982). People who report having meaningful interactions with other people are less likely to experience loneliness; conversely, lonely people report a lack of intimate self-disclosure with close friends (Solano, Batten, & Parish, 1982).

Women and men appear to experience loneliness with approximately the same frequency, yet women are more likely than men to label themselves as lonely. More of the lonely men deny their loneliness. Why this difference in honesty of self-appraisal? Primarily, research suggests, because a lonely man is less acceptable and more likely to be socially rejected than is a lonely woman (Borys & Perlman, 1985). Gender stereotypes hold that expressions of emotional weakness are less appropriate for men than for women, and the man who says he is lonely defies that expectation.

State loneliness is a more temporary experience, often caused by some dramatic change in one's life. Students, for example, often experience state loneliness when they enter college, leaving behind the familiarity of home and high school and entering a new and often bewildering environment. This loneliness often goes away as new social networks are established (Shaver, 1982).

Coping with loneliness depends in large measure on the factors to which the person attributes his or her unhappiness. Students who blame their own deficiencies for their loneliness are more likely to remain unhappy. The person who sees loneliness as only a temporary state is less likely to remain unhappy and may be more apt to take corrective actions. One of the best counters to loneliness is the establishment of meaningful relationships with friends. It is the presence of friends, rather than relatives or romantic partners, that most clearly distinguishes between the lonely college student and the contented college student (Cutrona, 1982).

It is often thought that age is related to loneliness and that old people are the most unhappy of all. However, research shows that this common assumption is not true, as Figure 9-1 indicates. In fact, reported loneliness seems to decrease as people get older, perhaps because older people have developed a more stable network of relationships. Younger people, in contrast, are often still trying to establish such networks, and experience loneliness in the process.

Reasons for Affiliation

Contacts with other people are often an antidote for loneliness, especially social loneliness. But what are the reasons for affiliation? What do we gain from social interaction that we cannot experience alone? **Social comparison theory,** introduced in Chapter Three, proposes that we look to other people as a way to evaluate our own attitudes and abilities. In the absence of objective measures of evaluation, social interaction provides a subjective measuring tool.

Affiliation also serves to reduce anxiety. We saw earlier that the initial reaction to isolation may be a state of extreme anxiety. If so, Stanley Schachter reasoned, perhaps the reverse is true as well: anxiety may lead to a desire for affiliation. In his initial study, Schachter (1959) told female introductory psychology students at the University of Minnesota that they would receive a series of electrical shocks. Subjects in the "high anxiety" condition were told that the shocks would be painful but would cause no permanent damage. Subjects in the "low anxiety" condition, in contrast, were led to expect virtually painless shocks that would feel, at worst, like a tickle. After receiving this description, the students were told that there would be a ten-minute delay while the equipment was set up. Each subject was allowed to choose whether she would wait by herself or with some of the other subjects in the same experiment. After the subjects had made their choices, the experiment was terminated. Schachter's concern was only with the choices that subjects would make, and no shocks were administered.

As Schachter predicted, the level of induced anxiety influenced the waiting preferences. Of the 32 subjects in the high-anxiety condition, 20 wanted to wait with other subjects; only 10 of the 30 subjects in the low-anxiety condition chose to wait with others. The adage "Misery loves company" was confirmed.

What is it about being with others that makes affiliation so desirable for highly anxious subjects? There are at least two possible explanations. First, the presence of others may serve as a distraction, allowing the subject to forget temporarily about the impending shocks. Alternatively, people in this situation may be unsure of their reactions and seek out other people as a means of social comparison. If the first explanation is true, then any other person would be

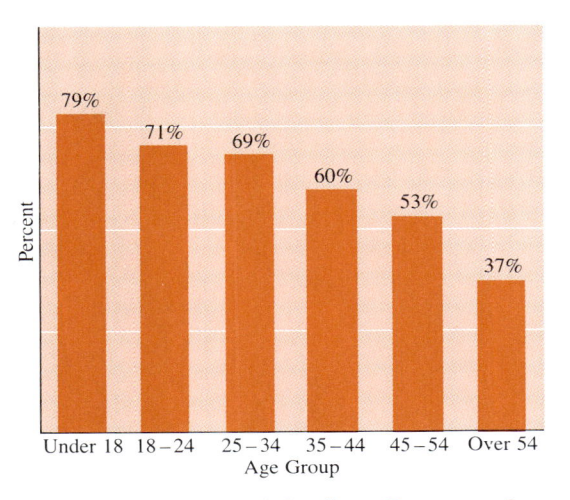

Figure 9-1 Age trends in loneliness: Percentage of people who say they feel lonely sometimes or often.

Photo 9–2 Does misery love company?

desirable. But if social comparison is critical, then it would be important to seek out people who were in a similar situation.

To test out these two explanations, Schachter (1959) conducted a second experiment. This time all subjects were told that they would receive painful shocks; hence all subjects were in a high-anxiety condition. Each subject was given the choice of waiting alone or with others, but the characteristics of the others were varied. Some subjects were given the choice of waiting alone or waiting with other female students who were taking part in the same experiment. Other subjects could wait either alone or with female students who were not participating in the experiment but instead were waiting to see their faculty advisers.

The results of the study were clear. Subjects who had the opportunity to wait with others in the same experiment showed a clear preference for doing so. In contrast, subjects who could wait with students not involved in the experiment showed a unanimous preference for waiting alone. These findings suggest that distraction is *not* an explanation of the link between anxiety and affiliation. Further, instead of concluding that misery loves company, Schachter suggests it is more appropriate to say that "misery loves miserable company."

A third explanation for Schachter's results does not require the company to be miserable—only to be in the same situation. Faced with an unfamiliar situation, people may seek cognitive clarity—in other words, they may want to know more about the situation. Babies, for example, often turn to their mothers when unexpected or novel events occur. In the same manner, college students faced with electrical shock may seek the company of others in order to appraise the situation (Shaver & Klinnert, 1982). More generally, people in a stressful situation tend to seek out someone who will help them to cope with the stress. In some cases, they may seek a very competent and intelligent person; in other cases, they may prefer a warm and supportive person (Rofé, 1984).

Electric shocks in a psychology laboratory are far removed from most people's lives. Can the relationship between stress and affiliative behavior be generalized to the more ordinary circumstances of daily life? Investigators have often considered this question in terms of the more general concept of **social support,** defined as the benefits that can be gained through interaction with others. As one way of exploring this relationship, Carolyn Cutrona (1986) asked college students at the University of Iowa to keep a daily record of social interactions and stressful experiences for 14 consecutive days. When she analyzed these records, Cutrona found a significant relationship between social interaction and stress. Behaviors reflecting a felt need for both emotional support and informational support were more likely to occur following stress than in the absence of stressful events. Thus when people are under stress, they do seek out other people, and for good reason. Other people, and the resources that they offer, may serve as a *buffer*, reducing the impact of the stressful event (Cohen & Wills, 1985).

Of course, people's reasons for affiliation are not limited to the reduction of stress and anxiety. People affiliate with others because they like them, enjoy their company, and share their interests. On other occasions, people may affiliate with others in order to gain approval or to develop an identity that can be achieved only in interaction with other people. Learning theories suggest that other people are reinforcing, serving as rewards in and of themselves. In summary, affiliation is motivated by a variety of needs and desires, each of which increases the likelihood of social interaction.

Affiliation Patterns and Social Networks

To understand patterns of affiliation, investigators have begun in their own backyards—on the college campuses where they are located. Bibb Latané and Liane Bidwell (1977), for example, observed people in a variety of locations on the Ohio State and University of North Carolina campuses, recording whether each person they observed was alone or in the presence of other people. Overall, about 60% of the people they saw were with at least one other person. Interestingly, women were much more likely to be with other people than men were, suggesting that, at least in public places, women may affiliate more than men.

Looking more closely at social interaction patterns, Ladd Wheeler and John Nezlek (1977) asked first-year college students to keep track of all interactions that they had during two-week periods in both the fall and the spring semesters. The advantage of this strategy over simple observation is that data could be collected for a single person over a longer period, and private as well as public affiliation patterns could be tapped. The possible disadvantage of this method is that the investigator had to rely on self-report data, whose shortcomings were discussed in Chapter Two. By limiting the interactions to those that lasted ten minutes or more, the investigators hoped to focus on situations in which affiliation was actually occurring, as opposed to the casual exchanges involved in such activities as getting a homework assignment and checking a book out of the library. Same-sex affiliation was more common among these students: 56% of their interactions were with a person of the same sex. During the first semester, the women students spent significantly more time engaged in some kind of interaction than the men; but by the second semester this difference had disappeared. As one explanation of this difference, Wheeler and Nezlek suggest that women may be more likely to look to social interaction as a way to deal with the initial stress of adjusting to college.

Patterns of affiliation are not random, of course. We systematically establish links with particular people whom we find rewarding, and we try to avoid contact with people whose companionship is less enjoyable. The term **social network** refers to those persons with whom an individual is in actual contact (Berscheid, 1985), and analysis of these networks looks at the question of "who" as well as "how often."

When people move to a new location, their social networks inevitably change. New people are added to the network and others may gradually be dropped. Entering college is one such point in most people's lives, although the experience may be quite different for the student who has moved away from home and into a dormitory than for the student who remains at home and commutes to the university. Robert Hays and Diana Oxley (1986), who studied these two types of experiences among first-year university students, found, not surprisingly, that the social networks of commuters were initially more intimate, as they maintained connections with old friends and relatives more easily. The resident students required more time to establish social networks, and the networks they eventually established included a much greater proportion of new acquaintances. Their networks were also more centered on campus activities and relaxation. The networks of male and female students differed in some respects. Women interacted more frequently and exchanged more informational and emotional support, a finding that is consistent with frequent reports of greater emotional expressiveness among women.

Little research on social networks has been done outside of the college campus. In one of the few studies to consider a broader range of people, Booth (1972) interviewed 800 adults in Nebraska. He found that although men and women reported having a similar number of close friends, women had closer and more frequent contact with their friends and relatives than men did. It is risky, of course, to conclude anything about basic gender differences, because the occupational statuses of the men and women in this sample were very different. Most of the men were employed outside the home, whereas the majority of the women were homemakers and may have had more flexible schedules that allowed them to develop and maintain friendships of a close and personal nature.

These studies begin to provide us with a picture of human social interaction. It is interesting to note how often we choose to be with someone of the same sex. Although opposite-sex interactions frequently draw more attention, affiliation with someone of the same sex is an obviously important aspect of many people's social life.

Attraction

So far we have considered why people choose to affiliate with other people, and we have looked at some of the general patterns of social interaction. Yet, given the general need for affiliation, how do people choose which people they want to be with? Why are they friendly with or attracted to some people, while they reject or dislike others? In this section we move from the general nature of affiliation to the specific reaction of attraction.

The Basis of Initial Attraction

What characteristics make people attractive to us? To understand the basis of initial attraction, unconfounded by past knowledge and experience, psychologists have often brought strangers together in the laboratory and studied the features that are associated with greater or lesser liking. On the basis of this research, we can say that the odds are in favor of our liking a person if that person—

1. has similar beliefs, values, and personality characteristics;
2. satisfies our needs;
3. is physically attractive;
4. is pleasant or agreeable;
5. reciprocates our liking; and
6. is in geographical proximity to us.

Let's consider each of these factors in turn.

Similarity of beliefs, values, and personality. We like people whose attitudes and values agree with ours, and we dislike those who disagree with us (Byrne, 1971). If their personalities are like ours, the attraction is even stronger. Most of the early studies that demonstrated this relationship were done in the laboratory and were based on descriptions of hypothetical persons. A subject might be told, for example, that another person shared his or her beliefs on 80% of the attitude issues on which both had been polled; in a comparison condition, the alleged similarity might be only 20%. In general, the former condition resulted in greater attraction toward the other person (hypothetical, in this case).

Field studies provide a broader view of this relationship. In an early field study, Theodore Newcomb (1961) gave male college students free housing if they agreed to fill out seemingly endless questionnaires about their attitudes and their liking for their housemates. The results of this massive study showed generally that men whose attitudes were similar at the beginning of the semester came to like each other more by the end of the testing period. More recently Kandel (1978) conducted an extensive questionnaire study with over 1,800 male and female adolescents aged 13–18. By comparing the attitudes and values of each student with those of his or her best friend, she was able to show strong support for the similarity relationship. Some areas of similarity were more important than others, however. Best friends were most apt to be similar with respect to such demographic variables as grade, sex, race, and age. Friends also tended to have similar attitudes toward drug use, although they did not always share attitudes toward parents and teachers.

Looking at a broader range of characteristics, Hill and Stull (1981) questioned college roommates representing both sexes, all years, and a variety of religious and ethnic backgrounds. Among female roommates, similarity in values was very important. Value similarity was very high among pairs who had chosen to be roommates, and it was also influential in predicting which assigned roommates decided to stay together. Sharing values with others was less important for men—additional evidence that women and men tend to define and experience friendship differently.

The relationship between interpersonal attraction and similarity is a two-sided coin. On the one hand, as the evidence described above has shown, people seem to like and feel attracted toward people who are similar to them. On the other hand, the relationship can also be explained by reference to the other side of the coin: people dislike those who are dissimilar to them. Milton Rosenbaum (1986) has argued that this is the stronger force in interpersonal encounters, suggesting that dissimilarity leads to repulsion. Those who are dissimilar to us represent threats; they challenge our beliefs and pose possible impediments to our goals. The motivation to avoid such people could in some cases be stronger than the need to find people who are similar.

People who are dissimilar to us are not always disliked, however. In fact, on some occasions we even *prefer* the dissimilar person. For example, if a person is stigmatized (Novak & Lerner, 1968) or is of lower status (Karuza & Brickman, 1978), we may prefer that person to be dissimilar to us in attitudes, perhaps because too much similarity to a less desirable person is threatening to our self-image. Furthermore, even our initial tendency to dislike those who are dissimilar to us can be modified, and often quite easily. Simply having the opportunity to predict a person's attitudes (Aderman, Bryant, & Donelsmith, 1978) or being allowed to discuss areas of disagreement (Brink, 1977) will substantially increase our liking for the initially dissimilar person.

Complementarity of need systems. There are also times when opposites attract. According to the theory of need **complementarity,** people choose relationships in which their basic needs can be mutually gratified (Winch, Ktsanes, & Ktsanes, 1954). Sometimes the result of such a choice is a pairing of apparent opposites, as when a very dominant person is attracted to a very submissive partner. At other times the opposition may be more apparent than real, as when women with traditional views of their own roles prefer men with traditionally masculine attributes (Seyfried & Hendrick, 1973). In this case, both partners believe in traditional sex roles, but the specific characteristics they favor in themselves are opposite to those they favor in their partners. There is some evidence that the complementarity principle operates in long-term relationships (Kerckhoff & Davis, 1962); however, it probably operates only on a few dimensions and in a limited number of situations (Levinger, Senn, & Jorgensen, 1970).

One reason for the ambiguous findings in this area is that investigators have failed to consider the total picture of needs in a relationship. Needs exist in various domains, and the resources that one person brings to the relationship may be exchanged for some virtue in another area (Foa, 1971). In an intriguing demonstration of this more complex pattern of needs, Harrison and Saeed (1977) examined 800 advertisements in the lonely-hearts column of a widely circulated weekly tabloid. By analyzing both what people offered (such as the "good company" offered by a "good-looking woman of high moral standards") and what they sought ("wealthy older man with good intentions"), these investigators discovered some interesting aspects of the exchange relationship in male/female pairs. For example, women were more likely to offer physical attractiveness, and men were more likely to seek it. In similar fashion, men were more likely to offer financial security and women to request it. Supporting the similarity principle, good-looking advertisers of both sexes sought a good-looking partner. Further, some evidence of the more complex exchanges that may occur was shown by the self-described attractive women who sought financially well-to-do men (see also Box 9–1).

Thus both similarity and complementarity may play some role in attraction. To date, however, the evidence for similarity is much stronger and more broadly based, applying to both same-sex and opposite-sex friendships in both laboratory and field settings. Complementarity, in contrast, has been found primarily in romantic heterosexual pairings, and we don't know how important it is either in same-sex friendships or in homosexual romantic pairs.

Physical attractiveness. Aristotle wrote that "beauty is a greater recommendation than any letter of introduction," and things have not changed much in the last 2,300 years. As we discussed in Chapter Four, physical appearance is one of the first things that we notice about another person. The vast amounts of

Box 9-1
Courtship in the personal column

Do heterosexual and homosexual persons look for the same qualities in a prospective partner? Kay Deaux and Randall Hanna (1984) considered this question by analyzing the same material that Harrison and Saeed (1977) used—namely, personal advertisements in newspapers. These investigators gathered 800 such ads, representing equal numbers of heterosexual females, homosexual females, heterosexual males, and homosexual males. Each ad was coded in terms of what the person requested and what was offered.

Heterosexuals and homosexuals did differ in some respects. In general, heterosexuals sought a broader range of characteristics, more often mentioning attractiveness, personality, hobbies, financial status, and religion than the homosexual advertisers. In contrast, homosexuals were more likely to seek particular sexual habits and characteristics.

In many respects, gender was more influential than sexual orientation. Men, whether homosexual or heterosexual, were more likely to seek physical attractiveness and to describe themselves in physical terms. Women were more likely to mention psychological characteristics when describing both what they offered and what they sought.

Looking just at the heterosexual advertisers, we find results similar to those of Harrison and Saeed (1977). Heterosexual women were most likely to offer physical attractiveness and to seek financial security, while heterosexual men offered financial status and security and provided objective physical descriptors.

Homosexual advertisers showed some interesting differences. Physical characteristics were much less important to homosexual women than to heterosexual women; the lesbians placed greater emphasis on hobbies, interests, and sincerity in the prospective relationship. Although physical appearance was downplayed by the homosexual women, it was emphasized by the homosexual men. The latter group mentioned physical characteristics most often, and personality factors seemed to be much less important than they were for the heterosexual men. Sexuality was also a more central issue for the male homosexuals than for any other group.

As we can see, interpersonal attraction is not a simple process. Both gender and sexual preference influence one's choices. What is highly important to one person may be merely incidental to another.

---

money spent on cosmetics, plastic surgery, diet foods, and contemporary fashions attest to the degree of concern people invest in presenting a favorable image.

Such investments seem to pay off, because there is an implicit assumption in our society that "what is beautiful is good" (Dion, Berscheid, & Walster, 1972). As one example, Karen Dion (1972) showed college women some photographs of children who had allegedly misbehaved. Some of the children were physically attractive and others were not. Particularly when the misbehavior was severe, the beautiful children were given the benefit of the doubt. Respondents tended to disregard the misbehavior of the attractive children, whereas less beautiful children who committed the same acts were called maladjusted and deviant. Even children themselves are aware of these differences: children as young as 3 years prefer pretty children to less attractive peers (Dion, 1977).

Interestingly, the reverse statement is true as well: What is good is beautiful. People we like for other reasons are often believed to have attractive physical features (Gross & Crofton, 1977). Junior high school students who are perceived to excel in athletic ability

Photo 9–3 We are beckoned by the physically attractive in the hope that their attractiveness will "rub off."

or academic ability, for example, are considered more attractive than their peers who are not so outstanding (Felson & Bohrnstedt, 1979).

One reason we are beckoned by the physically attractive lies in our hope that their attractiveness will "rub off" on us. Many years ago the sociologist W. W. Waller (1937) observed that we gain a great deal of prestige by being seen with an attractive person of the other sex. This "rating and dating" complex has been verified in more recent research. A man makes the most favorable impression on observers when he is accompanied by a good-looking woman. He is viewed most negatively when his female companion is physically unattractive (Sigall & Landy, 1973). Such "rub-off" effects may be one-sided, however. Although men gain in likability when their female partner is highly attractive, women do not necessarily receive equal benefits. Daniel Bar-Tal and Leonard Saxe (1976) showed subjects slides of presumably married couples, in which the husband and the wife varied in physical attractiveness. The unattractive man who was paired with an attractive wife was judged to have the highest income, the greatest professional success, and the highest intelligence. In contrast, the unattractive woman paired with an attractive husband gained no advantage by the pairing—she was judged solely on her own level of attractiveness.

Although women may not gain from having an attractive partner, physical attractiveness is not unimportant for the man himself. Harry Reis and his colleagues have found that the more attractive a man is, the more social interaction he has with women—and the less he has with other men. Somewhat surprisingly, the amount of a woman's social interaction is unrelated to her physical attractiveness. For both sexes, however, attractiveness is associated with the *quality* of social interactions: highly attractive people report more satisfaction and more pleasurable interactions (Reis, Nezlek, & Wheeler, 1980; Reis et al., 1982).

But what causes this sex difference, somewhat contrary to popular wisdom? At least part of the answer lies in the relationship between physical attractiveness and feelings of social competence. For men these two characteristics are related, and attractive men are likely to be more assertive and less fearful of women. The association is just the opposite among women: attractive women are less assertive and are less likely to initiate contacts with men.

Pleasant or agreeable characteristics. Not surprisingly, we like people who are nice or who do nice things. As we discussed in Chapter Four, personality characteristics vary in their likability, and we will be more attracted to someone who has positive traits than to someone who demonstrates more negative habits (Kaplan & Anderson, 1973). Beyond evaluating the characteristics of another person in and of themselves, however, we are also concerned with the interpersonal implications of those traits (Clore & Kerber, 1978). In other words, when we evaluate another person's characteristics, we give some consideration to what those traits or behaviors mean for us. For example, "considerate" not only is a favorable description of another person but also implies that we ourselves will receive some positive outcomes from interaction with that person. At the more negative pole, we tend to be least attracted to persons who can be described in terms that not only suggest negative aspects of their personality but imply negative consequences for us as well (such as "unappreciative" or "dishonest").

Reciprocal liking. We are attracted to people who like us. Heider's balance theory, presented in Chapter Seven, predicts, for example, that if Susan likes herself and Bonnie likes Susan, a cognitively balanced state will result in which Susan likes Bonnie in return. In other words, liking and disliking are often reciprocal. If members of a discussion group are told that other group members like them very much, they are most likely to choose those same members when asked to form smaller groups later in the experimental session (Backman & Secord, 1959). The opposite is also true: we tend to dislike those people who have indicated negative feelings toward us. Finally, our tendency toward balance can be taken one step further, as illustrated by the maxim "My enemy's enemy is my friend." Two persons who share in their dislike for a third person will tend to be more attracted to each other than those who do not share this bond (Aronson & Cope, 1968).

Propinquity. All else being equal, we tend to like people who live close to us better than those who are at some distance. This factor of **propinquity** has even been set to music, as in the song from *Finian's Rainbow* that says "When I'm not near the one I love, I love the one I'm near." More recently, Stephen Stills has advised us to love the one we're with. At a more scientific level, Festinger, Schachter, and Back (1950) found that residents of an apartment complex were more apt to like and interact with those who lived on the same floor of the building than with people who lived on other floors or in other buildings. Members of Air Force bomber crews develop closer relationships with co-workers who are stationed near them than with co-workers stationed a few yards away (Kipnis, 1957). And students in a classroom where alphabetical seating is required are more likely to report friendships with people whose names begin with the same letter than with those whose names are at some distance away in the class roll (Byrne, 1961).

Why is propinquity a factor in attraction? The effect may be due in part to simple familiarity. A mass of evidence indicates the existence of a **mere exposure effect**; that is, repeated exposure to the same stimulus leads to greater attraction toward that object (Harrison, 1977; Saegert, Swap, & Zajonc, 1973). The sense of familiarity that is created by frequent contact may be comforting and thereby increase attractiveness. Simply having another person respond to one's behavior—an event whose likelihood increases with the frequency of contact—may also make that person more attractive in our eyes (Davis, 1982). Frequency of interaction can also affect perceptions of similarity and thereby increase the attractiveness that we feel for another (Moreland & Zajonc, 1982). Even the anticipation of interaction seems to increase our liking for another person (Darley & Berscheid, 1967), particularly when the person is either initially disliked or ambivalently valued. As Tyler and Sears (1977) suggest, we may even come to like obnoxious people when we know that we must live with them.

Theoretical Models of Attraction

A variety of antecedent conditions influence interpersonal attraction. Psychologists have developed a number of theoretical models that help to explain why these and other factors are effective. The consistency models introduced in our discussion of attitude change (Chapter Seven), for example, suggest that attraction can develop as we seek consistency among attitudes toward various persons and issues.

Some of the other theoretical models rely on principles of reinforcement and exchange, introduced in Chapter One. Three of these models will be considered in more detail here: reinforcement/affect theory, social exchange theory, and interdependence theory.

Reinforcement/affect theory. Perhaps the most basic explanation of interpersonal attraction relies on the concept of reinforcement—that we like people who reward us and dislike people who punish us. Donn Byrne and Gerald Clore (1970) conceptualize interpersonal attraction as a basic learning process. This model assumes that most stimuli can be classified as rewards or punishment, and it assumes that rewarding stimuli elicit positive feelings (or affect) whereas punishing stimuli elicit negative feelings. Our evaluations of people or objects are, in turn, based on the degree of positive or negative affect we experience, and neutral stimuli that are associated with the affect will gain the capacity to produce similar feelings. Lott and Lott (1974) have proposed a similar model.

To look at this theory in more concrete terms, let's consider some of the factors we discussed previously. Having somebody do nice things for us, for example, would undoubtedly be a positive, rewarding experience. Byrne and Clore (1970) suggest that the reward value of such an experience creates positive affect and, in turn, leads us to evaluate positively (or like) the person associated with that reward. To take it one step further, they would also predict that other people and objects associated with that situation (for example, the place where the interaction occurred and other people present at the time) would also tend to be liked more because of the conditioning process. Byrne and his colleagues (Byrne, 1971) have marshaled an impressive array of support for this apparently simple principle.

Social exchange theory. **Social exchange theory** does not challenge the general assumption that reinforcement is an important basis of interpersonal attraction, but it goes beyond the simple reinforcement theory just discussed to consider *both* parties involved in the relationship. Attraction does, after all, involve two persons, and it seems reasonable to assume that we should consider how the two persons interact, rather than focus only on the characteristics of the other person while ignoring the perceiver.

Margaret Clark and Judson Mills suggest that an important distinction is to be made between *exchange* and *communal* relationships (Clark & Mills, 1979; Mills & Clark, 1982). Some relationships, such as those with strangers, acquaintances, or business associates, adhere to the principles of social exchange. Reciprocity is the rule in such relationships: what one gives to the relationship and what one gets from it are kept in balance. In other relationships, such as those with family members and close friends, people are more responsive to the other person's needs and less concerned with balancing every input and outcome. If someone you like is in trouble, for example, you may go to your friend's aid without expecting any compensation in return.

In a clever demonstration of the difference between exchange and communal relationships, Clark (1984) scheduled pairs of students for an experiment, the pairs consisting of either two friends or two strangers. The experimental task for the two subjects involved looking for specified sequences of numbers in a 15 × 26 matrix of numbers. The subjects were asked to take turns looking for a set of numbers and circling them when they were located, and the experimenter promised the participants a joint reward that they could divide as they wished. Two pens were available for the task, one with red ink and one with black, and the choice between these pens was the dependent variable of interest. In an exchange relationship, Clark reasoned, it would be important for the two participants to keep track of each other's contribution so that they could divide the reward according to input. How to keep track? By choosing a pen of a different color than one's partner had used. This kind of record keeping should be less important in a communal relationship, and the friends would be more likely to use the same pen. As Figure 9–2 shows, that was the outcome of the study.

Whereas participants in an exchange relationship are more likely to keep track of contributions and to reciprocate in kind, participants in a communal relationship are more likely to be tuned to the other person's needs. People in a communal relationship will, for example, check more often to see whether a partner needs help, uninfluenced by the possibility of reciprocation (Clark, Mills, & Powell, in press).

Interdependence theory. As we saw in Chapter One, the interdependence theory of John Thibaut

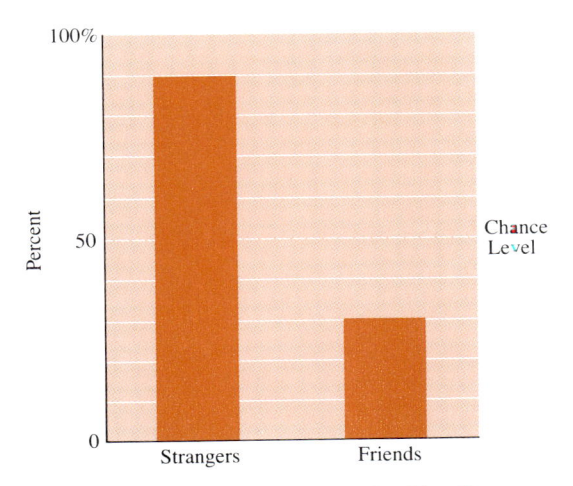

Figure 9–2 Record keeping in relationships: Percentage of subjects who chose to use a pen of a different color from that used by their partners (either strangers or friends)

and Harold Kelley is similar to social exchange theory in conceptualizing interaction in terms of costs and rewards (Kelley & Thibaut, 1978; Thibaut & Kelley, 1959). Interdependence theory is more detailed, however, about the interaction of two people's behaviors, framing these interdependencies in terms of an outcome matrix. Also important in this theory is the concept of a *comparison level*. The theory suggests that people compare the gains in a relationship against some baseline that they have come to expect. This *comparison level* is based on past experiences, and any present relationship will be judged as satisfactory only if it exceeds the comparison level. The comparison level can change over time; as you grow older, for example, you may demand more from a relationship than you did when you were a teenager. The comparison level is also specific to situations. Your calculations of *outcome value* (reward minus costs), for example, may differ considerably when you are deciding on a dentist and on a lover.

One other factor enters into the calculations of social exchange theory—the *comparison level for alternatives*. Imagine that you have been in a relationship for some time, a relationship that is generally good and exceeds your comparison level. Then you meet an exciting stranger, who promises far more rewards and fewer costs. What would you do? In all likelihood, you would experience some instability as you decided whether to go for the more attractive option. In contrast, if your current relationship offered few rewards and considerable costs, you might choose the exciting stranger with little hesitation.

This example underlines how important subjective evaluations are in the social exchange process. Rewards and costs are not objective standards that can be measured with a ruler. Rather, they depend on individual beliefs, on attributions about ourselves and others, and they are subject to constant change (Kelley, 1979). As a result, it may be difficult to assess exact outcomes in a complex interaction. Still, the general idea that we do consider such factors in the course of a relationship is very convincing.

Each of these three theories points to important aspects of the attraction process. At the most basic level, reinforcement theory tells us a great deal about the factors that will influence our attraction to another person. Most of the antecedents to attraction that we discussed earlier can, in fact, be handled by a simple reinforcement model. Yet, when we consider a more active interaction between two persons, additional factors are needed to explain interpersonal attraction. Social exchange theory and interdependence theory take us in that direction, considering both partners as necessary components of the explanation. With this in mind, let's consider some of the deeper relationships in which people become involved.

Close Relationships

The initial impression that we form of another person—whether that person is attractive or not attractive—is a critical starting point in any relationship. Yet it is only a starting point; a close relationship between two people involves far more than an initial attraction to each other (Berscheid, 1985). One important difference is that relationships develop over time, and cannot be characterized in terms of a single interaction. For this reason, the social-psychological analysis of close relationships was slow to develop. The laboratory tradition of social psychology, in which subjects participate in brief, one-time sessions, lends itself to the study of initial attraction but not to the study of continuing relationships. As psychologists have added other methods to their repertoire (see Chapter Two), the study of close relationships has progressed. Further, recognizing the principles of communication that we discussed in Chapter Five, psychologists have begun to look at relationships as an interactive phenomenon. Any relationship requires at least two people. Each brings his or her own set of characteristics to the relationship and both affects and is affected by the other person. Further, every relationship takes place in a physical and social context that can place constraints on its development (Kelley et al., 1983).

In this section we will look more closely at close relationships—at friendship and at love.

Friendship

What does it mean to be a friend? What do you expect of a friend that you would not anticipate from a casual acquaintance? Are some behaviors incompatible with friendship, so that their occurrence signals the end of the relationship? Such questions suggest that friendships are regulated by a set of informal rules that people recognize and adhere to. Why should such rules exist? For at least two reasons: first, to deal with common sources of conflict and difficulty; second, to keep up an expected level of reward. To identify just what the rules of friendship are, Michael Argyle and Monika Henderson (1984) interviewed students in four countries—England, Italy, Japan, and Hong Kong. They defined four criteria for a friendship rule: (*a*) people should generally agree that the behavior specified by the rule is important in a friendship; (*b*) the rule should be applied differently to current friends and to former friends; (*c*) failure to adhere to the rule should often be cited as a reason for the breakup of a friendship; and (*d*) the rule should differentiate behavior between close friends and not-so-close friends. Applying these criteria to their cross-cultural interviews, Argyle and Henderson identified six rules that people believe are central to friendship. They are shown in Figure 9–3, along with three other rules that met most of the criteria but failed to differentiate between close and less close friends.

Students entering college, particularly those whose attendance involves a move away from home, have ample opportunity to apply these rules to developing friendships. The assignment of a dormitory roommate often provides the first chance for a new friendship. Of course, some of these assignments are more successful than others, despite the best attempts of college administrators to match similar people. Little time seems to be required for roommates to decide

Each of the following rules is important to friendship, Argyle and Henderson (1984) learned. The first six rules met all of the criteria they established; the final three rules did not distinguish between close and less close friends, but met the other criteria for friendship.

1. Share news of success with a friend.
2. Show emotional support.
3. Volunteer help in time of need.
4. Strive to make a friend happy when in each other's company.
5. Trust and confide in each other.
6. Stand up for a friend in his or her absence.
7. Repay debts and favors.
8. Be tolerant of other friends.
9. Don't nag a friend.

Figure 9–3 The rules of friendship

whether a friendship will form. Studying the development of friendship over the course of the first year, John Berg (1984) discovered that the decision to continue to share a room during the second year could be predicted from reactions reported early in the first year. Among other factors, a student's perceived comparison level for alternatives was related to his or her later choice, in the way that interdependence theory would predict. Specifically, students who saw their current arrangement as a lot better than any other they could make were more likely to seek a continued relationship.

Pairs of people who become close friends act quite differently, right from the beginning, than do pairs of people who do not become friends (Hays, 1985). Dyads who do not become friends show a steady decline in contact. A developing friendship, in contrast, is characterized by an initial flurry of activity and then a gradual decline in the sheer amount of activity. This gradual decline in amount of interaction, explained in part by the probable increase in other activities during a student's first year at college, is accompanied by an *increase* in the intimacy or quality of the interaction. As we saw in the studies of affiliation, sex differences also emerge in the analysis of friendship development. Male friendships are more apt to evolve from shared activities, whereas female friendships depend more on verbal communication and self-disclosure (Hays, 1985). Characteristics other than sex distinguish friendship patterns as well. The individual who has a strong need for intimacy is more apt to develop friendships and is more likely to engage in self-disclosure with those friends. Individuals motivated by needs for power and dominance are more likely to seek a large-group context for activity rather than a dyadic interaction (McAdams, Healy, & Krause, 1984).

Conceptions and Measurement of Love

Love is different from friendship, most people believe. Romantic love often seems to develop quite rapidly, for example, while the course of friendship can be more gradual. Romantic love appears more fragile than friendship, and can have more negative consequences, such as suffering and frustration (Berscheid, 1985).

Basic to conceptions of love is the idea of caring. In a love relationship, behavior is often motivated by concern for the partner's interests rather than one's own. Primary concern with one's own needs seems to be more characteristic of casual attraction than of more intense love relationships (Steck et al., 1982).

The social psychologist Zick Rubin (1970, 1973) has developed two questionnaires to measure the separate states of liking and loving. Liking, in his conceptualization, is based primarily on affection and respect, while loving relies on intimacy, attachment, and care for the welfare of the other person. Some items from each scale are shown in Figure 9–4.

Love-Scale Items

1. If I could never be with _____, I would feel miserable.
2. I would forgive _____ for practically anything.
3. I feel that I can confide in _____ about virtually everything.

Liking-Scale Items

1. I think that _____ is unusually well adjusted.
2. Most people would react very favorably to _____ after a brief acquaintance.
3. _____ is the sort of person I myself would like to be.

Figure 9–4 Items in Rubin's love and liking scales. Scores on individual items can range from 1 to 9, with 9 always indicating the positive end of the continuum. Each scale contains nine items.

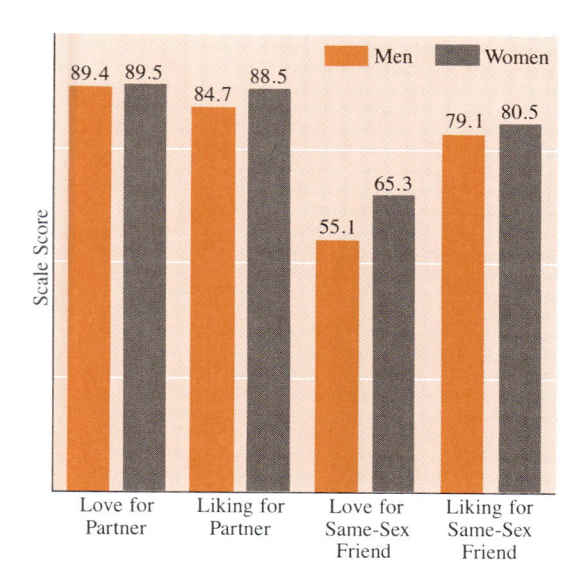

Figure 9–5 Love and liking for opposite-sex partners and same-sex partners

These two scales were presented to 158 couples at the University of Michigan who were dating but not engaged. They were asked to complete both the Love Scale and the Liking Scale with respect to their dating partner and then with respect to a close friend of the same sex. The average scores for the men and women in Rubin's study are shown in Figure 9–5, which shows that the love scores of men and women in regard to their respective dating partners were almost identical. However, women *liked* their dating partners significantly more than they were liked in return. This difference is due to the fact that women rated their partners higher on such task-oriented dimensions as intelligence and leadership potential. Men and women reported liking their same-sex friends equally, but women indicated greater love toward their same-sex friends than men did. Women's deeper involvement in same-sex associations is consistent with some research on affiliation patterns that we discussed earlier.

Rubin's work shows that there is a conceptual distinction between liking and romantic love. Other findings that suggest that these two measures differ include the finding that the two partners' scores were more closely related on the dimension of love than on the dimension of liking. In addition, Rubin found that the higher the partners' love scores, the more likely they were to expect that they would marry; liking scores, in contrast, were less strongly related to this prediction.

Although Rubin has developed a single scale for assessing love, other investigators suggest that love is not an unidimensional concept. One distinction drawn is between *passionate* (or romantic) *love* and *companionate love*. Passionate love is described as "a state of intense absorption in another. Sometimes 'lovers' are those who long for their partners and for complete fulfillment. Sometimes 'lovers' are those who are ecstatic at finally having attained their partners' love, and, momentarily, complete fulfillment. A state of intense physiological arousal" (Walster & Walster, 1978, p. 9).

A perhaps more familiar form of love is *companionate love*, defined as the affection we feel for those with whom our lives are deeply intertwined. In contrast to the sometimes fleeting state of romantic love, companionate love reflects longer-term relationships and may be a later stage in a romantic relationship.

John Alan Lee (1973) has suggested that love is

even more varied. He offers three primary types of love styles—romantic love, game-playing love, and friendship love—and three secondary styles of love—possessive love, logical love, and selfless love. Each of these styles is identified by a descriptive Greek or Latin label, and each can be assessed by specific questionnaire items developed by Clyde and Susan Hendrick (1986) and shown in Figure 9–6. People vary in their predisposition to experience these different kinds of love. And as people move from passionate to companionate love, they shift from *eros* to *storge* or *pragma*.

It should be noted that the sex of the lovers is not an implicit part of these definitions. Although social psychologists have tended to focus on the heterosexual relationship, love relationships between persons of the same sex may also be considered in this framework.

Eros: romantic, passionate love
- My lover and I have the right physical "chemistry" between us.
- My lover fits my ideal standards of physical beauty/handsomeness.

Ludus: game-playing love.
- I try to keep my lover a little uncertain about my commitment to him/her.
- I enjoy playing the "game of love" with a number of different partners.

Storge: friendship love
- My most satisfying love relationships have developed from good friendships.
- Love is really a deep friendship, not a mysterious, mystical emotion.

Pragma: logical love
- I consider what a person is going to become in life before I commit myself to him/her.
- One consideration in choosing a partner is how he/she will reflect on my career.

Mania: possessive, dependent love
- When my lover doesn't pay attention to me, I feel sick all over.
- I cannot relax if I suspect that my lover is with someone else.

Agape: selfless love
- I would rather suffer myself than let my lover suffer.
- Whatever I own is my lover's to use as he/she chooses.

Figure 9–6 Six styles of love

Mate Selection

It is said that in the 1960s and 1970s, the prerequisites for marriage in China were "four things that go round"—a bicycle, a watch, a fan, and a sewing machine. Now, with changes in the Chinese economy, the four things are more modern—a television set, a washing machine, a stereo, and a refrigerator, according to one news report (Bennett, 1985). Economic advantages, it is claimed, are the major attraction in a marriage partner.

Less materialistic types might claim that the choice of a partner is based more on personal than on financial characteristics. Certainly people are able to identify characteristics that they believe are valuable in a mate. A group of married persons, varying in age from 18 to 40, listed the following 10 characteristics as most important: being a good companion, consideration, honesty, affection, dependableness, intelligence, kindness, being understanding, being interesting to talk to, and loyalty (Buss & Barnes, 1986). Characteristics that they would not value in a mate included dominance, agnosticism, being a night owl, and being an early riser (the same people did not necessarily mention all of these features).

The principle of similarity, which we discussed earlier when we talked about initial impressions, is evidenced in mate selection as well. From the ethological tradition, the coupling of individuals based on resemblance on one or more characteristics is termed **assortative mating** (Buss, 1984). In other words, people do not mate randomly; they often seek mates who share common characteristics and who like to engage in similar activities. Some investigators, for example, have found that married couples are similar on such characteristics as susceptibility to boredom, desire to seek out experiences, and impulsivity (Lesnik-Oberstein & Cohen, 1984). Others have found that spouses tend to be similar in their choice of activities, their willingness to display intimacy, and the level of quarrelsomeness that they will tolerate (Buss, 1984). Of course, one might suspect that couples who do not share some commonalities will be less successful and hence may not still be around when a psychologist comes to question them. However, the fact that the degree of similarity stays constant over time is an indication that it is an important factor in initial selection (Buss, 1984).

Photo 9–4 Long-term commitment involves the willingness to maintain love.

Stages in the Development of Love

Although love at first sight can occur, the development of a close relationship takes place over time. As a general model, we can consider a relationship—any close relationship—to move from a fairly superficial stage to a deeper and more intimate bond (Kelley et al., 1983). In the first stage, which can be called acquaintanceship, two people begin to get to know each other. Initial impressions are made, and the two begin to interact. Many relationships never progress beyond this stage. The dental hygienist who cleans our teeth, the bus driver on our regular route, and the person we meet occasionally at a neighborhood party all exemplify this level of contact.

The movement from acquaintance to the actual building of a relationship constitutes a second stage. During this stage, increasing degrees of interdependence are established. The people involved discover aspects of each other through increasing interaction, and they become more willing to disclose information about themselves. The two partners in this stage of a relationship also begin to invest time and energy in the relationship, coordinating their activities with each other and anticipating rewarding future interactions.

Buildup is the third stage of a close relationship. Progress in this stage is not always smooth, as the partners face an unfolding set of circumstances and problems, some of which temporarily increase the tension between them. Finally, in the fourth stage, real commitment develops. Now the advantages of the relationship clearly outweigh the disadvantages. In some cases, commitment may develop as a result of "falling in love." In other cases, as in those societies in which arranged marriages are the rule, commitment may be the outcome of a formal agreement, after which emotional involvement and love can follow.

This four-stage model describes the development of a relationship in very general terms. To really understand how love develops, however, it may be necessary to consider separate elements of a relationship. Robert Sternberg (1986) suggests that love has three major elements—intimacy, passion, and commitment—and that these elements develop at different rates in the course of a relationship. (See Figure 9–7.) (Because this model has three elements, it is sometimes called the triangular model of love.) *Intimacy* represents the warmth and closeness in a relationship. It develops gradually over the course of a relationship, continuing to grow (although at a progressively slower rate) as the partners share experiences and feelings. *Passion* represents the hotter aspect of a relationship, as described earlier in terms of passionate (versus companionate) love. Passion typically develops very quickly but then, as the graph indicates, drops off as the couple become accustomed to each other. *Commitment* can be of two types. A short-term commitment involves the decision that one loves another person; a long-term commitment involves willingness to maintain that love. This aspect of love typically develops slowly at first, and then speeds up as the rewards and costs of the relationship become clear.

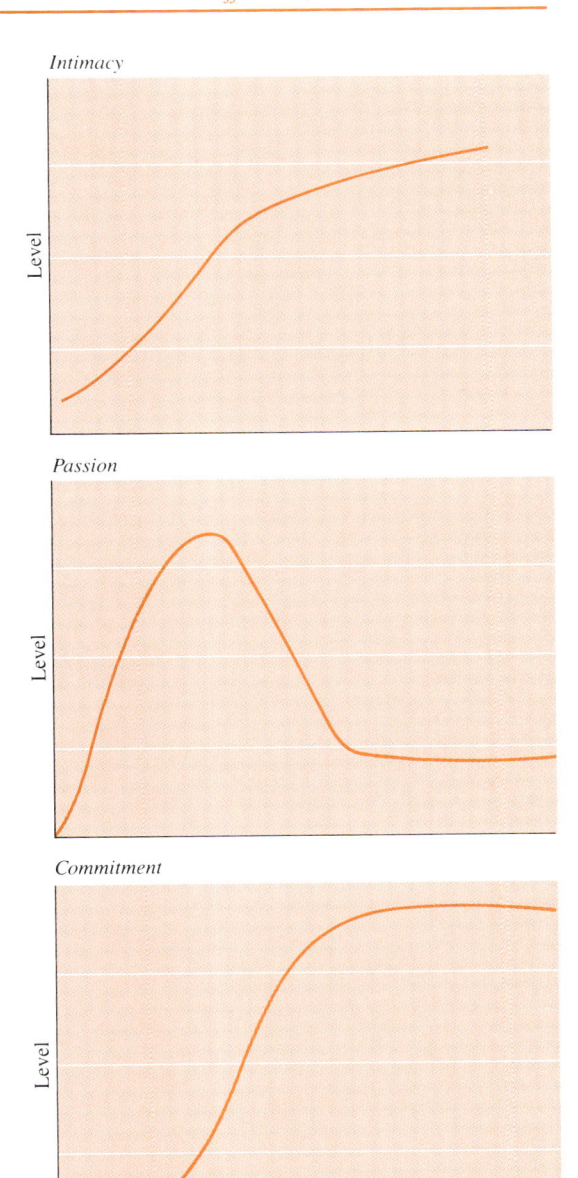

Figure 9–7 Changing ingredients: Aspects of love grow at different rates and vary in their ability to endure

What happens in the course of a relationship as two people develop a commitment to each other? Many behaviors and feelings change, as Figure 9–8 indicates.

An increase in trust is one of those changes. When we talk about trust, we can consider three separate ways in which a person views his or her partner (Rempel, Holmes, & Zanna, 1985). First, trust involves predictability, the ability to estimate what the person will do. Second, trust implies dependability: a partner develops certain assumptions about the internal characteristics and dispositions of his or her mate. Both predictability and dependability are based on past evidence and experience with the partner. Beyond these two elements, trust implies faith. In this case, a partner is looking ahead, confident that certain outcomes will come to pass. In a close relationship, love and happiness are closely linked to these three elements.

As a relationship develops and the partners become more closely involved with each other, a number of changes take place (Berscheid, 1985). Some of the changes are listed below.

1. Partners interact more often, for longer periods of time, in a widening array of settings.
2. People attempt to restore proximity when separated, and feel comforted when proximity is regained.
3. People open up to each other, disclosing secrets and sharing physical intimacies.
4. People become less inhibited, more willing to share positive and negative feelings and to praise and criticize each other.
5. People develop their own communication system.
6. People increase their ability to map and anticipate each other's views.
7. People begin to synchronize their goals and behavior.
8. People increase their investment in the relationship, increasing its importance in their life space.
9. People begin to feel that their separate interests are inextricably tied to the well-being of their relationship.
10. People increase their liking, trust, and love for each other.
11. People see the relationship as irreplaceable, or at least as unique.
12. People more and more relate to others as a couple rather than as individuals.

Figure 9–8 Characteristics of a relationship

partnership (see Box 9–2). Why do some relationships work out and others fail? Are there certain factors that influence the course of a relationship, and can we predict the positive and negative outcomes? It is to this side of the attraction coin that we now turn.

Falling Out of Love

The movies of the 1930s usually ended with boy and girl together. Although the Hollywood version of romance has changed even in Hollywood itself, it has surely never been true of all real-life relationships. People do meet and fall in love and live together or marry. Yet some of these people fall out of love, break off engagements, and separate or divorce. Jealousy can arise and threaten the foundations of a

Breaking Up Is Hard to Do

Many relationships that begin with the glow of romantic or passionate love do not go on to fulfill their initial promise; others endure and lead to marriage, children, and golden anniversaries. Can any patterns be detected in those relationships that break up versus those that last? To answer this question, Hill, Rubin, and Peplau (1976) conducted an exten-

Box 9-2
Jealousy

Jealousy. "Cruel as the grave," the Bible calls it. "The jaundice of the soul," John Dryden declared. And almost inevitable, according to the French writer La Rochefoucauld, who stated that "jealousy is always born together with love."

But is it inevitable? And just what is jealousy? As social psychologists have become more interested in the development of love and romance, they have also begun to look at the issue of jealousy. Most definitions of jealousy refer to an emotional state that is experienced when a person perceives that some other person (either real or imagined) poses a threat to an ongoing relationship with a partner.

Are some people more likely to be jealous than others? Recent research suggests that two factors are common to most jealous reactions: a desire for an exclusive relationship and feelings of inadequacy (White, 1981). These two factors are found in the jealousy experienced by both men and women, but the patterns of jealousy differ. A man's jealousy is often related to a low level of general self-esteem, to dependence on the partner as a source of self-esteem, and to traditionality of sex-role beliefs. A woman's jealousy is associated mainly with a strong dependence on the relationship itself—a belief that it is more rewarding than any available alternative (White, 1981).

Thus, for men, jealousy seems to be more closely related to issues of status, while for women the nature of the relationship is more crucial. These different emphases are also shown in a study that asked men and women to say how they would react to situations that were likely to create jealous feelings (Shettel-Neuber, Bryson, & Young, 1978). Men were more likely to say that they would get angry and involved in activities that would endanger the relationship; women were more apt to say that they would get depressed and do things to improve the relationship. Although jealousy may be nearly universal, then, it is not always experienced in the same way by women and men.

---

sive two-year study, following the course of 231 couples in the Boston area. At the end of the two-year period, 103 couples (45% of the original sample) had broken up; 65 others were still dating, 9 were engaged, 43 were married, and 11 could not be contacted.

To understand the process of breaking up, Hill and his colleagues first looked at the answers to the initial questionnaire that each couple had completed at the beginning of the two-year period. Were there any clues at that stage that could predict the course of the relationship? Not surprisingly, those couples who reported feeling closer in 1972 were more likely to be together in 1974. Yet those reported feelings were not a perfect predictor: many couples who reported feeling close at the initial testing still did break up during the subsequent two years. Consistent with our earlier discussion, scores on a love scale were more predictive than scores on a liking scale. In addition, the women's love scores were a better indicator of whether the relationship would last than the men's love scores. Thus, for some reason, the feelings of the woman in the relationship are a more sensitive index of the health of the relationship. Unrelated to the future success of the relationship were whether the couple had had sexual intercourse and whether they had lived together. A couple were equally likely to maintain a relationship whether or not they had engaged in these more intimate forms of interchange.

Photo 9–5 Many relationships do not fulfill their initial promise.

Similarity of the two partners, discussed earlier as an important factor in attraction, also was important among these Boston couples. As Table 9–1 indicates, similarities with respect to age, education, intelligence, and attractiveness were all greater for the couples who stayed together than for those who broke up. However, similarity of religion, sex role attitudes, and desired family size were not useful in predicting the long-term success of relationships. Nonetheless, couples were fairly well matched on each of these variables at the beginning of the study, suggesting that these factors are important in the initial selection of a partner.

Another important predictor of the success of the relationship was the man's need for power (Stewart & Rubin, 1976). As measured by stories told in response to TAT cards, need for power is conceptualized as a stable tendency to seek impact on others, either through direct action or through more subtle attempts at influence. Men who scored high in need for power in the Boston couples study were more likely to expect problems in the relationship and were more likely to express dissatisfaction with the relationship at the initial testing. True to the expectations of these men, a couple in which the man had a high need for power were much less likely to be together two years later. In fact, 50% of these relationships had broken up, compared with only 15% of those in which the man was low in the need for power. The women's need for power was measured as well, but their scores showed absolutely no association with the success or failure of the relationship.

To gain more understanding of the breakup process, Hill and his colleagues used a second method of data

Table 9-1 Relationship between similarity and breaking up: Correlations of partners' characteristics and attitudes two years later, by status

Characteristics and Attitudes of Partners	All Couples (N = 231)	Together Couples (N = 117)	Breakup Couples (N = 103)
CHARACTERISTICS			
Age	.19*	.38*	.13
Highest degree planned	.28*	.31*	.17
SAT, math	.22*	.31*	.11
SAT, verbal	.24*	.33*	.15
Physical attractiveness	.24*	.32*	.16
Father's educational level	.11	.12	.12
Height	.21*	.22†	.22†
Religion (% same)	51%*	51%*	52%*
ATTITUDES			
Sex-role traditionalism (10-item scale)	.47*	.50*	.41*
Favorability toward women's liberation	.38*	.36*	.43*
Approval of sex among "acquaintances"	.25*	.27*	.21†
Romanticism (6-item scale)	.20†	.21†	.15
Self-report of religiosity	.37*	.39*	.37*
Number of children wanted	.51*	.43*	.57*

* $p < .01$.
† $p < .05$.

collection: intensive interviews with some of the couples that had broken up. These interviews provided many new insights into the process of breaking up, even including such facts as when the breakup occurred. In view of the fact that the majority of the couples in this study were college students, it may not be surprising to learn that these relationships were most likely to break up at critical points in the school year—at the beginning of the fall semester and at the ends of the fall and spring semesters. These natural break points in the calendar year allowed couples to break up more easily, and the less involved partner in a relationship was more likely to take advantage of these natural break points to end the relationship. In contrast, when the partner who had reported being more involved chose to end the affair, the timing was more likely to be in the middle of the school year than at the end. For the less involved partner, the separation of a summer vacation may provide a good excuse for ending the relationship, testifying to the truth of La Rochefoucauld's maxim "Absence diminishes mediocre passions and increases great ones."

Most of the breakups were perceived to be somewhat one-sided: over 85% of both men and women reported that one person wanted to end the relationship more than the other. These perceptions were not totally accurate, however. Although there was considerable agreement in many cases, there was also a systematic bias in the reports. People were more likely to say that they were the one who wanted to break off the relationship than to say that their partner wished to do so. Such a strategy is, of course, self-protective: those partners who did the breaking up were considerably happier, less lonely, and less depressed (but more guilty) than those partners who were the "broken-up-with" ones.

Just who does the breaking up in the typical male/female couple? Although some cases are clearly mutual decisions, when one person initiates the split, it is more likely to be the woman. Zick Rubin and his colleagues (Rubin, Peplau, & Hill, 1978) have suggested that in our society men tend to fall in love more readily than women, and women fall out of love more readily than men. Although such an assertion contradicts many of the stereotypes of the romantic woman and the "strong, silent" man, the data do support the argument. An interesting by-product of men's greater unwillingness to end the relationship is found in the contact that the partners reported having after the breakup. If the man broke up the relationship, the couple were very likely to remain casual friends; however, if the woman was the one to end the relationship, it was apparently much more difficult for them to stay friends, and fewer than half the couples did so.

The end of an affair is probably less traumatic than the end of a marriage. Nevertheless, the factors that contribute to the breakup of short-term relationships have something in common with those that lead to the rupture of long-term bonds. Even in itself the breakup of an affair provides important continuity in our understanding of the development of love between two persons.

Inequity and Impermanence

Earlier we discussed the general principles of social exchange theories. **Equity theory** is another version of social exchange theory, and one that has particular application to the dissolution of relationships. According to equity theory, people in a relationship consider not only their own costs and rewards but also the costs and rewards for the other person (Hatfield & Traupmann, 1981; Walster, Walster, & Berscheid, 1978). Ideally, these two ratios are balanced. Equity theory suggests that people have some notion of what they deserve from a relationship, and this notion is based in part on what the other partner in the relationship is getting. The person who feels that the relationship is out of balance will become distressed and will try to restore the balance, either by actually altering the inputs and outcomes or by psychologically altering his or her perception of the gains and costs that both partners are experiencing.

One of the interesting predictions of equity theory is that people become dissatisfied whenever the relationship is out of balance—whether they are overbenefited or underbenefited in comparison with their partner. Thus, if the rewards I experience in a relationship are great and the costs are small, I will not necessarily be satisfied. If my partner's outcomes are either much greater or much less than mine, I will feel some distress.

The form that distress takes depends both on the sex of the partner and on the type of inequity. Both men and women report being angry when they perceive an inequitable relationship; men, however, are more likely to report being hurt and resentful, whereas women mention sadness and frustration. When they feel they are overbenefited, men report guilt; when they feel underbenefited, they express anger. Women are more likely to express anger when they are overbenefited; when underbenefited, they are more likely to become depressed (Sprecher, 1986).

Relationships that both partners perceive to be equitable are most likely to be successful ones (Davidson, 1984; Traupmann et al., 1981). In contrast, the perception of inequity can signal difficulty. For example, you might feel that you put a lot into a relationship, giving your partner emotional support and comfort but receiving little in return. If at the same time you felt that your partner was giving little to the relationship in exchange for your kindness, what would you do? Equity theory would predict that if the imbalance were too great, you would probably choose to end the relationship. In a test of this prediction, 511 men and women at the University of Wisconsin were interviewed about their relationships with their dating partners (Berscheid & Walster, 1978). At the initial testing each person was asked to evaluate his or her dating relationship in terms of the contributions and the benefits that each partner was receiving. For example, the person was asked to consider all the things that might contribute to a relationship (such as personality, emotional support, help in making decisions) and to rate his or her own contribution on a scale from +4 to −4. Subjects were then asked to make a similar rating of their partners' contributions. Each person was also asked to rate the benefits received from the relationship, such as love, excitement, security, or a good time, again for both the self and the partner. These four estimates enabled the investigators to determine how equitable the relationship was perceived to be.

Three months later, the people were interviewed again and asked whether they were still going out with the same partner and how long they expected the relationship to last. People who had reported equitable relationships at the earlier session were more likely to be still dating at the second testing period.

They were also more likely to predict that the relationship would last than were those persons who reported a less equitable relationship. Hence, although it may be difficult to measure accurately all the factors that contribute to a relationship, it seems clear that our willingness to stay in a relationship is directly related to our perceptions of its costs and benefits.

Marriage and Divorce

The breakup of an affair probably forestalls a marriage that would not have worked. Yet marriage is obviously not a guarantee of lifelong attraction. In the United States, for example, the divorce rate has been increasing quite rapidly in recent years. What happens in these more extended relationships to cause a split?

A number of personality and demographic factors have been associated with the likelihood of divorce (Newcomb & Bentler, 1981). For example, people who marry young are more likely to divorce. In terms of personality, people with high amounts of ambition and strong achievement needs tend to have less stable marriages. Among men, a need for orderliness is associated with divorce; ambition and intelligence are more common to divorced women.

Yet such static factors do not address the dynamics of a marital relationship. In fact, relationships are constantly changing, and it is in the shifting balance between two persons that marriage and divorce must be explored (Kelley et al., 1983).

George Levinger (1979) has offered a descriptive analysis of marital relationships based on the combination of attractions and barriers that are present. Some of the attractions that he identifies are material rewards, such as family income; others are either symbolic, such as status, or affectional, such as companionship and sexual enjoyment. Barriers are conceived of as the potential costs of divorcing, such as financial expenses, feelings toward children, and religious constraints. Finally, Levinger suggests that people also weigh the alternative attractions, a concept similar to Thibaut and Kelley's comparison level. Possible alternative attractions that a husband or wife might consider are the values of independence or a preferred companion or sexual partner. This framework is helpful in identifying some of the factors that may come into play when individuals decide whether to continue or to end a relationship. In general, we can predict that when the attractions of the present relationship decrease, the barriers to escape from the relationship diminish, and the strength of alternative attractions increases, then at that point an individual would choose to get out of the relationship.

The deterioration of a relationship is rarely sudden. Steve Duck (1982) has suggested that four distinct stages can be identified as a relationship dissolves. In the first, *intrapsychic* stage, the individual focuses on his or her partner, identifying causes of dissatisfaction and planning how to confront the partner with the problem. This confrontation occurs in the *dyadic* stage, and its outcome can be either reconciliation or a clearer determination to end the relationship. If the latter occurs, it is then publicized in the *social* stage. What was private now becomes public, and both partners will work on ways to save face, assign blame, and adjust their lives to a new status. Finally, in the *"grave-dressing"* phase, each partner devises an ending to the relationship and constructs a story about the events that led up to it. The stories may or may not be accurate, but they will guide future recollections and interpretations (Harvey, Flanary, & Morgan, in press).

In 1958 the psychologist Harry Harlow wrote: "So far as love or affection is concerned, psychologists have failed in their mission. The little we know about love does not transcend simple observations, and the little we write about it has been written better by poets and novelists" (1958, p. 673). We know a great deal more today than we did in 1958. Many more investigators have become interested in the topic of love, and the issue is no longer taboo. Furthermore, the wider variety of methodologies that are now being used by social psychologists make it possible to investigate complex and long-term relationships more fully.

Summary

Loneliness is a subjective experience, generally an unpleasant one. Emotional loneliness is caused by the lack of an intimate relationship with one person; social loneliness results from the lack of a broader social network.

The need to affiliate, or to be with others, is exceedingly strong in most people. Reasons for affiliation include the intrinsic value of companionship and the usefulness of other people in providing a standard for social comparison and self-evaluation. Under conditions of increased situational anxiety, there is a greater desire to be with others, particularly those who are in the same situation. Studies of affiliation patterns have provided descriptive data on the extent to which people choose to be alone or with others and how social networks develop over time.

Initial attraction to another person is influenced by the following factors: similarity of beliefs, values, and personality; complementarity of needs; physical attractiveness; pleasant or agreeable characteristics; reciprocal liking; and propinquity. Theories that have been proposed to explain interpersonal attraction include reinforcement/affect theory, social exchange theory, and interdependence theory.

Close relationships are far more complex than initial attraction, involving a long sequence of interactions between two people. Relationships between friends also involve a set of implicit rules that both partners are expected to follow.

Liking and loving are different emotions, and questionnaires have been developed to assess the two. Different kinds of love can also be identified and measured.

Love develops through a set of stages, from acquaintanceship through buildup to commitment. Love also involves a set of processes—intimacy, passion, and commitment—which develop at different rates.

People fall in love and people fall out of love. Initial feelings of intimacy and similarity of interests are related to breakups; perceptions of inequality in the relationship are also a factor. Even after couples marry, relationships continue to change. The decision to divorce has been represented as the result of an imbalance among attractions, barriers, and alternative attractions, and can also be described as a series of stages.

Glossary Terms

assortative mating
complementarity
equity theory
mere exposure effect
propinquity
social comparison theory
social exchange theory
social network
social support

Sexual relationship is an interpersonal relationship, and as such is subject to the same principles of interaction as are other relationships.
Lester A. Kirkendall & R. W. Libby

Custom controls the sexual impulse as it controls no other.
Margaret Sanger

Edna Manley: *The Trees Are Joyful*. National Gallery of Jamaica.

CHAPTER TEN

The Social Psychology of Sexual Behavior

I. The Study of Sexual Behavior
   Methods of Study
   Surveys of Sexual Activity
   Sexual Attitudes and Behaviors of College Students
II. Theoretical Issues in Sexual Behavior
   Psychoanalytic Theory of Sexuality
   Cognitive Aspects of Sexual Behavior
   Heterosexual and Homosexual Preferences
III. Sexual Behavior in Relationships
   Sexuality in Dating Relationships
   Sexuality in Long-Term Relationships
IV. Sexual Behavior and Contraception
V. Erotic Material and Sexual Arousal
   Definitions of Sexual Stimuli
   Physiological Responses to Erotic Stimuli
   Psychological Responses to Erotic Stimuli
   Behavioral Responses to Erotic Stimuli
VI. Summary

Sexual experiences are a part of human social interaction, and sexuality is an obvious part of our lives and of our culture. As romantic love develops and relationships are formed, sexuality generally becomes an issue to be confronted. Most of us remember our first sexual experience; many of us fantasize about future sexual encounters. People joke about sex, worry about sex, and enjoy sex.

At a broader societal level, popular treatments of sexuality become best-sellers, and sex-therapy clinics proliferate. Much of the advertising that appears in newspapers, in magazines, and on television capitalizes on our sexual desires, and in any major city, large numbers of movie theaters offer X-rated films exclusively. Sexual harassment becomes an issue for the courts to deal with.

It is not surprising, then, that the topic of sexual behavior finds a place in a social psychology text. It is an important part of human interaction, and it relates to our attitudes, to societal norms, and to basic learning processes as well. In this chapter we will consider a number of facets of sexual behavior: the frequency of various forms of sexual behavior, theoretical models concerning the development of sexual behavior, the role of sexuality in interpersonal relationships, issues of contraception and family planning, and the influence of erotic material on behavior.

The Study of Sexual Behavior

In the Victorian era, when Freud proposed that sexuality was central to human nature, shock waves resounded through the literate world. His ideas were considered not only revolutionary but immoral and evil. Some people still believe in the immorality of much sexual behavior; many others today, though not necessarily advocates of Freudian theory, nonetheless argue for the centrality of sexuality to human social behavior. Certainly it is difficult to avoid the topic of sex in newspapers, in magazines, or on the streets. Yet, despite our irrepressible sexual habits and their pervasive effects, sexual behavior was long a taboo topic for the social scientist. In the 1920s, for example, a professor was fired from the University of Minnesota because he approved a questionnaire on attitudes toward sex (which included such "unreasonable" questions as "Have you ever blown into the ear of a person of the opposite sex in order to arouse their passion?"). Only within the last 25 years have colleges and universities offered courses on human sexuality. Even today, investigators who are concerned with the area of sexual behavior often encounter forms of hostility and antagonism not experienced by those who conduct research on less controversial topics.

At the same time, many people are fascinated by the results of sex research, and findings are often quickly publicized and circulated in the mass media. Works by Kinsey and by Masters and Johnson, for example, became best-sellers even though they were written in a technical style and were intended mainly for the professional audience. Such popularity poses an additional problem for the sex researcher, in that findings may be taken for absolute truth when they reflect only a preliminary stage of understanding.

Methods of Study

The earliest scientific reports of sex were based primarily on the case history records of practicing psychiatrists. In addition to the obvious example of Sigmund Freud, the work of Havelock Ellis (1899/1936) at the turn of the century was based on clinical practice. Both men focused more on abnormal sexual functioning than on general descriptions of sexual behavior as a social phenomenon. More recent investigators have turned again to the case study method, now to investigate normal populations, and have shown how rich a source of data such studies can be (Abramson, 1984).

Apart from the clinical case history approach, how do investigators study human sexual behavior? Because sex is primarily a private behavior, some of the methods discussed in Chapter Two are not appropriate for this sort of research. The most common approach has been to use questionnaires and interviews to investigate the range and frequency of people's sexual activities. Kinsey's studies, for example, were based exclusively on this method. Kinsey conducted detailed interviews with a large sample of U.S. citizens (Kinsey, Pomeroy, & Martin, 1948; Kinsey et al., 1953). Similar procedures have continued to be used in recent years, with data often collected by questionnaires sent through the mail (Blumstein & Schwartz, 1983; Hunt, 1974). The primary advantage of this method, particularly when the questionnaires are anonymous, is that it allows respondents a considerable degree of privacy in discussing intimate aspects of their sex lives. Potentially embarrassing topics can be dealt with more easily when no face-to-face encounter is involved.

There are some problems with the survey method, however (Byrne & Byrne, 1977). One difficulty concerns the representativeness of the sample of subjects. Subjects in any survey are to some degree self-selected; in other words, after the investigator determines an initial sample, the selected subjects must agree to participate. Particularly in the area of sex research, it is probable that those people who agree to participate are not a random sample. Some people are quite willing to discuss or to describe their sexual experiences, while others are aghast at the very thought. Generalizing the results of surveys to the total population is therefore very risky. A second, related problem concerns the accuracy of the answers. As in any self-report measure, the investigator must be concerned with the accuracy of the subject's information. In the area of sex, where norms and values are so strong, the difficulties of accepting self-report data as completely accurate are particularly acute. On the one hand, people may be reluctant to report behavior that they suspect is not "normal"; on the other hand, some people may exaggerate their reported activities in order to appear exciting, progressive, or even normal in our age of high sexual pressures. Despite these limitations, however, the survey method will continue to be used when the concern is with describing normative patterns of sexual behavior.

A more recently adopted alternative to the survey method is the laboratory experiment. For example, investigators have conducted numerous studies in which subjects are exposed to a variety of erotic films and asked to indicate their reactions to the material or to engage in other forms of behavior, such as aggression toward a confederate. In some instances, most notably the work by Masters and Johnson (1966), subjects engage in intercourse in the laboratory setting. Such approaches gain the advantages of the experimental method but still have some problems (Bentler & Abramson, 1981). Volunteer bias is inevitable, because all potential subjects must be fully informed of the topic of the research before they decide whether to participate in the experiment. People who do not wish to watch pornographic films can choose not to participate, and those who do choose to participate are probably not a random sample. Further, the laboratory is a highly artificial setting for behaviors that typically occur in very private situations. Although this criticism has been applied to many areas of research, it is probably more severe in the case of sexual behavior.

Despite the problems and difficulties inherent in the study of sexual behavior, progress has been made in recent years. We are finally beginning to learn a good deal about sexual behavior—its frequency, its role in intimate relationships, and factors that affect its occurrence.

Surveys of Sexual Activity

Who engages in which types of sexual behavior under what circumstances? In seeking the answer to this question, we can look to the results of a number of survey studies completed during the past 30 to 40 years. The original, of course, was the work of Alfred Kinsey (Kinsey et al., 1948, 1953). A large-scale survey by Morton Hunt (1974) provided an update on Kinsey's data. More recently, Philip Blumstein and Pepper Schwartz (1983) conducted a series of intensive interviews designed to compare the sexual experiences of married and cohabiting heterosexual couples, lesbian couples, and gay male couples.

Kinsey's original investigations were pioneering efforts in the study of sex and their major findings are worth reviewing. A few preliminary comments are in order, however. We must always remember that Kinsey's subjects were volunteers selected from diverse sections of society; they were not selected in

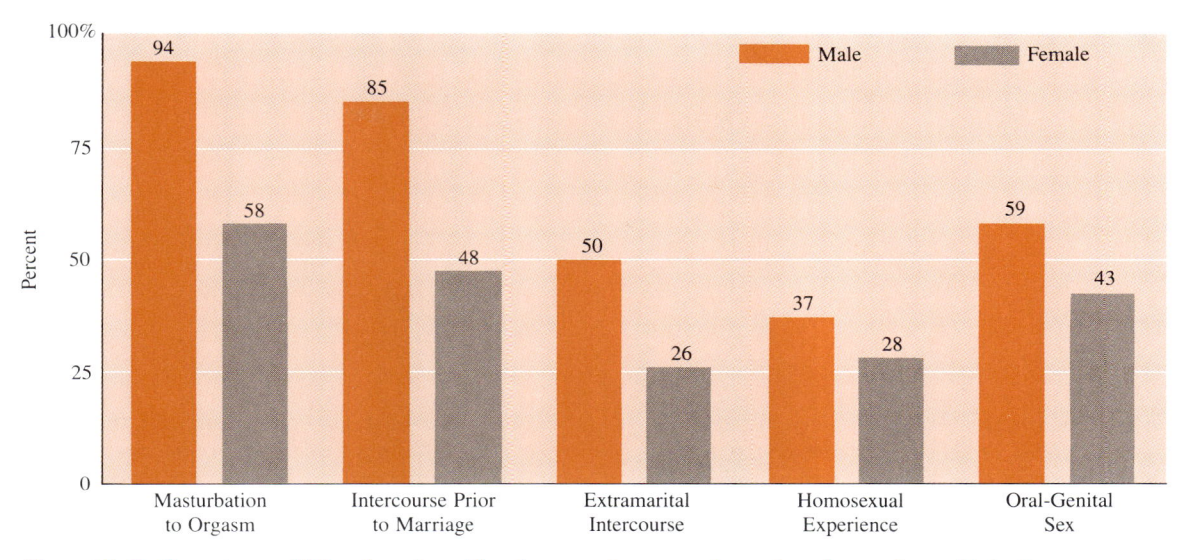

Figure 10-1 Percentages of Kinsey's male and female respondents reporting various forms of sexual behavior.

a fashion designed to ensure the representativeness of the sample. Moreover, the data were collected in face-to-face interviews, where subjects may have been reluctant to admit some behaviors. Yet, although there are many possible methodological artifacts in Kinsey's procedures, comparisons between his findings and those of other investigators have produced generally consistent outcomes.

Some of the more general findings of Kinsey and his associates are shown in Figure 10-1. As can be seen, during the late 1940s and early 1950s, when these data were collected, higher percentages of men than of women reported engaging in most sexual activities. It is also important to note that although a substantial number of people of both sexes (37% of the men, 28% of the women) reported having had at least one homosexual experience, relatively few people of either sex (4% of the men, 3% of the women) reported themselves as being exclusively homosexual.

Socioeconomic status was one of the most significant predictors of the sexual behavior of respondents of both sexes. College-educated people had begun most sexual practices later than people who did not eventually go to college. As adults, however, the college-educated men and women reported less inhibition in most sexual behaviors and were more likely to engage in masturbation, oral-genital sex, homosexuality, and a variety of coital positions. Although differences among religious denominations were not so striking, people who described themselves as nonreligious were more likely to masturbate, to pet to orgasm, and to have premarital coitus and extramarital affairs.

In the early 1970s, Morton Hunt (1974) conducted a survey of 2026 people in the United States, generally matching the U.S. adult population in regard to most demographic characteristics. This survey still is subject to some of the methodological problems discussed earlier, particularly in regard to subject self-selection, but the findings give us some indication of more recent sexual attitudes and behavior.

In considering people's expressed attitudes toward various forms of sexuality, Hunt did not have much basis for comparison, as Kinsey had considered only people's reported behavior, not their reported attitudes. Even without this comparison, however, Hunt's findings suggest a considerable degree of permissiveness in attitudes toward sexuality. For example, more than 75% of his sample believed that schools should teach sex education. The vast majority of the people surveyed believed that the man should not always be the one to initiate sexual intercourse, and nearly as many people reported that nonmarital sex was acceptable. Particular sexual practices, such as cunnilingus and fellatio, also were widely accepted.

What about the actual behavior reported by people in this survey? Hunt's data differ from Kinsey's in several respects. Extramarital intercourse, for example, decreased slightly for men (from 50% to 41%), while the incidence of extramarital intercourse remained fairly constant for women. Those who did engage in extramarital affairs, however, did so earlier in the marriage than did the people in Kinsey's sample. As a possibly related factor, we can consider the findings in regard to divorced persons (the frequency of divorce had doubled since the time of Kinsey's surveys). Hunt's divorced men and women both reported considerably more sexual activity than did the divorced persons in Kinsey's sample. In Hunt's sample, divorced men reported an average of 8.0 sexual partners a year, and divorced women reported an average of 3.5.

More women reported nonmarital sex in Hunt's sample (75%, compared with 48% in Kinsey's study), but there was little change in the incidence of nonmarital sex among the men. At the same time, fewer men reported going to prostitutes in the 1970s than in the 1940s and 1950s. The frequency of intercourse between marriage partners increased somewhat; for couples in the 26-to-35 age range, the average was 2.6 times a week, in comparison with the earlier figure of 2.0 times a week. One of the most striking differences was in the frequency of oral-genital contact. In parallel with the permissive attitudes that were expressed, more than two-thirds of the people had tried this form of sexual activity.

The incidence of homosexuality did not appear to have changed much since Kinsey's study. Hunt's findings were similar to Kinsey's: 6% of the men and 3% of the women reported having had a homosexual experience within the preceding year. The percentage of people in Hunt's study who reported having had at least one homosexual experience at some time was nearer to 25%.

In summary, Hunt's survey suggested that there had been some relaxation (1) of the pressures operating against sexual activity (particularly in the forms of sexuality), (2) in the sexual activities of women, and (3) in the sexual activity of divorced persons. At the same time, relatively little change had occurred in many areas between the 1940s and the 1970s, a finding that suggests that the apparent increase in sexuality in our society may have been only a change in expressed attitudes rather than a drastic shift in behavior.

More than 12,000 people completed a questionnaire developed by Blumstein and Schwartz (1983) to assess the attitudes and experiences of American couples in the domains of work, money, and sexuality. From this larger pool the investigators selected 300 couples who lived in one of three U.S. cities (Seattle, San Francisco, New York) for more intensive interviews. These 300 couples were of four types:

married heterosexual couples, cohabiting heterosexual couples, lesbian couples, and gay male couples. Both members of each couple were interviewed separately, and each interview took between two and a half and four hours to complete.

Frequency of sexual intercourse varied among these four types of couples. Gay men, for example, had sex more often in the early stage of a relationship than did other couples, but engaged in sex far less frequently than married couples after 10 years in the relationship. Lesbian women reported the lowest rate of sexual activity at all stages of the relationship. Among all groups, however, the amount of sexual activity declined as the duration of the relationship increased. Although respondents in all groups reported that they had not been sexually faithful to their partners, such reports were much more frequent among gay men (82%) than among members of the other groups (among whom the percentages varied between 21% and 33%). Overall, Blumstein and Schwartz conclude, the changes in sexual behavior have probably been less extreme than some people think, and the behaviors of women and men are shaped as much by their socialized gender roles as by their sexual preference.

Sexual Attitudes and Behaviors of College Students

We have looked at changes in the incidence of sexual behavior in the general population. Do the attitudes and behaviors of college students differ in any noticeable ways?

Early surveys (reviewed by Smigel and Seiden, 1968) found that approximately 45% of college men and 12% of college women approved of sexual activity among unmarried people. Later work by Reiss (1960, 1967), whose U.S. sample included both Black and White high school and college students in both northern and southern schools, indicated that sexual standards had become much more liberal. In 1959, when Reiss conducted his first study, nearly 70% of the men and 27% of the women said that sexual intercourse without marriage would be acceptable to them. By the 1970s, these numbers had shifted again, particularly among women. As many as 70% of college women in these more recent surveys said that nonmarital sexual intercourse would be acceptable to them under some conditions (Kaats & Davis, 1970; Nutt & Sedlacek, 1974).

Beliefs about the propriety of nonmarital sexual intercourse are one aspect of more general feelings about sexual permissiveness, which also include opinions about extramarital sex, prostitution, and casual sex. In one of the most recent surveys designed to tap the attitudes of college students, women were found to be more conservative than men on most of these issues (Hendrick et al., 1985). Women were less likely, for example, to agree that "Casual sex is acceptable" and more likely to say that "Sex is a sacred act." Sex differences were also found in other areas of sexual attitudes. Women, for example, were more likely to advocate individual responsibility for sexual behavior, and were more likely to endorse the importance of emotional communion.

People's attitudes may not always be expressed in

their behavior, however. What are the findings on the actual sexual behavior of college students?

James Curran (1975) asked 164 U.S. college students at a large, relatively conservative Midwestern university to complete a questionnaire about their sexual experience. Table 10-1 shows the results of his study, which looked at a large variety of sexual behaviors. As the table indicates, men and women did not differ greatly in respect to the majority of behaviors. The figures do suggest, however, that these college men and women may have experienced some sexual behaviors in different orders. More women had experienced cunnilingus and fellatio than had experienced intercourse, for example, while that pattern was reversed among men. These findings suggest that in the 1970s some women were enjoying various forms of sexual satisfaction while still remaining technically virgins. Thus the sequences of behaviors may have differed somewhat among men and women, but the overall frequencies of sexual behavior differed only slightly—a finding that suggests that a double standard of behavior may not have been pervasive in the college population.

The overall rates of intercourse for men and women, in this midwestern U.S. sample (44% for men and 37% for women) are somewhat lower than figures reported from other locales. Some other studies suggest that approximately 55% of college women and 75% of college men have engaged in sexual intercourse (King, Balswick, & Robinson, 1977). Similar studies done in Canada a few years earlier have shown rates of about 40% for women and 55% for men (Perlman, 1973).

The prevalence of sexual behavior among the single as well as among the married surely testifies to the importance of sex as one aspect of social interaction. Yet the frequency data, though interesting, tell us only *what* is being done, not *why*. What are the reasons for sexual behavior? What theoretical frameworks have been offered to explain sexuality?

Theoretical Issues in Sexual Behavior

Standards for sexual behavior vary widely. If we investigate various cultures, we find an incredible diversity of attitudes toward sexual behavior. In some cases, sex is seen as pleasurable, in others as innocuous, and in still others as potentially dangerous. Members of one society may say that sex is "the best thing in life," while other groups view sex as "a little like work" (Broude, 1975). How are these variations in attitudes toward sexual behavior explained?

Psychoanalytic Theory of Sexuality

Sigmund Freud was perhaps the first person to insist that sexuality is a basic part of the human personality (see Chapter One). In his theorizing at the turn of the century, Freud proposed that sexual energy is the basic motivator of human behavior, and he described a sequence of stages paralleling supposed changes in the location of sexual tension (Freud, 1938). Infantile sexuality centered on *oral* and then *anal* areas of the body, but at the age of 3 or so, the *genital*

Table 10–1 Sexual behavior among college students

Have you ever engaged in the following behavior with a member of the opposite sex?	Percentage of Men Saying Yes	Percentage of Women Saying Yes
1. One minute of continuous kissing on the lips?	86.4%	89.2%
2. Manual manipulation of clothed female breasts?	82.7	71.1
3. Manual manipulation of bare female breasts?	75.5	66.3
4. Manual manipulation of clothed female genitals?	76.4	67.5
5. Kissing nipples of female breast?	65.5	59.0
6. Manual manipulation of bare female genitals?	64.4	60.2
7. Manual manipulation of clothed male genitals?	57.3	51.8
8. Mutual manipulation of genitals?	55.5	50.6
9. Manual manipulation of bare male genitals?	50.0	51.8
10. Manual manipulation of female genitals until there were massive secretions?	49.1	50.6
11. Sexual intercourse, face to face?	43.6	37.3
12. Manual manipulation of male genitals to ejaculation?	37.3	41.0
13. Oral contact with female genitals?	31.8	42.2
14. Oral contact with male genitals?	30.9	42.2
15. Mutual manual manipulation of genitals to mutual orgasm?	30.9	26.5
16. Oral manipulation of male genitals?	30.0	38.6
17. Oral manipulation of female genitals?	30.0	41.0
18. Mutual oral-genital manipulation?	20.9	28.9
19. Sexual intercourse, entry from the rear?	14.5	22.9
20. Oral manipulation of male genitals to ejaculation?	22.7	26.5
21. Mutual oral manipulation of genitals to mutual orgasm?	13.6	12.0

area became central to the expression of sexuality. At this stage, too, Freud postulated critical differences between male and female development—differences that he believed contributed to significant variations in the sexual behavior of adult men and women. More specifically, Freud suggested that women could experience mature sexuality only through vaginal orgasms as a result of penetration by the penis. Freud considered other modes of achieving orgasm, such as direct clitoral stimulation, to reflect inadequate femininity, which he believed derived from the young girl's early penis envy. Although Freud believed that there was a physical as well as a psychological distinction between clitoral and vaginal orgasms, later research has shown that the two forms are identical, both as physiological events and in the sensation they produce (Masters & Johnson, 1966).

Freud also believed that his proposed sequence of the development of sexuality, including the famous oedipal period, was universal. In other words, he assumed that members of every culture and society go through the same sequence of events in the development of their sexuality. Although the socialization practices of various cultures may modify the expression of sexual energy, Freud for the most part believed that similar sexual motivations and conflicts would be found in every society.

Cognitive Aspects of Sexual Behavior

Many people disagree with Freud's theory of sexuality, but few deny that sexual behavior is basic to humans and animals alike. As a necessity for reproduction of the species, sexual intercourse is performed fairly instinctively, although the forms and cycles of sex vary among species (Daly & Wilson, 1978; Ford & Beach, 1951). In human beings, in particular, the variation in forms of sexual behavior is considerable, and it is difficult to account for these differences on the basis of instinct alone. Consequently, many recent theorists in the area of sexual behavior have begun to focus on cognitive factors that surround the choice and experience of sexuality.

As Paul Abramson (1983) states in explaining his model of the sexual system, "the underlying assumption in the present schema is that all decisions regarding sexual expression are controlled by a mechanism which has been represented as a cognitive structure." A careful examination of Figure 10–2 will show how this assumption works. Abramson assumes that a variety of factors influence the cognitive structure: parental standards, social norms, maturation, and previous sexual experience. For example, parents may instruct us in what is proper sexual behavior. Other norms and values may be learned from church or from peers. The process of maturation itself, especially the onset of puberty, can influence our beliefs about sexuality. And finally, actual sexual experience—whether fantasy, masturbation, or intercourse—plays an important role in our beliefs. From the sum of these experiences, we develop a set of principles about sexual behavior.

In other terms, these principles constitute a **script** for sexual behavior. Scripts, as we saw in Chapter Four, are conceptual representations of sequences of events that guide our behavior in relevant settings. People have beliefs about the kinds of sexual behavior that are appropriate, and these beliefs affect their actions. Scripts can change, of course, and some investigators have suggested that such changes are necessary before behavior can change (Reed & Weinberg, 1984). The scripts of young men and women, for example, differed more in the 1960s than they do today, and their different rates of sexual activity probably reflected the differences in their scripts. The script for men supported sexual activity, while the women's script said, "Nice girls don't." By the 1970s, many women were developing new scripts that more closely resembled men's, and the rates of sexual activity of the two sexes became more similar as well. Although it is difficult to establish cause and effect in this case, it is quite evident that cognitive factors are very much involved in sexual behavior. A variety of sexual stimulus cues, both internal and external, influence sexual behavior, and these cues are processed by the mediating cognitive structure. Hormones and the nervous system exert their internal influence, while a multitude of external stimuli are associated with sexuality.

Certain situations, such as those in which sexual permissiveness is fostered or in which alcohol or other drugs are being used, also encourage sexual expression. Neither internal nor external cues operate directly in most cases. Rather, the stimulus event is transformed into a mental image, which in turn influences sexual activity (Przybyla & Byrne, 1984).

This model of sexual behavior is admittedly complex, yet it rests on a couple of very simple assumptions. First, it assumes that we learn from past experience and that principles of learning can be applied as easily to sexual behavior as to other forms of social behavior. Second, it assumes that our cognitions about sexuality are important—in other words,

```
Input            Mediator         Sexual Stimulus Cues        Outcome

Maturation  ──►                ◄── Endocrinological
                                   Events

Social Norms ──►  Cognitive    ◄── Conditioned and
                  Structure        Unconditioned Stimuli  ──►  Sexual Expression
                                                               (Overt and Covert)
Internalized  ──►              ◄── Physiological Events
Parental Standards

Previous Sexual ──►            ◄── Situational Parameters
Experience
         ▲                                                          │
         └──────────────────────────────────────────────────────────┘
```

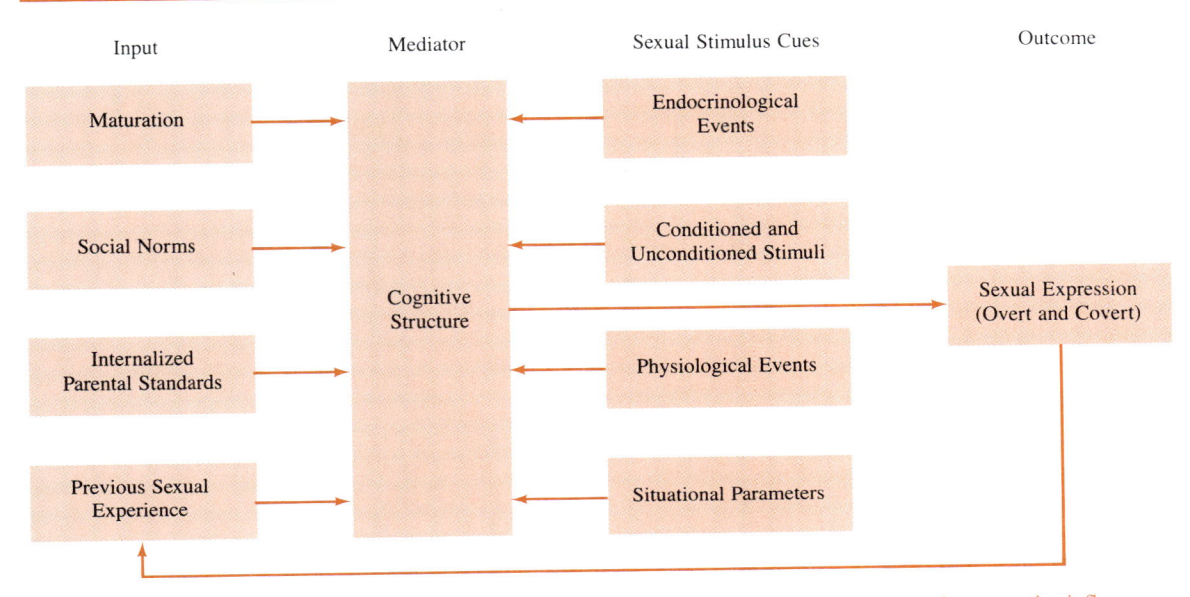

Figure 10–2 The sexual system. In this model proposed by Paul Abramson, cognitive structures have a major influence on sexual expression. The structures are formed on the basis of various inputs, and they, in turn, monitor various sexual stimulus cues to determine eventual sexual expression.

that sexual expression is not instinctual but rather is the outcome of rational thought. Freud would probably disagree with both assumptions, especially with the latter. Most current investigators of sexual behavior, however, have adopted some combination of learning and cognitive principles to explain sexual behavior (Byrne, 1977, 1982; Rook & Hammen, 1977), and the early findings appear to justify their assumptions.

Heterosexual and Homosexual Preferences

Evidence that learning plays an important part in our definition of and response to sexual stimuli is related to the issue of heterosexual versus homosexual behavior. Why do some people prefer sexual partners of the same sex to partners of the other sex? Before discussing this question, we must understand the distinction between gender identity and sexual preference. **Gender identity** refers to one's self-awareness of being male or female (Money & Ehrhardt, 1972). Early theories of homosexuality often assumed that the homosexual's gender identity was opposite to the biological sex. In other words, some argued that the male homosexual identified himself as a female and hence preferred a male sex partner. This *sex-role inversion* theory suggested that homosexuals dress, act, and behave as much like the other sex as possible. More recently it has been recognized that gender identity and *sexual preference* are quite distinct—that homosexuals have no confusion about their gender identity but simply prefer partners of the same sex.[1]

---

[1] **Transsexualism,** in contrast, refers to the case in which one's gender identity is in opposition to one's bodily appearance and sex organs. The writer James Morris, who became Jan Morris after a sex-change operation, described the feelings of a transsexual as follows: "I was born with the wrong body, being feminine by gender but male by sex, and I could achieve completeness only when the one was adjusted to the other" (Morris, 1974).

Although there is no society in which homosexual expression is the dominant form (Ford & Beach, 1951), homosexual behavior has been common throughout history. In early Greek times, Sappho, born on the island of Lesbos (from which the word *lesbian* is derived), wrote passionate love poems describing both homosexual and heterosexual love. Romans were fairly relaxed about all forms of sexual behavior, but with the advent of Christianity, the norms regarding sexual behavior became more restrictive. In the 19th century, Oscar Wilde was jailed and ruined, despite his creative output, when a court found him guilty of homosexual practices (Money & Tucker, 1975). Even in recent years, the majority of people in a national U.S. sample stated that homosexuality is sick and should be outlawed (Levitt & Klassen, 1974). In various parts of the United States, numerous initiatives have been proposed (and frequently passed) to limit the civil rights of homosexuals. The epidemic of AIDS (acquired immune deficiency syndrome), a deadly disease first believed to be associated only with homosexual practices, has intensified antihomosexual attitudes in many segments of the population, despite evidence that the disease is not specific to any one group.

The strong feelings aroused by indications of homosexuality and the disagreement about the causes of homosexual behavior obviously have a long history. Freud, for example, did not consider homosexuality an illness but was ambivalent about the normality of such behavior (see Box 10–1). In 1973, however, the American Psychiatric Association officially removed homosexuality from its list of mental

Photo 10–1 In response to the AIDS epidemic, advertisements for condoms have been directed to women as well as men.

disorders, thus endorsing the view that the choice of a sex partner of the same gender is no more an indication of mental illness than is choice of a partner of the other gender. More recently, an extensive investigation sponsored by the Kinsey Institute (Bell & Weinberg, 1978) indicates that people who prefer a same-sex partner are every bit as well adjusted, on the average, as a comparable sample of heterosexuals. The majority of the homosexuals studied were or had been involved in steady relationships (though often of shorter duration than those of heterosexuals), derived satisfaction from their jobs, had a wide circle of friends, and described themselves as "pretty happy."

Box 10–1
A letter from Freud

April 9, 1935

Dear Mrs. _____,

I gather from your letter that your son is a homosexual. I am most impressed by the fact that you do not mention this term yourself in your information about him. May I question you, why do you avoid it? Homosexuality is assuredly no advantage, but it is nothing to be ashamed of, no vice, no degradation, it cannot be classified as an illness; we consider it to be a variation of the sexual function produced by a certain arrest of sexual development. Many highly respectable individuals of ancient and modern times have been homosexuals, several of the greatest men among them (Plato, Michelangelo, Leonardo da Vinci, etc.). It is a great injustice to persecute homosexuality as a crime, and cruelty too. If you do not believe me, read the books of Havelock Ellis.

By asking me if I can help, you mean, I suppose, if I can abolish homosexuality and make normal heterosexuality take its place. The answer is, in a general way, we cannot promise to achieve it. In a certain number of cases we succeed in developing the blighted germs of heterosexual tendencies which are present in every homosexual; in the majority of cases it is no more possible. It is a question of the quality and age of the individual. The result of the treatment cannot be predicted.

What analysis can do for your son runs in a different line. If he is unhappy, neurotic, torn by conflicts, inhibited in his social life, analysis may bring him harmony, peace of mind, full efficiency, whether he remains a homosexual or gets changed. If you make up your mind he should have analysis with me (I don't expect you will!!) he has to come over to Vienna. I have no intention of leaving here. However, don't neglect to give me your answers.

Sincerely yours with kind wishes,

Sigmund Freud

The question still remains why some people prefer homosexuality while others prefer heterosexuality. A nature-versus-nurture debate has raged on this topic for many years, and for most of this period the nurturists have had the edge. Theorists from Freud (1930) to Masters and Johnson (1979) have proposed that critical experiences in childhood can determine adult sexual preference. Among the factors suggested to be responsible for homosexuality have been relationships with mothers and fathers, the nature of early sexual experiences, and peer relationships.

Michael Storms (1981) has also pointed to the importance of early experiences, suggesting that sexual orientation is a result of a temporal link between physiological development and social development. According to Storms, if sex drives develop fairly early, then erotic fantasies will be associated with the same-sex peer group. If the physiological drives develop at a later age, however, when social interaction with the other sex is more common, then erotic fantasies, and in turn behavior, will be heterosexual. Although this model stresses the importance of social factors, it also invokes a "nature" argument, because Storms suggests that sexual drives generally have their onset earlier in homosexuals.

The earlier reliance on "nurture" explanations is also questioned in the most recent report on homosexuality from the Kinsey Institute (Bell, Weinberg, & Hammersmith, 1981a, 1981b). After an intensive study of nearly 1000 male and female homosexuals and a comparison group of nearly 500 male and female heterosexuals in the San Francisco Bay area, Bell and his colleagues have questioned much of the conventional wisdom in this area. Their research did show some differences between homosexuals and heterosexuals in feelings toward mothers, toward fathers, and toward the parental relationship and in childhood conformity to traditional gender roles. However, using sophisticated statistical techniques to infer causality, they concluded that these differences did not cause adult sexual preference. Rather, they suggest that "by the time boys and girls reach adolescence, their sexual preference is likely to be already determined" (1981a, p. 186), and thus these socialization differences may reflect an already established sexual preference.

The recent Kinsey Institute findings also provide an interesting perspective on **bisexuality**—sexual attraction to and activity with members of both sexes in roughly equal measure. Freud (1930) believed that people are inherently bisexual. Similarly, Kinsey's original studies concluded that sexual choice is best represented as a continuum, from exclusively heterosexual at one end to exclusively homosexual at the other, with many people falling somewhere in between these extremes. Among the respondents in the recent Kinsey Institute study, 8% of the heterosexual men and 13% of the heterosexual women were best considered, on the basis of their self-reports, to be bisexual. Social learning and specific sexual experiences appeared to have been much more influential for people in this group than they had been for the exclusively homosexual people.

What kinds of experiences might be important in the development of bisexuality? Blumstein and Schwartz (1977) suggest three kinds of circumstances that are common influences: (1) experimentation in a friendship context (particularly common among women), (2) liberal hedonistic environments where group sex and other activities are explored, and (3) erotically based ideological positions in which sex represents one aspect of a more general philosophy of life. Other situations that may encourage or permit homosexual behavior by persons who generally consider themselves heterosexual include prisons, military camps, and prep schools, where heterosexual outlets are absent or severely limited. The influence of such circumstances underlines the contribution of social factors to sexuality without negating the contributions that biological factors may make.

Sexual Behavior in Relationships

Thus far we have considered sexual behavior from the perspective of the individual, looking at the frequency with which people report experiencing sexual activities and the theoretical issues involved in an individual's decisions about when and how to engage in sex. Yet it is clear that most sexual behavior is a shared experience—in other words, it is an important social and interpersonal activity. Let's look, then, at the role of sexuality in interpersonal relationships.

Sexuality in Dating Relationships

In Chapter Nine we discussed an extensive study of more than 200 dating couples in the Boston area, focusing on the ways in which partners fall in and out of love. The same study included an in-depth investigation of the sexual behavior of these couples and provides us with one of the most thorough reports on the nonmarital sexual behavior of college students in the 1970s (Peplau, Rubin, & Hill, 1977).

The majority of these couples were very positive about sexuality in a relationship. Not only did 80% of the couples believe that it was completely acceptable for couples who love each other to have intercourse, but their behavior was consistent with these expressed beliefs: 82% of the couples had had intercourse in their current relationship. This figure does not imply that the proportion of college students who are sexually intimate is this large; our earlier discussion of the frequency of sexual behavior among college students showed the percentage was somewhat lower. Among students who are "going with" someone, however, the incidence of sexual intimacy is substantial.

Although the majority of the students in the study had experienced intercourse with their current partner, 18% of the couples reported abstention. In these couples, it appeared that the woman was the primary source of restraint. Of the men, 64% reported that it was their partner's desire to abstain that kept them from engaging in sexual activity. Another reason for abstention in these couples, endorsed by nearly half of the men and women, was a fear of pregnancy. In addition, women said that sex would violate their ethical standards and that it was too early in the relationship to consider sexual activity. The religious background of the woman was also related to the sexual behavior of the couple. Approximately 27% of the Catholic women in the sample refrained from intercourse, compared with 16% of Jewish women and only 2% of Protestant women. Interestingly, the man's religious background had no effect on the presence or absence of sexual intercourse in the relationship.

Among the couples who had engaged in intercourse during their relationship, approximately half had done so within one month after the first date. Comparing these couples with the ones who had begun sexual activity at a later stage in the relationship, the investigators found that characteristics of the woman again were more closely related to the couple's activities than were characteristics of the man. As Table 10-2 indicates, the women in couples who had had sexual intercourse early reported themselves to be less religious, more oriented toward a career, less oriented toward the homemaker role, and higher in self-esteem as assessed by a variety of self-ratings.

The three types of couples observed in this study (those who abstained, those who engaged in sex fairly early in the relationship, and those who first engaged in sex at a later point in the relationship) viewed the relationship between sex and emotional intimacy in rather different ways. Abstaining couples had a traditional view of sexuality, and they believed that a permanent commitment of marriage was a necessary prerequisite for sexual behavior. The women in these relationships were typically virgins; the men may have had limited sexual experience in other relationships. Those couples who experienced sexual activity very early in the relationship, in contrast, indicated their approval of casual sex. They said that although love is desirable in a sexual relationship, sex without love is also acceptable. Often sexual intercourse served these couples as a means of devel-

Table 10-2 Characteristics of women in "early coitus" and "later coitus" couples

	Early Coitus (N = 90)	Later Coitus (N = 92)
Self-rating on religiosity (9-point scale)	3.4	4.2
Preference for being full-time housewife in 15 years (mean rank among 4)	2.8	2.3
Preference for being single career woman in 15 years (mean rank among 4)	3.0	3.5
Authoritarian submission (10 items)	1.8	2.3
Adherence to alternative lifestyle (9-point scale)	6.2	5.3
Self-ratings (all 9-point scales)		
Creative	6.4	5.9
Intelligent	7.0	6.6
Self-confident	5.8	5.0
Desirable as a date	6.8	6.2

NOTE: All early-late differences significant at $p < .05$ or better. Similar analyses for men failed to reach statistical significance. (Early = within one month of first date.)

SOURCE: American Psychological Association *Monitor*, April 1986.

oping emotional intimacy rather than as a means to express such feelings. Between these two extremes were the couples that the investigators termed *sexual moderates*. For these couples, sex occurred later in the relationship, after love and emotional intimacy had been established. Ethical considerations did not appear to delay the onset of sexual activity, but romantic concerns were a necessary element.

Despite the diversity in views toward sexuality among these three kinds of couples, the chances of the relationship's long-term success were equal for all three patterns. Two years after the initial interviews, an equal percentage of each type of couple had married (20%), had continued to date (34%), and had broken up (46%).

One final area of interest in this study concerns the differences between men's and women's attitudes toward sexuality. Men's attitudes toward sex in a casual relationship were somewhat more positive (a finding that is consistent with those of the attitude surveys discussed earlier), but both men and women agreed that sex was acceptable in a love relationship. Contrary to some assumptions, men did not differ from women in their attitudes toward the relation between love and sexual satisfaction in the relationship. Love was moderately correlated with sexual satisfaction in the reports of both sexes.

Perhaps the most striking difference between the sexes is seen in the issue of loss of virginity. Many commentators have suggested that the loss of virginity is a more important step for a woman than for a man (Bernard, 1975), and the findings of this study of Boston couples support that suggestion. Whether the man was a virgin before the couple entered the relationship was not related to the couple's feelings of commitment, but the woman's previous sexual status was associated with that commitment. Couples in which the woman had been a virgin before the existing relationship reported more love for each other and a greater probability of marriage. In addition, these women reported more closeness and greater satisfaction in the relationship than women who had experienced intercourse before. It is interesting, however, that the previous virginity of the woman had no long-term effect on the relationship: couples in which the woman had been a virgin before their relationship were no more likely to stay together than couples in which the woman had had prior sexual experience.

In summary, the nonmarital sexual behavior of college students covers a wide range of styles. Although sexual activity of any kind (such as petting

Photo 10–2 The association between sexual satisfaction and general satisfaction with the relationship is well documented.

or genital manipulation) is most likely to occur when there is a sense of equity in the relationship (Walster, Walster, & Traupmann, 1978), the actual experience of intercourse may happen early, late, or not at all. Its occurrence seems to have little to do with the long-term success of the relationship.

Sexuality in Long-Term Relationships

Although nonmarital sex appears to have little effect on the stability of dating relationships, we may ask whether it has any long-term effects. Specifically, does the premarital sexual experience of couples who do get married have any effect on their subsequent marital satisfaction? Ard (1974) asked this question of a sample of 161 couples who had been married about 20 years. Nearly half of these couples reported having had premarital intercourse with their future spouses. (This figure very closely approximates Kinsey's data but may prove surprising to some students. College students, when asked to estimate the extent of their parents' sexual activities, tend to grossly underestimate the levels of such activity, whether it is premarital, marital, or extramarital, as studies by Pocs and Godow, 1977, have shown.) When persons in Ard's sample of married couples were asked whether their premarital sexual experience—either intercourse or the lack of it—had had any effect on their marriages, the majority of couples in both groups reported that there was little effect. More people reported a favorable effect than an unfavorable effect, regardless of the level of activity, although wives who had not experienced premarital intercourse with their spouses were most inclined to report favorable effects of premarital abstention on subsequent marital happiness.

Within the marital relationship itself, sex is often believed to be a critical determinant of the couple's happiness. One observer concluded: "There are couples for whom the only good thing in marriage is sex. And there are sexless marriages which are satisfactory to husband and wife. But both these situations are rare. Usually in a discordant marriage the sex life is unsatisfactory, too" (Golden, 1971, p. 185).

The association between sexual satisfaction and general satisfaction with the relationship is well documented (Blumstein & Schwartz, 1983; Perlman & Abramson, 1982). Married people who were asked to monitor the frequency of their sexual intercourse for 35 days and then to rate their marital happiness reported a high relationship between the two; this finding suggests that sex and marital happiness do go together (Thornton, 1977). The same study found that marital happiness was negatively related to the frequency of reported arguments, as might be expected, and that the frequency of sex was negatively related to the frequency of arguments as well. More generally, Blumstein and Schwartz (1983) found that in all types of long-term relationships—heterosexual, lesbian, and gay—frequency of sex was related to sexual satisfaction, which in turn was related to satisfaction with the relationship. Infrequent sex was associated with conflict and general dissatisfaction with the relationship, particularly in heterosexual couples; this relationship was less pronounced among lesbian and gay couples. These connections are not surprising; nonetheless, it is important to remember that correlational data cannot demonstrate causality. Both the frequency of sex and the frequency of arguments may affect marital happiness; in turn, both of these factors may be affected by some third variable, such as job difficulties, health worries, or the presence of interfering relatives in the home.

Other factors are also related to sexual satisfaction and happiness with the relationship, according to the findings of Blumstein and Schwartz (1983). Partners reported being happier, for example, when they felt equally able both to initiate and to refuse sexual interaction. Sexual satisfaction was also related to perceptions of the partner's attractiveness, except in the case of the lesbian relationships. Again, however, one must be careful about assuming the direction of causality. Partners may find sex satisfying because they view their partner as attractive, or they may believe their partner is attractive because they enjoy their sexual relationship.

These studies indicate that sexual behavior is indeed an important aspect of most relationships. Although it surely is not the sole determinant of happiness and may be affected by many other kinds of behaviors and events, sexual behavior is nonetheless a central element in most people's ongoing relationships.

Sexual Behavior and Contraception

As everyone knows, sexual behavior may be more than an end in itself. It can also have future consequences—specifically, pregnancy and the birth of children. Or *does* everyone know? The dramatic increase in pregnancies among American teenagers, most of them unmarried (see Photo 10–3), suggests that the connection between sexual intercourse and

Photo 10-3 The reality of teenage pregnancy.

future pregnancy is not always recognized, at least at the time the intercourse occurs.

In 1978, 10% of all teenage women in the United States became pregnant—a total of more than 1 million women. Few of these young women (less than 20%) were married at the time of conception and many had not married by the time the child was born. Many of the women terminated the unwanted pregnancy by abortion—nearly 40%, according to figures collected by the Alan Guttmacher Institute (1981).

Unwanted pregnancies can be avoided if sexually active people use some form of contraception. But many people do not take such precautions. Of the respondents in one recent survey of sexually active 15–19-year-olds, 26% said that they never used contraceptives, and an additional 45% said they only sometimes took precautions. The use of contraceptives does increase with age: whereas 38% of the 15-year-olds said they never used contraceptives, only 15% of the 19-year-olds made that claim (Morrison, 1985). Nonetheless, neither age nor education guarantees that contraception will be practiced regularly. Even among a well-educated sample at a university with a service that provides information on birth control and freely dispenses contraceptives, fewer than a third of the students who acknowledged being sexually active practiced contraception regularly (Byrne, 1983). Some evidence suggests that college women are using less effective contraceptive methods now than they did some years earlier, despite an increase in the amount of sexual activity (Gerrard, 1982).

Why don't people who engage in sexual activity practice effective contraception? One reason is that teenagers often lack knowledge both of the facts of reproductive physiology and of the effectiveness of contraceptives. A third of the teenagers questioned in one study, for example, agreed that "if a girl truly doesn't want a baby, she won't get pregnant even though she may have sex without taking any birth control precautions" (Morrison, 1985, p. 543). Knowledge increases with sexual experience as well as with age. Further, children of higher socioeconomic classes are more likely to have accurate information than are those of lower socioeconomic classes (Morrison, 1985).

Lack of knowledge is not the only reason for failure to use contraceptives, however. Many women simply believe that "it can't happen to me." Ignoring the information on the increasing numbers of teenage pregnancies tirelessly reported by the media, these women exempt themselves from the general laws of probability. Some women do not use contraceptives because such use suggests premeditation, and they fear that their partner will think ill of them. The desire for spontaneity is often given as an explanation for failure to take precautions: they want to be able to tell themselves that they were "swept away" by passion. Other attitudes that discourage the use of contraceptives include the belief that contraception interferes with enjoyment, that it is morally wrong, and that it is the responsibility of one's partner rather than of oneself (Morrison, 1985). People may also find it too difficult, too expensive, or too embarrassing to buy contraceptives. Nearly a third of the people interviewed in most surveys give responses of this type. Finally, some teenage women—as many as 25% in some surveys—don't use contraceptives because they want to get pregnant (Morrison, 1985).

Donn Byrne (1983) has suggested that five steps occur in the decision to practice contraception: (1) acquiring factual information about contraception, (2) acknowledging the likelihood of engaging in sexual intercourse, (3) obtaining contraceptives, (4) communicating with the partner about contraception, and (5) practicing contraception. At each step of this sequence, a variety of social and psychological factors can affect the outcome. For the person who wishes to believe that sexual intercourse is an impulsive, romantic act, such a sequence of steps is probably unthinkable. Yet unless each of these steps is taken, unwanted pregnancy may well result.

One factor that affects this sequence is the person's general attitudes toward sexuality. Byrne (1977, 1983) has discussed individual differences in such attitudes, contrasting people who have generally positive attitudes about sexuality (termed erotophilics) with those who have generally negative attitudes (called erotophobics). These two types of people can be seen to differ at each point in the decision sequence (Fisher, Byrne, & White, 1983). Students enrolled in a course in human sexuality, for example, did more poorly on a midterm exam designed to assess their knowledge of contraception and other practices if they held negative attitudes toward sexuality. Erotophobic men underestimate the likelihood that they will engage in sexual activity; not surprisingly, they are also less likely to purchase contraceptive devices. People with more negative attitudes toward sexuality feel less comfortable discussing sexual issues with their partner.

The degree to which people feel guilt, or expect to feel guilt, about sexual activity is also related to their use of contraceptives. Sexually active women who score high on a measure of sex guilt are more likely than the low scorers to use either ineffective contraceptives or none at all (Gerrard, 1982). Women who have a high level of anxiety are less likely to use birth control pills than those women whose anxiety is lower, perhaps because the pill requires planning and acknowledgment of the likelihood of sexual activity. The highly anxious woman is more likely to rely on her partner to use a condom (Leary & Dobbins, 1983).

Overall, general attitudes toward sexuality affect a variety of behaviors that lead to effective contraception. Ironically, the people who find sex most troublesome may, through their own actions, increase the likelihood of unwanted pregnancy if they do engage in sexual activity.

Erotic Material and Sexual Arousal

As we noted earlier in discussing theoretical models of sexuality, external stimuli can affect sexual choices and behavior. Such influences are abundant in our society—in books, in films, and on television (see Box 10-2). But just what is sexually arousing? And how does sexual arousal affect other forms of behavior?

Definitions of Sexual Stimuli

Defining sexual stimuli is one of the most difficult tasks in this area of study. The terms *erotica* and *obscenity* have been used interchangeably, but they have somewhat different meanings. **Obscenity** is mainly a legal term (as is *insanity* in the mental health field). Originally *obscenity* referred to that which was considered publicly offensive and therefore proscribed—primarily derogatory statements about the church or government (Wilson, 1973). Sexual terms and activities came to be incorporated in the realm of obscenity around the middle of the 19th century; more recent developments in the United States have completed the process by limiting legal obscenity to the sexual realm (Bender, 1971). The U.S. Supreme Court set three criteria by which material could be judged obscene: (1) it tends to incite prurient interest in the average person, (2) it goes substantially beyond community standards with regard to the depiction of sex, and (3) it is without redeeming social value (Money & Athanasiou, 1973). Subsequent court cases, however, have demonstrated that these criteria are very difficult to pin down—even though some people may glibly claim that they "know obscenity when they see it."

Erotica is the term most often used by social scientists to refer to any visual or verbal material that is considered sexually arousing. This definition is still somewhat vague, reflecting the fact that relatively little work has been devoted to specifying the content of sexual stimuli (Diamond, 1980). Furthermore, material may be sexually arousing to one person and not to another. However, the definition of *erotica* does attempt to focus on the material as such and is an improvement over definitions that require an inference of prurient interest or social value.

Reactions to erotic material take a variety of forms. Some responses occur in the body, causing measurable physiological changes. People react to erotic material at a cognitive level as well, as in the case of fantasies. Further, exposure to erotic material may lead to certain forms of behavior, a matter that has practical as well as theoretical significance.

Physiological Responses to Erotic Stimuli

Several methods are used to determine physiological reactions to erotic stimuli. The reactions of sexual

Box 10–2
Sex and the media

How much sex is really portrayed in the media? Do best-selling novels and major motion pictures do well precisely because they contain a great deal of explicit sexuality? Has the sexual content of books and movies changed over the past three decades? Paul R. Abramson and Mindy B. Mechanic (1983) considered these questions in an analysis of the top five novels and top five motion pictures of 1959, 1969, and 1979. The subjects of their archival analysis are listed on the opposite page.

In books and in movies, people who engage in sex are generally young, single, attractive, and physically healthy. Rarely are these fictitious characters uninterested in sex or unable to perform, and almost never is there any evidence of concern about contraception. Movies, which are subject to specific moral codes and rating systems, generally depicted less sexual activity than the best-selling novels did.

Changes in sexual activity described in novels are evident over the 20-year period. Sex partners in the most recent books are depicted as having known each other for a shorter time and showing less romantic concern than those in the earlier novels. These modern partners are also less communicative. In the 1979 novels, 46% of the characters avoided both verbal and nonverbal communication after sex, but only 9% did so in the 1959 books.

Relatively few sexual scenes were found in any of the most popular movies, but the sexual episodes that were shown were more explicit in the most recent films. Certainly there were many highly sexual films in those years (for example, the film *10* in 1979), but they were not necessarily the most widely attended films. One interesting shift between 1959 and 1979 is the presence of alcohol and other intoxicants: in 1959, such substances were always part of the sex scenes, whereas they were absent from the best-attended films of later years.

continued

organs, for example, can be subjected to measurement. A device called the penile plethysmograph can be attached to the penis to measure its volume and size (Freund, Sedlacek, & Knob, 1965; Zuckerman, 1971), and the woman's responses can be measured by blood volume and pulse pressure in the genital area (Heiman, 1975). More recently, investigators have begun to use thermograms, which are essentially temperature maps of the body (Abramson et al., 1981). This method can be used to measure the responses of both men and women, so that they can be directly compared. Another advantage of the thermogram is that it is nonintrusive, allowing subjects more privacy and reducing recording errors. As an alternative to these more technological methods, other investigators have assessed physiological reactions simply by asking subjects how aroused they feel (Mosher, 1973; Schmidt, Sigusch, & Meyberg, 1969).

Most studies of physiological responses to erotic stimuli find that subjects do report sexual arousal. For example, in a study of German male college students, approximately 80% of the students who had observed sexually explicit photos reported that they had had an erection, and almost one-fifth reported the emission of some pre-ejaculatory fluid (Schmidt et al., 1969). In a later study that included female college students, most of the women reported some bodily reactions in the genital area (Schmidt & Sigusch, 1970). A study conducted with U.S. college students (Mosher, 1973) produced similar findings.

Although the physiological responses to erotic material are consistent, the effect seems to diminish over time, at least for the typical college student. A study done for the U.S. Commission on Obscenity and Pornography (Howard, Reifler, & Liptzin, 1971), for example, found that exposure to erotic material

Perhaps most striking in this analysis is the uniformly unrealistic presentation of sexuality that seems predominant in the popular media. People are not old, they are not married, they do not talk, and no one worries about the consequences. In reality, sexual behavior is far more varied than that.

Novels	Motion Pictures
1959*	**1959**
Dr. Zhivago (Pasternak)	*Auntie Mame*
Lolita (Nabokov)	*Some Like It Hot*
Exodus (Uris)	*Pillow Talk*
Lady Chatterley's Lover (Lawrence)	*Imitation of Life*
	Shaggy Dog
1969	**1969**
Portnoy's Complaint (Roth)	*The Love Bug*
The Godfather (Puzo)	*Funny Girl*
The Salzberg Connection (MacInnes)	*Bullitt*
The Love Machine (Susann)	*Butch Cassidy and the Sundance Kid*
Airport (Hailey)	*Romeo and Juliet*
1979	**1979**
The Women's Room (French)	*Superman*
Bloodline (Sheldon)	*Every Which Way but Loose*
The World According to Garp (Irving)	*Star Trek*
The Holcroft Convenant (Ludlum)	*Alien*
Scruples (Krantz)	*The Amityville Horror*

*Only four novels were included in the 1959 sample.

could be satiating. Each male subject, approximately 22 years of age, spent 90 minutes a day for three weeks alone in a room that contained a large and diverse collection of erotic materials, including books, photographs, and movies, as well as some nonerotic material. All measures—including both penile erections and self-ratings of arousal—decreased over time. Subjects spent less and less time with the erotic material and even resorted to reading *Reader's Digest*. The introduction of new erotic stimuli, however, heightened the response once more, suggesting that the satiation may be specific rather than general.

Sexual arousal can also occur without the presence of such erotic materials in the environment. Self-generated fantasies and other cognitive processes can lead to arousal, and their effects on physiological responses can be demonstrated in a laboratory setting (Greer, 1974). In such studies, subjects are asked to sit in a comfortable chair, to imagine a sexual scene, and to "turn themselves on" by doing so. Within two or three minutes, changes in physiological responses have been observed.

Psychological Responses to Erotic Stimuli

Responses to erotic material occur at a mental level as well as a physiological one. People often respond to erotic stimuli by engaging in sexual fantasies, for example, imagining future encounters or recalling past events. These cognitive reactions to erotic stimuli clearly are part of what is generally called sexual arousal.

The original Kinsey studies reported that women were less likely than men to be sexually aroused by erotic stimuli (Kinsey et al., 1953). Although this sex difference was accepted without question for many years, recent investigators find evidence to the contrary. Both men and women report sexual arousal in response to erotic stimuli, although certain qualitative aspects of the reported fantasies may differ. After undergraduate students agreed to be involved in an experiment dealing with sexual material, William Fisher and Donn Byrne (1978) asked them to watch a ten-minute film in which a couple undressed and engaged in heavy petting. Both sexes reported considerable arousal in response to the film, and the investigators found no sex differences in the responses. Interestingly, when the investigators varied the background description of the film—describing the couple variously as married, as a prostitute and client, and as casual acquaintances—both men and women reported being most aroused by the casual-sex theme.

Other investigators have simply asked subjects to relax completely for a short period and to fantasize about an erotic situation. Reported fantasies again reveal no quantitative differences between men and women, but there is some evidence that women's fantasies are more complex and emotionally richer than men's (Carlson & Coleman, 1977). Similarly, when men and women are asked to describe the thoughts and ideas they've had during sexual activity, women tend to report more imaginative fantasies, while men are more apt to think of past experiences and current behavior (McCauley & Swann, 1978). Women are also somewhat more likely to describe fantasies dealing with submission, whereas men's fantasies more often reveal performance concerns (Knafo & Jaffe, 1984). Again, however, the overall level of fantasy is no higher among men than among women. Thus Kinsey's conclusions seem to be no longer valid.

Not all responses to erotic stimuli are positive, however. Many people respond primarily with guilt. For such people, viewing erotic stimuli is more of an aversive experience; in fact, people who score high on a measure of sex guilt are less likely to view erotic material (Schill & Chapin, 1972) and show less physiological arousal when they are exposed to such material (Pagano & Kirschner, 1978). Guilt about sex is stronger among the older generation than the younger, a finding that may reflect some changes in general attitudes toward sex (Abramson & Imai-Marquez, 1982).

Sexual arousal can affect the ways we evaluate other people, particularly people with whom some sexual interactions can be imagined. For example, sexually aroused men rated photographs of women as more attractive than nonaroused men did (Stephan, Berscheid, & Walster, 1971). This perception of a woman's attractiveness was particularly strong when the men believed they would actually have a date with her. As might be expected in a primarily heterosexual, college-student population, the male subjects' ratings of attractiveness increased only when the photos were of women, not of other men (Griffitt, May, & Veitch, 1974). Presumably a similar study conducted with a homosexual population would find stronger effects for same-sex than for other-sex targets.

Sexual arousal and fantasy can be affected by a variety of factors. In one recent experiment some male and female subjects were given a vodka-and-tonic drink before they viewed erotic photographs from *Playboy, Playgirl, Penthouse,* and fashion magazines (McCarty, Diamond, & Kaye, 1982). Other subjects drank only tonic water. Subjects who had the alcohol reported more arousal and stronger fantasies than the "teetotalers." Consistent with earlier findings, no differences were found between the fantasy reactions of men and women. In an additional experimental manipulation, the researchers told half the subjects in each group that they would be drinking alcohol and told the other half that they would be drinking neutral tonic water. (Because vodka's taste is not distinctive, this deception was effective.) The manipulation had a strong effect. Subjects who thought they had been drinking alcohol reported stronger fantasies than subjects who thought their drink was only tonic, no matter what drink they actually had. The strongest fantasies of all were reported by those subjects who believed they had tonic but actually had alcohol—presumably because they could not readily explain the arousal caused by the alcohol and attributed it to the erotic photographs. (Recall the discussion of emotional labeling in Chapter Three.)

Behavioral Responses to Erotic Stimuli

Exposure to explicit sexual materials leads to a state of physiological arousal, to fantasy, and to more positive evaluation of sexual targets. But does it lead to increased sexual activity?

The assumption generally made is that exposure to erotic material will cause an increase in the sexual activity of the observer. Investigators have tried to test this assumption in the following way. First, the typical sexual activity of subjects (who volunteer for the study) is assessed through self-reports that describe their sexual activities during the previous week or month. Then the subjects are shown erotic materials (usually films), and later—perhaps a day later, perhaps a week—they are asked to report again on their sexual activities. The procedural problems in this methodology are probably apparent. The use of volunteers may mean that the sample contains too large a proportion of sensation-seeking subjects. The situation may have demand characteristics that influence the subjects to engage in or to report more sexual activity after watching the films. Nevertheless, the findings of these studies are still preferable to uninformed speculation.

Such studies demonstrate a relatively limited effect of erotic material on subsequent sexual behavior. By way of summary, we can report the following conclusions: (1) Sexual activity increases for only a brief period, such as on the night the subjects view the film (Cattell, Kawash, & DeYoung, 1972). (2) There are no reports of increased sexual activity over a prolonged period—say, 12 weeks—even in response to four viewings of sexually explicit films (Mann, Sidman, & Starr, 1971, 1973). (3) There is apparently no change in types of sexual activity (Amoroso et al., 1971). Donald Mosher (1973), in reviewing studies by himself and others, offers the generalization that "erotic films lead to increased sexual activity immediately following the films only if there is a well-established sexual pattern" (p. 109). And even those mild increases are not found in younger and less experienced viewers. Thus exposure to specifically erotic stimuli appears to have a relatively weak effect on subsequent sexual activity, at least under the conditions studied to date.

However, the effects of erotic material cannot be discussed fully without consideration of another possible link—that between sexual stimuli and aggressive behavior. Freud was one of the first to suggest that sexual behavior and aggression are closely linked. He stated that "the sexuality of most men shows an admixture of aggression, of a desire to subdue" (1938, p. 659). Recent psychoanalytic theory has continued to argue for this connection, as in the following statement: "Hostility, overt or hidden, is what generates and enhances sexual excitement, and its absence leads to sexual indifference and boredom" (Stoller, 1976, p. 903).

The U.S. President's Commission on Obscenity and Pornography (1970), appointed to determine whether there is in fact a link between erotic material and violence, concluded that there is not. Later research has modified that conclusion, however. Let us first consider the effects of nonaggressive erotic material—the kind of material on which the commission based its conclusions.

If a person has not been previously angered, exposure to erotic material seems to have no effect on aggression (Donnerstein, 1982); thus the commission's original conclusions are confirmed. When anger is involved, however, aggression and exposure to erotica seem to be related, although the linkage is a bit complex. In some cases, exposure to erotic material may actually inhibit the display of aggression. For example, Robert Baron and Paul Bell (1977) found that college men who had seen pictures of women in bathing suits, pictures of nude women, or pictures of acts of lovemaking were less aggressive than men who had seen neutral pictures of scenery. Men who read erotic literary passages, however, showed no decrease in aggression. This finding suggests that only some forms of erotica will inhibit aggression. Further research has shown that this inhibitory effect is also dependent on a very low level of provocation (Ramirez, Bryant, & Zillmann, 1982).

In contrast, more intense provocation or more arousing forms of erotic material—such as films depicting actual intercourse and oral and anal activities—will increase aggressive behavior (Donnerstein, Donnerstein, & Evans, 1975; Ramirez et al., 1982). Lengthy exposure to these more intense forms of erotic material has also been shown to have other effects, including more leniency in attitudes toward rape and greater callousness in attitudes toward women in general (Zillmann & Bryant, 1982). We will return to this topic in Chapter Eleven, when we discuss the influence of the media on aggressive behavior. For the time being, we must conclude that the relation between erotic material and aggressive behavior is more complex than the President's Commission realized and that erotic material can often cause an increase in aggressive behavior.

Summary

Sexual behavior is an important aspect of social interaction, although scientific study of the topic was considered taboo until fairly recently. Initial work in this area relied on case studies of clinical patients. More recent methods have also included survey research and laboratory experimentation.

Kinsey's landmark work provided information on the frequency with which U.S. adults engaged in various forms of sexual behavior. More recent investigators have updated Kinsey's information and found a gradual increase in the sexual behavior of U.S. adults, particularly women. Similar studies conducted with college students show that nonmarital sexual activity is fairly frequent.

Freud was among the first to insist that sexuality is a basic part of the human personality. His theories on infantile sexuality and the differences between male and female sexuality were influential for many years. Other theoretical discussions of sexuality point to the importance of cognitive factors. These theories stress the importance of socialization experiences and the role of learning in determining what situations and stimuli will be perceived as sexually arousing.

Explanations for the development of homosexual and heterosexual preferences have stressed both nature and nurture.

Bisexuals are people who engage in sexual behavior with persons of both sexes. Evidence suggests that learning and experience may play a larger role in bisexuality than in homosexuality.

Studies of sexual activity in dating relationships show little connection between the presence or absence of such activity and the future success of the relationship. Those couples who abstain, those who engage in sex in the early stage of a relationship, and those who engage in sex at later stages of a relationship do differ, however, in values and beliefs.

In long-term relationships, reports of happiness in the relationship are related to frequency of sexual activity for both heterosexual and homosexual couples. Other aspects of a relationship, such as amount of conflict and perceptions of equality, also relate to sexual satisfaction. Because these data are correlational, however, it is difficult to draw conclusions about the direction of causality.

An obvious consequence of sexual activity is pregnancy. Attitudes and behaviors in regard to birth control are related to more general attitudes toward sexuality.

Studies of the influence of erotic stimuli on sexual behavior must begin with a consideration of the distinction between the terms *obscenity* and *erotica*.

Responses to erotic material include physiological changes, fantasy, guilt, and an increase in the perceived attractiveness of other people. Actual sexual behavior may be affected by exposure to erotic stimuli, although the effects are fairly short-term.

Glossary Terms

bisexuality
erotica
gender identity
obscenity
script
transsexualism

You cannot shake hands with a clenched fist.
Indira Gandhi

One of television's great contributions is that it brought murder back into the home where it belongs.
Alfred Hitchcock

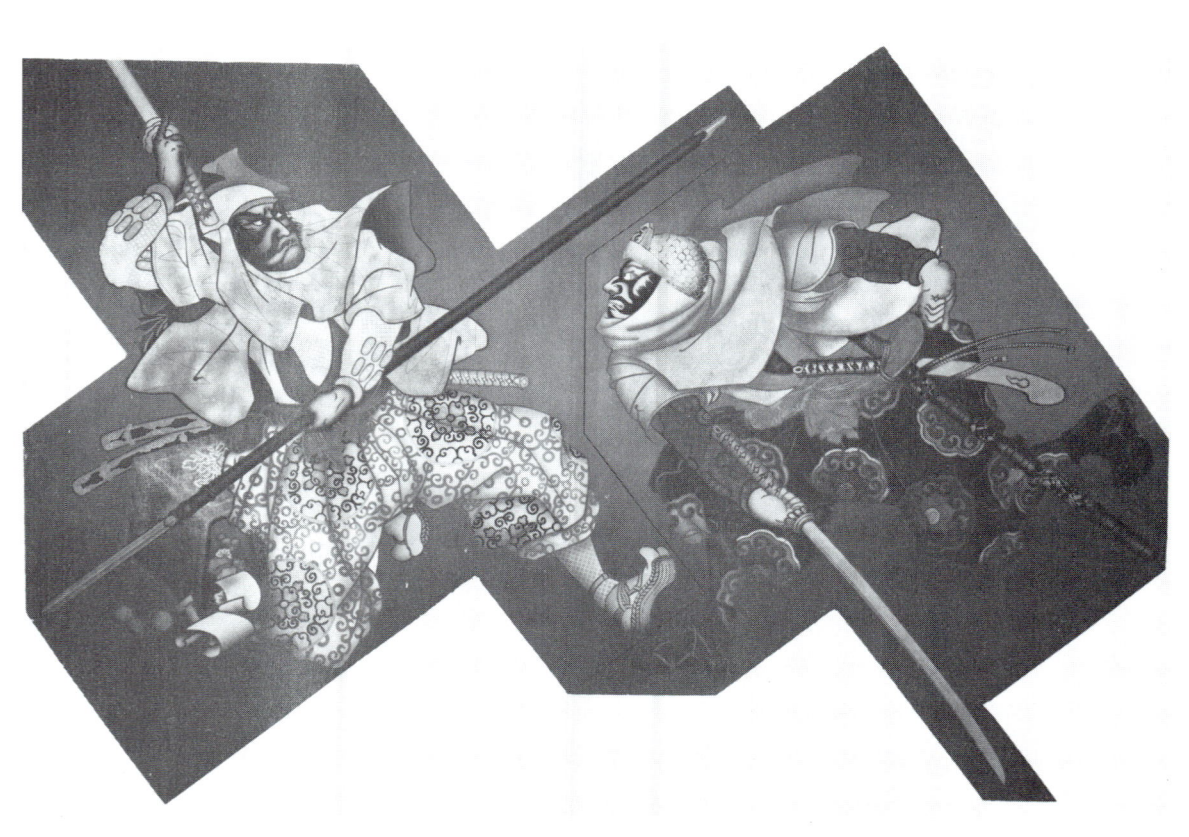

Larry Rivers: *Heroes of Chushingura*, 1974.

CHAPTER ELEVEN

Aggression & Violence

I. Aggression and Human Nature
   Definitions of Aggression
   Biological Explanations of Aggression
   Social Explanations of Aggression
II. Conditions That Influence Aggression
   Frustration
   Aggressive Cues: The Weapons Effect
   General Arousal
   Verbal and Physical Attack
   Third-Party Instigation
   Deindividuation
   Drugs and Alcohol
   Environmental Conditions
   Individual Differences in Aggressive Behavior
III. Violence and the Mass Media
   Television Violence and Aggression in Children
   Pornography and Aggression toward Women
IV. Violence in Society
   Violence in the Home
   Violence in the Streets
   Collective Violence
V. How Can Aggression Be Controlled?
VI. Summary

*D*uring the approximately 5600 years that humans have recorded their history, more than 14,600 wars have occurred, averaging out to nearly three wars per year throughout our history (Montagu, 1976). Places such as the Falkland Islands become known to most people only because of warfare. Since the beginning of the 20th century, more than 900,000 civilians in the United States have died as a result of criminal acts. In fact, among stable industrialized societies, the United States has the highest rates of homicide, assault, rape, and robbery. With great regularity one reads in the newspapers of parents abusing children, husbands and wives engaging in physical violence, and teenaged gangs attacking strangers who enter their neighborhoods.

One could easily conclude from these facts that violence and aggression are integral facets of human society. Indeed, some behavioral scientists assume that aggression is the natural result of a "killer instinct" in human nature. Claiming an evolutionary basis, the popular writer Robert Ardrey (1961) stated that "man is a predator whose natural instinct is to kill with a weapon." Other scientists, however, believe that aggression can be explained completely as a learned social behavior that is predictable and potentially controllable.

Interpretations of aggressive behavior are determined by theoretical viewpoints; and when we consider the nature of aggression, we find more than enough theories to go around. These theoretical perspectives differ in a variety of ways: in the extent to which they consider aggression innate or learned, in the extent to which the person, rather than situational factors, is considered influential, and in the proposed ways in which aggression might be controlled in the future. In this chapter we will look at several of these theories. In addition, we will consider what factors influence aggression. We ask, for example, how alcohol and drugs affect aggressive behavior, whether violence on television and in films affects the observer, how aggression is expressed in the home, and how violence might be controlled in the future.

Aggression and Human Nature

Few would argue that humans lack the capacity to behave in aggressive and antisocial ways, but there is a great deal of disagreement as to the reasons for human aggression. At an even more basic level, confusion exists as to just what it means to be aggressive. Although *aggression* is a term used often in everyday language, it can take on some very specific meanings when it is used by social scientists.

Definitions of Aggression

Numerous definitions of aggression have been suggested, and these definitions often reflect the theoretical assumptions of their proponents. Traditional psychoanalytic theory, for example, defines aggression as an underlying biological urge that must seek expression. The noted ethologist Konrad Lorenz describes aggression as "the fighting instinct in beast and man which is directed against members of the same species" (1966, p. ix). More behavioristic scientists recommend that we look at outward behaviors rather than infer inner drives and motives. Thus definitions of aggressive behavior can vary on a variety of dimensions, including the degrees to which they stress observable behaviors versus motives and intentions, consider immediate versus long-term consequences, and acknowledge psychological as well as physical effects (Krebs & Miller, 1985). In discussing general theoretical approaches to understanding aggressive behavior, we will see how different factors are emphasized.

For most of our discussion, however, we will rely on a definition of aggression that is accepted by most social psychologists: *"Aggression is any form of behavior directed toward the goal of harming or injuring another living being who is motivated to avoid such treatment"* (Baron, 1977, p. 7).

This definition has a number of important features. First of all, it limits aggression to those forms of behavior in which the person *intends* to harm a victim. If you accidentally knock someone over while riding your bicycle, for example, that would not be considered an act of aggression. Similarly, when a nurse gives a patient a routine injection, the intention is not to do harm, although pain may be involved. But what if the patient has just insulted the nurse, who then jams the needle in with unnecessary force? Certainly there is a component of aggression in this behavior. If an attempt to harm someone is unsuccessful—for example, if I try to hit someone but miss—that behavior, too, would be considered aggressive, because the intent was to inflict harm. Although it is often difficult to establish intention with complete certainty, as the proceedings of criminal trials well indicate, the concept of intentionality is important in distinguishing aggressive behavior from other forms of behavior that might lead to some harm.

Often, in everyday speech, people talk about an "aggressive manager" or an "aggressive salesperson." Generally, such descriptions refer to a person who is energetic, assertive, and eager to get ahead. These behaviors do not fit our definition of aggression, however, unless the particular manager or salesperson is deliberately trying to harm another person in the process of being successful.

Our working definition doesn't limit aggression to physical harm. Verbal insults are forms of aggression, and even refusal to give a person something he or she needs can be considered a form of aggression. Our definition does, however, limit aggression to those behaviors that involve other living beings, either human or animal. A person who kicks a wall is probably angry, but this behavior would not be considered aggressive according to our definition. Finally, instances of aggression are limited to those cases in which the other person would prefer to avoid the pain. Behaviors most clearly ruled out by this clause are those of a sadomasochistic nature.

In research practice, aggressive behavior has been studied in a wide variety of forms. Ethologists have observed the physical combat of animals in the wild, and social psychologists have considered the willingness of college students to administer shock to another student. Written stories have been analyzed for evidence of themes of violence, and court records have been collected for reports of assault and battery. Not all of these behaviors fully satisfy the definition of aggression that we have offered, at least insofar as intention must be proven. All of these forms of aggression, however, can be offered as evidence that humans have the capacity to express violence and to cause harm to one another.

But why do they do so? At the most general level, answers to that question fall into two general categories. On the one hand, many people have argued that aggression is so basic to human nature that it will inevitably find expression. Proponents of this point of view include psychoanalysts, ethologists, and sociobiologists. People who take a cultural perspective, on the other hand, see norms, learning, and socialization experiences as the source of aggressive behavior. Let's consider each of these general classes of explanation before considering more specific determinants of aggression.

Biological Explanations of Aggression

Sigmund Freud wrote: "The tendency to aggression is an innate, independent, instinctual disposition in man" (1930, p. 102). According to traditional psychoanalytic theory, aggressive energy is constantly generated by our bodily processes. For example, the intake of food leads to the generation of energy. Aggression is thus defined as an underlying urge that must seek expression. Like sexual urges, aggressive urges must be "released"—that is, expressed directly or indirectly. They can be discharged either in socially acceptable ways (such as a vigorous debate or an athletic activity) or in less socially acceptable ways (such as insults or fights). The destructive release of aggressive urges need not be directed against other people; it may be aimed toward the self, as in suicide. However it is discharged, aggression is considered to be innate and inevitable. In fact, Freud believed that one function of society is to keep natural aggression in check.

Some of Freud's successors—often called **neo-Freudians**—revised his theory, viewing aggression as more of a rational than an irrational process (Hartmann, Kris, & Loewenstein, 1949). According to the neo-Freudians, aggressive drives are healthy; they represent adaptations to the realities of the environment. Like Freud, however, most of these later theorists continued to believe that aggression develops from innate and instinctive forces.

A different biological view of aggression comes to us from the ethologists. **Ethology** is a subfield of biology concerned with the instincts and action patterns common to all members of a species operating in their natural habitat (Eibl-Eibesfeldt, 1970). Ethologists observe the normal behavior of fish, birds, and other animals in the field and try to identify similarities in and causes of their behavior. They often assume that these behaviors (or "action patterns") are under innate, or instinctual, control (Crook, 1973).

According to ethologists, the expression of any fixed action pattern depends on the accumulation of energy. But in order for this energy to be released, it must be triggered by an external stimulus, called a "releasing stimulus" (Hess, 1962). Ethologists use the concept of *releasers* (releasing stimuli) to explain the relationship between internal factors and external stimuli. Specifically, in explaining aggression, ethologists suggest that certain environmental cues allow an organism to express aggressive behavior. Essentially, this is a two-factor theory of the expression of aggression: it has an advantage over orthodox psychoanalytic theory and the neo-Freudian approaches in recognizing that environmental changes contribute to the aggressive response.

Aggression, according to Konrad Lorenz (1966), functions to preserve the species as well as the individual. In other words, aggression has survival value. Lorenz believes that an organism is far more aggressive toward its own species than toward other species. The basic purpose of such aggression is to keep members of the species separated—to give each member enough territory to survive. Intraspecies aggression also affects sexual selection and mating; the stronger are more likely to mate. Thus aggression ensures that the best and strongest animals will carry on the species.

In Lorenz's view, aggression becomes undesirable only when the species—the human species, for example—fails to develop the usual instinctual inhibitions against it. Intraspecies fights usually end not in death but rather in acts of appeasement by the loser (see Photo 11–1). According to Lorenz, all humans' troubles arise from their "being a basically harmless, omnivorous creature, lacking in natural weapons with which to kill [their] big prey, and, therefore, also devoid of the built-in safety devices which prevent 'professional' carnivores from abusing their killing power to destroy fellow members of their own species" (1966, p. 241). Lacking the innate ability to kill without weapons, the human species also has failed to evolve inhibitory mechanisms to prevent aggression. If humans had no weapons at their disposal, they wouldn't be equipped to kill members of their species. What if all killing of other people had to be done with our hands and teeth? Wouldn't that not only reduce the murder rate but also restrain our desire to kill?

Another theory that has developed from animal studies is **sociobiology,** defined by E. O. Wilson as the "systematic study of the biological basis of all social behavior" (1975, p. 4). As we saw in Chapter One, sociobiology is an extension of Darwinian evo-

Photo 11-1 The agony of defeat. The wolf on the left indicates by the positions of her ears and tail that she submits to the dominance of the wolf on the right.

lutionary theory. From this perspective, aggression has evolved because it is adaptive. More specifically, sociobiologists argue that such genetically based behaviors will be maintained by a population or society "if they increase the genetic fitness (i.e., reproductive success) of the individual or his close relatives who also carry the genes for that behavior" (Cunningham, 1981, p. 71). In the case of aggression, sociobiologists suggest that there is a biological advantage to be gained from being aggressive. To acquire more resources, for example, or to defend the resources one has, one might show aggressive behavior. If successful, the aggressive individual might thereby strengthen the position of his or her own group in relation to others. Thus, for the sociobiologist, aggressive behavior has a clear goal—to preserve one's own species and to increase its chances of future success.

At the same time, aggression as a competitive strategy has a number of disadvantages. It is a potentially costly strategy, in that severe injury or death can result, thereby making it impossible for the individual to transmit further genes to the next generation. Consequently, aggression may develop in a selective fashion, to be used in those circumstances where other methods of satisfying needs are not available or where the potential gains are considerable (Krebs & Miller, 1985).

Although the views of psychoanalysts, ethologists, and sociobiologists differ in some important respects, such as the role of the environment in contributing to aggressive behavior, they share some basic assumptions. Most important, all three positions consider aggression to be an innate, instinctual behavior and thus a basic part of the human condition. They may argue about when and where aggression will be displayed, but they all agree that it will be displayed. For the biological theorist, aggression always has existed and always will.

Social Explanations of Aggression

Many psychologists believe that although the aggressive behavior of lower animals can be explained by instinctual processes, the aggressive behavior of humans is not regulated by internal drives—rather, it is learned. The psychologist J. P. Scott has concluded that "all research findings point to the fact that there is no physiological evidence of any internal need or spontaneous driving force for fighting; that all stimulation for aggression comes eventually from forces present in the physical environment" (Scott, 1958, p. 98). If aggressive behavior is indeed learned, how does such learning take place? Proponents of this viewpoint have suggested two methods: instrumental learning and observational learning (Bandura, 1973).

The principle of **instrumental learning** says that any behavior that is reinforced, or rewarded, is more likely to occur in the future. Therefore, if a person acts aggressively and receives a reward for doing so, he or she is more likely to act aggressively on other occasions. The possible range of reinforcements for humans is broad. For example, social approval or increased status can act as a reinforcement of aggressive behavior (Geen & Stonner, 1971; Gentry, 1970). Money can act as a reinforcement for adults (Buss, 1971; Gaebelein, 1973), and candy has proved to be an effective reward for children (Walters & Brown, 1963). For the person who is extremely provoked, evidence of a victim's suffering can serve as a form of reinforcement (Baron, 1974; Feshbach, Stiles, & Bitter, 1967), suggesting a mechanism whereby mass executioners are able to carry out their activities.

Although many aggressive responses can be learned through direct reinforcement, most investigators believe that **observational learning**, or social **modeling**, is a more frequent method of acquiring aggressive behaviors. Specifically, we can learn new behaviors by observing the actions of other people (called *models*). Consider the following situation. A child in a nursery school is brought to a room and asked by an experimenter to play a game. The experimenter then takes the child to one corner of the room and shows him or her how to make pictures by using potato prints and colorful stickers. Soon thereafter, the experimenter brings an adult into the room and takes that person to another corner, where a mallet, a set of Tinker Toys, and an inflated Bobo doll are placed.

After the experimenter leaves the room, the adult begins to play with the "adult toys." In a nonaggressive condition, the adult plays quietly with the Tinker Toys for ten minutes. In an aggressive condition, the adult spends most of the time attacking the Bobo doll, hitting it, kicking it, pounding its nose, and yelling aggressive comments such as "Sock him in the nose!" Then the experimenter returns and takes the child to another room with another set of toys. After frustrating the child briefly by telling him or her that play with a favorite toy is not allowed, the experimenter gives the child an opportunity to play with any of the other toys in the room. These include aggressive toys (such as a Bobo doll, a mallet, and several dart guns) and nonaggressive toys (such as crayons, toy bears, a tea set, and plastic farm animals).

In this and similar experiments, Albert Bandura and his collaborators were interested in the ways in which the observation of an adult's aggressive behavior would affect a child's play choices (Bandura, Ross, & Ross, 1961, 1963a). The adult's behavior did have an effect (see Photo 11–2). Children who had watched an aggressive adult model were consistently more aggressive than those children who had watched a nonaggressive model. (They were also more aggressive than members of control groups, who had watched no model at all.)

But can the behavior of these children really be considered aggression? Recall that our definition limits aggression to behavior directed against another living being. A Bobo doll doesn't seem to qualify. Recent investigations have shown, however, that attacks directed toward a Bobo doll do relate to other forms of aggression. Nursery school children who behaved most violently toward the doll were also rated as being most aggressive in general by their teachers and their peers (Johnston et al., 1977).

Even if an attack on a Bobo doll cannot be considered true aggression, Bandura (1973) has argued for the importance of the experiments in demonstrating the ways in which aggressive behaviors can be acquired. He makes the important distinction between *learning* and *performance* of a response. Presumably, when children observe the attacks, they learn, or acquire, a response; subsequently, when interacting with human beings, they may *perform* the acquired response. Many studies with adults attest to the importance of modeling (Bandura, 1973). Although most adults know how to be aggressive, their willingness to do so is often based on the presence of an aggressive model. The model may not serve as an instructional source, but he or she can act as a *disinhibiting* factor—an example that says "It's all right to be aggressive in this situation."

Those who explain aggression as a learned response claim that if there are societies in which no aggressive behavior is manifested, one can conclude that learning, rather than instinct, plays a dominant role in aggression. A few such societies *do* exist. For example, in the United States and Canada, members of isolated communities such as the Amish, the Mennonites, and the Hutterites strive to achieve peaceful coexistence. The Hutterites advocate a life of pacifism; aggressive acts in their society go unrewarded (Eaton & Weil, 1955, cited in Bandura & Walters, 1963). Geoffrey Gorer (1968) has reviewed anthropological evidence of societies whose goal is peaceful isolation; these societies include the Arapesh of New Guinea, the Lepchas of Sikkim, and the Pygmies of central Africa.

The societies described by Gorer share several characteristics that facilitate the development and maintenance of nonaggressive behavior. First, they tend to exist in rather inaccessible places that other groups do not covet as a living area. Whenever other groups have invaded their territory, the members of these societies have responded by retreating into even more inaccessible areas. Second, members of these societies are oriented toward the concrete pleasures of life—such as eating, drinking, and sex—and an adequate supply of these pleasures apparently satisfies their needs. Achievement or power needs are not encouraged in children: "The model for the growing child is of concrete performance and frank enjoyment, not of metaphysical symbolic achievements or of ordeals to be surmounted" (Gorer, 1968, p. 34). Third, these societies make few distinctions between males and females. Although differences between men's and women's roles exist in each of

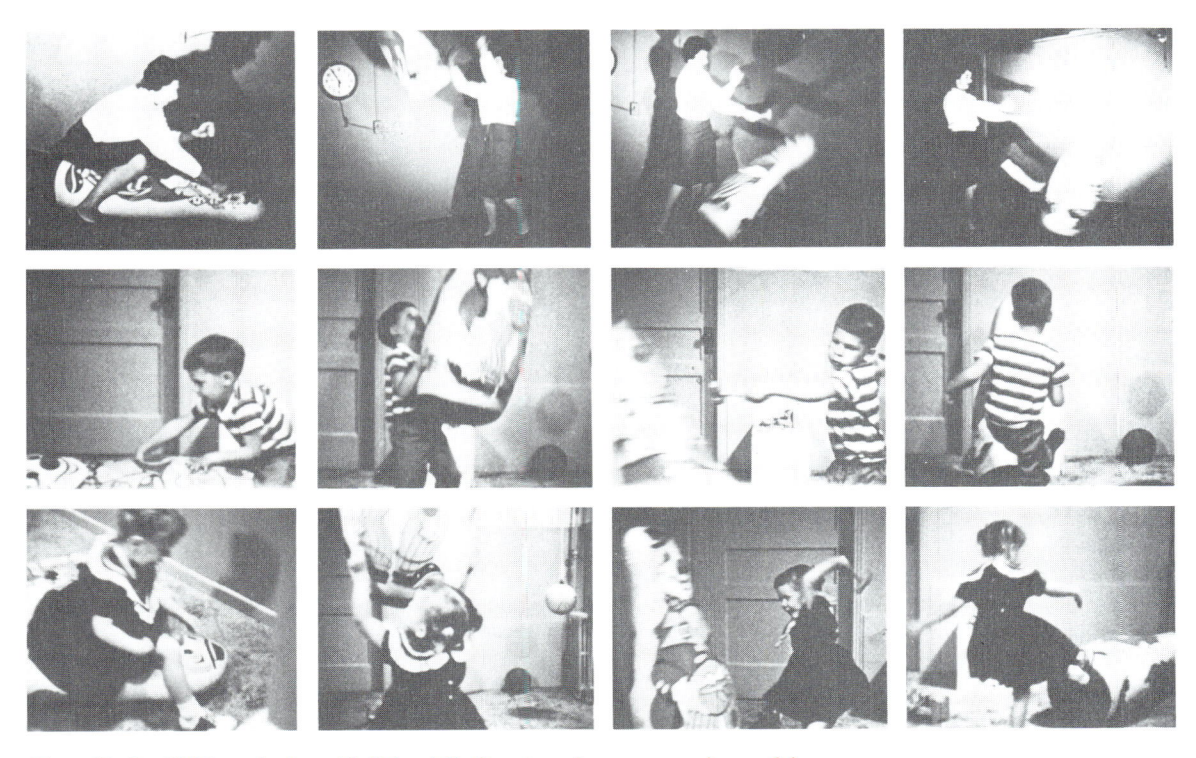

Photo 11-2 Children playing with Bobo doll after observing an aggressive model

these societies, no attempt is made to project (for instance) an image of brave, aggressive masculinity.

Although the majority of societies in the world exhibit some forms of aggression (Rohner, 1976), the existence of nonaggressive societies reminds us of the malleability of human nature and the great diversity in "normal" behaviors from one society to another (Eisenberg, 1972). Both within and between societies, a variety of conditions encourage or discourage the display of aggression. Any instinctual readiness to aggress can surely be modified by the learning experiences that occur.

Conditions That Influence Aggression

Both the biological and the social perspectives offer explanations for the fact that, at a general level, people tend to be capable of aggression. But given a propensity for aggression, when do people actually act in an aggressive manner? Social scientists have identified many conditions that increase the probability of aggressive behavior. Some of these conditions relate to the motivational or affective state that the person is experiencing. Other influences are external to the individual, a feature of the environment or the immediate circumstances. In this section we consider the range of factors that determine just how and when aggression will be displayed.

Frustration

In 1939 a group of psychologists at Yale University (Dollard et al., 1939) hypothesized that frustration causes aggression. More specifically, this **frustration-aggression hypothesis** postulated that "the occurrence of aggression always presupposes frustration" (N. E. Miller, 1941, pp. 337–338). Would any frustrating event inevitably lead to aggression? Not necessarily, argued Neal Miller, one of the developers of this hypothesis. "Frustration produces instigations to a number of different types of responses, one of which is an instigation to some form of aggression" (1941, p. 338). In summary, although these psychologists believed that aggression is always a consequence of some frustration, frustration may have other outcomes as well.

In their original formulation, the Yale theorists defined frustration as the state that emerges when circumstances interfere with a goal response: "an interference with the occurrence of an instigated goal-response at its proper time in the behavior sequence" (Dollard et al., 1939, p. 7). For example, a rat accustomed to running down a particular path for food might experience frustration if a door suddenly appeared in the middle of what had previously been a clear path.

To consider a human case of frustration, Russell Geen (1968) asked subjects to work on a jigsaw puzzle. In one condition (task frustration), the puzzle had no solution; in another condition (personal frustration), the task was solvable, but the experimenter's confederate continually interfered with students as they worked, preventing them from completing the puzzle. In both experimental conditions, subjects were more aggressive toward the confederate than the subjects in a control condition were.

Evidence derived from studies using both human and nonhuman subjects suggests that aggression *may* be caused by frustration (see Azrin, Hutchinson, & Hake, 1966; Rule & Percival, 1971). For example, Arnold Buss (1963) subjected college students to three types of frustration: failing a task, losing an opportunity to win money, and missing a chance to earn a better grade. Each type of frustration led to approximately the same level of aggression, and in each case the level of aggression was greater than in a control condition in which no frustration was experienced. Yet, the level of aggression exhibited was not very great in any case. Perhaps the aggression was minimal because it could not serve to overcome the cause of the frustration. Buss (1961, 1966) suggests that frustration and aggression may be linked only when the aggression has *instrumental value*—that is, when aggressive behavior will help to override the frustration. Other studies also have reported no increase in aggression as a result of the degrees of frustration produced in human subjects in the laboratory (Gentry, 1970; Taylor & Pisano, 1971).

Frustrations of a fairly mild nature are unlikely to result in aggression; in contrast, intense frustration often leads to aggressive behavior. A field study by Mary Harris (1974) suggests the importance of the level of frustration. Harris had her confederates purposely cut in ahead of people standing at different points in lines at theaters and grocery stores. If the confederate cut in ahead of the person who was second in line, that person tended to become quite aggressive (verbally), whereas a person who was twelfth in line exhibited many fewer aggressive reactions. Presumably, when you are close to the checkout counter or the ticket window, an interference is much more frustrating than when you still have a considerable way to go.

Aggressive responses also depend on how arbitrary the frustration is. In one demonstration of this relationship, Burstein and Worchel (1962) found that group members whose progress was impeded by a member who had a hearing problem were much less aggressive than those group members who had equal difficulty because one member appeared to be deliberately blocking the group's progress. Other studies have shown that frustration leads to aggression only when the goal blocking is not expected (Worchel, 1974).

It seems clear, on the basis of several decades of research that have followed the original Yale experiments, that frustration is not sufficient in itself to cause aggression in all cases. A most important mediator of the effect is anger (Krebs & Miller, 1985): does the frustration or the blocking of the goal cause the person to feel angry? In a further modification of the original hypothesis, Leonard Berkowitz (1965b, 1969, 1971) emphasizes the interaction between environmental cues and internal emotional states.

Berkowitz suggests that reaction to frustration creates "only a *readiness* for aggressive acts. Previously acquired aggressiveness habits can also establish this readiness" (1965b, p. 308). In other words, Berkowitz maintains that the occurrence of aggressive behavior is not solely dependent on frustration and that an intervening variable—a readiness—must be added to the chain.

According to Berkowitz, another important factor is the presence of aggressive cues in the environment that serve as triggers for the expression of aggression. Frustration creates readiness in the form of anger; stimulus cues actually elicit aggression. Furthermore, the cues themselves can increase the strength of the aggressive response, particularly when the aggressive response is impulsive (Zillmann, Katcher, & Milavsky, 1972). Although stimulus cues aren't always necessary for aggression to occur, Berkowitz would argue that they generally increase the probability of aggressive behavior.

Aggressive Cues: The Weapons Effect

Do aggressive cues really elicit aggressive behavior? A systematic research program conducted by Berkowitz and his colleagues at the University of Wisconsin has established considerable support for this position. In a typical experiment, a male college student is introduced to another subject, who in reality is a confederate of the experimenter. The confederate either angers the subject deliberately or treats him in a neutral manner. Immediately after this phase of the experiment, both persons watch a brief film clip—either a violent prizefight scene from the film *Champion* or a neutral film showing English canal boats or a track race. After watching the film clip, the subject is given an opportunity to administer electrical shocks to the accomplice. Using this basic paradigm, Berkowitz and his colleagues have developed a variety of tactics to create aggressive cues in the environment. In one experiment, for example, the accomplice was introduced either as a nonbelligerent speech major or as a physical education major who was interested in boxing. When the confederate was introduced as a boxer, the subjects administered more severe shocks (Berkowitz, 1965a). In another experiment, the confederate was introduced either as Kirk Anderson (presumably providing an associa-

Table 11–1 Mean number of shocks given to accomplice

Accomplice's Name	Aggressive Film Angered	Aggressive Film Nonangered	Track Film Angered	Track Film Nonangered
Kirk	6.09$_a$	1.73$_c$	4.18$_b$	1.54$_c$
Bob	4.55$_b$	1.45$_c$	4.00$_b$	1.64$_c$

NOTE: Cells having a subscript in common do not differ significantly (at the .05 level) by Duncan multiple range test.

tion with Kirk Douglas, who was the actor in the boxing film) or as Bob Anderson. Once again, the aggressive-cue value of the confederate affected the level of aggression displayed by the subject (see Table 11–1). As the table indicates, subjects gave the most shocks when they were angered, when they had watched an aggressive film, and when the accomplice had the same name as the boxer in the film. In addition, subjects who had been angered were always more aggressive than those who had not been angered.

Other experiments in this series have focused on the aggressive-cue value of weapons (Berkowitz & LePage, 1967). In one such experiment, male university students received either one or seven electrical shocks from a student (confederate) and then were given an opportunity to administer shocks in return. While some subjects participated in the study, a rifle and a revolver were placed on a nearby table; for other subjects, no objects were present. As one might expect, the subjects who had been shocked more by the confederate were apt to administer shocks in return. More important, the presence of the guns increased the average number of shocks administered from 4.67 to 6.07.

Some critics have suggested that the weapons effect may be due to demand characteristics (recall the discussion in Chapter Two). There is evidence that the presence of weapons is not sufficient if the person fails to interpret the weapons appropriately (Fraczek & Macaulay, 1971; Turner & Simons, 1974). Further, if the individual fears that a display of aggression will result in punishment or disapproval, the cues are less likely to be effective (Turner et al., 1977). Yet beyond these qualifications, there is still evidence that the sight of weapons may increase aggressive behavior. This finding has important practical implications. It suggests the dangers inherent in a society that allows the free display of dangerous weapons. As Berkowitz has phrased it, "Guns not only permit violence, they can stimulate it as well. The finger pulls the trigger, but the trigger may also be pulling the finger" (Berkowitz, 1968, p. 22). Differences between Canada and the United States are consistent with Berkowitz's position. In Canada, where firearms such as revolvers and submachine guns must be registered and may not be owned for purposes of "protection," the homicide rate is considerably lower than in the United States. However, there are other differences between these countries as well, and we cannot be certain that the availability of guns is a major cause of homicides. Imprisonment, for example, is more likely in Canada than in the United States, and such policies may also be related to the frequency of homicide.

General Arousal

The frustration-aggression model suggests that aggression is caused by a specific kind of emotional arousal—by anger that occurs when the attainment of a goal is blocked. Other models of aggression point to more general states of arousal that will increase the likelihood of aggressive behavior. These general models of arousal, which we discussed in regard to emotional expression in Chapter Three, are typified by Dolf Zillmann's **excitation transfer the-**

ory** (Zillmann, 1979). According to this theory, arousal generated in one situation may be transferred to and intensify a subsequent emotional state. More specifically, Zillmann suggests that the expression of aggression (or any other emotion, for that matter) depends on three factors: first, some learned dispositions or habits of the person; second, some source of energization or arousal; and third, the person's interpretation of the arousal state. Thus the way we interpret an event is important in determining whether we act aggressively. Zillmann has taken this analysis a step further, and suggests that energy may transfer from one situation to another. For example, imagine that you've just jogged five miles around a track. You're lying in the infield, recovering from the run, and a man yells an insult at you as he runs by. What would you do? If you had just settled down in the infield, you would probably do nothing. You might feel aroused, but you would attribute the arousal to your exercise. However, if the insult were hurled a few minutes later, you might no longer be thinking of the exercise—but some arousal might still remain. In this circumstance, that residual arousal could be transferred to the insulting incident, and you might react aggressively to your tormentor—more aggressively than if you had not just run five miles (Bryant & Zillmann, 1979).

Verbal and Physical Attack

Direct verbal and physical attacks are much more obvious influences on aggressive behavior. When someone yells at you for no apparent reason, are you likely to scream back? Or if someone walked up to you in the street and began to shove you, how would you react? In all probability, you would be tempted (and might well act) to retaliate with some form of verbal or physical aggression.

Attacks are a much more reliable provocation to aggressive behavior than frustration. For example, in the experiment in which Geen (1968) manipulated two types of frustration while students were working on a jigsaw puzzle, a third experimental condition was included in which the subjects were allowed to complete the puzzle (thus eliminating the possibility of frustration). At the completion of the task, however, the confederate proceeded to insult the subject, attacking both his intelligence and his motivation. Subsequent aggression toward the confederate was stronger in this condition than in either of the frustration conditions. In line with these findings, many laboratory investigations of aggressive behavior have included verbal attack prior to the assessment of aggression.

Stuart Taylor and his colleagues (Taylor, 1967; Taylor & Epstein, 1967) have also looked at the effect of direct attack on subsequent aggression. In their experiments, the subjects weren't asked to administer shocks to a passive learner; instead, they engaged in a two-person interaction in which both persons were allowed to administer shocks. (In actuality, the subject's opponent was a confederate of the experimenter or was fictitious—the subject was told that another person was returning the shocks, but in fact the schedule of shocks was arranged by the experimenter.) In general, these experiments provide clear evidence of reciprocity—subjects tended to match the level of shock that their opponent delivered. If the opponent continued to increase the level of shock, the subject also increased the intensity. Although the absolute level of shock can vary with certain factors—for example, both men and women are more reluctant to administer shock to a woman than to a man (Taylor & Epstein, 1967)—the general pattern of increases and decreases in response to the partner's pattern holds true.

We do not always retaliate immediately when we are attacked by another person. Remembering the discussion of attribution in Chapter Four, you may suspect that our explanations of an attacker's motives can affect our reactions. Did the person *intend* to harm us? Could he or she have foreseen the consequences of the action? The answers that we give to such questions do indeed affect our subsequent aggressive behavior (Ferguson & Rule, 1983).

In one demonstration of the role of attributions, college men received bursts of aversive noise from a male opponent (Dyck & Rule, 1978). The level of noise was described as either the typical amount administered by most people (high consensus) or an atypical amount (low consensus). A second variable that the experimenters manipulated was whether the opponent had any knowledge of the consequences of his action—whether he knew the type and level of noise that he was imposing on the subject. Both factors affected the amount of aggressive behavior that subjects showed. Less retaliation was shown when the behavior was believed to be typical (thus leading the attribution away from the particular individual) and when the subject believed that the opponent was not aware of the consequences of his actions.

Beliefs about the intentions of one's attacker are also important. We are more likely to retaliate if we believe an opponent intended to hurt us than if we think the person did not realize the pain that he or she was causing (Greenwell & Dengerink, 1973; Ohbuchi & Kambara, 1985). In fact, these beliefs are more influential than the actual harm suffered. Advance knowledge of mitigating circumstances is most effective in reducing a person's tendency to retaliate. Both verbal self-reports of anger and physiological measures of arousal show this deterrent effect. Information regarding possible mitigating circumstances is less effective, though, if it comes after the pain has been experienced. At this point, attributions of intent may already be formed and the later information cannot effectively counter the earlier impression (Johnson & Rule, 1986).

Third-Party Instigation

Aggression doesn't always occur when two persons are in isolation. Often witnesses and bystanders become involved in the interaction. At a prizefight, for example, members of the audience can enthusiastically urge their favorite to pulverize his opponent. Newspapers frequently report incidents in which pedestrians urge a potential suicide victim to jump (see Box 11–1). What are the effects of such third-party instigations on the frequency and intensity of aggressive behavior?

In the obedience experiments described in Chap-

Box 11–1
The baiting crowd

"A Puerto Rican handyman perched on a 10th floor ledge for an hour . . . as many persons in a crowd of 500 . . . shouted at him in Spanish and English to jump. Even as cries of 'Jump!' and 'Brinca!' rang out, policemen pulled the man to safety from the narrow ledge" (*New York Times,* quoted in Mann, 1981, p. 704).

Why would a crowd bait a person to commit suicide? This kind of incident doesn't happen very often, but when it does, serious questions are raised about human behavior. To understand more about this aspect of group behavior, Leon Mann (1981) analyzed newspaper reports of 21 cases in which a crowd was present when someone was attempting to commit suicide by jumping from a building, a bridge, or a tower. In 10 of these cases, the crowd had urged the person to jump.

Two factors were significantly associated with the baiting crowd. First, crowds were more likely to urge the victim on in evening hours—baiting was more common after six at night than earlier in the day. Second, baiting was less likely when the potential suicide victim was higher than the 12th floor of the building. In the few cases when bystanders were very close to the person, baiting did not occur.

Both nighttime and distance from the victim are factors that increase deindividuation. When people are farther away from a victim, aggression is more likely. (If the victim is too far away, however, potential hecklers may realize that their cries will not be heard.) Like distance, the cover of darkness increases anonymity, and, in this case, it made aggression more likely.

---

ter Eight, Stanley Milgram (1963, 1965, 1974) explored the effect of an experimenter's commands on the willingness of subjects (in this case, men in New Haven and Bridgeport, Connecticut) to administer shock to another person. In these studies, the effect of external pressure was clear: subjects who were prodded to be aggressive delivered much greater shock than subjects who acted alone.

Not all bystanders are so intrusive, however. What happens when a witness simply observes the aggressive behavior but neither urges nor condemns it? Richard Borden (1975) found that the effect of the observer depends in large part on the implicit values he or she conveys. For example, in one case, male subjects participating in the standard shock experiment were observed by either a male or a female student. Subjects who were observed by a man showed a significantly higher level of aggression than subjects who were observed by a woman. After the male observer left, the subjects reduced their level of aggression, whereas subjects' behavior was relatively unaffected by the departure of the woman. Why did the sex of the observer have an effect?

Borden hypothesized that the norms of our society implicitly suggest that men approve of violence whereas women are opposed to it. To test this hypothesis of implicit values, Borden conducted a second experiment in which the observer belonged either to a karate club (aggressive observer) or to a peace organization (pacifistic observer). In this case, the sex of the observer was also varied, so that both men and women assumed the aggressive and pacifistic roles. When the explicit values of the observer were controlled, the sex of the observer had no effect; however, the explicit values were influential. Subjects who were observed by a member of the karate club were more aggressive than subjects who were observed by a member of a peace organization. Once again, the departure of the aggressive instigator led to a decrease in shock levels, but the departure of the pacifist resulted in no increase in shocks.

Let's look at one more aspect of third-party instigation. Turning the tables slightly, let's look at how the aggressor can affect the instigator. Are instigators of aggression influenced by the degree to which someone follows their recommendations? Jacqueline Gaebelein has conducted a series of studies examining the behavior of the person who instigates aggression (Gaebelein, 1973, 1978; Gaebelein & Hay, 1974; Mander & Gaebelein, 1977; White & Gruber, 1982). Her studies show that instigators will urge more aggression if their recommendations are followed. In contrast, if that person refuses to be aggressive, the instigator will reduce his or her urgings. Thus cooperation in this situation would lead to an increasing level of violence, whereas noncooperation would tend to decrease the level of hostility. Another way to reduce the instigation is to involve the instigator directly in the situation, allowing that person to both give and receive shock directly. Instigators tend to "cool it" when they themselves are vulnerable to shock (Gaebelein & Hay, 1974).

In summary, direct urging by an observer or audience member will increase the amount of aggression a person displays. Furthermore, an observer who reflects aggressive values can cause increases in aggressive behavior. The instigator is not totally removed—his or her behavior is affected by the cooperation or noncooperation of the aggressor, and the instigations may wane when the recommended aggression is not forthcoming.

Deindividuation

When people can't be identified, they are more likely to perform antisocial acts. As we saw in Chapter Two, students who participated in a laboratory experiment that involved administering shock were more likely to be aggressive when they were completely disguised by hoods and sheets than when they were identified by name tags (Zimbardo, 1970). Other experiments have used similar manipulations of anonymity and have found that people are more likely to express both physical and verbal hostility when their own identity is not stressed (Cannavale, Scarr, & Pepitone, 1970; Festinger, Pepitone, & Newcomb, 1952; Mann, Newton, & Innes, 1982). In discussing **deindividuation**, Phillip Zimbardo (1970) has suggested that conditions that increase anonymity serve to minimize concerns with evaluation and thus weaken the normal controls that are based on guilt, shame, and fear. More recently, investigators have pointed to the concept of private self-awareness (see Chapter Three). When focus is shifted to external cues, private self-awareness decreases (Prentice-Dunn & Rogers, 1982). No longer as tuned to themselves, people seem more willing to engage in aggressive behavior.

The concept of deindividuation can be applied to the victim as well as to the aggressor. For example, Milgram (1965) found that people were more willing to administer electric shocks when they couldn't see the victim and when the victim couldn't see them. (Also see Box 11–1.) In some ways, aggression under these conditions is dehumanized—because people cannot see the consequences of their actions, these actions may be easier to perform. It is probably significant that the genocide of World World II involved gas chambers that could be controlled from a distance and that hoods are often placed over the heads of execution victims. Even when aggression is not severe (for example, honking your horn at a stalled driver in front of you), a driver who cannot see the "victim" (because a curtain is drawn across the rear window) will be more likely to honk at a stalled motorist (Turner, Layton, & Simons, 1975).

Drugs and Alcohol

Drugs and alcohol are widely used in our society. Popular wisdom suggests that alcohol facilitates aggression, and cartoons of the hostile drunk are common. Similarly, many people believe that marijuana has the opposite effect—that it tends to "mellow people out" and minimize any tendencies toward aggression. In this instance, the popular wisdom appears to be close to the mark, although research on the topic is still in an early stage. Stuart Taylor and his colleagues have conducted a series of studies in which various dosages of either alcohol or THC (tetrahydrocannabinol, the major active ingredient of marijuana) are administered to subjects before they participate in an aggression experiment (Shuntich & Taylor, 1972; Taylor & Gammon, 1975; Taylor et al., 1976). In the aggression situation, subjects compete against a partner in a reaction-time experiment; each player has an opportunity to shock the player who loses on a trial. These specific conditions are important to remember, because it appears that effects are found only when a person is provoked or attacked (Taylor, Gammon, & Capasso, 1976). What happens when alcohol or THC is present in the bloodstream of a potential attacker? As Figure 11–1 shows, the two substances have quite different effects. Although low doses of alcohol (0.5 ounce of alcohol per 40 pounds of body weight, or the equivalent of one cocktail) actually reduce the level of aggression (compared with a group that has had no alcohol), larger doses of alcohol (1.5 ounces per 40 pounds of body weight) have quite the opposite effect: subjects who had consumed large doses of alcohol gave substantially stronger shocks.

Marijuana has a different effect. Small amounts of THC (0.1 milligram per kilogram of body weight) had no effect on aggressive behavior, and larger doses (0.3 milligrams per kilogram of body weight) tended to suppress aggressive behavior. Still higher doses of marijuana (0.4 milligrams per kilogram) do not facilitate aggression either, but rather decrease the individual's willingness to retaliate against an aggressor (Myerscough & Taylor, 1985).

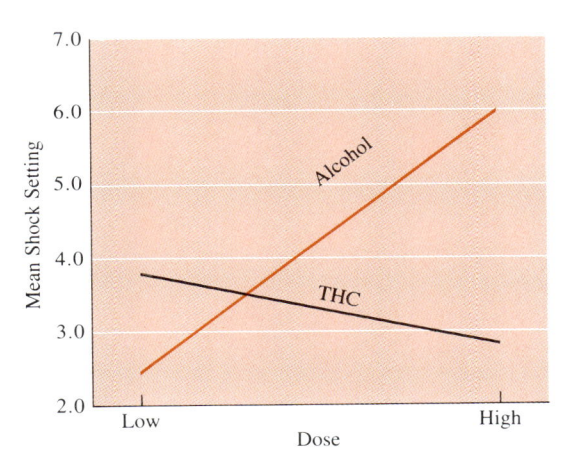

Figure 11–1 Mean shock setting as a function of high and low doses of alcohol and THC. Increasing the amount of alcohol in the system leads to greater aggression in the laboratory setting, while THC tends to have the opposite effect.

Environmental Conditions

Conditions in the environment often affect people's moods. For example, you may complain that you feel grouchy because the air conditioning in your room doesn't work on a hot day or because the noise of construction outside your window is distracting.

Can environmental conditions affect behavior as well? In Chapter Seventeen we will consider some ways in which the environment influences behavior. Here we will consider a more specific question: Can environmental conditions such as noise, air pollution, and extreme temperatures influence the likelihood that a person will act aggressively toward others?

Unpleasant levels of noise can lead to an increase in aggressive behavior. Subjects who are exposed to loud bursts of noise in a laboratory experiment, for example, will deliver significantly higher levels of shock to a partner than will subjects who are exposed to either low-level noise or no noise at all (Donnerstein & Wilson, 1976). In general, these increases in aggression are found only if subjects are provoked or angered. As in the case of alcohol, the external stimulus in itself is not sufficient to produce aggression. It does lower the threshold, however, so that when an instigation to aggression is present, the aggressive behavior is displayed more readily.

Unpleasant air quality—smog, smoke, haze—also affects the tendency toward aggression. Air quality can be assessed by measurement of the ozone level, an index of the level of pollutants in the air. Using this measure, James Rotton and James Frey (1985) conducted an archival study that revealed a relationship between weather and violent crime. As the ozone level increased, so did reports of family disturbances. With some regularity, days of high temperatures and low winds preceded violent episodes—a suggestive finding.

Many people have suggested a relationship between temperature and violence. During the extensive outbreak of civil disturbances in the United States in the 1960s, the mass media frequently emphasized the "long hot summer" effect. Heat was cited as a cause of riots. Indeed, the majority of disturbances did occur during summer (U.S. Riot Commission, 1968).

The actual relationship between temperature and aggressive behavior is not quite so simple, however, and the form of the relationship varies between laboratory and field settings. In a series of experiments, Robert Baron and his colleagues (Baron, 1972; Baron & Bell, 1975, 1976; Bell & Baron, 1976) found that under some conditions, heat increases the tendency toward aggression, even in subjects who haven't been angered; in other cases, however, higher temperatures seem to decrease the tendency toward aggression. Although the initial set of findings was somewhat confusing, Baron (1977) has provided an intriguing explanation that appears to incorporate all the findings: he suggests that aggression is mediated by the level of negative affect or discomfort that a person experiences and that the relation between this discomfort and aggression is curvilinear. In other words, at very low or very high levels of discomfort, aggression is minimized. Aggression is most likely at intermediate levels of discomfort.

This complex explanation has been supported by other laboratory findings. For example, Palamarek and Rule (1979) either insulted or did not insult college men in a room that was either fairly comfortable (about 73° F) or unreasonably warm (about 96° F). When they were given a choice of tasks to perform, the men who had been insulted were more likely to choose a task that allowed them to aggress against their partners when the temperature was comfortable, but they were less likely to choose the aggressive task when the room was excessively warm. Again, these results support the curvilinear interpretation: moderate arousal, caused by *either* insult or heat, leads to greater aggression, but when both factors are present *or* when both are absent, less aggression occurs.

An alternative explanation for these findings, however, has been suggested by Craig and Dona Anderson (1984). Subjects in the laboratory not only are aware that they are in an experiment, but in most cases are aware that the experiment has something to do with the effects of temperature (potential subjects must be informed about any risk or aversive conditions before they agree to participate). Consequently, the subject who experiences uncomfortably high temperatures and who is then given the opportunity to be aggressive toward another student may well guess what the experiment is all about. Having decided that the experimenter wanted to see if they would be more aggressive, these subjects may consciously resist the aggressive choice. Thus the curvilinear relationship reported by Baron and his colleagues could be an artifact of the experimental procedure.

The debate over the relationship between temperature and aggression has concerned data collected outside the laboratory as well. In one of the first tests of this relationship, Baron and Ransberger (1978) identified the instances of collective violence in the United States between 1967 and 1971. Then they

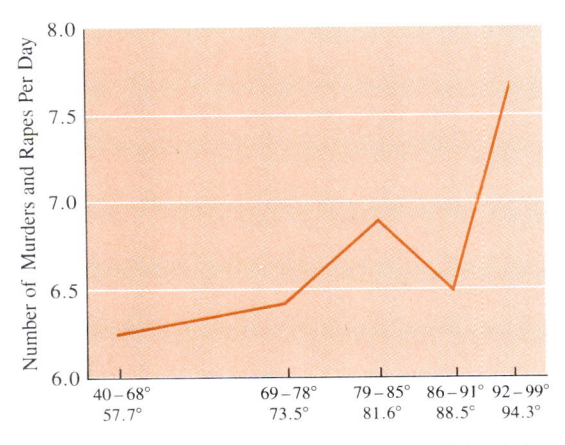

Figure 11-2 The relationship between aggressive crime (murder and rape) and maximum daily temperature

obtained records of the average temperatures on the days when the violence occurred. Their findings supported Baron's contention that temperature and aggression are related in a curvilinear manner: riots are more likely to occur as the days get hotter—but only up to a point.

This conclusion has not gone unchallenged. Carlsmith and Anderson (1979) suggested that Baron and Ransberger did not take account of the number of days in different temperature ranges. In other words, if 80-degree days are more common than 90-degree days, simple probability would lead us to expect more riots in the former periods than in the latter. By using simple probability theory, Carlsmith and Anderson calculated the likelihood of a riot for each temperature interval. Their results suggest a simple linear relation—the higher the temperature, the more likely a riot.

In further support for the linear argument, Craig and Dona Anderson (1984) collected data on temperatures and violent crimes—specifically, rape and murder—in Houston between 1980 and 1982. Their findings, shown in Figure 11-2, clearly support the contention that aggression and temperature are related in a reasonably direct linear fashion. To test the hypothesis further, these investigators considered the ratio of aggressive crimes to total crimes as it relates to temperature. Again they found a linear relationship, suggesting that it is aggressive crimes, rather than crimes in general, that increase when the temperature rises.

There is of course an upper limit to this relationship. At a temperature of 130 degrees, for example, few people would want to move, let alone be aggressive. Within the normal range of temperatures, however, aggression seems to rise with the temperature.

Individual Differences in Aggressive Behavior

Not all individuals are equally aggressive. Although we have been discussing conditions that will increase the probability that any individual will become more aggressive, it is also true that some people are generally more aggressive than others. In fact, there is evidence that individual differences in aggressive behavior are quite stable over time, particularly among men (Huesmann et al., 1984; Olweus, 1979, 1984b). Thus the eight-year-old boy who is named frequently by classmates as one who pushes and shoves other children is more likely to become, by the age of 30, a man with a record of criminal behavior, wife abuse, and traffic violations.

The reasons for this stability are a matter of disagreement. If you think back to our discussion of the nature of aggression, you may suspect that both biological and cultural explanations can be offered. And they have been. Some investigators have argued that there is substantial heritability in aggressive tendencies, using studies of twins to support their conclusions (Rushton et al., 1986). On the other side, one can find evidence that parents, peers, and the media provide a consistent context in which aggression is encouraged or discouraged, thus leading to stable reactions as well.

Questions of sex differences in aggressive behavior often are debated on this same ground. In an early review of the literature, Eleanor Maccoby and Carol Jacklin (1974) concluded that men are the more aggressive sex, and that the behavioral differences that are found may result from differences in biological readiness for aggressive behavior. More recent investigators are not so sure. Alice Eagly and Valerie Steffen (1986) have also concluded that men are more aggressive than women, but that the differences observed in social-psychological research are small and not always consistent. Sex differences are greater when the issue is physical aggression than when verbal and other types of psychological harm are considered. These investigators also find substantial differences between women and men in their beliefs about aggression. Women, for example, feel more guilty and anxious about behaving aggressively. They are also more concerned about the harm they may cause their victims, and more worried about possible danger to themselves. These beliefs, suggest Eagly and Steffen, may mediate the extent to which men and women consciously choose to behave aggressively. More generally, the variations in the observed patterns of aggression remind us of the importance of considering the specific situation when we try to understand and explain behavior.

Violence and the Mass Media

On March 30, 1981, John W. Hinckley, Jr. stood outside a Washington, D.C., hotel among a crowd of reporters and well-wishers waiting for President Ronald Reagan to appear. When the president came out of the hotel, Hinckley fired, wounding the president, his press secretary, and two other persons. Why did he do it? This disturbed young man apparently identified with the protagonist of the movie *Taxi Driver;* he is reported to have seen the movie more than a dozen times and to have fallen in love with an actress who had a featured role in the film. By shooting the president, he somehow thought, he could make part of the film's fiction become his own reality.

Some years earlier, a 15-year-old boy in Florida killed his 82-year-old neighbor for no apparent reason. The lawyers for the defendant claimed that the boy was legally insane at the time of the murder as a result of watching too much television. (Their defense was unsuccessful, however, and the boy was convicted of murder.)

Do presentations of violence in the media encourage the observer to act aggressively? Is aggression in our society greater than it would be if such presentations were not available? In this section we consider answers to that question, which has caused heated debate in academic circles as well as among the general public. Although newspapers can also be a source of influence (see Box 11–2), most of the debate has focused on two issues: (1) the influence of televised violence on aggressive behavior in children, and (2) the influence of pornographic films on aggression toward women.

Television Violence and Aggression in Children

In a small village in the Ivory Coast, an old African man watched a battery-powered television set at a local schoolhouse. After several hours of viewing mostly imported American programs, the man asked with some perplexity, "Why are whites always stabbing, shooting, and punching one another?" (Odino, 1986).

The prevalence of violence on television is not subject to dispute. The number of violent acts shown on prime-time television averages eight an hour. On children's Saturday morning cartoons, a violent act occurs every two minutes. It has been estimated that by age 16 the average child will have witnessed more than 13,000 killings on TV (Liebert & Schwartzberg, 1977).

The first evidence that witnessed aggression could lead to aggressive behavior came from Bandura's studies of children's behavior with a Bobo doll, discussed earlier. In some of these studies, the aggressive model was a live actor who was in the room with the child; in others, the model was shown on film or in the form of a cartoon character (Bandura et al., 1961, 1963a). In all cases, children who watched a model acting aggressively were more likely to engage in similar aggression against the Bobo doll.

In trying to learn more about the possible link between media violence and subsequent aggression,

Box 11–2
Is publicity fatal?

The sociologist David Phillips (1986) has spent many years investigating the relationship between activities ending in death, such as suicides, homicides, and automobile and airplane accidents, and newspaper coverage of violence. His questions are ones that many of us ask each other when an apparent rash of self-inflicted deaths follows the suicide of a well-known person. The method that Phillips employs to answer such questions is archival: he uses newspaper files as one source of data and available records of fatalities as another source.

Consider these studies of the impact of publicized suicide. In his first study, Phillips systematically gathered a list of suicide stories that appeared on the front page of the *New York Times* between 1947 and 1968. On November 1, 1965, for example, the *Times* reported the death of Daniel Burros, a leader of the Ku Klux Klan who committed suicide soon after a newspaper story revealed that he was Jewish. To assess the possible effect of this suicide story, Phillips obtained records of monthly suicide rates (for the United States as a whole) and compared the rates for the months before and after the publicized event with those of the same months in the preceding and following years. Phillips found that the number of suicides in the month of the story and the month immediately after exceeded predicted averages by nearly 60 suicides.

These methods are admittedly fairly crude. The stories recorded appeared only in local newspapers, while the suicide rate was calculated for the nation as a whole. Furthermore, monthly statistics provide a very global measure of a specific effect. Given these rough measures, it is all the more surprising that a relationship was found.

Phillips has gone further in his investigations, correcting some of the weaknesses in the first study. A study of patterns within California used the *Los Angeles Times* and the *San Francisco Chronicle* as sources of stories about suicides. In a clever extension of reasoning, Phillips considered two possible death patterns that could suggest suicide—noncommercial plane fatalities and motor vehicle accidents. In both cases, Phillips reasoned that individuals might make their intentional deaths appear accidental in order to protect families from shame and to avoid insurance problems.

continued

investigators adopted two strategies. First, they continued to do experiments, but they began to use actual film and television material rather than the more artificial Bobo-doll sequences. Second, many investigators have conducted field studies of actual television viewing patterns and used quasi-experimental designs to analyze the results.

Within the laboratory setting, investigators were able to define some of the factors that are related to the acquisition and display of aggressive behavior. For example, some investigators have suggested that aggressive behavior follows the viewing of filmed violence only if the film justifies the violence it shows (Berkowitz & Alioto, 1973). Other factors that appear important are the degree to which the observer identifies with the aggressor in the film, the initial aggressiveness of the observer, and the degree to which the villain has some redeeming features (Geen & Stonner, 1973; Liebert & Schwartzberg, 1977; Turner & Berkowitz, 1972).

A few experiments have been conducted in more natural settings outside of the laboratory. A boarding school in Belgium was one such site. During a designated "Movie Week," investigators manipulated the amount of violent content that was shown on television (Leyens et al., 1975). Teenaged boys who lived in four small dormitories at the boarding school were observed before Movie Week started, and their

The results of his analysis of motor vehicle accident fatalities is shown in the figure below. Of course, neither Phillips nor anyone else can know what was in the minds of the drivers who met their deaths in this way. Yet these studies demonstrate the power of a theory that allows one to predict relationships, sometimes between seemingly unrelated events, and then to test the validity of the theory with available data.

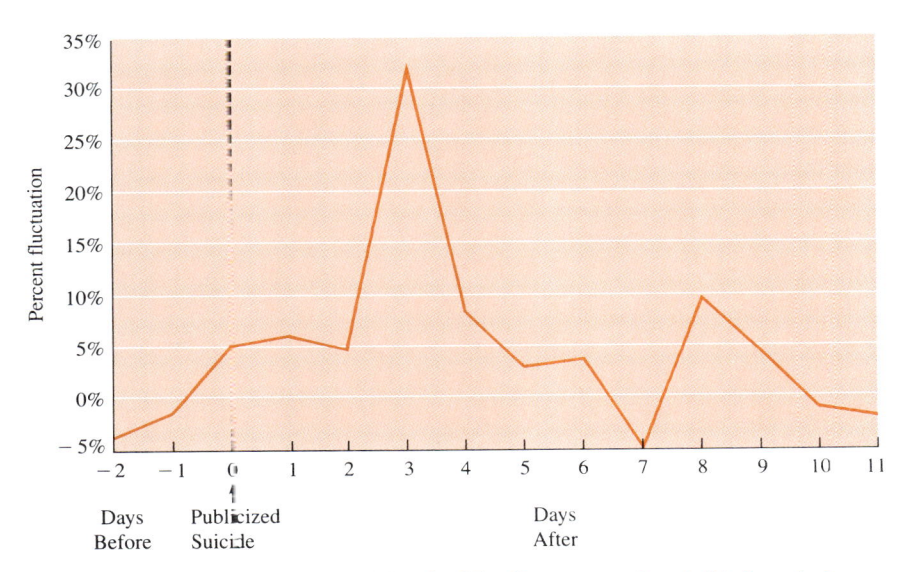

Daily fluctuation in motor vehicle accident fatalities for a two-week period before, during, and after publicized suicides

aggressive behavior was recorded. Aggressive behavior tended to be high in two of the dormitories and relatively low in the other two. During Movie Week, the television sets that the boys normally watched were disconnected and special movies were shown instead. Boys in two of the dormitories (one high in violence, one low) watched only films that were saturated with violence, including *Bonnie and Clyde, The Dirty Dozen,* and *Iwo Jima.* The residents of the other two dormitories saw nonviolent films such as *Lili* and *La Belle Américaine.* Observers then rated the amount of each boy's aggressive behavior during Movie Week and the following week.

Physical aggression increased among the boys who saw the violent films. The authors concluded that "the films evoked among the spectators the kind of aggression they had been exposed to" (Leyens et al., 1975, p. 353). Verbal aggression, however, increased only among the residents of the aggressive dormitory who were shown violent films. Residents of the nonaggressive dormitory who saw the violent films actually exhibited a decrease in verbal aggression. As might be expected, the effects of the films were much more extreme just after viewing than during later observation periods. Other studies conducted in the United States have produced similar findings (Parke et al., 1977).

Field studies, as we know, sacrifice some control,

Photo 11–3 By watching televised models, children learn sets of behavior that can later be imitated.

but they allow investigators to consider people's natural viewing habits. The basic strategy of these studies, many of which have been conducted in recent years, is to obtain information about the amount and type of television programming watched and to relate those data to some measure of an individual's aggressive behavior. Despite considerable debate, the bulk of the evidence from these studies supports a relationship between media violence and aggression: children who watch more violence on television are more aggressive (Freedman, 1984, 1986; Friedrich-Cofer & Huston, 1986; Roberts & Maccoby, 1985; Singer & Singer, 1981). This relationship has been observed not only in the United States but in Finland, Poland, and Australia as well (Eron, 1982).

If we had only this kind of correlational data, we could not be sure that media violence really causes aggression. Perhaps children who are more aggressive choose to watch more violent television fare. In fact, the direction of causality works both ways, as sophisticated longitudinal research designs have been able to demonstrate (Eron, 1982; Huesmann, Lagerspetz, & Eron, 1984). In these research designs, investigators first observe children as young as age 8 and assess their aggressiveness and the amount of time they spend viewing television. Then some years later, say when the subjects have reached age 18, the investigators again assess aggressiveness and amount of television watching. Applying statistical techniques, investigators can then determine whether the amount of television watched when the child is 8 is related to the amount of aggressive behavior shown at 18. These correlations are statistically significant, often more significant than the two measures assessed at the same point in time. In other words, the amount of time an 8-year-old watches television tells us more about how aggressive that child will be at 18 than it does about how aggressive the child is now (Eron, 1980). Such evidence does not show that television is the only cause of violence, but it has become quite clear that it is one cause.

Why does viewing televised violence have this effect? What psychological processes can explain this relationship? Observational learning is one explanation. In watching televised models, the child learns a set of behaviors that can later be imitated. The degree to which these behaviors are acquired and later displayed are affected by a number of factors. Children who believe that violent TV shows portray life as it really is, for example, are more likely to demonstrate aggressive behavior. The child who identifies strongly with the aggressive characters in a show is also more likely to be aggressive (Huesmann, Lagerspetz, & Eron, 1984).

Cognitive explanations can also be offered. Frequent observation of violence on TV may make aggression themes more accessible in memory. Recalling our discussion in Chapter Four, we can think of television as a kind of priming device. With such thoughts and schemas more readily available, the individual may be more likely to engage in behaviors with an aggressive tone. Then, too, frequent exposure to violent material may cause the individual to become desensitized, less concerned and anxious about the consequences of potentially harmful actions (Berkowitz, 1984).

On the basis of evidence collected through a variety of research methods, it seems reasonable to conclude that the viewing of violence on television can increase people's tendency to be aggressive, both immediately afterward and at some distance in the future. Yet it is also important to recognize that this link is not inevitable. Not all children who watch violence on TV will grow up to be aggressive adults. Furthermore, researchers have begun to explore the ways this link can be weakened (Singer & Singer, 1983). For example, if a child watches violence on television in the presence of an adult who condemns the violence, that child is less likely to behave aggressively in later situations (Hicks, 1968; Horton & Santogrossi, 1978). (On the other side of the coin, condoning or encouraging comments made by an adult can lead to more aggressive behavior by the child.) The behavior of children's peers may also be influential (Leyens, Herman, & Dunand, 1982). Leonard Eron (1982) has experimented with short training sessions in which children are helped to discriminate television fantasy from real-life events, learning, for example, how special effects are used to simulate violence. His findings are encouraging, suggesting that a year later children who had gone through the three-hour training session were less aggressive than a comparable group of children who had not had the training. Programs such as these may serve as important keys to the control of aggressive behavior.

Pornography and Aggression toward Women

During the past decade or two, pornographic material has become much more common, as scenes of rape, coercion, and the exercise of power pervade both books and films. We define **pornography** as a particular type of erotic material—material that combines elements of sexuality and aggression and in which force or coercion is used to accomplish the sexual act. What effect does this kind of material have on aggressive behavior toward other people, particularly toward women, who are usually portrayed as the victims of aggression?

A widely publicized study in Denmark considered the frequency of sex offenses before and after the removal of all restrictions on the sale of pornographic materials (Kutchinsky, 1973). The initial findings of this "natural experiment" suggested that sex crimes declined markedly, and the study gave rise to a "safety valve" theory (Kronhausen & Kronhausen, 1964). Thus it was argued that potential sex offenders may have obtained sufficient sexual satisfaction through the reading and viewing of pornographic materials. However, more recent figures from Denmark show an increase, rather than a decrease, in rape (Bachy, 1976). Because these data are correlational, we cannot be certain that the lifting of restrictions on pornography caused the increase in sex crimes in Denmark. These findings do, however, pose questions for the safety-valve theory.

More conclusive answers to the question of the relationship of pornography and violence come from the extensive research program of Edward Donnerstein and his colleagues (Donnerstein, 1982; Malamuth & Donnerstein, 1982). Their findings show very consistently that men who are exposed to pornographic materials will be more aggressive toward women in subsequent interactions. Let's consider one of these experiments by Donnerstein and Berkowitz (1981) in some detail.

Male college students believed they were participating in an experiment on stress and learning, in which they would be paired with either a male or a female student. In the initial stage of the experiment, they were asked to write an essay. Their partner then was asked to evaluate the essay, indicating a judgment by administering shocks to the subject. The partner gave a high number of shocks, indicating a negative evaluation. In the next stage of the experiment, the subjects were exposed to one of four films: a neutral talk-show interview, an erotic film depicting sexual intercourse with no aggressive content, or one of two pornographic films that combined aggression and sexuality, depicting a woman being slapped and sexually attacked. One of these pornographic films had a positive outcome, ending with the woman smiling at her attackers. In the other pornographic film, the outcome was negative, and the woman was clearly suffering at the end of the film. After viewing one of these films, the subject was returned to the "learning task" and given the opportunity to be aggressive toward (that is, to shock) his partner. Figure 11–3 shows the results of this experiment.

As Figure 11–3 shows, aggression levels varied markedly with the sex of the target. When the male subject was paired with another man, none of the sexual films aroused significantly more aggression than the neutral film. With a female partner, in contrast, both pornographic films dramatically increased the man's level of aggression. But what if the male subject had not been angered? Is a state of anger necessary for such a display of aggression against women? Donnerstein and Berkowitz (1981) conducted a second study to answer these questions.

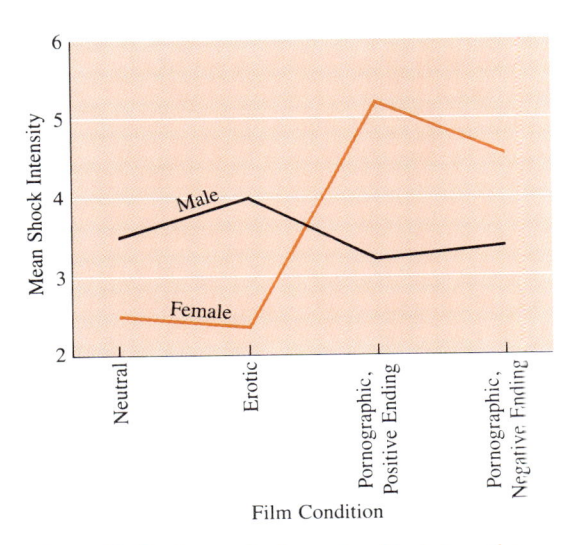

Figure 11–3 Aggression by male subjects toward a male or female partner after viewing neutral, erotic, or pornographic films

Using the same four films, they found that nonangered men did not act aggressively toward a female partner when the pornographic film had a negative ending. But when the pornographic film showed the woman enjoying the sexual violence, nonangered men were nearly as aggressive toward a female partner as were the men who had been angered.

Current research continues to demonstrate the negative effects of pornography on attitudes and behavior toward women. Men who listen to audiotapes depicting rape, for example, are more likely to believe that women get pleasure from being raped, more prone to have aggressive sexual fantasies, and more accepting of violence against women (Malamuth, 1981a, 1981b).

Men were also shown to be more accepting of interpersonal violence against women after watching commercially released violent-sexual films, such as *Swept Away* and *The Getaway* (Malamuth & Check, 1981). Not all men respond this way. Yet for some men, including men who have been convicted of rape, scenes of rape are more arousing than scenes of mutually consenting sex (Malamuth, 1981b; Quinsey, Chaplin, & Upfold, 1984).

Thus, to answer our earlier question, the effects of pornography on subsequent behavior appear to be quite strong. Exposure to pornographic materials leads to more aggressive behavior, and this aggression is, for the most part, directed against women.

Violence in Society

Questions about the effects of media violence have taken investigators out of the laboratory. In more naturalistic settings, they have found ample evidence of aggressive behavior. Between relatives at home, between strangers on the street, and between groups and nations in conflict, aggression is pervasive.

Violence in the Home

Apparently, when it comes to aggressive behavior, "there's no place like home." Well-publicized statistics on wife beating, spouse abuse, and child abuse testify to the frequency with which aggression occurs. In light of this evidence, some social scientists have described the family as the "cradle of violence" (Steinmetz & Straus, 1973).

Violence between romantic partners often begins long before the marriage ceremony. More than half of 500 university students in Kentucky who were asked to describe their dating relationships said that they had committed some physically abusive act toward their partners (Sigelman, Berry, & Wiles, 1984). As Table 11–2 shows, pushing and shoving were the most common forms of abuse. Women were more likely than men to slap a partner; they were also more likely to kick, hit, and bite, and to throw things at their partners. Despite these differences in form, the abuse in relationships was generally mutual. Those who reported being abusive also reported being abused.

Straus and his colleagues have conducted an extensive series of studies within the home setting to describe and explain the incidence of family violence (Steinmetz & Straus, 1974; Straus, 1973; Straus, Gelles, & Steinmetz, 1980). Their research shows that aggressive behavior in the family is extremely frequent, if not commonplace. In a study of more than 2000 married couples in the United States, these investigators found that more than 25% of the couples had engaged in some form of physical violence during their married life. Both husbands and wives engaged in acts of violence, but the rates for husbands were higher for the more harmful forms of violence, such as beating or using a knife or gun.

Comparisons of social-class differences tended to challenge some popular stereotypes. Although white-collar workers indicated less approval of marital violence than blue-collar workers did, the reported frequency of actual aggressive behavior did not vary much between the two groups. The fact that aggression between spouses is so common (and that such incidents are far more frequent than physical attacks between strangers or mere acquaintances) provides support for Straus's somber description of "the marriage license as a hitting license" (Straus, 1975).

Table 11–2 Percentage of male and female college students reporting having abused a heterosexual partner in various ways

	Sex of Abuser	
Action	Male	Female
Threw something	18%	27%
Pushed, shoved	42	29
Slapped	17	34
Kicked, hit, bit	9	18
Hit with some object (or tried to do so)	12	19
Beat up	3	1
Threatened with knife or gun	2	1
Used a knife or gun	<1	<1

Family violence is not restricted to adults. Children, too, become statistics of domestic violence. For example, a survey of university students revealed that more than half had experienced either actual or threatened physical punishment during their final year of high school (Straus, 1971). Reports of child beating have become increasingly prominent in recent years. Although parent/child aggression is an obvious problem in itself, there are also suggestions that the consequences of such aggression extend far beyond the immediate incident. For example, Owens and Straus (1975) report that persons who experience violence as children are more likely to favor violence as a means of achieving personal and political ends as adults. In other words, through learning and role modeling, people can perpetuate the aggressive behaviors they learned as children.

Violence in the Streets

Although the home is the most common site of violence, aggressive behavior in our society is by no means limited to the family. Reports of homicides, rapes, and other forms of aggression can be found daily in the newspapers, often as feature articles in some of the more sensational tabloids.

Acts of aggression are common even in the school classroom. The occurrence of bullying and harassment in the primary schools (grades 1 through 9) has been declared a serious problem in Norway, and a nationwide campaign has been developed to reduce the incidence of this form of aggression (Olweus, 1984a).

According to the Federal Bureau of Investigation and the Royal Canadian Mounted Police, crime rates in the United States and Canada have been increasing yearly. No single explanation accounts for these forms of aggression and violence. Although "individual criminal tendencies" may explain some occurrences, broader structural explanations are needed also. For example, Peggy Sanday (1981) has found that certain cultural groups are more likely to have a high incidence of rape than others. Looking at a sample of tribal societies, Sanday found that rape was most common in societies that had a large amount of interpersonal violence, generally supported male dominance, and encouraged separation of males and females. In contrast, societies that fostered greater equality between the sexes were likely to have a very low incidence of rape. Sanday's findings, though based on cultures quite different from our own, suggest that general cultural values may be related to particular forms of aggression and violence.

Exact figures on the incidence of aggression are difficult to obtain, particularly if one wants to make comparisons across countries. Reporting procedures, for example, may exaggerate crime rates in one country while underestimating them in another. Available statistics suggest, however, that the United States has the dubious distinction of leading most of the industrialized nations of the world in crimes of violence. Such evidence certainly testifies to the importance of understanding the causes of aggression and seeing the problem of aggression as more than an academic issue.

Collective Violence

Aggression is not confined to single individuals acting alone. Collective violence—violence between nations or between identifiable groups within a nation—has played a role in most civilizations. In the United States, for example, incidents of violence were frequent between 1879 and 1889, whereas rates were low in the following decade (Levy, 1969). Again, in the 1960s, collective violence was frequent in riots by young people, ghetto residents, and others. Canada, too, has had its share of collective violence. Canadians have rioted over unemployment in the 1930s, conscription in the 1940s and confederation in the 1960s and 1970s.

Why does collective violence occur? Davies (1962, 1969) has suggested that dissatisfaction occurs when a long period of rising prosperity is followed by a sharp drop in fortunes. The earlier increase in socioeconomic or political satisfaction leads people to expect the continuation of such improvements (thus producing a "curve of rising expectations"). When these expectations are frustrated, collective violence is more likely to occur. Economic trends in both the United States and Canada in the 1980s fit this general pattern, leading some to fear that collective violence will become more common.

Other theorists have developed Davies's ideas further, focusing on the concept of **relative deprivation.** According to this general theory, people compare their conditions with those of others (Crosby, 1976). Relative deprivation is "a feeling of discontent based on the belief that one is getting less than one deserves" (Martin, 1980). One feels *fraternal deprivation* when one compares one's own group with another group. For example, Blacks might compare their state with that of Whites, or women might make comparisons with men. *Egoistic deprivation* is felt when the comparison is made on a more individual level, as when you compare your general situation with that of a more prosperous friend.

A number of factors influence feelings of relative deprivation, among them a belief that one deserves a particular outcome and that one is not responsible for failure to achieve that outcome (Crosby, 1976). If a person feels deprived in relation to some other person or group, what does he or she do? Joanne Martin (1980) suggests that the actions depend on how optimistic or pessimistic a person is about the situation. A person who sees some grounds for hope may engage in self-improvement efforts at the individual level or constructive actions, such as voting, at the system level. If hopes are frustrated, however, less positive outcomes may result. An individual may turn to alcohol or drugs, or take part in collective violence.

There is considerable support for this theory, ranging from laboratory experiments to historical analyses of cases as disparate as the French Revolution and the civil-rights protests in the United States. In each case, the evidence suggests that it is not those groups that are most oppressed that engage in collective violence; rather, it is those that have reason to believe they should and could have something better. Or, as Tocqueville once commented, "evils which are patiently endured when they seem inevitable become intolerable when once the idea of escape from them is suggested" (quoted in Crosby, 1976, p. 85).

How Can Aggression Be Controlled?

Although some form of violence has always existed in our society, we can question whether aggression is inevitable. Can aggressive behavior be controlled or eliminated? The answer to this question depends on the assumptions one makes about the causes of aggression.

Theorists who believe that aggression is an innate characteristic of human beings are pessimistic about the possibilities of controlling aggressive behavior. As Freud grew older and witnessed the devastation of World War I, he became increasingly resigned to the inevitability of aggression. His postulation of a death instinct—a compulsion in all human beings "to return to the inorganic state out of which all living matter is formed" (Hall & Lindzey, 1968, p. 263)—represented the culmination of his pessimism. He saw aggression as a natural derivation of the death instinct.

Psychoanalysts who adopt this position see little chance of restraining our violent behaviors. Freud himself wrote that there is "no likelihood of our being able to suppress humanity's aggressive tendencies" (quoted in Bramson & Goethals, 1968, p. 76). However, two procedures may provide some hope. One, at an international level, is a combining of forces to restrain the aggressive actions of powerful nations. At an individual level, the development of the superego can serve as a way of restraining innate aggressive impulses. Additionally, neo-Freudians advocate participation in socially acceptable aggressive activities (sporting events, debates, and the like) as a way of releasing aggressive energy.

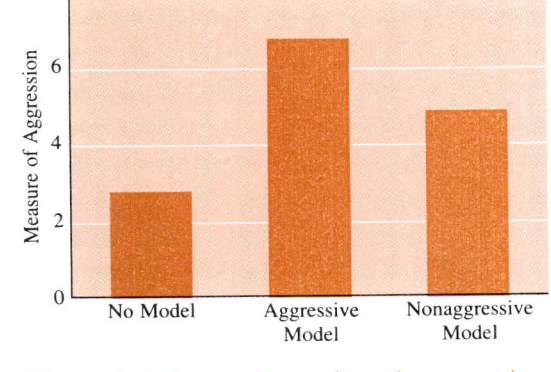

Ethologists and sociobiologists also believe that aggression is unlikely to be eliminated. To them, the task is one of channeling aggression into socially acceptable behaviors. Lorenz (1966), for example, believed that Olympic games, space races to Mars, and similar international competitions provide opportunities for the direction of aggressive behaviors into relatively harmless pursuits. The ethologists would encourage us to identify, and thereby control, the cues that trigger the expression of aggression.

For those who favor cultural explanations of aggressive behavior, possibilities for the control and reduction of violence are more numerous. Because they believe that environmental factors control the acquisition and maintenance of aggressive behaviors, they maintain that appropriate changes in environmental conditions can cause a decrease in aggression and violence. For example, social learning theorists suggest that observation of nonaggressive models leads to the acquisition of nonaggressive behavior. In an experiment demonstrating this effect, students watched a subject administer shocks to a "victim" before the students were given their turn

Figure 11–4 Impact of aggressive and nonaggressive models on overt aggression

(Baron & Kepner, 1970). As Figure 11–4 shows, the students who had observed an aggressive model administered more shocks to the "learner" than subjects who had not observed a model. In contrast, students who witnessed a restrained, nonaggressive model were less aggressive. Other investigators have found similar results (see Donnerstein & Donnerstein, 1977), although the success of the model in reducing an opponent's aggression may be an important qualification (Lando & Donnerstein, 1978). Even more important, research has shown that if both types of models are present, the nonaggressive model can effectively negate the influence of the aggressive model (Baron, 1971). Therefore, even if we cannot eliminate all aggressive models from our society, we may be able to reduce aggression by adding more nonaggressive models to the environment.

Learning theorists also advocate nonreinforcement of aggressive responses (Brown & Elliott, 1965). A person who is not rewarded for displays of aggression is less likely to acquire or maintain aggressive behaviors. Some people have also suggested that punishment or the threat of it may serve as a deterrent to aggressive behavior (see Box 11–3). Actual punishment may be an effective deterrent under certain conditions. Robert Baron (1977) suggests four necessary conditions: (1) the punishment must be predictable, (2) it must immediately follow the aggressive behavior, (3) it must be legitimized by

Box 11-3

Is capital punishment a deterrent to violent crime?

Policy makers have often argued about the possible deterrent effects of capital punishment. Advocates of capital punishment believe that the threat of the death sentence will reduce homicide; opponents suggest that such threats of punishment will have no noticeable effect. For the most part, these debates have been carried on in the absence of data.

David Phillips (1980) conducted an archival study that presents some relevant information. Using reports of murders and capital punishments recorded in London between 1858 and 1921, Phillips found that homicides decreased immediately after a well-publicized execution—and then they increased. As the accompanying graph shows, homicides decreased (by about 35%) during the period just after an execution. During subsequent weeks, however, homicides increased above the rate that would be expected, returning to the base rate about six weeks later.

Thus both advocates and opponents of capital punishment may have some basis for their beliefs. Capital punishment may serve as a deterrent in the short run, but the long-term effects are not evident—at least not in 19th-century England.

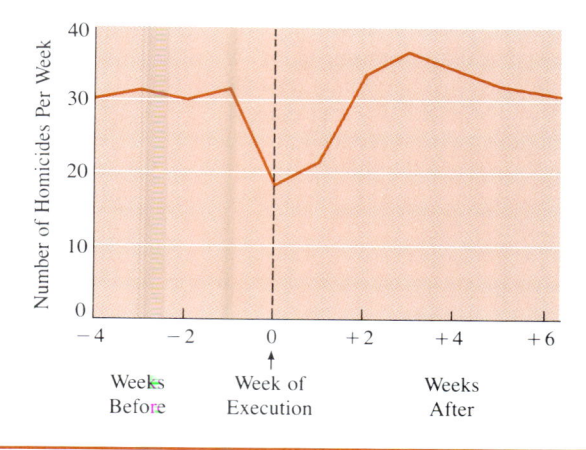

---

existing social norms, and (4) the persons administering the punishment should not be seen as aggressive models. If these conditions are not met, punishment could encourage aggression.

The conditions under which the *threat* of punishment can reduce aggression are perhaps even more limited. A threat appears to be effective only when the person who makes it is not terribly angry, when the expected punishment is very great and the probability of its delivery is high, and when the potential aggressor has relatively little to gain by being aggressive (Baron, 1977). These apparent limitations suggest that, in general, threat of punishment is not a very effective means of reducing aggressive behavior.

Investigators have pointed to incompatible responses as a third means of controlling violence. Basically, they suggest that because it is hard to do two things at once, the performance of violent acts should be reduced when conditions induce responses that are incompatible with the expression of aggression. Demonstrations of the effectiveness of this strategy have included the use of humorous cartoons (Baron & Ball, 1974) and conditions that foster empathy (Rule & Leger, 1976). In both cases subjects were less aggressive when an alternative response was available than when aggression was their only choice.

Information about mitigating circumstances can also reduce aggression. Explaining a person's aggressive behavior—providing reasons that suggest that the provocation was beyond the person's control—reduces the tendency to counterattack (Zillmann et al., 1975; Zillmann & Cantor, 1976). As we saw earlier, information about mitigating circumstances is particularly effective if it comes before the act of aggression. Of course, such explanations are not always available; to the extent that they can be introduced and accepted as reasonable, however, they allow people to choose to reduce their aggressive tendencies.

If frustration is believed to be a major determinant of aggression, then we might look to ways of reducing frustration as a means of controlling aggression. When Ransford (1968) interviewed Blacks living in the Watts area of Los Angeles in the 1960s, he found that those with intense feelings of dissatisfaction and frustration were more prone to violent action. The violence that accompanied Quebec's separatist movement was also attributed to social and economic frustrations. Community leaders can take numerous actions to reduce such frustrations: by providing better services, introducing human-relations training for police, and dealing directly with the causes of frustration, they could reduce aggression and violence.

Another suggested means of reducing aggression is catharsis. The term *catharsis* has a long history (Scheff & Bushnell, 1984). Aristotle first used the concept to explain the value of theater, arguing against Plato that dramatic catharsis could purge the audience of negative emotional experiences. Later Freud applied the term to a particular method of treating neurosis. As research psychologists use the term today, **catharsis** refers to the release of aggressive energy through the expression of aggressive emotions or through alternative forms of behavior. The role of catharsis in reducing aggressive behavior is stated clearly by Dollard and his colleagues: "The expression of any act of aggression is a catharsis that reduces the instigation to all other acts of aggression" (1939, p. 33). In other words, the concept of catharsis suggests that if you can get the anger off your chest, you will be less likely to behave aggressively on future occasions.

Proponents of the catharsis hypothesis have suggested that fantasy is one way in which aggression can be reduced. Although investigators have found that aggressive behavior can result in a decrease in aggressive fantasies (Murray & Feshbach, 1978), the more important possibility (if one is interested in controlling aggressive behavior)—that fantasies can serve to reduce aggressive behavior—has not received much support (Hartmann, 1969; Walters & Thomas, 1963). There is somewhat more support for the notion of behavioral catharsis—that the opportunity to express aggression at the time of frustration reduces subsequent aggressive behavior (Konečni, 1975). Behavioral catharsis, however, does not reduce the overall incidence of aggressive behavior—it simply controls the future expression at the cost of present violence.

A belief in innate aggressive tendencies might lead us to throw up our hands and say, "There's nothing to be done; war is inevitable and people are naturally violent." There is ample evidence, however, that aggressive behavior can be modified. Changes in a variety of factors, such as those reviewed here, can affect the occurrence of aggression. Even if such factors do not account for all aggressive behavior, they clearly account for a portion of it. These facts should not be overlooked as we seek a more peaceful human existence.

Summary

Definitions of aggression vary in accordance with one's theoretical perspective. For our discussion, we consider aggression to be any form of behavior that is directed toward the goal of harming or injuring another living being who is motivated to avoid such treatment.

Why are human beings aggressive? Answers to this question take two general forms, one stressing biological causes and the other emphasizing social factors. Biological explanations, offered by psychoanalysts, ethologists, and sociobiologists, stress the innate character of aggression. Proponents of socialization point to learning processes, such as reinforcement and modeling, to explain the development of aggressive behavior.

Many conditions can influence the occurrence of aggressive behavior. The experience of frustration when one is blocked from achieving a goal can lead to aggressive behavior if it arouses anger. Both the level of frustration and the intentions of the frustrating agent will influence this effect. Cues in the environment, such as weapons and firearms, increase the likelihood of aggression. So, too, do direct physical and verbal attacks. Instigation by a third party increases the tendency toward aggressive behavior.

Aggressive behavior is more likely to occur when the potential aggressor is not readily identifiable— when he or she is in a deindividuated state.

Moderate amounts of alcohol increase levels of aggressive behavior; marijuana, in contrast, acts as a deterrent. Environmental factors such as noise, air pollution, and heat can also affect the amount of aggression exhibited.

Individual differences in tendencies toward aggressive behavior are fairly stable over time. Men are somewhat more aggressive than women on the average, but sex differences in regard to aggression vary widely in different situations.

Depictions of violence in the mass media can lead to increases in aggressive behavior. Early experiments with children and Bobo dolls have been followed by more realistic laboratory studies and by longitudinal studies of actual television-viewing habits in children. All these studies point to a link between media violence and aggressive behavior.

Exposure to aggressive erotica (pornography) can increase aggressive behavior in men, particularly toward women.

Considerable violence occurs in the home, between spouses and between parents and children. Other forms of violence in our society include homicide and rape, as well as incidents of collective violence—violence between nations and between identifiable groups within a nation. The concept of relative deprivation has been used to explain why some groups decide to revolt or engage in collective violence.

Prospects for the control of aggression depend in large part on one's theoretical assumptions. A belief that aggression has an innate and instinctual basis leads to a relatively pessimistic outlook. Although aggression may be diverted into socially acceptable forms, its expression is seen as inevitable.

For those who favor social and cultural explanations of aggression, the control and eventual reduction of aggression seems more feasible. Suggested strategies for reducing aggression include the provision of nonaggressive models, nonreinforcement and punishment, incompatible responses, and information about mitigating circumstances.

Glossary Terms

catharsis
deindividuation
ethology
excitation transfer theory
frustration-aggression hypothesis
instrumental learning
modeling
neo-Freudians
observational learning
pornography
relative deprivation
sociobiology

If it is more blessed to give than to receive, then most of us are content to let the other fellow have the greater blessing.
Shailer Mathews

Giving is, indeed, more blessed than receiving, for having social credits is preferable to being socially indebted.
Peter Blau

Henry Moore: *Family Group*, 1946, Bronze. Hirshhorn Museum and Sculpture Garden, Smithsonian Institution. Gift of Joseph H. Hirshhorn, 1966.

CHAPTER TWELVE

Prosocial Behavior

This chapter was written by Carol K. Sigelman.

I. Prosocial Behavior and Human Nature
   Traditional Psychological Theories and Altruism
   Sociobiological Theory and Altruism
   Culture and Altruism
II. Why Do We Help? Models of Helping Behavior
   Helping as a Decision-Making Process
   Emotional Arousal and Empathy
   Norms
   Cost-Reward Analysis
   Decision-Making Models of Helping in Perspective
III. Situational Influences on Prosocial Behavior
   The Person in Need of Help
   The Influence of Other People
IV. Personal Influences on Prosocial Behavior
   Traits: The Search for the Good Samaritan
   Psychological States and Helping
V. Seeking and Receiving Help: The Recipient's Perspective
VI. Toward a Prosocial Society
   Encouraging Prosocial Behavior in Children
   Enlisting Support for Worthy Causes
   Legislating a Prosocial Society
VII. Summary

*O*ften it seems that all we read about in the newspapers is violence, war, and corruption. Yet people do behave in more likable ways. They join forces to accomplish positive goals; they do favors for one another; they support charities. Occasionally they even risk their lives to save others:

> A young man, late one Saturday evening, was driving by a dance hall just as the dance was ending and the crowd was beginning to spill out onto the sidewalk. He noticed a lot of people suddenly running toward an area. Then, as he recounts what happened, he saw "this dude carrying a girl by her hair, dragging her and punching her, punching her out like a beanbag." At that point he became involved: "I went over there and I grabbed the dude and I shoved him over and I said lay off the chick. So me and him started going at it. I told him to get out of here, man, look at her, man, the girl's mouth's all bleeding, she got her teeth knocked out, she got a handful of hair pulled out. Everybody was just standing around." [Huston et al., 1981, p. 17]

This vivid description of a rescue attempt raises many questions: Why did this young man help, and why did the other bystanders fail to help? What was his true motivation, and what was going on inside him as he sized up the situation and decided to take action? Whatever the answers, his act is a clear example of what this chapter is about: prosocial behavior. **Prosocial behavior** is usually defined as behavior that benefits others or has positive social consequences (Staub, 1978; Wispé, 1972). The term *prosocial* contrasts with the term *antisocial,* which applies to the aggressive and violent behaviors discussed in Chapter Eleven. A host of specific behaviors can be viewed as prosocial—intervention by a bystander, charity, courtesy, cooperation, donation, friendship, helping, rescue, sacrifice, sharing, sympathy. *Cooperation,* or working with others for mutual benefit, is an important prosocial behavior that will

Photo 12–1 On May 25, 1986, millions of people in the United States took part in "Hands across America" to raise money for the hungry and homeless. Did they have motives other than altruism?

be discussed in Chapter Sixteen. Here we emphasize **helping behavior,** or prosocial behavior that clearly benefits another person rather than oneself, especially intervention in emergencies.

Notice that prosocial behavior has been defined in terms of its consequences. Such a definition raises some questions. For example, if you unintentionally worsen the condition of an accident victim to whom you are administering first aid, have you acted in a prosocial manner? What if you clearly benefit someone by giving him or her money, but do so in order to get a favor in return? The act has positive social consequences, but wouldn't most of us call it a bribe rather than a prosocial act? Because of such problems, it is useful to consider not only the consequences of an act but the motives behind it. The clearest instances of prosocial behavior merit the term *altruism*. **Altruism** is a very special form of helping behavior that is voluntary, costly to the altruist, and motivated by something other than the anticipation of material or social reward (Walster & Piliavin, 1972). Some researchers insist that the primary motive is to improve the other's welfare (Batson & Coke, 1981). Altruism, then, is selfless rather than selfish, and the degree of altruism in a prosocial act can vary widely. One of the liveliest debates among psychologists interested in prosocial behavior centers on whether true altruism even exists. Using our young hero as an example, we may agree that he chose to intervene, and that he did so despite the risk of injury, but can we agree on his motivation? Perhaps it was not selfless concern for the victim; perhaps it was a need to live up to his image of a hero, a desire for adventure, or any of a variety of similarly self-centered motives.

The study of prosocial behavior started later than the study of antisocial behavior, but it soon became one of the most active areas in social psychology (Krebs & Miller, 1985). The behaviors studied have ranged from the merely considerate to the heroic—from picking up pencils, filling out questionnaires, and turning off the lights in parked cars to stopping a thief and helping the victim of an epileptic seizure. The emergencies staged by some researchers are so realistic and so intense that ethical issues arise about whether such research should even be done (see Chapter Two). Yet such research has much to say about people's behavior in emergencies.

We will begin our exploration of prosocial behavior by examining the challenge that the very idea of altruism poses to our understanding of human nature. Then we will look at what happens when an individual encounters a situation that calls for prosocial behavior and at some explanations that social psychologists have offered to account for prosocial acts. These explanatory models can help us to analyze a wide range of influences on prosocial behavior. Such influences include both factors in the situation, such as characteristics of the person in need and the presence of other people who could potentially help, and factors within the person, such as aspects of personality and moods of the moment. Throughout most of the chapter, we will be looking through the potential helper's eyes, but later we will shift our perspective to that of the recipient of help in order to understand why some prosocial acts are appreciated and others are not. Finally, we will try to apply what we have learned to the task of building a more prosocial society in the future.

Prosocial Behavior and Human Nature

There are many practical reasons for being interested in the study of prosocial behavior. Many of us believe that the world would be a better place if people were more prosocial, and we deplore the cases we read about in which a person in desperate need of help fails to receive it. For psychologists, however, part of the fascination of prosocial behavior is theoretical rather than practical. The very existence of prosocial behavior, especially altruism, poses a challenge to psychology. Many psychological theories assume that human beings are basically selfish. How, then, can those theories account for selfless actions? Is true altruism even possible? Yet remarkably heroic acts do occur. Is it conceivable that altruism is built into the very nature of human beings? These are perhaps the most important and fascinating questions in the study of prosocial behavior.

Traditional Psychological Theories and Altruism

Traditional psychological theories have a hard time explaining altruism. Freudian psychoanalytic theory, for example, rests on the assumption that human nature is instinctively selfish and aggressive. How, then, can it explain altruism? Not very easily. Some psychoanalytic theorists view altruism as a means of defending ourselves against our own internal conflicts and anxieties, but this approach seems to deny that we can genuinely care for others. Other psychoanalytic theorists have taken a more positive approach and tried to understand how positive influences in personality development can reduce the strength of selfish motives and lead us to internalize more selfless values (Ekstein, 1978).

Or consider learning theories, especially those that emphasize principles of reinforcement. A basic principle of reinforcement theory is that we repeat and strengthen those behaviors that result in positive consequences for us. How, then, can altruism increase in strength, or even exist, if it is associated with negative consequences such as loss of resources, injury, even death?

Some learning theorists have responded by denying that true altruism exists. What appears to be altruism, they say, is really **egoism,** or self-interest. Some argue that there are subtle rewards for seemingly altruistic acts (Gelfand & Hartmann, 1982). For example, people may feel better about themselves as a result of rushing to the rescue, or may expect rewards in the afterlife. It has also been argued that by adulthood we have learned to find prosocial behavior self-rewarding and no longer need external rewards to make such behavior worthwhile to us (Baumann, Cialdini, & Kenrick, 1981). Researchers acting within a reinforcement framework have tried to demonstrate that helping is in fact reinforcing to the helper (for example, R. F. Weiss et al., 1971).

Is selflessness really selfishness in disguise? Some of the arguments offered by learning theorists sound somewhat circular; that is, they seem to assume that, because the prosocial behavior occurred, its consequences *must* have been reinforcing. So strong is the belief that people act in their own self-interest that it is impossible for many psychologists to imagine an act that is not motivated by self-interest. Learning theorists do make a useful point when they note that the rewards for altruism may be subtle. It is hard to prove that no selfish motivation whatever existed in even the most heroic rescues. At the same time, demonstrations that prosocial behavior can be reinforcing do not prove that prosocial behavior is *always* reinforcing. Like psychoanalytic theorists, learning theorists still have difficulty explaining why people sometimes help others at huge costs to themselves and with little or no apparent reward.

Sociobiological Theory and Altruism

Sociobiology reaches further back in time to explain the development of altruism. As we saw in regard to aggressive behavior in Chapter Eleven, sociobiology relies on evolutionary theory and genetic inheritance to explain social behavior. Traditional evolutionary theory, as developed by Charles Darwin and others, has some problems in accounting for altruistic behavior. Darwin's "survival of the fittest" view says that if one's genes help one to survive and thus allow one to produce more offspring than less "fit" individuals, those genes will become more common in future generations of the species. But how could genes that predispose an individual to be altruistic be passed on with any frequency when altruists endanger their very survival for the sake of others?

Consider an especially puzzling example of altruism among social insects. Female worker bees (and ants and wasps as well) have evolved so that they are sterile. Instead of bearing their own offspring, they devote their lives to caring for the queen bee's offspring and even sacrifice their lives in defense of her hive. Such behavior is impossible to explain in terms of the survival of the fittest individuals. Sociobiologists have suggested, however, that it can be explained in terms of survival of the fittest *genes* (W. D. Hamilton, 1964; Trivers & Hare, 1976). As offspring of a single queen and as sisters, female workers share three-fourths of their genes in common with other workers and any future workers the queen may produce. (Male bees develop from unfertilized eggs and have only one set of chromosomes containing genes rather than the two sets that female bees, and humans of both sexes, have. As a result, all daughters of a queen receive exactly the same genetic material from their father, so that they are more alike genetically than they would be if both parents had two sets of chromosomes.) By contrast, if a worker were able to reproduce, she would pass on only half of her genes to her own offspring, just as human parents do. At this point sociobiologists introduce the concept of **kin selection,** or the selection over the course of evolution of characteristics or traits that contribute to the survival of the *kinship group's* genes. It is, they argue, the survival of genes, which are shared with relatives or kin, rather than the survival of individuals, that matters in evolution. The worker bees can actually pass on more of their genetic material to future generations by helping the queen to produce more sisters than they could by reproducing themselves. The genes that make worker bees sterile and altruistic do not improve their own chances of survival, but may have been selected through evolution because they enhance the survival of their kin. Similarly, when an animal dies to save its offspring or relatives, its genes are lost but the genes of the kinship group survive and perhaps become more prevalent in future generations.

This is a view that, like so many others, regards altruism as a matter of selfishness—in this case, an interest in passing on as much of the family's genetic formula as possible. Of course, no one is suggesting that bees, or even humans, consciously make decisions based on the probability that their actions will cause their genes to flourish. Sociobiologists are arguing that altruism could be built into the genetic code of humans and other animal species because it has been effective over time in increasing the survival of kin. As a result, genes that underlie altruistic tendencies would become more numerous in the species.

Kin selection might, if we accept the sociobiological assumptions, explain our willingness to help our kin, but why would anyone help a stranger? Dennis Krebs (1983) suggests that early humans may not have known for certain who their relatives were and so may have evolved to help those who *might* share their genes, members of their in-group, or people who were physically similar to themselves (see Morgan, 1985, for a demonstration that evolution could result in prosocial behavior toward fellow members of social groups that include nonkin). Still, this hypothesis does not explain why people would help dissimilar others or members of out-groups. Here the concept of **reciprocal altruism** has been introduced by sociobiologists (Trivers, 1971). You might risk your own safety to help a total stranger, the argument goes, if you anticipated some help in return—help that would pay you back for your original sacrifice and would benefit both of you in the long run. Here selection over the course of evolution favors those with genes that predispose them to altruism because in the long run altruistic acts are reciprocated and thus benefit the individual. Once again, then, altruism is interpreted as genetic self-interest.

By applying such concepts as kin selection and reciprocal altruism, sociobiologists paint an unsettling picture of human nature. Taken to its extreme, this view suggests that "we are survival machines—robot vehicles blindly programmed to preserve the selfish molecules known as genes" (Dawkins, 1976, p. ix). At the same time, sociobiology carries a positive message by suggesting that altruism is part of the basic biological nature of human beings, just as self-interest is (M. L. Hoffman, 1981).

How strong is the evidence for a biological basis of altruism? Martin Hoffman (1981) has drawn together a range of sociobiological and psychological evidence supporting the idea that altruism is part of human nature. Moreover, he proposes that the genetically influenced quality underlying altruism is **empathy,** or the vicarious experiencing of another's emotions, as when we shed tears with or feel the joy of our favorite movie stars. In support of this hypothesis, some fascinating studies indicate that humans are designed from birth to respond to the distress of their peers. One such study found that newborns became distressed by the cries of other newborns (G. B. Martin & Clark, 1982). And it was not just that any crying sound was irritating, for these newborns were not similarly upset by their own tape-recorded cries or by the cries of chimpanzees.

Some investigators suggest that individual differences in empathy and other prosocial tendencies among adults have a genetic basis (Matthews et al., 1981; Rushton et al., 1986). J. Phillipe Rushton and his colleagues found, for example, that identical twins, who have identical genes, are more similar to each other on questionnaires designed to assess altruism, empathy, and nurturance than are fraternal twins, who share about half of their genes. Rushton and his colleagues concluded that differences in genetic endowment among people have a considerable influence on differences in their tendencies to behave both prosocially and antisocially. Finally, as we shall see shortly, several researchers emphasize the role of empathic emotion as a motivator of altruistic behavior. Thus the concept of a genetic basis for altruism seems worth pursuing.

Culture and Altruism

We have ignored another important influence on human behavior: culture. Donald Campbell (1978, 1983) is one forceful critic of sociobiological views of altruism, arguing that biological evolution must favor selfishness as long as humans compete with one another. Campbell believes that *cultural* evolution is responsible for prosocial behavior, that societies have been more successful at adapting when they have developed ways of socializing their members to control their naturally selfish urges. Thus societies attempt to instill prosocial values in the young through child-rearing practices, religion, and education. Some societies provide more opportunities for learning to behave prosocially than others do, particularly by involving older children in the care of younger ones (Graves & Graves, 1983). As Daniel Batson (1983) notes, however, biological evolution and cultural evolution need not pull us in opposite directions. For example, kin selection may create a biologically based tendency to aid kin, and culture may then build on that foundation by urging people to extend their prosocial tendencies to non-kin. Religious teachings do, after all, encourage us to love our neighbors as ourselves and to act in a spirit of "brotherly love."

Such controversies over the origins—and even the possibility—of altruism are debates about the very nature of human beings. Psychoanalytic theory, reinforcement theory, and sociobiology all assume that humans are basically selfish and interpret altruistic behavior as basically selfish, too. No one denies that people sometimes behave in ways that seem very unselfish. The most heated debates center on the motives behind such behavior, with some theorists believing that the motives are ultimately egoistic or selfish, but others arguing that genuinely altruistic motivation based on empathy for fellow humans is possible. Similarly, some theorists believe that altruism is built into our biological nature, while others maintain that our biologically rooted tendency toward selfishness must be controlled by cultural influences that foster prosocial behavior. The issues are by no means resolved (see Zahn-Waxler, Cummings, & Iannoti, 1986).

Why Do We Help? Models of Helping Behavior

Think back to the young man described at the beginning of this chapter. Certainly the most important question to ask about him is why he rushed forward to help the woman being assaulted. Why do any of us help? As we shall see, many factors influence whether a person will act prosocially. Here we are concerned with the basic motivations and processes behind such behavior. In their attempts to explain why people help, social psychologists have emphasized that helping situations are decision-making situations and then have tried to show how both emotional and cognitive processes lead to decisions.

Helping as a Decision-Making Process

Three models of helping behavior (Latané & Darley, 1970; Piliavin et al., 1981; Schwartz, 1977) assume that people progress through steps in making a decision to help or not to help. All three emphasize *cognitive processes,* such as interpreting a situation and weighing the consequences of alternative actions. All also insist that the decision-making process involves not only rational cognition but also emotion. Helping situations arouse feelings in us (sympathy for the victim, distress at another person's suffering, feelings of moral obligation to act), and feelings serve to motivate behavior.

Jane Piliavin and her associates (1981), for example, have proposed an **arousal/cost-reward model** of helping in emergency situations that can be extended to nonemergencies as well. As in all models of helping, the first step is becoming aware of a need for help (Krebs & Miller, 1985). After all, no decision making is going to occur if you never even notice that an emergency is taking place. It is easier to become aware of the need for help if an emergency is clear, as when a victim screams for help or otherwise directly requests it. But many helping situations are ambiguous and may or may not be interpreted as emergencies (see Photo 12–2). The second step in the model is becoming emotionally aroused, and the third step is labeling that arousal. You may, for example, see a fight and become excited, but you are more likely to help if you attribute your arousal to concern for the victim's welfare than if you attribute it to the drink you had or the loud music you have been listening to. The fourth step involves a cost-reward analysis in which the consequences of helping or failing to help are cognitively weighed. Arousal serves to motivate action of some kind, and cost-benefit deliberations influence whether that action

Photo 12–2 As people come upon this scene, the man screams, "Get away from me!" Specific elements of the situation can be critical in determining whether people conclude that there is an emergency and a need for help

is direct intervention, escape from the situation, or something in between. Thus the final step in the Piliavin model is the making of a decision, the taking of a course of action.

To understand why people help, let us look more closely at three prominent elements in decision-making models of helping. First, we will consider arousal as a motivator of helping, and the specific kinds of emotions that are experienced in helping situations. Then we will consider the role of **norms,** or societal standards of behavior, in motivating helping. Finally, we will consider the process of weighing the costs and rewards of helping and of failing to help.

Emotional Arousal and Empathy

Several researchers have proposed that emotional arousal is the key motivator of helping behavior, especially in emergencies. Emergencies are by nature sudden and emotionally involving. Even watching someone drop a book may produce a mild form of arousal, such as a feeling of concern or distress at the sound of the book hitting the floor.

In their model of intervention in emergencies, Piliavin and her colleagues (1981) highlight the role of arousal in helping. They suggest that emergencies produce an arousal that bystanders are motivated to reduce. If a person is aroused to the point of panic and sees little chance of accomplishing anything positive, the most direct way to reduce arousal may be to escape from the situation. When the victim's need is clear and severe, however, and when it seems possible to be of aid without huge difficulties, one can reduce arousal by providing help.

Several studies show that emergencies are indeed physiologically arousing and, more important, that people who are more highly aroused are more likely to help or to help quickly. For example, Gaertner and Dovidio (1977) staged an emergency in which a stack of chairs apparently crashed down on a woman in the next room. Bystanders who had the fastest heart rates and reported that they felt the most upset intervened more quickly than those who were less aroused. The same study demonstrated, however, that arousal alone is not sufficient to motivate helping: the cognitive labeling of arousal is also important, as we saw in Chapters Three and Eleven. If helping is to occur, arousal must be attributed to the victim's plight rather than to something else. Bystanders who were given a placebo drug that they were told would arouse them were slower to help in an ambiguous emergency than were bystanders who were given a drug that supposedly would give them a dull headache and related symptoms but would not arouse them. Those given the "arousing" drug could attribute the arousal they felt when they heard the crash to the drug rather than to the crash. Thus emotional arousal, whatever its source, needs to be interpreted as some kind of response to the helping situation (Sterling & Gaertner, 1984).

But what specific kinds of emotional response do people in need evoke? Several theorists have emphasized one particular form of emotional reaction as the basis for helping behavior: *empathy* (Hoffman, 1981; Krebs, 1975; Coke, Batson, & McDavis, 1978; Eisenberg & Miller, 1987). The cognitive process of taking the perspective of a person in need is thought to produce an emotional response of empathy (Coke, Batson, & McDavis, 1978). Empathy then motivates us to reduce the distress of the person in need. Batson and his colleagues have also proposed that there is a critical distinction between empathic concern—an empathic focus on the distress of another person and the motivation to reduce it—and *personal* distress, or concern with one's *own* discomfort and the motivation to reduce it. On a scale they have used to measure emotional reactions to a victim's plight, adjectives reflecting empathy include *sympathetic, compassionate,* and *tender,* while reactions indicating personal distress include *alarmed* and *upset.* Notice that in the Piliavin arousal/cost-reward model, it is really personal distress that we are supposedly motivated to reduce. Batson suggests that empathic concern may provide a genuinely altruistic motivation for helping (Batson & Coke, 1981). He and his colleagues have tried to show that empathic concern exists, is separable from personal distress, and has different motivational properties from personal distress.

For example, they used placebo drugs to lead some women to think they were experiencing empathic concern and others to think they were experiencing personal distress as they watched a woman apparently being shocked in a learning experiment (Batson et al., 1981). Both groups of women were quite willing to help by taking some of the shocks themselves when they had no possibility of escaping the situation because they would have to stay and watch the victim take shocks if they failed to help. However, when escape was easy because they could leave the experiment, the women experiencing personal distress were egoistic rather than altruistic, escaping rather than helping. One can, after all, reduce one's own unpleasant distress more easily and quickly by escaping than by helping. By contrast, a large majority of those who experienced empathic concern continued to help spare the woman her agony even when they could easily have escaped and turned their backs on her (see Figure 12–1). Thus empathy, but not

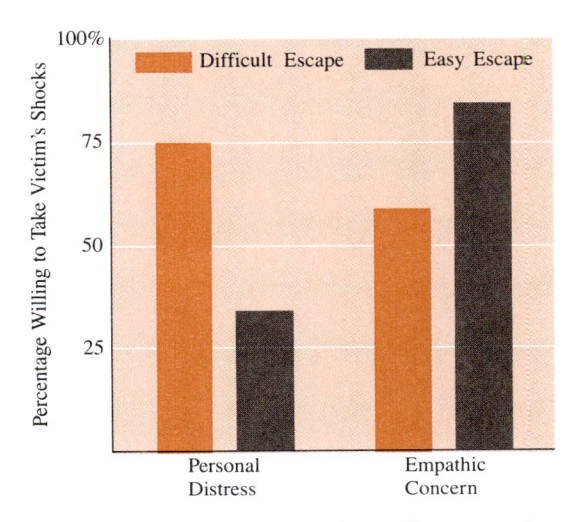

Figure 12–1 Empathy versus distress: Percentage of subjects who were willing to help a victim as a function of whether their arousal was labeled as personal distress or as empathic concern and of ease of escape from the situation

personal distress, appeared to arouse a genuinely altruistic motivation for helping, which the women could satisfy only by seeing the other woman's suffering end.

Can we conclude that empathic concern motivates genuinely altruistic helping? Not unless all possible egoistic motives are ruled out. What if the empathic helper is worried about being negatively evaluated by others if he or she fails to help? In response to criticism along these lines by Archer (1984), Batson and his colleagues compared students with high and low empathic arousal under conditions of high and low potential for negative social evaluation by others. College students who had been instructed to empathize with a young woman who expressed her loneliness and need for friends were more helpful than students who were instructed merely to process information about the victim's plight objectively—even when no one, including the victim, would ever know they failed to help, not just when looking bad in the eyes of others was a real threat (Fultz et al., 1986). In this study, then, self-centered concern with negative evaluations from others could not explain why empathic concern motivates helping. However, researchers have not yet ruled out an egoistic concern with avoiding one's own negative evaluations of oneself for failing to help or with gaining a sense of self-esteem from behaving prosocially. Indeed, some of Batson's own research has suggested that even highly empathic people betray egoistic motives on occasion, especially when helping is costly or escape from responsibility is easy (Batson et al., 1983, 1986). Yet empathy is a motivation for helping that is at least less selfish than a desire to escape unpleasant personal distress or to avoid the disapproval of others.

Slowly, then, researchers are beginning to understand the emotions we feel when someone needs our help. It is clear that emotional arousal motivates helping behavior—if that arousal is interpreted as due to an emergency situation or a victim's plight. Special attention has been given to the specific emotional reaction of empathy, for it implies a genuinely altruistic motivation for helping—a desire to reduce suffering that we, through our capacity for empathy, share with the person directly affected. Both empathic concern and personal distress can and do motivate helping behavior, for both are arousing. However, it is one thing to say that we help in order to reduce the distress of another person, and another to say that we help in order to get rid of our own unpleasant feelings of disgust, fear, and alarm. And when people are clearly experiencing empathy rather than personal distress, it is difficult to rule out the possibility that they are helping in order to maintain a positive self-image or to avoid the shame and guilt associated with failure to help. Thus those who emphasize the role of emotion in motivating helping behavior must continue to grapple with the issue of how much of that emotion is altruistic and how much is egoistic.

Norms

Normative explanations of helping behavior suggest that we help others because we have internalized *norms,* or societal standards for behavior, and are motivated to act in accordance with those norms. What norms are relevant to prosocial behavior? One is the **social-responsibility norm,** which states that we should help those who need help (Berkowitz & Daniels, 1963). People are indeed likely to help those who appear to be dependent on them. In many instances, however, highly needy individuals do not receive the help that the social-responsibility norm says they should receive. Most people endorse the norm verbally, but fewer act in accordance with it (Piliavin et al., 1981).

More powerful is the **reciprocity norm.** As Alvin Gouldner (1960) conceptualizes it, the reciprocity norm states that people should help those who have helped them and should not injure those who have helped them. This norm is closely related to *equity theory* (see Chapter Nine), which emphasizes the imbalance produced in a relationship when one person helps (or harms) another and the resulting need to restore equity. Gouldner argued that the norm of reciprocity is universal and essential to maintaining stable relationships among people.

There is no doubt that people often experience strong feelings of obligation to reciprocate when someone does them a favor. Indeed, prison inmates have been known to capitalize on the norm of reciprocity by trying to "buy" and dominate newcomers through the giving of gifts (McCorkle & Korn, 1954). The very power of the reciprocity norm may be one reason that recipients of help are sometimes resentful, as we will see later. Despite the power of this norm, however, it too sometimes fails to operate (for example, Schopler & Thompson, 1968).

Despite their plausibility, both of these normative explanations have been found wanting (see, for example, Latané & Darley, 1970; Schwartz, 1977). First, norms are so general that they may not tell us what to do in specific situations. Second, if most people in a society subscribe to such norms, how can norms explain individual differences in helping behavior? Third, two conflicting norms may seem equally applicable in a situation. The norm of social responsibility, for example, is contradicted by a norm that says "Don't meddle in other people's affairs." And finally, people's behavior often is inconsistent with social norms.

However, Shalom Schwartz has given new life to the normative approach to understanding prosocial behavior (Schwartz, 1973, 1977; Schwartz & Howard, 1981, 1984). Instead of focusing on general social norms, Schwartz and his colleagues have measured **personal norms,** or the individual's feelings of moral obligation to act in a given way in a given situation. Personal norms are a blend of cognition (expectations about one's behavior based on values) and emotion (anticipated feelings of self-satisfaction or dissatisfaction depending on how one acts). We develop personal norms in a specific helping situation; these feelings of obligation then motivate us to help; and we are then rewarded by the positive feeling that we have acted in accordance with our own moral standards. Whereas we may obey social norms to please society, we adhere to personal norms to please ourselves.

Let's try Schwartz's approach: "If a stranger to you needed a bone marrow transplant and you were a suitable donor, would you feel a moral obligation to donate bone marrow?" This question is a measure of one personal norm studied by Schwartz (1973). Notice that it asks not about generalized feelings of social responsibility but about a specific kind of obligation. Along with it in the survey were questions assessing respondents' tendencies to use defenses to neutralize their personal norms. Specifically, Schwartz measured people's tendencies to accept or deny responsibility for the welfare of others. Three months later, respondents received a mail request to donate bone marrow. People with a strong personal norm motivating them to donate marrow were indeed more likely to act in accordance with their beliefs than those without a strong sense of obligation—as long as they did not also have a strong tendency to deny responsibility for the welfare of others. Those who denied such responsibility sometimes felt an obligation to help, but when it came to deciding, they may have talked themselves out of feeling personally responsible for helping. For them, there was no relationship between the norm they verbalized and the way they acted.

In a wide range of studies by Schwartz and others, measures of personal norms, along with measures of defenses against those norms such as denial of responsibility, have proved very useful in predicting behavior. Schwartz's model is more complex than earlier normative explanations. It specifies how a motivation to help, in the form of a specific personal norm, is activated in a situation and then how defenses come into play to determine whether or not a personal norm is acted upon. It recognizes that people differ not only in their normative beliefs but also in their tendencies to act consistently with their beliefs. Schwartz has demonstrated that norms are useful after all in explaining why people act prosocially. Finally, he also draws our attention to the idea that living up to one's own personal standards can be intrinsically motivating, or can serve as its own reward. On occasion we may help because we are intrinsically motivated to do the right thing, not to reduce our own uncomfortable arousal (as in the Piliavin arousal/cost-reward model) and not to reduce the distress of another person (as in Batson's view).

Cost-Reward Analysis

A view of helping situations as decision-making situations focuses attention on the costs and rewards of deciding to help or not to help. In their arousal/cost-reward model of intervention in emergencies, Piliavin and her colleagues (1981), as already noted, emphasize that bystanders to emergencies are emotionally aroused and motivated to reduce that arousal. Decision-making processes enter in as bystanders evaluate the situation and attempt to reduce their arousal in the least costly way they can. An analysis of costs and rewards leads to a decision to help or not to help and influences the form that any assistance takes. This model assumes, as do several social-psychological theories, that people are generally motivated to increase the rewards of their actions and to decrease the costs. In emergencies and other helping situations, the focus is on costs, for the rewards are often few.

What costs are relevant? First, there are the almost inevitable *costs of helping:* effort and time expended, loss of resources, the risk of harm, possible embarrassment or disapproval by others, negative emotional reactions to interacting with the victim, and so on. Costs also include rewards one has to forgo in order to help (as when helping means missing an important appointment). To establish the *net* costs of helping, the bystander would subtract from these costs any potential rewards for helping: payments, social approval, increased self-esteem associated with being a helpful person and living up to personal norms, and so on.

The *costs of not helping* must also be considered. Piliavin and her colleagues (1981) break these costs down into personal costs and empathy costs. Personal costs of failing to help include such consequences as guilt, loss of self-esteem, and social disapproval. Empathy costs are tied to the knowledge that the victim will continue to suffer if no help is supplied.

It is essential to recognize that this cost-reward approach is concerned with costs and rewards as the potential helper perceives them. Faced with the assault described at the beginning of the chapter, for example, our heroic young man may have perceived himself as capable of taking on the attacker without suffering a scratch, while other bystanders may have figured it would be their last day on earth if they intervened. Not only do different people calculate costs differently, but all of us are motivated to distort costs and rewards when we face a difficult decision. One way out of the dilemma posed by an emergency in which the costs of helping and the costs of failure to help are both high is to use cognitive distortion (Piliavin et al., 1981). We might downplay the consequences of failing to help by thinking, "It's not so serious," or "Someone else will be right along to help." Magically, the costs of failing to help are lowered!

Many of the influences on prosocial behavior that we will discuss later in the chapter work by affecting perceptions of costs and rewards. Figure 12–2 summarizes the predictions that this model makes about the way a person is likely to respond when the costs of helping and the costs of not helping are either high or low. The model predicts, for example, that a person is most likely to help when the costs of helping are low but the costs of not helping are very high. By contrast, little help is to be expected if helping is likely to be very costly but no great cost is involved if one fails to help. Much research supports these predictions.

Decision-Making Models of Helping in Perspective

Perhaps this picture of how people decide whether to offer help seems too cold and calculating. The models of helping that we have considered do view

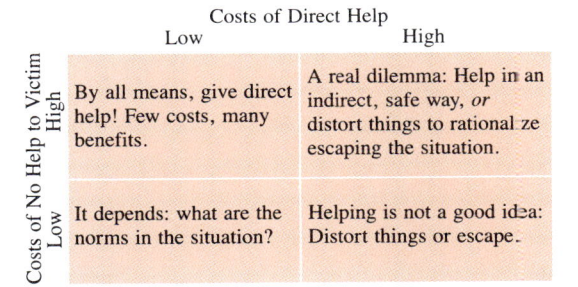

	Costs of Direct Help	
	Low	**High**
Costs of No Help to Victim — High	By all means, give direct help! Few costs, many benefits.	A real dilemma: Help in an indirect, safe way, *or* distort things to rationalize escaping the situation.
Costs of No Help to Victim — Low	It depends: what are the norms in the situation?	Helping is not a good idea: Distort things or escape.

Figure 12–2 Predicted effects of cost factors. Costs of helping and costs expected if the victim receives no help are considered in making a decision. The decision is especially difficult when both kinds of costs are high. In such situations, people sometimes throw cost considerations out the window and help impulsively

arousal or emotion as an important motivator of helping. Yet potential helpers are also seen as proceeding step by step through a decision-making process that starts with the perception of a need for help and ends, after a rational consideration of costs and rewards, in a decision. Let us correct this picture a bit. Bibb Latané and John Darley (1970) emphasize that decision-making steps may not occur one by one in a logical way. Emergencies, by their very nature, are dangerous, unusual, unique, unforeseen, and pressing. As a result, they produce arousal or stress that is not present in nonemergencies and that may interfere with rational decision making and action. The arousal/cost-reward model of Piliavin and her associates also emphasizes the arousing nature of emergencies and the interplay between emotion and cognition. Indeed, some emergencies are so clear and severe and so arousing that bystanders act impulsively, ignoring many cues in the situation, failing to weigh costs and rewards, and behaving in ways that look irrational to an outsider—very much as our heroic young man did. *Impulsive help,* as the term suggests, is quick help. Piliavin and her colleagues (1981) speculate that the impulse to act in dramatic emergencies may be innate but that we are socialized to pay closer attention to cost and reward factors in less compelling emergencies. Decision-making models of helping do not describe impulsive help very well. Nor do they fit situations in which we merely act out a well-rehearsed routine of helping (Schwartz, 1977), as when a parent routinely answers a child's questions about homework. Still, decision-making models fit many situations, emergencies and nonemergencies, when we are confronted by a new situation and unsure what to do.

We have now introduced three important aspects of the helping response: the motivational role of emotional arousal, particularly empathy with the person in need; the activation of norms relevant to helping and the motivation to act in accordance with internalized personal norms; and the cognitive processes involved in assessing a helping situation and weighing the costs of alternative actions. Armed with these basic concepts, we are now in a position to look more closely at influences on helping behavior. Like all social behavior, prosocial behavior is influenced by characteristics of the situation, characteristics of the person, and the interaction between situational and personal factors. Let us examine some of the situational and personal factors that make prosocial behavior more or less likely to occur.

Situational Influences on Prosocial Behavior

The situations in which prosocial behavior occurs vary widely, from emergencies to nonemergencies, from ambiguous situations to perfectly clear-cut ones. Accordingly, levels of arousal and empathy, relevant norms, and cost factors also vary widely from situation to situation. In exploring the impact of situational factors on helping, let us begin with what is usually the most prominent element in a helping situation: the person in need of help.

The Person in Need of Help

Characteristics and behaviors of the person in need of help are situational cues that potential helpers read as they interpret the situation and decide whether to help. Who receives help and who does not?

The nature of the need. By its very nature, helping is a response to a person in need, but the nature of the person's dependency on others influences the rate of helping behavior. Dependency can be a stable characteristic of a person (for example, a mentally retarded child) that elicits helpful responses from almost everyone. It can also result from a temporary plight (for example, a sprained ankle). Or, finally, dependency can be the function of a relationship between two people (for example, between parent and child). Leonard Berkowitz and his colleagues have demonstrated that if dependency is introduced into the relationship between two people—for instance, if a supervisor's rewards depend heavily on a worker's productivity—helping behavior is more likely to occur (Berkowitz, 1978; Berkowitz & Daniels, 1963). Thus the people who receive help seem to be the people who are dependent on others. However, potential helpers look closely at the nature of and reasons behind an individual's dependency.

First, potential helpers weigh the legitimacy of a recipient's need. Imagine how you would react if a woman approached you in the supermarket and asked for a dime to buy milk. Then imagine the same woman asking for a dime for frozen cookie dough. Bickman and Kamzan (1973) found that 58% of the shoppers who were asked for milk money responded but only 36% were willing to shell out for cookie dough. The more legitimate the need, the more help received.

Second, potential helpers are influenced by the causes of dependency or need. Suppose that you are approached by a fellow student in need of your class notes. Would you be more likely to help the student who claims to be unable to take good notes or the student who just skips class out of lack of motivation? Typically, you are more likely to help if the need is due to something uncontrollable, such as lack of ability or the professor's shortcomings, than if it is due to something more controllable, such as lack of effort (Weiner, 1980). Generally people who are dependent through no fault of their own are helped more than people who can be blamed for their dependency. Our attributions about the cause of dependency influence the nature of our emotional response. When we attribute need to uncontrollable factors, positive emotions such as empathy are aroused, and they in turn motivate helping. However, when we attribute need to controllable factors and hold a person responsible for his or her plight, negative emotions such as disgust and anger are aroused and motivate us to avoid the person (Reisenzein, 1986).

All of this is quite straightforward. The people who receive help are those who are dependent and whose need is legitimate, not their fault, and not under their control. But a puzzle arises: sometimes the people who should have the greatest claims on us for those very reasons are not given the help they deserve. Consider this finding: A person with a bandaged forearm receives more help picking up dropped envelopes than a nondisabled person, but a person with a bandaged forearm, an eye patch, and a scar receives no more help than a nondisabled person (Samerotte & Harris, 1976). The only way we can account for this curiosity is to consider the costs of helping. People often experience an aversion to people who are disabled, disfigured, or otherwise stigmatized, and may be reluctant to pay the extra "costs" of interacting with such individuals, despite their dependency. This is especially true when other costs of helping are high. For example, salespersons in shoe stores spent more time helping a customer who limped in with a broken heel than they did a "normal" customer when the store was almost empty, but slightly *less* time helping the more dependent person when the store was busy and the salesperson risked losing business (Schaps, 1972). Even the most dependent and worthy persons do not always elicit the help to which they seem entitled, especially as the perceived costs of helping escalate.

Relationship with the potential helper. We cannot consider the characteristics of the person in need in a vacuum; we must also take into account the relationship between that person and the potential helper. Relationships between relatives and friends imply mutual dependency and a special obligation to help (M.S. Clark, 1983). Indeed, studies of tornadoes and other disasters indicate that people tend to help family members first, then friends and neighbors, and finally strangers (Form & Nosow, 1958). Yet, even though intimate relationships are special, a brief acquaintance or familiarity is enough to increase the rate of helping (Latané & Darley, 1970; Pearce, 1980). As Box 12-1 shows, many people serve as informal helpers for people they do not know very well.

Those people with whom we have some relationship are seen as part of our "we-group." As Harvey Hornstein (1976) and others have suggested, we become more emotionally involved when someone in our we-group is in trouble and are therefore more motivated to help them than we do when the person in need is a total stranger. We may also view the rewards of helping and the costs of not helping such a person as greater than those involved in helping a stranger.

Similarity and attraction. The concept of a we-group suggests that we will be especially helpful to anyone who is similar to ourselves in some important way. Indeed, we generally are. For example, Krebs (1975) led subjects to believe that they were either similar or dissimilar to a person whom they watched receiving rewards and punishments in a roulette game. Those who believed themselves similar to the roulette player not only were more emotionally aroused as they watched but were more likely to help the person at a cost to themselves. The similarity of a foreign country to our own country also influences judgments of how deserving that country is of foreign aid (Taormina & Messick, 1983).

Similarity is, of course, a major basis for attrac-

Box 12-1
Informal helpers

"To be perfectly truthful, I regard myself as a B− hairdresser. But my business is booming. Mostly that's because I listen to people, care about their personal concerns, and try to be helpful. The guy down the street is really an A+ hairdresser—one of the best in town. But he's going to go out of business because he can't stand people and is incapable of listening sympathetically to *anyone's* problems" (Cowan, 1982, p. 390).

Psychologists and psychiatrists are not the only ones who help people with personal problems. Indeed, many people are hesitant to seek professional help and rely instead on a range of informal helpers, from friends to bartenders. Emory Cowan (1982) interviewed four informal helping groups: hairdressers, divorce lawyers, industrial supervisors, and bartenders. Of these groups, bartenders fielded the largest number of problems, but could deal with them only briefly because of the fast pace of their work. By contrast, hairdressers and divorce lawyers often had repeated "therapy sessions" with the same clients. Not surprisingly, job supervisors heard mostly about work-related problems. Hairdressers heard more about problems with children, health, and marriages. Interestingly bartenders were the only informal helpers who heard much about sexual problems, undoubtedly because alcohol tends to loosen the tongue. Most of these informal helpers felt comfortable in their roles and fairly effective as lay psychologists. Although little research has been done on the actual effectiveness of such informal helpers, they should be taken seriously, says Cowan, and even be offered training by psychologists in how to help more effectively.

---

tion to other people (see Chapter Nine). Not surprisingly, other aspects of attractiveness also influence helping responses. For example, pleasant people are helped more than unpleasant ones (Gross, Wallston, & Piliavin, 1975), and applications for graduate school left in phone booths are more likely to be returned if a physically attractive person's photo is attached than if a physically unattractive person's photo is attached (Benson, Karabenick, & Lerner, 1976).

If we generally help people who are similar to ourselves and attractive, are we more helpful to members of our own racial or ethnic group than to members of other groups? The extent to which Blacks and Whites help members of their own race or the other race has been examined intensively, and the evidence is a bit baffling (see Piliavin et al., 1981). Whites, for example, sometimes help Blacks less than they help Whites; sometimes help Blacks and Whites equally; and sometimes show reverse discrimination by helping Blacks more than they help

Whites. Similar inconsistencies are found in the helping behavior of Blacks. The simple help-those-who-are-similar rule does not hold up well here. Why not?

According to Irwin Katz (1981), the reactions of most White people toward Black people are ambivalent. That is, most Whites feel sympathetic toward Blacks and want to be unprejudiced, but at the same time have negative reactions toward Blacks. The result of ambivalent emotional responses is inconsistent and extreme behavioral reactions—for example, extra help to a highly worthy Black, but little help to an unworthy or otherwise unattractive Black. Most Whites would bend over backward to help Blacks, or at least would treat them equally to Whites, if denial of help to Blacks would smack of racial prejudice. However, if Whites can find an acceptable reason other than race for failing to help Blacks, the negative side of their ambivalence may win out. Consistent with this interpretation, Gaertner and Dovidio (1977) found that Whites helped Blacks as quickly as they helped Whites in an unambiguous emergency in which a fellow research participant was apparently struck by a stack of falling chairs and screamed out from the next room. In this clear emergency, failure to help the Black victim would be inexcusable and would seem racist. However, Whites helped Blacks less quickly than they helped Whites in an ambiguous emergency (the same crashing sounds, but no scream to signal injury). Here subjects may have been able to rationalize their failure to help along these lines: "It's not that I'm prejudiced against Blacks; it's just that this person does not seem to be in any serious trouble." Similarly, in small work groups, Whites helped Blacks as much as they helped Whites when it was clear that a difficult task created the need for help, but they discriminated against Blacks who asked for help because they had not tried hard enough (Frey & Gaertner, 1986). Whites may have reasoned that failure to help an unworthy Black was justifiable and thus managed to maintain their self-image as unprejudiced people despite their failure to help. Generally, we can expect Whites to be most helpful to Blacks when a failure to help would clearly mark them as bigots and least helpful to Blacks when they can avoid such costs by justifying their inaction on more acceptable grounds. Such prejudiced behavior is far more subtle than the overt racism of the past, but it is prejudice nonetheless.

Similarly, our ambivalent feelings toward disabled and other stigmatized individuals may explain why we sometimes go out of our way to help them and at other times fail to give them as much help as we give nonhandicapped people in the same situation (Katz, 1981). On the one hand, we feel sympathy and recognize that the norm of social responsibility should guide our behavior, but on the other hand, we are uncomfortable around such people and are motivated to avoid them. Again the result is inconsistent reactions.

As you can see, the answer to the question of who elicits help is complex. We do tend to help those who are dependent, especially when that dependency is legitimate and no fault of the victim. In addition, we are especially helpful to people we view as part of our we-group, people with whom we already have some relationship, people who are similar to ourselves, or people who are otherwise attractive to us. At the same time, ambivalent attitudes toward some people make for certain exceptions to these generalizations. Because of ambivalence, both disabled persons and members of racial minorities elicit their fair share of help or even extra help under some circumstances but less than their share of help under other circumstances. Even these exceptions to the general rules, then, demonstrate that characteristics of the person in need are important influences on prosocial behavior.

The Influence of Other People

At the heart of social psychology is the truth that people influence one another. If you witness an assault or some other emergency, other witnesses become part of the situation from your perspective. They can influence you not only through what they do in the situation but by their very presence.

The presence of others: The bystander effect. Some of the first and most exciting social-psychological research on helping behavior was inspired by a disturbing and puzzling incident in New York City in 1964. The stabbing of Kitty Genovese might have passed for "just another murder" except for some peculiar circumstances:

> For more than half an hour thirty-eight respectable, law-abiding citizens in Queens watched a killer stalk and stab a woman in three separate attacks in Kew Gardens.
>
> Twice the sound of their voices and the sudden glow of their bedroom lights interrupted him and frightened him off. Each time he returned, sought her out and stabbed her again. Not one person telephoned the police during the assault; one witness called after the woman was dead. [*New York Times,* March 27, 1964]

The New York community was appalled by this dramatic failure to help, appalled all the more because the number of potential helpers was so large. Was this a comment on big-city life, a sign that people had become apathetic and unconcerned for their fellow humans, or what? Bibb Latané and John Darley set out to find an explanation, suspecting that the very fact that so many witnesses were present may have contributed to Kitty Genovese's death.

In one of their early laboratory studies, Darley and Latané (1968) seated students in cubicles connected by an intercom system and asked them to discuss college life. Subjects were led to believe either that they were alone with another participant (who would soon be the victim of an epileptic seizure), or that there was one other witness besides themselves, or that there were four other witnesses. The victim explained that he had seizures, and then the next time he came on the air he had one, becoming incoherent and crying for help ("I'm gonna die-er-help-err-er-seizure-er"). Helping was less likely and slower as the number of potential helpers increased (see Figure 12–3). This, then, is the **bystander effect:** individuals are less likely to help when they are in the presence of other bystanders than when they are alone.

The bystander effect applies in nonemergencies as well. For example, groups of diners in restaurants leave smaller tips per person than do people eating alone (Freeman et al., 1975). After reviewing more than 50 studies, Latané and Nida (1981) concluded that the bystander effect is very consistent. On the average, in studies in which participants were either alone or in the presumed or actual presence of nonreactive confederates of the experimenter, 75% of the people who were alone helped, but only 53% of those in the presence of others did so.

But does this really mean that there is no safety in numbers? Even if each individual has a lower probability of helping when he or she is part of a group, isn't it likely that *somebody* in a group will provide help and that the victim will thus be helped more often by groups than by individuals? Not so, according to Latané and Nida. In studies in which bystanders are in full communication, the victim is actually less likely to get help as the number of potential helpers increases. When bystanders cannot communicate, victims are no better off in the hands

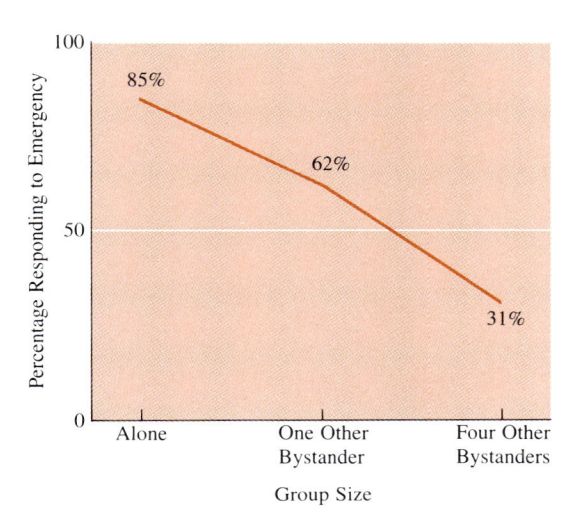

Figure 12–3 Percentage of subjects exposed to a "seizure" who intervened by the end of the taped emergency as a function of group size

of groups of bystanders than in the hands of an individual bystander. Thus the presence of others not only decreases the likelihood that an individual will help but may even decrease, though less consistently and powerfully, the probability that the victim will receive help.

What causes the bystander effect? Three social processes may account for it (Latané & Darley, 1970; Latané, Nida, & Wilson, 1981). Through a *social influence* process, bystanders look to others to help them interpret the situation and may conclude that the need for help is not so great if others do not seem alarmed or are not taking action. Second, *audience inhibition,* or what is also called evaluation apprehension (see Chapter Two), may contribute to the bystander effect if a bystander is worried about how others will evaluate his or her behavior. The risk of embarrassing oneself—for example, by acting as though there were an emergency when there is none—may inhibit helping. Or, in situations in which bystanders arrive at the scene of an accident after it has occurred and are not sure what caused it, potential helpers may even fear that arriving bystanders will mistakenly conclude that they caused the victim's plight if they get involved (Cacioppo, Petty, & Losch, 1986). Finally, there is the process called *diffusion of responsibility:* when several potential helpers are available, responsibility for acting is divided, and so each individual may be less likely to assume personal responsibility for acting. These three processes—social influence, audience inhibition, and diffusion of responsibility—all play a role in the bystander effect. A closer examination of how they work tells us much about when the bystander effect will occur and when it will not.

Social influence processes that affect a bystander's interpretation of the situation are more important in ambiguous emergencies than in clear and severe emergencies, where there is little need to rely on cues from other people to tell you that you have an emergency on your hands (Solomon, Solomon, & Stone, 1978). Indeed, in one study 100% rates of helping were obtained from groups of bystanders when a maintenance man fell and cried out in pain in the next room (R. D. Clark & Word, 1972). The presence of others inhibited helping only when the emergency was ambiguous (when the fall but not the cry was heard). If other bystanders are not passive but instead indicate by the expressions of alarm on their faces or by what they say that the situation is clearly an emergency, they can encourage the individual to view the situation as serious and to act (Bickman, 1979).

The audience inhibition process depends on the individual's believing that others will disapprove if he or she treats the situation as an emergency and takes action. When other bystanders seem unconcerned, a person may conclude that the group norm in the situation is inaction and worry about negative evaluations if he or she helps. In other emergencies, however, it may be clear that the group views helping as appropriate, and then a person may worry about what others will think if he or she *fails* to act. Schwartz and Gottlieb (1980) have argued that the critical thing is what an individual believes the group's norm is. If the cues in the situation suggest that help is appropriate, an audience of other bystanders will increase helping; but when helping appears to be inappropriate, an audience will inhibit helping. In fact, if a group is cohesive or close, helping rates may *increase* rather than decrease as group size increases, possibly because group members are more than usually motivated to conform to group norms of social responsibility (Rutkowski, Gruder, & Romer, 1983). In many studies of the bystander effect, people were strangers and probably concluded that they might be in an embarrassing position in the group if they intervened.

Finally, the diffusion of responsibility process appears to depend on whether responsibility is focused on individual bystanders and on whether they feel more competent to help than other bystanders. Leonard Bickman (1972), for example, found that the bystander effect was reduced when another bystander was supposedly in a different building from the one in which the subject and the victim were located and therefore could not easily intervene. Focusing responsibility on an individual—for example, asking him or her to guard your belongings against theft on a crowded beach—makes that person more likely to help than if he or she has no special obligation (Moriarty, 1975). On the other hand, an individual is likely to dodge personal responsibility for acting when another witness has special competence—for example, is a medical student who can be expected to be more capable and responsible in a medical emergency (Schwartz & Clausen, 1970).

In summary, the bystander effect is most likely to occur when all three processes are operating—when bystanders conclude from each other's impassive behavior that nothing is wrong, when they feel that the group's norm is one of inaction and fear negative evaluations if they act, and when they feel no special responsibility for acting because responsibility seems to be diffused among them. But the bystander effect can also be avoided. The social influence process by which other bystanders influence interpretations of the situation can be lessened if (1) someone in the group signals by expressions or words that an emergency is occurring, or (2) the incident is difficult to interpret as anything but an emergency. The audience inhibition process can be lessened if apprehension about being evaluated negatively for helping can be reduced, as when someone in the group reminds others of helping norms or when an existing group's norms already favor action over inaction. Diffusion of responsibility is less likely if bystanders have responsibility to act focused on them as individuals or feel that they are more capable of helping than others are. It is likely that one or more of the three processes underlying the bystander effect was at work the night Kitty Genovese was slain, but research indicates that there are limits to the bystander effect and ways to reduce its power. Indeed, many studies underscore people's willingness to get involved in emergencies. However, the Kitty Genovese incident can play itself out time and again if conditions favor the bystander effect.

The actions of others: Reinforcement and modeling. As we have just seen, other people, by their very presence, can influence the likelihood of a helping response. What those people do—their facial expressions, words, and deeds—can have an impact as well. A discussion of the influence of other people on helping behavior would not be complete without reference to more direct ways in which other people affect our prosocial behavior. Learning theories are highly relevant here. First, reinforcement and punishment are important sources of social influence. If you are reinforced by others for helping, you will help more in the future; if you are punished for your attempts to help, you will help less in the future (M. K. Moss & Page, 1972).

Learning theory also alerts us to the effects of observing models of helping behavior. Models can remind us of what is appropriate in a situation, show us how to be helpful, reduce our inhibitions against acting, or inform us of the consequences of acting (Aderman & Berkowitz, 1970). For example, if one bystander in a group of bystanders breaks the ice and begins to take action, others are likely to follow the leader (J. P. Wilson, 1976; J. P. Wilson & Petruska, 1984). We are especially likely to imitate a model of helping behavior if we see the model reinforced.

For instance, you may be more likely to volunteer to work with mentally retarded people if you have a friend who finds such work gratifying. Watching people *fail* to help influences us through the same basic learning processes. Part of the reason for the bystander effect is that other bystanders serve as models of inaction rather than action. Our own tendencies to help are influenced in many ways, good and bad, by the presence and actions of other people.

Personal Influences on Prosocial Behavior

Clearly situational influences on prosocial behavior are important. But don't some people have traits that make them more likely to be Good Samaritans than others are, regardless of the situation? Do more fleeting factors such as moods affect a person's willingness to help? Let us consider both the enduring traits and the psychological states of the potential helper.

Traits: The Search for the Good Samaritan

Mother Teresa of India, like the Good Samaritan in the Bible, is an altruist. She has devoted her life to serving poor and starving people everywhere. She has sought no reward for her efforts (though she has been honored with a Nobel prize). Surely she and those rare others like her would be the first to return a lost wallet or lend a stranger a dime. What makes some people more prosocial than others?

The search for a recipe for the Good Samaritan has been rather frustrating. For example, in their pioneering work, Latané and Darley (1970) tried to predict helping behavior on the basis of several paper-and-pencil personality tests and background variables. The only factor that seemed to matter was size of hometown. People who grew up in small towns were more helpful than those who grew up in more populous places. It looked for a time as though the search for the altruistic personality was futile.

Why was it so hard to find links between personal characteristics and prosocial behavior? For one thing, researchers often tried to predict helping behavior in a single situation on the basis of personal traits. The link between personality and helping becomes much stronger when *multiple* helping behaviors are measured and an overall index of helpfulness across situations is formed (Rushton, 1984). (This point should recall the discussion of attitudes and behavior in Chapter Six.) In addition, the search for personal predictors of helping has often gone on in the context of studies that are really designed to study situational influences on helping (Krebs & Miller, 1985). In compelling emergencies, for example, personality may not have much room to show itself because everyone is prompted to act (Piliavin et al., 1981). Finally, the type of helping behavior studied is important. Most studies done by social psychologists have focused on spontaneous, short-term helping acts toward strangers (for example, helping someone who drops a grocery bag). People who are willing to help in these situations are not necessarily the same people who would help friends and families, who would commit themselves to longer-term assistance, or who would plan in advance to offer help (Amato, 1985; Eagly & Crowley, 1986).

What personal characteristics *have* been linked to prosocial behavior? Several studies are in agreement with Latané and Darley (1970), finding lower rates of helping among city-raised people or city dwellers than among rural people in most everyday helping situations (for example, Amato, 1983; House & Wolf, 1978; and see Figure 12–4), though helping rates may vary widely among a city's neighborhoods (Korte, 1984). Stanley Milgram (1970) proposed the **urban-overload hypothesis** to account for the lower rate of helping sometimes found among urbanites. According to this hypothesis, city people must be selective in the face of high levels of stimulation; that sometimes means ignoring people in need, treating people brusquely, and being choosy about whom to help. (See Chapter Seventeen for a further discussion of this hypothesis.)

Another aspect of a person's background that is related to being a Good Samaritan is having parents who serve as models of altruism and instill concern for the welfare of others. When researchers interviewed people who had rescued Jews from the Nazis during World War II at great risk to their own lives, they found that almost all identified strongly with at least one parent who had high moral standards, was altruistic, and emphasized concern for others (London, 1970; Fogelman & Wiener, 1985). One rescuer said her parents taught her "not to make differences between people. We all have one God. It doesn't matter how much money you have, or anything"

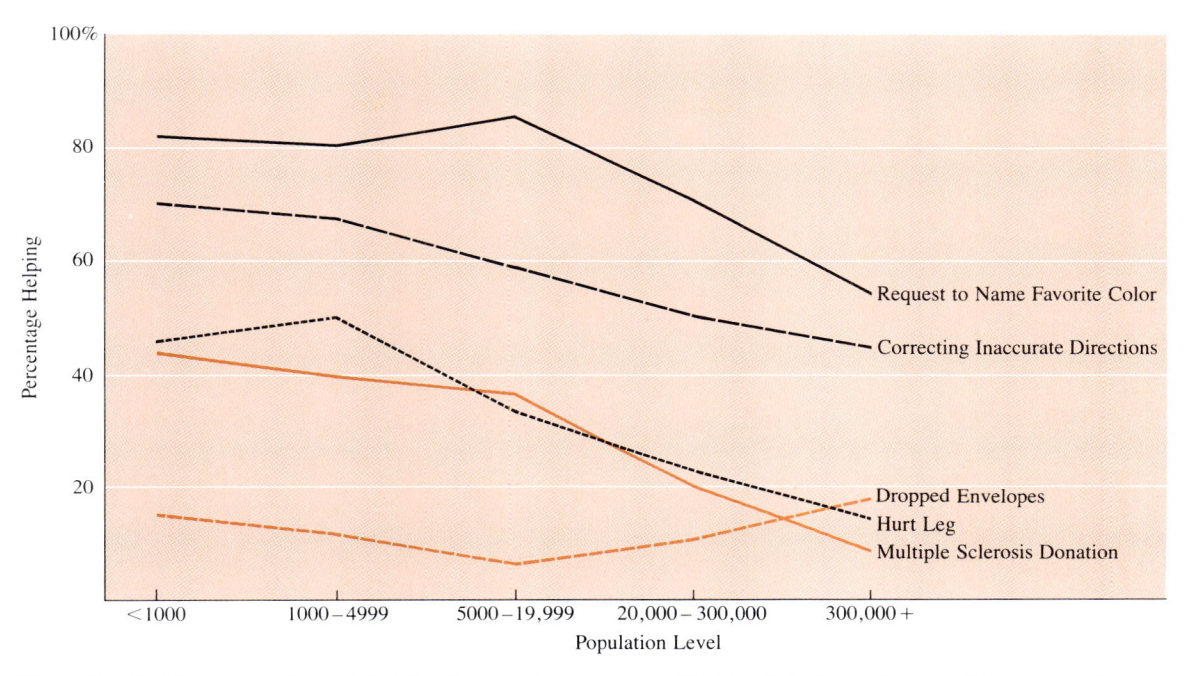

Figure 12-4 Percentages of people helping decrease for most types of helping behavior as the size of the community's population increases (Amato, 1983). Notice that the different requests also elicit different rates of helping across environments

(Fogelman & Wiener, 1985, p. 65). Experiences during childhood socialization, then, may underlie some of the differences among adults in their prosocial tendencies.

When we turn from background characteristics to personality traits, we see that people who are highly helpful seem to be highly moral and oriented toward the needs of others (Rushton, 1984). More mature and complex levels of moral judgment, which reflect a concern with broad principles of human justice rather than with self-interest, are associated with a greater willingness to help (Eisenberg-Berg, 1979; Erkut, Jaquette, & Staub, 1981). Just as those who emphasize the role of empathy in prosocial behavior would expect, the ability to take the perspectives of other people and the tendency to empathize with others predict helping behavior (Eisenberg & Miller, 1987; Underwood & Moore, 1982). Moreover, as the work of Schwartz (1977) on norms indicates, the people who tend to be most helpful are those who hold strong personal norms relevant to helping and who tend to ascribe responsibility for others' welfare to themselves rather than to deny such responsibility. Thus on several counts the Good Samaritan tends to be concerned about others rather than about the self. It is not yet clear, however, whether such traits make for a truly altruistic personality. It may be that highly moral and empathic people are simply motivated to maintain a self-image of themselves as good, responsible, and concerned (Batson et al., 1986).

Finally, willingness to help is related to one's sense of competence—both general self-esteem and confidence about handling a particular situation (Midlarsky, 1984). This was very evident in a comparison of people who actually intervened to stop criminals and control subjects of similar basic demographic characteristics (Huston et al., 1981). The emergencies these people faced were clearly dangerous ones, and all but one of these Good Samaritans was a man. Interveners proved to be taller and heavier than the control interviewees, viewed themselves as stronger, and were more likely to have had training in such relevant skills as lifesaving, first aid, and self-defense. In general, men rate themselves as more competent in the kinds of situations that social psychologists have used to study helping. As the study of criminal apprehension suggests, men see less danger for themselves in these situations (or in a more common situation such as giving a ride to a hitchhiker) and are therefore more likely to offer their help. A desire to appear heroic, long considered part of the male role, may motivate men to help in more dangerous situations, just as traditions of chivalry may be influential in more commonplace forms of help (Eagly & Crowley, 1986).

Shotland and Heinold (1985) compared the responses of students who had had a first aid course and students who had not to a very serious emergency in which blood was apparently gushing from an artery of a fallen worker. Here the more competent students were no more likely to intervene than the less competent ones, but there was a huge difference in the quality of the help they gave. Untrained students, perhaps because they were unsure of how to help, often helped indirectly by looking for someone who could help. Those with first aid training were more likely to help directly, and effectively, by applying pressure to the wound. Since arterial bleeding can cause death in a matter of minutes, victims had a far greater chance of surviving when competent bystanders were present.

Relationships between prosocial tendencies and the personal factors emphasized here—small-town background, parents who teach altruism, mature moral judgment, role-taking and empathy skills, personal norms and beliefs supportive of helping, and competence—have tended to be fairly weak and inconsistent. The problem is that helping situations vary so greatly that it may be unrealistic to expect the same traits to predict behavior in every situation. For example, self-defense skills that were highly relevant in the dangerous emergencies that Huston and his associates studied are likely to be irrelevant when the task is to fill out a questionnaire for a needy graduate student.

The moral is that characteristics of the situation and characteristics of the person interact in complex ways to influence behavior. To cite just one example, researchers identified students high and low in the trait of empathy and then asked them to volunteer to work with children who had a fictitious disorder called "neurological dysfunction syndrome" (Barnett, Feighny, & Esper, 1983). Highly empathic students volunteered more time than less empathic students did if the children were described as highly responsive to help. When the children were described as unresponsive to help, however, highly empathic students were actually *less* willing to work with them than students who scored low on the empathy measure, possibly because they were not sure that in this situation they could relieve their empathic concern successfully by helping (see Figure 12–5). The kind

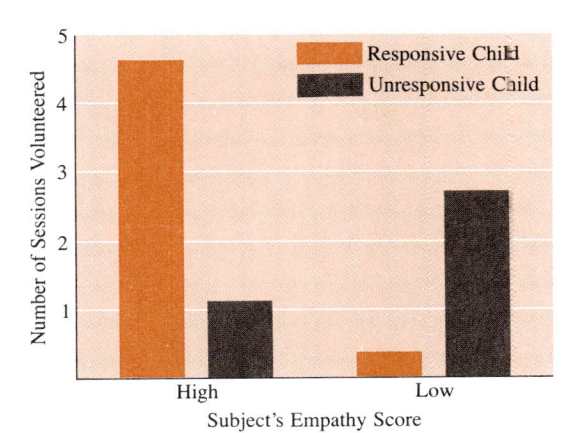

Figure 12–5 Personality and situation interact

of person who helps in one situation simply may not be the kind of person who helps in another situation. Yet some people still do seem to be more consistently prosocial across a range of situations than others are (see Rushton, 1984; and notice in Figure 12–5 that highly empathic students did tend to help more overall than less empathic ones). It is just that it may be futile to search for traits that predict Good Samaritanism in *all* situations.

Psychological States and Helping

Suppose you have had a wonderful day, with money, grades, love, and anything else your heart desires all coming your way. Do you want to spread happiness throughout the world, or do you jealously guard your good feelings against the risk that someone may spoil your good mood? What happens if you are in a bad mood? Temporary moods and feelings do affect prosocial behavior, but how?

Good moods. Alice Isen (1970) administered a battery of tests to teachers and college students, telling some that they had scored very well, others that they had performed poorly, and still others nothing at all. A fourth group was spared from taking the tests. The "successful" subjects were more likely than the others to help a woman struggling with an armful of books. Isen therefore spoke of a "warm glow of success," which makes people more likely to help. This effect has been documented many times. Even professional football players are more likely to help other players to their feet when their own teams are ahead than when they are behind (Berg, 1978).

Might good moods in general, even if they are not a result of recent success, do the same? Isen and Levin (1972) tried to find out. Students who were given free cookies in the library and students who had had no such good fortune were asked to volunteer for an experiment that required either aiding or distracting subjects. Beneficiaries of cookies were more willing than control subjects to help but less willing to distract people. This finding suggested that the good moods produced by cookies did not lead to compliance with just any request but increased helping behavior specifically. Even good weather can lift people's spirits and make them more helpful (Cunningham, 1979).

Why do good moods produce helpful behavior? In Isen's view, positive emotions produce positive thoughts. Happiness sets up a "loop" of positive cognitions, to which the happy person can add by engaging in prosocial behavior (Isen et al., 1978). If, in order to be helpful, subjects must do something unpleasant, they are less likely to help because helping would interfere with their good mood and break the chain of positive cognitions (Isen & Simmonds, 1978).

Bad moods. If a good mood makes helping more likely, does a bad mood, such as sadness or guilt, make it less likely? The answer is not that simple. Sometimes a bad mood does interfere with helping; at other times, though, it has no effect, and at still other times it actually *increases* helping behavior (see Dovidio, 1984; Rosenhan et al., 1981). There is support for the idea that either a good mood or a bad mood (compared to a more neutral mood) can increase prosocial behavior, but the link between a good mood and helping is far more consistent than the link between a bad mood and helping.

Let us start with some very consistent evidence that feelings of guilt (for example, over accidentally breaking someone's camera) motivate helping (Dovidio, 1984). Guilt due to a transgression leads to helping either the victim of the transgression or a third party who had nothing to do with the transgression. Naturally, it seemed to researchers that people were trying to atone for their sins or to restore their self-esteem by helping. But then it became clear that even *witnessing* harm-doing increased the motivation to help. Another explanation was needed. This finding led Robert Cialdini and his colleagues to propose a **negative-state relief model** of the relationship between bad moods and helping (Cialdini, Darby, & Vincent, 1973). According to this model, either doing or witnessing harm creates a negative emotional state, which the person is motivated to relieve. Helping is one way of erasing a bad mood, but it is not the only way. If people who are put in a bad mood as a result of either inflicting or witnessing harm have something good happen to them before an opportunity to help arises, they are less helpful than those subjects who are left in a bad mood (Cialdini, Darby, & Vincent, 1973). A positive experience is apparently enough to erase the bad mood; helping is no longer necessary. This finding suggests that helping behavior on the part of people in a bad mood is egoistic rather than altruistic. It is a means to the goal of feeling better (Manucia, Baumann, & Cialdini, 1984).

The negative-state relief model helped to clear up one source of confusion about the effects of a bad mood on helping. Cialdini and Kenrick (1976) noticed that the subjects of studies indicating that a bad mood increased helping were usually adults, whereas the subjects of studies indicating that a bad mood decreased helping were often children. They proposed that we come to learn during childhood that helping someone is a way to get relief from a negative mood. To the very young child who has not yet learned that helping can cure the blues, helping involves only a loss of rewards and is less likely to occur when the child is in a bad mood than otherwise. During the school years, children will be more helpful after being put in a bad mood only if they can get social approval by helping, not if their helping is anonymous (Kenrick, Baumann, & Cialdini, 1979). Finally, by high school age, helping has become self-rewarding and so will occur after a bad mood even when the individual expects no external reward. Helping, then, is one way for adolescents and adults, but not children, to obtain negative-state relief.

But a bad mood only sometimes increases helping even among adults. One reason for the variability is that people in a bad mood are very much affected by characteristics of the situation. For example, in one study (Weyant, 1978), adults in a bad mood were very likely to volunteer to help if helping was easy and potentially very beneficial (sitting in a donation booth for the American Cancer Society). However, they were unlikely to help if helping was costly or was for an unimportant cause (going from door to door to collect donations for Little League baseball). By contrast, people who were put in a good mood were not so greatly affected by the costs and benefits of helping and were generally more helpful than control subjects. The clarity of the need for help is also influential. People in a bad mood may be less likely to notice a need for help because they are wrapped up in their own woes; they may be more helpful only if a need is clearly pointed out to them (McMillen, Sanders, & Solomon, 1977). Apparently, then, people in a bad mood must perceive the need for help and must perceive helping as likely to improve their mood in order for a bad mood to increase helping behavior.

Finally, some of the confusion about the relationship between a bad mood and helping can be reduced if we consider more specifically what the individual is thinking about rather than only whether he or she is feeling good or bad. Researchers found that if students were instructed to imagine the feelings that would be experienced by a friend who was dying, they were more helpful than control subjects who thought neutral thoughts. However, if students were instructed to imagine *their own* reactions to the friend's dying, they were no more helpful than controls (Thompson, Cowen, & Rosenhan, 1980). In short,

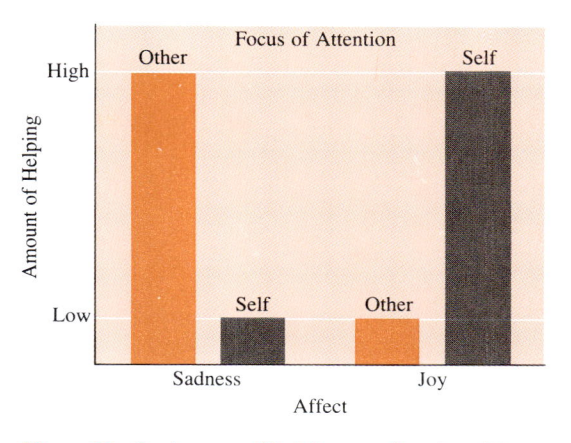

Figure 12–6 Amount of helping as a function of joy, sadness, and self versus other as focus of attention

it mattered what the person was sad about and thinking about while sad. Empathic sadness for the friend increased helping, but sadness for oneself did not. Extending this line of study to good moods, researchers found that happiness over the idea of being sent to Hawaii increased helping, while empathic joy at the thought of a friend's going to Hawaii actually decreased helping below the level for the control group that imagined more neutral events (Rosenhan, Salovey, & Hargis, 1981). The findings of these two studies are shown in Figure 12–6.

These studies suggest that the effects of moods on helping behavior depend on whether people are focusing their attention on themselves or on others—and on how they compare their own condition with that of the person in need of help. If you feel sad about your own state of affairs, you may think *you* are the one who needs help! You will therefore be less likely to help someone else than you would be if your thoughts were focused on the misfortunes of someone else. If you feel happiness for yourself, your good mood will promote helping. However, focusing on the good fortunes of others may make you envious or prompt you to think that other people are very well off in comparison with yourself and thus in no great need of help (Rosenhan, Salovey, & Hargis, 1981). Perhaps the most important implication of this research is that not just any bad mood, or for that matter any good mood, increases helping behavior. It is important to consider the role of the thoughts that accompany a mood.

Taking into account what a person is thinking about also helps to clear up some confusion about the relationship between being self-preoccupied and helping. Common sense suggests that the person who is self-preoccupied will be less attentive to another person's need for help. Indeed, being preoccupied with how you have done on an important test or otherwise doubting yourself decreases the tendency to help (Aderman & Berkowitz, 1983). But other evidence suggests that being made more aware of yourself as a person increases the tendency to see yourself as responsible for what happens to you and to other people, makes you more conscious of norms of appropriate behavior, and may therefore increase the tendency to help. For example, Mayer and associates (1985) increased self-awareness in some subjects by telling them that they had a very rare astrological configuration. These self-aware undergraduates were more likely to volunteer to distribute pamphlets to help elderly people than less self-aware subjects, though only when the request for help was made very clearly so that they noticed it. Focusing on oneself, then, is most likely to interfere with helping when it involves thinking about one's weaknesses or doubting one's abilities, and it is most likely to promote helping when it makes one more conscious of norms of responsible behavior (Gibbons & Wicklund, 1982).

All things considered, some seemingly baffling relationships between moods and helping make sense.

A good mood generally makes people more likely to help than they would normally be. It may do so by setting in motion a chain or loop of positive thoughts, which one can further by providing help. A negative mood sometimes increases and sometimes decreases the tendency to help. It is most likely to prompt helping when the potential helper, an adult rather than a child, has come to view prosocial behavior as a self-rewarding activity that can be effective in negative-state relief. In addition, the need for help must be clear so that the person in a bad mood notices it, and it must be possible to provide help at relatively little cost. And finally, when one's attention is focused on the troubles of others (rather than on one's own woes), or when attention is focused on the self in relation to norms of appropriate behavior (but one is not preoccupied with negative qualities of the self), help is more likely. Thus helping behavior is affected by the way a person is feeling *and* by what he or she is thinking about when a helping occasion arises.

Seeking and Receiving Help: The Recipient's Perspective

So far in this chapter, our focus has been on giving help rather than receiving it. Yet if our society has norms that call for giving help when it is needed, it also has norms that place a high value on self-reliance and independence. How do you feel when a back-seat driver "helps" you to remember to stop at red lights? When a classmate who is no more

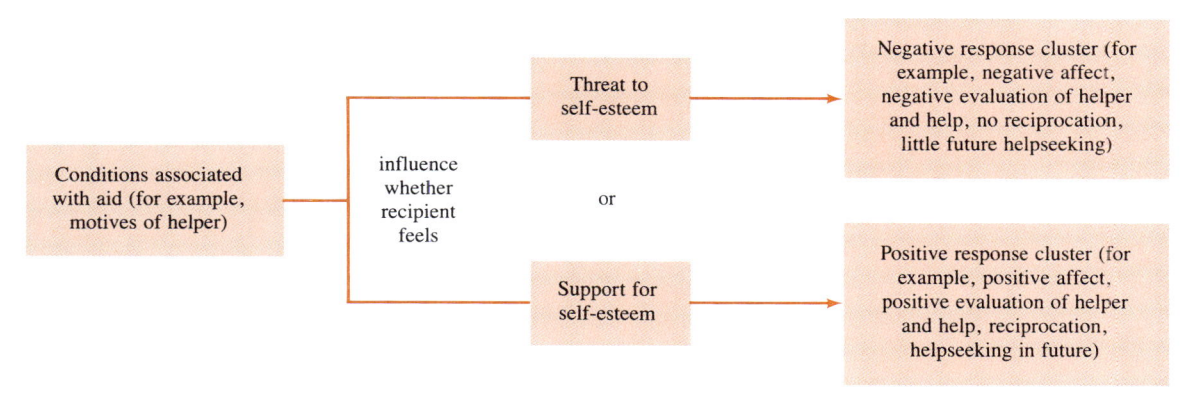

Figure 12-7 Recipient reactions to being helped. Reactions to receiving aid depend on whether the conditions of the aid threaten self-esteem or support it

capable than you are offers you help with your studies? Probably like screaming, "I'd rather do it myself!" Think too of the times when you have genuinely needed help but have been reluctant to seek it, as when you drive around hopelessly lost rather than stopping to ask for directions or just can't bring yourself to ask your professor a question. Seeking or receiving help sometimes means that you have to admit being needy, incompetent, and dependent on others rather than self-reliant. Just as helpers want to present themselves as good people, recipients of help want to avoid being seen as incompetent and dependent (Baumeister, 1982). In addition, because of the power of the norm of reciprocity, receiving help means feeling indebted and feeling pressured to reciprocate (Greenberg, 1980). Moreover, the recipient of help is "one down" in relation to the helper and is strongly motivated to restore equity or balance in the relationship (Hatfield & Sprecher, 1983). No wonder receiving help is a mixed blessing (Fisher, 1983)!

When does being the recipient of help make people uncomfortable and perhaps more likely to bite than shake the hand that feeds them? This question has special importance when we consider people who are frequently in the position of needing and receiving help—welfare recipients, disabled and elderly persons, and even countries dependent on aid from other nations.

One model of reactions to aid stresses that the critical determinant of whether help is appreciated or resented is the extent to which receiving it threatens self-esteem. As Figure 12-7 indicates, recipients of help can have one of two kinds of reactions, one positive and one negative (Fisher, Nadler, & Whitcher-Alagna, 1982). If help supports a person's self-esteem, positive reactions predominate. If help threatens self-esteem, however, the recipient will have negative feelings, dislike the helper and the help, be unlikely to reciprocate, and avoid seeking help again. When self-esteem is threatened, in other words, the recipient of help will show negative and defensive reactions that are aimed at restoring self-esteem. Just as both situational and personal factors influence helping behavior, they influence whether reactions to aid are positive or negative. Situational influences include characteristics of the donor, characteristics of the aid, and characteristics of the context surrounding the aid (Fisher, 1983).

First the donor. Recipients ask themselves why the donor helped them. In the foreign relations field, for example, if people in one nation view an aid-giving nation as having unacceptable policies or as being an enemy, aid from that nation is likely to be seen as manipulative and is less appreciated than aid from a friend (Gergen & Gergen, 1983). More generally, a favor that seems motivated by selfishness is less appreciated than one motivated by altruism

(Tesser, Gatewood, & Driver, 1968). Greenberg and Westcott (1983) have recently begun to explore the possibility that some people have "creditor" personalities and strive to keep others in their debt as a way of gaining power in a relationship. In addition, helpers who are more concerned with feeling effective than with being altruistic do not want to be paid back, for reciprocation would destroy the sense of superiority they gain by helping (Rosen et al., 1986).

It also makes a difference whether the helper is an intimate or a stranger. In *communal relationships* (discussed in Chapter Nine), helping one another is expected. Friends do not keep score on who has contributed what (M. S. Clark, 1984), and they do not expect immediate reciprocation for a favor. Indeed, they may resent it, for it implies that the score must be settled (Clark & Mills, 1979). It is in *exchange relationships*—businesslike relationships with such people as store clerks and strangers—that people keep score, expect a favor to be reciprocated immediately, and feel uncomfortably indebted if they cannot reciprocate.

So in many situations it is easier to accept help from a friend than from a stranger. But there are exceptions. For example, researchers compared students' reactions to help from a friend and from a stranger on either a very ego-involving task supposedly reflecting intelligence or a less involving task reflecting the operation of chance (Nadler, Fisher, & Ben-Itzhak, 1983). The most negative emotional reactions to being helped occurred among subjects who were helped repeatedly by friends on the ego-involving task. The most positive emotional reactions were to a friend's repeated help on a noninvolving task. In other words, self-esteem may be threatened when friends or similar others help on a task that is central to self-esteem.

Characteristics of the aid and the way it is given also influence recipients' reactions. Providing far more help than is needed will be resented, for example, and help that is appropriate to the difficulties faced by the recipient is more appreciated than help that is inappropriate (DePaulo, Brittingham, & Kaiser, 1983). It is unwise to force help on people, especially when it is unneeded and unwanted. However, there is an advantage in offering help when it is needed and can be freely accepted or rejected. More help is received and the helper is better liked when help is offered routinely than when it must be requested (Broll, Gross, & Piliavin, 1974). This same effect was demonstrated in a field experiment with welfare recipients, who obtained more needed social services when their caseworkers offered such services routinely than when recipients had to ask for them (Piliavin & Gross, 1977). The act of asking for help may be especially humiliating, and service providers may reduce negative reactions among their clients if they make it easier for clients to get help.

Finally, consider the context surrounding the helping act. Perhaps its most important feature is whether recipients have an opportunity to reciprocate. In one study, people in the United States, Sweden, and Japan played a gambling game in which another player gave them 10 chips that saved them from bankruptcy and eventually allowed them to win the game (Gergen et al., 1975). Consistently the helper was liked better if he asked for the 10 chips back than if he either wanted no repayment or demanded repayment with high interest. A favor that can never be repaid may be no favor at all. At least this seems true in businesslike exchange relationships. In cooperative interracial work groups, however, Stuart W. Cook and Michael P. Pelfrey (1985) found positive reactions to help despite a lack of opportunity to reciprocate. In such close (communal) groups, looking out for one another's welfare may come to be seen simply as part of the duty of a good group member.

Finally, some people feel more discomfort than others when they receive help. People with high self-esteem are especially likely to view needing or receiving help as threatening, perhaps because they are less often in the position of having to admit personal inadequacies (Nadler, Altman, & Fisher, 1979). People with high self-esteem tend to be strong believers in the norm of reciprocity, and they are especially uncomfortable seeking help when they know in advance that they will not be able to reciprocate it (Nadler et al., 1985; see Figure 12–8). Being in an inferior position is hard for people with high self-esteem to swallow. Yet reacting negatively to being helped sometimes has the positive benefit of motivating independent effort. Indeed, in one study people with high self-esteem who were given a hint on one problem-solving task did better on a second, unrelated task than those who had not been helped (DePaulo et al., 1981). It was as though they rose to the challenge of proving that they needed no help. Meanwhile, people with low self-esteem actually did worse on the second task if they had been helped than if they had not, suggesting that they may have seen receiving help as confirmation of their low opinions of themselves and lost the motivation to try on their own.

In summary, these findings illustrate why help is not always appreciated and have many practical implications. For example, to avoid negative reactions to their efforts, helpers in professional roles can convey genuine interest in the welfare of the client to prove that their motives are honorable; try to establish with the client a more communal relationship, in which mutual concern is emphasized, rather than the reciprocal transactions of an exchange relationship; offer needed help rather than making the client ask for it; ensure that the help is indeed appropriate to the client's needs; and give clients opportunities to reciprocate. They can be sensitive to the threat to self-esteem that aid implies, and they can try to boost the self-esteem of those who feel like failures to encourage them to make efforts to help themselves (Nadler & Mayseless, 1983). When help undermines the self-worth of people with problems, it only adds to their problems.

Toward a Prosocial Society

Although prosocial behavior is not always appreciated, and although some people believe we should value individual initiative and independence more highly than interdependence, most would agree that

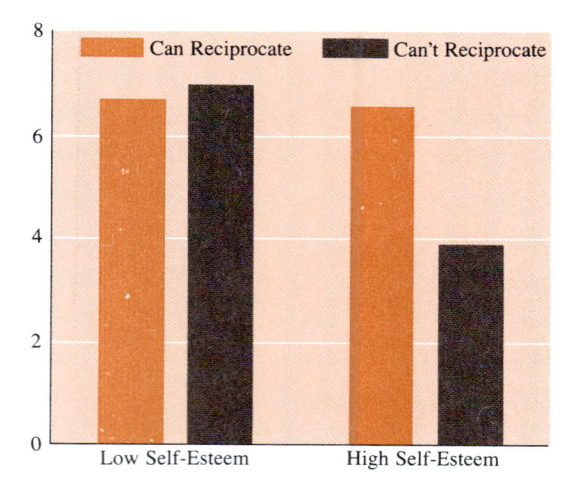

Figure 12-8 Self-esteem and help-seeking

the world would be a better place if whatever prosocial tendencies people have were strengthened. How might knowledge of prosocial behavior be applied to achieve this goal? Let us conclude by looking briefly at the tasks of fostering prosocial behavior in children, increasing support for charities, and legislating prosocial behavior.

Encouraging Prosocial Behavior in Children

As we saw earlier, children do not have to be taught to show at least simple forms of prosocial response. Newborns are distressed by the cries of other newborns. Older infants seem to show primitive forms of empathy and tendencies to share and help well before the age of 2 (M. L. Hoffman, 1975; Zahn-Waxler, Radke-Yarrow, & King, 1979). One 13-month-old, for example, recognized that an adult might cheer up a crying friend, but, still being somewhat egoistic, brought his own mother rather than the friend's mother to do the job (M. L. Hoffman, 1975). Children then become increasingly prosocial with age (see Eisenberg, 1986). Part of this developmental trend has little to do with the way children are raised. As children mature cognitively, they are increasingly able to take the perspectives of other people and, by adulthood, to help others on the basis of empathic concern (Underwood & Moore, 1982). Yet socialization experiences also play a role. For example, mothers of toddlers who are especially empathic point out the consequences for others of their children's behavior in a forceful way (Zahn-Waxler, Radke-Yarrow, & King, 1979; Radke-Yarrow & Zahn-Waxler, 1984). One- to three-year-olds who are abused at home react less with concern and comfort than with fear and aggression when peers are distressed, again suggesting that early socialization experiences can have an impact on a child's prosocial tendencies (Main & George, 1985).

Basic principles of learning can be used to encourage prosocial behavior among children. Children can be reinforced for their prosocial behavior. Indeed, before they develop internal motives for helping, children seem to rely on promises of external rewards to motivate them (Bar-Tal, Raviv, & Lesser, 1980). As we have also seen, models of prosocial behavior can strengthen prosocial behavior. Just as exposure to violence on television can increase aggression, exposure to prosocial television programs can increase prosocial behavior (Roberts & Maccoby, 1985; Rushton, 1979). Preaching charity can be as effective as modeling it, especially if the preaching is strongly stated and points out reasons for giving (Grusec, Saas-Korlsaak, & Simutis, 1978). The problems arise when parents preach charity but practice selfishness. Research suggests that children exposed to this kind of hypocrisy will do just what one might expect: preach charity but practice selfishness (Bryan & Walbek, 1970). Finally, since children sometimes are reluctant to help because they

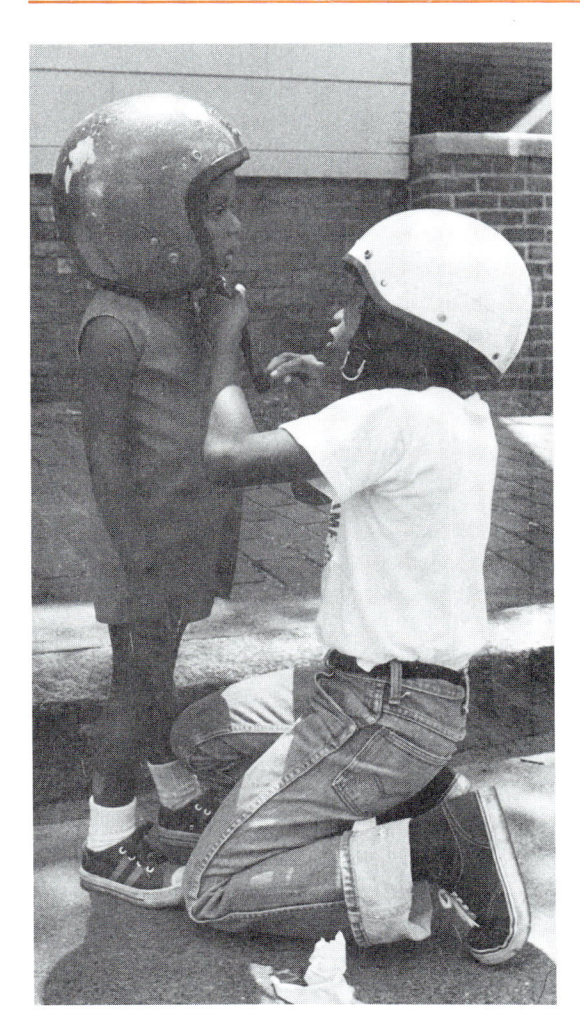

Photo 12-3 Children show signs of prosocial behavior early in life, and these tendencies strengthen as children develop

feel incompetent or fear disapproval (Midlarsky & Hannah, 1985), they may be more likely to help, and to help effectively, if they are taught how to handle common emergencies. Thus parents who recognize the importance of practicing what they preach and who also teach and reinforce their children's helpful acts will foster prosocial behavior.

Some psychologists have argued that competition and individual achievement are so highly valued in North America that children are trained to be competitive rather than cooperative (Bronfenbrenner, 1970). A comparison of Australian and Japanese children demonstrated that children in an individualistic culture are less likely to act in the interest of the whole group than to favor themselves, whereas children in a collectivist culture that emphasizes social harmony tend to favor the group (Mann, Radford, & Kanagawa, 1985). By providing more opportunities for children to cooperate and help each other at home and at school, we might correct the current imbalance in favor of individualism and competition.

Enlisting Support for Worthy Causes

Research on prosocial behavior also has much to say about how to encourage people to give to worthy charities. At a time when cutbacks in federal spending have increased the need for private giving, such hints are especially useful. Fund raisers can attempt to reduce the costs and increase the rewards of donating. Already they make it easy for people to give at the office and highlight the fact that donations are tax-deductible. It is no accident that neighbors are recruited as solicitors. The potential donor, susceptible to modeling, may think, "The Joneses are behind this cause, and look how rewarding it has been for them." Telethons may encourage giving by providing us with prestigious models of giving and by putting us in a good mood. In some campaigns, small gifts are given to potential donors, perhaps to make people feel obligated to reciprocate. In these and other ways, many of the influences on prosocial behavior discussed in this chapter can be applied quite directly to increase support for charities.

At the same time, research on the psychology of giving reveals that what may work with some potential donors may not work with others. Consider the case of getting people to donate blood—an act that few North Americans do with regularity. What sorts of appeals are likely to be most effective? Judging from recent research (Piliavin, Evans, & Callero, 1984), it may matter whether one is trying to recruit new donors or trying to keep repeaters coming back. Blood donors are at first influenced by external social pressures, such as being coaxed to the bloodmobile by a friend. They are more likely to donate blood when they believe their peers support such action (Foss, 1983). According to Jane Piliavin and her associates, however, people who have a good experience initially are more likely to return, and after three or four times they become "addicted" to giving blood, define themselves as people who give blood, and become intrinsically motivated to do so. Thus the motivation shifts from extrinsic to intrinsic over time—from, for example, not wanting to disappoint a friend to feeling a moral obligation to help. People who at first show little sign of being intrinsically motivated often fail to return, but they are more likely to do so if staff members at the blood center emphasize that people who give blood are altruistic people. "Rookies" may then begin to define themselves as altruistic donors.

This research suggests that what may work in recruiting first-time donors may not work with veterans. Indeed, this seems to be the case. Researchers found, for example, that pointing out to donors the benefits they themselves would receive by giving blood—a strategy that would be expected to work well on the basis of cost-reward models of helping—was less effective than appealing to altruistic motives in getting experienced blood donors to commit themselves to further donations (Paulhus, Shaffer, & Downing, 1977). This study found that first-time donors were not affected by either egoistic or altruistic appeals. Another study found that first-time donors were more likely to give blood if they were offered fast-food coupons and other prizes for doing so (Ferrari et al., 1985). Such carrots had no effect on experienced donors.

Perhaps most disturbing is evidence that if people are already intrinsically motivated to be altruistic, external rewards can actually undermine their motivation and make them less likely to help in the future. That is, people may start to say to themselves that they gave blood not because they are altruistic people who enjoy helping for its own sake but because they were pressured to give or rewarded for doing so. Ziva K. Kunda and Shalom H. Schwartz (1983) demonstrated the dangers of external reward by paying some students to tape course readings for a blind student while asking other students to do so without pay. Those who were paid later expressed a lesser sense of moral obligation to read for the blind in the future, at least when they were convinced by the experimenters that any dishonesty in their answers would be detected. When people are not already intrinsically motivated to donate, perhaps extra incentives for giving are a way to get things started.

When people are already intrinsically motivated, however, external rewards can backfire. In a perfect world, everyone would be motivated to give for the sake of giving, to be true to their own values. Until then, perhaps a bonus coupon here and there is not a bad idea!

Legislating a Prosocial Society

Kaplan (1978) has analyzed laws relevant to prosocial behavior in several countries. He finds lawmakers in North America quick to define and punish antisocial behavior but less concerned with punishing failures to help. True, we do punish people for failure to help in apprehending a criminal. We may also hold bystanders accountable if they have a special relationship to the victim; if they are responsible, even accidentally, for the victim's plight; or if they worsen the situation by intervening. But Kaplan would have you imagine sitting on a dock munching a sandwich as the person next to you falls in the water and screams for the nearby life preserver. Under most laws in the United States and Canada, you will suffer no legal penalty at all if you continue to chomp away at your sandwich and watch the person drown! Such countries as France and the Netherlands do hold bystanders accountable if they fail to help strangers in emergencies, and recently a few states (Massachusetts, Minnesota, Rhode Island, and Vermont) have passed "duty to assist" laws that impose a fine for failure to help in an emergency (Shotland, 1985).

Applying the cost-reward model of helping, we could increase helping not only by punishing failure to help but by reducing the costs and increasing the rewards of helping. Indeed, we already have "Good Samaritan" laws that protect doctors from liability when they stop to help injured motorists. "Crime Stoppers" programs allow people to call anonymously to report crimes so that they need not fear retaliation by the criminal and reward them for useful information (Rosenbaum & Lurigio, 1985). Still, our society's emphasis on individualism stands in the way of legislating prosocial behavior (J. A. Kaplan, 1978).

Increasing prosocial tendencies in children and adults takes work. The seeds of altruism may be built into our nature, but so are the seeds of selfishness and aggression. As Harvey Hornstein (1976) put it, "human beings are potentially the cruelest and kindest animals on earth" (p. 66).

Summary

Prosocial behavior—behavior that benefits others or has positive social consequences—takes many forms, including helping behavior and cooperation. The term *altruism* is reserved for prosocial acts whose motivation seems to be to benefit another person rather than to gain material or social rewards. Altruism poses a challenge to psychoanalytic and learning theories, for both assume that people are basically selfish. Sociobiological theory proposes that altruism may be built into our genetic makeup through kin selection and reciprocal altruism because such behavior contributes to the survival of genes. Cultural influences also strengthen prosocial tendencies.

Models explaining why we help others view helping as a step-by-step decision-making process that starts with an awareness of the need for help and involves emotional arousal and empathy, internalized norms, and considerations of costs and rewards. Emotional arousal motivates helping behavior, and empathic concern, which can be distinguished from personal distress, may be especially important as a motivator of altruism. Although such general norms as the social-responsibility norm and the reciprocity norm offer only partial explanations of helping, measuring the strength of personal norms, or feelings of moral obligation to engage in specific helping behaviors, along with the tendency to accept or deny responsibility for the welfare of others, has proven useful in predicting helping behavior. Finally, the costs of helping and the costs of the victim's failure to receive help are weighed in a helping situation, and such cost factors influence the likelihood of helping.

Among various situational influences on helping behavior are the characteristics of the person in need of help. Generally, the people who are most likely to receive help are those who are dependent, whose need is legitimate, and whose need is not their fault and not subject to their own control. In addition, we tend to help people with whom we already have a relationship, who are similar to ourselves, or who are otherwise attractive to us. Ambivalence toward disabled persons and members of minority groups results in some exceptions to these generalizations.

Other important situational influences are associated with the presence and actions of other bystanders. The bystander effect, which causes a person to be less likely to help when others are present than when he or she is alone, is brought about by three processes: social influence affecting interpretations of the situation, audience inhibition or evaluation apprehension, and diffusion of responsibility among potential helpers. The bystander effect can be countered if these processes cannot operate— for example, if the emergency is unambiguously an emergency, if people can expect social approval rather than social disapproval for helping, and if responsibility is focused on individual bystanders. Other people also influence us more directly by reinforcing and modeling helping behavior.

Personal influences on prosocial behavior include both traits and states. Particularly prosocial individuals tend to have small-town upbringings, parents who foster altruism, mature moral judgment, role-taking and empathy skills, personal norms supportive of helping, and competence, but it is difficult to identify traits that predict behavior in all situations. Being in a good mood consistently increases the likelihood of helping, while being in a bad mood does so mainly when the individual has come to learn that helping can result in negative-state relief, when the helping situation is such that it promises easy relief from the blues, when attention is focused on others' woes rather than one's own, or when the situation heightens self-awareness but not preoccupation with one's own failings.

Taking the perspective of the recipient of help

makes us realize that it is difficult to seek and receive help gracefully because of threats to self-esteem. Threats to self-esteem are reduced and help is more appreciated when recipients attribute selfless motives to the helper, have a communal relationship with the helper, receive help that is appropriate to their needs and is freely offered, and can reciprocate. People with high self-esteem are especially threatened by receiving help, but this response motivates them to succeed without it.

Knowledge of prosocial behavior can be used to build a more prosocial society. For example, although children become more prosocial with age as a result of cognitive maturation, they can be encouraged further through rewards, exposure to prosocial models, preaching (as long as adults do not practice selfishness while preaching charity), and opportunities to behave prosocially. Similarly, application of social-psychological findings can increase charitable giving and bystander intervention among adults.

norms
personal norms
prosocial behavior
reciprocal altruism
reciprocity norm
social-responsibility norm
sociobiology
urban-overload hypothesis

Glossary Terms

altruism
arousal/cost-reward model
bystander effect
egoism
empathy
helping behavior
kin selection
negative-state relief model

We must recognize that beneath the superficial classifications of sex and race the same potentialities exist.
Margaret Mead

Each individual ego is endowed from the beginning with its own peculiar dispositions and tendencies.
Sigmund Freud

Robert Frank: *Trolley–New Orleans*, 1955–1956, Gelatin silver print. Courtesy Pace/MacGill Gallery.

CHAPTER THIRTEEN

Group & Individual Differences

I. Similarities and Differences among Groups
   The Social-Psychological Tradition
   Overlapping Distributions
   Questions of Causality
II. Cross-Cultural Comparisons
   Universal or Culture-Specific?
   Some Research Examples
III. Demographic Categories
   Race and Ethnicity
   Gender
   Difficulties with Demographic Variables
IV. Personality Variables
   Authoritarianism: The Development of a Concept
   Alternative Approaches to Personality
V. Personality and Social Behavior
   Some Questions about Personality
   Some Questions about Situations
   Interaction between Personality and Situations
VI. Summary

*I*n *Gulliver's Travels,* the wandering Captain Gulliver visits a series of imaginary societies, encountering the Lilliputians, the Blefuscudeans, the Houyhnhnms, and a variety of other people and nations (Swift, 1726/1960). In each case, he finds a group of people whose appearance, values and behaviors differ radically from his own. In similar scenarios, science fiction writers describe human beings whose behaviors and thoughts are often quite different from those of the people we all know. Do these kinds of differences among groups represent mere fictional license, or do groups of people really differ in their behavior?

Many social psychologists assume that people are basically alike and that the primary causes of behavior are external to the person. This argument suggests that different situations produce different behaviors and that, given the same conditions, all people would generally have the ability to behave in the same way. In contrast, other observers of human behavior assume that various groups of people behave differently. For example, in the year 1909, newly inaugurated President William Howard Taft told a group of Black college students in Charlotte, North Carolina, "Your race is adapted to be a race of farmers, first, last and for all times" (quoted in Logan, 1957, p. 66). As we saw in earlier chapters, there are stereotypes of many groups. People maintain beliefs about men and women, Blacks and Whites, old people and young people, and the citizens of various countries. But to what extent do these beliefs reflect reality?

This chapter addresses that question. First we will look at the field of cross-cultural psychology, which attempts to determine the generality of basic psychological principles across a variety of countries and cultural groups. Then we will turn to the more specific factors of race and gender, asking whether they predict differences in social behavior.

The chapter will also explore the issue of personality differences. Although the categorization of people may begin at a highly visible level, most of us classify people in accordance with a system that goes beyond obvious physical characteristics such as gender or race. Implicit personality theories (discussed in Chapter Four) guide us in categorizing the people we know. For example, we may see Tony and Harriet as being very similar in their extroverted, friendly personalities, whereas Jeannette and Peter may be quiet and introverted. In trying to select workers for a community project, we may consider a dimension of efficiency and favor Alice and Al over Joan and Jim. In doing so, we are identifying a particular personality characteristic (efficiency), and we are assuming that personality can affect behavior (in this case, work on a community project).

Psychologists have attempted to conceptualize and measure systematically the ways individuals differ. Many of these differences have implications for social behavior, and we will look at some of these patterns. In addition, we will look at some of the broad issues involved in relating personality constructs to situational variables.

Similarities and Differences among Groups

Throughout recorded history, people have made comparisons between their own racial or geographical group and other groups. For example, Aristotle believed that Greece's benign climate enabled the Greeks to develop physical and mental characteristics that were superior to those of other Europeans. This *chauvinistic* stance (a belief that one's own group is better than other groups) is certainly not unique to Aristotle. When people make comparisons between their own country and other countries, between their own sex and the other sex, or between their own class and other classes, they tend to imply that their country, sex, and so on are superior. The possibility

of such biases is one of the issues that must concern the investigator of group differences. People often fail to recognize how strongly their own experience influences what they see.

When we consider possible differences among groups, several important issues arise. First, as a backdrop, there is the tradition of social psychology, which gives far more attention to situational factors than to person factors. A second issue is the nature of differences—are differences absolute, or are we simply talking about more or less? Third, and perhaps most important, we must consider the causes of any differences that are found. Let's review some of these issues in more detail before moving on to specific comparisons among groups.

The Social-Psychological Tradition

Social psychology traditionally traces its origin to the work of Kurt Lewin, who stressed the person's present psychological life space as a source of behavior (Lewin, 1935, 1936) and disdained past determinants. Although Lewin clearly recognized that both the person and the environment are important, most of his followers have tended to stress the environment rather than the person. Lewin's original formulation—B (behavior) $= f(P,E)$, where P and E represent the person and the environment, respectively—clearly shows that he himself regarded personality and individual differences as important.

As Robert Helmreich has pungently stated, "classic, laboratory social psychology has generally ignored individual differences, choosing to consider subjects as equivalent black boxes or as two-legged (generally white) rats from the same strain" (1975, p. 551). In other words, social psychologists did not give much thought to possible differences among individuals or groups. What was true of one group, they assumed, would probably be true of any other group.

This assumption has been challenged, however, as more and more social psychologists have begun to explore the nature of group differences at a variety of levels. Cross-cultural psychologists have asked whether behaviors observed in the United States can be generalized to people in other cultures. Within the United States, many people have begun to look at the role of gender, often questioning earlier assumptions that what was true of men must be true of women as well. Personality variables have begun to appear more frequently in the theorizing of social psychologists, and debates on their importance have been waged with increasing fervor.

Thus the assumption that the empirical relationships discovered in one laboratory from work with one kind of subject in one country or culture will be found among all people is no longer so widely held as it once was. Some social psychologists still hold to the "universal" position; but for many others, the patterns of variation among groups are important keys to understanding human social behavior.

Overlapping Distributions

Such terms as *cultural differences* and *sex differences* can be misleading. They tend to carry the assumption that there are differences to be found—and that is a question we should ask rather than a conclusion we can assume.

In looking for differences, investigators can become blind to similarities between members of different groups. Anthropologists use the term **exotic bias** to refer to the tendency of investigators to focus only on those aspects of a group or society that differ from their own society. North American social scientists visiting a South Seas island may first notice differences in style of dress and diet. If the society is a matrilineal one, in which status descends through women's lineage, this feature also may command the attention of investigators who are accustomed to a patrilineal system. However, aspects of the culture that correspond to the culture of the investigators may go unnoticed—since they aren't exotic or different, they may be taken for granted.

The effects of biases are not restricted to the anthropological field study. Whenever we set out to explore the ways in which two groups may differ (Blacks and Whites, or women and men, for example), we run the risk of ignoring the similarities between those groups, which may far outweigh the differences between them.

Even when we do observe differences between two identifiable groups, precautions are in order. For example, if you found a statistically significant sex difference in aggression, you wouldn't be able to assume that all men are more aggressive than all women. If you were to study aggressive behavior in young children, you would find many little girls who are potential sluggers and many young boys who tend to shy away from physical confrontation. This concept of *overlapping distributions* is illustrated in Figure 13-1. Most studies of differences between races, cultures, or sexes find this type of distribution. Although one group may differ from another, many people within each group do not fit the pattern.

Questions of Causality

Perhaps the most difficult problem of all in the study of possible differences between groups is that of determining why differences occur. Recalling our discussion of methods in Chapter Two, we can speak of the independent variable in an experiment as one that is manipulated by the experimenter and randomly assigned across conditions. In such experiments, it is reasonably safe to assume that the independent variable (for example, the number of bystanders present in an emergency) does not vary systematically with any other characteristics of the subjects. When our quasi-independent variable is race or sex or culture, however, we can't make such assumptions. The experimenter has not randomly assigned race, for example, and many other factors could be associated with such a characteristic. In seeking to determine what these other factors are, psychologists have encountered innumerable obstacles and have often become embroiled in controversy.

Traditionally, investigators have looked to hereditary factors as one possible cause of group differences and environmental factors as another possible cause. Hereditary explanations stress the importance of genetic factors and often assume the inevitability of observed group differences. Sociobiology pro-

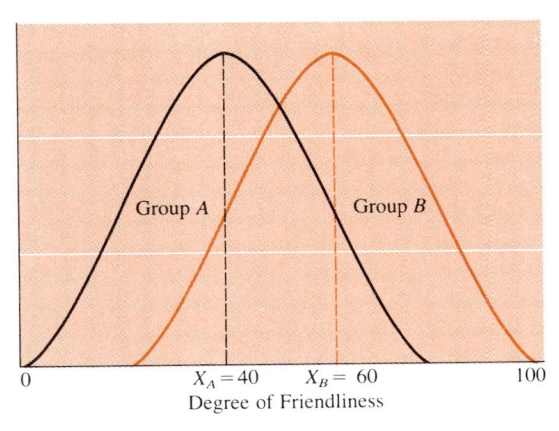

Figure 13-1 The concept of overlapping distributions. The curve on the left represents the distribution of "friendliness" scores for members of group A, and the curve on the right represents the scores for members of group B. Let's assume arbitrarily that the highest score is 100 and the lowest is 0. If we look at the group averages, indicated by X, we see that members of group B are, on the average, friendlier than members of group A; however, many members of group A have higher scores that some members of group B, and some members of group B are quite unfriendly. (Many members of A and B are alike in degree of friendliness.) Most psychological traits and social behaviors exhibit this kind of overlap when two groups are compared

vides one example of the hereditary perspective. Sociobiologists assume that sex differences in such behaviors as aggression and caring for children are genetically based. Other investigators with a biological bent have pointed to a variety of possible genetic and hormonal determinants of postulated differences between women and men in a variety of intellectual behaviors, such as verbal abilities and skill in problem solving (for example, Broverman et al., 1968).

Most questions of genetic determinants have been concerned with the issue of intelligence. During the 1970s, for example, considerable controversy surrounded the issue of racial differences in intelligence. Numerous studies indicate that Black children, on the average, score approximately 15 points lower than White children on standard IQ measures

(Loehlin, Lindzey, & Spuhler, 1975). Both "hereditarians" and "environmentalists" recognize the existence of such differences in test scores, but they do not agree on how the differences should be interpreted. For the genetically based interpreter, such differences are evidence of innate racial differences (Herrnstein, 1973; Jensen, 1973).

Similar hereditary arguments have been posed to explain assumed sex differences in intelligence, and were particularly popular in the early part of the century. As Stephanie Shields (1975) has vividly shown, these investigations were problematic. Shifts in theory regarding which area of the brain controlled intelligence were often followed by dramatic reversals in findings concerning which sex possessed a larger area of the supposed "seat of intelligence." According to these turn-of-the-century investigators, male dominance in social life was paralleled by, and indeed the result of, male superiority in intelligence. In subsequent years, some investigators took a different stance and assumed that there were no sex differences in intelligence. In fact, the standard Stanford-Binet test of intelligence was constructed so that only items showing no sex differences were included (McNemar, 1942).

Individual differences in specific personality traits have also been explained on the basis of genetic influence. The British psychologist Hans Eysenck (1967), for example, has defined introversion/extroversion as a basic personality dimension and has pointed to its roots in physiological processes. J. Phillipe Rushton and his colleagues (1986) argue that both aggressive and altruistic behaviors have a genetic basis, as discussed in Chapters Eleven and Twelve.

Other investigators have looked to socialization experiences for the causes of observed differences between groups. These explanations cover a broad range of factors, including economic and environmental conditions, specific socialization practices of parents, and more general issues of racism and sexism (to be discussed in Chapter Sixteen). Thus cultural differences may be seen as the result of different norms and cultural beliefs. Racial and ethnic differences may be explained by patterns of socialization, economic and social-class differences, or differences in reactions to the testing situation itself. Similarly, sex differences may be attributed to differences in the learning experiences of boys and girls and to the continued pervasiveness of **gender-role norms**—beliefs about appropriate behavior for women and men.

Rather than focus exclusively on either heredity or environment, many investigators prefer to consider the possible influence of both factors—although they may still differ considerably in the weight they attach to each factor. As just one example of this strategy, from hundreds that might be considered, we can look at a study by Richard Price and his colleagues (1982). These researchers studied 138 pairs of Swedish twins, as well as the spouses and children of those twins. Height, clearly a genetically based physical characteristic, was measured, as were a variety of personality traits. The twins and their relatives were much less similar in personality than in height. In fact, the authors suggest that personality was influenced mainly by environment, especially by influences outside the home (experiences not shared by the family as a whole).

Other studies have shown a stronger effect of heredity. Overall, however, it is probably safe to conclude that although both heredity and environment may be influential, environment and experience have more to do than heredity with determining the kinds of social behaviors discussed in this book.

Cross-Cultural Comparisons

Much of the research reported in this book has been based on samples of U.S. citizens. Social psychology is, in the words of one critic, both "culture bound and culture blind" (Berry, 1978). This focus may be attributed in part to an ethnocentric bias and in part to the fact that the majority of social psychologists are located in the United States: it is estimated that 80% of all psychologists who are living now or who ever have lived are from the United States (Triandis & Lambert, 1980).

Investigators from the United States too often generalize their findings to other cultures without much thought. For example, it is frequently assumed that people in the United States and Canada are quite similar in attitudes, behaviors, and values. However, the governments of these two countries differ, as do their basic constitutional premises and many of their social customs. In recent years, Canadians have pointed out that such differences do exist and that past generalizations are not warranted (Berry, 1974; Sadava, 1978). If there are important differences between these two neighboring countries, then it is easy to see how cultural differences can be quite substantial if we compare the United States with, for example, countries in Asia or Latin America.

It is the aim of cross-cultural psychology to study and understand these potential differences. More specifically, in the words of Harry Triandis, "cross-cultural psychology is concerned with the systematic study of behavior and experience as it occurs in different cultures, is influenced by culture, or results in changes in existing cultures" (1980, p. 1).

Universal or Culture-Specific?

Investigators outside the United States have often questioned how applicable the theories and principles of American social psychology are to their own countries. The French psychologist Serge Moscovici (1972), for example, has argued that the concept of equity theory (see Chapter Nine) is particular to capitalistic systems and plays only a small role in the interpersonal behavior of people who live under other forms of government. Similar arguments have been voiced regarding other U.S.-derived principles, such as those relating similarity and attraction and those dealing with the content of particular communications (Brislin, 1980).

Recognizing these potential problems, social scientists distinguish between what they call etic constructs and emic constructs. **Etic constructs** concern universal factors—those that hold across all the cultures we know or have investigated. For example, the concept of the family can be considered an etic construct, although the various forms of family life certainly vary across cultures (Triandis, 1977b). In contrast, **emic constructs** are culture-specific—they exist or have meaning only within a particular cultural framework. "Generation gap," for example, might have meaning only in the United States and in societies that are similar to the United States.

The problem arises when truly emic constructs are assumed to be etic—in other words, when findings from one culture are assumed to apply to the larger society. The term *pseudoetic* has been applied to this type of conclusion. One of the challenges confronting cross-cultural psychologists is the task of distinguishing the etic from the pseudoetic.

How does the cross-cultural psychologist go about making this distinction? There are no easy answers to this question, but some strategies are more productive than others. Of course, research has to be carried out in more than one culture in order to determine what they have in common. (As a general policy, investigators would be wise to study more than two cultures in order to get a better sense of what is common and what is different, as Segall [1986] and others have urged.)

It is important for the investigator exploring another culture to become familiar with that culture. Through this familiarization process, the investigator may realize that certain concepts taken for granted in one's own country are not assumed in the other country. For much the same reason, an experimenter cannot always take a methodology and apply it intact in another setting. Procedures may have different meanings in other countries; conditions designed to represent "crowding" in the United States, for example, might be seen as luxurious space in an overpopulated country.

Although the problems of cross-cultural research are considerable, the rewards may also be great. Cultures themselves may be considered as independent variables, so that the investigator has a far greater range of conditions than would be possible within a single setting (Mann, 1980). For example, investigators have studied patterns of gender-role development by looking at cultures that vary widely in the degree to which physical strength is required in the society's activities (Whiting & Edwards, 1973). With this range of variation, they have been able to conclude that gender roles of boys and girls become more divergent when physical strength is an important issue in a society.

By extending our horizons in these ways, we stand to gain a great deal more understanding of human behavior.

Some Research Examples

Cross-cultural psychologists have explored a great range of issues, from perception to cognition to emotion (Triandis & Lonner, 1980). Let us consider just a few examples.

As we saw in Chapter Five, facial expressions are an important form of nonverbal communication. Do such expressions constitute an etic principle? Extensive research suggests that expressions of emotions are indeed innate and universal (Izard, 1980). However, the *display rules* that govern the particular expression of an emotion vary widely among cultures, suggesting emic principles with regard to a particular expression.

A similar combination of etic and emic principles can be found in the social-distance literature. **Social distance** refers to the degree of acceptance or rejection of social interaction between members of diverse groups (Westie, 1953). Measures of social distance are often used to assess prejudice: investigators ask a person whether he or she would accept members of group *X* as close friends, as neighbors, as coworkers, and so forth. The more negatively people evaluate a particular group of people, the more social or psychological distance they will want to put between themselves and members of the specified group. Harry Triandis and his colleagues have found that information about occupation, race, religion, and nationality are all used by citizens throughout the world when they evaluate other people. The relative importance of these cues, however, varies among cultures. In the United States, for example, a person's race was found to be more important to people than that person's occupation or religion; in Germany, occupation and religion were more important influences on evaluation than race (Triandis, Davis, & Takezawa, 1965).

Kenneth Gergen and his colleagues have suggested that social exchange is a basic principle of human interaction (Gergen, Morse, & Gergen, 1980). Yet the actual resources that are exchanged and the principles by which fairness is assessed can vary

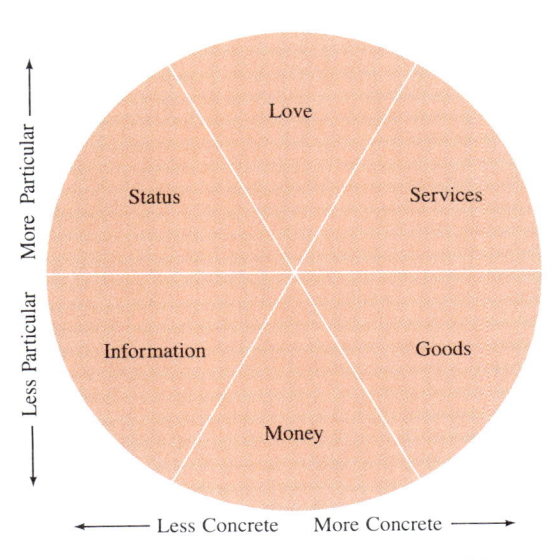

Figure 13–2 Basic classes of resources in social exchange

widely among cultures. Consider first the types of resources that we exchange with one another. Edna and Uriel Foa (1974) suggest that there are six basic classes of resources: status, love, services, information, money, and goods. These classes vary on two dimensions, as illustrated in Figure 13–2. First, a resource can vary from very concrete to less concrete (or more symbolic). Goods and services are considered concrete, for example, whereas status and information are more symbolic. Resources can also vary in the degree to which they are particularized, or identified with a particular individual. Love, for example, is a resource that is usually connected with a particular person, whereas money is a more generalized type of resource. According to Foa and Foa, resources that are adjacent to each other in the diagram should be most easily interchangeable, and their research supports this prediction. If we move to other cultures, however, we will probably find shifts in the preferences for certain sectors of the exchange pattern. Some societies stress the concreteness of rewards, while others stress particularism. Thus although the patterns of preference can vary, the overall structure of resources can probably be considered an etic construct.

The principles by which fairness is assessed in a culture relate to more general patterns within that culture, such as emphasis on collectivism versus individualism. Societies with a Chinese background, such as those of Hong Kong, Singapore, and Taiwan, tend to have a collectivist orientation, emphasizing the social environment, whereas such countries as the United States stress individualism and self-interest. Kwok Leung and Michael Bond (1984) suspected that people of these contrasting societies would use different principles in allocating rewards for performance. They predicted further that the status of the recipient as a member of the in-group or of the out-group would affect the reward patterns. To explore these possible differences, Leung and Bond asked Chinese and American students to evaluate the fairness of allocations given by a worker to either a friend or a stranger. In the scenario that students received, the worker used a principle either of equity (rewarding the person according to relative performance) or of equality (sharing the reward equally, with no reference to performance). As they predicted, Chinese students were much more sensitive to the distinction between friend and stranger. They used the equality principle for friends but the equity principle for strangers. The American students, in contrast, favored equity rather than equality with friends, seemingly showing less concern for the in-group solidarity that was important to the Chinese.

These Chinese and American students may have been using different cultural scripts to interpret the interaction. As Harry Triandis and his colleagues (1984) define it, a **cultural script** is a pattern of social interaction that is characteristic of a particular cultural group. As one example, Triandis points to the South African Black concept of *ubuntu,* a concern for the dignity of others and an obligation to give sympathy and help to those who need it. Among Hispanics, Triandis suggests, the concept of *simpatía* is a dominant cultural script. According to this script, people are generally perceived to be likable, attractive, and fun to be with. They are expected to be able to share in others' feelings and to strive for harmony in interpersonal relations. Operating on the basis of a *simpatía* script, Hispanics would be expected to be more positively oriented toward social interaction and to be more optimistic about the good tone of such interactions. To test this prediction, Triandis and his colleagues gave a set of questionnaires to Hispanic and non-Hispanic naval recruits, asking them to estimate the likelihood of a wide range of behaviors in a variety of interactive situations. Hispanics expected much more positive interactions, as the investigators had predicted. Triandis and his colleagues did not look at actual behavior in this study. If behavior follows the attitudes, however, one can expect Hispanics to approach interactions with more positive expectations, and to be less prone to competitive or critical interchanges.

Differences in cultural scripts can be very important for the person traveling to another country. Like the social psychologist, the traveler should not assume that all concepts are etic, but rather should be on the lookout for the emic.

Demographic Categories

Moving closer to home, in this section we will look at similarities and differences between groups of people within our own society. Specifically, we will ask whether people of different racial and ethnic groups differ and whether men and women differ, focusing on social behaviors. Both race and sex are considered *demographic* variables—categories that can be used to classify people on the basis of "vital statistics" such as age, geographic region, race, and sex. Such categorization systems are not perfect. Both scientists and citizens, for example, have often debated the means of classifying someone's racial status. (South Africa's distinction between Blacks and Coloureds is a graphic illustration of the political difficulties involved in this question.) Sex is somewhat clearer, although even here there are people whose physical and genetic characteristics may make them anomalous in the typical categorization systems. Although these are important questions, they are not our interest here. Instead, we will accept the categories as they are typically defined and will look to possible differences in social behaviors that parallel these distinctions.

Race and Ethnicity

Just as psychologists have tended to concentrate on people in the United States, so they have tended to focus on Whites. In an illustration of this trend, Robert Guthrie's (1976) summary of the history of psychological research is titled *Even the Rat Was White*. In this volume Guthrie deals not only with the assumptions made about the differences between Blacks and Whites but also with the often unrecognized contributions of Black psychologists to scientific knowledge.

Blacks are not the only group that is excluded when a culturally monolithic approach, to use a term suggested by Albert Ramirez (in press), is adopted. Members of other ethnic groups, such as Hispanics and Asian Americans, also fail to be recognized when a single perspective is emphasized.

Much of the research comparing ethnic groups, particularly Blacks and Whites, has focused on issues of intelligence, reflecting social and political concerns with education. Although this issue is somewhat outside the domain of social psychology, we should note that both heredity and environment contribute to intelligence. Neither contribution is easy to assess. In the case of environment, for example, even the same educational system may operate very differently for members of different ethnic groups, so that it is unwise to assume equivalence (Boykin, 1986; Ramirez, in press). With regard to the specific issue of Black intelligence, Scarr and Weinberg's conclusion seems most acceptable: "The social environment plays a dominant role in determining the average IQ level of Black children and . . . both social and genetic variables contribute to individual variation among them" (1976, p. 739).

More social-psychological in nature are investigations dealing with self-esteem (see Chapter Three). Some observers hypothesized that Blacks would have lower self-esteem than Whites as a result of continued experience with prejudice and discrimination. Similar predictions were made for Hispanic group members. Early research seemed to support this hypothesis (Gurin et al., 1969; Proshansky & Newton, 1968). In the 1970s, the emergence of the message that "Black is beautiful" in the United States suggested an alteration in this pattern, as Blacks began to adopt their own standards of evaluation. In the process of "becoming Black" (a process that Cross, 1980, calls "nigrescence"), self-esteem may increase. A variety of factors can influence measures of self-esteem among Blacks (as well as Whites). In reviewing a series of recent studies, Gray-Little and Appelbaum (1979) found that studies reporting higher self-esteem scores among White students than among Black students, as well as studies reporting no difference, were most apt to have been conducted at integrated schools. In contrast, studies conducted at segregated schools and desegregated schools with Black majorities generally indicated more positive self-concept scores among Black students than among Whites. Although the evidence is not conclusive, it appears that Black children in such schools may have a greater sense of internal control, even though they do not always find the atmosphere congenial (Epps, 1980).

As in cross-cultural research, investigators are often hampered by unfamiliarity with the group they are studying. Paradigms developed in a middle-class White culture may be no more appropriate to Black culture than they are to Hispanic or Asian cultures (Boykin, Franklin, & Yates, 1979; Ramirez, in press). Indeed, Afro-Americans in the United States can be characterized as using a different cultural script. A fundamental element of this script, A. Wade Boykin (1986) suggests, is "verve." By *verve* he means a preference for high levels of stimulation and energetic action, which can be contrasted with a less active European-American tradition.

James Jones (1979) has suggested five areas in which patterns of difference may emerge: time, rhythm, improvisation, oral expression, and spirituality (see Box 13–1).

To take a more concrete example, we can look at the area of nonverbal communication. As we saw in Chapter Five, differences have been observed in the amount of gazing behavior shown by Blacks and Whites as they talk or listen to someone else speak. Other nonverbal behaviors may reflect characteristic differences between Black and White society. Cooke (1980) has discussed a variety of hand gestures and stances that may be unique to the Black culture, communicating very specific meanings to the people involved. Although some of these gestures have made their way into other parts of the culture—such as "giving skin," now prominent in sports—they are aspects of the Black experience that typically have been ignored by social psychologists.

In trying to determine how racial group may relate to various forms of social behavior, investigators must always be aware that ethnicity is confounded with other variables (see Jones, 1983). In the United States, both Blacks and Hispanics typically have higher unemployment rates, lower incomes, lower education levels, poorer housing, and more health problems than Whites (Pettigrew, 1964). Blacks are subject to other pressures and practices of racism as well. Any and all of these factors can contribute to observed differences between groups. As a consequence of this multidetermined reality, we really know rather little about ethnic differences in social behavior.

Gender

Whereas social-psychological research on Blacks and Whites has been relatively sparse, research comparing women and men is abundant. Investigators have looked for sex differences in behavior since before the turn of the century. In those years, questions of possible differences in intelligence received the greatest attention. More recently, as society has debated the appropriate roles of women and men, academic investigators have looked for possible sex differences in social behaviors as well. Almost no area of social behavior has been exempt from this questioning, although some domains have been more popular than others. Sex differences in aggressive behavior, for example, have been a heated topic of debate. Many investigators agree that the two sexes differ in the display of aggression, but there is considerable disagreement as to how substantial that difference is (Maccoby & Jacklin, 1974; Eagly & Steffen, 1986). As we saw in Chapter Eleven, debates about the causes of such differences are also quite lively. Sociobiologists argue that male aggressiveness has a genetic basis, while proponents of socialization point out that aggressiveness is more discouraged in females than in males.

These debates have continued in regard to sex differences in prosocial behavior, as we saw in Chapter Twelve. In this case, analysis of the literature shows that men are more likely to offer help to strangers in short-term encounters and that women, perhaps because they are perceived to be more dependent, are more likely to receive such help. These sex differences, however, like those found in regard to aggressive behavior, are highly variable, appearing in some situations and not in others. Furthermore, the tendency of investigators to focus on some kinds of situations (such as one-time help to strangers) and to ignore others (such as long-term commitments of help to friends and relatives) introduces considerable risk in any interpretation of findings.

As we saw in our discussion of communication patterns in Chapter Five, men and women also differ in their nonverbal behaviors. In the amount and patterning of eye contact, in body position and gestures, in touching behavior, and in interpersonal distance, men and women exhibit reliable and often substantial differences (Henley, 1977; LaFrance & Mayo, 1978). In interpersonal interactions, women have greater facility in eliciting warmth, whereas men elicit anxiety (Weitz, 1976).

Beyond these differences in actual behavior, women have been found to be better judges of the affective, or emotional, state of other people (Hall, 1984, 1986). In other words, in situations that require another person's mood or intentions to be interpreted on the basis of nonverbal cues, women prove to be superior to men. However, there are limits to this superiority. If a message is very brief, women seem to lose their

Box 13–1
Understanding TRIOS

The psychologist James Jones (1979) suggests that an understanding of bicultural dynamics in the United States requires new concepts and theories. He offers TRIOS, a set of five dimensions that differ in Black and White experience. These dimensions are *T*ime, *R*hythm, *I*mprovisation, *O*ral expression, and *S*pirituality.

1. *Time* can be divided into units of various sizes, from the milliseconds used by physicists to the years and seasons calculated by ancient astronomers. People, too, differ in their perception and sense of time. Although psychologists have generally ignored the time dimension, looking instead at static moments in time, we might learn a great deal by studying the units people use in interpreting the flow of their life (McGrath & Kelly, 1986). As just one example, consider the difference between the executive who blocks time by a series of 15-minute appointments and the native of Trinidad who says that "any time is Trinidad time."

2. *Rhythm*, often a part of the Black stereotype, has a broader meaning than the musical patterns it describes. Related to time in Jones's definition, rhythm is seen as "an organization of time into recurring patterns" (p. 417). Ideas of rhythm can also be used to describe the relationship between individuals and social systems. Blacks and Whites may differ in their basic rhythms, and the introduction of a member of one group into the system of another may highlight these differences in tempo.

3. *Improvisation* can take many forms, from playground basketball to American jazz. Both of these particular examples are rooted in the Black experience. People improvise when they confront an unstable or unknown environment or when their own qualities are not the ones sought by a particular system. Jones suggests that "Black people could not have survived the American experience without improvi-

continued

---

advantage, suggesting that a certain minimal amount of information is necessary in order for the sex difference to appear (Rosenthal & DePaulo, 1979).

Sex differences also appear in the reception of deceptive messages. Women are more likely than men to believe a deceptive message; men tend to be quicker to grasp the true state of affairs that underlies a cover-up. On the other side of the coin, men tend to be less expressive than women, who convey their moods and sentiments more clearly than men do (Rosenthal & DePaulo, 1979).

Other sex differences that have been discussed earlier in this text include women's tendency to conform more than men in face-to-face interactions, and the evidence that women tend more than men to have friendships that emphasize conversation and self-disclosure. Many other examples could be cited to show that women and men do not always act the same. At the same time, sex differences are often elusive, conveying the impression that "now you see them, now you don't" (Deaux & Major, 1987). Men and women may show similar communication styles in one situation, for example, while differing considerably in another setting. Like racial differences, sex differences must be interpreted cautiously, and the investigator must recognize the limits that demographic variables impose.

Difficulties with Demographic Variables

The use of demographic variables to describe differences in social behavior can provide us with some useful information. At the same time, their use is ultimately limited, particularly when we seek *explanations* for any observed differences. Let's briefly consider some of these problems.

sation" (p. 423). Denied access to the dominant system, Blacks have been forced to improvise and develop new systems. Psychologists tend to focus on the dominant systems in their research, and they fail to notice many forms that differ from those dominant patterns.

4. *Oral expression* may form the basis for rich traditions when a group is excluded from the written exchange of a society. In Ireland, for example, traveling storytellers preserved accounts that might have been destroyed by warfare had they been written. The popular television series *Roots* depicted the important role that oral tradition played in African society. Oral expression requires personal contact and therefore engenders certain forms of communication while eschewing others (see Chapter Five). Language itself varies among groups in a society, and an oral tradition may emphasize different kinds of images and metaphors than a written tradition would (Boykin, 1986).

5. *Spirituality* is a topic that psychologists tend to avoid, but it is clearly central to the lives of many people. Whether one thinks in terms of a particular religious creed or a more general world view, spirituality may be as important to some lives as the notion of individual achievement is to others. To people of the Black culture, Boykin (1986) suggests, spirituality emphasizes the vitalistic rather than the mechanistic influences in life.

These five concepts—time, rhythm, improvisation, oral expression, and spirituality—are not the only dimensions of importance when we talk about differences between Blacks and Whites or among peoples of many other ethnic groups. Yet they do suggest some important perspectives that need to be taken into account when we look at members of different racial and ethnic groups.

First, neither race nor sex is a "pure" variable. In the case of race, possible genetic differences are submerged by differences in education, social class, and other aspects of lifestyle. Thus we say that race in the United States is *confounded* with other variables; that is, its effects can't be separated out. The Black person in the United States is, in Boykin's words (1986), in a triple quandary. Part of the Black experience is, as we have suggested, a particular cultural script. In addition, Black people (and other ethnic groups as well) have the experience of being a minority group within the dominant social structure. And third, Blacks and other minority groups also participate in the mainstream experience of the culture. Analyzing the degree to which each of these three streams of influence may have its effect on behavior is a truly impossible task.

Similarly, in the case of sex, possible genetic differences cannot be separated from the very strong influence of socialization. Few people would argue with the contention that boys and girls are raised quite differently and that early experiences are important in the development of adult differences. Opportunities, role models, and the specific reinforcements provided by parents, teachers, and peers all influence behavior. Sex is also embedded in the social structure. Men and women have different positions in society, and assumptions about appropriate gender roles differ markedly (Eagly, 1986). Women's roles often incorporate communal qualities, such as selflessness and concern for others. Men's roles, on the other hand, prescribe behaviors that demonstrate assertion and independence. Assumptions about the appropriate sphere of women's and men's activities can have substantial effects on the behaviors that are actually learned. As the philosopher John Stuart Mill stated more than 100 years ago, "I deny that any one knows, or can know, the nature of the two sexes, as long as they have only been seen in their present relation to one another." His message is still true today. Hence both race differences and sex differences, although they may be observed, are very difficult to explain.

A second limitation of the demographic approach is that the overlap between the two selected groups is often considerable (see Figure 13–1). Observed sex differences in aggression and conformity, for example, have been shown to account for relatively little of the total variation in people's behavior. In other words, the influence of race or sex, though statistically significant, may be practically quite small.

A third issue is that Blacks and Whites, and men and women, do not act in a vacuum. As we have seen in earlier chapters, people tend to form expectancies about other people, and in acting on these expectancies, they may confirm them. Gender-role norms—beliefs about appropriate behavior for women and men—are pervasive (Deaux & Major, 1987). Similar norms may affect interactions between Blacks and Whites. Thus social-interaction situations may actually create differences between women and men, or between Blacks and Whites, rather than being a neutral stage for their display.

Personality Variables

Because demographic variables can create as many questions as they answer, psychologists often prefer to look at differences among people in terms of psychological rather than demographic characteristics. The concept of personality differences has not been entirely absent from our earlier discussions. Chapter Three, for example, examined the characteristics of self-monitoring and self-consciousness. We looked at locus of control in Chapter Eight. And our extensive discussion of attitude change implies that there are individual differences in people's beliefs and values.

A major concern in the study of personality is the extent to which we can classify all individuals on a single dimension, as opposed to the extent to which each individual must be viewed as a unique combination of characteristics (Allport, 1937; Mischel, 1977; Murray, 1938). In taking the former approach, termed the **nomothetic approach,** investigators isolate a single dimension of concern and try to categorize people in terms of one variable. In other words, the focus is on one trait, and the assumption is that all people have some "amount" of that trait. For example, a researcher interested in the concept of achievement behavior may develop a scale to measure need for achievement. With this scale in hand, the researcher can assess people's achievement needs, eventually developing a rank ordering of people, from those who score very high on need for achievement to those who score very low. Then the researcher will try to determine how individuals with different scores on the measure will perform in selected situations.

In contrast, the **idiographic approach** to personality focuses on the interrelationship of events and characteristics within an individual—it centers attention on the person. Here the emphasis is not on making comparisons among individuals but rather on understanding the complexity of a single individual and the way in which the component parts of a person fit together. Idiographic personologists have also been more interested in the concept of choice and the ways in which individuals determine the environments in which they are found (Tyler, 1978). In other words, they are more interested in how people shape their environments than in how environments mold people.

The implications of these differences are numerous—they involve basic assumptions, methodologies, and goals—and the development of these positions goes far beyond the bounds of a social psychology textbook. For the social psychologist, the trait-centered (or nomothetic) approach has been dominant (to the extent that personality has been considered at all).

The number of personality traits that have been identified is staggering. Consider just a few: need for approval, sensation-seeking tendencies, achievement orientation, cognitive complexity, need for power, self-monitoring, locus of control, and self-esteem. Each of these dimensions has a method of measurement and a body of related research. From the array of possibilities, we have selected the concept of authoritarianism. Authoritarianism has a long history of study, and the concept has been applied in a wide variety of situations. It thus lends itself to a good case study of the relationship between personality and social behavior.

Authoritarianism: The Development of a Concept

The concept of authoritarianism was the product of a group of social scientists, led by T. W. Adorno and E. Frenkel-Brunswik, who attempted to assess degrees of anti-Semitism. Clearly prompted by events in Germany during the 1930s under the reign of Hitler, these investigators wanted to develop a general measure of individuals' susceptibility to antidemocratic ideology. The result of their effort was a measure of **authoritarianism,** popularly referred to as the F scale (*F* denoting Fascism). This concept initially was seen as a series of separate components, including anti-Semitism, ethnocentrism, and political and economic conservatism (Adorno et al., 1950). The developers of this measure believed that the characteristic they were assessing was a general one, not limited in its applications to any one group. Thus individuals who were anti-Semitic were also thought to be antagonistic toward Blacks, Hispanics, and other minority groups.

In developing their conceptualizations, the investigators relied on the theory of psychoanalysis and Freud's concepts of the ego, the superego, and the id (discussed in Chapter One). They postulated nine components of authoritarianism: conventionalism, authoritarian submission, authoritarian aggression, power and toughness, anti-intraception, superstition and stereotypy, destructiveness and cynicism, projectivity, and overconcern with sex. Each of these components is defined, with sample items from the original F scale, in Figure 13–3. Some items have been altered as the scale has gone through a set of

1. **Conventionalism.** *Rigid* adherence to and *over*emphasis on middle-class values, and overresponsiveness to contemporary *external* social pressure.
   Sample items: "A person who has bad manners, habits, and breeding can hardly expect to get along with decent people."
   "No sane, normal person could ever think of hurting a close friend or relative."

2. **Authoritarian submission.** An exaggerated, emotional need to submit to others; an uncritical acceptance of a strong leader who will make decisions.
   Sample items: "People should have a deep faith in a supernatural force higher than themselves to whom they give total allegiance and whose decisions they obey without question."
   "Obedience and respect for authority are the most important virtues children should learn."

3. **Authoritarian aggression.** Favoring condemnation, total rejection, stern discipline, and severe punishment as ways of dealing with people and forms of behavior that deviate from conventional values.
   Sample items: "Sex crimes, such as rape and attacks on children, deserve more than mere imprisonment; such criminals ought to be publicly whipped, or worse."
   "No insult to our honor should ever go unpunished."

4. **Anti-intraception.** Disapproval of a free emotional life, of the intellectual or theoretical, and of the impractical. Anti-intraceptive persons maintain a narrow range of consciousness; realization of their genuine feelings or self-awareness might threaten their adjustment. Hence they reject feelings, fantasies, and other subjective or "tender-minded" phenomena.
   Sample items: "When a person has a problem or worry, it is best not to think about it, but to keep busy with more cheerful things."
   "There are some things too intimate and personal to talk about even with one's closest friends."

5. **Superstition and stereotypy.** Superstition implies a tendency to shift responsibility from within the individual onto outside forces beyond one's control, particularly to mystical determinants. Stereotypy is the tendency to think in rigid, oversimplified categories, in unambiguous terms of black and white, particularly in the realm of psychological or social matters.
   Sample items: "It is entirely possible that this series of wars and conflicts will be ended once and for all by a world-destroying earthquake, flood, or other catastrophe."
   "Although many people may scoff, it may yet be shown that astrology can explain a lot of things."

6. **Power and toughness.** The aligning of oneself with power figures, thus gratifying both one's need to have power and the need to submit to power. Personal weakness is denied.
   Sample items: "What this country needs is fewer laws and agencies and more courageous, tireless, devoted leaders whom the people can put their faith in."
   "Too many people today are living in an unnatural, soft way; we should return to the fundamentals, to a more red-blooded, active way of life."

7. **Destructiveness and cynicism.** Rationalized aggression; for example, cynicism permits the authoritarian person to be aggressive because "everybody is doing it." The generalized hostility and vilification of the human by highly authoritarian persons permit them to justify their own aggressiveness.
   Sample item: "Human nature being what it is, there will always be war and conflict."

8. **Projectivity.** The disposition to believe that wild and dangerous things go on in the world. In the authoritarian personality, the undesirable impulses that cannot be admitted by the conscious ego tend to be projected onto minority groups and other vulnerable objects.
   Sample items: "The sexual orgies of the old Greeks and Romans are kid stuff compared to some of the goings-on in this country today, even in circles where people might least expect it."
   "Nowadays when so many different kinds of people move around so much and mix together so freely, people have to be especially careful to protect themselves against infection and disease."

9. **Sex.** Exaggerated concern with sexual goings-on and punitiveness toward violators of sexual mores.
   Sample items: "Homosexuality is a particularly rotten form of delinquency and ought to be severely punished."
   "No matter how they act on the surface, men are interested in women for only one reason."

Figure 13-3 **Components of authoritarianism**

Photo 13–1 Authoritarianism in action. A rigid belief in traditional standards and the acceptance of authority to enforce those standards may lead to extreme action, such as this gathering of the Ku Klux Klan

revisions, but the third and final version of the scale contains many of the items listed in Figure 13–3 (Cherry & Byrne, 1977).

Investigators were interested in determining (1) the conditions that might lead to the development of an authoritarian personality and (2) the characteristics that could accompany authoritarianism. In seeking answers to the first question, they turned to a consideration of the parents of highly authoritarian people. They found, for example, that highly authoritarian persons tend to have a more traditional family ideology, which includes strong parental control over family decisions, a clear-cut role for each parent, and restrictions on the rights of children to dissent. Less authoritarian persons preferred a more democratic family structure (Levinson & Huffman, 1955).

Hundreds of studies have been conducted in an effort to identify other characteristics of the authoritarian personality, and a broad picture of this personality has emerged. Prejudice, for example, has been shown repeatedly to relate to authoritarianism, from the time of the early studies that related F scores to a general measure of ethnocentrism to a host of later studies that consistently show the high-F person to be high in prejudice against minority groups. The findings are the same whether the focus is White prejudice against Blacks (Martin & Westie, 1959), Arab prejudice against Jews (Epstein, 1966), or Israeli prejudice against Arabs (Siegman, 1961).

Highly authoritarian persons are often uncomfortable in ambiguous situations (Zacker, 1973); in such situations, they try to impose a simplified structure. In their search for simplicity, authoritarian persons are reluctant to believe that "good people" can possess both good and bad attributes (Steiner & Johnson, 1963a).

Highly authoritarian people also avoid some kinds of situations. For example, they aren't likely to complete mail questionnaires sent by psychologists (Poor, 1967) or volunteer for psychological experiments (Rosenthal & Rosnow, 1975). This avoidance of personal involvement by high authoritarians is not limited to their interaction with psychologists. In a representative sample of adults interviewed in Philadelphia, authoritarians reported less interest in political affairs, less participation in politics and community activities, and more characteristic preferences for strong leaders (in other words, let someone else do it) than low authoritarians (Sanford, 1950). Such people are also more likely to attend church (M. B. Jones, 1958).

Preferences for political candidates can also be predicted by scores on the F scale: highly authoritarian people generally prefer the more conservative candidate (Hansen, 1978). In the 1980 U.S. presidential election, for example, supporters of Ronald Reagan had significantly higher F scores than did supporters of either Jimmy Carter or John Anderson (Byrne & Przybyla, 1980). Similar findings emerged in regard to the New York senatorial election: supporters of the Conservative party candidate (Alfonse D'Amato) were more authoritarian than supporters of either Jacob Javits (a Republican) or Elizabeth Holtzman (a Democrat).

Persons high in authoritarianism are also more supportive of specific military involvement by the government. During the Vietnam War, for example, students who actively protested the war scored lower in authoritarianism than students who supported U.S. involvement in Vietnam (Izzett, 1971). In a related study, an attitude scale in regard to Lieutenant William Calley and the My Lai massacre was constructed and administered, along with the F scale, to a group of college students (Fink, 1973). The subjects who believed that Calley's actions were excusable and that he should not have been court-martialed were more authoritarian than those who were critical of Calley's actions. Defenders of Calley during that period were more apt to believe that he had no choice but to obey orders and that therefore he was not personally responsible for the actions carried out under his instructions (Kelman, 1973). Such opinions are highly consistent with the general belief in authority that is held by the authoritarian personality.

In summary, the search for correlates of authoritarianism has given us a picture of a person who is generally conservative in political and social attitudes, deferent to authority, and prone to look askance at deviations from the conventional moral order.

Authoritarian behavior and situational factors. "Authoritarian deeds," as two investigators have noted, "have more social consequence than authoritarian thoughts" (Kirscht & Dillehay, 1967, p. 2). Therefore, it is important to look at specific behaviors and determine whether the authoritarian personality is as easily predictable as the neat pattern of correlates would suggest. First, we should consider situations that are likely to elicit differences in behavior between highly authoritarian and less authoritarian people. Logically, we should predict that behavioral differences would be most apparent in those areas that relate to the specific construct—for example, conformity to authority and judgments of right and wrong.

Overall, studies that have attempted to relate authoritarianism to conformity behavior have been inconsistent (Cherry & Byrne, 1977). To understand why, we must consider more carefully the source of pressure toward conformity. If that source is a clearly recognized authority figure, we might expect highly authoritarian persons to conform more readily than less authoritarian persons. In contrast, if the source of such pressure has little authority, is there really any reason to expect the authoritarian to exhibit substantial conformity? When we look at the evidence from this more reasoned perspective, the findings seem to fall into place. Highly authoritarian people are more conforming and less hostile to high-status sources than are people who are low on authoritarianism (Roberts & Jessor, 1958; Steiner & Johnson, 1963b).

Behavioral differences between high-authoritarian and low-authoritarian personalities have been observed in their perception of information. For example, Levy (1979) asked a sample of registered voters in Detroit to evaluate the evening news commentators (who at that time were Walter Cronkite on CBS, John Chancellor on NBC, and Harry Reasoner and Howard K. Smith on ABC) and to indicate how often they believed what their preferred source of information told them about race relations and Vietnam. Highly authoritarian listeners were much more likely to believe in the source that they had designated as an authority than less authoritarian listeners were.

High and low authoritarians also differ in their ability to recall information. Using one of the most famous trials of the 1970s, Garcia and Griffitt (1978) compared persons high and low in authoritarianism on their recall of evidence in the Patricia Hearst case. The subjects did not differ in the number of prosecution arguments they recalled; however, high authoritarians recalled significantly fewer arguments presented by the defense attorneys than low authoritarians did. Moreover, high authoritarians were more likely than low authoritarians to infer guilt.

Further studies indicate that high authoritarians may have a general bias against the defendant in a criminal trial. Not only are they more likely to recommend conviction, but they also are more influenced by incriminating evidence (Werner, Kagehiro, & Strube, 1982). In a mock trial situation, students who were asked to determine the guilt of a defendant presumably charged with robbery and murder heard evidence that had been obtained by wiretapping. In some cases, the judge declared the evidence inadmissible; in other cases, the evidence was allowed by the judge. When the wiretap evidence was incriminating, authoritarian "jurors" were more likely to be influenced by it, whether or not it had been declared admissible. When the wiretap evidence exonerated the defendant, in contrast, they were relatively uninfluenced by the information.

To summarize, high and low authoritarian persons do behave differently in some situations—but not all. As we will discuss in more detail later in this chapter, it is important to consider the characteristics of the situation as well as the characteristics of the person. Certain situations may trigger an authoritarian response; in such situations, the behavior of a high-F person will be predictably different from that of a low-F person. Other situations may simply be irrelevant to the authoritarian character; in those situations, personality characteristics may tell us nothing about the behaviors that might occur.

Alternative Approaches to Personality

As we suggested at the beginning of this chapter, investigators have been interested in a wide variety of personality characteristics. For the most part, these characteristics are represented as dimensions. In other words, people vary in the degree to which they have a particular characteristic, such as authoritarianism. Some may be highly authoritarian, some may be moderately authoritarian, and some may be very low in authoritarian tendencies. In contrast to this dimensional approach, Steve Gangestad and Mark Snyder (1985) suggest that some personality variables are best represented as discrete classes. Self-monitoring (see Chapter Three), they suggest, is one such variable: people are self-monitors or they are not. Personality variables that are regulated by genetic factors may be best represented in this dichotomous fashion. At our present stage of understanding personality, however, the dimensional approach is more useful.

Investigation of such traits as authoritarianism and self-monitoring, whether conceptualized as dimensions or as discrete classes, assumes a certain stability of personality. A person who has the trait is expected to exhibit certain kinds of behavior across a wide variety of situations—even though, as we have seen, the trait may not be called for uniformly by every situation. This kind of work tends to emphasize an individual's motives and needs, as is seen most vividly in the psychoanalytic assumptions in regard to authoritarianism. Traditional personality theorizing generally assumes the stability of traits (Pervin, 1985).

The growing emphasis on cognitive processes within social psychology, described most fully in Chapter Four, suggests an alternative interpretation of personality. From this perspective, the flexibility of personality is given more emphasis than its stability, and personality is considered to be dependent on the situational context. This approach focuses on the processes involved in personality, such as interpretation, inference, encoding, and recall (Cantor & Kihlstrom, 1981). The way in which people process information and the meaning that the information acquires become major predictors of their behavior. It is perhaps too early to know how successful these cognitive models will be in accounting for individual differences in the wide range of social behaviors. Their development, however, attests to the difficulty that some traditional measures of personality have had.

Personality and Social Behavior

Numerous failures lurk in the closets of personality psychology and social psychology. How can we explain the successes and failures—why something that works on one occasion may not work on another occasion? To answer this question, let us look at some of the basic issues that personality psychologists and social psychologists have been discussing (often with great intensity) in recent years.

Some Questions about Personality

Some years ago, many people became discouraged about our ability to predict behavior on the basis of personality, pointing to numerous failures and weak correlations (Mischel, 1968). In recent years, however, the picture has been more encouraging as psychologists have begun to analyze the role of personality traits more carefully.

The most common way to assess personality is to ask people to describe themselves, often using a scale that has been designed by psychologists to assess a particular characteristic. Yet questions have been raised about the accuracy of people's reports of their own behaviors (Fiske, 1978). Instead of asking people to state how dominant, authoritarian, or unique they are, some investigators argue strongly for straightforward observations of behavior. In other words, we should decide whether or not a person is friendly by observing the person's behavior in a variety of situations in which friendliness or unfriendliness may be displayed. As you might guess, the avoidance of this particular technique has not been based on rational grounds alone; it is obviously much more difficult to make a series of observations than to administer a simple paper-and-pencil questionnaire. Some investigators find that if they combine a variety of personality-assessment techniques—for example, biographical information, trait questionnaires, and behavioral sampling methods—they can predict actual behavior much more effectively than they can if they use only a single measure of personality (Alker & Owen, 1977).

When we try to assess the relation between personality and social behavior, we must be concerned equally with the method of assessing personality and with the kinds of social behavior that we are trying to understand. Sometimes an investigator will spend a great deal of time refining the personality instrument and then choose the social behavior with haste and little thought.

The issue at stake here is similar to the one faced by investigators of attitudes, who attempt to predict behavior from measures of individual attitudes. As we saw in Chapter Six, such predictions are possible, provided that certain factors are taken into account and certain pitfalls avoided. The same strategy can be applied here. For example, James Jaccard (1974, 1977) has suggested that personality measures should be related to multiple-act criteria but not to single-act criteria. In other words, if we measure a person's achievement motivation and set up a number of situations in which achievement traits may be exhibited, we should find that, overall, high-achievement individuals exhibit more achievement behavior than low-achievement individuals. In any single situation, in contrast, the results will probably not be so clear—some situations may result in little difference, whereas the behaviors shown in other situations may even be reversed. Seymour Epstein makes a similar point in arguing for the principle of aggregation (Epstein, 1979; Epstein & O'Brien, 1985). He points out that any single observation of behavior can involve considerable error and have limited generality. However, if we observe a person's behavior over a period of time, general personality measures become much more capable of predicting overall behavior.

Suppose that you think of your friend Joe as extroverted, outgoing, and friendly. Yet, at a party on one particular Thursday evening, Joe (for any of a number of reasons) stays pretty much to himself, talking to a few close friends and avoiding most of the other guests. As a personality psychologist who believes that your study of personality assessment should allow you to predict every single behavior, you may feel that your theory about Joe was wrong. It is more likely, however, that you will consider how Joe has acted in all the other situations in which you have seen him—you will keep your assessment of his character intact.

Can psychologists do better than that? Is it possible to predict all of the people all of the time? Kenrick and Springfield (1980) suggest that it is possible, but only if we recognize that various traits have differing degrees of relevance from one individual to another. These investigators asked each subject to select a personality dimension on which his or her behavior was most consistent. Not surprisingly, the particular dimensions selected differed widely among the subjects. However, in analyzing the selections of subjects individually, the investigators found that there was a consistency of reported behavior—one that was reported by subjects themselves and seen by their parents and friends.

Another way of viewing the issue of consistency is to think in terms of prototypes (see Chapter Four). Mischel and Peake (1982) have suggested that some behaviors are highly prototypic for a person. For example, if I want to evaluate how compulsive I am, I may think about the neatness of my bookshelves, the arrangement of my filing system, and the cleanliness of my kitchen—and ignore the state of my closet or the piles of junk in the basement. For me, then, the former behaviors would fit my prototype of compulsiveness, and one might expect greater consistency in those behaviors. I might exhibit less consistency in the latter behaviors because I do not consider them basic to my prototype of compulsiveness.

Thus the issue of consistency in personality and behavior is complicated, and analysis must consider the trait, the representativeness of the behavior, and the particular individual who is being assessed. In short, there is consistency in personality—and there is inconsistency. A Chinese philosopher would smile at the thought!

Some Questions about Situations

Another question raised in the debate about personality and behavior is the role of situations. Despite social psychologists' considerable involvement with the situational determinants of action, we do not have an adequate taxonomy of situations. Situations can vary on many dimensions: their location, the kinds of activities that go on, the number and kinds of people involved in them, to name only a few (Magnusson, 1981). In addition to these objective characteristics, we can also look at the way people perceive situations. From this more subjective perspective, we may ask people how similar various situations seem to them. Once again, we find greater consistency in behavior when we take this individual perspective into account (Lord, 1982).

In considering the influence of personality on

Photo 13–2 Situations may be strong or weak. In the structured (or strong) classroom setting pictured on the right, students taking an exam show little variation in their behavior. In contrast, unstructured (or weak) situations like the one above allow more room for individual personalities to have an effect

behavior, we also need to assess how "weak" or "strong" the situation is (Mischel, 1977). Strong situations, as Mark Snyder and William Ickes (1985) define them, are ones that "provide salient clues to guide behavior and have a fairly high degree of structure and definition" (p. 904). In a typical laboratory experiment, for example, the choices that a subject can make are typically quite restricted. In such cases, we might not expect personality differences to have much effect, because the possible behaviors are quite limited. In contrast, situations that are less structured (or "weak") allow for a much greater range of behavioral choices, and hence personality variations become more influential (Monson, Hesley, & Chernick, 1982).

To illustrate this distinction, compare the behavior of students in a classroom with their behavior in their own apartments or dormitory rooms. We would expect much more variation in the second situation than in the first, variation that would probably relate to many personality traits.

Another way to think about situations is to use the framework of social cognition. Situations can be categorized on the basis of prototypes—assumptions about the behaviors that are typical in the situation (Schutte, Kenrick, & Sadalla, 1985). There is a great deal of consensus as to the behaviors that are expected in some situations; other situations may elicit little agreement, and behavior can be expected to vary accordingly.

Finally, in thinking about situations, we need to consider individual choice (Snyder, 1981; Snyder & Ickes, 1985). Outside of the experimental setting, people are not randomly assigned to situations; rather, they choose to enter some situations and avoid others. Some people may frequent church socials while others seek out X-rated movies. The situations people choose probably indicate a great deal about their basic personality traits, and social psychologists are beginning to look more closely at such choices.

Interaction between Personality and Situations

The consensus that has evolved—confirming Kurt Lewin's early formulation—is that personalities *and* situations must be considered if human social behavior is to be thoroughly understood. This *interactionist* position probably represents the views of most social psychologists today (Blass, 1984). Yet controversy still surrounds the exact meaning of the term *interaction*. The interactionist position maintains that, in most instances, we can explain some behavior by considering only personalities and other behavior by considering only situations, but we can explain more behavior by considering the interface between personalities and situations. Many psychologists have come to adopt this position (Endler & Magnusson, 1976; Magnusson & Endler, 1977).

When we adopt the interactionist position, we begin to think of human behavior in more active terms (Endler & Magnusson, 1976). As we saw in Chapter Five, communication is not a stable process, nor is the interaction of any single individual with his or her environment. Situations constantly change, often in very subtle ways, and a person's behavior often relfects these subtle changes. Human behavior is more complex than we originally thought, and understanding that behavior is a far more exciting endeavor than we once imagined.

Summary

Social psychologists have traditionally been more interested in situational determinants of behavior than in individual differences among people. In recent years, however, interest in both group differences, such as race and sex, and individual personality differences has increased. When one compares members of different groups, one should be aware of the degree to which the distributions of scores overlap.

Issues of causality involve both hereditary and environmental explanations, although the latter are generally weighted more heavily.

Cross-cultural research attempts to determine how general our knowledge of human behavior is—whether our constructs are etic (truly universal) or emic (specific to a particular culture). Certainly it is evident that patterns of behavior vary in some ways from one culture to another, and the cultural script of a culture may be a key to understanding that variation.

Research comparing Blacks and Whites demonstrates the need for a broader understanding of human behavior. It is often difficult to interpret racial differences, however, because so many other factors vary with race.

Sex differences have been found in some social behaviors, including aggression, conformity, and nonverbal communication. Typically the differences are fairly small, however, and the patterns vary substantially across situations. In general, such demographic variables as race and sex are difficult to interpret. Race and sex are confounded with life experiences and are embedded in a social structure that assigns positions on the basis of race and sex.

Psychologists often prefer to describe people in terms of personality variables rather than demographic characteristics. The nomothetic approach to the study of personality stresses general dimensions and norms that apply to all people; the idiographic approach focuses on the interrelationship of events and characteristics within an individual.

The concept of authoritarianism was developed by a group of social scientists who wanted to understand anti-Semitism during World War II. They developed the F scale to measure authoritarianism and defined nine components of authoritarianism. High- and low-authoritarian people differ in many respects, including family ideology, political preferences, prejudice, and attitudes toward authority figures and defendants in criminal trials.

The relation between personality variables and social behavior is complex. How a trait is measured and to whom it is applied are important issues in understanding the consistency of personality. The situation must also be considered. According to the dominant interactionist view, personality and situations must be studied jointly.

Glossary Terms

authoritarianism
cultural script
emic constructs
etic constructs
exotic bias
gender-role norms
idiographic approach
nomothetic approach
social distance

No man is an island, entire of itself.
John Donne

It takes two flints to make a fire.
Louisa May Alcott

Fernando Botero: *Dancing in Columbia*, 1980. The Metropolitan Museum of Art, Anonymous Gift, 1983. (1983.251)

CHAPTER FOURTEEN

Behavior in Groups

I. The Influence of Other People
   The Effects of an Audience
   Social Facilitation
   The Coacting Audience
II. Group Composition and Structure
   Group Size
   Communication Networks
   Roles and Expectations
III. Interaction in Groups
   Group Performance
   The Perils of Groupthink
   The Polarizing Effects of Group Interaction
   Minority Group Influence
IV. Group Socialization
   Basic Processes
   Stages of Group Socialization
VI. Summary

*S*tuck in an elevator that is stalled between floors, seven strangers begin to notice one another, then start to compare reactions and share stories of past experiences, and then develop a plan of action to get out of the elevator. Returning for the second part of the marathon play *Nicholas Nickleby,* members of a theater audience who were formerly strangers begin to chat with their neighbors, share their box lunches, and cheer heroes and boo villains together. In both of these instances, individuals become involved with a group of persons, and their actions are influenced by the group.

In citing these examples, we are no longer focusing strictly on the individual but rather on the behavior of a number of persons. According to many people, this is the essence of social psychology. However, social psychologists often prefer to work at the level of the individual, stressing each person's perceptions, beliefs, and actions and ignoring the interaction that takes place in groups. Some social psychologists have even suggested that groups are not real. The late Floyd Allport used to say, "You can't stumble over a group," proposing that groups exist only in the minds of people. According to Allport, groups are no more than shared sets of values, ideas, thoughts, and habits that exist simultaneously in the minds of several persons. Others have argued just as impressively that groups are entities that should be treated as unitary objects in our environment (Durkheim, 1898; Warriner, 1956). Such advocates renounce the suggestion that all social behaviors can be explained adequately at the individual level; they stress the unique aspects of the group process in and of itself.

Clearly, one can adopt any of numerous perspectives on the way a situation may be influenced by the number of people involved in it. Most of us would probably agree that many of the activities of our lives involve other people. Football teams, families, faculties, and fishing crews all involve the interaction of a group of people. But groups also may be composed of individuals who don't come into close proximity with one another or see one another often. The national sales manager for Frisbees, for example, along with his or her field representatives, may constitute a group, even though their face-to-face contact may be infrequent.

Just what is a group? Not every collection of people can be considered a group. The term *aggregate* refers to collections of individuals who do not interact with one another. Persons standing on a street corner waiting for the light to change, the members of an audience at the latest Woody Allen movie, and, in many cases, students in a large college lecture hall—these people typically do not interact or share feelings to such a degree that they influence one another. However, as the case of the passengers in the stalled elevator illustrates, an aggregate can become a group.

Groups differ from aggregates in several respects. Whereas an aggregate has no particular structure, a group has some definite form of organization and its members have some relationship with one another. Groups are dynamic, whereas aggregates are more passive. Members of groups are aware of one another; the people in an aggregate are often oblivious of others who share the same space at the same time. As a working definition of groups, Joseph McGrath offers the following: "A group is an aggregation of two or more people who are to some degree in dynamic interrelation with one another" (1984, p. 8).

This definition can encompass many types of groups, from a small family to a large work group, from an experimental group that meets only once to a military unit that stays together for months or years. Some groups are, as McGrath (1984) has recognized, more "groupy" than others. In other words, some groups involve greater amounts of social interaction, exert more intense pressures on their members, or involve greater commitments to the group's function. In every case, however, the group process can be observed to exert an influence on the behavior of the individual members.

In this chapter we consider the ways in which groups act—how they perform, how members of groups communicate with one another, and how they draw together or split apart. First, however, let us turn our attention to a simpler question—how does the presence of other people influence the behavior of the individual?

The Influence of Other People

In the late nineteenth century an Indiana University psychologist named Norman Triplett became interested in the effects of other people on individual performance. In studying the records of the Racing Board of the League of American Wheelmen, Triplett observed that cyclists' times were faster when the cyclists were racing against each other than when they simply raced against a clock. On the basis of this observation, Triplett proposed a theory of *dynamogenesis*. Basically, his model suggested that the presence of other people acts as a stimulant to the performer. If such a model reflected reality, Triplett reasoned, it would hold for activities other than bicycle racing. Creating an analogy to bicycle racing, Triplett (1898) asked children to wind fishing reels and compared their performance when alone with their performance when another child was present. This experiment marks the earliest attempt to understand how the mere presence of other people—not necessarily acting as a group—can influence behavior. Considerable investigation has followed the initial venture by Triplett.

The Effects of an Audience

Often we act individually but at the same time are aware that others are watching us. For example, on entering a room full of strangers, we may be painfully (or gleefully) aware that many eyes are focused on us. A guest lecturer can present a talk and have no interaction with the members of the audience. How does awareness of an audience affect behavior?

Many people experience fear and anxiety in the presence of an audience. A survey of people's fears showed that speaking in front of a group is feared more than height, darkness, loneliness, sickness, and even death (Borden, 1980). On some occasions, however, the presence of an audience can give us an extra "charge." Athletes report that they perform better before a crowd than in an empty stadium (Davis, 1969), and many actors comment on the difference between playing for a full house and playing in a theater that is nearly empty. What accounts for these differences?

First of all, let us define the basic characteristics of the audience situation. The individual is acting or performing a behavior in the presence of a group of people; however, there is no direct interaction between the individual and the audience—rather, the members of the audience are passive observers of the action (Geen, 1980).

The influence of the audience depends on a number of factors. Bibb Latané (1981) has suggested three major factors: the number of people in the audience, the immediacy of the audience, and the strength (or status) of the members of the audience (see Figure 14–1). In describing his model of *social impact*, Latané uses the analogy of a light bulb. Just as the amount of light falling on a surface depends on the number of bulbs, their closeness to the surface, and the wattage, so does social impact represent the joint contribution of *numbers, immediacy,* and *strength*. How does each of these audience factors affect an individual's performance?

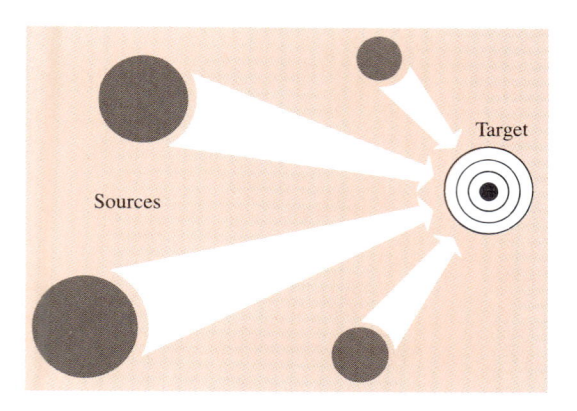

Figure 14–1 A model of social impact. The impact of an audience is determined by the number of sources (or circles, in this illustration), their strength (or size, in this illustration), and their immediacy, or nearness to the target

As the number of people in an audience increases, so does the impact of that audience. Although the exact form of this relationship is a matter of some dispute, most investigators would agree that an increase in the size of an audience has a greater effect when the audience is initially small (Latané, 1981; Tanford & Penrod, 1984). The difference between 3 and 4 observers, for example, would be much greater than the difference between 30 and 31. At some point, Sarah Tanford and Steven Penrod (1984) suggest, the addition of members to an audience will have no incremental effect at all, as an effective ceiling will have been reached.

Less powerful than the number of people, but still influential, are the immediacy and the strength of the audience (Latané, 1981; Mullen, 1985; Jackson, 1986). *Immediacy* refers to the proximity of an audi-

Photo 14–1 The impact of an audience depends on a variety of factors, including its size and distance from the performers.

ence to the target individual. Audiences that are physically present have more impact than those that are at some distance—for example, audiences that are separated from the performer by a one-way mirror through which only the audience can see.

Latané (1981) defines *strength* as the power, status, or resources of an audience. Demonstrating the influence of strength, Latané and Harkins (1976) found that students who expected to sing before an audience of high-status people reported more tension than those who expected a low-status audience.

Alone or in combination, these three factors can affect the degree of influence an audience exerts on us.

Social Facilitation

An audience can influence performance. But just what kinds of effects does an audience have? In some cases, an audience acts to increase the level of performance; in other cases, it decreases performance. Such contradictions beg for a theory. **Social facilitation,** a term coined by Floyd Allport (1920), refers to the improvement of individual performance in the presence of other people. (Remember, we are concerned with the effect of the *mere presence* of other people, not with interaction between a person and an audience.) In contrast, **social inhibition** refers to a decrease in an individual's performance in the presence of other people.

Many years after Allport made his observations, Robert Zajonc (1965) proposed a theoretical model to account for discrepant findings in regard to the effects of an audience. Relying on a drive model of learning, Zajonc suggested that the presence of others is a source of general arousal, or drive (see Figure 14–2). Such arousal occurs because other people can be unpredictable and so create feelings of uncer-

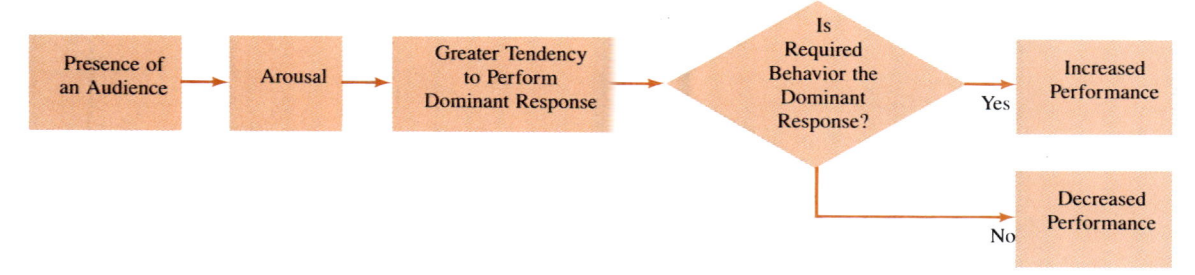

Figure 14-2 Arousal model of social facilitation

tainty in the individual. In the case of responses that are well learned (or *dominant,* in the terminology of the model), this drive results in increased levels of performance. In contrast, responses that are not well learned suffer from increased arousal, since well-learned responses interfere with their performance (Zajonc & Sales, 1966). For example, if you are asked to act in a community play, and it is your first experience with acting, the presence of an audience may be detrimental—you may drop lines, forget your entrance, or suffer a severe case of stage fright. In contrast, an experienced and well-rehearsed actor appearing before a similar audience should perform very well, because arousal leads to an increase in well-learned behaviors. Although the extent of these effects varies, this explanation, based on rather simple assumptions, can account for many of the findings regarding the effects of an audience on performance (Bond & Titus, 1983; Cottrell, 1972; Geen & Gange, 1977; Guerin, 1986; Schmitt et al., 1986).

Although there is considerable agreement that the presence of an audience can affect performance—sometimes for better, sometimes for worse—we are not totally sure why those effects occur. Zajonc himself assumes that the arousal properties of an audience are innate, or wired into the organism, and has, in fact, shown that cockroaches, as well as people, are subject to social facilitation effects. Yet other factors are also at work in this arousal state. Cottrell (1972), for example, argued that the presence of others is a *learned* source of drive. According to Cottrell, it is not the mere presence of others that causes arousal but rather the expectation that an audience will be judging one's performance. Consequently, if subjects are asked to perform in front of a group of people who are blindfolded, they should show less arousal than when they perform in front of a group of clear-sighted evaluators. Studies using this approach have supported the distinction, finding more arousal in subjects (and the predicted effects on performance of simple and complex tasks) when an audience is expected to be capable of evaluation (Cottrell et al., 1968; Guerin, 1986).

Others suggest that increased arousal is a result of conflict between possible responses and that distraction is an important mediator of social facilitation (Baron, 1986). This explanation is based on three assumptions. First, other people are distracting. In the presence of others, people may pay attention to incidental features of their appearance and dress, worry about the reactions that those people may have, or in other ways become distracted from the task at hand. Second, it is assumed that distraction leads to a conflict in attention. And third, attentional conflict creates a state of arousal. This arousal, it is assumed, will then lead to the predicted social facilitation effects: better performance of simple responses and worse performance of complex tasks.

Some other explanations for social facilitation effects rely on the concept of self-presentation, as introduced in Chapter Three. Confronted with an audience, a person may feel increasing pressure to present a positive front (Sanders, 1984). With simple tasks, the exertion of more effort in an attempt to present a positive front can lead to enhanced performance. When one is faced with a complex task, on the other hand, the frustrations of the task may be magnified, leading to embarrassment, withdrawal, or anxiety (Bond, 1982; Sanders, 1984).

None of the explanations offered is necessarily right in all circumstances. The state of arousal that leads to social facilitation effects may be caused by a variety of factors; although each one may be sufficient, no single cause may be a necessary condition. Despite the variety of explanations, however, each points to the same phenomenon: arousal leads to an increase in the performance of well-learned responses and a decrease in the performance of poorly learned responses. As Box 14–1 shows, these effects can be found as readily in the pool hall as in the psychology laboratory.

The Coacting Audience

So far, we have concentrated on the effects of a passive audience that merely observes while the actor performs. However, if we look back to the initial experiment of Triplett, we see that the audience was not passive; it performed a task. How does the situation involving the coacting audience differ from those we described earlier?

How would you react in the Triplett situation, winding a fishing reel and being acutely aware of the person next to you engaged in the same task? Many people, particularly in Western societies, would see the situation as a challenge and attempt to do better than their companion. These competitive attitudes were pointed out in early research by Dashiell (1930), who found that people in a coactive situation performed faster but less accurately than people working alone.

A coacting audience provides a basis for **social comparison** (see Chapter Three). By observing others' behavior, we can establish a basis for evaluating our own performance. If another person is doing somewhat better than we are, that person's performance may also serve as a competitive cue. As Triplett observed, performance often improves in these circumstances. But what if the other person is doing about the same, or even worse? Then the coacting audience seems to have little effect. There is also little effect when the other person is vastly superior; the person's great distance from us may make him or her an invalid source of comparison, and we will continue to perform at our standard rate (Seta, 1982).

Characteristics of the task and the situation also affect performance with a coacting audience. When the task is a simple or well-learned one, competition may improve performance, consistent with the predictions of social facilitation theory. On more complex or less familiar tasks, however, competition tends to impair performance. To counter this tendency, specific instructions encouraging cooperation on a complex task have been found to improve the performance of coactors (Laughlin & Jaccard, 1975).

Performers in a coacting audience also use one another as a source of new information. This modeling effect, discussed in earlier chapters, suggests that a performer can learn new responses simply by observing the other participants. If the other participants are successful in their actions, a person is

Box 14–1
Social facilitation in the poolroom

Do you ever play pool? What happens to your game when someone is watching? According to social facilitation theory, your performance should improve if you are a good player but should get worse if your typical play is only mediocre. James Michaels and his colleagues tested this prediction in the pool center of a college union (Michaels et al., 1982). During the initial stage of this study, observers unobtrusively watched the action and identified pairs of players who were either above average or below average in their play. During the second stage, teams of four observers stood next to the table where one of the pairs was playing and observed the next several rounds of play. Six pairs of above-average players and six pairs of below-average players were observed in this manner.

Did the presence of observers make a difference? Yes, and in exactly the way that social facilitation theory would predict. Above-average players increased their shot accuracy from 71% when not being closely observed to 80% when group members stood by. In contrast, below-average players got worse, their accuracy decreasing from 36% to 25%.

most likely to learn and perform these same responses (Bandura, 1965). At a sorority or fraternity rush party, for example, the would-be pledge may spend part of the time observing how other people interact with the group members, hoping to gain clues to the appropriate behavior.

Group Composition and Structure

A group, as we defined it earlier in this chapter, involves more than people performing the same activity at a particular time and place. Groups involve interaction, shared perceptions and experiences, the development of emotional or affective ties, and interdependent roles (DeLamater, 1974).

Not all groups are alike, however; they vary in at least as many ways as individuals do. One way in which groups differ is in their composition—in very loose terms, what does the group "look like"? How many people are in the group? Of what sex and ethnic identity are the members? Groups can also be characterized by their structure. **Group structure** refers to the system of roles, norms, and relationships among members which provides a framework for the group's functioning. Group structure holds a group together, accounting for some of the regularities in the behavior of group members (Forsyth, 1983). Leadership (to be discussed in Chapter Fifteen) is one such property. Other structural properties include the networks or channels of communication that are established in a group and the particular roles that certain members assume.

In this section we will consider one of the ways group composition can differ—in size—and two aspects of group structure, communication networks and roles and norms.

Group Size

Even within the limits of the definition of *group* that we introduced at the beginning of the chapter, it is possible to conceive of groups that range in size from a couple on their honeymoon to all the members of the U.S. Congress or the Canadian House of Commons. Most experimental research, however, has concentrated on small groups, generally varying from three to ten persons.

There have been some efforts to specify the "ideal size" of problem-solving groups. For example, P. E. Slater (1958) concluded that groups of five were the most effective for dealing with mental tasks in which group members collect and exchange information and make a decision based on evaluation of that information. Osborn (1957), the developer of brainstorming, suggested that the optimum size of such groups ranges from five to ten members.

Yet conclusions regarding the ideal size of problem-solving groups are inevitably oversimplifications. First, there are varying criteria for determining what is successful. Smaller groups may be more satisfying to participants, because the members have a chance to express their opinions fully. The addition of a few more members may add essential skills and make for a better solution to the task, but it can hurt members' participation and morale. Second, task structure can interact with group size. Some tasks require only one person, whereas other tasks can be performed only by several individuals. Third, the amount of structure in the group interacts with its size. Although groups composed of more than five persons are often less satisfying than small groups, larger groups can be effective without any major loss of morale when the task is structured. Furthermore, the circumstances and the duration of the group must be considered. In exotic and stressful environments, such as expeditionary stations in the Antarctic, larger groups appear to be more satisfying than smaller groups, perhaps because a larger group offers a greater variety of possibilities for interaction (Harrison & Connors, 1984).

The effects of group size are important in less exotic environments as well, such as a jury room. The traditional jury in England, the United States, and Canada consisted of 12 persons who must come to a unanimous decision. In 1966 Great Britain changed its policy to require agreement by only 10 of the 12. In 1970 the U.S. Supreme Court ruled that a jury of 6 people could do the job just as well as a jury of 12, citing research findings to support its decision (Wrightsman, 1987).

How does the size of a jury affect the decision it reaches? The answer to this question is not a simple one, and early research yielded inconsistent results (Hastie, Penrod, & Pennington, 1983; Wrightsman, 1987). Numerous models of decision making predict that the possibility of a hung jury—a jury that cannot reach a unanimous decision—increases as the size of the jury increases (for example, Tanford & Penrod, 1983). To test this possibility in controlled conditions, Norbert Kerr and Robert MacCoun (1985b) conducted a study using mock jurors (college students participating in an experiment rather than citizens drawn from a real jury pool). The subjects were assigned to mock juries consisting of 3, 6, or 12 people, given information about a set of armed robbery cases, and asked to deliberate on each of the cases for a maximum of ten minutes per case. Kerr and MacCoun were interested not only in the outcome of the deliberations but in the deliberation process itself.

The size of the group made a difference in this study, as Figure 14–3 shows. Larger groups, in this case 12 persons, were much more likely to fail to reach a unanimous verdict than were the 3-person mock juries. Looking in a more detailed way at the different types of cases, Kerr and MacCoun observed that the effect of group size was more pronounced when the case was a close one, in which prosecution and defense arguments were evenly balanced. Larger groups also took longer to reach their verdicts, in part because the small groups were much more likely to have unanimous opinions at the very beginning of the deliberation period.

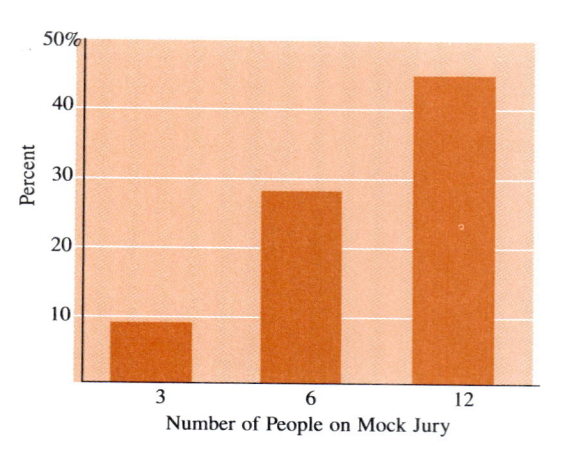

Figure 14–3 The effect of group size on jury decision making: The percentage of mock juries that failed to reach a unanimous decision

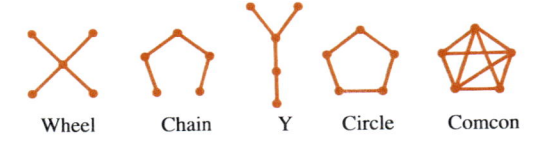

Figure 14-4 Some examples of communication networks. The dots represent positions of persons in the networks, and lines represent the primary channels of communication

As the results of this jury simulation study show, size is not merely a descriptive characteristic of a group but a factor that can influence group process as well.

Communication Networks

Group size is meaningless when group members have difficulty in communicating with one another. Real-world groups sometimes establish restricted channels through which messages may go. For example, members of a large faculty may not be allowed to speak about problems with the university president directly but instead may have to communicate through a dean. Personal feelings between individuals may affect communication channels; there may be two members of the church's board of deacons who "haven't spoken to each other for years." Location of some group members in a different building may inhibit communication between them. (In Chapter Seventeen, we consider in more detail the effects of the physical environment on social interaction.)

We refer to prescribed patterns of communication as **communication networks** (Shaw, 1964, 1978). A number of communication networks are represented schematically in Figure 14-4. Although these representations are abstract, it is relatively easy to think of concrete examples of each. On a football team, for example, the quarterback is generally the center of communication. Other players direct most of their comments to him, and he speaks to everyone on the team. This would be an example of the wheel. In the circle, each person can talk only to adjacent persons. The children's party game of "telephone" illustrates this pattern. Organizational hierarchies represent more complex communication networks; these networks often involve hundreds of people, but they can usually be broken down into these simpler patterns.

The form of a communication network is important because it determines the way the group functions. For example, the "wheel" gives great control to the person in the middle; he or she can communicate with each of the other four members, but they (in *peripheral positions*) can communicate only with the *central person* and not with each other. If such a communication network were established by the ground rules at the formation of a new group, the central-position person would probably emerge as the leader. In such cases, possession of information leads to power.

Both the "Y" and "chain" networks in Figure 14-4 also lead to centralized organization as the central person becomes pivotal. In contrast, "circle" networks do not facilitate the emergence of a dominant leader (Leavitt, 1951). In groups that have a "circle" communication network or a "comcon" network, in which every member is able to communicate with everyone else, it is impossible to predict which position will lead to leadership and dominance. In these networks, the individual personalities and skills of group members are the determining factors.

What effects do communication networks have on productivity? Which networks are most satisfying to group members? The second question can be answered simply. People prefer positions in which they have

Photo 14-2 On a football team, the quarterback is generally the center of the communication network

greater opportunities for communication and participation. "Silent" partners do not like to remain quiet. The central position in the "wheel," the "chain," and the "Y" is rated as a satisfying one, whereas the peripheral positions in these same networks are associated with poor morale (Leavitt, 1951). Networks that permit decentralized communication lead to higher morale for persons at all positions.

The efficiency of various communication networks depends on the task faced by the group. Centralized networks—such as a "wheel" or a "Y"—are most efficient when the task is a relatively simple one. The job gets done faster and fewer errors are made. When a problem becomes more complex, however, the advantages of such centralization are diminished. Routing all information through a central person becomes time-consuming and does not take advantage of the contributions that other members of the network might make. In this case, a circular network pattern is superior.

Although there is a tendency to think that the characteristics of the people in a group are of paramount importance, research clearly shows us that structural factors can be at least as influential on the group process. Communication networks (and their cousin the organization chart) have a major influence on the activities of a group, as do the tasks and problems in which a group engages.

Roles and Expectations

Chapter One introduced the concept of **role,** referring to the functions performed by a person who occupies a particular position within a particular context. Similarly, **role expectations** were defined as assumptions about the behavior of a person who occupies a particular role. When a group initially forms, the roles of individual members are often not very clearly defined. Sometimes a leader will have been designated in advance (a specific role that we will talk more about in Chapter Fifteen). More often, however, various roles emerge and develop in the course of group interaction—a process that is termed **role differentiation** (Forsyth, 1983). In contrast, when a group or organization has been functioning for some time, the roles tend to be quite clearly defined and a newcomer may be assigned to some previously defined position. In other words, roles are associated with particular positions rather than with persons (McGrath, 1984; Katz & Kahn, 1976).

As groups continue to develop, more generalized expectations about appropriate rules and procedures (called **norms**) develop as well. In Chapter Eight we described some of Muzafer Sherif's early experiments on the **autokinetic effect**—the apparent movement of a spot of light in an otherwise darkened room. One of the most interesting aspects of Sherif's research on this effect was its findings on the way group norms become established. The judgments made by subjects who were part of a group were much less variable than those made by people who were alone. In later research in this same vein, investigators have found that such norms persist even after the members who established the norm leave the group (Jacobs & Campbell, 1961). Your own participation in ongoing groups may provide additional insight on the persistence of norms.

As groups evolve, they almost inevitably develop hierarchies of authority. This tendency to organize on the basis of status distinctions seems a ubiquitous human tendency, even though the precise basis of the status assignment may vary from one group to another. The sociologist Joseph Berger and his colleagues have developed a model called **status characteristics theory** to explain how some of these organizing processes work (Berger, Rosenholtz, & Zelditch, 1980; Humphreys & Berger, 1981). According to this theory, differences in evaluations and beliefs about types of individuals become the basis for inequalities in social interaction. A status characteristic is a characteristic that occurs in two or more states or conditions, each of which is assigned its own value. In a college seminar, for example, intelligence may be considered a status characteristic, and those with more intelligence are accorded more status than those low in intelligence. In turn, certain expectations are attached to the performance of those who differ in status, in this case on the basis of intelligence. Berger would call this a *specific status characteristic* because it is directly relevant to the group task. *Diffuse status characteristics* are less directly linked to the task, but people may infer relevant characteristics on the basis of them. Race and sex operate in this fashion. People often assume, for example, that members of one identifiable group (such as men) have more skill in particular domains that could be relevant to the group task (such as mathematical ability or leadership skill). They then use this diffuse status characteristic as the basis for expectations about the performance of individuals who are members of those categories. These expectation states in turn lead to the development of particular hierarchies of authority within the group.

More than one type of status characteristic may exist in a group. For example, a work group might contain both women and men, and both skilled workers and unskilled workers. For the particular job, let us assume that people believe men to be better than women and skilled workers to be more talented than unskilled workers. In this case, a skilled female worker and an unskilled male worker would both represent cases of status inconsistency. In such instances, Humphreys and Berger (1981) predict, a state of relative equality is more likely to develop.

Gender is an interesting example of a diffuse status characteristic because the role expectations associated with male and female can be so pervasive. Just as people often assume that parents will contribute more effort to a family group than will children, so some people think that it is appropriate for men to contribute more to a group effort than women do. As the stereotype goes, men are more dominant, assertive, and competitive, whereas women are more passive, dependent, and weak. If these beliefs are common, Norbert Kerr and Robert MacCoun (1985a) reasoned, then people working in a dyad would be more likely to take a free ride—let their partner do more of the work—if the partner is a man than if the partner is a woman. In contrast, a man should be most reluctant to let his partner "carry him," because such behavior would contradict normative role beliefs. Setting up a two-person task that involved pumping air into a container and manipulating the information that subjects had about their partner's performance, Kerr and MacCoun found strong support for their predictions. Gender beliefs affected behavior, sorting even two-person groups into a status hierarchy.

Interaction in Groups

Composition and structure are for the most part static features of groups, but they can influence the dynamic processes that occur. In this section we look directly at the dynamics of group interaction: the processes that take place in groups and the performance of groups as they attempt to accomplish tasks.

Group Performance

A major question that group researchers have addressed is whether individuals working together in a group perform more successfully or efficiently than individuals working alone. The reason for such interest is not hard to discover: any organization seeking to maximize its output needs to know how to plan its division of labor. Although the question may seem simple and straightforward, the answer is more complex. It would be relatively simple if one could assume that all tasks performed by groups are similar. But they're not. Tasks differ in the kinds of behavior they require, the degree to which they encourage individual or group effort, their physical and intellectual demands, the criterion by which success is determined, and in numerous other ways as well (McGrath, 1984). To illustrate some of these possible variations, we consider two types of group activities: one that is concerned with the exertion of effort and another that focuses on problem-solving activities.

Exertion of effort. On a purely physical task, a group should perform better than an individual. Removal of debris from a California highway after a major mud slide, for example, should be more efficiently accomplished by five people working together than by a single person working alone. But, as it turns out, the increase in productivity would probably not be fivefold.

When in a group, individuals often slack off. The term **social loafing** has been applied to this effect, the decrease in individual effort that occurs when people work in groups. Investigators have known about this effect since the early part of the century, when a French professor of agricultural engineering named Max Ringelmann conducted a series of studies on the performance of human workers (Kravitz & Martin, 1986). Ringelmann wanted to assess the relative efficiency of humans, oxen, and machinery in pulling and pushing loads. In the course of his investigations, he had occasion to compare the performance of people working alone with those working as part of a group, and he found evidence of lesser performance in group conditions.

Ringelmann's primary explanation for this effect pointed to the lack of coordination that may exist when several individuals work concurrently. More

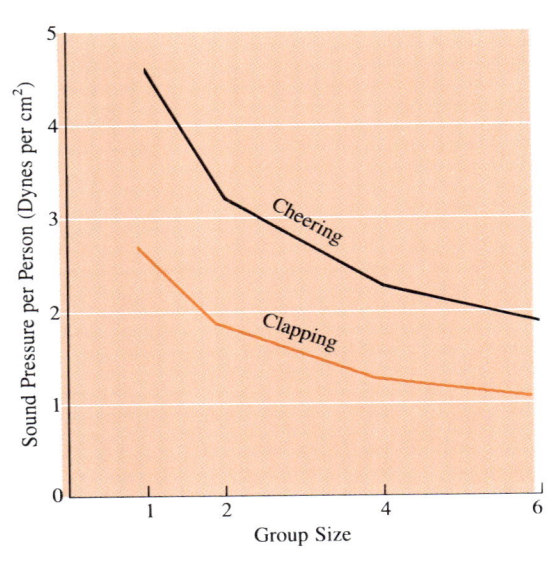

Figure 14–5 The influence of group size on individual performance

recent investigators have paid greater attention to the motivational loss that group participation may cause. Bibb Latané and his colleagues have conducted a number of studies to demonstrate the scope of these effects (Latané, Williams, & Harkins, 1979). In one study, students participating in a laboratory experiment were asked either to cheer or to clap as loud as they could. Each student performed this task a number of times—sometimes alone, sometimes with one other student, sometimes in a group of four, and sometimes in a group of six. In each case, the investigators were able to record the sound produced by each individual. Further, subjects all wore headsets and blindfolds so that they could not tell what the other people in the group were doing. As Figure 14–5 shows, groups produced social loafing: individual effort dropped precipitously as group size increased.

Why does social loafing occur? One explanation concerns the lack of identifiability in a group (Williams, Harkins, & Latané, 1981). People in a group may feel that they can "hide in the crowd": a lack of effort will not be detected. In support of this explanation, Kipling Williams and his colleagues found that subjects who were told that their individual output would be identified did not show the social loafing effect.

Another explanation for social loafing concerns one's beliefs about what others in the group will do. If people think that their co-workers are going to loaf, then they may decide, in an application of equity principles, that they might as well cut back on their effort as well (Jackson & Harkins, 1985). Because many of us have experience in groups in which not every member does his or her share, this expectation may be fairly common. If specific information is provided to a person about the expected exertion of others, however, the social loafing effect is eliminated.

The contribution of individuals to the group product can be improved in other ways as well. Making the job more difficult, for example, results in increased overall performance (Harkins & Petty, 1982; Jackson & Williams, 1985). People also are able to counter the social loafing tendency if the task is personally involving. Thus students who worked on a problem that they believed had consequences for future academic procedures in their institution did not loaf, whereas loafing was in evidence when the consequences of their effort would be felt only by students at a school in another part of the country (Brickner, Harkins, & Ostrom, 1986).

Problem solving. The term *problem solving* refers to a wide variety of tasks, varying from counting dots to solving the problems faced by the managements of large business organizations. The requirements of these tasks frequently vary. Some tasks are easily divisible, so that the overall problem can be broken down into specialized subtasks, each of which may be performed by one person. Other tasks cannot be broken down into subtasks. Even when subtasks can be defined, they may or may not be obvious to the participants; if they aren't obvious, considerable judgment and negotiation may precede the actual problem-solving attempt (Steiner, 1972).

One problem-solving task that cannot be easily divided into subtasks is known as the Tower of Hanoi, an exercise in which disks of various diameters must be rearranged on a series of pegs, one move at a time. In a classic study, Marjorie E. Shaw (1932) used puzzles and problems similar to this one to compare group and individual problem solving. Subjects worked either in five groups of four persons each or as individuals. In solving such problems, 5 individuals out of 63 produced correct solutions (8%), compared with 8 out of 15 groups (53%). The groups took about 1½ times as long to solve the problems, however. The cost in person-hours was thus greater in the groups. Shaw concluded that the major advantage of the group was its ability to recognize and reject incorrect solutions and suggestions.

Brainstorming is a group problem-solving task in which subtasks may be developed but are not immediately apparent. About 30 years ago, an advertising executive named Osborn (1957) began to advocate brainstorming as a device by which groups could devise new or creative solutions to difficult problems. The ground rules for brainstorming are shown in Figure 14–6. Such a technique can be applied to

---

1. Given a problem to solve, all group members are encouraged to express whatever solutions and ideas come to mind, regardless of how preposterous or impractical they may seem.
2. All reactions are recorded.
3. No suggestion or solution can be evaluated until all ideas have been expressed. Ideally, participants should be led to believe that no suggestions will be evaluated at the brainstorming session.
4. The elaboration of one person's ideas by another is encouraged.

Figure 14–6 Rules for brainstorming

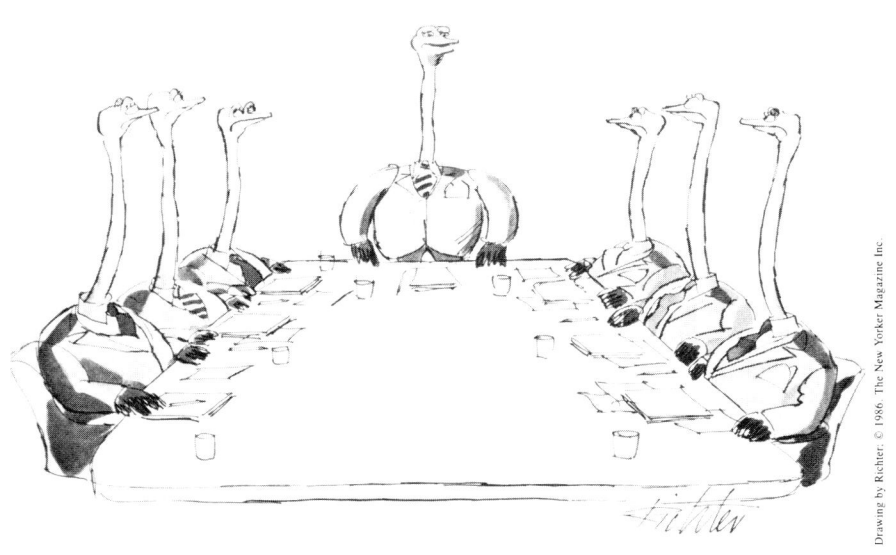

"The motion has been made and seconded that we stick our heads in the sand."

a wide range of problems. For example, an advertising agency might use brainstorming to develop a new slogan, a government agency might use it to predict the effects of a policy change, or a school board might use it to discover ways of handling a financial deficit.

Osborn claimed great success with the brainstorming procedure. Empirical evaluations, however, are more equivocal. For example, Taylor, Berry, and Block (1958) found that the number of suggestions made by groups did exceed the number made by any given individual working alone. However, when the suggestions of four separate individuals operating under brainstorming instructions were combined, they produced almost twice as many ideas per unit of time as did the face-to-face brainstorming groups of four persons each. This was also true when the subjects were research scientists who had worked together to solve problems (Dunnette, Campbell, & Jaastad, 1963). Lamm and Trommsdorff (1973) have summarized brainstorming research in the following way: "The empirical evidence clearly indicates that subjects brainstorming in small groups produce fewer ideas than the same number of subjects brainstorming individually. Less clear evidence is available on measures of quality, uniqueness, and variety" (p. 361).

Much of the research on brainstorming groups has been criticized because it brings together individuals who do not know one another—individuals who, for the purpose of the experiment, are formed into "groups," which are then disbanded (Bouchard, 1972). Members of such groups might be reluctant to express some of their wild flights of fancy in front of strangers, even under ground rules that prohibit criticism of any idea. Moreover, such transitory groups may not be highly motivated. Training and practice can improve the performance of brainstorming groups (Cohen, Whitmyre, & Funk, 1960; Parnes & Meadow, 1959). One of the critical factors may be the degree to which separate subtasks can be defined. If members are selected who readily select subtasks or areas of specialization, group brainstorming may not involve the mismanagement of time that is often claimed for it.

To summarize the work on group problem solving, we must consider both the task and the nature of the individuals engaged in the task. Under many circumstances, a group may be better able than an individual to solve a problem—for example, when a task can be divided into subtasks and individuals' skills can be matched with those particular subtasks (Steiner, 1972). However, when the division of tasks is unspecified or when the members of a group lack the necessary skills, group performance may fall well below its potential (and even below the level of an individual performing the task alone).

The Perils of Groupthink

The group, as we have described it so far, appears to be a rational creation: individuals come together, seek the best solution to a problem, and proceed to perform tasks to the best of their ability. Experience tells us, however, that such an ideal state does not always exist. Groups often make bad decisions and then go on to defend those decisions with ardor. The social psychologist Irving Janis, in analyzing a number of case studies in which government policy makers made serious errors, coined the term **groupthink,** which he defines as "a mode of thinking that people engage in when they are deeply involved in a cohesive in-group, when the members' strivings for unanimity override their motivation to realistically appraise alternative courses of action" (Janis, 1972, p. 9). More recently, Janis has defined *groupthink* more simply as a tendency to seek concurrence (Longley & Pruitt, 1980).

Among the situations (or fiascoes, to use Janis's own term) analyzed were the U.S. invasion of the Bay of Pigs in Cuba, U.S. involvement in North Korea, the escalation of the Vietnam War, and the lack of preparedness on the part of the United States for the attack on Pearl Harbor during World War II. When is groupthink most likely to occur?

Janis identifies five conditions that are likely to foster groupthink; they are shown in Figure 14–7. The first condition is **cohesiveness,** which can be defined as the sum total of all the forces attracting members to a group (Cartwright, 1968). The variable of closeness has also been described as a "we-feeling" and a positive emotional climate. Groups in which members like one another and want to remain in one another's presence are cohesive; groups in which members are unattracted to one another and groups that are breaking up are said to be low in cohesiveness.

The spirit of closeness—or lack of it—in a group can have an important effect on the behavior of its members. For example, sportswriters are fond of observing that certain athletic teams have the "best material" or "personnel" but that they "just can't put it together." In such cases, it is likely that the absence of closeness—or even the presence of hostilities among team members—is influential in the team's less-than-expected performance.

Highly cohesive groups are more likely than less cohesive groups to agree on a common goal (Schachter et al., 1951). Uniformity is stressed in cohesive groups, and members of cohesive groups are more likely to change their opinions in the direction of their fellow members' opinions than are members of less cohesive groups (Back, 1951; Lott & Lott, 1961). When you like the other members of a group, you

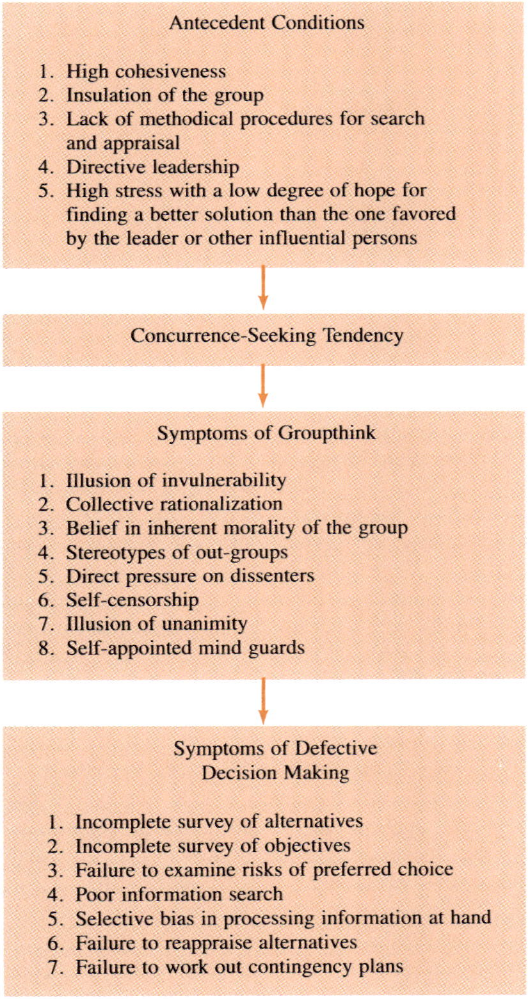

Antecedent Conditions

1. High cohesiveness
2. Insulation of the group
3. Lack of methodical procedures for search and appraisal
4. Directive leadership
5. High stress with a low degree of hope for finding a better solution than the one favored by the leader or other influential persons

↓

Concurrence-Seeking Tendency

↓

Symptoms of Groupthink

1. Illusion of invulnerability
2. Collective rationalization
3. Belief in inherent morality of the group
4. Stereotypes of out-groups
5. Direct pressure on dissenters
6. Self-censorship
7. Illusion of unanimity
8. Self-appointed mind guards

↓

Symptoms of Defective Decision Making

1. Incomplete survey of alternatives
2. Incomplete survey of objectives
3. Failure to examine risks of preferred choice
4. Poor information search
5. Selective bias in processing information at hand
6. Failure to reappraise alternatives
7. Failure to work out contingency plans

Figure 14–7 A model of groupthink

may have a greater tendency to go along with their opinions, believing that harmony will enhance the good feelings among you.

Although cohesiveness is probably the most important single factor in the tendency to succumb to groupthink, other conditions also foster a tendency to seek concurrence. Groups that are isolated from the judgments of qualified outsiders are likely victims. Add a highly directive leader, in a context where procedures for debate are not established, and groupthink becomes even more likely. Finally, immediate pressures to reach a solution will intensify the tendency toward groupthink (or the concurrence-seeking tendency). Janis goes on to describe symptoms that are typical of the groupthink situation, also shown in Figure 14–7. Among these symptoms is the emergence of "mind guards"—members who protect the group from information that might shatter its complacency. Finally, Janis describes the characteristics of the decision-making process thought to take place in this situation, a process that generally is highly selective in both information search and the evaluation of alternatives.

In a constructive vein, Janis goes on to suggest ways in which groupthink can be prevented. A leader should encourage dissidence, call on each member of the group to be critical, and reinforce members who voice criticism of a favored plan. Furthermore, a leader should not present a favored plan at the outset; initially, he or she should describe a problem, not recommend a solution. Finally, Janis suggests that routine procedures should be established by which several independent groups could work on one problem. With such dispersion of energies, it is unlikely that a consensus will develop prematurely. Of course, in order to reach a final decision, the groups must merge.

Although the analysis that Janis offers seems to be applicable to many situations, investigators have had some difficulty subjecting the full analysis to empirical test (Longley & Pruitt, 1980). Some features of the theory have been supported, however.

Experiments that have varied the type of leadership style find support for Janis's assumption that directive leaders are more apt to produce symptoms of groupthink. In one study, for example, groups led by a directive leader were more apt to endorse a defective decision when selecting a drug for public distribution (McDonaugh, 1986). In another study, groups headed by a leader whose style discouraged participation made less use of available facts and suggested few solutions for the group's problem (Flowers, 1977).

One archival study used the public statements of leading decision makers involved in five U.S. foreign-policy crises, three of which Janis described as examples of groupthink (Tetlock, 1979). Consistent with Janis's hypothesis, groupthink decision makers made more positive references to the United States and to its allies than did the nongroupthink participants. Moreover, groupthink policy makers were more simplistic in their perceptions of the basic issues. However, in contrast to Janis's suggestion, groupthink members were no more negative than nongroupthink members toward Communist states and their allies.

Although many aspects of the groupthink model remain to be clarified, it offers a fascinating perspective on group decision making.

The Polarizing Effects of Group Interaction

Observations of group discussions reveal that pressures toward uniformity (or concurrence-seeking tendencies) often occur during the decision-making process (Festinger, 1950). In a classic study of the group problem-solving process, Stanley Schachter (1951) arranged for one member of a group to maintain a position on a discussion topic that was quite at odds with the positions of the other group members. Initially, this person, who was called a *deviate* because of his position on the issue, received a great deal of attention. Other members directed more of their communications toward him than toward one another. However, after it began to be clear that his position on the topic was not going to shift, the others terminated their communications to him and concentrated on resolving their own minor differences.

One very strong outcome of group discussions is a *polarization* of responses; that is, the consensus judgments and opinions resulting from group participation are more extreme than those of the individual participants beforehand (Myers & Lamm, 1976). Initial research in this area focused on the specific question of whether groups are more or less conservative in their decisions than individuals are. This question generated more than a decade of research on what was termed the *risky shift*. This research began with the initial finding by James Stoner (1961) that group decisions were riskier than individual decisions, countering the common belief that groups tend to be more conservative than their individual members. (The view that groups are less productive and produce less satisfactory solutions than individuals still pervades popular wisdom—consider the description of a camel as "a horse designed by a committee.")

Most of the research studies that followed Stoner's

employed the choice-dilemma questionnaire developed by Kogan and Wallach (1964), one item of which is shown in Figure 14–8. Note that the definition of a risky choice is rather specific in this figure. Subjects are not asked whether they would recommend a risky or a conservative decision; instead, they are asked to estimate what the odds for success would have to be in order for them to choose a risky action. In the typical risky-shift experiment, members of a group respond to the questionnaire individually. Then they form a group to discuss each hypothetical choice and arrive at a unanimous group decision. Each subject is then asked to go back over each item on the questionnaire and, once again, indicate an individual decision. Most studies that used this method found that group decisions were indeed riskier, and a variety of theoretical formulations were offered to explain this initially unpredicted finding.

More recently, investigators have realized that although group discussion often produces a shift in individual opinions, such a shift is not necessarily in the direction of greater risk. If the initial opinions of the group tend toward conservatism, then the shift resulting from group discussion will be toward a more extreme conservative opinion (Fraser, 1971; Myers & Bishop, 1970). Therefore, the term **group polarization** has effectively replaced the term *risky shift* as a general description of this particular phenomenon.

Given the apparent pervasiveness of group polarization, we should ask *why* such polarization occurs. What causes the members of a group to shift their opinions toward an extreme position? Three general kinds of explanations have been offered. These

Mr. A., an electrical engineer who is married and has one child, has been working for a large electronics corporation since graduating from college five years ago. He is assured of a lifetime job with a modest, though adequate, salary and liberal pension benefits upon retirement. On the other hand, it is very unlikely that his salary will increase much before he retires. While attending a convention, Mr. A. is offered a job with a small, newly founded company which has a highly uncertain future. The new job would pay more to start and would offer the possibility of a share in the ownership if the company survived the competition of the larger firms.

Imagine that you are advising Mr. A. Listed below are several probabilities or odds of the new company proving financially sound. *Please check the lowest probability that you would consider acceptable to make it worthwhile for Mr. A. to take the new job.*

_____ The chances are 1 in 10 that the company will prove financially sound.
_____ The chances are 3 in 10 that the company will prove financially sound.
_____ The chances are 5 in 10 that the company will prove financially sound.
_____ The chances are 7 in 10 that the company will prove financially sound.
_____ The chances are 9 in 10 that the company will prove financially sound.
_____ Place a check here if you think Mr. A. should *not* take the new job no matter what the probabilities.

Figure 14–8 A choice-dilemma questionnaire item

explanations are based on interpersonal comparisons, informational influence, and social identification.

According to the *interpersonal comparison* explanation, individuals in a group assess the opinions of others and move to a position of perceived agreement. Motives suggested for this behavior include the desire for a favorable evaluation by others and a concern for self-presentation. This explanation focuses on the characteristics of the group members, not on information that might develop in the course of group discussion. The interpersonal-comparison explanation suggests that "group polarization is a source effect, not a message effect" (Myers & Lamm, 1976, p. 613). One variation of this position is the "climb on the bandwagon" effect, believed to be particularly evident when members of the group expect future interactions with one another in other settings (Andrews & Johnson, 1971).

Shifts in opinions motivated by interpersonal comparison are most likely to occur in situations that are personally involving (Isenberg, 1986). When basic values are engaged and when the issue is emotionally charged, these source effects should be most potent.

Informational influence explanations stress the cognitive learning that results from exposure to persuasive arguments during the course of group discussion. Here the emphasis is on the actual content (or the "message") of the group discussion and on the degree to which members are persuaded by the new information presented. This persuasion may involve mutual reinforcement. For example, Myers and Bishop (1971) found that 76% of the arguments in a group supported the position held by most of the members. Therefore, a shift toward extremity occurs because the tendency to accept dominant positions is reinforced by statements of attitudes that reflect one's own attitudes.

Group members do not adopt a more extreme position solely because of the arguments to which they are exposed. When they hear such arguments, they generally process the information, rehearse their own arguments, and then actively commit themselves to the position of the group.

Persuasive argumentation appears to carry more weight than interpersonal comparison as an explanation for group polarization effects, although the two factors frequently act in concert (Isenberg, 1986). Its influence is likely to be particularly strong when a decision calls for rationality, requiring group members to deal with many factual or logical components.

A third explanation for group polarization effects emphasizes the identity of the group itself. Although proponents of the social identification explanation do not dispute the influence of interpersonal comparison and informational influence, they stress the necessity for individuals to consider themselves part of a specifiable group (Mackie, 1986; Turner, 1982). According to this explanation, members of a group first categorize themselves in terms of their group membership. Having established this social identity, they then associate certain characteristics with their group membership, including particular attitudinal positions. Further, there is evidence that these positions are often perceived to be more extreme than they actually are, and these perceptions lay the groundwork for the group polarization effect. From this perspective, conformity is the major mechanism accounting for polarization shifts, as individuals seek to adopt the positions represented by their group. Without group identity, however, no polarization effects would be expected.

In summary, group polarization effects are indeed real. Whether these effects cause a group to become open to more conservative or more risky shifts depends on the initial opinions of the majority of group members.

Minority Group Influence

Not all members of a group necessarily identify with the group as a whole. Sometimes particular policies may cause some members of the group to feel at odds with the group goals. On other occasions, visible signs may cause one or more members of a group to stand out from the others. As we saw in Chapter Four, certain characteristics of individuals may make them salient—easily distinguishable from the other members of the group. Blacks in a predominantly White organization, for example, or women in predominantly male organizations may be viewed by members of the majority as a recognizable subgroup. Further, as Rosabeth Moss Kanter (1977) has described, people whom others view as different may become more aware of the characteristics that distinguish them from the majority, and thus come to define themselves as a minority.

A person may be in the minority for more than one reason. Anne Maass and her colleagues have made a distinction between "single" and "double" minorities (Maass, Clark, & Haberkorn, 1982). In their terms, a "single" minority is someone who deviates from the majority only in terms of belief. As an example, they suggest the American antiwar students of the mid-1960s, most of whom were members of the White middle class. A "double" minority is a person who differs both in beliefs and in category, such as a member of the Black Panthers during the same period.

The person who is in the minority by virtue of some ascribed characteristic, such as race or gender, has little choice about being seen as a minority, at least initially. In stating their beliefs, these minority members may choose to increase or decrease the distance between themselves and the dominant group. A person who is similar to the majority in ascribed characteristics but differs in values may not be accorded minority status so quickly. Whatever the basis of minority status, the member of the minority must choose whether to adopt the goals and principles of the majority, to try to influence the majority, or to leave the group. In some cases, however, if the constraints in a situation are strong, leaving the group may not be an easy alternative. It is not easy for Black Americans, for example, to withdraw completely from the White system, though they may be able to avoid full participation in it.

Students of social influence have long recognized the possibility of discrepant views among members of a group. In Chapter Eight, for example, we saw how a minority could be influenced by the majority, as the naive individuals in a group frequently conformed to the majority members' judgments of lengths of lines even though those judgments were incorrect. Recognition that a minority can also exert influence on a majority has been slower to develop (Mugny, 1982; Moscovici, 1976, 1985).

How can a minority influence a majority? Some investigators believe that minority and majority influence operate in much the same way (Latané & Wolf, 1981; Tanford & Penrod, 1984). Recalling the model of social impact discussed earlier in this chapter, we can think of minority influence as being determined by the strength, the immediacy, and the number of minority group members. According to this view, a minority will be more effective when its members have higher status or greater ability, when they are closer to the majority in space or time, and when their numbers are larger.

Other investigators believe that members of minority groups need to engage in specific behavior patterns in order to influence the majority position. According to the French psychologist Serge Moscovici (1976, 1985), a leading proponent of this perspective, the success of a minority depends on the inferences that members of the majority group make about the minority members and their alternative position. A minority that presents a united front may cause the majority to attribute strong beliefs and commitment to the minority group. Having made such an inference, the majority group will be less resistant to change. In order for the minority group to create this impression, Moscovici suggests, the *behavioral style* of the members is important. According to Moscovici, they should appear to be consistent, to be invested in their position, to have autonomy and to be able to stand up for their beliefs, to be somewhat rigid, and to be fair.

A minority that states its position consistently is generally more successful in influencing the majority (Nemeth, 1979). However, particular situational factors can moderate this effect (Mugny, 1975; Wolf, 1979), and on some occasions a negotiating style may be more effective than inflexible presentation. Sometimes, for example, an active and consistent minority may "go too far," alienating the majority and resulting in exclusion of the minority from the group—becoming a definite out-group in the eyes of the majority (Di Giacomo, 1980).

Agreement with a minority position appears to differ from agreement with a majority in other important respects. The conformity exhibited in agreement with the majority position is more apt to be a public phenomenon. Minority influence, in contrast, has a greater effect on private, internalized attitudes and beliefs (Maass & Clark, 1984). Why should these differences occur? Charlan Nemeth (1986) suggests that exposure to persistent minority views engenders greater thought about the issue. More specifically, she predicts that people who encounter a minority position think about more aspects of the situation; they entertain divergent thoughts and consider novel solutions. Responses to a majority argument, in contrast, are believed to be more limited, converging on the proposed solution quite quickly. Testing this prediction, Nemeth and Wachtler (1983) arranged for groups of college students to work on a creative problem-solving task with some confederates of the experimenter assigned to each group. In the "majority" condition, groups consisted of two subjects and four confederates; in the "minority" condition, the ratio was reversed. Although in each case the confederates offered the same solution to the problem, the responses of the subjects differed. Whereas subjects in the majority condition tended to go along with the confederates' solutions, subjects in the minority group discovered many more possible solutions to the problems. It is also interesting to note that subjects in the majority condition reported feeling more awkward in a postexperimental questionnaire than did subjects in the minority condition. This finding suggests that majority pressure produced some stress on group members.

The relative influence of majorities and minorities is an important question for those who wish to know how a group functions. At different points in time, of course, an individual may be part of the minority as well as the majority. Recognition of the potential of minority influence is particularly important, however, in helping to understand how social change can occur.

Group Socialization

So far, most of the discussion has focused on intact groups, studied at one particular time and often brought together by the social psychologist for one occasion. In actuality, groups are not static. People join groups and they leave them; groups accept members and they reject them. To truly understand the nature of groups, we need to look more closely at the process of socialization and at the changes that occur in the composition of groups and the status of members.

The social psychologists Richard Moreland and John Levine (1982) have provided an insightful account of the process of group socialization, and we will rely on their model as we discuss the relation between groups and their members.

Basic Processes

People belong to many kinds of groups—sports teams, fraternities and sororities, church groups, political parties, and work groups, to name only a few. Although groups differ in focus and purpose, within any group we can spot a number of common characteristics. According to Moreland and Levine (1982), three processes are basic to group socialization: evaluation, commitment, and role transitions.

1. *Evaluation.* Evaluation is a process by which members of the group assess the rewards that members and the group as a whole provide. In evaluating a group, for example, you might consider what you get out of it, what it costs you, and how important the group goals are to you. Further, recalling the ideas of social exchange theory (see Chapter Nine), you might also compare the rewards of the group with the possibilities for rewards in other groups. Would you rather be in sorority A or sorority B? Would you rather be a member of the chess club or of the skydiving club?

Members of a group also make such assessments about individual members. Does Blair really make a contribution to our group? Is Sonny fun to have around? These evaluation processes continue through the life of a group and can incorporate many different dimensions. Furthermore, these evaluations take into account past rewards and costs and expected future rewards and costs as well. For example, a manager might look at her team and decide that although Robin has been an important contributor in the past, his ability to contribute to the next project is doubtful. Once again, these evaluations will probably take into account people now outside the group who might be recruited for membership.

2. *Commitment.* If the individual or the members of a group evaluate the relationship as a positive or rewarding one, then commitment is likely to result. As Moreland and Levine state, "groups are more committed to individuals who help them attain group

goals, and individuals are more committed to groups that help them satisfy personal needs" (1982, p. 145). In making such a commitment, both the group and the individual again take into account a variety of temporal perspectives—past, present, and expected future rewards, as well as a comparison with other situations that might offer more. The more rewarding the present member or group and the less rewarding other available groups, the greater the commitment.

Commitment has a number of consequences, some of which we discussed in describing the group interaction process. Here we can point to four specific consequences: (1) consensus agreement on the group goals and values, (2) positive affective ties, both of the individual to the group and of the group to the individual, (3) a willingness to exert effort on behalf of the group or the individual, and (4) a desire for continuance of membership in the group (Moreland & Levine, 1982). Again we look at these consequences from two perspectives—from that of the individual who is committed to the group and from that of the group that is committed to the individual member.

3. *Role transitions*. Groups are not stable over time, and the role of any individual within the group can change. We may think of the various roles as lying on a dimension from nonmembers at one end to full members at the other end. A nonmember of a bowling team, for example, could be either someone who has never joined or someone who quit the team last month. Full members of a group are those who are closely identified with the group and are fully established in their roles. In between these two extremes, we can think about so-called quasi members—newcomers to the group who are not yet fully accepted or marginal members who have lost some of their former status.

As the group changes over time, individual members may have different roles within the group. Often the transition from one role to another is marked by formal ceremonies, or rites of passage. Bar mitzvahs and bat mitzvahs, for example, mark the transition of Jewish children to adulthood. Other role transitions may be marked in more personal ways. On becoming a member of an honorary society, for example, you may be toasted by your friends at a party. After getting promoted to a more desirable team in the organization, you may buy yourself a present. These and other activities may serve as markers of a social-psychological transition in the life of a group.

Stages of Group Socialization

Having considered the major processes that occur in the life of a group and in the lives of its members, let us turn to the actual process of group socialization. As Figure 14–9 shows, we can think of the life span of a group as consisting of five general periods, with four specific points marking the transitions between stages. As we analyze each of these stages, you may want to think about your own experiences in groups as possible illustrations of the process. Bear in mind that this curve is only a general model—the exact shape of the curve may vary.

	Prospective Member	New Member	Full Member	Marginal Member	Ex-Member
	INVESTIGATION	**SOCIALIZATION**	**MAINTENANCE**	**RESOCIALIZATION**	**REMEMBRANCE**
	Recruitment Reconnaissance	Accommodation Assimilation	Role Negotiation	Accommodation Assimilation	Tradition Reminiscence

Commitment →

ENTRY — ACCEPTANCE — DIVERGENCE — EXIT

Time →

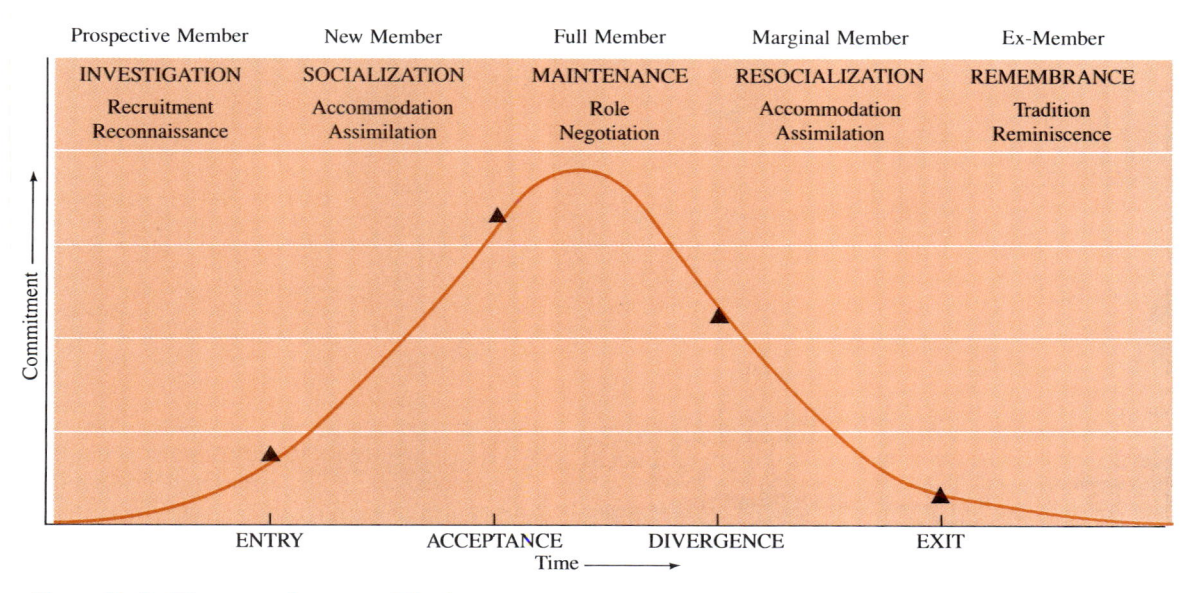

Figure 14–9 The stages of group socialization

1. *Investigation.* Fraternity or sorority rush provides an excellent example of the investigation stage. From the perspective of the individual who wants to join a group, the rush period is one of reconnaissance. As the person goes through rush, he or she is assessing the various groups, trying to decide which one would be most compatible with personal needs and values. Individuals' reasons for joining a group can vary widely, of course, as will their actual choice of a group. Some of these differences can be related to the person's prior experience with groups. The reconnaissance activities of first-year college students, for example, are influenced by the positive or negative experiences they have had with groups in high school (Pavelchak, Moreland, & Levine, 1986). Students whose high school experiences were generally positive try harder to identify potentially desirable college groups. Students who have had little past experience with groups are at a disadvantage as they try to evaluate the potential satisfaction that a college group will offer. Not only are their reconnaissance activities less extensive, but they are also likely to be overly optimistic in assessing the rewards that a group may offer.

At the same time that individuals are assessing the potential value of group membership, groups are engaging in recruitment activities, looking for persons who will "fit in" with their goals and activities. Fraternities and sororities, for example, use various criteria to decide on the suitability of a prospective member. Not all groups are as formal and closed, of course. Many groups do very little evaluation at this stage and are willing to accept anyone who wishes to be a member. Political organizations, for example, are relatively open groups. A group's willingness to accept new members depends in part on its past success. Successful groups are often more restrictive in their policies toward new recruits. Unsuccessful groups, in contrast, often actively seek new members. A good example of this latter state is seen in the famous study by Leon Festinger and his colleagues (1956), who investigated the behavior of a group that predicted the end of the world on a particular date. When the prediction proved false, members of this group became active proselytizers, seeking new recruits wherever they could find them.

2. *Entry.* The entry stage (indicated by the first triangle in Figure 14–9) marks the role transition

between investigation and socialization. At this point the individual moves from being a prospective member to being a new member of the group. In formal groups, this transition is usually marked by some kind of ceremony or initiation rite, designed in part to increase the member's commitment to the group. In less formal groups, this transition may occur without much notice, and the commitment to and by the group may be weaker as a result.

3. *Socialization*. During the period of socialization the individual and the group attempt to merge their respective goals and norms. The group attempts to assimilate the individual, instructing the person in its ways, its rituals, its procedures, and its expectations. At the same time, the individual may attempt to shape the group so that it is compatible with his or her own needs.

This socialization period varies in length and can take many forms. In the sorority or fraternity, for example, the pledge period represents a stage of socialization. Many corporations have an initial training program for prospective managers that serves much the same function. In less formal organizations, the socialization stage may be less clearly defined but still can be viewed in terms of gradual assimilation of the member to the group and gradual accommodation of the group to the new member.

4. *Acceptance*. Acceptance marks the transition between being a new member and being a full member, or between being an outsider and an insider within the group. At this point, as the curve in Figure 14–9 indicates, commitment of the group to the member and commitment of the member to the group are both high. Again, rites of passage often mark this second transition. The full benefits of the group are now available to the member, and questions of loyalty or contribution are no longer raised.

5. *Maintenance*. Role negotiation is most clearly seen during the maintenance period of a group. Now a full member, the individual tries to see where he or she will fit most clearly into the structure of the organization. At the same time, the group is trying to restructure itself, taking into account the potential contributions of the new member. Leadership roles evolve in this stage (see Chapter Fifteen), and members of the group negotiate complex and interdependent relationships with one another.

6. *Divergence*. Role negotiation is not always successful. Sometimes workable relationships do not develop; in other cases, relationships that once worked are altered by the addition of new members to the group. When the group no longer satisfies the individual, or the individual no longer satisfies the group, a third transition point (termed "divergence") is marked. Sometimes this transition is expected. For example, when you graduated from high school and went to college, your departure (at least in part) from your group of high school friends was an expected divergence. Similarly, when you graduate from college, memberships in college clubs or activities will be predictably terminated. In these cases, movement on the curve in Figure 14–9 is toward exit.

In other cases, the divergence is unexpected. An individual who veers from the group position on some important issue may be labeled a deviant by the group, and that person's status in the group will be questioned. From the individual's perspective, the group has changed, and the commitment that the individual feels toward the group diminishes.

7. *Resocialization.* If the divergence was expected, resocialization efforts are usually minimal. Instead, both the group and the member may engage in efforts to prepare for the eventual exit of the member. Going-away parties, for example, are one means of preparing for a transition that is inevitable.

If the divergence was unexpected, efforts at resocialization may be much stronger. As we saw earlier, responses to a deviant often involve a great deal of attention and communication in attempts to change the person's position so that it will be more consistent with the group's (Schachter, 1951). Both the individual and the group may negotiate and compromise, trying to regain the prior levels of commitment. Should these efforts be successful, the individual will return to full membership status, essentially moving backward on the curve shown in Figure 14-9. If the efforts are unsuccessful, then this individual, like the expected divergent, will move toward the exit transition point.

8. *Exit.* At the point of exit, the individual's and the group's commitment to each other have diminished. An evaluation of the rewards of the situation has led to a conclusion that such rewards are minimal, either in themselves or in comparison with the rewards that another group or another member would offer. The exit transition may be executed very quickly, as when an employee resigns or is fired outright. In other cases, negotiating this transition point takes more time as both the individual and the group prepare for the new situation. The individual may show a gradual decline in his or her commitment to the group—first missing a few meetings, then failing to carry out some responsibilities, then being a member in name only. On the other side, the group will gradually shift the individual to a marginal position where there is less involvement in decisions and less interaction with members.

Rites of passage may mark the exit transition as well. Retirement ceremonies mark the end of service for the employee. Angry public statements are sometimes made by the individual who has been expelled from the group. These events, like the rites that preceded them, testify to the importance of such transition points in the relationships between individuals and groups.

9. *Remembrance.* Finally, when the relationship between the individual and the group has been severed, there is a period of remembrance. The individual reminisces (with either favorable or unfavorable thoughts) about his or her relationship to that group and what it means for the future. From the group's perspective, recall of events involving that person often take the form of tradition. "Remember what Todd did when we . . ." may be the basis of consolidating the memories of Todd, either favorable or unfavorable, depending on the basis of the exit. Although commitment is now weak or absent, evaluations of the member or the group persist and provide a basis for future evaluations by groups and by prospective members.

This model of group socialization can be applied to nearly every kind of group, from formal to informal, from large to small, from short-lived to long-lived. Although the lengths of various stages and the forms of various transition points vary, the model captures important aspects of the socialization process in every group.

Summary

A group is defined as two or more people who interrelate in some dynamic way. In contrast to an aggregate, a collection of people who do not interrelate, groups have structure, organization, and relationships among the members.

Other people may influence our behavior, even when we are not part of a group. The *social impact* of an audience is determined by the number of people, their status, and their immediacy to the target.

The drive theory of *social facilitation* suggests that the presence of others is a source of general arousal that will result in increased performance of simple or well-learned responses and decreased performance of more complex tasks. A variety of social and cognitive concerns can lead to greater arousal. Other explanations of social facilitation point to the distractive aspects of an audience and to the self-presentation concerns of the performer.

Coacting audiences create a feeling of competition. In addition, they provide a source of modeling and of social comparison.

Groups vary in composition—for example, their size and the identity of their members—and in structure—the systems of roles and norms that hold a group together. The size of a group is a composition variable that has attracted a great deal of interest, including its practical implications for jury size.

Communication networks are one feature of group structure. These networks affect both the performance of the group and the satisfaction of its members. Role expectations and norms develop in all groups, and authority hierarchies are seemingly inevitable as well. Often these hierarchies are based on *status characteristics,* which may or may not be related to the specific group project.

Whether a group will perform better than an individual depends both on the nature of the task and on the characteristics of individual members. On tasks requiring physical exertion, *social loafing* is often observed, as individuals exert less effort in the group than they would alone.

Groupthink, defined as a tendency of members to seek concurrence, illustrates the process by which groups may come to poor decisions. Several conditions encourage the development of groupthink; perhaps the most important factor is a high degree of *cohesiveness,* or "we-feeling."

In general, group interaction tends to lead to a *polarization* of responses: opinions resulting from group discussion are more extreme than the opinions of individuals prior to the group discussion. Interpersonal comparison, informational influence, and social identification are three explanations for the group polarization effect.

Not all members of a group feel equally committed to the group. A minority group may form within the larger group because of shared beliefs or characteristics. Such groups can influence the majority, primarily through the display of a consistent behavioral style. It is thought that minority influence is more potent at the private level of acceptance, whereas majority influence affects public conformity.

Over the life span of a group, three processes appear particularly important: evaluation, commitment, and role transition. The socialization of a group can be described in terms of five general periods, separated by four specific transition points. These periods and the transition points are investigation, entry, socialization, acceptance, maintenance, divergence, resocialization, exit, and remembrance. Both the individual and the group engage in characteristic activities at each stage of this socialization process.

social facilitation
social inhibition
social loafing
status characteristics theory

Glossary Terms

autokinetic effect
cohesiveness
communication networks
group polarization
group structure
groupthink
norms
role
role differentiation
role expectations
social comparison

*The question "Who ought to be boss?" is like asking
"Who ought to be the tenor in the quartet?" Obviously,
the man who can sing tenor.*
Henry Ford

*You can take people as far as they will go, not as far
as you would like them to go.*
Jeannette Rankin

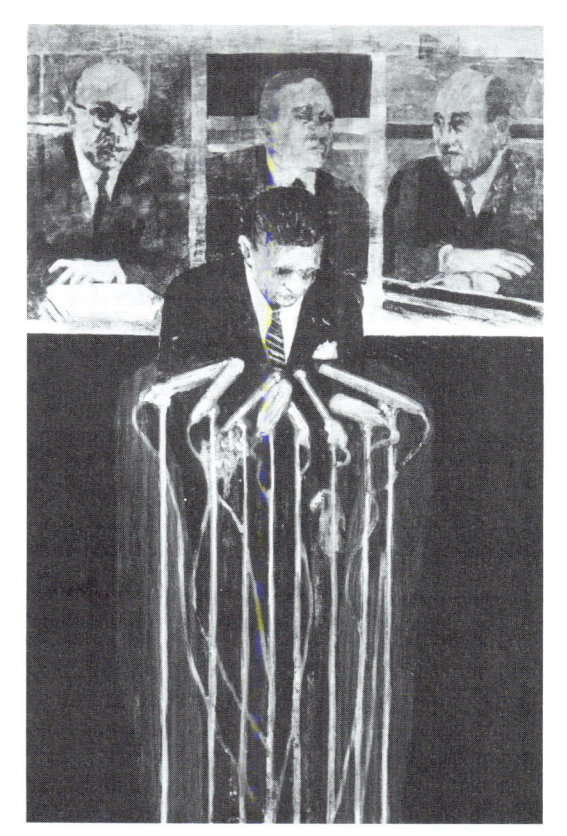

James Gill: *In His Image*, 1965. Photo by Frank J. Thomas.

CHAPTER FIFTEEN

Leadership

I. The Search for Leadership Traits
   Do Leaders Possess Certain Traits?
   The "Great Man" Theory of Leadership
   Where Is the "Great Woman" Theory?
II. What Do Leaders Do?
   Dimensions of Leadership
   Assessing Leaders' Behaviors
III. Contingency Models of Leadership
   Elements of Fiedler's Contingency Model
   Putting the Elements Together
   Leaders and Situations: Matches and Mismatches
IV. The Interaction of Leaders and Followers
   Perceptions of Leadership
   Reactions to a Leader's Behavior
   How Followers Influence Leaders
V. Summary

*G*roups, as we have described them, are collections of people interacting and working together toward a common goal. Yet not all members of a group play the same role in directing the group toward that goal. In nearly every group, whether it is a wolf pack or a human society, a single individual or group of individuals takes greater responsibility for getting things done.

Leadership has long been a topic of wide interest. Business firms and consulting organizations sponsor leadership training workshops in an attempt to instill the qualities of leadership in the novice manager. National magazines declare a vacuum of leadership in the country and search for potential leaders of the future. Social and organizational psychologists have, over the years, continued to explore the question of **leadership**—that "process of influence between a leader and followers to attain group, organizational, or societal goals" (Hollander, 1985, p. 486).

Many of the psychological concepts that we have examined earlier in this book are related to leadership—social influence and power, for example, as discussed in Chapter Eight. However, the leadership role cannot be fully described by any single set of processes; indeed, many writers have resorted to the more magical quality of *charisma* in their attempts to explain how leaders differ from the rest of us.

The study of leadership has changed from a search for simplicity to a recognition of complexity. In early attempts to study leadership, researchers tried to identify the qualities that "made" a leader—characteristics that all leaders, but no followers, possessed. Implicit in this approach was the assumption that certain traits—or even a single trait—would guarantee the emergence of a leader, whether it be the election of a captain of the church bowling team, the promotion of a company vice-president, or the selection of a jury foreman. But that simple approach didn't work. It failed to recognize the numerous functions that leaders play, the variety of tasks performed by groups, and the characteristics of the system in which leaders and groups operate. More complex analyses that followed took into account some of these broader issues.

In this chapter we will explore the issues of leadership, considering what it means to lead, what it means to follow, and how leaders and followers influence each other.

The Search for Leadership Traits

What makes one person a successful leader, while another person fails in the same position? How have some revolutionary leaders—for example, Napoleon, Hitler, and Mao Zedong—been able to control the destinies of millions of people, while other leaders come and go? Why does one person consistently become the class president, the director of the local city council, or the occupant of other leadership positions? Patterns of this kind have led people to look for the limited set of traits or characteristics that distinguish the leader from the follower.

Do Leaders Possess Certain Traits?

The earliest approach to studying leadership, and one that is still used to a small extent today, was to find a group of leaders and followers, give them a series of personality measures, and try to determine which characteristics distinguish the leaders from the followers. Although researchers were initially enthusiastic about this approach, it has become considerably less popular in recent years.

Disillusionment with this approach resulted in part from the rather simplified assumptions that were made. Often, for example, investigators assumed that a single characteristic would be sufficient to separate leaders from followers. For example, Bird (1940) analyzed the results of 20 studies that had considered 79 leadership traits. In these studies, leadership was usually defined in terms of school activities, but with great variation in the settings; for example, they included student councils, scout troops, speech and drama groups, and athletic teams. Bird found little consistency in the results from one study to another. Of the 79 traits, 51 made a difference in only one study each. Although the lack of consistency resulted partly from the use of different but almost synonymous terms in different studies (for instance, *more reliable* versus *more accurate in work*), the general result was a disappointment for those who assumed that leaders were somehow "special" in regard to many traits. High degrees of only four characteristics—intelligence, initiative, sense of humor, and extroversion—were identified often enough in leaders for Bird to consider them "general traits of leadership" (1940, p. 380).

Later reviews of studies of leadership characteristics (Jenkins, 1947; Stogdill, 1948) tended to arrive at the same conclusion: there is no single trait that consistently characterizes leaders. Even high intelligence, which many academic investigators assumed should be a mark of the successful leader, did not turn out to be of overwhelming importance as a general leadership trait. For example, Mann's (1959) review concludes: "Considering independent studies as the unit of research, the positive association between intelligence and leadership is found to be highly significant. . . . However, the magnitude of the relationship is less impressive; no correlation reported exceeds .50 and the median *r* [correlation coefficient] is roughly .25" (p. 248). In other words, although intelligence is frequently related to good leadership, the association is quite weak.

Abraham Korman (1968), in his review of managerial performance, suggested that although the intelligence levels of first-line supervisors could be related to their performance levels, there was little connection between intelligence and the success of higher-level managers. In part, the lack of connection between intelligence and performance of leaders at higher levels may be the result of a selection process: at these levels, perhaps all managers have relatively high intelligence, and so other variables become more important in determining leadership. Gibb (1969) suggested that if there is too much discrepancy between a potential leader's intelligence and the intelligence of other group members, his or her success in initiating and maintaining leadership is hampered. Leaders can be too bright for their followers. "The evidence suggests that every increment of intelligence means wiser government, but that the crowd prefers to be ill-governed by people it can understand" (Gibb, 1969, p. 218). In short, available evidence does not support the assumption that any *single* variable—be it a personality trait such as extroversion, a demographic variable such as height or age, or a cognitive characteristic such as intelligence—distinguishes leaders from followers.

To conclude that no single trait distinguishes leaders from followers (or, to phrase the statement slightly differently, distinguishes more effective leaders from less effective leaders) is not to say that some people are not more likely than others to assume leadership positions and to function effectively in those positions. In fact, evidence from common experience as well as laboratory experimentation suggests that certain people do "float to the top" more often than they would be expected to do by chance.

To assess this phenomenon in the laboratory, investigators use what is called a rotation design. In a rotation design, each subject participates in a variety of groups and never interacts with the same person more than once. In the most extensive form of rotation design, the tasks on which each group works differ as well. By looking at the pattern of leadership that emerges in all of these conditions, researchers can draw some conclusions about the consistency with which certain individuals become leaders. Doing just such an analysis, David Kenny and Stephen Zaccaro (1983) found that leadership is very stable in such situations. The same individuals tended to emerge as leaders, despite differences in group composition and task. Just what traits characterized these leaders is not known, however. Perhaps a characteristic such as behavioral flexibility, rather than any stable personality trait, is the key to understanding consistency in leadership.

A specific cluster of personality traits that predicts leadership in one setting may not be relevant in a different setting. A study by McClelland and Boyatzis (1982) provides one example of this variation. On the basis of previous research, these investigators identified a pattern of motives that are characteristic of effective managers: a high need for power, a lower need for affiliation, and high self-control. Managers high in power motivation are interested in having impact on others; managers lower in affiliation are less concerned about being disliked when unpopular decisions must be made; and high self-control allows the person to be organized and disciplined in his or her actions.

After assessing a group of male managers on these characteristics in the late 1950s, the investigators then checked back 8 and 16 years later to determine the progress of the managers within the company.

Men who had had the defined pattern of scores in earlier years were significantly more likely to be at higher levels of management in the later periods—but only if they were in nontechnical fields, such as customer services, marketing, accounting, and personnel. In contrast, the pattern was not at all predictive of the advancement of managers in technical fields, such as engineering and construction.

Trait approaches should not be abandoned entirely. The early "simple and sovereign" approach, however, has been replaced by a more complex version of trait models, which recognizes the interaction of persons and situations (and echoes the message of Chapter Thirteen).

The "Great Man" Theory of Leadership

The "great man" theory of leadership, in its boldest form, proposes that major events in national and international affairs are influenced by the people who hold positions of leadership "and that all factors in history, save great men, are inconsequential" (Hook, 1955, p. 14). Perhaps the greatest exponent of the "great man" theory was the historian Thomas Carlyle, who believed that genius would exert its influence wherever it was found.

A sudden act by a great leader could, according to this theory, change the fate of a nation. Thus Germany became overtly nationalistic and belligerent in the 1930s solely because Adolf Hitler was in power; had there been no Hitler, says the theory, there would have been no World War II. The extreme form of the theory would go on to propose that, had a "great man" been in power in Great Britain or the United States at that time, World War II could have been averted in spite of Hitler's belligerence. Implicit in the "great man" theory is the assumption that leaders possess *charisma,* a set of personality characteristics that facilitate the accomplishment of their goals, even in the face of great obstacles.

Can this theory of leadership be tested by relating the personal qualities of ruling monarchs to the extent of growth or decline in their countries during their reign? Frederick Adams Wood (1913), an early-20th-century American historian, thought so. He made a detailed study of 386 rulers in 14 Western European countries who lived between A.D. 1000 and the time of the French Revolution. All the rulers whom he studied had absolute power over their kingdoms. Each was classified as strong, weak, or mediocre on the basis of knowledge about his or her intellectual and personal characteristics (presumably independent of the strength or weakness of the nation at that time). The condition of each country was also classified by whether it exhibited a state of prosperity, a state of decline, or no clear indication of either. (This classification was based on the country's economic and political status, not on its artistic, educational, or scientific development.)

Wood found a relation between the monarchs' personalities and the state of their countries: "Strong, mediocre, and weak monarchs are associated with strong, mediocre, and weak periods respectively" (1913, p. 246). Although the correlation coefficient was reasonably strong (between + .60 and + .70), as with an correlation, we cannot infer a direct relation between cause and effect. However, Wood clearly favors the interpretation that strong leaders cause their countries to flourish. It is equally possible, though, that a state of prosperity in a country permits brilliant rulers to emerge or to reign successfully with little strain. The interpretation that Wood favors can also be doubted because of the problems in establishing independent and objective measurements of the quality of a monarch and his or her country's development. King Charles I of England is an example. It is not enough that King Charles lost his crown and his head; the final indignity is that Wood called him two-faced and obstinate. Yet other observers, as Hook notes, might describe Charles as "shrewd and principled." Although we admire Wood's exhaustive approach to the study of "great men," we must conclude that his data do not permit an answer to his question.

An opposing viewpoint: The Zeitgeist and social determinism. A strong rebuttal to the "great man" theory is found in approaches that place emphasis on social forces, social movements, and changing social values as determinants of historic events. *Zeitgeist* means "spirit of the times" or "temper of the times." According to the Zeitgeist theory of history, leaders are like actors who play out the roles designed for them by broad social forces. This theory sees the leader's temperament, motives, and ability as having little real influence in the face of social movements. As Victor Hugo wrote, "there is nothing in this world so powerful as an idea whose time has come"—a statement reflecting the perspective of the Zeitgeist, or social determinism.

Which is more nearly correct, the "great man" or the Zeitgeist theory? Study of the history of scientific discovery gives rather weak support to the "great man" hypothesis. Although certain scientists rise notably above their peers, an analysis by Dean Simonton (1979) of scientific accomplishments suggests that sheer chance and the influence of the Zeitgeist (and of previous technological discoveries) are more important determinants of scientific eminence than personal qualities.

Can the conflict between the "great man" theory and the Zeitgeist hypothesis be resolved? We have emphasized throughout this book that no one theory is always correct and that conflicting theories can each make a contribution to the understanding of complex social phenomena. Simonton (1979) concurs with this point in his analysis of scientific eminence, and Hook believes the "great man" plays a unique and decisive role "only where the historical situation permits major *alternative* paths of development" (1955, p. 109). Even if Christopher Columbus had not set sail in 1492, another explorer would have "discovered" the New World soon thereafter. The forces at work gave no alternative. Only when choices exist does the great man or woman influence history.

What may arise out of a clash between a particular leader and his times is a new set of values; for example, one effect of the nonviolent protest for Black rights led by Martin Luther King, Jr., was the consciousness among many Whites that certain cit-

Box 15-1
Long-term success of revolutionary leaders

The social psychologists Peter Suedfeld and A. Dennis Rank (1976) hypothesized that during the phase of initial struggle, revolutionary leaders would need to be cognitively simple—categorical and single-minded in their approach to problems. After the revolution, however, the successful leader might need a broader, more complex view of the world. In an archival study, these investigators tested their hypothesis by analyzing the prerevolution and postrevolution writings of 19 leaders throughout history.

Their hypothesis was supported. Leaders who continued to be prominent after the revolution (such as Cromwell in England, Thomas Jefferson in the United States, Lenin and Stalin in Russia, and Castro in Cuba) showed a shift toward greater complexity. Their themes became more varied and their ideas more complex. In contrast, leaders who did not continue in power after the revolution (such as Alexander Hamilton in the United States, Trotsky in Russia, and Guevara in Cuba) showed little change in their more single-minded statements.

---

izens in the United States were being unfairly treated. This effect cannot be attributed to the man alone or to his times; it resulted from a creative interaction between the two (Elkind, 1971).

Furthermore, both times and people change. Flexibility, as we suggested earlier, may be a key element. The most successful revolutionary leaders, for example, are those who are able to make the transition from the outsider position before the revolution to the insider position afterward (see Box 15-1).

Where Is the "Great Woman" Theory?

Throughout history there have been famous women leaders as well as famous men. The queens of France, Russia, and England can be matched with more recent counterparts such as Corazon Aquino, Indira Gandhi, and Margaret Thatcher. Yet most of the research on leadership has focused primarily or entirely on men as leaders. Indeed, a major bibliography of leadership research (Bass, 1981) does not even include sex in the index, although other variables such as race, age, and social class have numerous references. In the past, some researchers have justified this gap by pointing to the absence of women leaders in business, industry, politics, and academics, although the absence of women in these positions has never been as total as some commentators suggest. Accompanying this lack of attention is evidence that pervasive stereotypes exist to the effect that women do not make good leaders (Massengill & DiMarco, 1979; Shein, 1973, 1975). To the extent that women's leadership abilities are considered, it is often assumed that their style is quite different from that of men; women are said to focus on the social needs of the group rather than on its tasks (Dion, 1985). Thus a common assumption in the trait approach to leadership is that masculinity is one of the characteristics essential to the good leader.

With the increasing appearance of women in leadership positions in many fields, it is clear that the assumed sex differences in leadership ability should be tested. Although the results of such comparisons are not always clear, it is certainly true that differences between male and female leaders are far less frequent than might be supposed (S. M. Brown, 1979; Dion, 1985; Hollander & Yoder, 1980). Particularly when one studies actual leaders who have emerged naturally in their roles (rather than being assigned in the context of a laboratory experiment), differences between the leadership behaviors of women and men are not very apparent (Hollander, 1985). Thus, for people who choose to be leaders, individual leadership qualities may be more important than gender.

Yet even if the behaviors of women and men in leadership positions are similar, they may be eval-

Photo 15–1 Increasing numbers of women in leadership positions, such as Corazon Aquino of the Philippines, challenge earlier assumptions about women's lack of leadership abilities.

uated differently. For example, Jago and Vroom (1982) found that men who were perceived to be autocratic managers were evaluated favorably by group members, whereas autocratic women were viewed negatively. Participative styles of leadership were rated favorably, whether the manager was male or female. Thus male leaders may have greater latitude in their behaviors, being able to gain acceptance from subordinates by a variety of practices. Women, in contrast, may have fewer acceptable options and hence may be more constricted in the behaviors they can display.

When we assess male and female leadership behavior, it is important to consider the context in which that behavior is exercised. Independent of what the leader does, actions of both subordinates and superiors can influence the evaluations that result. If those actions are expressed differently toward women and men, then different leadership behaviors may result. If a truly identical situation were to prevail, then men and women might well be evaluated in the same way.

Virginia Brown and Florence Geis (1984) considered two factors that they believed would influence the evaluation of leadership performance: the legitimation of a leader's behavior by an authority and support expressed for the leader by the group members. In their study, subjects were asked to watch a videotape showing five graduate students engaged in a problem-solving task. One of the students—a man for half of the subjects, a woman for the other half—was specifically designated leader of the group. In some cases, the film also showed a professor endorsing this person's selection as leader, expressing confidence in the student's ability to lead the group. In other cases, this segment of the film was omitted. The researchers manipulated two conditions of group support, again by varying the film. In the positive support case, group members were shown giving a variety of nonverbal cues of support, such as nods, smiles, and vocal animation. In the negative support case, group members expressed doubt and occasional disapproval, knitting their brows, frowning, and exchanging dubious glances with one another. In addition, one evaluative comment (either approval or disapproval, according to the condition) was expressed by a group member when the leader was momentarily out of the room. Thus, with this combination of conditions, the investigators were able to learn whether legitimation and social support would have the same effect on the evaluation of a male and female leader. As Figure 15–1 shows, they did. When there is both legitimation and social support, both men and women are evaluated favorably; when there is neither legitimation nor social support, both men and women are evaluated less favorably.

Thus to question whether men or women make better leaders is, like the search for single traits that make good leaders, not terribly productive. Leadership needs to be analyzed in terms of both the behaviors that are believed to be effective in gaining respect and authority and the situations in which those behaviors are displayed.

What Do Leaders Do?

The relative futility of the quest for distinguishing traits of leaders had several ramifications. One was a rethinking of the difference between a designated leader and a person who exercised leadership (Stogdill, 1974). During the 1940s and 1950s, research focused on the *functions* of leaders. The result of these efforts was a new focus on *influence* as the salient aspect of leadership.

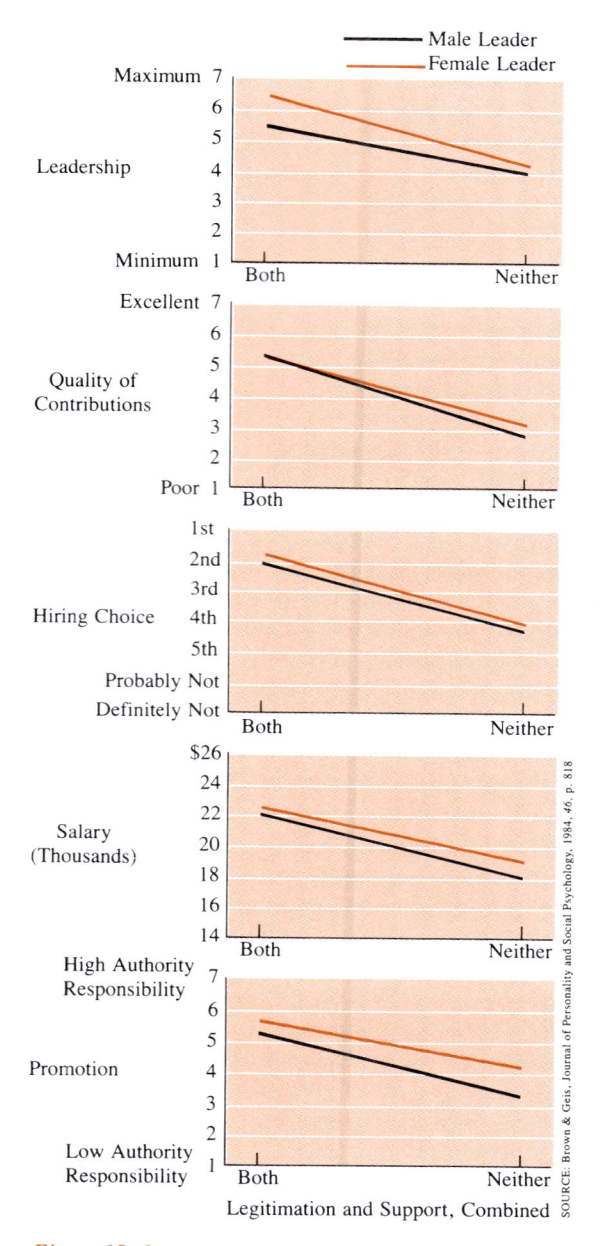

Figure 15-1
Evaluations of male and female leaders on five dimensions

SOURCE: Brown & Geis, Journal of Personality and Social Psychology, 1984, 46, p. 818

From this viewpoint, almost every member of every group has some leadership responsibility. Certainly all members of a football team have some such function—even the water carrier, if the provided refreshment really renews energy, effort, and efficiency. Of course, some group members exert much more influence toward goal attainment than others do. Members of a group, team, or organization can often be rank-ordered according to the amount of influence they exert on each aspect of the group's task. For a football team, the coaching staff and the quarterback may exert the most influence when it comes to selecting plays that are successful in moving the team toward the goal line. When inspiration and motivation are considered, some other player may be more important.

Dimensions of Leadership

In studying the functions of leadership, investigators examined what kinds of things leaders actually do. For example, the U.S. Army adopted 11 "principles of leadership" (Carter, 1952), which Gibb (1969, p. 228) has converted into seven possible behaviors: (1) performing professional and technical specialties, (2) knowing subordinates and showing consideration for them, (3) keeping channels of communication open, (4) accepting personal responsibility and setting an example, (5) initiating and directing action, (6) training people as a team, and (7) making decisions. Similarly, the survey by the Ohio State leadership group (Hemphill & Coons, 1950) pro-

Box 15-2
Nine proposed dimensions of leader behavior

1. ***Initiation.*** Described by the frequency with which a leader originates, facilitates, or resists new ideas and new practices.
2. ***Membership.*** Described by the frequency with which a leader mixes with the group, stresses informal interaction between himself or herself and members, or interchanges personal services with members.
3. ***Representation.*** Described by the frequency with which the leader defends his or her group against attack, advances the interests of the group, and acts on behalf of the group.
4. ***Integration.*** Described by the frequency with which a leader subordinates individual behavior, encourages pleasant group atmosphere, reduces conflict between members, or promotes individual adjustment to the group.
5. ***Organization.*** Described by the frequency with which the leader defines or structures his or her own work, the work of other members, or the relationships among members in the performance of their work.
6. ***Domination.*** Described by the frequency with which the leader restricts individuals or the group in action, decision making, or expression of opinion.
7. ***Communication.*** Described by the frequency with which a leader provides information to members, seeks information from them, facilitates exchange of information, or shows awareness of affairs pertaining to the group.
8. ***Recognition.*** Described by the frequency with which a leader engages in behavior that expresses approval or disapproval of group members.
9. ***Production.*** Described by the frequency with which a leader sets levels of effort or achievement or prods members for greater effort or achievement.

---

posed nine basic dimensions of the leader's behavior; these are listed in Box 15-2.

So much for analysis; what does a leader actually do? Halpin and Winer (1952) set out to identify empirically the dimensions of a leader's behavior. After constructing questionnaire items and administering them to various sets of group members, the Ohio State researchers did a factor analysis of the responses (Stogdill, 1963). Two major factors of leadership, or clusters of behaviors, emerged: consideration and initiating structure. These two factors are independent of each other; in other words, a person's standing on one dimension is not related to his or her standing on the other.

Consideration reflects the extent to which the leader shows behavior that is "indicative of friendship, mutual trust, respect, and warmth" in relationships with the other group members (Halpin, 1966, p. 86). Genuine consideration by the leader reflects an awareness of the needs of each member of the group. Leaders high in this behavioral characteristic encourage their co-workers to communicate with them and to share their feelings (Korman, 1966). In Halpin and Winer's study, consideration accounted for almost half of the variability in behavior among leaders.

Initiating structure refers to "the leader's behavior in delineating the relationship between himself and members of the work group and in endeavoring to establish well-defined patterns of organization, channels of communication, and methods of procedure" (Halpin, 1966, p. 86). Thus initiating structure refers to the leader's task of getting the group moving toward its designated goal. (A part of initiating structure may be identifying and agreeing on the goal.) Initiating structure accounted for about one-third of the variability among leaders.

Other analyses of leadership have produced sim-

Table 15-1 The leader behavior description questionnaire

Initiating Structure	Consideration
1. Makes his or her attitudes clear to the staff.	1. Does personal favors for staff members.
2. Tries out new ideas with the staff.	2. Does little things to make it pleasant to be a member of the staff.
3. Rules with an iron hand.[a]	
4. Criticizes poor work.	3. Is easy to understand.
5. Speaks in a manner not to be questioned.	4. Finds time to listen to staff members.
6. Assigns staff members to particular tasks.	5. Keeps to him- or herself.[a]
7. Works without a plan.[a]	6. Looks out for the personal welfare of individual staff members.
8. Maintains definite standards of performance.	7. Refuses to explain his or her actions.[a]
9. Emphasizes the meeting of deadlines.	8. Acts without consulting the staff.[a]
10. Encourages the use of uniform procedures.	9. Is low to accept new ideas.[a]
11. Makes sure that his or her part in the organization is understood by all members.	10. Treats all staff members as equals.
12. Asks that staff members follow standard rules and regulations.	11. Is willing to make changes.
	12. Is friendly and approachable.
13. Lets staff members know what is expected of them.	13. Makes staff members feel at ease when talking with them.
14. Sees to it that staff members are working up to capacity.	14. Puts suggestions made by the staff into operation.
15. Sees to it that the work of staff members is coordinated.	15. Gets staff approval on important matters before going ahead.

Each item is answered by checking one of five adverbs: *always, often, occasionally, seldom,* or *never.*
[a]Scored negatively.

---

ilar results. Bales (1953), for example, has concluded that leadership has two functions: *task orientation* (or thrust to achieve the group's goals) and *socioemotional orientation* (support of group members' morale and cohesiveness). Because the results of studies by Bales (1958) and others have been independently confirmed, we conclude that *initiating structure* and *consideration* (or similar factors) are two major dimensions of leadership behavior, not simply mutually exclusive leadership patterns (Gibb, 1969). In other words, the leadership process generally involves both of the leadership dimensions or orientations, and people may exhibit both in various degrees.

Assessing Leaders' Behaviors

The most common method of assessing a leader's behavior is to ask the group members to rate him or her on a set of descriptive statements, reproduced in Table 15-1. These statements form the Leader Behavior Description Questionnaire (LBDQ), devised by the Personnel Research Board at Ohio State University (Halpin, 1966; Schriesheim & Kerr, 1974; Stogdill, 1963, 1969).

In any organized group—whether it is a professional hockey team, the teaching staff at an elementary school, or a firefighting crew for an oil company—the leader's behavior can be evaluated in terms of initiating structure and consideration. It may be difficult for the same person to fulfill both of these functions successfully in a single setting. The achievement-oriented leader must often be critical of the group members' ideas or actions; such a leader may constantly turn the members' attention back toward the goal when they digress. At the same time, another member of the organization may become the group-maintenance expert, concerned with arbitrating task-oriented disputes, relieving tensions, and giving every person a pat on the back or a chance to be heard. However, sometimes a particular behavior may achieve both functions; a leader who helps

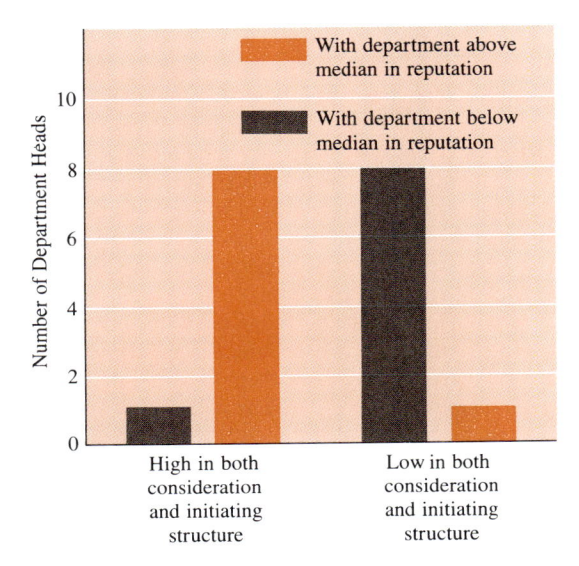

Figure 15–2 Relation between the reputation achieved by college departments and the consideration and initiating-structure scores of department heads taken conjunctively

a group solve a difficult problem may also, by that action, develop solidarity and raise morale (Cartwright & Zander, 1968).

In general, the challenges of successfully fulfilling both leadership functions are considerable. (You may wish to consider, for example, how many presidents of the United States or prime ministers of Canada were successful in "getting the country moving again" at the same time that they were "bringing people together.") However, although the combination of behaviors may be difficult, leaders are rated as being most effective when they rank high on both dimensions (Stogdill, 1974).

Group performance level is related to leadership-skill ratings. For example, pupils of Canadian teachers who were rated highly on both consideration and initiating structure scored higher on provincewide examinations (Greenfield & Andrews, 1961). Even the rank of the school principals on these two dimensions was related to the performance of the students (Keeler & Andrews, 1963). In another study, faculty members at a liberal arts college were asked to name the five departments in the college that had the reputation of being the best led or administered and the five departments that were least well administered (Hemphill, 1955). They then rated the head of their own department on the LBDQ. As shown in Figure 15–2, the department's administrative rating was consistent with the ratings that its faculty gave their department head. In an entirely different setting, Korean War aircraft commanders were rated on overall effectiveness by their superiors (including a performance assessment of each commander's group), while their crews completed the LBDQ (Halpin, 1953, 1954). Once again, the relation between leadership effectiveness rating and group performance level held. Of the nine commanders who were rated in the upper 10% of overall effectiveness by their superiors, eight were above the mean on both consideration and initiating structure, according to their crews. Of the ten commanders who were rated least effective, more fell below the mean than above the mean on both dimensions of leader behavior.

Despite the results of the preceding studies, some questions remain. Stogdill summarizes the findings of these studies as follows: "The significance of consideration and structure is to be explained, not in terms of leadership, but in terms of followership. The two patterns of behavior emerge as important, not because they are exhibited by the leader, but because they produce differential effects on the behavior and expectations of followers" (1974, p. 141). (We will consider the important role that followers play in a later section of this chapter.) Others

> **Box 15-3**
> Leadership: The case of presidential effectiveness
>
> In recent U.S. history, presidents have often been in trouble. Elected with mandates of varying strengths, presidents inevitably decline in popularity as their terms progress. Every modern U.S. president has been endorsed less favorably at the end of his term than he was at the beginning.
>
> Why are evaluations of presidential effectiveness so negative? The most popular explanation is a dispositional one, reflecting the **fundamental attribution error** (see Chapter Four). Both the citizens and the media are most likely to explain events in terms of the person—in this case, in terms of the president. In contrast to this dispositional explanation, Lawrence Wrightsman (1982) has suggested that we consider the nature of the task as well as the character of the president.
>
> The modern presidency is far more complex than its predecessors were. For example, F. D. Roosevelt had a White house staff of 37, whereas recent presidents have had staffs of as many as 600. The media now play a much more important role, highlighting even minor actions of an incumbent president. The numbers of government agencies and private lobbyists have both increased as well. Perhaps this increasing complexity means that no single person can do the job well. The person who does well on some aspects of the job may be a dismal failure at others—and all failures will undoubtedly be noted by at least some segments of the population!
>
> Wrightsman (1985) has suggested that ten task dimensions are central to presidential leadership:
>
> 1. Persuading the nation
> 2. Providing moral leadership
>
> *continued*

have argued that the LBDQ does not provide ratings of actual leader behavior but instead reflects the *implicit leadership theories* of the person doing the rating (Lord et al., 1978; Rush, Thomas, & Lord, 1977). According to this explanation, most of us have an idea of what "appropriate" leadership behavior is. Thus even with minimal information about the leader, we will give high ratings on dimensions of leader behavior when performance is good and low ratings when performance is poor. Such an explanation does not mean that real leader behaviors are not the source of *some* of the findings for the LBDQ ratings, but it does caution us against assuming that the questionnaire ratings are a completely accurate representation of behavior. One obvious solution to the problem of whether ratings reflect actual behavior or people's ideas about ideal leader behavior is to observe actual leadership behavior, rather than to rely solely on questionnaire ratings by group members. Although this approach is difficult and time-consuming, it is necessary if we are fully to understand the dynamics of leadership behavior.

Contingency Models of Leadership

A functional approach to leadership, although an improvement in some respects over the analyses that stressed single traits, still does not permit us to understand leadership behavior. Most current investigators believe that it is necessary to look at both the leader's behavior and the situation in which leadership is exercised. In other words, these new models of leadership assume that the effectiveness of any

3. Appearing "presidential"
4. Identifying goals and priorities
5. Maintaining the ongoing activities of the executive branch
6. Getting legislation passed
7. Determining and conducting foreign policy
8. Managing the White House staff
9. Crisis decision making
10. Providing political-party leadership

In the spirit of Fiedler's contingency model, Wrightsman suggests that both situational and personal factors determine effective leadership. Consider the fourth goal, for example. Identification of priorities may be easier in a situation in which the electoral mandate was strong or at a time when conflicts within the country are minimal. On the personal side, identification of priorities may be easier for the leader who has strong internal values, who has considerable experience in government, or who can easily see the "big picture." If *either* the situation is not right *or* the leader is not able to define priorities, effectiveness will be low.

We can also identify in these ten dimensions aspects that may be incompatible. For example, to maintain the ongoing activities of the executive branch, a president may need to be concerned with detail and bureaucracy. In contrast, identifying goals may require the sacrifice of detail for the broader picture. Rarely will a single individual have both sets of skills developed to a high degree.

What can be done? There are no easy answers, no quick resolutions. Recognition that task and situation are indispensable elements of leadership, however, allows a clearer conception of what presidential effectiveness can be.

particular leadership style is *contingent upon* the circumstances or conditions in which that particular group finds itself. Hence the term *contingency models,* a general perspective that can be applied to presidential effectiveness as well as small group performance (see Box 15–3).

Several contingency models have been developed, each emphasizing a distinctive set of leadership behaviors and situational factors (for example, House, 1971; Vroom & Yetton, 1973). Here we will focus on the model developed by Fred Fiedler (1967), perhaps the most prominent contingency model.

Elements of Fiedler's Contingency Model

There are four basic components in Fiedler's contingency model. One refers to the personality of the leader, whereas the other three describe characteristics of the situation in which the leader must lead. To Fiedler the personality component means leadership style, which has been defined as "the underlying need-structure of the individual that motivates his behavior in various leadership situations" (Graen et al., 1970, p. 286). Leadership style is assessed by the extent of the leader's esteem or liking for his or her "least preferred co-worker," called the LPC measure. Each leader is asked to think of all the people with whom he or she has ever worked and then to select the one with whom it has been most difficult to cooperate. This person is the "least preferred co-worker," or LPC. The leader is then given a set of bipolar rating scales and is asked to rate this least preferred co-worker on each of the dimensions listed. Examples of these dimensions include pleasant/unpleasant, friendly/unfriendly, and rejecting/accepting (Fiedler, 1967).

The LPC score may be thought of as an indication of a leader's emotional reaction to people with whom he or she could not work well (Fiedler, 1972). Low-LPC leaders, who rate their least preferred co-worker quite negatively, are considered to be task-oriented administrators, who gain satisfaction and self-esteem from the group's completion of its tasks, even if the leader personally must suffer unpleasant interpersonal relationships to get the tasks completed. For these leaders, a poorly performing co-worker is a major threat to self-esteem. In contrast, high-LPC leaders (who rate their best preferred co-worker more favorably) are more concerned about interpersonal relationships. To high-LPC leaders, satisfaction comes from happy group relationships; they are more relaxed, compliant, and nondirective. Low performance by a co-worker is not terribly threatening, and hence that worker is not rated so negatively. Thus high-LPC and low-LPC leaders seek to satisfy different basic needs in a group. In a review of the LPC research, Rice (1978) describes the two types of leaders as differing in their basic value orientation. High-LPC leaders value interpersonal success more than low-LPC leaders do, and they tend to base a wide range of judgments about themselves, others, and the environment on interpersonal success. Low-LPC leaders, in contrast, value task success more than high-LPC leaders do, and their judgments are correspondingly based on task considerations.

As we noted before, contingency models emphasize the importance of the interaction between the style of the leader and the characteristics of the situation. Thus contingency models must have a way of accessing the favorability of a situation for particular types of leaders. For Fiedler, the favorability of a situation depends on the degree to which the situation allows a leader to exert influence and control over group members (Rice & Kastenbaum, 1983). Situational favorability, defined in this model as situational control, is said to depend on three specific factors: (1) leader/member relations, (2) task structure, and (3) leader position power. Although one can imagine other factors that might affect the favorability of situations, these are the three elements that Fiedler has chosen to use in his particular model of leadership contingency. Let's consider what each of these factors designates.

1. *Leader/member relations*. The leader's personal relations with members of his or her organization can range from very good to very poor. Some leaders are liked and respected by their group, whereas others may be disliked, distrusted, or even completely rejected. Fiedler proposes that this general group atmosphere is the most important single factor determining the leader's influence in a small group (Fiedler, 1964).

2. *Task structure*. The amount of structure in the task that the group has been assigned, often on an order "from above," can vary widely. Some tasks have a great deal of *goal clarity;* that is, the requirements of the task are clearly known or programmed. For example, the factory team assembling a car or a refrigerator has little doubt about what it is sup-

posed to do. Other tasks, such as those of ad hoc committees, policy-making groups, and creative groups, often lack goal clarity and structure—no one knows exactly what the group's purposes are or how the group should proceed. A second element of task structure concerns *solution specificity*—that is, whether there is more than one way to complete the task. A third element of task structure is *decision verifiability:* once a decision has been made, how clearly does the group know that the decision is a correct one? All these aspects of task structure play a role in determining the effectiveness of different types of leaders.

3. *Position power.* A third major component of the contingency model is the power and authority inherent in the leadership position. Does the leader have the authority to hire and fire? Can the leader reward persons by giving raises in pay or status, or is he or she limited in means of regulating the behavior of group members? Does the organization back up the leader's authority? For example, the person in charge of a group of volunteer workers in a political campaign would ordinarily have little position power over the volunteers. A football coach, an owner of a small business, and a police chief will often carry high degrees of position power.

Putting the Elements Together

Now that we have defined each of the four components of Fiedler's contingency model—leadership style and the three factors that determine the favorability of the situation—how do we fit the parts together? For purposes of simplification and analysis, Fiedler considers each of the last three components to be dichotomous. Leader/member relationships are either good or poor; task structure is either clear or unclear; and position power is either strong or weak. Because there are two categories in each of these situational components, we may conceive of a system of eight classifications ($2 \times 2 \times 2$), which would encompass all the possible combinations. Fiedler has arranged these eight classifications on a dimension of favorability to the leader, as shown in Figure 15–3, on the basis of his specific assumptions about the importance of each classification.

Favorable situations, in this model, are defined as conditions that permit the leader to exert a great deal of influence on the group. From this perspective, good leader/member relations, strong position power, and clear task structure are considered favorable conditions. In contrast, poor leader/member relations, an unstructured task, and weak position power are considered unfavorable conditions.

This is only the first part of the story, however. The second part concerns how the personality style of the leader relates to the different conditions of favorability. Fiedler hypothesizes that low-LPC leaders (the task-oriented, controlling types) are most effective under conditions that are either *very favorable* (classes I, II, and III) or *very unfavorable* (classes VII and VIII). In other words, the low-LPC leader is most effective when he or she has either a great deal of influence and power or almost no influence

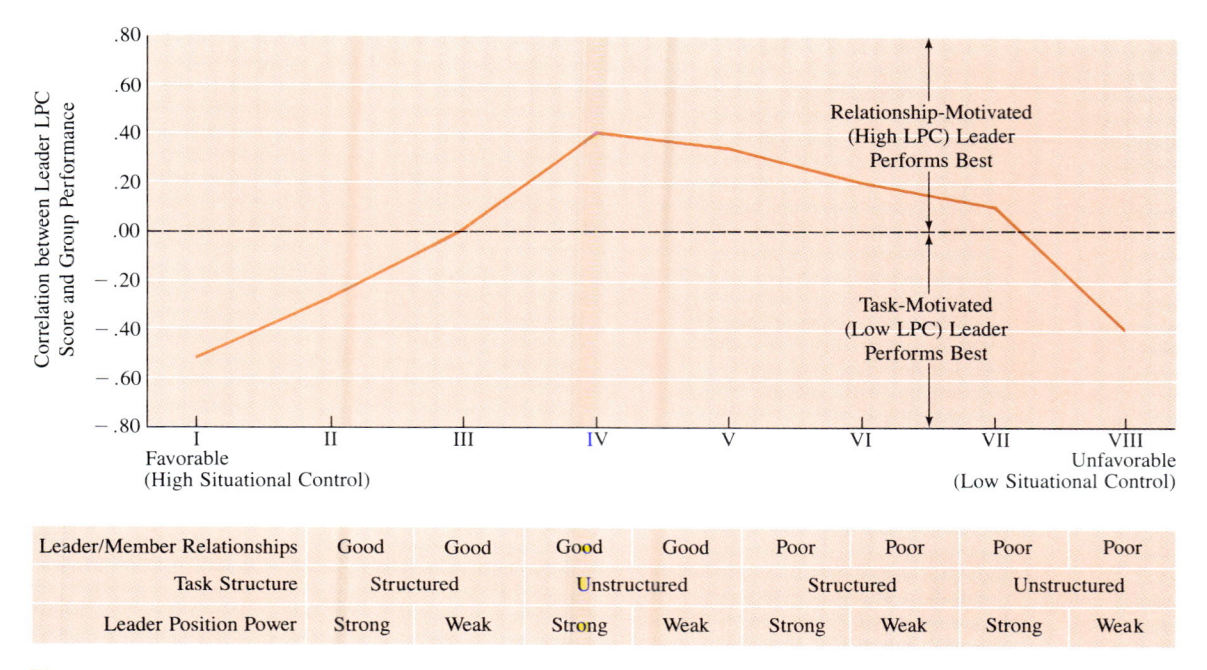

Figure 15–3 The contingency model of leadership, showing the relationship between leadership style and group performance

or power. In contrast, high-LPC leaders (the relationship-oriented types) are most effective under conditions that are *moderately favorable* or *unfavorable* and in which the leader's influence and power are mixed or moderate (classes IV, V, VI). These predictions are shown in Figure 15–3, where the correlations between leader LPC score and group performance are graphed.

Many studies have supported Fiedler's contingency model of leadership (Chemers, 1983; Strube & Garcia, 1981). In one of the strongest of these studies, West Point cadets were assembled in four-man groups that differed in leader position power, leader/member relations, and LPC scores (Chemers & Skrzypek, 1972). The investigators designated the leaders and asked each group to perform one structured and one unstructured task. These investigations found that the eight conditions of favorability and the LPC scores corresponded almost perfectly to the model. In a more limited test of the model, focusing only on class II, Schneier (1978) observed students enrolled in a personnel management course and allowed leaders to emerge naturally. As Fiedler's model would predict, those persons who emerged as leaders had lower LPC scores than the average group member; in fact, in 74% of the groups, the eventual leader had the lowest score among the four or five persons in the group. It is also of interest that this study found similar patterns for both male and female leaders, thus extending the general validity of the model. Although Fiedler's contingency theory has an impressive degree of support, some studies have failed to fit the model. As most of the nonsupporting studies have been done in field settings, additional determinants of situational favorability may be important in more complex settings (Peters, Hartke, & Pohlmann, 1985).

The most basic conclusion of Fiedler's massive

research program is that there is no such thing as a good leader for all situations. For example, consider a laboratory group in a chemistry class where the task structure is very clear (the instructor has made a definite assignment) but the position power of the group leader is weak (he or she has little authority to make decisions or assign grades). Who would be the best type of leader in this situation? It would depend on the leader/member relations, defining the group as either a class II or a class VI. If leader/member relations were good, a task-oriented leader (with a low LPC score) would probably do the best job. In contrast, if leader/member relations were poor, a high-LPC leader should elicit a better performance from the group. Just these kinds of comparisons have been made in testing the model. For example, high school basketball teams (defined as having a structured task and weak position power) with good relationships between the captain and the other team members win more games if the captain is a task-oriented leader (Fiedler, 1964). You might want to analyze some of the groups that you belong to in terms of these dimensions and consider how the style of the leader leads to effective or ineffective performance of your group.

Leaders and Situations: Matches and Mismatches

What if a leader with one style is in a group situation that is most suitable for the other style of leadership? More specifically, what if a high-LPC leader is in a situation that gives a great deal of control to the leader, or if a low-LPC leader is in a situation that allows only moderate control? Martin Chemers and his colleagues (1985) predicted that such leaders would experience a great deal of stress that would be manifested in physical symptoms and in decreased job performance. To test their hypothesis, these investigators asked 51 administrators at the University of Utah to complete a series of questionnaires about their job and their health. In addition, they filled out a measure of LPC, on the basis of which the investigators categorized them as high- or low-LPC leaders. Figure 15–4 shows the findings in regard to physical symptoms—the numbers of illnesses and health problems the administrators reported they had experienced during the preceding six months. As predicted, leaders who were in unfavorable situations, as defined by Fiedler's model, were more likely to report symptoms of ill health than were leaders who were in situations favorable to their leadership style. Reported days of absence due to illness followed the same pattern, as did the amount of stress that the administrators said they experienced in their jobs.

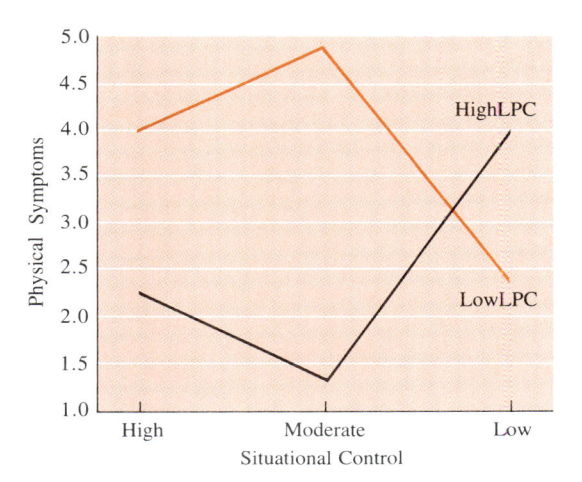

Figure 15–4 Mean number of physical health symptoms reported by high- and low-LPC (least preferred coworker) administrators at each level of situational control

If a leader experiences this kind of stress and is not effective, what should be done? Should one try to change the leader or the situation? Fiedler believes it is more fruitful to try to change the leader's work environment than to try to change his or her personality or leadership style. To help leaders make these changes, Fiedler and his colleagues (Fiedler, Chemers, & Mahar, 1976) have developed a leadership training program called Leader Match, which helps leaders define and create situations in which they are most effective. For example, a leader can volunteer for structured or ambiguous task assignments and thus achieve the preferred level of task structure; power in a group can be shifted according to autocratic or participatory principles; and a leader can influence leader/member relationships by either socializing or remaining aloof. Fiedler reports that in a series of validation studies using Army cadets, middle managers, police sergeants, and leaders of Latin American volunteer public health organizations, leaders trained by the Leader Match system were found to be consistently more effective than untrained control-group leaders (Fiedler, 1978). Although this approach probably represents a more direct attack on the problem of training effective leaders, other social scientists report that the application of positive reinforcement, dissonance, reactance, and other psychological principles can be successful in modifying the personality and behavior of the leader (Varela, 1969). In fact, the distinction between leadership style and specific leader behaviors may not be as clear as Fiedler's model suggests, and consequently certain changes may alter the characteristics of both the leader's personality *and* the leader's group situations.

The Interaction of Leaders and Followers

Leadership is not a one-way street. As Fillmore Sanford noted nearly 40 years ago, "not only is it the follower who accepts or rejects leadership, but it is the follower who *perceives* both the leader and the situation and who reacts in terms of what he perceives" (1950, p. 4). Any complete understanding of leadership must therefore include knowledge of followers as well as leaders—knowledge of how the followers perceive the leader and how their behavior may alter the leader's behavior. This is a much more process-oriented approach than that of the contingency model. Like the critics who rejected the Shannon and Weaver model of communication (see Chapter Five), critics of the traditional models of leadership emphasize *process* and *transaction* in their attempt to define their topic of study.

Perceptions of Leadership

Although the investigator of leadership may specify certain dimensions of leadership and manipulate those dimensions with some precision in the laboratory, it

"I believe in keeping things simple and to the point."

does not necessarily follow that people will perceive leaders according to those dimensions. Jeffrey Pfeffer (1978), in fact, suggests that leadership may be an ephemeral phenomenon—that much of what we call leadership is based on the attributions of observers rather than on any real behavior of the designated leader. Pfeffer argues that in any real organization there are innumerable constraints on the leader's effectiveness. In analyzing the effects of individual mayors on city budgets, for example, Salancik and Pfeffer (1977) found that characteristics of the government structure and the particular year had more influence on budget allocations than the individuals who occupied the position of mayor.

Despite evidence to the contrary, we tend to think that the leader's personality is important. Why? Pfeffer suggests that we attribute events to the leader because the leader is a more visible cause; the environment may be so complex that it is difficult to pinpoint environmental causes of events. As an example, the manager of a professional baseball or football team often serves as a scapegoat when the team is performing poorly. It's unlikely that the owner would fire the whole team, or even a substantial portion of it, even if there were evidence that many players were performing poorly. In contrast, it's easy, if not always effective, to focus on the manager as the cause of the poor performance.

Recalling our discussion of implicit personality theories and schemas in Chapter Four, we may think about the kinds of images people have of leaders. These images may or may not be based on actual performance, but it is likely that they influence the evaluation of any particular leader. Foti and her colleagues, for example, have found that people have rather clear **prototypes** of the effective political leader (Foti, Fraser, & Lord, 1982). Characteristics associated with an *effective* political leader differ from those associated with the more general category of political leader in a number of respects. For example, the effective political leader is viewed as more intelligent, as displaying better judgment, and as more sympathetic to the problems of the poor, more likely to side with the average citizen, and more likely to have a well-defined program for moving the country ahead. In another comparison, this time between political leaders and the even more general category of leader, other characteristics differentiated the two categories. Political leaders were seen as more likely to be religious and more sympathetic to the poor than leaders in general were.

It is quite likely that there are also distinct prototypes for other types of leaders—for religious leaders, for athletic coaches, and for business executives. Knowing more about the content of these prototypes might allow us to understand how subordinates evaluate their leaders in different settings.

Reactions to a Leader's Behavior

Followers may base their reaction to a leader's behavior on the extent to which the leader's behavior fits their prototype of a good leader. Other factors, such as the style of leadership the leader displays, can affect the reactions of subordinates as well. Earlier we discussed the dimensions of consideration and initiating structure as they affect overall group performance. Group performance, it was reported, was generally best when the leader was high on both dimensions. Individual reactions of group members are also affected by variations on these dimensions. In one laboratory experiment, college students interacted with a leader who was either warm or cold and either directive or nondirective, so that each student confronted one of four distinct types of leadership condition (Tjosvold, 1984). When the leader was both warm and directive (corresponding to a high rating on both consideration and initiating structure), subjects were most motivated to complete a subsequent task, outperforming all other groups. Warmth of the leader in itself, whatever the leader's directive qualities, also created positive feelings in the subordinates. Under these conditions, the followers reported feeling more open toward the leader, more satisfied with the leader, and more willing to work for the leader in the future.

The basis of a leader's authority—whether the leader was appointed by some outside agent or elected by the members—can also influence the reactions of subordinates. In general, it appears that an elected leader will create a greater sense of responsibility and higher expectations in subordinates (Hollander, 1985). In such cases, the leader must be competent and the group must be successful in order for the group to endorse his or her performance. For the appointed leader, either individual competence *or* group success may be sufficient for group endorsement. Further, research by Hollander and Julian (1970, 1978) suggests that the elected leader is also more apt to be deposed—for example, when group failure violates the expectations that were held.

Followers evaluate their leaders not only by outcomes but by procedures as well. Hence it is important that the followers see the actions of the leader as fair. Laboratory studies show that outcomes and procedures are equally important. In an experiment by Tyler and Caine (1981), residents of Evanston, Illinois, were asked to evaluate the actions of a hypothetical councilman with regard to a controversial housing rule. Residents were given information on how the councilman voted (the outcome) and the basis for his decision. In the unfair condition, the vote was described as being based solely on the councilman's personal feelings about the issue. In the fair condition, the vote was presumably based on the feedback received at a town meeting. As Figure 15–5 shows, both outcome and procedure affected

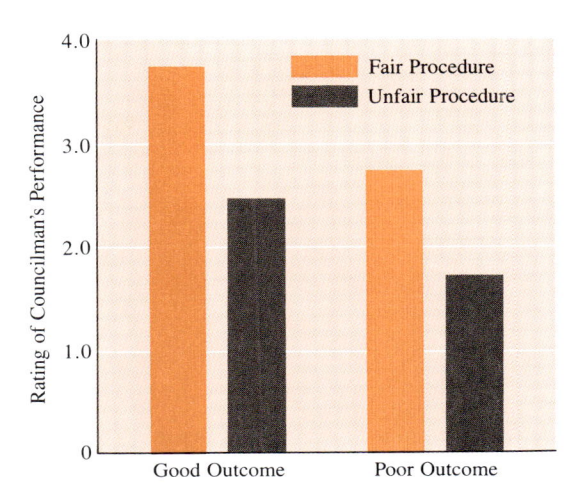

Figure 15-5 Effects of procedure and outcome on the evaluation of a leader

subjects' ratings of the councilman's performance. Thus, even when the outcome was good—in other words, consistent with the respondent's own views—performance was devalued if the procedure by which that outcome was reached was perceived to be unfair.

Although these subjects took both outcome and fairness into account when evaluating the leader, further studies by Tyler and Caine suggest that fairness is more important than outcome in some situations. Asking students to evaluate actual political leaders and actions of the government, these investigators found that perceptions of fairness outweighed the value of the outcome. In other words, although people are capable of taking both factors into account, actual judgments of leaders depend more on perceptions of justice in the actions of those leaders. Anecdotal support of this conclusion is found in a statement by former British Prime Minister Harold Macmillan, who was asked to evaluate the performance of General Eisenhower during World War II. The one indispensable quality that Eisenhower had, according to Macmillan, was fairness (Hollander, 1985).

Perceptions of the leader affect future actions by group members. For example, suppose that the members of a group perceive the leader's behavior to be inequitable. Perhaps the leader takes more of the credit for a group performance than he or she deserves, or perhaps when salaries are determined, the leader allocates an unfairly small proportion of the total resources to the group and a large proportion to himself or herself. Not surprisingly, followers in such a situation reduce their endorsement of the leader (Hollander & Julian, 1970; Michener & Lawler, 1975). They may also go further—acting on their perceptions of inequity by revolting against the leader and forming coalitions to counter the leader's behavior (Lawler & Thompson, 1978). Such revolts are much more likely to occur when the group members see the leader as responsible for the inequitable decision, rather than when the responsibility can be attributed to someone else—for example, when organizational policy is seen as constraining the leader's options (Lawler & Thompson, 1978). Group members may even choose to depose their leader. Although a crisis may temporarily increase the influence of the leader, particularly if that leader was elected by the group, continued failure will lead to dissatisfaction and an eventual ouster, if the group has the power to depose the leader (Hollander, Fallon, & Edwards, 1977).

How Followers Influence Leaders

It is clear that a good leader must pay attention to reactions of the group members. Karl Weick (1978) has suggested that a good leader should act as a medium, able to take in messages of various types from various sources and to reflect an understanding of those messages in subsequent behavior.

Even if the leader is not aware of all the messages coming from subordinates and the general system, these messages can still significantly influence the leader's behavior. For example, Fodor (1978) found that supervisors adopted a more authoritarian style of control when they were faced with a stressful situation than when the situation involved less stress. Other studies have shown that situational demands will cause different effects, depending on the personality of the leader. When the situational demands of the situation increase, task-oriented leaders show less structure and instead begin to increase their consideration and concern for people. In the same situation, interaction-oriented leaders show a decrease in social behaviors and an increased concern for task considerations (Stogdill, 1974).

Leadership is not a static process. There is a constant interchange between leaders and followers (Katz & Kahn, 1978), and each is influenced by the other in an ongoing process. Neither events nor leadership styles are static, and the shifting patterns in an organizational setting provide a fascinating testing ground for the social scientist interested in dynamic, transactional processes.

Summary

Studies to determine the characteristics that distinguish leaders from nonleaders have produced inconsistent findings. Although no single leadership trait has been identified, some people do consistently become leaders in group situations while others do not.

Attempts to explain the emergence of great political leaders have considered both the charismatic qualities of the leader and the Zeitgeist, or the temper of the times.

The question of whether women and men differ in leadership abilities has been difficult to answer, as efforts to resolve it have been confounded by stereotypes of the two sexes, biased evaluations of performance, and situational variations. Evidence suggests, however, that there are few differences between women and men when legitimation and group support are equivalent and when one looks at leaders who have emerged in a natural (as opposed to an experimental) context.

Designated leaders of groups have two major functions: initiating structure and consideration. *Initiating structure* refers to the leader's behavior in identifying the group's goal and moving the group toward the goal. *Consideration* refers to the leader's concern with relationships between himself or herself and other group members. Leaders are rated as more effective when they are considered to fill both functions well.

Fiedler's contingency theory of leadership emphasizes that there is no one successful type of leader. The four basic components of Fiedler's model are the personality of the leader, leader/member relations, task structure, and position power. Depending on the favorability of the situation, either a task-oriented or an interaction-oriented leader may be more effective. Changes in the situation may allow a particular leader to become more effective.

Leaders and followers must be viewed as interacting if group behavior is to be understood. The attributions that subordinates make about the leader's behavior will affect the group process and can alter the leader's behavior as well.

Glossary Terms

consideration
fundamental attribution error
leadership
initiating structure
prototype

You're going to find racism everyplace. In fact, I have never lived a day in my life that in some way—some small way, somewhere—someone didn't remind me that I'm Black.
Henry Aaron

We were wedded together on the basis of mutual work and goals.
Judy Chicago

Hiroji Kubota, Magnum Photos Inc.

CHAPTER SIXTEEN

Intergroup Relations

I. Prejudice and Discrimination
         Racism
         Sexism
         Causes of Prejudice and Discrimination
  II. In-Groups and Out-Groups
         Categorization and Social Identity
         Views of the In-Group and Out-Group
 III. Strategies of Interaction
         Cooperation and Competition
         Bargaining and Negotiation
         Third-Party Intervention
 IV. Reduction of Intergroup Conflict
         Superordinate Goals
         Intergroup Contact
         Reduction of Threat
  V. Summary

*G*roups form to achieve goals. In the process, the group establishes its own identity, distinguishing itself and its members from other groups with other members. Yet just as individuals are not isolated, neither are groups, and when groups come in contact with each other, conflict often results.

Examples of such conflict are all too numerous, both in literature and in reality. Shakespeare's Montagues and Capulets find more modern descendants in the 19th-century Hatfields and McCoys, who waged a 50-year feud over the theft of some pigs. Wars between the Spartans and the Athenians are echoed in current conflicts, whether they be between the United States and the Soviet Union, the Iranians and the Iraqis, or numerous other parties to international conflict. Within many Western countries, labor and management exemplify two groups that must continually negotiate to achieve their sometimes shared and often opposing goals. Evidence of such negotiations can be seen in groups as diverse as professional athletes, steel and auto workers, and elementary school teachers, each engaged in recurrent negotiations with their respective managers. In other cases, negotiation may be less formal but the conflicts as great or greater, as in relations among Whites, Blacks, and other ethnic groups or between women and men.

These situations of conflict and potential conflict, so readily found in our society, present a real challenge to those who wish to understand human behavior. As the late British psychologist Henri Tajfel stated, "intergroup relations represent in their enormous scope one of the most difficult and complex knots of problems which we confront in our times" (1982, p. 1). It is those problems that we will consider in this chapter.

First, however, we should specify exactly what is meant by the term **intergroup behavior.** Following the lead of Muzafer and Carolyn Sherif (1979), we offer the following definition: "Whenever individuals belonging to one group interact, collectively or individually, with another group or its members in terms of their group identification, we have an instance of intergroup behavior" (p. 9). The emphasis on *group* in this definition is important, for it alerts us to some of the critical issues in the study of intergroup relations. If I as an individual dislike management or am frustrated by my boss, this would not be an example of intergroup relations. However, if I as a union member take up particular issues with my boss, conscious both of my union membership and of his or her role as a representative of management, then *intergroup relations* would be an appropriate term. In other words, individual actions may be an important part of intergroup relations *if* those actions are influenced by the stance or values of some larger group.

In trying to understand the process of intergroup relations, we begin by analyzing the attitudes that people hold toward members of identifiable groups—and in particular the evidence of prejudice and discrimination. Then we will turn to the issue of social identity, looking at how groups define themselves in relation to other groups. Strategies of interaction between groups will be considered, including cooperation, competition, negotiation, and third-party intervention. Finally, on a more optimistic note, we will consider how conflict can be reduced, reviewing some of the strategies that have proved successful in different arenas.

Prejudice and Discrimination

Consider the following case:

> Aloysius Maloney has grown up in Grates Cove, C.B., Newfoundland, one of the many poor fishing villages of the province. His father, a fisherman, was lost at sea. His mother receives only a small welfare check in addition to the family allowance for the family's livelihood. Aloysius is very intelligent and desperately wants to go to a university on the mainland. But a university admissions officer tells him that he can't be admitted to the university because the academic quality of his school is so low. "Everybody knows that Newfoundland's schools are so inferior that no one from that province could survive in college," he is told.

In this example, behavior toward a particular individual is being influenced by general attitudes that are held about groups of people. Prejudice and discrimination, although the terms are often used interchangeably, are actually two distinct concepts. **Prejudice** refers to an intolerant, unfair, or unfavorable attitude toward another group of people (Harding et al., 1969). Typically, prejudice implies an affective or emotional response to a particular group of people (Brewer & Kramer, 1985). **Discrimination** refers to specific behaviors toward members of that group which are unfair in comparison with behavior toward members of other groups. Refusing admission to a student from Newfoundland while accepting an equally qualified student from Ontario, for example, would be discriminatory behavior.

To illustrate the ways in which prejudice and discrimination operate, we will consider two pervasive "isms": racism and sexism.

Racism

The U.S. Commission on Civil Rights has defined **racism** as "any attitude, action, or institutional structure which subordinates a person because of his or her color" (1969, p. 1). Such a definition incorporates both negative attitudes and discriminatory behavior, and acknowledges that racism can exist on either an individual or an institutional level.

"We don't discriminate on the basis of age, sex, religion, color or national origin—we just don't hire Scorpios."

Examples of racism are unfortunately all too numerous. In February 1987 the *New York Times* reported that in the previous two years there had been 45 cases of arson and cross burning in the United States after minority families had moved into mostly white neighborhoods (Williams, 1987). Hundreds of acts of vandalism and intimidation were reported as well.

During World War II, shortly after the Japanese attack on Pearl Harbor, pressure built in the United States to evacuate Japanese-Americans from the West Coast of the United States and confine them to internment camps in the interior. Both the mass media and government officials insisted that these Japanese-Americans, two-thirds of whom were U.S. citizens, were a threat to the country's security. Early in 1942, more than 110,000 Japanese-Americans were moved to hastily constructed camps, where they were detained for three years. Similarly, thousands of Japanese-Canadians in British Columbia were uprooted and resettled in the interior. Most of them lost their homes, farms, and businesses in the process.

In both Great Britain and Canada, attitudes and behaviors toward settlers from India and Pakistan frequently reflect extreme prejudice and discrimination. In South Africa, a minority of Europeans live in domination over a majority of Africans, and segregation of the races is virtually total. Although some policies are at last changing, Africans have been punished for staying overnight in White areas, are jailed for holding meetings and forming political parties, and must produce pass permits on demand to members of the ruling police force. Few newspapers are allowed to print articles critical of the ruling Nationalist party, and it was not until 1975 that the government permitted any television in South Africa.

Although examples of racism are numerous throughout the world, we will focus on the research dealing with Blacks and Whites in the United States because this situation has been studied most extensively. Such an emphasis does not imply, however, that other ethnic groups do not also experience prejudice and discrimination. Hispanics, for example, experience many of the same consequences as do Blacks, though the larger society is generally less aware of their problems (Ramirez, in press).

Some forms of prejudice and discrimination have been reduced or eliminated in recent years. School segregation was ruled unconstitutional by the U.S. Supreme Court in the historic 1954 *Brown* vs. *Board of Education* decision, and affirmative action poli-

Photo 16-1 This beach in Durban, South Africa, is restricted for use by Whites only.

cies in the United States and elsewhere have mandated equal treatment regardless of color. Yet it has been argued that racist values have not really changed. Although it may be less socially acceptable to show blatant racism than it once was, those underlying attitudes can be expressed on issues that are relevant to ethnic groups, such as affirmative action and law and order. **Symbolic racism,** from this perspective, is a "blend of antiblack affect and . . . traditional moral values embodied in the Protestant ethic" (Kinder & Sears, 1981, p. 416). It has its roots, Sears and Kinder argue, in early-learned racial fears and stereotypes and in fundamental feelings about social morality and propriety (Kinder & Sears, 1981; Sears & Kinder, 1985). Individuals who hold such deep-seated attitudes are likely to oppose issues that promise equality for the races not because their personal self-interest is at stake (as in the case of parents of school-aged children who would be affected by desegregation) but rather because of more general racist attitudes.

If it is true that symbolic racism has replaced more overt forms of racism, then investigators need to be more subtle in designing measures that will identify prejudice and discrimination when they exist (Crosby, Bromley, & Saxe, 1980). A variety of such measures have been tested. Borrowing from the methodologies of cognitive psychology, Samuel Gaertner and John McLaughlin (1983) used a reaction-time task in which subjects were asked to respond yes or no to the pairing of a positive or negative adjective with the category Blacks or Whites. If they thought a particular pair was meaningful, they were asked to press a button labeled "yes"; if they thought the pair was not meaningful, they were asked to press another button labeled "no." The assumption the investigators made, based on previous work in cognitive psychology, was that subjects would respond more quickly if the pair represented an existent attitude, and less rapidly if the trait was not typically associated with the group. The results of this experiment, graphed separately for individuals who had previously been assessed as high and low on racial prejudice, are shown in Figure 16–1. As the graph indicates, there was no real difference in reaction times to negative words, whether paired with the category Blacks or Whites. Positive words, in contrast, were responded to much more rapidly when they were paired with Whites than with Blacks. Thus whereas contemporary college students may no longer associate Blacks with such terms as *lazy, stupid,* and *welfare,* they are more likely to think of Whites in association with such words as *ambitious, clean,* and *smart.* It is also interesting to note that the reactions of students high and low in prejudice did not differ. This similarity suggests that although some individuals may not express their attitudes overtly on a questionnaire assessing prejudice, their underlying beliefs may still reflect a differential evaluation of Blacks and Whites.

Some investigators have argued that prejudice or rejection results largely from perceived dissimilarity in values (Rokeach, 1968, 1979; Rokeach & Mezei, 1966). According to this belief-similarity hypothesis, a White person who rejects Blacks does so not because the people are Black but rather because it is assumed that Blacks have different values. In one

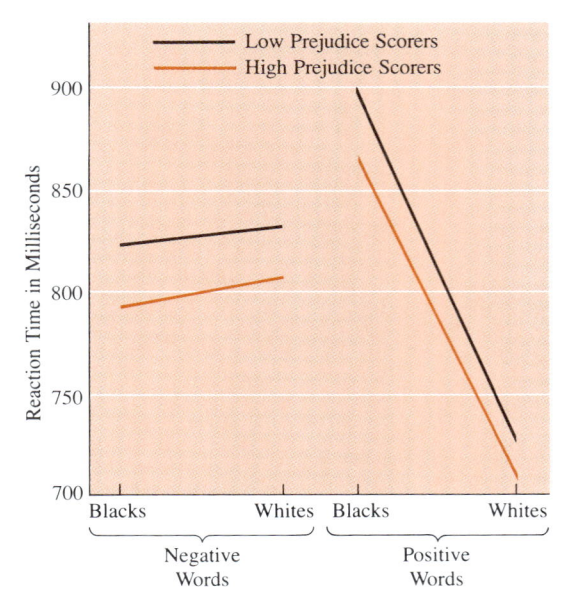

Figure 16–1 Mean reaction time of high and low prejudice scoring subjects to Blacks and Whites paired with negative and positive words

recent test of this hypothesis, speech styles were used as a cue to assumptions about cultural background and values (McKirnan, Smith, & Hamayan, 1983). Subjects in this experiment, all of whom were White, lower-middle-class college students, listened to a short tape of a speaker talking about Chicago. The speaker, who was identified by the investigators as being Black or White, spoke in what is termed "Black English vernacular" or in standard English. (In actuality, the speaker was a Black graduate student who spoke easily in both dialects.) To understand the difference in these two forms of speech, contrast these two sentences:

1. Sports would be my thang, but the teams in Chicago ain't 'bout nothing.
2. I like to follow sports, except Chicago teams are always so bad.

After listening to the brief tape, subjects gave the speaker an overall evaluation and rated the speaker on perceived similarity and desirability of social contact (the researchers used a measure of social distance as described in Chapter Thirteen). Analysis of these ratings supported the belief-similarity hypothesis. Specifically, the speaker was rated more positively when he sounded like the subjects themselves—all of whom, it should be recalled, were White—and the effect of racial label was minimal.

Although these results support the contention that belief similarity outweighs racial attitudes, other investigators are not so sure. Using the terminology of the early 1960s, the social psychologist Harry Triandis forcefully stated, "People do not exclude other people from their neighborhood . . . because the other people have different [values], but they do exclude them because they are Negroes" (1961, p. 186).

Both views have some truth, as prejudice and discrimination depend on the type of behavior being considered. For some issues, such as whether one is willing to work with a person, evidence suggests that beliefs are more important than the person's race. For other behaviors, such as accepting a person as close kin by marriage, race is more influential than beliefs (Moe, Nacoste, & Insko, 1981). Social pressure accounts for some of these effects: when social pressure favors discrimination, the effect of race is stronger than the effect of beliefs. In contrast, when such pressure is weak, beliefs may be a more important determinant of attitudes.

Not all would agree that racism exists, despite substantial evidence that the phenomenon is persistent and real. In evaluating the opportunities that Black people have in U.S. society, for example, many

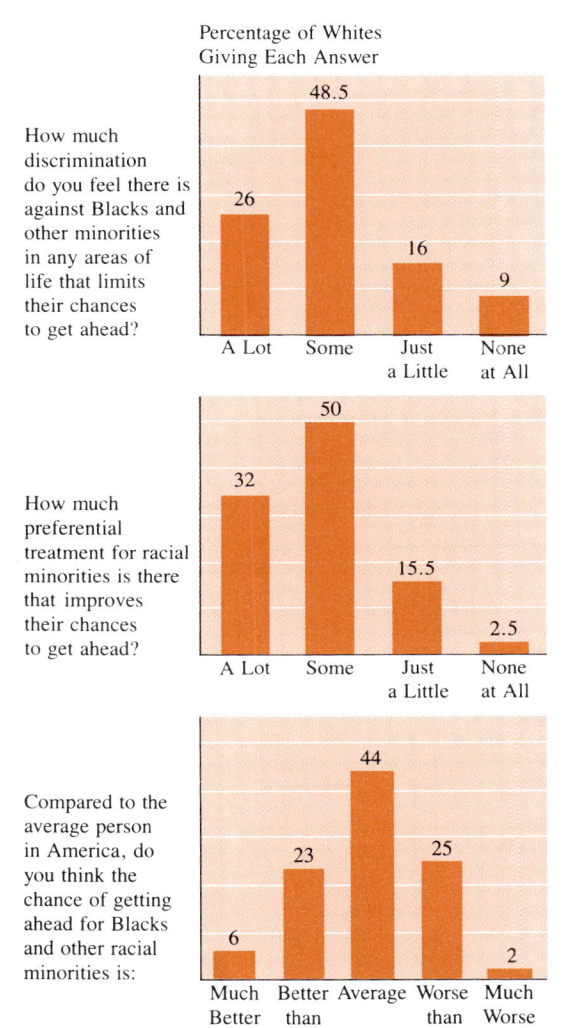

Figure 16–2 White perceptions of Black opportunity

Whites feel that racial minorities already receive preferential treatment (see Figure 16–2). Yet these opinions, gathered in a survey of more than 1800 U.S. citizens, coexist with other beliefs that there is some discrimination against Blacks, as Figure 16–2 also shows (Kluegel & Smith, 1986). Beliefs about economic equality, argue James Kluegel and Eliot Smith (1986) are heavily influenced by the country's dominant ideology, which in the United States endorses the belief that individual effort can create opportunity. Thus those who work hard will profit, and, in a reversal of the argument, those who are economically deprived must not have worked so hard. Many White citizens see their own opportunities as plentiful and regard the U.S. opportunity structure as a fair one. In considering an issue such as poverty, for example, Whites therefore tend to deny structural causes for such a state. Consequently, when seeking explanations for the cause of Black poverty, Whites often see the other person's position in the stratification system as the result of individual ability and effort—or the lack thereof. Further, as a result of such beliefs, Whites may feel that specific affirmative action programs are not needed, given the equality of opportunity that they believe exists.

Blacks themselves are less likely to believe that opportunities for Blacks are substantial, and almost twice as many Blacks as Whites (50% versus 26%) believe they have not had a fair chance to make the most of themselves. At the same time, Blacks generally adhere to the dominant ideology, that hard work prevails, underlining the contradiction between values that often exists (see Chapter Six).

Racism is not just a matter of individual prejudices and attitudes. At the national level, the laws and practices of a society can enforce and perpetuate discrimination against one group by another. In South Africa, as we noted earlier, a wide-ranging body of laws and restrictions keeps Black South Africans separate from the ruling White minority. Until fairly recently, the Untouchables in India were controlled by a similar set of policies and long-standing norms; members of that group were not allowed to participate freely in the society. Similarly, in the United States, numerous policies have kept Blacks "separate but equal" and perpetuated institutional racism. Although many of these policies have changed in recent years, it is clear that racism still exists and that the larger social structure is as important a factor in racism as individual attitudes of prejudice (Wellman, 1977).

Sexism

The concept of sexism is similar to racism, incorporating both attitudes and actions that treat one group as subordinate to another. In the case of **sexism,** however, the prejudice and discrimination are directed against people by virtue of their gender rather than their color or ethnic identity.

As in the case of beliefs about Blacks and Whites, people generally associate different characteristics with women and men. A **stereotype,** as discussed in Chapter Four, is a kind of schema or set of ideas associated with the members of an identifiable group. Many investigators have asked groups of people to describe what the average man and the average woman are like. The personality characteristics that are ascribed to men and women typically fall into two general groups—one collection of traits representing competence and independence (men) and a second group focusing on warmth and expressiveness

Table 16-1 Stereotypes of men and women: probability judgments

Characteristic	Judgment[a] Men	Women
TRAIT		
Independent	.78	.58
Competitive	.82	.64
Warm	.66	.77
Emotional	.56	.84
ROLE BEHAVIORS		
Financial provider	.83	.47
Takes initiative with opposite sex	.82	.54
Takes care of children	.50	.85
Cooks meals	.42	.83
PHYSICAL CHARACTERISTICS		
Muscular	.64	.36
Deep voice	.73	.30
Graceful	.45	.68
Small-boned	.39	.62

(women) (Broverman et al., 1972; Spence, Helmreich, & Stapp, 1974). These beliefs have considerable generality across cultures, having been observed in both North and South America, Europe, Australia, and parts of the Middle East (Williams & Best, 1982).

Although it might be argued that these two patterns—competence and expressiveness—are different but do not represent more favorable or less favorable impressions, other evidence suggests that the picture is not so optimistic. Consider the results of a study by Inge Broverman and her colleagues (1970). These authors asked 79 practicing mental health clinicians (clinical psychologists, psychiatrists, and social workers) to describe the characteristics of one of three types of persons: a normal adult male, a normal adult female, and a normal adult person with sex unspecified. The clinicians were asked to characterize the healthy, mature, socially competent person in each category. The results, not particularly encouraging if sexual equality is our goal, were quite clear-cut. Both male and female clinicians saw the healthy adult male and the healthy adult person as nearly synonymous; the healthy adult female, in contrast, was significantly different from the healthy adult person. For example, both the healthy adult person and the healthy adult male were described by adjectives from the competency cluster (*independent, active, competitive*), whereas the healthy adult female was seen as possessing far less of each of these characteristics. The healthy adult female was viewed as more submissive, more concerned about her appearance, and more excitable in minor crises— a set of characteristics not attached to either the healthy adult or the healthy male.

Personality traits are not the only characteristics associated with men and women. Gender stereotypes also include beliefs about the role behaviors in which men and women can be expected to engage and the physical characteristics that they possess, as shown in Table 16-1. In this case, people were asked to estimate the probability that an average man or an average woman would possess each characteristic. Two things are notable about these figures. First of all, in each category some characteristics are associated more strongly with women than with men and others are linked more closely to men than to women, illustrating the different stereotypes that people have. At the same time, it is not an all-or-none situation. Although people generally think that a woman is more likely to be emotional than a man, people generally think that a reasonable proportion of men are emotional too. In other words, stereotypes about gender are probabilistic estimates, not either/or certainties.

Representations of women and men in the media can reflect assumptions about their characteristics. In a fascinating exploration of media presentations, Dane Archer and his colleagues (1983) explored the phenomenon of "face-ism," or the degree of facial prominence in visual representations. In any photograph or artistic portrait, it is possible to calculate the percentage of the vertical dimension that is occupied by the head to obtain an index of relative facial prominence. Several types of visual images, including newspaper and magazine photographs, classic artwork, and drawings by college students, were measured in this way. In nearly every case, the measurements showed greater facial prominence accorded to men than to women. In other words, depictions of men give greater attention to the head, while representations of women show relatively more of the body. As these investigators suggest, the visual representations may indicate the relative emphasis that our culture places on mental life for men and physical appearance for women. Photo 16–2 provides one example of face-ism.

These visual representations are a rather subtle form of discrimination between the sexes; other actions are much more blatant and the evidence for differential treatment is substantial. In a study of performance evaluation, for example, subjects who viewed the successful performance of a man attributed that performance to ability, while subjects observing a woman perform at an equivalent level believed luck to be more responsible for the outcome (Deaux & Emswiller, 1974). Clerks in a department store have been observed to give priority to a man if both a male and a female customer are waiting for service (Zinkhan & Stoiadin, 1984).

In employment categories, women are underrepresented in nearly all professional and prestige occupations. The kinds of behaviors that women often encounter as they attempt to prepare themselves for these occupations constitute one obstacle. For example, Harris (1970) reports the following responses given by male faculty members to female applicants for doctoral work: "You're so cute, I can't see you as a professor of anything"; "Any woman who has got this far has got to be a kook. There are already too many women in this department"; "I know you're competent, and your thesis advisor knows you're competent. The question in our minds is are you really serious about what you're doing?" and "Why don't you find a rich husband and give this all up?" (p. 285).

Numerous studies have documented the existence of bias in hiring women. For example, Fidell (1970) sent a number of academic résumés to heads of psychology departments at major U.S. universities and asked each head to evaluate the applicant as a potential professor in that department. Two forms—identical except for sex of applicant—were used, each going to half of the selected chairpersons. The results showed that men were generally offered a higher position than women (that is, associate professor rather than assistant professor), despite the equality of their backgrounds. Lest we infer that only psychologists are biased, it should be noted that Lewin and Duchan (1971) found similar results in physics departments.

Beliefs about women's opportunities, like beliefs

Photo 16–2 Face-ism in a postcard photo of President Ronald Reagan and Nancy Reagan.

about the opportunities for Blacks and other ethnic minorities, are linked to more general values and ideologies (Kluegel & Smith, 1986). In the case of women, gender-role traditionalism plays a major role in addition to the dominant ideology that links effort and rewards. These beliefs have more influence on a person's judgment of discrimination and opportunity structures than do more immediate issues, such as one's own self-interest. Married men, for example, are not more supportive of policies that would reduce job discrimination than are single men, despite some financial advantages for doing so. Again, these findings testify to the pervasiveness of both racism and sexism as general values.

However, people are more aware of discrimination and limited opportunities in the case of women than they are in the case of Blacks. Not only do people tend to see more evidence of discrimination against women than against Blacks, but they also believe there is more preferential treatment and hence more general opportunity for Blacks than for women (Kluegel & Smith, 1986). Available statistics on such indicators as unemployment and education argue against these beliefs. Then why the beliefs? One reason, Kluegel and Smith suggest, is the segregation of U.S. society. Many Whites know little about the life of Blacks, and may have very little day-to-day contact with them. Thus their information about opportunity for Blacks is based not on direct experience but rather on potentially selective accounts in the media or by friends. The lives of men and women, in contrast, are generally intermeshed, and information is probably more readily available. Discrimination is therefore much more likely to be observed in the case of women than in the case of Blacks.

Racism and sexism are not the only examples of prejudice and discrimination by members of one group toward members of another group. In Canada, for example, views of the dominant English-speaking groups toward the French-Canadians are often prejudicial, and evidence of discrimination has been shown. Studies of the career advancement of civil servants have shown that French-speaking Canadians make less money, on the average, than English-speaking Canadians when factors of age, education, and seniority are equivalent (Beattie & Spencer, 1971). In the United States, one recent study showed that observers tend to discriminate against Vietnam veterans in hiring recommendations, citing a higher likelihood of psychological problems (Bordieri & Drehmer, 1984). And in many societies, ageism—discrimination against the elderly—is both a social reality and a political issue. Older people are evaluated more negatively, particularly on measures of competence (Kite & Johnson, 1987) and face discrimination in employment and other arenas.

Causes of Prejudice and Discrimination

Many theories have been advanced to explain why prejudice and discrimination occur. Gordon Allport, in his classic book *The Nature of Prejudice* (1958), identified six types or levels of analysis that have been applied: historical and economic, sociocultural, situational, psychodynamic, phenomenological, and the earned reputation. Let us briefly consider each of these.

Historical and economic emphasis. The historian reminds us that we cannot fully understand the causes of prejudice without studying the background of the relevant conflicts, and it is a sad fact that most prejudices have a long history. Anti-Black prejudice in the United States, for example, has its roots in slavery and the slave owner's treatment of Black families, in the exploitation of Blacks by carpetbaggers, and in the failure of Reconstruction in the South after the Civil War.

Some historically oriented theories of prejudice emphasize economic factors. For example, advocates of the theories of Karl Marx see prejudice as a way of letting the rulers exploit the laboring class. As Cox has stated, "race prejudice is a social attitude propagated among the public by an exploiting class for the purpose of stigmatizing some group as inferior so that the exploitation of either the group itself or its resources may both be justified" (1948, p. 393). In the treatment of Black slaves before the U.S. Civil War, of Oriental immigrants in California at the turn of the century, and of Chinese laborers brought in to build the Canadian Pacific Railroad we see classic examples of the haves vilifying the have-nots.

In emphasizing broad patterns, the historical and economic explanations provide useful background for understanding prejudice and discrimination. Social psychologists, however, prefer more "micro" explanations.

Sociocultural emphasis. Sociologists and anthropologists emphasize sociocultural factors as determinants of prejudice and discrimination. Among these sociocultural factors are (1) the phenomena of increased urbanization, mechanization, and complexity, (2) the upward mobility of certain groups, (3) the increased emphasis on competence and train-

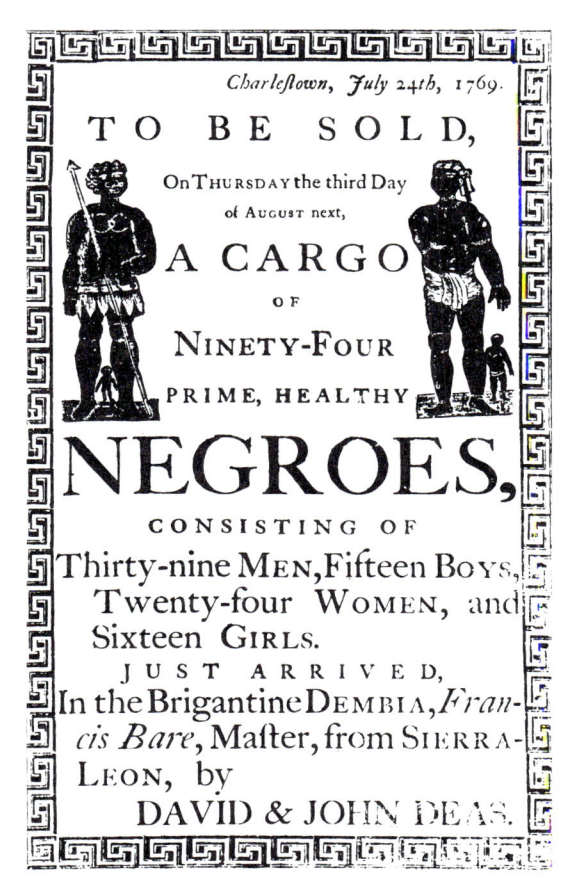

Photo 16-3 The treatment of Black slaves before the Civil War is one example of the exploitation of one group by another for economic reasons.

ing, the scarcity of jobs, and the competition to get them, (4) the increase in population in the face of a limited amount of usable land and a lack of adequate housing, (5) the inability of many people to develop internal standards, leading to reliance on others (individuals, organizations, the mass media, or advertising) and a conforming type of behavior, and (6) changes in the role and function of the family, with concomitant changes in standards of morality.

These explanations all emphasize the effects that social change can have on a society, and suggest that the uncertainty experienced in times of change is expressed in hostility toward groups whose values and customs seem different from what one is accustomed to.

Situational emphasis. Let us now turn to explanations that operate at a more individual level—those that begin to deal with the question of why some people are prejudiced while others are not. The situational emphasis is the most social-psychological in nature, focusing on current forces in the environment as the cause of prejudice. Conformity to others is a strong influence on prejudice, according to this form of analysis. During the 1960s in the U.S. South, for example, many restaurant owners claimed that they themselves were not prejudiced but that their customers would object if they allowed Blacks to be served.

Changes over time in stereotypes of racial or national groups often reflect this situational emphasis. During World War II, U.S. citizens were exposed to government propaganda that led to an adoption of negative stereotypes of the Japanese and the Germans and to favorable stereotypes of allies, including the Russians. Early in the war most U.S. citizens described the Russians as hard-working and brave. In 1948, as postwar conflicts between the two great powers emerged, the stereotypes were quite different. Although "hard-working" was still considered an appropriate description of the Russians, more people in the United States in 1948 believed that Russians were cruel. In a world where the Soviet Union was no longer an ally but an adversary, assumptions about the nature of Russians had changed. In recent years a different change has begun to take place in regard to the assumptions held by many U.S. citizens about mainland Chinese: negative attitudes are moderating with the advent of rapprochement and Coca-Cola franchises in China.

Psychodynamic emphasis. The psychodynamic view sees prejudice as a result of the prejudiced person's own conflicts and maladjustments. Psychodynamic theories of prejudice take two approaches. One assumes that prejudice is rooted in the human condition, because frustration is inevitable in human life. Frustration and deprivation lead to hostile impulses, "which if not controlled are likely to discharge against ethnic minorities" (Allport, 1958, p. 209). In this interpretation, we can see the frustration-aggression hypothesis (discussed in Chapter Eleven) finding its place in the explanation of discrimination. **Scapegoating**—the displacement of hostility onto less powerful groups—is hypothesized to result from frustration when the original source of the frustration is not available for attack or is not attackable for other reasons. Lynching of Blacks, burning of synagogues, and other assaults on representatives of minority groups are instances of such behavior.

A second approach assumes that prejudice develops only in people who have a personality defect or a weak character structure. This approach does not accept prejudice as normal; it postulates that prejudice is the result of the strong anxieties and insecurities of neurotic persons.

The original research on the authoritarian personality, as discussed in Chapter Thirteen, was based on this type of psychoanalytic model. According to T. W. Adorno and his colleagues, the authoritarian personality results from a strict and rigid superego, a primitive id, and a weak ego structure (Sanford, 1956), which lead to predictable patterns of behavior toward minority groups.

Phenomenological emphasis. According to the phenomenological emphasis, the individual's perception of the world is more important than any objective features of that world. Unlike the psychodynamic view, which stresses more durable personality characteristics, the phenomenological emphasis stresses the immediate perceptions of a person. As we saw in Chapter Four, there are many possible interpretations of a single event. Interpretations can be influenced by a variety of factors: past experience, the behavior of other people in the same situation, selective attendance to certain aspects of the situation. For example, the assertive behavior of a woman, seen in the context of more passive women, may be interpreted as "too aggressive" and "pushy," even though the behavior may be comparable to that of a man in the same situation. Discriminatory behavior may follow. In contrast, previous experience with that same woman, or comparison of her behavior with that of others in a similar situation, might result in quite different behavior on our part. In other words, the phenomenological interpretation of prejudice and discrimination emphasizes immediate influences and pays little attention to broad historical factors.

Emphasis on earned reputation. All the previous approaches have localized the source of prejudice in the observer. They have failed to consider that minority groups, by their behavior or characteristics, may precipitate the negative feelings that are directed toward them. The *earned reputation* theory postulates that minority groups possess characteristics that provoke dislike and hostility. There is some evidence to support this theory. For example, Triandis and Vassiliou, in a study of people from Greece and the United States, conclude: "The present data suggest that there is a 'kernel of truth' in most stereotypes *when they are elicited from people who have first-hand knowledge of the group being stereotyped*" (1967, p. 324). A careful review by Brigham (1971) concludes that ethnic stereotypes can have a "kernel of truth" in the sense that different groups of respondents agree on which traits identify a particular object group. Furthermore, at least in some cases, these beliefs about the characteristics of members of another group may be relatively accurate (McCauley & Stitt, 1978).

Each of these explanations of prejudice has some merits, but none is sufficient to explain every case: a phenomenon as pervasive as prejudice has many sources. Hence we must acknowledge the multiple causes of prejudice, while realizing that attempts to identify specific causes for individual cases of prejudice are helpful.

In-Groups and Out-Groups

In considering prejudice and discrimination, we were looking at the consequences of intergroup relations in very broad terms, considering how people in general react to certain identifiable groups, such as Blacks and women. In taking this perspective, we were also emphasizing some of the *outcomes* of intergroup relations. But what are the *processes* involved? How do groups view themselves and how do they look at other groups? In this section we consider some of the specific processes that almost inevitably emerge when groups come in contact with one another.

Categorization and Social Identity

Many of the cognitive processes discussed in Chapter Four, by describing how experience is translated into mental representations, have been used to explain how groups gain a definition (Stephan, 1985). As David Wilder has stated, "on the simplest level, groups may be defined as categories of persons subject to the same principles of organization and inference attributed to any category" (1986, p. 293). Thus from this perspective, the processes of attention, encoding, and retrieval explain how a group comes to associate certain characteristics with itself and, similarly, how certain attributes come to be associated with other groups.

The act of categorization itself leads people to assume similarity among the members of a category. Even when the distinctions between groups are arbitrary, people tend to minimize the differences they see among members of the same group and to accentuate the differences between members of two different groups (Wilder, 1986; Brewer & Kramer, 1985).

Although an outside observer tends to see group membership as relatively homogeneous, members of groups find more heterogeneity in their membership. For example, when members of a sorority were asked to describe members of their own sorority and members of another sorority, they saw much greater similarity among members of the other sorority. In other words, they were more willing to use a common stereotypic category in judging members of the other sorority, while seeing greater diversity among the members of their own group (Linville, 1982).

Differences between views of in-groups and out-groups may reflect different levels of categorization (Park & Rothbart, 1982). In judging members of a group that we do not know very well, we may see them all mainly as members of "group X," with a common set of attributes. In contrast, when we view our own group members, whom we know much better, we may use a finer level of categorization to distinguish among the different types of group members.

The mere presence of another group can make members more aware of their own group identity. To understand how this process works, imagine that you are a student at Rutgers University participating in a psychology experiment on verbal learning. As you sit down at a table in the experimental room (a rather cluttered room with many objects that seem out of place in a laboratory), you notice a pennant on the wall in front of you. Without thinking a great deal about it, you go on to the experimental task, which requires you to look at a series of 50 words and then, after a brief interval, look at another list of words and identify those words that you saw earlier.

The critical elements in this experiment, designed by David Wilder and Peter Shapiro (1984), are (*a*) the pennant, which was a manipulation of group salience, and (*b*) the particular words, which were the dependent variable used to assess group identity. Three different pennants were used: a Rutgers pennant (to make the in-group salient), a Princeton pennant (to make a relevant out-group salient), and a New York Yankees pennant (presumably an irrelevant out-group). The final list of words contained words relevant to each of these groups. Wilder and Shapiro hypothesized that making either the in-group (Rutgers) or a *relevant* out-group (Princeton) salient would lead the Rutgers students to select more words related to Rutgers than they would if their group identity had not been activated. As Figure 16–3 shows, that was the case. In fact, Rutgers students who were confronted with signs of a relevant out-group (in this case, Princeton) were almost as likely to think in terms of their in-group as they were when their in-group was made salient directly by a Rutgers pennant.

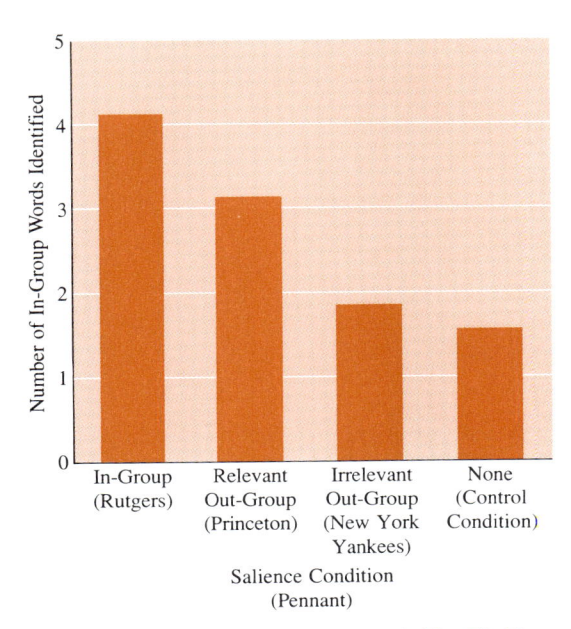

Figure 16-3 Number of in-group words identified in four conditions

Although cognitive principles of categorization can explain some aspects of intergroup relations, most researchers would agree that it is important to consider motivational issues as well. "Social categorization entails much more than the cognitive classification of events, objects, or people. It is a process impregnated by values, culture and social representations" (Tajfel & Forgas, cited in Brewer & Kramer, 1985, p. 224). This perspective suggests that members of groups do more than simply note the differences between their in-group and the out-group. They attempt to emphasize the differences, and take actions that will discriminate in favor of their own group. The resulting social competition exacerbates the distinctions further, creating an ever-increasing sense of *we* and *they*. Such a strategy is particularly likely for a group member who has experienced some personal failure (Meindl & Lerner, 1984). In one experiment, for example, English-speaking Canadian students who had just inadvertently caused an accident in a psychologist's laboratory were asked to respond to opinions expressed by a French-speaking Canadian. In contrast to students who did not commit the transgression, these students responded in ways that suggested a rejection of equal status and an endorsement of favored treatment for English-speaking Canadians.

Views of the In-Group and Out-Group

In intergroup relations, the in-group's views often serve as a reference point by which an out-group is judged. This phenomenon is known as **ethnocentrism**. As originally defined by the sociologist William Sumner in 1906, ethnocentrism is the "view of things in which one's own group is the center of everything, and all others are scaled and rated with reference to it" (quoted in Brewer, 1986, p. 88). In a descriptive passage, Sumner goes on to say: "Each group nourishes its own pride and vanity, boasts itself superior, exalts its own divinities, and looks with contempt on outsiders. Each group thinks its own folkways the only right ones, and if it observes that other groups have other folkways, these excite its scorn" (quoted in Brewer, 1986, p. 88).

Many behaviors were associated with ethnocentrism, in Sumner's view, as summarized in Table 16-2. For the in-group, the evaluations are positive and the behaviors indicate loyalty to the group goals. Values and behaviors in regard to the out-group, in marked contrast, indicate negative evaluations, rejection, and fear.

Subsequent research has shown ethnocentrism to be somewhat more complex than Sumner so elo-

Table 16–2 Facets of ethnocentrism

Orientations toward In-Group	Orientations toward Out-Group
See selves as virtuous and superior	See out-group as contemptible, immoral, and inferior
See own standards of value as universal, intrinsically true	Rejection of out-group values
See selves as strong	See out-group as weak
Sanctions against theft	Sanctions for theft
Sanctions against murder	Sanctions for murder
Cooperative relations with other group members	Absence of cooperation
Obedience to authorities	Absence of obedience
Willingness to retain membership in group	Rejection of membership
Willingness to fight and die for group	Virtue in killing out-group members in warfare
	Maintenance of social distance
	Negative affect, hate
	Use as bad examples in training children
	Blame for in-group troubles
	Distrust and fear

quently described it. Sometimes there is a decided in-group bias, reflecting Sumner's position. Cross-cultural studies, for example, have shown that there appears to be a universal tendency to view one's own group as morally superior and more worthy of trust (Brewer, 1986). On other dimensions, however, in-groups do not describe the out-group in more negative terms than those they use to describe themselves (Brewer, 1986; Tajfel, 1982). In some cases, members of an in-group recognize that their own position is less favorable than the out-group's. Rather than deny that distinction, the in-group instead simply chooses to minimize the difference between the two groups, seeing them as less dissimilar than outsiders perhaps would.

Because an in-group recognizes that it is not necessarily better on *all* dimensions, there is often a tendency to choose for comparison those dimensions that favor one's in-group over the out-group. In concluding a discussion of this issue, Brewer accordingly suggests that "perhaps the essence of ethnocentrism is this tendency to expect that the out-group will share the in-group's definition of the conflict or distinction between them and will be willing to make comparisons in terms that favor the in-group" (1986, p. 101).

Ethnocentric views lead not only to negative evaluations of an out-group but also to biased explanations for their actions. As a general rule, group members are guilty of what Thomas Pettigrew (1979) has termed the ultimate attribution error (recall discussions in Chapter Four). In this pattern, in-group members attribute their own desirable behaviors to internal and stable factors while citing transitory factors to explain desirable behaviors of the out-group. Just the reverse pattern is evidenced when undesirable behaviors are at issue.

Members of different groups also offer different explanations for their basis of differentiation. Students at two universities in Hong Kong, for example, offered different explanations for the differences between their two schools (Hewstone, Bond, & Wan, 1983). Asked to explain why graduates of Hong Kong University are placed more highly in the city's work force, Hong Kong University students suggested that they were more adaptable to the needs of Hong Kong society, whereas students at the Chinese University of Hong Kong believed that Hong Kong students had more connections that outweighed simple merit.

In Great Britain, Hewstone and Jaspars (1982) asked both Black (mostly West Indian) and White male working-class adolescents to answer questions about race-related situations. For example, one item on the questionnaire stated: "Many more Black people than White people get arrested on suspicion charges." The boys were then asked to what degree this situation (a true one) was the result of (1) Black people's making more trouble than White people and (2) the police's being racist. Other questions dealt with unemployment rates, proportion of managerial jobs, and educational opportunities. Black subjects tended very strongly to see White representatives of "the system" as the chief cause of racial discrimination. White subjects tended to divide the blame evenly, although they saw Blacks as more responsible and Whites as less responsible than the Black subjects did.

In Chapter Eight we discussed forms of power that may be in effect between two individuals. In intergroup relations, issues of power also come into play (Apfelbaum, 1979). Often, though not always, two groups confront each other with different levels of power and potential influence or with different kinds of power. In labor/management conflicts, for example, management typically has the financial resources, but labor can shut down operations. Unequal power has certain effects on each of the groups in question, perhaps more notably on the group with lesser power. Often the group with lesser power is more aware of the power and status differentials (Tajfel, 1982).

Early in the study of intergroup relations, Kurt Lewin observed that "the privileged group . . . usually offers its members more and hinders them less than does the less privileged group," further noting that "the member of the underprivileged group is more hampered by his group belongingness" (quoted in Apfelbaum, 1979, pp. 194–195). More recent research has suggested that differences in status between two groups will increase the tendency in both groups toward in-group bias—particularly if the difference in status is perceived as unreasonable or illegitimate (Tajfel, 1982). Thus power differences between groups may affect one's perceptions both of one's own group and of the other group, typically accentuating actual differences that exist between two interacting groups.

Strategies of Interaction

Groups can deal with each other in many ways. The situation itself may foster certain approaches; for example, certain situations encourage cooperation between groups, while others, where resources are limited, engender competition. Often groups approach situations with very different goals in mind, and one group's success may mean the other group's failure. In such situations, negotiation and bargaining often become necessary, aimed at resolving conflicts in such a way that both groups will be at least partly satisfied with the outcome. Groups cannot always resolve their conflicts, however, and sometimes a third party must be brought into the situation to work for a resolution.

In this section we will discuss these various strategies of interaction. Some of the studies of these strategies and processes have been done with a minimal situation—with two-person "groups," called dyads. Yet, even though these studies do not match the complexity of intergroup relations, they can point out some fundamental aspects of the interaction process.

Cooperation and Competition

Cooperation and competition are two very different approaches to interaction, whether we are considering the interaction between two individuals or two groups. **Cooperation** can be defined as working together for mutual benefit. **Competition,** in contrast, is activity directed toward achieving a goal that only one of the persons or groups can obtain.

Whether an individual or group chooses to cooperate or to compete depends in large part on the *reward structures* inherent in the situation. Reward structures are characteristics of the situation that "set the stage," influencing the kinds of actions that will be taken. There are three basic types of reward structures: a cooperative reward structure, a competitive reward structure, and an individualistic reward structure.

In the **cooperative reward structure,** the goals of the situation are linked so that one individual or group can attain its goals only if the other individuals or groups attain theirs. (Morton Deutsch, 1973, has used the term *promotive interdependence* to describe this kind of situation.) In the contrasting **competitive reward structure,** the participants' goals are negatively linked, so that success by one party necessarily means failure for the other. (Deutsch's term for this situation is *contrient interdependence*.) More graphically describing the distinction between these two situations, Deutsch has stated: "In a cooperative situation the goals are so linked that everybody 'sinks or swims' together, while in the competitive situation if one swims, the other must sink" (1973, p. 20). A third type of reward structure, the **individualistic reward structure,** operates when individual or group goals are independent of one another—that is, what one group does has no influence on what the other group does.

The distinctions among these three kinds of reward structures may be clearer if we shift to the familiar situation of the college classroom and grading procedures. If a professor announces that grades will be determined on a curve, and that 15% of students will receive A's no matter what the absolute scores are, that professor is setting up a competitive reward structure. The success of one student in attaining an A actually decreases the chances that another student will receive an A. An even stronger example—and a more competitive reward structure—is the case in which the professor says that only one A will be given. The professor might set up a cooperative reward structure by developing team projects. In this case, the professor might say that grades were dependent on the group's efforts—if the group did well, everyone in the group would get an A, and if the group did poorly, everyone in the group would suffer accordingly. Finally, as an example of the individualistic reward structure, the professor might say, "I reward competent work. If you complete your assignments successfully, you will receive an A. There are no curves or quotas; in fact, I would be happy to see all of you produce high-quality work and receive A's." In this case students' outcomes are not interdependent, since reward attainment by one has no effect on the probability of reward attainment by another.

The prevailing reward structure can sharply alter the behavior of people in a situation. Some researchers, convinced of the advantages of cooperation, have tried to alter reward structures in some public schools. In one case, there was a concern about the consequences of racially integrating the schools in Austin, Texas. Attempting to avoid a situation in which minority students would become one separate group and White students another, competing for the same rewards, Elliot Aronson and his colleagues developed the *jigsaw method* of learning (Aronson et al., 1978).

In one demonstration, fifth-graders were asked to study the biography of Joseph Pulitzer. In the jigsaw classroom, students were divided into heterogeneous, multiethnic teams. Each child on the team was given one section of the material on Pulitzer and, after mastering it, had to teach it to the others in the group. Thus, each child depended on others in the group for parts of the "jigsaw."

In studies conducted over six-week periods, the jigsaw method was compared with traditional classrooms run by teachers identified as good teachers by their colleagues (to put the jigsaw method to the hardest test). The experiments were preceded by workshops to train teachers and by "team building" exercises to help students put aside their competitive motives. The teams met for about 40–45 minutes a day, at least three times a week.

At the end of the six-week period, comparisons between jigsaw classes and control classes showed the following results: (1) jigsaw students grew to like their groupmates, (2) Anglo and Black children, although not Mexican-Americans, developed more favorable attitudes toward school, (3) students' self-esteem increased, (4) Black and Mexican-American students tended to master more material, while Anglo students did no worse in the jigsaw classes than in traditional ones, and (5) children in the jigsaw groups were more likely to express cooperative attitudes and to see their classmates as learning resources. Thus the jigsaw method changed the reward structure in the class, substituting a cooperative goal for what might have been intergroup rivalry.

Competitive reward structures, in contrast, foster intergroup rivalry. A graphic example of these consequences is seen in the classic field study at Robber's Cave conducted by Muzafer Sherif and his associates (Sherif, 1966; Sherif et al., 1961).

The boys at Robber's Cave were a normal group of 11- and 12-year-olds attending a summer camp and taking part in its typical swimming, hiking, and camping-out activities. What was different about this camp—and what the boys did not know—was that it was staffed by researchers who observed their behavior and specifically structured the situation. Two groups of boys were brought to separate cabins on the first day of camp, unaware that the other group existed. To develop cohesiveness within each group, the researchers planned activities that required the boys to cooperate for mutual benefit (for example, camping out or cleaning up a beach). The boys soon came to recognize one another's strengths and weaknesses; leaders emerged on the basis of their contributions to the group. Each group developed a name for itself (the "Rattlers" and the "Eagles"), group jokes, standards for behavior, and sanctions for those who "got out of line." Thus, during this phase, the reward structure between groups was essentially an individualistic one: what one group did had no effect on the other group—in fact, each group was totally unaware of the other's existence.

Then the researchers shifted to a competitive reward structure. They created intergroup conflict by bringing the two groups together and creating situations in which only one group would win—for example, by setting up tournaments with desirable prizes for only one group. When the groups were brought together for this series of contests, fair play was replaced by an ethic akin to that of the former Green Bay Packer coach Vince Lombardi: "Winning isn't everything, it's the only thing." The groups began to call each other derogatory names, pick fights, and raid each other's camp. "Rattlers" downgraded all "Eagles," and vice versa, to the extent that neither group desired further contact with the other group. Muzafer Sherif remarked that a neutral observer who had no knowledge of what had happened would have assumed that the boys were "wicked, disturbed and vicious bunches of youngsters" (1966, p 58).

We will return to the boys of Robber's Cave later. For the moment, however, it is important to point out how easily intergroup conflict can begin. Competitive reward structures often foster the development of such conflict, mandating that rewards given to one group will automatically be unavailable to the other. The social psychologist Morton Deutsch (1973), who has extensively studied the workings of cooperative and competitive groups, has identified three likely consequences of the competitive situation.

First, communication between competitive groups is unreliable and impoverished. Available communication channels either are not used or are used in a way to deliberately mislead the other group. Consequently, neither group trusts the information it receives from the other.

Second, perceptions of the other group are distorted, as the discussion of in-groups and out-groups suggested. Groups see their own behavior toward the other group as benevolent while viewing the actions of the other group as hostile and ill intentioned. Suspicion of the other's motives may lead in turn to negative responses to any request made by the other group and to a greater willingness to exploit the other group's needs.

Finally, groups in competition develop the belief that the only way to resolve the conflict is for one side to impose a solution through the use of superior force. Each side tries to enhance its own power and minimize the legitimacy of the other group. In this process, the scope of the conflict is often expanded, moving from a specific issue to a concern with moral principles and general superiority.

On the surface, it sounds easy to avoid intergroup conflict: simply substitute a cooperative reward structure for a competitive one, and groups will work in harmony. But the solution is not that simple. Often there is a real conflict between group interests, as a shortage of resources makes it impossible for both groups to achieve what they want. In industry, labor unions often want higher wages, while managers want to lower costs. In warfare, both nations may want a single piece of territory. In other cases, religious or cultural values may be inherently contradictory. In fact, most conflicts between groups involve elements of both cooperation and competition—the parties must cooperate with each other in order to achieve at least a portion of their own goals. (Such interactions are often called *mixed-motive* interactions.) Bargaining and negotiation become the means for attempting resolution and compromise.

Bargaining and Negotiation

Bargaining and *negotiation* are terms that are used often, both in conversation and in media reports. We may talk about bargaining with a car dealer for a good price, for example, or reporters may keep us abreast of the latest negotiations in the Mideast. Although there is some tendency to use the term *bargaining* when we talk about interactions between individuals and *negotiation* when we talk about larger social units, such as unions or nations, we will consider the terms interchangeable. **Bargaining** (or negotiation) is defined as "the process whereby two or more parties attempt to settle what each shall give and take, or perform and receive, in a transaction between them" (Rubin & Brown, 1975, p. 2).

The core of a bargaining relationship is that at least two parties are involved and that the interests of these two parties conflict with regard to one or more issues (Rubin & Brown, 1975). In labor/management negotiations, for example, the two parties may disagree on a number of issues—wages, fringe benefits, hours, or job security, to name only a few.

To begin to negotiate, both parties must voluntarily enter into the bargaining relationship. If one group refuses to negotiate, then no bargaining can take place. If a teacher's union goes on strike, for example, but the board of education refuses to hear the union's demands, then intergroup conflict is at a stalemate, and bargaining cannot begin (see Box 16–1 for two perspectives on strikes).

Once both parties have agreed to negotiate, the give-and-take process of bargaining can begin. If the issues that separate the two parties are numerous, the bargaining process can be extremely complex, although the stages in the process may be predictable. Dean Pruitt (1981, p. 14) has listed six steps in the negotiating process:

1. Agreement about the need to negotiate.
2. Agreement on a set of objectives and principles (for example, in arms-control negotiations, the principle that the agreement should permit neither side to coerce the other).
3. Agreement on certain rules of conduct.
4. Defining the issues and setting up an agenda.
5. Agreement on a formula (in other words, agreement in principle).
6. Agreement on implementing details.

Reflecting on examples of international negotiation, such as those in the Mideast or those conducted at the end of the Vietnam War, one can recall incidents that marked the bargaining at each of these stages.

A variety of activities take place during the course of bargaining (Rubin & Brown, 1975). Each side presents demands or proposals, which in turn are evaluated by the other party. Often counterproposals

Box 16–1
Two perspectives on strikes

How do strikes affect labor and management? In this classic consequence of intergroup conflict, both groups have a stake in reaching the best agreement. Two studies give us some information about the effects of a strike on the perceptions of each side.

The U.S. auto industry has a coordinated collective bargaining arrangement, whereby a strike is conducted at only one of the "big three" automakers (Ford, General Motors, and Chrysler) but the agreement reached in that settlement is generally applicable to all three companies. The existence of such an arrangement allowed the psychologists Ross Stagner and Boaz Eflal (1982) to conduct a quasi-experimental study of the effects of a strike on attitudes of union members, comparing workers at the plant that went on strike with those at the plants that did not. Actually being on strike made a substantial difference. Strikers evaluated both their union and their leadership more positively than nonstrikers did, and they were more willing to engage in union activities. During the strike, the striking workers showed more militant and negative attitudes toward management; after the strike, they were more satisfied with the settlement package. Thus actual involvement in the strike intensified positive attitudes toward the in-group and negative attitudes toward the out-group, demonstrating some of the effects of intergroup conflict that we discussed earlier.

What does management think about strikes? We do not have a parallel study that considers attitudes of management toward workers. However, a study by Shirom (1982) gives us some insight into the reactions of managers to a strike settlement and their beliefs about its "goodness" as a resolution of the conflict. In this study, Shirom questioned 51 management negotiators, each of whom had been involved in a strike in which at least 100 workers participated. Under what conditions did the managers think the strike had been advantageous to their side? Two factors stood out: the size of the striking work force and the ability of management to keep the plant in operation during the strike. With a large work force or with continued operation, managers tended to rate the settlement as advantageous. Perhaps surprisingly, the duration of the strike, which should be related to costs, did not appear to influence managers' opinions.

Both of these studies indicate that the outcome of bargaining is not totally objective. Although it is possible to make objective statements about dollars or territories, reactions to agreements have a strong psychological component as well.

---

follow, accompanied perhaps by some concessions, and the process is characterized by a sequence of such exchanges. Usually there is some division or exchange of resources. For example, in a labor/management dispute, labor may agree to accept a somewhat lower wage increase in return for greater job security.

Although the basic bargaining process can be described rather simply, a great many factors affect its outcome, and social scientists have invested considerable effort in the attempt to understand more about particular characteristics of the bargaining process. (For summaries of this work, see Miller & Crandall, 1980; Pruitt, 1981; Rubin & Brown, 1975). Let us look at just some of the factors that can play a part in this complex process.

The nature of the demands that each party makes—both their size and their timing—can affect the ultimate outcome of the bargaining process. If an agreement is eventually reached, the party that makes larger initial demands and smaller concessions generally achieves a larger outcome (Pruitt, 1981). However, if both parties make lower initial demands and faster concessions, resolution is usually achieved more rapidly. There are some exceptions to this seemingly obvious statement. If one party makes extremely low demands or concedes very quickly, agreement is more difficult to reach (Bartos, 1974; Hamner, 1974). Presumably the other party in this case decides that it will do much better to sit and wait for additional concessions, without feeling a need to make any concessions of its own (Pruitt, 1981).

In formal bargaining situations, each group is often represented by one selected individual, who is termed the *representative bargainer*. For example, the union president may represent the total union membership, and management may similarly appoint one individual to represent the broader management group. In general, studies of this process show that representative bargainers are more competitive, make smaller concessions, and are less likely to reach agreements than individual bargainers who are representing only themselves (Davis, Laughlin, & Komorita, 1976). Surveillance of the representative bargainer by his or her constituents intensifies this effect. In a laboratory study of bargaining, some bargainers were told that their behavior would be constantly observed by the "owner" of the company, who was seated behind a one-way mirror (Carnevale, Pruitt, & Britton, 1979). In other cases, bargainers were told that the "owners" would receive only a final report on the negotiated agreement. Surveillance made a difference. When they believed they were being observed, bargainers made more statements about their own role, made more threats and putdowns of the other negotiator, and were less likely to indicate an understanding of the other bargainer's priorities. Surveillance affected not only the behavior of the bargainers but the outcome of the negotiations as well. Bargainers under surveillance settled for lower profits than bargainers who were not being observed.

Accountability to one's constituents can have similar effects. Knowing that one is accountable may make a bargainer reluctant to give in, fearing to be perceived as a loser by the constituency. "Saving face" becomes more important than achieving a good agreement (Brown, 1977). Bargainers who are held accountable engage in more pressure tactics and gain lower outcomes (Carnevale, Pruitt, & Seilheimer, 1981). Interestingly, however, this pattern holds only when the bargainers have face-to-face contact with each other. Perhaps the greater range of nonverbal communication possible in the face-to-face situation (see Chapter Five) creates stronger messages of dominance and thus impedes the bargaining process.

Many other factors can affect the bargaining process. The personalities of individual bargainers, for example, may facilitate or hinder the process (see Rubin & Brown, 1975). Different kinds of strategies and different types of communication will alter the process as well (Putnam & Jones, 1982). Events external to the bargainers themselves that create stress and tension make bargaining more difficult and outcomes less favorable (Hopmann & Walcott, 1977). Publicity in the mass media, for example, can "leak" critical information, narrowing bargainers' options.

At least two general kinds of agreements can be reached in a bargaining process (Pruitt, 1982). In the *compromise*, both parties concede to a middle ground on some obvious dimension. For example, if the teacher's union wants salaries of $20,000 a year and the school board initially offers $16,000, a settlement of $18,000 would represent a compromise agreement. Alternatively, compromise agreements may involve trade-offs, whereby one party concedes in one area while the other concedes in another. For example, the school board might hold fast on salaries while agreeing to the teachers' demands for job security.

A second type of agreement is the **integrative agreement,** one that reconciles both parties' interests and thus yields a high payoff for both groups. In general, the basis for integrative agreements is less obvious initially and may require the development of new alternatives. In this respect, integrative agreements are like creative problem solving (Pruitt, 1982). Both compromise and integrative agreements have been termed "win/win" outcomes (Filley, 1975), in that both parties in the conflict may gain in the eventual resolution.

Third-Party Intervention

Conflicting groups frequently fail to reach an agreement. In such cases, a third party is often sought to reconcile or to mediate their differences. **Mediation** is defined as "third-party assistance to two or more disputing parties who are trying to reach agreement" (Pruitt & Kressel, 1985, p. 1). Mediators are found in divorce courts, labor-management negotiations, and community disputes, and the technique of mediation is increasingly being put to use. Mediators even have a professional association, the Society for Professionals in Dispute Resolution, which was founded in 1973 (Pruitt & Kressel, 1985).

Once mediation is expected, the bargaining process often slows down. In what has been described as a "chilling effect," bargainers tend to resist making additional concessions until the third party has arrived. Why should this happen? One speculation is that the bargaining groups, hesitant to lose face, resist making final concessions until the mediator has arrived, at which point an external attribution will be available. More practically, some have suggested that bargaining groups expect an arbitrator to "split the difference"—hence any advance weakening of their position will make their final settlement less. Both of these reasons may help to explain why movement toward an agreement when third-party intervention is expected is slower when the conflict of interest is large rather than small (Hiltrop & Rubin, 1982)—there is less "face" to be lost and more payoff to be gained by moving slowly.

Mediation is unlikely to be effective when the relationship between the two bargaining groups is poor. Nor are the chances for successful resolution very high when resources are scarce. Under such conditions, the likelihood of finding a mutually acceptable compromise is not very high. Conversely, mediation is most likely to be successful when both parties are highly motivated to settle the case and when they are committed to the mediation process. And in general, clients are likely to be satisfied with the mediation process, as most studies show satisfaction rates of 75% or higher (Kressel & Pruitt, 1985).

To create pressure toward agreement, a successful mediator needs to possess certain characteristics and to adopt particular strategies. Primary among the personal characteristics are trustworthiness and perceived ability (Rubin & Brown, 1975)—traits that have been found to be effective source characteristics in research on attitude change (see Chapter Seven). Deborah Kolb (1985) suggests that successful mediators use specific techniques of impression management, such as those discussed in Chapter Three. Thus the mediator attempts to convey an impression of legitimacy, of social position, and of expertise in order to gain the confidence of both parties and to win acceptance for the proposed solution. A good mediator will also tailor tactics to the particular situational demands, consistent with interaction principles introduced by contingency theories of leadership (Chapter Fifteen). A mediator may approach a group that is experiencing considerable hostility, for example, with humor and rather directive tactics; nondirective techniques, in contrast, will be used when bargainers are inexperienced and lack expertise (Carnevale & Pegnetter, 1985). In summary, there is no single set of mediation tactics that guarantees success.

Reduction of Intergroup Conflict

Bargaining and negotiation are formal procedures that may be used to reduce intergroup conflict when both parties recognize the disagreement and are willing to enter into negotiations in order to resolve the conflict. These procedures work best when specific issues can be defined and the parties are interested in resolving those issues.

Other cases of intergroup conflict are less easily resolved (see Box 16–2). Sometimes the issues are not capable of being limited in such a way that bargaining may proceed. At other times the groups may have no formal relationship with each other, so that specific negotiation is very difficult. In the case of Black/White relations in the United States, for example, intergroup conflict is both less defined and more general than a bargaining situation could handle.

For those concerned with intergroup relations, it is important to identify situations that will prevent conflict as well as to develop means for its reduction. In this section we will consider a variety of principles and procedures that have been found effective in decreasing intergroup conflict.

Superordinate Goals

When we left the boys at Robber's Cave, they were "wicked, disturbed and vicious"—the outcome of a competitive reward structure that had been fashioned by the researchers. These investigators did not wish to let the state of intergroup conflict persist, and they tried by a variety of methods to reduce the hostilities (Sherif, 1966; Sherif et al., 1961). Several strategies were tried and found wanting. The boys attended religious services that emphasized love and cooperation, but this appeal to moral values did not stop them from going right back to their warlike strategies when the services ended. Introduction of a third group, which served as "a common enemy," only widened

> **Box 16-2**
> Intergroup conflict in Northern Ireland
>
> The centuries-old conflict between Ireland and Britain has pitted both political factions and religious denominations against each other. The division of Ireland in 1921 into the predominantly Catholic southern Republic of Ireland and the predominantly Protestant Northern Ireland etched those differences more sharply. Northern Ireland is among the poorest of countries, plagued by poverty, unemployment, and poor housing (Trew & McWhirter, 1982).
>
> The modern era of conflict in Northern Ireland is often dated from 1969, when reactions to housing discrimination led to riots and the subsequent intervention of the British Army. According to statistics collected between 1969 and 1976, more than 1500 people were killed and another 17,800 injured in the fighting. Terrorism has become a major issue (Alexander & O'Day, 1984).
>
> Whether one is Protestant or Catholic, one's religious affiliation is a source of social identity in Northern Ireland. As we discussed earlier, visible signs, such as sex and race, facilitate in-group/out-group distinctions. In Northern Ireland, the basis of distinguishing Catholic from Protestant is more subtle, and outsiders find it difficult initially to make the distinctions. Group identity cues include surnames, location of residence, and school attended. Using only these three pieces of information, both Protestant and Catholic students in Ulster (Northern Ireland) agreed on the categorization of individuals described to them (Stringer & Cook, 1985).
>
> Northern Ireland is a dramatic arena for exploring many aspects of intergroup relations (Heskin, 1980). The level of stress experienced by many people of this country is more intense than that found in less turbulent areas, and the tests of effective strategies for reducing intergroup conflict are more demanding. Certainly the country presents a challenge for those who would try to understand and to improve the state of intergroup relations.

the scope of conflict. Conferences between the leaders of the two groups were rejected, because concessions by the leaders would be interpreted by their followers as traitorous sellouts of the groups' interests. Intergroup contact under pleasant circumstances, such as going to the movies or shooting off fireworks on the Fourth of July, only provided more opportunities for the expression of hostility.

The resolution of this conflict was finally made possible through the introduction of a **superordinate goal**—an important goal that could be achieved only through cooperation. First, the researchers arranged for a breakdown in the water-supply line. The boys joined forces in order to find the leak, but they resumed their conflict when the crisis had passed. The researchers then instigated a series of such joint efforts to achieve a superordinate goal: the groups pooled their money to rent a movie, and they used a rope to pull and start the food-supply truck. As a cumulative effect of these joint projects, the groups became friendlier with each other, began to see strengths in each other, and developed friendships across group lines. In fact, the majority of the boys chose to return home on the same bus, and the group that had won $5 as a prize used the money to treat the other group.

One thing that a superordinate goal does is to change the salient group identity. Rather than identifying themselves as "Rattlers" or "Eagles," the boys at Robber's Cave presumably began to think of themselves as members of a common group. Within the laboratory, Roderick Kramer and Marilynn Brewer (1984) have shown that people are more cooperative when a superordinate group identity is emphasized than when differentiating group memberships are stressed.

An important element in the effectiveness of

superordinate goals is the success of the group in achieving that goal. Groups with a previous history of competition who work together on a project and fail may like each other less than they did before work on the superordinate project began. As Stephen Worchel cautions "anyone wishing to reduce intergroup conflict through intergroup cooperation must pay careful attention to the conditions surrounding the cooperative encounter" (1986, p. 297).

Intergroup Contact

Can simple contact between two groups lead to improvement of intergroup relations? Many people have made the optimistic assumption that if two racial or religious groups could be brought together, the antagonism often expressed by each group toward the other would erode, and positive attitudes would develop. This, in essence, is the **intergroup contact hypothesis**.

The optimism expressed by this hypothesis needs to be qualified. Contact between groups does not always reduce conflict; on some occasions, intergroup contact can result in increased antagonism. If outcomes are to be positive, a number of conditions need to be met (Amir, 1976; Cook, 1970; Miller & Brewer, 1984; Stephan, 1985). First, the situation needs to provide what can be called acquaintance potential. In other words, people need to have the opportunity actually to interact with one another, and thus to discover that some of their beliefs may have been in error. Casual or superficial contact—such as between two persons who work on the same floor of a building but have no real interaction—has little effect on intergroup attitudes.

Second, the interaction must provide disconfirming information about the negative traits believed to be characteristic of the other group. If one has contact with a typical or representative member of the other group who simply confirms the stereotypes that were held, then positive change is unlikely (Wilder, 1984).

Third, the relative status of participants in a contact situation is important. Positive change is more likely to occur when members of the two groups occupy the same social status. In other words, equal status implies equal power among the people who interact (Ramirez, 1977). In the school setting, for example, Albert Ramirez (in press) has found that Chicano high school students report much less prejudice and discrimination when Chicanos occupy some of the leadership positions in the school than when administrative positions are dominated by Anglos.

The importance of equal status has been demonstrated even in the laboratory. In one such experiment, two groups first worked separately on a task and then joined with each other for work on a cooperative task (Norvell & Worchel, 1981). To examine the effect of "historical" status differences, the experimenters created two conditions. In one condition both groups were told that they had done equally well on the first task, so that they had equal status. In the other condition both groups were told that one of the groups (group *A*) had done better on the first task, so that the two groups had unequal status. In the second, cooperative phase of the experiment, the researchers introduced an additional factor. In half of the cases in which a winner had been declared, the experimenters gave additional information to the other group (group *B*), thus redressing the balance of their status. Similarly, in half of the cases in which no winner had been declared, the experimenters gave additional information to members of one of the subgroups—information that would be useful in performance on the second task—thus creating a new imbalance in their relative power within the larger group. How did these manipulations of status affect people's liking for members of the other group? Figure 16–4 provides the answers.

In the no-winner/no-additional-information condition, equal status increased attraction to members of the other group. In contrast, when an "historical imbalance" existed (based on the previous group experience), it was necessary to restore the balance between the two groups in order for greater attraction to result. One other interesting finding that emerged from the study concerned perceptions of fairness. None of the groups felt that it was particularly fair for the experimenter to provide additional information to one of the groups during the second, cooperative task, even if the purpose was to rebalance the status difference between the two groups. Yet this perception of unfairness did not prevent members from changing their perceptions of the out-group, as Figure 16–4 shows. Norvell and Worchel (1981) speculate that affirmative action programs may have similar effects: although members of the in-group do not see affirmative action programs as fair, the increased contact that results from such programs may lead to more positive intergroup attitudes.

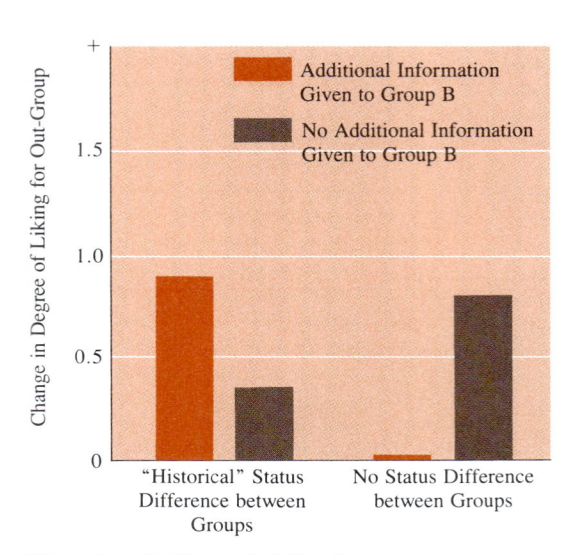

Figure 16–4 Change in liking for an out-group as a function of previous status difference between groups and additional information provided to one of the groups

Investigators today are generally far more cautious about claiming positive effects for the intergroup contact hypothesis than they were 25 years ago. As Tajfel (1982) has stated, the change may reflect a "loss of innocence." Intergroup contact can have positive or negative results, depending on the conditions that surround the contact. Equal status, a need for cooperation, a social climate that favors intergroup contact, and rewards from the contact itself all work to support the intergroup contact hypothesis. In contrast, situations that foster competition, produce frustration, or emphasize status differences between the participants tend to strengthen rather than reduce prejudice between two groups.

Reduction of Threat

In the area of international relations, interactions between major powers—for example, the United States and the Soviet Union—deal not at the level of individual contact but rather at the level of the perceived balance of power between the nations. Considering the arms race in particular, we can search for a strategy to reduce this particular form of intergroup conflict. The psychologist Charles Osgood (1966, 1974) has offered one such strategy, which he terms **GRIT**—standing for "graduated and reciprocated initiatives in tension reduction." The basic principles of this strategy are as follows:

1. Set the atmosphere for conciliation by stating your intention to reduce tension through subsequent acts, indicating the advantages for the other party in reciprocating.
2. Publicly announce each unilateral initiative in advance, indicating that it is part of a general strategy.
3. With each announcement, invite some form of reciprocation.
4. Carry out each initiative as announced, without requiring reciprocation.
5. Continue the initiatives for some time, even in the absence of reciprocation.
6. Make each initiative unambiguous and open to verification.
7. Initiatives should be risky and vulnerable to exploitation, but they should not reduce the capacity to retaliate with nuclear weapons if an attack is launched.
8. Also maintain capacity to retaliate with conventional arms.
9. Once the other party begins to reciprocate, the initiator should reciprocate as well, exposing itself to at least as much, or slightly more, vulnerability.
10. Diversify unilateral initiatives by type of action and geographical location.

Osgood's GRIT strategy is based on a belief that the arms race must be deescalated. His recommended procedure is a gradual one, with the initiating party maintaining strength while gradually reducing the level of conflict. During the initial stages of this sequence, the aim is to put pressure on the target party, both through one's own actions and, presumably, through a buildup of world public support. Later stages in the sequence (for example, steps 4, 5, and 6) are intended to establish an image of credibility and predictability. Later stages—assuming the initial stages are successful—incorporate a mixture of resistance and yielding.

The ultimate success of this model cannot be tested experimentally; it must await the actions of world leaders. Nonetheless, considerable laboratory experimentation has supported the validity of many of the points (Lindskold, 1986). Laboratory research also suggests, however, that participants in intense conflict are often reluctant to use conciliatory techniques, preferring to rely on threat instead (Deutsch, Canavan, & Rubin, 1971). If we may generalize from such research to the current world situation, it seems unlikely that GRIT will be adopted as a means of managing conflict.

Summary

Intergroup behavior occurs whenever individuals belonging to one group interact, collectively or individually, with another group or its members in terms of their group identification. Examples of intergroup behavior are numerous, including ethnic relations, labor/management negotiations, and international conflict.

Prejudice refers to an intolerant attitude toward a group of people; *discrimination* refers to specific unfair behaviors toward members of that group.

Racism is a particular form of prejudice and discrimination, directed toward an ethnic group. Although overt discrimination on the basis of race has been reduced, racism still is expressed in symbolic forms. Attitudes toward minority groups and the opportunities available to them are influenced by belief similarity and by endorsement of the dominant ideology that relates hard work to rewards.

Sexism is a similar form of prejudice, but in this case the behavior is directed against a person by virtue of gender rather than race. Prejudice toward women is related to stereotypic beliefs about the characteristics that men and women typically possess. Much more than Blacks and other groups, however, women are widely perceived to suffer discrimination.

Many theories have attempted to explain prejudice. These theories, differing in their level of analysis and the factors considered relevant, emphasize historical and economic factors, sociocultural factors, situational factors, psychodynamic characteristics, phenomenological perceptions, and the earned reputation of the target group.

Cognitive principles of categorization explain some of the phenomena that characterize in-group/out-group relations. In-groups and out-groups have predictable views of one another, demonstrating an ethnocentrism that emphasizes the moral superiority of the in-group and the failings and danger of the out-group.

There are three basic types of reward structures: cooperative, competitive, and individualistic. Competitive reward structures are most apt to lead to intergroup conflict.

Bargaining is a process used to reduce conflict and resolve differences between groups. A variety of conditions can affect the outcome of the bargaining process, including the timing and size of demands, the accountability of a representative bargainer to his or her constituents, and surveillance by the constituency. Often a third party must be called in when bargaining parties cannot resolve their differences.

Numerous strategies have been used to reduce or avoid intergroup conflict. Establishing a *superordinate goal* is one such strategy. The *intergroup contact hypothesis* suggests that simple contact will reduce antagonism. Research has suggested that the contact process is more complicated, and its success depends on a variety of factors.

GRIT (graduated and reciprocated initiatives in tension reduction) is one strategy that has been suggested for the problem of arms control.

Glossary Terms

bargaining
competition
competitive reward structure

cooperation
cooperative reward structure
discrimination
ethnocentrism
GRIT
individualistic reward structure
integrative agreement
intergroup behavior
intergroup contact hypothesis
mediation
prejudice
racism
scapegoating
sexism
stereotype
superordinate goal
symbolic racism

We shape our buildings and afterwards our buildings shape us.
Winston Churchill

Living organisms never submit passively to the impact of environmental forces.
René Dubos

Jeffrey Blankfort, Jeroboam, Inc.

CHAPTER SEVENTEEN

Interpersonal Behavior & the Physical Environment

This chapter was written by Eric Sundstrom.

I. Ambient Environment
    Temperature
    Noise
    Air Pollution
    Illumination
II. Settings for Conversation
    Pleasant Places
    Seating Arrangements
    Psychological Barriers
    Layout of Classrooms
III. Architecture and Interaction
    Proximity and Attraction
    Residential Design and Social Overload
    Overload in Open-Space Schools
IV. Privacy
    Theories of Privacy
    Privacy in Open-Plan Offices
V. Crowding
    Crowding and Social Pathology
    Models of Crowding
VI. Attachment to Places
    Territories
    Home Environments
    Workplaces
    Neighborhoods
    Public Spaces
VII. Summary

*F*or many years philosophers, psychologists, and other experts have debated the effect of the physical environment on human behavior. Some have argued that the climate, the layout of cities, the architecture of buildings, the arrangement of rooms, and other aspects of the environment have a powerful and decisive influence on human behavior. This view has been called **environmental determinism,** or, if it refers just to the influence of buildings, *architectural determinism*. One proponent likened buildings to molds into which organized social processes are cast, and to the "stony skeleton of social life" (Youtz, 1929, p. 60). Social psychologists have also claimed that architecture can influence patterns of social interaction (Festinger, Schachter, & Back, 1950).

Critics of environmental determinism argue that we do not react passively to our physical surroundings but actively mold our settings to suit our purposes or alter our behavior to cope with our environments (Franck, 1984; Lipman, 1969). After all, inert buildings cannot actively influence our behavior. And physical environments are only part of our wider context, so they encompass just a few of the many factors that figure in our perceptions, choices, and decisions. According to these views, physical environments do not determine behavior, but at most have an indirect influence.

This chapter explores theory and evidence concerning connections between physical settings and interpersonal behavior. In the first section we examine the indirect influences of the ambient environment on such behaviors as aggression, altruism, and attraction. The next four sections explore the environment as a context for interpersonal interaction; they discuss the arrangement of rooms for conversation, the importance of physical accessibility in friendships and groups, and the role of physical settings in privacy and crowding. The symbolic aspects of the physical environment are explored next, followed by a discussion of territorial attachment to places.

As a whole, the chapter suggests that the physical environment enters into interpersonal behavior in many ways. Physical settings emerge as sources of stress, contexts for conversation, constraints on personal accessibility, symbols of self-identity and status, sources of distraction, resources for privacy, boundaries around neighborhoods, and more.

Ambient Environment

The **ambient environment** includes some of the most dynamic qualities of the physical setting—temperature, sound, air quality, and light. These aspects of the environment can indirectly influence interpersonal behavior through effects on comfort or mood or through contributions to arousal, stress, or overload.

One possible effect of the ambient environment involves **arousal,** a generalized state of physiological and psychological excitation. Exposure to uncomfortably warm temperatures or to moderately loud noise can increase a person's arousal, at least temporarily (Sundstrom, 1986a). Arousal, in turn, can make people unusually sensitive to certain interpersonal situations (as in the case of aggression, discussed in Chapter Eleven).

Inhospitable ambient conditions, such as very loud noise or extreme heat, can also produce stress. **Stress** is usually defined as a physiological and psychological response to demand, challenge, threat, or adversity, which includes mobilization of capacities for coping (McGrath, 1970; Selye, 1971; Sundstrom, 1986a). Environmental sources of stress are most disturbing when they are intense and uncontrollable (Baum, Singer, & Baum, 1981). The degree of stress produced by the environment, however, depends on the subjective judgment that it threatens comfort or well-being (Cohen, 1980b).

Environmental stress has an important influence on social behavior because the arousal it engenders can lead to overreaction to some social cues and insensitivity to others. Stress can decrease sensitivity to interpersonal cues in at least three ways. First, people under stress sometimes exhibit a *narrowing of attention,* focusing on the cues most salient to their immediate goals and overlooking others (Hockey, 1970; Solly, 1969). Second, a source of stress may create overload, an amount of stimulation or information that exceeds the individual's capacities. To cope with overload a person may set priorities and then ignore the "low-priority inputs" (Milgram, 1970; Miller, 1964). Third, stress may exact a psychic cost through the effort expended in trying to cope, which can diminish an individual's cognitive capacities (Cohen, 1980a).

A pedestrian on a sidewalk, for example, may

experience stress as a consequence of the loud noise from passing traffic, the afternoon heat, the polluted air, and the bustling crowds. In consequence, the pedestrian may overlook or ignore a person nearby who has just dropped a load of packages. The same pedestrian may react with exaggerated anger at an accidental collision with someone walking in the opposite direction.

The impact of environmental stress depends on **adaptation,** or responses that allow organisms to adjust to their environments (Dubos, 1980). One such response is *perceptual adaptation,* a change in perception after continued exposure to an environment (Wohlwill, 1974). Someone who lives near a busy freeway, for example, hears a constant din of passing traffic. It may seem loud at first, but in time becomes part of the background and is no longer consciously noticed. Similarly, most people are unable to smell a strong odor for more than a few seconds. As a result of such adaptation, environmental stressors may seem most intense to newcomers to a physical setting.

Through perceptual adaptation each of us establishes a personal standard for evaluating environments, called an **adaptation level.** The urbanite who visits a suburb, for example, may find it quiet, at least by urban standards. But a visitor from a farm, accustomed to more peaceful surroundings, may experience the same suburb as noisy. Individual standards of comparison, or adaptation levels, develop through continued exposure to an environment (Helson, 1964). Figure 17–1 illustrates the results of a study in which people from different environments

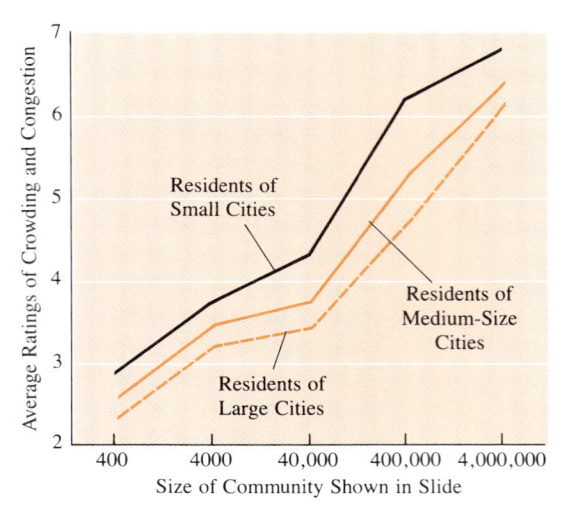

Figure 17–1 Average ratings of crowding and congestion of scenes in communities of different sizes, by residents of small, medium-sized, and large cities.

rated the amount of crowding and congestion depicted in a series of scenes photographed in communities of different sizes. Residents of large cities rated the scenes less crowded than did residents of small cities (Wohlwill & Kohn, 1973).

Despite our ability to adapt to potentially stressful environments, we may still suffer adverse effects from them—the *aftereffects of stressors*—even after the source of stress is gone. One experiment showed that people working in the presence of loud, unpredictable, uncontrollable noise could perform clerical tasks with unimpaired speed and accuracy. When they went to a different, quiet room to work, however, they caught fewer errors in proofreading a manuscript and showed less persistence in a task designed to assess their tolerance for frustration (Glass & Singer, 1972). Later research confirmed the adverse aftereffects of unpredictable, uncontrollable noise, and found that other stressors had similar effects (Cohen, 1980a).

Aftereffects of stressors may indirectly influence interpersonal behavior. Even after an environmental stressor has ceased, insensitivity to social cues, for example, may linger. And because of adaptation, such effects may occur without conscious awareness. So such stressors as heat and noise can have interpersonal effects during and after exposure, perhaps unnoticed by those involved.

Temperature

Heat can create discomfort, arousal, or stress, depending on the ambient temperature, the relative humidity, and other factors (Sundstrom, 1986a). As a consequence of discomfort or mild arousal due to heat, people may react with unusual violence to provocation or frustration (see the discussion in Chapter Eleven).

Research concerning violent crime corroborates the folk wisdom that links high temperatures with aggression. When two geographers reviewed literature on the connection between weather and crime, they found that such studies had been published as early as 1833 (Harries & Stadler, 1983). They analyzed 4,309 cases of aggravated assault reported to the Dallas police from March through October 1980 in conjunction with weather reports from the Dallas–Fort Worth Airport. A daily index of "thermal discomfort" based on ambient temperature and dew point temperature (related to humidity) was significantly correlated with the frequency of aggravated assault in Dallas. Assaults became more frequent as the temperature and humidity climbed. (Assaults were also more frequent on weekends and in the summer.) A similar study of violent crime in Chicago found the rates of criminal assault (homicide, rape, battery, armed robbery) correlated with the ambient temperature. Data from Houston revealed a similar correlation, with rates of murder and rape highest on the hottest days (Anderson & Anderson, 1984). DeFronzo (1984) analyzed aggregate data on seven serious forms of violent crime from the Federal Bureau of Investigation's *Uniform Crime Reports*, along with climatic data from the 142 largest metropolitan areas. Rates of burglary and homicide were modestly but significantly correlated with the number of days of the year when temperatures rose above 90°F.

Rising temperatures may even make drivers more prone to honk their horns. Robert Baron (1976) observed drivers on warm summer days (83°F) and on cooler days as they waited behind a car that remained stopped at an intersection after the light turned green. On warm days, more honking was done by drivers of cars with windows open (which presumably did not have air conditioners operating), and they honked more quickly than on cooler days. Researchers observed drivers in Phoenix, Arizona, behind the car of an accomplice who remained stopped in the one-lane exit of an intersection when the light turned green (Kenrick & MacFarlane, 1986). Observations took place from April through August, when outdoor temperatures sometimes ranged well above 100°F. The researchers used daily records of temperature and humidity to calculate an index of thermal discomfort. As the index rose, drivers honked more quickly, spent more time honking, and honked a greater number of times (see Figure 17–2). The hottest temperatures brought the most honking. At temperatures above 100°F, one-third of drivers who

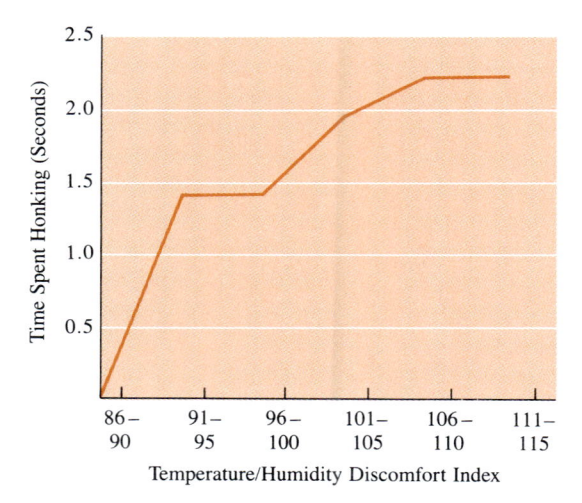

Figure 17–2 Average amount of time drivers spent honking their horns behind a car stopped at a green light in Phoenix, Arizona, as a function of a temperature/humidity discomfort index.

used their horns leaned on them for more than half of the duration of the green light. This never happened at temperatures below 90°F.

Some social psychologists theorized that uncomfortable heat also leads to disliking. In two similar studies, groups of volunteers performed simple tasks for 45 minutes in either a comfortable or "hot" environmental chamber (100°F with 60% relative humidity). They read the dossier of a stranger, including a picture, a biographical sketch, and an attitude scale the stranger had supposedly completed. Participants liked the absent stranger less in the "hot" condition than in the comfortable condition (Griffitt, 1970; Griffitt & Veitch, 1971). Later studies failed to find adverse effects of temperature on liking for a stranger when participants believed the stranger was in the next room and had just given them either a compliment or an insult (Bell & Baron, 1974, 1976).

Other research suggests a **shared stress effect:** people who share stressful environments feel attracted to one another. In an experiment to investigate reactions to an actual person, rather than a hypothetical stranger, in adverse conditions, researchers used loud noise instead of heat as the stressor and exposed volunteers to stressful or comfortable conditions (Kenrick & Johnson, 1979). Half of the participants in each condition indicated how much they liked an actual person in the same room; half responded to a dossier of an absent stranger. Consistent with the shared stress hypothesis, a real person was liked better by participants in the stressful environment than by those who were in the comfortable environment. As in the earlier studies, participants liked the bogus stranger less in stressful conditions than in comfortable ones. (This study lasted less than an hour, so it does not tell us whether the shared stress effect occurs during longer exposures to stressful environments.)

Noise

Noise, or unwanted sound, can influence interpersonal interactions through its capacity to create arousal, stress, or overload (Sundstrom, 1986a). Loud bursts of noise, for example, were found to be associated with physiological arousal, although the effect disappeared within a few minutes through adaptation (Glass & Singer, 1972).

Exposure to loud noise led the participants in a management simulation to assign lower salaries to fictitious applicants for a job (Sauser, Arauz, & Chambers, 1978). Loud noise also decreases the likelihood of altruism. For instance, in a staged incident a pedestrian dropped packages near a construction area during jackhammer noise of varying loudness. Fewer passers-by stopped to help in noisy conditions, especially when the noise was very loud

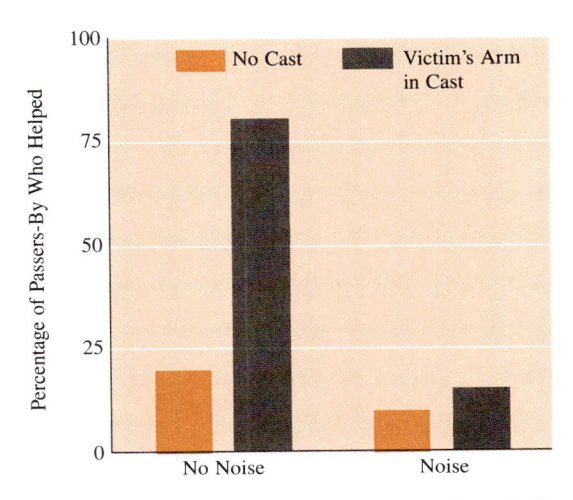

Figure 17-3 Percentage of passers-by stopping to help a pedestrian who had dropped books while either wearing an arm cast or without a cast, in quiet or noisy conditions. Noise apparently deterred altruism and led passers-by to overlook the arm cast.

(Page, 1977). Other studies found similar results (Wiener, 1976; Yinon & Bizman, 1980). Participants in a laboratory study worked on a task while exposed to loud or soft noise. When they finished and began to leave, a student asked for help in a project that involved doing arithmetic. Those exposed to loud noise helped less (Sherrod & Downs, 1974).

Lower rates of altruism in noisy conditions may reflect overload: noise may occupy so much of an individual's attention that little remains for someone who needs help (Cohen, 1978). To test this idea, researchers staged incidents on a city street in which a pedestrian dropped a box of books. In half of the incidents the pedestrian's arm was in a cast. Sometimes a noisy power lawn mower with no muffler was running nearby; at other times it was quiet. In relative quiet, passers-by helped more when the pedestrian's arm was in the cast. But passers-by who were exposed to the loud noise helped less, regardless of the cast (Mathews & Canon, 1975; see Figure 17-3). Loud noise apparently led people to overlook or ignore an important social cue in a brief encounter with a stranger.

Noise does seem to promote inattention to social cues. Researchers showed color slides to students as they learned lists of nonsense syllables in either quiet or noisy conditions (Cohen & Lezak, 1977). The slides depicted people in everyday activities or in dangerous situations. One slide showed a man paying for oil at a gas station; another showed a man trying to rob the same gas station. When unexpectedly quizzed about the slides, participants in the noisy conditions described fewer of the dangerous situations. In another experiment, researchers placed "novel objects," including a female research assistant holding a large yellow teddy bear, near a sidewalk. Pedestrians who had passed two such objects were interviewed when traffic noise was either quiet or loud. Fewer pedestrians noticed the novel objects in noisy conditions. Pedestrians also walked faster in loud noise (Korte & Grant, 1980).

Noise, like heat, increases the chances of aggression. In one study volunteers saw a film depicting violent or nonviolent acts. Then while exposed to noisy or quiet conditions they had an ostensible opportunity to give electric shocks to another person (an accomplice who did not actually receive the shocks). Participants gave more shocks in the noisy conditions (Geen & O'Neal, 1969). Other studies found similar effects of noise (Geen, 1978; Konecni, 1975). In another laboratory, volunteers heard random bursts of noise, either loud or soft, and then had an ostensible opportunity to give another person an electric shock. Participants who had been insulted and exposed to loud noise gave more intense "shocks" than those in other conditions. Half of the participants in each condition, however, had access to a button they believed would stop the noise, so that they had a sense of control. Unlike those for whom noise was uncontrollable, participants who believed they had control over the loud noise did not react by giving more intense shocks, even though they did not use the button (Donnerstein & Wilson, 1976).

Air Pollution

Many large cities in the United States and Canada have "unhealthy" air because of pollution, according to government reports. **Air pollution** is the presence in the air of any dust, mist, vapor, fiber, or gas other than its natural constituents. We know little about the effects of air pollution on human behavior, especially interpersonal behavior (Evans & Jacobs, 1982). Air pollution may influence social behavior indirectly, however, through physiological effects or psychological stress. One study, for instance, found cigarette smoke associated with degraded performance on tests of cognitive abilities (Oborne, 1983), which in interpersonal situations might be manifested as decreased sensitivity to social cues. Air pollution may also influence social activities through the tendency to discourage outdoor recreation. (For example, Chapko and Solomon, 1976, reported a decline in attendance at a New York City zoo and an aquarium as air pollution rose to unhealthful levels.)

The effects of a noxious odor on liking are similar to those of uncomfortable heat or noise. Volunteers in a laboratory room were exposed to an extremely unpleasant chemical odor or to no odor, and asked for ratings of liking for a stranger (Rotton et al., 1978). In the first of two studies participants believed the stranger was in the next room (where the unpleasant odor would easily penetrate). Those exposed to the odor gave higher ratings of liking for the stranger—apparently an example of the *shared stress effect*. In the second study the experimenter told each participant that he or she was "the only person being interviewed that evening" (p. 64) and would probably never meet the stranger. Participants exposed to the noxious odor in these circumstances liked the stranger less than those exposed to no odor, as in other studies of environmental stressors that used the "bogus stranger" technique.

Pollution from cigarette smoke brings annoyance, disliking for smokers, and even overt hostility among nonsmokers. Louis Harris and Associates (1980) reported that 35% of a sample of U.S. office workers said they smoked. Of the nonsmoking majority, 26% said it bothered them "a great deal" when co-workers smoked near them. Nonsmokers expressed less liking for a person who smoked in their presence than for the same person when he or she did not smoke (Bleda & Sandman, 1977). Similarly, people fled public benches in a shopping mall faster after their personal space was invaded if the invader smoked (Bleda & Bleda, 1978). Volunteers administered higher levels of aversive noise to another person when they were exposed to cigarette smoke, whether they had been provoked or not (Jones & Bogat, 1978). Similarly, participants in a mock physiological experiment gave more "hostile" evaluations of the researchers when someone in the room had smoked, even a bystander (Zillman, Baron, & Tamborini, 1981). Negative reactions to people in the presence of cigarette smoke could reflect physiological reactions as well as annoyance.

Illumination

An unusual experiment found a connection between the intensity of illumination and loudness of conversation. Researchers systematically varied the lighting in areas outside classrooms where students gathered and recorded the noise level of their conversations. It grew quieter as the lights dimmed. People apparently hushed their voices in low levels of illumination and spoke more loudly as lighting became brighter (Sanders, Gustanski, & Lawton, 1976). Louder talk may reflect the effects of arousal by the bright light. Or dim light may bring a feeling of intimacy, reflected in a lowering of voices to discuss personal topics.

Pedestrians invited to participate in an opinion survey agreed to answer more questions as the amount of sunlight increased (Cunningham, 1979). They became less agreeable as less sunlight reached the ground.

Dim lighting has sometimes contributed to conditions of anonymity, in which people have acted with relative lack of inhibition. Participants in one experiment had an opportunity to give electric shocks, sometimes in dimmed lighting while dressed in hoods and robes designed to hide their identities (Zimbardo, 1970, described in Chapter Two). Those in "deindividuated" conditions gave more shock than participants without hoods and robes who wore name tags under bright lights. In a more extreme experiment, some participants entered a well-lit room and others entered a completely dark room. Researchers told those in the dark condition that each would leave separately and never see the others. All groups included both men and women; they had no special instructions except that they would remain together in the room for an hour. Tape recordings and interviews revealed very different behavior when the room was dark than when it was illuminated. Those in the dark explored their environment and chatted at first. But after awhile conversation usually faded as the students began to interact physically. Over 90% said they deliberately touched one another, and nearly half said they hugged. Most (80%) said they became sexually aroused. Those in the well-lit room, in contrast, stayed at a polite distance and talked sedately (Gergen, Gergen, & Barton, 1973).

Settings for Conversation

The appearance and layout of a room, especially the seating arrangement, may affect the quality of conversations through their influence on mood, comfort, or interpersonal distance. This section discusses pleasant settings for conversation, seating arrangements for dyads and small groups, psychological barriers between conversants, and the layout of classrooms.

Pleasant Places

In a test of the idea that pleasant settings lead to positive responses to people, volunteers took part in interviews in one of three rooms. The "average" room, a professor's office, appeared well kept but showed signs of the occupant's work. The "beautiful" room had carpeted floors, ample lighting, attractive furniture, and tasteful decorations. At the other extreme, the "ugly" room looked like a janitor's storeroom. It had gray walls, windows half-covered with dirty shades, and lighting from an unshaded overhead bulb. Pails, mops, and brooms lined the walls, and the bare floor badly needed cleaning. Interviewees each rated 10 photographs of faces on "fatigue versus energy," "displeasure versus well-being," and other properties. As expected, they gave most positive ratings in the "beautiful" room and most negative ratings in the "ugly" room (Maslow & Mintz, 1956). One of the researchers unobtrusively observed the two interviewers, and reported that they finished their interviews more quickly in the "ugly" room. They even gave lower ratings of the photos in the "ugly" room (Mintz, 1956).

Renovated classrooms can have similar effects. Two identical 40-seat classrooms had gray walls, white chairs, and a sterile appearance. One was painted in attractive colors and decorated with posters, area rugs, plants, and other items. Each of two introductory psychology classes used one of the rooms for half of a term, then switched. The students made higher grades in the remodeled room, and the two teachers received higher ratings (they had not heard the hypothesis). Rates of participation in class discussions, however, did not differ in the two rooms (Wollin & Montagne, 1981), perhaps because of the identical row-and-column seating arrangements.

Other research suggests an indirect connection between pleasant places and positive responses to people. Volunteers viewed color slides of professors' offices in which the appearance and decoration varied. When such items as a potted plant and aquarium were present, the students indicated that they would feel more welcome and more comfortable in the office (Campbell, 1979). Participants in another project listed either the positive or the negative features of their residences. Then on leaving the session they encountered another student (an accomplice) who asked for help in a project that involved doing arithmetic problems. Those who had focused on positive features of their residences helped more. A second experiment revealed a similar effect on altruism after participants viewed color slides of attractive or unattractive settings (Sherrod et al., 1977).

Seating Arrangements

Besides the appearance of a room, the arrangement of chairs and other furniture can play a role in interpersonal interactions, primarily through their influence on conversation distance. In friendly conversation, for example, people in the United States and Canada seem to prefer interpersonal distances between 1½ and 4 feet, within *personal distance*. Edward T. Hall (1959, 1966) observed that we choose smaller distances—less than 1½ feet—for highly emotional encounters; this is *intimate distance*. More formal discussions occur at *social distance*—4 to 12 feet. Only speeches or meetings with public figures call for distances greater than 12 feet, or *public distance* (Altman & Vinsel, 1980). (Chapter Five discusses interpersonal distance and eye contact in greater detail.) To talk while seated at tables, people typically choose adjacent chairs at the corners, facing at a 90° angle from each other (Sommer, 1959). This arrangement allows a choice of whether or not to make eye contact. People prefer to sit face to face rather than side by side unless the face-to-face distance is greater than about 5½ feet (Sommer, 1962a, 1962b).

Seating arrangements conducive to conversation place people within comfortable distance, facing toward each other directly enough for convenient eye contact. Osmond ((1957) called these **sociopetal spaces** (similar to *centripetal*), and suggested that such environments increase the chances of conversation. Hall (1966) wrote that if a "receptionist is less than ten feet from another person, even a stranger, she will be sufficiently involved to be virtually compelled to talk" (p. 123).

A new geriatrics ward for women at a Saskatchewan hospital provides an example of sociopetal space. The cheerfully decorated, newly furnished wardroom was the showplace of the hospital. But the patients seemed depressed, and sat in their new chairs staring morosely into space. The hospital's consultants noticed that the chairs were lined up along the walls, side by side, all facing the center of the large room (Sommer & Ross, 1958). They persuaded the staff to rearrange the chairs into circles around small tables. The patients protested at first, but after a few weeks the frequency of their conversations had nearly doubled.

In a more formal experiment, students entered a well-furnished room in pairs to listen to music and give opinions about it. They sat in chairs oriented directly toward each other, or at angles of 90° or 180°. The chairs stood 3 to 9 feet apart, within "personal" or "social" distance. While the participants waited for the music to begin, observers surreptitiously recorded affiliative behaviors, such as the number of statements made and the amount of positive verbal content. The more directly the chairs faced, the more affiliative the students acted (Mehrabian & Diamond, 1971a). In a similar experiment groups of four strangers chose their own seats in a room that allowed various seating arrangements. The more directly the participants faced each other, the more time they spent talking (Mehrabian & Diamond, 1971b).

"Sociofugal" settings discourage conversation among people within conversational distance by making eye contact difficult (Osmond, 1957). Waiting areas in airports, for example, usually have chairs bolted to the floor in rows facing in the same direction. Chairs facing toward each other are typically too far apart for comfortable conversation, as Photo 17–1 shows. Other such spaces include bus depots, some classrooms, and reception areas in clinics, personnel offices, and hospitals. These arrangements may represent deliberate attempts to deter unwanted

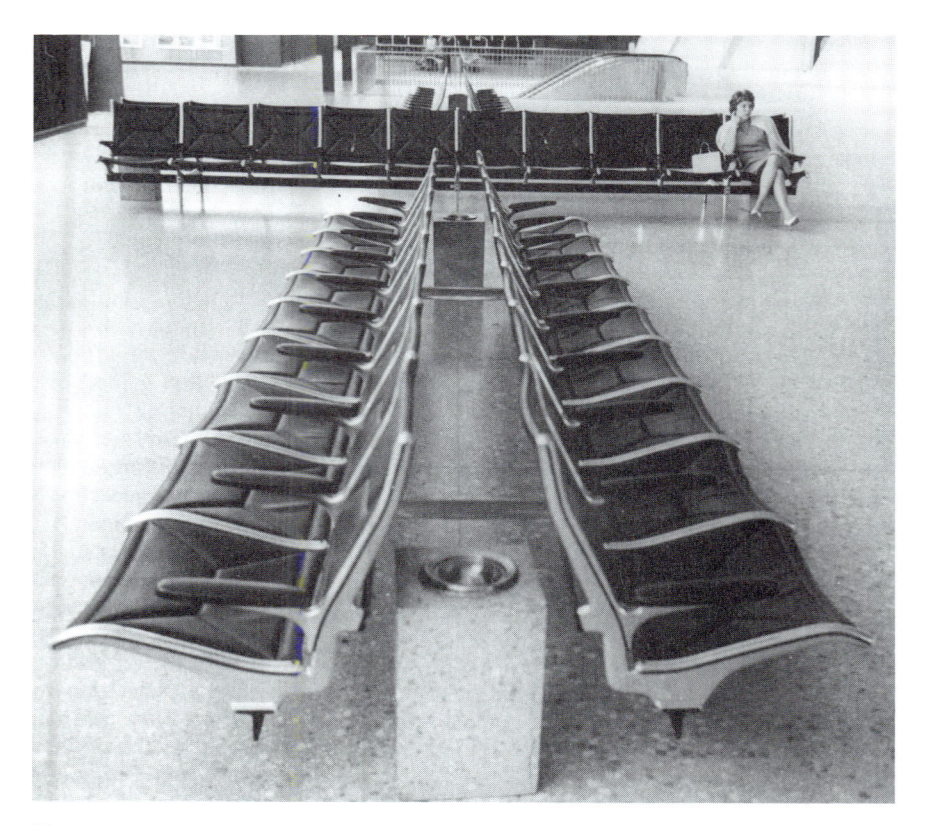

Photo 17-1 Sociofugal space. Waiting areas, such as this airport concourse, deter conversation through arrangements of chairs bolted in rigid rows facing in different directions.

conversation among strangers, to allow occupants to go about their business without feeling compelled to talk to neighbors. In places where people go to seek conversation—such as cafeterias and cocktail lounges—groups of chairs are usually arranged around small tables or in circles.

People who try to talk in environments unsuited to conversation experience discomfort, and may even blame it on each other. Participants in a laboratory experiment indicated discomfort with seating arrangements that left interpersonal distances of 12 feet, especially for conversations about personal topics (Scott, 1984). In another experiment volunteers held conversations from uncomfortably distant chairs—11 feet apart—or from chairs placed at a comfortable distance. As expected, those in the distant arrangement felt ill at ease. And even though they had no choice regarding interpersonal distance, participants in the distant condition held their partners responsible for their own negative feelings (Aiello & Thompson, 1980). Perhaps people in "sociofugal" settings misconstrue the distance created by the environment as aloofness on the part of the occupants.

Conversation in small groups parallels opportunities for eye contact. In groups of ten people seated around a circular table, Steinzor (1950) recorded the initiator of each comment and the next person to speak. Responses usually came from across the table,

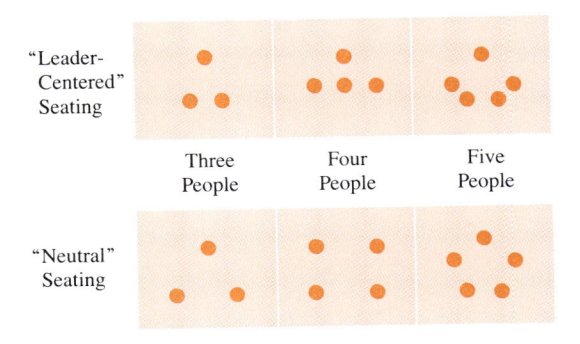

Figure 17–4 Leader-centered and neutral seating arrangements for group discussions by three, four, and five people. Those seated in the neutral arrangement showed greater consensus and performed better on a laboratory task.

seldom from people one or two seats away from the speaker, and tended to involve people who could easily make eye contact. Other studies found the so-called Steinzor effect in a natural setting (Silverstein & Stang, 1976) and in the laboratory (Baker, 1984; Howells & Becker, 1962; Ward, 1968).

A group's leader tends to occupy the head of the table, if it has one. The members of 12-person mock juries, for instance, sat at rectangular tables with five chairs on the long sides and one at each end. The groups typically chose leaders from those seated in the end chairs, in positions that permitted easy eye contact with all members of the group. Occupants of end positions received higher ratings on influence in the group, and participated more than other members in the discussions (Strodtbeck & Hook, 1961). In other studies, observers attributed greater influence to the occupants of seats at the end of a table (Pellegrini, 1971), and occupants of end seats at rectangular tables received most nominations as leader (Altemeyer & Jones, 1974) and highest ratings on leadership (Bass & Klubeck, 1952). However, prospective leaders preferred visible seats (Heckel, 1973), and people who chose visible positions had relatively high scores on dominance (Hare & Bales, 1963) and locus of control (Hiers & Heckel, 1977). Besides reflecting a deliberate choice by an aspiring leader, a location at the head of the table may reflect the choice of other seats by other members of the group attempting to designate a leader. Lecuyer (1976) reported that groups typically reserved the end or corner seat for the leader. On the other hand, a highly visible seat may expose its occupant to subtle pressures from other members of the group to participate in the discussion.

Leaders can dominate discussions from prominent, highly visible seats. In a comparison of five-person groups seated at rectangular or circular tables, assigned leaders sat at the end of the rectangular table. Leaders participated more than other members of the groups at rectangular tables, but not at circular tables. Leaders at rectangular tables also devoted a greater proportion of their comments to the task, and spent less time on socioemotional issues, than the leaders at circular tables (Lecuyer, 1976). In another study, groups of three, four, or five persons sat in "neutral" arrangements or "leader-centered" arrangements that made one position more visible than the others, as shown in Figure 17–4. Groups in the neutral arrangements showed greater consensus and performed better on a complex task than those in leader-centered arrangements (Cummings, Huber, & Arendt, 1974).

Psychological Barriers

Holding a conversation across a table or desk can signal psychological distance. In commercial and government offices, visitors typically sit across the desk from the occupant, and university professors and visitors usually do not have a desk between them, perhaps in a deliberate attempt to minimize social distance (Joiner, 1976; Campbell, 1980). Students have rated professors whose offices had desk-between arrangements less easy to find outside of class and less likely to give individual attention than those whose offices had open arrangements (Zweigenhaft, 1976). The professors with the desk-between arrangement were also older and had higher rank; their offices apparently mirrored social distance. Volunteers who viewed color slides of offices said they would feel less comfortable and less welcome in desk-between arrangements than in open arrangements, and rated the occupant as less friendly (Campbell, 1979; Morrow & McElroy, 1981). A physician, in contrast, reported more patients "ill at ease" in interviews on the same side of the desk than on opposite sides (Coleman, 1968). Anxious interviewees in another study rated the interviewer as more friendly when they were separated by a desk; the less anxious ones saw the interviewer as more pleasant and agreeable with no desk in between (Widgery & Stackpole, 1972). Apparently the psychological distance of an interview across a desk can comfort an anxious interviewee.

A desk may connote greater psychological distance than a table. When students rated a professor depicted in a line drawing as seated either at a small conference table or at a desk across from a student, they saw the seating position at the desk as more formal and the professor seated there as less nurturing and less skilled in human relations (Becker, Gield, & Froggat, 1983).

Layout of Classrooms

Researchers introduced a sociopetal seating arrangement and a "soft" appearance in a university classroom to encourage participation in discussions. Before renovation the classroom resembled those at many large universities, with rows of plastic desk-arm chairs facing toward two large tables and a blackboard. After renovation the room had three-tiered benches lined with fabric-covered cushions, arranged in a hexagon. Wooden paneling concealed sharp corners; adjustable lighting and decorative items had been added. Ten classes of up to 20 students each were observed in the new "soft" classroom. An average of 79% of the students participated in the class discussions, compared with 37% in rooms similar to the experimental room before its renovation (Sommer & Olsen, 1980). The higher rates of participation in the redesigned classroom confirm the findings concerning sociopetal seating arrangements.

Students seated in the front and center of a traditional classroom tend to participate most. In one classroom with chairs arranged in rows and columns, students in the middle of the front rows participated twice as much as those seated near the ends of the last row, as shown in Figure 17–5 (Sommer, 1967). Other researchers reported similar results (Adams, 1969; Koneya, 1976; MacPherson, 1984).

Higher levels of participation in the front-center seats could stem from ease of eye contact and proximity to the instructor. Students may choose these seats to take an active role in class (Koneya, 1976). Or perhaps students in these seats feel compelled to

	Instructor	
57%	61%	57%
37%	54%	37%
41%	51%	41%
31%	48%	31%

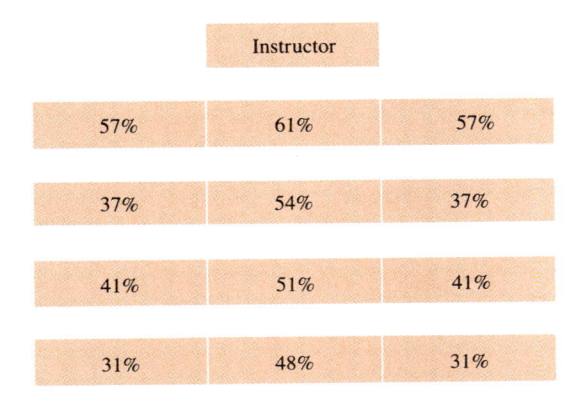

Figure 17–5 Participation in classroom discussions as a function of seating position.

participate because of the greater opportunity for eye contact with the instructor. Interviews in a New Zealand school revealed deliberate choices of seats: students who wanted to concentrate on academic matters selected seats near the front of the room; those who valued interactions with other students and preferred relative freedom from control by the teacher selected seats in back (MacPherson, 1984). Among students who first selected their own seats, then later sat in randomly assigned seats, those at the front of the room participated most in discussions even after random assignment (Levine et al., 1980). These findings probably reflect both individual choices of seats and pressures to participate in locations near the instructor.

Students seated in the front-center section of a classroom sometimes obtain relatively higher grades (Becker et al., 1973; Sommer, 1974). Levine and his colleagues (1980) found highest grades in the front half of the room only when students selected their own seats. But in another classroom where students had been randomly assigned seats, those in the center section earned better grades (Stires, 1980). Better performance in the center of the room may stem from *social facilitation,* or the motivating effects of neighbors (Knowles, 1982). The choice of a seat in the center of the room may also reflect a desire to avoid the distractions at the periphery (Mac-Pherson, 1984). In very large lecture halls, the motivating effect of neighbors and the minimal distractions in the center of the room may outweigh the importance of ease of eye contact with the instructor in the front seats.

Architecture and Interaction

Beyond the appearance and arrangement of rooms, the physical environment enters into social behavior through the layout and design of buildings and the resulting accessibility of residences and workplaces. In this section we review the connections of the architecture of buildings with interpersonal attraction, social overload, and the development of groups.

Proximity and Attraction

Advocates of architectural determinism substantiated their views by citing correlations of physical proximity—or **propinquity**—and friendship. Research has consistently shown that we tend to converse with the occupants of residences or work stations near our own, and choose our friends from among our neighbors. Consider the results of a field study of friendships in Westgate West, a housing complex for married students (Festinger, Schachter, & Back, 1950). The two-story buildings had five similar apartments on each floor, with all doors facing in the same direction. Couples on the waiting list received apartments as vacancies arose, so they had no choice in their location. Couples who were asked to name the three others with whom they socialized most generally named residents of the same floor of the same building. They named 41% of all the next-door neighbors they could have mentioned and 22% of the possible choices two doors away. Couples on second floors often named those on the first floor who lived near the stairs. They apparently befriended those with whom the buildings afforded most opportunities to interact.

Proximity is correlated with interaction and friendship in other settings as well. Among residents of suburbs, gatherings and friendships typically involve neighbors from the same block (Gans, 1967; Whyte, 1956). Residents of apartment buildings generally have acquaintances or friends in nearby apartments (Bochner et al., 1976; Ebbesen, Kjos, & Konecni, 1976; Nahemow & Lawton, 1975). Office workers tend to choose partners for conversation and friends among co-workers at nearby work stations (Conrath, 1973; Gullahorn, 1952; Homans, 1954) and students usually select friends from neighboring seats in classrooms (Byrne, 1961). In a class at a police academy where seats had been assigned alphabetically, 45% of the trainees chose friends whose last names began with letters adjacent in the alphabet (Segal, 1974)! Figure 17–6 shows the results of a study of 297 office employees who worked on the same floor of a high-rise office building: the closer the desks were, the greater the likelihood of friendship was.

People in homogeneous populations new to their environments seem especially likely to select friends

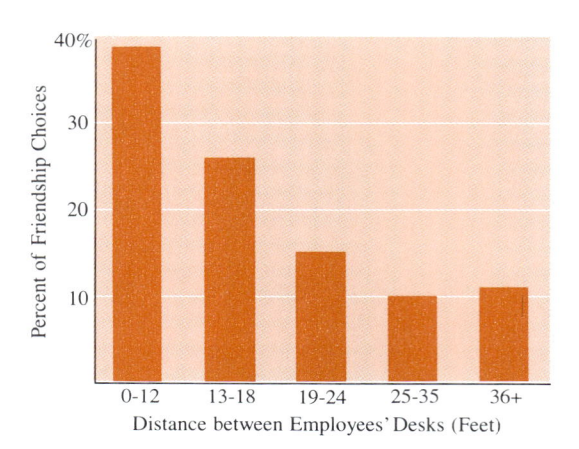

Figure 17–6 Percentage of friendship choices among co-workers as a function of the distance between desks in an office.

on the basis of proximity. Newcomers can easily become acquainted with their neighbors, and may initially choose them for friends. Students who moved into a dormitory, for example, formed friendships on the basis of proximity during the first few weeks, but later sought friends with similar attitudes (Newcomb, 1961). In populations similar in age, education, socioeconomic background, or other characteristics, neighbors may be compatible enough for sustained friendship. In heterogeneous populations people may have to go farther to find others with similar outlooks. Friendships in an established neighborhood in Ann Arbor, for example, became more frequent with increasing proximity of residences, but also involved people with similar backgrounds and preferences (Athanasiou & Yoshioka, 1973). Most of the residents of three high-rise buildings had friends in the same building, usually of similar age and race (Nahemow & Lawton, 1975). However, proximity gave opportunities for friendship among people with disparate backgrounds who might not otherwise have become acquainted. Proximity also creates the possibility of conflict. When residents of an apartment complex in California named the couples they liked least and most, it was found that those they liked least lived even closer than those they liked most (Ebbesen et al., 1976).

The relationship between proximity and interaction depends on the architecture. For instance, houses in courts or cul-de-sacs face toward one another, and residents come and go via the same pathways, so they have many opportunities to become acquainted. Married students who lived in U-shaped courts tended to choose friends in their own courts, rarely in adjacent courts whose houses face in the opposite direction (Festinger et al., 1950). In two other studies, residents of cul-de-sacs knew a greater proportion of their neighbors than residents of through streets (Brown & Werner, 1985; Mayo, 1979). Indoor cul-de-sacs seem to operate the same way. Clerical workers in open-plan offices worked in a large area with 200 co-workers or in walled areas containing about 30 workers. Two-thirds of friendship choices in smaller areas were reciprocated, compared with 38% in the large area (Wells, 1965). In three U.S. Air Force barracks, partitions divided the bunks into clusters of six. Occupants of the divided barracks spent more time talking with fewer people than in three identical buildings with no partitions (Blake et al., 1956).

Occasionally people drawn together by proximity develop into *small groups*. In the Westgate housing project, for example, the residents of a few of the U-shaped courts formed cohesive social groups (Festinger et al., 1950). Among office workers who made friends with neighbors at work, some formed small, informal groups that shared leisure activities (Gullahorn, 1952; Homans, 1950, 1954). However, groups developed only among a fraction of those who interacted with others in residences or work spaces in close proximity to their own.

Residential Design and Social Overload

Some environments provide more opportunities for interaction than occupants want or can tolerate—and foster social overload. For instance, residents of 14-story apartment towers (housing 110 families each) encounter more people in the lobby, elevator, or stairs than do residents of 3-story buildings housing 12 families each (McCarthy & Saegert, 1979). High-rise dwellers encounter more people they don't recognize in their buildings, feel less safe there, and have less confidence that neighbors will come to their aid.

One way of avoiding social overload in heavily populated settings is to withdraw from social contact. This strategy may partly explain why student residents of two- to four-story dormitories reported having more friends in their dormitories than residents of a ten-story "megadorm" that housed 1,000 students (Holahan & Wilcox, 1978). Not surprisingly, megadorm residents also reported lower satisfaction with their living environments.

Buildings can foster social overload through their layout as well as their size. New first-year students at the State University of New York at Stony Brook moved into double bedrooms of about the same size—roughly 150 square feet of floor space per person—in two types of buildings. The rooms were comparable, and the buildings housed about the same numbers of students per floor. As Figure 17–7 shows,

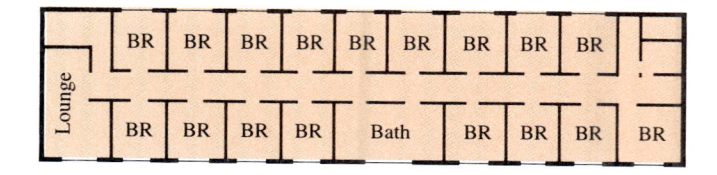

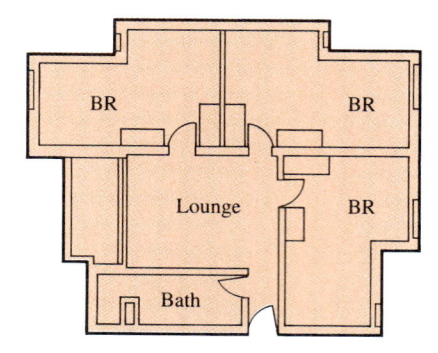

Figure 17–7 Floor plans of corridor-design and suite-design dormitories.

however, the floor plans differed substantially. Students entered rooms in *corridor-design dormitories* from long, double-loaded corridors that served 33 other students who shared the same bathroom and lounge. Students reached their rooms in *suite-design dormitories* through small lounges that served clusters of three bedrooms, and shared bathrooms with only five other students (Baum & Valins, 1977). Residents of corridor-design dormitories complained of more unwanted social contact and expressed a greater desire to avoid people than those in the suite-design dorms. This finding seemed to reflect the greater accessibility of students to their neighbors in the corridor-design dorms. When residents stepped outside their doors, they could run into any of more than 30 other residents of the same floor. In contrast, when the residents of suites left their rooms, they could expect to encounter five suitemates. Corridor residents with rooms near the bathroom especially suffered, as they occupied the center of the traffic pattern.

Corridor residents spent less time in the dormitories than suite residents, probably to avoid social overload. Suite residents, in contrast, did much of their studying in the dorms and carried on other nonsocial activities there. Suite residents were often seen in hallways and lounges, where most social encounters occurred. Corridor residents kept to their rooms for nonsocial activities, apparently to avoid unwanted social contact (Valins & Baum, 1977).

Corridor residents' withdrawal extended beyond the dormitories. In a laboratory study that compared the reactions of first-year students from the two types of dormitories, students arrived in a waiting room where one other student already sat (an accomplice of the researchers). Corridor residents sat farther away, looked less toward the student's face, and initiated fewer conversations than suite residents did. In groups, corridor residents showed less inclination than suite residents to rely on consensus (Baum, Harpin, & Valins, 1975). On another campus, corridor and suite residents each worked in groups with two other people (actually accomplices), who either included them in the discussion or ignored them. In contrast to suite residents, corridor residents indicated greater comfort when they were ignored (Reichner, 1979).

Unfortunately for corridor residents, withdrawal probably did little to reduce overload—avoiding eye contact and conversation could hardly change the numbers of people in the hallways. So perhaps they experienced repeated stress from an uncontrollable source. Such circumstances can lead to **learned helplessness** (see Chapter Eight), which occurs when the individual believes he or she cannot influence what happens, quits trying, and becomes depressed.

To find out whether corridor residents developed learned helplessness, researchers conducted a study involving first-year students who had been randomly assigned to either suite- or corridor-design dormitories (Baum, Aiello, & Calesnick, 1978). During the students' first, third, or seventh weeks on campus, they took part in a game that allowed a cooperative response, a competitive response, or withdrawal (a sign of helplessness). Corridor residents made more competitive and fewer cooperative responses than suite residents. By the end of the seventh week suite residents exhibited more cooperation. As expected, corridor residents increasingly resorted to withdrawal. Corridor residents explained that their competitive responses expressed disliking, and their withdrawal meant something like "I don't really care what happens with the game."

Fortunately, problems created by corridor-design dormitories have architectural solutions (Baum & Davis, 1980). As an alternative to the long-corridor (40 students) and short-corridor (20 students) designs, a long corridor was divided to create a modified-corridor design with a lounge entered through doors from both sides (see Figure 17–8). Students from long, short, and modified corridors completed surveys and were observed for 15 weeks. After awhile the residents of long corridors, unlike those on short and modified corridors, began to report unwanted social contact, to avoid other students in the dormitory, and to close their doors. They also avoided social interaction when they were invited to a laboratory. The architectural intervention apparently insulated residents from the social overload typical of the long corridors.

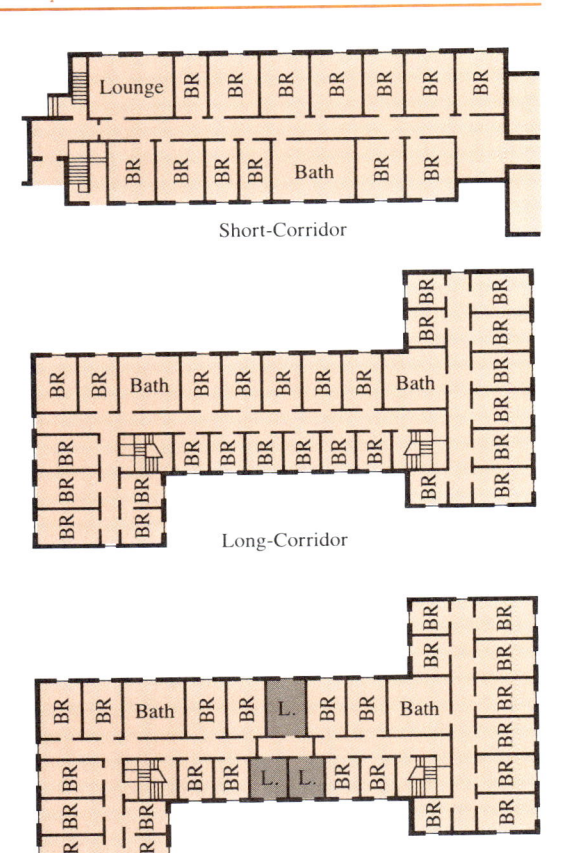

Figure 17–8 In dormitory rooms arranged in the *short-corridor* design (top), residents experienced little of the crowding and social overload found in the *long-corridor* design (center), where 40 students shared two bathrooms. In a *modified-corridor design*, one long corridor was divided at the center by a lounge formed from three former bedrooms and a section of the hallway (bottom; lounge shaded). As hoped, residents of the modified corridor experienced little of the unwanted social contact usually found in a long corridor.

Overload in Open-Space Schools

The design of the physical environment can foster social overload in schools as well as in residential settings. This is perhaps most apparent in **open-space schools,** which, like open-plan offices, have few interior walls or partitions. An innovation of the late 1960s, they comprised over half of the schools constructed in the United States from 1967 to 1970 and represented part of a wider trend toward a more "open," less structured approach to education (Weinstein, 1979).

Research on the impact of open-space schools has been plagued by weakness in both internal and external validity (see Chapter Two). Some studies have compared schools in different districts, where the populations of students also differ. Sometimes teachers have been able to choose between open-space and conventional arrangements, so differences between types of schools may reflect the individual teachers' personalities. Worse, the effects of architectural openness have often been difficult to separate from effects of curriculum or teaching (Ahrentzen et al., 1982). However, there are some consistent findings.

Open-space schools leave teachers accessible to interaction with their peers and exposed to the noise and distraction of other classes that share a single large space. Teachers in open-space schools report more aural distraction, visual distraction, crowding, and noise than those working in more traditional settings (Ahrentzen et al., 1982; Weinstein, 1979), but also more frequent contacts with other teachers (Ahrentzen & Evans, 1984; Weinstein, 1979). In managing open classrooms, teachers restrict their class activities to avoid distracting other classes (Ahrentzen & Evans, 1984) and introduce more frequent and more prolonged transitions between activities (Cotterell, 1984).

Students in open-space schools and conventional schools show no consistent differences in academic achievement, on average. Students with difficulties in reading or with lower IQs, however, sometimes suffer in open-space schools. Students in open-space schools tend to interact more with teachers and other students, move around more, and engage in a wider variety of activities (Weinstein, 1979). One study found students in open classrooms more familiar with school norms—they knew the school rules, knew what to do and where to go—perhaps because of teachers' efforts. The same students, however, said they had more academic problems—more of them found schoolwork difficult, made mistakes, did the wrong work, were unable to answer teachers' questions (Cotterell, 1984). All of these findings suggest that students in open-space schools experience more stimulation and input from more sources than students in conventional classrooms—and those whose capacities are strained by the added demands may also experience difficulties.

Privacy

Definitions of **privacy** emphasize control over information (Margulis, 1977; Westin, 1967) or regulation of interpersonal interaction (Altman & Chemers, 1980; see Sundstrom, 1986b). One well-accepted definition of privacy is the selective control over access to the self or group (Altman, 1975, 1976). Privacy often involves the manipulation of the physical environment to limit the accessibility of individuals or groups. Students in dormitories, for example, can open their doors to invite visitors in and open their curtains to see and be seen, or close doors and curtains to retreat.

"Hello, I'm taking a poll on how people feel about invasion of their privacy . . ."

Theories of Privacy

Some theories say privacy contributes to our personal *autonomy* (Beardsley, 1971). Erving Goffman's theory of *self-presentation* (1959) suggests that when we have an audience, we maintain appearances and try to manage the impressions of ourselves formed by others (see Chapter Three). But in "back regions" inaccessible to outsiders, we relax and pay less attention to impression management. In large, open offices, for example, "someone is always likely to be present before whom an impression of industriousness must be maintained; in a small office all pretense of work and decorous behavior can be dropped when the boss is out" (p. 26). Kelvin (1973) theorized that privacy insulates us from unwanted audiences, who might hold us accountable to standards of acceptable behavior. Privacy allows control over others' knowledge of our actions, providing a "positive limitation of the power of others" (p. 260).

Privacy allows us to control our involvement in social interaction, according to Irwin Altman's theory of **privacy regulation.** Altman points out that our desires for interaction change from time to time, but we try to maintain an optimal level of social contact:

> If a person desires a lot of interaction with another person and gets only a little, then he feels lonely, isolated or cut off. And if he actually receives more interaction than he originally desires, then he feels intruded upon, crowded, or overloaded. However, what is too much, too little, or ideal shifts with time and circumstances, so what is optimum depends on where one is on the continuum of desired privacy. If I want to be alone, a colleague who comes into my office and talks for fifteen minutes is intruding and staying too long. If I want to interact with others, then the same fifteen minute conversation may be far too brief. [1975, p. 25]

According to this theory, whenever we want more or less interaction than we are experiencing, we use *privacy-regulation mechanisms* to try to achieve the optimum. These mechanisms include personal space (discussed in Chapter Five), territory (discussed later in this chapter), verbal and nonverbal behavior, and uses of the physical environment. Responses in corridor- and suite-design dormitories illustrate uses of physical settings: students invited social contact by studying in the lounges, where social encounters often occurred. They limited their accessibility by retreating into their rooms and shutting the doors. The suite design proved better for regulating social interaction, however, perhaps because semiprivate lounges separated the rooms from public corridors.

According to Altman's theory, failure to achieve privacy can lead to stress and other problems. As expected, first-year students living in dormitories at the University of Utah who dropped out of school within 18 months for nonacademic reasons had failed to adopt the strategies of privacy regulation used by successful students. These first-year students were asked whether they did such things as shut the door to their room, find a quiet place, arrange the room for privacy, or use the bathroom at a quiet time. Dropouts used fewer means of regulating interaction than students who stayed in school, and found them less effective (Vinsel et al., 1980).

Architects sometimes use a theory of privacy based on a hierarchy of species in which physical boundaries define concentric zones of accessibility (see Zimring, 1982). *Public spaces*—such as sidewalks, plazas, and malls—have few barriers to public access, and serve as thoroughfares. *Semipublic spaces*—such as stores, shops, restaurants, and reception areas of hotels—have physical boundaries to differentiate them, but users can easily gain access to them. *Semiprivate spaces* have physical barriers to limit public access, such as walls, fences, doors, or gates, as in athletic clubs, office buildings, and lounges in suite-design dormitories. *Private spaces* provide most seclusion, as in bedrooms, private offices, and bathrooms. Areas of varying accessibility give a range of settings to match the needs of individuals or groups for control over interaction. Secluded spaces allow solitary or intimate activities free from observation or interruption (Westin, 1967); accessible spaces permit many public activities (Jacobs, 1970). This theory implies that environments deter privacy—and perhaps create social overload—through insufficient physical separation of people whose activities interfere with one another. Problems arise especially where private spaces open directly into public spaces, as in corridor-design dormitories, or where few private spaces exist.

Privacy in Open-Plan Offices

People who work in **open-plan offices** have trouble finding privacy. This type of office evolved from the German *Burolandschaft*, or "office landscape," in which employees of all ranks work in large, open areas with few walls, their work spaces separated mainly by office furniture and potted plants (see Photo 17–2). Advocates claimed that workers communicate best when they can easily see one another, especially if they are located near counterparts in the flow of work. They criticized conventional offices, arguing that walls impede communication, unnecessarily emphasize status, and erode motivation. "Office landscapes" appeared in the United States in the late 1960s and soon evolved to incorporate shoulder-high, interlocking partitions to separate work stations (Pile, 1978). By the late 1970s about one-third of office workers in the United States worked in open-plan offices (Harris & Associates, 1980).

Workers in open-plan offices consistently report less privacy, on average, than do workers in offices

Photo 17–2 In open-plan offices such as this throughout Canada, Europe, and the United States, workers sit at desks in large, open areas containing few walls—separated by office furniture, potted plants, and interlocking, movable partitions. Designed to improve comunication, such offices make informal conversation convenient, but occupants complain of noise and lack of privacy.

with more enclosed work spaces. In a survey of 519 employees in 15 open offices, for instance, two-thirds complained of disturbance in concentration; other complaints concerned noise, lack of privacy, and difficulty holding confidential conversations (Nemecek & Grandjean, 1973). A majority, however, said open offices aided "personal contacts" and made communication easier. In another study, employees at a corporate office completed a survey before and after moving into a new open-plan facility. They reported a decline in privacy, especially troublesome for managers, who needed privacy for confidential conversations. Acoustical measurements confirmed that the managers' work spaces had lower *speech privacy* (ability to converse without being understood outside the work space). This open-plan office brought no improvement in communication (Sundstrom, Herbert, & Brown, 1982). Other studies also found open-plan offices deficient in privacy (Boyce, 1974; Hedge, 1982; Hundert & Greenfield, 1969). When a group moved to open offices, informal conversation often became easier, but confidential conversation and feedback from supervisors suffered (Sundstrom, 1986a).

Open-plan offices also created problems at community colleges, where faculty had either private offices, two-person offices, or open-plan offices (Becker, Gield, Gaylin, & Sayer, 1983). Of the professors in open-plan offices, 84% expressed dissatisfaction with their privacy, compared with 11% in private offices. Professors in open-plan offices complained of interruption and distraction; they said the lack of privacy affected the topics discussed and their ability to praise or criticize students. More professors in open-plan offices said they worked elsewhere. Students felt less free to drop in at open-plan offices—and said professors were less likely to be there—than at private or shared offices.

Privacy in offices depends on enclosure of individual work stations. In one study, office workers rated their work spaces and permitted the researchers to measure such physical features as the number of sides of the work space bounded by walls, partitions, or barriers at least six feet high. Privacy increased with enclosure (see Figure 17–9). Walled offices with doors had most privacy (Sundstrom, Town, Brown, Forman, & McGee, 1982). Privacy in turn is associated with satisfaction with the job (Ferguson & Weisman, 1986; Sundstrom, Burt, & Kamp, 1980).

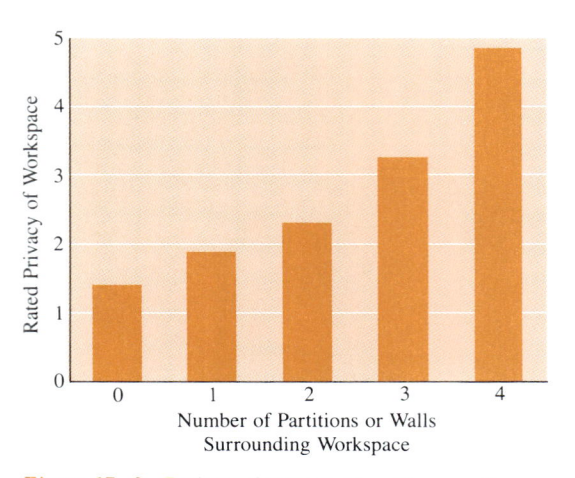

Figure 17–9 Ratings of privacy of work spaces by office employees as a function of number of sides of their work space bounded by a wall or barrier at least six feet high

Crowding

In a way, the opposite of privacy is **crowding,** a form of stress that sometimes occurs in densely populated environments. You may experience crowding in an elevator jammed with passengers, on a downtown sidewalk at rush hour, near a bargain table at a department store, or in the lobby of a theater at a popular movie. But as a form of stress, crowding is subjective—so your reactions may differ from someone else's. High **population density,** defined as the number of people per unit of space or the amount of space per person, is not necessarily synonymous with crowding. Indeed, we often seek densely populated environments for pleasure and stimulation, as when we go to cocktail parties, football games, concerts, revivals, and political rallies. In a crowd we even find *anonymity,* a form of privacy (Westin, 1967). According to one social psychologist, high population density intensifies our emotional reactions, whether positive or negative (Freedman, 1975). The **density intensity hypothesis** suggests that the presence of a crowd actually enhances an already positive experience, such as watching the home team in a championship, but makes an unpleasant experience worse. Being in a densely populated environment, however, can be a stressful experience in itself.

Crowding and Social Pathology

Early research tested the **social pathology hypothesis**—the idea that high population density brings disease, delinquency, crime, insanity, and other social ills. Evidence in support of this idea at first consisted of studies that found correlations between gross population density—the number of people per acre or census tract—and rates of crime, mental illness, and other social pathologies (Zlutnick & Altman, 1972). This research had a critical flaw, however: it overlooked the fact that it is often poor people who live in densely populated areas of cities. Pathologies found in such areas may result from poverty. Research that took this possibility into account failed to support the social pathology hypothesis. An analysis of census data from Chicago revealed that the number of persons per acre correlated with rates of death,

Photo 17–3 An example of high population density.

tuberculosis, infant mortality, public assistance, and juvenile delinquency (Winsborough, 1965). But when such factors as occupation, income, education, ethnicity, and quality of housing were statistically controlled, the relationships disappeared or became negative.

Research with nonhuman species supports the social pathology hypothesis. In one of the best-known studies, John Calhoun (1962) placed 48 Norway rats in a pen with four chambers, of which two had only one entrance and the others had two entrances. He provided sufficient food and water and allowed the population to reproduce without restriction. The colony increased to 80 animals. The crowded rats began to exhibit serious abnormalities in nest building, courting, mating, rearing of the young, and social organization. Some males became aggressive and disregarded the ritualized signals of submission that usually end a fight. Individuals maintained territories by force. Females often neglected their young, and up to 75% of the infant rats died. More pathologies occurred in the two most accessible pens, called the *behavioral sink*. Autopsies revealed signs of prolonged stress, such as enlarged adrenal glands.

In another study, Sika deer on an island near the coast of Maryland had developed an unusually high density of about 300 deer, or one deer per acre. During the winter two years later over half of the herd died, even though food was plentiful. Autopsies showed signs of prolonged stress. More deer died the next winter, and the herd stabilized at around 80 (Christian, Flyger, & Davis, 1960). Similar signs of stress and pathology have been associated with high population density in many species (Freedman, 1972).

Studies of urban human populations which controlled for family income have found little or no connection between density and social pathologies. Researchers reported, for instance, that the number of persons per room within dwellings correlated with mortality, public assistance, and juvenile delinquency in Chicago—even after they controlled for socioeconomic status and ethnicity—but the correlations were small (Galle, Gove, & McPherson, 1972). Another study of Chicago census data showed similar weak correlations (Galle & Gove, 1979). Other research, however, failed to find even weak connections between household density and social pathologies in New York City (Freedman, Heshka, & Levy,

1975) and Toronto (Booth, 1976; Kirmeyer, 1978). Hong Kong's population density far exceeds those of cities in the United States and Canada, but its rates of crime and other social pathologies have been far lower (Michelson, 1970).

Research in prisons does show a connection between high population density and some types of pathology. Prison inmates housed in open dormitories with 27 or more other prisoners expressed more negative reactions to the housing than those in single or double rooms, and they had most complaints about illness; those in single cells had fewest negative reactions and lowest rates of illness (Cox, Paulus, & McCain, 1984). In Atlanta, complaints of illness increased as the number of prisoners per cell rose from one to six. In Texas, maximum security prisons with large populations (an average of 1700) had ten times more suicides, 78% more psychiatric commitments, and three times more deaths than prisons with smaller populations (an average of 830) but similar housing conditions. And at a small psychiatric prison in Texas, the reported death rate was significantly related ($r = +.81$) to the prison's population the same year, as shown in Figure 17–10 (Paulus, McCain, & Cox, 1978).

Models of Crowding

Why are rates of illness and death elevated in crowded prisons and not in crowded cities? One answer concerns the types of settings in which people experience high population density. Daniel Stokols theorized that crowding is most intense and difficult to

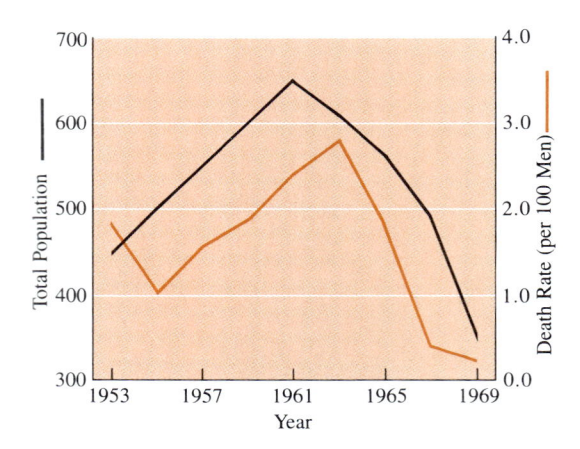

Figure 17–10 Total annual population of a psychiatric prison and annual rate of deaths per 100 prisoners

resolve in *primary environments,* such as residences or workplaces, where "an individual spends much time, relates to others on a personal basis, and engages in a wide range of personally important activities" (1976, p. 73). Here interpersonal sources of stress such as overload or "thwarting" seriously threaten an individual's sense of well-being and may be difficult to avoid (Zlutnick & Altman, 1972). By contrast, encounters in *secondary environments*—such as shopping centers, stores, and sidewalks—are relatively transitory, anonymous, and inconsequential. Here crowding occurs in brief episodes, generally with strangers, in places where an individual does not expect to exert much control in any case. Consistent with these ideas, residents of San Francisco indicated much greater tolerance for crowding in their neighborhoods than in their residences (Loo & Ong, 1984).

Another answer is that crowding seems to be most difficult to tolerate in settings that provide few resources for coping or opportunities for escape. For instance, residents of crowded dwellings who had places at home to be alone had less trouble with high household density than those without such places to go to (Verbrugge & Taylor, 1980). So it is understandable that we find little social pathology in urban

Table 17-1 Models of crowding

Model of Crowding	Experience in High Population Density	Immediate Reactions	Long-Term Consequences
Overload	Overstimulation or excess cognitive load from too many people, close interpersonal proximity	Withdrawal; avoidance of social contact; inattention to social cues	With continued social overload, habitual withdrawal from social contact
Arousal	Physiological, psychological arousal (from close interpersonal proximity, fear, uncertainty)	Improved performance of simple tasks; degraded performance of complex or difficult tasks	None predicted
Interference	Frustration from people constraining behavior, interfering with activities, or blocking access to resources	Negative feelings, hostility	Increased likelihood of violent, aggressive response to provocation
Control	Inability to control sources of overload, interference	Psychological stress	With persistent failure to achieve personal control, learned helplessness
Privacy regulation	Inability to optimize individual level of interpersonal interaction	Use of privacy-regulation mechanisms to reduce social contact (personal space, territory, nonverbal communication)	With persistent failure of privacy regulation, severe stress, loss of personal identity

environments—where residents have many resources for dealing with high density—and serious pathology in crowded prison cells, from which there is no escape.

A third answer is that the intensity of crowding depends on both the particular sources of stress in high density and the individual's ability to cope with them. Stress in densely populated settings can come from multiple sources. In the *interaction-demand model* proposed by Andrew Baum and Paul Paulus (1987), stress from increasing numbers of people and decreasing interpersonal distances in high-density settings is said to involve *uncertainty* (and lack of control), *cognitive load,* and *goal interference.* These sources of crowding reflect processes hypothesized by several earlier models—overload, arousal, interference, control, and privacy regulation—outlined in Table 17-1.

Overload models suggest that densely populated settings bring interactions with too many people or with too much immediacy, which can create overstimulation and strain cognitive capacities (Cohen, 1978). Shoppers in a store, for example, noticed fewer details as the store grew more crowded (Saegert, Macintosh, & West, 1975). Perhaps to avoid overload, people crowded together in laboratories avoided eye contact and withdrew (Greenberg & Firestone, 1977; Sundstrom, 1975a). Even in *anticipation* of being crowded, people shunned interaction with one or two others in a large waiting room (Baum & Greenberg, 1975; Baum & Koman, 1976).

Research on students "tripled" in dormitory rooms designed for two gave results consistent with overload models of crowding. Students assigned two roommates understandably experienced more crowding than those assigned one roommate in similar rooms. Tripled women experienced especially intense crowding, apparently because they tried to cope by spending extra time interacting with roommates. Tripled men, in contrast, tended to withdraw, behavior that seemed to mitigate their experience of crowding. After a semester, tripled students performed more poorly on complex tasks in a laboratory, as overload models predicted. Tripled women had unusually frequent health problems, consistent with their intense experience of crowding (Hopstock, Aiello, & Baum, 1979). Other research found lower grades among tripled students, despite their greater withdrawal (Glassman et al., 1978, see also Karlin, Rosen, & Epstein, 1979). "Tripled" roommates often formed a coalition of two students and one "isolate," who had particularly severe problems (Aiello, Baum, & Gormley, 1981; Baum, Shapiro, Murray, & Wideman, 1979; Reddy et al., 1981). The coalitions could reflect a reliance on supportive social relationships, which tend to act as buffers against stress (Switzer & Taylor, 1983).

A variant of the overload model, the **urban overload hypothesis,** says that city dwellers adapt to daily experience of crowds and other sources of stress by shunning involvement with other people (Korte, 1980; McCauley & Taylor, 1976). Unfortunately, this idea is difficult to test. Stanley Milgram (1970) found urbanites less willing than suburbanites to help strangers who asked for aid. However, the differences could reflect the norms of cities, or the personalities of people who choose to live there, as much as they reflect withdrawal to minimize overload.

To avoid comparing urban and suburban populations, some investigators have identified "high-input" and "low-input" areas within both cities and rural towns by measuring noise, automobile traffic, and pedestrian traffic (Korte, Ypma, & Toppen, 1975). They find that a person who acts like a stranger in need of assistance receives more help in low-input areas of both cities and small towns. In three other towns researchers measured the density of pedestrian traffic in selected locations, and in varying densities dropped stamped, addressed letters. As density increased, so did the proportion of passersby who ignored the letters (Kammann, Thomson, & Irwin, 1979). Similarly, city dwellers who lived on streets containing stores reported more crowding and avoided interaction on sidewalks and in public places more than those on streets without stores (Baum, Davis, & Aiello, 1978). Earlier research had found that people made less eye contact with strangers in cities than in suburbs or small towns (McCauley & Newman, 1977). To find out how the same people behaved in both city and suburb, researchers observed suburbanites who commuted to a busy area of Philadelphia (McCauley, Coleman, & DeFusco, 1978). The observers stood in train stations in the city in the mornings and in suburban stations in the evenings and recorded the number of people leaving the trains who returned their gaze. As the overload hypothesis predicted, fewer commuters made eye contact in the city.

Arousal models of crowding suggest that densely populated settings bring physiological and psychological arousal. Very high densities in laboratory rooms (think of a crowded concert) do produce signs of elevated arousal: increased skin conductance (Aiello, Epstein, & Karlin, 1975), blood pressure, and heart rate (Evans, 1979). Urine samples collected from riders of Swedish commuter trains showed increasing levels of epinephrine with increasing densities in cars (Singer, Lundberg, & Frankenhaeuser, 1978). Prisoners also had higher blood pressure in relatively crowded quarters (Paulus, McCain, & Cox, 1978).

Arousal in crowded conditions may stem from the discomfort of close interpersonal proximity and inappropriate *immediacy* of other people (Evans, 1978) or from uncertainty or even fear of harm (Paulus, 1980). Whether stress occurs, however, may depend on *attributions* concerning the source of arousal. Crowding may accompany the labeling of the situation as unpleasant (Patterson, 1976), or the attribution of the arousal to the other people or the crowded setting, and not to something else (Aiello, Thompson, & Brodzinsky, 1983; Worchel & Teddlie, 1976).

Through arousal, crowding can influence performance. The *arousal hypothesis* suggests that performance increases with arousal up to a point, but thereafter decreases (Sundstrom, 1986a). Simple tasks are thought to have higher optimum levels of arousal than complex ones (recall the discussion of *social facilitation* in Chapter Fourteen). So if crowding stimulates arousal, it should facilitate performance of simple tasks but hinder performance of complex tasks. Early laboratory experiments failed to find effects of density on performance. Groups of volunteers sat in crowded rooms and worked math problems, marked certain letters in a text, formed words from letters, and did other chores for several hours.

They did no better or worse than groups in more comfortable densities (Freedman, Klevansky, & Ehrlich, 1971; Ross et al., 1973; Stokols et al., 1973; see Baum & Paulus, 1987). Later, more complex tasks did show the expected decrement in performance. Volunteers traced a three-dimensional maze more poorly in crowded conditions (Paulus et al., 1976; see also Paulus, 1980; Paulus & Mathews, 1980). Similarly, volunteers made more errors in two concurrent tasks in high density (Evans, 1979).

According to *interference models* of crowding, people in densely populated settings constrain our behavior, interfere with our activities, impede the achievement of goals, and cause frustration (Schopler & Stockdale, 1978; Stokols, 1976; Sundstrom, 1975b). *Behavioral constraint* occurs when the mere presence of others hinders the completion of activities, as in a waiting line at the checkout counter of a store (Montano & Adamopoulos, 1984). *Interference* can involve physical obstruction, as in exiting a crowded subway. In either case, the model predicts negative feelings, hostility, and even aggression toward others. For example, children in a play area acted more aggressively as their numbers increased (Hutt & Vaizey, 1966). In laboratory experiments with adults, members of all-male groups generally reacted negatively to others in high density, but all-female groups showed positive reactions (Sundstrom, 1978). In a task sensitive to physical interference, people in cramped quarters got in one another's way and worked inefficiently (Heller, Groff, & Solomon, 1977). When volunteers in another experiment searched a file cabinet for certain items, increased group size produced the expected drop in performance. Payment by piece rate improved performance in high density, at a cost of greater stress (McCallum et al., 1979).

According to the *control* model of crowding, stress arises from an inability to influence events in high-density settings (Rodin & Baum, 1978). Threats to personal control can involve restricted space, excessive immediacy, and—most important—unmanageable numbers of people (Baron & Rodin, 1978). The model predicts greater crowding as personal control decreases, even if density remains constant. For example, passengers on an elevator with four other people (confederates in the experiment) experienced greater crowding when they had been maneuvered away from the control panel than when they stood near it (Rodin, Solomon, & Metcalf, 1978). Passengers on Swedish commuter trains who boarded at the first stop reported less distress and had less epinephrine in their urine than those who boarded at midroute—apparently because of the greater control in choosing a seat at the first stop (Singer et al., 1978). In a laboratory experiment, groups of women worked in cramped or spacious conditions. Some were told they could leave at any time, so that they might have a sense of control. Later, those exposed to high density with no control did more poorly than the others on measures of tolerance for frustration. Also consistent with the control model, the posting of large signs in the lobby of a prison giving directions to telephones and water fountains and other instructions was followed by a decline in reports of crowding among visitors (Wener & Kaminoff, 1983).

Similarly, information about a high-density situation in a laboratory reduced crowding (Baum, Fisher, & Solomon, 1981).

The control model implies that chronic failure to achieve personal control promotes *learned helplessness,* as in the long-corridor dormitories. Consistent with this model, children from crowded three-room apartments showed little persistence in working a solvable puzzle after trying an unsolvable one (Rodin, 1976). Besides passivity, learned helplessness includes depression, which could partly account for high rates of suicide in crowded prisons.

According to Irwin Altman's (1975) theory of *privacy regulation,* excessive social contact prompts coping—through withdrawal, avoidance of nonverbal immediacy, territorial behavior, and other tactics. If efforts at boundary control meet with repeated failure, the individual experiences chronic stress and eventual erosion of self-identity. These effects could also contribute to the pathologies found in crowded prisons.

Attachment to Places

This section discusses attachment to physical settings and its role in organizing social interaction and relationships. We begin by exploring the idea that humans have territories, and then discuss home environments, workplaces, neighborhoods, and public places.

Territories

A **territory** constitutes a zone of control and influence. According to Altman's theory of privacy regulation, territories serve to organize interpersonal relationships and provide a basis for regulating social contact. The use of the term *territory* to describe an attachment to a place, however, invokes an ethological model of human behavior.

To an ethologist, the term *territory* refers to a specific place that an animal marks or identifies with a call, a scent, or some other sign, and uses for nesting and as a base for hunting or foraging. If another member of the same species crosses the boundary, a confrontation ensues—with posturing, threatening gestures, or even ritualized combat. The intruder usually retreats. Not all species exhibit territorial behavior, however, and territorial species vary greatly in their instinctive patterns of behavior (see Wynne-Edwards, 1962).

Territoriality serves many functions that promote the survival of a species. It ensures dispersion of families evenly over a habitat, which in turn minimizes overgrazing and overhunting. It provides nesting sites for the rearing of young; it provides a basis for social organization (Carpenter, 1958). One ethologist who observed free-ranging domestic cats noted that when two individuals met outside their territories, the animal with lower rank in the local dominance hierarchy usually retreated. In their own territories, however, residents nearly always drove away intruders, even those of higher rank in the dominance hierarchy (Leyhausen, 1965). Such **territorial dominance** permits even low-ranked animals to keep territories.

Are humans territorial? Some people claim we are, and argue that human violence stems in part from instinctive responses to territorial encroachment (Ardrey, 1966; Lorenz, 1966; see Chapter Eleven). We do claim places, but in more complex ways than nonhuman species. For instance, if we are among the territorial species, we are unique in entertaining guests (Edney, 1974). Although observations of nonhuman territoriality obviously cannot be generalized directly to humans, our behavior is still analogous to territoriality. We maintain homes and apartments, work at assigned work stations, and temporarily lay claim to tables in restaurants, spaces in parks, benches at bus stops, and portions of other public places. Anybody who has strayed into a farmer's field only to confront the owner's shotgun will probably think twice before completely dismissing the idea that humans have territories.

Humans do seem to exhibit a form of territorial dominance, in that we dominate encounters on our own turf. A physician noticed, for instance, that patients appeared submissive in his office but acted assertive and confident when he called at their homes (Coleman, 1968). An experiment in a college dormitory also demonstrated territorial dominance. Pairs of students debated in one student's room about the appropriate jail sentence for a fictional criminal. One argued for the prosecution, the other for the defense. Whether they prosecuted or defended, those in their own rooms argued more persuasively and spent more time talking than their visitors (Martindale, 1971).

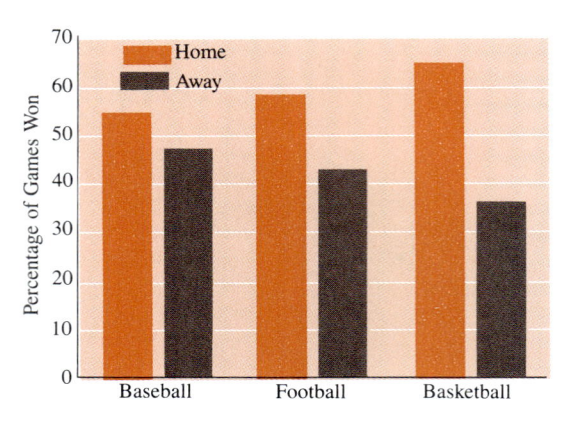

Figure 17–11 Percentages of "home" and "away" games won by professional baseball, football, and basketball teams during the 1979–80 season

In another dormitory, pairs consisting of a resident and a visitor worked on a cooperative task in the resident's room. Half of the pairs held similar attitudes and half held dissimilar attitudes. Among pairs with dissimilar attitudes, residents exerted more "dominant speech patterns," as expected. When attitudes were similar, however, the residents deferred to the visitors in the cooperative task, exhibiting a "hospitality effect" (Conroy & Sundstrom, 1977). A later study explored territorial dominance in triads of college men, in which one had a low score on dominance, one had a moderate score, and one had a high score. The triads worked together on a problem-solving task in one member's room. Regardless of the resident's own score on dominance, the average triad's solution reflected greater influence by the resident than by either visitor (Taylor & Lanni, 1982).

Perhaps territorial dominance contributes to the well-known *home-field advantage* in competitive sports. In 1979–80, for instance, baseball, football, and basketball teams won significantly more games in their home fields or arenas than away from home. Figure 17–11 shows the record of professional teams, which reveals a pronounced home-field advantage in basketball. College football and baseball teams also won more games at home than on the road (Hirt & Kimble, 1981; Schwartz & Barsky, 1977). Home fields may constitute territories because of home teams' frequent use and control of them. If so, perhaps the visiting teams feel inhibited or intimidated, or the home team feels assertive or confident on its own turf. But the home team has other advantages. For one thing, its members know the quirks of the playing field. For another, the visiting team may suffer fatigue from traveling (Schwartz & Barsky, 1977). The home team can also benefit from the behavior of its fans. To investigate this phenomenon, Greer (1983) analyzed the performance of college men's basketball teams during the five minutes following sustained protests involving concerted booing and shouting by fans. All of 15 episodes during two playing seasons represented support for the home team. Most involved protests at referees' calls favoring the visiting team. After these episodes, performance improved among home teams but declined among visitors. Debate continues over the reasons for the home-field advantage.

If we are territorial, humans have more than one kind of territory. Irwin Altman (1975) identifies three types of territories (see Table 17–2), in a typology supported by subsequent research (Brown, 1987; Taylor & Stough, 1978). **Primary territories** are places "owned and exclusively used by individuals or groups, . . . clearly identified as theirs by others, . . . controlled on a relatively permanent basis, and . . . central to the day-to-day lives of the occupants" (p. 112). We use our primary territories, such as homes and private offices, for long periods of time, and decorate or modify them to express individual or collective identity. These places provide privacy for solitude and intimacy (Taylor & Ferguson, 1980). **Secondary territories** consist of areas claimed and used by groups, who try to maintain control over

Table 17–2 Three types of territories

Type of Territory	Occupants	Pattern of Use	Control and Privacy	Examples
Primary	Individual, family	Regular, frequent use; long-term occupancy; personally important activities	High degree of control over access; high level of privacy	Bedroom; family residence; private office
Secondary	Group	Regular use by group members	Moderate control over access by nonmembers	Neighborhood bar, church, park; meeting room; fraternity house; apartment building
Public	Individual, group	Temporary use for limited periods	Limited control; little if any privacy	Table at restaurant, bench at bus stop, seat in theater or classroom

Source: Adapted from Altman, 1975.

access to their turf. Regular users of neighborhood bars, for instance, sometimes claim them as territories and discourage outsiders by glaring or making hostile remarks (Cavan, 1963). Juvenile gangs claim zones of cities (Van Vliet, 1983). Fraternities, clubs, congregations, and other groups maintain zones of controlled access. Individuals temporarily claim small **public territories** in spaces available to practically anyone, such as outdoor benches, telephone booths, public beaches, and tables at libraries or parks. Such places often have norms concerning users and their behavior. Some restaurants, for example, turn away customers without shoes; others refuse to admit men without jacket and tie (though waiters usually have extras available). Public territories generally allow very little privacy.

Some writers define **interaction territories** as areas immediately surrounding two or more people holding a conversation (Lyman & Scott, 1967). Analogous to "personal space" for individuals, these areas resemble invisible bubbles that last only as long as the conversations within them. People usually hesitate to invade interaction territories; those who do intrude show signs of discomfort and submissiveness. The "permeability" of an interaction territory depends on such things as the size of the group, their apparent status, and their race (Cheyne & Efran, 1972; Brown, 1981; Efran & Cheyne, 1972, 1973, 1974; Knowles, 1972, 1973).

Home Environments

Home environments represent more than zones of control; they also express our identities and relationships with the larger community. The location, size, design, and other features of a home symbolize social status (Duncan, 1986), group membership (Altman & Gauvain, 1981), and self-identity (Dovey, 1986). Homes embody our connections with past and future (Werner, Altman, & Oxley, 1986). One study found commitment to the residence associated with physical definition of boundaries: residents of houses surrounded by fences, hedges, retaining walls, and other borders were found to have lived there longer, intended to stay longer, and answered their doorbells faster than their neighbors whose boundaries were less clearly defined (Edney, 1972). Other research found affiliation with neighborhood or community associated with decoration of houses and yards. Residents with strongest social ties to the neighborhood had most decorations (Greenbaum & Greenbaum, 1981). Of 139 suburban homes studied, more of those on blocks or cul-de-sacs with greater affiliation and contact among residents were decorated for Halloween and Christmas (Brown & Werner, 1985).

Use of the physical environment to express self-identity—or **personalization**—represents a form of commitment to a place and perhaps an expression of territorial control. In dormitory rooms at a large university, researchers counted such things as posters, rugs, stereos, and other personal objects, and identified students who had left the university for non-academic reasons (Hansen & Altman, 1976). They found that dropouts had displayed fewer personal items than students who remained on campus. Another study in the same dormitories found a greater number of personal objects in the rooms of students who later dropped out than in the rooms of those who stayed, but the dropouts' markers, unlike those of students who stayed in school, concerned other localities, such as former residences (Vinsel et al., 1980).

Families divide their homes into zones for privacy and shared activities. Researchers identified four types of space among 45 families with two to four children (Sebba & Churchman, 1983). *Public* areas—including all hallways and bathrooms, almost all living rooms, and about a third of all kitchens—belonged to the entire family. All members of a family used *jurisdiction* areas, but recognized them as the domain of one member; these areas comprised 56% of kitchens, where mothers had responsibility. *Shared* areas belonged to subgroups, and included all parents' bedrooms and some bedrooms used by two or three children. *Individual* areas included single bedrooms and some parents' studies. The four types of areas resemble the concentric zones of accessibility discussed earlier, but depend on family norms as much as on physical boundaries and barriers (see Altman, Nelson, & Lett, 1972). Some families maintain a *privacy gradient:* they receive acquaintances in the living room, allow friends in the dining room, but invite only close friends and relatives into the kitchen (Fisher, Bell, & Baum, 1984).

When a group shares living quarters, its success may depend on orderly use of the environment consistent with the group's structure and activities—and a failure to establish territorial patterns may be associated with failure of the group (Altman, Taylor, & Wheeler, 1971). In several groups confined to institutions, members' use of the environment reflected the group's dominance hierarchy. On a mental ward, high-ranked members of a group of patients tended to move freely about the entire ward, while those of lesser rank claimed specific places (Esser et al., 1964). In a prison, highly dominant members of a group of inmates had access to most space and had the most desirable bunks (Austin & Bates, 1974). In a reform school, dominant members of a group of boys also occupied the most desirable places—as long as the group's membership remained stable. When the group changed (two highly dominant boys left and two new boys entered), the whole group's territorial behavior dropped. The boys roved about instead of using specific locations; the tendency for dominant boys to use desirable places disappeared. At the same time, cottage supervisors reported a 50% increase in incidents of aggression. Within a few weeks aggression subsided and territorial behavior resumed as the group regained its equilibrium (Sundstrom & Altman, 1974).

Workplaces

Offices and factories do not always have places for workers to call their own. In some factories employees go to different work stations each day; their only zones of control are lockers. But in some offices people have as much control as over their environments at home (Sundstrom, 1986a, 1987). In offices with individually assigned work stations, or **work spaces,** the highest satisfaction with the environment is associated with personalization of the work space—display of photographs, posters, rugs, and other personal belongings (Brill, 1984).

Personalization can serve as a **status marker,** or a physical feature of a work space that signals the occupant's standing or formal rank in the organization (Konar & Sundstrom, 1986). The offices of corporate executives often reflect their status; a promotion brings a larger office with more and better furniture. A study of 529 office workers investigated some of the traditional symbols of status—including private office, closable door, large work space, large or expensive desk, and capacity for personalization—and found them most prevalent among people with supervisory responsibility. These workers reported greatest satisfaction with their environments in work spaces they saw as commensurate with their status (Konar et al., 1982).

Neighborhoods

Perhaps the most controversial ideas about physical characteristics of neighborhoods concern their connections with crime. Oscar Newman (1972) studied architectural correlates of crime in public housing projects in New York City and found that rates of robbery rose with the number of stories per building

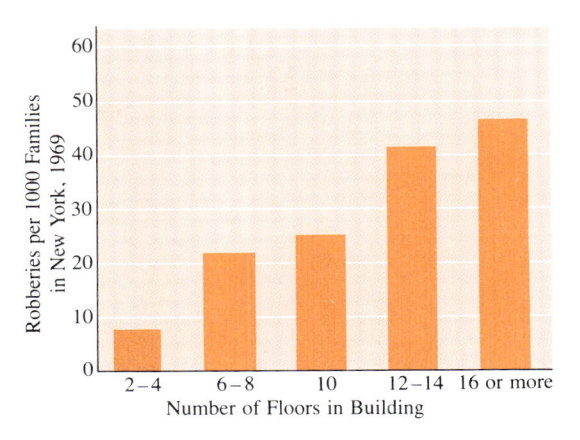

Figure 17-12 Rate of robberies in public housing in New York City per 1000 families as a function of the number of stories per building. A controversial theory that links architecture and crime suggests that residents of high-rise buildings have more difficulty regulating access to their buildings as neighbors become too numerous to recognize and distinguish from outsiders.

(Figure 17-12). Robberies in high-rise buildings consisted mainly of muggings in public areas—especially elevators, halls, and lobbies—not easily visible to residents or passers-by. To discourage such crime, Newman advocated defensible space in apartment buildings: entrances and public areas should be so arranged that they would be subject to *natural surveillance,* and buildings should be physically subdivided into *zones of territorial influence*—areas small enough to allow local residents to recognize one another and to distinguish outsiders.

Newman cited the infamous Pruitt-Igoe housing project in St. Louis as an example of nondefensible space. It opened in the 1950s: 33 buildings, each 11 stories tall, with a total of 2,764 apartments for low-income families. Within a few years it had become a crime-ridden wreck and a haven for derelicts, and nearly 70% of the apartments were vacant. Eventually the city demolished it. Its failure probably reflects its location in a slum and the design of the buildings, whose large size made recognition of outsiders difficult. The towers stood on featureless grounds that lacked even symbolic boundaries, and each had several entrances through which people could come and go unseen by residents. One building, however, differed. Construction workers had erected a chain-link fence around it to protect building materials, and residents persuaded them to leave it. Two years later the building had 80% less vandalism than the others, and over 95% of its apartments were occupied. The fence apparently limited access by outsiders and created a zone of control (Newman, 1972).

Later studies found some of the expected links between architecture and crime. Investigators reported twice the rate of theft in six- to ten-story dormitories as in three- to four-story dormitories, and found that residents of the smaller buildings knew their neighbors better (Bynum & Purri, 1984). Other investigators examined suburban single-family residences that had been burglarized and compared them with nonburglarized homes (Brown & Altman, 1983). Burglarized homes had fewer visible signs of occupancy, such as automobiles in the driveways or lawn sprinklers operating. Nonburglarized homes had more symbolic barriers, such as address signs and hedges, and more actual barriers, such as fences, and permitted better surveillance by neighbors.

Territorial control in neighborhoods depends as much on the social context as on the architecture. When residents of urban blocks were asked to rate the effectiveness of territorial displays such as shrubbery and lawn furniture, they saw real barriers such as fences as deterrents to intrusion, but those who lived in cohesive neighborhoods saw the displays as more effective (Brower, Dockett, & Taylor, 1983). Other researchers surveyed 448 families on city blocks where people "help each other" or go their own way (Taylor, Gottfredson, & Brower, 1981). Residents of cohesive blocks had fewer problems with vandalism, littering, troublemakers, and other intrusions in territories near their homes. Such problems occurred more often in low-income districts of rental properties than in middle-income districts of owner-occupied homes.

Territorial displays reflect residents' perceptions of personal control. Elderly residents whose homes had physically defined boundaries or outdoor decorations felt relatively safe from crime (Pollock & Patterson, 1980; Patterson, 1978). Among elderly women living in a large city, those who were fearful of crime perceived that they had little territorial control and little personal control over events or ability to predict them (Normoyle & Lavrakas, 1984).

It has been suggested that the closer we get to home, the greater our sense of territorial control (Taylor & Brower, 1986). This model of "near-home" territories incorporates a gradient of increasing desire for control in increasingly "central" settings. As Figure 17–13 indicates, desired control is greatest in the home and successively less on porch, yard, sidewalk, block, and neighborhood. Perceived threat increases with decreasing centrality, reaching a maximum in dangerous parts of the city. Each step represents a boundary—perceived by the resident, and perhaps defined physically.

According to this theory, when we face insufficient or threatened control in near-home territories,

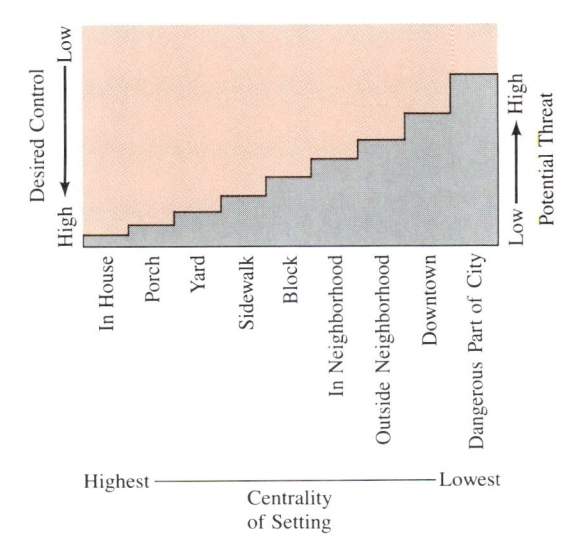

Figure 17-13 Gradient of desired control and potential threat in "near-home" territories

we can react in three ways. One involves *expansion or reassertion* of territorial control, as in a neighborhood that responds to loitering teenagers and a rash of purse snatching by forming an organization and helping police remove the troublemakers. The second strategy, *bulwarking*, involves the addition or reinforcement of physical barriers, as in a neighborhood that blocks a through street to create a cul-de-sac and adds a gate and guardhouse at the entry. The third strategy is *retreat*, as in neighborhoods where residents react to littering and vandalism in their front yards by redefining them as part of the sidewalks, abandoning them, and withdrawing. Expansion strengthens the social order underlying territorial control, but bulwarking isolates existing problems, and retreat may encourage decay of the social and physical order of the neighborhood (see Taylor, 1982).

Public Spaces

In choosing public territories, we seem to prefer a polite distance between ourselves and other users. Observations in a library, for example, revealed that students who entered alone usually sat at tables by themselves (64%). Those who sat at tables already occupied by other students usually took the most distant chair (diagonally across the table). Users of other libraries maximized their distance from other people or their belongings (Sommer, 1966) and stayed longest at tables where nobody else sat (Becker, 1973).

Occupants of public territories signal their claims nonverbally. A study in a game arcade, for example, found that newcomers claimed machines by touching or manipulating them. Users reacted to prospective intrusion with prolonged touching of their machines (Werner, Brown, & Damron, 1981).

A sense of control over a public territory depends on the length of time the occupant has been there. In a campus snack bar, a confederate approached people who had been seated for varying lengths of time and said, "Excuse me, but you are sitting in my seat." Those who had been seated for only a few minutes tended to leave apologetically, but those who had been there longer resisted displacement (Sommer, 1969). On a beach, the longer a party of people had been there, the larger the area they viewed as "theirs" (Edney & Jordan-Edney, 1974).

People sometimes assert a continuing claim to a public space by leaving personal belongings while they are absent. To investigate such **territorial markers,** Sommer (1969) left a newspaper, a paperback book, or a sweater to reserve a chair at the campus snack bar. Someone sat in a marked chair during only 14% of the trials. Another experiment in a crowded study hall involved various types of

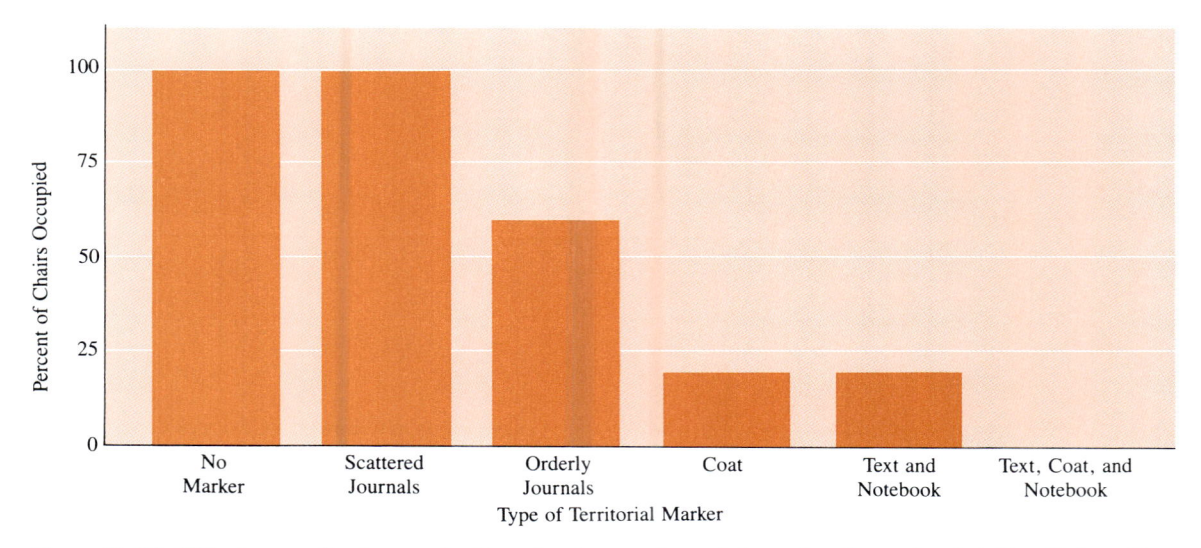

Figure 17–14 Effectiveness of various territorial markers in reserving a chair at a heavily used study hall, as indicated by the percentage of chairs occupied by another student

markers, as shown in Figure 17–14. On several evenings an observer recorded how much time elapsed before someone sat in a marked chair and a randomly chosen unmarked chair. After an average of 20 minutes an unmarked chair had an occupant. In contrast, a sport coat, notebook, and textbook held a marked chair for the whole evening (Sommer & Becker, 1969). In a bar where all tables were occupied and people were waiting, a jacket with a briefcase or bookbag deterred users from taking a temporarily vacant table, but the markers proved more effective if they appeared to belong to a man than if they appeared to belong to a woman. Markers deterred would-be users of peripheral tables more than tables with "high interaction potential" (Shaffer & Sadowski, 1975; see also Becker & Conglio, 1975).

Holding a public territory depends more on the restraint shown by potential users than on the active defense of territorial claims. When a would-be user approaches a marked chair, he or she usually asks a neighbor whether it is taken. But neighbors seldom defend territorial claims in the occupant's absence unless the prospective user has asked (Sommer & Becker, 1969). People sometimes use their own belongings to mark absent neighbors' territories, but only the exceptional neighbor will challenge an intruder (Hoppe, Greene, & Kenny, 1972).

Even the "owner" of a public territory may hesitate to confront an intruder (Becker & Mayo, 1971). In a study conducted in a classroom during a break in a long class, an invader took a seat that another student had occupied. Only 27% of invaded students confronted the invader and asked for their seats back, although those whose chairs were in the center of the room were more likely to defend them (Haber, 1980). Fortunately, such invasions of public territories probably occur infrequently—except perhaps by social psychologists.

Summary

Debate over *environmental determinism* questions whether climate, geography, and architecture can influence behavior. Research described in this chapter suggests that physical settings enter into interpersonal behavior in many ways: as sources of stress, contexts for conversation, constraints on interpersonal accessibility, sources of distraction, symbols of identity and status, boundaries around neighborhoods, and others.

The *ambient environment*—including temperature, air quality, sound, and light—can stimulate *arousal* or even lead to *stress*. Environmental sources of stress, such as loud noise, are evaluated against personal standards of judgment called *adaptation levels*. Environmental stressors can lead to overload and can have delayed adverse psychological effects. However, stressors are most disturbing when they are first encountered; after continued exposure to a stressor, a person can become accustomed to it through *adaptation* in perceptions.

Uncomfortably warm temperatures are associated with increased rates of violent crime and other expressions of hostility. Loud, uncontrollable *noise* decreases altruism and attention to some social cues, and increases responsiveness to provocation. *Air pollution* from cigarette smoke has been associated with disliking and negative evaluations of smokers, and even hostility in a laboratory experiment. Voice levels tend to be louder in bright light than in dim light.

Architecture enters into social behavior by providing pleasing environments, in which people respond favorably to one another. *Sociopetal spaces* encourage conversation through seating arrangements that bring people into comfortable conversational distance, facing each other directly enough to allow eye contact. A desk or table between conversants adds psychological distance to an encounter.

Participation in classrooms is greatest in the front and center seats, where eye contact between student and instructor is most likely, and in center sections of the room, locations that lend themselves to social facilitation. People usually choose friends from among those whose residences or work spaces are closest to their own, apparently because *propinquity* provides convenient opportunities for interaction. Residential design can create too much social contact, however, as in dormitories that incorporate long corridors with central bathrooms and lounges. Occupants of corridor-design dormitories have reported unwanted interaction, and have demonstrated social withdrawal and even signs of *learned helplessness*.

The physical environment provides a resource for regulating and organizing interpersonal interaction and for obtaining *privacy*. Privacy contributes to autonomy and control over self-presentation. Mechanisms of *privacy regulation*, such as territory and personal space, allow an individual to optimize his or her level of involvement with other people. According to the theory of a *hierarchy of spaces*—public, semipublic, semiprivate, and private—an individual obtains greatest privacy in spaces least accessible to others. Privacy in offices is associated with physical enclosure of work spaces. Workers in *open-plan offices* have reported dissatisfaction with the lack of privacy. Teachers in *open-space schools* report greater interaction, more noise, and more distraction, and devote more time to classroom management.

Crowding, a form of stress, can occur in conditions of high *population density,* when people are concentrated in a relatively small space. At one time high density in large cities was thought to foster disease, crime, and mental illness. But evidence for the *social pathology hypothesis* came from weak correlational studies and research on nonhumans. Rigorous studies of urban populations find little connection between density and pathology. Research in prisons, however, has found density to be associated with illness, psychiatric commitments, and even death rates.

Theorists have identified several sources of stress in high density, including overload, arousal, interference, and lack of personal control. According to the *urban overload hypothesis,* city dwellers react to congestion by avoiding involvement with people. High density can stimulate arousal, which if prolonged can have adverse effects on health. Interference by other people in crowded conditions may increase the chances of aggression; lack of personal control can lead to learned helplessness. General theories of crowding suggest that when these sources of stress coincide, crowding can adversely affect physical health and performance.

We form attachments to places by claiming *territories,* analogous to the bounded regions claimed and defended by certain nonhuman animals. Human attachments to places, however, are complex and involve several types of territories. A *primary territory* is central to the individual's daily life and allows considerable control. Here the occupant has an advantage in a competitive encounter—a phenomenon called *territorial dominance*. A *secondary territory* is controlled by a group, which regulates access by outsiders. A *public territory,* temporarily claimed in a public place, gives its occupants little control. An *interaction territory* surrounds a conversation in progress, and passers-by hesitate to intrude.

Home environments signal our past, present, and future relationships with the community through exterior appearance, decoration, and demarcation of boundaries. Individual identity is expressed through *personalization*. Interior arrangements of a residence may reflect a gradient of privacy, with some areas accessible to outsiders and others reserved for intimate encounters. Territorial patterns among the members of a group who share an environment depend on the group's dominance hierarchy. In work environments, characteristics of an individual *work space* and *status markers* signal the occupant's rank or standing in the organization. In neighborhoods, the design of the environment can lessen the likelihood of crime through "defensible space" that incorporates clearly marked boundaries, subdivided areas small enough so that residents can recognize one another, and opportunities for surveillance. In public places we select temporary territories far from others and claim them through *territorial markers*—belongings left while we are absent. Such markers may or may not be respected.

Glossary Terms

adaptation
adaptation level

air pollution
ambient environment
arousal
crowding
density intensity hypothesis
environmental determinism
interaction territory
learned helplessness
noise
open-plan office
open-space school
personalization
population density
primary territory
privacy
privacy regulation
propinquity
public territory
secondary territory
shared stress effect
social pathology hypothesis
sociopetal spaces
status marker
stress
territorial dominance
territorial marker
territory
urban overload hypothesis
work space

*Research that produces nothing but books
will not suffice.*
Kurt Lewin

One faces the future with one's past.
Pearl S. Buck

Paul Klee, *Mural from the Temple of Longing Thither*, 1922. The Metropolitan Museum of Art, The Berggruen Klee Collection, 1984. (1984.315.33)

CHAPTER EIGHTEEN

Social Psychology & Society

I. Pure Science or Applied Science—or Both?
    The Waxing and Waning of Applied Interests
    Kurt Lewin and Action Research
II. Health Care and Medical Practice
    Causes of Illness
    Identification of Medical Problems
    Prevention of Illness
    Treatment of Illness
III. Energy Use
    Conservation Strategies
    Social Traps
IV. The Legal System
    Setting Bail
    Jury Selection
    Trial Procedures
V. From Problems to Solutions
    Documenting Problems
    Evaluating Solutions
    Strategies for Change
VI. Summary

Social psychology has discovered a great deal about human behavior—how people love and hate, how they help and harm, how they perceive as individuals, and how they relate in groups. However, the more cynical reader may still ask, "What good does this knowledge do?" After all, much of the research of social psychology has been conducted in laboratories, in a rarefied atmosphere removed from the currents of everyday life. Yet astronomy laboratories have put people on the moon, biological laboratories have developed vaccines to prevent polio, and physics laboratories have produced nuclear energy, with both good and ill effects. Can social psychology match this record of contribution to society?

Some people argue that social psychology has done little. Virulent critics claim that social psychology *can't* do anything—that it has little to contribute to solving the problems of society. But there is evidence to the contrary. Although errors have been made and applications have not been as rapid as many people would like, there is substantial evidence of social-psychological contributions to understanding and solving social issues. And the potential for contribution is even greater.

Many people have recognized the need for social-psychological contributions. Although technological developments in the past several decades have been tremendous, it often seems that humanity has made little headway over centuries. Yet we may be on the brink of changing that assessment—of using social psychology not to control people but to help them run their own lives in more profitable ways. In his presidential address to the American Psychological Association, George A. Miller (1970) urged an extension of this view. He said, "I can imagine nothing that we could do that would be more relevant to human welfare, and nothing that could pose a greater challenge to the next generation of psychologists, than to discover how best to give psychology away" (p. 21).

Miller, reflecting a theme of this book, notes that each of us makes assumptions about human nature. All people routinely "practice psychology" as they attempt to cope with the problems of their everyday lives. But, Miller states, they could practice it better if they knew which assumptions were scientifically verified—if the valid principles of psychology were "given away" to them. For some social psychologists Miller's words have served as a beacon. Throughout this textbook we have tried to show how psychological knowledge can be applied to your own behavior—not only to interpersonal behaviors but also to the larger problems that our societies face now and in the future. The aim is an ambitious one, to be sure, but the potential consequences are substantial and possibly even critical to our future.

Pure Science or Applied Science —or Both?

The ideal of social scientists applying their knowledge to the solution of social problems sounds quite sensible. You may be surprised, however, to learn that many social psychologists have not tried to put their findings to any practical use. Moreover, considerable debate and controversy have raged about whether social psychologists *should* become involved in applied research, much less in social intervention. Some basic-research scientists have felt that it is not part of their role as scientists to point out the practical value of their findings. In fact, some have held that "the pursuit of scientific knowledge is a good activity in its own right, and even better since scientific knowledge is an absolute good apart from its consequences" (Baumrin, 1970, p. 74). This position has been commonly called *knowledge for knowledge's sake*. Other basic scientists, although they do not doubt that scientific findings will eventually prove useful, argue that application at this time is premature. Applied scientists, in contrast, advocate that science should study human problems now in order to work out solutions and determine what the consequences of any action might be. Although arguments have flourished between these two polar positions, social psychology has, throughout its history, produced representatives of both camps, as well as individuals who conduct both basic and applied research, either simultaneously or in alternation. The brief look at the history of social psychology in the next section will confirm this statement.

The Waxing and Waning of Applied Interests

The earliest work in social psychology consisted mainly of laboratory ventures. Although the problems were often inspired by real-world events, the objective was to understand basic principles rather than to solve real-world problems. Throughout the first 40 years of this century, research encompassed both laboratory and field settings, although the laboratory took increasing precedence in the work of many social psychologists.

During World War II, social psychology blossomed and was very often applied as well. Much of the early work on attitude change, as developed by the Yale Communication Research Program (see Chapter Seven), was aimed at very practical problem solving—how to maintain good morale and high performance in soldiers during the war. During this same period, Kurt Lewin was making major and highly influential contributions to the field of social psychology, and his program of *action research* (which we will discuss in more detail) was explicitly aimed at fusing basic and applied research into a single pursuit.

Despite Lewin's effort, however, many of his followers became more and more attracted to the laboratory. The research of the 1950s and 1960s focused increasingly on developing sophisticated theoretical models within a laboratory setting and disdained application (Ring, 1967). In part this shift reflected a belief among social psychologists that the more rigorously controlled laboratory experiments they conducted, the more credibility would accrue to the discipline. In other words, the more controlled and "pure" the research was, the more scientific its practitioners could claim to be. Other external factors also played a part in this retreat to the ivory tower during the 1950s and early 1960s. Universities tend to reward the specialist—particularly the specialist who is highly productive in terms of papers and reports. Practical problems, in contrast, often require a more interdisciplinary emphasis and a much greater span of time for completion than the more controlled laboratory experiment. During this period, applied psychologists more often worked in industry or for government organizations, whereas theoretically oriented psychologists remained in the university. Communication between the two camps was, unfortunately, often meager at best.

In the past decade or two, the pendulum has shifted again, and more and more investigators direct at least some of their attention to field settings (Rodin, 1985). Again there is more than one reason for the shift.

The social and political activism of the 1960s and 1970s challenged many academics to think beyond the ivory tower. Many of society's problems whose implications for psychology seemed evident—such as population growth, school desegregation, policy decisions—were not easily solved with the existent laboratory-based research findings. In real-world settings, as Robert Kahn (1981) noted, people are "playing for keeps," and traditional experimental procedures could not capture this urgency.

Although many social psychologists continue to engage primarily in laboratory research, many others have involved themselves to an increasing degree in the field. Armed with new statistical and methodological techniques and confronting a broader range of concepts and issues, these investigators have made important discoveries about social behavior in society. Lewin's legacy is having a rebirth.

Kurt Lewin and Action Research

Kurt Lewin was probably the strongest early advocate of combining applied and theoretical social psychology within a single structure. In developing his **field theory** (discussed in Chapter One), he argued that behavior must always be viewed in relation to the environment. And although he was a passionate defender of the importance of theory, he also argued that theory must deal with those variables in society that make a difference (Cartwright, 1978).

Lewin's statement that there is nothing so practical as a good theory has often served as the byword of the social-psychological enterprise. Yet, ironically, the context of this statement is often ignored, as investigators justify their exclusive laboratory experimentation and exclusion of practical problems. The full text of Lewin's statement gives a much more revealing picture of his beliefs:

> [Close cooperation between theoretical and applied psychology] can be accomplished . . . if the theorist does not look toward applied problems with highbrow aversion or with a fear of social problems, and if the applied psychologist realizes that there is nothing so practical as a good theory. [1951, p. 169]

Thus, although Kurt Lewin was interested in the development of theories, he was also interested in *doing* something with them. Lewin tried to resolve social conflicts such as marital friction, management/worker disputes, and the psychosociological problems of minority groups.

To describe his work, Lewin coined the term **action research**, defined as research whose goal is the understanding or solution of social problems. Action research is considered a process of "analysis, fact-finding or evaluation; and then a repetition of this whole circle of activities; indeed, a spiral of such circles" (Sanford, 1970, p. 4). In short, the action researcher obtains data about an organization, feeds these data into the organization, measures the change that occurs, and then repeats the process.

Lewin noted that community organizations and agencies that are concerned with eliminating and preventing social problems are often unsuccessful, no matter how hard they seem to try. His goal was to transform such goodwill into organized, efficient action by helping community groups answer three questions: (1) What is the present situation? (2) What are the dangers? And, most important of all, (3) What shall be done?

Lewin's goals were indeed lofty. They were to encourage social psychologists to focus on significant problems, to develop solid social-psychological theory, and to act as change and intervention agents as well. Perhaps it is not surprising that such an ambitious program could not be realized in his lifetime. Yet, as we shall see, the roots were good ones, and although the soil was inhospitable for some period and germination was slow, the products of Lewin's ideas are finally beginning to flourish.

As social psychologists go back and forth between laboratory and field settings, they gain increasing understanding of the determinants of human behavior and the contexts in which that behavior occurs. And just as the control and precision of the laboratory can help to isolate particular cause-and-effect relationships, so the context and complications of the field can help to define the concepts that need to be explored (Rodin, 1985). As Lewin claimed, the process indeed goes in both directions.

In recent years, social psychologists have tested the applicability of their knowledge in a wide variety of settings: health care, energy conservation, judicial processes, consumer protection, school desegregation, and the like. The list is lengthy, and we can deal with only a few of these issues. But these selections will, we hope, show that social psychology can and does contribute to society. In effect, they answer the question "But what good is it?"

Health Care and Medical Practice

Health care is a major industry in many countries and a major concern in most countries throughout the world. In the United States, for example, more than 10% of personal income is spent for health care, and the health industry is the largest service industry in the country (S. E. Taylor, 1978). In developing countries, health care often focuses on the young and on problems concerning birth and malnutrition. In more developed countries where zero population growth exists, more and more concern is focusing on the diseases of adults and the problems of the elderly.

Traditionally, problems of health were the province of medical personnel—of the doctors, nurses, and paramedics whose training is geared specifically toward health and illness. More recently, contributions from many other disciplines have been recognized, and the field of **behavioral medicine** has developed. Most simply, behavioral medicine is a field that integrates behavioral and biomedical science, focuses on health and illness, and concerns itself with the application of knowledge to the prevention, diagnosis, and treatment of illness.

Changing patterns of disease made it necessary to go beyond the traditional biomedical model of health (Krantz, Grunberg, & Baum, 1985). In the early part of this century, infectious diseases such as tuberculosis were the primary cause of death. Today people are more likely to die of cardiovascular disorders and cancer, both of which are influenced by behavioral and environmental factors. People choose to smoke, thereby increasing their risk of heart problems and lung cancer. People eat too much or eat the wrong kinds of foods, increasing their susceptibility to coronary problems. Thus medical factors alone are not enough to cure, much less prevent, the onset of today's predominant diseases.

Behavioral medicine is an interdisciplinary field, and social psychologists are not alone in contributing to it. However, social psychology's contributions—both actual and potential—are considerable, ranging from analysis of the causes of illness and the recognition by patients that they are ill to the procedures whereby services are delivered (S. E. Taylor, 1978). We will consider just a sample of the research done by social psychologists, looking at examples in four general categories: the causes of illness, the identification of illness, the prevention of illness (or the maintenance of health), and the treatment of illness.

Causes of Illness

The causes of physical and mental illness are numerous and vary from one disease to another. Causes of disease may be external to the person, residing in environmental conditions, or they may be rooted in individual biological conditions or behavior patterns.

Environmental causes of disease have frequently been the focus of public attention in recent years.

Possible effects of radiation from atomic bomb tests in Nevada have led citizens of St. George, Utah, to file suit against the government. Some years ago, a hotel in Philadelphia became famous as the site of "Legionnaire's disease." Pollution standards for industry have been widely debated as scientists learn more about the harmful effects of various chemical substances. In some cases, environmental events have direct, measurable effects on physical health. In other cases, environmental events may have their initial impact on people's psychological sense of well-being, which in turn can affect their physical health. Such was the case at Three Mile Island, Pennsylvania.

Following the initial accident at the nuclear power plant at Three Mile Island, decisions had to be made about the best method of removing the radioactive gas trapped inside the installation. After considerable debate, it was decided to vent the gas directly into the atmosphere. Contributing to this decision, in addition to the physical scientists, were social psychologists who had been assessing stress in the residents of Three Mile Island (Baum, Fleming, & Singer, 1982). Their recommendation was based in part on psychological findings showing that chronic stress (such as would be predicted if the release of gas continued over an extended period) is more debilitating than acute stress, which focuses on a limited point in time.

To study residents' reactions to these events, Andrew Baum and his colleagues collected a variety of measures from the residents at four times: before the venting took place, during the venting period, three to five days after the venting, and again six weeks after the venting period. As a basis of comparison, the researchers also surveyed residents of Frederick, Maryland, a town 80 miles away that was similar in many respects to Three Mile Island. Among the measures collected were self-reports of somatic stress—the degree to which the residents reported being bothered by a variety of physical symptoms. Figure 18–1 shows the results of this study. As the graph indicates, residents of Three Mile Island reported more physical stress symptoms at all four points in time than citizens in Frederick, Maryland. However, the graph also indicates that the frequency of reported symptoms was most intense before the venting began and decreased later.

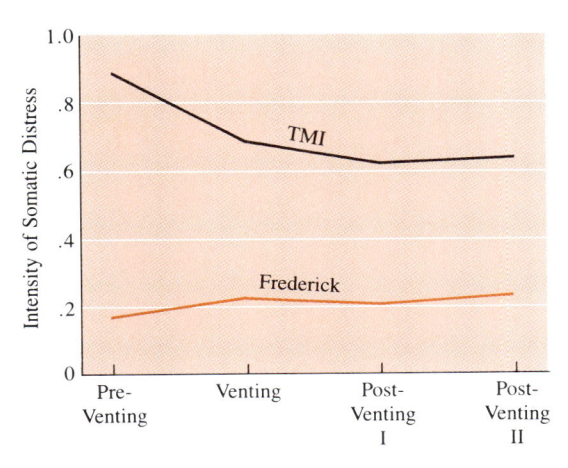

Figure 18–1 Somatic distress among citizens of Three Mile Island and citizens of Frederick, Maryland

In interpreting such data, one needs to be concerned about self-reports. Aware of the publicity and the researchers' interest, Three Mile Island residents could have inflated their reports of the symptoms they were actually feeling. However, other information collected by Baum and his colleagues suggests that the self-reports may be reliable. Both performance on a proofreading task and biochemical measures of stress showed similar patterns.

People's lifestyles can predispose them to certain forms of illness. Cigarette smoking is a prime example of how habits and behaviors can lead to illness.

People begin to smoke for many reasons; peer-group pressure, for example, is a strong influence on adolescents (Eiser & van der Pligt, 1984; McAlister, Krosnick, & Milburn, 1984). Other kinds of substance abuse are also influenced by the immediate context. Military personnel who used heroin in Vietnam, for example, were often able to give up the drug when they returned to their home environment. Similarly, other behavioral choices that may predispose one to illness—to avoid exercise, to drink excessive alcohol, or to have a poor diet—may be influenced by the social group with which one identifies and interacts.

Particular types of individuals are more likely to suffer certain illnesses. One of the most popular areas of investigation has been the study of people who show the **Type A behavior pattern**—a set of behaviors associated with increased risk of coronary heart disease. Among the behaviors that constitute the Type A pattern are intense achievement strivings, strong tendencies to challenge and compete with others, impatience with slowness, and frequent hostility (Matthews, 1982).

In opposition to the Type A pattern are Type B people, who generally show an absence of the Type A characteristics. Type A people, in contrast to Type B people, have been found to overestimate the passage of time, imagining a specified period of time to be longer than it actually is. Type A people are also likely to be more aggressive when they are frustrated and to react negatively to situations in which they have no control (Glass, 1977). Individuals characterized by the Type A pattern seek more performance challenges than do Type B people. Furthermore, once engaged in a challenging task, Type A's try to increase the activity and the demands. In an experiment conducted by Deems Ortega and Janet Pipal (1984), Type A and Type B subjects (assessed earlier by a questionnaire) first engaged in a 15-minute period of relaxation exercises, no activity (these subjects were termed the passive group), or active performance of a task. After this period, they were allowed to choose their desired level of challenge for a forthcoming task. As Figure 18–2 shows, the two types of people reacted quite differently. The more active Type A people had been, the more challenge they sought in the next task. Type B people, in contrast, showed a more compensatory type of response: the more active they had been earlier, the less activity they sought afterward.

Michael Strube (1986), suggests that Type A and Type B people differ primarily in the value that they place on productivity and success. Not only do Type A's place more value on these outcomes, but they also have a greater desire for self-appraisal. This difference is most apparent in situations that create uncertainty about one's abilities. A situation in which the individual lacks control is one such case. Similarly, when performance feedback is absent or inconsistent, uncertainty will occur. Under such conditions, Type A people will exert more effort in order to satisfy their need for self-appraisal.

Understanding *why* Type A people engage in the behaviors they do is an important first step in attempting to modify those behaviors that increase the risk of coronary disease. Social psychologists are contributing to these efforts, along with specialists from several other disciplines.

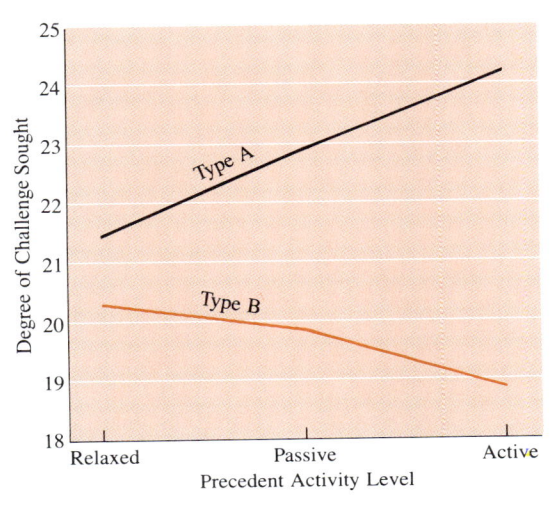

Figure 18-2 Degree of challenge sought by Type A and Type B subjects who had previously been relaxed, passive, or active

Identification of Medical Problems

Identification of a medical problem requires at least two steps: first, the prospective patient must recognize that there is a problem and seek medical help, and second, the medical personnel must make a correct diagnosis. In both phases, principles of social psychology may be applied.

Recognition of physical symptoms may vary from individual to individual. Recalling the concept of private self-consciousness, introduced in Chapter Three, we find that people who score high on this dimension are more likely to detect physical symptoms (Scheier, Carver, & Gibbons, 1979). Situations that focus attention on the body may lead to an increased awareness of physical problems (Pennebaker, 1982). As just one example, national publicity given to public figures (such as Betty Ford) with breast cancer may make the individual woman more prone to perform self-examinations and/or seek medical expertise.

Awareness of one's symptoms does not always lead to an immediate search for medical attention. Often the factors to which a person attributes a disability hinder the quest (Rodin, 1978; S.E. Taylor, 1982). A person may notice strange pigmentation of the skin, for example, but simply dismiss it as a bad case of sunburn rather than a potential skin cancer. Frequent stomach pains may be self-diagnosed as a minor case of nerves rather than a severe ulcer.

Judgments of the severity of a medical problem are biased when the illness is one's own; these judgments are also influenced by beliefs about the prevalence of the illness in question. In one study that investigated these factors, college students who participated in a study of health issues were told that they did or did not have a particular (and in truth nonexistent) enzyme deficiency (Jemmott, Ditto, & Croyle, 1986). Half of the subjects in each group were led to believe that 4 of every 5 people had the same deficiency, so that they received the impression that the presumed condition was very common. The other half of the subjects learned that the deficiency occurred in only 1 of 5 people, so that to them it seemed relatively rare. Both of these kinds of information, one concerning personal relevance and the other about the prevalence of the illness, influenced judgments of the severity of the condition. People who believed relatively few people had the deficiency considered it a less serious threat to health than did those who thought many people had it. Further, those who believed that they themselves had the condition rated it as significantly less serious than did people who had not been diagnosed as having the condition. This kind of defensiveness about one's own health, like the behavior of the person who ignores a persistent cough or dismisses a potential skin cancer, causes serious delays in the search for treatment, often leading to more serious disease.

Attributional processes may also come into play when the doctor makes a diagnosis (Snyder & Mentzer, 1978). As one example, consider the availability heuristic, which was discussed in Chapter Four. This principle of judgment suggests that people estimate the probability of an event on the basis of the psychological availability of that event (Tversky & Kahneman, 1973). In other words, if a number of cases of a particular symptom are readily in mind (such as cyanide poisoning, perhaps), then a physician may be predisposed to make that diagnosis quite readily—even if the likelihood of that condition is quite low.

The judgments of medical personnel may also be influenced by prevailing stereotypes. For example, Barbara Wallston and her colleagues found that nurses have generally negative perceptions of alcoholics (DeVellis, Wallston, & Wallston, 1978). When asked to evaluate an alcoholic patient, nurses responded much more negatively than they did to patients with other illnesses of comparable severity. Sex discrimination has been shown in hospital wards as well. Licensed practical nurses were asked to rate male and female patients who had identical illnesses. Nurses viewed the female patients more negatively and considered them less mentally healthy than the men—even though the illnesses were primarily physical rather than psychological.

Prevention of Illness

Illness can sometimes be relatively easy to prevent if a simple physical intervention is involved. Tooth decay, for example, has decreased dramatically with the addition of fluoride to the water supply. When changes in behavior and lifestyle are required, in contrast, prevention is much more difficult to achieve. There are at least two major obstacles (Krantz, Grunberg, & Baum, 1985). First, the threats posed by such things as smoking, poor eating habits, and lack of exercise often seem remote in comparison with the immediate gratifications they provide. And as learning theorists have shown, immediate rewards and punishments are typically much more effective than delayed outcomes. A second difficulty is the degree to which social behaviors are enacted in context and supported by the environment. Individuals who smoke, for example, often have friends and family who smoke and who support the activity (Eiser & van der Pligt, 1984; McAlister, Krosnick, & Milburn, 1984). This context produces resistance to any change directed at the individual alone.

Successful prevention programs need to deal with both of these obstacles, emphasizing short-term gains and creating a broad context of support.

As an example of a broad-scale intervention program aimed at preventing one particular health-threatening behavior, consider the antismoking program conducted by Richard Evans and his colleagues at the University of Houston (Evans et al., 1978, 1981). The goal of this program was to train adolescents to resist social pressures to begin smoking. Thus, rather than trying to get adults who are already addicted to cigarettes to stop smoking, this program focused on young people who hadn't yet started.

In initial interviews with a group of fifth-, sixth-, and seventh-grade students, the investigators learned that most of the children believed that smoking was dangerous to their long-range health. Nevertheless, more immediate pressures in the environment often encouraged them to smoke. Three pressures that were particularly strong were peer influence, parents who smoked, and media presentations of smokers.

To counteract these specific pressures, Evans and his colleagues designed a program to help children deal with the situation. Through a structured videotaped presentation, children were presented with information about the dangers of smoking, as well as illustrations of the pressures that peers, parents, and media can exert. Sessions followed in which students discussed each of these points, with posters placed in the room to remind students of the filmed messages.

To determine the effectiveness of the program, the investigators used not only self-reports of smoking behavior but also a saliva test that can detect the presence of nicotine in the body. The results of this multifaceted approach are encouraging. Ten weeks later, only 10% of students in the treatment group had begun to smoke, compared with 18% of students in a control group. Thus, although the treatment did not prevent all students from beginning to smoke, it reduced the number by almost 50%. Further, analysis of the behavior of students in this same school system three years later suggested that the campaign was an effective deterrent to smoking.

Social networks and systems not only serve to encourage or discourage specific preventive health behaviors. In addition, as we discussed in Chapter Nine, other people can serve as a general source of social support, and such support seems to offer a buffer against the stresses of life (Cohen & Wills, 1985). As a consequence, people who have a strong social network are less likely to become ill. There are several ways in which social support may serve this preventive function (Rodin, 1985). At the most immediate level, the presence of supportive networks may reduce anxiety and physiological stress. At a secondary level, friends can provide useful information about health and disease. Friends can also serve a diagnostic function, pointing out problems that the person has ignored or denied.

Just as some people, such as those with the Type A behavior pattern, are more prone to illness, so other types of people are more resistant to stress and illness. **Hardiness** is one characterization of such people, defined by Suzanne Kobasa as "a constellation of personality characteristics that function as a resistance resource in the encounter with stressful life events" (Kobasa, Maddi, & Kahn, 1982, p. 169). More specifically, hardy people have three general characteristics: a sense of commitment to their lives; a belief that they can control events; and a view of change as a positive challenge (Kobasa, 1979). Each of these characteristics helps the hardy person to cope with stressful events and therefore lowers the person's susceptibility to illness.

Another measure that is even more directly related to preventive health behavior is the concept of health locus of control. In Chapter Eight we discussed the general concept of **locus of control**, referring to the

> **Box 18–1**
> Sample items from a scale measuring health locus of control
>
> 1. People who take care of themselves stay healthy.
> 2. Many times illness results from carelessness.
> 3. Regular doctor check-ups are a key to health.
> 4. Basic health principles prevent illness.
> 5. I can cure myself when sick.

belief that events are internally or externally controlled. **Health locus of control** is a more specific form of this concept, referring to people's beliefs that they can exert control over their state of health or illness (an internal health locus of control) or that prevention of illness is beyond their control (external health locus of control).

Richard Lau has developed a scale to measure this specific form of perceived control (Lau, 1982). Some sample items from the scale are listed in Box 18–1. Individuals who score high on this dimension believe that they can exert control over their state of health, and they engage in a variety of preventive behaviors. For example, they are likely to eat properly, get regular exercise, and control their weight. Such people are also more likely to stop smoking, to use effective birth control, and generally to have more extensive knowledge about disease (Abella & Heslin, 1984; Lau, 1982; Wallston & Wallston, 1978). Individuals who score low on the health-locus-of-control scale are less likely to take these actions, perhaps because they believe that one's own activities have little effect on the ultimate state of health or illness.

Treatment of Illness

The medical model suggests that there is a recommended treatment or procedure that will cure or alleviate almost any illness. Yet the success of that treatment often depends on the willingness of the patient to comply with the prescribed regimen—to take the pills, to show up for chemotherapy treatments, to observe dietary restrictions, and the like. Here social-psychological factors have a major role to play.

A first task of the medical practitioner is to convey information to the patient—information that presumably will affect the patient's compliance. Yet too often the practitioner volunteers too little information and the patient asks too few questions, with the result that the potential treatment program encounters real problems (DiMatteo & DiNicola, 1982).

Providing the patient with sufficient information about his or her illness and treatment is one means of reducing stress. In one study patients who were given both information and particular techniques for coping with stress recovered more rapidly than patients who were less involved in the process (Langer, Janis, & Wolfer, 1975). Even in less severe or nonemergency situations, such as giving blood, having both information and choice (for example, choosing which arm to use for the blood donation) will reduce the stress (Mills & Krantz, 1979).

The way a physician presents information—whether possible negative outcomes are stressed—can affect the patient's perception of the risks involved and thus the amount of stress the patient experiences. In a situation designed to be analogous to this physician–patient interaction, Russell Jones and his colleagues gave subjects in a laboratory experiment information about the likelihood of being assigned to one of two tasks (Jones, Howard, & Haley, 1984). The two tasks differed in desirability: one task promised money as a reward for accuracy and the other threatened punishment for inaccuracy. The probability of these two outcomes was varied, so that the likelihood of assignment to one task was either 20%, 50%, or 80%, and the likelihood of assignment to the other task was the correspondent 80%, 50%, or

20%. In their instructions to the subjects, the experimenters stressed either the likelihood of the positive outcome (whatever the level) or the probability of the negative outcome.

If people were totally rational in their decision making, this difference in emphasis should have no effect, as the probability would be the same no matter which alternative was emphasized. Yet when subjects were asked, after a few intervening activities, to estimate the probability that they would be assigned to the undesirable task, their answers showed a bias, as Figure 18–3 indicates. Subjects were consistently more likely to believe in the likelihood of the positive outcome when their instructions had emphasized the desirable outcome, even though the objective probability was the same when the undesirable outcome was stressed. Even when the objective probability of the desirable event was 80%, for example, an emphasis on negative consequences reduced the subjective estimate to a 50–50 proposition. Thus the physician's choice of words can dramatically affect the patient's understanding of information.

Other aspects of the communication process are important as well. For example, it may be important for the physician to be able to decode the patient's nonverbal messages (as discussed in Chapter Five), especially messages that convey fear and resistance. Physicians also need to be aware of the nonverbal messages that they themselves are sending, because patients may rely more heavily on such messages—particularly when the verbal message is garbed in technical jargon not understood by the average patient.

In general, the more satisfied patients are with the quality of their interaction with their physician, the

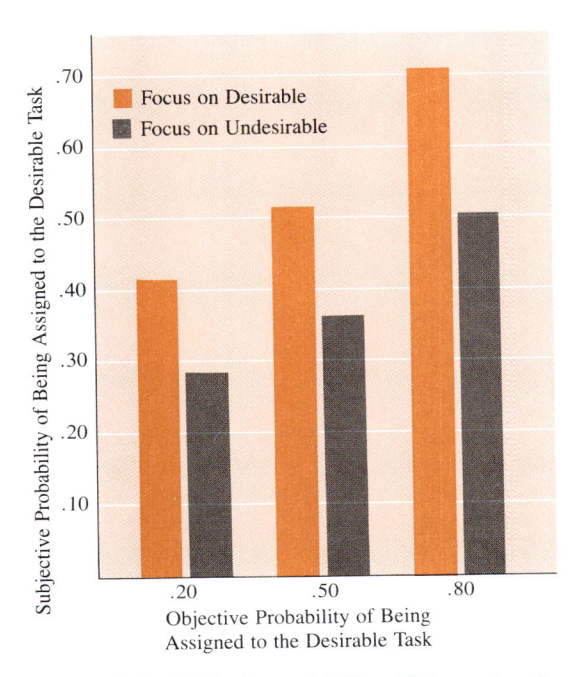

Figure 18–3 Subjective probability of being assigned to the desirable task as a function of objective probability and focus of instructions

more likely they are to comply with his or her recommendations (Krantz, Grunberg, & Baum, 1985). Recovery can be affected by a variety of other factors as well—even the view from the hospital window! In Chapter Seventeen we noted many of the ways in which the physical environment can affect behavior. One investigator has found that hospital patients' recoveries are related to whether their room looks out at trees or at a brick wall (Ulrich, 1984). Patients who viewed a brick wall were released from the hospital an average of one day later and were reported by nurses to appear substantially more depressed than patients who had a more scenic view.

The rate at which patients recover from surgery or illness is also influenced by their beliefs about their condition. Women recovering from surgery for breast cancer, for example, adjust better when they believe that there is some possibility of exercising control over their future condition—control exercised either by themselves or by a physician (Taylor,

Lichtman, & Wood, 1984). Shelley Taylor (1983) suggests that the ability to gain a sense of control or mastery over events is one of three processes involved in successful recovery from life-threatening events, such as heart attacks or cancer surgery. Gaining information, following prescribed treatment, taking dietary precautions in the future—these and other strategies allow the patient some sense of control. A second process that characterizes successful adjustment is a search for meaning in the experience— why did it happen and what does it mean for the future? Finally, patients try to restore a sense of self-esteem, which is often threatened by surgery or illness. Social comparison sometimes helps in this case, as patients seek out examples of others who are worse off than they. Such downward comparisons (for example, "I'm really much better off than she is") can bolster one's own sense of self. The patients whose recoveries are more successful also choose dimensions of self-evaluation on which they can feel good. Some of the beliefs reflected in these processes may be illusionary, based less on fact than on hope. Yet for the patient recovering from severe illness, hope may pave the way for constructive action that will increase the chance of recovery.

In summary, social psychology has much to contribute to the field of behavioral medicine. Until recently, the concern of medicine was technological advancement, a trend that "created an array of tools with which to do things *to* people, thus resulting in less and less time to do things *with* people" (Wexler, 1976, p. 276). Although technological advances are still important, increasing recognition is being given to the human element and to the psychological processes that mediate between health and illness.

Energy Use

When the Arab countries imposed an oil embargo in 1973–1974, many people began to recognize that energy use was an important societal issue. Although public belief in the possibility of severe shortages has vacillated as oil has become more readily available, most scientists assume that there will eventually be an energy shortage. Some of the solutions to this potential shortage are outside the province of the social sciences: developing alternative sources of fuel, for example, is a problem for geologists, chemists, and engineers. Yet the adoption of these new technologies is a question of human behavior, as are efforts to conserve energy sources now available.

Conservation Strategies

What are the possible solutions to the energy problem? Some people say that the political process is the only means of solution, with controls enforced by an external authority. *Mutually-agreed-upon coercion* is the term used by Garrett Hardin (1968). Others argue that voluntary conservation is the preferred approach. The strategy that one advocates depends in part on the way one explains the problem (Belk, Painter, & Semenik, 1981). Those who attribute the energy shortage to actions by the government, by oil producers, or by the oil companies are most apt to favor government pressure as a solution—either pressure directed at the oil companies or restrictions imposed by the government on the population. In contrast, people who see energy shortages as caused by the actions of the general public are more likely to favor voluntary conservation as a solution.

Social psychologists have focused their efforts on the development of effective conservation strategies. Among the techniques that they have studied are information campaigns, commitment, and feedback. Information campaigns have had mixed results. In Britain, for example, a "Save It" campaign stressed that excessive consumption of energy today would lead to future shortages (Gaskell & Ellis, 1982). Coupled with this general message were specific suggestions for reducing energy use, such as installing insulation, turning down thermostats, and turning off unnecessary lights. As measured both by self-reports and by the purchase of certain energy-saving devices, the British campaign was successful. Other information campaigns have been less successful, however. Sometimes the information does not reach the intended audience; when it does, the recipients may be unresponsive to the message (Stern & Aronson, 1984).

As we saw in Chapter Seven, neither attitudes nor behaviors always change in response to persuasive messages. Recognizing the range of obstacles intervening between message and action, social scientists have suggested various strategies for increasing the effectiveness of information campaigns (Costanzo et al., 1986). Among these strategies are techniques for increasing the probability that the message will be heard and understood. Messages that are directed at the individual consumer, for example, are more effective than those aimed at a general audience. An individual home audit is one way to accomplish this goal (Yates & Aronson, 1983). In such audits, a person knowledgeable about energy conservation uses the customer's own bill to explain particular points and provides specific case examples of people who have done exceptionally well in conserving energy.

Even if communication is tailored to provide specific information about energy use, however, it may not be effective. Clive Seligman and his colleagues administered a survey about energy that included questions related to beliefs about science, the legitimacy of the energy crisis, efforts to conserve energy, and concern for personal comfort (Seligman et al., 1979). People's concern for their own comfort was found to be closely related to their energy use. For example, one of the items on the questionnaire was "It's essential to *my* health and well-being for the house to be air-conditioned all summer." Another item was "While others might tolerate turning off the air conditioner in the summer, my own need for being cool is high." People who agreed with statements such as these were unlikely to show strong conservation behavior, even if they endorsed the reality of the energy shortage.

To supplement information campaigns, social psychologists have used the principles of commitment and feedback to encourage energy conservation. In one study, for example, a group of homeowners committed themselves to reduce energy consumption, both of natural gas for heat in the winter and of electricity for air conditioning in the summer (Pallak & Cummings, 1976). Half of the homeowners were told that their efforts would be made public—their names would be listed in the paper—and the remaining participants were assured that they would not be personally identified. Public commitment proved to be a more effective incentive than either private commitment or no commitment at all (there was a control group that had no communication with the experimenters). In a further exploration, the same researchers asked an additional group of subjects to keep an energy log, monitoring appliance use, thermostat settings, and utility-meter readings. This procedure proved nearly as effective as the public-commitment condition, a result that suggests the value of self-controlled procedures.

Monitoring procedures that provide direct feedback to the consumer can be effective in reducing energy consumption (Becker, 1978; Seligman & Darley, 1977). Having information readily available on just how well you're doing in your efforts can be much more effective than shutting off lights or turning down the air conditioner without knowing whether your efforts are really making a difference. Specific goals are useful as well. Lee Becker (1978) gave families a goal of 20% reduction in electricity use during a period of several weeks in the summer and provided feedback as well. Although those families did not quite meet the goal, their energy consumption did decrease by nearly 15%. In contrast, a group given a relatively easy goal of 2% reduction showed little change in energy use, not differing from a control group that had no goal.

A campaign in Australia used principles of cognitive dissonance (as described in Chapter Seven) to encourage conservation (Kantola, Syme, & Campbell, 1984). The investigators first assessed people's attitudes toward energy conservation and then selected for further study those who believed that energy conservation was an important responsibility. In a manipulation of dissonance, the investigators then pointed out to some of the individuals that there was a discrepancy between their stated attitudes and their actual energy consumption (as determined by readings of home electric meters). Other individuals were given either information about their past use of electricity, tips for conservation, or no additional information. During the two-week period following the manipulation, people whose attention had explicitly been drawn to the inconsistency between their attitudes and their behavior used less energy than any of the other groups, as Figure 18–4 indicates. After four weeks, however, the effectiveness of the dissonance manipulation had diminished. Frequent reminders may be necessary for long-term behavioral change.

Borrowing from learning and reinforcement models, other investigators have explored the use of financial incentives for reduced energy consumption. This straightforward approach, based on an economic model of human behavior, assumes that rewarded behavior will be maintained whereas behavior that is punished or not rewarded will decrease (Platt, 1973). Using this approach, Lou McClelland and Stuart Cook (1980) set up a contest among groups

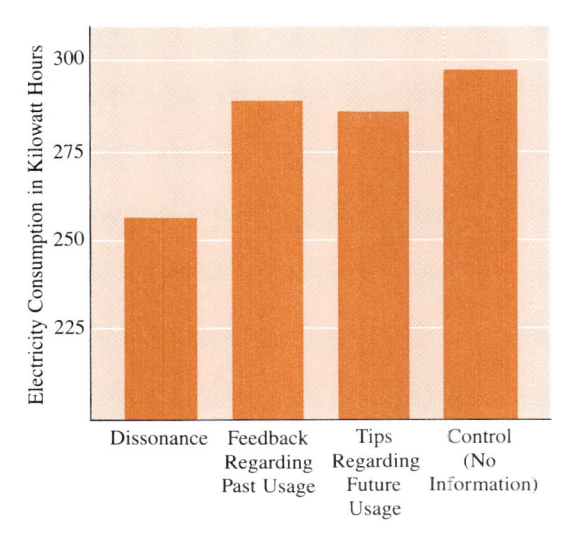

Figure 18-4 Electricity consumed by subjects in four conditions during the two weeks following manipulation of dissonance or provision of information on energy use

of apartment residents in a University of Colorado housing complex. In each of a series of two-week periods, the group that had conserved the most energy won $80 to use as it wished. The results of this competition were positive: over a 12-week period, energy savings averaged over 6%. It was clear that "money talks." In designing a large-scale energy-saving plan, however, it would be important to consider whether the incentives awarded for energy savings exceeded the savings themselves! Furthermore, there are some serious questions as to whether energy-saving behavior will continue once the rewards are removed, and even the money itself (assuming the amounts are conservative) may lose its appeal after a short time (McClelland & Canter, 1978).

Social Traps

Energy conservation, on a national or international scale, depends on more than a single individual's effort. This interrelationship between the individual's behavior and the consequences for society has become a focus of interest in recent years. Garrett Hardin (1968) highlighted this issue with his analysis of the tragedy of the commons, a problem with no technical solution. Consider the following example. A number of people are raising cattle in a common pasture. For years, perhaps centuries, the pasture has provided more than enough food for all the cattle. Any number of events—poaching, disease, war—serve to control the human and cattle populations so that each herder may maintain his or her herd without infringing on the stock of others. Yet at some point this utopia ends, and the land no longer supports all the cattle. How does this change come about? Assume that each herder, wanting to maximize profit, raises as many cattle as possible for the meat or milk or hides that they provide. A single herder decides to add one additional animal to the stock. That herder realizes considerable profit from the addition. The common pasture, at the same time, has to be divided more ways—yet our individual herder notices less loss than gain. Eventually, however, as many herders increase their herds, the commons becomes depleted. Or, as Hardin has stated, "freedom in a commons brings ruin to all" (1968, p. 1244).

Influenced by Hardin, social scientists study what is termed a social trap. As described by John Platt (1973), a **social trap** is a situation that provides immediate individual incentives for behaviors that in the long run have unfortunate consequences for society if those behaviors are performed by large numbers of people. In the short run, each individual benefits; in the long run, the society suffers. Many of the problems of energy conservation can be related to this dilemma. Individuals benefit from air-conditioned temperatures of 70° in summer and from heated temperatures of 70° in winter, but the ultimate outcome when hundreds and thousands of individuals adopt that policy is a heavy use of energy and an eventual shortage for everyone.

Such problems are essentially human problems, and they require human solutions. Early research suggests that neither information alone nor the knowledge of interdependence will be effective in reducing the exploitation of a resource. More promising results have been obtained when communication is encouraged and when subjects develop a sense of participating in the determination of how the resource is to be managed. Such solutions will have to be developed if we are to halt the depletion of common resources.

The Legal System

More than 12 million crimes were reported in the United States in 1979 (Greenberg & Ruback, 1982). Figures for other years and other countries vary but in all cases indicate the extent of the criminal justice problem. Unreported crimes magnify these numbers. The criminal justice system is a complex one, involving various levels of jurisdiction (federal, state or provincial, and local) and a variety of agencies (including police, courts, attorneys, corrections officers), as well as the plaintiffs, defendants, and witnesses involved in individual cases. Within this complex setting, social psychologists have taken a growing interest in the processes of the legal system.

Psychologists have become involved in a number of areas. In the most general terms, we can consider three basic areas: substantive law, the legal process, and the legal system (Monahan & Loftus, 1982). In the area of *substantive law,* psychologists have begun to test some of the basic assumptions underlying legal codes and conventions. For example, should children be allowed to testify in criminal cases? Are they able to distinguish fact from fantasy, and would their testimony be reliable? In 1979 the U.S. Supreme Court stated that "most children, even in adolescence, simply are not able to make sound judgments concerning many decisions" (quoted in Monahan & Loftus, 1982, p. 443). Psychologists have begun to test some of these assumptions, using data from both developmental psychology and cognitive psychology to assess children's capacities for understanding and decision making.

Research directed at the *legal process* is concerned with the actual proceedings of conflict resolution. A major interest in this area is the trial process itself—characteristics of jurors and defendants, rules of evidence and procedures for decision making, and jury deliberation. By far the greatest amount of work by social psychologists has been centered in this area. A third focus of psychological research is the *legal system* itself: what factors affect sentencing decisions, how does the parole system operate, and what are the interactions between the criminal justice system and the mental health system?

It is not surprising that social psychologists have been intrigued by the operation of the legal system.

Law functions in an interpersonal context, and many of the processes that occur can be interpreted in accordance with basic social-psychological principles. Greenberg and Ruback (1982) have interpreted a wide range of legal phenomena in terms of two basic theoretical models: attribution theory and social exchange theory.

In making attributions, people are trying to explain why a particular event occurred (see Chapter Four). Let's think about just a few of the ways this process could occur in the legal system. If you saw one person hit another, would you choose to call the police? Part of your decision to help (see Chapter Twelve) would be based on your explanation of the event. Were the two persons just friends who were kidding around? Or was one person a mugger, intent on robbing the other? Attributions continue to be made throughout the legal process. In setting bond, a judge makes some inferences about the character of the accused. In listening to testimony, jurors make inferences about the characters of the plaintiff, the defendant, and other witnesses. In deciding on parole, parole boards make assumptions about the character of the convicted person and try to predict future behavior.

Social exchange theory (see Chapter One) can also be used to interpret many of the interactions in the legal system. In plea bargaining, for example, an exchange between the prosecutor and the defendant may take place: "If I reduce the charge, will you agree to testify against X?" In determining a sentence, a judge may try to follow a principle of equity (see Chapter Nine), ensuring that the penalty imposed on the convicted criminal matches the damage done to the victim. These and many other examples testify to the relevance of social-psychological theory to the criminal justice system.

Because the applications of psychology to the law have been so numerous, we can discuss only a few examples in depth. We will limit our discussion to three general issues: the setting of bail, the process of jury selection, and procedures in the trial process itself.

Setting Bail

After a suspect has been arrested, he or she must appear before a judge for what is termed the "initial appearance." For minor offenses, the judge may decide the case at that time. For a traffic violation, for example, the case is usually decided quickly and a fine often levied. For more serious offenses, this initial appearance may be the occasion for the judge to set bail, an exchange in which the accused puts up a certain amount of money in return for release from custody until a final hearing takes place (Greenberg & Ruback, 1982; Wrightsman, 1987).

How is the amount of bail determined? Ebbe Ebbesen and Vladimir Konečni (1975) used two methodological approaches in their attempts to answer this question. In the first study, they used a classic experimental design, manipulating the levels of four variables that they believed might be important: the prior record of the accused, the local community ties of the accused, the amount of bail recommended by the prosecuting attorney, and the amount of bail recommended by the defense attorney. Municipal and superior court judges in California were asked to make recommendations for bail after reading case descriptions that varied each of these factors. In their second study, these investigators used the field study method: observers attended bail hearings and recorded the events that took place, including the actual levels of the four variables that had been manipulated in the earlier study. The observers kept records of other kinds of information as well, including the age and sex of the accused and the severity of the crime (these variables had been held constant in the experimental study).

What factors were important in the judges' decisions? In the experimental study, three of the four factors emerged as important determinants. Most important were the local ties of the defendant to the community. When the accused was described as having lived in the area for four to six years, being employed in the area, and having family there, bail was set at a significantly lower level than when local ties were weak (living in the area only a couple of months, unemployed, and with family in another part of the state). Also important were the recommendations of the prosecuting attorney and the prior record of the accused. Higher bail was recommended if the prosecuting attorney had asked for higher bail and if the accused had a prior criminal record. In this experiment, the recommendation of the defense attorney had no effect.

The second study, based on actual bail decisions, showed somewhat different results and underlines the importance of testing experimental findings in a less controlled setting. In this real-life setting, the judges' decisions on bail were influenced primarily by the recommendations of the prosecuting attorney. Much weaker was the influence of the defense attorney's recommendation, and local ties and prior record had no direct effect at all. Both the presence of local ties and the severity of the crime did play an indirect role, however, influencing the recommendation that the prosecuting attorney made. In more severe crimes, prosecuting attorneys requested higher bails, and higher bails were awarded. Somewhat surprisingly, local ties worked in just the opposite direction than in the previous experimental study: when the accused person had strong local ties, prosecuting attorneys tended to recommend higher bail than when such ties were weak.

This study shows quite clearly just what factors affect the bail-setting process. Further, it testifies to the importance of multiple strategies in research and the need for social psychologists to move outside the laboratory in their search for accurate diagnoses of social problems.

Jury Selection

The selection of a jury for any particular trial begins as a process of random selection, as some number of people are called to court from a list of eligible jurors. (Even that original list is not totally representative of the population, however, because certain requirements must be met. For example, jurors must be 18 or older, understand English, and have no felony record.) From this larger group, 12 persons (plus some number of alternates) are selected for the actual jury, after an examination procedure

Photo 18-1 Many elements of a typical trial have been studied by social psychologists.

that is known as *voir dire*. In the voir dire, the presiding judge or the opposing attorneys question prospective jurors and are allowed to remove certain potential jurors from the case, either without a stated reason (a peremptory challenge) or by citing apparent evidence of bias (a challenge for cause) (Hans & Vidmar, 1982; Wrightsman, 1987). In the latter case, in particular, there is an assumption that the court will be able to differentiate between the biased and the unbiased—an assumption that seems questionable (Hans & Vidmar, 1982).

Beginning in the early 1970s, some social psychologists began to consult with defense teams in the selection of a jury. The aim of these efforts was to select a jury that would be sympathetic to the cause of the defense and hence would make acquittal of the defendant more likely. Lawyers have always engaged in this strategy during the voir dire process, basing their selections on *implicit personality theories* (as discussed in Chapter Four) that relate particular personal characteristics to likely juror judgments. It is unclear whether these implicit theories have much support; evidence to date suggests only limited effectiveness.

Social scientists have contributed more sophisticated methods of assessing attitudes and values to the jury selection process. Among their techniques are extensive community surveys, interviews with individuals who are acquainted with prospective jurors, and analysis of both verbal and nonverbal responses made by potential jurors during the voir dire process (Hans & Vidmar, 1982). This increased repertoire of measurement tools has led some observers to conclude that systematic jury selection can influence the outcome of any case. Yet at most, the scientific evidence suggests that the success of the selection techniques depends on the particular type of case. Jury selection may be more useful when demographic characteristics can be closely linked to attitudes toward a particular issue, such as drug use or political violations, than in a murder case in which the personality-attitude links are less evident (Hans & Vidmar, 1982).

More relevant to a murder case than such demographic characteristics as age or sex are people's attitudes toward the death penalty. In capital-punishment cases it has often been the policy to exclude jurors who state in advance that they are unwilling to impose a death penalty. (The juries that result from this exclusion are called "death qualified" juries.) A number of people in both the legal and the social science communities have suggested that exclusion of such jurors may result in a "conviction prone" jury rather than a neutral one. Phoebe Ellsworth and her colleagues have recently conducted two studies that test this assumption, and the studies have been cited in recent California court decisions.

In the first of two studies (Fitzgerald & Ellsworth, 1984), over 800 eligible jurors in California were contacted by telephone and asked to assume that they were on a jury that was to decide on a sentence for a convicted defendant. They were then asked about their willingness to vote for the death penalty, as well as their attitudes about other aspects of the trial process. About 17% of this sample said they would never vote for the death penalty, a position that would make them unacceptable for jury service in capital cases. The people who voiced this opinion were not a random sample, however. Significantly more women than men, and significantly more Blacks than Whites, would be excluded from capital cases on this basis. In addition, jurors who were opposed to capital punishment differed from other respondents in several other ways. In contrast to the death-qualified jurors, these excluded jurors were less punitive, less mistrustful of the defense, and more concerned with maintaining guarantees of due process. Thus the death-qualification procedure would seem to create a jury that is not totally representative of the citizenry.

Pursuing this question further, Cowan, Thompson, and Ellsworth (1984) contacted a random group of adults who were eligible for jury service and designed a jury-simulation experiment in the laboratory. Two types of 12-person juries were formed: one in which all members were death-qualified and one in which at least two members were opposed to the death penalty (mixed juries). Each mock jury watched a 2½-hour videotape of a homicide trial, gave an initial verdict, and then deliberated as a group for an hour. The results of the study again show the pattern of differences between the juror who is death-qualified and the one who is not. Both in their initial ballot and after the group deliberation, death-qualified jurors were more likely to vote guilty. Furthermore, analysis of the deliberations of the two types of groups showed that mixed juries seem to benefit from their diversity of opinion. Members of these mock juries were more critical of witnesses and better able to remember the evidence, although they were also less satisfied with their jury experience. These two studies are important contributions by social scientists to an understanding of jury selection.

Yet despite the clarity of these research findings, a 1986 U.S. Supreme Court decision upheld the use of death-qualified jurors. In an opinion written by Justice (now Chief Justice) William H. Rehnquist, the Court dismissed the social science data on the grounds that simulation studies do not necessarily predict the behavior of actual jurors. As this outcome illustrates, the findings of social scientists' socially relevant research are not always accepted by the institutions in question.

Trial Procedures

Many of the procedures that occur during a typical trial have been subjected to scrutiny by social psychologists. Judges' instructions, the use of confessions, and the form of opening statements by prosecution and defense attorneys are only a few of the topics investigated.

In their opening statements, both attorneys introduce themselves and their clients and provide the jury with a broad overview of their cases. Although the stated purpose of these opening statements is mainly informational, they can serve a persuasive function as well, influencing the jury to be favorable to a particular verdict (Lind & Ke, 1985). In one study of the effectiveness of opening statements, mock jurors in a simulated trial heard one of two types of opening statement from both the prosecuting attorney and the defense attorney (Pyszczynski & Wrightsman, 1981). In the brief opening statement, only a short introduction was given, in which the attorney promised that convincing evidence would be provided later. In the extensive opening statement, a full summary of the evidence was presented. After the opening statements by both lawyers, the mock jurors then read a full transcript of a criminal trial and made judgments about the defendant's guilt or innocence. Did the form of the attorneys' opening statements affect the final verdicts? Figure 18–5 shows the results. The effectiveness of a particular strategy on the part of one attorney depends on the strategy used by the other. Verdicts of guilty were least likely when the defense attorney made a lengthy opening statement and the prosecuting attorney spoke only briefly. In general, the authors suggest that jurors may be influenced by the first strong presentation they receive.

There is a risk for the defense attorney, however, in making an extensive opening statement if he or she promises evidence that is not subsequently provided. In a second study, Pyszczynski and his colleagues set up three different conditions (Pyszczynski et al., 1981). In one condition the defense attorney promised in the opening statement that convincing evidence of innocence would be provided. In a second condition the same promise was made, but later in the trial the prosecutor pointed out to the jury that the promise had not been fulfilled. In a third (control) condition neither the promise nor the reminder

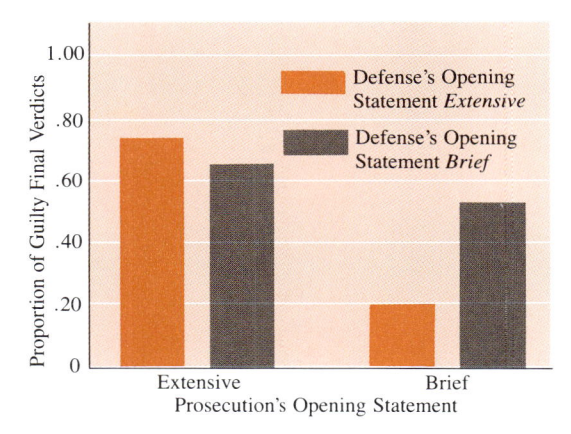

Figure 18–5 Proportion of guilty verdicts by length of prosecution's opening statement

was included. A promise of convincing evidence did influence the mock jurors, making them more favorable toward the defendant. However, when the prosecution reminded jurors that the promise had not been fulfilled, the effectiveness of the promise diminished sharply.

Another question that has been addressed in jury research is the use of coerced confessions. The U.S. Supreme Court has ruled that only voluntary confessions may be admitted as evidence; coerced confessions have been ruled out. Within the legal system, coercion has been defined primarily in terms of a threat of harm. But what if coercion takes the form of the promise of some reward? To explore some of the issues surrounding confessions, Saul Kassin and Lawrence Wrightsman (1980) presented mock jurors with a trial transcript that included testimony about the defendant's confession. In some cases, testimony showed that the defendant had confessed voluntarily; in other cases, the confession had been made in response to either a threat or a promise of leniency. In a control group, no evidence of a confession was presented. The results showed that subjects were willing to discount a confession if it had been made under threat. However, a confession made under the promise of leniency was treated in the same manner as a voluntary confession, leading to a greater likelihood of a guilty verdict. Further studies have shown that even explicit instructions by the judge to discount coerced confessions do not diminish the effect when the coercion is positive in nature (Kassin & Wrightsman, 1985).

Social psychologists have been active in a great many other areas of law. Accuracy of eyewitness testimony has been one major area of interest (Penrod, Loftus, & Winkler, 1982; Wells, 1985). Other investigators have focused on the processes of group deliberation, a topic that was considered in Chapter Fourteen. Some of these investigations have dealt mainly with theoretical issues that *might* be relevant to judicial proceedings; others have been aimed at more directly applicable features of the process. There has been a great deal of debate about the degree to which psychology can contribute to the law (Loh, 1984; McCloskey, Egeth, & McKenna, 1986; Saks & Baron, 1980). Too often, it is suggested, psychologists have been concerned solely with the trial process, when in fact fewer than 5% of cases actually go to trial. As in all areas of applied research, it is important for the investigator to establish ties with practitioners in the field. For research to be most useful, the acquired wisdom of the practitioner must be used both to shape questions and to interpret findings in a truly interdisciplinary approach to the problems.

From Problems to Solutions

Health, energy conservation, and law are all areas of concern to applied social psychologists. But are they necessarily social problems? Leonard Bickman and his associates have suggested that four criteria are needed to define a situation as a social problem (Ovcharchyn-Devitt et al., 1981). First, the situation must exert a negative impact on some people. Sec-

Photo 18-2 The social sciences greatly contributed to such landmark cases as *Brown* v. *Board of Education*.

ond, one must consider the number of people who are affected. Generally, the more people affected, the more serious the social problem. Third, Bickman and his colleagues suggest that we consider the "intractability" of the problem. Social problems, unlike temporary situations that may be unpleasant, generally have a long history, and many previous solutions may have been attempted. Fourth, a social problem is defined by consensus—the society as a whole, or some significant portion of it, agrees that a particular situation is a problem.

Using these criteria, we can point to a number of certifiable social problems. In the 1950s, desegregation gained widespread attention as just such a social problem. The social sciences contributed evidence in the landmark case of *Brown* v. *Board of Education*, decided by the U.S. Supreme Court in 1954. The role of the social sciences in this field, described in more detail in Box 18-2, illustrates each of the aspects of social problems and social change that we will discuss here: documenting a problem, evaluating solutions to that problem, and developing strategies for social change.

Documenting Problems

Identifying a situation as a social problem is only the first stage in problem solving. Once a problem is recognized, it must be analyzed carefully so that solutions that fit the problem can be devised. In the model for research on social problems that Bickman and his colleagues have proposed (see Figure 18-6), at least five kinds of information are believed to be necessary to document a social problem. A general scenario of the situation is suggested as a first step so that the investigator will understand exactly what is happening. For example, in studying the effects of affirmative action in the steel industry, investigators would want to know how and when women were hired, what groups within the steel mills might be sources of discriminatory actions, and what impact the policies were having both on women and on other workers (see Deaux & Ullman, 1983).

Having become familiar with the basic situation, the investigator should then gather more specific information about the group of people affected by the problem and how great the impact of the problem

Box 18–2
Segregation: problems and solutions

An early and very famous example of research aimed at documenting existing problems is the work of Clark and Clark (1947), who administered projective tests to Blacks and Whites and demonstrated the effects of social prejudice. In the famous *Brown* v. *Board of Education* case of 1954, Kenneth Clark testified to the court as follows:

> I have reached the conclusion . . . that discrimination, prejudice, and segregation have definitely detrimental effects on the personality development of the Negro child. The essence of this detrimental effect is a confusion in the child's concept of his own self-esteem—basic feelings of inferiority, conflict, confusion in his self-image, resentment, hostility towards himself, and hostility towards Whites [Kluger, 1976, p. 353].

As those familiar with U.S. history know, the result of this case was the order to desegregate schools in the United States, under the assumption that separate educational facilities are inherently unequal. The Clarks and other investigators had defined a problem—racial prejudice. Yet it is important to note that although they advocated a particular solution, their research had focused on the problem, not on the effectiveness of various solutions.

Later assessments have, in fact, suggested that the solution was far less beneficial than proponents had hoped (Gerard, 1983). Walter Stephan (1978) has systematically reviewed the evidence for desegregation in terms of the hypotheses implicitly or explicitly offered by social scientists in their testimony during the *Brown* v. *Board of Education* case. Disappointingly, he concludes that desegregation generally has not

continued

---

is. Other environmental and interpersonal factors need to be explored, as the causes of most social problems are complex. Finally, an investigator should gather as much information as possible on the causes of the problem.

There is danger in defining problems too broadly. As Karl Weick (1984) has suggested, conceptualizing social problems on a massive scale can generate excessive stress and stretch the limits of rational problem-solving efforts. As an alternative, Weick recommends a strategy aimed at the "small win"—"a concrete, complete, implemented outcome of moderate importance" (1984, p. 43). It is easier to achieve a series of such goals than to complete a single large project, and the small wins may have substantially greater effects in the long run because of their diffuse nature.

Once a problem is defined, solutions can be attempted. They may focus on either the society, the group, or the individual, depending on the nature of the problem. Solutions to problems regarding legal procedures, for example, would be best directed at the practicing judges and lawyers who implement those procedures. Recommendations for improved health practices, in contrast, might be aimed at the general public. The appropriateness of the devised solution must in turn, according to the model in Figure 18–6, be reevaluated in terms of the initial problem criteria.

Evaluating Solutions

Most often the solution to a social problem is devised by politicians, bureaucrats, and other persons directly involved in the problem. In the past, social scientists were often content to maintain their roles as citizens and observe the outcomes of such programs. But in 1969 Donald Campbell issued a challenge:

reduced the prejudices of Whites and Blacks toward each other and that the self-esteem of Blacks has rarely increased in desegregated schools. However, achievement levels of Blacks have increased in desegregated schools, providing support for the decision if not for all the hypothesized effects of desegregation. In this review, however, Stephan is careful to note that these conclusions are tentative. Much of the research had problems, and rarely were either the conditions of desegregation or the measures of effects constant across conditions.

Although evaluations of desegregation programs as a whole indicate that the predicted goals were not always achieved, continuing research on segregation and integration in the classroom can provide new insights (Patchen, 1982; Schofield, 1982). In discovering what particular conditions are associated with successful integration, social scientists can provide information that will facilitate positive changes. Investigators have discovered that the *intergroup contact hypothesis*, which suggests that simply bringing two groups together will reduce prejudice (see Chapter Sixteen), must be qualified by several conditions. Among the necessary conditions are equal status of the groups, cooperative interdependence on tasks, and egalitarian norms (Brewer & Miller, 1984). Other investigators have found that Black students who have had prior interracial experience in their neighborhoods, friendship groups, or high schools adjust more easily to predominantly White colleges (Graham, Baker, & Wapner, 1985).

In summary, the research on desegregation illustrates both the strengths and the limitations of social science's contributions to the solution of social problems. The documentation of a problem is relatively easy. Yet the scope of the problems makes solutions difficult to find, and progress is often better gauged by a focus on the steps achieved than by exclusive attention to the steps yet to be taken.

The United States and other modern nations should be ready for an experimental approach to social reform, an approach in which we try out new programs designed to cure specific social problems, in which we learn whether or not these programs are effective, and in which we retain, imitate, modify, or discard them on the basis of apparent effectiveness on the multiple imperfect criteria available. [p. 409]

In effect, he argued for an experimenting society, and in the years since his challenge, evaluation research has become one of the most active fields of social science.

The term **evaluation research** has been used in many ways, but a basic definition of the term is "research which is aimed at assessing or evaluating the effects of a given social action or program" (Hornstein, 1975, p. 214). This strategy has been applied to a myriad of areas: college courses, mental health programs, compensatory education, and income maintenance, for example. It is applicable to virtually any other social program, large or small, in which the effects of action or change can be measured. The evaluation program can serve a few persons or a few million people; it can focus on a single classroom, an entire nation, or several nations; it can last a few hours or go on indefinitely (Weiss, 1972).

The aim of evaluation research is quite simple but the process itself can be quite complex. Carol Weiss (1972), in her definition of evaluation research, begins to hint at some of these complexities: "The purpose of evaluation research is to measure the effects of a program against the goals it set out to accomplish as a means of contributing to subsequent decision making about the program and improving future programming" (p. 4). Evaluation research must begin with specific questions, phrased in terms of the goals

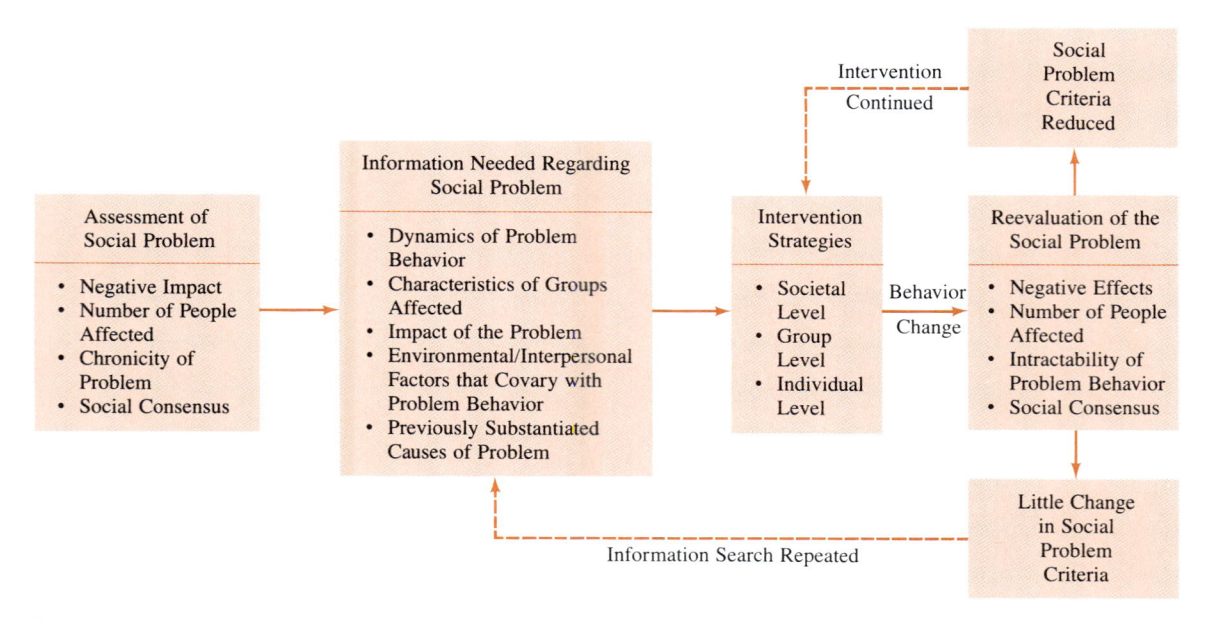

Figure 18–6 Stages in research on social problems

that an organization has set for itself. Again, this process may appear to be a simple matter, but in practice it often turns out to be more complex. "Program goals are often hazy, ambiguous, hard to pin down" (Weiss, 1972, p. 25). Officials of a program may have a general sense that they want their program to be better, but exactly how they want it to be better is often left vague and undefined. "Better" or "more modern" or "more effective" is a general description that must be translated into specific criteria before the evaluation research can proceed.

As one example, the announced goals of Operation Head Start, a program in compensatory education conducted in the United States during the late 1960s, were to compensate for the alleged educational disadvantages that caused poor children to have difficulties when they entered the first grades of school (Rossi & Williams, 1972). Yet the major evaluation showed that the program produced no noticeable improvement in cognitive skills. If the specific goal was a concrete improvement in cognitive skills, then the program evaluation, for the most part, showed the program to be a failure. However, in the swirl of controversy that surrounded this project (Hellmuth, 1970; Williams & Evans, 1972), many advocates argued that other goals were established by the project—for example, the physical health of the children may have been improved. Alternatively, cognitive skills may have improved in ways not tapped by the measures used. These controversies illustrate some of the problems involved in the specification of goals in a social program—and the care that the evaluation researcher must take to specify the exact objectives and to devise appropriate methods of measuring the outcomes of the program.

Once the exact objectives are specified, an evaluation-research program must devise methods to measure the desired effects. In such an effort, a vast arsenal of methods (as discussed in Chapter Two) may be used—interviews, questionnaires, existing records, observations, and any other available forms of data that appear to be relevant to the questions posed. Often, however, a true experiment, whether of a laboratory or field variety, is impossible. As a result, methodologists, most notably Donald Campbell and his colleagues, have been active in developing a number of **quasi-experimental research** designs that will approximate some of the experimental controls while allowing for the "messiness" of real live data (see Campbell & Stanley, 1966). As Figure 18–7 indicates, considerable precautions must be taken when data are evaluated. Because the investigator has little control over most of the independent variables and only some control over the data collection (the dependent variables), alternative explanations for the effects observed must be considered carefully.

Still another feature of evaluation research is that it takes place in what Weiss (1972) has called a "turbulent setting." Social psychologists accustomed to the calm of their laboratory may find the activity of an on-site evaluation somewhat disquieting. Furthermore, the evaluation research project is often of secondary concern to the members of the organization that is being evaluated. In most cases, these people are concerned mainly with giving service or producing a product and not with the needs of the researchers. They may, in fact, find the investigators' presence an annoyance or an inconvenience. Evaluation itself may affect the behavior of the personnel. Personality conflicts may develop between the researcher and key personnel; the organization may suffer a crisis in some other aspect of its operation, which in turn will affect the evaluation program; or the program itself may change during the course of its operation as a result of other pressures and needs. These are only some of the factors that make evaluation research a much more "turbulent" arena than the more traditional social psychology setting.

Yet, despite the difficulties of evaluation research, its benefits can be substantial. Only when we know how existing programs are actually working can we begin to develop better solutions to society's problems.

Strategies for Change

Research can help to define the problem and evaluate alternative solutions. But the change process itself may go beyond research. As Hornstein (1975) has observed, the individual can confront a social problem and ask, "Is more information needed?" If the answer is yes, then research such as we have discussed can be conducted. However, if the answer is "No, we have enough information" or even "Yes, more information is needed, but we don't have time to get it," then direct social change may be the chosen route.

Three major types of change strategies are (1) the empirical-rational strategy, (2) the normative-reeducative strategy, and (3) the power-coercive strategy.

The **empirical-rational strategy** assumes that people are rational and that they will act on the basis of the best information available. Therefore, in order to improve people's ability to make decisions, one need only present them with the facts. This strategy clearly is congenial to many Western values, such as willpower and educability. Because of our belief in this strategy, we maintain public schools, write letters to our legislators, read newspapers regularly, and give money for cancer research. Of course, there are limits to our acceptance of this strategy; that is, we also smoke, drive at excessive speeds, refuse to exercise, and often pick a new car by kicking its tires and slamming its doors instead of consulting a con-

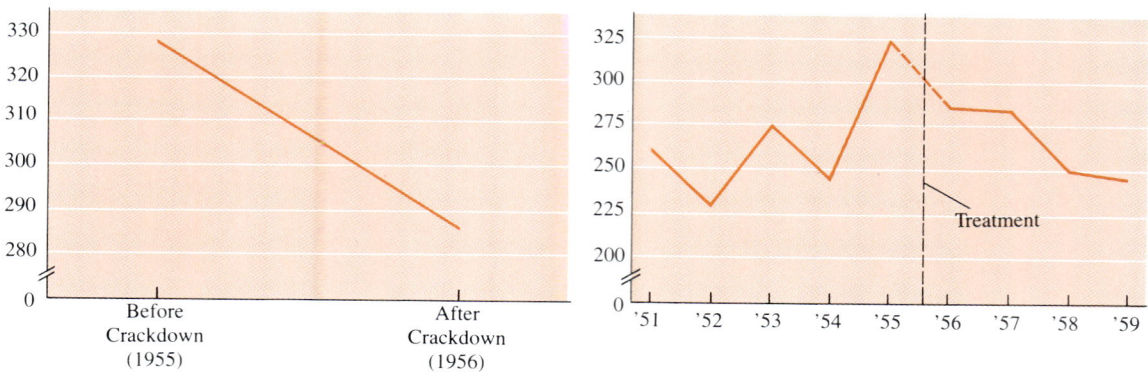

566 Chapter Eighteen

Figure 18–7 Reforms as experiments. Donald T. Campbell, distinguished social scientist, makes a strong appeal for an experimental approach to social reform. He presents several research designs for evaluating specific programs of social amelioration, one of which is the interrupted time-series design. A convenient illustration comes from the 1955 Connecticut crackdown on speeding. After a record high of traffic fatalities in 1955, the governor instituted a severe crackdown on speeding. At the end of one year of such enforcement, there had been 284 traffic deaths, compared with 324 the year before. These results are shown in the left-hand graph above, with a deliberate effort to make them look impressive. The right-hand graph includes the same data as the graph to the left, except that those data are presented as part of an extended time series. Campbell acknowledges that the crackdown did have some beneficial effects, but he advocates the exploration of as many rival hypotheses as possible to explain the decline in traffic fatalities from 1955 to 1956. For example, 1956 might have been a particularly dry year, with fewer accidents due to rain or snow. There might have been a dramatic increase in use of seat belts. At least part of the 1956 drop is the product of the 1955 extremity. (It is probable that the unusually high rate in 1955 caused the crackdown, rather than, or in addition to, the crackdown's causing the 1956 drop.) Campbell asks for a public demand for hardheaded evaluation and for education about the problems and possibilities involved in the use of socially relevant data.

sumer-guide magazine. In short, we often act irrationally; hard facts have limited power to change behavior.

Expert testimony in front of government committees represents a form of empirical-rational strategy. To take the argument a step further, one could easily argue that all governmental research is based on the empirical-rational strategy; that is, government agencies fund research that will produce facts, which can then be disseminated for the purpose of effecting change.

The **normative-reeducative strategy** assumes that people are intelligent and rational, but it also assumes that they are bound up in their own particular culture. As a result, they have definite behavioral response patterns that are based on attitudes, values, traditions, and relationships with others. Before trying to change a person, group, or community, the change agent must take these cultural or normative determinants into account.

Kurt Lewin was one of the first to use the normative-reeducative strategy in efforts to resolve social conflicts (Lewin, 1948). Many police training programs that have developed since the 1970s reflect the normative-reeducative strategy. In response to riots and accusations of police brutality, analyses of activities by the police were conducted in many communities. Time-and-motion studies revealed that less than 20% of the working hours of police officers was spent in law-enforcement activities, whereas increasing portions of time were spent in a wide range of social-service activities. Morton Bard (1970) has referred to the New York City police as a "human resource agency without parallel" and has pointed out that "maintaining order and providing interpersonal service—not law enforcement and crime suppression—are what modern police work is all about" (p. 129). Social scientists rediscovered what the police already knew—that crime in the streets is much less common than crime *off* the streets. One of the riskiest activities for police officers is handling family disputes (Driscoll, Meyer, & Schanie, 1973). In brief, the police were being trained in traditional law enforcement or property surveillance but were being called on to serve a wide range of social-service functions.

A normative-reeducative strategy was developed for police officers. Social scientists began riding in patrol cars, observing training programs, and generally acquainting themselves with the norms of law enforcement. Actual entry into the system was slow. Social psychologists first performed specific services for the police, such as improving the ways of selecting new recruits. Next came lectures and sensitivity training that dealt with such matters as the emotionally disturbed, ways to deal with aggression, and the general area of interpersonal relations (Diamond & Lobitz, 1973). Gradually the social scientists became more involved in all aspects of police training—and more acceptable in the eyes of the police (Carlson, Thayer, & Germann, 1971).

The normative-reeducative process moves slowly; change depends on a great deal of agreement and collaboration between the agents of change and the people in the selected system. But there have been payoffs. Bard (1970) has trained a special squad of patrol officers in the use of mediation and referral in handling domestic disturbances. This project has been highly successful in preventing homicides, reducing the number of assaults and arrests, and preventing injury to the police themselves. A central characteristic of this approach has been the predictability of change, which has been in the desired direction and has been approved by both the change agents and the police.

The **power-coercive strategy** differs from the first two in its use of political, economic, and social power. Federal legislation of civil rights has moved integration forward in the United States and has promoted bilingualism in Canada; labor strikes have affected economic policies; and boycotts have changed discriminatory hiring practices. Similarly, Martin Luther King, Jr., César Chavez, and Saul Alinsky became famous for their power-coercive strategies in their quests for constructive change (Sharp, 1970, 1971).

In employing power-coercive methods, change agents have been concerned primarily with nonviolent strategies of change. Opposition to violent strategies is based on at least two principles. One is that the use of violence means denying human worth and that even the most favorable short-term outcome does not justify violent methods. A second reason is that violent strategies introduce much more unpredictability into a social system than nonviolent approaches do (Fairweather, 1972). *Predictability* in this context refers to (1) whether one accomplishes one's desired goals, (2) how long one's accomplishments last, and (3) whether any unexpected negative side effects result. Evaluated according to these three criteria, nonviolent strategies are found to be much more effective in establishing planned change throughout a broad social system.

Some social scientists argue that violent strategies may be successful as well. William Gamson (1975) analyzed the outcomes of a sample of 53 groups that sought change in the United States during the late 19th and early 20th centuries and concluded that violence was often a successful tactic when it was used by groups that had a sense of confidence and a rising sense of power. Gamson's advocacy of violence as a successful tactic is qualified, however. He finds it used successfully when it is a secondary tactic, backing up primary nonviolent power-coercive strategies such as strikes, bargaining, and propaganda. "Violence, in short, is the spice of protest, not the meat and potatoes" (Gamson, 1974, p. 39).

Nonviolent power-coercive methods have brought about much planned social change during the past few decades. Demonstrations have been accompanied by legal sanctions and class-action suits. One of the more interesting aspects of the power-coercive strategy is that it can take many forms. The case history described in Box 18–3 summarizes an unusually innovative approach to problem resolution by one of the masters of the power-coercive strategy.

Despite their frequent effectiveness, power-coercive strategies are seldom sufficient change methods in and of themselves. Often they must be coupled with a normative-reeducative approach to maximize change. In fact, in most social-change endeavors, there will be occasion to use all three of these strategies in various ways at various times. Indeed, it is most difficult to use only one strategy. Yet, to be successful, the change agent must be aware of which strategy is being used, as well as how others perceive the strategy.

Just as the form of social change can vary, so the role of the social scientist can vary in relation to the change process. Harvey Hornstein (1975) has discussed three roles that the change agent may play: the expert, the collaborator, and the advocate.

As an expert, the social scientist does not collaborate directly with the change makers but instead offers advice from a distance. In such a role, the social scientist is most influential in the early stages of the change process, when plans are being formulated. Any single social scientist may, of course, be only one voice among many recommending directions or procedures for change. Many experts are called to testify at congressional hearings, for example, and the final decision represents some composite of the testimony of these experts, political pressures, and other factors.

As Lewin recognized early on, many of the motivational problems that may occur in the expert relationship are minimized when the social scientist takes a *collaborative* role. Indeed, it has been argued that "the adaptation of research findings is primarily determined by the motivational by-products of collaboration rather than by the technical expertise of a research effort" (Hornstein, 1975, p. 223). Kurt Lewin's concept of action research exemplified the collaborative relationship between the social scientist and the target of change. Technical expertise is

> **Box 18-3**
> Use of power-coercive strategies
>
> The late Saul Alinsky was one of the foremost organizers of community action groups; he trained such minority-group leaders as César Chavez, who organized California's agricultural workers and then precipitated a national consumer boycott against California grapes. Alinsky was a proponent of the power-coercive strategy and used this strategy in quite a variety of ways. One of the more novel uses of this approach was his battle with Eastman Kodak in Rochester, New York. Following a Rochester race riot that was due partly to a conflict over Kodak's inadequate training and job programs for Blacks, the local churches invited Alinsky to work in their Black ghetto. He accepted and soon founded a community action group called FIGHT (Freedom, Integration, God, Honor, Today). Instead of depending on community action tactics such as picketing and demonstrating, FIGHT began soliciting stock proxies from churches, individuals, and organizations as a direct power challenge to Kodak's policies. Enough proxies were turned over to FIGHT to enable the group to force Kodak to improve its policies concerning minority groups.

not sufficient in this kind of relationship; in addition, the social scientist must have interpersonal skills to help the group move toward its goal.

In both expert and collaborative relationships, the agent of change (the social scientist) and the object of change (the organization) tend to agree on the goals to be pursued. In an advocate relationship, in contrast, the social scientist may disavow collaboration and instead pursue a path of action aimed at changing the organization from outside. This role of the change agent is most evident in the use of the power-coercive strategy, although the extent of involvement and the forms of power used may vary widely.

The work of the social psychologist Hannah Levin (1970) exemplifies the advocate role. While working as a consultant to a community health center, Levin was dismayed to find that the people who lived near the health center had little or no say in its operation. The health authorities told the people that they could have an advisory board, but those who actually administered the health program would have to be physicians. However, the people wanted the operating policies to be determined by the local residents. In the confrontation that followed, Levin became a professional advocate for the people. Levin and the people's groups were informed that they could advise, or even participate, but not control. The health authorities were unable to see the difference between participation and control. According to Levin, the people's retort was "If you don't see any real difference between participation and control, then you can participate and the community will control!" (1970, p. 123). Through Levin's advocacy, the people were able to establish influence over the policies of the health center. One outcome of community control was a shift in priorities from programs that emphasized treatment of suicidal and acutely disturbed patients to programs that focused on young people.

Although most social psychologists believe that their research will eventually have practical applications, many resist applying current knowledge to current problems. Our knowledge is imperfect and our understanding inadequate, they claim. Yet, as we have seen, some other social psychologists are much more inclined to apply our findings now, believing that we already have a good deal of basic technology to use in the solution of social problems. Jacobo Varela (1971, 1978) has been perhaps the most passionate advocate of such a **social technology.** From his background in engineering, Varela moved to the social sciences, attempting to use many of the same strategies but with a different set of tools. His arguments are persuasive:

> The fact is that we already have most of the technology we need to solve an enormous range of social problems, from personal miseries to organizational conflict, from the marriage bed to the conference table. If we wait for pure

research to come up with real-world answers, though, we will be waiting for Godot.... Engineers and physical scientists cannot wait for theoretical perfection. If the Romans had waited for the elegance of the Verrazano-Narrows Bridge instead of fooling around with stone arches, the course of civilization would have changed. The Roman arches had their faults, but they have lasted nineteen centuries. [1978, p. 84]

Many would disagree with Varela's analysis. Yet, just as there are many methods for doing research, there are also many responses to the outcomes of research, and no single response or tactic has an exclusive claim on the truth. It is imperative that social psychologists continue to do basic theory-oriented research, both in the laboratory and in natural settings, for such research will add to our knowledge and form the basis for future social technologies. At some point, however, we may be obligated to use the knowledge that we have in the solution of social problems. And many would argue that the time has come.

Summary

The contributions of social psychology do not stop with an increase in theoretical understanding of human behavior. Social-psychological knowledge has been applied to the solution of a variety of social problems. This emphasis on application began early in the tradition of social psychology, with Kurt Lewin's concept of action research. Although social psychologists became more interested in pure laboratory research during the 1950s and 1960s, much more applied research has been conducted in recent years. In addition, field settings have been used to test and extend basic theory as well. Three significant areas of applied social research are health care, energy conservation, and the legal system.

Behavioral medicine is a field that integrates behavioral and biomedical science. Social psychologists are studying many aspects of illness, including causes, identification, prevention, and treatment. Causes of illness may be internal to the person (as exemplified by the *Type A behavior pattern*) or may, as in the case of Three Mile Island, be a result of environmental stressors. Identification of illness, both by the patient and by the physician, illustrates basic psychological principles of social cognition and attribution. Prevention of illness has been studied in a number of ways, including the general traits of *hardiness* and *health locus of control*. Programs to discourage cigarette smoking are another example of social-psychological principles in practice. Treatment of illness is influenced by the ways in which physicians present information and the satisfaction that a patient feels with his or her interactions with the physician.

Studies of energy use have tried to identify effective conservation strategies. Information campaigns are popular but not always effective. Personalized messages help. Also effective are tactics that require public commitment to the goal of conservation and that provide feedback on actual energy use. Other psychological principles, such as cognitive dissonance and incentives, have been used successfully as well.

Psychologists have also looked at *social traps*, situations that provide immediate rewards to individuals for behaviors that may have negative consequences for a society in the long run.

In applying their knowledge to an understanding of the legal system, social psychologists have looked at substantive law, the legal process, and the legal system itself. Many basic principles, such as attribution theory and social exchange theory, can be applied throughout the legal system. The specific processes that have been studied include the setting of bail, the process of jury selection, and procedures in the trial process itself.

Social psychology can contribute to the process of social change in three ways: by documenting problems that exist, by estimating the costs and benefits of alternative kinds of change, and by providing the means for change.

Social scientists may also be involved in the process of change itself. Three strategies for planned change are the *empirical-rational strategy,* the *normative-reeducative strategy,* and the *power-coercive strategy.* The empirical-rational strategy is based on the assumption that people will act on the best available information and hence focuses on dissemination of information as a means to change. Those who use the normative-reeducative strategy assume that our behavior is based on attitudes, values, and interpersonal relationships, and they take these factors into account when planning change. The power-coercive strategy uses political, social, and economic pressures to bring about desired social change.

The social scientist can take one of three roles in the change process: that of an expert, a collaborator, or an advocate. These roles vary in their level of involvement with the change process itself. *Social technology* is the application of social science principles to the solution of social problems.

Glossary Terms

action research
behavioral medicine
empirical-rational strategy
evaluation research
field theory
hardiness
health locus of control
locus of control
normative-reeducative strategy
power-coercive strategy
quasi-experimental research
social technology
social trap
Type A behavior pattern

GLOSSARY

Action research Research whose goal is the understanding or solution of social problems.

Adaptation Processes that allow people to adjust to their surroundings, including shifts in perception of an environment with continued exposure, such as decreased sensitivity to loud noise.

Adaptation level Personal standard of comparison used to make judgments of noise, crowding, and other properties of the physical and social environment.

Air pollution Gas, dust, mist, vapor, or fiber present in the air in addition to its natural constituents.

Altruism A special form of helping behavior that is voluntary, costly, and motivated by something other than the expectation of reward.

Ambient environment Changeable qualities of one's immediate surroundings, including temperature, humidity, air quality, sounds, and light.

Anchor A reference point that is used in making judgments.

Androgyny A term referring to a high degree of masculine (or agentic) traits and a high degree of feminine (or communal) traits; currently used by investigators to refer to psychological, rather than physical, characteristics.

Anticonformity Behavior that is directly antithetical to the normative group expectations. Also called counterconformity.

Archival research Analysis of existing documents or records, especially those contained in public archives.

Arousal A generalized state of physiological and psychological excitation.

Arousal: cost-reward model (of helping) A model that predicts that people will help if they become aware of a need for help, experience physiological arousal, label that arousal as a response to the victim, and decide that cost and reward factors favor intervention.

Assimilation effects In social-judgment theory, shifts in judgments toward an anchor point.

Assortative mating The nonrandom coupling of individuals based on resemblance of one or more characteristics.

Authoritarianism A basic personality dimension that includes a set of organized beliefs, values, and preferences, including submission to authority, identification with authority, denial of feelings, and cynicism.

Autokinetic effect The tendency for a stationary light, when viewed in an otherwise completely dark room, to appear to be moving.

Balance theory A theory of attitude change based on the principle of consistency among elements in a relationship. Heider, who proposed this model, stated that unbalanced states produce tension, which a person will try to reduce by changing some attitude.

Bargaining The process whereby two or more parties try to settle what each shall give and take, or perform and receive, in a transaction between them.

Behavioral medicine A field that integrates behavioral and biomedical science, focuses on health and illness, and is concerned with the application of knowledge to the prevention, diagnosis, and treatment of illness.

Behaviorism A theoretical perspective made prominent by John B. Watson in which explanations of behavior emphasize external stimuli and learning processes.

Belief in a just world A belief that there is an appropriate fit between what people do and what happens to them.

Bisexuality Engaging in sexual behavior with both sexes during similar periods of time.

Bystander effect The finding that a person is less likely to provide help when in the presence of witnesses than when alone.

Catharsis Release of aggressive energy through the expression of aggressive emotions or through alternative forms of behavior.

Causal attribution The process of explaining events, or inferring their causes.

Causal schema A conception of the way two or more causal factors interact in relation to a particular kind of effect; an assumed pattern of data in a complete analysis-of-variance framework.

Central trait A personal characteristic that strongly influences a perceiver's impressions of the person possessing the trait.

Cognition Knowledge acquired through experience.

Cognitive dissonance theory A theory of attitude change developed by Leon Festinger and based on the principle of consistency. Cognitive dissonance exists when two cognitions contradict each other. Such dissonance is uncomfortable, and it is predicted that a person will reduce dissonance by one of several means—for example, by changing an attitude.

Cognitive structure A set of principles and processes that organizes cognitive experience.

Cohesiveness The attractiveness that a group has for its members and that the members have for one another; the force that holds a group together.

Communication networks Representations of the acceptable paths of communication between persons in a group or organization.

Competition Activity directed toward achieving a goal that only one of the persons or groups can obtain.

Competitive reward structure A reward structure in which not all people striving for a reward can attain it and in which movement toward the goal by one person decreases the chance that others will attain that goal.

Complementarity A principle to explain interpersonal attraction; refers to a pairing of different (and sometimes opposite) needs, such as dominance and submission.

Compliance Behavior in accordance with a direct request.

Conformity Yielding to group pressures when no direct request to comply is made.

Consideration A dimension of leadership; the leader's concern with relationships between himself or herself and other group members and the maintenance of group morale and cohesiveness.

Construct A concept, defined in terms of observable events, used by a theory to account for regularities or relationships in data.

Contrast effect In social-judgment theory, a shift in judgment away from an anchor point.

Cooperation Working together for mutual benefit; a prosocial behavior.

Cooperative reward structure A reward structure in which everyone in the group must achieve the reward in order for it to be attained by any one participant. Each person's efforts advance the group's chances.

Correlational method A study of the interrelation between two or more sets of events. Such a method does not allow conclusions about the causal relation between the two events.

Crowding A form of stress that sometimes occurs in conditions of high population density. (A related term, *crowded,* is used to refer to situations in which population density is high.)

Cultural script A pattern of social interaction that is characteristic of a particular cultural group.

Debriefing Discussion conducted at the end of an experiment in which the experimenter reveals the complete procedures to subject and explains the reasons for any

Glossary 575

deception that may have occurred.

Defense mechanisms Devices used by the ego, operating at an unconscious level, that transform libidinal impulses into less threatening expression.

Deindividuation A state of relative anonymity, in which a group member does not feel singled out or identifiable.

Demand characteristics The perceptual cues, both explicit and implicit, that communicate what behavior is expected in a situation.

Density intensity hypothesis The proposition that the presence of a crowd enhances positive experiences and makes unpleasant experiences worse.

Dependent variable A variable whose changes are considered to be consequences, or effects, of changes in other (independent) variables.

Discrimination Any behavior that reflects acceptance or rejection of a person solely on the basis of membership in a particular group.

Display rules Socially learned rules for controlling the expression of emotions.

Distributive justice A principle of social exchange theory that says one's rewards should be proportional to one's investments.

Door-in-the-face effect A technique in which compliance with a request follows an initial refusal of a larger request.

Ego In Freudian theory, that part of the personality that is oriented toward acting reasonably and realistically; the "executive" part of personality.

Egoism Self-interest or behavior that is motivated by selfish concerns (as contrasted with altruism).

Emblems Body gestures that are substitutes for the spoken word.

Emic Referring to culture-specific constructs that have meaning only within a particular cultural framework.

Empathy The vicarious experience of another person's perceptions and feelings.

Empirical rational strategy A strategy of planned change that holds that publishing the facts that support change is sufficient to initiate that change.

Environmental determinism The view that environmental characteristics, such as the climate or the layout of a city, can influence behavior.

Equity theory A theory that specifies how people evaluate relative contributions to a relationship. Specifically, the theory suggests that ratios of inputs and outcomes should be equal for both participants.

Erotica Visual or verbal material that is considered sexually arousing.

Ethnocentrism The tendency to judge other people or groups by the standards of one's own group.

Ethology The study of the behavior of animals in their natural settings.

Etic Referring to universal factors; constructs that are not culture-specific.

Evaluation apprehension A concern on the part of a subject in a study that he or she is performing correctly and will be positively evaluated by the researcher.

Evaluation research Research that assesses or evaluates the effects of a particular social action or program.

Excitation transfer theory A theory that suggests that arousal generated in one situation may transfer and intensify a subsequent emotional state.

Exotic bias A tendency, in observing another group or society, to focus on aspects that differ from one's own group or society and to ignore similar features.

Experimental realism Arrangement of the events of an experiment so that they will seem convincing and have the maximum possible impact on the subjects. This is sometimes accomplished through deception.

Experimenter expectancies Beliefs held by the experimenter and reflected in his or her behavior that may cause changes or distortions in the results of an experiment.

External validity The "generalizability" of a research finding (for example, to other populations, settings, treatment arrangements, or measurement arrangements).

Facial affect program The connection between an emotional experience and a particular pattern of facial muscles.

False consensus bias The belief that others share one's attitudes and behaviors.

Field theory A social-psychological perspective developed by Kurt Lewin that proposes that one's social behavior is a function not only of one's own attitudes, personality, and other intrapersonal factors but also of one's environment, or "field."

Foot-in-the-door effect A psychological effect whereby compliance with a small request makes it more likely that the person will comply with a larger (and less desirable) request.

Frustration-aggression hypothesis A theory that assumes that aggression is always motivated by frustration, although frustration may have other consequences as well.

Functional theory A theory of attitude change that emphasizes the basis of attitudes in different individual needs. To change someone's attitude, one must understand why that attitude is held.

Fundamental attribution error The tendency of observers to overemphasize the actor as a cause of events.

Gender identity One's self-awareness of being male or female.

Gender-role norms Beliefs about appropriate behavior for women and men.

GRIT Graduated and reciprocated initiatives in tension reduction; a strategy of arms reduction proposed by the psychologist Charles Osgood.

Group polarization A shift in opinions by members of a group toward a more extreme position.

Group structure The system of roles, norms, and relationships among members that exist in a group.

Groupthink A mode of thinking in which group members' strivings for unanimity override their motivation to realistically appraise alternative courses of action; a tendency to seek concurrence.

Hardiness A constellation of personality characteristics that function as a resistance resource in encounters with stressful life events.

Health locus of control A personality dimension—the belief that one can exert control over one's health (internal health locus of control) or that prevention of illness is beyond one's control (external health locus of control).

Hedonic relevance The extent to which a person's actions are rewarding or costly to the observer.

Helping behavior A form of prosocial behavior that benefits another person more than oneself; as distinct from prosocial cooperation in which mutual benefit is gained.

Heuristics Mental shortcuts that reduce complex problem solving to simpler judgmental operations.

Hypothesis A tentative explanation of a relationship between variables, or a supposition that a relationship may exist. A hypothesis generates some scientific method (such as an experiment) that seeks to confirm or disprove the hypothesis.

Id In Freudian theory, a set of drives that is the repository of our basic unsocialized impulses, including sex and aggression.

Idiographic Approach to the study of personality that focuses on the interrelationship of events and characteristics within a single individual.

Illusory correlation An overestimation of the strength of a relationship between two variables. Variables may not be related at all, or the relationship may be much weaker than believed.

Illustrators Nonverbal behaviors that are directly linked with spoken language.

Implicit personality theories Assumptions people make that two or more personality traits are related so that, if a person has one of the traits, it is believed that he or she will have another one as well.

Impression management The conscious or unconscious attempt to control images that are projected in real or imagined social interactions.

Independent variable A variable that is manipulated in an experiment; a variable whose changes are considered to be the cause of changes in another (dependent) variable.

Individualistic reward structure A reward structure in which goal attainment by one participant has no effect on the probability of goal attainment by others.

Initiating structure A dimension of leadership; the leader's behavior in identifying the group's goal and moving the group toward its goal.

Instrumental learning A type of learning in which a response is followed by a reward or reinforcement, resulting in an increase in the frequency of the response.

Integrative agreement An agreement that reconciles the interests of both parties in a negotiation, yielding high payoff for both groups.

Interaction A joint effect of two or more variables such that the effect of one variable is different for various levels of the other variables.

Interaction territory The area immediately surrounding two or more people as they engage in conversation, which passers-by hesitate to enter.

Intergroup behavior The interaction of members of one group with members of another group, where such interaction is based on the group identification of the individuals.

Intergroup contact hypothesis The assumption that prejudice will be reduced and favorable attitudes will develop when members of two groups with negative attitudes toward each other are brought together.

Internal validity The conclusiveness with which the effects of the independent variables are established in a scientific investigation, as opposed to the possibility that some confounding variable(s) may have caused the observed results.

Interview A research method that involves asking another person a set of questions according to a predetermined schedule and recording the answers.

Kinesics A scheme developed by Birdwhistell for classifying body motions, intended to parallel linguistic categories.

Kin selection In sociobiology, the concept that genes will become more common in a species if they contribute to the survival of relatives, even if those genes decrease the individual's chances of survival. Used to argue that altruism might be biologically based.

Leadership The process of influence between a leader and followers to attain group, organizational, or societal goals.

Learned helplessness The belief that one's outcomes are independent of one's actions, learned through exposure to situations in which outcomes are noncontingent and resulting in behavior deficits and feelings of depression.

Life space In field theory, the person plus his or her environment, all of which is viewed as one set of interdependent factors.

Likert scale A method of attitude measurement in which people indicate their agreement or disagreement with a set of declarative statements.

Locus of control A person's belief that events are within his or her own control (internal) or that outside forces are in control (external).

Main effect The effect that levels of a single independent variable have on a dependent variable, not considering any other variables that may be affecting the results.

Manipulation check One or more questions posed to the subject(s) by the experimenter to assess the effectiveness of the experimental manipulation.

Mediation Third-party assistance to two or more disputing parties who are trying to reach an agreement.

Mere exposure effect The finding that repeated exposure to an object results in greater attraction to that object.

Modeling The tendency for a person to reproduce the action, attitudes, and emotional responses exhibited by a real-life or symbolic model. Also called "observational learning."

Mundane realism Arrangement of the events in an experiment so that they seem as similar as possible to normal, everyday occurrences.

Negative-state-relief model A hypothesis explaining the relation between negative moods and helping behavior as a learned way of escaping negative psychological states.

Neo-Freudians Followers of Freud who depart in various ways from some of Freud's doctrines.

Noise Unwanted sound, which can be stressful if it is loud, unpredictable, and uncontrollable.

Nomothetic Approach to the study of personality that focuses on differences between people on a single norm or dimension selected by an investigator.

Normative reeducative strategy A strategy of planned change that assumes that, before trying to change a person or group, one must take the cultural or normative factors into account (such as the past history of the person or group.)

Norms Socially defined and enforced standards of behavior that concern the way a person should interpret the world and/or behave in it.

Obedience A special form of compliance in which behavior is performed in response to a direct order.

Objective self-awareness A psychological state in which individuals focus their attention on and evaluate aspects of their self-concepts, particularly discrepancies between "real" self and "ideal" self.

Obscenity That which is considered offensive to the mass populace and therefore proscribed. Recent definitions have limited the meaning of *obscenity* to offensive sexual materials.

Observational learning A type of learning in which responses are acquired simply by observing the actions of others.

Open-plan office A style of office design in which work spaces occupy large areas, undivided by walls but separated by furniture, plants, and moveable partitions.

Open-space school A style of school building in which several different classes occupy large areas divided by few walls.

Paralanguage Vocalizations which are not language but which convey meaning; examples include pitch and rhythm, laughing and yawning.

Participant observer An investigator in a field study who participates in the activities of the group being observed and maintains records of the group members' behaviors.

Personalism The perceived intentionality of a person's behavior; the degree to which a perceiver believes that another's behavior is directed at him or her.

Personalization Deliberate adornment, decoration, or modification of an environment by its occupants to reflect their identities or personalities.

Personal norms An individual's feelings of obligation to act in a given way in a particular situation; more specific and more predictive of behavior than general social norms.

Phenomenological approach A point of view in social psychology stating that the environment, as the person perceives it, is an important influence on behavior.

Philosophies of human nature Expectations that people possess certain qualities and will behave in certain ways.

Population density The number of persons or other animals per unit of space, or units of space per person; for example, people per acre in a city or square feet per person in a room.

Pornography Erotic material which combines elements of sexuality and aggression and in which force or coercion is used to accomplish the sexual act.

Power coercive strategy A strategy that uses either violent or nonviolent pressures (lobbying, petitions, strikes, riots, and so on) to bring about social change.

Prejudice An unjustified evaluative reaction to a member of a racial, ethnic, or other group, which results solely from the person's membership in that group; an intolerant, unfair, or unfavorable attitude toward another group of people.

Primacy effect The tendency for the first information received to have the predominant effect on one's judgments or opinions about persons, objects, or issues.

Primary territory Area or space that is central to the life of an individual or group, owned or controlled on a relatively permanent basis, and used for personally important activities.

Priming The effects of a prior context on the retrieval of information.

Privacy Selective control over access to oneself or one's group, including control over information and personal accessibility to other people.

Privacy regulation The use of verbal and nonverbal behaviors, including uses of the physical environment, to optimize one's level of involvement with other people.

Propinquity Proximity or geographical closeness.

Prosocial behavior Behavior that has positive social consequences and improves the physical or psychological well-being of another person or persons.

Prototype An abstract set of features commonly associated with members of a category.

Psychoanalytic theory A theory of personality and social behavior developed by Sigmund Freud on the basis of psychotherapeutic experiences.

Public territory Area in a public place that is temporarily claimed and used by an individual or group, such as a table at a library or space on a beach.

Quasi-experimental research Social research in which the investigator does not have full experimental control over the independent variable but does have extensive control over how, when, and for whom the dependent variable is measured.

Questionnaire survey A research method in which the experimenter supplies written questions to the subject, who provides written answers.

Racial identity One's sense of belonging to a particular racial or ethnic group.

Racism Any attitude, action, or institutional structure that subordinates a person because of his or her color or race.

Randomization Assignment of conditions (for instance, assignment of subjects to treatment conditions) in a completely random manner—that is, a manner determined entirely by chance.

Reactance A motivational state that is aroused whenever a person feels that his or her freedom to choose an object is severely limited and that results in the object's increased desirability.

Reciprocal altruism In sociobiology, the concept that natural selection would favor those with genes predisposing them to altruism because altruistic acts are eventually reciprocated and thus benefit the individual. Used to argue that altruism might be biologically based.

Reciprocity norm A standard of behavior that says that people should help, and should refrain from injuring, those who have helped them.

Reinforcement A consequence of a response that increases the probability that the response will be made again under the same stimulus conditions.

Relative deprivation One's perceived state in relation to the perceived state of others or in relation to unfulfilled expectations.

Reliability Consistency of measurement. Stability of scores over time, equivalence of scores on two forms of a test, and similarity of two raters' scoring of the same behavior are examples of three different kinds of reliability.

Response An alteration in a person's behavior that results from an external or internal stimulus.

Role The socially defined pattern of behaviors expected of an individual who is assigned a certain social function, such as spouse, clergyman, or baseball umpire.

Role differentiation The emergence and development of roles in the course of group interaction.

Role expectations Assumptions about the behavior of a person who holds a particular role.

Salience The distinctiveness of a stimulus relative to the context.

Scapegoating The displacement of hostility onto less powerful groups when the source of frustration is not available for attack or not attackable for other reasons.

Schema An organized configuration of knowledge, derived from past experience, that we use to interpret our experience.

Script The conceptual representation of a stereotyped event sequence.

Secondary territory Physical space claimed by a group, which controls its accessibility and use by outsiders, such as a fraternity house or church building.

Selective exposure Seeking out information that supports one's attitudes and beliefs and avoiding information that is inconsistent with that attitudinal position.

Self-concept The totality of an individual's thoughts and feelings having reference to the self as an object.

Self-consciousness A disposition to focus attention inward on the self. Two forms are private self-consciousness and public self-consciousness.

Self-disclosure The revealing of personal information about the self; self-revelation.

Self-esteem The evaluation of oneself in either positive or negative terms.

Self-fulfilling prophecy The process whereby a perceiver's beliefs about a target person can elicit behavior from the target person that will confirm the expectancy.

Self-handicapping strategy Any action or choice of performance setting that enhances the opportunity to externalize failure and to internalize success.

Self-monitoring The use of cues from other people's self-presentations in controlling one's own self-presentation. High self-monitoring individuals use their well-developed self-presentational skills for purposes of impression management in social relations.

Self-perception theory A theory that proposes that we infer our attitudes, emotions, and other internal states from observing our own behavior.

Self-presentation The process of impression management as it deals with aspects of the self (see **impression management**).

Self-schema A set of cognitive generalizations about the self that organizes and guides the processing of self-related information.

Self-serving attribution bias The tendency to accept greater personal responsibility for positive outcomes than for negative outcomes.

Semantic differential technique A method of attitude measurement in which people rate a concept on a series of bipolar adjective scales.

Sexism Prejudice and discrimination directed against people by virtue of their sex.

Shared stress effect A tendency for people who are together in a stressful environment to feel attracted to one another.

Simulation A research method that attempts to imitate some crucial aspects of a real-world situation in order to gain more understanding of the underlying mechanisms that operate in that situation.

Social comparison theory A theory that proposes we use other people as sources for comparison so that we can evaluate our own attitudes and abilities.

Social distance The degree of physical, social, or psychological closeness to members of an ethnic, racial, or religious group that a person finds acceptable.

Social exchange theory A general theoretical model that conceptualizes relationships in terms of rewards and costs to the participants.

Social facilitation The state in which the presence of others improves the quality of an individual's performance.

Social inhibition A decline in individual performance in the presence of other people.

Socialization A process of acquiring behaviors that are considered appropriate by society.

Social judgment theory A theory of attitude change that emphasizes the individual's perception and judgment of a persuasive communication. Central concepts in this theory are anchors, assimilation and contrast effects, and latitudes of acceptance, rejection, and noncommitment.

Social learning theory A theory that proposes that social behavior develops as a result of observing others and of being rewarded for certain acts.

Social loafing A decrease in individual effort when people work in groups as compared to when they work alone.

Social network The set of people with whom an individual is in actual contact.

Social pathology hypothesis The idea that high population density leads to social ills, such as disease, deviance, and crime.

Social-responsibility norm A standard of behavior that dictates that people should help persons who are dependent or in need of help.

Social support Benefits that can be gained through interaction with others.

Social technology The application of social science principles to the solution of social problems.

Social theory A belief about how and in what ways variables in the social environment go together.

Social trap A situation that provides immediate individual incentives for behaviors that in the long run may have negative consequences for society if large numbers of people perform the behaviors.

Sociobiology A new discipline concerned with identifying biological and genetic bases for social behavior in animals and humans.

Sociopetal spaces Physical settings that encourage interpersonal interaction through seating arrangements that place people within comfortable conversation distances facing one another.

Status characteristics theory A theory of group process proposing that differences in evaluation and beliefs about types of individuals become the basis for inequalities in social interaction.

Status marker Physical symbol or indication of an individual's rank in an organization or relative standing in a social system, especially in work environments, such as size of an office.

Stereotype A schema about members of an identifiable group.

Stimulus Any event, internal or external to the person, that brings about an alteration in that person's behavior.

Stimulus discrimination The process of making distinctions between similar stimuli.

Stimulus generalization A process whereby, after a person learns to make a certain response to a certain stimulus, other similar but previously ineffective stimuli will also elicit that response.

Stress A physiological and psychological reaction to a demand, threat, challenge, or adversity involving arousal and mobilization of capacities for coping.

Superego In Freudian theory, the part of personality oriented toward doing what is morally proper; the conscience. The superego includes one's ego ideal, or ideal self-image.

Superordinate goal An important goal that can be achieved only through cooperation.

Symbolic interaction A theory that deals with the importance of interactions between oneself and other people, stressing that the sense of self is a product of social interaction.

Symbolic racism A blend of anti-Black affect and traditional moral values embodied in the Protestant ethic; underlying attitudes that support racist positions.

Territorial dominance Phenomenon in which an individual dominates interactions with others when in his or her own territory.

Territorial marker Object used to claim and reserve space in a publicly available area when a person is temporarily absent.

Territory A physical zone of control and influence. In nonhuman species, a specific region that an animal marks with scents or calls, uses for nesting or foraging, and defends against intruders of the same species.

Transsexualism A gender identity opposite to one's bodily appearance and sexual organs. A person with male sex organs whose gender identity is female, or vice versa, is a transsexual.

Type A behavior pattern A set of behaviors associated with increased risk for coronary heart disease.

Unobtrusive measures A measurement that can be made without the knowledge of the person being studied. An unobtrusive measure is also nonreactive.

Urban overload hypothesis The idea that city-dwellers react to excessive stimulation by avoiding interpersonal involvement.

Vividness The intensity or emotional interest of a stimulus.

Work space Work station in an office or factory assigned to a single individual.

REFERENCES

Abbey, A., Dunkel-Schetter, C., & Brickman, P. (1983). Handling the stress of looking for a job in law school: The relationship between intrinsic motivation, internal attributions, relations with others, and happiness. *Basic and Applied Social Psychology, 4*, 263–278.

Abella, R., & Heslin, R. (1984). Health, locus of control, values, and the behavior of family and friends: An integrated approach to understanding preventative health behavior. *Basic and Applied Social Psychology, 5*, 283–293.

Abelson, R. P. (1981). Psychological status of the script concept. *American Psychologist, 36*, 715–729.

Abelson, R. P., & Rosenberg, M. J. (1958). Symbolic psychologic: A model of attitudinal cognition. *Behavioral Science, 3*, 1–13.

Abramson, L. Y., Seligman, M. E. P., & Teasdale, J. D. (1978). Learned helplessness in humans: Critique and reformulation. *Journal of Abnormal Psychology, 87*, 49–74.

Abramson, P. R. (1983). Implications of the sexual systems. In D. Byrne & W. Fisher (Eds.) *Adolescents, sex, and contraception*. Hillsdale, NJ: Erlbaum.

Abramson, P. R. (1984). *Sarah: A sexual biography*. Albany, NY: State University of New York Press.

Abramson, P. R., & Imai-Marquez, J. (1982). The Japanese-American: A cross-cultural, cross-sectional study of sex guilt. *Journal of Research in Personality, 16*, 227–237.

Abramson, P. R., & Mechanic, M. B. (1983). Sex and the media: Three decades of best selling books and major motion pictures. *Archives of Sexual Behavior, 12*, 185–206.

Abramson, P. R., Perry, L. B., Seeley, T. T., Seeley, D. M., & Rothblatt, A. B. (1981). Thermographic measurement of sexual arousal: A discriminant validity analysis. *Archives of Sexual Behavior, 10*, 171–176.

Adams, R. S. (1969). Location as a feature of instructional interaction. *Merrill-Palmer Quarterly, 15*, 309–321.

Aderman, D., & Berkowitz, L. (1983). Self-concern and the unwillingness to be helpful. *Social Psychology Quarterly, 46*, 293–301.

Aderman, D., Bryant, F. B., & Donelsmith, D. E. (1978). Prediction as a means of inducing tolerance. *Journal of Research in Personality, 12*, 172–178.

Adorno, T. W., Frenkel-Brunswik, E., Levinson, D., & Sanford, N. (1950). *The authoritarian personality*. New York: Harper.

Ahrentzen, S., & Evans, G. W. (1984). Distraction, privacy, and classroom design. *Environment and Behavior, 16*, 437–454.

Ahrentzen, S., Jue, G. M., Skorpanich, M. A., & Evans, G. W. (1982). School environments and stress. In G. W. Evans (Ed.), *Environmental stress*, (pp. 224–225). New York: Cambridge University Press.

Aiello, J. R. (1977a). A further look at equilibrium theory: Visual interaction as a function of interpersonal distance. *Environmental Psychology and Nonverbal Behavior, 1*, 122–140.

Aiello, J. R. (1977b). Visual interaction at extended distances. *Personality and Social Psychology Bulletin, 3*, 83–86.

Aiello, J. R., Baum, A., & Gormley, F. P. (1981). Social determinants of residential crowding stress. *Personality and Social Psychology Bulletin, 7*, 643–649.

Aiello, J. R., Epstein, Y. M., & Karlin, R. A. (1975). Effects of crowding on electrodermal activity. *Sociological Symposium, 14*, 43–57.

Aiello, J. R., & Thompson, D. E. (1980). When compensation fails: Mediating effects of sex and locus of control at extended interaction distances. *Basic and Applied Social Psychology, 1*, 65–82.

Aiello, J. R., Thompson, D. E., & Brodzinsky, D. M. (1983). How funny is crowding anyway? Effects of room size, group size, and the introduction of humor. *Basic and Applied Social Psychology, 4*, 193–207.

Ajzen, I. (1986). From intentions to actions: A theory of planned behavior. In J. Kuhl & J. Beckman (Eds.), *Action-control: From cognition to behavior*. New York: Springer.

Ajzen, I., & Fishbein, M. (1980). *Understanding attitudes and predicting social behavior*. Englewood Cliffs, NJ: Prentice-Hall.

Alan Guttmacher Institute. (1981). *Teenage pregnancy: The problem that hasn't gone away*. New York: Alan Guttmacher Institute.

Alexander, Y., & O'Day, A. (1984). *Terrorism in Ireland*. London: Croom Helm.

Alker, H. A., & Owen, D. W. (1977). Biographical, trait and behavioral-sampling predictions of performance in a stressful life setting. *Journal of Personality and Social Psychology, 35*, 717–723.

Allport, F. H. (1920). The influence of the group upon association and thought. *Journal of Experimental Psychology, 3*, 159–182.

Allport, G. W. (1937). *Personality: A psychological interpretation*. New York: Holt.

Allport, G. W. (1958). *The nature of prejudice.* Garden City, NY: Doubleday Anchor. (Originally published, 1954.)

Allport, G. W. (1962). The general and the unique in psychological science. *Journal of Personality, 30,* 405–422.

Allport, G. W. (1985). The historical background of social psychology. In G. Lindzey & E. Aronson (Eds.), *Handbook of social psychology* (Vol. 1) (3rd ed.) (pp. 1–46). New York: Random House.

Altemeyer, R. A., & Jones, K. (1974). Sexual identity, physical attractiveness, and seating position as determinants of influence in discussion groups. *Canadian Journal of Behavioural Science, 6,* 357–375.

Altman, I. (1973). Reciprocity of interpersonal exchange. *Journal of the Theory of Social Behaviour, 3,* 249–261.

Altman, I. (1975). *The environment and social behavior: Privacy, personal space, territory, and crowding.* Pacific Grove, CA: Brooks/Cole.

Altman, I. (1976). Privacy: A conceptual analysis. *Environment and Behavior, 8,* 7–29.

Altman, I., & Chemers, M. (1980). *Culture and environment.* Pacific Grove, CA: Brooks/Cole.

Altman, I., & Gauvain, M. (1986). A cross-cultural and dialectic analysis of homes. In L. Liben, A. Patterson, & N. Newcombe (Eds.), *Spatial representation and behavior across the life span* (pp. 283–319). New York: Academic Press.

Altman, I., Nelson, P., & Lett, E. (1972). The ecology of home environments. In *Catalogue of Selected Documents in Psychology.* Washington, D.C.: American Psychological Association.

Altman, I., Taylor, D., & Wheeler, L. (1971). Ecological aspects of group behavior in isolation. *Journal of Applied Social Psychology, 1,* 76–100.

Altman, I., & Vinsel, A. (1980). Personal space: An analysis of E. T. Hall's proxemics framework. In I. Altman & J. Wohlwill (Eds.), *Human behavior and environment: Advances in theory and research* (Vol. 2) (pp. 181–254). New York: Plenum.

Amato, P. R. (1983). Helping behavior in urban and rural environments: Field studies based on a taxonomic organization of helping episodes. *Journal of Personality and Social Psychology, 45,* 571–586.

Amato, P. R. (1985). An investigation of planned helping behavior. *Journal of Research in Personality, 19,* 232–252.

American Psychological Association. (1973). *Ethical principles in the conduct of research with human participants.* Washington, D.C.: American Psychological Association.

Amir, Y. (1976). The role of intergroup contact in change of prejudice and ethnic relations. In P. A. Katz (Ed.), *Towards the elimination of racism.* New York: Pergamon Press.

Amoroso, D. M., Brown, M., Pruesse, M., Ware, E. E., & Pilkey, D. W. (1971). An investigation of behavioral, psychological, and physiological reactions to pornographic stimuli. *Technical Reports of the Commission on Obscenity and Pornography* (Vol. 8). Washington, D.C.: U.S. Government Printing Office.

Andersen, S. M., Lazowski, L. E., & Donisi, M. (1986). Salience and self-inference: The role of biased recollections in self-inference processes. *Social Cognition, 4,* 75–95.

Anderson, C. A., & Anderson, D. C. (1984). Ambient temperature and violent crime: Tests of the linear and curvilinear hypotheses. *Journal of Personality and Social Psychology, 46,* 91–97.

Anderson, C. A., & Sechler, E. S. (1986). Effects of explanation and counterexplanation on the development and use of social theories. *Journal of Personality and Social Psychology, 50,* 24–34.

Anderson, N. H. (1965). Averaging versus adding as a stimulus-combination rule in impression formation. *Journal of Experimental Psychology, 70,* 394–400.

Anderson, N. H. (1968). Likableness ratings of 555 personality-trait words. *Journal of Personality and Social Psychology, 9,* 272–279.

Anderson, N. H. (1974). Cognitive algebra: Integration theory applied to social attribution. In L. Berkowitz (Ed.), *Advances in experimental social psychology* (Vol. 7). New York: Academic Press.

Andrews, I. R., & Johnson, D. L. (1971). Small-group polarization of judgments. *Psychonomic Science, 24,* 191–192.

Apfelbaum, E. (1979). Relations of domination and movements for liberation: An analysis of power between groups. In W. G. Austin & S. Worchel (Eds.), *The social psychology of intergroup relations.* Pacific Grove, CA: Brooks/Cole.

Archer, D., Iritani, B., Kimes, D. D., & Barrios, M. (1983). Face-ism: Five studies of sex differences in facial prominence. *Journal of Personality and Social Psychology, 45,* 725–735.

Archer, R. L. (1984). The farmer and the cowman should be friends: An attempt at reconciliation with Batson, Coke, and Pych. *Journal of Personality and Social Psychology, 46,* 709–711.

Ard, B. N., Jr. (1974). Premarital sexual experience: A longitudinal study. *Journal of Sex Research, 10,* 32–39.

Ardrey, R. (1961). *African genesis.* New York: Delta Books.

Ardrey, R. (1966). *The territorial imperative.* New York: Atheneum.

Argyle, M., & Dean, J. (1965). Eye contact, distance, and affiliation. *Sociometry, 28,* 289–304.

Argyle, M., & Henderson, M. (1984). The rules of friendship. *Journal of Social and Personal Relationships, 1,* 211–237.

Argyle, M., & Ingham, R. (1972). Gaze, mutual gaze, and proximity. *Semiotica, 6,* 32–49.

Arkin, R., Cooper, H., & Kolditz, T. (1980). A statistical review of the literature concerning the self-serving attribution bias in interpersonal influence situations. *Journal of Personality, 48,* 435–448.

Aronson, E., Blaney, N., Stephan, C., Sikes, J., & Snapp, M. (1978). *The jigsaw classroom.* Beverly Hills, CA: Sage.

Aronson, E., Brewer, M., & Carlsmith, J. M. (1985). Experimentation in social psychology. In G. Lindzey & E. Aronson (Eds.), *Handbook of social psychology* (Vol. 1) (3rd ed.) (pp. 441–486). New York: Random House.

Aronson, E., & Cope, V. (1968). My enemy's enemy is my friend. *Journal of Personality and Social Psychology, 8,* 8–12.

Aronson, E., & Mills, J. (1959). The effect of severity of initiation on liking for a group. *Journal of Abnormal and Social Psychology, 59,* 177–181.

Asch, S. E. (1946). Forming impressions of personality. *Journal of Abnormal and Social Psychology, 41,* 258–290.

Asch, S. E. (1951). Effects of group pressure upon the modification and distortion of judgments. In H. Guetzkow (Ed.), *Groups, leadership, and men.* Pittsburgh: Carnegie Press.

Asch, S. E. (1956). Studies of independence and conformity: A minority of one against a unanimous majority. *Psychological Monographs, 70* (9, Whole No. 416).

Asch, S. E. (1958). Effects of group pressure upon modification and distortion of judgments. In E. E. Maccoby, T. M. Newcomb, & E. L. Hartley (Eds.), *Readings in social psychology* (3rd ed.). New York: Holt, Rinehart & Winston.

Athanasiou, R., & Yoshioka, G. A. (1973). The spatial character of friendship formation. *Environment and Behavior, 5*, 43–65.

Atkins, A., Deaux, K., & Bieri, J. (1967). Latitude of acceptance and attitude change: Empirical evidence for a reformulation. *Journal of Personality and Social Psychology, 6*, 47–54.

Austin, J. L. (1962). *How to do things with words.* Oxford: Oxford University Press.

Austin, W. T., & Bates, F. L. (1974). Ethological indicators of dominance and territory in a human captive population. *Social Forces, 52*, 447–455.

Axsom, D., & Cooper, J. (1985). Cognitive dissonance and psychotherapy: The role of effort justification in inducing weight loss. *Journal of Experimental Social Psychology, 21*, 149–160.

Azrin, N. H., Hutchinson, R. R., & Hake, D. F. (1966). Attack, avoidance, and escape reactions to aversive shock. *Journal of Experimental Analysis of Behavior, 9*, 191–204.

Bachy, V. (1976). Danish "permissiveness" revisited. *Journal of Communication, 26*, 40–43.

Back, K. W. (1951). Influence through social communication. *Journal of Abnormal and Social Psychology, 46*, 9–23.

Back, K. W. (1972). *Beyond words: The story of sensitivity training and the encounter movement.* New York: Russell Sage Foundation.

Backman, C. W., & Secord, P. F. (1959). The effect of perceived liking on interpersonal attraction. *Human Relations, 12*, 379–384.

Baker, P. M. (1984). Seeing is behaving: Visibility and participation in small groups. *Environment and Behavior, 16*, 159–184.

Bales, R. F. (1953). The equilibrium problem in small groups. In T. Parsons, R. F. Bales, & E. A. Shils (Eds.), *Working papers in the theory of action.* Glencoe, IL: Free Press.

Bales, R. F. (1958). Task roles and social roles in problem-solving groups. In E. E. Maccoby, T. M. Newcomb, & E. L. Hartley (Eds.), *Readings in social psychology* (3rd ed.). New York: Holt, Rinehart & Winston.

Bandura, A. (1965). Vicarious processes: A case of no-trial learning. In L. Berkowitz (Ed.), *Advances in experimental social psychology* (Vol. 2). New York: Academic Press.

Bandura, A. (1973). *Aggression: A social-learning analysis.* Englewood Cliffs, NJ: Prentice-Hall.

Bandura, A. (1977). *Social learning theory.* Englewood Cliffs, NJ: Prentice-Hall.

Bandura, A., Ross, D., & Ross, S. (1961). Transmission of aggression through imitation of aggressive models. *Journal of Abnormal and Social Psychology, 63*, 575–582.

Bandura, A., Ross, D., & Ross, S. (1963). Imitation of film-mediated aggressive models. *Journal of Abnormal and Social Psychology, 66*, 3–11.

Bandura, A., & Walters, R. (1963). *Social learning and personality development.* New York: Holt, Rinehart & Winston.

Bard, M. (1970). Alternatives to traditional law enforcement. In F. F. Korten, S. W. Cook, & J. I. Lacey (Eds.), *Psychology and the problems of society.* Washington, D.C.: American Psychological Association.

Barker, R. G., & Schoggen, P. (1973). *Qualities of community life.* San Francisco: Jossey-Bass.

Barnett, M. A., Feighny, K. M., & Esper, J. A. (1983). Effects of anticipated victim responsiveness and empathy upon volunteering. *Journal of Social Psychology, 119*, 211–218.

Baron, R. A. (1971). Reducing the influence of an aggressive model: The restraining effects of discrepant modeling cues. *Journal of Personality and Social Psychology, 20*, 240–245.

Baron, R. A. (1972). Aggression as a function of ambient temperature and prior anger arousal. *Journal of Personality and Social Psychology, 21*, 183–189.

Baron, R. A. (1974). Aggression as a function of victim's pain cues, level of prior anger arousal, and exposure to an aggressive model. *Journal of Personality and Social Psychology, 29*, 117–124.

Baron, R. A. (1976). The reduction of human aggression: A field study of the influence of incompatible reactions. *Journal of Applied Social Psychology, 6*, 260–274.

Baron, R. A. (1977). *Human aggression.* New York: Plenum.

Baron, R. A., & Ball, R. L. (1974). The aggression-inhibiting influence of nonhostile humor. *Journal of Experimental Social Psychology, 10*, 23–33.

Baron, R. A., & Bell, P. A. (1975). Aggression and heat: Mediating effects of prior provocation and exposure to an aggressive model. *Journal of Personality and Social Psychology, 31*, 825–832.

Baron, R. A., & Bell, P. A. (1976). Aggression and heat: The influence of ambient temperature, negative affect, and a cooling drink on physical aggression. *Journal of Personality and Social Psychology, 33*, 245–255.

Baron, R. A., & Bell, P. A. (1977). Sexual arousal and aggression by males: Effects of type of erotic stimuli and prior provocation. *Journal of Personality and Social Psychology, 35*, 79–87.

Baron, R. A., & Kepner, C. R. (1970). Model's behavior and attraction toward the model as determinants of adult aggressive behavior. *Journal of Personality and Social Psychology, 14*, 335–344.

Baron, R. A., & Ransberger, V. M. (1978). Ambient temperature and the occurrence of collective violence: The "long hot summer" revisited. *Journal of Personality and Social Psychology, 36*, 351–360.

Baron, R. M., & Rodin, J. (1978). Perceived control and crowding stress: Processes mediating the impact of spatial and social density. In A. Baum & Y. Epstein (Eds.), *Human response to crowding.* Hillsdale, NJ: Erlbaum.

Baron, R. S. (1986). Distraction-conflict theory: Progress and problems. *Advances in Experimental Social Psychology, 19*, 1–40.

Bar-Tal, D. (1976). *Prosocial behavior: Theory and research.* Washington, D.C.: Hemisphere (distributed by Halsted Press).

Bar-Tal, D., Raviv, A., & Lesser, T. (1980). The development of altruistic behavior: Empirical evidence. *Developmental Psychology, 16*, 516–524.

Bar-Tal, D., & Saxe, L. (1976). Perceptions of similarly and dissimilarly attractive couples and individuals. *Journal of Personality and Social Psychology, 33*, 772–781.

Bartos, O. J. (1974). *Process and outcome in negotiation.* New York: Columbia University Press.

Bass, B. M. (1981). *Stogdill's handbook of leadership* (Rev. ed.). New York: Free Press.

Bass, B., & Klubeck, S. (1952). Effects of seating arrangement on leaderless group discussions. *Journal of Abnormal and Social Psychology, 47*, 724–727.

Batson, C. D. (1983). Sociobiology and the role of religion in promoting prosocial behavior: An alternative view. *Journal of Personality and Social Psychology, 45*, 1380–1385.

Batson, C. D., Bolen, M. H., Cross, J. A., & Neuringer-Benefiel, H. E. (1986). Where is the altruism in the altruistic personality? *Journal of Personality and Social Psychology, 50*, 212–220.

Batson, C. D., & Coke, J. S. (1981). Empathy: A source of altruistic motivation for helping? In J. P. Rushton & R. M. Sorrentino (Eds.), *Altruism and helping behavior: Social, personality, and developmental perspectives*. Hillsdale, NJ: Erlbaum.

Batson, C. D., Duncan, B. D., Ackerman, P., Buckley, T., & Birch, K. (1981). Is empathic emotion a source of altruistic motivation? *Journal of Personality and Social Psychology, 40,* 290–302.

Batson, C. D., O'Quin, K., Fultz, J., Vanderplas, M., & Isen, A. M. (1983). Influence of self-reported distress and empathy on egoistic versus altruistic motivation to help. *Journal of Personality and Social Psychology, 45,* 706–718.

Bauer, R. A. (1970). Self-confidence and persuasibility: One more time. *Journal of Marketing Research, 7,* 256–258.

Baum, A., Aiello, J. R., & Calesnick, L. E. (1978). Crowding and personal control: Social density and the development of learned helplessness. *Journal of Personality and Social Psychology, 36,* 1000–1011.

Baum, A., & Davis, G. E. (1980). Reducing the stress of high-density living: An architectural intervention. *Journal of Personality and Social Psychology, 38,* 471–481.

Baum, A., Davis, G. E., & Aiello, J. R. (1978). Crowding and neighborhood mediation of urban density. *Journal of Population, 1,* 266–279.

Baum, A., Fisher, J. D., & Solomon, S. (1981). Type of information, familiarity, and the reduction of crowding stress. *Journal of Personality and Social Psychology, 40,* 11–23.

Baum, A., Fleming, R., & Singer, J. E. (1982). Stress at Three Mile Island: Applying psychological impact analysis. In L. Bickman (Ed.), *Applied social psychology annual* (Vol. 3). Beverly Hills, CA: Sage.

Baum, A., & Greenberg, C. I. (1975). Waiting for a crowd: The behavioral and perceptual effects of anticipated crowding. *Journal of Personality and Social Psychology, 32,* 671–679.

Baum, A., Harpin, R. E., & Valins, S. (1975). The role of group phenomena in the experience of crowding. *Environment and Behavior, 7,* 185–198.

Baum, A., & Koman, S. (1976). Differential response to anticipated crowding: Psychological effects of social and spatial density. *Journal of Personality and Social Psychology, 34,* 526–536.

Baum, A., & Paulus, P. (1987). Crowding. In D. Stokols & I. Altman (Eds.), *Handbook of environmental psychology*. New York: Wiley.

Baum, A., Shapiro, A., Murray, D., & Wideman, M. (1979). Interpersonal mediation of perceived crowding and control in residential dyads and triads. *Journal of Applied Social Psychology, 9,* 491–507.

Baum, A., Singer, J., & Baum, C. (1981). Stress and the environment. *Journal of Social Issues, 37*(1), 4–35.

Baum, A., & Valins, S. (1977). *Architecture and social behavior: Psychological studies of social density*. Hillsdale, NJ: Erlbaum.

Baum, A., & Valins, S. (1979). Architectural mediation of residential density and control: Crowding and the regulation of social contact. In L. Berkowitz (Ed.), *Advances in experimental social psychology* (Vol. 12). New York: Academic Press.

Baumann, D. J., Cialdini, R. B., & Kenrick, D. T. (1981). Altruism as hedonism: Helping and self-gratification as equivalent responses. *Journal of Personality and Social Psychology, 40,* 1039–1046.

Baumeister, R. F. (1987). How the self became a problem: A psychological review of historical research. *Journal of Personality and Social Psychology, 52,* 163–176.

Baumeister, R. F., & Jones, E. E. (1978). When self-presentation is constrained by the target's knowledge: Consistency and compensation. *Journal of Personality and Social Psychology, 36,* 608–618.

Baumrin, B. H. (1970). The immorality of irrelevance: The social role of science. In F. F. Korten, S. W. Cook, & J. I. Lacey (Eds.), *Psychology and the problems of society*. Washington, D.C.: American Psychological Association.

Beardsley, E. L. (1971). Privacy: Autonomy and selective disclosure. In J. R. Pennock & J. W. Chapman (Eds.), *Privacy* (pp. 56–70). New York: Atherton.

Beattie, C., & Spencer, B. G. (1971). Career attainment in Canadian bureaucracies: Unscrambling the effects of age, seniority, education, and ethnic linguistic factors in salary. *American Journal of Sociology, 77,* 472–490.

Becker, F. D. (1973). Study of spatial markers. *Journal of Personality and Social Psychology, 26,* 439–445.

Becker, F. D., & Conglio, C. (1975). Environmental messages: Personalization and territory. *Humanitas, 11,* 55–74.

Becker, F. D., Gield, B., & Froggat, C. (1983). Seating position and impression formation in an office setting. *Journal of Environmental Psychology, 3,* 253–261.

Becker, F. D., Gield, B., Gaylin, K., & Sayer, S. (1983). Office design in a community college: Effect on work and communication patterns. *Environment and Behavior, 15,* 699–726.

Becker, F. D., & Mayo, C. (1971). Delineating personal distance and territoriality. *Environment and Behavior, 3,* 375–381.

Becker, F. D., Sommer, R., Bee, J., & Oxley, B. (1973). College classroom ecology. *Sociometry, 36,* 514–525.

Becker, L. J. (1978). Joint effect of feedback and goal setting on performance: A field study of residential energy conservation. *Journal of Applied Psychology, 63,* 428–433.

Belk, R., Painter, J., & Semenik, R. (1981). Preferred solutions to the energy crisis as a function of causal attributions. *Journal of Consumer Research, 8,* 306–312.

Bell, A. P., & Weinberg, M. S. (1978). *Homosexualities: A study of diversity among men and women*. New York: Simon and Schuster.

Bell, A. P., Weinberg, M. S., & Hammersmith, S. K. (1981a). *Sexual preference: Its development in men and women*. Bloomington: Indiana University Press.

Bell, A. P., Weinberg, M. S., & Hammersmith, S. K. (1981b). *Sexual preference: Its development in men and women. Statistical appendix*. Bloomington: Indiana University Press.

Bell, P. A., & Baron, R. A. (1974). Effects of heat, noise, and provocation on retaliatory evaluative behavior. *Bulletin of the Psychonomic Society, 4,* 479–481.

Bell, P. A., & Baron, R. A. (1976). Aggression and heat: The mediating role of negative affect. *Journal of Applied Social Psychology, 6,* 18–30.

Bem, D. J. (1967). Self-perception: An alternative interpretation of cognitive dissonance phenomena. *Psychological Review, 1967, 74,* 183–200.

Bem, D. J. (1972). Self-perception theory. In L. Berkowitz (Ed.), *Advances in experimental social psychology* (Vol. 6). New York: Academic Press.

Bender, P. (1971). Definition of "obscene" under existing law. *Technical Reports of the Commission on Obscenity and Pornography* (Vol. 2). Washington, D.C.: U.S. Government Printing Office.

Bennett, A. (1985). In today's China, road to romance begins at the bank. *Wall Street Journal*, October 4, 1985, pp. 1, 7.

Benson, P. L., Karabenick, S. A., & Lerner, R. M. (1976). Pretty pleases: The effects of physical attractiveness, race, and sex on receiving help. *Journal of Experimental Social Psychology*, *12*, 409–415.

Bentler, P. M., & Abramson, P. R. (1981). The science of sex research: Some methodological considerations. *Archives of Sexual Behavior*, *10*, 225–251.

Berg, B. (1978). Helping behavior on the gridiron: It helps if you're winning. *Psychological Reports*, *42*, 531–534.

Berg, J. H. (1984). Development of friendship between roommates. *Journal of Personality and Social Psychology*, *46*, 346–356.

Berger, J., Rosenholtz, S. J., & Zelditch, M., Jr. (1980). Status organizing processes. *Annual Review of Sociology*, *6*, 479–508.

Berglas, S., & Jones, E. E. (1978). Drug choice as an externalization strategy in response to noncontingent success. *Journal of Personality and Social Psychology*, *36*, 405–417.

Berkowitz, L. (1965a). Some aspects of observed aggression. *Journal of Personality and Social Psychology*, *2*, 359–369.

Berkowitz, L. (1965b). The concept of aggressive drive: Some additional considerations. In L. Berkowitz (Ed.), *Advances in experimental social psychology* (Vol. 2). New York: Academic Press.

Berkowitz, L. (1968). Impulse, aggression, and the gun. *Psychology Today*, *2*(4), 18–22.

Berkowitz, L. (1969). The frustration-aggression hypothesis revisited. In L. Berkowitz (Ed.), *Roots of aggression: A re-examination of the frustration-aggression hypothesis*. New York: Atherton.

Berkowitz, L. (1971). The contagion of violence: An S-R mediational analysis of some effects of observed aggression. In W. Arnold & M. Page (Eds.), *Nebraska Symposium on Motivation* (Vol. 18). Lincoln: University of Nebraska Press.

Berkowitz, L. (1984). Some effects of thoughts on anti- and prosocial influences of media events: A cognitive-neoassociation analysis. *Psychological Bulletin*, *95*, 410–427.

Berkowitz, L., & Alioto, J. T. (1973). The meaning of an observed event as a determinant of its aggressive consequences. *Journal of Personality and Social Psychology*, *28*, 206–217.

Berkowitz, L., & Daniels, L. R. (1963). Responsibility and dependency. *Journal of Abnormal and Social Psychology*, *66*, 664–669.

Berkowitz, L., & LePage, A. (1967). Weapons as aggression-eliciting stimuli. *Journal of Personality and Social Psychology*, *7*, 202–207.

Berkun, M. M. (1964). Performance decrement under psychological stress. *Human Factors*, *6*, 21–30.

Bernard, J. (1975). *Women, wives, mothers*. Chicago: Aldine.

Berry, D. S., & McArthur, L. Z. (1985). Some components and consequences of a babyface. *Journal of Personality and Social Psychology*, *48*, 312–323.

Berry, D. S., & McArthur, L. Z. (1986). Perceiving character in faces: The impact of age-related craniofacial changes on social perception. *Psychological Bulletin*, *100*, 3–18.

Berry, J. W. (1974). Canadian psychology: Some social and applied emphases. *Canadian Psychologist*, *15*, 132–139.

Berry, J. W. (1978). Social psychology: Comparative, societal and universal. *Canadian Psychological Review*, *19*, 93–104.

Berscheid, E. (1966). Opinion change and communicator-communicatee similarity and dissimilarity. *Journal of Personality and Social Psychology*, *4*, 670–680.

Berscheid, E. (1985). Interpersonal attraction. In G. Lindzey & E. Aronson (Eds.), *Handbook of social psychology*, (Vol. II) (3rd ed.) (pp. 413–484). New York: Random House.

Berscheid, E., Graziano, W., Monson, T., & Dermer, M. (1976). Outcome dependency: Attention, attribution and attraction. *Journal of Personality and Social Psychology*, *34*, 978–989.

Berscheid, E., & Walster, E. (1978). *Interpersonal attraction* (2nd ed.). Reading, MA: Addison-Wesley.

Beveridge, W. I. B. (1964). *The art of scientific investigation*. London: Mercury.

Bickman, L. (1972). Social influence and diffusion of responsibility in an emergency. *Journal of Experimental Social Psychology*, *8*, 438–445.

Bickman, L., & Kamzan, M. (1973). The effect of race and need on helping behavior. *Journal of Social Psychology*, *89*, 73–77.

Biddle, B. J., & Thomas, E. J. (Eds.). (1966). *Role theory: Concepts and research*. New York: Wiley.

Bird, C. (1940). *Social psychology*. New York: Appleton-Century-Crofts.

Birdwhistell, R. L. (1978). *Kinesics and context*. Philadelphia: University of Pennsylvania Press.

Blake, R., Rhead, C., Wedge, B., & Mouton, J. (1956). Housing architecture and social interaction. *Sociometry*, *19*, 133–139.

Blass, T. (1984). Social psychology and personality: Toward a convergence. *Journal of Personality and Social Psychology*, *47*, 1013–1027.

Bleda, P., & Bleda, E. (1978). Effects of sex and smoking on reactions to spatial invasion at a shopping mall. *Journal of Social Psychology*, *104*, 311–312.

Bleda, P., & Sandman, P. H. (1977). In smoke's way: Socioemotional reactions to another's smoking. *Journal of Applied Psychology*, *62*, 452–458.

Blumstein, P. W., & Schwartz, P. (1977). Bisexuality: Some social psychological issues. *Journal of Social Issues*, *33*(2), 30–45.

Blumstein, P. W., & Schwartz, P. (1983). *American couples*. New York: Morrow.

Bochner, S., Duncan, R., Kennedy, E., & Orr, F. (1976). Acquaintance links between residents of a high rise building: An application of the "small world" method. *Journal of Social Psychology*, *100*, 277–284.

Bohrnstedt, G. W., & Fisher, G. A. (1986). The effects of recalled childhood and adolescent relationships compared to current role performances on young adults' affective functioning. *Social Psychology Quarterly*, *49*, 19–32.

Bond, C. F., Jr. (1982). Social facilitation: A self-presentational view. *Journal of Personality and Social Psychology*, *42*, 1042–1050.

Bond, C. F., Jr., & Titus, L. J. (1983). Social facilitation: A meta-analysis of 241 studies. *Psychological Bulletin*, *94*, 265–292.

Bond, M. H., & Cheung, T. (1983). College students' spontaneous self-concept: The effect of culture among respondents in Hong Kong, Japan, and the United States. *Journal of Cross-Cultural Psychology*, *14*, 153–171.

Booth, A. (1972). Sex and social participation. *American Sociological Review*, *37*, 183–192.

Booth, A. (1976). *Urban crowding and its consequences*. New York: Praeger.

Borden, R. J. (1975). Witnessed aggression: Influence of an observer's sex and values on aggressive responding. *Journal of Personality and Social Psychology*, *31*, 567–573.

Borden, R. J. (1980). Audience influence. In P. B. Paulus (Ed.), *Psychology of group influence*. Hillsdale, NJ: Erlbaum.

Bordieri, J. E., & Drehmer, D. E. (1984). Vietnam veterans: Fighting the employment war. *Journal of Applied Social Psychology, 14*, 341–347.

Borys, S., & Perlman, D. (1985). Gender differences in loneliness. *Personality and Social Psychology Bulletin, 11*, 63–74.

Bouchard, T. J., Jr. (1972). Training, motivation, and personality as determinants of the effectiveness of brainstorming groups and individuals. *Journal of Applied Psychology, 56*, 324–331.

Boyce, P. (1974). Users' assessments of a landscaped office. *Journal of Architectural Research, 3*(3), 44–62.

Boykin, A. W. (1986). The triple quandary and the schooling of Afro-American children. In U. Neisser (Ed.), *The school achievement of minority children: New perspectives*. Hillsdale, NJ: Erlbaum.

Boykin, A. W., Franklin, A. J., & Yates, J. F. (Eds.). (1979). *Research directions of black psychologists*. New York: Russell Sage Foundation.

Bramson, L., & Goethals, G. W. (Eds.). (1968). *War* (Rev. ed.). New York: Basic Books.

Brehm, J. W. (1966). *A theory of psychological reactance*. New York: Academic Press.

Brehm, S. S., & Brehm, J. W. (1981). *Psychological reactance: A theory of freedom and control*. New York: Academic Press.

Brehm, J. W., Stires, L. K., Sensenig, J., & Shaban, J. (1966). The attractiveness of an eliminated choice alternative. *Journal of Experimental Social Psychology, 2*, 301–313.

Brewer, M. B. (1986). The role of ethnocentrism in intergroup conflict. In S. Worchel & W. G. Austin (Eds.), *Psychology of intergroup relations* (2nd ed.) (pp. 88–102). Chicago: Nelson-Hall.

Brewer, M., Dull, V., & Lui, L. (1981). Perceptions of the elderly: Stereotypes as prototypes. *Journal of Personality and Social Psychology, 41*, 656–670.

Brewer, M. B., & Kramer, R. M. (1985). The psychology of intergroup attitudes and behavior. *Annual review of psychology, 36*, 219–243.

Brewer, M. B., & Miller, N. (1984). Beyond the contact hypothesis: Theoretical perspectives on desegregation. In N. Miller & M. B. Brewer (Eds.), *Groups in contact: The psychology of desegregation* (pp. 281–302). Orlando: Academic Press.

Brickner, M. A., Harkins, S. G., & Ostrom, T. M. (1986). Effects of personal involvement: Thought-provoking implications for social loafing. *Journal of Personality and Social Psychology, 51*, 763–769.

Brigham, J. C. (1971). Ethnic stereotypes. *Psychological Bulletin, 76*, 15–38.

Brill, M. (1984). *Using office design to increase productivity*, (Vol. 1). Buffalo, NY: Workplace Design and Productivity, Inc.

Brink, J. H. (1977). Effect of interpersonal communication on attraction. *Journal of Personality and Social Psychology, 35*, 783–790.

Brislin, R. W. (1980). Introduction to social psychology. In H. C. Triandis & R. W. Brislin (Eds.), *Handbook of cross-cultural psychology: Social psychology* (Vol. 5). Boston: Allyn & Bacon.

Broll, L., Gross, A. E., & Piliavin, I. M. (1974). Effects of offered and requested help on help-seeking and reactions to being helped. *Journal of Applied Social Psychology, 4*, 244–258.

Bronfenbrenner, U. (1970). *Two worlds of childhood: U.S. and U.S.S.R.* NY: Russell Sage Foundation.

Broude, G. J. (1975). Norms of premarital sexual behavior: A cross-cultural study. *Ethos, 3*, 381–402.

Broverman, D. M., Klaiber, E. L., Kobayashi, Y., & Vogel, W. (1968). Roles of activation and inhibition in sex differences in cognitive abilities. *Psychological Review, 75*, 23–50.

Broverman, I. K., Broverman, D. M., Clarkson, F. E., Rosenkrantz, P. S., & Vogel, S. R. (1970). Sex-role stereotypes and clinical judgements of mental health. *Journal of Consulting and Clinical Psychology, 34*, 1–7.

Broverman, I. K., Vogel, S. R., Broverman, D. M., Clarkson, F. E., & Rosenkrantz, P. S. (1972). Sex-role stereotypes: A current appraisal. *Journal of Social Issues, 28*(2), 59–78.

Brower, S., Dockett, K., & Taylor, R. B. (1983). Residents' perceptions of territorial features and perceived local threat. *Environment and Behavior, 15*, 419–437.

Brown, B. B. (1987). Territoriality. In D. Stokols and I. Altman (Eds.), *Handbook of environmental psychology*. New York: Wiley.

Brown, B. B., & Altman, I. (1983). Territoriality, defensible space, and residential burglary: An environmental analysis. *Journal of Environmental Psychology, 3*, 203–220.

Brown, B. B., & Werner, C. (1985). Social cohesiveness, territoriality, and holiday decorations: The influence of cul-de-sacs. *Environment and Behavior, 17*, 539–565.

Brown, B. R. (1977). Face-saving and face-restoration in negotiation. In D. Druckman (Ed.), *Negotiations: Social-psychological perspectives*. Beverly Hills, CA: Sage.

Brown, C. E. (1981). Shared space invasion and race. *Personality and Social Psychology Bulletin, 7*, 103–108.

Brown, P., & Elliott, R. (1965). Control of aggression in a nursery school class. *Journal of Experimental Child Psychology, 2*, 103–107.

Brown, R. (1965). *Social psychology*. New York: Free Press.

Brown, R. (1986). *Social psychology. The second edition*. New York: Free Press.

Brown, S. M. (1979). Male versus female leaders: A comparison of empirical studies. *Sex Roles, 5*, 595–611.

Brown, V., & Geis, F. L. (1984). Turning lead into gold: Evaluations of men and women leaders and the alchemy of social consensus. *Journal of Personality and Social Psychology, 46*, 811–824.

Bryan, J. H., & Walbek, N. (1970). The impact of words and deeds concerning altruism upon children. *Child Development, 41*, 747–757.

Bryant, J., & Zillmann, D. (1979). The effect of the intensification of annoyance through residual excitation from unrelated prior stimulation on substantially delayed hostile behavior. *Journal of Experimental Social Psychology, 15*, 470–480.

Buckhout, R. (1980). Nearly 2,000 witnesses can be wrong. *Bulletin of the Psychonomic Society, 16*, 307–310.

Bugental, D. E., Kaswan, J. E., & Love, L. R. (1970). Perception of contradictory meanings conveyed by verbal and nonverbal channels. *Journal of Personality and Social Psychology, 16*, 647–655.

Bugental, D. E., Love, L. R., & Gianetto, R. M. (1971). Perfidious feminine faces. *Journal of Personality and Social Psychology, 17*, 314–318.

Burger, J. M. (1986). Increasing compliance by improving the deal: The that's-not-all technique. *Journal of Personality and Social Psychology, 51*, 277–283.

Burstein, E., & Worchel, P. (1962). Arbitrariness of frustration and its consequences for aggression in a social situation. *Journal of Personality, 30*, 528–540.

Buss, A. H. (1961). *The psychology of aggression*. New York: Wiley.
Buss, A. H. (1963). Physical aggression in relation to different frustrations. *Journal of Abnormal and Social Psychology, 67*, 1–7.
Buss, A. H. (1967). Instrumentality of aggression, feedback, and frustration as determinants of physical aggression. *Journal of Personality and Social Psychology, 3*, 153–162.
Buss, A. H. (1971). Aggression pays. In J. L. Singer (Ed.), *The control of aggression and violence*. New York: Academic Press.
Buss, D. M. (1984). Toward a psychology of the person-environment (PE) correlation: The role of spouse selection. *Journal of Personality and Social Psychology, 47*, 361–377.
Buss, D. M., & Barnes, M. (1986). Preferences in human mate selection. *Journal of Personality and Social Psychology, 50*, 559–570.
Buss, D. M., & Craik, K. H. (1983). Contemporary worldviews: Personal and policy implications. *Journal of Applied Social Psychology, 13*, 259–280.
Bynum, T. S., & Purri, D. M. (1984). Crime and architectural style: An examination of the environmental design hypothesis. *Criminal Justice and Behavior, 11*, 179–196.
Byrne, D. (1961). The influence of propinquity and opportunities for interaction on classroom relationships. *Human Relations, 14*, 63–70.
Byrne, D. (1971). *The attraction paradigm*. New York: Academic Press.
Byrne, D. (1977). Social psychology and the study of sexual behavior. *Personality and Social Psychology Bulletin, 3*, 3–30.
Byrne, D. (1982). Predicting human sexual behavior. In A. G. Kraut (Ed.), *The G. Stanley Hall lecture series* (Vol. 2). Washington, DC: American Psychological Association.
Byrne, D. (1983). Sex without contraception. In D. Byrne & W. A. Fisher (Eds.), *Adolescents, sex, and contraception*. Hillsdale, NJ: Erlbaum.
Byrne, D., & Byrne, L. A. (1977). *Exploring human sexuality*. New York: Thomas Y. Crowell.
Byrne, D., & Clore, G. L. (1970). A reinforcement model of evaluative responses. *Personality: An International Journal, 1*, 103–128.
Byrne, D., & Przybyla, D. P. J. (1980). Authoritarianism and political preferences in 1980. *Bulletin of the Psychonomic Society, 16*, 471–472.
Cacioppo, J. T., & Petty, R. E. (1982). The need for cognition. *Journal of Personality and Social Psychology, 42*, 116–131.
Cacioppo, J. T., Petty, R. E., & Kao, C. (1984). The efficient assessment of need for cognition. *Journal of Personality and Assessment, 48*, 306–307.
Cacioppo, J. T., Petty, R. E., & Losch, M. E. (1986). Attributions of responsibility for helping and doing harm: Evidence for confusion of responsibility. *Journal of Personality and Social Psychology, 50*, 100–105.
Caldwell, D. F., & O'Reilly, C. A., III. (1982). Boundary spanning and individual performance: The impact of self-monitoring. *Journal of Applied Psychology, 67*, 124–127.
Calhoun, J. B. (1962). Population density and social pathology. *Scientific American, 206*(2), 139–148.
Campbell, A., Converse, P. E., & Rogers, W. L. (1976). *The quality of American life: Perceptions, evaluations, and satisfactions*. New York: Russell Sage Foundation.
Campbell, D. E. (1979). Interior office design and visitor response. *Journal of Applied Psychology, 64*, 648–653.
Campbell, D. E. (1980). Professors and their offices: A survey of person-behavior-environment relationships. In R. Stough & A. Wandersman (Eds.), *Optimizing environments: Research, practice and policy* (pp. 227–237). Washington, DC: Environmental Design Research Association.
Campbell, D. T. (1969). Reforms as experiments. *American Psychologist, 24*, 409–429.
Campbell, D. T. (1978). On the genetics of altruism and the counter-hedonic components of human culture. In L. Wispe (Ed.), *Altruism, sympathy, and helping: Psychological and sociological principles*. New York: Academic Press.
Campbell, D. T. (1983). The two distinct routes beyond kin selection to ultrasociality: Implications for humanities and social sciences. In D. L. Bridgeman (Ed.), *The nature of prosocial development: Interdisciplinary theories and strategies*. New York: Academic Press.
Campbell, D. T., & Stanley, J. C. (1966). *Experimental and quasi-experimental designs for research*. Chicago: Rand McNally.
Campbell, J. D., Tesser, A., & Fairey, P. J. (1986). Conformity and attention to the stimulus: Some temporal and contextual dynamics. *Journal of Personality and Social Psychology, 51*, 315–324.
Cannavale, F. J., Scarr, H. A., & Pepitone, A. (1970). Deindividuation in the small group: Further evidence. *Journal of Personality and Social Psychology, 16*, 141–147.
Cantor, N. (1981). A cognitive-social approach to personality. In N. Cantor & J. F. Kihlstrom (Eds.), *Personality, cognition, and social interaction* (pp. 23–44). Hillsdale, NJ: Erlbaum.
Cantor, N., & Kihlstrom, J. F. (1981). *Personality, cognition, and social interaction*. Hillsdale, NJ: Erlbaum.
Cantor, N., Mischel, W., & Schwartz, J. C. (1982). A prototype analysis of psychological situations. *Cognitive Psychology, 14*, 45–77.
Caporael, L. R. (1981). The paralanguage of caregiving: Baby talk to the institutionalized aged. *Journal of Personality and Social Psychology, 40*, 876–884.
Carlsmith, J. M., & Anderson, C. A. (1979). Ambient temperature and the occurrence of collective violence: A new analysis. *Journal of Personality and Social Psychology, 37*, 337–344.
Carlsmith, J. M., Ellsworth, P. C., & Aronson, E. (1976). *Methods of research in social psychology*. Reading, MA: Addison-Wesley.
Carlson, E. R., & Coleman, C. E. H. (1977). Experiential and motivational determinants of the richness of an induced sexual fantasy. *Journal of Personality, 45*, 528–542.
Carlson, H., Thayer, R. E., & Germann, A. C. (1971). Social attitudes and personality differences among members of two kinds of police departments (innovative vs. traditional) and students. *Journal of Criminal Law, Criminology and Police Science, 62*, 564–567.
Carnevale, P. J. D., & Pegnetter, R. (1985). The selection of mediation tactics in public sector disputes: A contingency analysis. *Journal of Social Issues, 41*(2), 65–81.
Carnevale, P. J. D., Pruitt, D. G., & Britton, S. D. (1979). Looking tough: The negotiator under constituent surveillance. *Personality and Social Psychology Bulletin, 5*, 118–121.
Carnevale, P. J. D., Pruitt, D. G., & Seilheimer, S. D. (1981). Looking and competing: Accountability and visual access in integrative bargaining. *Journal of Personality and Social Psychology, 40*, 111–120.

Caron, A. H. (1979). First-time exposure to television: Effects on Inuit children's cultural images. *Communication Research, 6,* 135–154.

Carpenter, C. R. (1958). Territoriality: A review of concepts and problems. In A. Roe & G. Simpson (Eds.), *Behavior and evolution.* New Haven: Yale University Press.

Carr, S. J., & Dabbs, J. M., Jr. (1974). The effects of lighting, distance and intimacy of topic on verbal and visual behavior. *Sociometry, 37,* 592–600.

Carter, J. H. (1952). Military leadership. *Military Review, 32,* 14–18.

Cartwright, D. (1968). The nature of group cohesiveness. In D. Cartwright & A. Zander (Eds.), *Group dynamics: Research and theory* (3rd ed.). New York: Harper & Row.

Cartwright, D. (1978). Theory and practice. *Journal of Social Issues, 34*(4), 168–180.

Cartwright, D., & Zander, A. (Eds.). (1968). *Group dynamics: Research and theory* (3rd ed.). New York: Harper & Row.

Carver, C. S. (1979). A cybernetic model of self-attention processes. *Journal of Personality and Social Psychology, 37,* 1251–1281.

Carver, C. S., & Scheier, M. F. (1982). Control theory: A useful conceptual framework for personality–social, clinical, and health psychology. *Psychological Bulletin, 92,* 111–135.

Cary, M. S. (1978). The role of gaze in the initiation of conversation. *Social Psychology, 41,* 269–271.

Cash, T. F., Begley, P. J., McCown, D. A., & Weise, B. C. (1975). When counselors are seen but not heard: Initial impact of physical attractiveness. *Journal of Counseling Psychology, 22,* 273–279.

Cash, T. F., Cash, D. W., & Butters, J. W. (1983). "Mirror, mirror, on the wall...?": Contrast effects and self-evaluations of physical attractiveness. *Personality and Social Psychology Bulletin, 9,* 351–358.

Cash, T. F., Kehr, J. A., Polyson, J., & Freeman, V. (1977). Role of physical attractiveness in peer attribution of psychological disturbance. *Journal of Consulting and Clinical Psychology, 45,* 987–993.

Castore, C. H., & DeNinno, J. A. (1977). Investigations in the social comparison of attitudes. In J. M. Suls & R. L. Miller (Eds.), *Social comparison processes: Theoretical and empirical perspectives.* Washington, D.C.: Halsted.

Cattell, R. B., Kawash, G. F., & DeYoung, G. E. (1972). Validation of objective measures of ergic tension: Response of the sex erg to visual stimulation. *Journal of Experimental Research in Personality, 6,* 76–83.

Cavan, S. (1963). Interaction in home territories. *Berkeley Journal of Sociology, 8,* 17–32.

Chaiken, S. (1979). Communicator physical attractiveness and persuasion. *Journal of Personality and Social Psychology, 37,* 1387–1397.

Chaiken, S., & Eagly, A. H. (1976). Communication modality as a determinant of message persuasiveness and message comprehensibility. *Journal of Personality and Social Psychology, 34,* 605–614.

Chaiken, S., & Eagly, A. H. (1983). Communication modality as a determinant of persuasion: The role of communicator salience. *Journal of Personality and Social Psychology, 45,* 241–256.

Chaiken, S., & Stangor, C. (1987). Attitudes and attitude change. *Annual Review of Psychology, 38,* 575–630.

Chapko, M. K., & Solomon, H. (1976). Air pollution and recreational behavior. *Journal of Social Psychology, 100,* 149–150.

Chapman, L. J. (1967). Illusory correlation in observational report. *Journal of Verbal Learning and Verbal Behavior, 6,* 151–155.

Chemers, M. M. (1983). Leadership theory and research: A systems-process integration. In P. B. Paulus (Ed.), *Basic group processes* (pp. 9–39). New York: Springer-Verlag.

Chemers, M. M., Hays, R. B., Rhodewalt, F., & Wysocki, J. (1985). A person-environment analysis of job stress: A contingency model explanation. *Journal of Personality and Social Psychology, 49,* 628–635.

Chemers, M. M., & Skrzypek, G. J. (1972). An experimental test of the Contingency Model of leadership effectiveness. *Journal of Personality and Social Psychology, 24,* 172–177.

Cherry, F., & Byrne, D. (1977). Authoritarianism. In T. Blass (Ed.), *Personality variables in social behavior.* Hillsdale, NJ: Erlbaum.

Cheyne, J. A., & Efran, M. G. (1972). The effect of spatial and interpersonal variables on the invasion of group controlled territories. *Sociometry, 35,* 477–489.

Christian, J. J., Flyger, V., & Davis, D. E. (1960). Factors in the mass mortality of a herd of Sika deer, Cervus nippon. *Chesapeake Science, 1,* 79–95.

Cialdini, R. B. (1985). *Influence: Science and practice.* Glenview, IL: Scott, Foresman.

Cialdini, R. B., Borden, R. J., Thorne, A., Walker, M. R., & Freeman, S. (1976). Basking in reflected glory: Three (football) field studies. *Journal of Personality and Social Psychology, 34,* 366–375.

Cialdini, R. B., Cacioppo, J. T., Bassett, R., & Miller, J. A. (1978). Low-ball procedure for producing compliance: Commitment then cost. *Journal of Personality and Social Psychology, 36,* 463–476.

Cialdini, R. B., Darby, B. L., & Vincent, J. E. (1973). Transgression and altruism: A case for hedonism. *Journal of Experimental Social Psychology, 9,* 502–516.

Cialdini, R. B., & Kenrick, D. T. (1976). Altruism as hedonism: A social developmental perspective on the relationship of negative mood state and helping. *Journal of Personality and Social Psychology, 34,* 907–914.

Cialdini, R. B., Levy, A., Herman, P., & Evenbeck, S. (1973). Attitudinal politics: The strategy of moderation. *Journal of Personality and Social Psychology, 25,* 100–108.

Cialdini, R. B., Levy, A., Herman, P., Kozlowski, L., & Petty, R. E. (1976). Elastic shifts of opinion: Determinants of direction and durability. *Journal of Personality and Social Psychology, 34,* 663–672.

Cialdini, R. B., Vincent, J. E., Lewis, S. K., Catalan, J., Wheeler, D., & Darby, B. L. (1975). A reciprocal concessions procedure for inducing compliance: The door-in-the-face technique. *Journal of Personality and Social Psychology, 21,* 206–215.

Clark, H. H. (1985). Language use and language users. In G. Lindzey and E. Aronson (Eds.), *Handbook of social psychology,* (Vol. II) (3rd ed.) (pp. 179–231). New York: Random House.

Clark, K. B., & Clark, M. P. (1947). Racial identification and preference in Negro children. In T. M. Newcomb & E. L. Hartley (Eds.), *Readings in social psychology.* New York: Holt.

Clark, M. S. (1983). Reactions to aid in communal and exchange relationships. In J. D. Fisher, A. Nadler, & B. M. DePaulo (Eds.), *New directions in helping* (Vol. 1). *Recipient reactions to aid.* New York: Academic Press.

Clark, M. S. (1984). Record keeping in two types of relationships. *Journal of Personality and Social Psychology, 47,* 549–557.

Clark, M. S., & Mills, J. (1979). Interpersonal attraction in exchange and communal relationships. *Journal of Personality and Social Psychology, 37,* 12–24.

Clark, M. S., Mills, J., & Powell, M. C. (in press). Keeping track of needs in communal and exchange relationships. *Journal of Personality and Social Psychology.*

Clark, R. D., III, & Word, L. E. (1972). Why don't bystanders help? Because of ambiguity? *Journal of Personality and Social Psychology, 24,* 392–400.

Clark, R. D., III, & Word, L. E. (1974). Where is the apathetic bystander? Situational characteristics of the emergency. *Journal of Personality and Social Psychology, 29,* 279–287.

Clee, M. A., & Wicklund, R. A. (1980). Consumer behavior and psychological reactance. *Journal of Consumer Research, 6,* 389–405.

Clore, G. L., & Kerber, K. W. (1978). *Toward an affective theory of attraction and trait attribution.* Unpublished manuscript, University of Illinois, Champaign.

Clore, G. L., Wiggins, N. H., & Itkin, S. (1975). Gain and loss in attraction: Attributions from nonverbal behavior. *Journal of Personality and Social Psychology, 31,* 706–712.

Cohen, C. E. (1981). Person categories and social perception: Testing some boundaries of the processing effects of prior knowledge. *Journal of Personality and Social Psychology, 40,* 441–452.

Cohen, D., Whitmyre, J. W., & Funk, W. H. (1960). Effect of group cohesiveness and training upon creative thinking. *Journal of Applied Psychology, 44,* 319–322.

Cohen, S. (1978). Environmental load and the allocation of attention. In A. Baum, J. E. Singer, & S. Valins (Eds.), *Advances in environmental psychology.* Hillsdale, NJ: Erlbaum.

Cohen, S. (1980a). The aftereffects of stress on human performance and social behavior: A review of research and theory. *Psychological Bulletin, 88,* 82–108.

Cohen, S. (1980b). Cognitive processes as determinants of environmental stress. In I. Sarason & C. Spielberger (Eds.), *Stress and anxiety* (Vol. 7). Washington, D.C.: Hemisphere.

Cohen, S., & Lezak, A. (1977). Noise and attentiveness to social cues. *Environment and Behavior, 9,* 559–572.

Cohen, S., & Spacapan, S. (1978). The aftereffects of stress: An attentional interpretation. *Environmental Psychology and Nonverbal Behavior, 3,* 43–57.

Cohen, S., & Wills, T. A. (1985). Stress, social support, and the buffering hypothesis. *Psychological Bulletin, 98,* 310–357.

Coke, J. S., Batson, C. D., & McDavis, K. (1978). Empathic mediation of helping: A two-stage model. *Journal of Personality and Social Psychology, 36,* 752–766.

Coleman, A. D. (1968). Territoriality in man: A comparison of behavior in home and hospital. *American Journal of Orthopsychiatry, 38,* 464–468.

Collins, B. E. (1970). *Social psychology.* Reading, MA: Addison-Wesley.

Collins, B. E. (1974). Four components of the Rotter Internal-External scale: Belief in a difficult world, a just world, a predictable world, and a politically responsive world. *Journal of Personality and Social Psychology, 29,* 381–391.

Conrath, D. W. (1973). Communication patterns, organizational structure, and man: Some relationships. *Human Factors, 15,* 459–470.

Conroy, J., & Sundstrom, E. (1977). Territorial dominance in a dyadic conversation as a function of similarity of opinion. *Journal of Personality and Social Psychology, 35,* 570–576.

Cook, S. W. (1970). Motives in a conceptual analysis of attitude-related behavior. In W. J. Arnold & D. Levine (Eds.), *Nebraska symposium on motivation, 1969.* Lincoln: University of Nebraska Press.

Cook, S. W. (1976). Ethical issues in the conduct of research in social relations. In C. Selltiz, L. S. Wrightsman, & S. W. Cook (Eds.), *Research methods in social relations* (3rd ed.). New York: Holt, Rinehart & Winston.

Cook, S. W., & Pelfrey, M. (1985). Reactions to being helped in cooperating interracial groups: A context effect. *Journal of Personality and Social Psychology, 49,* 1231–1245.

Cook, T. D., & Campbell, D. T. (Eds.). (1979). *The design and analysis of quasi-experiments for field settings.* Chicago: Rand McNally.

Cooke, B. G. (1980). Nonverbal communication among Afro-Americans: An initial classification. In R. L. Jones (Ed.), *Black psychology* (2nd ed.). New York: Harper & Row.

Cooley, C. H. (1902/1964). *Human nature and the social order.* New York: Schocken Books.

Cooper, J. (1976). Deception and role playing: In telling the good guys from the bad guys. *American Psychologist, 31,* 605–610.

Cooper, J., & Fazio, R. H. (1984). A new look at dissonance theory. *Advances in Experimental Social Psychology, 17,* 229–266.

Costanzo, M., Archer, D., Aronson, E., & Pettigrew, T. (1986). Energy conservation behavior: The difficult path from information to action. *American Psychologist, 41,* 521–528.

Costanzo, P. R. (1970). Conformity development as a function of self-blame. *Journal of Personality and Social Psychology, 14,* 366–374.

Cota, A. A., & Dion, K. L. (1986). Salience of gender and sex composition of ad hoc groups: An experimental test of distinctiveness theory. *Journal of Personality and Social Psychology, 50,* 770–776.

Cotterell, J. L. (1984). Effects of school architectural design on student and teacher anxiety. *Environment and Behavior, 16,* 455–479.

Cottrell, N. B. (1972). Social facilitation. In C. G. McClintock (Ed.), *Experimental social psychology.* New York: Holt.

Cottrell, N. B., Wack, D. L., Sekerak, G. J., & Rittle, R. H. (1968). Social facilitation of dominant responses by the presence of an audience and the mere presence of others. *Journal of Personality and Social Psychology, 9,* 245–250.

Cowan, C. L., Thompson, W. C., & Ellsworth, P. C. (1984). The effects of death qualification on jurors' predisposition to convict and on the quality of deliberation. *Law and Human Behavior, 8,* 53–79.

Cowan, E. L. (1982). Help is where you find it: Four informal helping groups. *American Psychologist, 37,* 385–395.

Cox, O. C. (1948). *Caste, class, and race.* New York: Doubleday.

Cox, V. C., Paulus, P. B., & McCain, G. (1984). Prison crowding research. *American Psychologist, 39,* 1148–1160.

Cozby, P. C. (1973). Self-disclosure: A literature review. *Psychological Bulletin, 79,* 73–91.

Crook, J. H. (1973). The nature and function of territorial aggression. In M. F. A. Montagu (Ed.), *Man and aggression* (2nd ed.). New York: Oxford University Press.

Crosby, F. (1976). A model of egoistical relative deprivation. *Psychological Review, 83*, 85–113.

Crosby, F., Bromley, S., & Saxe, L. (1980). Recent unobtrusive studies of black and white discrimination and prejudice: A literature review. *Psychological Bulletin, 87*, 546–563.

Cross, W. E., Jr. (1980). Models of psychological Nigrescence: A literature review. In R. L. Jones (Ed.), *Black psychology* (2nd ed.). New York: Harper & Row.

Croyle, R. T., & Cooper, J. (1983). Dissonance arousal: Physiological evidence. *Journal of Personality and Social Psychology, 45*, 782–791.

Crusco, A. H., & Wetzel, C. G. (1984). The Midas touch: The effects of interpersonal touch on restaurant tipping. *Personality and Social Psychology Bulletin, 10*, 512–517.

Crutchfield, R. S. (1955). Conformity and character. *American Psychologist, 10*, 191–198.

Csikszentmihalyi, M., & Figurski, T. J. (1982). Self-awareness and aversive experience in everyday life. *Journal of Personality, 50*, 15–28.

Cummings, L. L., Huber, G. P., & Arendt, E. (1974). Effects of size and spatial arrangements on group decision making. *Academy of Management Journal, 17*, 460–475.

Cunningham, M. R. (1979). Weather, mood, and helping behavior: Quasi-experiments with the Sunshine Samaritan. *Journal of Personality and Social Psychology, 37*, 1947–1956.

Cunningham, M. R. (1981). Sociobiology as a supplementary paradigm for social psychological research. In L. Wheeler (Ed.), *Review of personality and social psychology* (Vol. 2). Beverly Hills, CA: Sage.

Curran, J. P. (1975). Convergence toward a single sexual standard? *Social Behavior and Personality, 3*, 189–195.

Curtis, R. C., & Miller, K. (1986). Believing another likes or dislikes you: Behaviors making the beliefs come true. *Journal of Personality and Social Psychology, 51*, 284–290.

Cutrona, C. E. (1982). Transition to college: Loneliness and the process of social adjustment. In L. A. Peplau & D. Perlman (Eds.), *Loneliness: A sourcebook of current theory, research and therapy*. New York: Wiley.

Cutrona, C. E. (1986). Behavioral manifestations of social support: A microanalytic investigation. *Journal of Personality and Social Psychology, 51*, 201–208.

Daly, M., & Wilson, M. (1978). *Sex, evolution and behavior*. Scituate, MA: Duxbury Press.

Danheiser, P. R., & Graziano, W. G. (1982). Self-monitoring and cooperation as a self-presentational strategy. *Journal of Personality and Social Psychology, 42*, 497–505.

Darley, J. M., & Berscheid, E. (1967). Increased liking as a result of the anticipation of personal contact. *Human Relations, 20*, 29–39.

Darley, J. M., & Fazio, R. H. (1980). Expectancy confirmation processes arising in the social interaction sequence. *American Psychologist, 35*, 867–881.

Darley, J. M., & Gross, P. H. (1983). A hypothesis-confirming bias in labeling effects. *Journal of Personality and Social Psychology, 44*, 20–33.

Darley, J. M., & Latané, B. (1968). Bystander intervention in emergencies: Diffusion of responsibility. *Journal of Personality and Social Psychology, 8*, 377–383.

Darwin, C. (1872). *The expression of the emotions in man and animals*. London: John Murray.

Dashiell, J. F. (1930). An experimental analysis of some group effects. *Journal of Abnormal and Social Psychology, 25*, 190–199.

Davidson, B. (1984). A test of equity theory for marital adjustment. *Social Psychology Quarterly, 47*, 36–42.

Davidson, L. R., & Duberman, L. (1982). Friendship: Communication and interactional patterns in same-sex dyads. *Sex Roles, 8*, 809–822.

Davies, J. C. (1962). Toward a theory of revolution. *American Sociological Review, 27*, 5–19.

Davies, J. C. (1969). The J-curve of rising and declining satisfactions as a cause of great revolutions and a contained rebellion. In H. D. Graham & T. R. Gurr (Eds.), *Violence in America*. New York: New American Library.

Davis, D. (1982). Determinants of responsiveness in dyadic interactions. In W. Ickes & E. S. Knowles (Eds.), *Personality, roles, and social behavior*. New York: Springer-Verlag.

Davis, J. H. (1969). *Group performance*. Reading, MA: Addison-Wesley.

Davis, J. H., Bray, R. M., & Holt, R. W. (1976). The empirical study of social decision processes in juries. In J. L. Tapp & F. J. Levine (Eds.), *Law, justice and the individual in society*. New York: Holt, Rinehart & Winston.

Davis, J. H., Laughlin, P. R., & Komorita, S. S. (1976). The social psychology of small groups: Cooperative and mixed motive interaction. In M. R. Rosenzweig & L. W. Porter (Eds.), *Annual review of psychology, 27*, 501–542.

Dawes, R. M., & Smith, T. L. (1985). Attitude and opinion measurement. In G. Lindzey & E. Aronson (Eds.), *Handbook of social psychology* (Vol. 1) (3rd ed.). New York: Random House.

Dawkins, R. (1976). *The selfish gene*. Oxford: Oxford University Press.

Dean, L. M., Willis, F. N., & Hewitt, J. (1975). Initial interaction distance among individuals equal and unequal in military rank. *Journal of Personality and Social Psychology, 32*, 294–299.

Deaux, K. (1968). Variations in warning, information preference, and anticipatory attitude change. *Journal of Personality and Social Psychology, 9*, 157–161.

Deaux, K. (1976). Sex: A perspective on the attribution process. In J. H. Harvey, W. J. Ickes, & R. F. Kidd (Eds.), *New directions in attribution research* (Vol. 1). Hillsdale, NJ: Erlbaum.

Deaux, K. (1984). From individual differences to social categories: Analysis of a decade's research on gender. *American Psychologist, 39*, 105–116.

Deaux, K., & Emswiller, T. (1974). Explanations of successful performance on sex-linked tasks: What is skill for the male is luck for the female. *Journal of Personality and Social Psychology, 29*, 80–85.

Deaux, K., & Hanna, R. (1984). Courtship in the personals column: The influence of gender and sexual orientation. *Sex Roles, 11*, 363–375.

Deaux, K., & Lewis, L. L. (1983). Components of gender stereotypes. *Psychological Documents, 13*, 25. (Ms. No. 2583).

Deaux, K., & Major, B. (in press). Putting gender into context: An interactive model of gender-related behavior. *Psychological Review*.

Deaux, K., & Ullman, J. C. (1983). *Women of steel: Female blue-collar employment in the basic steel industry*. New York: Praeger.

Deaux, K., Winton, W., Crowley, M., & Lewis, L. L. (1985). Level of categorization and content of gender stereotypes. *Social Cognition, 3*, 145–167.

DeFronzo, J. (1984). Climate and crime: Tests of an FBI assumption. *Environment and Behavior, 16*, 185–210.

DeGree, C. E., & Snyder, C. R. (1985). Adler's psychology (of use) today: Personal history of traumatic life events as a self-handicapping strategy. *Journal of Personality and Social Psychology, 48*, 1512–1519.

DeJong, W. (1979). An examination of self-perception mediation of the foot-in-the-door effect. *Journal of Personality and Social Psychology, 37*, 2221–2239.

DeJong, W., & Kleck, R. E. (1986). The social psychological effects of overweight. In C. P. Herman, M. P. Zanna, & E.T. Higgins (Eds.), *Physical appearance, stigma, and social behavior: The Ontario symposium, Volume 3* (pp. 65–87). Hillsdale, NJ: Erlbaum.

DeLamater, J. (1974). A definition of "group." *Small Group Behavior, 5*, 30–44.

Dembroski, T. M., Lasater, T. M., & Ramirez, A. (1978). Communicator similarity, fear arousing communications, and compliance with health care recommendations. *Journal of Applied Social Psychology, 8*, 254–269.

DePaulo, B. M., Brittingham, G. L., & Kaiser, M. K. (1983). Receiving competence-relevant help: Effects on reciprocity, affect, and sensitivity to the helper's nonverbally expressed needs. *Journal of Personality and Social Psychology, 45*, 1045–1060.

DePaulo, B. M., Brown, P. L., Ishii, S., & Fisher, J. D. (1981). Help that works: The effects of aid on subsequent task performance. *Journal of Personality and Social Psychology, 41*, 478–487.

DePaulo, B. M., Lanier, K., & Davis, T. (1983). Detecting the deceit of the motivated liar. *Journal of Personality and Social Psychology, 45*, 1096–1103.

DePaulo, B. M., Rosenthal, R., Eisenstat, R. A., Rogers, P. L., & Finkelstein, S. (1978). Decoding discrepant nonverbal cues. *Journal of Personality and Social Psychology, 36*, 313–323.

DePaulo, B. M., Stone, J. I., & Lassiter, G. D. (1985). Telling ingratiating lies: Effects of target sex and target attractiveness on verbal and nonverbal deceptive success. *Journal of Personality and Social Psychology, 48*, 1191–1203.

Deutsch, M. (1968). Field theory in social psychology. In G. Lindzey & E. Aronson (Eds.), *Handbook of social psychology* (Vol. I) (2nd ed.). Reading, MA: Addison-Wesley.

Deutsch, M. (1973). *The resolution of conflict: Constructive and destructive processes.* New Haven: Yale University Press.

Deutsch, M., Canavan, D., & Rubin, J. (1971). The effects of size of conflict and sex of experimenter on interpersonal bargaining. *Journal of Experimental Social Psychology, 7*, 258–267.

Deutsch, M., & Gerard, H. B. (1955). A study of normative and informational social influences upon individual judgment. *Journal of Abnormal and Social Psychology, 51*, 629–636.

DeVellis, B. M., Wallston, B. S., & Wallston, K. A. (1978). Stereotyping: A threat to individualized patient care. In M. Miller & B. Flynn (Eds.), *Current issues in nursing* (Vol. 2).

Diamond, I. (1980). Pornography and repression: A reconsideration of "who" and "what." *Signs, 5*, 686–701.

Diamond, M. J., & Lobitz, W. C. (1973). When familiarity breeds respect: The effects of the experimental depolarization program on police and student attitudes toward each other. *Journal of Social Issues, 29*(4), 95–109.

Di Giacomo, J.-P. (1980). Intergroup alliances and rejections within a protest movement (analysis of the social representations). *European Journal of Social Psychology, 10*, 329–344.

DiMatteo, M. R., & DiNicola, D. D. (1982). *Achieving patient compliance: The psychology of the medical practitioner's role.* New York: Pergamon.

Dion, K. (1972). Physical attractiveness and evaluation of children's transgressions. *Journal of Personality and Social Psychology, 24*, 207–213.

Dion, K. K. (1977). The incentive value of physical attractiveness for young children. *Personality and Social Psychology Bulletin, 3*, 67–70.

Dion, K. K. (1986). Stereotyping based on physical attractiveness: Issues and conceptual perspectives. In C. P. Herman, M. P. Zanna, & E.T. Higgins (Eds.), *Physical appearance, stigma, and social behavior: The Ontario symposium, Volume 3* (pp. 7–21). Hillsdale, NJ: Erlbaum.

Dion, K. K., Berscheid, E., & Walster, E. (1972). What is beautiful is good. *Journal of Personality and Social Psychology, 24*, 285–290.

Dion, K. L. (1985). Sex, gender, and groups: Selected issues. In V. E. O'Leary, R. K. Unger, & B. S. Wallston (Eds.), *Women, gender, and social psychology* (pp. 293–347). Hillsdale, NJ: Erlbaum.

Dipboye, R. L., Arvey, R. D., & Terpstra, D. E. (1977). Sex and physical attractiveness of raters and applicants as determinants of resume evaluations. *Journal of Applied Psychology, 62*, 288–294.

Dipboye, R. L., Fromkin, H. L., & Wiback, K. (1975). Relative importance of applicant sex, attractiveness, and scholastic standing in evaluation of job applicant resumes. *Journal of Applied Psychology, 60*, 39–45.

Dollard, J., Doob, L. W., Miller, N. E., Mowrer, O. H., & Sears, R. R. (1939). *Frustration and aggression.* New Haven: Yale University Press.

Donnerstein, E. (1982). Erotica and human aggression. In R. G. Geen & E. Donnerstein (Eds.), *Aggression: Theoretical and empirical reviews.* New York: Academic Press.

Donnerstein, E., & Berkowitz, L. (1981). Victim reactions in aggressive erotic films as a factor in violence against women. *Journal of Personality and Social Psychology, 41*, 710–724.

Donnerstein, E., Donnerstein, M., & Evans, R. (1975). Erotic stimuli and aggression: Facilitation or inhibition. *Journal of Personality and Social Psychology, 32*, 237–244.

Donnerstein, E., & Wilson, D. W. (1976). The effects of noise and perceived control upon ongoing and subsequent aggressive behavior. *Journal of Personality and Social Psychology, 34*, 774–781.

Donnerstein, M., & Donnerstein, E. (1977). Modeling in the control of interracial aggression: The problem of generality. *Journal of Personality, 45*, 100–116.

Doob, L. W. (1947). The behavior of attitudes. *Psychological Review, 54*, 135–156.

Dovey, K. (1986). Home and homelessness. In I. Altman & C. Werner (Eds.), *Home environments. Human behavior and environment: Advances in theory and research* (Vol. 8) (pp. 33–64). New York: Plenum.

Dovidio, J. F. (1984). Helping behavior and altruism: An empirical and conceptual overview. In L. Berkowitz (Ed.), *Advances in experimental social psychology* (Vol. 17). Orlando, FL: Academic Press.

Dovidio, J. F., Evans, N., & Tyler, R. B. (1986). Racial stereotypes: The contents of their cognitive representations. *Journal of Experimental Social Psychology, 22*, 22–37.

Dreiser, T. (1929). *A gallery of women*. New York: Boni and Liveright.

Driscoll, J. M., Meyer, R. G., & Schanie, C. F. (1973). Training police in family crisis intervention. *Journal of Applied Behavioral Science, 9*, 62–81.

Dubos, R. (1980). *Man adapting* (2nd ed.). New Haven: Yale University Press.

Duck, S. (1982). A topography of relationship disengagement and dissolution. In S. W. Duck (Ed.), *Personal relationships 4: Dissolving personal relationships*. New York: Academic Press.

Dumont, J. P. C., & Robertson, R. M. (1986). Neuronal circuits: An evolutionary perspective. *Science, 233*, 849–852.

Duncan, J. S. (1986). The house as symbol of social structure: Notes on the language of objects among collectivistic groups. In I. Altman & C. Werner (Eds.), *Home environments. Human behavior and environment: Advances in theory and research* (Vol. 8) (pp. 133–151). New York: Plenum.

Duncan, S. (1969). Nonverbal communication. *Psychological Bulletin, 72*, 118–137.

Duncan, S., Jr., & Fiske, D. W. (1977). *Face-to-face interaction*. Hillsdale, NJ: Erlbaum.

Dunnette, M. D., Campbell, J., & Jaastad, K. (1963). The effect of group participation on brainstorming effectiveness for two industrial samples. *Journal of Applied Psychology, 47*, 30–37.

Durkheim, E. (1898). Représentations individuelles et représentations collectives. *Revue de Métaphysique, 6*, 274–302. (In D. F. Pocock [trans.], *Sociology and philosophy*, New York: Free Press, 1953.)

Duval, S., Duval, V. H., & Neely, R. (1979). Self-focus, felt responsibility, and helping behavior. *Journal of Personality and Social Psychology, 37*, 1769–1778.

Duval, S., & Wicklund, R. A. (1972). *A theory of objective self-awareness*. New York: Academic Press.

Dyck, R. J., & Rule, B. G. (1978). Effect of retaliation on causal attributions concerning attack. *Journal of Personality and Social Psychology, 36*, 521–529.

Eagly, A. H. (1986). *Sex differences in social behavior: A social-role interpretation*. Hillsdale, NJ: Erlbaum.

Eagly, A. H., & Carli, L. L. (1981). Sex of researchers and sex-typed communications as determinants of sex differences in influenceability: A meta-analysis of social influence studies. *Psychological Bulletin, 90*, 1–20.

Eagly, A. H., & Chaiken, S. (1984). Cognitive theories of persuasion. *Advances in Experimental Social Psychology, 17*, 267–359.

Eagly, A. H., Chaiken, S., & Wood, W. (1981). An attribution analysis of persuasion. In J. Harvey, W. C. Ickes, & R. F. Kidd (Eds.), *New directions in attribution theory* (Vol. 3). Hillsdale, NJ: Erlbaum.

Eagly, A. H., & Crowley, M. (1986). Gender and helping behavior: A meta-analytic review of the social psychological literature. *Psychological Bulletin, 100*, 283–308.

Eagly, A. H., & Steffen, V. J. (1986). Gender and aggressive behavior: A meta-analytic review of the social psychological literature. *Psychological Bulletin, 100*, 309–330.

Eagly, A. H., & Telaak, K. (1972). Width of the latitude of acceptance as a determinant of attitude change. *Journal of Personality and Social Psychology, 23*, 388–397.

Eagly, A. H., & Warren, R. (1976). Intelligence, comprehension and opinion change. *Journal of Personality, 44*, 226–242.

Ebbesen, E., Kjos, G., & Konecni, V. (1976). Spatial ecology: Its effects on the choice of friends and enemies. *Journal of Experimental Social Psychology, 12*, 505–518.

Ebbesen, E. B., & Konecni, V. J. (1975). Decision making and information integration in the courts: The setting of bail. *Journal of Personality and Social Psychology, 32*, 805–821.

Edney, J. J. (1972). Property, possession, and performance: A field study in human territoriality. *Journal of Applied Social Psychology, 2*, 275–282.

Edney, J. J. (1974). Human territoriality. *Psychological Bulletin, 81*, 959–975.

Edney, J. J., & Jordon-Edney, N. L. (1974). Territorial spacing on a beach. *Sociometry, 37*, 92–104.

Efran, M. G., & Cheyne, J. A. (1972). The study of movement and affect in territorial behavior. *Man-Environment Systems, 3*, 348–350.

Efran, M. G., & Cheyne, J. A. (1973). Shared space: The cooperative control of spatial areas by two interacting individuals. *Canadian Journal of Behavioural Science, 5*, 201–210.

Efran, M. G., & Cheyne, J. A. (1974). Affective concomitants of the invasion of shared space: Behavioral, physiological, and verbal indicators. *Journal of Personality and Social Psychology, 29*, 219–226.

Eibl-Eibesfeldt, I. (1970). *Ethology: The biology of behavior* (E. Klinghammer, trans.). New York: Holt, Rinehart & Winston.

Eisenberg, L. (1972). The *human* nature of human nature. *Science, 176*, 123–128.

Eisenberg, N. (1986). *Altruistic emotion, cognition, and behavior*. Hillsdale, NJ: Erlbaum.

Eisenberg, N., & Miller, P. A. (1987). The relation of empathy to prosocial and related behaviors. *Psychological Bulletin, 101*, 91–119.

Eisenberg-Berg, N. (1979). Relationship of prosocial moral reasoning to altruism, political liberalism, and intelligence. *Developmental Psychology, 15*, 87–89.

Eiser, J. R., & van der Pligt, J. (1984). Attitudinal and social factors in adolescent smoking: In search of peer group influence. *Journal of Applied Social Psychology, 14*, 348–363.

Ekman, P. (1972). Universals and cultural differences in facial expressions of emotion. In J. K. Cole (Ed.), *Nebraska symposium on motivation* (Vol. 19). Lincoln: University of Nebraska Press.

Ekman, P. (Ed.) (1982). *Emotion in the human face* (2nd ed.). Cambridge: Cambridge University Press.

Ekman, P. (1985). *Telling lies*. New York: Berkley Books.

Ekman, P., & Friesen, W. V. (1972). Hand movements. *Journal of Communication, 22*, 353–374.

Ekman, P., & Friesen, W. V. (1974). Detecting deception from body or face. *Journal of Personality and Social Psychology, 29*, 288–298.

Ekman, P., & Friesen, W. V. (1975). *Unmasking the face*. Englewood Cliffs, NJ: Prentice-Hall.

Ekman, P., Friesen, W. V., & Scherer, K. B. (1976). Body movement and voice pitch in deceptive interaction. *Semiotica, 16*, 23–27.

Ekstein, R. (1978). Psychoanalysis, sympathy, and altruism. In L. Wispé (Ed.), *Altruism, sympathy, and helping: Psychological and sociological principles*. New York: Academic Press.

Elkind, D. (1971). Praise and imitation. *Saturday Review*, January 16, pp. 51ff.

Ellis, H. (1936). *Studies in the psychology of sex.* New York: Random House. (Originally published, 1899.)

Ellis, R. A., & Taylor, M. S. (1983). Role of self-esteem within the job search process. *Journal of Applied Psychology, 68,* 632-640.

Ellsworth, P. C. (1977). From abstract ideas to concrete instances: Some guidelines for choosing natural research settings. *American Psychologist, 32,* 604-615.

Ellsworth, P. C., Carlsmith, J. M., & Henson, A. (1972). The stare as a stimulus to flight in human subjects: A series of field experiments. *Journal of Personality and Social Psychology, 21,* 302-311.

Endler, N. S., & Magnusson, D. (1976). Toward an interactional psychology of personality. *Psychological Bulletin, 83,* 956-974.

Epps, E. G. (1980). The impact of school desegregation on aspirations, self-concepts and other aspects of personality. In R. L. Jones (Ed.), *Black psychology* (2nd ed.). New York: Harper & Row.

Epstein, R. (1966). Aggression toward outgroups as a function of authoritarianism and imitation of aggressive models. *Journal of Personality and Social Psychology, 3,* 574-579.

Epstein, S. (1979). The stability of behavior: I. On predicting most of the people much of the time. *Journal of Personality and Social Psychology, 37,* 1097-1126.

Epstein, S., & O'Brien, E. J. (1985). The person-situation debate in historical and current perspective. *Psychological Bulletin, 98,* 513-537.

Erkut, S., Jaquette, D. S., & Staub, E. (1981). Moral judgment-situation interaction as a basis for predicting prosocial behavior. *Journal of Personality, 49,* 1-14.

Eron, L. D. (1980). Prescription for reduction of aggression. *American Psychologist, 35,* 244-252.

Eron, L. D. (1982). Parent-child interaction, television violence, and aggression of children. *American Psychologist, 37,* 197-211.

Esser, A. H., Chamberlain, A. S., Chapple, E., & Kline, N. S. (1964). Territoriality of patients on a research ward. In J. Worris (Ed.), *Recent advances in biological psychiatry.* New York: Plenum.

Evans, G. W. (1978). Human spatial behavior: The arousal model. In A. Baum & Y. Epstein (Eds.), *Human response to crowding.* Hillsdale, NJ: Erlbaum.

Evans, G. W. (1979). Behavioral and physiological consequences of crowding in humans. *Journal of Applied Social Psychology, 9,* 27-46.

Evans, G. W., & Jacobs, S. V. (1982). Air pollution and human behavior. *Journal of Social Issues, 37*(1), 95-125.

Evans, R. I., Rozelle, R. M., Maxwell, S. E., Raines, B. E., Dill, C. A., Guthrie, T. J., Henderson, A. H., & Hill, P. C. (1981). Social modeling films to deter smoking in adolescents: Results of a three-year field investigation. *Journal of Applied Psychology, 66,* 399-414.

Evans, R. I., Rozelle, R. M., Mittelmark, M. B., Hansen, W. B., Bane, A. L., & Havis, J. (1978). Deterring the onset of smoking in children: Knowledge of immediate physiological effects and coping with peer pressure, media pressure, and parent modeling. *Journal of Applied Social Psychology, 8,* 126-135.

Exline, R. V. (1971). Visual interaction: The glances of power and preference. In J. K. Cole (Ed.), *Nebraska symposium on motivation* (Vol. 19). Lincoln: University of Nebraska Press.

Exline, R. V., Ellyson, S. L., & Long, B. (1975). Visual behavior as an aspect of power role relationships. In P. Pliner, L. Krames, & T. Alloway (Eds.), *Nonverbal communication of aggression* (Vol. 2). New York: Plenum.

Exline, R., & Winters, L. (1965). Affective relations and mutual glances in dyads. In S. Tomkins & C. Izard (Eds.), *Affect, cognition, and personality.* New York: Springer.

Eysenck, H. J. (1967). *The biological basis of personality.* Springfield, IL: Charles C Thomas.

Fairweather, G. W. (1972). *Social change: The challenge to survival.* Morristown, NJ: General Learning Press.

Fazio, R. H. (1986). How do attitudes guide behavior? In R. M. Sorrentino & E. T. Higgins (Eds.), *Handbook of motivation and cognition: Foundations of social behavior.* New York: Guilford Press.

Fazio, R. H., Herr, P. M., & Olney, T. J. (1984). Attitude accessibility following a self-perception process. *Journal of Personality and Social Psychology, 47,* 277-286.

Fazio, R. H., Lenn, T. M., & Effrein, E. A. (1983/1984). Spontaneous attitude formation. *Social Cognition, 2,* 217-234.

Fazio, R. H., Sanbonmatsu, D. M., Powell, M. C., & Kardes, F. R. (1986). On the automatic activation of attitudes. *Journal of Personality and Social Psychology, 50,* 229-238.

Fazio, R. H., Sherman, S. J., & Herr, P. M. (1982). The feature-positive effect in the self-perception process: Does not doing matter as much as doing? *Journal of Personality and Social Psychology, 42,* 404-411.

Fazio, R. H., & Williams, C. J. (1986). Attitude accessibility as a moderator of the attitude-perception and attitude-behavior relations: An investigation of the 1984 Presidential election. *Journal of Personality and Social Psychology, 51,* 505-514.

Feild, H. S. (1978). Attitudes toward rape: A comparative analysis of police, rapists, crisis counselors, and citizens. *Journal of Personality and Social Psychology, 36,* 156-179.

Feldman-Summers, S. (1977). Implications of the buck-passing phenomenon for reactance theory. *Journal of Personality, 45,* 543-553.

Felson, R. B. (1985). Reflected appraisal and the development of self. *Social Psychology Quarterly, 48,* 71-78.

Felson, R. B., & Bohrnstedt, G. W. (1979). "Are the good beautiful or the beautiful good?" The relationship between children's perceptions of ability and perceptions of physical attractiveness. *Social Psychology Quarterly, 42,* 386-392.

Felson, R. B., & Reed, M. D. (1986). Reference groups and self-appraisals of academic ability and performance. *Social Psychology Quarterly, 49,* 103-109.

Fenigstein, A. (1979). Self-consciousness, self-attention, and social interaction. *Journal of Personality and Social Psychology, 37,* 75-86.

Fenigstein, A., Scheier, M., & Buss, A. (1975). Public and private self-consciousness: Assessment and theory. *Journal of Consulting and Clinical Psychology, 43,* 522-527.

Ferguson, G. S., & Weisman, G. D. (1986). Alternative approaches to the assessment of employee satisfaction within the office environment. In J. Wineman (Ed.), *Behavioral issues in office design* (pp. 85-108). New York: Van Nostrand Reinhold.

Ferguson, T. J., & Rule, B. G. (1983). An attributional perspective on anger and aggression. In E. Donnerstein & R. G. Geen (Eds.), *Aggression: Theoretical and empirical reviews.* New York: Academic Press.

Ferrari, J. R., Barone, R. C., Jason, L. A., & Rose, T. (1985). The use of incentives to increase blood donations. *Journal of Social Psychology, 125,* 791–793.

Feshbach, S., Stiles, W. B., & Bitter, E. (1967). The reinforcing effect of witnessing aggression. *Journal of Experimental Research in Personality, 2,* 133–139.

Festinger, L. (1950). Informal social communication. *Psychological Review, 57,* 271–282.

Festinger, L. (1954). A theory of social comparison processes. *Human Relations, 7,* 117–140.

Festinger, L. (1957). *A theory of cognitive dissonance.* Stanford, CA: Stanford University Press.

Festinger, L., & Carlsmith, J. M. (1959). Cognitive consequences of forced compliance. *Journal of Abnormal and Social Psychology, 58,* 203–210.

Festinger, L., Pepitone, A., & Newcomb, T. (1952). Some consequences of deindividuation in a group. *Journal of Abnormal and Social Psychology, 47,* 382–389.

Festinger, L., Riecken, H., & Schachter, S. (1956). *When prophecy fails.* Minneapolis: University of Minnesota Press.

Festinger, L., Schachter, S., & Back, K. (1950). *Social pressures in informal groups: A study of human factors in housing.* New York: Harper.

Fidell, L. S. (1970). Empirical verification of sex discrimination in hiring practices in psychology. *American Psychologist, 25,* 1094–1098.

Fiedler, F. E. (1964). A contingency model of leadership effectiveness. In L. Berkowitz (Ed.), *Advances in experimental social psychology* (Vol. 1). New York: Academic Press.

Fiedler, F. E. (1967). *A theory of leadership effectiveness.* New York: McGraw-Hill.

Fiedler, F. E. (1972). Personality, motivational systems, and behavior of High and Low LPC persons. *Human Relations, 25,* 391–412.

Fiedler, F. E. (1978). Recent developments in research on the contingency model. In L. Berkowitz (Ed.), *Group processes.* New York: Academic Press.

Fiedler, F. E., Chemers, M. M., & Mahar, L. (1976). *Improving leadership effectiveness: The leader match concept.* New York: Wiley.

Filley, A. (1975). *Interpersonal conflict resolution.* Glenview, IL: Scott, Foresman.

Fine, M., & Bowers, C. (1984). Racial self-identification: The effects of social history and gender. *Journal of Applied Social Psychology, 14,* 136–146.

Fink, H. C. (1973). Attitudes toward the Calley-My Lai case, authoritarianism and political beliefs. Paper presented at meeting of Eastern Psychological Association, Washington, D.C., May.

Fishbein, M., & Ajzen, I. (1975). *Belief, attitude, intention, and behavior: An introduction to theory and research.* Reading, MA: Addison-Wesley.

Fisher, J. D. (1983). Recipient reactions to aid: The parameters of the field. In J. D. Fisher, A. Nadler, & B. M. DePaulo (Eds.), *New directions in helping* (Vol. 1). *Recipient reactions to aid.* New York: Academic Press.

Fisher, J. D., Bell, P. A., & Baum, A. (1984). *Environmental psychology* (2nd ed). New York: Holt, Rinehart & Winston.

Fisher, J. D., Nadler, A., & Whitcher-Alagna, S. (1982). Recipient reactions to aid. *Psychological Bulletin, 91,* 27–54.

Fisher, J. D., Rytting, M., & Heslin, R. (1976). Hands touching hands: Affective and evaluative effects of an interpersonal touch. *Sociometry, 39,* 416–421.

Fisher, W. A., & Byrne, D. (1978). Sex differences in response to erotica: Love versus lust? *Journal of Personality and Social Psychology, 36,* 117–125.

Fisher, W. A., Byrne, D., & White, L. A. (1983). Emotional barriers to contraception. In D. Byrne & W. A. Fisher (Eds.), *Adolescents, sex, and contraception* (pp. 207–239). Hillsdale, NJ: Erlbaum.

Fiske, D. W. (1978). *Strategies for personality research: The observation versus interpretation of behaviors.* San Francisco: Jossey-Bass.

Fiske, S. T., Fischhoff, B., & Milburn, M. A. (1983). Images of nuclear war: An introduction. *Journal of Social Issues, 39* (1), 1–6.

Fiske, S. T., & Taylor, S. E. (1984). *Social cognition.* Reading, MA: Addison-Wesley.

Fitzgerald, R., & Ellsworth, P. C. (1984). Due process vs. crime control: Death qualification and jury attitudes. *Law and Human Behavior, 8,* 31–51.

Flowers, M. L. (1977). A laboratory test of some implications of Janis's groupthink hypothesis. *Journal of Personality and Social Psychology, 35,* 888–896.

Foa, E. B., & Foa, U. G. (1974). *Social structure of the mind.* Springfield, IL: Charles C Thomas.

Foa, U. G. (1971). Interpersonal and economic resources. *Science, 171,* 345–351.

Fodor, E. M. (1978). Simulated work climate as an influence on choice of leadership style. *Personality and Social Psychology Bulletin, 4,* 111–114.

Fogelman, E., & Wiener, V. L. (1985). The few, the brave, the noble. *Psychology Today, 19*(8), 61–65.

Fong, G. T., & Markus, H. (1982). Self-schemas and judgments about others. *Social Cognition, 1,* 191–204.

Ford, C., & Beach, F. A. (1951). *Patterns of sexual behavior.* New York: Paul Hoeber.

Form, W. H., & Nosow, S. (1958). *Community in disaster.* New York: Harper.

Forsyth, D. R. (1983). *An introduction to group dynamics.* Pacific Grove, CA: Brooks/Cole.

Forward, J., Canter, R., & Kirsch, N. (1976). Role-enactment and deception methodologies: Alternative paradigms? *American Psychologist, 31,* 595–604.

Foss, R. D. (1983). Community norms and blood donation. *Journal of Applied Social Psychology, 13,* 281–290.

Foti, R. J., Fraser, S. L., & Lord, R. G. (1982). Effects of leadership labels and prototypes on perceptions of political leaders. *Journal of Applied Psychology, 67,* 326–333.

Fraczek, A., & Macaulay, J. R. (1971). Some personality factors in reaction to aggressive stimuli. *Journal of Personality, 39,* 163–177.

Franck, K. A. (1984). Exorcising the ghost of physical determinism. *Environment and Behavior, 16,* 411–435.

Franzoi, S. L. (1983). Self-concept differences as a function of private self-consciousness and social anxiety. *Journal of Research in Personality, 17,* 275–287.

Franzoi, S. L., & Brewer, L. C. (1984). The experience of self-awareness and its relation to level of self-consciousness: An experiential sampling study. *Journal of Research in Personality, 18,* 522–540.

Fraser, C. (1971). Group risk-taking and group polarization. *European Journal of Social Psychology, 1,* 493–510.

Freedman, J. L. (1972). The effects of population density on humans. In J. T. Fawcett (Ed.), *Psychological perspectives on population.* New York: Basic Books.

Freedman, J. L. (1975). *Crowding and behavior.* San Francisco: Freeman.

Freedman, J. L. (1984). Effect of television violence on aggressiveness. *Psychological Bulletin, 96,* 227–246.

Freedman, J. L. (1986). Television violence and aggression: A rejoinder. *Psychological Bulletin, 100,* 372–378.

Freedman, J. L., & Fraser, S. C. (1966). Compliance without pressure: The foot-in-the-door technique. *Journal of Personality and Social Psychology, 4,* 195–202.

Freedman, J. L., Heshka, S., & Levy, A. (1975). Population density and pathology: Is there a relationship? *Journal of Experimental Social Psychology, 11,* 539–552.

Freedman, J. L., Klevansky, S., & Ehrlich, P. R. (1971). The effect of crowding on human task performance. *Journal of Applied Social Psychology, 1,* 7–25.

Freedman, R. (1986). *Beauty bound.* Lexington, MA: Lexington Books.

French, J. R. P., Jr., & Raven, B. H. (1959). The bases of social power. In D. Cartwright (Ed.), *Studies in social power.* Ann Arbor: University of Michigan Press.

Frenkel, O. J., & Doob, A. N. (1976). Post-decision dissonance at the polling booth. *Canadian Journal of Behavioural Science, 8,* 347–350.

Freud, E. L. (Ed.) (1960). *Letters to Sigmund Freud.* New York: Basic Books.

Freud, S. (1930). *Civilization and its discontents.* London: Hogarth Press.

Freud, S. (1938). Three contributions to the theory of sex. In A. A. Brill (Ed.), *The basic writings of Sigmund Freud.* New York: Random House.

Freud, S. (1959). Fragment of an analysis of a case of hysteria. In *Collected papers* (Vol. 3). New York: Basic Books. (Originally published, 1905.)

Freund, K., Sedlacek, F., & Knob, K. (1965). A simple transducer for mechanical plethysmography of the male genital. *Journal of the Experimental Analysis of Behavior, 8,* 169–170.

Frey, D. (1986). Recent research on selective exposure to information. *Advances in Experimental Social Psychology, 19,* 41–80.

Frey, D. L., & Gaertner, S. L. (1986). Helping and the avoidance of inappropriate interracial behavior: A strategy that perpetuates a nonprejudiced self-image. *Journal of Personality and Social Psychology, 50,* 1083–1090.

Friedrich-Cofer, L., & Huston, A. C. (1986). Television violence and aggression: The debate continues. *Psychological Bulletin, 100,* 364–371.

Fultz, J., Batson, C. D., Fortenbach, V. A., McCarthy, P. M., & Varney, L. L. (1986). Social evaluation and the empathy-altruism hypothesis. *Journal of Personality and Social Psychology, 50,* 761–769.

Gaebelein, J. W. (1973). Third party instigation of aggression: An experimental approach. *Journal of Personality and Social Psychology, 27,* 389–395.

Gaebelein, J. W. (1978). Third party instigated aggression as a function of attack pattern and a nonaggressive response option. *Journal of Research in Personality, 12,* 274–283.

Gaebelein, J. W., & Hay, W. M. (1974). Third party instigation of aggression as a function of attack and vulnerability. *Journal of Research in Personality, 7,* 324–333.

Gaertner, S. L., & Dovidio, J. F. (1977). The subtlety of white racism, arousal, and helping behavior. *Journal of Personality and Social Psychology, 35,* 691–707.

Gaertner, S. L., & McLaughlin, J. P. (1983). Racial stereotypes: Associations and ascriptions of positive and negative characteristics. *Social Psychology Quarterly, 46,* 23–30.

Galle, O. R., & Gove, W. R. (1979). Crowding and behavior in Chicago, 1940–1970. In J. R. Aiello & A. Baum (Eds.), *Residential crowding and design* (pp. 23–39). New York: Plenum.

Galle, O. R., Gove, W. R., & McPherson, J. M. (1972). Population density and pathology: What are the relations for man? *Science, 176,* 23–30.

Gamson, W. A. (1974). Violence and political power: The meek don't make it. *Psychology Today, 8*(2), 35–41.

Gamson, W. A. (1975). *The strategy of social protest.* Homewood, IL: Dorsey.

Gangestad, S., & Snyder, M. (1985). "To carve nature at its joints": On the existence of discrete classes in personality. *Psychological Review, 92,* 317–349.

Gans, H. J. (1967). *The Levittowners: Ways of life and politics in a new suburban community.* New York: Pantheon.

Garcia, L. T., & Griffitt, W. (1978). Evaluation and recall of evidence: Authoritarianism and the Patty Hearst case. *Journal of Research in Personality, 12,* 57–67.

Gaskell, G., & Ellis, P. (1982). Energy conservation: A psychological perspective on a multidisciplinary phenomenon. In P. Stringer (Ed.), *Confronting social issues: Applications of social psychology* (Vol. 1) (pp. 103–122). London: Academic Press.

Geen, R. G. (1968). Effects of frustration, attack and prior training in aggressiveness upon aggressive behavior. *Journal of Personality and Social Psychology, 9,* 316–321.

Geen, R. G. (1978). Effects of attack and uncontrollable noise on aggression. *Journal of Research in Personality, 12,* 15–29.

Geen, R. G. (1980). The effect of being observed on performance. In P. B. Paulus (Ed.), *Psychology of group influence.* Hillsdale, NJ: Erlbaum.

Geen, R. G., & Gange, J. J. (1977). Drive theory of social facilitation: Twelve years of theory and research. *Psychological Bulletin, 84,* 1267–1288.

Geen, R. G., & O'Neal, E. C. (1969). Activation of cue-elicited aggression by general arousal. *Journal of Personality and Social Psychology, 11,* 289–292.

Geen, R. G., & Stonner, D. (1971). Effects of aggressiveness habit strength on behavior in the presence of aggression-related stimuli. *Journal of Personality and Social Psychology, 17,* 149–153.

Geer, J. H. (1974). *Cognitive factors in sexual arousal—toward an amalgam of research strategies.* Paper presented at meeting of American Psychological Association, New Orleans, August.

Gekas, V. (1982). The self-concept. *Annual Review of Sociology, 8,* 1–33.

Gekas, V., & Schwalbe, M. L. (1983). Beyond the looking-glass self: Social structure and efficacy-based self-esteem. *Social Psychology Quarterly, 46,* 77–88.

Gelfand, D. M., & Hartmann, D. P. (1982). Response consequences and attributions: Two contributors to prosocial behavior. In N. Eisenberg (Ed.), *The development of prosocial behavior.* New York: Academic Press.

Geller, D. M. (1978). Involvement in role-playing simulations: A demonstration with studies on obedience. *Journal of Personality and Social Psychology, 36,* 219–235.

Gentry, W. D. (1970). Effects of frustration, attack, and prior aggressive training on overt aggression and vascular processes. *Journal of Personality and Social Psychology, 16,* 718–725.

Georgoudi, M., & Rosnow, R. L. (1985). Notes toward a contextualist understanding of social psychology. *Personality and Social Psychology Bulletin, 11,* 5–22.

Gerard, H. B. (1983). School desegregation: The social science role. *American Psychologist, 38,* 869–877.

Gerbasi, K. C., Zuckerman, M., & Reis, H. T. (1977). Justice needs a new blindfold: A review of mock jury research. *Psychological Bulletin, 84,* 323–345.

Gergen, K. J. (1985). The social constructionist movement in modern psychology. *American Psychologist, 40,* 266–275.

Gergen, K. J., Ellsworth, P., Maslach, C., & Seipel, M. (1975). Obligation, donor resources, and reactions to aid in three cultures. *Journal of Personality and Social Psychology, 31,* 390–400.

Gergen, K. J., Gergen, M. M., & Barton, W. H. (1973). Deviance in the dark. *Psychology Today,* October, 129–130.

Gergen, K. J., Morse, S. J., & Gergen, M. M. (1980). Behavior exchange in cross-cultural perspective. In H. C. Triandis & W. W. Lambert (Eds.), *Handbook of cross-cultural psychology. Vol. 5: Social psychology.* Boston: Allyn & Bacon.

Gergen, M. M., & Gergen, K. J. (1983). Interpretive dimensions of international aid. In A. Nadler, J. D. Fisher, & B. M. DePaulo (Eds.), *New directions in helping.* (Vol. 3) *Applied perspectives on help-seeking and receiving.* New York: Academic Press.

Gerrard, M. (1982). Sex, sex guilt, and contraceptive use. *Journal of Personality and Social Psychology, 42,* 153–158.

Gibb, C. A. (1969). Leadership. In G. Lindzey & E. Aronson (Eds.), *Handbook of social psychology* (Vol. 4) (2nd ed.). Reading, MA: Addison-Wesley.

Gibbons, F., & Wicklund, R. (1982). Self-focused attention and helping behavior. *Journal of Personality and Social Psychology, 43,* 462–474.

Glass, D. (1977). *Behavior patterns, stress, and coronary disease.* Hillsdale, NJ: Erlbaum.

Glass, D. C., & Singer, J. E. (1972). *Urban stress.* New York: Academic Press.

Glassman, J. B., Burkhart, B. R., Grant, R. D., & Vallery, G. C. (1978). Density, expectation and extended task performance: An experiment in the natural environment. *Environment and Behavior, 10,* 299–315.

Godfrey, D. K., Jones, E. E., & Lord, C. G. (1986). Self-promotion is not ingratiating. *Journal of Personality and Social Psychology, 50,* 106–115.

Goethals, G. R. (1986). Social comparison theory: Psychology from the lost and found. *Personality and Social Psychology Bulletin, 12,* 261–278.

Goethals, G. R., & Darley, J. M. (1977). Social comparison theory: An attributional approach. In J. M. Suls & R. L. Miller (Eds.), *Social comparison processes: Theoretical and empirical perspectives.* Washington, D.C.: Halsted-Wiley.

Goffman, E. (1955). On face-work: An analysis of ritual elements in social interaction. *Psychiatry, 18,* 213–231.

Goffman, E. (1959). *The presentation of self in everyday life.* Garden City, NY: Doubleday.

Goffman, E. (1967). *Interaction ritual: Essays on face-to-face behavior.* Garden City, NY: Doubleday.

Golden, J. (1971). Roundtable: Marital discord and sex. *Medical Aspects of Human Sexuality, 1,* 160–190.

Gorer, G. (1968). Man has no "killer" instinct. In M.F.A. Montague (Ed.), *Man and aggression.* New York: Oxford University Press.

Gould, S. J. (1986). Cardboard Darwinism. *New York Review of Books,* September 25, pp. 47–54.

Gouldner, A. W. (1960). The norm of reciprocity: A preliminary statement. *American Sociological Review, 25,* 161–178.

Grabitz-Gneich, G. (1971). Some restrictive conditions for the occurrence of psychological reactance. *Journal of Personality and Social Psychology, 19,* 188–196.

Grady, K. E. (1977). *Sex as a social label: The illusion of sex differences.* Unpublished doctoral dissertation, City University of New York.

Graen, G., Alvares, K., Orris, J. B., & Martella, J. A. (1970). Contingency model of leadership effectiveness: Antecedent and evidential results. *Psychological Bulletin, 74,* 284–296.

Graham, C., Baker, R. W., & Wapner, S. (1985). Prior interracial experience and Black student transition into predominantly White colleges. *Journal of Personality and Social Psychology, 47,* 1146–1154.

Graham, J. A., & Heywood, S. (1975). The effects of elimination of hand gestures and of verbal codability on speech performance. *European Journal of Social Psychology, 5,* 189–195.

Granberg, D., & Brent, E. (1983). When prophecy bends: The preference-expectation link in U.S. Presidential elections, 1952–1980. *Journal of Personality and Social Psychology, 45,* 477–491.

Graves, N. B., & Graves, T. D. (1983). The cultural context of prosocial development: An ecological model. In D. L. Bridgemen (Ed.), *The nature of prosocial development: Interdisciplinary theories and strategies.* New York: Academic Press.

Gray-Little, B., & Appelbaum, M. I. (1979). Instrumentality effects in the assessment of racial differences in self-esteem. *Journal of Personality and Social Psychology, 37,* 1221–1229.

Greenbaum, P. E., & Greenbaum, D. S. (1981). Territorial personalization: Group identity and social interaction in a Slavic-American neighborhood. *Environment and Behavior, 13,* 574–589.

Greenberg, C., & Firestone, I. J. (1977). Compensatory responses to crowding: Effects of personal space intrusion and privacy reduction. *Journal of Personality and Social Psychology, 35,* 637–644.

Greenberg, J., & Pyszczynski, T. (1985). The effect of an overheard ethnic slur on evaluations of the target: How to spread a social disease. *Journal of Experimental Social Psychology, 21,* 61–72.

Greenberg, M. S. (1980). A theory of indebtedness. In K. J. Gergen, M. S. Greenberg, & R. H. Willis (Eds.), *Social exchange: Advances in theory and research.* New York: Plenum.

Greenberg, M. S., & Ruback, R. B. (1982). *Social psychology of the criminal justice system.* Pacific Grove, CA: Brooks/Cole.

Greenberg, M. S., & Westcott, D. R. (1983). Indebtedness as a mediator of reactions to aid. In J. D. Fisher, A. Nadler, & B. M. DePaulo (Eds.), *New directions in helping.* (Vol. 1) *Recipient reactions to aid.* New York: Academic Press.

Greenfield, T. B., & Andrews, J. H. M. (1961). Teacher leader behavior. *Alberta Journal of Educational Research, 7,* 92–102.

Greenwald, A. G., & Pratkanis, A. R. (1984). The self. In R. S. Wyer & T. K. Srull (Eds.), *The handbook of social cognition* (Vol. 3). Hillsdale, NJ: Erlbaum.

Greenwell, J., & Dengerink, H. A. (1973). The role of perceived versus actual attack in human physical aggression. *Journal of Personality and Social Psychology, 26*, 66–71.

Greenwood, J. D. (1983). Role-playing as an experimental strategy in social psychology. *European Journal of Social Psychology, 13*, 235–254.

Greer, D. L. (1983). Spectator booing and the home advantage: A study of social influence in the basketball arena. *Social Psychology Quarterly, 46*, 252–261.

Grice, H. P. (1975). Logic and conversation. In P. Cole & J. L. Morgan (Eds.), *Syntax and semantics 3: Speech acts* (pp. 41–58). New York: Academic Press.

Griffitt, W. (1970). Environmental effects on interpersonal affective behavior: Ambient effective temperature and attraction. *Journal of Personality and Social Psychology, 15*, 240–244.

Griffitt, W., May, J., & Veitch, R. (1974). Sexual stimulation and interpersonal behavior: Heterosexual evaluative responses, visual behavior, and physical proximity. *Journal of Personality and Social Psychology, 30*, 367–377.

Griffitt, W., & Veitch, R. (1971). Hot and crowded: Influences of population density on interpersonal affective behavior. *Journal of Personality and Social Psychology, 17*, 92–98.

Gross, A. E., & Crofton, C. (1977). What is good is beautiful. *Sociometry, 40*, 85–90.

Gross, A. E., & Fleming, I. (1982). Twenty years of deception in social psychology. *Personality and Social Psychology Bulletin, 8*, 402–408.

Gross, A. E., Wallston, B. S., & Piliavin, I. M. (1975). Beneficiary attractiveness and cost as determinants of responses to routine requests for help. *Sociometry, 38*, 131–140.

Grujic, L., & Libby, W. L., Jr. (1978). *Nonverbal aspects of verbal behavior in French Canadian French-English bilinguals.* Paper presented at the meeting of the American Psychological Association, Toronto, September.

Grusec, J. E., Saas-Korlsaak, P., & Simutis, Z. M. (1978). The role of example and moral exhortation in the training of altruism. *Child Development, 49*, 920–923.

Grush, J. E., McKeough, K. L., & Ahlering, R. F. (1978). Extrapolating laboratory exposure research to actual political elections. *Journal of Personality and Social Psychology, 36*, 257–270.

Grush, J. E., & Schershing, C. (1978). *The impact of personal wealth on political elections: What has the Supreme Court wrought?* Paper presented at meeting of Midwestern Psychological Association, Chicago, May.

Guerin, B. (1986). Mere presence effects in humans: A review. *Journal of Experimental Social Psychology, 22*, 38–77.

Gullahorn, J. T. (1952). Distance and friendship as factors in the gross interaction matrix. *Sociometry, 15*, 123–134.

Gurin, P., Gurin, G., Lao, R. C., & Beattie, M. (1969). Internal-external control in the motivational dynamics of Negro youth. *Journal of Social Issues, 25*(3), 29–53.

Guthrie, R. V. (1976). *Even the rat was white: A historical view of psychology.* New York: Harper & Row.

Haber, G. M. (1980). Territorial invasion in the classroom. *Environment and Behavior, 12*, 17–31.

Haines, H., & Vaughan, G. M. (1979). Was 1898 a "great date" in the history of experimental social psychology? *Journal of the History of the Behavioral Sciences, 15*, 323–332.

Hall, C. S., & Lindzey, G. (1968). The relevance of Freudian psychology and related viewpoints for the social sciences. In G. Lindzey & E. Aronson (Eds.), *Handbook of social psychology* (Vol. 1) (2nd ed.). Reading, MA: Addison-Wesley.

Hall, C. S., & Lindzey, G. (1978). *Theories of personality* (3rd ed.). New York: Wiley.

Hall, E. T. (1959). *The silent language.* New York: Doubleday.

Hall, E. T. (1966). *The hidden dimension.* Garden City, NY: Doubleday.

Hall, J. A. (1984). *Nonverbal sex differences: Communication accuracy and expressive style.* Baltimore: Johns Hopkins University Press.

Hall, J. A. (1986). On explaining gender differences: The case of nonverbal communication. In P. Shaver (Ed.), *Review of personality and social psychology* (Vol. 7). Beverly Hills, CA: Sage.

Halpin, A. W. (1953). Studies in aircrew composition: III. In *The combat leader behavior of B-29 aircraft commanders.* Washington, D.C.: Human Factors Operations Research Laboratory, Bolling Air Force Base, September.

Halpin, A. W. (1954). The leadership behavior and combat performances of airplane commanders. *Journal of Abnormal and Social Psychology, 49*, 19–22.

Halpin, A. W. (1966). *Theory and research in administration.* New York: Macmillan.

Halpin, A. W., & Winer, B. J. (1952). *The leadership behavior of the airplane commander.* Columbus: Research Foundation, Ohio State University. (Mimeographed.)

Hamilton, D. L. (1979). A cognitive-attributional analysis of stereotyping. In L. Berkowitz (Ed.), *Advances in experimental social psychology* (Vol. 12). New York: Academic Press.

Hamilton, D. L. (Ed.). (1981). *Cognitive processes in stereotyping and intergroup behavior.* Hillsdale, NJ: Erlbaum.

Hamilton, D. L., Dugan, P. M., & Trolier, T. K. (1985). The formation of stereotypic beliefs: Further evidence for distinctiveness-based illusory correlation. *Journal of Personality and Social Psychology, 48*, 5–17.

Hamilton, D. L., & Gifford, R. K. (1976). Illusory correlation in interpersonal perception: A cognitive basis of stereotypic judgments. *Journal of Experimental Social Psychology, 12*, 392–407.

Hamilton, W. D. (1964). The genetical evolution of social behavior, I & II. *Journal of Theoretical Biology, 7*, 1–52.

Hamner, W. C. (1974). Effects of bargaining strategy and pressure to reach agreement in a stalemated negotiation. *Journal of Personality and Social Psychology, 30*, 458–467.

Haney, C., Banks, C., & Zimbardo, P. (1973). Interpersonal dynamics in a simulated prison. *International Journal of Criminology and Penology, 1*, 69–97.

Hans, V. P., & Vidmar, N. (1982). Jury selection. In N. L. Kerr & R. M. Bray (Eds.), *The psychology of the courtroom.* New York: Academic Press.

Hansen, W. B., & Altman, I. (1976). Decorating personal places: A descriptive analysis. *Environment and Behavior, 8*, 491–504.

Hanson, D. J. (1978). Authoritarianism as a variable in political research. In H. J. Eysenck & G. D. Wilson (Eds.), *The psychological basis of ideology.* Baltimore: University Park Press.

Hardin, G. (1968). The tragedy of the commons. *Science, 162*, 1243–1248.

Harding, J., Proshansky, H., Kutner, B., & Chein, I. (1969). Prejudice and ethnic relations. In G. Lindzey & E. Aronson (Eds.), *Handbook of social psychology* (Vol. 5) (2nd ed.). Reading, MA: Addison-Wesley.

Hare, A. P., & Bales, R. F. (1963). Seating position in small group discussion. *Sociometry, 26*, 480–486.

Harkins, S. G., & Petty, R. E. (1983). Effects of task difficulty and task uniqueness on social loafing. *Journal of Personality and Social Psychology, 43,* 1214–1229.

Harlow, H. F. (1958). The nature of love. *American Psychologist, 13,* 673–685.

Harries, K. D., & Stadler, S. J. (1983). Determinism revisited: Assault and heat stress in Dallas, 1980. *Environment and Behavior, 15,* 235–256.

Harris, A. S. (1970). The second sex in academe. *American Association of University Professors Bulletin, 56,* 283–295.

Harris, L., & Associates (1980). *The Steelcase national study of office environments, II: Comfort and productivity in the office of the 80's.* Grand Rapids, MI: Steelcase, Inc.

Harris, M. B. (1974). Mediators between frustration and aggression in a field experiment. *Journal of Experimental Social Psychology, 10,* 561–571.

Harris, M. J., & Rosenthal, R. (1985). Mediation of interpersonal expectancy effects: 31 meta-analyses. *Psychological Bulletin, 97,* 363–386.

Harrison, A. A. (1977). Mere exposure. In L. Berkowitz (Ed.), *Advances in experimental social psychology.* New York: Academic Press.

Harrison, A. A., & Connors, M. M. (1984). Groups in exotic environments. *Advances in Experimental Social Psychology, 18,* 49–87.

Harrison, A. A., & Saeed, L. (1977). Let's make a deal: An analysis of revelations and stipulations in lonely hearts advertisements. *Journal of Personality and Social Psychology, 35,* 257–264.

Hartmann, D. (1969). Influence of symbolically modeled instrumental aggression and pain cues on aggressive behavior. *Journal of Personality and Social Psychology, 11,* 280–288.

Hartmann, H., Kris, E., & Loewenstein, R. M. (1949). Notes on a theory of aggression. *Psychoanalytic Study of the Child, 3–4,* 9–36.

Harvey, J. H., Flanary, R., & Morgan, M. (in press). Vivid memories of vivid loves gone by. *Journal of Social and Personal Relationships.*

Hass, R. G. (1975). Persuasion or moderation? Two experiments on anticipatory belief change. *Journal of Personality and Social Psychology, 31,* 1155–1162.

Hass, R. G. (1984). Perspective taking and self-awareness: Drawing an E on your forehead. *Journal of Personality and Social Psychology, 46,* 788–798.

Hass, R. G., & Mann, R. W. (1976). Anticipatory belief change: Persuasion or impression management? *Journal of Personality and Social Psychology, 34,* 105–111.

Hastie, R. (1981). Schematic principles in human memory. In E. T. Higgins, C. P. Herman, & M. P. Zanna (Eds.), *Social cognition: The Ontario symposium* (Vol. 1). Hillsdale, NJ: Erlbaum.

Hastie, R. (1984). Causes and effects of causal attributions. *Journal of Personality and Social Psychology, 46,* 44–56.

Hastie, R., Penrod, S. D., & Pennington, N. (1983). *Inside the jury.* Cambridge, MA: Harvard University Press.

Hatfield, E., & Sprecher, S. (1983). Equity theory and recipient reactions to aid. In J. D. Fisher, A. Nadler, & B. M. DePaulo (Eds.), *New directions in helping* (Vol. 1). *Recipient reactions to aid.* New York: Academic Press.

Hatfield, E., & Traupmann, J. (1981). Intimate relationships: A perspective from equity theory. In S. Duck & R. Gilmour (Eds.), *Personal relationships I: Studying personal relationships.* New York: Academic Press.

Hayduk, L. A. (1983). Personal space: Where we now stand. *Psychological Bulletin, 94,* 293–335.

Hays, R. B. (1985). A longitudinal study of friendship development. *Journal of Personality and Social Psychology, 48,* 909–924.

Hays, R. B., & Oxley, D. (1986). Social network development and functioning during a life transition. *Journal of Personality and Social Psychology, 50,* 305–313.

Heckel, R. V. (1973). Leadership and voluntary seating choice. *Psychological Reports, 32,* 141–142.

Hedge, A. (1982). The open-plan office: A systematic investigation of employee reactions to their work environment. *Environment and Behavior, 14,* 519–542.

Heider, F. (1944). Social perception and phenomenal causality. *Psychological Review, 51,* 358–374.

Heider, F. (1946). Attitudes and cognitive organization. *Journal of Psychology, 21,* 107–112.

Heider, F. (1958). *The psychology of interpersonal relations.* New York: Wiley.

Heilman, M. E., & Guzzo, R. A. (1978). The perceived cause of work success as a mediator of sex discrimination in organizations. *Organizational Behavior and Human Performance, 21,* 346–357.

Heiman, J. R. (1975). The physiology of erotica: Women's sexual arousal. *Psychology Today, 8*(11), 90–94.

Heller, J., Groff, B. D., & Solomon, S. H. (1977). Toward an understanding of crowding: The role of physical interaction. *Journal of Personality and Social Psychology, 35,* 183–190.

Hellmuth, J. (Ed.). (1970). *Disadvantaged child* (Vol. 3). *Compensatory education: A national debate.* New York: Brunner/Mazel.

Helmreich, R. (1975). Applied social psychology: The unfulfilled promise. *Personality and Social Psychology Bulletin, 1,* 548–560.

Helson, H. (1964). *Adaptation-level theory: An experimental and systematic approach to behavior.* New York: Harper & Row.

Hemphill, J. K. (1955). Leadership behavior associated with the administrative reputation of college departments. *Journal of Educational Psychology, 46,* 385–401.

Hemphill, J. K., & Coons, A. E. (1950). *Leader behavior description.* Personnel Research Board, Ohio State University.

Hendrick, C. (1977). Role-playing as a methodology for social research: A symposium. *Personality and Social Psychology Bulletin, 3,* 454.

Hendrick, C., & Hendrick, S. (1986). A theory and method of love. *Journal of Personality and Social Psychology, 50,* 392–402.

Hendrick, C., & Jones, R. A. (1972). *The nature of theory and research in social psychology.* New York: Academic Press.

Hendrick, S., Hendrick, C., Slapion-Foote, M. J., & Foote, F. H. (1985). Gender differences in sexual attitudes. *Journal of Personality and Social Psychology, 48,* 1630–1642.

Henley, N. M. (1977). *Body politics: Power, sex, and nonverbal communication.* Englewood Cliffs, NJ: Prentice-Hall.

Herek, G. M. (1986). The instrumentality of attitudes: Toward a neofunctional theory. *Journal of Social Issues, 42* (2), 99–114.

Herman, C. P., Zanna, M. P., & Higgins, E. T. (Eds.). (1986). *Physical appearance, stigma, and social behavior: The Ontario Symposium, Volume 3.* Hillsdale, NJ: Erlbaum.

Herrnstein, R. (1973). *IQ in the meritocracy.* Boston: Atlantic Monthly Press and Little, Brown.

Heskin, K. (1980). *Northern Ireland: A psychological analysis.* New York: Columbia University Press.

Hess, E. H. (1962). Ethology. In R. Brown, E. Galanter, E. H. Hess, & G. Mandler, *New directions in psychology.* New York: Holt.

Hewstone, M., Bond, M. H., & Wan, K.-C. (1983). Social facts and social attributions: The explanation of intergroup differences in Hong Kong. *Social Cognitions, 2,* 142–157.

Hewstone, M., & Jaspars, J. (1982). Explanations for racial discrimination: The effect of group discussion on intergroup attributions. *European Journal of Social Psychology, 12,* 1–16.

Hicks, D. (1968). Short- and long-term retention of affectively-varied modeled behavior. *Psychonomic Science, 11,* 369–370.

Hiers, J. M., & Heckel, R. V. (1977). Seating choice, leadership, and locus of control. *Journal of Social Psychology, 103,* 313–314.

Higbee, K. L. (1969). Fifteen years of fear arousal: Research on threat appeals: 1953–1968. *Psychological Bulletin, 72,* 426–444.

Higgins, E. T. (1981). The "communication game": Implications for social cognition and persuasion. In. E. T. Higgins, C. P. Herman, & M. P. Zanna (Eds.), *Social cognition: The Ontario symposium, Vol. 1* (pp. 343–392). Hillsdale, NJ: Erlbaum.

Higgins, E. T. (in press). Self-discrepancy: A theory relating self and affect. *Psychological Review.*

Higgins, E. T., & Bargh, J. A. (1987). Social cognition and social perception. *Annual Review of Psychology, 38,* 369–425.

Higgins, E. T., & King, G. (1981). Accessibility of social constructs: Information-processing consequences of individual and contextual variability. In N. Cantor & J. F. Kihlstrom (Eds.), *Personality, cognition, and social interaction* (pp. 69–121). Hillsdale, NJ: Erlbaum.

Higgins, E. T., & McCann, C. D. (1984). Social encoding and subsequent attitudes, impressions, and memory: "Context-driven" and motivational aspects of processing. *Journal of Personality and Social Psychology, 47,* 26–39.

Higgins, E. T., Rholes, C. R., & Jones, C. R. (1977). Category accessibility and impression formation. *Journal of Experimental Social Psychology, 13,* 141–154.

Hill, C. T., Rubin, Z., & Peplau, L. A. (1976). Breakups before marriage: The end of 103 affairs. *Journal of Social Issues, 32*(1), 147–168.

Hill, C. T., & Stull, D. E. (1981). Sex differences in effects of social and value similarity in same-sex friendship. *Journal of Personality and Social Psychology, 41,* 488–502.

Hills, L. R. (1973). The cruel rules of social life. *Newsweek,* October 1, p. 15.

Hilton, J. L., & Darley, J. M. (1985). Constructing other persons: A limit on the effect. *Journal of Experimental Social Psychology, 21,* 1–18.

Hiltrop, J. M., & Rubin, J. Z. (1982). Effects of intervention mode and conflict of interest on dispute resolution. *Journal of Personality and Social Psychology, 42,* 665–672.

Himmelfarb, S., & Eagly, A. H. (1974). Orientations to the study of attitudes and their change. In S. Himmelfarb & A. H. Eagly (Eds.), *Readings in attitude change.* New York: Wiley.

Hirt, E., & Kimble, C. E. (1981). *The home-field advantage in sports: Differences and correlates.* Paper presented at meeting of Midwestern Psychological Association, Detroit, May.

Hockey, G. R. (1970). Effect of loud noise on attentional selectivity. *Quarterly Journal of Experimental Psychology, 22,* 28–36.

Hoelter, J. W. (1984). Relative effects of significant others on self-evaluation. *Social Psychology Quarterly, 47,* 255–262.

Hoelter, J. W. (1986). The relationship between specific and global evaluations of self: A comparison of several models. *Social Psychology Quarterly, 49,* 129–141.

Hoffman, M. L. (1975). Developmental synthesis of affect and cognition and its implications for altruistic motivation. *Developmental Psychology, 11,* 607–622.

Hoffman, M. L. (1981). Is altruism part of human nature? *Journal of Personality and Social Psychology, 40,* 121–137.

Holahan, C. J., & Wilcox, B. L. (1978). Residential satisfaction and friendship formation in high- and low-rise student housing: An interactional analysis. *Journal of Educational Psychology, 70,* 237–241.

Hollander, E. P. (1985). Leadership and power. In G. Lindzey & E. Aronson (Eds.), *Handbook of social psychology* (3rd ed.) (pp. 485–537). New York: Random House.

Hollander, E. P., Fallon, B. J., & Edwards, M. T. (1977). Some aspects of influence and acceptability for appointed and elected group leaders. *Journal of Psychology, 95,* 289–296.

Hollander, E. P., & Julian, J. W. (1970). Studies in leader legitimacy, influence, and innovation. In L. Berkowitz (Ed.), *Advances in experimental social psychology* (Vol. 5). New York: Academic Press.

Hollander, E. P., & Julian, J. W. (1978). A further look at leader legitimacy, influence, and innovation. In L. Berkowitz (Ed.), *Group processes.* New York: Academic Press.

Hollander, E. P., & Yoder, J. (1980). Some issues in comparing women and men as leaders. *Basic and Applied Social Psychology, 1,* 267–280.

Homans, G. C. (1950). *The human group.* New York: Harcourt, Brace & World.

Homans, G. C. (1954). The cash posters. *American Sociological Review, 19,* 724–733.

Homans, G. C. (1958). Social behavior and exchange. *American Journal of Sociology, 63,* 597–606.

Homans, G. C. (1970). The relevance of psychology to the explanation of social phenomena. In R. Borger & F. Cioffi (Eds.), *Explanation in the behavioral sciences.* Cambridge, England: Cambridge University Press.

Homans, G. C. (1974). *Social behavior: Its elementary forms* (Rev. ed.). New York: Harcourt Brace Jovanovich.

Hook, S. (1955). *The hero in history.* Boston: Beacon Press.

Hopmann, P. T., & Walcott, C. (1977). The impact of external stresses and tensions on negotiations. In D. Druckman (Ed.), *Negotiations: Social-psychological perspectives.* Beverly Hills, CA: Sage.

Hoppe, R. A., Greene, M. S., & Kenny, J. W. (1972). Territorial markers: Additional findings. *Journal of Social Psychology, 88,* 305–306.

Hopstock, P. J., Aiello, J. R., & Baum, A. (1979). Residential crowding research. In J. R. Aiello & A. Baum (Eds.), *Residential crowding and design* (pp. 9–21). New York: Plenum.

Hornstein, G. A. (1985). Intimacy in conversational style as a function of the degree of closeness between members of a dyad. *Journal of Personality and Social Psychology, 49,* 671–681.

Hornstein, H. A. (1975). Social psychology as social intervention. In M. Deutsch & H. A. Hornstein (Eds.), *Applying social psychology: Implications for research, practice, and training.* Hillsdale, NJ: Erlbaum.

Hornstein, H. A. (1976). *Cruelty and kindness: A new look at aggression and altruism.* Englewood Cliffs, NJ: Prentice-Hall.

Horton, R. W., & Santogrossi, D. A. (1978). The effect of adult commentary on reducing the influence of televised violence. *Personality and Social Psychology Bulletin, 4*, 337–340.

House, J. S., & Wolf, S. (1978). Effects of urban residence on interpersonal trust and helping behavior. *Journal of Personality and Social Psychology, 36*, 1029–1043.

House, R. J. (1971). A path-goal theory of leader effectiveness. *Administrative Science Quarterly, 16*, 321–338.

Hovland, C., Harvey, O. J., & Sherif, M. (1957). Assimilation and contrast effects in reactions to communication and attitude change. *Journal of Abnormal and Social Psychology, 55*, 244–252.

Hovland, C., Janis, I., & Kelley, H. H. (1953). *Communication and persuasion.* New Haven: Yale University Press.

Hovland, C. I., & Weiss, W. (1951). The influence of source credibility on communication effectiveness. *Public Opinion Quarterly, 15*, 635–650.

Howard, J. L., Reifler, C. B., & Liptzin, M. B. (1971). Effects of exposure to pornography. In *Technical report of the Commission on Obscenity and Pornography* (Vol. 8). Washington, D.C.: U.S. Government Printing Office.

Howells, L. T., & Becker, S. W. (1962). Seating arrangement and leadership emergence. *Journal of Abnormal and Social Psychology, 64*, 148–150.

Huesmann, L. R., Eron, L. D., Lefkowitz, M. M., & Walder, L. O. (1984). Stability of aggression over time and generations. *Developmental Psychology, 20*, 1120–1134.

Huesmann, L. R., Lagerspetz, K., & Eron, L. D. (1984). Intervening variables in the TV violence-aggression relation: Evidence from two countries. *Developmental Psychology, 20*, 746–775.

Humphreys, P., & Berger, J. (1981). Theoretical consequences of the status characteristics formulation. *American Journal of Sociology, 86*, 953–983.

Hundert, A. J., & Greenfield, N. (1969). Physical space and organizational behavior: A study of an office landscape. In *Proceedings, 77th annual convention, American Psychological Association,* pp. 601–602.

Hunt, M. (1974). *Sexual behavior in the 1970's.* Chicago: Playboy Press.

Hunt, M. (1985). *Profiles of social research: The scientific study of human interactions.* New York: Russell Sage Foundation.

Huston, T. L., Ruggiero, M., Conner, R., & Geis, G. (1981). Bystander intervention into crime: A study based on naturally-occurring episodes. *Social Psychology Quarterly, 44*, 14–23.

Hutt, C., & Vaizey, M. (1966). Differential effects of group density on social behavior. *Nature, 209*, 1371–1372.

Insko, C. A. (1965). Verbal reinforcement of attitude. *Journal of Personality and Social Psychology, 2*, 621–623.

Insko, C. A. (1981). Balance theory and phenomenology. In R. Petty, T. Ostrom, & T. Brock (Eds.), *Cognitive responses in persuasion.* Hillsdale, NJ: Erlbaum.

Insko, C. A. (1984). Balance theory, the Jordan paradigm, and the Wiest tetrahedron. *Advances in Experimental Social Psychology, 18*, 89–140.

Insko, C. A., Smith, R. H., Alicke, M. D., Wade, J., & Taylor, S. (1985). Conformity and group size: The concern with being right and the concern with being liked. *Personality and Social Psychology Bulletin, 11*, 41–50.

Isen, A. M. (1970). Success, failure, attention and reactions to others: The warm glow of success. *Journal of Personality and Social Psychology, 15*, 294–301

Isen, A. M., & Daubman, K. A. (1984). The influence of affect on categorization. *Journal of Personality and Social Psychology, 47*, 1206–1217.

Isen, A. M., & Levin, P. F. (1972). Effect of feeling good on helping: Cookies and kindness. *Journal of Personality and Social Psychology, 21*, 384–388.

Isen, A.M., Shalker, T. E., Clark, M., & Karp, L. (1978). Affect, accessibility of material in memory, and behavior: A cognitive loop? *Journal of Personality and Social Psychology, 36*, 1–12.

Isen, A. M., & Simmonds, S. F. (1978). The effect of feeling good on a helping task that is incompatible with good mood. *Social Psychology Quarterly, 41*, 346–349.

Isenberg, D. J. (1986). Group polarization: A critical review and meta-analysis. *Journal of Personality and Social Psychology, 50*, 1141–1151.

Iyengar, S., Kinder, D. R., Peters, M. D., & Krosnick, J. A. (1984). The evening news and Presidential evaluations. *Journal of Personality and Social Psychology, 46*, 778–787.

Izard, C. E. (1969). The emotions and emotion constructs in personality and culture research. In R. B. Cattell (Ed.), *Handbook of modern personality theory.* Chicago: Aldine.

Izard, C. E. (1980). Cross-cultural perspectives on emotion and emotion communication. In H. C. Triandis & W. Lonner (Eds.), *Handbook of cross-cultural psychology. Vol. 3: Basic processes.* Boston: Allyn & Bacon.

Izzett, R. (1971). Authoritarianism and attitudes toward the Vietnam War as reflected in behavioral and self-report measures. *Journal of Personality and Social Psychology, 17*, 145–148.

Jaccard, J. J. (1974). Predicting social behavior from personality traits. *Journal of Research in Personality, 7*, 358–367.

Jaccard, J. J. (1977). Personality and behavioral prediction: An analysis of behavioral criterion measures. In L. Kahle & D. Fiske (Eds.), *Methods for studying person-situation interactions.* San Francisco: Jossey-Bass.

Jackson, J. M. (1986). In defense of social impact theory: Comment on Mullen. *Journal of Personality and Social Psychology, 50*, 511–513.

Jackson, J. M., & Harkins, S. G. (1985). Equity in effort: An explanation of the social loafing effect. *Journal of Personality and Social Psychology, 49*, 1199–1206.

Jackson, J. M., & Williams, K. D. (1985). Social loafing on difficult tasks: Working collectively can improve performance. *Journal of Personality and Social Psychology, 49*, 937–942.

Jacobs, J. (1970). The uses of sidewalks: Contact. In H. Proshansky, W. Ittelson, & L. Rivlin (Eds.), *Environmental psychology* (pp. 312–319). New York: Holt, Rinehart & Winston.

Jacobs, R. C., & Campbell, D. T. (1961). The perpetuation of an arbitrary tradition through several generations of a laboratory microculture. *Journal of Abnormal and Social Psychology, 62*, 649–658.

Jago, A. G., & Vroom, V. H. (1982). Sex differences in the incidence and evaluation of participative leader behavior. *Journal of Applied Psychology, 67*, 776–783.

Jahoda, G. (1986). Nature, culture and social psychology. *European Journal of Social Psychology, 16*, 17–30.

James, R. (1959). Status and competence of jurors. *American Journal of Sociology, 64*, 563–570.

James, W. (1890). *The principles of psychology* (Vols. 1 and 2). New York: Holt.

Janis, I. L. (1972). *Victims of groupthink.* Boston: Houghton Mifflin.

Janis, I. L., & Feshbach, S. (1953). Effects of fear-arousing communications. *Journal of Abnormal and Social Psychology, 48,* 78–92.

Janis, I. L., & Field, P. B. (1959). Sex differences and personality factors related to persuasibility. In I. L. Janis, C. I. Hovland, P. B. Field, H. Linton, E. Graham, A. R. Cohen, D. Rife, R. P. Abelson, G. S. Lesser, & B. T. King (Eds.), *Personality and persuasibility.* New Haven: Yale University Press.

Jellison, J. M., & Green, J. (1981). A self-presentation approach to the fundamental attribution error: The norm of internality. *Journal of Personality and Social Psychology, 40,* 643–649.

Jellison, J. M., Jackson-White, R., Bruder, R. A., & Martyna, W. (1975). Achievement behavior: A situational interpretation. *Sex Roles, 1,* 369–384.

Jemmott, J. B., III, Ditto, P. H., & Croyle, R. T. (1986). Judging health status: Effects of perceived prevalence and personal relevance. *Journal of Personality and Social Psychology, 50,* 899–905.

Jenkins, W. O. (1947). A review of leadership studies with particular reference to military problems. *Psychological Bulletin, 44,* 54–79.

Jensen, A. R. (1973). *Educability and group differences.* New York: Basic Books.

Johnson, H. G., Ekman, P., & Friesen, W. V. (1975). Communicative body movements: American emblems. *Semiotica, 15,* 335–353.

Johnson, T. E., & Rule, B. G. (1986). Mitigating circumstance information, censure, and aggression. *Journal of Personality and Social Psychology, 50,* 537–542.

Johnston, A., DeLuca, D., Murtaugh, K., & Diener, E. (1977). Validation of a laboratory play measure of child aggression. *Child Development, 48,* 324–327.

Joiner, D. (1976). Social ritual and architectural space. In H. Proshansky, W. Ittelson, & L. Rivlin (Eds.), *Environmental psychology* (2nd ed.) (pp. 224–241). New York: Holt, Rinehart & Winston.

Jones, E. E. (1985). Major developments in social psychology during the past five decades. In G. Lindzey & E. Aronson (Eds.), *Handbook of social psychology* (Vol. 1) (3rd ed.) (pp. 47–107). New York: Random House.

Jones, E. E. (1986). Interpreting interpersonal behavior: The effects of expectancies. *Science, 234,* 41–46.

Jones, E. E., & Baumeister, R. (1976). The self-monitor looks at the ingratiator. *Journal of Personality, 44,* 654–674.

Jones, E. E., & Davis, K. E. (1965). From acts to dispositions: The attribution process in person perception. In L. Berkowitz (Ed.), *Advances in experimental social psychology* (Vol. 2). New York: Academic Press.

Jones, E. E., Farina, A., Hastorf, A. H., Markus, H., Miller, D. T., & Scott, R. A. (1984). *Social stigma: The psychology of marked relationships.* New York: Freeman.

Jones, E. E., Gergen, K. J., & Jones, R. G. (1963). Tactics of ingratiation among leaders and subordinates in a status hierarchy. *Psychological Monographs, 77,* (Whole No. 566).

Jones, E. E., Kanouse, D. E., Kelley, H. H., Nisbett, R. E., Valins, S., & Weiner, B. (1972). *Attribution: Perceiving the causes of behavior.* Morristown, NJ: General Learning Press.

Jones, E. E., & McGillis, D. (1976). Correspondent inferences and the attribution cube: A comparative reappraisal. In J. H. Harvey, W. J. Ickes, & R. F. Kidd (Eds.), *New directions in attribution research* (Vol. 1). Hillsdale, NJ: Erlbaum.

Jones, E. E., & Pittman, T. S. (1982). Toward a general theory of strategic self presentation. In J. Suls (Ed.), *Psychological perspectives on the self.* Hillsdale, NJ: Erlbaum.

Jones, E. E., Rhodewalt, F., Berglas, S., & Skelton, J. A. (1981). Effects of strategic self-presentation on subsequent self-esteem. *Journal of Personality and Social Psychology, 41,* 407–421.

Jones, E. E., & Wortman, C. B. (1973). *Ingratiation: An attributional approach.* Morristown, NJ: General Learning Press.

Jones, J. M. (1979). Conceptual and strategic issues in the relationship of Black psychology to American social science. In A. W. Boykin, A. J. Franklin, & J. F. Yates (Eds.), *Research directions of Black psychologists.* New York: Russell Sage Foundation.

Jones, J. M. (1983). The concept of race in social psychology: From color to culture. In L. Wheeler & P. Shaver (Eds.), *Review of personality and social psychology* (Vol. 4). Beverly Hills, CA: Sage.

Jones, J. W., & Bogat, A. (1978). Air pollution and human aggression. *Psychological Reports, 43,* 721–722.

Jones, M. B. (1958). Religious values and authoritarian tendency. *Journal of Social Psychology, 45,* 83–89.

Jones, R. A., Howard, P. H., & Haley, J. V. (1984). Probability distortions and outcome desirability: Experimental verification of medical folklore. *Journal of Applied Social Psychology, 14,* 319–333.

Jones, W. H., Freemon, J. E., & Goswick, R. A. (1981). The persistence of loneliness: Self and other determinants. *Journal of Personality, 49,* 27–48.

Jourard, S. M. (1971). *Self-disclosure.* New York: Wiley.

Jussim, L. (1986). Self-fulfilling prophecies: A theoretical and integrative review. *Psychological Review, 93,* 429–445.

Kaats, G. R., & Davis, K. E. (1970). The dynamics of sexual behavior of college students. *Journal of Marriage and the Family, 32,* 390–399.

Kahn, R. (1981). *Work and health.* New York: Wiley.

Kammann, R., Thomson, R., & Irwin, R. (1979). Unhelpful behavior in the streets: City size or immediate pedestrian density. *Environment and Behavior, 11,* 245–250.

Kandel, D. B. (1978). Similarity in real-life adolescent friendship pairs. *Journal of Personality and Social Psychology, 36,* 306-312.

Kanter, R. M. (1977). *Men and women of the corporation.* New York: Basic Books.

Kantola, S. J., Syme, G. J., & Campbell, N. A. (1984). Cognitive dissonance and energy conservation. *Journal of Applied Psychology, 69,* 416–421.

Kaplan, J. A. (1978). A legal look at prosocial behavior: What can happen if one tries to help or fails to help another. In L. Wispé (Ed.), *Altruism, sympathy, and helping: Psychological and sociological principles.* New York: Academic Press.

Kaplan, M. F., & Anderson, N. H. (1973). Information integration theory and reinforcement theory as approaches to interpersonal attraction. *Journal of Personality and Social Psychology, 28,* 301–312.

Karlin, R. A., Rosen, L. S., & Epstein, Y. M. (1979). Three into two doesn't go: A follow-up on the effects of overcrowded dormitory rooms. *Personality and Social Psychology Bulletin, 5,* 391–395.

Karlins, M., & Abelson, H. I. (1970). *How opinions and attitudes are changed* (2nd ed.). New York: Springer.

Karuza, J., Jr., & Brickman, P. (1978). *Preference for similar and dissimilar others as a function of status.* Paper presented at meeting of Midwestern Psychological Association, Chicago, May.

Kassin, S. M., & Wrightsman, L. S. (1980). Prior confessions and mock juror verdicts. *Journal of Applied Social Psychology, 10,* 133–146.

Kassin, S. M., & Wrightsman, L. S. (1985). Confession evidence. In S. M. Kassin & L. S. Wrightsman (Eds.), *The psychology of evidence and trial procedure* (pp. 67–94). Beverly Hills, CA: Sage.

Katz, D. (1960). The functional approach to the study of attitudes. *Public Opinion Quarterly, 24,* 163–204.

Katz, D., & Kahn, R. L. (1976). *The social psychology of organizations* (2nd ed.). New York: Wiley.

Katz, D., & Stotland, E. (1959). A preliminary statement to a theory of attitude structure and change. In S. Koch (Ed.), *Psychology: A study of a science* (Vol. 3). New York: McGraw-Hill.

Katz, I. (1981). *Stigma: A social psychological analysis.* Hillsdale, NJ.: Erlbaum.

Katz, P. A. (1986). Gender identity: Development and consequences. In R. D. Ashmore & F. K. Del Boca (Eds.), *The social psychology of female-male relations* (pp. 21–67). New York: Academic Press.

Kauffman, D. R., & Steiner, I. D. (1968). Conformity as an ingratiation technique. *Journal of Experimental Social Psychology, 4,* 404–414.

Kaufmann, H. (1973). *Social psychology: The study of human interaction.* New York: Holt, Rinehart & Winston.

Keeler, B. T., & Andrews, J. H. M. (1963). Leader behavior of principals, staff morale, and productivity. *Alberta Journal of Educational Research, 9,* 179–191.

Kelley, H. H. (1950). The warm-cold variable in first impressions of persons. *Journal of Personality, 18,* 431–439.

Kelley, H. H. (1967). Attribution theory in social psychology. In D. Levine (Ed.), *Nebraska symposium on motivation, 1967* (Vol. 15). Lincoln: University of Nebraska Press.

Kelley, H. H. (1972). Causal schemata and the attribution process. In E. E. Jones, D. Kanouse, H. H. Kelley, R. E. Nisbett, S. Valins, & B. Weiner (Eds.), *Attribution: Perceiving the causes of behavior.* Morristown, NJ: General Learning Press.

Kelley, H. H. (1979). *Personal relationships: Their structures and processes.* Hillsdale, NJ: Erlbaum.

Kelley, H. H., Berscheid, E., Christensen, A., Harvey, J. H., Huston, T. L., Levinger, G., McClintock, E., Peplau, L. A., & Peterson, D. R. (1983). *Close relationships.* New York: Freeman.

Kelley, H. H., & Thibaut, J. W. (1978). *Interpersonal relations: A theory of interdependence.* New York: Wiley-Interscience.

Kelly, G. A. (1955). *A theory of personality: The psychology of personal constructs* (2 vols.). New York: Norton.

Kelman, H. C. (1968). *A time to speak: On human values and social research.* San Francisco: Jossey-Bass.

Kelman, H. C. (1973). Violence without moral restraint: Reflections on the dehumanization of victims and victimizers. *Journal of Social Issues, 29* (4), 25–61.

Kelvin, P. (1973). A social-psychological examination of privacy. *British Journal of Social and Clinical Psychology, 12,* 248–261.

Kenny, D. A., & Zaccaro, S. J. (1983). An estimate of variance due to traits in leadership. *Journal of Applied Psychology, 68,* 678–685.

Kenrick, D. T., Baumann, D. J., & Cialdini, R. B. (1979). A step in the socialization of altruism as hedonism: Effects of negative mood on children's generosity under public and private conditions. *Journal of Personality and Social Psychology, 37,* 747–755.

Kenrick, D. T., & Johnson, G. A. (1979). Interpersonal attraction in aversive environments: A problem for the classical conditioning paradigm? *Journal of Personality and Social Psychology, 37,* 572–579.

Kenrick, D. T., & MacFarlane, S. W. (1986). Ambient temperature and horn honking: A field study of the heat/aggression relationship. *Environment and Behavior, 18,* 179–191.

Kenrick, D. T., & Springfield, D. O. (1980). Personality traits and the eye of the beholder: Crossing some traditional philosophical boundaries in the search for consistency in all of the people. *Psychological Review, 87,* 88–104.

Kerckhoff, A. C., & Davis, K. E. (1962). Value consensus and need complementarity in mate selection. *American Sociological Review, 27,* 295–303.

Kerr, N., Atkin, R., Stasser, G., Meek, D., Holt, R., & Davis, J. (1976). Guilt beyond a reasonable doubt: Effects of concept definition and assigned rule on the judgments of mock jurors. *Journal of Personality and Social Psychology, 34,* 282–294.

Kerr, N. L., & MacCoun, R. J. (1985a). Role expectations in social dilemmas: Sex roles and task motivation in groups. *Journal of Personality and Social Psychology, 49,* 1547–1556.

Kerr, N. L., & MacCoun, R. J. (1985b). The effects of jury size and polling method on process and product of jury deliberation. *Journal of Personality and Social Psychology, 48,* 349–363.

Kessler, S. J., & McKenna, W. (1978). *Gender: An ethnomethodological approach.* New York: Wiley.

Kihlstrom, J. F., & Cantor, N. (1984). Mental representations of the self. *Advances in Experimental Social Psychology, 17,* 2–47.

Kimble, C. E., & Forte, R. (1978). *Simulated and real eye contact as a function of emotional intensity and message positivity.* Paper presented at meeting of Midwestern Psychological Association, Chicago, May.

Kimble, G. A. (1961). *Hilgard and Marquis's conditioning and learning.* New York: Appleton-Century-Crofts.

Kinder, D. R. (1978). Political person perception: The asymmetrical influence of sentiment and choice on perceptions of political candidates. *Journal of Personality and Social Psychology, 36,* 859–871.

Kinder, D. R., & Sears, D. O. (1981). Prejudice and politics: Symbolic racism versus racial threats to the good life. *Journal of Personality and Social Psychology, 40,* 414–431.

King, K., Balswick, J. O., & Robinson, I. E. (1977). The continuing premarital sexual revolution among college females. *Journal of Marriage and the Family, 39,* 455–459.

Kinsey, A. C., Pomeroy, W. B., & Martin, C. E. (1948). *Sexual behavior in the human male.* Philadelphia: Saunders.

Kinsey, A. C., Pomeroy, W. B., Martin, C. E., & Gebhard, P. H. (1953). *Sexual behavior in the human female.* Philadelphia: Saunders.

Kipnis, D. M. (1957). Interaction between members of bomber crews as a determinant of sociometric choice. *Human Relations, 10,* 263–270.

Kirmeyer, S. I. (1978). Urban density and pathology: A review of research. *Environment and Behavior, 10*, 247–269.

Kirscht, J. P., & Dillehay, R. C. (1967). *Dimensions of authoritarianism: A review of research and theory.* Lexington: University of Kentucky Press.

Kitcher, P. (1985). *Vaulting ambition.* Cambridge, MA: MIT Press.

Kite, M., & Johnson, B. (1987). *Comparative stereotypes of younger and older adults: A meta-analysis.* Unpublished manuscript, Purdue University.

Kleinke, C. L. (1986). Gaze and eye contact: A research review. *Psychological Bulletin, 100*, 78–100.

Kleinke, C. L., Bustos, A. A., Meeker, F. B., & Staneski, R. A. (1973). Effects of self-attributed and other-attributed gaze on interpersonal evaluations between males and females. *Journal of Experimental Social Psychology, 9*, 154–163.

Kluegel, J. R., & Smith, E. R. (1986). *Beliefs about inequality.* New York: Aldine de Gruyter.

Kluger, R. (1976). *Simple justice.* New York: Knopf.

Knafo, D., & Jaffe, Y. (1984). Sexual fantasizing in males and females. *Journal of Research in Personality, 18*, 451–462.

Knapp, M. L. (1978). *Nonverbal communication in human interaction* (2nd ed.). New York: Holt, Rinehart & Winston.

Knapp, M. L., Hart, R. P., & Dennis, H. S. (1974). An exploration of deception as a communication construct. *Human Communication Research, 1*, 15–29.

Knowles, E. S. (1972). Boundaries around social space: Dyadic responses to an invader. *Environment and Behavior, 4*, 437–445.

Knowles, E. S. (1973). Boundaries around group interaction: The effect of group size and member status on boundary permeability. *Journal of Personality and Social Psychology, 26*, 327–331.

Knowles, E. S. (1982). A comment on the study of classroom ecology: A lament for the good old days. *Personality and Social Psychology Bulletin, 8*, 357–361.

Knowles, E. S., & Brickner, M. A. (1981). Social cohesion effects on spatial cohesion. *Personality and Social Psychology Bulletin, 7*, 309–313.

Knox, R. E., & Inkster, J. A. (1968). Postdecision dissonance at post time. *Journal of Personality and Social Psychology, 8*, 319–323.

Kobasa, S. C. (1979). Stressful life events, personality, and health: An inquiry into hardiness. *Journal of Personality and Social Psychology, 37*, 1–11.

Kobasa, S. C., Maddi, S. R., & Kahn, S. (1982). Hardiness and health: A prospective study. *Journal of Personality and Social Psychology, 42*, 168–177.

Kogan, N., & Wallach, M. A. (1964). *Risk-taking: A study in cognition and personality.* New York: Holt.

Kolb, D. M. (1985). To be a mediator: Expressive tactics in mediation. *Journal of Social Issues, 41* (2), 11–26.

Konar, E., & Sundstrom, E. (1986). Status demarcation and office design. In J. Wineman (Ed.), *Behavioral issues in office design* (pp. 203–223). New York: Van Nostrand Rinehold.

Konar, E., Sundstrom, E., Brady, K., Mandel, D., & Rice, R. (1982). Status demarcation in the office. *Environment and Behavior, 14*, 561–580.

Konecni, V. J. (1975a). The mediation of aggressive behavior: Arousal level versus anger and cognitive labeling. *Journal of Personality and Social Psychology, 32*, 706–712.

Konecni, V. J. (1975b). Annoyance, type and duration of postannoyance activity, and aggression: The "cathartic" effect. *Journal of Experimental Psychology: General, 104*, 76–102.

Koneya, M. (1976). Location and interaction in row-and-column seating arrangements. *Environment and Behavior, 8*, 265–282.

Korman, A. K. (1966). "Consideration," "initiating structure," and organizational criteria—A review. *Personnel Psychology, 19*, 349–361.

Korman, A. K. (1968). The prediction of managerial performance: A review. *Personnel Psychology, 21*, 295–322.

Korte, C. (1980). Urban-nonurban differences in social behavior and social psychological models of urban impact. *Journal of Social Issues, 36*(3), 29–54.

Korte, C. (1984). The helpfulness of urban villagers. In E. Staub, D. Bar-Tal, J. Karylowski, & J. Reykowski (Eds.), *The development and maintenance of prosocial behavior: International perspectives.* New York: Plenum.

Korte, C., & Grant, R. (1980). Traffic noise, environmental awareness, and pedestrian behavior. *Environment and Behavior, 12*, 408–420.

Korte, C., Ypma, I., & Toppen, A. (1975). Helpfulness in Dutch society as a function of urbanization and environmental input level. *Journal of Personality and Social Psychology, 32*, 996–1003.

Kramer, R. M., & Brewer, M. B. (1984). Effects of group identity on resource use in a simulated commons dilemma. *Journal of Personality and Social Psychology, 46*, 1044–1057.

Krantz, D. S., Grunberg, N. E., & Baum, A. (1985). Health psychology. *Annual Review of Psychology, 36*, 349–393.

Krauss, R. M., Curran, N. M., & Ferleger, N. (1983). Expressive conventions and the cross-cultural perception of emotion. *Basic and Applied Social Psychology, 4*, 295–305.

Krauss, R. M., & Glucksberg, S. (1977). Social and nonsocial speech. *Scientific American, 236*, 100–105.

Kraut, R. E. (1973). Effects of social labeling on giving to charity. *Journal of Experimental Social Psychology, 9*, 551–562.

Kraut, R. E., & Johnston, R. (1979). Social and emotional messages of smiling: An ethological approach. *Journal of Personality and Social Psychology, 37*, 1539–1553.

Kraut, R. E., & Poe, D. (1980). On the line: The deception judgments of customs inspectors and laymen. *Journal of Personality and Social Psychology, 39*, 784–798.

Kravitz, D. A., & Martin, B. (1986). Ringelmann rediscovered: The original article. *Journal of Personality and Social Psychology, 50*, 936–941.

Krebs, D. (1975). Empathy and altruism. *Journal of Personality and Social Psychology, 32*, 1134–1146.

Krebs, D. (1983). Commentary and critique: Sociobiological approaches to prosocial development. In D. L. Bridgeman (Ed.), *The nature of prosocial development: Interdisciplinary theories and strategies.* New York: Academic Press.

Krebs, D. L., & Miller, D. T. (1985). Altruism and aggression. In G. Lindzey & E. Aronson (Eds.), *Handbook of social psychology* (Vol. II) (3rd ed.) (pp. 1–71). New York: Random House.

Kressel, K., & Pruitt, D. G. (1985). Themes in the mediation of social conflict. *Journal of Social Issues, 41* (2), 179–198.

Kronhausen, E., & Kronhausen, P. (1964). *Pornography and the law* (Rev. ed.). New York: Ballantine.

Kunda, Z., & Schwartz, S. H. (1983). Undermining intrinsic moral motivation: External reward and self-presentation. *Journal of Personality and Social Psychology, 45*, 763–771.

Kutchinsky, B. (1973). The effect of easy availability of pornography on the incidence of sex crimes: The Danish experience. *Journal of Social Issues, 29*(3), 163–181.

Kutner, B., Wilkins, C., & Yarrow, P. R. (1952). Verbal attitudes and overt behavior involving racial prejudice. *Journal of Abnormal and Social Psychology, 47*, 649–652.

LaFrance, M., & Mayo, C. (1976). Racial differences in gaze behavior during conversations: Two systematic observational studies. *Journal of Personality and Social Psychology, 33*, 547–552.

LaFrance, M., & Mayo, C. (1978). *Moving bodies: Nonverbal communication in social relationships.* Pacific Grove, CA: Brooks/Cole.

Lalljee, M., Watson, M., & White, P. (1982). Explanations, attributions, and the social context of unexpected behavior. *European Journal of Social Psychology, 12*, 17–29.

Lamm, H., & Trommsdorff, G. (1973). Group versus individual performance on tasks requiring ideational proficiency (brainstorming): A review. *European Journal of Social Psychology, 3*, 361–388.

Landman, J., & Manis, M. (1983). Social cognition: Some historical and theoretical perspectives. *Advances in Experimental Social Psychology, 16*, 49–123.

Lando, H. A., & Donnerstein, E. (1978). The effects of a model's success or failure on subsequent aggressive behavior. *Journal of Research in Personality, 12*, 225–234.

Landy, D., & Sigall, H. (1974). Beauty is talent: Task evaluation as a function of the performer's physical attractiveness. *Journal of Personality and Social Psychology, 29*, 299–304.

Langer, E. J. (1975). The illusion of control. *Journal of Personality and Social Psychology, 32*, 311–328.

Langer, E. J. (1978a). The psychology of chance. *Journal for the Theory of Social Behaviour, 7*, 185–207.

Langer, E. J. (1978b). Rethinking the role of thought in social interaction. In J. H. Harvey, W. J. Ickes, & R. F. Kidd (Eds.), *New directions in attribution research* (Vol. 2). Hillsdale, NJ: Erlbaum.

Langer, E. J. (1983). *The psychology of control.* Beverly Hills: Sage.

Langer, E. J., & Benevento, A. (1978). Self-induced dependence. *Journal of Personality and Social Psychology, 36*, 886–893.

Langer, E., Blank, A., & Chanowitz, B. (1978). The mindlessness of ostensibly thoughtful action: The role of "placebic" information in interpersonal interaction. *Journal of Personality and Social Psychology, 36*, 635–642.

Langer, E., Janis, I., & Wolfer, J. (1975). Reduction of psychological stress in surgical patients. *Journal of Experimental Social Psychology, 11*, 155–165.

Langer, E. J., & Rodin, J. (1976). The effects of choice and enhanced personal responsibility for the aged: A field experiment in an institutional setting. *Journal of Personality and Social Psychology, 34*, 191–198.

Langer, E. J., & Roth, J. (1975). Heads I win, tails it's chance: The illusion of control as a function of the sequence of outcomes in a purely chance task. *Journal of Personality and Social Psychology, 32*, 951–955.

Langlois, J. H. (1986). From the eye of the beholder to behavioral reality: Development of social behaviors and social relations as a function of physical attractiveness. In C. P. Herman, M. P. Zanna, & E. T. Higgins (Eds.), *Physical appearance, stigma, and social behavior: The Ontario symposium, Vol. 3* (pp. 23–51). Hillsdale, NJ: Erlbaum.

LaPiere, R. T. (1934). Attitude and actions. *Social Forces, 13*, 230–237.

Latané, B. (Ed.). (1966). Studies in social comparison. *Journal of Experimental Social Psychology, Supplement No. 1.*

Latané, B. (1981). The psychology of social impact. *American Psychologist, 36*, 343–356.

Latané, B., & Bidwell, L. D. (1977). Sex and affiliation in college cafeterias. *Personality and Social Psychology Bulletin, 3*, 571–574.

Latané, B., & Darley, J. (1970). *The unresponsive bystander: Why doesn't he help?* New York: Appleton-Century-Crofts.

Latané, B., & Harkins, S. (1976). Cross-modality matches suggest anticipated stage fright as multiplicative function of audience size and status. *Perception and Psychophysics, 20*, 482–488.

Latané, B., & Nida, S. A. (1981). Ten years of research on group size and helping. *Psychological Bulletin, 89*, 308–324.

Latané, B., Nida, S. A., & Wilson, D. W. (1981). The effects of group size on helping behavior. In J. P. Rushton & R. M. Sorrentino (Eds.), *Altruism and helping behavior: Social, personality, and developmental perspectives.* Hillsdale, NJ: Erlbaum.

Latané, B., Williams, K., & Harkins, S. (1979). Many hands make light the work: The causes and consequences of social loafing. *Journal of Personality and Social Psychology, 37*, 822–832.

Latané, B., & Wolf, S. (1981). The social impact of majorities and minorities. *Psychological Review, 88*, 438–453.

Lau, R. R. (1982). Origins of health locus of control beliefs. *Journal of Personality and Social Psychology, 42*, 322–334.

Laughlin, P. R., & Jaccard, J. J. (1975). Social facilitation and observational learning of individuals and cooperative pairs. *Journal of Personality and Social Psychology, 32*, 873–879.

Lawler, E. J., & Thompson, M. E. (1978). Impact of leader responsibility for inequity on subordinate revolts. *Social Psychology, 41*, 264–268.

Leary, M. R., & Dobbins, S. E. (1983). Social anxiety, sexual behavior, and contraceptive use. *Journal of Personality and Social Psychology, 45*, 1347–1354.

Leary, M. R., Wheeler, D. S., & Jenkins, T. B. (1986). Aspects of identity and behavioral preference: Studies of occupational and recreational choice. *Social Psychology Quarterly, 49*, 11–18.

Leavitt, H. J. (1951). Some effects of certain communication patterns on group performance. *Journal of Abnormal and Social Psychology, 46*, 38–50.

LeBon, G. (1896). *The crowd.* London: Ernest Benn.

Lécuyer, R. (1976). Social organization and spatial organization. *Human Relations, 29*, 1045–1060.

Lee, J. A. (1973). *The colors of love: An exploration of the ways of loving.* Don Mills, Ont.: New Press.

Lerner, M. J. (1966). *The unjust consequences of the need to believe in a just world.* Paper presented at meeting of American Psychological Association, New York, September.

Lerner, M. J. (1975). The justice motive in social behavior. *Journal of Social Issues, 31*(3), 1–19.

Lerner, M. J. (1977). The justice motive: Some hypotheses as to its origins and forms. *Journal of Personality, 45*, 1–52.

Lerner, M. J., Miller, D. T., & Holmes, J. G. (1976). Deserving and the emergence of forms of justice. In L. Berkowitz & E. Walster (Eds.), *Advances in experimental social psychology* (Vol. 9). New York: Academic Press.

Lesnik-Oberstein, M., & Cohen, L. (1984). Cognitive style, sensation seeking, and assortative mating. *Journal of Personality and Social Psychology, 46*, 112–117.

Leung, K., & Bond, M. H. (1984). The impact of cultural collectivism on reward allocation. *Journal of Personality and Social Psychology, 47*, 793–804.

Leventhal, H. (1970). Findings and theory in the study of fear communications. In L. Berkowitz (Ed.), *Advances in experimental social psychology* (Vol. 5). New York: Academic Press.

Levin, H. (1970). Psychologist to the powerless. In F. F. Korten, S. W. Cook, & J. I. Lacey (Eds.), *Psychology and the problems of society*. Washington, D.C.: American Psychological Association.

Levine, D. W., O'Neal, E., Garwood, S. G., & McDonald, P. J. (1980). Classroom ecology: The effects of seating position on grades and participation. *Personality and Social Psychology Bulletin, 6*, 409–412.

Levine, R. A., & Campbell, D. T. (1972). *Theories of conflict, ethnic attitudes, and group behavior*. New York: Wiley.

Levinger, G. (1979). A social psychological perspective on marital dissolution. In G. Levinger & O. C. Moles (Eds.), *Divorce and separation*. New York: Basic Books.

Levinger, G., Senn, D. J., & Jorgensen, B. W. (1970). Progress toward permanence in courtship: A test of the Kerckhoff-Davis hypotheses. *Sociometry, 33*, 427–443.

Levinson, D. J., & Huffman, P. E. (1955). Traditional family ideology and its relation to personality. *Journal of Personality, 23*, 251–273.

Levitt, E., & Klassen, A. (1974). Public attitudes toward homosexuality: Part of the 1970 national survey by the Institute for Sex Research. *Journal of Homosexuality, 1*, 29–43.

Levy, S. G. (1969). A 150-year study of political violence in the United States. In H. D. Graham & T. R. Gurr (Eds.), *Violence in America*. New York: New American Library.

Levy, S. G. (1979). Authoritarianism and information processing. *Bulletin of the Psychonomic Society, 13*, 240–242.

Lewin, A. Y., & Duchan, L. (1971). Women in academia. *Science, 173*, 892–895.

Lewin, K. (1935). *A dynamic theory of personality*. New York: McGraw-Hill.

Lewin, K. (1936). *Principles of topological psychology*. New York: McGraw-Hill.

Lewin, K. (1938). The conceptual representation and measurement of psychological forces. *Contributions to Psychological Theory*, (Vol. I) (No. 4). Durham, NC: Duke University Press.

Lewin, K. (1948). *Resolving social conflicts*. New York: Harper.

Lewin, K. (1951). *Field theory in social science*. New York: Harper.

Leyens, J.-P., Camino, L., Parke, R. D., & Berkowitz, L. (1975). Effects of movie violence on aggression in a field setting as a function of group dominance and cohesion. *Journal of Personality and Social Psychology, 32*, 346–360.

Leyens, J.-P., Herman, G., & Dunand, M. (1982). The influence of an audience upon the reactions to filmed violence. *European Journal of Social Psychology, 12*, 131–142.

Leyhausen, P. (1965). The communal organization of solitary mammals. *Symposium of the Zoological Society of London, 14*, 249–253.

Lieberman, S. (1965). The effects of changes of roles on the attitudes of role occupants. In H. Proshansky & B. Seidenberg (Eds.), *Basic studies in social psychology*. New York: Holt, Rinehart & Winston.

Liebert, R. M., & Schwartzberg, N. S. (1977). Effects of mass media. In M. R. Rosenzweig & L. W. Porter (Eds.), *Annual review of psychology* (Vol. 28). Palo Alto, CA: Annual Reviews.

Likert, R. (1932). A technique for the measurement of attitudes. *Archives of Psychology*, No. 140.

Lind, E. A., & Ke, G. Y. (1985). Opening and closing statements. In S. M. Kassin & L. S. Wrightsman (Eds.), *The psychology of evidence and trial procedure* (pp. 229–252). Beverly Hills, CA: Sage.

Lindskold, S. (1986). GRIT: Reducing distrust through carefully introduced conciliation. In S. Worchel & W. G. Austin (Eds.), *Psychology of intergroup relations* (2nd ed.) (pp. 305–322). Chicago: Nelson-Hall.

Linville, P. W. (1982). The complexity-extremity effect and age-based stereotyping. *Journal of Personality and Social Psychology, 42*, 193–211.

Linville, P. W. (1985). Self-complexity and affective extremity: Don't put all of your eggs in one cognitive basket. *Social Cognition, 3*, 94–120.

Linville, P. W. (1987). Self-complexity as a cognitive buffer against stress-related illness and depression. *Journal of Personality and Social Psychology, 52*, 663–676.

Lipman, A. (1969). The architectural belief system and social behavior. *British Journal of Sociology, 20*, 190–204.

Lippa, R. (1976). Expressive control and the leakage of dispositional introversion-extraversion during role-played teaching. *Journal of Personality, 44*, 541–559.

Lippa, R. (1978). The effect of expressive control on expressive consistency and on the relation between expressive behavior and personality. *Journal of Personality, 46*, 438–461.

Lippmann, W. (1922). *Public opinion*. New York: Harcourt, Brace and World.

Litman-Adizes, T., Raven, B. H., & Fontaine, G. (1978). Consequences of social power and causal attribution for compliance as seen by powerholder and target. *Personality and Social Psychology Bulletin, 4*, 260–264.

Loehlin, J., Lindzey, G., & Spuhler, J. N. (1975). *Race differences in intelligence*. San Francisco: Freeman.

Loftus, E. F. (1979). *Eyewitness testimony*. Cambridge, MA: Harvard University Press.

Logan, R. W. (1957). *The Negro in the United States*. Princeton, NJ: Van Nostrand.

Loh, W. D. (1984). *Social research in the judicial process*. New York: Russell Sage Foundation.

London, P. (1970). The rescuers: Motivational hypotheses about Christians who saved Jews from the Nazis. In J. Macaulay & L. Berkowitz (Eds.), *Altruism and helping behavior: Social psychological studies of some antecedents and consequences*. New York: Academic Press.

Longley, J., & Pruitt, D. G. (1980). Groupthink: A critique of Janis's theory. In L. Wheeler (Ed.), *Review of personality and social psychology* (Vol. 1). Beverly Hills, CA: Sage.

Loo, C., & Ong, P. (1984). Crowding perceptions, attitudes, and consequences among the Chinese. *Environment and Behavior, 16*, 55–87.

Lord, C. G. (1982). Predicting behavioral consistency from an individual's perception of situational similarities. *Journal of Personality and Social Psychology, 42*, 1076–1088.

Lord, R. G., Binning, J. F., Rush, M. C., & Thomas, J. C. (1978). The effect of performance cues and leader behavior on questionnaire ratings of leadership behavior. *Organizational Behavior and Human Performance, 21*, 27–39.

Lorenz, K. (1966). *On aggression*. New York: Harcourt, Brace & World.

Lott, A. J., & Lott, B. E. (1961). Group cohesiveness, communication level, and conformity. *Journal of Abnormal and Social Psychology, 62,* 408–412.

Lott, A. J., & Lott, B. E. (1974). The role of reward in the formation of positive interpersonal attitudes. In T. L. Huston (Ed.), *Foundations of interpersonal attraction.* New York: Academic Press.

Lott, B., & Lott, A. J. (1985). Learning theory in contemporary social psychology. In G. Lindzey & E. Aronson (Eds.), *Handbook of social psychology* (Vol. 1) (3rd ed.) (pp. 109–135). New York: Random House.

Lott, D. F., & Sommer, R. (1967). Seating arrangements and status. *Journal of Personality and Social Psychology, 7,* 90–94.

Lumsdaine, A., & Janis, I. (1953). Resistance to counterpropaganda produced by a one-sided versus a two-sided propaganda presentation. *Public Opinion Quarterly, 17,* 311–318.

Lyman, S. M., & Scott, M. B. (1967). Territoriality: A neglected sociological dimension. *Social Problems, 15,* 236–249.

Maass, A., & Clark, R. D., III. (1984). Hidden impact of minorities: Fifteen years of minority influence research. *Psychological Bulletin, 95,* 428–450.

Maass, A., Clark, R. D., III, & Haberkorn, G. (1982). The effects of differential ascribed category membership and norms on minority influence. *European Journal of Social Psychology, 12,* 89–104.

Maccoby, E. E., & Jacklin, C. N. (1974). *The psychology of sex differences.* Stanford: Stanford University Press.

Mackie, D. M. (1986). Social identification effects in group polarization. *Journal of Personality and Social Psychology, 50,* 720–728.

MacPherson, J. (1984). Environments and interaction in row-and-column classrooms. *Environment and Behavior, 16,* 481–502.

Maddux, J. E., & Rogers, R. W. (1983). Protection motivation and self-efficacy: A revised theory of fear appeals and attitude change. *Journal of Experimental Social Psychology, 19,* 469–479.

Magnusson, D. (Ed.). (1981). *Toward a psychology of situations: An interactional perspective.* Hillsdale, NJ: Erlbaum.

Magnusson, D., & Endler, N. S. (Eds.). (1977). *Personality at the crossroads: Current issues in interactional psychology.* Hillsdale, NJ: Erlbaum.

Main, M., & George, C. (1985). Responses of abused and disadvantaged toddlers to distress in agemates: A study in the day care setting. *Developmental Psychology, 21,* 407–412.

Major, B. (1980). Information acquisition and attribution processes. *Journal of Personality and Social Psychology, 39,* 1010–1023.

Major, B. (1981). Gender patterns in touching behavior. In C. Mayo & N. M. Henley (Eds.), *Gender and nonverbal behavior.* New York: Springer-Verlag.

Major, B., & Heslin, R. (1982). Perceptions of same-sex and cross-sex reciprocal touch: It's better to give than to receive. *Journal of Nonverbal Behavior, 3,* 148–163.

Malamuth, N. M. (1981a). Rape fantasies as a function of exposure to violent sexual stimuli. *Archives of Sexual Behavior, 10,* 33–47.

Malamuth, N. M. (1981b). Rape proclivity among males. *Journal of Social Issues, 37*(4), 138–157.

Malamuth, N. M., & Check, J. V. P. (1981). The effects of mass media exposure on acceptance of violence against women: A field experiment. *Journal of Research in Personality, 15,* 436–446.

Malamuth, N. M., & Donnerstein, E. (1982). The effects of aggressive-pornographic mass media stimuli. In L. Berkowitz (Ed.), *Advances in experimental social psychology* (Vol. 15). New York: Academic Press.

Mander, A. M., & Gaebelein, J. W. (1977). Third party instigation of aggression as a function of noncooperation and veto power. *Journal of Research in Personality, 11,* 475–486.

Mann, J., Sidman, J., & Starr, S. (1973). Evaluating social consequences of erotic films: An experimental approach. *Journal of Social Issues, 29*(3), 113–131.

Mann, L. (1980). Cross-cultural studies of small groups. In H. C. Triandis & R. W. Brislin (Eds.), *Handbook of cross-cultural psychology* (Vol. 5). *Social psychology.* Boston: Allyn & Bacon.

Mann, L. (1981). The baiting crowd in episodes of threatened suicide. *Journal of Personality and Social Psychology, 41,* 703–709.

Mann, L., Newton, J. W., & Innes, J. M. (1982). A test between deindividuation and emergent norm theories of crowd aggression. *Journal of Personality and Social Psychology, 42,* 260–272.

Mann, L., Radford, M., & Kanagawa, C. (1985). Cross-cultural differences in children's use of decision rules: A comparison between Japan and Australia. *Journal of Personality and Social Psychology, 49,* 1557–1564.

Mann, R. D. (1959). A review of the relationship between personality and performance in small groups. *Psychological Bulletin, 56,* 241–270.

Manucia, G. K., Baumann, D. J., & Cialdini, R. B. (1984). Mood influences on helping: Direct effects or side effects? *Journal of Personality and Social Psychology, 46,* 357–364.

Margulis, S. T. (1977). Conceptions of privacy: Current status and next steps. *Journal of Social Issues, 33*(3), 5–21.

Markus, H. (1977). Self-schemata and processing information about the self. *Journal of Personality and Social Psychology, 35,* 63–78.

Markus, H., Crane, M., Bernstein, S., & Siladi, M. (1982). Self-schemas and gender. *Journal of Personality and Social Psychology, 42,* 38–50.

Markus, H., & Nurius, P. (1986). Possible selves. *American Psychologist, 41,* 954–969.

Markus, H., Smith, J., & Moreland, R. L. (1985). Role of the self-concept in the perception of others. *Journal of Personality and Social Psychology, 49,* 1494–1512.

Markus, H., & Zajonc, R. B. (1985). The cognitive perspective in social psychology. In G. Lindzey & E. Aronson (Eds.), *Handbook of social psychology* (Vol. 1) (3rd ed.) (pp. 137–230). New York: Random House.

Martin, G. B., & Clark, R. D., III. (1982). Distress crying in neonates: Species and peer specificity. *Developmental Psychology, 18,* 3–9.

Martin, J. (1980). Relative deprivation: A theory of distributive injustice for an era of shrinking resources. In *Research in organizational behavior* (Vol. 3). Greenwich, CN: JAI Press.

Martin, J., & Westie, F. (1959). The tolerant personality. *American Sociological Review, 24,* 521–528.

Martindale, D. A. (1971). Territorial dominance behavior in dyadic verbal interactions. *Proceedings, 79th Annual Convention, American Psychological Association, 6,* 305–306.

Maslow, A. H., & Mintz, N. L. (1956). Effects of esthetic surroundings: I. Initial effects of three esthetic conditions upon perceiving "energy" and "well-being" in faces. *Journal of Psychology, 41,* 247–254.

Massengill, D., & DiMarco, N. (1979). Sex-role stereotypes and requisite management characteristics: A current replication. *Sex Roles, 5,* 561–570.

Masters, W. H., & Johnson, V. E. (1966). *Human sexual response.* Boston: Little, Brown.

Masters, W. H., & Johnson, V. E. (1979). *Homosexuality in perspective*. Boston: Little, Brown.

Mathews, K. E., Jr., & Canon, L. K. (1975). Environmental noise level as a determinant of helping behavior. *Journal of Personality and Social Psychology, 32*, 571–577.

Matthews, K. A. (1982). Psychological perspectives on the Type A behavior pattern. *Psychological Bulletin, 91*, 293–323.

Matthews, K. A., Batson, C. D., Horn, J., & Rosenman, R. H. (1981). "Principles in his nature which interest him in the fortune of others ...": The heritability of empathic concern for others. *Journal of Personality, 49*, 237–247.

Mayer, F. S., Duval, S., Holtz, R., & Bowman, C. (1985). Self-focus, helping request salience, felt responsibility, and helping behavior. *Personality and Social Psychology Bulletin, 11*, 133–144.

Maynard, D. W., & Zimmerman, D. H. (1984). Topical talk, ritual and the social organization of relationships. *Social Psychology Quarterly, 47*, 301–316.

Mayo, J. M. (1979). Effects of street forms on suburban neighboring behavior. *Environment and Behavior, 11*, 375–397.

McAdams, D. P., Healy, S., & Krause, S. (1984). Social motives and patterns of friendship. *Journal of Personality and Social Psychology, 47*, 828–838.

McAlister, A. L., Krosnick, J. A., & Milburn, M. A. (1984). Causes of adolescent cigarette smoking: Tests of a structural equation model. *Social Psychology Quarterly, 47*, 24–36.

McArthur, L. A. (1972). The how and what of why: Some determinants of consequences of causal attribution. *Journal of Personality and Social Psychology, 22*, 171–193.

McArthur, L. Z. (1982). Judging a book by its cover: A cognitive analysis of the relationship between physical appearance and stereotyping. In A. H. Hastorf & A. M. Isen (Eds.), *Cognitive social psychology* (pp. 149–211). New York: Elsevier/North Holland.

McArthur, L. Z., & Apatow, K. (1983/1984). Impressions of baby-faced adults. *Social Cognition, 2*, 315–342.

McArthur, L. Z., & Baron, R. M. (1983). Toward an ecological theory of social perception. *Psychological Review, 90*, 215–238.

McCallum, R. C., Rusbult, C., Hong, C., Walden, T., & Schopler, J. (1979). The effects of resource availability and importance of behavior upon the experience of crowding. *Journal of Personality and Social Psychology, 37*, 1304–1313.

McCarthy, D., & Saegert, S. (1979). Residential density, social overload, and social withdrawal. *Human Ecology, 6*, 253–272.

McCarty, D., Diamond, W., & Kaye, M. (1982). Alcohol, sexual arousal, and the transfer of excitation. *Journal of Personality and Social Psychology, 42*, 977–988.

McCauley, C., Coleman, G., & DeFusco, P. (1978). Commuters' eye contact with strangers in city and suburban train stations: Evidence of short-term adaptation in interpersonal overload in the city. *Environmental Psychology and Nonverbal Behavior, 2*, 215–225.

McCauley, C., Durham, M., Copley, J. B., & Johnson, J. P. (1985). Patients' perceptions of treatment for kidney failure: The impact of personal experience on population predictions. *Journal of Experimental Social Psychology, 21*, 138–148.

McCauley, C., & Newman, J. (1977). Eye contact with strangers in city, suburb, and small town. *Environment and Behavior, 9*, 547.

McCauley, C., & Stitt, C. L. (1978). An individual and quantitative measure of stereotypes. *Journal of Personality and Social Psychology, 36*, 929–940.

McCauley, C., & Swann, C. P. (1978). Male-female differences in sexual fantasy. *Journal of Research in Personality, 12*, 76–86.

McCauley, C., & Taylor, J. (1976). Is there overload of acquaintances in the city? *Environmental Psychology and Nonverbal Behavior, 1*, 41–55.

McClelland, D. C., & Boyatzis, R. E. (1982). Leadership motive pattern and long-term success in management. *Journal of Applied Psychology, 67*, 737–743.

McClelland, L., & Canter, R. J. (1978). Psychological research on energy conservation: Context, approaches, methods. In J. Singer, S. Valins, & A. Baum (Eds.), *Advances in environmental psychology*. Hillsdale, NJ: Erlbaum.

McClelland, L., & Cook, S. W. (1980). Promoting energy conservation in master-metered apartments through group financial incentives. *Journal of Applied Social Psychology, 10*, 19–31.

McClintock, C. G. (1958). Personality syndromes and attitude change. *Journal of Personality, 26*, 479–493.

McCloskey, M., Egeth, H., & McKenna, J. (1986). The experimental psychologist in court: The ethics of expert testimony. *Law and Human Behavior, 10*, 1–14.

McCorkle, L. W., & Korn, R.R. (1954). Resocialization within walls. *Academy of Political and Social Science, 293*, 88–98.

McDonaugh, G. R. (1986). *An investigation of the effects of moral judgment level and leadership style on effective decision making*. Unpublished Master's thesis, Purdue University.

McGhee, P. E., & Teevan, R. C. (1967). Conformity behavior and need for affiliation. *Journal of Social Psychology, 72*, 117–121.

McGinniss, J. (1970). *The selling of the President, 1968*. New York: Pocket Books.

McGrath, J. E. (1984). *Groups: Interaction and performance*. Englewood Cliffs, NJ: Prentice-Hall.

McGrath, J. E., & Kelly, J. R. (1986). *Time and human interaction*. New York: Guilford Press.

McGrath, J. E., Martin, J., & Kulka, R. A. (1982). *Judgment calls in research*. Beverly Hills: Sage.

McGuire, W. J. (1964). Inducing resistance to persuasion. In L. Berkowitz (Ed.), *Advances in experimental social psychology*, (Vol. 1). New York: Academic Press.

McGuire, W. J. (1968a). Personality and attitude change: A theoretical housing. In A. G. Greenwald, T. C. Brock, & T. M. Ostrom (Eds.), *Psychological foundations of attitudes*. New York: Academic Press.

McGuire, W. J. (1968b). Personality and susceptibility to social influence. In E. F. Borgatta & W. W. Lambert (Eds.), *Handbook of personality theory and research*. Chicago: Rand McNally.

McGuire, W. J. (1973). The yin and yang of progress in social psychology: Seven koan. *Journal of Personality and Social Psychology, 26*, 446–456.

McGuire, W. J. (1984). Perspectivism: A look back at the future. *Contemporary Social Psychology, 10*, 19–39.

McGuire, W. J. (1985). Attitudes and attitude change. In G. Lindzey & E. Aronson (Eds.), *Handbook of social psychology* (Vol. 2) (3rd ed.). New York: Random House.

McGuire, W. J., & McGuire, C. V. (1981). The spontaneous self-concept as affected by personal distinctiveness. In M. D. Lynch, A. A. Norem-Hebeisen, & K. J. Gergen (Eds.), *Self-concept: Advances in theory and research*. Cambridge, MA: Ballinger.

McGuire, W. J., & Millman, S. (1965). Anticipatory belief lowering following forewarning of a persuasive attack. *Journal of Personality and Social Psychology, 2*, 471–479.

McGuire, W. J., & Padawer-Singer, A. (1976). Trait salience in the spontaneous self-concept. *Journal of Personality and Social Psychology, 33*, 743–754.

McGuire, W. J., & Papageorgis, D. (1962). Effectiveness of forewarning in developing resistance to persuasion. *Public Opinion Quarterly, 26*, 24–34.

McKirnan, D. J., Smith, C. E., & Hamayan, E. V. (1983). A sociolinguistic approach to the belief-similarity model of racial attitudes. *Journal of Experimental Social Psychology, 19*, 434–447.

McMillen, D. L., Sanders, D. Y., & Solomon, G. S. (1977). Self-esteem, attentiveness, and helping behavior. *Personality and Social Psychology Bulletin, 3*, 257–261.

McNemar, Q. (1942). *The revision of the Stanford-Binet scale: An analysis of the standardization data*. Boston: Houghton Mifflin.

Mead, G. H. (1934). *Mind, self, and society*. (C. W. Morris, Ed.) Chicago: University of Chicago Press.

Mehlman, R. C., & Snyder, C. R. (1985). Excuse theory: A test of the self-protective role of attributions. *Journal of Personality and Social Psychology, 49*, 994–1001.

Mehrabian, A. (1969a). Some referents and measures of nonverbal behavior. *Behavioral Research Methods and Instrumentation, 1*, 203–207.

Mehrabian, A. (1969b). Significance of posture and position in the communication of attitude and status relationships. *Psychological Bulletin, 71*, 359–372.

Mehrabian, A. (1972). *Nonverbal communication*. Chicago: Aldine-Atherton.

Mehrabian, A., & Diamond, S. (1971a). Effects of furniture arrangement, props, and personality on social interaction. *Journal of Personality and Social Psychology, 20*, 18–30.

Mehrabian, A., & Diamond, S. (1971b). Seating arrangement and conversation. *Sociometry, 34*, 281–289.

Mehrabian, A., & Weiner, M. (1967). Decoding of inconsistent communications. *Journal of Personality and Social Psychology, 6*, 109–114.

Meindl, J. R., & Lerner, M. J. (1984). Exacerbation of extreme responses to an out-group. *Journal of Personality and Social Psychology, 47*, 71–84.

Meyer, W.-U., & Starke, E. (1982). Own ability in relation to self-concept of ability: A field study of information-seeking. *Personality and Social Psychology Bulletin, 8*, 501–507.

Michaels, J. W., Blommel, J. M., Brocato, R. M., Linkous, R. A., & Rowe, J. S. (1982). Social facilitation and inhibition in a natural setting. *Replications in Social Psychology, 2*, 21–24.

Michelson, W. (1970). *Man and his urban environment: A sociological approach*. Reading, MA: Addison-Wesley.

Michener, H. A., & Lawler, E. J. (1975). The endorsement of formal leaders: An integrative model. *Journal of Personality and Social Psychology, 31*, 216–223.

Midlarsky, E. (1984). Competence and helping: Notes toward a model. In E. Staub, D. Bar-Tal, J. Karylowski, & J. Reykowski (Eds.), *The development and maintenance of prosocial behavior: International perspectives*. New York: Plenum.

Midlarsky, E., & Hannah, M. E. (1985). Competence, reticence, and helping by children and adolescents. *Developmental Psychology, 21*, 534–541.

Milgram, S. (1963). Behavioral study of obedience. *Journal of Abnormal and Social Psychology, 67*, 371–378.

Milgram, S. (1965). Some conditions of obedience and disobedience to authority. *Human Relations, 18*, 57–76.

Milgram, S. (1970). The experience of living in cities. *Science, 167*, 1461–1468.

Milgram, S. (1974). *Obedience to authority*. New York: Harper & Row.

Milgram, S. (1978). The experience of living in cities. *Science, 167*, 1461–1468.

Milgram, S., Mann, L., & Harter, S. (1965). The lost-letter technique of social research. *Public Opinion Quarterly, 29*, 437–438.

Millar, M. G., & Tesser, A. (1986). Effects of affective and cognitive focus on the attitude-behavior relation. *Journal of Personality and Social Psychology, 51*, 270–276.

Miller, A. G. (1972). Role playing: An alternative to deception? A review of the evidence. *American Psychologist, 27*, 623–636.

Miller, A. G. (1986). *The obedience experiments: A case study of controversy in social science*. New York: Praeger.

Miller, C., & Crandall, R. (1980). Bargaining and negotiation. In P. B. Paulus (Ed.), *Psychology of group influence*. Hillsdale, NJ: Erlbaum.

Miller, C. T. (1984). Self-schemas, gender, and social comparison: A clarification of the related attributes hypothesis. *Journal of Personality and Social Psychology, 46*, 1222–1229.

Miller, D. T., Norman, S. A., & Wright, E. (1978). Distortion in person perception as a consequence of the need for effective control. *Journal of Personality and Social Psychology, 36*, 598–607.

Miller, D. T., & Turnbull, W. (1986). Expectancies and interpersonal processes. *Annual Review of Psychology, 37*, 233–256.

Miller, G. A. (1969). Psychology as a means of promoting human welfare. *American Psychologist, 24*, 1063–1075. (Reprinted in F. F. Korten, S. W. Cook, & J. I. Lacey [Eds.] (1970). *Psychology and the problems of society*. Washington, D.C.: American Psychological Association.)

Miller, J. G. (1964). Adjusting to overloads of information. In R. Waggoner & D. Carek (Eds.), *Disorders of Communication* (Vol. 42) (pp. 87–100). Baltimore: Williams & Wilkins.

Miller, J. G. (1984). Culture and the development of everyday social explanation. *Journal of Personality and Social Psychology, 46*, 961–978.

Miller, L. E., & Grush, J. E. (1986). Individual differences in attitudinal versus normative determination of behavior. *Journal of Experimental Social Psychology, 22*, 190–202.

Miller, N. (1965). Involvement and dogmatism as inhibitors of attitude change. *Journal of Experimental Social Psychology, 1*, 121–132.

Miller, N., & Brewer, M. B. (Eds.). (1984). *Groups in contact: The psychology of desegregation*. Orlando, FL: Academic Press.

Miller, N. E. (1941). The frustration-aggression hypothesis. *Psychological Review, 48*, 337–342.

Miller, N. E., & Dollard, J. (1941). *Social learning and imitation*. New Haven: Yale University Press.

Mills, J., & Clark, M. S. (1982). Exchange and communal relationships. In L. Wheeler (Ed.), *Review of personality and social psychology* (Vol. 3). Beverly Hills, CA: Sage.

Mills, R. T., & Krantz, D. S. (1979). Information, choice, and reactions to stress: A field experiment in a blood bank with laboratory analogue. *Journal of Personality and Social Psychology, 37*, 608–620.

Mintz, N. L. (1956). Effects of esthetic surroundings: II. Prolonged and repeated experience in a "beautiful" and an "ugly" room. *Journal of Psychology, 41*, 459–466.

Mirels, H. L. (1970). Dimensions of internal versus external control. *Journal of Consulting and Clinical Psychology, 34*, 226–228.

Mischel, W. (1968). *Personality and assessment.* New York: Wiley.

Mischel, W. (1977). On the future of personality measurement. *American Psychologist, 32*, 246–254.

Mischel, W., & Peake, P. K. (1982). Beyond déja vu in the search for cross-situational consistency. *Psychological Review, 89*, 730–755.

Mita, T. H., Dermer, M., & Knight, J. (1977). Reversed facial images and the mere-exposure hypothesis. *Journal of Personality and Social Psychology, 35*, 597–601.

Moe, J. L., Nacoste, R. W., & Insko, C. A. (1981). Belief versus race as determinants of discrimination: A study of Southern adolescents in 1966 and 1979. *Journal of Personality and Social Psychology, 41*, 1031–1050.

Monahan, J., & Loftus, E. F. (1982). The psychology of law. In M. R. Rosenzweig & L. W. Porter (Eds.), *Annual review of psychology* (Vol. 33). Palo Alto, CA: Annual Reviews.

Money, J., & Athanasiou, R. (1973). Pornography: Review and bibliographic annotations. *American Journal of Obstetrics and Gynecology, 115*, 130–146.

Money, J., & Ehrhardt, A. A. (1977). *Man and woman; boy and girl.* Baltimore: Johns Hopkins Press.

Money, J., & Tucker, P. (1975). *Sexual signatures: On being a man or a woman.* Boston: Little, Brown.

Monson, T. C., Hesley, J. W., & Chernick, L. (1982). Specifying when personality traits can and cannot predict behavior: An alternative to abandoning the attempt to predict single act criteria. *Journal of Personality and Social Psychology, 43*, 385–399.

Montagu, A. (1976). *The nature of human aggression.* New York: Oxford University Press.

Montano, D., & Adamopoulos, J. (1984). The perception of crowding in interpersonal situations: Affective and behavioral responses. *Environment and Behavior, 16*, 643–666.

Moreland, R. L., & Levine, J. M. (1982). Socialization in small groups: Temporal changes in individual-group relations. In L. Berkowitz (Ed.), *Advances in experimental social psychology* (Vol. 15). New York: Academic Press.

Moreland, R. L., & Zajonc, R. B. (1982). Exposure effects in person perception: Familiarity, similarity, and attraction. *Journal of Experimental Social Psychology, 18*, 395–415.

Morgan, C. J. (1985). Natural selection for altruism in structured populations. *Ethology and Sociobiology, 6*, 211–218.

Morgan, M. (1982). Television and adolescents' sex role stereotypes: A longitudinal study. *Journal of Personality and Social Psychology, 43*, 947–955.

Moriarty, T. (1975). Crime, commitment and the responsive bystander: Two field experiments. *Journal of Personality and Social Psychology, 31*, 370–376.

Morris, J. (1974). *Conundrum.* New York: Harcourt Brace Jovanovich.

Morrison, D. M. (1985). Adolescent contraceptive behavior: A review. *Psychological Bulletin, 98*, 538–568.

Morrow, P. C., & McElroy, J. C. (1981). Interior office design and visitor response: A constructive replication. *Journal of Applied Psychology, 66*, 646–650.

Morton, T. L. (1978). Intimacy and reciprocity of exchange: A comparison of spouses and strangers. *Journal of Personality and Social Psychology, 36*, 72–81.

Moscovici, S. (1972). Society and theory in social psychology. In J. Israel & H. Tajfel (Eds.), *The context of social psychology: A critical assessment.* New York: Academic Press.

Moscovici, S. (1976). *Social influence and social change.* New York: Academic Press.

Moscovici, S. (1985). Social influence and conformity. In G. Lindzey & E. Aronson (Eds.). *Handbook of social psychology* (Vol. II) (3rd ed.) (pp. 347–412). New York: Random House.

Mosher, D. L. (1973). Sex differences, sex experience, sex guilt, and explicitly sexual films. *Journal of Social Issues, 29*(3), 95–112.

Moss, M. K., & Page, R. A. (1972). Reinforcment and helping behavior. *Journal of Applied Social Psychology, 2*, 360–371.

Mowen, J. C., & Cialdini, R. B. (1980). On implementing the door-in-the-face compliance technique in a business context. *Journal of Marketing Research, 17*, 253–258.

Mueller, C. W., & Donnerstein, E. (1981). Film-facilitated arousal and prosocial behavior. *Journal of Experimental Social Psychology, 17*, 31–41.

Mueller, J. H. (1982). Self-awareness and access to material rated as self-descriptive or nondescriptive. *Bulletin of the Psychonomic Society, 19*, 323–326.

Mugny, G. (1975). Negotiations, image of the other and the process of minority influence. *European Journal of Social Psychology, 5*, 209–229.

Mugny, G. (1982). *The power of minorities.* London: Academic Press.

Mullen, B. (1985). Strength and immediacy of sources: A meta-analytic evaluation of the forgotten elements of social impact theory. *Journal of Personality and Social Psychology, 48*, 1458–1466.

Mullen, B., Atkins, J. L., Champion, D. S., Edwards, C., Hardy, D., Story, J. E., & Vanderklok, M. (1985). The false consensus effect: A meta-analysis of 115 hypothesis tests. *Journal of Experimental Social Psychology, 21*, 262–283.

Mullen, B., Futrell, D., Stairs, D., Tice, D. M., Baumeister, R. F., Dawson, K. E., Riordan, C. A., Radloff, C. E., Goethals, G. R., Kennedy, J. G., & Rosenfeld, P. (1986). Newscasters' facial expressions and voting behavior of viewers: Can a smile elect a President? *Journal of Personality and Social Psychology, 51*, 291–295.

Mullen, B., & Suls, J. (1982). "Know thyself": Stressful life changes and the ameliorative effect of private self-consciousness. *Journal of Experimental Social Psychology, 18*, 43–55.

Murray, H. A. (1938). *Explorations in personality.* New York: Oxford University Press.

Murray, J., & Feshbach, S. (1978). Let's not throw the baby out with the bathwater: The catharsis hypothesis revisited. *Journal of Personality, 46*, 462–473.

Myers, D. G., & Bishop, G. D. (1970). Discussion effects on racial attitudes. *Science, 169*, 778–789.

Myers, D. G., & Bishop, G. D. (1971). Enhancement of dominant attitudes in group discussion. *Journal of Personality and Social Psychology, 20*, 386–391.

Myers, D. G., & Kaplan, M. F. (1976). Group-induced polarization in simulated juries. *Personality and Social Psychology Bulletin, 2*, 63–66.

Myers, D. G., & Lamm, H. (1976). The group polarization phenomenon. *Psychological Bulletin, 83*, 602–627.

Myerscough, R., & Taylor, S. (1985). The effects of marijuana on human physical aggression. *Journal of Personality and Social Psychology, 49,* 1541–1546.

Nadler, A., Altman, A., & Fisher, J. D. (1979). Helping is not enough: Recipient's reactions to aid as a function of positive and negative information about self. *Journal of Personality, 47,* 615–628.

Nadler, A., Fisher, J. D., & Ben-Itzhak, S. (1983). With a little help from my friend: Reaction to receiving prolonged vs. one-act help from a friend or stranger, as a function of centrality. *Journal of Personality and Social Psychology, 44,* 310–321.

Nadler, A., & Mayseless, O. (1983). Recipient self-esteem and reactions to help. In J. D. Fisher, A. Nadler, & B. M. DePaulo (Eds.), *New directions in helping* (Vol. 1). *Recipient reactions to aid.* New York: Academic Press.

Nadler, A., Mayseless, O., Peri, N., & Chemerinski, A. (1985). Effects of opportunity to reciprocate and self-esteem on help-seeking behavior. *Journal of Personality, 53,* 23–35.

Nahemow, L., & Lawton, M. P. (1975). Similarity and propinquity in friendship formation. *Journal of Personality and Social Psychology, 33,* 205–213.

Nemecek, J., & Grandjean, E. (1973). Results of an ergonomic investigation of large-space offices. *Human Factors, 15,* 111–224.

Nemeth, C. (1979). The role of an active minority in intergroup relations. In W. G. Austin & S. Worchel (Eds.), *The social psychology of intergroup relations.* Pacific Grove, CA: Brooks/Cole.

Nemeth, C. J. (1986). Differential contributions of majority and minority influence. *Psychological Review, 93,* 23–32.

Nemeth, C. J., & Wachtler, J. (1983). Creative problem solving as a result of majority vs. minority influence. *European Journal of Social Psychology, 13,* 45–55.

Newcomb, M. D. (1986). Nuclear attitudes and reactions: Associations with depression, drug use, and quality of life. *Journal of Personality and Social Psychology, 50,* 906–920.

Newcomb, M. D., & Bentler, P. M. (1981). Marital breakdown. In S. Duck & R. Gilmour (Eds.), *Personal relationships 3: Personal relationships in disorder.* New York: Academic Press.

Newcomb, T. M. (1961). *The acquaintance process.* New York: Holt, Rinehart & Winston.

Newman, O. (1972). *Defensible space: Crime prevention through urban design.* New York: Macmillan.

Newtson, D. (1974). Dispositional inference from effects of actions: Effects chosen and effects foregone. *Journal of Experimental Psychology, 10,* 489–496.

Nisbett, R. E., Krantz, D. H., Jepson, C., & Kunda, Z. (1983). The use of statistical heuristics in everyday inductive reasoning. *Psychological Review, 90,* 339–363.

Nisbett, R. E., & Kunda, Z. (1985). Perception of social distributions. *Journal of Personality and Social Psychology, 48,* 297–311.

Nizer, L. (1973). *The implosion conspiracy.* New York: Doubleday.

Noller, P. (1984). *Nonverbal communication and marital interaction.* Oxford, England: Pergamon.

Normoyle, J., & Lavrakas, P. J. (1984). Fear of crime in elderly women: Perceptions of control, predictability, and territoriality. *Personality and Social Psychology Bulletin, 10,* 191–202.

Norvell, N., & Worchel, S. (1981). A reexamination of the relation between equal status contact and intergroup attraction. *Journal of Personality and Social Psychology, 41,* 902–908.

Novak, D., & Lerner, M. J. (1968). Rejection as a consequence of perceived similarity. *Journal of Personality and Social Psychology, 9,* 147–152.

Nutt, R. L., & Sedlacek, W. E. (1974). Freshman sexual attitudes and behavior. *Journal of College Student Personnel, 15,* 346–351.

Oborne, D. J. (1983). Cognitive effects of passive smoking. *Ergonomics, 26,* 1163–1171.

Odino, J. (1986). African nations struggle to make television their own. *New York Times,* December 28.

Ohbuchi, K., & Kambara, T. (1985). Attacker's intent and awareness of outcome, impression management, and retaliation. *Journal of Experimental Social Psychology, 21,* 321–330.

Olweus, D. (1979). Stability of aggressive reaction patterns in males: A review. *Psychological Bulletin, 86,* 852–875.

Olweus, D. (1984a). *Bullying and harassment among school children in Scandinavia: Research and a nationwide campaign in Norway.* Unpublished manuscript.

Olweus, D. (1984b). Development of stable aggressive reaction patterns in males. In R. Blanchard & C. Blanchard (Eds.), *Advances in aggression research* (Vol. 1) (pp. 103–137). New York: Academic Press.

Orne, M. T. (1969). Demand characteristics and the concept of quasi-controls. In R. Rosenthal & R. Rosnow (Eds.), *Artifact in behavior research.* New York: Academic Press.

Orne, M. T., & Holland, C. C. (1968). On the ecological validity of laboratory deceptions. *International Journal of Psychiatry, 6,* 282–293.

Ortega, D. F., & Pipal, J. E. (1984). Challenge seeking and the Type A coronary-prone behavior pattern. *Journal of Personality and Social Psychology, 46,* 1328–1334.

Orvis, B. R., Cunningham, J. D., & Kelley, H. H. (1957). A closer examination of causal inference: The role of consensus, distinctiveness, and consistency information. *Journal of Personality and Social Psychology, 29,* 426–434.

Osborn, A. F. (1957). *Applied imagination.* New York: Scribner.

Osgood, C. E. (1966). *Perspective in foreign policy.* Palo Alto, CA: Pacific Books.

Osgood, C. E. (1974). *GRIT for MBFR: A proposal for unfreezing force-level postures in Europe.* Unpublished manuscript, University of Illinois.

Osgood, C. E., Suci, G. J., & Tannenbaum, P. H. (1957). *The measurement of meaning.* Urbana: University of Illinois Press.

Oskamp, S. (1977). *Attitudes and opinions.* Englewood Cliffs, NJ: Prentice-Hall.

Osmond, H. (1957). Function as the basis of psychiatric ward design. *Mental Hospitals, 8,* 23–30.

O'Sullivan, M., Ekman, P., Friesen, W., & Scherer, K. (1985). What you say and how you say it: The contribution of speech content and voice quality to judgments of others. *Journal of Personality and Social Psychology, 48,* 54–62.

Ovcharchyn-Devitt, C., Calby, P., Carswell, L., Perkowitz, W., Scruggs, B., Turpin, R., & Bickman, L. (1981). Approaches towards social problems: A conceptual model. *Basic and Applied Social Psychology, 2,* 275–287.

Owens, D. J., & Straus, M. A. (1975). The social structure of violence in childhood and approval of violence as an adult. *Aggressive Behavior, 1,* 193–211.

Pagano, M., & Kirschner, N. M. (1978). Sex guilt, sexual arousal, and urinary acid phosphatase output. *Journal of Research in Personality, 12,* 68–75.

Page, R. (1977). Noise and helping behavior. *Environment and Behavior, 9,* 311–334.

Palamarek, D. L., & Rule, B. G. (1979). The effects of ambient temperature and insult on the motivation to retaliate or escape. *Motivation and Emotion, 3*, 83-92.

Pallak, M. S., & Cummings, W. (1976). Commitment and voluntary energy conservation. *Personality and Social Psychology Bulletin, 2*, 27-30.

Park, B., & Rothbart, M. (1982). Perception of out-group homogeneity and levels of social categorization: Memory for the subordinate attributes of in-group and out-group members. *Journal of Personality and Social Psychology, 42*, 1051-1068.

Parke, R. D., Berkowitz, L., Leyens, J.-P., West, S. G., & Sebastian, R. J. (1977). Some effects of violent and nonviolent movies on the behavior of juvenile delinquents. In L. Berkowitz (Ed.), *Advances in experimental social psychology* (Vol. 10). New York: Academic Press.

Parnes, S. J., & Meadow, A. (1959). Effects of "brainstorming" instructions on creative problem solving by trained and untrained subjects. *Journal of Educational Psychology, 50*, 171-176.

Patchen, M. (1982). *Black-white contact in schools.* West Lafayette, IN: Purdue University Press.

Patterson, A. H. (1978). Territorial behavior and fear of crime in the elderly. *Environmental Psychology and Nonverbal Behavior, 2*, 131-144.

Patterson, M. L. (1976). An arousal model of interpersonal intimacy. *Psychological Review, 83*, 235-245.

Patterson, M. L. (1982). A sequential function model of verbal exchange. *Psychological Review, 89*, 231-249.

Patterson, M. L. (1983). *Nonverbal behavior: A functional perspective.* New York: Springer-Verlag.

Patterson, M. L., Mullens, S., & Romano, J. (1971). Compensatory reactions to spatial intrusion. *Sociometry, 34*, 114-121.

Patterson, M. L., Roth, C. P., & Schenk, C. (1979). Seating arrangement, activity and sex differences in small group crowding. *Personality and Social Psychology Bulletin, 5*, 100-103.

Patzer, G. L. (1985). *The physical attractiveness phenomena.* New York: Plenum.

Paulhus, D. L., Shaffer, D. R., & Downing, L. L. (1977). Effects of making blood donor motives salient upon donor retention: A field experiment. *Personality and Social Psychology Bulletin, 3*, 99-102.

Paulus, P. B. (1980). Crowding. In P. B. Paulus (Ed.), *Psychology of group influence.* Hillsdale, NJ: Erlbaum.

Paulus, P. B., Annis, A. B., Seta, J., Schkade, J., & Matthews, R. B. (1976). Density does affect task performance. *Journal of Personality and Social Psychology, 34*, 248-253.

Paulus, P. B., Cox, V., McCain, G., & Chandler, J. (1975). Some effects of crowding in a prison environment. *Journal of Applied Social Psychology, 5*, 86-91.

Paulus, P. B., & Matthews, R. W. (1980). When density affects task performance. *Personality and Social Psychology Bulletin, 6*, 119-124.

Paulus, P., McCain, G., & Cox, V. (1978). Death rates, psychiatric commitments, blood pressure, and perceived crowding as a function of institutional crowding. *Environmental Psychology and Nonverbal Behavior, 3*, 107-116.

Pavelchak, M. A., Moreland, R. L., & Levine, J. M. (1986). Effects of prior group memberships on subsequent reconnaissance activities. *Journal of Personality and Social Psychology, 50*, 56-66.

Pearce, P. L. (1980). Strangers, travelers, and Greyhound terminals: A study of small-scale helping behaviors. *Journal of Personality and Social Psychology, 38*, 935-940.

Pelligrini, R. J. (1971). Some effects of seating position on social perception. *Psychological Reports, 28*, 887-893.

Pennebaker, J. W. (1982). *The psychology of physical symptoms.* New York: Springer-Verlag.

Penrod, S., Loftus, E., & Winkler, J. (1982). The reliability of eyewitness testimony: A psychological perspective. In N. L. Kerr & R. M. Bray (Eds.), *The psychology of the courtroom* (pp. 119-168). New York: Academic Press.

Pepitone, A. (1981). Lessons from the history of social psychology. *American Psychologist, 36*, 972-985.

Peplau, L. A., Miceli, M., & Morasch, B. (1982). Loneliness and self-evaluation. In L. A. Peplau & D. Perlman (Eds.), *Loneliness: A sourcebook of current theory, research and therapy.* New York: Wiley.

Peplau, L. A., & Perlman, D. (Eds.). (1982). *Loneliness: A sourcebook of current theory, research and therapy.* New York: Wiley.

Peplau, L. A., Rubin, Z., & Hill, C. T. (1977). Sexual intimacy in dating relationships. *Journal of Social Issues, 33*(2), 86-109.

Perlman, D. (1973). The sexual standards of Canadian university students. In D. Koulack & D. Perlman (Eds.), *Readings in social psychology: Focus on Canada.* Toronto: Wiley.

Perlman, S. D., & Abramson, P. R. (1982). Sexual satisfaction among married and cohabiting individuals. *Journal of Consulting and Clinical Psychology, 50*, 458-460.

Pervin, L. A. (1985). Personality: Current controversies, issues, and directions. *Annual Review of Psychology, 36*, 83-114.

Peters, L. H., Hartke, D. D., & Pohlmann, J. T. (1985). Fiedler's contingency theory of leadership: An application of the meta-analysis procedures of Schmidt and Hunter. *Psychological Bulletin, 97*, 274-285.

Peterson, C., & Seligman, M. E. P. (1984). Causal explanations as a risk factor for depression: Theory and evidence. *Psychological Review, 91*, 347-374.

Peterson, P. D., & Koulack, D. (1969). Attitude change as a function of latitudes of acceptance and rejection. *Journal of Personality and Social Psychology, 11*, 309-311.

Pettigrew, T. F. (1964). *A profile of the Negro American.* Princeton, NJ: Van Nostrand.

Pettigrew, T. F. (1979). The ultimate attribution error: Extending Allport's cognitive analysis of prejudice. *Personality and Social Psychology Bulletin, 5*, 461-476.

Petty, R. E., & Brock, T. C. (1976). Effects of responding or not responding to hecklers on audience agreement with a speaker. *Journal of Applied Social Psychology, 6*, 1-17.

Petty, R. E., & Cacioppo, J. T. (1977). Forewarning, cognitive responding, and resistance to persuasion. *Journal of Personality and Social Psychology, 35*, 645-655.

Petty, R. E., & Cacioppo, J. T. (1981). *Attitudes and persuasion: Classic and contemporary approaches.* Dubuque, IO: William C. Brown.

Petty, R. E., & Cacioppo, J. T. (1986). The elaboration likelihood model of persuasion. *Advances in Experimental Social Psychology, 19*, 123-205.

Petty, R. E., Wells, G. L., & Brock, T. C. (1976). Distraction can enhance or reduce yielding to propaganda: Thought disruption versus effort justification. *Journal of Personality and Social Psychology, 34*, 874-884.

Pfeffer, J. (1978). The ambiguity of leadership. In M. W. McCall,

Jr., & M. M. Lombardo (Eds.), *Leadership: Where else can we go?* Durham, NC: Duke University Press.

Phares, E. J. (1976). *Locus of control in personality*. Morristown, NJ: General Learning Press.

Phillips, D. P. (1970). *Dying as a form of social behavior*. (Doctoral dissertation, Princeton University). Ann Arbor, MI: University Microfilms, No. 70-19, 799.

Phillips, D. P. (1972). Deathday and birthday: An unexpected connection. In J. M. Tanur (Ed.), *Statistics: A guide to the unknown*. San Francisco: Holden-Day.

Phillips, D. P. (1980). The deterrent effect of capital punishment: New evidence on an old controversy. *American Journal of Sociology, 86,* 139–148.

Phillips, D. P. (1986). Natural experiments on the effects of mass media violence on fatal aggression: Strengths and weaknesses of a new approach. *Advances in Experimental Social Psychology, 19,* 207–250.

Pile, J. (1978). *Open office planning: A handbook for interior designers and architects*. New York: Whitney Library of Design.

Piliavin, I. M., & Gross, A. E. (1977). The effects of separation of services and income maintenance on AFDC recipients' perceptions and use of social services: Results of a field experiment. *Social Service Review, 9,* 389–406.

Piliavin, J. A., Dovidio, J. F., Gaertner, S. L., & Clark, R. D., III. (1981). *Emergency intervention*. New York: Academic Press.

Piliavin, J. A., Evans, D. E., & Callero, P. (1984). Learning to "give to unnamed strangers": The process of commitment to regular blood donation. In E. Staub, D. Bar-Tal, J. Karylowski, & J. Reykowski (Eds.), *The development and maintenance of prosocial behavior: International perspectives*. New York: Plenum.

Pittenger, J. B., & Baskett, L. M. (1984). Facial self-perception: Its relation to objective appearance and self-concept. *Bulletin of the Psychonomic Society, 22,* 167–170.

Platt, J. (1973). Social traps. *American Psychologist, 28,* 641–651.

Pocs, O., & Godow, A. G. (1977). Can students view parents as sexual beings? In D. Byrne & L. Byrne (Eds.), *Exploring human sexuality*. York: Crowell.

Podsakoff, P. M., & Schriesheim, C. A. (1985). Field studies of French and Raven's bases of power: Critique, reanalysis, and suggestions for future research. *Psychological Bulletin, 97,* 387–411.

Pollock, L. M., & Patterson, A. H. (1980). Territoriality and fear of crime in elderly and nonelderly homeowners. *Journal of Social Psychology, 111,* 119–129.

Poor, D. (1967). *Social psychology of questionnaires*. Unpublished bachelor's thesis, Harvard University. (Cited in R. Rosenthal & R. L. Rosnow [Eds.], *Artifact in behavioral research*. New York: Academic Press, 1969.)

Post, D. L. (1980). Floyd H. Allport and the launching of modern social psychology. *Journal of the History of the Behavioral Sciences, 16,* 369–376.

Prentice-Dunn, S., & Rogers, R. W. (1982). Effects of public and private self-awareness on deindividuation and aggression. *Journal of Personality and Social Psychology, 43,* 505–513.

Price, R. A., Vandenberg, S. G., Iyer, H., & Williams, J. S. (1982). Components of variation in normal personality. *Journal of Personality and Social Psychology, 43,* 328–340.

Proshansky, H., & Newton, P. (1968). The nature and meaning of Negro self-identity. In M. Deutsch, I. Katz, & A. R. Jensen (Eds.), *Social class, race, and psychological development*. New York: Holt, Rinehart & Winston.

Pruitt, D. G. (1981). *Negotiation behavior*. New York: Academic Press.

Pruitt, D. G. (1982). *Integrative agreements: Nature and antecedents*. Unpublished manuscript.

Pruitt, D. G., & Kressel, K. (1985). The mediation of social conflict: An introduction. *Journal of Social Issues, 41* (2), 1–10.

Pryor, J. B., & Merluzzi, T. V. (1985). The role of expertise in processing social interaction scripts. *Journal of Experimental Social Psychology, 21,* 362–379.

Przybyla, D. P. J., & Byrne, D. (1984). The mediating role of cognitive processes in self-reported sexual arousal. *Journal of Research in Personality, 18,* 54–63.

Putnam, L. L., & Jones, T. S. (1982). The role of communication in bargaining. *Human Communication Research, 8,* 262–280.

Pyszczynski, T., Greenberg, J., Mack, D., & Wrightsman, L. S. (1981). Opening statements in a jury trial: The effect of promising more than the evidence can show. *Journal of Applied Social Psychology, 11,* 434–444.

Pyszczynski, T. A., & Wrightsman, L. S. (1981). The effects of opening statements on mock jurors' verdicts in a simulated criminal trial. *Journal of Applied Social Psychology, 11,* 301–313.

Quinsey, V. L., Chaplin, T. C., & Upfold, D. (1984). Sexual arousal to nonsexual violence and sadomasochistic themes among rapists and non-sex-offenders. *Journal of Consulting and Clinical Psychology, 52,* 651–657.

Radke-Yarrow, M., & Zahn-Waxler, C. (1984). Roots, motives, and patterns in children's prosocial behavior. In E. Staub, D. Bar-Tal, J. Karylowski, & J. Reykowski (Eds.), *The development and maintenance of prosocial behavior: International perspectives*. New York: Plenum.

Radloff, R., & Helmreich, R. (1968). *Groups under stress: Psychological research in SEALAB II*. New York: Irvington.

Ramirez, A. (1977). Chicano power and interracial group relations. In J. L. Martinez (Ed.), *Chicano psychology*. New York: Academic Press.

Ramirez, A. (in press). Racism towards Hispanics: The culturally monolithic society. In P. Katz & D. Taylor (Eds.), *Toward the elimination of racism: Profiles in controversy*.

Ramirez, J., Bryant, J., & Zillmann, D. (1982). Effects of erotica on retaliatory behavior as a function of level of prior provocation. *Journal of Personality and Social Psychology, 43,* 971–978.

Ransford, H. E. (1968). Isolation, powerlessness, and violence: A study of attitudes and participation in the Watts riot. *American Journal of Sociology, 73,* 581–591.

Raps, C. S., Peterson, C., Jonas, M., & Seligman, M. E. P. (1982). Patient behavior in hospitals: Helplessness, reactance, or both? *Journal of Personality and Social Psychology, 42,* 1036–1041.

Reddy, D. M., Baum, A., Fleming, R., & Aiello, J. R. (1981). Mediation of social density by coalition formation. *Journal of Applied Social Psychology, 11,* 529–537.

Reed, D., & Weinberg, M. S. (1984). Premarital coitus: Developing and established sexual scripts. *Social Psychology Quarterly, 47,* 129–138.

Reichner, R. F. (1979). Differential responses to being ignored: The effects of architectural design and social density on interpersonal behavior. *Journal of Applied Social Psychology, 9,* 13–26.

Reingen, P. H. (1982). Test of a list procedure for inducing compliance with a request to donate money. *Journal of Applied Psychology, 67,* 110–118.

Reis, H. T., Nezlek, J., & Wheeler, L. (1980). Physical attractiveness in social interaction. *Journal of Personality and Social Psychology, 38*, 604–617.

Reis, H. T., Wheeler, L., Spiegel, N., Kernis, M., Nezlek, J., & Perri, M. (1982). Physical attractiveness in social interaction, II: Why does appearance affect social experience? *Journal of Personality and Social Psychology, 43*, 979–996.

Reisenzein, R. (1986). A structural equation analysis of Weiner's attribution-affect model of helping behavior. *Journal of Personality and Social Psychology, 50*, 1123–1133.

Reiss, I. (1960). *Premarital sexual standards in America.* New York: Free Press.

Reiss, I. (1967). *The social context of premarital sexual permissiveness.* New York: Holt, Rinehart & Winston.

Rempel, J. K., Holmes, J. G., & Zanna, M. P. (1985). Trust in close relationships. *Journal of Personality and Social Psychology, 49*, 95–112.

Rhodewalt, F. (in press). Self-presentation and the phenomenal self: On the stability and malleability of self-conceptions. In R. Baumeister (Ed.), *Private and public selves.* New York: Springer-Verlag.

Rhodewalt, F., & Agustsdottir, S. (1986). Effects of self-presentation on the phenomenal self. *Journal of Personality and Social Psychology, 50*, 47–55.

Rhodewalt, F., Saltzman, A. T., & Wittmer, J. (1984). Self-handicapping among competitive athletes: The role of practice in self-esteem protection. *Basic and Applied Social Psychology, 5*, 197–209.

Rice, R. W., & Kastenbaum, D. R. (1983). The contingency model of leadership: Some current issues. *Basic and Applied Social Psychology, 4*, 373–392.

Ring, K. (1967). Experimental social psychology: Some sober questions about frivolous values. *Journal of Experimental Social Psychology, 1967, 3*, 113–123.

Rinn, W. E. (1984). The neuropsychology of facial expression: A review of the neurological and psychological mechanisms for producing facial expressions. *Psychological Bulletin, 95*, 52–77.

Roberts, A. H., & Jessor, R. (1958). Authoritarianism, punitiveness, and perceived social status. *Journal of Abnormal and Social Psychology, 56*, 311–314.

Roberts, D. F., & Maccoby, N. (1985). Effects of mass communication. In G. Lindzey & E. Aronson (Eds.), *Handbook of social psychology* (Vol. II) (3rd ed.) (pp. 539–598). New York: Random House.

Roberts, J. V. (1985). The attitude-memory relationship after 40 years: A meta-analysis of the literature. *Basic and Applied Social Psychology, 6*, 221–241.

Roberts, J. V., & Herman, C. P. (1986). The psychology of height: An empirical review. In C. P. Herman, M. P. Zanna, & E. T. Higgins (Eds.), *Physical appearance, stigma, and social behavior: The Ontario symposium, Volume 3* (pp. 113–140). Hillsdale, NJ: Erlbaum.

Rodin, J. (1976). Density, perceived choice, and response to controllable and uncontrollable outcomes. *Journal of Experimental Social Psychology, 12*, 564–578.

Rodin, J. (1978). Somatopsychics and attribution. *Personality and Social Psychology Bulletin, 4*, 531–540.

Rodin, J. (1985). The application of social psychology. In G. Lindzey & E. Aronson (Eds.), *Handbook of social psychology*, (Vol. II) (3rd ed.) (pp. 805–881). New York: Random House.

Rodin, J., & Baum, A. (1978). Crowding and helplessness: Potential consequences of density and loss of control. In A. Baum & Y. Epstein (Eds.), *Human response to crowding.* Hillsdale, NJ: Erlbaum.

Rodin, J., & Langer, E. J. (1977). Long-term effects of a control-relevant intervention with the institutionalized aged. *Journal of Personality and Social Psychology, 35*, 897–902.

Rodin, J., Solomon, S. K., & Metcalf, J. (1978). Role of control in mediating perceptions of density. *Journal of Personality and Social Psychology, 36*, 988–999.

Rofé, Y. (1984). Stress and affiliation: A utility theory. *Psychological Review, 91*, 235–250.

Rogers, C. R. (1957). A note on the "nature of man." *Journal of Counseling Psychology, 4*, 199–203.

Rogers, L. E., & Farace, R. V. (1975). Analysis of relational communication in dyads: New measurement procedures. *Human Communication Research, 1*, 222–239.

Rogers, R. W. (1975). A protection motivation theory of fear appeals and attitude change. *Journal of Psychology, 91*, 93–114.

Rohner, R. P. (1976). *A worldwide study of sex differences in aggression: A universalist perspective.* Paper presented at meeting of Eastern Psychological Association, New York, April.

Rokeach, M. (1968). *Beliefs, attitudes, and values.* San Francisco: Jossey-Bass.

Rokeach, M. (1970). Faith, hope, bigotry. *Psychology Today, 3*(11), 33–37ff.

Rokeach, M. (1973). *The nature of human values.* New York: Free Press.

Rokeach, M. (1979). Some unresolved issues in theories of beliefs, attitudes, and values. *Nebraska Symposium on Motivation, 27*, 261–304.

Rokeach, M., & Mezei, L. (1966). Race and shared belief as factors in social choice. *Science, 151*, 167–172.

Rook, K. S., & Hammen, C. L. (1977). A cognitive perspective on the experience of sexual arousal. *Journal of Social Issues, 33*(2), 7–29.

Rosen, S., Tomarelli, M. M., Kidda, M. L., Jr., & Medvin, N. (1986). Effects of motive for helping, recipient's inability to reciprocate, and sex on devaluation of the recipient's competence. *Journal of Personality and Social Psychology, 50*, 729–736.

Rosenbaum, D. P., & Lurigio, D. P. (1985). Crime stoppers: Paying the price. *Psychology Today, 19*(6), 56–61.

Rosenbaum, M. E. (1986). The repulsion hypothesis: On the nondevelopment of relationships. *Journal of Personality and Social Psychology, 51*, 1156–1166.

Rosenberg, M. (1979). *Conceiving the self.* New York: Basic Books.

Rosenberg, S., & Gara, M. A. (1985). The multiplicity of personal identity. *Review of Personality and Social Psychology, 6*, 87–113.

Rosenberg, S., & Jones, R. A. (1972). A method for investigating and representing a person's implicit theory of personality: Theodore Dreiser's view of people. *Journal of Personality and Social Psychology, 22*, 372–386.

Rosenberg, S., Nelson, C., & Vivekanathan, P. S. (1968). A multidimensional approach to the structure of personality impressions. *Journal of Personality and Social Psychology, 39*, 283–294.

Rosenberg, S., & Sedlak, A. (1972). Structural representations of implicit personality theory. In L. Berkowitz (Ed.), *Advances in experimental social psychology* (Vol. 6). New York: Academic Press.

Rosenfeld, H. M. (1965). Effect of an approval-seeking induction on interpersonal proximity. *Psychological Reports, 17*, 120–122.

Rosenhan, D. L., Karylowski, J., Salovey, P., & Hargis, K. (1981).

Emotion and altruism. In J. P. Rushton & R. M. Sorrentino (Eds.), *Altruism and helping behavior: Social, personality, and developmental perspectives*. Hillsdale, NJ: Erlbaum.

Rosenhan, D. L., Salovey, P., & Hargis, K. (1981). The joys of helping: Focus of attention mediates the impact of positive affect on altruism. *Journal of Personality and Social Psychology, 40*, 899–905.

Rosenthal, R. (1966). *Experimenter effects in behavioral research*. New York: Appleton-Century-Crofts.

Rosenthal, R., & DePaulo, B. M. (1979). Sex differences in eavesdropping on nonverbal cues. *Journal of Personality and Social Psychology, 37*, 273–285.

Rosenthal, R., & Jacobson, L. (1968). *Pygmalion in the classroom: Teacher expectation and intellectual development*. New York: Holt, Rinehart & Winston.

Rosenthal, R., & Rosnow, R. L. (1975). *The volunteer subject*. New York: Wiley.

Rosow, I. The social effects of the physical environment. *Journal of the American Institute of Planners, 27*, 127–133.

Ross, L., Greene, D., & House, P. (1977). The "false consensus effect": An egocentric bias in social perception and attribution processes. *Journal of Experimental Social Psychology, 13*, 279–301.

Ross, L. D., Amabile, T. M., & Steinmetz, J. L. (1977). Social roles, social control, and biases in social-perception processes. *Journal of Personality and Social Psychology, 35*, 485–494.

Ross, M., Layton, B., Erickson, B., & Schopler, J. (1973). Affect, facial regard, and reactions to crowding. *Journal of Personality and Social Psychology, 28*, 69–76.

Ross, M., McFarland, C., Conway, M., & Zanna, M. P. (1983). Reciprocal relation between attitudes and behavior recall: Committing people to newly formed attitudes. *Journal of Personality and Social Psychology, 45*, 257–267.

Rossi, P. H., & Williams, W. (Eds.). (1972). *Evaluating social programs: Theory, practice, and politics*. New York: Seminar Press.

Rothbart, M., & Park, B. (1986). On the confirmability and disconfirmability of trait concepts. *Journal of Personality and Social Psychology, 50*, 131–142.

Rotter, J. B. (1966). Generalized expectancies for internal versus external control of reinforcement. *Psychological Monographs, 80*(1, Whole No. 609).

Rotter, J. B., Chance, J., & Phares, E. J. (Eds.) (1972). *Applications of a social learning theory of personality*. New York: Holt, Rinehart & Winston.

Rotton, J., Barry, T., Frey, J., & Soler, E. (1978). Air pollution and interpersonal attraction. *Journal of Applied Social Psychology, 8*, 57–71.

Rotton, J., & Frey, J. (1985). Air pollution, weather, and violent crimes: Concomitant time-series analysis of archival data. *Journal of Personality and Social Psychology, 49*, 1207–1220.

Rubenstein, C., & Shaver, P. (1982). The experience of loneliness. In L. A. Peplau & D. Perlman (Eds.), *Loneliness: A sourcebook of current theory, research, and therapy*. New York: Wiley.

Rubin, J. Z., & Brown, B. R. (1975). *The social psychology of bargaining and negotiation*. New York: Academic Press.

Rubin, Z. (1970). Measurement of romantic love. *Journal of Personality and Social Psychology, 16*, 265–273.

Rubin, Z. (1973). *Liking and loving: An invitation to social psychology*. New York: Holt, Rinehart & Winston.

Rubin, Z., Peplau, L. A., & Hill, C. T. (1978). *Loving and leaving: Sex differences in romantic attachments*. Unpublished manuscript, Brandeis University.

Rugg, E. A. (1975). *Social research practices opinion survey: Summary of results*. Unpublished paper, George Peabody College.

Rule, B. G., Bisanz, G. L., & Kohn, M. (1985). Anatomy of a persuasion schema: Targets, goals, and strategies. *Journal of Personality and Social Psychology, 48*, 1127–1140.

Rule, B. G., & Leger, G. J. (1976). Pain cues and differing functions of aggression. *Canadian Journal of Behavioural Science, 8*, 213–222.

Rule, B. G., & Percival, E. (1971). The effects of frustration and attack on physical aggression. *Journal of Experimental Research in Personality, 5*, 111–118.

Runkel, P. J., & McGrath, J. E. (1972). *Research on human behavior: A systematic guide to method*. New York: Holt, Rinehart & Winston.

Rush, M. C., Thomas, J. C., & Lord, R. G. (1977). Implicit leadership theory: A potential threat to the internal validity of leader behavior questionnaires. *Organizational Behavior and Human Performance, 20*, 93–110.

Rushton, J. P. (1979). Effects of prosocial television and film material on the behavior of viewers. In L. Berkowitz (Ed.), *Advances in experimental social psychology* (Vol. 12). New York: Academic Press.

Rushton, J. P. (1984). The altruistic personality: Evidence from laboratory, naturalistic, and self-report perspectives. In E. Staub, D. Bar-Tal, J. Karylowski, & J. Reykowski (Eds.), *The development and maintenance of prosocial behavior: International perspectives*. New York: Plenum.

Rushton, J. P., Fulker, D. W., Neale, M. C., Nias, D. K. B., & Eysenck, H. J. (1986). Altruism and aggression: The heritability of individual differences. *Journal of Personality and Social Psychology, 50*, 1192–1198.

Russell, D., Cutrona, C. E., Rose, J., & Yurko, K. (1984). Social and emotional loneliness: An examination of Weiss's typology of loneliness. *Journal of Personality and Social Psychology, 46*, 1313–1321.

Russo, N. F. (1975). Eye contact, interpersonal distance, and the equilibrium theory. *Journal of Personality and Social Psychology, 31*, 497–502.

Rutkowski, G. K., Gruder, C. L., & Romer, D. (1983). Group cohesiveness, social norms, and bystander intervention. *Journal of Personality and Social Psychology, 44*, 545–552.

Ryan, W. (1971). *Blaming the victim*. New York: Pantheon.

Sacks, H., Schegloff, E., & Jefferson, G. (1974). A simplest systematics for the organization of turn-taking in conversation. *Language, 50*, 696–735.

Sadava, S. W. (1978). Teaching social psychology: A Canadian dilemma. *Canadian Psychological Review, 19*, 145–151.

Saegert, S., MacIntosh, B., & West, S. (1975). Two studies of crowding in urban spaces. *Environment and Behavior, 7*, 159–184.

Saegert, S. C., Swap, W., & Zajonc, R. B. (1973). Exposure, context, and interpersonal attraction. *Journal of Personality and Social Psychology, 25*, 234–242.

Saks, M. J., & Baron, C. H. (Eds.). (1980). *The use/nonuse/misuse of applied social research*. Cambridge, MA: Abt Books.

Salancik, G. R., & Pfeffer, J. (1977). Constraints on administrator discretion: The limited influence of mayors on city budgets. *Urban Affairs Quarterly, 12*, 475–496.

Salinger, J. D. (1953). *The catcher in the rye*. New York: Signet.

Samerotte, G. C., & Harris, M. B. (1976). Some factors influencing helping: The effects of a handicap, responsibility, and requesting help. *Journal of Social Psychology, 98*, 39–45.

Sanday, P. R. (1981). The socio-cultural context of rape: A cross-cultural study. *Journal of Social Issues, 37*(4), 5–27.

Sanders, G. S. (1984). Self-presentation and drive in social facilitation. *Journal of Experimental Social Psychology, 20*, 312–322.

Sanders, M., Gustanski, J., & Lawton, M. (1976). Effect of ambient illumination on noise level of groups. *Journal of Applied Psychology, 59*, 527–528.

Sanford, F. H. (1950). *Authoritarianism and leadership.* Philadelphia: Institute for Research in Human Relations.

Sanford, N. (1956). The approach of the authoritarian personality. In J. L. McCary (Ed.), *Psychology of personality.* New York: Grove Press.

Sanford, N. (1970). Whatever happened to action research? *Journal of Social Issues, 26*(4), 3–23.

Sauser, W. I., Arauz, C. G., & Chambers, R. M. (1978). Exploring the relationship between level of office noise and salary recommendations: A preliminary research note. *Journal of Management, 4*, 57–63.

Scarr, S., & Weinberg, R. A. (1976). IQ test performance of black children adopted by white families. *American Psychologist, 31*, 726–739.

Schachter, S. (1951). Deviation, rejection, and communication. *Journal of Abnormal and Social Psychology, 46*, 190–207.

Schachter, S. (1959). *The psychology of affiliation.* Stanford, CA: Stanford University Press.

Schachter, S., Ellertson, N., McBride, D., & Gregory, D. (1951). An experimental study of cohesiveness and productivity. *Human Relations, 4*, 229–238.

Schachter, S., & Singer, J. (1962). Cognitive, social, and physiological determinants of emotional state. *Psychological Review, 69*, 379–399.

Schaps, E. (1972). Cost, dependency, and helping. *Journal of Personality and Social Psychology, 21*, 74–78.

Scheff, T. J., & Bushnell, D. D. (1984). A theory of catharsis. *Journal of Research in Personality, 18*, 238–264.

Scheier, M. F., & Carver, C. S. (1980). Individual differences in self-concept and self-process. In D. M. Wegner & R. R. Vallacher (Eds.), *The self in social psychology.* New York: Oxford University Press.

Scheier, M. F., & Carver, S. C. (1981). Private and public aspects of self. In L. Wheeler (Ed.), *Review of personality and social psychology* (Vol. 2). Beverly Hills, CA: Sage.

Scheier, M. F., Carver, C. S., & Gibbons, F. X. (1979). Self-directed attention, awareness of bodily states and suggestibility. *Journal of Personality and Social Psychology, 37*, 1576–1588.

Schein, E. H. (1957). Reaction patterns to severe chronic stress in American army prisoners of war of the Chinese. *Journal of Social Issues, 13*(3), 21–30.

Schiffrin, D. (1977). Opening encounters. *American Sociological Review, 42*, 679–691.

Schill, T., & Chapin, J. (1972). Sex guilt and males' preference for reading erotic literature. *Journal of Consulting and Clinical Psychology, 39*, 516.

Schlenker, B. R. (1980). *Impression management: The self-concept, social identity, and interpersonal relations.* Pacific Grove, CA: Brooks/Cole.

Schlenker, B. R., & Forsyth, D. R. (1977). On the ethics of psychological research. *Journal of Experimental Social Psychology, 13*, 369–396.

Schlosberg, H. (1954). Three dimensions of emotion. *Psychological Review, 61*, 81–88.

Schmidt, G., & Sigusch, V. (1970). Sex differences in responses to psychosexual stimulation by film and slides. *Journal of Sex Research, 6*, 268–283.

Schmidt, G., Sigusch, V., & Meyberg, V. (1969). Psychosexual stimulation in men: Emotional reactions, changes of sex behavior, and measures of conservative attitudes. *Journal of Sex Research, 5*, 199–217.

Schmitt, B. H., Gilovich, T., Goore, N., & Joseph, L. (1986). Mere presence and social facilitation: One more time. *Journal of Experimental Social Psychology, 22*, 242–248.

Schneider, D. J. (1973). Implicit personality theory: A review. *Psychological Bulletin, 79*, 294–309.

Schneier, C. E. (1978). The contingency model of leadership: An extension of emergent leadership and leader's sex. *Organizational Behavior and Human Performance, 21*, 220–239.

Schofield, J. W. (1982). *Black and white in school: Trust, tension, or tolerance?* New York: Praeger.

Schopler, J., & Stockdale, J. (1977). An interference analysis of crowding. *Environmental Psychology and Nonverbal Behavior, 4*, 171–186.

Schopler, J., & Thompson, V. D. (1968). Role of attribution processes in mediating amount of reciprocity for a favor. *Journal of Personality and Social Psychology, 10*, 243–250.

Schriesheim, C., & Kerr, S. (1974). Psychometric properties of the Ohio State leadership scales. *Psychological Bulletin, 81*, 756–765.

Schulz, R., & Barefoot, J. (1974). Nonverbal responses and affiliative conflict theory. *British Journal of Social and Clinical Psychology, 13*, 237–243.

Schuman, H., & Kalton, G. (1985). Survey methods. In G. Lindzey & E. Aronson (Eds.), *Handbook of social psychology* (Vol. 1) (3rd ed.) (pp. 635–697). New York: Random House.

Schutte, N. S., Kenrick, D. T., & Sadalla, E. K. (1985). The search for predictable settings: Situational prototypes, constraint, and behavioral variation. *Journal of Personality and Social Psychology, 49*, 121–128.

Schwartz, B., & Barsky, S. F. (1977). The home advantage. *Social Forces, 53*, 641–661.

Schwartz, G. E. (1982). Psychophysiological patterning and emotion revisited: A systems perspective. In C. Izard (Ed.), *Measuring emotion in infants and children.* Cambridge, England: Cambridge University Press.

Schwartz, S. H. (1973). Normative explanations of helping behavior: A critique, proposal, and empirical test. *Journal of Experimental Social Psychology, 9*, 349–364.

Schwartz, S. H. (1977). Normative influences on altruism. In L. Berkowitz (Ed.), *Advances in experimental social psychology* (Vol. 10). New York: Academic Press.

Schwartz, S. H., & Clausen, G. T. (1970). Responsibility, norms, and helping in an emergency. *Journal of Personality and Social Psychology, 16*, 299–310.

Schwartz, S. H., & Gottlieb, A. (1980). Bystander anonymity and reactions to emergencies. *Journal of Personality and Social Psychology, 39*, 418–430.

Schwartz, S. H., & Gottlieb, A. (1981). Participants' postexperimental reactions and the ethics of bystander research. *Journal of Experimental Social Psychology, 17*, 396–407.

Schwartz, S. H., & Howard, J. A. (1981). A normative decision-making model of altruism. In J. P. Rushton & R. M. Sorrentino

(Eds.), *Altruism and helping behavior: Social, personality, and developmental perspectives.* Hillsdale, NJ: Erlbaum.

Schwartz, S. H., & Howard, J. A. (1984). Internalized values as motivators of altruism. In E. Staub, D. Bar-Tal, J. Karylowski, & J. Reykowski (Eds.), *The development and maintenance of prosocial behavior: International perspectives.* New York: Plenum.

Scott, J. A. (1984). Comfort and seating distance in living rooms: The relationship of interactants and topic of conversation. *Environment and Behavior, 16,* 35–54.

Scott, J. P. (1958). *Aggression.* Chicago: University of Chicago Press.

Scott, R. L. (1977). Communication as an intentional, social system. *Human Communication Research, 3,* 258–267.

Searle, J. (1979). *Expression and meaning: Studies in the theory of speech acts.* Cambridge: Cambridge University Press.

Sears, D. O. (1986). College sophomores in the laboratory: Influences of a narrow data base on social psychology's view of human nature. *Journal of Personality and Social Psychology, 51,* 515–530.

Sears, D. O., & Kinder, D. R. (1985). Whites' opposition to busing: On conceptualizing and operationalizing group conflict. *Journal of Personality and Social Psychology, 48,* 1141–1147.

Sebba, R., & Churchman, A. (1983). Territories and territoriality in the home. *Environment and Behavior, 15,* 191–210.

Segal, M. W. (1974). Alphabet and attraction: An unobtrusive measure of the effect of propinquity in a field setting. *Journal of Personality and Social Psychology, 30,* 654–657.

Segall, M. H. (1986). Culture and behavior: Psychology in global perspective. *Annual Review of Psychology, 37,* 523–564.

Selby, J. W., Calhoun, L. G., & Brock, T. A. (1977). Sex differences in the social perception of rape victims. *Personality and Social Psychology Bulletin, 3,* 412–415.

Seligman, C., & Darley, J. M. (1977). Feedback as a means of decreasing residential energy consumption. *Journal of Applied Psychology, 62,* 363–368.

Seligman, C., Finegan, J. E., Hazlewood, J. D., & Wilkinson, M. (1985). Manipulating attributions for profit: A field test of the effects of attributions on behavior. *Social Cognition, 3,* 313–321.

Seligman, C., Kriss, M., Darley, J. M., Fazio, R. H., Becker, L. J., & Pryor, J. B. (1979). Predicting summer energy consumption from homeowners' attitudes. *Journal of Applied Social Psychology, 9,* 70–90.

Seligman, M. E. P. (1975). *Helplessness: On depression, development, and death.* San Francisco: Freeman.

Seligman, M. E. P., & Schulman, P. (1986). Explanatory style as a predictor of productivity and quitting among life insurance sales agents. *Journal of Personality and Social Psychology, 50,* 832–838.

Selltiz, C., Wrightsman, L. S., & Cook, S. W. (1976). *Research methods in social relations* (3rd ed.). New York: Holt, Rinehart & Winston.

Selye, H. (1971). The evolution of the stress concept. In L. Levi (Ed.), *Society, stress, and disease* (Vol. I). London: Oxford University Press.

Seta, J. J. (1982). The impact of comparison processes on coactor's task performance. *Journal of Personality and Social Psychology, 42,* 281–291.

Seyfried, B. A., & Hendrick, C. (1973). When do opposites attract? When they are opposite in sex and sex-role attitudes. *Journal of Personality and Social Psychology, 25,* 15–20.

Shaffer, D. R., & Sadowski, C. (1975). This table is mine: Respect for marked barroom tables as a function of gender of spatial marker and desirability of locale. *Sociometry, 38,* 408–419.

Shamir, B. (1986). Self-esteem and the psychological impact of unemployment. *Social Psychology Quarterly, 49,* 61–72.

Shannon, C., & Weaver, W. (1949). *The mathematical theory of communication.* Urbana: University of Illinois Press.

Shapiro, P. N., & Penrod, S. (1986). Meta-analysis of facial identification studies. *Psychological Bulletin, 100,* 139–156.

Sharp, G. (1970). *Exploring nonviolent alternatives.* Boston: Porter Sargent.

Sharp, G. (1971). *The politics of nonviolent action.* Philadelphia: Pilgrim Press.

Shaver, P. (1982). *State and trait loneliness during the transition into college.* Paper presented at Nags Head Conference on Social Interaction, North Carolina.

Shaver, P., & Klinnert, M. (1982). Schachter's theories of affiliation and emotion: Implications of developmental research. In L. Wheeler (Ed.), *Review of personality and social psychology* (Vol. 3). Beverly Hills, CA: Sage.

Shaw, M. E. (1932). A comparison of individuals and small groups in the rational solution of complex problems. *American Journal of Psychology, 44,* 491–504.

Shaw, M. E. (1964). Communication networks. In L. Berkowitz (Ed.), *Advances in experimental social psychology* (Vol. 1). New York: Academic Press.

Shaw, M. E. (1978). Communication networks fourteen years later. In L. Berkowitz (Ed.), *Group processes.* New York: Academic Press.

Shaw, M. E., & Costanzo, P. R. (1982). *Theories of social psychology* (2nd ed.). New York: McGraw-Hill.

Shedler, J., & Manis, M. (1986). Can the availability heuristic explain vividness effects? *Journal of Personality and Social Psychology, 51,* 26–36.

Shein, V. E. (1973). The relationship between sex-role stereotypes and requisite management characteristics. *Journal of Applied Psychology, 54,* 95–100.

Shein, V. E. (1975). Relationships between sex-role stereotypes and requisite management characteristics among female managers. *Journal of Applied Psychology, 60,* 340–344.

Sherif, C. W., Sherif, M., & Nebergall, R. E. (1965). *Attitude and attitude change: The social judgment approach.* Philadelphia: Saunders.

Sherif, M. (1935). A study of some social factors in perception. *Archives of Psychology, 27,* No. 187, 1–60.

Sherif, M. (1966). *In common predicament: Social psychology of intergroup conflict and cooperation.* Boston: Houghton Mifflin.

Sherif, M., Harvey, O. J., White, B. J., Hood, W. E., & Sherif, C. W. (1961). *Intergroup conflict and cooperation: The Robber's Cave experiment.* Norman: University of Oklahoma Book Exchange.

Sherif, M., & Hovland, C. (1961). *Social judgment.* New Haven: Yale University Press.

Sherif, M., & Sherif, C. W. (1979). Research on intergroup relations. In W. G. Austin & S. Worchel (Eds.), *The social psychology of intergroup relations.* Pacific Grove, CA: Brooks/Cole.

Sherrod, D. R., Armstrong, D., Hewitt, J., Madonia, B., Speno, S., & Teruya, D. (1977). Environmental attention, affect and altruism. *Journal of Applied Social Psychology, 7,* 359–371.

Sherrod, D. R., & Downs, R. (1974). Environmental determinants of altruism: The effects of stimulus overload and perceived control on helping. *Journal of Experimental Social Psychology, 10,* 468–479.

Shettel-Neuber, J., Bryson, J. B., & Young, L. E. (1978). Physical attractiveness of the "other person" and jealousy. *Personality and Social Psychology Bulletin, 4,* 612–615.

Shields, S. A. (1975). Functionalism, Darwinism, and the psychology of women. *American Psychologist, 30,* 739–754.

Shirom, A. (1982). Strike characteristics as determinants of strike settlements: A chief negotiator's viewpoint. *Journal of Applied Psychology, 67,* 45–52.

Shotland, R. L. (1985). When bystanders just stand by. *Psychology Today, 19*(6), 50–55.

Shotland, R. L., & Heinold, W. D. (1985). Bystander response to arterial bleeding: Helping skills, the decision-making process, and differentiating the helping response. *Journal of Personality and Social Psychology, 49,* 347–356.

Shotland, R. L., & Straw, M. K. (1976). Bystander responses to an assault: When a man attacks a woman. *Journal of Personality and Social Psychology, 34,* 990–999.

Shuntich, R. J., & Taylor, S. P. (1972). The effects of alcohol on human physical aggression. *Journal of Experimental Research in Personality, 6,* 34–38.

Siegman, A. W. (1961). A cross-cultural investigation of the relationship between ethnic prejudice, authoritarian ideology, and personality. *Journal of Abnormal and Social Psychology, 63,* 654–655.

Siegman, A. W., & Reynolds, M. A. (1983). Self-monitoring and speech in feigned and unfeigned lying. *Journal of Personality and Social Psychology, 45,* 1325–1333.

Sigall, H., & Landy, D. (1973). Radiating beauty: The effects of having a physically attractive partner on person perception. *Journal of Personality and Social Psychology, 28,* 218–224.

Sigall, H. E., Aronson, E., & Van Hoose, T. (1970). The cooperative subject: Myth or reality? *Journal of Experimental Social Psychology, 6,* 1–10.

Sigelman, C. K., Berry, C. J., & Wiles, K. A. (1984). Violence in college students' dating relationships. *Journal of Applied Social Psychology, 5,* 530–548.

Silverman, I. (1977). Why social psychology fails. *Canadian Psychological Review, 18,* 353–358.

Silverstein, C. H., & Stang, D. J. (1976). Seating position and interaction in triads. *Sociometry, 39,* 166–170.

Silverthorne, C. P., & Mazmanian, L. (1975). The effects of heckling and media of presentation on the impact of a persuasive communication. *Journal of Social Psychology, 96,* 229–236.

Simonton, D. K. (1979). Multiple discovery and invention: Zeitgeist, genius, or chance? *Journal of Personality and Social Psychology, 37,* 1603–1616.

Singer, J. E., Lundberg, U., & Frankenhaeuser, M. (1978). Stress on the train: A study of urban commuting. In A. Baum & J. E. Singer (Eds.), *Advances in environmental psychology* (Vol. 1). Hillsdale, NJ: Erlbaum.

Singer, J. L., & Singer, D. G. (1981). *Television, imagination, and aggression: A study of preschoolers' play.* Hillsdale, NJ: Erlbaum.

Singer, J. L., & Singer, D. G. (1983). Psychologists look at television: Cognitive, developmental, personality, and social policy implications. *American Psychologist, 38,* 826–834.

Skinner, B. F. (1971). *Beyond freedom and dignity.* New York: Knopf.

Slater, P. E. (1958). Contrasting correlates of group size. *Sociometry, 25,* 129–139.

Sloan, L. R., Love, R. E., & Ostrom, T. M. (1974). Political heckling: Who really loses? *Journal of Personality and Social Psychology, 30,* 518–525.

Smigel, E. O., & Seiden, R. (1968). The decline and fall of the double standard. *Annals of the American Academy of Political and Social Sciences, 376,* 1–14.

Smith, M. B., Bruner, J. S., & White, R. W. (1956). *Opinions and personality.* New York: Wiley.

Smith, R. E., Keating, J. P., Hester, R. K., & Mitchell, H. E. (1976). Role and justice considerations in the attribution of responsibility to a rape victim. *Journal of Research in Personality, 10,* 346–357.

Snyder, C. R., Higgins, R. L., & Stucky, R. J. (1983). *Excuses: Masquerades in search of grace.* New York: Wiley/Interscience.

Snyder, C. R., Lassegard, M., & Ford, C. E. (1986). Distancing after group success and failure: Basking in reflected glory and cutting off reflected failure. *Journal of Personality and Social Psychology, 51,* 382–388.

Snyder, M. (1979). Self-monitoring processes. In L. Berkowitz (Ed.), *Advances in experimental social psychology* (Vol. 12). New York: Academic Press.

Snyder, M. (1981). On the influence of individuals on situations. In N. Cantor & J. F. Kihlstrom (Eds.), *Personality, cognition, and social interaction.* Hillsdale, NJ: Erlbaum.

Snyder, M. (1984). When belief creates reality. *Advances in Experimental Social Psychology, 18,* 247–305.

Snyder, M. (1987). *Public and private realities: The psychology of self-monitoring.* New York: W. H. Freeman.

Snyder, M., & DeBono, K. G. (1985). Appeals to image and claims about quality: Understanding the psychology of advertising. *Journal of Personality and Social Psychology, 49,* 586–597.

Snyder, M., & Gangestad, S. (1986). On the nature of self-monitoring: Matters of assessment, matters of validity. *Journal of Personality and Social Psychology, 51,* 125–139.

Snyder, M., & Ickes, W. (1985). Personality and social behavior. In G. Lindzey & E. Aronson (Eds.), *Handbook of social psychology* (Vol. 2) (3rd ed.). New York: Random House.

Snyder, M., & Monson, T. C. (1975). Persons, situations, and the control of social behavior. *Journal of Personality and Social Psychology, 32,* 637–644.

Snyder, M., & Swann, W. B., Jr. (1978). Behavioral confirmation in social interaction: From social perception to social reality. *Journal of Experimental Social Psychology, 14,* 148–162.

Snyder, M., Tanke, E. D., & Berscheid, E. (1977). Social perception and interpersonal behavior: On the self-fulfilling nature of social stereotypes. *Journal of Personality and Social Psychology, 35,* 656–666.

Snyder, M. L., & Mentzer, S. (1978). Social psychological perspectives on the physician's feelings and behavior. *Personality and Social Psychology Bulletin, 4,* 541–547.

Solano, C. H., Batten, P. G., & Parish, E. A. (1982). Loneliness and patterns of self-disclosure. *Journal of Personality and Social Psychology, 43,* 524–531.

Solly, C. M. (1969). Effects of stress on perceptual attention. In B. P. Rourke (Ed.), *Explorations in the psychology of stress and anxiety.* Toronto: Longmans Canada.

Solomon, L. Z., Solomon, H., & Stone, R. (1978). Helping as a function of number of bystanders and ambiguity of emergency. *Personality and Social Psychology Bulletin, 4,* 318–321.

Sommer, R. (1959). Studies in personal space. *Sociometry, 22,* 247–260.
Sommer, R. (1962a). The distance for comfortable conversation: A further study. *Sociometry, 25,* 111–116.
Sommer, R. (1962b). Personal space. *American Institute of Architects Journal, 38*(6), 81–83.
Sommer, R. (1966). The ecology of privacy. *Library Quarterly, 36,* 234–248.
Sommer, R. (1967). Classroom ecology. *Journal of Applied Behavioral Science, 3,* 489–503.
Sommer, R. (1969). *Personal space: The behavioral basis of design.* Englewood Cliffs, NJ: Prentice-Hall.
Sommer, R. (1974). *Tight spaces.* Englewood Cliffs, NJ: Prentice-Hall.
Sommer, R., & Becker, F. D. (1969). Territorial defense and the good neighbor. *Journal of Personality and Social Psychology, 11,* 85–92.
Sommer, R., & Olsen, H. (1980). The soft classroom. *Environment and Behavior, 12,* 3–16.
Sommer, R., & Ross, H. (1958). Social interaction on a geriatrics ward. *International Journal of Social Psychiatry, 4,* 128–133.
Sommers, S. (1984). Reported emotions and conventions of emotionality among college students. *Journal of Personality and Social Psychology, 46,* 207–215.
Sorrentino, R. M., & Boutilier, R. G. (1974). Evaluation of a victim as a function of fate similarity/dissimilarity. *Journal of Experimental Social Psychology, 10,* 84–93.
Spears, R., van der Pligt, J., & Eiser, J. R. (1985). Illusory correlation in the perception of group attitudes. *Journal of Personality and Social Psychology, 48,* 863–875.
Spence, J. T. (1985). Gender identity and its implications for concepts of masculinity and femininity. In T. Sondregger (Ed.), *Nebraska symposium on motivation.* Lincoln: University of Nebraska Press.
Spence, J. T., Helmreich, R., & Stapp, J. (1974). The Personal Attributes Questionnaire: A measure of sex-role stereotypes and masculinity-femininity. *JSAS Catalog of Selected Documents in Psychology, 4,* 127.
Sprecher, S. (1986). The relation between inequity and emotions in close relationships. *Social Psychology Quarterly, 49,* 309–321.
Staats, A. W. (1967). An outline of an integrated learning theory of attitude formation and function. In M. Fishbein (Ed.), *Readings in attitude theory and measurement.* New York: Wiley.
Stagner, R., & Eflal, B. (1982). Internal union dynamics during a strike: A quasi-experimental study. *Journal of Applied Psychology, 67,* 37–44.
Staub, E. (Ed.). (1978). *Positive social behavior and morality* (Vol. 1). *Social and personal development.* New York: Academic Press.
Steck, L., Levitan, D., McLane, D., & Kelley, H. H. (1982). Care, need, and conceptions of love. *Journal of Personality and Social Psychology, 43,* 481–491.
Steele, C. M., Southwick, L. L., & Critchlow, B. (1981). Dissonance and alcohol: Drinking your troubles away. *Journal of Personality and Social Psychology, 41,* 831–846.
Steiner, I. D. (1972). *Group process and productivity.* New York: Academic Press.
Steiner, I. D., & Johnson, H. (1963a). Authoritarianism and "tolerance of trait inconsistency." *Journal of Abnormal and Social Psychology, 67,* 388–391.
Steiner, I. D., & Johnson, H. H. (1963b). Authoritarianism and conformity. *Sociometry, 26,* 21–34.
Steinmetz, S. K., & Straus, M. A. (1973). The family as cradle of violence. *Society (formerly Trans/Action), 10,* 50–56.
Steinmetz, S. K., & Straus, M. A. (Eds). (1974). *Violence in the family.* New York: Dodd, Mead.
Steinzor, B. (1950). The spatial factor in face-to-face discussion groups. *Journal of Abnormal and Social Psychology, 45,* 522–555.
Stephan, W., Berscheid, E., & Walster, E. (1971). Sexual arousal and heterosexual perception. *Journal of Personality and Social Psychology, 20,* 93–101.
Stephan, W. G. (1978). School desegregation: An evaluation of predictions made in Brown v. The Board of Education. *Psychological Bulletin, 85,* 217–238.
Stephan, W. G. (1985). Intergroup relations. In G. Lindzey & E. Aronson (Eds.), *Handbook of social psychology* (Vol. II) (3rd ed.) (pp. 599–658). New York: Random House.
Sterling, B., & Gaertner, S. L. (1984). The attribution of arousal and emergency helping: A bidirectional process. *Journal of Experimental Social Psychology, 20,* 586–596.
Stern, P. C., & Aronson, E. (Eds.) (1984). *Energy use: The human dimension.* New York: Freeman.
Sternberg, R. J. (1986). A triangular theory of love. *Psychological Review, 93,* 119–135.
Stewart, A. J., & Rubin, Z. (1976). The power motive in dating couples. *Journal of Personality and Social Psychology, 34,* 305–309.
Stier, D. S., & Hall, J. A. (1984). Gender differences in touch: An empirical and theoretical review. *Journal of Personality and Social Psychology, 47,* 440–459.
Stires, L. K. (1980). Classroom seating location, student grades, and attitudes: Environment or self-selection? *Environment and Behavior, 12,* 241–254.
Stogdill, R. M. (1948). Personal factors associated with leadership. *Journal of Psychology, 23,* 36–71.
Stogdill, R. M. (1963). *Manual for the Leader Behavior Description Questionnaire—Form XII.* Bureau of Business Research, Ohio State University.
Stogdill, R. M. (1969). Validity of leader behavior descriptions. *Personnel Psychology, 22,* 153–158.
Stogdill, R. M. (1974). *Handbook of leadership: A survey of theory and research.* New York: Free Press.
Stokols, D. (1976). The experience of crowding in primary and secondary environments. *Environment and Behavior, 8,* 49–86.
Stokols, D. (1978). Typology of crowding experiences. In A. Baum & Y. Epstein (Eds.), *Human response to crowding.* Hillsdale, NJ: Erlbaum.
Stokols, D., Rall, M., Pinner, B., & Schopler, J. (1973). Physical, social, and personal determinants of the perception of crowding. *Environment and Behavior, 5,* 87–115.
Stoller, R. J. (1976). Sexual excitement. *Archives of General Psychiatry, 33,* 899–909.
Stoner, J. A. F. (1961). *A comparison of individual and group decisions involving risk.* Unpublished Master's thesis, School of Industrial Management, M.I.T.
Storms, M. D. (1981). A theory of erotic orientation development. *Psychological Review, 88,* 340–353.
Straus, M. (1971). Some social antecedents of physical punishment: A linkage theory interpretation. *Journal of Marriage and the Family, 33,* 658–663.
Straus, M. A. (1973). A general systems theory approach to a theory of violence between family members. *Social Science Information, 12,* 105–125.

Straus, M. A. (1975). *The marriage license as a hitting license: Social instigation of physical aggression in the family.* Paper presented at meeting of American Psychological Association, Chicago, September.

Straus, M. A., Gelles, R. J., & Steinmetz, S. K. (1980). *Behind closed doors: Violence in the American family.* New York: Doubleday.

Streufert, S., Castore, C. H., & Kliger, S. C. (1967). *A tactical and negotiations game: Rationale, method, and analysis.* Technical Report No. 1, Purdue University, Office of Naval Research.

Strickland, B. R. (1977). Internal-external control of reinforcement. In T. Blass (Ed.), *Personality variables in social behaviors.* Hillsdale, NJ: Erlbaum.

Stringer, M., & Cook, N. M. (1985). The effects of limited and conflicting stereotypic information on group categorization in Northern Ireland. *Journal of Applied Social Psychology, 15,* 399–407.

Strodtbeck, F. (1951). Husband-wife interaction over revealed differences. *American Sociological Review, 16,* 468–473.

Strodtbeck, F., & Hook, H. (1961). The social dimensions of a 12-man jury table. *Sociometry, 24,* 397–415.

Strodtbeck, F., James, R., & Hawkins, C. (1957). Social status in jury deliberations. *American Sociological Review, 22,* 713–718.

Strodtbeck, F., & Mann, R. (1956). Sex role differentiation in jury deliberations. *Sociometry, 19,* 3–11.

Strube, M. J. (1986). *Toward a theory of Type A behavior.* Paper presented at meeting of Midwestern Psychological Association, May 1986, Chicago.

Strube, M. J. (in press). A self-appraisal model of the Type A behavior pattern. In R. Hogan & W. Jones (Eds.), *Perspectives in personality: Theory, measurement and interpersonal dynamics.* Greenwich, CT: JAI Press.

Strube, M. J., & Garcia, J. E. (1981). A meta-analytic investigation of Fiedler's contingency model of leadership effectiveness. *Psychological Bulletin, 90,* 307–321.

Stryker, S. (1982). Identity salience and role performance: The relevance of symbolic interaction theory for family research. In M. Rosenberg & H. B. Kaplan (Eds.), *Social psychology of the self-concept* (pp. 200–208). Arlington Heights, IL: Harlan Davidson.

Stryker, S., & Statham, A. (1985). Symbolic interaction and role theory. In G. Lindzey & E. Aronson (Eds.), *Handbook of social psychology* (Vol. 1) (3rd ed.) (pp. 311–378). New York: Random House.

Suedfeld, P. (1982). Aloneness as a healing experience. In L. A. Peplau & D. Perlman (Eds.), *Loneliness: A sourcebook of current theory, research and therapy.* New York: Wiley.

Suedfeld, P., & Rank, A. D. (1976). Revolutionary leaders: Long-term success as a function of changes in conceptual complexity. *Journal of Personality and Social Psychology, 34,* 169–178.

Sullivan, H. S. (1953). *The interpersonal theory of psychiatry.* New York: Norton.

Suls, J., Gaes, G., & Gastorf, J. (1979). Evaluating a sex-related ability: Comparison with same-, opposite-, and combined-sex norms. *Journal of Research in Personality, 13,* 294–304.

Suls, J. M., & Miller, R. L. (Eds.). (1977). *Social comparison processes: Theoretical and empirical perspectives.* Washington, D.C.: Halsted-Wiley.

Sundstrom, E. (1975a). An experimental study of crowding: Effects of room-size, intrusion, and goal-blocking on nonverbal behavior, self-disclosure, and self-reported stress. *Journal of Personality and Social Psychology, 32,* 645–654.

Sundstrom, E. (1975b). Toward an interpersonal model of crowding. *Sociological Symposium, 14,* 124–144.

Sundstrom, E. (1978). Crowding as a sequential process: Review of research on the effects of population density on humans. In A. Baum & Y. Epstein (Eds.), *Human response to crowding.* Hillsdale, NJ: Erlbaum.

Sundstrom, E. (1986a). *Work places: The psychology of the physical environment in offices and factories.* New York: Cambridge University Press.

Sundstrom, E. (1986b). Privacy in the office. In J. Wineman (Ed.), *Behavioral issues in office design* (pp. 177–201). New York: Van Nostrand Rinehold.

Sundstrom, E. (1987). Work environments: Offices and factories. In D. Stokols and I. Altman (Eds.), *Handbook of environmental psychology.* New York: Wiley.

Sundstrom, E., & Altman, I. (1974). Field study of territorial behavior and dominance. *Journal of Personality and Social Psychology, 30,* 115–124.

Sundstrom, E., & Altman, I. (1976). Personal space and interpersonal relationships: Research review and theoretical model. *Human Ecology, 4,* 47–67.

Sundstrom, E., Burt, R., & Kamp, D. (1980). Privacy at work: Architectural correlates of job satisfaction and job performance. *Academy of Management Journal, 23*(1), 101–117.

Sundstrom, E., Herbert, R. K., & Brown, D. (1982). Privacy and communication in an open plan office: A case study. *Environment and Behavior, 14,* 379–392.

Sundstrom, E., Town, J., Brown, D., Forman, A., & McGee, C. (1982). Physical enclosure, type of job, and privacy in the office. *Environment and Behavior, 14,* 543–559.

Swann, W. B., Jr. (1984). Quest for accuracy in person perception: A matter of pragmatics. *Psychological Review, 91,* 457–477.

Swann, W. B., Jr. (1986). The self as architect of social reality. In B. R. Schlenker (Ed.), *The self and social life* (pp. 100–125). New York: McGraw-Hill.

Swann, W. B., Jr., & Ely, R. J. (1984). A battle of wills: Self-verification versus behavioral confirmation. *Journal of Personality and Social Psychology, 46,* 1287–1302.

Sweeney, P. D., Anderson, K., & Bailey, S. (1986). Attributional style in depression: A meta-analytic review. *Journal of Personality and Social Psychology, 50,* 974–991.

Sweeney, P. D., & Gruber, K. L. (1984). Selective exposure: Voter information preferences and the Watergate affair. *Journal of Personality and Social Psychology, 46,* 1208–1221.

Swift, J. (1960). *Gulliver's travels.* New York: New American Library. (Originally published, 1726.)

Switzer R., & Taylor, R. B. (1983). Sociability versus privacy of residential choice: Impacts of personality and local social ties. *Basic and Applied Social Psychology, 4,* 123–136.

Symonds, M. (1975). Victims of violence: Psychological effects and aftereffects. *American Journal of Psychoanalysis, 35,* 19–26.

Szent-Györgyi, A. (1971). Looking back. *Perspectives in Biology and Medicine, 15,* 1–6.

Szybillo, G. J., & Heslin, R. (1973). Resistance to persuasion: Inoculation theory in a marketing context. *Journal of Marketing Research, 10,* 396–403.

Tajfel, H. (1982). Social psychology of intergroup relations. In M. R. Rosenzweig & L. W. Porter (Eds.), *Annual review of psychology* (Vol. 33). Palo Alto, CA: Annual Reviews.

Tanford, S., & Penrod, S. (1983). Computer modeling of influence in the jury: The role of the consistent juror. *Social Psychology Quarterly, 46,* 200–212.

Tanford, S., & Penrod, S. (1984). Social influence model: A formal integration of research on majority and minority influence processes. *Psychological Bulletin, 95,* 189–225.

Taormina, R. J., & Messick, D. M. (1983). Deservingness for foreign aid: Effects of need, similarity, and estimated effectiveness. *Journal of Applied Social Psychology, 13,* 371–391.

Taylor, D. W., Berry, P. C., & Block, C. H. (1982). Does group participation when using brainstorming facilitate or inhibit creative thinking? *Administrative Science Quarterly, 3,* 23–47.

Taylor, R. B. (1982). Neighborhood physical environment and stress. In G. Evans (Ed.), *Environmental stress* (pp. 286–324). New York: Cambridge University Press.

Taylor, R. B., & Brower, S. (1986). Home and near-home territories. In I. Altman & C. Werner (Eds.), *Home environments. Human behavior and environment: Advances in theory and research* (Vol. 8) (pp. 183–212). New York: Plenum.

Taylor, R. B., & Ferguson, G. (1980). Solitude and intimacy: Privacy experiences and the role of territoriality. *Journal of Nonverbal Behavior, 4,* 227–239.

Taylor, R. B., Gottfredson, S. D., & Brower, S. (1981). Territorial cognitions and social climate in urban neighborhoods. *Basic and Applied Social Psychology, 2,* 289–303.

Taylor, R. B., & Lanni, J. C. (1982). Territorial dominance: The influence of the resident advantage in triadic decision making. *Journal of Personality and Social Psychology, 41,* 909–915.

Taylor, R. B., & Stough, R. R. (1978). Territorial cognition: Assessing Altman's typology. *Journal of Personality and Social Psychology, 36,* 418–423.

Taylor, S. E. (1978). A developing role for social psychology in medicine and medical practice. *Personality and Social Psychology Bulletin, 4,* 515–523.

Taylor, S. E. (1982). Social cognition and health. *Personality and Social Psychology Bulletin, 8,* 549–562.

Taylor, S. E. (1983). Adjustment to threatening events: A theory of cognitive adaptation. *American Psychologist, 38,* 1161–1173.

Taylor, S. E., Lichtman, R. R., & Wood, J. V. (1984). Attributions, beliefs about control, and adjustment to breast cancer. *Journal of Personality and Social Psychology, 46,* 489–502.

Taylor, S. E., & Thompson, S. C. (1982). Stalking the elusive "vividness" effect. *Psychological Review, 89,* 155–181.

Taylor, S. P. (1967). Aggressive behavior and physiological arousal as a function of provocation and the tendency to inhibit aggression. *Journal of Personality, 35,* 297–310.

Taylor, S. P., & Epstein, S. (1967). Aggression as a function of the interaction of sex of the aggressor and the sex of the victim. *Journal of Personality, 35,* 474–486.

Taylor, S., & Gammon, C. B. (1975). Effects of type and dose of alcohol on human physical aggression. *Journal of Personality and Social Psychology, 32,* 169–175.

Taylor, S. P., Gammon, C. B., & Capasso, D. R. (1976). Aggression as a function of the interaction of alcohol and threat. *Journal of Personality and Social Psychology, 34,* 938–941.

Taylor, S. P., & Pisano, R. (1971). Physical aggression as a function of frustration and physical attack. *Journal of Social Psychology, 84,* 261–267.

Taylor, S. P., Vardaris, R. M., Rawtich, A. B., Gammon, C. B., Cranston, J. W., & Lubetkin, A. I. (1976). The effects of alcohol and delta-9-tetrahydrocannabinol on human physical aggression. *Aggressive Behavior, 2,* 153–161.

Tesser, A., Gatewood, R., & Driver, M. (1968). Some determinants of gratitude. *Journal of Personality and Social Psychology, 9,* 233–236.

Tetlock, P. E. (1979). Identifying victims of groupthink from public statements of decision makers. *Journal of Personality and Social Psychology, 37,* 1314–1324.

Tetlock, P. E. (1981). Pre-to-post election shifts in presidential rhetoric: Impression management or cognitive adjustment? *Journal of Personality and Social Psychology, 41,* 207–212.

Tetlock P. E. (1984). Cognitive style and political belief systems in the British House of Commons. *Journal of Personality and Social Psychology, 46,* 365–375.

Tetlock, P. E. (1986). A value pluralism model of ideological reasoning. *Journal of Personality and Social Psychology, 50,* 819–827.

Tetlock, P. E., Bernzweig, J., & Gallant, J. L. (1985). Supreme Court decision making: Cognitive style as a predictor of ideological consistency of voting. *Journal of Personality and Social Psychology, 48,* 1227–1239.

Tetlock, P. E., & Manstead, A. S. R. (1985). Impression management versus intrapsychic explanations in social psychology: A useful dichotomy? *Psychological Review, 92,* 59–77.

Thibaut, J. W., & Kelley, H. H. (1959). *The social psychology of groups.* New York: Wiley.

Thompson, W. C., Cowan, C. L., & Rosenhan, D. L. (1980). Focus of attention mediates the impact of negative affect on altruism. *Journal of Personality and Social Psychology, 38,* 291–300.

Thornton, B. (1977). Toward a linear prediction model of marital happiness. *Personality and Social Psychology Bulletin, 3,* 674–676.

Tjosvold, D. (1984). Effects of leader warmth and directiveness on subordinate performance on a subsequent task. *Journal of Applied Psychology, 69,* 422–427.

Trager, G. L. (1958). Paralanguage: A first approximation. *Studies in Linguistics, 13,* 1–12.

Traupmann, J., Petersen, R., Utne, M., & Hatfield, E. (1981). Measuring equity in intimate relationships. *Applied Psychological Measurement, 5,* 467–480.

Trew, K., & McWhirter, L. (1982). Conflict in Northern Ireland: A research perspective. In P. Stringer (Ed.), *Confronting social issues: Applications of social psychology* (Vol. 2) (pp. 195–214). London: Academic Press.

Triandis, H. C. (1961). A note on Rokeach's theory of prejudice. *Journal of Abnormal and Social Psychology, 62,* 184–186.

Triandis, H. C. (1977). *Some universals of social behavior.* Address presented at meeting of American Psychological Association, San Francisco, August.

Triandis, H. C. (1980). Introduction. In H. C. Triandis & W. W. Lambert (Eds.), *Handbook of cross-cultural psychology, 1, Perspectives.* Boston: Allyn & Bacon.

Triandis, H. C., Davis, E. E., & Takezawa, S. I. (1965). Some determinants of social distance among American, German, and Japanese students. *Journal of Personality and Social Psychology, 2,* 540–551.

Triandis, H. C., & Lambert, W. W. (Eds.) (1980). *Handbook of cross-cultural psychology, 1, Perspectives.* Boston: Allyn & Bacon.

Triandis, H. C., & Lonner, W. (Eds.) (1980). *Handbook of cross-cultural psychology, 3, Basic processes.* Boston: Allyn & Bacon.

Triandis, H. C., Marin, G., Lisansky, J., & Betancourt, H. (1984) *Simpatía* as a cultural script of Hispanics. *Journal of Personality and Social Psychology, 47,* 1363–1375.

Triandis, H. C., & Vassiliou, V. (1967). Frequency of contact and stereotyping. *Journal of Personality and Social Psychology, 7,* 316–328.

Triplett, N. (1898). The dynamogenic factors in pacemaking and competition. *American Journal of Psychology, 9,* 507–533.

Trivers, R. L. (1971). The evolution of reciprocal altruism. *Quarterly Review of Biology, 46,* 35–57.

Trivers, R. L., & Hare, H. (1976). Haplodiploidy and the evolution of the social insects. *Science, 191,* 249–263.

Trope, Y., & Ben-Yair, E. (1982). Task construction and persistence as means for self-assessment of abilities. *Journal of Personality and Social Psychology, 42,* 637–645.

Tucker, L. A. (1983). Muscular strength and mental health. *Journal of Personality and Social Psychology, 45,* 1355–1360.

Tunnell, G. B. (1977). Three dimensions of naturalness: An expanded definition of field research. *Psychological Bulletin, 84,* 426–437.

Turner, C. W., & Berkowitz, L. (1972). Identification with film aggressor (covert role taking) and reactions to film violence. *Journal of Personality and Social Psychology, 21,* 256–264.

Turner, C. W., Layton, J. F., & Simons, L. S. (1975). Naturalistic studies of aggressive behavior: Aggressive stimuli, victim visibility, and horn honking. *Journal of Personality and Social Psychology, 31,* 1098–1107.

Turner, C. W., & Simons, L. S. (1974). Effects of subject sophistication and evaluation apprehension on aggressive responses to weapons. *Journal of Personality and Social Psychology, 30,* 341–348.

Turner, C. W., Simons, L. S., Berkowitz, L., & Frodi, A. (1977). The stimulating and inhibiting effects of weapons on aggressive behavior. *Aggressive Behavior, 3,* 355–378.

Turner, J. C. (1982). Toward a cognitive redefinition of the social group. In H. Tajfel (Ed.), *Social identity and intergroup relations* (pp. 15–40). Cambridge, England: Cambridge University Press.

Tversky, A., & Kahneman, D. (1973). Availability: A heuristic for judging frequency and probability. *Cognitive Psychology, 5,* 207–232.

Tversky, A., & Kahneman, D. (1974). Judgment under uncertainty. Heuristics and biases. *Science, 815,* 1124–1131.

Tyler, L. (1978). *Individuality: Human possibilities and personal choice in the psychological development of men and women.* San Francisco: Jossey-Bass.

Tyler, T. R., & Caine, A. (1981). The influence of outcomes and procedures on satisfaction with formal leaders. *Journal of Personality and Social Psychology, 41,* 642–655.

Tyler, T. R., & Sears, D. O. (1977). Coming to like obnoxious people when we must live with them. *Journal of Personality and Social Psychology, 35,* 200–211.

Ulrich, R. S. (1984). View through a window may influence recovery from surgery. *Science, 224,* 420–421.

Underwood, B., & Moore, B. (1982). Perspective-taking and altruism. *Psychological Bulletin, 91,* 143–173.

U.S. Commission on Civil Rights. (1969). *Racism in America and how to combat it.* Washington, D.C.: U.S. Government Printing Office.

U.S. President's Commission on Obscenity and Pornography. (1971). *Report.* Washington, D.C.: U.S. Government Printing Office.

U.S. Riot Commission. (1968). *Report of the National Advisory Commission on Civil Disorders.* New York: Bantam Books.

Valle, V. A., & Frieze, I. H. (1976). Stability of causal attributions in changing expectations for success. *Journal of Personality and Social Psychology, 33,* 579–587.

Van Vliet, W. (1983). Exploring the fourth environment: An examination of the home range of city and suburban teenagers. *Environment and Behavior, 15,* 567–588.

Varela, J. A. (1969). Aplicación de hallazgos provenientes de las ciencias sociales. *Revista Interamericana de Psicología, 3,* 45–52.

Varela, J. A. (1978). Solving human problems with human science. *Human Nature,* October, 84–90.

Verbrugge, L. M., & Taylor, R. B. (1980). Consequences of population density and size. *Urban Affairs Quarterly, 16,* 135–160.

Vinsel, A., Brown, B. B., Altman, I., & Foss, C. (1980). Privacy regulation, territorial displays, and effectiveness of individual functioning. *Journal of Personality and Social Psychology, 39,* 1104–1115.

von Baeyer, C. L., Sherk, D. L., & Zanna, M. P. (1981). Impression management in the job interview: When the female applicant meets the male (chauvinist) interviewer. *Personality and Social Psychology Bulletin, 7,* 45–51.

Vroom, V. H., & Yetton, P. W. (1973). *Leadership and decision-making.* Pittsburgh: University of Pittsburgh Press.

Waller, W. W. (1937). The rating and dating complex. *American Sociological Review, 2,* 727–737.

Wallston, B. S., & Wallston, K. A. (1978). Locus of control and health: A review of the literature. *Health Education Monographs, 6,* 107–117.

Walster, E., Aronson, E., & Abrahams, D. (1966). On increasing the persuasiveness of a low prestige communicator. *Journal of Experimental Social Psychology, 2,* 325–342.

Walster, E., & Walster, G. W. (1978). *Love.* Reading, MA: Addison-Wesley.

Walster, E., Walster, G. W., & Berscheid, E. (1978). *Equity: Theory and research.* Boston: Allyn & Bacon.

Walster, E., Walster, G. W., & Traupmann, J. (1978). Equity and premarital sex. *Journal of Personality and Social Psychology, 36,* 82–92.

Walters, R., & Thomas, E. (1963). Enhancement of punitiveness by visual and audiovisual displays. *Canadian Journal of Psychology, 17,* 244–255.

Walters, R. H., & Brown, M. (1963). Studies of reinforcement of aggression. III. Transfer of responses to an interpersonal situation. *Child Development, 34,* 536–571.

Ward, C. (1968). Seating arrangement and leadership emergence in small group discussions. *Journal of Social Psychology, 74,* 83–90.

Warriner, C. H. (1956). Groups are real: A reaffirmation. *American Sociological Review, 21,* 549–554.

Watson, R. I., Jr. (1973). Investigation into deindividuation using a cross-cultural survey technique. *Journal of Personality and Social Psychology, 25,* 342–345.

Waxler, N. E., & Mishler, E. G. (1978). Experimental studies of families. In L. Berkowitz (Ed.), *Group processes.* New York: Academic Press.

Webb, E. J., Campbell, D. T., Schwartz, R. D., & Sechrest, L. (1966). *Unobtrusive measures: Nonreactive research in the social sciences.* Chicago: Rand McNally.

Weber, R., & Crocker, J. (1983). Cognitive processes in the revision of stereotypic beliefs. *Journal of Personality and Social Psychology, 45,* 961–977.

Wegner, D. M., & Vallacher, R. R. (1977). *Implicit psychology:*

An introduction to social cognition. New York: Oxford University Press.
Weick, K. (1978). The spines of leaders. In M. W. McCall, Jr., & M. M. Lombardo (Eds.), *Leadership: Where else can we go?* Durham, NC: Duke University Press.
Weick, K. E. (1984). Small wins: Redefining the scale of social problems. *American Psychologist, 39,* 40–49.
Weigel, R. H., Vernon, D. T. A., & Tognacci, L. N. (1974). Specificity of the attitude as a determinant of attitude-behavior congruence. *Journal of Personality and Social Psychology, 30,* 724–728.
Weiner, B. (Ed.). (1974). *Achievement motivation and attribution theory.* Morristown, NJ: General Learning Press.
Weiner, B. (1980). A cognitive (attribution)-emotion-action model of motivated behavior: An analysis of judgments of help-giving. *Journal of Personality and Social Psychology, 39,* 186–200.
Weiner, B., Frieze, I., Kukla, A., Reed, L., Rest, S., & Rosenbaum, R. M. (1972). Perceiving the causes of success and failure. In E. E. Jones, D. E. Kanouse, H. H. Kelley, R. E. Nisbett, S. Valins, & B. Weiner, *Attribution: Perceiving the causes of behavior.* Morristown, NJ: General Learning Press.
Weinstein, C. S. (1979). The physical environment of the school: A review of the research. *Review of Educational Research, 49,* 577–610.
Weiss, C. H. (1972). *Evaluation research: Methods for assessing program effectiveness.* Englewood Cliffs, NJ: Prentice-Hall.
Weiss, R. F., Buchanan, W., Altstatt, L., & Lombardo, J. P. (1971). Altruism is rewarding. *Science, 171,* 1262–1263.
Weiss, R. S. (1973). *Loneliness: The experience of emotional and social isolation.* Cambridge, MA: M.I.T. Press.
Weitz, S. (1976). Sex differences in nonverbal communication. *Sex Roles, 2,* 175–184.
Wellman, D. T. (1977). *Portraits of White racism.* New York: Cambridge University Press.
Wells, B. W. P. (1965). The psycho-social influence of building environments: Sociometric findings in large and small office spaces. *Building Science, 1,* 153–165.
Wells, G. L. (1985). The eyewitness. In S. M. Kassin & L. S. Wrightsman (Eds.), *The psychology of evidence and trial procedure* (pp. 43–66). Beverly Hills, CA: Sage.
Wells, G. L., & Loftus, E. F. (Eds.). (1984). *Eyewitness testimony.* Cambridge, England: Cambridge University Press.
Wells, G. L., & Murray, D. M. (1984). Eyewitness confidence. In G. L. Wells & E. F. Loftus (Eds.), *Eyewitness testimony* (pp. 155–170). Cambridge, England: Cambridge University Press.
Wener, R., & Kaminoff, R. D. (1983). Improving environmental information. Effects of signs on perceived crowding and behavior. *Environment and Behavior, 15,* 3–20.
Werner, C., Altman, I., & Oxley, D. (1986). Temporal aspects of homes: A transactional perspective. In I. Altman & C. Werner (Eds.), *Home environments. Human behavior and environment: Advances in theory and research* (Vol. 8) (pp. 8–32). New York: Plenum.
Werner, C., Brown, B. B., & Damron, G. (1981). Territorial marking in a game arcade. *Journal of Personality and Social Psychology, 41,* 1094–1104.
Werner, C. M., Kagehiro, D. K., & Strube, M. J. (1982). Conviction proneness and the authoritarian juror: Inability to disregard information or attitudinal bias? *Journal of Applied Psychology, 67,* 629–636.

West, S. G., & Gunn, S. P. (1978). Some issues of ethics and social psychology. *American Psychologist, 33,* 30–38.
Westie, F. R. (1953). A technique for the measurement of race attitudes. *American Sociological Review, 18,* 73–78.
Westin, A. (1967). *Privacy and freedom.* New York: Atheneum.
Wexler, M. (1976). The behavioral sciences in medical education: A view from psychology. *American Psychologist, 31,* 275–283.
Weyant, J. M. (1978). Effects of mood states, costs, and benefits on helping. *Journal of Personality and Social Psychology, 36,* 1169–1176.
Wheeler, L., Koestner, R., & Driver, R. E. (1982). Related attributes in the choice of comparison others: It's there, but it isn't all there is. *Journal of Experimental Social Psychology, 18,* 489–500.
Wheeler, L., & Nezlek, J. (1977). Sex differences in social participation. *Journal of Personality and Social Psychology, 35,* 742–754.
Whitcher, S. J., & Fisher, J. D. (1979). Multidimensional reaction to therapeutic touch in a hospital setting. *Journal of Personality and Social Psychology, 37,* 87–96.
White, G. L. (1981). Some correlates of romantic jealousy. *Journal of Personality, 49,* 129–147.
White, J. W., & Gruber, K. J. (1982). Instigative aggression as a function of past experience and target characteristics. *Journal of Personality and Social Psychology, 42,* 1069–1075.
Whitehead, G. I., III, Smith, S. H., & Eichhorn, J. A. (1982). The effect of subject's race and other's race on judgments of causality for success and failure. *Journal of Personality, 50,* 193–202.
Whiting, B., & Edwards, C. P. (1973). A cross-cultural analysis of sex differences in the behavior of children aged three through eleven. *Journal of Social Psychology, 91,* 171–188.
Whyte, W. H., Jr. (1956). *The organization man.* New York: Simon & Schuster.
Wicker, A. W. (1979). *An introduction to ecological psychology.* Pacific Grove, CA: Brooks/Cole.
Wicklund, R. A. (1975). Objective self-awareness. In L. Berkowitz (Ed.), *Advances in experimental social psychology* (Vol. 8). New York: Academic Press.
Wicklund, R. A., & Frey, D. (1980). Self-awareness theory: When the self makes a difference. In D. M. Wegner & R. R. Vallacher (Eds.), *The self in social psychology.* New York: Oxford University Press.
Widgery, R., & Stackpole, C. (1972). Desk position, interview anxiety, and interviewer credibility: An example of cognitive balance. *Journal of Counseling Psychology, 19,* 173–177.
Wiemann, J. M., & Knapp, M. L. (1975). Turn-taking in conversations. *Journal of Communication, 25,* 75–92.
Wiener, F. (1976). Altruism, ambience and action: The effects of rural and urban rearing on helping behavior. *Journal of Personality and Social Psychology, 34,* 112–124.
Wilder, D. A. (1977). Perception of groups, size of opposition and social influence. *Journal of Experimental Social Psychology, 13,* 253–268.
Wilder, D. A. (1984). Intergroup contact: The typical member and the exception to the rule. *Journal of Experimental Social Psychology, 20,* 177–194.
Wilder, D. A. (1986). Social categorization: Implications for creation and reduction of intergroup bias. *Advances in Experimental Social Psychology, 19,* 291–355.
Wilder, D. A., & Shapiro, P. N. (1984). Role of out-group cues in

determining social identity. *Journal of Personality and Social Psychology, 47,* 342–348.

Williams, J. E., & Best, D. L. (1982). *Measuring sex stereotypes: A thirty nation study.* Beverly Hills, CA: Sage.

Williams, K., Harkins, S., & Latané, B. (1981). Identifiability as a deterrent to social loafing: Two cheering experiments. *Journal of Personality and Social Psychology, 40,* 303–311.

Williams, L. (1987). Report traces 45 cases of attacks on minorities. *New York Times,* February 15, p. 22.

Williams, W., & Evans, J. W. (1972). The politics of evaluation: The case of Head Start. In P. H. Rossi & W. Williams (Eds.), *Evaluating social programs: Theory, practice, and politics.* New York: Seminar Press.

Wilson, E. O. (1975). *Sociobiology: The new synthesis.* Cambridge, MA: Belknap Press of Harvard University Press.

Wilson, J. P. (1976). Motivation, modeling, and altruism: A person x situation analysis. *Journal of Personality and Social Psychology, 34,* 1078–1086.

Wilson, J. P., & Petruska, R. (1984). Motivation, model attributes, and prosocial behavior. *Journal of Personality and Social Psychology, 46,* 458–468.

Wilson, T. D., & Dunn, D. S. (1986). Effects of introspection on attitude-behavior consistency: Analyzing reasons versus focusing on feelings. *Journal of Experimental Social Psychology, 22,* 249–263.

Wilson, T. D., & Linville, P. W. (1985). Improving the performance of college freshmen with attributional techniques. *Journal of Personality and Social Psychology, 49,* 287–293.

Wilson, W. C. (1973). Pornography: The emergence of a social issue and the beginning of psychological study. *Journal of Social Issues, 29,* 7–17.

Winch, R. F., Ktsanes, T., & Ktsanes, V. (1954). The theory of complementary needs in mate selection: An analytic and descriptive study. *American Sociological Review, 19,* 241–249.

Winsborough, H. (1965). The social consequences of high population density. *Law and Contemporary Problems, 30,* 120–126.

Wishner, J. (1960). Reanalysis of "impressions of personality." *Psychological Review, 67,* 96–112.

Wispé, L. G. (1972). Positive forms of social behavior: An overview. *Journal of Social Issues, 28,* 1–19.

Wohlwill, H., & Kohn, I. (1973). The environment as experienced by the migrant: An adaptation-level view. *Representative Research in Social Psychology, 4,* 135–164.

Wohlwill, J. F. (1974). Human adaptation to levels of environmental stimulation. *Human Ecology, 2,* 127–147.

Wolf, S. (1979). Behavioural style and group cohesiveness as sources of minority influence. *European Journal of Social Psychology, 9,* 381–395.

Wollin, D. D., & Montagne, M. (1981). College classroom environment. *Environment and Behavior, 13,* 707–716.

Wood, F. A. (1913). *The influence of monarchs.* New York: Macmillan.

Worchel, S. (1974). The effect of three types of arbitrary thwarting on the instigation to aggression. *Journal of Personality, 42,* 301–318.

Worchel, S. (1986). The role of cooperation in reducing intergroup conflict. In S. Worchel & W. G. Austin (Eds.), *Psychology of intergroup relations* (2nd ed.) (pp. 288–304). Chicago: Nelson-Hall.

Worchel, S., Arnold, S., & Baker, M. (1975). The effects of censorship on attitude change: The influence of censor and communication characteristics. *Journal of Applied Social Psychology, 5,* 227–239.

Worchel, S., & Teddlie, C. (1976). The experience of crowding: A two-factor theory. *Journal of Personality and Social Psychology, 34,* 30–40.

Wortman, C. B., & Brehm, J. W. (1975). Responses to uncontrollable outcomes: An integration of reactance theory and the learned helplessness model. In L. Berkowitz (Ed.), *Advances in experimental social psychology* (Vol. 8). New York: Academic Press.

Wright, M. H., Zautra, A. J., & Braver, S. L. (1985). Distortion in control attributions for real life events. *Journal of Research in Personality, 19,* 54–71.

Wrightsman, L. S. (1964). Measurement of philosophies of human nature. *Psychological Reports, 14,* 743–751.

Wrightsman, L. S. (1985). The social psychology of U.S. presidential effectiveness. In S. Oskamp (Ed.), *Applied social psychology annual* (Vol. 6) (pp. 161–184). Newbury Park, CA: Sage.

Wrightsman, L. S. (1987). *Psychology and the legal system.* Pacific Grove, CA: Brooks/Cole.

Wyer, R. S., Jr., & Srull, T. K. (1981). Category accessibility: Some theoretical and empirical issues concerning the processing of social stimulus information. In E. T. Higgins, C. P. Herman, & M. P. Zanna (Eds.), *Social cognition: The Ontario symposium* (Vol. 1). Hillsdale, NJ: Erlbaum.

Wynne-Edwards, V. (1962). *Animal dispersion in relation to social behavior.* New York: Hafner.

Yarkin, K. L., Town, J. P., & Wallston, B. S. (1982). Blacks and women must try harder: Stimulus person's race and sex attributions of causality. *Personality and Social Psychology Bulletin, 8,* 21–24.

Yarmey, A. D., & Johnson, J. (1982). Evidence for the self as an imaginal prototype. *Journal of Research in Personality, 16,* 238–243.

Yates, S., & Aronson, E. (1983). A social-psychological perspective on energy conservation in residential buildings. *American Psychologist, 38,* 435–444.

Yinon, Y., & Bizman, A. (1980). Noise, success, and failure as determinants of helping behavior. *Personality and Social Psychology Bulletin, 6,* 125–130.

Youtz, P. N. (1929). *Sounding stones of architecture.* New York: W. W. Norton.

Zacker, J. (1973). Authoritarian avoidance of ambiguity. *Psychological Reports, 33,* 901–902.

Zahn-Waxler, C., Cummings, E. M., & Iannoti, R. J. (Eds.). (1986). *Altruism and aggression: Social and biological origins.* New York: Cambridge University Press.

Zahn-Waxler, C., Radke-Yarrow, M., & King, R. A. (1979). Child rearing and children's prosocial initiations toward victims of distress. *Child Development, 50,* 319–330.

Zajonc, R. B. (1965). Social facilitation. *Science, 149,* 269–274.

Zajonc, R. B. (1968). Attitudinal effects of mere exposure. *Journal of Personality and Social Psychology Monograph Supplement, 9*(2, Part 2), 2–27.

Zajonc, R. B. (1980). Cognition and social cognition: A historical perspective. In L. Festinger (Ed.), *Retrospections on social psychology* (pp. 180–204). New York: Oxford University Press.

Zajonc, R. B., & Sales, S. (1966). Social facilitation of dominant subordinate responses. *Journal of Experimental Social Psychology, 2,* 160–168.

Zanna, M., Goethals, G., & Hill, J. (1975). Evaluating a sex-related ability: Social comparison with similar others and standard setters. *Journal of Experimental Social Psychology, 11*, 86–93.

Zillmann, D. (1978). Attribution and misattribution of excitatory reactions. In J. H. Harvey, W. J. Ickes, & R. F. Kidd (Eds.), *New directions in attribution research* (Vol. 2). Hillsdale, NJ: Erlbaum.

Zillmann, D. (1979). *Hostility and aggression.* Hillsdale, NJ: Erlbaum.

Zillmann, D., Baron, R. A., & Tamborini, R. (1981). Social costs of smoking: Effects of tobacco smoke on hostile behavior. *Journal of Applied Social Psychology, 11*, 548–561.

Zillmann, D., & Bryant, J. (1982). Pornography, sexual callousness, and the trivialization of rape. *Journal of Communication,* Autumn.

Zillmann, D., Bryant, J., Cantor, J. R., & Day, K. D. (1975). Irrelevance of mitigating circumstances in retaliatory behavior at high levels of excitation. *Journal of Research in Personality, 9*, 282–293.

Zillmann, D., & Cantor, J. R. (1976). Effect of timing of information about mitigating circumstances on emotional responses to provocation and retaliatory behavior. *Journal of Experimental Social Psychology, 12*, 38–55.

Zillmann, D., Katcher, A., & Milavsky, B. (1972). Excitation transfer from physical exercise to subsequent aggressive behavior. *Journal of Experimental Social Psychology, 8*, 247–259.

Zimbardo, P. G. (1970). The human choice: Individuation, reason, and order versus deindividuation, impulse, and chaos. In W. J. Arnold & D. Levine (Eds.), *Nebraska Symposium on Motivation, 1969.* Lincoln: University of Nebraska Press.

Zimring, C. (1982). The built environment as a source of psychological stress: Impacts of buildings and cities on satisfaction and behavior. In G. Evans (Ed.), *Environmental stress* (pp. 151–178). New York: Cambridge University Press.

Zinkhan, G. M., & Stoiadin, L. F. (1984). Impact of sex role stereotypes on service priority in department stores. *Journal of Applied Psychology, 69*, 691–693.

Zlutnick, S., & Altman, I. (1972). Crowding and human behavior. In J. F. Wohlwill & D. Carson (Eds.), *Environment and the social sciences.* Washington, D.C.: American Psychological Association.

Zuckerman, M. (1971). Physiological measures of sexual arousal in the human. *Psychological Bulletin, 75*, 297–329.

Zuckerman, M. (1979). Attribution of success and failure revisited, or: The motivational bias is alive and well in attribution theory. *Journal of Personality, 47*, 245–287.

Zuckerman, M., DePaulo, B. M., & Rosenthal, R. (1981). Verbal and nonverbal communication of deception. In L. Berkowitz (Ed.), *Advances in experimental social psychology* (Vol. 14). New York: Academic Press.

Zuckerman, M., Lazzaro, M. M., & Waldgeir, D. (1979). Undermining effects of the foot-in-the-door technique with extrinsic rewards. *Journal of Applied Social Psychology, 9*, 292–296.

Zweigenhaft, R. L. (1976). Personal space in the faculty office: Desk placement and the student-faculty interaction. *Journal of Applied Psychology, 61*, 529–532.

AUTHOR INDEX

Abbey, A., 80–81
Abella, R., 548
Abelson, H. I., 189
Abelson, R. P., 106, 196–197
Abrahams, D., 187
Abramson, L. Y., 234
Abramson, P. R., 273, 274, 280, 288, 292, 294
Ackerman, P., 344
Adamopoulos, J., 523
Adams, R. S., 508
Aderman, D., 248–249, 357, 364
Adler, A., 86
Adorno, T. W., 108, 391, 474
Agustsdottir, S., 87
Ahlering, R. F., 194
Ahrentzen, S., 514
Aiello, J. R., 146, 234–235, 506, 512, 522, 523
Ajzen, I., 176–177
Alexander, Y., 488
Alicke, M. D., 215
Alioto, J. T., 320
Alker, H. A., 397
Allport, F. H., 6, 7, 404, 407
Allport, G. W., 4, 6, 103, 160, 390, 472–473, 474
Altemeyer, R. A., 507
Altman, A., 367
Altman, I., 149, 505, 514, 515–516, 518, 520, 524, 525, 526, 527, 528, 530
Altstatt, L., 339
Alvares, K., 449
Amabile, T. M., 120
Amato, P. R., 358
American Psychological Association, 56
Amir, Y., 489
Amoroso, D. M., 295
Anderson, C. A., 103–104, 317, 499
Anderson, D. C., 317, 499
Anderson, K., 79–80
Anderson, N. H., 99–100, 252
Anderson, S. M., 70
Andrews, I. R., 424
Andrews, J. H. M., 447

Annis, A. B., 523
Apatow, K., 95–96
Apfelbaum, E., 479
Appelbaum, M. I., 386
Arauz, C. G., 500
Archer, D., 470, 551
Archer, R. L., 345
Ard, B. N., Jr., 287
Ardrey, R., 300, 525
Arendt, E., 507
Argyle, M., 134, 144–146, 256–257
Arkin, R., 79
Armstrong, D., 504
Arnold, S., 232
Aronson, E., 36, 38, 39, 42, 50, 56, 187, 202, 252, 481, 551
Arvey, R. D., 96–97
Asch, S. E., 97–98, 212–214
Athanasiou, R., 291, 510
Atkins, A., 195
Atkins, J. L., 115
Austin, J. L., 130
Austin, W. T., 528
Axsom, D., 202
Azrin, N. H., 308

Bachy, V., 324
Back, K., 252, 496, 509, 511
Back, K. W., 420
Backman, C. W., 252
Bailey, S., 79–80
Baker, M., 232
Baker, P. M., 507
Baker, R. W., 563
Bales, R. F., 446, 507
Ball, R. L., 331
Balswick, J. O., 278
Bandura, A., 17–18, 305–306, 319, 411
Bane, A. L., 546–547
Banks, C., 48–49
Bard, M., 567
Barefoot, J., 145
Bargh, J. A., 106, 112
Barker, R. G., 45
Barnes, M., 259

Barnett, M. A., 360
Baron, C. H., 560
Baron, R. A., 296, 301, 305, 316–317, 329–331, 499, 500, 503, 524
Baron, R. M., 95
Baron, R. S., 408
Barone, R. C., 370
Barrios, M., 470
Barry, T., 502
Barsky, S. F., 526
Bar-Tal, D., 251, 368
Bartlett, F. C., 105
Barton, W. H., 503
Bartos, O. J., 485
Baskett, L. M., 76
Bass, B., 507
Bass, B. M., 441
Bassett, R., 219
Bates, F. L., 528
Batson, C. D., 337, 341, 344–345, 347, 359
Batten, P. G., 242
Bauer, R. A., 191
Baum, A., 234–235, 497, 512, 513, 521, 522, 523, 524, 528, 542, 543, 546, 549
Baum, C., 497
Baumann, D. J., 339, 362
Baumeister, R. F., 67, 84, 88, 169, 365
Baumrin, B. H., 539
Beach, F. A., 279, 282
Beardsley, E. L., 515
Beattie, C., 472
Beattie, M., 230, 386
Becker, F. D., 508, 517, 531, 532
Becker, L. J., 551, 552
Becker, S. W., 507
Bee, J., 509
Begley, P. J., 97
Belk, R., 550
Bell, A. P., 282, 283–284
Bell, P. A., 296, 316, 500, 528
Bem, D. J., 69
Bender, P., 291
Benevento, A., 235–236

Ben-Itzhak, S., 366
Bennett, A., 259
Benson, P. L., 352
Bentler, P. M., 267, 274
Ben-Yair, E., 78
Berg, B., 361
Berg, J. H., 257
Berger, J., 415–416
Berglas, S., 85–87
Berkowitz, L., 309–310, 320, 323, 324–325, 346, 350, 357, 364
Bernard, J., 286
Bernstein, S., 65
Bernzweig, J., 47
Berry, C. J., 326
Berry, J. W., 95–96, 381
Berry, P. C., 419
Berscheid, E., 88, 153, 188, 246, 250, 253, 256, 257, 260–261, 262, 266–267, 294
Best, D. L., 469
Betancourt, H., 384
Bettleheim, B., 224
Beveridge, W. I. B., 30, 32
Bickman, L., 350, 355–356, 560–561
Biddle, B. J., 13
Bidwell, L. D., 246
Bieri, J., 195
Binning, J. F., 448
Birch, K., 344
Bird, C., 437
Birdwhistell, R. L., 138
Bisanz, G. L., 184
Bishop, G. D., 423–424
Bitter, E., 305
Bizman, A., 501
Blake, R., 511
Blaney, N., 481
Blass, T., 400
Bleda, E., 502
Bleda, P., 502
Block, C. H., 419
Blommel, J. M., 410
Blumstein, P., 284, 288
Blumstein, P. W., 273, 274, 276–277
Bochner, S., 510
Bogat, A., 502
Bohrnstedt, G. W., 75, 251
Bolen, M. H., 345, 359
Bond, C. F., Jr., 408–409
Bond, M. H., 68, 383, 478
Booth, A., 247, 520
Borden, R. J., 86, 313, 406
Bordieri, J. E., 472
Borys, S., 242
Bouchard, T. J., Jr., 419
Boutilier, R. G., 123–124
Bowers, C., 67
Bowman, C., 364
Boyatzis, R. E., 438
Boyce, P., 517
Boykin, A. W., 385, 386, 389
Brady, K., 529
Bramson, L., 329

Braver, S. L., 227
Brehm, J. W., 231–232, 234
Brehm, S. S., 231–232
Brent, E., 198
Brewer, M. B., 36, 38, 42, 73, 109, 463, 476–478, 488, 489, 563
Brickman, P., 80–81, 248
Brickner, M. A., 418
Brigham, J. C., 475
Brill, M., 529
Brink, J. H., 249
Brislin, R. W., 381
Brittingham, G. L., 366
Britton, S. D., 485
Brocato, R. M., 410
Brock, T. A., 123
Brock, T. C., 190–191
Brodzinsky, D. M., 523
Broll, L., 366
Bromley, S., 465
Bronfenbrenner, U., 369
Broude, G. J., 278
Broverman, D. M., 379, 469
Broverman, I. K., 469
Brower, S., 530
Brown, B. B., 511, 516, 526, 527, 528, 530, 531
Brown, B. R., 483, 484, 485, 487
Brown, C. E., 527
Brown, D., 517, 518
Brown, M., 295, 305
Brown, P., 329
Brown, P. L., 367
Brown, R., 130–131
Brown, S. M., 441
Brown, V., 443
Bruder, R. A., 85
Bruner, J. S., 203
Bryan, J. H., 368
Bryant, F. B., 248–249
Bryant, J., 296, 311, 331
Bryson, J. B., 263
Buchanan, W., 339
Buckhout, R., 100
Buckley, T., 344
Bugental, D. E., 143–144
Burger, J. M., 219
Burkhart, B. R., 522
Burnstein, E., 309
Burt, R., 518
Bushnell, D. D., 331
Buss, A. H., 73, 74, 305, 308
Buss, D. M., 171–173, 259–260
Bustos, A. A., 132
Butters, J. W., 76
Bynum, T. S., 530
Byrne, D., 247, 252, 253–254, 273–274, 280, 281, 289–290, 294, 393, 394, 510
Byrne, L. A., 273–274

Cacioppo, J. T., 187, 189–190, 192–193, 206–207, 219, 355
Caine, A., 456

Calby, P., 560–561
Caldwell, D. F., 90
Calesnick, L. E., 234–235, 512
Calhoun, J. B., 519
Calhoun, L. G., 123
Callero, P., 370
Camino, L., 320–321
Campbell, A., 50–51
Campbell, D. E., 504, 508
Campbell, D. T., 38–39, 40, 42, 48, 54, 341, 415, 562–563, 564–565, 566
Campbell, J., 419
Campbell, J. D., 216
Campbell, N. A., 202–203, 552
Canavan, D., 491
Cannavale, F. J., 314
Canon, L. K., 501
Canter, R., 50
Canter, R. J., 553
Cantor, J. R., 331
Cantor, N., 64, 105, 396
Capasso, D. R., 315
Caporael, L. R., 131
Carli, L. L., 191, 216
Carlsmith, J. M., 36, 38, 42, 50, 56, 135, 200, 317
Carlson, E. R., 294
Carlson, H., 567
Carnevale, P. J. D., 485, 487
Caron, A. H., 168
Carpenter, C. F., 525
Carr, S. J., 145
Carswell, L., 560–561
Carter, J. H., 444
Cartwright, D., 420, 447, 540
Carver, C. S., 72–73, 545
Carver, S. C., 88
Cary, M. S., 134
Cash, D. W., 76
Cash, T. F., 76, 97
Castore, C. H., 49, 78
Catalan, J., 218
Cattell, R. B., 295
Cavan, S., 527
Chaiken, S., 171, 173, 177, 187–188, 190, 192–193
Chamberlain, A. S., 528
Chambers, R. M., 500
Champion, D. S., 115
Chance, J., 231
Chapin, J., 294
Chapko, M. K., 502
Chaplin, T. C., 325
Chapman, L. J., 110
Chapple, E., 528
Check, J. V. P., 325
Chein, I., 463
Chemerinski, A., 367
Chemers, M., 514
Chemers, M. M., 452, 453, 454
Chernick, L., 399
Cherry, F., 393, 394
Cheung, T., 68
Cheyne, J. A., 527

Christensen, A., 256, 260-261, 267
Christian, J. J., 519
Churchman, A., 528
Cialdini, R. B., 86, 205-206, 218-219, 339, 362
Clark, H. H., 129, 147, 148
Clark, K. B., 67, 562
Clark, M., 361
Clark, M. P., 67, 562
Clark, M. S., 254, 351, 366
Clark, R. D., 111, 341, 342-344, 346, 347-349, 352, 355, 358, 425, 426
Clarkson, F. E., 469
Clausen, G. T., 356
Clee, M. A., 232
Clore, G. L., 139, 252, 253-254
Cohen, D., 419
Cohen, L., 260
Cohen, S., 113, 245, 497, 498, 501, 521, 547
Coke, J. S., 337, 344
Coleman, A. D., 508, 525
Coleman, C. E. H., 294
Coleman, G., 522
Collins, B. E., 216, 230
Conglio, C., 532
Conner, R., 336, 360
Connors, M. M., 412
Conrath, D. W., 510
Conroy, J., 526
Converse, P. E., 50-51
Conway, M., 207
Cook, N. M., 488
Cook, S., 42, 43
Cook, S. W., 56, 367, 489, 552-553
Cooke, B. G., 386
Cooley, C. H., 15, 63
Coons, A. E., 444-445
Cooper, H., 79
Cooper, J., 50, 200-202
Cope, V., 252
Copley, J. B., 42-43
Costanzo, M., 551
Costanzo, P. R., 10, 11, 12, 16, 21, 216
Cota, A. A., 68
Cotterell, J. L., 514
Cotterell, N. B., 408
Cowan, C. L., 558
Cowan, E. L., 352
Cowen, C. L., 363
Cox, O. C., 472
Cox, V., 523
Cox, V. C., 520
Cozby, P. C., 149
Craik, K. H., 171-173
Crandall, R., 484
Crane, M., 65
Critchlow, B., 201
Crocker, J., 109
Crofton, C., 250
Crook, J. H., 303
Crosby, F., 328, 465
Cross, J. A., 345, 359
Cross, W. E., Jr., 386

Crowley, M., 109, 358, 360
Croyle, R. T., 201, 545
Crusco, A. H., 139
Crutchfield, R. S., 216
Csikszentmihalyi, M., 71
Cummings, E. M., 342
Cummings, L. L., 507
Cummings, W., 552
Cunningham, J. D., 116-117
Cunningham, M. R., 304, 361, 503
Curran, J. P., 136-137, 278-279
Curtis, R. C., 154
Cutrona, C. E., 242, 243, 245

Dabbs, J. M., Jr., 145
Daly, M., 279
Damron, G., 531
Danheiser, P. R., 89
Daniels, L. R., 346, 350
Darby, B. L., 218, 362
Darley, J., 342, 346, 349, 351
Darley, J. M., 32, 36-38, 55-56, 78, 153, 155, 253, 354-355, 358, 551, 552
Darwin, C., 136, 339
Dashiell, J. F., 409
Daubman, K. A., 112
Davidson, B., 266
Davidson, L. R., 149
Davies, J. C., 327
Davis, D., 253
Davis, D. E., 519
Davis, E. E., 383
Davis, G. E., 513, 522
Davis, J. H., 406, 485
Davis, K. E., 118, 120-121, 249, 277
Davis, T., 152
Dawes, R. M., 162, 164, 175
Dawkins, R., 340
Dawson, K. E., 169
Day, K. D., 331
Dean, J., 144-146
Dean, L. M., 143
Deaux, K., 31, 84, 109, 122, 155, 195, 205, 250, 388, 390, 470, 561
DeBono, K. G., 192, 204
DeFronzo, J., 499
DeFusco, P., 522
DeGree, C. E., 86
DeJong, W., 95, 217-218
DeLamater, J., 411
DeLuca, D., 306
Dembroski, T. M., 188
Dengerink, H. A., 312
DeNinno, J. A., 78
Dennis, H. S., 151
DePaulo, B. M., 143, 152, 366, 367, 388
Dermer, M., 88
Deutsch, M., 9, 214, 480, 482, 491
DeVellis, B. M., 546
DeYoung, G. E., 295
Diamond, I., 291
Diamond, M. J., 567
Diamond, S., 505
Diamond, W., 294-295

Diener, E., 306
Di Giacomo, J. P., 426
Dill, C. A., 546-547
Dillehay, R. C., 394
DiMarco, N., 441
DiMatteo, M. R., 548
DiNicola, D. D., 548
Dion, K. K., 95, 250
Dion, K. L., 68, 441
Dipboye, R. L., 96-97
Ditto, P. H., 545
Dobbins, S. E., 290
Dockett, K., 530
Dollard, J., 6, 8, 16-17, 19, 307-308, 331
Donelsmith, D. E., 248-249
Donisi, M., 70
Donnerstein, E., 296, 316, 324-325, 329, 502
Donnerstein, M., 296, 329
Doob, A. N., 33, 203
Doob, L. W., 19, 165, 307-308, 331
Dovey, K., 527
Dovidio, J. F., 108, 342-344, 346, 347-349, 352-353, 358, 362
Downing, L. L., 370
Downs, R., 501
Drehmer, D. E., 472
Dreiser, T., 102-104
Driscoll, J. M., 567
Driver, M., 366
Driver, R. E., 78
Duberman, L., 149
Dubos, R., 498
Duchan, L., 470
Duck, S., 268
Dugan, P. M., 110
Dull, V., 109
Dumont, J. P. C., 25
Dunand, M., 323
Duncan, B. D., 344
Duncan, J. S., 527
Duncan, R., 510
Duncan, S., 133
Duncan, S., Jr., 147
Dunkel-Schetter, C., 80-81
Dunn, D. S., 179-180
Dunnette, M. D., 419
Durham, M., 42-43
Durkheim, E., 7, 404
Duval, S., 71-72, 364
Duval, V. H., 72
Dyck, R. J., 312

Eagly, A. H., 161, 187-188, 190, 191-193, 216, 318, 358, 360, 387, 389
Ebbesen, E., 510, 511
Ebbesen, E. B., 555-556
Edney, J. J., 525, 527, 531
Edwards, C., 115
Edwards, C. P., 382
Edwards, M. T., 457
Effrein, E. A., 165
Eflal, B., 484

Efran, M. G., 527
Egeth, H., 560
Ehrhardt, A. A., 281
Ehrlich, P. R., 523
Eibl-Eibesfeldt, I., 303
Eichhorn, J. A., 122
Eisenberg, L., 307
Eisenberg, N., 344, 359, 368
Eisenberg-Berg, N., 359
Eisenstat, R. A., 143
Eiser, J. R., 110, 166, 544, 546
Ekman, P., 136–137, 138, 143, 151, 153
Ekstein, R., 338
Elkind, D., 441
Ellertson, N., 420
Elliott, R., 329
Ellis, H., 273
Elllis, P., 551
Ellis, R. A., 75–76
Ellsworth, P. C., 50, 54, 56, 135, 366, 558
Ellyson, S. L., 132–133
Elms, A., 224
Ely, R. J., 155
Emswiller, T., 470
Endler, N. S., 400
Epps, E. G., 386
Epstein, R., 393
Epstein, S., 311–312, 397
Epstein, Y. M., 522
Erickson, B., 523
Erkut, S., 359
Eron, L. D., 318, 322–323
Esper, J. A., 360
Esser, A. H., 528
Evanbeck, S., 205–206
Evans, D. E., 370
Evans, G. W., 502, 514, 523
Evans, J. W., 564
Evans, N., 108
Evans, R., 296
Evans, R. I., 546–547
Exline, R. V., 132–133, 135
Eysenck, H. S., 341, 380

Fairey, P. J., 216
Fairweather, G. W., 567
Fallon, B. J., 457
Farace, R. V., 149
Farina, A., 67, 97
Fazio, R. H., 70, 153, 165, 178–179, 200–201, 551
Feighny, K. M., 360
Feild, H. S., 123
Feldman-Summers, S., 232
Felson, R. B., 68, 76, 251
Fenigstein, A., 73, 74
Ferguson, G. S., 518, 526
Ferguson, T. J., 312
Ferleger, N., 136–137
Ferrari, J. R., 370
Feshbach, S., 188–189, 305, 331
Festinger, L., 6, 31, 33, 78, 199–200, 252, 314, 422, 429, 496, 509, 511
Fidell, L. S., 470

Fiedler, F. E., 449–454
Field, P. B., 191
Figurski, T. J., 71
Filley, A., 486
Fine, M., 67
Finegan, J. E., 40–41
Fink, H. C., 394
Finkelstein, S., 143
Firestone, I. J., 521
Fischhoff, B., 160
Fishbein, M., 176–177
Fisher, G. A., 75
Fisher, J. D., 140–141, 365, 366, 367, 524, 528
Fisher, W. A., 290, 294
Fiske, D. W., 147, 397
Fiske, S. T., 21, 72, 111, 160
Fitzgerald, R., 558
Flanary, R., 268
Fleming, I., 57
Fleming, R., 522, 543
Flowers, M. L., 422
Flyger, V., 519
Foa, E. B., 383
Foa, U. G., 249, 383
Fodor, E. M., 458
Fogelman, E., 358–359
Fong, G. T., 105
Fontaine, G., 221
Foote, F. H., 227
Ford, C. E., 86, 279, 282
Form, W. H., 351
Forman, A., 518
Forsyth, D. R., 56, 411, 415
Forte, R., 135
Fortenbach, V. A., 345
Forward, J., 50
Foss, C., 516, 528
Foss, R. D., 370
Foti, R. J., 455
Fraczek, A., 310
Franck, K. A., 496
Frankenhaeuser, M., 523, 524
Franklin, A. J., 386
Franzoi, S. L., 73
Fraser, C., 31, 34, 423
Fraser, S. C., 217
Fraser, S. L., 455
Freedman, J. L., 31, 95, 217, 322, 518, 519, 523
Freeman, S., 86
Freeman, V., 97
Freemon, J. E., 242
French, J. R. P., Jr., 221
Frenkel, O. J., 203
Frenkel-Brunswik, E., 391, 474
Freud, E. L., 102
Freud, S., 7, 8, 150, 272, 273, 278–279, 283, 284, 302–303, 331, 391
Freund, K., 292
Frey, D., 71, 202
Frey, D. L., 353
Frey, J., 316, 502
Friedrich-Cofer, L., 322

Friesen, W., 143
Friesen, W. V., 136, 138, 151
Frieze, I. H., 121
Frodi, A., 310
Froggat, C., 508
Fromkin, H. L., 97
Fulker, D. W., 341, 380
Fultz, J., 345
Funk, W. H., 419
Futrell, D., 169

Gaebelein, J. W., 305, 314
Gaertner, S. L., 342–344, 346, 347–349, 352–353, 358, 465–466
Gaes, G., 78
Gallant, J. L., 47
Galle, O. R., 519
Gammon, C. B., 315
Gamson, W. A., 568
Gange, J. J., 408
Gangestad, S., 88, 396
Gans, H. J., 510
Gara, M. A., 65
Garcia, J. E., 452
Garcia, L. T., 395
Garwood, S. G., 509
Gaskell, G., 551
Gastorf, J., 78
Gatewood, R., 366
Gauvain, M., 527
Gaylin, K., 517
Gebhard, P. H., 273, 274, 293
Geen, R. G., 305, 308, 311, 320, 406, 408, 501
Geis, F. L., 443
Geis, G., 336, 360
Gekas, V., 64, 75
Gelfand, D. M., 338
Geller, D. M., 50
Gelles, R. J., 326
Gentry, W. D., 305, 308
George, C., 368
Georgoudi, M., 11
Gerard, H. B., 214, 562
Gergen, K., 503
Gergen, K. J., 11, 83, 365, 366, 383
Gergen, M. M., 365, 383, 503
Germann, A. C., 567
Gerrard, M., 289, 290
Gianetto, R. M., 143–144
Gibb, C. A., 438, 444, 446
Gibbons, F., 364
Gibbons, F. X., 73, 545
Gield, B., 508, 517
Gifford, R. K., 110
Gilovich, T., 408
Glass, D., 544
Glass, D. C., 228, 498, 500
Glassman, J. B., 522
Glucksberg, S., 129
Godfrey, D. K., 83
Godow, A. G., 287
Goethals, G. R., 78, 169
Goethals, G. W., 329

Goffman, E., 81, 90, 515
Golden, J., 288
Goore, N., 408
Gorer, G., 306
Gormley, F. P., 522
Goswick, R. A., 242
Gottfredson, S. D., 530
Gottlieb, A., 56, 356
Gould, S. J., 25
Gouldner, A. W., 346
Gove, W. R., 519
Grabitz-Gneich, G., 232
Grady, K. E., 95
Graen, G., 449
Graham, C., 563
Graham, J. A., 138
Granberg, D., 198
Grandjean, E., 517
Grant, R., 501
Grant, R. D., 522
Graves, N. B., 341
Graves, T. D., 341
Gray-Little, B., 386
Graziano, W., 88, 89
Green, J., 120
Greenbaum, D. S., 527
Greenbaum, P. E., 527
Greenberg, C., 521
Greenberg, C. I., 521
Greenberg, J., 110–111, 559
Greenberg, M. S., 365, 366, 554, 555
Greene, D., 115
Greene, M. S., 532
Greenfield, N., 517
Greenfield, T. B., 447
Greenwald, A. G., 64
Greenwell, J., 312
Greenwood, J. D., 50
Greer, D. L., 293, 526
Gregory, D., 420
Grice, H. P., 148
Griffitt, W., 294, 395, 500
Groff, B. D., 523
Gross, A. E., 33, 55–56, 57, 250, 352, 366
Gross, P. H., 36–38, 155
Gruber, K. J., 314
Gruber, K. L., 173–174
Gruder, C. L., 356
Grujic, L., 147
Grunberg, N. E., 542, 546, 549
Grusec, J. E., 368
Grush, J. E., 177, 194
Guerin, B., 408
Gullahorn, J. T., 510, 511
Gunn, S. P., 57
Gurin, G., 230, 386
Gurin, P., 230, 386
Gustanski, J., 503
Guthrie, R. V., 385
Guthrie, T. J., 546–547
Guzzo, R. A., 122

Haber, G. M., 532

Haberkorn, G., 425
Hake, D. F., 308
Haley, J. V., 548
Hall, C. S., 10, 328
Hall, E. T., 141–142, 504, 505
Hall, J. A., 387
Halpin, A. W., 445, 446, 447
Hamayan, E. V., 446
Hamilton, D. L., 108, 110
Hamilton, W. D., 339
Hammen, C. L., 281
Hammersmith, S. K., 283–284
Hamner, W. C., 485
Haney, C., 48–49
Hanna, R., 250
Hannah, M. E., 369
Hans, V. P., 557–558
Hansen, D. J., 394
Hansen, W. B., 528, 546–547
Hardin, G., 550, 553
Harding, J., 463
Hardy, D., 115
Hare, A. P., 507
Hare, H., 339
Hargis, K., 362, 363
Harkins, S., 407, 417–418
Harlow, H. F., 268
Harpin, R. E., 512
Harries, K. D., 499
Harris, A. S., 470
Harris, L., 502, 516
Harris, M. B., 308, 351
Harris, M. J., 153–154
Harrison, A. A., 249–250, 253, 412
Hart, R. P., 151
Harter, S., 163–164
Hartke, D. D., 452
Hartmann, D., 331
Hartmann, D. P., 338
Hartmann, H., 302
Harvey, J. H., 256, 260–261, 267, 268
Harvey, O. J., 196, 481–482, 487–488
Hass, R. G., 74, 206
Hastie, R., 105, 119, 412
Hastorf, A. H., 67, 97
Hatfield, E., 266, 365
Havis, J., 546–547
Hay, W. M., 314
Hayduk, L. A., 142
Hays, R. B., 246, 257, 453
Hazlewood, J. D., 40–41
Healy, S., 257
Heckel, R. V., 507
Hedge, A., 517
Hegel, G. W. F., 6
Heider, F., 6, 79, 115–116, 120, 121, 197–198
Heilman, M. E., 122
Heiman, J. R., 292
Heinold, W. D., 360
Heller, J., 523
Hellmuth, J., 564
Helmreich, R., 44–45, 377–378, 469
Helson, H., 498

Hemphill, J. K., 444–445, 447
Henderson, A. H., 546–547
Henderson, M., 256–257
Hendrick, C., 10, 50, 249, 259, 277
Hendrick, S., 259, 277
Henley, N. M., 133, 139, 387
Henson, A., 135
Herbert, R. K., 517
Herek, G. M., 203–205
Herman, C. P., 67, 95, 96
Herman, G., 323
Herman, P., 205–206
Herr, P. M., 70, 178
Herrnstein, R., 380
Heshka, S., 519
Heskin, K., 488
Hesley, J. W., 399
Heslin, R., 140–141, 207, 548
Hess, E. H., 303
Hester, R. K., 123
Hewitt, J., 143, 504
Hewstone, M., 478, 479
Heywood, S., 138
Hicks, D., 323
Hiers, J. M., 507
Higbee, K. L., 189
Higgins, E. T., 66, 67, 72, 86, 106, 112–113, 114, 129
Higgins, T., 76
Hill, C. T., 248, 263–266, 285–286
Hill, J., 78
Hill, P. C., 546–547
Hills, L. R., 230–231
Hilton, J. L., 155
Hiltrop, J. M., 486
Himmelfarb, S., 161
Hirt, E., 526
Hockey, G. R., 497
Hoelter, J. W., 64, 75
Hoffman, M. L., 340–341, 344, 368
Holahan, C. J., 511
Holland, C. C., 225
Hollander, E. P., 436, 441, 456–457
Holmes, J. G., 123, 262
Holtz, R., 364
Homans, G. C., 16, 18, 510, 511
Hong, C., 524
Hood, W. E., 481–482, 487–488
Hook, H., 507
Hook, S., 439–440
Hopman, P. T., 485
Hoppe, R. A., 532
Hopstock, P. J., 522
Horn, J., 341
Horner, M. S., 31
Hornstein, H. A., 149, 351, 371, 563, 565, 568
Horton, R. W., 323
House, J. S., 358
House, P., 115
House, R. J., 449
Hovland, C., 9, 185–187, 194–196
Howard, J. A., 346
Howard, J. L., 292–293

Howard, P. H., 548
Howells, L. T., 507
Huber, G. P., 507
Huesman, L. R., 318, 322–323
Huffman, P. E., 393
Hull, C., 32
Humphreys, P., 415–416
Hundert, A. J., 517
Hunt, M., 32, 273, 274–276
Huston, A. C., 322
Huston, T. L., 256, 260–261, 267, 336, 360
Hutchinson, R. R., 308
Hutt, C., 523

Iannoti, R. J., 342
Ickes, W., 399
Imai-Marquez, J., 294
Ingham, R., 134
Inkster, J. A., 203
Innes, J. M., 314
Insko, C. A., 166–167, 198, 215, 467
Iritani, B., 470
Irwin, R., 522
Isen, A. M., 112, 345, 361
Isenberg, D. J., 424
Ishii, S., 367
Itkin, S., 139
Iyengar, S., 168–169
Iyer, H., 380–381
Izard, C. E., 136, 383
Izzett, R., 394

Jaastad, K., 419
Jaccard, J., 397
Jaccard, J. J., 409
Jacklin, C. N., 318, 387
Jackson, J. M., 406, 418
Jackson-White, R., 85
Jacobs, J., 516
Jacobs, R. C., 415
Jacobs, S. V., 502
Jacobson, L., 154–155
Jaffe, Y., 294
Jago, A. G., 442
Jahoda, G., 26
James, W., 63, 66
Janis, I., 185–187, 548
Janis, I. L., 188–189, 191, 206, 420–422
Jaquette, D. S., 359
Jason, L. A., 320
Jaspars, J., 479
Jefferson, G., 147
Jellison, J. M., 85, 120
Jemmott, J. B., 111, 545
Jenkins, W. O., 66, 437
Jenson, A. R., 380
Jepson, C., 115
Jessor, R., 395
Johnson, B., 472
Johnson, D. L., 424
Johnson, G. A., 500
Johnson, H., 393

Johnson, H. G., 138
Johnson, H. H., 395
Johnson, J., 65
Johnson, J. P., 42–43
Johnson, T. E., 312
Johnson, V. E., 273, 274, 279, 283
Johnston, A., 306
Johnston, R., 137
Joiner, D., 508
Jonas, M., 234
Jones, C. R., 113
Jones, E. E., 9, 18, 67, 80, 83–84, 85–87, 88, 97, 118–119, 120–121, 153, 155
Jones, J. M., 386, 388–389, 502
Jones, K., 507
Jones, M. B., 394
Jones, R. A., 10, 102–103, 548
Jones, R. G., 83
Jones, T. S., 485
Jones, W. H., 242
Jordan-Edney, N. L., 531
Jorgensen, B. W., 249
Joseph, L., 408
Jourard, S. M., 149
Jue, G. M., 514
Julian, J. W., 456
Jussim, L., 155

Kaats, G. R., 277
Kagehiro, D. K., 395
Kahn, R., 540
Kahn, R. L., 415, 458
Kahn, S., 547
Kahneman, D., 114, 546
Kaiser, M. K., 366
Kalton, G., 52
Kambara, T., 312
Kaminoff, R. D., 524
Kammann, R., 522
Kamp, D., 518
Kamzan, M., 350
Kanagawa, C., 369
Kandel, D. B., 248
Kanouse, D. E., 80
Kanter, R. M., 425
Kantola, S. J., 202–203, 552
Kao, C., 193
Kaplan, J. A., 371
Kaplan, M. F., 252
Karabenick, S. A., 352
Kardes, F. R., 178
Karlin, R. A., 522
Karlins, M., 189
Karp, L., 361
Karuza, J., Jr., 248
Karylowski, J., 362
Kassin, S. M., 560
Kastenbaum, D. R., 450
Kaswan, J. E., 143–144
Katcher, A., 309
Katz, D., 67, 161, 203, 415, 458
Katz, I., 352, 353
Kauffman, D. R., 83

Kaufmann, H., 17
Kawash, G. F., 295
Kaye, M., 294–295
Ke, G. Y., 559
Keating, J. P., 123
Keeler, B. T., 447
Kehr, J. A., 97
Kelley, H. H., 6, 18–19, 26, 80, 98, 116–117, 119, 121, 185–187, 255–256, 257, 260–261, 267, 268
Kelly, G. A., 104
Kelly, J. R., 388
Kelman, H. C., 42, 50, 56, 394
Kelvin, P., 515
Kennedy, E., 510
Kennedy, J. G., 169
Kenny, D. A., 438
Kenny, J. W., 532
Kenrick, D. T., 105, 339, 362, 398, 399, 499, 500
Kepner, C. R., 329
Kerber, K. W., 252
Kerckhoff, A. C., 249
Kernis, M., 251
Kerr, N. L., 412, 416
Kerr, S., 446
Kessler, S. J., 95
Kidda, M. L., Jr., 366
Kihlstrom, J. F., 64, 396
Kimble, C. E., 135, 526
Kimble, G. A., 15
Kimes, D. D., 470
Kinder, D. R., 168–169, 198, 465
King, G., 113
King, K., 72, 278
King, M. L., Jr., 124
King, R. A., 368
Kinsey, A. C., 273, 274–275, 284, 293, 294
Kipnis, D. M., 252
Kirmeyer, S. I., 520
Kirsch, N., 50
Kirschner, N. M., 294
Kirscht, J. P., 394
Kitcher, P., 25
Kite, M., 472
Kjos, G., 510, 511
Klaiber, E. L., 379
Klassen, A., 282
Kleinke, C. L., 132, 135
Kleck, R. E., 95
Klevanski, S., 523
Kliger, S. C., 49
Kline, N. S., 528
Klinnert, M., 245
Klubeck, S., 507
Kluegel, J. R., 467–468, 471
Kluger, R., 562
Knafo, D., 294
Knapp, M. L., 131, 147, 151
Knob, K., 292
Knowles, E. S., 509, 527
Knox, R. E., 203
Kobasa, S. C., 547

Kobayashi, Y., 379
Koestner, R., 78
Koffka, K., 20
Kogan, N., 423
Kohler, W., 20
Kohn, I., 498
Kohn, M., 184
Kolb, D. M., 487
Kolditz, T., 79
Koman, S., 521
Komorita, S. S., 485
Konar, E., 529
Konecni, V., 510, 511
Konecni, V. J., 332, 501, 555–556
Koneya, M., 508
Korman, A. K., 437–438, 445
Korn, R. R., 346
Korte, C., 358, 501, 522
Koulack, D., 195, 196
Kozlowski, L., 205–206
Kramer, R. M., 463, 476–477, 488
Krantz, D. H., 115
Krantz, D. S., 542, 546, 548, 549
Krause, S., 257
Krauss, R. M., 129, 136–137
Kraut, R. E., 137, 152, 218
Kravitz, D. A., 417
Krebs, D., 340, 351
Krebs, D. L., 301, 304, 309, 337, 342, 344, 358
Kressel, K., 486
Kris, E., 302
Kriss, M., 551
Kronhausen, E., 324
Kronhausen, P., 324
Krosnick, J. A., 168–169, 544, 546
Ktsanes, I., 249
Ktsanes, V., 249
Kukla, A., 121
Kukla, R. A., 53–54
Kunda, Z., 115
Kunda, Z. K., 370
Kutchinsky, B., 324
Kutner, B., 174, 463

LaFrance, M., 131, 134–135, 387
Lagerspetz, K., 322–323
Lalljee, M., 119
Lambert, W. W., 381
Lamm, H., 419, 422–423
Landman, J., 21
Lando, H. A., 329
Landy, D., 97, 251
Langer, E., 548
Langer, E. J., 69, 220, 226–230, 235–236
Langlois, J. H., 95
Lanier, K., 152
Lanni, J. C., 526
Lao, R. C., 230, 386
LaPiere, R. T., 174
Lasater, T. M., 188
Lassegard, M., 86
Lassiter, G. D., 152
Latané, B., 32, 78, 246, 342, 346, 349,

Latané, B. (continued)
 351, 354–355, 358, 406–407, 417, 425
Lau, R. R., 548
Laughlin, P. R., 409, 485
Lavrakas, P. J., 530
Lawler, E. J., 457
Lawton, M., 503
Lawton, M. P., 510
Layton, B., 523
Layton, J. F., 315
Lazowski, L. E., 70
Lazzaro, M. M., 218
Leary, M. R., 66, 290
Leavitt, H. J., 413–414
LeBon, G., 7, 33
Lecuyer, R., 507
Lee, J. A., 258–259
Lefkowitz, M. M., 318
Leger, G. J., 331
Lenn, T. M., 165
LePage, A., 310
Lepper, M. R., 104
Lerner, M., 123–124, 248, 477
Lerner, R. M., 352
Lesnik-Oberstein, M., 260
Lesser, T., 268
Lett, E., 525
Leung, K., 284
Leventhal, H., 189
Levin, H., 569
Levin, P. F., 361
Levine, D. W., 509
Levine, J. M., 427–429
Levinger, G., 249, 256, 260–261, 267–268
Levinson, D., 391, 474
Levinson, D. J., 393
Levintan, D., 257
Levitt, E., 282
Levy, A., 205–206, 519
Levy, S. G., 327, 395
Lewin, A. Y., 470
Lewin, K., 6, 8, 9, 21, 22–23, 54, 377, 400, 539–541, 566, 568
Lewis, L., 109
Lewis, S. K., 218
Leyens, J.-P., 320–321, 323
Leyhausen, P., 525
Lezak, A., 501
Libby, W. L., 147
Lichtman, R. R., 550
Lieberman, S., 14
Liebert, R. M., 319, 320
Likert, R., 153
Lind, E. A., 559
Lindskold, S., 491
Lindzey, G., 6, 10, 328, 379–380
Linkous, R. A., 410
Linville, P. W., 66, 80, 476
Lipman, A., 496
Lippa, R., 85
Lippitt, R., 6
Lippmann, W., 108

Liptzin, M. B., 292–293
Lisansky, J., 384
Litman-Adizes, T., 221
Lobitz, W. C., 557
Loehlin, J., 379–380
Loewenstein, R. M., 302

Maccoby, E. E., 318, 387
Maccoby, N., 168, 322, 368
MacCoun, R. J., 412, 416
MacFarlane, S. W., 499
MacIntosh, B., 521
Mack, D., 559
Mackie, D. M., 424
MacPherson, J., 508, 509
Maddi, S. R., 547
Maddux, J. E., 189
Madonia, B., 504
Magnusson, D., 398, 400
Mahar, L., 454
Main, M., 368
Major, B., 84, 116–117, 141, 155, 388, 390
Malamuth, N. M., 324–325
Mandel, D., 529
Mander, A. M., 314
Manis, M., 21, 112
Mann, J., 295
Mann, L., 163–164, 313, 314, 369, 382
Mann, R. D., 437
Mann, R. W., 206
Manstead, A. S. R., 82
Manucia, G. K., 362
Margulis, S. T., 514
Markus, H., 21, 64–65, 66, 67, 76, 97, 105, 106
Martella, J. A., 449
Martin, B., 417
Martin, C. E., 273, 274, 293
Martin, G., 384
Martin, G. B., 341
Martin, J., 53–54, 328, 393
Martindale, D. A., 525
Martyna, W., 85
Maslach, C., 366
Maslow, A. H., 504
Massengill, D., 441
Masters, W. H., 273, 274, 279, 283
Mathews, K. E., Jr., 501
Matthews, K. A., 341, 544
Matthews, R. B., 523
Maxwell, S. E., 546–547
May, J., 294
Mayer, F. S., 364
Maynard, D. W., 147–148
Mayo, C., 134–135, 387, 532
Mayo, C. W., 131
Mayo, J. M., 511
Mayseless, O., 367
Mazmanian, L., 191
McAdams, D. P., 257
McAlister, A. L., 544, 546
McArthur, L. A., 95, 96, 116–117
McBride, D., 420

McCain, G., 520, 523
McCallum, R. C., 524
McCann, C. D., 113
McCarthy, D., 511
McCarthy, P. M., 345
McCarty, D., 294-295
McCauley, C., 42-43, 294, 475, 522
McClelland, D. C., 438
McClelland, L., 552-553
McClintock, C. G., 204
McClintock, E., 256, 260-261, 267
McCloskey, M., 560
McCorkle, L. W., 346
McCrown, D. A., 97
McDavis, K., 344
McDonald, P. J., 509
McDonaugh, G. R., 422
McElroy, J. C., 508
McFarland, C., 207
McGee, C., 518
McGhee, P. E., 216
McGillis, D., 118
McGinniss, J., 187
McGrath, J. E., 26, 53-54, 388, 405, 415, 417, 497
McGuire, C. V., 68
McGuire, W. J., 11, 30, 31, 32, 68, 161, 164, 165, 186, 191, 205-206
McKenna, J., 560
McKenna, W., 95
McKeough, K. L., 194
McKirnan, D. J., 466
McLane, D., 257
McLaughlin, J. P., 465-466
McMillen, D. L., 363
McNemar, Q., 380
McPherson, J. M., 519
McWhirter, L., 488
Mead, G. H., 6, 8, 12, 15, 63, 90
Meadow, A., 419
Mechanic, M. B., 292
Medvin, N., 366
Meeker, F. B., 132
Mehlman, R. C., 86
Mehrabian, A., 139, 142, 143, 144, 505
Meindl, J. R., 477
Mentzer, S., 546
Merluzzi, T., 107
Messick, D. M., 351
Metcalf, J., 228, 524
Meyberg, V., 292
Meyer, R. G., 567
Meyer, W.-U., 78
Mezei, L., 466
Miceli, M., 242
Michaels, J. W., 410
Michelson, W., 520
Michener, H. A., 457
Midlarski, E., 359, 369
Milavsky, B., 309
Milburn, M. A., 160, 544, 546
Milgram, S., 163-164, 222-225, 313, 314, 358, 497, 522
Millar, M. G., 180

Miller, A. G., 50, 224
Miller, C., 484
Miller, D. T., 67, 97, 123, 153, 155, 228, 301, 304, 309, 337, 342, 358
Miller, G. A., 538-539
Miller, J. A., 219
Miller, J. G., 120, 497
Miller, K., 154
Miller, L. E., 177
Miller, N., 196, 489, 563
Miller, N. E., 6, 16-17, 19, 307-308, 331
Miller, P. A., 344, 359
Miller, R. L., 78
Millman, S., 205
Mills, J., 202, 254, 366
Mills, R. T., 548
Mintz, N. L., 504
Mirels, H. L., 230
Mischels, W., 105, 390, 397, 398-399
Mitchell, H. E., 123
Mittelmark, M. B., 546-547
Moe, J. L., 467
Monahan, J., 554
Money, J., 281, 282, 291
Monson, T., 88-89
Monson, T. C., 399
Montagne, M., 504
Montagu, A., 300
Montano, D., 523
Moore, B., 359, 368
Morasch, B., 242
Moreland, R. L., 105, 253, 427-429
Morgan, C. J., 340
Morgan, M., 168, 268
Moriarty, T., 356
Morris, J., 281
Morrison, D. M., 289-290
Morrow, P. C., 508
Morse, S. J., 383
Morton, T. L., 149
Moscovici, S., 215, 381, 425-426
Mosher, D. L., 292, 295
Moss, M. K., 357
Mouton, J., 511
Mowen, J. C., 218-219
Mowrer, O. H., 19, 307-308, 331
Mueller, J. H., 73
Mugny, G., 425-426
Mullen, B., 73, 115, 169, 406
Mullens, S., 145
Murray, D., 522
Murray, D. M., 100
Murray, H. A., 390
Murray, J., 331
Murtaugh, K., 306
Myers, D. G., 422-424
Myerscough, R., 315

Nacoste, R. W., 467
Nadler, A., 365, 366, 367
Nahemow, L., 510
Neale, M. C., 341, 380
Nebergall, R. E., 194-195
Neely, R., 72

Nelson, C., 98
Nelson, P., 528
Nemecek, J., 517
Nemeth, C., 426
Neuringer-Benefiel, H. E., 345, 359
Newcomb, M. D., 173, 267
Newcomb, T., 33, 314
Newcomb, T. M., 45, 248, 510
Newman, J., 522
Newman, O., 529-530
Newton, J. W., 314
Netwon, P., 386
Newtson, D., 118
Nezlek, J., 246, 251
Nias, D. K. B., 341, 380
Nida, S. A., 354-355
Nisbett, R. E., 80, 115
Nizer, L., 150-151
Noller, P., 149-150
Norman, S. A., 228
Normoyle, J., 530
Norvell, N., 489-490
Nosow, S., 351
Novak, D., 248
Nurius, P., 66, 76
Nutt, R. L., 277

Oborne, D. J., 502
O'Brien, E. J., 397
O'Day, A., 488
Odino, J., 319
Ohbuchi, K., 312
Olney, T. J., 178
Olsen, H., 508
Olweus, D., 318, 327
O'Neal, E., 509
O'Neal, E. C., 501
Ong, P., 520
O'Quin, K., 345
O'Reilly, C. A., 111, 90
Orne, M. T., 39, 225
Orr, F., 510
Orris, J. B., 449
Ortega, D. F., 544
Orvis, B. R., 116-117
Osborne, A. F., 411, 418-419
Osgood, C. E., 144, 163, 491
Oskamp, S., 161
Osmond, H., 505
Ostrom, T. M., 191, 418
O'Sullivan, M., 143
Ovcharchyn-Devitt, C., 560-561
Owen, D. W., 397
Owens, D. J., 326
Oxley, B., 509
Oxley, D., 246, 527

Padawer-Singer, A., 68
Pagano, M., 294
Page, R., 167, 501
Page, R. A., 357
Painter, J., 550
Palamarek, D. L., 316-317
Pallak, M. S., 552

Index

Papageorgis, D., 205
Parish, E. A., 242
Park, B., 98–99, 476
Parke, R. D., 320–321
Parnes, S. J., 419
Patchen, M., 563
Patterson, A. H., 530
Patterson, M. L., 132–136, 145, 146, 523
Patzer, G. L., 95
Paulhus, D. L., 370
Paulus, P. B., 520, 521, 523
Pavelchak, M. A., 429
Pavlov, I., 16, 165
Peake, P. K., 398
Pearce, P. L., 351
Pegnetter, R., 487
Pelfrey, M. P., 367
Pelligrini, R. J., 507
Pennebaker, J. W., 545
Pennington, N., 412
Penrod, S., 101, 215, 406, 560
Penrod, S. D., 412, 425
Pepitone, A., 7, 9, 26, 33, 314
Peplau, L. A., 241, 242, 256, 260–261, 263–266, 267, 285–286
Percival, E., 308
Peri, N., 367
Perkowitz, W., 560–561
Perlman, D., 241, 242, 278
Perlman, S. D., 288
Perri, M., 251
Perry, L. B., 292
Pervin, L. A., 396
Peters, L. H., 452
Peters, M. D., 168–169
Petersen, R., 266
Peterson, C., 234
Peterson, D. R., 256, 260–261, 267
Peterson, P. D., 195, 196
Petruska, R., 357
Pettigrew, T., 551
Pettigrew, T. F., 386, 478
Petty, R. F., 187, 189–191, 192–193, 205–207, 355, 418
Pfeffer, J., 455
Phares, E. J., 230, 231
Phillips, D. P., 5, 320, 330
Pile, J., 516
Piliavin, I. M., 352, 366
Piliavin, J. A., 337, 342–344, 346, 347–349, 352, 358, 370
Pilkey, D. W., 295
Pinner, B., 523
Pipal, J. E., 544
Pisano, R., 308
Pittenger, J. B., 76
Pittman, T. S., 83–84
Platt, J., 522, 533
Pocs, O., 287
Podsakoff, P. M., 221
Poe, D., 152
Pohlmann, J. T., 452
Pollock, L. M., 530
Polyson, J., 97

Pomeroy, W. B., 273, 274, 293
Poor, D., 393
Post, D. L., 7
Powell, M. C., 178, 254
Pratkanis, A. R., 64
Prentice-Dunn, S., 314
Price, R. A., 380–381
Proshansky, H., 386, 463
Pruesse, M., 295
Pruitt, D. G., 420–421, 483, 484, 485, 486
Pryor, J., 107
Pryor, J. B., 551
Przybyla, D. P. J., 280, 394
Purri, D. M., 530
Putnam, L. L., 485
Pyszczynski, T. A., 110–111, 559

Quinsey, V. L., 325

Radford, M., 369
Radke-Yarrow, M., 368
Radloff, C. E., 169
Radloff, R., 44–45
Raines, B. E., 546–547
Rall, M., 523
Ramirez, A., 188, 385, 386, 464, 489
Ramirez, J., 296
Rank, A. D., 441
Ransberger, V. M., 317
Ransford, H. E., 331
Raps, C. S., 234
Raven, B. H., 221
Raviv, A., 368
Reddy, D. M., 522
Reed, D., 280
Reed, L., 121
Reed, M. D., 68
Reichner, R. F., 512
Reifler, C. B., 292–293
Reis, H. T., 251
Reisenzein, R., 350
Reiss, I., 277
Rempel, J. K., 262
Rest, S., 121
Reynolds, M. A., 151–152
Rhead, C., 511
Rhodewalt, F., 86–87, 453
Rholes, C. R., 113
Rice, R., 529
Rice, R. W., 450
Riechen, H., 31, 429
Ring, K., 540
Rinn, W. E., 136
Riordan, C. A., 169
Rittle, R. H., 408
Roberts, A. H., 395
Roberts, D. F., 168, 322, 368
Roberts, J. V., 95, 96, 173
Robertson, R. M., 25
Robinson, I. E., 278
Rodin, J., 228–230, 234, 524, 540, 541, 545, 547
Rofé, Y., 245
Rogers, C. R., 102

Rogers, L. E., 149
Rogers, P. L., 143
Rogers, R. W., 189, 314
Rogers, W. L., 50–51
Rohner, R. P., 307
Rokeach, M., 161, 466
Romano, J., 145
Romer, D., 356
Rook, K. S., 281
Rose, J., 242
Rose, T., 370
Rosen, L. S., 522
Rosen, S., 366
Rosenbaum, D. P., 371
Rosenbaum, M. E., 248
Rosenbaum, R. M., 121
Rosenberg, M., 66
Rosenberg, M. J., 196–197
Rosenberg, S., 63, 65, 74, 76, 98, 102–103
Rosenfeld, H. M., 142
Rosenfeld, P., 169
Rosenhan, D. L., 362, 363
Rosenholtz, S. J., 415
Rosenkrantz, P. S., 469
Rosenman, R. H., 341
Rosenthal, R., 40, 143, 152–155, 388, 393
Rosnow, R. L., 11, 393
Ross, D., 305–306
Ross, H., 505
Ross, L., 104, 115
Ross, L. D., 120
Ross, M., 207, 523
Ross, S., 305–306
Rossi, P. H., 564
Roth, J., 227
Rothbart, M., 98–99, 476
Rothblatt, A. B., 292
Rotter, J. B., 230–231
Rotton, J., 316, 502
Rowe, J. S., 410
Rozelle, R. M., 546–547
Ruback, R. B., 554, 555
Rubenstein, C., 241
Rubin, J. Z., 483, 484, 485, 486, 487, 491
Rubin, Z., 135, 257–258, 263–266, 285–286
Rubinstein, C., 242
Rugg, E. A., 56
Ruggiero, M., 336, 360
Rule, B. G., 184, 308, 312, 316–317, 331
Runkel, P. J., 26
Rusbult, C., 524
Rush, M. C., 448
Rushton, J. P., 318, 341, 358, 359, 361, 368, 380
Russell, D., 242
Russo, N. F., 145
Rutkowski, G. K., 356
Ryan, W., 123
Rytting, M., 140

Saas-Korlsaak, P., 368
Sacks, H., 147

Sadalla, E. K., 105, 399
Sadava, S. W., 381
Sadowski, C., 532
Saeed, L., 249–250
Saegert, S. C., 253, 511, 521
Saks, M. J., 560
Salancik, G. R., 453
Sales, S., 408
Salinger, J. D., 241
Salovey, P., 362, 363
Saltzman, A. T., 86–87
Samerotte, G. C., 351
Sanbonmatsu, D. M., 178
Sanday, P. R., 327
Sanders, D. Y., 363
Sanders, G. S., 408–409
Sanders, M., 503
Sandman, P. H., 502
Sanford, F. H., 394, 454
Sanford, N., 391, 474, 541
Santogrossi, D. A., 323
Sauser, W. I., 500
Saxe, L., 251, 465
Sayer, S., 517
Scarr, H. A., 314
Scarr, S., 385
Schachter, S., 31, 77, 240, 243–245, 252, 420, 429, 431, 496, 509, 511
Schanie, C. F., 567
Schaps, E., 351
Scheff, T. J., 331
Schegloff, E., 147
Scheier, M. F., 72–73, 74, 88, 545
Schein, E. H., 215
Scherer, K., 143
Scherer, K. B., 151
Schersching, C., 194
Schiffrin, D., 147
Schill, T., 294
Schkade, J., 523
Schlenker, B. R., 56, 81–82
Schlosberg, H., 144
Schmidt, G., 292
Schmitt, B. H., 408
Schneider, D. J., 102
Schneier, C. E., 452
Schofield, J. W., 563
Schoggen, P., 45
Schopler, J., 346, 523, 524
Schriesheim, C. A., 221, 446
Schulman, P., 81
Schulz, R., 145
Schuman, H., 52
Schutte, N. S., 105, 399
Schwalbe, M. L., 64, 75
Schwartz, B., 526
Schwartz, G. E., 136
Schwartz, J. C., 105
Schwartz, P., 273, 274, 276–277, 284, 288
Schwartz, R. D., 48, 54
Schwartz, S. H., 56, 342, 346–347, 349, 356, 359, 370
Schwartzberg, N. S., 319, 320
Scott, J. A., 506

Scott, J. P., 305
Scott, M. B., 527
Scott, R. A., 67, 97
Scott, R. L., 129
Scruggs, B., 560–561
Searle, J., 131
Sears, D. O., 39, 253, 465
Sears, R. R., 19, 307–308, 331
Sebastian, R. J., 321
Sebba, R., 528
Sechler, E. S., 103–104
Sechrest, L., 48, 54
Secord, P. F., 252
Sedlacek, F., 292
Sedlack, A., 102
Sedlack, W. E., 277
Seeley, D. M., 292
Seeley, T. T., 292
Segal, M. W., 510
Segall, M. H., 382
Seiden, R., 277
Seilheimer, S. D., 485
Seipel, M., 366
Sekerak, G. J., 408
Selby, J. W., 123
Seligman, C., 40–41, 81, 551, 552
Seligman, M. E. P., 233–234
Selltiz, C., 42
Selye, H., 497
Semenik, R., 550
Senn, D. J., 249
Sensenig, J., 232
Seta, J. J., 409, 523
Seyfried, B. A., 249
Shaban, J., 232
Shaffer, D. R., 370, 532
Shalker, T. E., 361
Shamir, B., 76
Shannon, C., 129
Shapiro, A., 522
Shapiro, P. N., 101, 476
Sharp, G., 567
Shaver, P., 241, 242
Shaw, M. E., 10, 11, 12, 16, 21, 413, 418
Shedler, J., 112
Shein, V. E., 441
Sherif, C. W., 194–195, 462, 481–482, 487–488
Sherif, M., 6, 8, 22, 194–196, 213–214, 415, 462, 481–482, 487–488
Sherk, D. L., 84
Sherman, S. J., 70
Sherrod, D. R., 501, 504
Shettel-Neuber, J., 263
Shirom, A., 484
Shotland, R. L., 360, 371
Shuntich, R. J., 315
Sidman, J., 295
Siegman, A. W., 151–152, 393
Sigall, H., 97, 251
Sigall, H. E., 39
Sigelman, C. K., 326
Sigusch, V., 292
Sikes, J., 481

Siladi, M., 65
Silverman, I., 30
Silverstein, C. H., 507
Silverthorne, C. P., 191
Simmonds, S. F., 361
Simons, L. S., 310, 315
Simonton, D. K., 440
Simultis, Z. M., 368
Singer, D. G., 322–323
Singer, J., 77, 497
Singer, J. E., 228, 498, 500, 523, 524, 543
Singer, J. L., 322–323
Skelton, J. A., 87
Skinner, B. F., 15, 69, 226
Skorpanich, M. A., 514
Skrzypek, G. J., 452
Slapion-Foote, M. J., 277
Slater, P. E., 411
Sloan, L. R., 191
Smigel, E. O., 277
Smith, C. E., 466
Smith, E. R., 467–468, 471
Smith, J., 105
Smith, M. B., 203
Smith, R. E., 123
Smith, R. H., 215
Smith, S. H., 122
Smith, T. L., 162, 164, 175
Snapp, M., 481
Snyder, M., 86, 87–89, 153, 154, 192, 204, 396, 399
Snyder, M. L., 546
Solano, C. H., 242
Soler, E., 502
Solly, C. M., 497
Soloman, G. S., 363
Soloman, H., 355, 502
Soloman, L. Z., 355
Soloman, S. H., 523
Soloman, S. K., 228, 524
Sommer, R., 142–143, 505, 508, 509, 531, 532
Sommers, S., 76
Sorrentino, R. M., 123–124
Southwick, L. L., 201
Spears, R., 110
Spence, J. T., 67, 469
Spencer, B. G., 472
Speno, S., 504
Spiegel, N., 251
Sprecher, S., 266, 365
Springfield, D. O., 398
Spuhler, J. N., 379–380
Srull, T. K., 72, 113
Staats, A. W., 165
Stackpole, C., 508
Stadler, S. J., 499
Stagner, R., 484
Stairs, D., 169
Staneski, R. A., 132
Stang, D. J., 507
Stangor, C., 171, 173, 177, 192–193
Stanley, J. C., 38–39, 40, 42, 565
Stapp, J., 469

Starke, E., 78
Starr, S., 295
Statham, A., 12
Staub, E., 336, 359
Steck, L., 257
Steele, C. M., 201
Steffen, V. J., 318, 387
Steiner, I. D., 83, 393, 395, 418, 420
Steinmetz, J. L., 120
Steinmetz, S. K., 326
Steinzor, B., 506
Stephan, C., 481
Stephan, W., 294
Stephan, W. C., 475
Stephan, W. G., 489, 562–563
Sterling, B., 344
Stern, P. C., 551
Sternberg, R. J., 261
Stewart, A. J., 264
Stier, D. S., 141
Stiles, W. B., 305
Stires, L. K., 232, 509
Stitt, C. L., 475
Stockdale, J., 523
Stogdill, R. M., 437, 443, 445, 446, 447, 457
Stoiadin, L. F., 470
Stokols, D., 520, 523
Stoller, R. J., 296
Stone, J. I., 152
Stone, R., 355
Stoner, J. A. F., 422
Stonner, D., 305, 320
Storms, M. D., 283
Story, J. E., 115
Stotland, E., 161
Stough, R. R., 526
Straus, M. A., 326
Streufert, S., 49
Strickland, B. R., 230
Stringer, M., 488
Strodtbeck, F., 507
Strube, M. J., 395, 452, 544
Stryker, S., 12, 65
Stucky, R. J., 86
Stull, D. E., 248
Suci, G. J., 144, 163
Suedfeld, P., 240–241, 441
Sullivan, H. S., 63, 90
Suls, J., 73
Suls, J. M., 78
Sundstrom, E., 479, 499, 500, 514, 517, 518, 521, 523, 526, 528, 529
Swann, C. P., 294
Swann, W. B., Jr., 82, 101, 153, 154, 155
Swap, W., 253
Sweeney, P. D., 79–80, 173–174
Swift, J., 376
Switzer, R., 522
Syme, G. J., 202–203, 552
Symonds, M., 123
Szeny-Gyorgyi, A., 54
Szybillo, G. W., 207

Tajfel, H., 462, 478, 479, 490
Takezawa, S. I., 383
Tamborini, R., 503
Tanford, S., 215, 406, 412, 425
Tanke, E. D., 153
Tannenbaum, P. H., 144, 163
Taormina, R. J., 351
Taylor, D., 528
Taylor, D. W., 419
Taylor, J., 522
Taylor, M. S., 75–76
Taylor, R. B., 520, 522, 526, 530, 531
Taylor, S., 215
Taylor, S. E., 21, 72, 111–112, 542, 545, 549–550
Taylor, S. P., 308, 311–312, 315
Taynor, J., 31
Teasdale, J. D., 234
Teddlie, C., 523
Teevan, R. C., 216
Telaak, K., 196
Terpstra, D. E., 97
Teruya, D., 504
Tesser, A., 180, 216, 366
Tetlock, P. E., 47, 82, 89, 170–171, 422
Thayer, R. E., 567
Thibaut, J. W., 6, 18–19, 26, 254–256, 268
Thomas, E., 331
Thomas, E. J., 13
Thomas, J. C., 448
Thomas, W. I., 6
Thompson, D. E., 506, 523
Thompson, M. E., 457
Thompson, S. C., 112
Thompson, V. D., 346
Thompson, W. C., 363, 558
Thomson, R., 522
Thorne, A., 86
Thornton, B., 288
Tice, D. M., 169
Titus, L. J., 408
Tjosvold, D., 456
Tognacci, L. N., 175
Tomarelli, M. M., 366
Toppen, A., 522
Town, J., 518
Town, J. P., 122
Trager, G. L., 131
Traupmann, J., 266, 286–287
Trew, K., 488
Triandis, H. C., 381, 382, 383, 384, 467, 475
Triplett, N., 6–7, 405, 409
Trivers, R. L., 339, 340
Trolier, T. K., 110
Trommsdorff, G., 419
Trope, Y., 78
Tucker, L. A., 75
Tucker, P., 282
Tunnell, G. B., 34
Turnbull, W., 153, 155
Turner, C. W., 310, 315, 320
Turner, J. C., 424

Turpin, R., 560–561
Tversky, A., 114, 546
Tyler, L., 391
Tyler, R. B., 108
Tyler, T. R., 253, 456

Ullman, J. C., 561
Ulrich, R. S., 549
Underwood, B., 359, 368
Upfold, D., 325
U.S. Commission on Civil Rights, 463
U.S. President's Commission on Obscenity and Pornography, 296
U.S. Riot Commission, 316
Utne, M., 266

Vaizey, M., 523
Valins, S., 80, 512
Vallacher, R. R., 102
Valle, V. A., 121
Vallery, G. C., 522
Vandenberg, S. G., 380–381
Vanderklok, M., 115
Vanderplas, M., 345
van der Plight, J., 110, 166, 544, 546
Van Hoose, T., 39
Van Vliet, W., 527
Varela, J., 569–570
Varela, J. A., 454
Varney, L. L., 345
Vassiliou, V., 475
Veitch, R., 294, 500
Verbrugge, L. M., 520
Vernon, D. T. A., 175
Vidmar, N., 557–558
Vincent, J. E., 218, 362
Vinsel, A., 505, 516, 528
Vivekanathan, P. S., 98
Vogel, S. R., 469
Vogel, W., 379
vonBaeyer, C. L., 84
Vroom, V. H., 442, 449

Wachtler, J., 426
Wack, D. L., 408
Wade, J., 215
Walbeck, N., 368
Walcott, C., 485
Walden, T., 524
Walder, L. O., 318
Waldgeir, D., 218
Walker, M. R., 56
Wallach, M. A., 423
Waller, W. W., 251
Wallston, K. A., 546, 548
Wallston, S. S., 122, 352, 546, 548
Walster, E., 187, 250, 258, 266–267, 286–287, 294, 337
Walster, G. W., 258, 266, 286–287
Walters, R., 306, 331
Walters, R. H., 305
Wan, K.-C., 478
Wapner, S., 563
Ward, C., 507

Ware, E. E., 295
Warren, R., 192
Warriner, C. H., 404
Watson, J. B., 7, 15
Watson, M., 119
Watson, R., Jr., 35
Weaver, W., 129
Webb, E. J., 48, 54
Weber, R., 109
Wedge, B., 511
Wegner, D. M., 102
Weick, K., 457
Weick, K. E., 562
Weigel, R. H., 175
Weinberg, M. S., 280, 282, 283–284
Weinberg, R. A., 385
Weiner, B., 80, 121, 122–123, 143, 350
Weinstein, C. S., 514
Weise, B. C., 97
Weisman, G. D., 518
Weiss, C., 563–564, 565
Weiss, R. F., 339
Weiss, R. S., 241–242
Weiss, W., 187
Weitz, S., 387
Wellman, D. T., 468
Wells, B. W. P., 511
Wells, G. L., 100, 190, 560
Wener, R., 524
Werner, C., 511, 527
Werner, C. M., 395, 531
West, S., 521
West, S. G., 57, 321
Westcott, D. R., 336
Westie, F., 393
Westie, F. R., 383
Westin, A., 514, 516, 518
Wetzel, C. G., 139
Wexler, M., 550
Weyant, J. M., 363
Wheeler, D., 218
Wheeler, L., 66, 78, 246, 251, 528
Whitcher, S. J., 140–141
Whitcher-Alagna, S., 365
White, B. J., 481–482, 487–488
White, G. L., 263
White, J. W., 314
White, L. A., 290
White, P., 119

White, R. W., 203
Whitehead, G. I., 111, 122
Whiting, B., 382
Whitmyer, J. W., 419
Whyte, W. H., Jr., 510
Wiback, K., 97
Wicklund, R. A., 71–72, 232, 364
Wideman, M., 522
Widgery, R., 508
Wiemann, J. M., 147
Wiener, F., 501
Wiener, V. L., 358–359
Wiggins, N. H., 139
Wilcox, B. L., 511
Wilder, D. A., 215, 475–476, 489
Wiles, K. A., 326
Wilkins, C., 174
Wilkinson, M., 40–41
Williams, C. J., 179
Williams, J. E., 469
Williams, J. S., 380–381
Williams, K., 417–418

Williams, L., 464
Williams, W., 564
Willis, F. N., 143
Wills, T. A., 245, 547
Wilson, D. W., 316, 355, 502
Wilson, E. O., 25, 303
Wilson, J. P., 357
Wilson, M., 279
Wilson, T. D., 80, 179–180
Wilson, W. C., 291
Winch, R. F., 249
Winer, B. J., 445
Winkler, J., 560
Winsborough, H., 519
Winters, L., 135
Winton, W., 109
Wishner, J., 98
Wispé, L. G., 336
Wittmer, J., 86–87
Wohlwill, H., 498
Wohlwill, J. F., 498
Wolf, S., 358, 425–426
Wolfer, J., 548
Wollin, D. D., 504
Wood, F. A., 439–440
Wood, J. V., 550

Wood, W., 187
Worchel, P., 309
Worchel, S., 232, 489–490, 523
Word, L. E., 355
Wortman, C. B., 83, 234
Wright, E., 228
Wright, M. H., 227
Wrightsman, L. S., 42, 102–103, 412, 448–449, 555, 557, 559, 560
Wyer, R. S., Jr., 72, 113
Wynne-Edwards, V., 525
Wysocki, J., 453

Yarkin, K. L., 122
Yarmey, A. D., 65
Yarrow, P. R., 174
Yates, J. F., 386
Yates, S., 551
Yetton, P. W., 449
Yinon, Y., 501
Yoder, J., 441
Yoshioka, G. A., 510
Young, L. E., 263
Youtz, P. N., 496
Ypma, I., 522
Yurko, K., 242

Zaccaro, S. J., 438
Zacker, J., 393
Zahn-Waxler, C., 342, 368
Zajonc, R. B., 21, 22, 106, 194, 253, 407–408
Zander, A., 447
Zanna, M., 67, 78
Zanna, M. P., 84, 207, 262
Zautra, A. J., 227
Zelditch, M., Jr., 415
Zillmann, D., 77, 296, 309, 310–311, 331, 503
Zimbardo, P. G., 34, 36, 38, 48–49, 314, 503
Zimmerman, D. H., 147–148
Zimring, C., 516
Zinkhan, G. M., 470
Zlutnick, S., 518, 520
Zuckerman, M., 79, 152, 218, 292
Zweigenhaft, R. L., 508

SUBJECT INDEX

Action research, 541, 542
Adaptation, 498
 definition of, 498
 level, 498
 perceptual, 498
Adding versus averaging, in impression formation, 99–100
Additive model, 99–100
Advocate role, by social scientist, 569
Affiliation, 243–247
 anxiety and, 243–245
 reasons for, 243–245
 same-sex, 246
Aggregate, distinguished from group, 404–405
Aggression, 300–333 (*see also* Violence)
 and anonymity, 34–35, 313–315
 and audience effects, 312–314
 control of, 328–332
 cross-cultural comparisons, 35, 306
 and cues, 309–310
 definitions of, 301–302
 and drugs and alcohol, 315
 environmental factors in, 315–318, 499, 500, 501
 erotic material and, 296
 ethological theory, 302–304
 and frustration, 33, 307–309
 and heat, 316–318, 499–500
 hereditary determinants of, 302–304
 high temperatures and, 316–318, 499–500
 individual differences in, 318
 instigators of, 307–325
 mass media and, 319–325
 and noise, 316, 500–502
 physical, 311–312
 in psychoanalytic theory, 8, 301
 and responses to pornography, 323–325
 sex differences in, 318, 387
 and sexual stimuli, 323–325
 in social-learning theory, 304–307
 and sociobiology, 25, 303–304
 and television watching, 319–323
 and territorial behavior, 525

Aggression (*continued*)
 theoretical positions on, 300
 third-party instigation of, 312–314
 verbal, 311–312
Air pollution, 502–503
Alcohol:
 and aggression, 315
 and dissonance reduction, 201
Alcoholics, nurses' reactions to, 546
Alinsky, Saul, 567, 569
Allport, Floyd, 6, 7
Aloneness, distinguished from loneliness, 241
Altruism (*see also* Prosocial behavior):
 cultural influences of, 341–342
 definition of, 337
 distinguished from prosocial behavior, 337
 psychological theories of, 338–339
 sociobiological theory of, 339–341
Analogy, use of, in hypothesis generation, 31
Anchor, in social judgment theory, 194
Anticipatory attitude change, 205–206
Anticonformity, 214–215
Anxiety, and affiliation, 243–245
Applications, of social psychology, 537–571
Arapesh of New Guinea, 306
Architecture, and effects on social behavior, 509–514
Archival research, 47–48
 advantages, 47–48
 disadvantages, 48
 in studying aggression, 316–323
Aristotle, 249
Arms race, 489–490
Arousal, 497
 and aggression, 310–311
 and social facilitation, 343–346, 407–408
 hypotheses, 523
 models, 522
Arousal model of intimacy, 144–146
Asch situation, 212–214

Assimilation effects, in social-judgment theory, 194
Association, as statistical measure, 55
Assortative mating, 259–260
Assumptions about human nature, 24–26
 and philosophies of human nature, 101–103
Attachment to places, 524–532
Attitude change:
 anticipatory, 205–206
 balance theory, 196–199
 cognitive dissonance theory, 199–203
 consistency theories, 196–199
 regarding energy usage, 202–203, 551
 functional theories, 203–205
 learning theories, 185–186
 the process of, 185–193
 social-judgment theory, 194–196
 stimulus-response theory, 185–186
Attitudes, 160–181
 anti-Black, 463, 466, 472–475
 behavioral intentions, 176–178
 and behavior regarding energy conservation, 551–552
 versus behaviors, 174–180
 beliefs and, 173–176
 central role in social psychology, 160
 components of, 161–162
 definition of, 247
 development of, 164–170
 of jurors, 556–560
 measurement of, 162–164
 nature of, 160–164
 opinions and, 161
 as predictors of behavior, 174–180
 of sexual behavior, 275–278, 286, 290–291
 structure of, 170–174
Attraction, interpersonal, 247–255
 and complementarity of needs, 249
 definition of, 247
 homosexuals versus heterosexuals, 250
 physical attractiveness and, 249–251
 propinquity and, 252–253
 and prosocial behavior, 351–353

639

Attraction, interpersonal *(continued)*
    reciprocal liking and, 252
    and similarity, 247–249
    theoretical explanations of, 253–255
Attribution process, 79–81, 116–123, 478, 523
    ability/luck attributions, 121
    actors versus observers, 122
    basic assumptions, 79–81
    bias in attribution process, 79
    of causes, 79, 115–123
    correspondent inference in, 118–119
    definition of, 79
    dispositional versus situational causes, 79, 115–117, 119
    in doctor's diagnosis, 546
    hedonic relevance in, 120
    and legal system, 555, 559
    personalism in, 121
    regarding physical symptoms, 545–546
    self-serving, 79, 121–122
    in success and failure, 121–122
    of Whites and Blacks, 122
Audience:
    characteristics of, 406
    coaching, 409–411
    effects of, 312–314, 406–411
Audience inhibition, as explanation of bystander intervention, 355
Authoritarianism, 474
    and behavior, 394–395
    development of the concept, 391–394
    dimensions of, 392
    and leadership, 458
    measurement of concept, 391
    research on, 393–395
    and situational factors, 394–395
Authoritarian personality, 391–394, 474
Autokinetic effect, 213–214, 415
Averaging model, 99–100

Bail setting, 555–556
Balance theory, 196–199
    and reciprocal liking, 252
Bargaining, 483–486
    definition of, 483
Basking in reflected glory, 86
Battered children, 326
Behavioral intentions, 176–178
Behavioral medicine, 542
"Behavioral sink," 519
Behaviorism, 7
Belief in a "just world," 123–124
Belief-similarity hypothesis, 466–467
Beliefs:
    about energy use, 551
    and illness recovery, 549–550
    B = f(P, E), 9, 377
Biases:
    in attribution process, 79
    knowledge bias, 187
    reporting bias, 187
    in social cognition, 114–115
Bilingualism, 147
    and nonverbal behavior, 147

Bisexuality, 284
Blacks, 122, 467–468
    differences from Whites, 385–386, 388
    and gaze differences, 134–135
    and intelligence, 385
    self-concept in, 385–386
    treatment by social psychologists, 385
Bobo doll, 305–307
Body movements, 137–139
Brainstorming, 418–419
    criticisms of research on, 419
Breaking up, 262–266
Brown v. Board of Education, 561, 562–563
Bystander effects, 354–357
    definition, 354
    explanations of, 355
    in nonemergency situations, 355–356
    social-influence process, 355
Bystanders, 354–357

Calley, Lt. William, 222, 394
Capital punishment, 330
Carlyle, Thomas, and "great man" theory of leadership, 439
Carnegie, Dale, 102
Carroll, Lewis, 130
Case study, intensive, 31
    in study of sexual behavior, 31, 273
Catcher in the Rye, 241
Category-based expectancies, 119
Catharsis, 331
Caulfield, Holden, 241
Causal attribution, 79, 115–124
    and belief in a just world, 123–124
    causal schema, 116–118
    correspondent inference, 118–119
    covariation in, 116–118
    Kelley's model of, 116–117
    multiple-necessary-cause model, 117–118
    multiple-sufficient-cause model, 117
    overestimation of dispositional causes in, 119–121
    success and failure, 121–123
Causal schema, 116–118
    in success and failure, 121–123
    types of information, 116
Central tendency, as statistic, 55
Central traits, 97–100
Change agents, 565–568
Channel, in communication process, 129, 130–143
Charisma, 436
Charities, enlisting support for, 369–371
Children:
    antismoking campaign with, 543–544, 546–547
    battered, 326
    and effects of television violence, 319–323
    encouraging prosocial behavior in, 370–371
    and frustration-aggression hypothesis, 309, 310
    and modeling aggression, 305–307

Choice dilemma questionnaire, 423
Cigarette smoking, 543–544, 546–547
Circumscribed accuracy, 101
Classical conditioning model, applied to acquisition of attitudes, 165
Classrooms, 504
    layout of, 508–509
Coaching audience, 409–411
Cognitive adjustment, 89
Cognitive consistency theories, 22
Cognitive dissonance theory, 199–203
    and energy use, 552
Cognitive structure, 21, 280–281
Cognitive theory, 20–23
    basic assumptions and concepts, 20–22, 24
    contributions to social psychology, 22–23
Cohesiveness, of a group, 420–421
Collaborator role, as change agent, 568–569
Collective violence, 327–328
Columbus, Christopher, 440
Communal relationships, versus exchange relationships, 254, 366
Communication, 128–157
    and bargaining, 484–485
    channels of, 130–143
    combining channels of, 143–144
    among competitive groups, 482
    conversation, 146–150
    deceptive, 150–152
    definition of, 128
    dimensions of, 144
    and gaze, 132–136
    marital, 149–150
    meaning of, 128–130
    models of, 129–130, 144–146
    networks, 413–414
    nonverbal, 132–141, 147
    one-sided versus two-sided, 189–190
    process of, 129
    and self-disclosure, 149
    and social interaction, 152–155
Communication Research Program (Yale University), 186–192
Comparison level, 255
    and comparison level of alternative, 255, 257
    in social-exchange theory, 255
Competition:
    characteristics of competitive situation, 480
    competitive reward structure, 480
    versus cooperation, 480–483
    definition, 480
Complementarity of need systems, 249
Compliance, 216–221
    distinction with conformity, 216–217
    door-in-the-face effect, 218–219
    foot-in-the-door technique, 217–218
    generality of, 220–221
    inducing compliance, 220–221, 548
    low-ball procedure, 219

Compliance *(continued)*
  with medical advice, 548
  "mindless," 220–221
Compromise, in negotiation, 485–486
Confessions, coerced, 560
Confidentiality, of data, 58
Conflict, intergroup, 480–483, 484, 487–489
Conformity:
  Asch situation, 212–214
  autokinetic effect and, 213–214
  beliefs versus behavior in, 216–217
  definition, 213
  distinguished from compliance, 216–217
  group size and, 215
  issues in the study of, 214–216
  opposite of, 214–215
  and personality, 216
  sex differences in, 216
  situational influences in, 214–216
Conscience, 8
Consideration, as leadership quality, 445, 446
Consistency theories, 196–199
Constructs, 10, 104
  in George Kelly's theory, 104
Contingency theory of leadership, 448–453
Contraception, 288–291
  and attitudes toward sexuality, 290–291
  and decision to use, 290
Contrast effects, in social judgment theory, 194
Control, 226–236
  belief in, 227–230
  density and, 523–524
  illusion of, 226–228
  individual differences in perceptions, 230
  learned helplessness and, 233–235
  locus of control, 230
  over public territory, 523–524
  reactions to loss of, by patients, 230–236
  and recovery in hospital patients, 550
  by residents of home for aged, 228–230
  self-induced dependent behavior and, 235–236
  sense of, 226–230, 524, 550
Conversation, 146–150
  in close relationships, 148–150
  patterns of, 146–148
  settings for, 503–508
Conversational implicature, 148
"Conviction-prone" jury, 558–559
Cooley, Charles, 15, 63
Cooperation:
  and attitude change, 482
  versus competition, 480–483
  cooperative reward structure, 480
  definition, 336
  and jigsaw method, 481
Cooperative principle, 148
Correlational method, 35
Correspondent inference, 118–119
Cost/reward analysis, in decision to help, 347–348

Counterconformity, *see* Anticonformity
Covariation principle, in attribution of cause, 116–118
Cross-cultural studies, 35, 381–385
  of anonymity and antisocial behavior, 35
  comparisons of violence rates, 35
Crowding, 518–524
  definition of, 518
  in laboratory, 44–46
  models of, 520–524
  in neighborhoods, 519–520
  population density and, 518
  research on, 520
  and social pathology, 520–522
  theories of, 520–524
Crowds, and aggression, 313
Cues, aggressive, 303, 309–310
Culture, effects of, 341

"Death dip," 5
Death instinct, 328
Debriefing, 58, 225
Deception, 150–152
Deceptive communication, 150–152
  detection of, 152
  lying, 151–152
Decision making, in emergencies, 355–356
Defense mechanisms, 8
Deindividuation, 33, 314–315, 503
  and aggression, 314–315
  in baiting crowds, 33, 313
Demand characteristics, 39, 167, 310
Demographic categories, 385–390
Density, 518, 523–524 *(see also* Crowding)
Dental care, 188–189
Dependent variable, 36
Desegregated schools, 561, 562–563
Destination, in communication process, 129
Differences, measure of, 55
Diffusion of responsibility, as explanation of bystander intervention, 355–356
Discrimination *(see also* Racism):
  against Blacks, 467–468
  causes of, 472–475
  definition, 463
  against French-Canadians, 471–472
  against Japanese-Americans and Japanese-Canadians, 464
Display rules, 137, 383
Dissonance reduction, *see* Cognitive dissonance theory
Distance zones, 141–142, 505
Distinctiveness, 112
Distributive justice, 18
Divorce, 267–268
Documenting social problems, 561–563
Dollard, John, 6, 8
Door-in-the-face effect, 218–219
Dormitory design, 511–513, 525
  and cooperation/competition, 512–513, 522
  and learned helplessness, 512
  and residents' reactions, 512, 521, 525

Dormitory design *(continued)*
  and social overload, 511, 521
Dreiser, Theodore, 103–104
Drugs and alcohol, and aggression, 315
Dryden, John, 263
Dyadic interaction, 18, 257
Dynamogenesis, 405

Earned reputation theory, and prejudice, 475
Eddy, Mary Baker, 102
Effectance, 64
Ego, 8
Ego involvement, in social-judgment theory of attitude change, 196–196
Egoism, 338–339
Eichmann, Adolf, 222
Emblems, as nonverbal acts, 138–139
Emic versus etic constructs, 381–384
Emotions, arousal of, and empathy, 343–346
Empathy, 341, 344–346
Empirical-rational strategy, 565–566
Encoding, 111–113
Energy use, 202–203, 550–553
  attitudes and, 551
  conservation strategies, 550–552
  monitoring and, 552
  persuasion and, 552–553
Environment, 495–535
  ambient, 497–503
  primary versus secondary, 520
  privacy in, 514–518
  and social behavior, 315–318
  and stress, 497, 498, 500
Environmental determinism, 496
Environmental stressors, 497, 498, 500
Equilibrium model of intimacy, 144–146
Equity theory, 346
  as applied to breakup of a relationship, 266–267
Erhard, Werner, 102
Erotica, 291
Erotic material:
  and aggression, 296
  and arousal, 291–296
  behavioral responses to, 295–296
  fantasies and, 293–295
  guilt as a reaction to, 294
  physiological responses to, 291–293
  psychological responses to, 293–295
Ethics, in research, 56–58
Ethnic differences in gaze, 134–135
Ethnicity, 385–387
Ethnocentrism, 477
  facets of, 478
Ethology, and aggression, 302–304
Evaluation apprehension, 39
Evaluation research, 563–565
Exchange relationships, versus communal relationships, 254, 366
Excitation-transfer theory, in aggression, 310–311
Exemplification, 84

Exotic bias, 378
Experimental realism, versus mundane realism, 38
Experimenter expectancies, 40
Expert role, as change agent, 568
External validity, 38–39
Eye contact, see Gaze
Eyewitness testimony, 100–101

"Face-ism," 470–471
Face-work, 82
Facial affect program, 136
Facial electromyography, 136
Facial expression, 136–137
False consensus bias, 115
Fear-arousing appeal, 188–189
Feedback, 129
Festinger, Leon, 6
Field experiment, 34, 40–42
  advantages, 41
  of anonymity and antisocial behavior, 34
  disadvantages, 41–42
  ethics, 56–58
Field study, 44–47
  advantages, 46
  disadvantages, 46–47
  ethics, 56–58
Field theory, 8, 9
Finian's Rainbow, 252
Foot-in-the-door effect, 31, 217–218
Forced compliance, 199–200
Freud, Sigmund, 8
Freudian theory, see Psychoanalytic theory
Friendship, and propinquity, 256–257
Frustration, 33, 307–309
Frustration-aggression hypothesis, 307–309, 310
  and control of aggression, 331
Functional theories, of attitude change, 203–205
Fundamental attribution error, 120
  applied to views of U.S. presidents, 448

Gallery of Women, 103–104
Gaze, 132–136
  ethnic differences in, 134–135
  functions of, 132–136
  and interpersonal distance, 146
  and status differences, 132–133, 135
Gender, see Sex
Gender identity, 67, 281
Gender-role norms, 380
General systems theory, 9
Genovese, Kitty, 354
Gestalt theory, 20–21
Gestures, 137–139
Global accuracy, 101
Good Samaritan, 357–361
"Great man" theory, of leadership, 439–441
"Great woman" theory, of leadership, 441–443
GRIT, 491

Group:
  cohesiveness, 356
  communication networks, 413–414
  communication opportunities, 413–414
  composition, 411–416
  definition of, 405
  distinguished from aggregate, 404–405
  dynamics, 405, 416–427
  performance, 416–420, 447
  polarization, 422–424
  problem solving, 418–420
  relations/roles, 414–416
  size, 215, 411–413
  socialization, 427–432
  structure, 411–416
Group differences (see also Sex differences):
  causes of, 379–381
  cross-cultural, 381–385
  environment as cause, 379–381
  heredity as cause, 379–381
  racial, 385–390
  sex, 387–390
  traditional social psychological view on, 377–378
Group socialization, 427–432
  basic process of, 427–428
  stages of, 428–432
Groupthink, 420–422

Hardiness, 547
Health care, 542–550
Health locus of control, 547–548
Heat, and aggression/violence, 316–318, 499–500
Hedonic relevance, in attribution of causes of behavior, 120–121
Hedonism, in social exchange theory, 18
Heider, Fritz, 6, 120
Helping behavior, 337 (see also Prosocial behavior)
Heredity, and aggression, 302–304
Heuristics, 114–115, 193
  availability, 114–115
  in judging persuasion, 193
  representativeness, 114
  statistical, 115
Hinckley, John W., Jr., 319
Historical versus contemporary emphasis, in theories in social psychology, 23
Hitler, Adolf, 437, 439
Home environments, 527–528
"Home field" advantage, 526
Homosexuality, 281–284
  determinants of, 284
  early experiences in determining, 283–284
  and personal ads, 250
Hull, Clark, 32
Human Relations Area Files, 35
Hutterites, 306
Hypotheses, 11, 30–36
  formulation of, 30–32
  possibility of disconfirming, 54

Hypotheses (continued)
  testing of, 32–36
Hypothetico-deductive method, 31

Id, 8
Idiographic approach, 103, 390–391
Illness:
  causes of, 542–544
  detection of medical problems in, 545–546
  prevention of, 546–548
  treatment of, 548–550
Illocution, 130–131
Illumination, 503
Illusion of control, 226–228
Illusory correlation, 110
Illustrators, in nonverbal behavior, 138
Implicit personality theory, 102–103
Implied presence, 4
Impression formation, 94–101
  accuracy of, 100–101
  adding versus averaging, 99–100
  central traits in, 97–100
  physical appearance in, 95–97
Impression management, 81–82, 206 (see also Self-presentation)
  and third-party mediators, 487
Impression organization, 101–111
  schemas, prototypes, and scripts, 104–108
  stereotypes, 108–111
  theories of, 102–104
Independence, as opposite of conformity, 214–215
Independent variable, 36
Individual differences, in traditional social-psychological view, 377–378
Individualistic reward structure, 384, 480
Individual versus social structure, in theories in social psychology, 24
Informational influence, 214, 424
Informed consent, 57
Ingratiation, 83
In-group versus out-group, 475–479
  differences in categorization between, 476
  differences in power between, 479
  and ethnocentrism, 477–478
Initiating structure, as leadership quality, 445, 446
Instrumental learning, 305
Integrative agreement, 486
Integrative complexity, 47, 170–171
Intentions, in definition of aggression, 301
Interaction, statistical, 56
Interaction, strategies of, 479–480
Interdependence theory, as explanation of attraction, 254–255
Intergroup behavior:
  between Blacks and Whites, 467–468, 479, 481
  conflict, 480–483, 484, 487–489
  and conflict in Ireland, 488
  contact, 481–482, 487–490

Intergroup behavior (continued)
　definition of, 462–463
　in-groups and out-groups, 475–479
　intergroup-contact hypothesis, 489–490
　intergroup relations, 461–493
　rivalry, 480–483
Internal validity, 40
Internal versus external events, in theories in social psychology, 24
International relations, 490–491
Interpersonal communication, see Communication
Interpersonal distance, 141–143
　distance zones, 141–142
Interventions in natural settings, see Quasi-experimental research
Interview survey, 51
Intimidation, 83
Invasion of privacy, 57

Jealousy, 263
Jigsaw method, of learning, 481
Journals, in social psychology, 6
Judgment, dimensions of, 163
Jury, 556–560
　"death-qualified," 558–559
　deliberations, 558
　selection of, 556–558
　size of, 412

Kelley, Harold, 6, 18–19
"Kernel of truth" hypothesis, 475
Kinesics, 138
　kinemes, 138
　kinemorphs, 138
King, Martin Luther, Jr., 124, 567
Kin selection, 340

Laboratory experiment, 34, 36–40
　advantages, 38
　on anonymity and antisocial behavior, 34
　disadvantages, 38–40
　ethics of, 56–58
　independent and dependent variables in, 36
　manipulation check, 37–38
　randomization in, 37
　in study of sexual behavior, 274
Language, 130–131
La Rochefoucauld, Count, 263, 265
Latitude of acceptance, 194–196
Latitude of noncommitment, 194–195
Latitude of rejection, 194–196
Leader Behavior Description Questionnaire (LBDQ), 446, 447, 448
Leader match, 454
Leaders, 435–459
　assigned versus self-selected, 441
　behavior of, 443–448
　designated, 456
　distinguished from followers, 437, 438
　effective versus ineffective, 447, 451–453, 455
　followers' effects on, 457–458

Leaders (continued)
　functions of, 443–445
　and intelligence, 438
　interaction of, and followers, 456–458
　and personality traits, 436–439
　reactions to behavior of, 456–458
　revolutionary, 436–437, 441
　and seating patterns, 507
　traits of, 436–439
Leadership, 435–459 (see also Leaders)
　contingency theory of, 448–453
　definition of, 436
　dimensions of, 444–446
　functions of, 443–444
　"great man" theory of, 439–441
　"great woman" theory of, 441–443
　implicit theories of, 448
　perceptions of, 454–456
　and presidential effectiveness, 448–449
　search for traits of, 436–439
　task-oriented versus interaction-oriented, 448–453, 458
　trait approach, 436–439
　Zeitgeist theory of, 440–441
Learned helplessness, 233–235, 512, 524
Learning theory, 15–20
　basic assumptions and concepts, 15–16
　contributions to social psychology, 19–20
　social exchange theory, 18–19
　social learning theory, 16–18
"Least preferred coworker" (LPC), 449–453
Legal system, 554–560
"Legionnaires' disease," 543
Lepchas of Sikkim, 306
Lewin, Kurt, 6, 8–9, 539–540
　and action research, 540–542
　and field theory, 8, 9
　as founder of social psychology, 8
　research strategy of, 541–452
　and resolving social conflicts, 566–567
Life space, psychological, 9, 377
Likert method of summated ratings, 163
Liking relationship, 197–198
Liking scale, 258
Lindzey, Gardner, 6
Locus of control, 230–231
　health, 547–548
Locution, 130
Loneliness, 241–243
　emotional versus social, 241–242
　trait versus state distinction, 242
"Looking-glass self," 15, 63
"Lost-letter technique," 163–164
Love:
　companionate, 258
　conceptions of, 257–259
　definitions of, 257
　development of, 260–262
　falling out of, 262–268
　measurement of romantic, 257–259

Love (continued)
　passionate, 258, 261
　romantic, 257
　stages in development of, 260–262
Love Scale, 258
Low-ball procedure, 219
Lying, 151–152

Main effect, 56
Manipulation check, 37
Marijuana, and aggression, 315
Marital relationships, 267–268
　predicting success of, 267
　sexuality in, 287–288
Marx, Karl, 472
Mass media, and violence, 319–325
Mate selection, 259–260
McDougall, William, 6, 7
Mead, George Herbert, 6, 8, 12, 63
Measurement, of attitudes, 162–164
Media, the:
　effects of, on attitudes, 167–170
　and portrayal of sex, 292–293
Mediation, 486–487
Medium, the, effects of, in attitude change, 190
Mental processing, 21
Mental representation, 21
"Mere exposure" effect, 194, 253
Message:
　in attitude change, 188–190
　fear-arousing, 188–189
Methods, in social psychology, 36–53
　archival research, 47–48
　correlational method, 35
　cross-cultural investigation, 35
　ethics in, 56–58, 224–225
　field experiment, 40–42
　field study, 44–47
　laboratory experiment, 36–40
　major, 36–53
　quasi-experimental research, 42–44
　role playing, 48–50
　selection of, 54–55
　simulation research and role playing, 48–50
　in studying sexual behavior, 53
　surveys and interviews, 50–53
Miller, Neal, 6
"Mindless" compliance, 220–221
"Minitheories," 11
Minority:
　influence of, 424–427
　majority's reaction to, 426
　"single" versus "double," 425
Modeling, 17
　of aggressive behavior, 305–306
　of prosocial behavior, 357
Moods:
　and helping, 361–364
　negative-state-relief model, 362
Morphemes, 130
Mother Teresa, 357
Multiple identities, 65

Multiple sufficient-cause model versus multiple necessary-cause model, 117–118
Murchison, Carl, 6
Mutual gaze, see Gaze

Negotiation, 483–486
 steps in process, 483
Neighborhoods, 529–530
Neo-Freudians, 302
"Nigrescence," 386
Phillips, David, 5
Noise, 129, 500–502
 and aggression, 501–502
 definition, 129
Nomothetic approach, 103, 390
Noncommon effect, 118
Noncontingency, 233
Nonverbal communication, 132–141
Normative influence, 214
Normative-reeducative strategy, 566–567
Norms, 13, 343
 gender-role norms, 380
 personal norms, 346–347
 and prosocial behavior, 346–347
 reciprocity norm, 346
 social responsibility norm, 346
Northern Ireland, 488

Obedience, 222–225
 criticisms of research on, 224
 destructive obedience, 222–224
 ethical concerns of research on, 224–225
 Milgram's study of, 222–225
 situational determinants of, 223–225
Objective self-awareness, 71
Obscenity, 291
Observational learning, 18, 305
"Open-plan offices," 516–517
Open-space schools, 513–515
Operant conditioning, and attitude acquisition, 166–167
Operation Head Start, 564
Opinions, 161
Orgasms, types of, in Freudian theory, 279
Outcome value, in social-exchange theory, 255
Overlapping distributions, principle of, 378–379
 applied to sex differences and race differences, 390
Overload, 511–514

Paralanguage, 130–131
Participant observer, 45
Personal distance, 504–506, 508
Personalism, in attribution of causes of behavior, 121
Personality:
 and conformity, 216
 differences, 390–396
 and helping behavior, 359–364
 relationship to social behavior, 396–400
 self-reports of, 397
 traits, 396

Personalization, 527
Personal norms, 346–347
Perspectivism, 11
Persuasion:
 central and peripheral routes to, 192–193
 elements of, 186–192
 resistance to, 190–192, 206–207
Phenomenological emphasis, 21
 and prejudice, 474
Phillips, David, 5
Philosophies of human nature, 101–103
Phonemes, 130
Physical attack:
 and aggression, 311–312
 within family, 325–326
Physical attractiveness, 95–97, 249–251
 effects of physically attractive partner, 251
 in impression formation, 95–97
Physical environment, 495–535
 and medical recovery, 549
 privacy and, 514–518
 and stress, 497, 498, 500
Plethysmograph, 292
Polarization, as result of group interaction, 422–424
Police officers, 567
Pornography, aggressive responses to, 323–325
Power:
 bases of, 221
 forms of, 221
 between in-groups and out-groups, 479
Power-coercive strategy, 221, 567–568
Prejudice:
 as an attitude, 466
 and authoritarianism, 474
 and belief-similarity hypothesis, 466–467
 causes of, 472–475
 definition of, 463
Premarital sexual relationships, 277–279, 284–287
Presence of others, see Affiliation; Audience
Presidential effectiveness, U.S., 448–449
Priming effect, in recall, 72, 113
Prison-simulation experiment, 48–49
Privacy, 514–518
 definition of, 514
 in open-plan offices, 516–517
 regulation mechanisms, 515–516, 524
 theories of, 515–516
Problem solving, 418–420
 brainstorming, 418–419
 by groups versus individuals, 418–420
Propinquity, 252–253, 509–511
Prosocial behavior, 336–367
 cultural influences of, 341–342
 definition of, 336
 examples of, 336
 and human nature, 338–342
 models of, 342–349

Prosocial behavior (continued)
 psychological theories of, 338–339
 psychological traits as predictors of, 357–364
 recipients of help, 350–353, 364–367
 situational influences on, 349–357
 social influence and, 355
 sociobiology and, 339–341
Prosocial society, 367–371
Prototype, 104–108
 of effective leaders, 455
 in impression organization, 104–108
Proximity, and friendship, 509–511
Pruitt-Igoe housing project, 529–530
Psychoanalytic theory, 7, 8
 on control of aggression, 8, 301
 explanation of sex differences, 278–279
 relationship to social psychology, 8
 of sexuality, 278–279
"Psycho-logic," 196–197
Psychological reactance, see Reactance, psychological
Psychological states, and helping, 361–364
Public spaces, see Territoriality and territories
Punishment:
 capital, 330
 as deterrent, 329–330
 threat of, 330
Pygmies of Central Africa, 306

Quasi-experimental research, 42–44
 advantages, 43
 cause-and-effect relationships, 565
 disadvantages, 43–44
 and policy decisions, 564–565
Questionnaire survey, 51

Race, as a "pure" variable, 385, 389
Racial differences, in intelligence, 385
Racial identity, 67
Racism, 463–468
 causes of, 466, 472–475
 definition of, 463
 examples of, 464
 parallels with sexism, 471
 and stereotypes, 465
 symbolic, 465
Randomization, 37
Reactance, psychological, 231–233
Reactor, in ingratiation, 83
Reasoned action, 176–178
Receiver, in communication process, 129
Recipients of help:
 needs of, 350–351
 opportunity to reciprocate, 365, 367
 reactions of, 365
 relationship with potential helper, 351, 365–366
Reciprocal altruism, 340
Reciprocity norm, 346
Reflected appraisals, 63
Reinforcement, 16
 in prosocial behavior, 357

Reinforcement/affect theory, as explanation of attraction, 253–254
Reinforcement contingencies, 69
Relational analysis, 149
Relative deprivation, 328
"Releasing stimulus," in ethology, 303
Reliability, 46
Response, 16
Reward structure, 480
Risky shift, 422–423
Robbers Cave experiment, 481–482, 487–488
Role, 12, 414
  conflict, 13–14
  differentiation, 415
  expectations, 12, 414–416
  transitions, 428
Role playing, see Simulation and role playing
Role theory:
  basic assumptions and concepts, 12–14
  contributions to social psychology, 14–15
Roosevelt, F. D., 448
Ross, Edmund, 6, 7

"Safety valve" theory, 324
Salinger, J. D., 241
Sampling procedure, 52
Sappho, 282
Scapegoating, 474
Schema, 21, 64, 104–108, 116–118
  causal, 116–118
  in impression organization, 104–108
  for sexual behavior, 280
Sealab II, 44–46
Selective exposure, 173–174, 202
Self, 62–91
  concepts of the, 64–66
  dealing with, 73–81
  definition of, 63
  evaluation of, 77–81
  multiple selves, 65
  nature of, 63–68
  presentation of, 81–90
  real versus ideal, 76–77
  social selves, 62
  theories of the, 63–64
Self-awareness, 15, 69–73, 314
  individual differences in, 73
  objective, 71
  states of, 71–73
Self-concept, 15, 63–66
  definition of, 63
Self-consciousness, 73
  and identification of medical problems, 73
  private versus public, 73–74
  Self Consciousness Scale, 73
Self-definition, influences on, 66–69
Self-disclosure, 149
Self-discrepancies, 15
Self-efficacy, 64, 189
Self-esteem, 74–76
  and emotions, 76–77
  related to masculinity, 74

Self-fulfilling prophecy, 153–155
Self-handicapping strategies, 85–87
Self-induced dependence, 235–236
Self-monitoring, 15, 87–90
  and attitude-behavior consistency, 192
  Self-Monitoring Scale, 88
Self-perception, 69–70, 178
Self-presentation, 15
  goals of, 82–85
  impression management and, 81–82, 90
  individual differences in, 87–90
  maintaining face in, 82
  presentation of self in everyday life, 82
  self-handicapping strategies in, 85–87
  and social facilitation, 408–409
  tactics of, 83–87
  in U.S. presidents, 89
Self-promotion, 83–84
Self-report, of sexual behavior, 274
Self-schema, 64
Self-serving attribution bias, 79
Semantic analysis, 130–131
Semantic differential technique, 163–164
Sex, as a "pure" variable, 385, 389
Sex differences:
  in affiliation, 247
  in aggression, 318, 387
  in attitudes toward sexuality, 275–278, 286
  in attraction after gaze, 135
  in body language, 139–140
  in breaking up a relationship, 263, 265
  in conformity, 216
  in detection of deception, 152
  in evaluations of success and failure as leaders, 441–443
  in expressing feelings, 263
  in extramarital sexual affairs, 275–277
  in eye contact, 135
  in Freud's theory, 279
  in friendship patterns, 388
  in gaze, 135
  in homosexual experience, 277
  in interaction, 387
  in jealousy, 263
  in judging the emotional state of others, 387, 546
  in leadership ability, 441–443
  in liking and loving, 197–198, 263
  in "lonely hearts" advertisements, 250
  in nurses' evaluations, 546
  in perceiving nonverbal cues, 139–140, 152
  in perception of leaders, 441–442
  in ratings of performance, 441–442
  in reactions to disturbance in a relationship, 263–265
  in representations by the media, 470–471
  in response to touch, 139–141
  in self-disclosure, 388
  and sex-role activity, 468–469
  in sexual arousal, 292, 294
  in social influence, 216
  in stereotypes, 468–469
  in treatment by clerks, 470

Sex guilt, 290
Sexism, 468–472
  in hiring, 470
  parallels with racism, 471
Sex-role inversion, 281
Sex roles, see Gender-role norms
Sexual arousal:
  and aggression, 296
  from erotic material, 291–296
Sexual behavior, 272–291
  among college students, 277–279, 284–286
  and contraception, 288–291
  early study of, 273
  first courses in, 272–273
  frequency of, 275–279
  heterosexual and homosexual, 277, 281–284
  Hunt's study of, 275
  Kinsey's study of, 273, 274–275
  methods in the study of, 53, 273–274
  misconceptions about, 289
  in relationships, 284–288
  sexual attitudes and, 275–278, 286, 290–291
  surveys of, 274–277
  taboos about studying, 272–273
  theories of, 278–284
Sexual preference, distinguished from gender identity, 281
Shared stress effect, 500, 502
Sherif, Muzafer, 6, 8
Simulation and role playing, 48–50
  advantages, 50
  disadvantages, 50
  as research method, 48–50
Situation:
  effect of, 349–357
  interaction of personality and, 394–395
  and personality, 394–395, 398–399
  "strong" versus "weak," 399
Size:
  of a group, 215, 411–413
  of jury, 412
Skinner, B. F., 226
Social cognition, 21, 101–114
  and attribution process, 116–123
  encoding, 111–113
  errors and biases, 114–115
  heuristics in, 114–115
  schemas, prototypes, and scripts, 104–108
  storage and retrieval, 113–114
Social comparison, 243–244, 409
Social-comparison theory, 78, 243
"Social cruel rules," 231
Social distance, as etic concept, 383
Social-exchange theory, 18–19, 254–255
  as applied to legal system, 555
  as explanation for affiliation, 383
  as explanation of attraction, 254
  and hedonism, 18
Social facilitation, 7, 407–410, 509
Social impact, 406–407

Social-influence process:
  effects of audience, 355
  as explanation of bystander intervention, 355
  by minority groups, 424–427
  sex differences in, 216
Social inhibition, 407
Social interaction, and communication, 152–155
Socialization, 7, 8
Social judgment theory, of attitude change, 194–196
Social-learning theory, 16–18
  and control of aggression, 304–307
  and development of attitudes, 167
Social loafing, 417–418
Social network, 246–247
Social-pathology hypothesis, 518–520
Social psychology:
  and action research, 541–542
  applications of, 537–571
  history of, 5–10
  methods in, 36–53
  theories in, 2–27
Social register, 131
Social-responsibility norm, 346
Social support, 245
Social technology, 569–570
Social theory, 103–104
Social traps, 553–554
Sociobiology:
  and aggression, 25, 303–304
  and prosocial behavior/altruism, 25, 339–341
"Sociopetal" spaces, 505
Source, in communication theory, 129
State-trait distinction, 242
Status characteristics theory, 415–416
  diffuse, 415
  specific, 415
Status differences:
  in eye contact, 132–133, 135
  in interpersonal distance, 142–143
  and liking, 139
  in nonverbal behavior, 139
Stereotypes, 468–469
  about Chinese, 474
  definition, 468
  and racism, 108
  about Russians, 473–474
  use of group stereotypes in forming impressions, 108–111
Stills, Stephen, 252
Stimulus, 15
  discrimination, 16

Stimulus *(continued)*
  generalization, 16
  sexual, 291
Stimulus-response theory, 15
Storage and retrieval, of social cognitions, 113–114
Strategies for change, 565–568
Suicide, 320–321
Sullivan, Harry Stack, 63
Sumner, William Graham, 477
Superego, 8
Superordinate goal, 487–489
Supplication, 84
Surveys and interviews, 50–53
  advantages, 52–53
  disadvantages, 53
  interview survey, 51
  questionnaire survey, 51
  in study of sexual behavior, 53, 274–277
Symbolic interactionism, 8
Symbolic racism, 465

Tarde, Gabriel, 6
Target-based expectancies, 119
Television, and violence, 319–323
Temperature, ambient, and aggression, 316–318, 499–500
Territoriality and territories:
  definitions of 525
  dominance, 525
  interaction and, 527
  markers, 531
  public, 527, 528, 531–532
  temporary, in public places, 527, 528
  types of, 526–527
"That's not all" technique, 219
Theories, in social psychology, 2–27
  assumptions about human nature, 24–26
  characteristics of good, 11
  cognitive theory, 20–23
  comparison of, 23–26
  definition of, 10
  field theory, 8, 9
  Gestalt theory, 20, 21
  learning theory, 15–20
  psychoanalytic theory, 7, 8
  reinforcement theory, 15–20
  role theory, 12–15
  sociobiological theory, 25, 339–341
Thermograms, 292
Thibaut, John, 6, 18–19
Third-party instigation of aggression, 312–314
Third-party intervention, 486–487

Thomas, W. I., 6
Threat, reduction of, 490–491
Three Mile Island, nuclear accident at, 543
Through the Looking Glass, 130
Touch, 139–141
Tragedy of the commons, 553
Transmitter, in communications process, 129
Transsexualism, 281
Trial process, 556–560
  bail setting and, 555–556
  jury selection, 556–558
  jury size, 412
  opening statement, 559–560
  procedures, 559–560
Triangulation, as research strategy, 54
TRIOS, as conception of Black-White differences, 388
Triplett, Norman, 6–7
Type A behavior pattern, 544

Unidirectional drive upward, 78
Unit relationship, 197
Units of analysis, in theories in social psychology, 23
Unobtrusive measures, 47
Urban-overload hypothesis, 358, 522
Utterance, 130

Value pluralism, 171
Variability, as statistical measure, 55
Verbal attack, and aggression, 311–312
Violence:
  collective, 327–328
  in the home, 325–326
  and the mass media, 319–325
  in Northern Ireland, 488
  in society, 325–328
  on television, 319–323
Virginity, loss of, 286
Visual dominance behavior, 135
Vividness, of a stimulus, 111–112

War, incidence of, 300
Weapons:
  cue value of, 310
  "weapons effect," 310
Weighted averaging model, 100
Wilde, Oscar, 282
Workplaces, 528–529

Zeitgeist, and leadership, 440–441
Znaniecki, F., 6

CREDITS

These pages constitute an extension of the copyright page.

We have made every effort to trace the ownership of all copyrighted material and to secure permission from copyright holders. In the event of any question arising as to the use of any material, we will be happy to make the necessary corrections in future printings.

CHAPTER TWO
35, Table 2–2 from "Investigation into Deindividuation Using a Cross-Cultural Survey Technique," by R. I. Watson, Jr., *Journal of Personality and Social Psychology,* 1973, *25,* 342–345. Copyright 1973 by the American Psychological Association. Reprinted by permission. **45,** Figure 2–2 from "Groups Under Stress: Psychological Research in SEALAB II," by R. Radloff and R. Helmreich. Copyright 1968 by Irvington Publishers, Inc. **47,** Figure 2–3 from "Supreme Court Decision Making: Cognitive Style as a Predictor of Ideological Consistency of Voting," by P. E. Tetlock, J. Bernzeig, and J. L. Gallant, *Journal of Personality and Social Psychology,* 1985, *48,* 1227–1239. Copyright 1985 by the American Psychological Association. Reprinted by permission. **52,** Figure 2–4 from "The Quality of American Life: Perceptions, Evaluations, and Satisfactions," by A. Campbell, P. E. Converse, and W. L. Rogers. Copyright 1976 by the Russell Sage Foundation. Reprinted by permission. **56,** Figure 2–5 from "A Hypothesis-Confirming Bias in Labelling Effects," by J. J. Darley and P. H. Gross, *Journal of Personality and Social Psychology,* 1983, *44,* 20–33. Copyright 1983 by the American Psychological Association. Reprinted by permission.

CHAPTER THREE
68, Figure 3–1 adapted from "Effects of Household Sex Composition on the Salience of One's Gender in the Spontaneous Self-Concept," by W. J. McGuire, C. V. McGuire, and W. Winton, *Journal of Experimental Social Psychology,* 1979, *15,* 77–90. Used by permission of the authors and Academic Press. **81,** Figure 3–4 from "Improving the Performance of College Freshmen with Attributional Techniques," by T. D. Wilson, and P. W. Linville, *Journal of Personality and Social Psychology,* 1985, *49,* 287–293. Copyright 1985 by the American Psychological Association. Reprinted by permission. **90,** Figure 3–5 from "Persons, Situations, and the Control of Social Behavior," M. Snyder and T. C. Monson, *Journal of Personality and Social Psychology,* 1975, *32,* 637–644. Copyright 1985 by the American Psychological Association. Reprinted by permission.

CHAPTER FOUR
96, Figure 4–1 from "Impressions of Baby-faced Adults," by L. Z. McArthur and K. Apatow, *Social Cognition,* 1983/1984, *2,* 315–342. Reprinted by permission. **99,** Table 4–1 adapted from "Ratings of Likableness, Meaningfulness, and Likableness Variances for 555 Common Personality Traits Arranged in Order of Decreasing Likableness," by N. H. Anderson, *Journal of Personality and Social Psychology,* 1968, *9,* 272–279. Copyright 1968 by the American Psychological Association. Reprinted by permission. **104,** Table 4–3 from "A Method for Investigating and Representing a Person's Implicit Theory of Personality," by S. Rosenberg and R. Jones, *Journal of Personality and Social Psychology,* 1972, *22,* 327–386. Copyright 1972 by the American Psychological Association. Reprinted by permission. **121,** Figure 4–3 adapted from B. Weiner, I. Frieze, A. Kukla, L. Red, S. Rest, and R. M. Rosenbaum, "Perceiving the Causes of Success and Failure." In *Attribution: Perceiving the Causes of Behavior,* by E. E. Jones, D. E. Karouse, H. H. Kelley, R. E. Nisbett, S. Valins, and B. Weiner. Copyright 1971 by General Learning Corporation. Used with permission of Silver Burdett Company.

CHAPTER FIVE
129, Figure 5–1 adapted from *The Mathematical Theory of Communication,* by C. Shannon and W. Weaver. Copyright 1949 by the University of Illinois Press. Reprinted by permission. **146,** Figure 5–4 adapted from "A Further Look at Equilibrium Theory: Visual Interaction as a Function of Interpersonal Distance," by J. R. Aiello, *Environmental Psychology and Nonverbal Behavior,* 1977, *1,* 122–140. Copyright 1977 by the American Psychological Association. Reprinted by permission. **148,** Figure 5–5 adapted from "An Arousal Model of Interpersonal Intimacy," by M. L. Patterson, *Psychological Review,* 1976, *83,* 235–245. Copyright 1976 by the American Psychological Association. Reprinted by permission.

CHAPTER SIX
171, Figure 6–4 from "Cognitive Style and Political Belief Systems in the British House of Commons," by P. E. Tetlock, *Journal of Personality and Social Psychology,* 1984, *46,* 365–375. Copyright 1984 by the American Psychological Association. Reprinted by permission. **186,** Table 7–1 from "Anatomy of a Persuasion Schema: Targets, Goals, and Strategies," by B.G. Rule, G. Bisanz, and M. Kohn, *Journal of Personality and Social Psychology,* 1985, *48,* 1127–1140. Copyright 1981 by the American Psychological Association. Reprinted by permission.

CHAPTER SEVEN
190, Figure 7–2 based on "The Need for Cognition," by J. T. Cacioppo and R. E. Petty, *Journal of Personality and Social Psychology,* 1982, *42,* 116–131. Copyright 1982 by the American Psychological Association. **195,** Figure 7–3 from "Width of the Latitude of Acceptance as a Determinant of Attitude Change," by A. Eagly and K. Telaak, *Journal of Personality and Social Psychology,* 1972, *23,* 388–397. Copyright 1972 by the American Psychological Association. Reprinted by permission. **198,** Figure 7–4 from "The Concepts of Balance, Congruity, and Dissonance," by R. B. Zajonc, *Public Opinion Quarterly,* 1960, *24,* 280–296. Copyright 1960 by Columbia University Press. Used by permission. **207,** Figure 7–7 adapted from "Inducing Resistance to Persuasion," by W. J. McGuire. In L. Berkowitz (Eds.), *Advances in Experimental Social Psychology,* Vol. 1. Copyright 1964 by Academic Press. Adapted by permission.

CHAPTER EIGHT
224, Table 8–2 adapted from "Behavioral Study of Obedience," by S. Milgram, *Journal of Personality and Social Psychology,* 1963, *67,* 371–378. Copyright 1963 by the American Psychological Association. Reprinted by permission. **228,** Figure 8–2 adapted from "Distortion in Control Attributions for Real Life Events," by M. H. Wright and A. J. Zautra, *Journal of Research in Personality,* 1985, *19,* 54–71. Copyright 1985 by Academic Press.

CHAPTER NINE
243, Figure 9–1 adapted from "The Friendship Bond: PT's Survey Report on Friendship in America," by M. B. Parlee, *Psychology Today,* 1977, *3,* 372–381. **255,** Figure 9–2 adapted from "Record Keeping in Two Types of Relationships," by M. S. Clark, *Journal of Personality and Social Psychology,* 1984, *47,* 549–557. Copyright 1984 by the American Psychological Association. **257,** Figure 9–3 adapted from "The Rules of Friendship," by M. Argyle and M. Henderson, *Journal of Social and Personal Relationships,* 1984, *1,* 211–237. **258** and **259,** Figures 9–4 and 9–5 adapted from "Measurement of Romantic Love," by Z. Rubin, *Journal of Personality and Social Psychology,* 1970, *16,* 267–268. Copyright 1970 by the American Psychological Association. **259,** Figure 9–6 from "A Theory and Method of Love," by C. Hendrick and S. Hendrick, *Journal of Personality and Social Psychology,* 1986, *50,* 392–402. Copyright 1986 by the American Psychological Association. Reprinted by permission. **261,** Figure 9–7 from "Changing Ingredients," *The New York Times,* September 10, 1985. Copyright © 1985 by The New York Times Company. Reprinted by permission. **265,** Table 9–1 adapted from "Breakups before Marriage: The End of 103 Affairs," by C. T. Hill, L. Rubin, and L. A. Peplau, *Journal of Social Issues,* 1976, *32,* 147–168. Copyright 1976 by the Society for the Psychological Study of Social Issues. Adapted by permission.

CHAPTER TEN
279, Table 10–1 from "Convergence toward a Single Sexual Standard," by J. P. Curran, *Social Behavior and Personality,* 1975, *3,* 189–195. Reprinted by permission. **281,** Table 10–2 from *The Sexual System: A Theory of Human Sexual Behavior,* by P. R. Abramson. Copyright 1981 by Academic Press. Reprinted by permission. **286,** Table 10–2 from "Sexual Intimacy in Dating Relationships," by L. A. Peplau, Z. Rubin, and C. T. Hill, *Journal of Social Issues,* 1977 *33*(2), 86–109. Reprinted by permission.

CHAPTER ELEVEN
310, Table 11–1 from "Film Violence and Cue Properties of Available Targets," by L. Berkowitz and R. G. Geen, *Journal of Personality and Social Psychology,* 1966, *3,* 525–530. **315,** Figure 11–1 from "The Effects of Alcohol and Delta-9-Tetrahydrocannabinol on Human Physical Aggression," by S. P. Taylor, R. M. Vardaris, A. B. Rawtich, C. B. Gammon, J. W. Cranston, and A. I. Lubetkin, *Aggressive Behavior,* 1976, *2*(2). Copyright 1976 by Alan R. Liss, Inc. Reprinted by permission. **318,** Figure 11–2 from "Ambient Temperature and Violent Crime," by C. A. Anderson and D. C. Anderson, *Journal of Personality and Social Psychology,* 1984, *46,* 91–97. Copyright 1984 by the American Psychological Association. Reprinted by permission. **321,** Table from "Natural Experiments on the Effects of Mass Media Violence on Fatal Aggression: Strengths and Weaknesses of a New Approach," by D. P. Phillips, *Advances in Experimental Social Psychology,* 1986, *19,* 207–250. (Originally from D. P. Phillips, "Suicide, Motor Vehicles and the Mass Media: Evidence Toward a Theory of Suggestion," *American Journal of Sociology,* 1979, *84,* 1150–1174). **325,** Figure 11–3 from "Victim Reactions in Aggressive Erotic Films as a Factor in Violence Against Women," by E. Donnerstein and L. Berkowitz, *Journal of Personality and Social Psychology,* 1981, *41,* 710–724. Copyright 1981 by the American Psychological Association. Reprinted by permission. **326,** Table 11–2 from "Violence in College Students' Dating Relationships," by C. K. Sigelman, C. J. Berry, and K. A. Wiles, *Journal of Applied Social Psychology,* 1984, *5,* 530–548. Copyright 1984 by V. H. Winston and Sons, Inc. **329,** Figure 11–4 from "Model's Behavior and Attraction Toward the Model as Determinants of Adult Aggressive Behavior," by R. A. Baron and C. R. Kepner, *Journal of Personality and Social Psychology,* 1970, *14,* 335–344. Copyright 1970 by the American Psychological Association. Reprinted by permission.

CHAPTER TWELVE
359, Figure 12–4 adapted from "Helping Behavior in Urban and Rural Environments: Field Studies Based on a Taxonomic Organization of Helping Episodes," by P. R. Amato, *Journal of Personality and Social Psychology,* 1983, *45,* 571–586. Copyright 1983 by the American Psychological Association. Reprinted by permission. **361,** Figure 12–5 adapted from "Effects of Anticipated Victim Responsiveness and Empathy upon Volunteering," by M. A. Barnett, K. M. Feighny, and J. A. Esper, *Journal of Social Psychology,* 1983, *119,* 211–218. **363,** Figure 12–6 adapted from "The Joys of Helping: Focus of Attention Mediates the Impact of Positive Affect on Altruism," by D. L. Rosenhan, P. Salovey, and K. Hargis, *Journal of Personality and Social Psychology,* 1981, *40,* 899–904. Copyright 1981 by the American Psychological Association. Reprinted by permission.

CHAPTER FOURTEEN
412, Figure 14–3 adapted from "The Effects of Jury Size and Polling Method on Process and Product of Jury Deliberation," by N. L. Kerr and R. J. MacCoun, *Journal of Personality and Social Psychology,* 1985, *48,* 349–363. Copyright 1985 by the American Psychological Association. **417,** Figure 14–5 adapted from "Many Hands Make Light the Work: The Causes and Consequences of Social Loafing," by B. Latané, K. Williams, and S. Harkins, *Journal of Personality and Social Psychology,* 1979, *37,* 822–832. Copyright 1979 by the American Psychological Association. Reprinted by permission. **421,** Figure 14–7 reprinted with permission of The Free Press, a Division of Macmillan, Inc. From *Decision Making: A Psychological Analysis of Conflict, Choice, and Commitment,* by Irving L. Janis and Leon Man. Copyright © 1977 by The Free Press. **423,** Figure 14–8 from *Risk Taking: A Study in Cognition and Personality,* by Nathan Kogan and Michael Wallach. Copyright © 1964 by Holt, Rinehart and Winston. Reprinted by permission of Holt, Rinehart and Winston, CBS College Publishing.

CHAPTER FIFTEEN

444, Figure 15–1 adapted from "Turning Lead into Gold: Evaluations of Men and Women Leaders and the Alchemy of Social Consensus," *Journal of Personality and Social Psychology,* 1984, *46,* 811–824. Copyright 1984 by the American Psychological Association. **445,** Table 15–1 adapted from *Leadership Behavior Description,* by J. K. Hemphill and A. E. Coons, Personnel Research Board, Ohio State University. Used by permission. Copyright 1984 by the American Psychological Association. Adapted by permission. **447,** Figure 15–2 adapted from "Leadership Behavior Associated with the Administrative Reputation of College Departments," by J. K. Hemphill, *Journal of Educational Psychology,* 1955, *46,*(7), 385–401. Reprinted by permission of Abrahams Magazine Service. **452,** Figure 15–3 from "Recent Developments in Research on the Contingency Model," by F. E. Fiedler. In L. Berkowitz (Ed.), *Group Processes.* Copyright 1978 by Academic Press. Reprinted by permission. **453,** Figure 15–4 from "A Person Environment Analysis of Job Stress: A Contingency Model Explanation," by M. M. Chemers, R. B. Hays, F. Rhodewalt, and J. Wysocki, *Journal of Personality and Social Psychology,* 1985, *49,* 628–635. Copyright 1985 by the American Psychological Association. Reprinted by permission.

CHAPTER SIXTEEN

466, Figure 16–1 from "Racial Stereotypes: Associations and Ascriptions of Positive and Negative Characteristics," by S. L. Gaertner and J. P. McLaughlin, 1983, *Social Psychology Quarterly, 46,* 23–30. Copyright 1984 by the American Sociological Association. Reprinted by permission of the author. **469,** Table 16–1 from "Individual Differences to Social Categories: Analysis of a Decade's Research on Gender," by K. Deaux, *American Psychologist,* 1984, *39,* 105–116. Copyright 1984 by the American Psychological Association. Reprinted by permission.

CHAPTER SEVENTEEN

498, Figure 17–1 adapted from "The Environment as Experienced by the Migrant: An Adaption Level View," by J. Wohlwill and I. Kohn, *Representative Research in Social Psychology,* 1973, 135–164. Reprinted by permission. **500,** Figure 17–2 from D. T. Kenrick and S. W. MacFarlane, "Ambient Temperature and Horn Honking: A Field Study of the Heat," *Environment and Behavior, 10,* 247–269. Copyright © 1986 by Environment and Behavior. Reprinted by permission of Sage Publications, Inc. **501,** Figure 17–3 adapted from "Environmental Noise Level as a Determinant of Helping Behavior," by K. Mathews and L. Canon, 1975, *Journal of Personality and Social Psychology, 32,* 571–577. Copyright 1975 by the American Psychological Association. **507,** Figure 17–4 adapted from "Effects of Size and Spatial Arrangements on Group Decision Making," by L. L. Cummings, G. P. Huber, and E. Arendt, *Academy of Management Journal,* 1974, *17*(3), 460–475. **509,** Figure 17–5 from "Classroom Ecology," by R. Sommer, *Journal of Applied Behavioral Science,* 1967, *3*(4), 489–503. Copyright 1978, NTL Institute. **510,** Figure 17–6 from "The Psycho-Social Influence of Building Environments: Sociometric Findings in Large and Small Office Spaces," by B. W. P. Wells, *Building Science,* 1965, *1,* 153–165. **512,** Figure 17–7 from *Architecture and Social Behavior: Psychological Studies of Social Density,* by A. Baum and S. Valins. Copyright © 1977 by Lawrence Erlbaum and Associates, Inc. Reprinted with permission. **513,** Figure 17–8 from "Reducing the Stress of High-Density Living: An Architectural Intervention," by A. Baum and G. Davis, *Journal of Personality and Social Psychology,* 1980, *38,* 471–478. Copyright 1980 by the American Psychological Association. Reprinted by permission. **518,** Figure 17–9 from "Physical Enclosure, Type of Job, and Privacy in the Office," by E. Sundstrom, J. Town, D. Brown, A. Forman, and C. McGee, *Environment and Behavior,* 1982, *14*(5), 543–559. **520,** Figure 17–10 "Death Rates, Psychiatric Commitments, Blood Pressure, and Perceived Crowding as a Function of Institutional Crowding," by P. B. Paulus, G. McCain and V. Cox, *Environmental Psychology and Nonverbal Behavior,* 3(2), 107–116. *Copyright* 1978 by Human Sciences Press, New York. Reprinted by permission. **526,** Figure 17–11 adapted from "The Home-Field Advantage in Sports: Differences and Correlates." Unpublished paper presented at the annual conference of the Midwestern Psychological Association, Detroit, 1981. **529,** Figure 17–12 from *Defensible Space,* by O. Newman. Copyright © 1972, 1973 by Oscar Newman. Reprinted by permission of Macmillan Publishing Co., Inc. And The Architectural Press Ltd. **531,** Figure 17–13 adapted from "Home and Near-Home Territories," by R. B. Taylor and S. Brower. In I. Altman and C. Werner (Eds.), *Home Environments: Human Behavior and Environment: Advances in Theory and Research,* 1966, Vol. 8, 183–212. Copyright 1986 by Plenum Publishing Corporation. Reprinted by permission. **532,** Figure 17–14 adapted from "Territorial Defense and the Good Neighbor," by R. Sommer and F. Becker, *Journal of Personality and Social Psychology,* 1968, *11,* 85–92. copyright 1969 by the American Psychological Association.

CHAPTER EIGHTEEN

543, Figure 18–1 from "Stress at Three Mile Island: Applying Psychological Impact Analysis," by A. Baum, R. Fleming, and J. E. Singer. In L. Bickman (Ed.), *Applied Social Psychology Annual,* Vol. 3. Copyright 1982 by Sage Publications, Inc. Reprinted by permission. **545,** Figure 18–2 adapted from "Challenge Seeking and the Type A Coronary-Prone Behavior Pattern," by D. F. Ortega and J. E. Pipal, *Journal of Personality and Social Psychology,* 1984, *46,* 1328–1334. Copyright 1984 by the American Psychological Association. Reprinted by permission. **549,** Figure 18–3 adapted from "Distortions and Outcome Desirability: Experimental Verification of Medical Folklore," by R. A. Jones, P. H. Howard, and J. V. Haley, 1984, *Journal of Applied Psychology,* 1984, *69,* 319–333. Copyright 1984 by the American Psychological Association. **553,** Figure 18–4 adapted from "Cognitive Dissonance and Energy Conservation," by S. J. Kantola, G. J. Syme, and N. A. Campbell, *Journal of Applied Psychology,* 1984, *69,* 416–421. Copyright 1984 by the American Psychological Association. Reprinted by permission. **559,** Figure 18–5 adapted from "The Effects of Opening Statements on Mock Jurors' Verdicts in a Simulated Criminal Trial," by T. A. Pyszcznski and L. Wrightsman, *Journal of Applied Social Psychology,* 1981, *11,* 301–313. Copyright 1981 by V. H. Winston and Sons, Inc. **564,** Figure 18–6 adapted from "Approaches toward Social Problems: A Conceptual Model," by C. Ovenarchyn-Devitt, P. Colby, L. Carswell, W. Perkowitz, B. Scruggs, R. Turpin, and L. Bickman, *Basic and Applied Social Psychology,* 1981, *2,* 275–287. Copyright © 1981 by Lawrence Erlbaum Associates, Inc. Reprinted by permission. **566,** Figure 18–7 adapted from "Reforms as Experiments," by D. T. Campbell, *American Psychologist,* 1969, *24,*(4), 409–429. Copyright 1969 by the American Psychological Association.

PHOTO CREDITS

CHAPTER ONE. 9, AP/Wide World Photos; **17,** National Library of Medicine; **22,** Ken Karp/Omni-Photo Communications, Inc.; **23,** Leonard Freed/Magnum Photos, Inc.

CHAPTER TWO. 49, © Prof. Philip G. Zimbardo, Department of Psychology, Stanford University; **51,** Owen Franken/Stock, Boston.

CHAPTER THREE. 70, Robert V. Eckert Jr./EKM-Nepenthe; **82,** © Richard Stine; **88,** Cathy Cheney/EKM-Nepenthe.

CHAPTER FOUR. 97, Gilles Press/Magnum Photos, Inc.; **106,** Mike Douglas/The Image Works; **124,** Ben Shahn: *Martin Luther King, Jr.*, 1968, New Jersey State Museum Collection, Trenton, Gift of Mrs. Robert Graff.

CHAPTER FIVE. 140, Michael Grecco/Stock, Boston; **142** Abigail Heyman/Archive Pictures, Inc.

CHAPTER SIX. 166, Charles Gatewood/The Image Works; **172,** AP/Wide World Photos.

CHAPTER SEVEN. 185, Robert Pacheco/EKM-Nepenthe; **188,** Courtesy The National Council on Alcoholism, New York.

CHAPTER EIGHT. 223, © Stanley Milgram 1965; **226,** Alan Carey/The Image Works; **229,** Ken Kerp/Omni-Photo Communications, Inc.; **233,** Culver Pictures, Inc.

CHAPTER NINE. 241, Patsy Davidson/The Image Works; **244,** Isabel Bishop: *Idle Conversation*, Geoffrey Clements Photography, collection of the Whitney Museum of American Art, NY; **251,** Drawing from *The Gibson Book: A Collection of the Published Works of Charles Dana Gibson*, © 1906; **260,** Janice Fullman/The Picture Cube; **263,** Lynne Jaeger Weinstein/Woodfin Camp & Associates.

CHAPTER TEN. 282, Courtesy Saatchi & Saatchi Compton Inc.; **287,** Abigail Heyman/Archive Pictures Inc., **289,** Courtesy The Children's Defense Fund.

CHAPTER ELEVEN. 304, Photo by T. M. Huffman. Printed with permission of Wolf Park, Battle Ground, Indiana. **307,** from "Imitation of Film-Mediated Aggressive Models," by A. Bandura, D. Ross, and S. A. Ross, *Journal of Abnormal and Social Psychology*, 1963, *66*, 3–11. Copyright 1963 by the American Psychological Association. Reprinted by permission; **322,** Michael Weisbrot and Family/Stock, Boston.

CHAPTER TWELVE. 337, John Griffin/The Image Works; **343,** Harry Wilks/Stock, Boston; **369,** Elizabeth Hamlin/Stock, Boston.

CHAPTER THIRTEEN. 393, Rebecca Chao/Archive Pictures Inc; **399,** Ellis Herwig/Stock, Boston; **399,** Gale Zucker/Stock, Boston.

CHAPTER FOURTEEN. 407, Elizabeth Hamlin/Stock, Boston; **410,** Patricia Hollander Gross/Stock, Boston; **414,** © George T. Kruse.

CHAPTER FIFTEEN. 442, AP/Wide World Photos.

CHAPTER SIXTEEN. 465, John F. Conn/Black Star; **473,** The Granger Collection.

CHAPTER SEVENTEEN. 506, Bob Adelman/Magnum Photos, Inc. **517,** Ellis Herwig/Stock, Boston; **519,** Red Grooms: *Loft on 25th Street*, 1965–1966. Hirshhorn Museum and Sculpture Garden, Smithsonian Institution.

CHAPTER EIGHTEEN. 557, Michael O'Brien/Archive Pictures Inc.; **561,** Burt Glinn/Magnum Photos Inc.

To the owner of this book:

We hope that you have enjoyed *Social Psychology (Fifth Edition)* as much as we have enjoyed writing it. We'd like to know as much about your experiences with the book as you care to offer. Only through your comments and the comments of others can we learn how to make *Social Psychology* a better book for future readers.

School: _____ Your instructor's name: _____

1. What did you like most about *Social Psychology (Fifth Edition)*? _____

   _____

   _____

2. What did you like least about the book? _____

   _____

3. Were all of the chapters of the book assigned for you to read? _____

   If not, which ones weren't? _____

4. If you used the Glossary, how helpful was it as an aid in understanding psychological concepts and terms? _____

   _____

5. Did you use the Study Guide? _____

   If so, please tell us what component was most useful (terms, short answer questions, multiple-choice items, or other components):

   _____

6. In the space below, or in a separate letter, please let us know what other comments about the book you'd like to make. (For example, were any chapters *or* concepts particularly difficult?) We'd be delighted to hear from you!

Optional:

Your name: _____ Date: _____

May Brooks/Cole quote you, either in promotion for *Social Psychology (Fifth Edition)* or in future publishing ventures?

Yes _____ No _____

Sincerely,

Kay Deaux
Lawrence S. Wrightsman

FOLD HERE

BUSINESS REPLY MAIL
FIRST CLASS   PERMIT NO. 353   PACIFIC GROVE, CA

POSTAGE WILL BE PAID BY ADDRESSEE

ATT: Dr. Kay Deaux and Dr. Lawrence S. Wrightsman

Brooks/Cole Publishing Company
511 Forest Lodge Road
Pacific Grove, California 93950-9968

NO POSTAGE
NECESSARY
IF MAILED
IN THE
UNITED STATES

FOLD HERE